gitude East from London

ZEN OCEAN

OR

N.Cape

SEA

Land seen in 1773

BEERINGS STRAITS

S. Laurence I.

SEA OF ANADIR

Tschukski

Ioanko L.

Anadir R.

Anadirskoi Ostrog

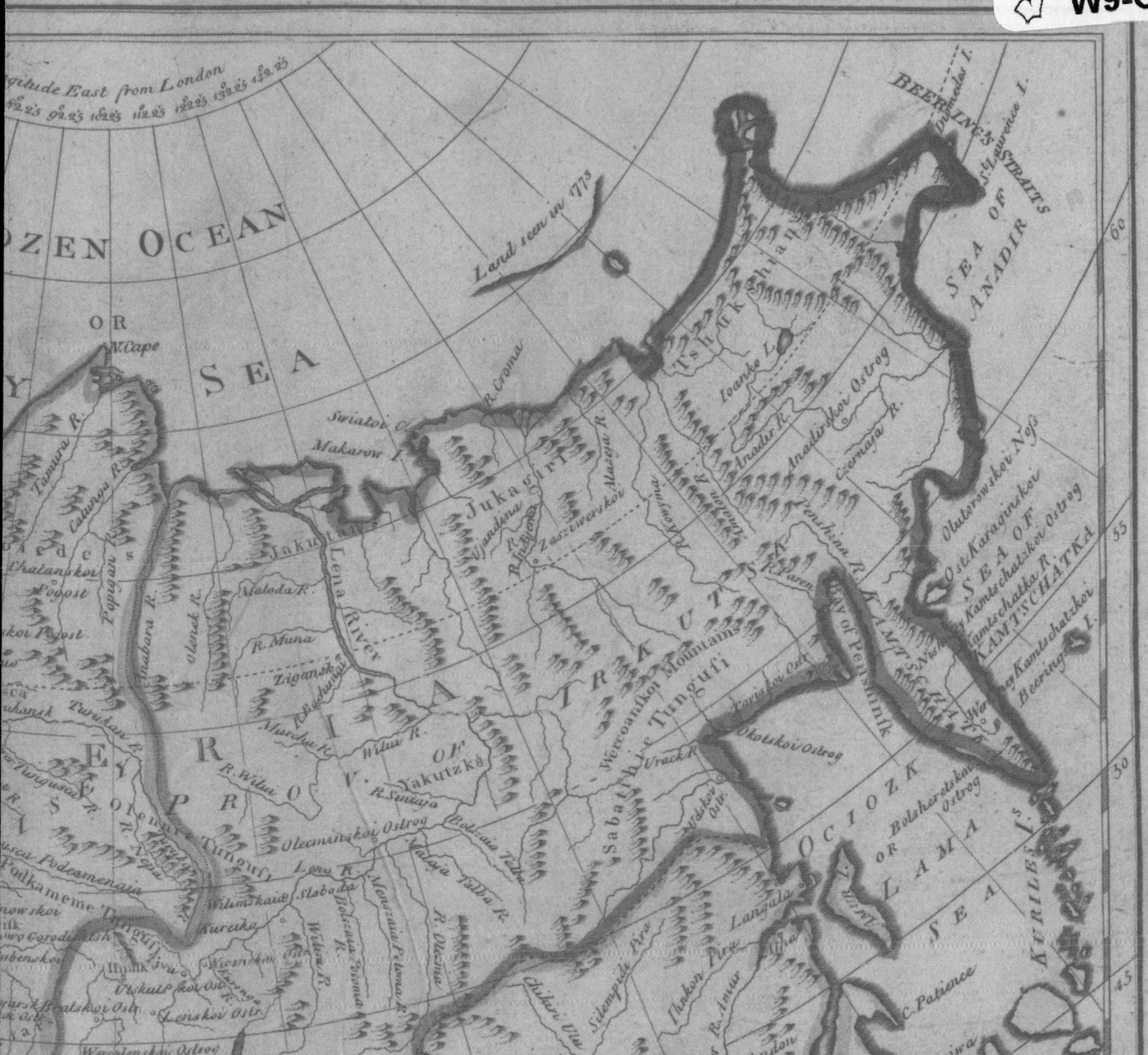

Swiatoi C.

Makarow I.

R. Croma

Jukagiri

Lena River

Jakutzk

Oloturowskoi Noss

Ost. Karaginskoi

SEA OF KAMTSCHATKA

Beering I.

Ziganska

R. Muna

R. Wilui

PROV. OF Yakutzka

Olecminskoi Ostrog

Wercoanskoi Mountains

Tungusi

Okotskoi Ostrog

Bay of Penschinsk

Bolsheretskoi Ostrog

OCIOZK OR LAMA SEA

KURILES I.

Irkutzk

Baikal L.

Selenginsk

C. Patience

C. Aniwa

Black C.

Saghalien Ula

Merghen

Tsitsicar

JESO I.

C. Eroen

Str. of Tessoi

COREA

Sugaar

Nanlin

CHINESE TARTARY

SANDY DESART

COREA GULF

Canazava

Oki

NIPHON

SIKOCO I.

KIUSU I.

Kiko

Kinkitao

PEKIN

CHINA

Yellow R.

Changte

Chinan

30

35

40

45

50

55

60

177 23

187 23

197 23

207 23

ENCYCLOPEDIA OF
RUSSIAN HISTORY

EDITORIAL BOARD

ENCYCLOPEDIA OF
RUSSIAN HISTORY

VOLUME 2: E-L

JAMES R. MILLAR, EDITOR IN CHIEF

Encyclopedia of Russian History

James R. Millar

For more information, contact
Macmillan Reference USA
300 Park Avenue South, 9th Floor
New York, NY 10010
Or you can visit our Internet site at
http://www.gale.com

LIBRARY OF CONGRESS CATALOGING-IN-PUBLICATION DATA

Encyclopedia of Russian history / James R. Millar, editor in chief.
p. cm.
Includes bibliographical references and index.
ISBN 0-02-865693-8 (set hardcover) — ISBN 0-02-865694-6 (v. 1) — ISBN 0-02-865695-4 (v. 2) — ISBN 0-02-865696-2 (v. 3) — ISBN 0-02-865697-0 (v. 4)
1. Russia—History—Encyclopedias. 2. Soviet Union—History—Encyclopedias. 3. Russia (Federation)—History—Encyclopedias. I. Millar, James R., 1936-

DK14.E53 2003
947'.003—dc21 2003014389

This title is also available as an e-book.
ISBN 0-02-865907-4 (set)
Contact your Gale sales representative for ordering information.

Printed in the United States of America
10 9 8 7 6 5 4 3 2 1

EARLY RUSSIA *See* KIEVAN RUS; MUSCOVY; NOVGOROD THE GREAT.

ECONOMIC GROWTH, EXTENSIVE

In the quantitative analysis of aggregate economic development, modern economists commonly distinguish extensive from intensive growth. Extensive economic growth comes from the expansion of ordinary inputs of labor, reproducible capital (i.e., machines and livestock) and natural resources. Intensive growth, by contrast, involves increased effectiveness, quality, or efficiency of these inputs—usually measured as a growth of total factor productivity.

The early development of the USSR was primarily of the extensive sort. Increased application of labor inputs came from reduced unemployment, use of women previously engaged within the household, diminished leisure (e.g., communist sabbaticals or *subotniki*), and forced or prison labor. Increased capital investments were a result of forced savings of the population, taxes and compulsory loans, deferred consumption, and a small and varying amount of foreign investment in the country. Natural resources were expanded by new mines and arable acreage, most notably the "virgin lands" opened up in semiarid zones of Kazakhstan during the 1950s. But shifting resources from the backward peasant sector to modern industry, as well as to borrowed technology, also accounted for some intensive growth.

During the 1950s total growth of gross domestic product (GDP) was an impressive 5.7 percent annually, adjusted for inflation, of which approximately 3.3 percent came from increased inputs and only about 2.4 percent from increased productivity. Growth rates declined to 5.1 percent during the 1960s, 3.2 percent during the 1970s, and a mere 1.9 percent during the 1980s. Less than 1 percent of these growth rates came from intensive sources. The increased share of extensive sources meant that growth could not be sustained for several reasons. Population growth was slowing in Russia. Most of the increased labor supplies came from the less educated populations of Soviet Central Asia, where industrial productivity was considerably lower than in the traditional heartland of Russia and Ukraine. These Muslim populations did not move readily to, or were not welcome in, the most productive areas of the USSR,

such as the Baltic states. Some economists, including Martin Weitzman and Stanley Fischer, attributed the slowdown to the difficulty of substituting new investments for labor, as well. Depletion of oil and ore fields also played a role in reduced growth.

For systemic reasons, the Soviet command economy could not develop the new goods, higher quality, and innovative processes that increasingly characterized the economies of the developed West. Nor could it keep up with the newly industrializing economies of southeast Asia, which by the 1980s displayed higher growth rates, predominantly from intensive sources.

See also: ECONOMIC GROWTH, IMPERIAL; ECONOMIC GROWTH, INTENSIVE; ECONOMIC GROWTH, SOVIET

BIBLIOGRAPHY

Gregory, Paul R., and Stuart, Robert C. (1986). *Soviet Economic Structure and Performance,* 3rd rev. ed. New York: Harper & Row.

Gregory, Paul R., and Stuart, Robert C. (1999). *Comparative Economics Systems,* 6th ed. Boston: Houghton Mifflin.

MARTIN C. SPECHLER

ECONOMIC GROWTH, IMPERIAL

The economic development of the Russian Empire can be traced back to the reign of Peter the Great (1682–1725), who was determined to industrialize Russia by borrowing contemporary technology from Western Europe and attracting foreign specialists. While military considerations played an important role in this drive, they combined with vast natural resources and large labor pool to develop an increasingly modern industrial sector by eighteenth-century standards. The less progressive policies of Peter's successors lead to a growing gap between Russia and its industrializing European competitors that became evident in the nineteenth century. Peter's most significant policy was his entrenchment of serfdom in the village, which was abolished in 1861. After the Crimean War (1854–1856), especially during the tenure of the Minister of Finance Count Sergei Witte (1892–1903), recognition of the dangers of the economic gap bolstered the accelerated industrialization of the Russian Empire. Large government investments in the rail network development expanded the transportation network from 2,000 kilometers in 1861 to more than 70,000 kilometers in 1913. This development helped to open up the iron and coal resources of the Southern regions (Ukraine) and facilitated the marketing of wheat, the major export commodity of the Russian empire. A vibrant textile industry grew in Moscow, and metalworking blossomed in St. Petersburg.

Government policy favored the influx of foreign capital, primarily from England, France, and Belgium, which were attracted by Russia's vast economic potential. The stabilized ruble exchange rate allowed Russia to join the international gold standard in 1897. The expansion of domestic heavy industries was promoted by government protectionist policies such as high tariffs, profit guarantees, tax reductions and exemptions, and government orders at high prices to insure domestic demand. The ministry of finance was the major agent in this strategy. Bureaucratic intervention into economic matters and bribery were among the numerous limitations on the development of a modern entrepreneurial class in Russia. More recent data suggest that the state was not as pervasive in Russian economic life as was originally thought. Budgetary subsidies were modest, and tariffs and indirect taxes were levied strictly for revenue purposes and played little role in the industrial policy. Russia had active commodity markets and was active in world markets. The state did not engage in economic planning, and both product and factor prices were set by markets. The creation of industrial trusts and syndicates in the early years of the twentieth century implied the existence of some monopolies in Russia.

The success of Russian industrialization before 1917 was evident, but agricultural progress was more modest (agriculture continued to account for more than half the national product). During the industrialization era, the share of agriculture fell from 58 percent in 1885 to 51 percent in 1913. Russian agriculture was characterized by feudal elements and serfdom that provided few incentives for investment, productivity improvements, or better management. Russian serfs had to work the landlords' land (called *barshchina*) or make in–kind or monetary payments from their crops (*obrok*). Peasant land prior to 1861 was held communally and was periodically redistributed. Agricultural reforms were modest or too late to prevent what many contemporary observers feel was a deepening agrarian crisis. The Emancipation Act of 1861 provided the peasants with juridical freedom and transferred to them about half the landholdings of the landed aristocracy. However, peasants had to "redeem" (buy) their allotted plots of land. The size of land allotments was very small, and backward, unproductive communal agriculture remained the main organizational form in villages. While the production and marketing of grain increased substantially after the Emancipation Act of 1861, the primary objective of the Russian emancipation was not to create a modern agriculture, but to prevent revolts, preserve the aristocracy, and retain state control of agriculture.

Many observers feel that the agrarian crisis was one of the causes of the Revolution of 1905, which necessitated further reforms by the tsarist government. The reforms introduced in 1906 and 1910 by Peter Stolypin allowed the peasants to own land and cultivate it in consolidated plots rather than in small, frequently separated strips. The Stolypin reforms weakened communal agriculture and created the base for a class of small peasant proprietors. These reforms were considered long overdue, and they had a positive effect on the development of agriculture. In spite of persistent regional differences, peasant living standards rose, and productivity and per capita output increased. Overall, agricultural growth during the post–emancipation period was much like that of Western Europe. In spite of the late removal of serfdom, there is evidence of significant peasant mobility, and the completion of an extensive rail network greatly facilitated the marketing of grain. Regional price dispersion fell as transportation costs were lowered, and agricultural marketing and land rents were, in fact, dictated by normal market principles.

Despite scholarly controversy concerning the consequences of active government intervention in economy, the late tsarist era after 1880 is characterized by the significant acceleration of the output growth rate. Between the 1860s and 1880s the average annual rate of growth of net national product was 1.8 percent, while for the period thereafter, up to the 1909–1913 period, the rate of economic growth was 3.3 percent. At the same time, Russia experienced significant population growth, which put the Russian empire in the group of poorer West European countries in per capita terms. Russian economic growth was largely the consequence of the relatively rapid rate of growth of population (1.6% from 1885 to 1913) and labor force (1.7% from 1885 to 1913), pointing to the extensive character of the growth. Less reliable data on the tsarist capital stock suggests that roughly two–thirds of the growth of Russian output was accounted for by the growth of conventional labor and capital inputs. With respect to structural change, the decline in the shares of agriculture (from 58% in 1885 to 51% in 1913) and expansion of industry, construction, and transportation (from 23% in 1885 to 32% in 1913) suggests that the Russian economy had indeed embarked on a path of modern economic growth.

Russia's economic power was concentrated in agriculture. In 1861 Russia produced more grain than any other country and was surpassed only by the United States in 1913 (123,000 versus 146,000 metric tons). On a per capita basis, however, Russia ranked well behind major grain producers (the United States and Germany) and was close to the level of such countries as France and Austria–Hungary. Russia's industrial base was even weaker. In 1861 the country was a minor producer of essential industrial commodities such as coal, iron, and steel, and still lagged behind the major industrial powers in 1913. Russia began its modern era with a per capita output that was 50 percent that of France and Germany and 15 percent that of England and the United States. On per capita basis, in 1913 Russia was a poor European country ranking well below Spain, Italy, and Austria–Hungary. The relative backwardness of the Russian empire is explained by rapid population growth and slow output growth in the years before the 1880s. Russia's output growth figures do not paint a picture of a collapsing economy, but rather of an economy that was either catching up or holding its own with the most industrialized countries of the era.

Data on human capital development (in particular, literacy data) suggest that Russia was still a socially backward nation at the turn of the century. In 1897 the illiteracy rate was 72 percent; in 1913 it was still as high as 60 percent, with urban literacy almost three times that of rural literacy. By contrast, in 1900 the illiteracy rate in the United States was 11 percent. Despite this fact, after 1880 investment in primary education rose, and primary school enrollment increased considerably. While Russia's birth and death rates began to decline after 1889, birth rates were still at premodern levels at the time of the 1917 revolution.

Foreign investment played a substantial role in the industrialization of Russia, since the domestic production of capital equipment was limited. In addition to importing technology and equipment, the Russian economy was also aided by the receipt of foreign savings to finance Russian capital formation along with domestic savings. Russia was a large debtor country during the period from 1880 to 1913, receiving significant capital influx from France, England, and Belgium. It accounted for 15 percent of world international debt by 1913. Foreign capital accounted for nearly 40 percent of Russian industrial investment, 15 to 20 percent of total investment, and about 2 percent of Russian output at the end of tsarist era. The Russian empire was more dependent upon foreign capital in both magnitude and duration than either the United States or Japan during their periods of dependence. The large foreign investments in Russia were a sign of confidence in its potential and responded to traditional signals such as profits sufficient to offset risk.

See also: AGRICULTURE; BARSHCHINA; INDUSTRIALIZATION; OBROK; PEASANT ECONOMY; PETER I; SERFDOM

BIBLIOGRAPHY

Gatrell, Peter. (1986). *The Tsarist Economy, 1850–1917.* New York: St. Martin's Press.

Gregory, Paul R. (1994). *Before Command: An Economic History of Russia from Emancipation to the First Five Year Plan.* Princeton, NJ: Princeton University Press.

PAUL R. GREGORY

ECONOMIC GROWTH, INTENSIVE

Increases in aggregate economic activity, or growth, may be generated by adding more labor and capital or by improving skills and technology. Development economists call the latter "intensive growth" because labor and capital work harder. Growth is driven by enhanced productivity (higher output per unit of input) rather than augmented factor supplies. Theory predicts that all growth in a steady-state, long-run equilibrium will be attributable to technological progress (intensive growth). Developing nations may initially grow faster than this "golden mean" rate, benefiting both from rapid capital accumulation (capital deepening) and technological catch-up, but must converge to the golden mean thereafter. During the 1970s many Marxist economists hypothesized that socialist economies were not bound by these neoclassical principles. They forecasted that extensive growth (increased factor supply) would be replaced by socialist–intensive methods ensuring superior performance, but they were mistaken: Growth fell below zero in 1989, heralding the collapse of the Soviet Union two years later.

See also: ECONOMIC GROWTH, EXTENSIVE; ECONOMIC GROWTH, SOVIET

BIBLIOGRAPHY

Abramowitz, M. (1986). "Catching Up, Forging Ahead, and Falling Behind." *Journal of Economic History* 46: 385–406.

Domar, Evsei. (1957). *Essays in the Theory of Economic Growth.* New York: Oxford University Press.

Krugman, P. (1994). "The Myth of Asia's Miracle." *Foreign Affairs* 73:62-78.

Solow, R. (1957). "Technical Change and the Aggregate Production Function." *Review of Economics and Statistics* 39(3):312-320.

STEVEN ROSEFIELDE

ECONOMIC GROWTH, SOVIET

During the first decade of Soviet rule and up to 1929, the Soviet economy struggled to recover from the damages of World War I, the Revolution, and the civil war, and then to find its way through policy zigzags of the young and inexperienced Soviet leadership. It is commonly accepted that during this decade of the 1920s the Soviet economy more or less managed to regain the level of national product of 1913, the last prewar year. In 1929 the Soviet Union embarked upon a strategy of rapid economic growth focused mainly on industrialization. The main institutional instrument used in order to implement growth was the Five-Year Plan, the key economic tool of the centrally planned system.

The record of Soviet growth since 1928 and the main factors that contributed to it are presented in Table 1. The data reflect mostly Western estimates, based partly on Soviet official data following adjustments to conform to Western definitions and methodology as well as to accuracy. One major methodological difference related to the national product was that, following Marxist teaching, the concept of Net National Product (NNP), the main Soviet aggregate measure for national income, did not include the value of most services, considered nonproductive.

One of the main goals of Soviet communist leadership was rapid economic growth that would equal and eventually surpass the West. The primary aim was to demonstrate the superiority of the communist economic system and growth strategy, based on the teachings of Marx and Lenin, over capitalism. The goal was needed also in order to build a sufficient military power base to avert the perceived military threat of the capitalist world in general, initially that of Nazi Germany. Indeed the rates of growth of Soviet GNP were initially, during the 1930s and the first Five-Year Plans, exceptionally high by international comparisons for that period; this made the Soviet model a showcase for imitation to many developing countries that became independent in the aftermath of World War II. While the Soviet growth rates were still high during the 1950s and 1960s, they were already matched or exceeded at that time by countries such as Germany and Japan, as well as a number of developing countries. The decade of the 1940s, with the devastation of World War II, witnessed stagnation at first and slow growth during the reconstruction efforts later. Growth somewhat accelerated in the aftermath of the death of Josef Stalin, but from the 1960s onward the rates of economic growth began to fall, declining continuously throughout the rest of the Soviet period down to near zero just before the dissolution of the USSR at the end of 1991. Various efforts at economic reform in order to reverse this trend largely failed. As a result, the entire postwar growth record declined further by international comparisons to below that of most groups of developed as well as developing countries, especially a number of East Asian and Latin American countries. While many developed market economies suffered from business cycles and oscillations in growth rates, they experienced sustained economic growth in the long run. Per contra the fall in Soviet growth rates proved to be terminal. Thus, although during the early decades the Soviet economy grew fast enough in order to catch up and narrow the gap with the developed countries, during its last decades it fell behind and the gap widened. The growth record with respect to GNP per capita, followed a similar trend of high rates of growth initially, but declined in later decades (Table 1). While in 1928 the Soviet level of GDP per capita stood around 20 percent of that of the United States, it reached about 30 percent in 1990, probably the best record in terms of comparisons with other Western economies. Throughout the period, the share of private consumption in GNP was lower than in most other nonsocialist countries. Consumption levels did go up significantly from very low levels during the two decades or so following Stalin's death. Also, throughout most of the period, there were relatively high public expenditures of education and health services, which helped to raise the comparative level of welfare and the quality of life. The failure of the communist regime to achieve sustained economic growth on a converging path with developed countries is no doubt the most important reason for the fall of the economy.

Table 1.

Growth, Productivity and Consumption 1928–1990
(AVERAGE ANNUAL GROWTH RATES)

Period/Category	1928–1990	1928–1940	1940–1950	1950–1960	1960–1970	1970–1980	1980–1985	1986–1990
GNP	3.2	5.8	2.2	5.2	4.9	2.5	1.8	1.3
Population	1.2	2.1	-0.8	1.8	1.3	0.9	0.9	0.9
GNP per Capita	2.0	3.6	3.0	3.3	3.6	1.6	0.9	0.4
Employment	1.4	3.9	0.3	1.6	1.8	1.4	0.7	0.1
Capital	5.7*	9.0	0.4	9.5	8.0	7.4	6.2	..
Total Factor Productivity (TFP)	0.5*	1.7	2	0.4	0.5	-1.2	-1.0	..
Consumption	3.2	3.5	3.3	5.2	5.2	3.4	1.9	2.2
Consumption per Capita	2.1	1.4	2.5	3.3	3.9	2.5	1.0	1.3

*1928–1985.

SOURCE: Ofer, 1987; Laurie Kurtzweg, "Trends in Soviet Gross National Product" in United States Congress, Joint Economic Committee. *Gorbachev's Economic Plans,* Vol. 1, Washington D.C., pp. 126–165; James Noren and Laurie Kurtzweg, "The Soviet Economy Unravels: 1985–91" in United States Congress, Joint Economic Committee. *The Former Soviet Union in Transition,* Vol. 1, Washington D.C. pp. 8–33, 1993; Angus Maddison. *Monitoring the World Economy 1820–1992,* OECD, Paris, 1995; Angus Maddison, *The World Economy : A Millennial Perspective,* OECD, Paris, 2000.

The growth record of the Soviet Union—its initial success and eventual failure—is a joint outcome of the selected growth strategy and the system of central planning, including almost full state ownership of the means of production. The centrally planned system was more effective at the start in mobilizing all needed resources, and directing them to the goals of industrialization and growth. The system is also characterized by using commands instead of incentives and decentralized initiatives: emphasis on fulfillment of quantitative production targets rather than on improvements in quality, technology, and efficiency, routine expansion instead of creativity, and rigidity and "more of the same" instead of flexibility—a very high cost for any change. Some of the above characteristics, while advantageous at the start, turned out to be obstacles when the economy developed and became more complex. Other features, such as difficulties in creating indigenous technological innovations, were less harmful initially, when technology could be transferred from abroad, but more of a hindrance later when more domestic efforts were needed.

The Soviet communist growth strategy, following Marxian doctrine, was based on high rates of investment and a rapid buildup of capital stock. High rates of investment come at the expense of lower shares of consumption, sacrificed at the beginning in exchange for hopes of abundance in the future. Central planning, state ownership, and the dictatorship of the proletariat were the necessary tools needed to impose such sacrifices. Next the regime mobilized the maximum possible number of able-bodied men and women to the labor force. A model of growth based mostly on maximum mobilization of capital and labor is called "extensive." The increase in output is achieved mainly through the increase in the amounts of inputs. Under an alternative "intensive" model, most of the increase in output is achieved through improvements in the utilization of a given amount of inputs. These include technological changes and improvements in management, organization, and networks, termed *total factor productivity* (TFP). The mobilization of capital in the Soviet growth model assumed that the newly installed equipment would embody also the most advanced technology. While this was the case to some extent during the first decade, with heavy borrowing of technology from abroad, the failure to generate indigenous civilian technology, as well as the mounting inefficiencies of central planning, diminished, eliminated, and turned negative the intensive contribution (TFP) to Soviet growth. Only during the 1930s TFP was significant and accounted for about 30 percent of total growth. Soviet leaders and economists were aware of the efficiency failure and tried to reverse it through many reforms but to no avail.

The problem with extensive growth is that the ability to mobilize more labor and capital is being exhausted over time; furthermore, in both cases early efforts to mobilize more resources backfire by reducing their availability in the future. Labor was mobilized from the start, by moving millions of people from farms to the cities, by obliging all able-bodied, especially women, to join the active labor force, and by limiting the number of people employed in services, forcing families to self-supply services during after-work hours. Very low wages compelled all adult members of the family to seek work. Table 1 illustrates that until the 1980s employment grew by a higher rate than the population, indicating a growing rate of labor force participation, achieving at the time one of the highest rates, especially for women, in the world. However, the table also shows that over time the rate of growth of employment declined, from nearly 4 percent per year from 1928 to 1940 to almost zero during the late 1980s. In the Soviet Union, birthrates declined far beyond the normal rates accompanying modernization everywhere. This was due to the heavy pressure on women to work outside the household, provide services in off-work hours, and raise children in small, densely inhabited, and poorly equipped apartments. In this way larger labor inputs early on resulted in fewer additions to the labor force in later years, thereby contributing to declining growth. During the 1980s employment increased at even a slower rate than the population.

A similar process affected capital accumulation. Because a labor force grows naturally by modest rates, the main vehicle of growth is capital (equipment and construction). This is especially true if the rate of efficiency growth is modest or near zero, as was the case most of the time in the USSR. It follows that the share of investment out of the national product must increase over time in order to assure a steady growth rate of the capital stock. An increased share of investment leaves less for improvements in consumption, in the supply of social services, and for defense. Indeed the share of (gross) investment increased in the Soviet Union to more than 30 percent of GNP, and this kept down the rate of growth of the capital stock and thus of output. Furthermore, with the earlier drying up of increments of labor, Soviet growth was driven for a time, still extensively, by capital alone. This in turn forced the system to always substitute capital for labor, a difficult task by itself, more so when no new technology is offered. The outcome was further decline in productivity of capital and of growth.

The early mobilization of labor and capital inputs at the cost of their future decline is part of a general policy of haste by the Soviet leadership, which was frustrated by declining growth, the inability to provide for defense and other needs, and the failure of partial reforms. In addition to the above, there were also overuses of natural resources, over-pumping of oil at the expense of future output, neglect of maintenance of infrastructure and of the capital stock, and imposition of taut plans that forced producers to cut corners and neglect longer-term considerations. Initally this policy of haste produced some incremental growth but at a cost of lower growth later. The results of the policy of haste spilled over to the transition period in the form of major obstacles for renewed economic growth.

The heavy military burden was another significant factor adversely affecting Soviet growth. Early on the Soviet Union was threatened and then attacked by Germany, and following World War II engaged in the Cold War. Throughout the entire period it had to match the military capabilities of larger and more advanced economies, hence to set aside a higher share of its output for defense. During the Soviet system's last decades this share grew to around 15 percent of GNP. This amount was unprecedented in peacetime. The real defense burden was even heavier than shown by the figures because the defense effort forced the leaders to give priority to defense, in both routine production and in technological efforts, thereby disrupting civilian production and depriving it of significant technological innovation.

Additional causes of declining growth over time were the deterioration of work motivation and discipline, increasing corruption and illegal activities, declining improvements in the standard of living, and weakening legitimization of the regime. Collective agriculture, the cornerstone of the communist system, became the millstone around its neck.

See also: ECONOMIC GROWTH, EXTENSIVE; ECONOMIC GROWTH, INTENSIVE; FIVE-YEAR PLANS; INDUSTRIALIZATION, RAPID; MARXISM; NET MATERIAL PRODUCT

BIBLIOGRAPHY

Bergson, Abram. (1961). *The Real National Income of Soviet Russia since 1928.* Cambridge, MA: Harvard University Press.

Domar, Evsey. (1957). "A Soviet Model of Growth." In *Essays in the Theory of Economic Growth.* New York: Oxford University Press.

Easterly, William, and Fischer, Stanley. (1995). "The Soviet Economic Decline: Historical and Republican Data." *World Bank Economic Review* 9(3):341–371.

Maddison, Angus. (2001). *The World Economy: A Millennial Perspective.* Paris: Development Centre of the Organisation for Economic Co-operation and Development.

Nove, Alec. (1993). *Economic History of the USSR, 1917–1991,* rev. ed. New York: Penguin.

Ofer, Gur. (1987). "Soviet Economic Growth, 1928–1985." *Journal of Economic Literature* 25(4):1767–1833.

Ofer, Gur. (1996). "Decelerating Economic Growth under Socialism: The Soviet Case." In *The Wealth of Nations in the Twentieth Century: The Policies and Institutional Determinants of Economic Development,* ed. Ramon Myers. Stanford, CA: Hoover Institution Press.

GUR OFER

ECONOMIC REFORM COMMISSION

The State Commission on Economic Reform, chaired by economist and vice premier Leonid Abalkin, was created in July 1989. The first fruit of its work was a background report written for a conference on radical economic reform held October 30–November 1, 1989, in Moscow. This document was very radical by soviet standards. It argued, "We are not talking about improving the existing economic mechanism, nor about merely replacing its outdated parts. One internally consistent system must be dismantled and replaced by another one, also internally consistent and thus incompatible with the previous one."

In April 1990 Abalkin and Yuri Maslyukov (chairman of Gosplan) presented to the Presidential Council a program for a rapid transition to the market. This program drew attention to the costs involved in economic reform (e.g., open inflation, decline in production, closing of inefficient enterprises, fall in living standards, increased inequality). Most likely the program was rejected because of its honesty in discussing the costs of rapid marketization. The program officially adopted in May was substantially more conservative.

From May to August of 1990 two teams were working on economic reform programs, one headed by Abalkin and one headed by Stanislav Shatalin. The latter produced the Five-Hundred-Day Plan. Mikhail Gorbachev did not commit himself to either. He asked Abel Aganbegyan to merge the two documents. This compromise was adopted at the Congress of People's Deputies in December 1990. Abalkin was dissatisfied by these events and resigned effective February 1991.

See also: GORBACHEV, MIKHAIL SERGEYEVICH

BIBLIOGRAPHY

Ellman, Michael, and Kontorovich, Vladimir, eds. (1998). *The Destruction of the Soviet Economic System: An Insiders' History.* Armonk, NY: M. E.Sharpe.

Hough, Jerry. (1997). *Democratization and Revolution in the USSR, 1985–1991.* Washington, DC: Brookings Institution Press.

MICHAEL ELLMAN

ECONOMISM

The label applied to a group of moderate Russian Social Democrats at the end of the nineteenth and the beginning of the twentieth century.

An offshoot of the legal Marxists, the economist group emphasized the role of practical activity among industrial workers. According to their theories, activism at the rank-and-file level would lead to social change: Agitation for a ten–hour day, limitation on fines for petty infractions, better sanitation in the workplace, and so forth would ignite conflict with tsarist officialdom. Class conflict would provoke revolutionary political demands and eventually lead to a bourgeois–liberal revolution, which all Russian Marxists of the time thought necessary before the advent of socialism. For the time being, though, these economist Marxists were willing to follow worker demands rather than impose an explicitly socialist agenda on the laboring class. Workers involved themselves in strikes, mutual aid societies, and consumer and educational societies to raise their class consciousness. Thus this faction criticized the leading role assigned to the revolutionary intelligentsia by scientific Marxists such as Georgy Plekhanov and Pavel Axelrod.

Organized as the Union of Social Democrats Abroad, the economists published the newspaper *Rabochaia Mysl* from 1897 to 1902 in St. Petersburg, Berlin, and Warsaw. While mostly concerned with worker grievances and local conditions, this newspaper (at first produced by St. Petersburg workers) did bring out a "Separate Supplement" in issue 7, written by Konstantin Takhtarev, that was critical of the more radical Marxists. The economists also sponsored the journal with a more political and theoretical character: *Rabochee Delo,* published from 1899 to 1902 in Switzerland. Economism is sometimes linked to the leading German revisionist Marxist Eduard Bernstein (1850–1932).

In 1899 one of the economists, Yekaterina Kuskova, wrote a "Credo," which came to the attention of Vladimir Ilich Lenin, who penned a protest the same year. That group's practical and local emphasis continued to be attacked, somewhat unfairly, by Lenin and his supporters in *Iskra* (Spark) and later in "What Is to Be Done?" (1902). Lenin argued that the opportunist notions of economism, as opposed to his revolutionary activism, justified a split in Russian Social Democracy the following year.

Several of the leading economists, for example, Sergei Prokopovich, later became liberals, like the more famous legal Marxist Peter Struve. Both Prokopovich and Kuskova became anticommunists and participated in an emergency relief committee during the 1920–1921 famine. Soon afterward they were arrested in the general crackdown on Lenin's opponents.

See also: LENIN, VLADIMIR ILICH; MARXISM

BIBLIOGRAPHY

Harding, Neil. (1977). *Lenin's Political Thought,* vol. 1. London: Macmillan.

Lenin, Vladimir Ilich. (1978). *Collected Works,* vol. 4. Moscow: Progress Publishers.

MARTIN C. SPECHLER

ECONOMY, POST-SOVIET

Establishing a market economy and achieving strong economic growth remained Russia's primary concerns for more than a decade after the breakup of the Soviet Union in 1991. By the middle of the decade, Russia had made considerable progress toward creating the institutions of a market economy. Although the process of privatization was flawed, a vast shift of property rights away from the state toward individuals and the corporate sector occurred. The main success of economic reforms were macroeconomic stabilization (gaining control over the inflation, relative reduction of government deficit, and so forth) as well as initial steps toward creating a modern financial system for allocating funds according to market criteria. The banking system was privatized, and both debt and equity markets emerged. There was an effort to use primarily domestic markets to finance the government debt.

In contrast to other ex-Soviet countries in Central Europe, Russia could not quickly overcome the initial output decline at the beginning of market reforms. Russia's economy contracted for five years as the reformers appointed by President Boris Yeltsin hesitated over the implementation of the basic foundations of a market economy. Russia achieved a slight recovery in 1997 (GDP growth of 1%), but stubborn budget deficits and the country's poor business climate made it vulnerable when the global financial crisis began in 1997. The August 1998 financial crisis signaled the fragility of the Russian market economy and the difficulties policymakers encountered under imperfect market conditions.

The crisis sent the entire banking system into chaos. Many banks became insolvent and shut down. Others were taken over by the government and heavily subsidized. The crisis culminated in August 1998 with depreciation of the ruble, a debt default by the government, and a sharp deterioration in living standards for most of the population. For the year 1998, GDP experienced a 5 percent decline. The economy rebounded in 1999 and 2000 (GDP grew by 5.4% in 1999 and 8.3% in 2000), primarily due to the weak ruble and a surging trade surplus fueled by rising world oil prices. This recovery, along with renewed government effort in 2000 to advance lagging structural reforms, raised business and investor confidence concerning Russia's future prospects. GDP is expected to grow by over 5.5 percent in 2001 and average 3–4 percent (depending on world oil prices) from 2002 through 2005. In 2003 Russia remained heavily dependent on exports of commodities, particularly oil, natural gas, metals, and timber, which accounted for over 80 percent of its exports, leaving the country vulnerable to swings in world prices. Macroeconomic stability and the improved business climate can easily deteriorate with changes in export commodity prices and excessive ruble appreciation. Additionally, inflation remained high according to international standards: From 1992 to 2000, Russia's average annual rate of inflation was 38 percent. Russia's agricultural sector remained beset by uncertainty over land ownership rights, which discouraged needed investment and restructuring. The industrial base was increasingly dilapidated and needed to be replaced or modernized if the country was to achieve sustainable economic growth.

Three basic factors caused Russia's transition difficulties, including the absence of broad-based political support for reform, inability to close the gap between available public resources and government spending, and inability to push forward systematically with structural reforms. Russia's second president, Vladimir Putin, elected in March 2000, advocated a strong state and market economy, but the success of his agenda was challenged by his reliance on security forces and ex-KGB associates, the lack of progress on legal reform, widespread corruption, and the ongoing war in Chechnya. Despite tax reform, the black market continued to account for a substantial share of GDP. In addition, Putin presented balanced budgets, enacted a flat 13 percent personal income tax, replaced the head of the giant Gazprom natural gas monopoly with a personally loyal executive, and pushed through a reform plan for the natural electricity monopoly. The fiscal burden improved. The cabinet enacted a new program for economic reform in July 2000, but progress was undermined by the lack of banking reform and the large state presence in the economy. After the 1998 crisis, banking services once again became concentrated in the state-owned banks, which lend mainly to the business sector. In 2000 state banks strengthened their dominant role in the sector, benefiting from special privileges such as preferential funding sources, capital injections, and implicit state guarantees. Cumulative foreign direct investment since 1991 amounted to $17.6 billion by July 2001, compared with over $350 billion in China during the same period. A new law on foreign investments enacted in July 1999 granted national treatment to foreign investors except in sectors involving national security. Foreigners were allowed to establish wholly owned companies (although the registration process can be cumbersome) and take part in the privatization process. An ongoing concern of foreign investors was property rights protection: Government intervention increased in scope as the enforcement agencies and officials in the attorney general's office attempted to re-examine privatization outcomes. The most significant barriers to foreign investment and sustainable economic growth continued to be the weak rule of law, poor infrastructure, legal uncertainty, widespread corruption and crime, capital flight, and brain drain (skilled professionals emigrating from Russia).

See also: BLACK MARKET; FOREIGN DEBT; PUTIN, VLADIMIR VLADIMIROVICH; RUSSIAN FEDERATION

BIBLIOGRAPHY

Gregory, Paul R., and Stuart, Robert C. (2001). *Russian and Soviet Economic Performance and Structure.* Boston, MA: Addison Wesley.

Gustafson, Thane. (1999). *Capitalism Russian-style.* Cambridge, UK: Cambridge University Press.

PAUL R. GREGORY

ECONOMY, TSARIST

The economy of the Russian Empire in the early twentieth century was a complicated hybrid of traditional peasant agriculture and modern industry. The empire's rapidly growing population (126 million in 1897, nearly 170 million by 1914) was overwhelmingly rural. Only about 15 percent of the population lived in towns, and fewer than 10 percent worked in industry. Agriculture, the largest sector of the economy, provided the livelihood for 80 percent of the population and was dominated by peasants, whose traditional household economies were extremely inefficient compared to agriculture in Western Europe or the United States. But small islands of modern industrial capitalism, brought into being by state policy, coexisted with the primitive rural economy. Spurts of rapid industrialization in the 1890s and in the years before World War I created high rates of economic growth and increased national wealth but also set in motion destabilizing social changes. Despite its islands of modernity, the Russian Empire lagged far behind advanced capitalist countries like Great Britain and Germany, and was unable to bear the economic strains of World War I.

The country's agricultural backwardness was rooted in the economic and cultural consequences of serfdom, and it was reinforced by the government's conservative policies before the Revolution of 1905. The Emancipation Act of 1861, while nominally freeing the peasantry from bondage, sought to limit change by shoring up the village communes. In most places the commune continued to control the amount of land allotted to each household. Land allotments were divided into scattered strips and subject to periodic redistribution based on the number of workers in each household; and it was very difficult for individual peasants to leave the commune entirely and move into another area of the economy, although increasing numbers worked as seasonal labor outside their villages (*otkhodniki*). Rapid population growth only worsened the situation, for as the number of peasants increased, the size of land allotments diminished, creating a sense of land hunger.

Most peasants lived as their ancestors had, at or near the margin of subsistence. Agricultural productivity was constrained by the peasantry's lack of capital and knowledge or inclination to use modern technology and equipment; most still sowed, harvested, and threshed by hand, and half used a primitive wooden plow. In 1901 a third of peasant households did not have a horse. Poverty was widespread in the countryside. Items such as meat and vegetable oil were rarely seen on the table of a typical peasant household.

After the 1905 revolution the government of Peter Stolypin (minister of the interior, later premier) enacted a series of laws designed to reform agriculture by decreasing the power of the village communes: Individual peasant heads of households were permitted to withdraw from the commune and claim private ownership of their allotment land; compulsory repartitioning of the land was abolished and peasants could petition for consolidation of their scattered strips of land into a single holding. However, bureaucratic processes moved slowly. When World War I began, only about one-quarter of the peasants had secured individual ownership of their allotment land and only 10 percent had consolidated their strips. While these changes allowed some peasants (the so-called kulaks) to adopt modern practices and become prosperous, Russian agriculture remained backward and underemployment in the countryside remained the rule. In increasing numbers peasants took out passports for seasonal work, many performing unskilled jobs in industry.

Industrialization accelerated in the 1890s, pushed forward by extensive state intervention under the guidance of Finance Minister Sergei Witte. He used subsidies and direct investment to stimulate expansion of heavy industry, imposed high taxes and tariffs, and put Russia on the gold standard in order to win large-scale foreign investment.

Although the process slowed from 1900 through the 1905 revolution, it soon picked up again and was very strong from 1910 to the outbreak of the war. The rate of growth in the 1890s is estimated to have been an impressive 8 percent a year. While the growth rate after 1910 was slightly lower (about 6%), the process of economic development was broader and the government's role diminished.

Railroad construction, so critical to economic development, increased greatly toward the end of the nineteenth century with the construction of the Trans-Siberian Railroad and then rose another 20 percent from 1903 to 1914. Although the number of miles of track per square mile and per capita was the lowest in Europe, the railroad-building boom stimulated great expansion in the related industries of iron and steel, coal, and machine building.

Industrial production came to be concentrated in large plants constructed during the period of rapid industrialization. In 1914, 56 percent of the employees in manufacturing worked in enterprises that employed five hundred or more workers, and 40 percent in plants employing one thousand or more workers. Such large-scale production frequently incorporated the most up-to-date technology. In a number of key industries production was concentrated in a few large oligopolies.

Starting in the later 1890s foreign investment became an important factor in the economy. In 1914 it amounted to one-third of total capital investment in Russian industry, most of it in mining, metallurgy, banking, and textiles. France, England, and Germany were the primary sources of foreign capital. Foreign trade policy was dominated by protectionism. Tariffs just before the war averaged an astonishing 30 to 38 percent of the aggregate value of imports, two to six times higher than in the world's most developed economies. Predictably, this led to higher prices.

Russia was highly dependent on Western imports of manufactured goods, largely from Germany. Raw materials, such as cotton, wool, silk, and nonferrous metals, comprised about 50 percent of all imports. Exports were dominated by grains and other foodstuffs (55% of the total). Russia was the world's largest grain exporter, supplying Western Europe with about one-third of its wheat imports and about 50 percent of its other grains.

The productivity of labor was extremely low because of the deficient capital endowment per worker. In 1913 horsepower per industrial worker in Russia was about 60 percent of that per worker in England and one-third the level per an American worker. In addition, many industrial workers were still connected to their villages and spent part of their time farming. Because of these factors the costs of production were considerably higher in Russian industry than in Western Europe.

Russian workers faced wretched working conditions and long hours with little social protection. Wages were so low that virtually the entire income of a household went to pay for basic necessities. Living space was meager and miserable, and there were few if any educational opportunities. In the face of these circumstances, some turned to self-help, and the cooperative movement made rapid advances. Many workers began to organize despite the restrictions on trade unions even after the Revolution of 1905. The labor movement renewed its efforts in the years before the war, combining political and economic demands. From 1912 strikes rose dramatically until in the first half of 1914 almost 1.5 million workers went on strike.

The tsarist economy collapsed under the strain of World War I, inhibited by political as well as economic limitations from meeting the demands of total economic mobilization and undermined by bad fiscal policy that led to destructive inflation. But part of the collapse must be traced to prewar roots. Chief among these was the still unresolved legacy of the old serf system: an agricultural system that was inefficient and inflexible, lacking in capital and technology, heavily taxed, and, as a result, unable to provide a reasonable standard of living for a rapidly growing population. Of near equal importance were the consequences of the rapid industrialization in the two decades before the war. Industrialization created the possibility of escaping the limits of the agricultural system, but the way it was carried out imposed most of the costs on the common people and uprooted peasants from the old society before the institutions and policies of a new society had been created.

See also: AGRICULTURE; GRAIN TRADE; KULAKS; INDUSTRIALIZATION, RAPID; PEASANTRY; STOLYPIN, PETER ARKADIEVICH; TRADE UNIONS; WITTE, SERGEI YULIEVICH

BIBLIOGRAPHY

Dobb, Maurice H. (1948). *Soviet Economic Development since 1917.* New York: International Publishers.

Gerschenkron, Alexander. (1962). *Economic Backwardness in Historical Perspective.* Cambridge, MA: Harvard University Press.

Gregory, Paul R. (1994). *Before Command: An Economic History of Russia from Emancipation to the First Five-Year Plan.* Princeton, NJ: Princeton University Press.

Mosse, Werner E. (1996). *An Economic History of Russia, 1856–1914.* London: Tauris.

CAROL GAYLE
WILLIAM MOSKOFF

EDINONACHALIE

The one-person management principle used in the Soviet economy to assign responsibility for the operation and performance of economic units, from industrial enterprises and R&D institutes to ministries and state committees.

Under edinonachalie, the head (*rukovoditel* or *edinonachalnik*) of each administrative unit issued all directives and took full responsibility for the results the organization achieved. Edinonachalie was a key feature of the Soviet management system from the beginning of central planning in the early 1930s. It did not literally mean, however, that one person made every decision. In industrial ministries, major manufacturing plants, and other large organizations, deputies or other subordinates who specialized in one or another sphere of operations were authorized to make decisions in their designated areas of expertise on behalf of the head of the organization. Moreover, although fully responsible for the organization's performance, the edinonachalnik was obliged to work with a consultative group of deputies, department heads, workers, and other technical personnel. This group could make decisions and give advice, but their decisions could only be implemented by the edinonachalnik, who, in both principle and practice, was free to ignore their advice.

Edinonachalie made enterprise managers responsible for the collective of workers and the outcome of the production process because it gave them the authority to direct the capital, material, and labor resources of the firm within the constraints of the targets and norms in the annual enterprise plan (*techpromfinplan*). Since the plan was law in the Soviet economy, this identified the manager as the person to punish if the plan was not fulfilled.

The concentration of decision-making authority and responsibility in the hands of the head of the administrative unit was based upon a strict hierarchical order. Subordinates to the edinonachalnik could not deal directly with higher authorities, although they could report to higher authorities that their superior was violating laws or rules.

See also: ENTERPRISE, SOVIET; TECHPROMFINPLAN

BIBLIOGRAPHY

Kuromiya, Hiroaki. (1984). "*Edinonchalie* and the Soviet Industrial Manager, 1928–1937." *Soviet Studies* 36:185–204.

Kushnirsky, Fyodor. (1982). *Soviet Economic Planning, 1965–1980.* Boulder, CO: Westview Press.

Malle, Silvana. (1985). *The Economic Organization of War Communism, 1918–1921.* Cambridge, UK: Cambridge University Press.

SUSAN J. LINZ

EDUCATION

Education and literacy were highly politicized issues in both Imperial and Soviet Russia, tied closely to issues of modernization and the social order. The development of an industrialized society and modern state bureaucracy required large numbers of literate and educated citizens. During the Imperial period, state officials faced what one scholar has dubbed "the dilemma of education": how to utilize education without undermining Russia's autocratic government. During the early Soviet period, on the other hand, the Bolsheviks attempted to use the education system as a tool of social engineering, as they attempted to invert the old social hierarchy. In both cases, the questions of which citizens should be educated and what type of education they should receive were as important as the actual material they were to be taught.

THE EDUCATION SYSTEM IN IMPERIAL RUSSIA, 1700–1917

Before 1700, Russia had no secular educational system. Literacy, defined here as the ability to comprehend unfamiliar texts, was generally taught in the home. Although there was a considerable spike upwards in literacy in seventeenth-century Muscovy, the overall percentage of literate Russians remained low. In 1700 no more than 13 percent of the urban male population could read—for male peasants, the rate was between 2 and 4 percent.

The Communist Party brought free education and mass literacy to the Soviet people. © DAVID TURNLEY/CORBIS

This was well below Western European literacy rates, which exceeded 50 percent among urban men. The hostility of many Orthodox officials towards education and the absence of a substantial urban class of burghers and artisans were two factors that contributed to Russia's comparatively low literacy rates.

Like many aspects of Russian society, the educational system was introduced and developed by the state. Peter I opened the first secular schools—institutes for training specialists, such as navigators and doctors—as part of his plan to turn Russia into a modern state. A number of important institutions, such as Moscow University (1755), were created in the next decades, but it was not until 1786 that a ruler (Catherine II) attempted to create a regular system of primary and secondary schools.

This was only the first of many such plans initiated by successive tsars. The frequent reorganization of the school system was disruptive, and since new types of schools were opened in addition to, rather than in place of, existing schools, the situation became quite chaotic over time. This confusion was compounded by the fact that many schools lay outside the jurisdiction of the Ministry of Education, which was created in 1802. Other state ministries regularly opened their own schools, ranging from technical institutes to primary schools, and the Holy Synod sponsored extensive networks of parochial schools. As a result, there were sixty-seven different types of primary schools in Russia in 1914.

Most schools fell into one of three categories: primary, secondary, or higher education. Primary schools were intended to provide students with basic literacy, numeracy, and a smattering of general knowledge. As late as 1911, less than 20 percent of primary school students went on to further study. Many secondary schools were also terminal, often with a vocational emphasis. Other secondary schools, such as gymnasia, prepared students for higher education. Higher education encompassed a variety of institutions, including universities and professional institutes.

From Peter I onward, the Russian state devoted a disproportionate amount of its educational spending on higher education. This was partly due to the pressing need for specialists, and partly because these institutions catered to social and economic elites. Ambitious plans notwithstanding, Russia developed a top-heavy educational system, which produced a relatively small number of well-educated individuals, but which failed to offer any educational opportunities to most Russians until the end of the nineteenth century. The number of primary school students in Russia grew from 450,000 in 1856 to 1 million in 1878 to 6.6 million in 1911; even then, there were still not enough spaces for all who wanted to enroll.

Access to education was, as a rule, better in cities and large towns than in rural areas, though it was still limited in even the largest cities until the 1870s. In 1911, 67 percent of urban youth aged eight to eleven were enrolled in primary schools (75% of boys, 59% of girls). In the countryside, the school system developed more slowly. Many rural schools opened before the 1870s were short-lived, and it was only in the 1890s that a concerted effort began to establish an extensive network of permanent rural schools. In 1911, 41 percent of rural children aged eight to eleven were enrolled in primary school (58% of boys, 24% of girls). Peasants in different areas had different attitudes about education, and there has been some dispute about how useful literacy was considered by rural populations.

The better access to education in urban areas is reflected in literacy statistics. The literacy rate among the urban population (over age nine) was roughly 21 percent in 1797 (29% of men, 12% of women); 40 percent in 1847 (50% of men, 28% of women); 58 percent in 1897; and 70 percent in 1917 (80% of men, 61% of women). In rural areas, the literacy rate was 6 percent in 1797 (6% of men, 5% of women); 12 percent in 1847 (16% of men, 9% of women); 26 percent in 1897; and 38 percent in 1917 (53% of men, 23% of women).

SOCIAL AND CULTURAL ASPECTS OF IMPERIAL EDUCATION POLICIES

While military and economic needs forced the Russian state to create an educational system, social and political considerations also played a role in shaping it. Tsars and their advisers carefully considered who should be educated, how long they should study, and what they should be taught. Above all, they were concerned about the educational policy's impact on Russia's political system and social hierarchy, both of which they wanted to preserve.

This was evident in the higher educational system, which was shaped to a degree by the tsars' desire to maintain social order and the nobility's support. Special institutes, such as the Corp of Cadets (1731), were created exclusively for the sons of hereditary nobles. While non-nobles were not barred from higher education (with a few exceptions), the very nature of the Russian school system made it difficult for such students to qualify for advanced institutions. Escalating student fees at gymnasia and universities in the nineteenth century provided an additional barrier.

Just as the nobility's position had to be defended, the lower classes had to be protected from "too much knowledge." Nicholas I and his Education Minister Sergei Uvarov (1831–1849) believed that excessive education would only create dissatisfaction among the peasantry. Accordingly, they placed strict limits on the curriculum and duration of rural primary schools. But they also increased the number of such schools, since they understood that basic literacy was of social and economic value. Uvarov, like many other Russian pedagogues, saw education as an opportunity to instill in young Russians loyalty to the tsar and proper moral values. A centrally controlled school inspectorate was created to ensure that teachers were imparting the right values to their students. All textbooks also required state approval.

Schools were used in other ways to maintain or modify the social order. A separate school system was created for Russia's Jews, and strict limits were placed on the number of Jewish students admitted into higher educational institutions. In the annexed Western provinces, schools were used as a weapon in the aggressive Russification campaign of the 1890s. And while most primary and secondary schools were coeducational, higher educational institutions were not. Separate women's institutes were only opened in 1876, and Russia's first coed university, the private Shaniavsky University, was established in 1908.

In order to prevent the circulation of subversive ideas, the state placed strict limits on private and philanthropic educational endeavors. In the 1830s all private educational institutions and tutors were placed under state supervision. The activities of volunteer movements trying to provide adult education, such as the Sunday School Move-

Moscow State University—the Soviet Harvard—rises above the Lenin Hills. © PAUL ALMASY/CORBIS

ment (1859–1862), were severely constrained, though zemstvos (local governmental bodies) were later allowed more leeway in this area. Alarm over the proliferation of unofficial (and illegal) peasant schools helped motivate the state's expansion of its rural education system in the 1890s.

Ironically, it was the educated elite the state had created that ultimately challenged the tsar's authority. Discontent became widespread in the 1840s, as large segments of educated society came to see state policies as retrograde and harmful to the peasantry. Frustrated by the conservative bureaucracy's disregard of their ideas, many educated Russians began to question the legitimacy of the autocratic form of government, with a small number of them becoming revolutionaries. This was one reason why the tsarist government found itself with little support among educated Russians in February 1917.

Even as educated society was becoming estranged from the autocracy, its members were growing distant from the masses they wished to help. As educated Russians adopted Western values and ideas, a vast cultural and social divide developed between them and the mostly uneducated peasantry, which largely retained traditional beliefs and culture. The growth of the education system in the last decades before 1917 was starting to bridge this gap, but the inability of these groups to understand one another contributed to the violence and chaos of 1917. Scholars debate whether a more rapid introduction of mass education into late Imperial Russia would have stabilized or further destabilized the existing order.

EDUCATION IN THE SOVIET UNION

While the Bolsheviks shared their tsarist predecessors' belief in education's potential social and political power, they had a different agenda: swift industrialization, social change, and the dissemination of socialist values. Although they lacked an educational policy upon seizing power, the Bolsheviks pledged to make education accessible to all, coeducational at all levels, and to achieve full literacy.

The Russian Republic's educational system was placed under the control of the Russian Commissariat of Enlightenment (*Narodnyi kommisariat prosveshcheniia,* or Narkompros), a republic-level institution created in October 1917. Its first leader was Anatoly Lunacharsky (r. 1917–1929). Like all Soviet institutions, Narkompros was controlled by the Communist Party. Before 1920, however, it had little authority. Many instructors had supported the Provisional Government's moderate reform program, and they refused to cooperate with the Bolsheviks. During the civil war (1918–1921), education was under the control of local authorities.

After 1920, Narkompros' officials tried to implement the ideas of progressive pedagogues, such as John Dewey, in primary and secondary schools. Their attempts were largely unsuccessful, hampered by a lack of funds and teacher opposition. Narkompros also faced challenges from the economic commissariats, which eventually took control of vocational education. This was the first round in a decades-long debate over the roles of general and vocational education. Teachers were frequently harassed by members of the Leninist Youth League (Komsomol).

Bolshevik higher educational policies were even more ambitious. Most members of educated society did not support the communists. Bolshevik leaders responded by creating a "red intelligentsia" to replace them. The children of "socially alien" groups were largely excluded from higher education, their places taken by young, poorly educated workers and peasants, known as *vydvizhentsy.* The number of technical institutes was expanded to accommodate the rapid growth of industry. A network of communist higher educational institutions was also opened. The influx of vydvizhentsy into higher education, and the persecution of "socially alien" teachers and students at all levels, climaxed during the cultural revolution (1928–1932). It has been argued that the vydvizhentsy, many of whom rose to prominent positions, provided an important base of support for Stalin's regime.

After 1932, experimental approaches were abandoned in favor of more practical teaching methods. Primary schools were returned to a more traditional curriculum, class-based preferences ended, and the separate communist educational system eliminated. The minimum duration of schooling was raised from four to seven years. Schools were now open to all students, though children whose parents were arrested faced serious discrimination until Stalin's death in 1953. Most of Narkompros' functions were transferred to the new Ministry of Education in 1946.

By the late 1950s, all children had access to a free education. Social mobility was possible on the basis of merit, although inequalities still existed. Children of the emerging Soviet elites often had access to superior secondary schools, which prepared them for higher education. Members of some non-Russian ethnic minorities had spaces reserved for them at prestigious higher educational institutions, as part of the Soviet Union's unique affirmative action program. After the 1950s, however, unofficial quotas again limited Jewish students' access to higher education.

There were also numerous adult education programs in the Soviet Union. These ranged from utopian attempts to train artists during the civil war to ongoing literacy campaigns. Literacy rates continued their steady rise after 1917 (88% in 1939, and 98% in 1959). Adult education programs were run by many groups, including the trade unions and the Red Army.

Soviet schools were expected to teach students loyalty to the state and instill them with socialist values; teachers who did otherwise were liable to arrest or dismissal. Political material was a constant part of Soviet curricula. In some periods, it was restricted mainly to the social sciences and obligatory study of Marxism-Leninism. During Stalin's rule, however, almost every subject was politicized. Rote memorization was common and student creativity discouraged.

Despite its flaws, the Soviet educational system achieved some impressive successes. The heavily subsidized system produced millions of well-trained professionals and scientists in its last decades. After 1984 the state began to loosen its grip on education, allowing teachers some flexibility. These tentative steps were quickly overtaken by events, however. Since 1991 the Russian school system has faced serious funding problems and declining facilities. Control of education has been transferred to regional authorities.

See also: ACADEMY OF ARTS; ACADEMY OF SCIENCE; HIGHER PARTY SCHOOL; LANGUAGE LAWS; LUNARCHSKY, ANATOLY VASILIEVICH; NATIONAL LIBRARY OF RUSSIA; RUSSIAN STATE LIBRARY

BIBLIOGRAPHY

Black, J. L. (1979). *Citizens for the Fatherland: Education, Educators, and Pedagogical Ideals in Eighteenth Century Russia.* Boulder, CO: East European Quarterly.

Brooks, Jeffrey. (1985). *When Russia Learned to Read: Literacy and Popular Culture, 1861–1917.* Princeton, NJ: Princeton University Press.

David-Fox, Michael. (1997). *Revolution of the Mind: Higher Learning Among the Bolsheviks, 1918–1929.* Ithaca: Cornell University Press.

Dunstan, John, ed. (1992). *Soviet Education under Perestroika.* London: Routledge.

Eklof, Ben. (1986). *Russian Peasant Schools: Officialdom, Village Culture, and Popular Pedagogy, 1861–1914.* Berkeley: University of California Press.

Fitzpatrick, Sheila. (1979). *Education and Social Mobility in the Soviet Union, 1921–1934.* Cambridge, UK: Cambridge University Press.

Hans, Nicholas. (1964). *History of Russian Educational Policy, 1701–1917.* New York: Russell & Russell, Inc.

Holmes, Larry E. (1991). *The Kremlin and the Schoolhouse: Reforming Education in Soviet Russia, 1917–1931.* Bloomington: Indiana University Press.

Kassow, Samuel D. (1989). *Students, Professors, and the State in Tsarist Russia.* Berkeley: University of California Press.

Marker, Gary. (1990). "Literacy and Literacy Texts in Muscovy: A Reconsideration." *Slavic Review* 49(1): 74–84.

Matthews, Mervyn. (1982). *Education in the Soviet Union: Policies and Education Since Stalin.* London: Allen & Unwin.

McClelland, James C. (1979). *Autocrats and Academics: Education, Culture, and Society in Tsarist Russia.* Chicago: University of Chicago Press.

Mironov, Boris N. (1991). "The Development of Literacy in Russia and the USSR from the Tenth to the Twentieth Centuries." *History of Education Quarterly* 31(2): 229–251.

Sinel, Allen. (1973). *The Classroom and the Chancellery: State Educational Reform in Russia under Count Dmitry Tolstoi.* Cambridge, MA: Harvard University Press.

Webber, Stephen L. (2000). *School, Reform, and Society in the New Russia.* New York: St. Martin's Press.

Whittaker, Cynthia H. (1984). *The Origins of Modern Russian Education: An Intellectual Biography of Count Sergei Uvarov.* DeKalb: Northern Illinois University Press.

BRIAN KASSOF

EHRENBURG, ILYA GRIGOROVICH

(1891–1967), poet, journalist, novelist.

Ilya Grigorovich Ehrenburg was an enigma. Essentially Western in taste, he was at times the spokesman for the Soviet Union, the great anti-Western power of his age. He involved himself with Bolsheviks beginning in 1907, writing pamphlets and doing some organizational work, and then, after his arrest, fled to Paris, where he would spend most of the next thirty years. In the introduction to his first major work, and probably his life's best work, the satirical novel *Julio Jurentino* (1922), his good friend Nikolai Bukharin described Ehrenburg's liminal existence, saying that he was not a Bolshevik, but "a man of broad vision, with a deep insight into the Western European way of life, a sharp eye, and an acid tongue" (Goldberg, 1984, p. 5). These characteristics probably kept him alive during the Josef Stalin years, along with his service to the USSR as a war correspondent and spokesman in the anticosmopolitan campaign. Arguably, his most important service to the USSR came in the period after Stalin's death, when his novel *The Thaw* (1956) deviated from the norms of Socialist Realism. His activities in Writer's Union politics consistently pushed a kind of socialist literature (and life) "with a human face," and his memoirs, printed serially during the early 1960s, were culled by thaw-generation youth for inspiration. When Stalin was alive, Ehrenburg may well have proven a coward. After his death, he proved much more courageous than most.

See also: BUKHARIN, NIKOLAI IVANOVICH; JEWS; WORLD WAR II

BIBLIOGRAPHY

Goldberg, Anatol. (1984). *Ilya Ehrenburg: Writing, Politics, and the Art of Survival.* London: Weidenfeld and Nicolson.

Johnson, Priscilla. (1965). *Khrushchev and the Arts: The Politics of Soviet Culture, 1962–1964.* Cambridge, MA: M.I.T. Press.

JOHN PATRICK FARRELL

EISENSTEIN, SERGEI MIKHAILOVICH

(1898–1948), film director, film theorist, teacher, arts administrator, and producer.

Sergei Eisenstein, born in Riga, was the most accomplished of Russia's first generation of Soviet filmmakers. Eisenstein both benefited from the communist system of state patronage and suffered the frustrations and dangers all artists faced in functioning under state control.

Acclaimed film director Sergei Eisenstein. ARCHIVE PHOTOS, INC. REPRODUCED BY PERMISSION.

The October Revolution and the civil war allowed Eisenstein to embark on a career in theater and film. His first moving picture was *Glumov's Diary,* a short piece for a theatrical adaptation of an Alexander Ostrovsky comedy. Between 1924 and 1929 he made four feature-length films on revolutionary themes and with revolutionary cinematic techniques: *The Strike* (1924), *The Battleship Potemkin* (1926), *October* (1928), and *The General Line* (also known as *The Old and the New,* 1929). In *Potemkin* Eisenstein developed the rapid editing and dynamic shot composition known as *montage. Potemkin* made Eisenstein world-famous, but at the same time he became embroiled in polemics with others in the Soviet film community over the purpose of cinema in "the building of socialism." Eisenstein believed that film should educate rather than just entertain, but he also believed that avant-garde methods could be educational in socialist society. This support for avant-garde experimentation would be used against him during the far more dangerous cultural politics of the 1930s. His last two films of the 1920s, *The General Line* and *October,* were influenced by the increasing interference of powerful political leaders. All of Eisenstein's Russian films were state commissions, but Eisenstein never joined the Communist Party, and he continued to experiment even as he began to accommodate himself to political reality.

From 1929 to 1932 Eisenstein traveled abroad and had a stint in Hollywood. None of his three projects for Paramount Pictures, however, was put into production. The wealthy socialist writer Upton Sinclair rescued him from the impasse by offering to fund a film about Mexico, *Qué Viva México!* Eisenstein thrived in Mexico, but Sinclair became disgruntled when filming ran months over schedule and rumors of sexual escapades reached him. When Stalin threatened to banish Eisenstein permanently if he did not return to the Soviet Union, Sinclair seized the opportunity to pull the plug on *Qué Viva México!* Eisenstein never recovered the year's worth of footage and he was haunted by the loss for the rest of his life.

The Moscow that Eisenstein found on his return in May 1932 was more constricted and impoverished than the city he had left. His polemics of the 1920s were not forgotten, and Eisenstein was criticized by party hacks and old friends alike for being out of step and a formalist, which is to say he cared more about experiments with cinematic form than with making films "accessible to the masses." Political attacks on the director culminated in 1937, at the height of the Great Terror, as Eisenstein was nearing completion of *Bezhin Meadow*, his first film since returning from abroad. Boris Shumyatsky, chief of the Soviet film industry, had the production halted; he proceeded to denounce Eisenstein to the Central Committee and then directly to Stalin, inviting a death sentence on the filmmaker. After barely surviving this attack, and after ten years of blocked film projects, Eisenstein wrote the required self-criticism and was given the opportunity to make a historical film. *Alexander Nevsky*, a medieval military encounter between Russians and Germans, would become his most popular film; however, Eisenstein was ashamed of it, and except for its "battle on the ice," it is generally considered to be his least interesting in technical and intellectual terms. The success of *Alexander Nevsky* catapulted him to the highest of inner circles; he won both the Order of Lenin and, in 1941, the newly created Stalin Prize. Then, in a restructuring of the film industry, Eisenstein was made Artistic Director of Mosfilm, a prestigious and powerful position.

In 1941, just months before World War II began in Russia, Eisenstein accepted a state commission to make a film about the sixteenth-century tsar, Ivan the Terrible. He worked on *Ivan the Terrible* for the next six years, eventually completing only two parts of the planned trilogy. Eisenstein's masterpiece, *Ivan the Terrible* is a complex film containing a number of coordinated and conflicting narratives and networks of imagery that portray Ivan as a great leader, historically destined to found the Russian state but personally doomed by the murderous means he had used. *Part I* (1945) received a Stalin Prize, *Part II* (1946, released 1958) did not please Stalin and was banned.

Eisenstein was one of few practicing film directors to develop an important body of theoretical writing about cinema. In the 1920s he wrote about the psychological effect of montage on the viewer; the technique was intended to both startle the viewer into an awareness of the constructed nature of the work and to shape the viewing experience. During the 1930s, when he was barred from filmmaking, Eisenstein wrote and taught. A gifted teacher, he relied on his wide reading and sense of humor to draw students into the creative process. Work on *Ivan the Terrible* in the 1940s stimulated his most productive period of writing. He produced several volumes of theoretical works in *Method* and *Nonindifferent Nature*, as well as a large volume of memoirs. This work developed his earlier concept of montage by broadening its scope to include sound and color as well as imagery within the shot.

By nature Eisenstein was a private and cautious man. He could be charming and charismatic as well as serious and demanding, but these were public masks; he guarded his private life. It seems clear that he had sexual relationships with both men and women but also that these affairs were rare and short-lived; he consulted with psychoanalysts on several occasions about his bisexuality in the 1920s and 1930s. In 1934, just after a law was passed making male homosexuality illegal in the Soviet Union, Eisenstein married his good friend and assistant, Pera Atasheva. It is fair to say that Eisenstein's sexuality was a source of some dissatisfaction for him and that his private life in general brought him considerable pain. He suffered from periodic bouts of serious depression and from the 1930s onward his health was also threatened by heart disease and influenza.

Eisenstein suffered a serious heart attack just hours after finishing Part II of *Ivan the Terrible.* He never recovered the strength to return to film production, but he wrote extensively until the night of February 11, 1948, when he suffered a fatal heart attack.

See also: CENSORSHIP; MOTION PICTURES

BIBLIOGRAPHY

Bordwell, David. (1994). *The Cinema of Eisenstein.* Cambridge, MA: Harvard University Press.

Bulgakowa, Oksana. (2001). *Sergei Eisenstein: A Biography.* San Francisco: PotemkinPress.

Neuberger, Joan. (2003). *Ivan the Terrible: The Film Companion.* London: I. B. Tauris.

Taylor, Richard. (2002). *The Battleship Potemkin: The Film Companion.* London: I. B. Tauris.

Taylor, Richard. (2002). *October.* London: British Film Institute.

JOAN NEUBERGER

ELECTORAL COMMISSION

Electoral commissions play a large role in the organization and holding of elections under Russia's so-called guided democracy. They exist at four fundamental levels: precincts (approximately 95,000), territorial (TIK, 2,700), regional (RIK), and central (TsIK). There are also municipal commissions in some of the large cities, and there are district commissions for elections to the State Duma (around 190 to 225 districts according to Duma elections, minus those falling on a region's borders).

The central, regional, and territorial commissions are permanent bodies with four-year terms. The district and precinct commissions are organized one to three months before elections, and curtail their activity ten days after the publication of results.

The electoral commissions have from three to fifteen voting members, at least half of whom are appointed based on nominations by electoral associations with fractions in the Duma and by the regional legislatures. Half of the members of the regional electoral commissions are appointed by the regional executive, the other half by the legislative assembly. This means that for all practical matters the electoral commissions are under the control of the executive power. Parties, blocs, and candidates participating in elections may appoint one member of the electoral commission with consultative rights in the commission at their level and the levels below them. The precinct and territorial commissions are organized by the regional commissions with the participation of local government.

A new form of central electoral commission arose in 1993, when it was necessary to hold parliamentary elections and vote on a constitution in a short time. Officials considered the election deadlines unrealistic. At that time the president named all members of the commission and its chair. The central electoral commission has fifteen members and is organized on an equal footing by the Duma, the Federation Council, and the president. The central commission is essentially a Soviet institution, with the actual power, including control over the numerous apparatuses, concentrated in the hands of the chair. Between 2001 and 2003, an electoral vertical was established whereby the central commission can directly influence the lower-level commissions. The central commission names at least two members of the regional commission and nominates candidates for its head. Moreover, in the future the regional electoral commissions may be disbanded in favor of central commission representation (this mechanism was tested in 2003 with the Krasnoyarsk Krai electoral commission). The role of the central commission, and also of the Kremlin, in regional and local elections has grown significantly. The central commission's authority to interpret ambiguous legal clauses enables it to punish and pardon candidates, parties, electoral associations, and mass media organizations. As a bureaucratic structure, the central electoral commission has turned into a highly influential election ministry with an enormous budget and powerful leverage in relation to other federal and regional power structures and the entire political life of the country.

See also: DUMA; PRESIDENCY

BIBLIOGRAPHY

McFaul, Michael. (2001). *Russia's Unfinished Revolution: Political Change from Gorbachev to Putin.* Ithaca, NY: Cornell University Press.

McFaul, Michael, and Markov, Sergi. (1993). *The Troubled Birth of Russian Democracy: Parties, Personalities, and Programs.* Stanford, CA: Hoover Institution Press.

McFaul, Michael; Petrov, Nikolai; and Ryabov, Andrei, eds. (1999). *Primer on Russia's 1999 Duma Elections.* Washington, DC: Carnegie Endowment for International Peace.

Reddaway, Peter, and Glinski, Dmitri. (2001). *The Tragedy of Russia's Reforms: Market Bolshevism against Democracy.* Washington, DC: U.S. Institute of Peace Press.

NIKOLAI PETROV

ELECTRICITY GRID

In 1920, Lenin famously said, "Communism equals Soviet power plus electrification of the whole country." He created the State Commission for Electrification of Russia (GOELRO) to achieve this, and the expansion of electricity generation and transmission became a core element in Soviet modernization. Total output rose from 8.4 billion kilowatt hours in 1930, to 49 billion in 1940 and 290 billion in 1960. After World War II the Soviet Union became the second largest electricity generator in the world, with the United States occupying first place. The soviets built the world's largest hydroelectric plant, in Krasnoyarsk in 1954, and the world's first nuclear power reactor, in Obninsk.

Electrification had reached 80 percent of all villages by the 1960s, and half of the rail track was electrified. Power stations also provided steam heating for neighboring districts, accounting for one-third of the nation's heating. This may have been efficient from the power-generation point of view, but there was no effort to meter customers or conserve energy. By 1960 the Soviet Union had 167,000 kilometers of high transmission lines (35 kilovolts and higher). This grew to 600,000 kilometers by 1975. Initially, there were ten regional grids, which by the 1970s were gradually combined into a unified national grid that handled 75 percent of total electricity output. In 1976 the Soviet grid was connected to that of East Europe (the members of Comecon).

The Soviet power supply continued to expand steadily, even as economic growth slowed. Output increased from 741 billion kilowatt hours in 1970 to 1,728 billion in 1990, with the USSR accounting for 17 percent of global electricity output. Still, capacity failed to keep pace with the gargantuan appetites of Soviet industry, and regional coverage was uneven, since most of the fossil fuels were located in the north and east, whereas the major population centers and industry were in the west. Twenty percent of the energy was consumed in transporting the coal, gas, and fuel-oil to thermal power stations located near industrial zones. In the early 1970s, when nuclear plants accounted for just two percent of total electricity output, the government launched an ambitious program to expand nuclear power. This plan was halted for more than a decade by the 1986 Chernobyl accident. In 1990 the Russia Federation generated 1,082 billion kilowatt hours, a figure that had fallen to 835 billion by 2000. Of that total, 15 percent was from nuclear plants and 18 percent from hydro stations, the rest was from thermal plants using half coal and half natural gas for fuel.

In 1992 the electricity system was turned into a joint stock company, the Unified Energy Systems of Russia (RAO EES). Blocks of shares in RAO EES were sold to its workers and the public for vouchers in 1994, and subsequently were sold to domestic and foreign investors, but the government held onto a controlling 53 percent stake in EES. Some regional producers were separated from EES, but the latter still accounted for 73 percent of Russian generating capacity and 85 percent of electricity distribution in 2000.

Electricity prices were held down by the government in order to subsidize industrial and domestic consumers. This meant most of the regional energy companies that made up EES ran at a loss, and could not invest in new capacity or energy conservation. By 1999, the situation was critical: EES was losing $1 billion on annual revenues of $7 billion. Former privatization chief Anatoly Chubais was appointed head of EES, and he proposed privatizing some of EES's more lucrative regional producers to the highest bidder. The remaining operations would be restructured into five to seven generation companies, which would be spun off as independent companies. A wholesale market in electricity would be introduced, and retail prices would be allowed to rise by 100 percent by 2005. The grid and dispatcher service would be returned to state ownership. Amid objections from consumers, who objected to higher prices, and from foreign investors in EES, who feared their shares would be diluted, the plan was adopted in 2002.

See also: CHERNOBYL; CHUBAIS, ANATOLY BORISOVICH

BIBLIOGRAPHY

Ebel, Robert. (1994). *Energy Choices in Russia.* Washington, DC: Center for Strategic and International Studies.

EES web site: <http://www.rao-ees.ru/en>.

PETER RUTLAND

ELIZABETH

(1709–1762), empress of Russia, 1741–1762, one of the "Russian matriarchate" or "Amazon autocratrixes," that is, women rulers from Catherine I through Catherine II, 1725–1796

Daughter of Peter I and Catherine I, grand princess and crown princess from 1709 to 1741, Elizabeth (Elizaveta Petrovna) was the second of ten offspring to reach maturity. She was born in the Moscow suburb of Kolomenskoye on December 29, 1709, the same day a Moscow parade celebrated the Poltava victory. Elizabeth grew up carefree with her sister Anna (1708–1728). Doted on by both parents, the girls received training in European languages, social skills, and Russian traditions of singing, religious instruction, and dancing. Anna married Duke Karl Friedrich of Holstein-Gottorp in 1727 and died in Holstein giving birth to Karl Peter Ulrich (the future Peter III). Elizabeth never married officially or traveled abroad, her illegitimate birth obstructing royal matches. Because she wrote little and left no diary, her inner thoughts are not well-known.

Hints of a political role came after her mother's short reign when Elizabeth was named to the joint regency for young Peter II, whose favor she briefly enjoyed. But when he died childless in 1730 she

Portrait of Empress Elizabeth Petrovna by Pierre Duflos.

was overlooked in the surprise selection of Anna Ivanovna. Under Anna she was kept under surveillance, her yearly allowance cut to 30,000 rubles, and only Biron's influence prevented commitment to a convent. At Aleksandrovka near Moscow she indulged in amorous relationships with Alexander Buturlin, Alexei Shubin, and the Ukrainian chorister Alexei Razumovsky. During Elizabeth's reign male favoritism flourished; some of her preferred men assumed broad cultural and artistic functions—for instance, Ivan Shuvalov (1717–1797), a well-read Francophile who cofounded Moscow University and the Imperial Russian Academy of Fine Arts in the 1750s.

Anna Ivanovna was succeeded in October 1740 by infant Ivan VI of the Brunswick branch of Romanovs who reigned under several fragile regencies, the last headed by his mother, Anna Leopoldovna (1718–1746). This Anna represented the Miloslavsky/Brunswick branch, whereas Elizabeth personified the Naryshkin/Petrine branch. Elizabeth naturally worried the inept regency regime, which she led her partisans in the guards to overthrow on December 5–6, 1741, with aid from the French and Swedish ambassadors (Sweden had declared war on Russia in July 1741 ostensibly in support of Elizabeth). The bloodless coup was deftly accomplished, the regent and her family arrested and banished, and Elizabeth's claims explicated on the basis of legitimacy and blood kinship. Though Elizabeth's accession unleashed public condemnation of both Annas as agents of foreign domination, it also reaffirmed the primacy of Petrine traditions and conquests, promising to restore Petrine glory and to counter Swedish invasion, which brought Russian gains in Finland by the Peace of Åbo in August 1743.

Elizabeth was crowned in Moscow in spring 1742 amid huge celebrations spanning several months; she demonstratively crowned herself. With Petrine, classical feminine, and "restorationist" rhetoric, Elizabeth's regime resembled Anna Ivanovna's in that it pursued an active foreign policy, witnessed complicated court rivalries and further attempts to resolve the succession issue, and made the imperial court a center of European cultural activities. In 1742 the empress, lacking offspring, brought her nephew from Holstein to be converted to Orthodoxy, renamed, and designated crown prince Peter Fyodorovich. In 1744 she found him a German bride, Sophia of Anhalt-Zerbst, the future Catherine II. The teenage consorts married in August 1745, and hopes for a male heir came true only in 1754. Elizabeth took charge of Grand Prince Pavel Petrovich. Nevertheless, the "Young Court" rivaled Elizabeth's in competition over dynastic and succession concerns.

While retaining ultimate authority, Elizabeth restored the primacy of the Senate in policymaking, exercised a consultative style of administration, and assembled a government comprising veteran statesmen, such as cosmopolitan Chancellor Alexei Bestuzhev-Ryumin and newly elevated aristocrats like the brothers Petr and Alexander Shuvalov (and their younger cousin Ivan Shuvalov), Mikhail and Roman Vorontsov, Alexei and Kirill Razumovsky, and court surgeon Armand Lestocq. Her reign generally avoided political repression, but she took revenge on the Lopukhin family, descendents of Peter I's first wife, by having them tortured and exiled in 1743 for loose talk about the Brunswick family and its superior rights. Later she abolished the death penalty in practice. Lestocq and Bestuzhev-Ryumin, who was succeeded as chancellor by Mikhail Vorontsov, fell into disgrace for alleged intrigues, although Catherine II later pardoned both.

In cultural policy Elizabeth patronized many, including Mikhail Lomonosov, Alexander Sumarokov, Vasily Tredyakovsky, and the Volkov brothers, all active in literature and the arts. Foreign architects, composers, and literary figures such as Bartolomeo Rastrelli, Francesco Araja, and Jakob von Stählin also enjoyed Elizabeth's support. Her love of pageantry resulted in Petersburg's first professional public theater in 1756. Indeed, the empress set a personal example by frequently attending the theater, and her court became famous for elaborate festivities amid luxurious settings, such as Rastrelli's new Winter Palace and the Catherine Palace at Tsarskoye Selo. Elizabeth loved fancy dress and followed European fashion, although she was criticized by Grand Princess Catherine for quixotic transvestite balls and crudely dictating other ladies'style and attire. Other covert critics such as Prince Mikhail Shcherbatov accused Elizabeth of accelerating the "corruption of manners" by pandering to a culture of corrupt excess, an inevitable accusation from disgruntled aristocrats amid the costly ongoing Europeanization of a cosmopolitan high society. The Shuvalov brothers introduced significant innovations in financial policy that fueled economic and fiscal growth and reinstituted recodification of law.

Elizabeth followed Petrine precedent in foreign policy, a field she took special interest in, although critics alleged her geographical ignorance and laziness. Without firing a shot, Russia helped conclude the war of the Austrian succession (1740–1748), but during this conflict Elizabeth and Chancellor Bestuzhev-Ryumin became convinced that Prussian aggression threatened Russia's security. Hence alliance with Austria became the fulcrum of Elizabethan foreign policy, inevitably entangling Russia in the reversal of alliances in 1756 that exploded in the worldwide Seven Years' War (1756–1763). This complex conflict pitted Russia, Austria, and France against Prussia and Britain, but Russia did not fight longtime trading partner Britain. Russia held its own against Prussia, conquered East Prussia, and even briefly occupied Berlin in 1760. The war was directed by a new institution, the Conference at the Imperial Court, for Elizabeth's declining health limited her personal attention to state affairs. The war dragged on too long, and the belligerents began looking for a way out when Elizabeth's sudden death on Christmas Day (December 25, 1761) brought her nephew Peter III to power. He was determined to break ranks and to ally with Prussia, despite Elizabeth's antagonism to King Frederick II. So just as Elizabeth's reign started with a perversely declared war, so it ended abruptly with Russia's early withdrawal from a European-wide conflict and Peter III's declaration of war on longtime ally Denmark. Elizabeth personified Russia's post-Petrine eminence and further emergence as a European power with aspirations for cultural achievement.

See also: ANNA IVANOVNA; BESTUZHEV-RYUMIN, ALEXEI PETROVICH; PETER I; SEVEN YEARS' WAR

BIBLIOGRAPHY

Alexander, John T. (1989). *Catherine the Great: Life and Legend.* New York: Oxford University Press.

Anisimov, Evgeny. (1995). *Empress Elizabeth: Her Reign and Her Russia*, ed. and tr. John T. Alexander. Gulf Breeze, FL: Academic International.

Hughes, Lindsey. (2002). *Peter the Great: A Biography.* New Haven, CT: Yale University Press.

Naumov, Viktor Petrovich. (1996). "Empress Elizabeth I, 1741–1762." In *The Emperors and Empresses of Russia: Rediscovering the Romanovs*, ed. and comp. Donald J. Raleigh and A. A. Iskenderov. Armonk, NY: M. E. Sharpe.

Shcherbatov, M. M. (1969). *On the Corruption of Morals in Russia*, ed. and tr. Anthony Lentin. Cambridge, UK: Cambridge University Press.

Wortman, Richard. (1995). *Scenarios of Power: Myth and Ceremony in Russian Monarchy*, vol. 1. Princeton, NJ: Princeton University Press.

JOHN T. ALEXANDER

EMANCIPATION ACT

The Emancipation Act was issued by the Russian Emperor Alexander II on March 3, 1861. By this act all peasants, or serfs, were set free from personal dependence on their landlords, acquired civil rights, and were granted participation in social and economic activities as free citizens.

The importance of emancipation cannot be overestimated. However, emancipation can be understood only by taking into consideration the history of serfdom in Russia. If in early modern Europe different institutions successfully emerged to represent the interests of different classes (e.g., universities, guilds, and corporations) against the state's absolutist tendencies, in Russia the state won over its competitors and took the form of autocracy. Despite the absolutist state's takeover in early modern Europe, it never encroached on the individual rights of its subjects to the extent that the Russian autocracy did. Indeed, autocracy presupposed that no right existed until it was granted and thus all subjects were slaves until the tsar decided otherwise.

As the process of state centralization proceeded in Russia, external sources of income (for instance, wars and territorial growth) were more or less exhausted by the seventeenth century, and the state switched its attention to its internal resources. Hence the continuous attempts to immobilize peasants and make them easily accessible as taxpayers. The Law Code of 1649 completed the process of immobilization declaring "eternal and hereditary attachment" of peasants to the land. Thus the Russian term for "serf" goes back to this attachment to the land more than to personal dependence on the master. Later in the eighteenth century it became possible to sell serfs without the land. Afterwards the only difference between the serf and the slave was that the serf had a household on the land of his master.

At the time of emancipation, serfdom constituted the core of Russian economic and social life. Its abolition undermined the basis of the autocratic state in the eyes of the vast majority of nobles as well as peasants. Those few in favor of the reform were not numerous: landlords running modernized enterprises and hindered by the absence of a free labor force and competition, together with liberal and radical thinkers (often landless). For peasants, the interpretation of emancipation ranged from a call for total anarchy, arbitrary redistribution of land, and revenge on their masters, to disbelief and disregard of the emancipation as impossible.

Thus Alexander II had to strike a balance between contradictory interests of different groups of nobility and the threat of peasant riots. The text of the act makes this balancing visible. The emperor openly acknowledged the inequality among his subjects and said that traditional relations between the nobility and the peasantry based on the "benevolence of the noblemen" and "affectionate submission on the part of the peasants" had become degraded. Under these circumstances, acting as a promoter of the good of all his subjects, Alexander II made an effort to introduce a "new organization of peasant life."

To pay homage to the class of his main supporters, in the document Alexander stresses the devotion and goodwill of his nobility, their readiness "to make sacrifices for the welfare of the country," and his hope for their future cooperation. In return he promises to help them in the form of loans and transfer of debts. On the other hand, serfs should be warned and reminded of their obligations toward those in power. "Some were concerned about the freedom and unconcerned about obligations" reads the document. The Emperor cites the Bible that "every individual is subject to a higher authority" and concludes that "what legally belongs to nobles cannot be taken from them without adequate compensation," or punishment will surely follow.

The state initiative for emancipation indicates that the state planned to be the first to benefit from it. Though several of Alexander's predecessors touched upon the question of peasant reform, none of them was in such a desperate situation domestically or internationally as to pursue unprecedented measures and push the reform ahead. The Crimean War (1853–1856) became the point of revelation because Russia faced the threat not only of financial collapse but of losing its position as a great power among European countries. The reform should have become a source of economic and military mobilization and thus kept the state equal among equals in Europe as well as eliminate the remnants of postwar chaos in its social life. However, the emancipation changed the structure of society in a way that demanded its total reconstruction. A series of liberal reforms followed, and the question of whether the Emperor ever planned to go that far remains open for historians.

The emancipation meant that all peasants became "free rural inhabitants" with full rights. The nobles retained their property rights on land while granting the peasants "perpetual use of their domicile in return of specified obligations," that is, peasants should work for their landlords as they used to work before. These temporal arrangements would last for two years, during which redemption fees for land would be paid and the peasant would become an owner of his plot. In general the Emancipation Act was followed by Regulations on Peasants Set Free in seventeen articles that explained the procedure of land redistribution and new organization of peasant life in detail.

Because peasants became free citizens, emancipation had far-reaching economic consequences. The organization of rural life changed when the peasant community—not the landlord—was responsible for taxation and administrative and police order. The community became a self-governing entity when rural property-holders were able to elect their representatives for participation in administrative bodies at the higher level as well as for the local court. To resolve conflicts arising between the nobles and the peasants, community justices were introduced locally, and special officials mediated these conflicts.

Emancipation destroyed class boundaries and opened the way for further development of capitalist relations and a market economy. Those who were not able to pay the redemption fee and buy their land entered the market as a free labor force promoting further industrialization. Moreover, it had a great psychological impact on the general public, because, in principle at least, there remained no underprivileged classes, and formal civil equality was established. A new generation was to follow—not slaves but citizens.

See also: ALEXANDER II; LAW CODE OF 1649; PEASANTRY; SERFDOM; SLAVERY

BIBLIOGRAPHY

"The Emancipation Manifesto, March 3 1861." (2003). <http://www.dur.ac.uk/~dml0www/emancipn.html>

Emmons, Terrence. (1968). *The Russian Landed Gentry and the Peasant Emancipation of 1861*. Cambridge, UK: Cambridge University Press..

Emmons Terrence, ed. (1970). *Emancipation of the Russian Serfs*. New York: International Thomson Publishing.

Field, Daniel. (1976). *The End of Serfdom: Nobility and Bureaucracy in Russia, 1855–1861*. Cambridge, MA: Harvard University Press.

Hellie, Richard. (1982). *Slavery in Russia, 1450–1725*. Chicago: University of Chicago Press.

Seton-Watson, Hugh. (1967). *The Russian Empire, 1801–1917*. Oxford: Oxford University Press.

Julia Ulyannikova

EMPIRE, USSR AS

The understanding of the concept of empire depends on time and space. During the nineteenth century the terms *empire* and *imperialism* were associated with the spread of progress by countries claiming to represent civilized forms of existence. By the end of World War II the emergent superpowers, the United States and the USSR, adhered to an anti-imperialist, anti-empire ideology and thereby ended the colonial empires of countries such as Britain and France.

According to Leninist thought, empire and imperialism represented the highest and last stages of capitalist development after which socialism would emerge. Therefore the Soviet leadership never considered the multinational USSR, the leader of socialist revolution, to be an empire. This Leninist ideological definition of empire, while providing a framework for comprehending the Soviet leadership's approach to governing, fails to describe the dynamics of the USSR as an empire. As shown by Dominic Lieven (2000), a country must fulfill several criteria to be considered an empire. It must be continental in scale, governing a range of different peoples, represent a great culture or ideology with more than local hegemony, exercise great economic and military might on more than a regional level, and arguably govern without the consent of the people. According to these criteria the USSR was indeed an empire, however not without certain characteristics distinguishing it from other empires, such as the British, Ottoman, or Hapsburg.

The USSR was the world's largest country, extending from Europe in the west to China and the Pacific in the east, its southern borders touching the boundaries of the Middle East. Given this geographic position, Moscow was a player in three of the world's most important regions. The Soviet Union's population consisted of hundreds of different peoples speaking a myriad of languages and practicing different religions, including Judaism, Orthodoxy, Catholicism, Protestantism, and Sunni and Shia Islam. Such diversity was reminiscent of the great British and French maritime empires.

Josef Stalin's brutal industrialization policies and victory in World War II paved the way for the Soviet Union's emergence as a superpower with global reach and influence. The Soviet economy was the second largest in the world despite its many deficiencies and supported a huge military industrial complex, which by the 1960s had enabled the

USSR to attain nuclear parity with the United States while maintaining the largest armed forces in the world.

Ideological power accompanied this military and economic might. The Cold War between the USSR and the United States was rooted in alternative visions of modernity. Whereas the United States held that liberal democracy and capitalism ultimately represented the end of history, the Soviet Union believed that an additional stage, that of communism, represented the true end of history. Many across the globe found Soviet communism's claims of representing a truly egalitarian and therefore more humane society attractive. In other words, the ideological and cultural power of the USSR exercised global influence.

In the midst of war and revolution many areas of the former tsarist empire became independent. With the exception of Finland, Estonia, Lithuania, Latvia, and parts of Poland, the Bolsheviks, through the effective and brutal use of force and coercion and under the banner of progressive Soviet communism, resurrected the empire they once called "Prison of the Peoples." In 1940 Stalin invaded and occupied the Baltic States, which subsequently, according to Soviet propaganda, voluntarily became part of the USSR. Until the late 1980s during the reform process of Mikhail Gorbachev, the Soviet leadership governed without the direct consent of the people.

LAND-BASED EMPIRE

The Soviet Union was a land-based empire encompassing all the territories of its tsarist predecessor—except Poland and Finland—while adding other areas such as western Ukraine and Bessarabia. The dynamics of a land-based empire differ greatly from those of maritime empires, such as the British and French. Before embarking on maritime empire building, countries such as Britain, France, and Spain already had a relatively solidified national identity. In tsarist Russia, empire and nation building commenced at roughly the same time, thereby blurring empire and nation. To determine where Russia the nation ended and where the empire began was difficult. This theme would continue in the Soviet era.

Given the geographical distance between the metropole and its maritime empire, a clear division remained between colonized, most of whom were of different races and cultures, and colonizer, and therefore the question of assimilation of different peoples under a single supranational ideology or symbol never arose. The metropolitan British identity was neither created nor adjusted to include the peoples of the vast empire ruled by London. In tsarist Russia the emperor and the crown represented the supranational entity to which the various peoples of the empire were to pledge their loyalty. Here, terminology is important. Two words for the English equivalent of "Russian" exist. When discussing anything related to Russian ethnicity, such as a person or the language, the word *russky* is used. However the empire, its institutions and the dynasty, were called *rossysky*, which carried a civil meaning designed to include everyone from Baltic German to Tatar. The emperor himself was known not as the "russky" tsar, but *vserossysky* (All-Russian).

The Soviet leadership faced the same problems of governing and assimilation associated with a multiethnic land empire. While Soviet nationality policy, in other words how Soviet leaders approached governing this large and diverse empire, varied over time, its goals never did. They were (a) to maintain the country's territorial integrity and domestic security; (b) to support the monopolistic hold on power of the Communist Party of the Soviet Union (CPSU); and (c) create a supranational Soviet identity, reminiscent of the civil rossysky. On one hand the Soviet leadership in line with Marxist–Leninist thought believed that nationalism, the death knell for any multinational empire, was a phenomenon inherent to capitalism and the bourgeois classes. Therefore, with the advent of socialism, broadly defined working class interests would triumph over national loyalties. In short, socialism makes nationalism redundant. On the other hand, the reality of governing a multiethnic empire required the Soviet leadership to pursue several policies reminiscent of a traditional imperial polity, such as deportations of whole peoples, playing one ethnic group against another, and drawing boundaries designed to maintain the supremacy of the central power.

Unlike previous empires, the USSR was a federation that had fifteen republics at the time of its dissolution in 1991. Confident in the relatively speedy victory of socialism and communism over capitalism, in the 1920s the Soviet leadership followed a very accommodating policy in regard to nationalities. Along with the creation of a federation that institutionalized national identities, the new Soviet authorities supported the spread and strengthening of non-Russian cultures, languages,

Union of Soviet Socialist Republics in 1985. XNR PRODUCTIONS. THE GALE GROUP

and identities. In areas where a national identity already existed, such as Ukraine, Georgia, and Armenia, great ethnic cultural autonomy was allowed. In areas where no national identity yet existed, as in Central Asia, Soviet ethnographers worked to create peoples and national borders, based on cultural and economic considerations. The Soviet drawing of borders is comparable to the creation of states by European imperial powers in Africa and the Middle East. Each created republic had identical state, bureaucratic, and educational structures, an Academy of Sciences, and other institutions whose responsibility was the maintenance and strengthening of the national identity as well as propagation of Marxist–Leninist teachings. Therefore the Soviet Union supported and gave birth to national identities, whereas other land-based empires, such as the Ottoman and Habsburg, fought against them. At the same time the central Soviet authorities recruited indigenous people in the non-Russian republics to serve in local, republican, and even all-union institutions.

Alongside nation building went social and economic modernization, and a requirement for the emergence of socialism, which would bring an end to strong national feelings. Unlike French and British colonial rule, the Soviets made dramatic changes of the societies and peoples of the USSR—one of the main thrusts of their nationality policy. While Central Asia and the Caucasus were the most economically and socially "backward," through rapid industrialization and collectivization of peasant land all societies of the USSR endured dramatic change, surpassing the extent to which France and Britain had affected their colonial possessions. Importantly, the Soviets strove to modernize Russia, which many regarded to be the imperial power. There is no such analogy in regard to the maritime European empires, whose metropole was considered to be at the forefront of modernization and civilization.

The rule of Josef Stalin brought changes to this policy. Regarding cultural autonomy a threat to the integrity of the Soviet state, Stalin imposed very strong central control over the constituent republics and appointed Russians to many of the high posts in the non-Russian republics. The biggest change, however, was in regard to the position of the Russian people within Soviet ideology. The Russians were now portrayed as the elder brother of the Soviet peoples whose culture and language provided the means for achieving communist modernity. Appreciation and love of Russian culture and language was no longer regarded as a threat to Soviet identity, but rather a reflection of loyalty to it.

From Stalin's death to the collapse of the USSR, Soviet nationality policy was an amalgamation of the policies followed during the first thirty-five years of Soviet power. The peoples of the non-Russian republics again filled positions in republican institutions. Through access to higher education, privilege, and the opportunity to exercise power within their republican or local domain, the central leadership created a sizeable and reliable body of non-Russian cadres who, with their knowledge of the local languages and cultures, ruled the non-Russian parts of the empire under the umbrella of the CPSU. However, Great Russians, meaning Russians, Ukrainians, or Belarusians, usually occupied military and intelligence service positions.

The Soviet command economy centered in Moscow limited the power of the local and republican authorities. Through allocation of economic resources, goods, and infrastructure, the central Soviet authorities wielded a great degree of real power throughout the USSR. Moreover, in traditional imperial style, Moscow exploited the natural resources of all republics, such as Russian oil and natural gas and Uzbek cotton, to fulfill all-union policies even to the detriment of the individual republic.

The problem of assimilation of varied peoples and the creation of a supranational identity remained. After the death of Stalin, the Soviet leadership realized that ethnic national feelings in the USSR were not dissipating and in some cases were strengthening. The Soviet leadership's response was essentially the promotion of a two-tiered identity. On one level it spoke of the flourishing of national identities and cultures. The leadership stressed, however, that this flourishing took place within a Soviet framework in which the people's primary loyalty was to the Soviet identity and homeland. In other words, enjoyment of one's national culture and language was not a barrier to having supreme loyalty to the progressive supranational Soviet identity.

Nevertheless the existence of national feelings continued to worry the Soviet leadership. During the late 1950s it adopted a new language policy, at the heart of which was expansion of Russian language teaching. The hope was that acquisition of Russian language and therefore culture would bring with it the spread and strengthening of a Soviet identity. The issue of language is always sensitive in the imperial framework. Attempts by a land-based empire to impose a single language frequently results in enflaming national feelings among the people whose native tongue is not the imperial one. Yet every land-based empire, especially one the size of the USSR, needs a lingua franca in order to govern and ease the challenges of administration.

RUSSIA AND THE SOVIET EMPIRE

One of the more contentious issues concerns the extent to which the Soviet Union was a Russian empire. The USSR did exist in the space of the former tsarist empire. The Russian language was the lingua franca. From Stalin onwards the Russians and their high culture were portrayed as progressive and therefore the starting point on the path toward the modern Soviet identity. Great Russians held the vast majority of powerful positions in the center, as well as sensitive posts in the non-Russian republics. Many people in the non-Russian republics regarded the USSR and Soviet identity to be only a different form of Russian imperialism dating from the tsarist period.

On the other hand the Soviets destroyed two symbols of Russian identity—the tsar and the peasantry—while emasculating the other, the Russian Orthodox Church. During the 1920s Lenin and other Bolsheviks, seeing Russian nationalism as the biggest internal threat to the Soviet state, worked to contain it. The Russian Soviet Federated Socialist Republic, by far the largest of the republics of the USSR whose population equaled all of the others combined, had no separate Communist Party and appropriate institutions in contrast to all of the other republics. The Soviet regime used Russian high culture and symbols, but in a sanitized form designed to construct and strengthen a Soviet identity. The Russian people suffered just as much as the other peoples from the crimes of the Soviet regime, especially under Stalin. Already by the 1950s Russian nationalism was on the rise. The Soviet regime was blamed for destroying Russian culture and Russia itself through its reckless exploitation of land and natural resources in pursuit of Soviet goals. In the closing years of the USSR the symbols of Russian identity, the tsarist tricolor flag and the double-headed eagle, were commonly seen, while cities and streets regained their prerevolutionary Russian names. For many Russians, a distinction existed between Russian and Soviet identity.

COLLAPSE OF THE SOVIET EMPIRE

Debate continues over the causes of the collapse of the USSR and specifically the extent to which Soviet handling of its multiethnic empire was responsible for it. The Soviet federal structure, although leaving real power in Moscow, nevertheless institutionalized and therefore strengthened national identities, which are lethal to any multinational empire. Yet the goal of nationality policy was the creation of a supranational Soviet identity. Despite this contradiction, Soviet nationality policy when compared to that of other imperial polities enjoyed a relative degree of success. By encouraging dependence on the state and protecting the educational and occupational interests of the local political elite and educated middle class, the central Soviet leadership blunted aspirations to independent nationhood and integrated groups within the Soviet infrastructure. While the use of local elites to govern the periphery is a traditional imperial practice, providing a degree of legitimacy to the imperial power, Soviet non-Russian elites achieved powerful positions within their respective republics, wielding power unattainable by the colonized local populations in the French and British empires.

Ideological power is as strong as its ability to deliver what it promises. Disillusionment with the unfulfilled economic promises of the Soviet ideology weakened loyalty to the Soviet identity. Gorbachev's economic policies only worsened the economic situation. At the same time, Gorbachev ended the CPSU's monopoly on power. Faced with growing popular dissatisfaction with the economic situation and loss of guarantee of power through the CPSU, regional and local political figures became nationalists when the national platform seemed to be the only way for them to retain power as the imperial center, the CPSU, weakened.

Russia itself led the charge against the Soviet center, thereby creating a unique situation. The country that many people inside and outside the USSR considered to be the imperial power, revolted against what it regarded to be the imperial power, the CPSU and central Soviet control over Russia, leading to the collapse of one of the world's great land-based empires.

See also: COLONIAL EXPANSION; COLONIALISM; NATIONALITIES POLICIES, SOVIET; NATIONALITIES POLICIES, TSARIST; UNION OF SOVIET SOCIALIST REPUBLICS

BIBLIOGRAPHY

Barkey, Karen, and Von Hagen, Mark, eds. (1997). *After Empire.* London: Westview Press.

Dawisha, Karen, and Parrott, Bruce, eds. (1997). *The End of Empire? The Transformation of the USSR in Comparative Perspective.* London: M. E. Sharpe.

Lieven, Dominic. (2000). *Empire.* London: John Murray.

Nahaylo, Bohdan, and Swoboda, Victor. (1990). *Soviet Disunion.* London: Penguin.

Pipes, Richard. (1964). *The Formation of the Soviet Union.* London: Harvard University Press.

Rezun, Miron, ed. (1992). *Nationalism and the Breakup of an Empire: Russia and Its Periphery.* Westport, CT: Praeger.

Rudolph, Richard, and Good, David, eds. (1992). *Nationalism and Empire: The Habsburg Empire and the Soviet Union.* New York: St. Martin's Press.

Suny, Ronald. (1993). *The Revenge of the Past: Nationalism, Revolution, and the Collapse of the Soviet Union.* Stanford, CA: Stanford University Press.

Szporluk, Roman. (2000). *Russia, Ukraine, and the Breakup of the Soviet Union.* Stanford, CA: Hoover Institution Press.

ZHAND P. SHAKIBI

ENGELS, FRIEDRICH

(1820–1895), German socialist theoretician; close collaborator of Karl Marx.

Friedrich Engels is remembered primarily as the close friend and intellectual collaborator of Karl Marx, who was the most important socialist thinker and arguably the most important social theorist of the nineteenth century. Engels must be regarded as a significant intellectual figure in his own right. Engels's writings exerted a strong influence on Soviet Marxist-Leninist ideology. Engels was born in Barmen in 1820, two and a half years after Marx. Ironically, Friedrich Engels worked for decades as the manager of enterprises in his family's firm of Ermen and Engels; this necessitated his move to Manchester in 1850. Engels contributed substantially to the financial support of Marx and his family. He survived Marx by twelve years, during an important period in the growth of the socialist movement when Engels served as the most respected spokesman for Marxist theory.

In recent decades there has been a lively debate over the degree of divergence between Marx's thought and that of Engels, and therefore over whether the general scheme of interpretation known as "historical materialism" or "dialectical materialism" was primarily constructed by Engels or accorded with the main thrust of Marx's intellectual efforts. George Lichtheim and Shlomo Avineri, distinguished scholars who have written about Marx, see Engels as having given a rigid cast to Marxist theory in order to make it seem more scientific, thus implicitly denying the creative role of human imagination and labor that had been emphasized by Marx. On the other hand, some works, such as those by J. D. Hunley and Manfred Steger, emphasize the fundamental points of agreement between Marx and Engels. The controversy remains unresolved and facts point to both convergence and divergence: Marx and Engels coauthored some major essays, including *The Communist Manifesto,* and Engels made an explicit effort to give Marxism the character of a set of scientific laws of purportedly general validity. The well-known laws of the dialectic, which became the touchstones of philosophical orthodoxy in Soviet Marxism-Leninism, were drawn directly from Engels's writings.

See also: DIALECTICAL MATERIALISM; MARXISM

BIBLIOGRAPHY

Carver, Terrell. (1989). *Friedrich Engels: His Life and Thought.* London: Macmillan.

Hunley, J. D. (1991). *The Life and Thought of Friedrich Engels: A Reinterpretation.* New Haven, CT: Yale University Press.

Steger, Manfred B., and Carver, Terrell, eds. (1999). *Engels after Marx.* University Park: Pennsylvania State University Press.

ALFRED B. EVANS JR.

ENLIGHTENMENT, IMPACT OF

The Enlightenment is traditionally defined as an intellectual movement characterized by religious skepticism, secularism, and liberal values, rooted in a belief in the power of human reason liberated from the constraints of blind faith and arbitrary authority, and opposed by the retrograde anti-Enlightenment. Originated with the French *philosophes,* especially Charles de Secondant Montesquieu (1689–1755), Denis Diderot (1713–1784), François Marie Arouet de Voltaire (1684–1778), and Jean-Jacques Rousseau (1712–1778), the Enlightenment quickly spread through Europe and the American colonies. It reached Russia in the mid–eighteenth century, peaking during the reign of Catherine II (1762–1796) and becoming one of the most important components of the country's Westernization and modernization.

The impact of the Enlightenment in Russia is generally described in terms of its reception and accommodation of the ideas of the philosophes. These ideas spurred new scientific and secular approaches to culture and government that laid the foundation of Russia's modern intellectual and political culture. In addition to greater intellectual exchange with Europe, the Enlightenment brought Russia institutions of science and scholarship, arts and theater, the print revolution, and new forms of sociability, such as learned and charitable societies, clubs, and Masonic lodges. The Enlightenment created a new generation of Russian scientists, scholars, and men of letters (i.e., Mikhail Lomonosov, Nikolai Novikov, Alexander Radishchev, and Nikolai Karamzin). The Enlightenment also brought about an intense secularization that significantly diminished the role of religion and theology and transformed the monarchy into an enlightened absolutism.

The actual impact of the Enlightenment in Russia was limited and inconsistent, however. While the writings of the philosophes were widely translated and read, Russian audiences were more interested in their novels than in their philosophical or political treatises. Policy makers preferred German cameralism and political science. Catherine's self-proclaimed adherence to the principles of the philosophes was rather patchy, which prompted widespread accusations that she had created the image of philosopher on the throne to dupe the European public. The progress of science, education, and literature as well as the formation of the public sphere owed more to government tutelage than independent initiative. Most Russian champions of Enlightenment were profoundly religious. Thus, criticism of the Orthodox Church was virtually nonexistent; anticlerical statements were directed primarily against Catholicism, the old foe of Russian Orthodoxy. Some of the new forms of sociability, such as Masonic lodges, served as venues not only for liberal discussion, but also for the exercises in occultism, alchemy, and criticism of the philosophes. The Enlightenment in Russia was preoccupied with superficial cultural forms rather than content.

The traditional picture outlined above needs to be revised in light of new studies of the European Enlightenment since the 1970s. Enlightenment is no longer identified as a uniform school of thought dominated by the philosophes. Instead it is understood as a complex phenomenon, a series of debates at the core of which lay the process of discovery and proactive and critical involvement of the individual in both private and public life. This concept softens the binary divides between the secular and the religious, the realms of private initiative and established public authority, and, in many cases, the conventional antithesis between Enlightenment and anti-Enlightenment.

One may interpret the Enlightenment in Russia more comprehensively and less exclusively as a process of discovering contemporary European culture and adapting it to Russian realities that produced a uniquely Russian national Enlightenment. An analysis of enlightened despotism need not be preoccupied with the balance between Enlightenment and despotism and can focus instead on the reformer's own understanding of the best interests of the nation. For example, it was political, demographic, and economic considerations rather than an anticlerical ideology that drove Catherine's policy of secularization. There is no need to limit discussions of the public debate to evaluations of whether or not it conformed to the standards of religious skepticism. Contemporary discussions of the difference between true and false Enlightenment demonstrate that religious education and faith, along with patriotism, were viewed as the key elements of true Enlightenment, while religious toleration was touted as a traditional Orthodox value. Instead of emphasizing the dichotomy between adoption of cultural institutions and reception of ideas, twenty-first century scholarship looks at institutions as the infrastructure of Enlightenment that created economic, social, and political mechanisms crucial for the spread of ideas.

See also: CATHERINE II; FREEMASONRY; ORTHODOXY

BIBLIOGRAPHY

De Madariaga, Isabel. (1999). *Politics and Culture in Eighteenth-Century Russia: Collected Essays.* New York: Longman.

Dixon, Simon. (1999). *The Modernisation of Russia, 1676–1825.* Cambridge, UK: Cambridge University Press.

Gross, Anthony Glenn, ed. (1983). *Russia and the West in the Eighteenth Century.* Newtonville, MA: Oriental Research Partners.

Smith, Douglas. (1999). *Working the Rough Stone: Freemasonry and Society in Eighteenth-Century Russia.* DeKalb: Northern Illinois University Press.

Wirtschafter, Elise Kimerling. (2003). *The Play of Ideas in Russian Enlightenment Theater.* DeKalb: Northern Illinois University Press.

OLGA TSAPINA

ENSERFMENT

Enserfment refers to the broad historical process that made the free Russian peasantry into serfs, abasing them further into near-slaves, then emancipating them from their slavelike status and finally freeing them so that they could move and conduct their lives with the same rights as other free men in the Russian Empire. This process took place over the course of nearly five hundred years, between the 1450s and 1906. Almost certainly enserfment would not have occurred had not 10 percent of the population been slaves. Also, it could not have reached the depths of human abasement had not the service state been present to legislate and enforce it.

The homeland of the Great Russians, the land between the Volga and the Oka (the so-called Volga-Oka mesopotamia), is a very poor place. There are almost no natural resources of any kind (gold, silver, copper, iron, building stone, coal), the three-inch-thick *podzol* soil is not hospitable to agriculture, as is the climate (excessive precipitation and a short growing season). Until the Slavs moved into the area in the eleventh through the thirteenth centuries, the indigenous Finns and Balts were sparsely settled and lived neolithic lives hunting and fishing. This area could not support a dense population, and any prolonged catastrophe reduced the population further, creating the perception of a labor shortage. The protracted civil war over the Moscow throne between 1425 and 1453 created a labor shortage perception.

At the time the population was free (with the exception of the slaves), with everyone able to move about as they wished. Because population densities were so low and agriculture was extensive (peasants cleared land by the slash-and-burn process, farmed it for three years, exhausted its fertility, and moved on to another plot), land ownership was not prized. Government officials and military personnel made their livings by collecting taxes and fees (which can be levied from a semi-sedentary population) and looting in warfare, not by trying to collect rent from lands tilled by settled farmers. Monasteries were different: In about 1350 they had moved out of towns (because of the Black Death, inter alia) into the countryside and entered the land ownership business, raising and selling grain. They recruited peasants to work for them by offering lower tax rates than peasants could get by living on their own lands. The civil war disrupted this process, and some monasteries, which had granted some peasants small loans as part of the recruitment package, found that they had difficulty collecting those loans. Consequently a few individual monasteries petitioned the government to forbid indebted peasants from moving at any time other than around St. George's Day (November 26). St. George's Day was the time of the pre-Christian, pagan end of the agricultural year, akin to the U.S. holiday, Thanksgiving. The monasteries believed that they could collect the debts owed to them at that time before the peasants moved somewhere else.

This small beginning—involving a handful of monasteries and only their indebted peasants—initiated the enserfment process. It is possible that the government rationalized its action because not paying a debt was a crime (a tort, in those times); thus, forbidding peasant debtors from moving was a crime-prevention measure. Also note that this was the normal time for peasants to move: The agricultural year was over, and the ground was probably frozen (the average temperature was -4 degrees Celsius), so that transportation was more convenient than at any other time of year, when there might be deep snow, floods, mud, drought, and so on.

For unknown reasons this fundamentally trivial measure was extended to all peasants in the Law Code (*Sudebnik*) of 1497. Similar limitations on peasant mobility were present in neighboring political jurisdictions, and there may have been a contagion effect. It also may have been viewed as a general convenience, for that is when peasants tended to move anyway. As far as is known, there were no contemporary protests against the introduction of St. George's Day, and in the nineteenth century the peasants had sayings stating that a reintroduction of St. George's Day would be tantamount to emancipation. The 1497 language was repeated in the *Sudebnik* of 1550, with the addition of verbiage reflecting the introduction of the three-field system of agriculture: Peasants who had sown an autumn field and then moved on St. George's Day had the right to return to harvest the grain when it was ripe.

Chaos with its inherent disruption of labor supplies caused the next major advance in the enserfment process: the introduction of the "forbidden years." Ivan IV's mad oprichnina (1565–1572) caused up to 85 percent depopulation of certain areas of old Muscovy. Recent state expansion and annexations encouraged peasants disconcerted by oprichnina chaos to flee for the first time to areas north of the Volga, to the newly annexed Kazan and Astrakhan khanates, and to areas south of the Oka in the steppe that the government was beginning to secure. In addition to the chaos caused by oprichnina military actions, Ivan had given lords control over their peasants, allowing them "to collect as much rent in one year as formerly they had collected in ten." His statement ordering peasants "to obey their lords in everything" also began the abasement of the serfs by making them subject to landlord control. Yet other elements entered the picture. The service state had converted most of the land fund in the Volga-Oka mesopotamia and in the Novgorod region into service landholdings (*pomestie*) to support its provincial cavalry, the middle service class. These servicemen could not render service without peasants on their pomestie lands to pay them regular rent. Finding their landholdings being depopulated, a handful of cavalrymen petitioned that the right of peasants to move on St. George's Day be annulled. The government granted these few requests, and called the times when peasants could not move "forbidden years." Like St. George's Day, the forbidden years initially applied to only a few situations, but in 1592 (again for precisely unknown reasons) they were applied temporarily to all peasants.

That should have completed the enserfment process. However, there were two reservations. First, it was explicitly stated that the forbidden years were temporary (although they did not actually end until 1906). Second, the government imposed a five-year statute of limitations on the enforcement of the forbidden years. Historians assume that this was done to benefit large, privileged landowners who could conceal peasants for five years on various estates so that their legal possessors (typically middle-service-class cavalrymen) could not find them and file suit for their return. Moreover, there was the issue of colonial expansion: The government wanted the areas north of the Volga, south of the Oka in the steppe, and along the Middle and South Volga eastward into the Urals and Siberia settled. It even had its own agents to recruit peasants into these areas, typically with the promise of half-taxation. Those running the expansion of the Muscovite state did not want their sparse frontier populations diminished by the forcible return of fugitive peasants to Volga-Oka mesopotamia. Thus they also supported the five-year statute of limitations on the filing of suits for the recovery of fugitive serfs.

The Time of Troubles provided a breathing spell in the enserfment process. Events occurred relevant to enserfment, but they had no long-term impact—with the possible exception of Vasily Shuisky's near-equation of serfs with slaves in 1607. After the country had recovered from the Troubles and from the Smolensk War (1632–1634), the middle-service class sensed that the new Romanov dynasty was weak and thus susceptible to pressure. In 1637 the cavalrymen began a remarkable petition campaign for the repeal of the statute of limitations on the filing of suits for the recovery of fugitive peasants. This in some respects was modeled after a campaign by townsmen to compel the binding of their fellows to their places of residence because of the collective nature of the tax system: When one family moved away, those remaining had to bear the burden imposed by the collective tax system until the next census was taken. For the townsmen the reference point typically was 1613, the end of the Time of Troubles. For the cavalrymen petitioners, the reference points were two: the statute of limitations and the documents (censuses, pomestie land allotments) proving where peasants lived. The middle-service-class petitioners pointed out that the powerful (i.e., contumacious) people were recruiting their peasants, concealing them for five years, and then using the fugitives to recruit others to flee. The petitioners, who had 5.6 peasant households apiece, alleged that the solution to their diminishing ability to render military service because of their ongoing losses of labor would be to repeal the statute of limitations. The government's response was to extend the statute of limitations from five to nine years. Another petition in 1641 extended it from nine to fifteen years. A petition of 1645 elicited the promise that the statute of limitations would be repealed once a census was taken to show where the peasants were living.

The census was taken in 1646 and 1647 but no action was taken. The government was being run by Boris Morozov, whose extensive estate records reveal that he was recruiting others lords' peasants in these years. Morozov and his corrupt accomplices got their comeuppance after riots in Moscow, which spread to a dozen other towns, led to their overthrow and to demands by the urban mob for a codification of the law. Tsar Alexis appointed the Odoyevsky Commission, which drafted the Law Code of 1649 (*ulozhenie*). It was debated and approved with significant amendments by the Assembly of the Land of 1648–1649. Part of the amendments involved the enserfment, especially the repeal of the forbidden years. Henceforth all peasants were subject to return to wherever they or their forbears were registered. This measure applied to all peasants, both those on the lands of private lords and the church (seignorial peasants) and those on lands belonging to the tsar, the state, and the peasants themselves (later known as state peasants). The land cadastre of 1626, the census of 1646–1647, and pomestie allotment documents were mentioned, but almost any other official documents would do as well. Aside from the issue of documentation, the other major enserfment issue was what to do with runaways, especially males and females who belonged to different lords and got married. The solutions were simple and logical: The Orthodox Church did not permit the breaking up of marriages, so the Law Code of 1649 decreed that the lord who had received a fugitive lost the couple to the lord from whom the fugitive had fled. If they wed as fugitives on "neutral ground," then the lord-claimants cast lots; the winner got the couple and paid the loser for his lost serf.

The Law Code did not resolve the issue of fugitives, because of the intense shortage of labor in Muscovy. After 1649 the government began to penalize recipients of fugitives by confiscating an additional serf in addition to the fugitive received. This had no impact, so it was raised to two. This in turn had no impact, so it was raised to four. At this point would-be recipients of fugitive serfs began to turn them away. Peter I took this one step further by proclaiming the death penalty for those who received the fugitive serfs, but it is not known whether anyone was actually executed.

The Law Code of 1649 opened the door to the next stage of enserfment. Lords wanted the peasants converted into slaves who could be disposed of as they wished (willed, sold, given away, moved). This contradicted the idea that serfs existed to support the provincial cavalry. The Law Code permitted landowners to move their serfs around, whereas landholders had to leave them where they were so that the next cavalry serviceman would have rent payers when the pomestie was assigned to him. The extent to which (or even whether) serfs were sold like slaves before 1700 is still being debated.

The issue was resolved during the reign of Peter I by two measures. First, in 1714 the service landholding and hereditary estate (*votchina*) were made equal under the law. Second, the introduction of the soul tax in 1719 made the lord responsible for his serfs' taxes and gave him much greater control over his subjects, especially after the collection of the soul tax commenced in 1724. In the same year, peasants were required to have a pass from their owners to travel. This was strengthened in 1722, and again in 1724. That serfs were becoming marketable was reflected in the April 15, 1721, ban on the sale of individual serfs. Whether the ban was ever enforced is unknown. The fact that it probably was not was reflected in a law of 1771 forbidding the public sale of serfs (the private sale of serfs was permitted) and a 1792 decree forbidding an auctioneer to use a gavel in serf auctions, indicating that the 1771 law was not observed either.

After 1725 the descent of seignorial serfs into slavery accelerated. In 1601 Godunov had required owners to feed their slaves, and in 1734 Anna extended this to serfs. In 1760 lords were allowed to banish serfs to Siberia. This was undoubtedly done to try to ensure calm in the villages. That this primarily concerned younger serfs (who could have been sent into the army) is reflected in the fact that owners received military recruit credit for such exiles.

A tragic date in Russian history was February 18, 1762, when Peter III abolished all service requirements for estate owners. This permitted serfowners to supervise (and abuse) their serfs personally. Thus it is probably not accidental that five years later, in 1767, Catherine II forbade serfs to petition against their owners. Catherine, supposedly enlightened, opposed to serfdom, and in favor of free labor, gave away 800,000 serfs to private owners during her reign. The year 1796 was the zenith of serfdom.

Paul tried to undo everything his mother Catherine had done. This extended to serfdom. In 1797 he forbade lords to force their peasants to work on Sunday, suggested that peasants could only be compelled to work three days per week, and that they should have the other three days to work for themselves. Paul was assassinated before he could do more.

His son Alexander I wanted to do something about serfdom, but became preoccupied with Napoleon and then went insane. He was informed by Nikolai Karamzin in 1811 that the Russian Empire rested on two pillars, autocracy and serfdom. Emancipation increasingly became the topic of public discussion. After suppressing the libertarian Decembrists in 1725, Nicholas I wanted to do something about serfdom and appointed ten committees to study the issue. His successor, Alexander II, took the loss of the Crimean War to mean that Russia, including the institution of serfdom, needed reforming. His philosophy was "better from above than below." Using Nicholas I's "enlightened bureaucrats," who had studied serfdom for years, Alexander II proclaimed the emancipation of the serfs in 1861, but this only freed the serfs from their slavelike dependence on their masters. They were then bound to their communes. State serfs were freed separately, in 1863. The seignorial serfs had to pay for their freedom, that is, the state was unwilling to expropriate the serfowners and simultaneously feared the consequences of a landless emancipation.

The serfs were finally freed in 1906, when they were released from control by their communes, the redemption dues were cancelled, and corporal punishment for serfs was abolished. Thus, all peasants were free for the first time since 1450.

See also: EMANCIPATION ACT; LAW CODE OF 1649; PEASANTRY; PODZOL; POMESTIE; SUDEBANK OF 1497; SUDEBANK OF 1550; SERFDOM; SLAVERY

BIBLIOGRAPHY

Blum, Jerome. (1961). *Lord and Peasant in Russia: From the Ninth to the Nineteenth Century.* Princeton, NJ: Princeton University Press.

Hellie, Richard. (1967, 1970). *Muscovite Society.* Chicago: The University of Chicago College Syllabus Division.

Hellie, Richard. (1971). *Enserfment and Military Change in Muscovy.* Chicago: University of Chicago Press.

Hellie, Richard, tr. and ed. (1988). *The Muscovite Law Code (Ulozhenie) of 1649.* Irvine, CA: Charles Schlacks, Publisher.

Kolchin, Peter. (1987). *Unfree Labor. American Slavery and Russian Serfdom.* Cambridge, MA: Harvard University Press.

Robinson, Geroid Tanquery. (1932). *Rural Russia under the Old Regime.* New York: Longmans.

Zaionchkovsky, P. A. (1978). *The Abolition of Serfdom in Russia.* Gulf Breeze, FL: Academic International Press.

RICHARD HELLIE

ENTERPRISE, SOVIET

Soviet industrial enterprises (*predpryatie*), occupying the lowest level of the economic bureaucracy, were responsible for producing the goods desired by planners, as specified in the *techpromfinplan* (technical-industrial financial plan) received by the enterprise each year. Owned by the state, headed by a director, and governed by the principle of one-person management (*edinonachalie*), each Soviet enterprise was subordinate to an industrial ministry. For example, enterprises producing shoes and clothing were subordinate to the Ministry of Light Industry; enterprises producing bricks and mortar, to the Ministry of Construction Materials; enterprises producing tractors, to the Ministry of Tractor and Agricultural Machine Building. Enterprises producing military goods were subordinate to the Ministry of Defense Industry. In some cases, enterprises subordinate to the Ministry of Defense Industry also produced civilian goods—for example, all products using electronic components were produced in military production enterprises. Many enterprises producing civilian goods and subordinate to a civilian industrial ministry had a special department, Department No. 1, responsible for military-related production (e.g., chemical producers making paint for military equipment or buildings, clothing producers making uniforms and other military wear, shoe producers making military footwear). While the enterprise was subordinate to the civilian industrial ministry, Department No. 1 reported to the appropriate purchasing department in the Ministry of Defense.

During the 1970s industrial enterprises were grouped into production associations (*obedinenya*) to facilitate planning. The creation of industrial or production associations was intended to improve the economic coordination between planners and producers. By establishing horizontal or vertical mergers of enterprises working in related activities, planning officials could focus on long-term or aggregate planning tasks, leaving the management of the obedinenya to resolve problems related to routine operations of individual firms. In effect the obedinenya simply added a management layer to the economic bureaucracy because the industrial enterprise remained the basic unit of production in the Soviet economy.

Soviet industrial enterprises were involved in formulating and implementing the annual plan. During plan formulation, enterprises provided information about the material and technical supplies needed to fulfill a targeted level and assortment of production, and updated accounts of productive capacity. Because planning policy favored taut plans (i.e., plans with output targets high relative to input allocations and the firm's productivity capacity), output targets based on previous plan fulfillment (i.e., the "ratchet effect" or "planning from the achieved level"), and large monetary bonuses for managers if output targets were fulfilled, Soviet enterprise managers were motivated to establish a safety factor by over-ordering inputs and under-reporting productive capacity during the plan formulation process. Similarly, during plan implementation, they were motivated to sacrifice quality in order to meet quantity targets or to falsify plan fulfillment documents if quantity targets were not met. In some instances managers would petition for a correction in the plan targets that would reduce the output requirements for a particular plan period (month, quarter, or year). In such instances they apparently expected that their future plan targets would be revised upward. In the current period, if plan targets were lowered for one firm, planning officials redistributed the output to other firms in the form of higher output targets, so that the annual plan targets would be met for the industrial ministry.

Unlike enterprises in market economies, Soviet enterprises were not concerned with costs of production. The prices firms paid for materials and labor were fixed by central authorities, as were the prices they received for the goods they produced. Based on average cost rather than marginal cost of production, and not including capital charges, the centrally determined prices did not reflect scarcity, and were not adjusted to capture changes in supply or demand. Because prices were fixed, and cost considerations were less important than fulfilling quantity targets in the reward structure, Soviet enterprises were not concerned about profits. Profits and profitability norms were specified in the annual enterprise plan, but did not signal the same information about the successful operation and performance of the firm that they do in a market economy. Typically, failure to earn profits was an accounting outcome rather than a performance outcome, and resulted in the planning authorities providing subsidies to the firm.

The operation and performance of Soviet enterprises was monitored by planning authorities using the financial plan component of the annual techpromfinplan. The financial plan corresponded to the input and output plans, documenting the flow of materials and goods between firms, as well as wage payments, planned cost reductions, and the like. Financial accounts for the sending and receiving firms in any transaction were adjusted by the state bank (Gosbank) to match the flow of materials or goods. Furniture manufacturers, for example, were given output targets for each item in their assortment of production—tables, chairs, benches, cabinets, bookshelves. The plan further specified the input allocations associated with each item. Gosbank debited the accounts of the furniture manufacturer when the designated inputs were received and credited the accounts of the supplying firms. Planned transactions did not involve the exchange of cash between firms. Gosbank provided cash to the enterprise each month to pay wages; the maximum amount that an enterprise could withdraw from Gosbank was based on the planned number of employees and the centrally determined wages. Cash disbursements for wage payments were strictly controlled to preclude enterprise directors from acting independently from planners' preferences. Financial control was further exercised by planners in that Gosbank only provided short-term credit if specified in the annual enterprise plan. This system of financial supervision was called ruble control (*kontrol rublem*).

See also: EDINONACHALIE; GOSBANK; MONETARY SYSTEM, SOVIET; RUBLE CONTROL; TECHPROMFINPLAN

BIBLIOGRAPHY

Berliner, Joseph S. (1957). *Factory and Manager in the USSR.* Cambridge, MA: Harvard University Press.

Freris, Andrew. (1984). *The Soviet Industrial Enterprise.* New York: St. Martin's Press.

Granick, David. (1954). *Management of the Industrial Firm in the USSR.* New York: Columbia University Press.

Linz, Susan J., and Martin, Robert E. (1982). "Soviet Enterprise Behavior under Uncertainty." *Journal of Comparative Economics* 6:24–36.

SUSAN J. LINZ

ENVIRONMENTALISM

Environmental protection in Russia traces its roots to seventeenth-century hunting preserves and Peter the Great's efforts to protect some of the country's forests and rivers. But environmentalism, in the sense of an intellectual or popular movement in support of conservation or environmental protection, began during the second half of the nineteenth century and scored some important victories during the late tsarist and early soviet periods. The movement lost most of its momentum during the Stalin years but revived during the 1960s and 1970s, peaking during the era of perestroika. After a decline during the early 1990s, environmentalism showed a resurgence later in the decade.

EARLY HISTORY

Sergei Aksakov's extremely popular fishing and hunting guides (1847 and 1851) awakened the reading public to the extent and importance of central Russia's natural areas and helped popularize outdoor pursuits. As the membership in hunting societies grew in subsequent decades, so did awareness of the precipitous decline in populations of game species. Articles in hunting journals and the more widely circulated "thick" journals sounded the alarm about this issue. Provincial observers also began to note the rapid loss of forest resources. Noble landowners, facing straitened financial circumstances after the abolition of serfdom, were selling timber to earn ready cash. Anton Chekhov, among others, lamented the loss of wildlife habitats and the damage to rivers that resulted from widespread deforestation. By the late 1880s the outcry led to the enactment of the Forest Code (1888) and hunting regulations (1892). These laws had little effect, but their existence testifies to the emergence of a Russian conservation movement.

In contrast to the environmentalism around the same time in the United States and England, the main impetus for the movement in Russia came from scientists rather than amateur naturalists, poets, or politicians. Russian scientists were pioneers in the fledgling field of ecology, particularly the study of plant communities and ecosystems. While they shared with western environmentalists an aesthetic appreciation for natural beauty, they were especially keen about the need to preserve whole landscapes and ecosystems. During the early twentieth century when the Russian conservation movement began to press for the creation of na-

Half of the livestock in Muslumovo have leukemia, but their meat and milk are still consumed. © GYORI ANTOINE/CORBIS SYGMA

ture preserves, it did not adopt the U.S. model of national parks designed to preserve places of extraordinary beauty for recreational purposes. Instead, Russian scientists sought to preserve large tracts of representative landscapes and keep them off limits except to scientists who would use them as laboratories for ecological observation. They called these tracts *zapovedniks*, a word derived from the religious term for "commandments" and connoting something forbidden or inviolate. The Permanent Commission on Nature Preservation, organized in 1912 under the auspices of the Russian Geographical Society, proposed the creation of a network of zapovedniks in 1917, shortly before the Bolshevik Revolution. Its primary author was the geologist Venyamin Semenov-Tian-Shansky (1870–1942). His brother, Andrei (1866–1942), a renowned entomologist, was an important proponent of the project, along with the botanist Ivan Borodin (1847–1930), head of the Permanent Commission, and the zoologist Grigory Kozhevnikov (1866–1933), who had first articulated the need for inviolate nature preserves.

These scientists also sought to popularize a conservation ethic among the populace, especially among young people. Despite their many educational efforts, however, they were unable to build a mass conservation movement. This was at least partly because their insistence on keeping the nature preserves off limits to the public prevented them from capitalizing on the direct experience and visceral affection that U.S. national parks inspire in so many visitors.

SOVIET PERIOD

The early Bolshevik regime enacted a number of conservation measures, including one to establish zapovedniks in 1921. The politicization of all aspects of scientific and public activity during the 1920s, together with war, economic crisis, and local anarchy, threatened conservation efforts and made it difficult to protect nature preserves from exploitation. In 1924 conservation scientists established the All-Russian Society for Conservation (VOOP) in order to build a broad based environmental movement. VOOP organized popular events such as Arbor Day and Bird Day, which attracted 45,000 young naturalists in 1927, and began publishing the magazine *Conservation* (*Okhrana prirody*) in 1928, with a circulation of 3,000. An All-Russian Congress for Conservation was convened in 1929, and an All-Soviet Congress in 1933. By this time conservationists had lost their optimism, overwhelmed by the Stalinist emphasis on conquering nature in the name of rapid industrial development. The government whittled away at the idea of inviolate zapovedniks over the ensuing decades, turning some into game reserves, others into breeding grounds for selected species, and opening still others to mining, logging, and agriculture. In 1950 the government proposed to turn over more than 85 percent of the protected territories to the agriculture and timber ministries.

Environmentalism of a grassroots and broad-based variety finally began to develop after Stalin's death. VOOP had expanded to some nineteen million members, but it existed primarily to funnel extorted dues into dubious land-reclamation schemes. The real impetus for environmentalism came during the early 1960s in response to a plan to build a large pulp and paper combine on Lake Baikal. Scientists once again spearheaded the outcry against the plan, which soon included journalists, famous authors, and others who could reach a broad national and international audience. The combine opened in 1967, but environmentalists gained a symbolic victory when the government promised to take extraordinary measures to protect the lake. Similar grassroots movements arose during the 1970s and early 1980s to protest pollution in the Volga River, the drying up of the Aral Sea, river-diversion projects, and other threats to environmental health.

Under Leonid Brezhnev, environmentalists were able to air some of their grievances in the press, especially in letters to the editors of mass-circulation newspapers. As long as they did not attack the idea of economic growth or other underpinnings of soviet ideology, they were fairly free to voice their opinions. By and large, the environmentalists called for improvements in the central planning system and more Communist Party attention to environmental problems, not systemic changes. Their arguments took the form of cheerleading for beloved places rather than condemnations of the exploitation of natural resources, and it became difficult to distinguish environmentalism from local chauvinism. In contrast to its counterpart in the West, environmentalism in the Soviet Union was often closely aligned with right-wing nationalist politics. Furthermore, environmental activism had little impact on economic planners. Although, as official propagandists boasted, the country had many progressive environmental laws, few of them were enforced. Activists were further hampered by official secrecy about the extent of environmental problems. In 1978 a manuscript entitled "The Destruction of Nature in the Soviet Union" by Boris Komarov (pseudonym of Ze'ev Wolfson, a specialist in environmental policy) was smuggled out and published abroad.

Environmentalism left the margins of soviet society and took center stage in the period of glasnost. After the Chernobyl disaster in 1986, everyone became aware of the threat soviet industry posed for the environment and public health, and also of the need for full disclosure of relevant information. Environmental issues galvanized local movements against the central government, and nationalist overtones in the environmental rhetoric fanned the flames. In Estonia, protests in 1987 against a phosphorite mine grew into a full–blown independence movement. Environmental issues also helped initiate general political opposition in Latvia, Lithuania, Kazakhstan, and elsewhere. Environmentalists began to win real victories, closing or halting production on some fifty nuclear plants and many large construction projects. There were thousands of grassroots environmental groups in the country by 1991, and the Greens were second only to religious groups in the degree of public trust they enjoyed.

POST-SOVIET ACTIVISM

After 1991 the influence of Russian environmental organizations declined. As the central government consolidated its power, public attention turned to pressing economic matters, and pollution problems decreased as a result of the closing of many factories in the post-Soviet depression. Later in the decade the government became openly hostile to environmental activism. It arrested two whistleblowers, Alexander Nikitin and Grigory Pasko, who revealed information about radioactive pollution from nuclear submarines. President Vladimir Putin dissolved the State Committee on the Environment in 2000 and gave its portfolio to the Natural Resources Ministry.

Environmental organizations survived by becoming professionalized nongovernmental organizations (NGOs) on the Western model, seeking funding from foreign foundations and appealing to world opinion rather than cultivating local memberships. Among the most influential of these are the Center for Russian Environmental Policy under the direction of Alexei Yablokov (former environmental adviser to Boris Yeltsin), the St. Petersburg Clean Baltic Coalition, the Baikal Environmental Wave, the Russian branch of the Worldwide Fund for Wildlife (WWF), and Green Cross International, of which Mikhail Gorbachev became president in 1993. A few radical environmental groups emerged during the early 1990s, notably the Rainbow Keepers and Eco-Defense, which promote more fundamental societal change. Beginning during the late 1990s, there was a revival of grassroots activism on local issues of air and water quality, animal welfare, nature education, and protection of sacred lands. Such efforts rely on local members and on the resources of preexisting (i.e., Soviet-era) institutions and networks, and they tend to cultivate local bureaucrats and political leaders.

See also: CHERNOBYL; RUSSIAN GEOGRAPHICAL SOCIETY; THICK JOURNALS

BIBLIOGRAPHY

Goldman, Marshall I. (1972). *Environmental Pollution in the Soviet Union: The Spoils of Progress.* Cambridge, MA: MIT Press.

Henry, Laura. (2002). "Two Paths to a Greener Future: Environmentalism and Civil Society Development in Russia." *Demokratizatsiya* 10(2):184–206.

Komarov, Boris (Ze'ev Wolfson). (1978). *The Destruction of Nature in the Soviet Union.* London: Pluto Press.

Pryde, Philip R. (1991). *Environmental Management in the Soviet Union.* Cambridge UK: Cambridge University Press.

Stewart, John Massey, ed. (1992). *The Soviet Environment: Problems, Policies and Politics.* Cambridge, UK: Cambridge University Press.

Weiner, Douglas R. (1988). *Models of Nature: Ecology, Conservation, and Cultural Revolution in Soviet Russia.* Bloomington: Indiana University Press.

Weiner, Douglas R. (1999). *A Little Corner of Freedom: Russian Nature Protection from Stalin to Gorbachev.* Berkeley: University of California Press.

Yanitsky, Oleg. (1999). "The Environmental Movement in a Hostile Context: The Case of Russia." *International Sociology* 14(2):157–172.

Ziegler, Charles E. (1987). *Environmental Policy in the USSR.* Amherst: University of Massachusetts Press.

RACHEL MAY

EPARKHYA *See* DIOCESE.

EPISCOPATE

The episcopate of the Russian Orthodox Church (Moscow Patriarchate) encompasses the whole body of bishops who govern dioceses and supervise clergy, as well as perform and administer church sacraments. The episcopate is drawn exclusively from the ranks of the celibate "black" clergy, although widowers who take monastic vows may also be recruited. The patriarch of Moscow and All Russia and the ecclesiastical ranks below him—metropolitans, archbishops, bishops, and hegumens—comprise the leadership of the church. The patriarch and metropolitans hold power over the church hierarchy and carry on the debates that produce (or resist) change within the church.

Eastern Orthodoxy is widely believed to have been introduced in Kievan Rus in 988 C.E. At first the Russian church was governed by metropolitans appointed by the patriarchate of Constantinople from the Greek clergy active in the Rus lands. When the Russian church gained its independence from Constantinople in 1448, Metropolitan Jonas, resident in the outpost of Moscow, was given the title of metropolitan of Moscow and All Russia. Metropolitan Job of Moscow became the first Russian patriarch in 1589, thereby establishing the Russian church's independence from Greek Orthodoxy.

The close link between ecclesiastical and temporal authorities in Russia reflected Byzantine cultural influence. The alliance between church and state ended with the reign of Peter the Great (1682-1725). Seeing the Russian Orthodox Church as a conservative body frustrating his attempts to modernize the empire, he did not appoint a successor when Patriarch Adrian died in 1700 and in his place appointed a bishop more open to Westernization. In 1721 Peter abolished the patriarchate and appointed a collegial board of bishops, the Holy Synod, to replace it. This body was subject to civil authority and similar in both structure and status to other departments of the state.

The reigns of Peter III (1762-1763) and Catherine II (1762-1796) brought Peter the Great's reforms to their logical conclusion, confiscating the church's properties and subjecting it administratively to the state. A (lay) over procurator was empowered to supervise the church, appointing important officials and directing the activities of the Holy Synod. The full extent of the over–procurator's control was realized under the conservative Konstantin Pobedonostsev (1880–1905), who kept the episcopate in submission.

The calls for reform during Tsar Nicholas II's reign (1894–1917) included demands for an end to state control of the church. By and large the bishops were dissatisfied with the Holy Synod and the role played by the over-procurator. Nicholas II responded by granting the church greater independence in 1905 and agreeing to allow a council that church officials anticipated would result in the liberalization of the church. In 1917, when the council was finally convened, it called for the restoration of the patriarchate and church sovereignty, and decentralization of church administration.

The October Revolution brought a radical change in the status of the episcopate. The Bolsheviks implemented a policy of unequivocal hostility toward Orthodoxy, fueled by the atheism of Marxist–Leninist doctrine and also by the church's legacy as defender of the imperial government. Bishops were a special target and, along with priests, monks, nuns, and laypersons, were persecuted on any pretext. Nearly the entire episcopate was executed or died in labor camps. In 1939 only four bishops remained free. Throughout the Soviet period, the number of bishops rose and fell according to the whims of the communist regime's religious policy.

While initially the episcopate was hostile to the Bolsheviks, the sustained persecution of believers made it apparent that if the church wished to survive as an institution it would have to change its position. In 1927 Patriarch Sergei, speaking for the church, issued a "Declaration of Loyalty" to the Soviet Motherland, "whose joys and successes are our joys and successes, and whose setbacks are our setbacks" This capitulation began one of the most controversial chapters in the episcopate's history. The Soviet authorities appointed all of the church's important officials and unseated any who challenged their rule. The regime and the church leadership worked together to root out schismatic groups and sects. Meanwhile, prelates assured the international community that accusations of religious persecution were merely anti-Soviet propaganda.

The reinstitutionalization of the Orthodox Church during the perestroika years marked the end of the episcopate's subordination to the atheist regime. The Orthodox Church figured prominently in discussions about the renewal and regeneration of Soviet society. In post-communist Russia, the patriarch and other Orthodox dignitaries became high-profile public figures. The episcopate has influenced political debate, most notably the deliberations on new religious legislation during the mid- and late 1990s. The end of communism also produced new challenges for the episcopate. Schismatic movements, competition from other faiths, and reformist priests have created divisions and threatened the Orthodox Church's preeminence.

See also: CHRISTIANIZATION; JOB, PATRIARCH; KIEVAN RUS; ORTHODOXY; PATRIARCHATE RUSSIAN ORTHODOX CHURCH

BIBLIOGRAPHY

Ellis, Jane. (1986). *The Russian Orthodox Church: A Contemporary History.* London: Routledge.

Gudziak, Borys A. (1998). *Crisis and Reform: The Kyivan Metropolitanate, the Patriarchate of Constantinople, and the Genesis of the Union of Brest.* Cambridge, MA: Harvard University Press.

Hosking, Geoffrey. (1998). *Russia: People and Empire, 1552–1917.* Cambridge, MA: Harvard University Press.

Knox, Zoe. (2003). "The Symphonic Ideal: The Moscow Patriarchate's Post-Soviet Leadership." *Europe–Asia Studies* 55:575–596.

ZOE KNOX

ESTATE *See* SOSLOVIE.

ESTONIA AND ESTONIANS

Estonia covers the area from 57.40° to 59.40° N and 21.50° to 28.12° E, bordered on the north by the Gulf of Finland, on the east by Russia, on the south by Latvia, and on the west by the Baltic Sea. Its area is 17,462 square miles (45,222 square kilometers), and its capital is Tallinn (population 400,378 in 2000). The estimated population of Estonia in 2003 was 1,356,000, including 351,178 ethnic Russians. Outside the country there are approximately 160,000 Estonians, among them 46,390 in the Russian Federation.

The Estonian constitution separates church and state. According to the census of 2000, there were 152,237 Lutherans (of whom 145,718 were Estonians), 143,557 Orthodox Chrsistians (104,698 of them Russians), 6,009 Baptists, and 5,745 Roman Catholics. Non-Christian religions included Islam (1,387 Muslims), Estonian native religion (1,058), Buddhism (622), and Judaism (257).

The Estonian language belongs to the Baltic-Finnic branch of the Finno-Ugric languages of the Uralic language family. The first book in Estonian was printed in 1525. According to the 2000 census, 99.1 percent of Estonians considered Estonian their mother tongue.

The Estonian constitution, adopted in 1992, vests political supremacy in a unicameral parliament, the Riigikogu, with 101 members elected by proportional representation for four-year terms. The Riigikogu makes all major political decisions, such as enacting legislation, electing the president and prime minister, during the longevity of governments, preparing the state budget, and making treaties with foreign countries. The head of state and supreme commander of the armed forces is the president, who is elected to not more than two consecutive five-year terms. The president is elected by a two-thirds majority of the Riigikogu. If no candidate receives two-thirds, the process moves to the Electoral College, made up of the members of Riigikogu and representatives of local government.

The Estonian economy is mainly industrial. The dominant branches are the food, timber, textile, and clothing industries, but transportation, wholesaling, retailing, and real estate are also significant. The importance of agriculture is diminishing, but historically it was the most important branch of Estonian economy. The main fields of agriculture are cattle and pig keeping and raising of crops and potatoes. In 2001 there were 85,300 agricultural households in Estonia.

The earliest settlements in Estonia date to the Mesolithic Age (9000 B.C.E.). Its Neolithic Age continued from 4900 B.C.E. to 1800 B.C.E., its Bronze Age until 500 B.C.E., and the Iron Age until the beginning of the thirteenth century. After a struggle for independence between 1208 and 1227, Estonia was conquered by the Danes and Germans. It territory was divided between Denmark (Tallinn and northern Estonia), the Teutonic Knights (southwestern Estonia), and the bishoprics of Saare-Lääne

Estonia, 1992 © MARYLAND CARTOGRAPHICS. REPRINTED WITH PERMISSION

(western Estonia and the islands) and Tartu (southeastern Estonia). In 1346 the Danish crown sold northern Estonia to the Teutonic Order. During the Livonian Wars (1558–1583), Ivan the Terrible invaded Old Livonia (now Estonia and Latvia). The largest of the Estonian islands, Saaremaa, became the property of the Danish king, northern Estonia capitulated to Sweden, and the southern part of present-day Estonia to Poland. By the Truce of Altmark (1629) Poland surrendered southern Estonia to Sweden. In 1645 Sweden obtained Saaremaa from Denmark. At the beginning of the eighteenth century, Peter the Great of Russia defeated Charles XII of Sweden in the Great Northern War, and, by the Peace of Nystad (1721), obtained Estonia, which he had occupied in 1710. Between 1816 and 1819, serfdom was abolished in Estonia. This led to an improved economic situation and the cultural development of the Estonian people, who constituted most of the class of peasants by that time. Between 1860 and 1880 there was an Estonian national awakening, the beginning of a modern Estonian nation. Estonians began to publish national newspapers, organized all-Estonian song festivals, and developed literature, education, and the arts. In the late nineteenth century, a wave of Russification, initiated by the tsarist government, reached Estonia. Estonian politicians demanded radical political changes during the revolution of 1905, but the Russian authorities responded with repressions. After the February Revolution in Russia, the Provisional Government allowed Estonia's territorial unification as one province (until then it had been divided into the Estonia and Livonia guberniyas).

On February 24, 1918, Estonia declared its independence. Its War of Independence (1918–1920) concluded with Soviet Russia recognizing its independence in the Tartu Peace Treaty signed on February 2, 1920. In 1939 the Nazi-Soviet Pact (also known as the Molotov-Ribbentrop Pact) assigned Estonia to the Soviet sphere of influence. Soviet troops occupied the Estonian Republic in June 1940 and incorporated it into the USSR. During the first year of the Soviet regime, 2,000 Estonian citizens were executed and 19,000 deported, more than half of them in June 1941. During the period 1941–1944, Estonia was occupied by Germany.

At the end of World War II there were nearly 100,000 Estonian refugees in the West. An anti-Soviet guerilla movement was active from 1944 through the mid-1950s. In March 1949, during the collectivization campaign, more than 20,000 Estonians were deported to Siberia. Throughout the Soviet period, a directed migration of population from Russia was conducted, mainly into Tallinn and the industrial region of northeastern Estonia. The 1970s and the first half of the 1980s comprised the most intense period of Russification. At the end of the 1980s, a new wave of national awakening began in Estonia, accompanied by political struggle to regain independence. On August 20, 1991, Estonia proclaimed its independence from the Soviet Union, and in September 1991 it was admitted to the United Nations.

See also: GREAT NORTHERN WAR; LATVIA AND LATVIANS; LIVONIAN WAR; NATIONALITIES POLICIES, SOVIET; NATIONALITIES POLICIES, TSARIST; WORLD WAR II

BIBLIOGRAPHY

Clemens, Walter C., Jr. (1991). *Baltic Independence and Russian Empire.* New York: St. Martin's Press.

Pettai, Vello A. (1996). "Estonia." In *Estonia, Latvia, and Lithuania: Country Studies*, ed. Walter R. Iwaskiw. Washington, DC: Federal Research Division, Library of Congress.

Raun, Toivo U. (2001). *Estonia and the Estonians.* Stanford, CA: Hoover Institution Press.

Taagepera, Rein. (1993). *Estonia: Return to Independence.* Boulder, CO: Westview Press.

ART LEETE

ETHIOPIAN CIVIL WAR

The Ethiopian civil war, between the Ethiopian government and nationalists from Eritrea (an Ethiopian province along the Red Sea), has raged off and on and has been tightly interconnected with Ethiopia's internal political problems and conflict with neighboring Somalia. In the 1880s Italy captured Eritrea. By 1952 Ethiopia regained control, but eight years later, in 1961, Eritrean nationalists demanded independence from Ethiopia. When the Ethiopian government rejected this demand, civil war erupted.

The civil war was a symptom of profound changes within Ethiopia, involving a confrontation between traditional and modern forces that changed the nature of the Ethiopian state. The last fourteen years of Haile Selassie's reign (1960–1974) witnessed growing opposition to his regime. Ethiopians demanded better living conditions for the poor and an end to government corruption. In 1972 and 1973, severe drought led to famine in the northeastern part of Ethiopia. Haile Selassie's critics claimed that the government ignored victims of the famine. In 1974 Ethiopian military leaders under Lieutenant Colonel Mengistu Haile-Mariam seized the government and removed Haile Selassie from power.

The Ogaden region of southeastern Ethiopia also became a trouble spot, beginning in the 1960s. The government of neighboring Somalia claimed the region, which the Ethiopian Emperor Menelik had conquered in the 1890s. Many Somali people had always lived there, and they revolted against Ethiopian rule. In the 1970s fighting broke out between Ethiopia and Somalia over the Ogaden region.

Until then, Ethiopia had enjoyed U.S. support, while the Soviet Union had sided with its rival, Somalia. In fact, in the space of just four years (1974–1978), the USSR concluded a Treaty of Friendship and Cooperation with Somalia, Ethiopia experienced a revolution in 1974, and the Soviet Union dramatically shifted massive support from Somalia to Ethiopia and then played a key part in the military defeat of its former ally in the Ogaden conflict of 1977–1978. During the conflict, about fifty Soviet ships passed through the Suez Canal to the port of Assab to unload fighter aircraft, tanks, artillery, and munitions—an estimated 60,000 tons of hardware—for delivery to Mengistu's regime.

After the 1974 revolution, the new military government under Mengistu adopted socialist policies and established close relations with the Soviet Union. The government began large-scale land reform, breaking up huge estates of the former nobility. The government claimed ownership of this land and turned it into farmland. But the military leaders also killed many of their Ethiopian opponents, further alienating former U.S. supporters who opposed the human rights abuses.

Eritrean rebels stepped up their separatist efforts after the 1974 revolution. Mengistu's regime invaded rebel-held Eritrea several times, but failed to regain control. Ethiopia's conflict with Eritrea also had a strong East-West dimension. The Soviet Union, along with some Arab states, advocated complete independence for Eritrea. In a speech to the United Nations, the Soviet delegate rejected the federalist compromise solution advocated by the United States, claiming that the Eritrean people had not given their consent. Soviet scholars also backed Ethiopia's claim to Eritrea on both historical and economic grounds. They noted that the Soviet Union had favored Ethiopian access to the Eritrean port of Assab as early as 1946. Despite an influx of Soviet military aid after 1977, Mengistu's counterinsurgency effort in Eritrea progressed slowly. Talks between the two sides continued well into the 1980s. The war ended in 1991 with Eritrea's independence; however, conflict between the two countries persisted for more than a decade. In June 2000, the two countries signed a cessation of hostilities agreement, and a United Nations peacekeeping force of more than 4,300 military personnel was dispatched later that year.

BIBLIOGRAPHY

Albright, David E. (1980). *Communism in Africa.* Bloomington: Indiana University Press.

Feuchtwanger, E. J., and Nailor, Peter. (1981). *The Soviet Union and the Third World.* New York: St. Martin's-Press.

Human Rights Watch Organization. (2003). *Eritrea and Ethiopia: The Horn of Africa War: Mass Expulsions and the Nationality Issue, June 1998–April 2002.* New York: Human Rights Watch.

Korn, David A. (1986). *Ethiopia, the United States, and the Soviet Union.* Carbondale: Southern Illinois University Press.

JOHANNA GRANVILLE

ETHNOGRAPHY, RUSSIAN AND SOVIET

Russian ethnography took shape as a distinct field of scholarship in the mid-nineteenth century, but the creation of ethnographic knowledge in Russia dates back at least to Kievan Rus. The *Russian Primary Chronicle* abounds with information about Slavic tribes and neighboring peoples, while later medieval and early modern Russian writings provide accounts of the peoples of Siberia and the Far North. It was only in the period following the reforms of Peter the Great (d. 1725), however, that the population of the empire was studied using explicitly scientific methods. In the 1730s Vasily Tatishchev disseminated Russia's first ethnographic survey, thereby legitimizing the notion of peoples and their cultures as objects of systematic scientific inquiry. From the 1730s to the 1770s the Russian Academy of Sciences sponsored two major expeditions dedicated to the study of the empire. Led by Gerhard Friedrich Miller and Peter Pallas, the academic expeditions covered a vast expanse from Siberia to the Caucasus to the Far North and, drawing on the talents of numerous dedicated scholars, amassed an enormous amount of ethnographic information and physical artifacts. But for all their achievements as ethnographers, eighteenth-century scholars viewed the study of cultural diversity as merely one component of a broadly defined natural science.

FOLKLORE AND THE SEARCH FOR NATIONAL IDENTITY

During the last decades of the eighteenth century Russian scholars began to turn their attention to folklore. Publishers of folk songs in the 1790s, such as Mikhail Popov and Nikolai Lvov, claimed that their collections were of value not only for entertainment but also as relics of ancient times and as sources of insight into the national spirit. By 1820 several significant folklore collections had appeared, including the Kirsha Danilov collection of folk epics, and the first efforts to collect folklore among the common people had begun under the patronage of Count Nikolai Rumiantsev. As Russian intellectuals struggled in the 1820s to define *narodnost,* the

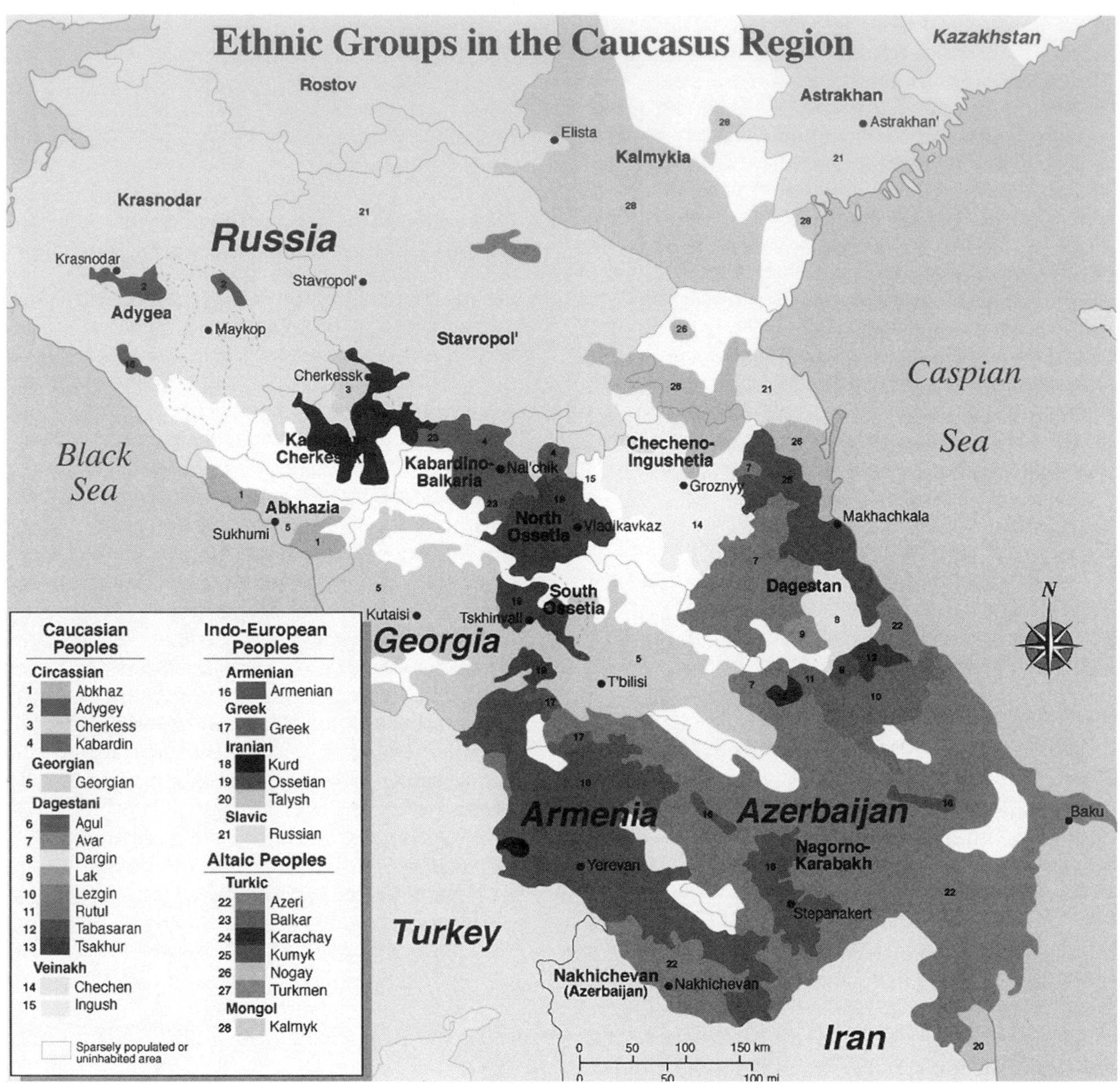

The Caucasus region is one of the most ethnically diverse areas in the former Russian empire. © MAPS.COM/CORBIS

national spirit, they turned increasingly to folklore for inspiration. Peter Kireyevsky assembled the largest folk song collection, drawing on an extensive network of contributors, including Alexander Pushkin, Nikolai Gogol, and other prominent writers. While Kireyevsky's songs were not published during his lifetime, other folklorists in the 1830s and 1840s, such as Ivan Snegarev, Ivan Sakharov, Vladimir Dal, and Alexander Tereshchenko, put out collections that enjoyed considerable success with the reading public despite their often dubious authenticity.

ETHNOGRAPHY AS A DISCIPLINE

Geographic exploration and folklore, the two main branches of ethnographic research up to this point, came together in the Ethnographic Division of the Russian Geographical Society, the founding of which in 1845 marks the emergence of ethnography as a distinct academic field. In its first years the society considered two well-developed conceptions of ethnography as a scholarly discipline. The eminent scientist Karl Ernst von Baer proposed that the Ethnographic Division study primarily the smaller and less-developed populations of the empire, paying particular attention to the role of environment and heredity. In contrast, Nikolai Nadezhdin, a well-known editor, literary critic, and historian, advocated a science of nationality dedicated to describing the full range of cultural, intellectual, and physical features that make up national identity. First priority, he felt, should go to the study of the Russian people. After replacing Baer as chair of the Ethnographic Division in 1847, Nadezhdin launched a major survey of the Russian provinces based on a specially designed questionnaire. The materials generated were published by the Ethnographic Division in its journal *Ethnographic Anthology* (*Etnografichesky sbornik*), the first periodical in Russian specifically devoted to ethnography, and were used for several major collections of Russian folklore.

In the 1860s a second major center of ethnographic study arose in Moscow with the founding of the Society of Friends of Natural History, Anthropology, and Ethnography (known by its Russian initials, OLEAE). Dedicated explicitly to the popularization of science, the society inaugurated its ethnographic endeavors in 1867 with a major exhibition representing most of the peoples of the Russian Empire as well as neighboring Slavic nationalities.

During the 1860s and 1870s ethnographic studies in Russia flourished and diversified. The Russian Geographical Society in St. Petersburg and OLEAE in Moscow sponsored expeditions, subsidized the work of provincial scholars, and published major ethnographic works. At the same time regional schools began to take root, particularly in Siberia and Ukraine. Landmark collections appeared in folklore studies, such as Alexander Afanasev's folktales, Vladimir Dal's proverbs and dictionary, Kireevsky's folksongs, and Pavel Rybnikov's folk epics (*byliny*). As new texts accumulated, scholars such as Fedor Buslaev, Alexander Veselovsky, Vsevolod Miller, and Alexander Pypin developed sophisticated methods of analysis that drew on European comparative philology, setting in place a distinctive tradition of Russian folklore studies.

The abolition of serfdom in 1861 sparked an upsurge of interest in peasant life and customary law. Nikolai Kalachov, Peter Efimenko, Alexandra Efimenko, and S.V. Pakhman undertook major studies of customary law among Russian and non-Russian peasants, while the Russian Geographical Society formed a special commission on the topic in the 1870s and generated data through the dissemination of a large survey. The vast literature on customary law was cataloged and summarized by Yevgeny Iakushkin in a three-volume bibliography. Alongside the study of customary law, ethnographers probed peasant social organization, with emphasis on the redistributional land commune.

THE PROFESSIONALIZATION OF ETHNOGRAPHY

While ethnographers in the 1860s through the 1880s produced an enormous quantity of important work, the boundaries and methods of ethnography as a discipline remained fluid and ill-defined. Not only did ethnography overlap with a number of other pursuits, such as philology, history, legal studies, and belle-lettres, but the field itself was distinctly under-theorized—descriptive studies were pursued as an end in themselves, with little attempt to integrate the data generated into broader theoretical schemes. During the 1880s and 1890s, however, ethnography began to establish itself on a more solid academic footing. New journals appeared, most notably the *Ethnographic Review* (*Etnograficheskoe obozrenie*) distributed by OLEAE and the Russian Geographical Society's *Living Antiquity* (*Zhivaia starina*). Instruction in ethnography, albeit rather haphazard, began to appear at the major universities. Museum ethnography also moved forward with the transformation, under the direction of Vasily Radlov, of the old Kunstkamara in St. Petersburg into a Museum of Anthropology and Ethnography, and the founding around the turn of the twentieth century of the Ethnographic Division of the Russian Museum.

By the 1890s theoretical influences from Western Europe, particularly anthropological evolutionism, had begun to exert a stronger influence on Russian scholars. Nikolai Kharuzin, a prominent young Moscow ethnographer, made evolutionist theory the centerpiece of his textbook on ethnography, the first of its kind in Russia. In the field, Lev Shternberg, a political exile turned ethnographer, claimed to find among the Giliak people (Nivkhi) of Sakhalin Island confirmation of the practice of group marriage as postulated by the evolutionist theorist Henry Lewis Morgan and Friedrich Engels. With the growing theoretical influence of Western anthropology came increased contacts. Shternberg and his fellow exiles Vladimir Bogoraz-Tan and Vladimir Iokhelson participated in the Jessup North Pacific Expedition sponsored by the American Museum of Natural History in New York under the direction of Franz Boas. Upon his return from exile, Shternberg was hired by Radlov of the Museum of Anthropology and Ethnography in St. Petersburg, and made use of his friendship with Boas to cultivate a fruitful collaboration with the museum in New York.

SOVIET PERIOD

The Russian Revolution presented both opportunities and dangers for the field of ethnography. On the eve of the February Revolution of 1917 a Commission for the Study of the Ethnic Composition of the Borderlands (KIPS) was established under the auspices of the Academy of Sciences. While initially established to aid the Russian effort in World War I, KIPS found a niche under the Bolshevik regime, which welcomed the collaboration of ethnographers in coping with the immense ethnic diversity of the Soviet state. During the 1920s KIPS ethnographers played a major role in defining the ethnic composition of the Soviet Union. The 1920s also saw the emergence of the first comprehensive programs of professional training in ethnography at Leningrad and Moscow universities.

In the late 1920s, however, "bourgeois" ethnography became a target of attack by radical Marxist activists. After a dramatic confrontation in April 1929, key ethnographic institutions were disbanded and ethnography itself was reclassified as a subfield of history devoted exclusively to the study of prehistoric peoples. Nevertheless ethnographers such as Sergei Tokarev and Nina Gagin-Torn continued to produce substantive scholarly works during the 1930s, while others collaborated with state institutions in conducting censuses and resolving practical issues of nationality policy. Soviet ethnographers and anthropologists were also called upon to repudiate Nazi racial ideology. Like many other fields, ethnography was badly shaken by the trials and purges of the 1930s. By the end of the decade many leading ethnographers had been executed or imprisoned in the gulag.

After World War II Soviet ethnography revived. Sergei Tolstov of the Academy of Sciences in Moscow was instrumental in drawing together a cadre of talented scholars, revitalizing professional training, and regaining for the field the autonomous status it had previously enjoyed. By the 1960s Soviet ethnography was a thriving profession whose central and local institutions produced a wealth of publications, sponsored numerous expeditions, and trained large numbers of talented students. Ideological constraints persisted, however, as ethnographers were often called upon to document a priori the successes of soviet nationality policy. As a rule ethnographers were expected to show a stark contrast between a dark past and a present tarnished in places by lingering survivals but well on the way toward the bright communist future. Rather than confront the exigencies of the present day, however, many ethnographers chose to linger in the past. Much of the most substantive work produced in the 1950s and 1960s was historical in nature, with the topic of ethnogenesis, or the origins of peoples, enjoying particular popularity. The 1970s, however, brought a renewed emphasis on contemporary ethnic processes. Yuly Bromlei, director of the Institute of Ethnography in Moscow, put forth his theory of ethnos, which attempted to show how ethnicity continued to be a vital force even as the peoples of the Soviet Union drew together (*sblizhenie*) in a process that would ultimately lead to their merging (*slyanie*) into a new form of human collectivity—the Soviet nation. Bromlei's theory remained the guiding doctrine of the field through the 1980s as social processes, such as intermarriage, geographical mobility, and bilingualism seemed to support the model of the merging of the peoples. However, much of the practical work of ethnographers, particularly on the local level, had the effect of solidifying and reinforcing the symbolic attributes of ethnic consciousness. The flowering of ethnic nationalism in the late 1980s and early 1990s took place on ground well prepared by the work of Soviet ethnographers.

See also: ACADEMY OF SCIENCES; BYLINA; FOLKLORE; FOLK MUSIC; PRIMARY CHRONICLE; NATION AND NATIONALITY; NATIONALITIES POLICIES, SOVIET; NATIONALITIES POLICIES, TSARIST; RUSSIAN GEOGRAPHICAL SOCIETY

BIBLIOGRAPHY

Grant, Bruce. (1995). *In the Soviet House of Culture: A Century of Perestroikas.* Princeton, NJ: Princeton University Press.

Hirsch, Francine. (1997). "The Soviet Union as a Work-in-Progress: Ethnographers and the Category 'Nationality' in the 1926, 1937 and 1939 Censuses." *Slavic Review* 52(2):251–278.

Knight, Nathaniel. (1998). "Science, Empire and Nationality: Ethnography in the Russian Geographical Society, 1845–1855." In *Imperial Russia: New Histories for the Empire,* ed. Jane Burbank and David Ransel. Bloomington: Indiana University Press.

Knight, Nathaniel. (1999). "Ethnicity, Nationality and the Masses: Narodnost and Modernity in Imperial Russia." In *Russian Modernity,* ed. David Hoffmann and Yanni Kotsonis. New York: Macmillan/St. Martin's.

Slezkine, Yuri. (1994). *Arctic Mirrors: Russia and the Small Peoples of the North.* Ithaca, NY: Cornell University Press.

NATHANIEL KNIGHT

EVENKI

The Evenki are the most geographically wide-ranging native people of Russia, occupying a territory from west of the Yenisey River to the Pacific Ocean, and from near the Arctic Ocean to northern China. One of Russia's northern peoples, they number about thirty thousand. Traditionally many Evenki pursued hunting, using small herds of domesticated reindeer mainly for transport and milk. Some groups focused more on fishing, whereas in northerly areas larger-scale reindeer husbandry was pursued. Largely nomadic, Evenki lived in groups of a few households, gathering annually in larger groups to trade news and goods, arrange marriages, and so forth.

The Evenki language is part of the Manchu-Tungus language group. Its four dialects differ substantially, a fact ignored by the soviets when they introduced Evenki textbooks based on the central dialect, which were barely intelligible to those in the East. Evenki cosmology includes a number of worlds; and their shamans negotiate between these worlds. Indeed, the word *shaman* derives from the Evenki samanil, their name for such spiritual leaders. Shamans were severely repressed during the Soviet period; the possibility of revitalizing shamanism proved a common trope for cultural revival among Evenki in early post-Soviet years.

Russian traders began to penetrate Evenki homelands in the mid-seventeenth century. Prior to this, southern Evenki had carried on trade relations with the Chinese. Russians subjected Evenki to a fur tax (*yasak*), and held hostages to ensure its payment. The Soviet government brought new forms of control, organizing Evenki into collective farms, arresting rich herders, and settling nomads to the extent possible. Families were often sundered, as adults remained with the reindeer herds while children attended compulsory school. Children were not taught their own language or how to pursue traditional activities. Inadequate schooling, racism, and apathy have hindered their ability to pursue nontraditional activities. In some areas, mining and smelting have removed substantial pastures and hunting grounds through environmental degradation. Hydropower projects have also challenged traditional activities by appropriating portions of Evenki territory.

Since the demise of the Soviet Union, Evenki reindeer herds have suffered serious decline. At the same time substantial numbers of families took the opportunity provided by new laws to leave state-owned farms and establish small, family based hunting and herding operations. However, lack of government support has made the survival of these enterprises almost impossible. Evenki are battling this predicament through the establishment of quasipolitical organizations, mainly at the regional level, to pursue their rights.

See also: NATIONALITIES POLICIES, SOVIET; NATIONALITIES POLICIES, TSARIST; NORTHERN PEOPLES

BIBLIOGRAPHY

Anderson, David. (2000). "The Evenkis of Central Siberia." In *Endangered Peoples of the Arctic. Struggles to Survive and Thrive,* ed. Milton M. Freeman. Westport, CT: Greenwood Press.

Anderson, David. (2000). *Identity and Ecology in Arctic Siberia. The Number One Reindeer Brigade.* Oxford: Oxford University Press.

Fondahl, Gail. (1998). *Gaining Ground? Evenkis, Land, and Reform in Southeastern Siberia.* Boston, MA: Allyn and Bacon.

GAIL A. FONDAHL

FABERGÉ, PETER CARL

(1846–1920), jeweler to the Russian imperial court; creator of the stunning Easter eggs, holiday gifts to Nicholas II and his family.

Peter Carl Fabergé was born in 1846 in St. Petersburg, the son of a master goldsmith. The French surname of the future jeweler derives from his family's Huguenot background; they left France during the seventeenth century, moving eastward from Germany to the Baltic before settling in Russia. Peter Carl, also called Carl Gustavovich in keeping with the Russian patronymic tradition, was educated in the local German-language school and later attended commercial courses at the Dresden Handelsschule. The combination of his astonishing craftsmanship and cosmopolitanism gave him entry to all European royal houses.

In 1861 young Carl set out on his requisite Grand Tour of the continent. He developed an abiding interest in renaissance and baroque designs and was especially influenced by the French rococo of the eighteenth century. His mastery of fine detail and ability to work in a variety of precious metals and jewels, including hardstone carving, contributed to his unique *style Fabergé.* In addition to his legendary eggs, whose matching of the delicacy of fine jewelry with technological innovations was epitomized by the miniature Trans-Siberian train that chugged through one of them, his *oeuvre* ranged from carved animals to icons to cigarette cases. His clients, primarily from the pan-European aristocracy, knew that he could be trusted not to repeat the specific designs they requested.

Fabergé matched his exquisite style with a finely honed business acumen. From his renowned establishment in St. Petersburg on Bolshaya Morskaya Street, he published catalogs of his *objets d'art.* Employing the finest craftsmen, he expanded his enterprise to Moscow, drawing the attention of serious art collectors from Bangkok to Boston; special exhibitions held around the world continue to attract by the thousands. He left Russia in 1918 and died in Lausanne, Switzerland, in 1920. Fabergé lies buried alongside his wife in Cannes.

See also: FRENCH INFLUENCE IN RUSSIA; ST. PETERSBURG

BIBLIOGRAPHY

Von Habsburg, Géza. (2000). *Fabergé: Imperial Craftsman and his World,* with contributions by Alexander Von

Solodkoff and Robert Bianchi. London: Booth-Clibborn Editions.

Louise McReynolds

FAMILY CODE OF 1926

In 1926 the Soviet government affirmed a new Code on Marriage, the Family, and Guardianship to replace the 1918 version. Adopted after extensive and often heated nationwide debate, the new Code addressed several social issues: the lack of protection for women after divorce; the large number of homeless orphans (*besprizorniki*); the incompatibility of divorce and common property within the peasant household; and the mutual obligations of cohabiting, unmarried partners.

The new Code promoted both individual freedom and greater protection for the vulnerable. It simplified the divorce procedure in the 1918 version even further by transferring contested divorces from the courts to local statistical bureaus. Either spouse could register a divorce without the partner's consent or even knowledge. This provision removed the law's last vestige of authority over the dissolution of marriage, circumscribing both the power of law and the marital tie. The Code recognized de facto marriage (cohabitation) as the juridical equal of civil (registered) marriage, thus undercutting the need to marry "legally." It provided a definition of de facto "marriage" based on cohabitation, a joint household, mutual upbringing of children, and third party recognition. It established joint property between spouses, thus providing housewives material protection after divorce. It abolished the controversial practice of "collective" paternity featured in the 1918 Family Code. If a woman had sexual relations with several men and could not identify the father of her child, a judge would assign paternity (and future child support payments) to one man only. The Code incorporated an April 1926 decree that reversed the prohibition on adoption and encouraged peasant families to adopt homeless orphans, who were to be fully integrated into the peasant household and entitled to land. It set a time limit on alimony to one year for the disabled and provided six months of alimony for the needy or unemployed. It also created a wider circle of family obligations by expanding the base of alimony recipients to include children, parents, siblings, and grandparents.

See also: FAMILY CODE ON MARRIAGE, THE FAMILY, AND GUARDIANSHIP; FAMILY EDICT OF 1944; FAMILY LAWS OF 1936; MARRIAGE AND FAMILY LIFE

BIBLIOGRAPHY

Farnsworth, Beatrice. (1978). "Bolshevik Alternatives and the Soviet Family: The 1926 Marriage Law Debate." In *Women in Russia,* eds. Dorothy Atkinson, Alexander Dallin, Gail Warshovsky Lapidus. Sussex, UK: Harvester Press.

Goldman, Wendy. (1984). "Freedom and Its Consequences: The Debate on the Soviet Family Code of 1926." *Russian History* 11(4):362–388.

Goldman, Wendy. (1991). "Working-Class Women and the 'Withering-Away' of the Family: Popular Responses to Family Policy." In *Russia in the Era of NEP: Explorations in Soviet Society and Culture,* eds. Sheila Fitzpatrick, Alexander Rabinowitch, Richard Stites. Bloomington: Indiana University Press.

Lapidus, Gail Warshovsky. (1978). *Women in Soviet Society.* Berkeley: University of California Press.

Quigley, John. (1979). "The 1926 Soviet Family Code: Retreat from Free Love." *Soviet Union* 6(2):166–74.

Wendy Goldman

FAMILY CODE ON MARRIAGE, THE FAMILY, AND GUARDIANSHIP

The Russian Central Executive Committee of Soviets ratified the Code on Marriage, the Family, and Guardianship in October 1918, one year after the Bolsheviks took power. Alexander Goikhbarg, the young author of the Code, expected that family law would soon be outmoded and "the fetters of husband and wife" unnecessary. Goikhbarg and other revolutionary jurists believed children, the elderly, and the disabled would be supported under socialism by the state; housework would be socialized and waged; and women would no longer be economically dependent on men. The family, stripped of its social functions, would "wither away," replaced by "free unions" based on mutual love and respect. The Code aimed to provide a transitional legal framework for that short period in which legal duties and protections were still necessary.

Prerevolutionary jurists had attempted throughout the late nineteenth century to reform Russia's strict laws on marriage and divorce, but achieved little success. Up to 1917, Russian law recognized the right of religious authorities to control marriage and divorce. Women were accorded few rights by either church or state. According to state law, a wife owed her husband complete obedience. She was compelled to live with him, take his name, and assume his social status. Up to 1914, a woman was unable to take a job, get an education, or execute a bill of exchange without her husband's consent. A father held almost unconditional power over his children. Only children from a legally recognized marriage were considered legitimate, and illegitimate children had no legal rights or recourse. Up to 1902, when the state enacted limited reforms, a father could recognize an illegitimate child only by special imperial consent. The Russian Orthodox Church considered marriage a holy sacrament, and divorce was almost impossible. It was permissible only in cases of adultery (witnessed by two people), impotence, exile, or unexplained and prolonged absence. In cases of adultery or impotence, the responsible party was permanently forbidden to remarry.

The 1918 Code swept away centuries of patriarchal and ecclesiastical power and established a new vision based on individual rights and gender equality. It was predated by two brief decrees enacted in December 1917 that substituted civil for religious marriage and established divorce at the request of either spouse. The 1918 Code incorporated and elaborated on these two decrees. It abolished the inferior legal status of women and created equality under the law. It eliminated the validity of religious marriage and gave legal status to civil marriage only, creating a network of local statistical bureaus (ZAGS) for the registration of marriage, divorce, birth, and death. The Code established no-grounds divorce at the request of either spouse. It abolished the juridical concept of "illegitimacy" and entitled all children to parental support. If a woman could not identify the father of her child, a judge assigned paternal obligations to all the men she had sexual relations with, thus creating a "collective of fathers." It forbade adoption of orphans by individual families in favor of state guardianship: jurists feared adoption, in a largely agrarian society, would allow peasants to exploit children as unpaid labor. The Code also sharply restricted the duties and obligations of the marital bond. Marriage did not create community of property between spouses: a woman retained full control of her earnings after marriage, and neither spouse had any claim on the property of the other. Although the Code provided an unlimited term of alimony for either gender, support was limited to the disabled poor. The Code presumed that both spouses, married or divorced, would support themselves.

The 1918 Code was very advanced for its time. Comparable legislation on equal rights and divorce would not be passed in Europe or the United States until the end of the twentieth century. Yet many Soviet jurists believed that the Code was not "socialist" but "transitional" legislation. Goikhbarg, like many revolutionary jurists, expected that law, like marriage, the family, and the state, would soon "wither away."

The Code had a significant effect on the population, both rural and urban. By 1925, Soviet citizens had widely adopted civil marriage and divorce. The USSR displayed a higher divorce rate than any European country, with fifteen divorces for every one hundred marriages. The divorce rate was higher in the cities than in the rural areas, and highest in Moscow and Leningrad. In Moscow, there was one divorce for every two marriages. Soviet workers, women in particular, suffered high unemployment during the 1920s, and divorce proved a special hardship for women who were unable to find work. Peasant families found it difficult to reconcile customary law with the autonomous property provisions of the Code. After extensive debate, Soviet jurists enacted a new Family Code in 1926 to redress these and other problems.

See also: FAMILY CODE OF 1926; FAMILY EDICT OF 1944, FAMILY LAWS OF 1936; MARRIAGE AND FAMILY LIFE

BIBLIOGRAPHY

Berman, Harold. (1963). *Justice in the USSR: An Interpretation of Soviet Law.* Cambridge, MA: Harvard University Press.

Goldman, Wendy. (1993). *Women, the State and Revolution: Soviet Family Policy, 1917–1936.* New York: Cambridge University Press.

Hazard, John. (1969). *Communists and Their Law.* Chicago: University of Chicago Press.

Stites, Richard. (1978). *The Women's Liberation Movement in Russia: Feminism, Nihilism and Bolshevism, 1860–1930.* Princeton, NJ: Princeton University Press.

Wood, Elizabeth. (1997). *The Baba and the Comrade: Gender and Politics in Revolutionary Russia.* Bloomington: Indiana University Press.

WENDY GOLDMAN

FAMILY EDICT OF 1944

This decree of the Presidium of the Supreme Soviet claimed to "protect motherhood and childhood." Amid deep concern for wartime manpower losses and social dislocation, the decree sought to increase natality and reinforce marriage.

The law's best–known provisions rewarded prolific mothers and made divorce more difficult to obtain; its pro–natalism and support for marriage reinforced prewar trends apparent in the Family Laws of 1936. Pro–natalist measures included family allowances paid to mothers regardless of marital status, extended maternity leave, protective labor legislation for pregnant and nursing women, and an ambitious plan to expand the network of childcare services and consumer products for children. Bearers of ten or more living children were honored as "Mother–heroines."

Other provisions tightened marital bonds by making divorce more onerous. Proceedings now took place in open court, with both parties present and the court obligated to attempt reconciliation. The intent to divorce was published in the newspaper, and fines increased substantially. Reversing the 1926 Family Code, only registered (not common–law) marriages were now officially recognized. The state also reestablished the notion of illegitimacy: only children of registered marriages could take their father's name and receive paternal child support.

The legislation had no significant lasting effect on birth or divorce rates. Despite its ambitious goals, promises of augmented childcare services and consumer goods went unfulfilled, given postwar economic devastation and prioritization of defense and heavy industries. The law's greatest significance was perhaps as a manifestation of the ongoing Soviet effort to imbue private life with public priorities.

See also: FAMILY CODE OF 1926; FAMILY CODE ON MARRIAGE, THE FAMILY, AND GUARDIANSHIP; FAMILY LAWS OF 1936

BIBLIOGRAPHY

Bucher, Greta. (2000). "Struggling to Survive: Soviet Women in the Postwar Years." *Journal of Women's History* 12(1):137–159.

Field, Deborah. (1998). "Irreconcilable Differences: Divorce and Conceptions of Private Life in the Khrushchev Era." *Russian Review* 57(4):599–613.

REBECCA BALMAS NEARY

FAMILY FARM *See* KHUTOR.

FAMILY LAWS OF 1936

In 1936, the Soviet state enacted several laws that sharply departed from previous legislation. The Soviet Union had been the first country in the world to legalize abortion in 1920, offering women free abortion services in certified hospitals. In 1936, however, the Central Executive Committee outlawed abortion. Anyone who performed the operation was liable to a minimum of two years in prison, and a woman who received an abortion was subject to high fines after the first offense. The new law offered monetary incentives for childbearing, providing stipends for new mothers, progressive bonuses for women with many children, and longer maternity leave for white-collar workers. The criminalization of abortion reflected growing anxiety among health workers, managers, and state officials over the rising number of abortions, the falling birth rate, the shortage of labor, and the possibility of war.

The law also made divorce more difficult and stiffened criminal penalties for men who refused to pay alimony or child support. It required both spouses to appear to register a divorce and increased costs for the first divorce to fifty rubles, 150 rubles for the second, and three hundred rubles for the third. It set minimum levels for child support at one–third of a defendant's salary for one child, fifty percent for two children, and sixty percent for three or more, increasing the penalty for nonpayment to two years in prison.

The law was part of a longer and larger public campaign to promote "family responsibility" and to reverse almost two decades of revolutionary juridical thinking. In April 1935, the Council of People's Commissars (Sovnarkom) granted the courts sweeping new powers to try and sentence children aged twelve and older as adults; this resulted in mass arrests and imprisonment of teenagers, mostly for petty theft. In May 1935 the local Commissions on the Affairs of Minors were abolished, and responsibility for all juvenile crime was shifted to the courts. Punishment replaced an earlier commitment to pedagogical correction. The 1936 laws also marked a turn in attitudes toward law and family. Jurists condemned as "legal nihilism" earlier notions that the law and the family would "wither away." Many legal theorists of the

1920s, including Yevgeny Pashukanis and Nikolai Krylenko, were arrested and shot.

See also: FAMILY CODE OF 1926; FAMILY CODE ON MARRIAGE, THE FAMILY, AND GUARDIANSHIP; FAMILY EDICT OF 1944

BIBLIOGRAPHY

Goldman, Wendy. (1991). "Women, Abortion, and the State, 1917–1936." In *Russia's Women: Accommodation, Resistance, Transformation,* eds. Barbara Clements, Barbara Engel, Christine Worobec. Berkeley: University of California Press.

Goldman, Wendy. (1993). *Women, the State, and Revolution: Soviet Family Policy and Social Life, 1917–1936.* New York: Cambridge University Press.

Sharlet, Robert. (1984). "Pashukanis and the Withering-Away of Law in the USSR." In *Cultural Revolution in Russia, 1928–31,* ed. Sheila Fitzpatrick. Bloomington: Indiana University Press.

WENDY GOLDMAN

FAMINE OF 1891–1892

The famine of 1891–1892 was one of the most severe agricultural crises to strike Russia during the nineteenth century. In the spring of 1891 a serious drought caused crops to fail along the Volga and in many other grain-producing provinces. The disaster came on the heels of a series of poor harvests, its impact worsened by endemic peasant poverty and low productivity. The population of the affected areas had few reserves of food and faced the prospect of mass starvation.

Beginning in the summer of 1891, the imperial Russian government organized an extensive relief campaign. It disbursed almost 150 million rubles to the stricken provinces, working closely with the zemstvos, institutions of local self-government responsible for aiding victims of food shortages. The ministry of internal affairs established food supply conferences to coordinate government and zemstvo efforts to find and distribute available grain supplies. When massive backlogs of grain shipments snarled the railroads and threatened the timely delivery of food, the government dispatched a special agent to remedy the situation. The heir to the throne, the future Nicholas II, chaired a committee designed to encourage and focus charitable efforts. Many public-spirited Russians—Leo Tolstoy, Anton Chekhov, Vladimir Korolenko and others—rushed into the countryside on their own initiative, setting up a large network of private soup kitchens and medical aid stations.

The relief campaign was remarkably successful. More than 12 million people received aid, and starvation was largely averted. Mortality for 1892 rose in the sixteen famine provinces—about 400,000 deaths above normal—much of it due to a simultaneous cholera epidemic. But compared to contemporary Indian and later Soviet famines, this loss of life was minimal. Still, the famine aroused public opinion. Many blamed the government's economic policies for causing the disaster, and its relief efforts were often unfairly criticized. Consequently, the famine proved to be an important turning point in Russian history, beginning a new wave of opposition to the tsarist regime.

See also: FAMINE OF 1921–1922; FAMINE OF 1932–1933; FAMINE OF 1946

BIBLIOGRAPHY

Robbins, Richard G., Jr. (1975). *Famine in Russia, 1891–1892: The Imperial Government Responds to a Crisis.* New York: Columbia University Press.

Simms, James Y., Jr. (1977). "The Crisis of Russian Agriculture at the End of the Nineteenth Century: A Different View." *Slavic Review* 36:377–398.

Wheatcroft, S.G. (1992). "The 1891–92 Famine in Russia: Toward a More Detailed Analysis of its Scale and Demographic Significance." In *Economy and Society in Russia and the Soviet Union, 1860–1930: Essays for Olga Crisp,* eds. Linda Edmondson and Peter Waldron. New York: St. Martin's Press.

RICHARD G. ROBBINS JR.

FAMINE OF 1921–1922

This devastating famine, comparable only to that of 1932 and 1933, most seriously affected the Volga provinces, Ukraine, and the Urals, and to a lesser extent several other regions, from late 1920 to mid-1923. At its peak in the summer of 1922, some thirty million people were starving (statistics from this period are uncertain), in towns as well as villages. One of the largest relief efforts in history, including foreign and Soviet agencies, reached most of these people despite enormous logistical and ideological obstacles.

Severe droughts in 1920 and especially 1921, as well as locusts and other natural disasters, most directly caused the famine. One-fourth of the crops failed overall, and many other areas had low yields. Agrarian developments during World War I and the Civil War also contributed to the crisis. The peasants' subdivision of landlord estates, the collapse of industrial production, and massive inflation led increasing numbers of peasants to orient production toward subsistence. From 1918 to 1920, many peasants sold or bartered food to townspeople despite Bolshevik efforts against private trade, but these sales declined because of requisitions by tsarist and provisional governments, the German-Austrian occupation in Ukraine, and the White armies and Bolsheviks, which depleted peasants' grain reserves. With insufficient seed, draft forces, and deteriorating equipment, peasants in 1921 succeeded in planting only two-thirds to three-fourths of the cropland farmed prior to the wars and much less in some regions. Yet even this would not have caused the disaster that occurred without the droughts of 1920 and 1921.

The Bolshevik government responded to the 1920 drought by ceasing requisitions from the central provinces and, in February 1921, by forming a commission for aiding agriculture in the affected regions, distributing food relief and seed, and importing grain. By late May 1921 it was clear that the country was in the midst of a second drought even more severe than that of 1920. Peasants resorted to eating weeds and other food surrogates, and cannibalism, trying to save their seed for the fall planting. Thousands of peasants fled from famine districts to Ukraine and other regions, often with government assistance, which sometimes spread famine conditions.

During the summer of 1921, the Bolshevik government distributed limited seed and food relief to famine regions, often by curtailing rationed supplies to towns, and appealed for food relief at home and abroad. Many groups responded. The International Red Cross set up an International Committee for Russian Relief, under the leadership of Fridtjof Nansen. Other agencies offering help included the International Committee of Workers' Aid, the American Friends Service Committee, and the Jewish Joint Distribution Committee.

By far most aid came from the American Relief Administration (ARA), headed by Herbert Hoover. In the Riga agreement of August 1921, the Bolsheviks allowed the ARA to distribute its own relief. Investigation of the Volga region led the ARA to attempt to aid as many people as possible until the 1922 harvest. Hoover persuaded the U.S. Congress to allocate $20 million for food supplies; these were shipped and distributed in a "corn campaign," conducted from January to August of 1922, which had to overcome the catastrophic disrepair of the railroads and the incompetence and ideologically motivated resistance of some local and central government officials. By the summer of 1921, some eleven million people received food from foreign relief agencies.

The ARA also organized medical aid and international food remittances, many sent to Ukraine. In October ARA personnel went to Ukraine and found famine conditions that the Moscow Bolsheviks had not mentioned, as well as a Ukrainian government that refused to accept the Riga agreement. Only after negotiations in December was Ukraine brought into the relief effort. The ARA and other groups also provided medical aid that reached more people than the food relief.

By the summer of 1922, Soviet government food relief had reached some five million people in the Volga, Ukraine, and elsewhere. Many ordinary Soviet citizens also contributed to famine relief. Soviet and foreign seed aid supported a 1922 harvest. Although grown on an area about 20 percent smaller than that of 1921, the 1922 harvest was much larger than that of the previous year because normal rainfall had returned. Still, famine conditions continued in many regions and especially among abandoned children (*besprizorniki*). The ARA continued relief into mid-1923 against intrusive Soviet efforts to limit its operations. A few small relief programs continued, but the 1923 harvest basically ended the famine.

Estimates of famine mortality vary, with the most widely accepted being five million deaths, most resulting from typhus and other epidemics spread by refugees. So vast was the famine that the combined relief efforts at their peak in the summer of 1922 encompassed at most two-thirds of famine victims, despite substantial imports. The ARA imported some 740,000 tons of food; the Bolshevik government supplied more than one million tons of grain.

The famine weakened armed resistance to the Bolshevik regime, and some argue that this was intentionally manipulated. It also, however, delayed national economic recovery for at least two years. The fact that Vladimir Lenin and other Soviet leaders agreed (however ambivalently) to foreign relief indicated a fundamental shift in their attitude toward the peasants and their orientation toward private production. This shift was reflected in the New Economic Policy of 1921, which legalized free trade and abolished the requisition policies of the Civil War and in the regime's food imports during famines in 1924 and 1928. The 1921 famine also convinced Soviet leaders that Soviet agriculture needed significant modernization, which underlay the decision to collectivize agriculture nine years later.

See also: AMERICAN RELIEF ADMINISTRATION; FAMINE OF 1891–1892; FAMINE OF 1932–1933; FAMINE OF 1946

BIBLIOGRAPHY

Edmondson, Charles M. (1977). "The Politics of Hunger: The Soviet Response to Famine, 1921." *Soviet Studies* XXIX (4):506–518.

Patenaude, Bertrand M. (2002). *The Big Show in Bololand: The American Relief Expedition to Soviet Russia in the Famine of 1921.* Stanford, CA: Stanford University Press.

MARK B. TAUGER

FAMINE OF 1932–1933

The famine began in the winter of 1931 and 1932, peaked between the fall of 1932 and the summer of 1933, and subsided with the 1933 harvest. Mortality was highest in rural areas of Ukraine, the North Caucasus, and the central and southern Volga Basin, but increased in most rural and even urban areas.

The famine affected all of Soviet society. Not only peasants, but also industrial workers and other townspeople desperately sought to supplement their inadequate food rations. Officials and managers responsible for production, transport, and distribution faced disastrous labor conditions from the subsistence crisis. The OGPU (Soviet security police), grain procurement agencies, and Soviet leaders, in their efforts to obtain grain and other supplies from the villages at all costs, minimized or ignored the pleas and starving conditions of the peasants.

The causes of the famine are disputed. The conventional view, that it was a human-made famine imposed by Joseph Stalin on Ukraine and certain other regions to suppress nationalist opposition, has been challenged. Conclusive new evidence shows that the harvests of 1931 and especially 1932 were much smaller than claimed by the Soviet government or later memoir and eyewitness accounts, that they were reduced by natural disasters, and that famine mortality was not limited to specific national regions or even to rural areas. New sources also show that the regime had inadequate reserves yet provided peasants limited famine relief, including relief from imported sources, in addition to supplying more than forty million people in towns, the army, and others on the rationing system in 1932–1933.

The famine developed in the wake of collectivization campaigns in 1930 and 1931 that reorganized most villages into collective or state farms. By this means the regime sought to increase food production and procurement to feed towns and industrial sites, which were growing rapidly because of the First Five-Year Plan and were dependent on government rationing systems, and to export in order to earn hard currency for purchases of producer goods. Collectivization allowed procurement agencies to obtain substantially more grain from the villages than during the 1920s, even considering what the peasants would have sold voluntarily. This left many peasants short of food as early as 1930. A drought in 1931 in the Volga region, Ukraine, the Urals, Siberia, Kazakhstan, and elsewhere reduced the harvest drastically. Yet the authorities procured more from this harvest than from that of 1930 (22.8 million tons vs. 22.1 million tons), often taking the last reserves from many farms. Peasants were left in desperate circumstances, and their mortality increased. Hundreds of thousands fled the drought regions seeking food.

Soviet leaders acknowledged the drought and returned grain to farms for food and seed. They introduced new labor organization rules in the collective farms to reduce evasion of responsibility for farm work. Laws in May 1932 legalized private trade in food products in an effort to increase production and improve urban food supplies. Unfortunately, 1932 was worse than 1931. Weakened by starvation and often resentful of procurements and collectivization, some peasants worked poorly or not at all. The new labor system encountered confusion and resistance and often had little effect. Crops were planted later than in previous years and with less seed. A complex of natural disasters—drought, heavy rains, infestations, soil exhaustion—drastically reduced the harvest. Yet agricultural and statistical authorities minimized or overlooked these problems and projected output matching or even exceeding that of 1931.

The harvest shortfall became evident early: July procurements were only 470,000 tons compared to 950,000 tons in July 1931. Statistical and OGPU reports convinced Stalin and other Soviet leaders that the 1932 harvest was normal and that procurements collapsed because peasants withheld grain from procurements to sell on the free market at astronomical prices and because local officials mismanaged procurements. The leadership changed its approach from incentives to extreme coercion in procurements and distribution. One part of this shift was the decree of August 7 that imposed harsh penalties for "theft of socialist property." In the following year, in the Russian republic alone, more than 200,000 people were arrested and more than 8,000 executed under this law. Simultaneously, the authorities conducted an intensive procurement campaign that lasted into the spring of 1933 in some regions. Procurement agents came from towns almost as famished as the villages, and their desperation led them to irrational actions they found difficult to explain in memoirs written later. They dug up peasants' yards to find concealed hoards, though the amounts they found were miniscule; they took prepared meals away from peasants. Starving peasants (and to a lesser extent townspeople) tried to survive on surrogates, and some resorted to cannibalism.

The authorities repeatedly reduced procurement quotas, ultimately obtaining fifteen percent less grain from the 1932 harvest (18.5 million tons) than from the 1931 harvest, but at a much greater cost in life and disruption. Even with reduced procurements, the small harvest left practically nothing to be sold on the market. By January 1933, most of the USSR was in a state of famine, and millions of peasants and townspeople fled their homes seeking subsistence. The Politburo attempted to control this situation by establishing an internal passport system, by directives to prevent starving peasants from fleeing the main agricultural regions and return to their farms those who had fled, and by establishing political departments in the state farms and machine-tractor stations to remove opposition officials and improve work organization.

The regime allocated much more food for relief and seed from the 1932 harvest, 5.7 million tons, than it had from the 1931 harvest, with rations doled out to peasants in return for their work. Still, farm work in the spring and summer of 1933 proceeded under desperate conditions, and many peasants died of starvation or related diseases while working. Moreover, the regime exported more than 300,000 tons of grain during the first half of 1933 to meet contractual commitments and cover loan payments. Purchasing countries received diplomatic reports about the famine but did not raise the issue and continued imports at dumping-level prices. Soviet officials at all levels denied the famine publicly, refused aid from foreign organizations, and tried to concealed the famine from foreign visitors.

Improved agricultural conditions and desperate work by all concerned led to a substantially greater harvest in 1933 that ended the famine in most areas by the fall of 1933. Estimates of mortality range from five million to eight million lives, mostly peasants but also townspeople and others, yet government aid in supplies, equipment, and organizational measures helped agriculture to recover and produce large harvests soon after the famine. This tragedy could have been substantially mitigated had Soviet leaders been less distrustful of and hostile toward the peasants, more skeptical of their own personnel and knowledge, and more open to outside aid.

See also: AGRICULTURE; FAMINE OF 1891–1892; FAMINE OF 1921–1922

BIBLIOGRAPHY

Conquest, Robert. (1986). *Harvest of Sorrow.* New York: Oxford University Press.

Osokina, Elena. (2000). *Our Daily Bread: Socialist Distribution and the Art of Survival in Stalin's Russia.* Armonk, NY: M.E. Sharpe.

Tauger, Mark. (2001). "Natural Disaster and Human Actions in the Soviet Famine of 1931–1933." *The Carl Beck Papers in Russian and East European Studies,* no. 1506. Pittsburgh: Center for Russian and East European Studies, University of Pittsburgh.

MARK B. TAUGER

FAMINE OF 1946

In 1946, the devastation of World War II and a severe drought that engulfed most of the major grain producing areas of the country, including Ukraine, Moldavia, the lower and middle Volga, Rostov oblast, and the central black earth zone, resulted in a poor harvest in the Soviet Union. Shortage of workforce, machinery, and livestock exacerbated the situation. Despite food shortages and malnutrition in the countryside in the spring of 1946, the Soviet government enforced unrealistic procurement quotas while exporting grain to Eastern Europe and France. Toward the end of 1946, the government lowered procurement plans in drought areas but raised quotas in other parts of the country in order to compensate for the shortfall. The authorities provided grain loans to collective farms and opened kitchens and children's houses, but the relief was administered inconsistently and belatedly. As a result, approximately two million people died from famine and related diseases in 1946 and 1947. The mortality rate peaked in the summer of 1947. The famine contributed to mass flight from the countryside to the cities and was followed by the arbitrary purging of peasants labeled "kulaks" from the countryside.

Despite its major political and social implications, this famine had not been studied until the 1990s, largely because the Soviet government ignored its existence. Even in confidential government documents, officials avoided mention of hunger or starvation, employing euphemisms suggesting difficulties with provisions. The central authorities advanced the image of a heroic postwar rebuilding process and a smooth transition to peacetime.

See also: FAMINE OF 1891–1892; FAMINE OF 1921–1922; FAMINE OF 1932–1933

BIBLIOGRAPHY

Ellman, Michael. (2000). "The 1947 Soviet Famine and the Entitlement Approach to Famines." *Cambridge Journal of Economics* 24:603–630.

Volkov, Ivan Mefodievich. (1992). "The Drought and Famine of 1946–47." *Russian Studies in History* 31:31–60.

NICHOLAS GANSON

FAR EASTERN REGION

The easternmost extremity of the Russian Federation is a vast territory with a sparse and declining population. It comprises 6.2 million square kilometers (2,394,000 square miles), or more than 36 percent of the country, but holds barely seven million residents, or less than 5 percent of the population. Given the inclement climate and poor transportation infrastructure in the north, residents are concentrated near the southern border with China, many living along the Amur River and the Pacific coast. Russians reached the coast during the seventeenth century; only in 1861 did they establish the city of Vladivostok after securing control over the southeastern maritime zone through a treaty with China. Construction of the Trans-Siberian railroad from the 1890s onward brought increased settlement. The Soviet state continued to rely on prison labor and exiles as well as military garrisons to develop the region, although at times it succeeded in drawing young settlers and workers with material incentives. During the 1990s incentives were ended, and many began to leave the region.

The Russian Far East is rich in natural resources, but fear of neighboring countries has affected their development and use. After accepting migrants and welcoming trade during the 1930s and 1940s, the Kremlin, led by Josef Stalin, expelled the Chinese and deported the Koreans to Central Asia. At great cost, the Far East sent marine products to European Russia in return for industrial goods. A brief rise in Sino-Soviet trade during the 1950s was followed by a massive military buildup that forced Moscow to spend much more on the area. Plans for exporting vast quantities of coal and lumber to Japan in return for investment in infrastructure were only partly realized before bilateral relations deteriorated at the end of the 1970s. Huge cost overruns meant that during the early 1980s, when authorities announced the completion of the Baikal-Amur Mainline railroad to extend development northward, even funds for maintenance could not be found. During the 1990s local elites diverted marine and lumber products to exports without paying taxes to Moscow. None of these approaches to the use of natural resources proved efficient for sustained development. During the early twenty-first century, Russians hoped that oil and gas projects, especially offshore by Sakhalin Island, would fuel the region's prosperity, yet fear of foreign control continued to leave investors uncertain of their prospects.

The Russian Far East has the potential to become part of the emerging Northeast Asian region, drawing together China, Japan, South Korea, and eventually North Korea. First, it would need to resolve tensions between the ten regional administrations, which pressed local agendas during the 1990s, and Moscow, which made efforts at recentralization. While there was a brief fear of the local governments banding together to restore the Far Eastern Republic of the early 1920s and gain substantial autonomy, the pendulum tilted toward Moscow; a presidential representative resided in Khabarovsk. Second, territorial disputes with China and Japan must be further resolved, stabilizing tensions over the border. Third, Russia must become confident of the balance of power in the region, overcoming fear that China or another country will dominate. Finally, plans for economic development need firm backing in Moscow, which must recognize that only by opening its eastern border to the outside world can it secure its future as a country facing both the developed European Union and the dynamic Asia-Pacific.

See also: BAIKAL-AMUR MAGISTRAL RAILWAY; CHINA, RELATIONS WITH; GEOGRAPHY; TRANS-SIBERIAN RAILWAY

BIBLIOGRAPHY

Bradshaw, Michael J., ed. (2001). *The Russian Far East and Pacific Asia: Unfulfilled Potential.* Richmond, UK: Curzon.

Minakir, Pavel A., and Freeze, Gregory L., eds. (1994). *The Russian Far East: An Economic Handbook.* Armonk, NY: M.E. Sharpe.

Stephan, John J. (1994). *The Russian Far East: A History.* Stanford, CA: Stanford University Press.

GILBERT ROZMAN

FATHERLAND-ALL RUSSIA

"Fatherland-All Russia" (*Otechestvo–Vsya Rossiya*, or OVR) was an alternative "ruling party," a bloc formed in the summer of 1999 in order to seize power from the weakening Kremlin. The first step towards organization was the formation of the bloc called Fatherland, a political structure created by Moscow mayor Yuri Luzhkov, who had presidential ambitions. Established and registered on December 19, 1998, a full year before Duma elections, Fatherland brought together a number of organizations that appealed to patriotism or paternalism. These included the Congress of Russian Communities (which later left it) and the "Power" movement, as well as the political wing of the reformist trade unions (*profsoyuzy*), "Union of Labor" and Women of Russia. It also included a handful of influential heads of Luzhkov-oriented regions: Karelia, Komi, Mordvinia, Udmurtia, and the Arkhangelsk, Moscow, Murmansk, Nizhegorod, Novosibirsk, and Yaroslavl oblasts. Prospective politicians, often the mayors of centers, headed the ubiquitous regional branches. This often led to conflict, when two or three local organizations simultaneously claimed to be the area's regional branch. The material base of "Fatherland" was provided by a powerful consortium of of financial and industrial groups known as the "Moscow clan."

Established three months later, the "All Russia" bloc became an alternative gubernatorial political project. The bloc included another dozen influential regional heads, including the leaders of Tatarstan, Bashkortostan, Petersburg, Irkutsk oblast, among others, as well as a few regional speakers. The mayor of St. Petersburg, Vladimir Yakovlev, became chair of the bloc. Four and a half months before the elections, despite the opposition of the Kremlin, the two powerful gubernatorial blocs were able to unite, advancing the recently retired prime minister, Yevgeny Primakov, as their leader. Soon after their formation, they were joined by a large contingent of the Agrarian Party of Russia, which did not see a future in continuing its association with Zyuganov's Communist Party.

Fatherland–All Russia, united not so much by ideology as by a foretaste of full assumption of power, announced an eclectic program. Its main slogan, "Trust only deeds," drew the voter's attention to powerful politicians united under the bloc's banners and to authoritarian governors. The overall agenda of the bloc, including the continuity of ruling power, social peace, and rejection of revolutionary shocks, were combined with concrete programmatic elaborations concerning key questions of economy, politics, and social development. These elaborations went through a series of discussions and were summarized in the form "Notices for the president." At the core of OVR's propaganda campaign was the juxtaposition of its candidates with the ruling Kremlin command, along with criticism of Yeltsin and his entourage, an identification of the "family" as the locus of corruption, and allegations of the government's secrecy and incompetence.

A crucial moment in the campaign, and the beginning of the end of OVR as a "party of future power," was a series of explosions in residential areas of Moscow and other cities, and the beginning of a new war in the northern Caucasus. People no longer wanted the economic and social improvements promised by OVR; instead, they wanted the safety and protection provided by a strong government. Although the complex and clumsy propaganda machine of OVR continued to attack Yeltsin, a social question based on new principles took hold and was answered in large part by the new prime minister, Vladimir Putin. The extremely strong public relations campaign of the Kremlin against OVR played its part as well.

In the end, OVR received 13.3 percent of the votes (third place), losing by nearly half to the KPRF and to the Unity Party that had been created shortly before the elections and had campaigned as a party of regional power. Moreover, nearly half the OVR votes came from four regions whose elites remained loyal to the bloc: Moscow, Moscow oblast, Tatarstan, and Bashkiria. In these regions, the bloc brought forth most of its candidates in districts where they already enjoyed a distinct majority. In the Duma, OVR formed the OVR faction (which delegates from Fatherland joined) and the delegate group called "Regions of Russia," which opposed the Kremlin for a while. In the absence of ideology and the disagreements associated with it, this factionalism could not continue for long. Beginning in mid-2000, a long process of unification took place, and in December 2000, Unity, Fatherland, and All Russia officially merged into the party "Unity and Fatherland" ("United Russia") with three co-chairs: Sergei Shoygu, Yuri Luzhkov, and Mintimir Shaymiev. Two weeks later, the new party was registered with the Ministry of Justice.

See also: LUZHKOV, YURI MIKHAILOVICH; PRIMAKOV, YEVGENY MAXIMOVICH; UNITY (MEDVED PARTY); WOMEN OF RUSSIA BLOC

BIBLIOGRAPHY

McFaul, Michael. (2001). *Russia's Unfinished Revolution: Political Change from Gorbachev to Putin.* Ithaca, NY: Cornell University Press.

McFaul, Michael, and Markov, Sergei. (1993). *The Troubled Birth of Russian Democracy: Parties, Personalities, and Programs.* Stanford, CA: Hoover Institution Press.

McFaul, Michael; Petrov, Nikolai; and Ryabov, Andrei, eds. (1999). *Primer on Russia's 1999 Duma Elections.* Washington, DC: Carnegie Endowment for International Peace.

Reddaway, Peter, and Glinski, Dmitri. (2001). *The Tragedy of Russia's Reforms: Market Bolshevism against Democracy.* Washington, DC: U.S. Institute of Peace Press.

NIKOLAI PETROV

FEAST BOOKS

Special paraliturgical books that register the annual commemorative meals in a monastic community throughout the calendar year.

Formally the Feast books are similar to Western late medieval anniversary books in parishes and brotherhoods. The Russian term for "feast book" is *kormovye kniga,* literally "feeding book." *Kormy,* "feedings," in memory of the deceased, correspond functionally and genetically to anniversary meals in Byzantine monasteries as well as in Western communities. The Russian term reflects the idea that by means of the donation, on the basis of which the meal is established, the monks become guests of the donor. "Feeding" the monks equals alms to the poor, in return for which the monks offer their liturgical services. *Kormy* were the most representative and most expensive form of commemoration in Muscovite Russia. Regular *kormy* usually took place on the anniversary of death or on the name day of the deceased. In earlier times, the dates of *kormy* were registered within the *Ustav,* the liturgical Rule. Probably as early as the beginning of the sixteenth century, monasteries began to register the dates separately in special Feast Books, but the preserved manuscripts derive only from the last third of that century and from the seventeenth century. The entries range from brief notation of date and name of the commemorated person to elaborate detail concerning donor and donation, the food to be served, and the burial place within the monastery. Some Feast Books additionally specify the menu throughout the year and contain instructions concerning discipline of the brethren, services, distribution of alms, and related matters.

See also: DONATION BOOKS; SOROKOUST

BIBLIOGRAPHY

Steindorff, Ludwig. (1995). "Commemoration and Administrative Techniques in Muscovite Monasteries." *Russian History/Histoire Russe* 22:433–454.

LUDWIG STEINDORFF

FEBRUARY REVOLUTION

The February Revolution (which, according to New Style dates, actually took place in March) developed out of a wave of industrial strikes in Petrograd from

January to March 1917. It gathered force when workers at Russia's largest factory were locked out on March 7 and when women workers at a few factories, angered by the food shortages, marched out from their factories on March 8 demanding bread. Men at nearby factories joined them, and over the next two days antigovernment demonstrations grew to include most of the industrial work force. By March 10 they were joined by students and broad sections of the urban lower and middle classes. Soldiers who were called out to help break up demonstrations acted with reluctance. The government's ordering of troops to fire into the crowds on March 11 broke the fragile bonds of discipline among the soldiers, who were mostly recent draftees with the same grievances as the demonstrators. A revolt by one detachment of the Volynsky Guard Regiment the morning of March 12 (February 27 O.S.) quickly spread to other regiments. By midday the government lost control of the means of armed coercion and collapsed.

To this point the revolution had been mainly a popular revolt, with little leadership. What there was came from socialist activists at the factory level and from individuals who emerged as organizers of factory demonstrations and leaders in attacks on police stations and other symbols of authority. The revolutionary parties, whose main leaders were in exile, played few leadership roles before March 12. But leadership was necessary to consolidate the revolution that had taken place in the streets. Two groups stepped forward on March 12. One was a group of Duma leaders who had watched the events of the preceding days, concerned about their implications for the war effort but also realizing that this might offer the long-sought opportunity to force Tsar Nicholas II to reform the government. That evening they formed a "Temporary Committee of the State Duma," which would take governmental responsibility in Petrograd. They opened negotiations with the army high command to secure its support in forcing Nicholas to make concessions. The involvement of these respected public figures proved vital in the following days.

At the same time, a multiparty group of socialist intellectuals met at the Duma building and led workers and soldiers in the formation of the Petrograd Soviet of Workers' and Soldiers' Deputies. This was a more avowedly revolutionary body, committed to making the street revolt into a sweeping social and economic as well as political revolution. The Duma Committee and the Petrograd Soviet leaders immediately, if warily, began to cooperate to consolidate the February Revolution and to form a new government. On March 15 they announced formation of a Provisional Government that would govern Russia until a new governmental system could be created by a Constituent Assembly, which was to be elected by universal franchise. The same day Nicholas II gave way to the reality of events and the pressures from his army commanders, and abdicated. News of the revolution in Petrograd sparked mostly peaceful revolutions in the cities and towns of Russia. New city governments, drawn primarily from liberal circles of educated society, replaced the old government authorities, while alongside them local soviets of workers and soldiers deputies sprang up.

The new government was drawn primarily from the liberal political leadership of the country. Its head, the minister-president, was Prince G. E. Lvov, a well-known liberal. The socialist Petrograd Soviet leaders promised to support the new government insofar as it pursued policies of which they approved. This political situation, however, was very unstable. The existence of the Petrograd Soviet alongside the Provisional Government robbed the latter of much of its actual authority, giving rise to what quickly was dubbed "dual-authority" (*dvoyevlastie*). The government had the generally recognized official authority and responsibility but not the effective power, while the Soviet had the actual power but not responsibility for governing. This situation emerged because the Soviet commanded the primary loyalty of the industrial workers and garrison soldiers, the main bases of power in Petrograd, and could call on this support in a conflict with the government.

The February Revolution resulted not merely in the overthrow of the monarchy and creation of a new government, but in an unleashing of popular self-assertion and the formation of thousands of organizations dedicated to expressing popular aspirations. Factory committees, soldiers' committees, trade and professional unions, cultural clubs, minority nationalist organizations, feminist groups, householders' associations, and other organizations were created to safeguard and advance the interests and hopes of the population in its varied identities. These became a major force in the later unfolding of the revolution as they asserted themselves and as political parties and leaders struggled to articulate their demands and win their allegiance. Gaining control over popular activism became one of the key tasks of the political elites and would-be leaders of the revolution.

As the new political system was unstable, it took some time for the main contours of power to become clear. While political parties remained important, three broad political blocs quickly emerged: liberals, moderate socialists, and radical left socialists. The liberals, represented especially by the Cadet Party (Constitutional Democrats), dominated the first Provisional Government and then shared it in coalition with the moderate socialists from May to October. The moderate socialists—the Mensheviks and Socialist Revolutionaries (SRs) predominantly—were the main force in the Petrograd and most other soviets around the country. The radical left—Bolsheviks, left-wing Mensheviks, and SRs, anarchists—were at first a small minority voice, but soon grew as the alternative to the "coalition" of liberals and moderate socialists when the Provisional Government failed to satisfy popular aspirations. Socialism was the overwhelming political position in 1917, and therefore the conflict between the moderate and radical socialists determined the main course of politics in 1917.

The moderate socialists, primarily Mensheviks and SRs, took form first. A key development here was the return of a group of socialist exiles from Siberia in March. Under the leadership of Irakli Tsereteli, a Georgian Menshevik, they established the policy of Revolutionary Defensism as the basic policy of the Petrograd Soviet (and, in fact, for most soviets in the country). Revolutionary Defensism spoke to the desire of the populace for an end to the war by calling for a general negotiated peace based on the principle of self-determination of nations and without annexations or indemnities. At the same time it addressed still strong patriotism by calling for continued defense of the country until this peace could be achieved. The Revolutionary Defensists also were willing to cooperate with the liberals in the Provisional Government, and beginning in May some of their leaders entered the government in what was called "coalition" governments—that is, ones with liberals and socialists, after massive antiwar demonstrations underscored the weakness of the government and strength of the Soviet.

A radical left opposition to these policies existed from the beginning, but received a major reinforcement by the return of political exiles from Western Europe. The most important of these proved to be Vladimir Lenin, who electrified politics on his return in April by denouncing not only the government, but also the policy of the dominant Revolutionary Defensists. This made the Bolsheviks relatively impotent in the optimistic mood of the spring of 1917, but positioned them to receive the support of the dissatisfied sections of the population in the summer and fall as the policies of the Revolutionary Defensists and the Provisional Government failed to find a way out of the war or to solve domestic problems.

The Provisional Government initiated important and far-reaching reforms, especially in areas of civil rights and individual and group freedoms. However, the new leadership faced almost unsolvable problems. The desire for peace was immense, and failure to make progress on ending the war undermined both the Provisional Government and the Revolutionary Defensist leaders of the Petrograd Soviet. This problem was compounded by an enormously unpopular, and unsuccessful, military offensive in the summer, which drove the soldiers and many others leftward politically. The government also failed to move swiftly to meet the peasantry's expectations for land reform. During the summer and early fall the economy deteriorated rapidly, food and other goods became ever scarcer, crime rose, and other social and economic problems multiplied, along with rising social tensions. Demands for autonomy or even separatism grew among some of the national minorities. The cumulative problems gave rise by June to a call for "All Power to the Soviets," a call for a more radical, soviet-based, government that would act more vigorously to end the war and solve the many problems. This resulted in massive street demonstrations in favor of soviet power in July (the "July Days"). This in turn was followed by an attack on the government from the right on September 9–13, the unsuccessful putsch by General Lavr Kornilov. Meanwhile, the Provisional Government was unstable, undergoing fundamental restructuring (accompanied by violence and major crises) in May, July, and September. During one of these Alexander Kerensky, a moderate socialist, became head of the government on July 21.

By September the radicals were winning reelections to the leadership of soviets, workers' and soldiers' committees, and other popular institutions. The Kornilov Affair gave an enormous boost of support for the Bolsheviks and radical left. Bolshevik-led coalitions took the leadership of the Petrograd Soviet—the most important political institution in the country—and soviets in Moscow and elsewhere. This, in addition to the increasing social problems and tensions, prepared the ground for the October Revolution.

See also: APRIL THESES; BOLSHEVISM; KORNILOV AFFAIR; LENIN, VLADIMIR ILICH; MENSHEVIKS; NICHOLAS II; OCTOBER REVOLUTION; REVOLUTION OF 1905

BIBLIOGRAPHY

Acton, Edward; Cherniaev, Vladimir I.; Rosenberg, William G., eds. (1997). *Critical Companion to the Russian Revolution, 1914–1921.* Bloomington: Indiana University Press.

Browder, Robert Paul, and Kerensky, Alexander F., eds. (1961). *The Russian Provisional Government, 1917: Documents.* 3 vols. Stanford, CA: Stanford University Press.

Frankel, Edith Rogovin; Frankel, Jonathan; and Knei-Paz, Baruch, eds. (1992). *Revolution in Russia: Reassessments of 1917.* Cambridge, UK: Cambridge University Press.

Hasegawa, Tsuyoshi. (1981). *The February Revolution: Petrograd 1917.* Seattle: University of Washington Press.

Koenker, Diane, and Rosenberg, William G. (1989). *Strikes and Revolution in Russia, 1917.* Princeton, NJ: Princeton University Press.

Lieven, Dominic. (1994). *Nicholas II: Twilight of the Empire.* New York: St. Martin's Press.

Rabinowitch, Alexander. (1968). *Prelude to Revolution: The Petrograd Bolsheviks and the July 1917 Uprising.* Bloomington: Indiana University Press.

Rabinowitch, Alexander. (1976). *The Bolsheviks Come to Power: The Revolution of 1917 in Petrograd.* New York: Norton.

Rosenberg, William G. (1974). *Liberals in the Russian Revolution: The Constitutional Democratic Party, 1917–1921.* Princeton, NJ: Princeton University Press.

Service, Robert, ed. (1992). *Society and Politics in the Russian Revolution.* Basingstoke and London: Macmillan.

Smith, S.A. (1983). *Red Petrograd: Revolution in the Factories, 1917–18.* Cambridge, UK: Cambridge University Press, 1983.

Suny, Ronald Grigor. (1972). *The Baku Commune, 1917–1918: Class and Nationality in the Russian Revolution.* Princeton, NJ: Princeton University Press.

Wade, Rex A. (2000). *The Russian Revolution: 1917.* Cambridge, UK: Cambridge University Press.

Wildman, Allan K. (1980, 1987). *The End of the Russian Imperial Army, Vol I: The Old Army and the Soldiers' Revolt (March–April 1917); Vol II: The End of the Russian Imperial Army: The Road to Soviet Power and Peace.* Princeton, NJ: Princeton University Press.

REX A. WADE

FEDERAL ASSEMBLY

For most of the Soviet period, Russia's legislature was a ceremonial, rubber stamp body called the Supreme Soviet. Under Mikhail Gorbachev, however, Russia's legislative structures underwent dramatic reform, becoming an arena for competitive elections and debates on major policy issues.

From May 1990 until September 1993, the Russian legislature consisted of the Russian Soviet Federated Socialist Republic (RSFSR) Congress of People's Deputies and a smaller body called the Supreme Soviet, which was the full-time working parliament. On September 21, 1993, President Boris Yeltsin dissolved the RSFSR Congress and Supreme Soviet after a protracted political confrontation with its members over constitutional and policy issues. He further decreed that elections to a new bicameral parliament called the Federal Assembly would be held in December 1993. This parliamentary structure was to be given constitutional status through a national referendum on a new constitution to be held simultaneously with the parliamentary elections. The elections and referendum took place on December 12, 1993, and on January 11, 1994, the newly elected deputies convened in Moscow for the opening of the new Federal Assembly.

The 1993 constitution provides for a mixed presidential-parliamentary system with a directly elected president and a prime minister approved by parliament. The lower chamber of the bicameral Federal Assembly is called the State Duma, and the upper chamber is the Federation Council. The president appoints the prime minister, and the Duma votes whether to confirm the appointment. The president has wide legislative powers, including the powers of veto and decree. Decrees (*ukazy*) carry the force of law, but may not violate existing law. A decree remains in effect until the parliament enacts legislation that supersedes it. The Federal Assembly may override a presidential veto by a two-thirds vote of each chamber.

The Duma may deny the government its confidence. Upon the first vote of no confidence in the government, the president may ignore the parliament's action. But the president must either dismiss the government or dissolve the Duma if the Duma votes no confidence a second time within three months. The prime minister may submit a motion of confidence to the Duma, which, if defeated by the Duma, leads the president to decide whether to dismiss the government or dissolve the Duma.

The president may not dissolve the Duma within one year of its election, nor during a state of emergency or national state of martial law, nor within six months of a presidential election. Parliament does have the right to remove the president by impeachment, but the constitution requires that both chambers, the Supreme Court, and the Constitutional Court concur with the charges.

Legislation originates in the Duma and, if passed, is sent to the Federation Council. If the Federation Council approves the legislation or fails to examine it within fourteen days, the legislation is sent to the president to be signed. If the Federation Council rejects the legislation, the two houses may form a commission to resolve differences. However, the Duma may override a Federation Council veto by a two-thirds vote. Following final action by the Federal Assembly, legislation is sent to the president, who must sign or veto the legislation.

ELECTIONS

The electoral system used in the December 1993 Duma elections was put into effect by presidential decree, but its essential features have been preserved under subsequent legislation. Duma elections employ a mixed system of proportional representation and single-member districts. Half of the Duma's 450 seats are allocated proportionately to registered parties that receive at least five percent of the vote in a single nationwide electoral district. The other 225 deputies are elected in single-round plurality elections in single-member districts.

Unlike the Duma, the Federation Council has changed significantly in the manner in which its members are chosen. The Constitution provides that two individuals from each of Russia's eighty-nine constituent territorial subjects, representing the legislative and executive branches of each region, are to be chosen as members of the Federation Council. The membership of the 1994–1995 chamber was chosen by popular election. A 1995 law provided, however, that thereafter the two members would be the head of the executive branch and the head of the legislature in each territorial subject. Therefore the members of the Federation Council were part-time members of the chamber and full-time officials in their home regions. Typically they traveled to Moscow for a few days every month for brief parliamentary sessions.

During the summer of 2000, President Vladimir Putin again changed the method for selecting Federation Chamber members. Under the new law he sponsored, all members were to be full-time delegates chosen by the chief executive officers and the legislative assemblies of the eighty-nine territorial subjects. The members chosen do not need to reside in the region sending them, allowing regions to send prominent businesspeople, retired military officers, and influential politicians as their representatives. The changeover was complete by the end of 2001.

Most observers believe that the system for selecting members of the Federation Council is likely to evolve further. Many advocate holding direct elections of senators, as in the United States. One difficulty with this is the constitutional provision stipulating that the two senators from each region represent the executive and legislative branches.

LEGISLATIVE-EXECUTIVE RELATIONS

Over the 1994–1995 and 1996–1999 terms of the State Duma, no party or coalition held a clear majority. However, in both Dumas, deputies opposed to President Yeltsin held a majority. Vetoes were frequent, and in 1999 the Duma came within fourteen votes of passing a motion to remove Yeltsin through impeachment. Nonetheless, behind-the-scenes bargaining over legislation was the norm. The chairman of the Duma in 1994 and 1995, Ivan Rybkin, was a communist but took a cooperative approach to his dealings with the executive branch, as did his successor as chairman, Gennady Seleznev, also a communist. On some highly contentious issues, such as the privatization of land, the branches were deadlocked. On many other issues, however, president and parliament were able to reach agreement. Overall, the president eventually signed about three-quarters of the laws passed by the Duma between 1994 and 1999.

The December 1999 parliamentary election and President Yeltsin's subsequent resignation resulted in a substantial change in legislative-executive relations. The Duma that convened in January 2000 was far friendlier to the president, and President Putin proved to be skillful in managing his relations with the Duma. By mid-2001 a coalition of four pro-Kremlin political factions had come to dominate the chamber, and the president was successful in passing an ambitious reform agenda. Much legislation that had been stalled under Yeltsin, including land privatization, cleared both chambers. So did many other laws, including a new

Labor Code, pension reform, simplified rules for business licensing and regulation, and ratification of the START-II treaty.

INTERNAL ORGANIZATION

In the Duma, political factions exercise substantial collective power over agenda-setting, organization, and procedures. The chamber's steering body is the Council of the Duma, which is made up of the leaders of each of the party factions (i.e., each party clearing the five percent threshold in the party list vote) as well as the heads of each organized deputy group possessing at least thirty-five members. The Council of the Duma forges the political compromises needed to reach agreement on important legislation. In addition, the leaders of the factions decide among themselves on the distribution of chairpersonships of the standing committees. Committee chairpersonships are distributed in rough proportion to factional strength, although under Putin, pro-presidential factions control the most influential committees. The Duma is not divided into "majority" and "minority" coalitions, although some evolution in that direction began in 2001.

The Federation Council lacks a system of political factions and is organized around its chairman and standing committees. The 2000 reform has led to significant changes in the way the chamber operates. A pro-Putin caucus, called "Federation," with approximately one hundred members, came to dominate the legislative proceedings in 2001. One of its members, a Putin ally named Sergei Mironov, was elected chairman of the chamber in December 2001. President Putin's legislative reforms began to sail through the chamber with almost no opposition. "Federation" was dissolved in January 2002, but the chamber remained strongly supportive of President Putin's program.

THE FEDERAL ASSEMBLY IN PERSPECTIVE

The 1993 constitution gives the president preponderant power in the political system. However, the electoral system that uses party-list voting for half the seats in the Duma, combined with the president's interest in seeking legislative legitimacy for his policy agenda, has allowed the parliament to exercise greater influence than President Yeltsin had originally anticipated. During his first two years, President Putin succeeded in marginalizing political opposition in both chambers and securing parliament's support for his legislative program, which included measures strengthening the central government vis-à-vis the regions and laws intended to improve the climate for investors and entrepreneurs. However, each chamber has developed a capacity for deliberation and decision making that may make parliament a more effective counterweight to future presidents. Therefore it is likely that the role of the Federal Assembly in the political system will continue to evolve.

See also: CONGRESS OF PEOPLE'S DEPUTIES; DUMA; GORBACHEV, MIKHAIL SERGEYEVICH; PUTIN, VLADIMIR VLADIMIROVICH; SUPREME SOVIET; YELTSIN, BORIS NIKOLAYEVICH

BIBLIOGRAPHY

Chaisty, Paul. (2001). "Legislative Politics in Russia." In *Contemporary Russian Politics: A Reader*, ed. Archie Brown. Oxford, UK: Oxford University Press.

McFaul, Michael. (2001). *Russia's Unfinished Revolution: Political Change from Gorbachev to Putin.* Ithaca, NY: Cornell University Press.

Remington, Thomas F. (2001). *The Russian Parliament: Institutional Evolution in a Transitional Regime, 1989–1999.* New Haven, CT: Yale University Press.

Smith, Steven, and Remington, Thomas F. (2001) *The Politics of Institutional Choice: Formation of the Russian State Duma.* Princeton, NJ: Princeton University Press.

THOMAS F. REMINGTON

FEDERALISM

The Russian Federation, as its name implies, is a federated political entity. However, this concept continues to evolve and is periodically challenged by a variety of political forces. Even if using one of the simpler definitions of federalism—that of "self rule plus shared rule" within a country—the Russian case defies easy classification.

According to the Russian constitution, there are eighty-nine distinct territorial entities within the Russian Federation, with some based on ethnic groups and others on territorial foundations. How these entities fit together in the Russian political system is a result of more than a decade of negotiation and practice. After all, the initial challenge was that while the Russian Socialist Federated Soviet Republic (RSFSR) was called a federation during the Soviet period, it was a unitary system in practice. Thus, at the time of independence in 1991, each of these political units had to renegotiate its standing within the new state, which eventually developed a system referred to as "assymetrical federalism." A number of the ethnic–based republics, for example, sought greater autonomy, or outright independence.

The Federation Treaty of March 1992 was the first step in formally resolving the question of powers and rights within the federated system. By the end of that year, all but Chechnya and Tatarstan signed the agreement, and the abstention of these two republics raised questions of a possible splintering of the Russian Federation. With the adoption of the new Russian constitution in December 1993, however, the Federation Treaty was enshrined in the main legal basis of the country. Beginning in 1994, the government in Moscow worked out an agreement with Tatarstan, as well as treaties with the other republics of the Russian Federation, leaving the Chechen Republic as the sole holdout. Indeed, that part of the Russian Federation remains contested and in the early twenty-first century is mired in a bloody conflict.

There are several key issues that continue to confront the federal structure in Russia. First, there are questions concerning basic budgetary and taxation rights. Are the regions able to create their own financial bases from which to fund specific projects? From education policies to economic development plans, problems exist as to what the republics can do. Second, there remains a problem of resource management on the national level. This is particularly important in the energy and strategic mineral fields. For example, control over energy deposits in the Yamalo–Nenets okrug was contested by that entity, the Tiumen oblast within which it is located, and the government in Moscow. Third, there are questions about the actual political power of regional governors. During the late–Yeltsin era, there was a tendency for the federal government to appoint regional officials in order to better control them from the center. Since that time, however, these officials are elected, and a few of these have begun to exercise real authority in their specific regions. In addition, the Federal Council, the upper chamber of the Russian legislature (similar to the U.S. Senate), is designed to represent the interests of these various subnational entities.

Given the vast territorial expanse of the Russian Federation, as well as the ethnic diversity of the regions, political leaders in Russia at least support the idea of a federated political system. However, the history of unitary control, both during tsarist and Soviet times, has yielded a legacy within the bureaucracy and administration that is difficult to change. In addition, the specific conditions and needs of each region undoubtedly dictate the specific level of authority that may be attained throughout the country. Most analysts and experts suggest that "federalism" in the Russian Federation will remain a multi–level system that will continue to see variations from region to region.

See also: FEDERATION TREATIES; NATIONALITIES POLICIES, SOVIET; PEOPLE'S COMMISSARIAT OF NATIONALITIES; RUSSIAN SOVIET FEDERATED SOCIALIST REPUBLIC

BIBLIOGRAPHY

Kahn, Jeffrey. (2002). *Federalism, Democratization, and the Rule of Law in Russia.* New York: Oxford University Press.

Kempton, Daniel R., and Clark, Terry D., eds. (2002). *Unity of Separation: Center–Periphery Relations in the Former Soviet Union.* Westport, CT: Praeger.

Ross, Cameron. (2003). *Federalism and Democratization in Post–Communist Russia.* Manchester, UK: Manchester University Press.

Stoner–Weiss, Kathryn. (2002). "Soviet Solutions to Post–Soviet Problems: Has Vladimir Putin Really Strengthened the Federal Center?" *PONARS [Program on New Approaches to Russian Security] Policy Memo No. 283,* October.

Walker, Edward W. (1995). "Designing Center–Region Relations in the New Russia." *East European Constitutional Review* 4(1): 54-60.

ROGER KANGAS

FEDERAL PROPERTY FUND

The State Property Committee agency charged with receiving and overseeing privatization of state enterprises designated for privatization began operations in October 1992 (under Anatoly Chubais) in what became a large–scale sale of state enterprises. The first stage was voucher privatization. Vouchers were sent to every man, woman, and child in Russia. These voucher checks could be used to purchase shares in what had previously been state enterprises. Or they could be invested in managed mutual funds or sold on the secondary market.

Enterprises slated for privatization were transferred to the Federal Property Fund. The initial stage of privatization excluded enterprises of national significance, such and oil and electric generation and those of military or strategic significance. Large scale, non-military enterprises were transferred subsequently in 1994–1995 and many were auctioned off under what was called the "loans for shares" program. When enterprises were transferred to the Federal Property Fund they were required to be converted into open joint stock companies before privatization. The Federal Property Fund was to oversee this transformation and supervise the privatization process.

In the end the Federal Property Fund participated in the largest privatization program in economic history, one that was replete with insider advantages, corruption, bribery, and scandalous underpayment by the ultimate owners. Privatization was also incomplete because the government maintained either a majority ownership or "golden shares" that allowed a veto over management decisions.

See also: PRIVATIZATION

BIBLIOGRAPHY

Gregory, Paul R., and Stuart, Robert C. (2001). *Russian and Soviet Economic Performance and Structure,* 7th ed. New York: Addison Wesley.

Hedlund, Stefan. (1999). *Russia's "Market" Economy: A Bad Case of Predatory Capitalism.* London: UCL Press.

JAMES R. MILLAR

FEDERATION TREATIES

On March 13, 1992, representatives of eighteen of Russia's twenty ethnic republics initialed a treaty of federation with the Russian federal government. Two republics—Chechnya and Tatarstan—refused to sign. A separate agreement was initialed by representatives of Russia's oblasts and *kraya* (administrative divisions) that same week, followed several days later by a third agreement with the country's autonomous *okruga* (territorial divisions) and the Jewish Autonomous Oblast. On March 31, 1992, the three treaties, which would be collectively referred to as the "Federation Treaty," were formally signed into law. After the formal separation of the Chechen and Ingush Republics was ratified by the Sixth Congress of Peoples' Deputies in April 1992, the number of republics under Russian constitutional law rose to twenty-one. While Ingushetia signed the Treaty upon its establishment, Chechnya refused to do so, asserting that it had declared formal independence in November 1991.

The April 1992 Treaty provided for a complicated and vague division of powers between the federal government and Russia's eighty-nine "subjects of the federation." It also required as many as one hundred enabling laws, most of which were never adopted. Symbolically, the most important provision was the Treaty's designation of the ethnic republics, but not the Russian Federation's other constituent units (oblasts, *kraya,* and autonomous *okruga*), as "sovereign," although it was not clear what legal rights, if any, "sovereign" status entailed. Some advocates of the republics argued that it implied a right to refuse to join the federation as well as a right of unilateral secession. Unlike the USSR constitution in effect at the time of the dissolution of the Soviet Union in December 1991, however, Russia's Federation Treaty of 1992 made no reference to a right of secession for the republics. Nor did federal authorities agree that the republics had a right to refuse to join the federation. The Treaty also stipulated that the constitutions of the republics had to conform to the federal constitution.

The intent of the drafters of the April 1992 had been to include the Treaty's provisions in a new constitution for the Russian Federation. However, the text of the Treaty was left out of the Russian Constitution of December 12, 1993, although Article 11.3 stated that the distribution of federal and regional powers is governed by "this Constitution, the Federation Treaty, and other treaties (*dogovory*) that delineate objects of jurisdiction and powers." Article 1, Part 2, of the constitution added that "should the provisions of the Federation Treaty . . . contravene those of the Constitution of the Federation, the provisions of the Constitution of the Russian Federation shall apply." In effect, the terms of the Federation Treaty were superseded by the federation provisions in the new constitution, which did not identify the republics as sovereign and was unequivocal in denying the subjects of the federation a unilateral right of secession.

While the Treaty had limited legal significance, its signing in early 1992 helped ameliorate some of the tension between the Russian federal government and the republics in the wake of the dissolution of the USSR. It also provided President Boris Yeltsin with an important political victory. But it left many critical issues unresolved, particularly the legal status of Chechnya and Tatarstan. In February 1994, Tatarstan agreed to become a constituent unit of the Russian Federation pursuant to the terms of a bilateral treaty. Chechnya would continue to refuse to join the federation, however, a position that led to war between the Russian federal government and supporters of Chechen independence later that year.

See also: CONSTITUTION OF 1993; FEDERALISM; RUSSIAN SOVIET FEDERATED SOCIALIST REPUBLIC

BIBLIOGRAPHY

Ahdieh, Robert B. (1997). *Russia's Constitutional Revolution: Legal Consciousness and the Transition to Democracy.* University Park: Pennsylvania State University Press.

Lapidus, Gail W., and Walker, Edward W. (1995). "Nationalism, Regionalism, and Federalism: Center-Periphery Relations in Post-Communist Russia." In *The New Russia: Troubled Transformation,* ed. Gail W. Lapidus. Boulder, CO: Westview Press.

EDWARD W. WALKER

FELDMAN, GRIGORY ALEXANDROVICH

(1884–1958), a pioneer in the mathematical study of economic growth.

Grigory Alexandrovich Feldman, an electrical engineer by profession, worked in Gosplan from 1923 until 1931. His report to the committee for long-term planning of Gosplan, entitled "On the Theory of the Rates of Growth of the National Income," was published in 1928 and became the basis for the committee's preliminary draft of a long-term plan. However, Feldman soon came under attack for his ideas on the politically sensitive subject of socialist industrialization and use of mathematics in the heroic atmosphere of those times. His numerical targets, though supported by the head of the committee, proved too optimistic and could not be realized. After some tendentious criticism, Feldman's career never recovered. Even his later work on growth in the United States, an early interest of his, could not be published. He apparently spent several years in labor camps before being released, quite sick, in 1953.

Feldman's two-sector growth model was based on the macroeconomic concepts of Karl Marx. Feldman first demonstrated that the higher the aggregate growth of an economy, the more capital had to be devoted to the producers' goods sector. Net investment would have to be proportional to the existing allocation of capital. The greater the capacity to produce capital goods, the faster the economy could grow, according to the model. Capital-output ratios in the two sectors could be minimized by working several shifts. This early growth model, however, ignored likely scarcities of food, foreign exchange, and skilled labor that would result when growth accelerated.

See also: ECONOMIC GROWTH, SOVIET; GOSPLAN

BIBLIOGRAPHY

Domar, Evsey D. (1957). *Essays in the Theory of Economic Growth.* New York: Oxford University Press.

Ellman, Michael. (1990). "Grigorii Alexandrovic Fel'dman." In *Problems of the Planned Economy,* eds. John Eatwell, Murray Milgate, and Peter Newman. New York: Norton.

MARTIN C. SPECHLER

FELDSHER

Medical assistant.

Feldshers first appeared in Russia during the eighteenth century, when they served as medical assistants in urban hospitals or as army corpspeople. During the nineteenth century they played a major role in rural medical systems. The law restricted them to practice under a physician's direct supervision; many were nevertheless assigned to run remote clinics on their own because of the dearth of physicians in the countryside. Forced by circumstances to tolerate such independent feldsher practice, known as "feldsherism," leading physicians adamantly opposed granting it legal sanction. "Feldsherism" remained a contentious issue as well as a widespread practice well into the 1920s.

During the 1870s, many provincial zemstvos established feldsher schools in order to raise feldshers' overall qualifications. Opening feldsher practice to women in 1871 brought growing numbers of urban women with gymnasium training into these schools. By the twentieth century, the qualifications of these newer feldshers and feldsher-midwives had improved dramatically. As of 1914 there were more than 20,000 civilian feldshers in Russia. Most served in rural areas, but one-third worked for urban hospitals, railroads, schools, and factories.

The publication in 1891 of the newspaper *Feldsher* sparked the appearance of a feldsher professional movement. In 1906, local feldsher societies formed a national Union of Societies of Physicians' Assistants, which published the newspaper *Feldshersky vestnik* (Feldsher Herald) and lobbied on feldshers' behalf. During the revolutions of 1905 and 1917, most feldshers identified with moderate socialist parties. In 1918 the Union was dissolved; its members entered the industrial medical union *Vsemediksantrud.*

The Soviet regime ceased training feldshers altogether in 1924, focusing instead on midwives and nurses. Feldsher training was resumed in 1937, and feldshers continue to serve as auxiliary medical personnel in Russia.

See also: HEALTH CARE SERVICES, IMPERIAL; HEALTH CARE SERVICES, SOVIET

BIBLIOGRAPHY

Ramer, Samuel C. (1976). "Who Was the Russian Feldsher?" *Bulletin of the History of Medicine* 50:213–225.

Ramer, Samuel C. (1996). "Professionalism and Politics: The Russian Feldsher Movement, 1891–1918." In *Russia's Missing Middle Class: The Professions in Russian History*, ed. Harley D. Balzer. Armonk, NY: M. E. Sharpe.

SAMUEL C. RAMER

FELLOW TRAVELERS

Intellectuals sympathetic to the Bolshevik cause and later to the Soviet Union as a socialist state.

The term *fellow traveler* (*poputchiki*) was used by Vladimir Lenin and other Bolsheviks to describe those who agreed with the principles of socialism but did not accept the entire Bolshevik program. Lenin attacked these "petty-bourgeois fellow travelers" for their weak understanding of theory and tactics, and for leading workers away from revolution. Leon Trotsky, in 1918, described the Left Socialist Revolutionaries in similar terms because of their vacillation on the October Revolution.

The pejorative sense of the term gave way in 1924, when Trotsky argued that fellow travelers in literature could be useful for the young Soviet state. He used the term to describe non-party writers who could serve the cause of revolution even though they were not proletarians. In *Literature and Revolution*, Trotsky argued that non-party intellectuals were no longer a serious threat and could be guided toward a proletarian view of the world. This was followed by a Central Committee resolution in 1925 refusing to prefer one faction or theory of literature over any other.

The groups and individuals defined as fellow travelers during the 1920s constituted a flourishing artistic and literary culture that produced the best Soviet literature of the decade. The most famous group was the Serapion Brotherhood, whose membership included Konstantin Fedin, Yevgeny Zamyatin, and Vsevolod V. Ivanov. These authors believed that literature should be free from outside control, but were generally sympathetic to the goals of the revolution. Others, perhaps less favorably inclined toward the Bolsheviks but nonetheless counted as fellow travelers, were Boris Pilnyak, Isaac Babel, and Mikhail Bulgakov.

By the late 1920s, fellow travelers were coming under increasing pressure from groups claiming to represent the proletariat, such as the Russian Association of Proletarian Writers (RAPP). In 1932, all independent organizations for writers and artists disappeared and the Writers' Union was created. Fellow travelers were required to either join the union and follow its rules or stop publishing.

By the end of 1920s, the term "fellow traveler" had been taken up in other countries as a designation for people sympathetic to the Soviet Union and especially for intellectuals who publicly expressed support for Stalin. Romain Rolland and George Bernard Shaw, for instance, praised the Soviet Union and saw it as a real alternative to western political systems. In the post–World War II era, "fellow traveler" became a term of derision, applied by conservatives to people who were communists in all but party affiliation. Albert Einstein, for example, was called a "dupe and a fellow traveler" by *Time* magazine in 1949 for his outspoken belief in socialism.

See also: CULTURAL REVOLUTION; RUSSIAN ASSOCIATION OF PROLETARIAN WRITERS; SERAPION BROTHERS; UNION OF SOVIET WRITERS

BIBLIOGRAPHY

Canute, David. (1988). *The Fellow-Travellers: Intellectual Friends of Communism.* New Haven, CT: Yale University Press.

Maguire, Robert. (1987). *Red Virgin Soil: Soviet Literature in the 1920s.* Ithaca, NY: Cornell University Press.

KARL E. LOEWENSTEIN

FEMINISM

Feminism in Russia first developed during the 1850s, following the disastrous Crimean War and the accession of Alexander II. At a time of political ferment over the nation's future, an intense debate arose within educated society over the dependent status of women and inherited assumptions about their capacities and their roles. The idea of women's emancipation was readily linked to peasant emancipation, plans for which were being publicly debated during these years. If one section of the population—enserfed peasants—could be liberated, why not women too, half the human race? Many activists in the women's movement over the next half-century pinpointed the 1850s and 1860s as the moment when women first challenged their own subordinate legal status, inferior education, exclusion from all but menial paid employment, and vulnerability to sexual exploitation, as well as the complex web of convention and sanction that restricted their everyday lives. A number of women writers—and some radical male writers—had already addressed these themes a generation earlier, but always as individuals. It was only during the 1850s that a women's movement, dedicated to change, could coalesce.

Unlike women in many western countries, Russian upper- and middle-class women kept their property upon marriage and were not forced into financial dependence on their husbands. However, even propertied women were disadvantaged by inferior inheritance rights; despite their financial autonomy, the law required that they obey their husbands and live in the marital home unless given formal permission to leave. In an abusive marriage a woman could apply to the courts for legal separation, but this was a tortuous process and available only to the relatively well-to-do. The vast majority of Russian women in this period were peasants; before 1861 many were serfs. Even after peasant emancipation their status in the family was subordinate, particularly as young women. They were valued in the village for their ability to work—in the fields and in the household—and to produce and raise children. Few had time to think about the possibilities of an alternative life or about their own lack of rights or status. It was feminists and female radicals who first set out to improve women's personal rights and establish their legal and actual autonomy, though the prevailing social conservatism on gender issues and the extreme limitations on political campaigning impeded any meaningful legislative change until the last years of tsarist rule.

Feminist ideas in Russia were inspired not only by social and political change at home, but equally by the emerging women's movement in the West (particularly North America, Britain, and France) in this period. Russian feminists established lasting contacts with their western counterparts and read western literature on the "woman question." Most considered themselves "westernizers" rather than "slavophiles" in the contemporary political-cultural controversy over Russia and its future. The word "feminism" itself was rarely used in Russia or elsewhere, and even when it gained wider currency toward the end of the century, it most often had a pejorative connotation, both for conservative and radical opponents of reformist women's movements, and for feminists too. Before 1905 they called themselves "activists in the women's movement" (*deyatelnitsy zhenskogo dvizheniya*). During the 1905 Revolution, when the movement was politicized, the most uncompromising became "equal-righters" (*ravnopravki*), emphasizing the struggle for social equality overall, not just for women. After 1917 feminist activists either emigrated or were silenced, and for the entire Soviet period feminism was branded a "bourgeois deviation."

RADICAL ALTERNATIVES TO FEMINISM

Like feminists, revolutionary women and men espoused sexual equality. But they fiercely rejected feminism, insisting that women's liberation must be part of a wider social revolution. Feminists, they claimed, based their appeal to women by driving a wedge between men and women of the oppressed classes struggling for their rights. Feminists denied the radical claim that they were motivated only by their own "selfish" ends, and saw themselves working for Russia's "renewal" and "regeneration," for the betterment of the whole population.

Although a socialist women's movement developed in Russia (as elsewhere) around 1900, both populist and Marxist revolutionary groups were antagonistic to separate work among women, and only well after 1900 was it possible for Bolshevik women (such as Alexandra Kollontai, Inessa Armand, and Nadezhdaya Krupskaya, Lenin's wife) to address women's issues specifically within their party organization. Though dubbed a "Bolshevik feminist" by later western historians, Kollontai herself was one of the most outspoken critics of reformist feminism—and the very concept of feminism—before and after 1917.

Soviet communism declared gender equality, as celebrated in this 1961 postcard, reading "Glory to Soviet Women!"

Disagreements between feminist reformers and radicals were present from the beginning. At first these conflicts were more over lifestyle than politics. Reformers observed existing social codes (dress, comportment, family obligations, respectability). Many, though not all, came from well-to-do gentry backgrounds and had no need to earn a living. Radicals, often of gentry origin too, were in conscious revolt against family and social propriety. They wore cropped hair and simple, unadorned clothing, smoked in public, and called themselves "nihilists" (*nigilistki*). Whether in financial need or not (many were), nihilists joined urban "communes," or set up their own. For a few years there was some contact (including individual friendships) between nihilists and feminists, focusing on attempts to set up an employment bureau for women and cooperative workshops providing employment and essential skills for themselves and other women. This collaboration foundered during the mid-1860s; within a few years many nihilist women had moved into illegal populist groups whose aim was the liberation of the "Russian people," the *narod.* In their own estimation, by the early 1870s the radicals had left the "woman question" behind.

FEMINIST CAMPAIGNING

The reformers were dedicated to working within the system. They raised petitions, lobbied ministers, and exploited personal connections to reach influential figures, many of them already sympathetic to feminist ideas. Of necessity, they focused on philanthropy and higher education. Philanthropy was the one form of public activity then open to women, an acknowledged extension of their "caring" role within the family. It aimed both to encourage self-sufficiency in the beneficiaries and to give their organizers practical experience of public administration. Feminist philanthropists ran their enterprises, as far as was possible, democratically and with minimal regulation. Most successful was a Society to Provide Cheap Lodgings (founded in 1861 and by 1880 a major charity) in St. Petersburg. Another society provided refuges for poor women. A major feminist preoccupation, particularly important in a rapidly urbanizing society, was to provide poorer women with alternatives to prostitution.

Campaigns for higher education were a new departure, but still within a familiar realm—woman as educator of her children—a role that became increasingly important in Russia's drive to "modernize." Feminists received support from individual professors and even university administrations. Persistent lobbying of government led to permission for public lectures for women (1869), then preparatory courses and finally university-level courses (1872 in Moscow), all existing on public goodwill, organization, and funding. Medical courses (for "learned midwives") were opened to women in St Petersburg (1872), extended to full medical courses in 1876. In 1878 the first Higher Courses for Women opened in St. Petersburg, followed by Moscow, Kiev, and Kazan. Though outside the university system, with no rights to state service and rank as given to men, these courses were effectively women's universities. Feminist campaigners also provided financial resources to students needing assistance, setting up a charity to raise money for the Higher Courses in 1878.

The campaign for higher education and specialist training was critically important for radical women too. Radicals' increasing identification with "the people" inspired them to train for professions that could be of direct use, principally teaching and medicine. During the early 1870s dozens of radical women (along with nonpolitical women in search of professional education not then available in Russia) went abroad to study, especially to Zurich, where the university was willing to admit them. Some radicals completed their training; others were drawn into Russian émigré political circles, abandoned their studies, and soon returned to Russia as active revolutionaries.

Feminism—like all reform movements in Russia during the 1870s—suffered in the increasingly repressive political environment. All independent initiatives, legal or illegal, came under suspicion: these included a feminist publishing cooperative founded during the mid-1860s, fundraising activities, proposals to form women's groups, and so forth. Alexander II's assassination in 1881 brought further misfortune. Several of the terrorist leaders were women, former *nigilistki,* and in the wholesale assault on liberalism following the murder, feminists were tarred with the same brush. The reaction after 1881 proved almost fatal. Expansion of higher education was halted; some courses were closed. Feminists ceased campaigning, and all avenues for action were barred. Only during the mid-1890s could feminists begin to regroup, but under strict supervision, and always limited by law to education and philanthropy.

POLITICAL ACTION

Before 1900 Russian feminism had no overt political agenda. For some activists this was a matter of choice, for many others a frustrating restriction. In several, though not all, western countries women's suffrage had been a focal point of feminist aspirations since the 1850s and 1860s. When rural zemstvos and municipal dumas were set up in Russia in the 1860s, propertied women received limited proxy rights to vote for the assemblies' representatives, but legal political activity—by either gender—was not permitted. Indeed, no national legislature existed before 1906, when the tsar was forced by revolutionary upheaval to create the State Duma. It was during the build up of this opposition movement, from the early 1900s, that Russian feminism began to address political issues, not only women's suffrage, but calls for civil rights and equality before the law for all citizens.

After Bloody Sunday (January 9, 1905), feminist activists began to organize, linking their cause with that of the liberal and moderate socialist Liberation Movement. Besides existing women's societies, such as the Russian Women's Mutual Philanthropic Society (*Russkoye zhenskoye vzaimnoblagotvoritelnoye obshchestvo,* established in 1895), new organizations sprang up. Most directly political was the All-Russian Union of Equal Rights for Women (*Vserossysky soyuz ravnopraviya zhenshchin*), dedicated to a wide program of social and political reform, including universal suffrage without distinction of gender, religion, or nationality. It quickly affiliated itself with the Union of Unions (*Soyuz soyuzov*). Feminist support for the Liberation Movement was unmatched by the movement's support for women's political rights, and much of the union's propaganda during 1905 was directed as much at the liberal opposition as at the government. Unlike the latter, however, many liberals were gradually persuaded by the feminist claim, and support increased significantly in the years of reaction that followed. The government refused to consider women's suffrage at any point.

The women's union—though itself overwhelmingly middle-class and professional—was greatly encouraged by women's participation in workers' strikes during the mid-1890s and, particularly, women's involvement in working-class action in 1904 and 1905. After 1905, however, feminists were increasingly challenged by revolutionary socialists in a competition to "win" working–class women to their cause. Prominent Bolsheviks such as Kollontai had finally convinced their party leaders of working–class women's revolutionary potential. During the last years of tsarist rule, when the labor movement overall was becoming increasingly active, Kollontai and her comrades benefited from the feminists' failure to make any headway in the mass organization of women, a failure exacerbated after the outbreak of World War I by the feminists' stalwart support for the war effort. It was the Bolsheviks, not the feminists, who capitalized on the war's catastrophic impact on the lives of working–class women and men.

With the outbreak of the February Revolution of 1917, the feminist campaign resumed, and initial opposition from the Provisional Government was easily overcome. In the electoral law for the Constituent Assembly, women were fully enfranchised. Before it was swept away by the Bolsheviks, the Provisional Government initiated several projects to give women equal opportunities and pay in public services, and full rights to practice as lawyers. It also proposed to transform the higher courses into women's universities; in the event, the courses were fully incorporated into existing universities by the Bolsheviks in 1918.

During the 1920s, with "bourgeois feminism" silenced, women's liberation was sponsored by the Bolsheviks, under a special Women's Department of the Communist Party (*Zhenotdel*). In 1930 the Zhenotdel was abruptly dismantled and the "woman question" prematurely declared "solved."

See also: KOLLONTAI, ALEXANDRA MIKHAILOVNA; KRUPSKAYA, NADEZHDA KONSTANTINOVNA; MARRIAGE AND FAMILY LIFE; ZHENOTDEL

BIBLIOGRAPHY

Atkinson, Dorothy; Dallin, Alexander; and Warshofsky, Lapidus, eds. (1977). *Women in Russia.* Stanford, CA: Stanford University Press.

Clements, Barbara Evans. (1979). *Bolshevik Feminist: The Life of Aleksandra Kollontai.* Bloomington: Indiana University Press.

Clements, Barbara Evans; Engel, Barbara Alpern; and Worobec, Christine, D., eds. (1991). *Russia's Women: Accommodation, Resistance, Transformation.* Berkeley: University of California Press.

Edmondson, Linda. (1984). *Feminism in Russia, 1900-1917.* Stanford, CA: Stanford University Press.

Edmondson, Linda, ed. (1992). *Women and Society in Russia and the Soviet Union.* Cambridge, UK: Cambridge University Press.

Engel, Barbara Alpern. (1983). *Mothers and Daughters: Women of the Intelligentsia in Nineteenth–Century Russia.* Cambridge, UK: Cambridge University Press.

Farnsworth, Beatrice, and Viola, Lynne, eds. (1992). *Russian Peasant Women.* Oxford: Oxford University Press.

Glickman, Rose L. (1984). *Russian Factory Women: Workplace and Society, 1880-1914.* Berkeley: University of California Press.

Noonan, Norma Corigliano, and Nechemias, Carol, eds. (2001). *Encyclopedia of Russian Women's Movements.* Westport, CT: Greenwood Press.

Norton, Barbara T., and Gheith, Jehanne, M., eds. (2001). *An Improper Profession: Women, Gender, and Journalism in Late Imperial Russia.* Durham, NC: Duke University Press.

Stites, Richard. (1978). *The Women's Liberation Movement in Russia: Feminism, Nihilism, and Bolshevism, 1860-1930.* Princeton, NJ: Princeton University Press.

LINDA EDMONDSON

FERGHANA VALLEY

A triangular basin with rich soil and abundant water resources from the Syr Darya River, modern canals, and the Kayrakkum Reservoir; the Ferghana Valley (Russian: *Ferganskaia dolina*; Uzbek: *Fargona ravnina*) is situated primarily in Uzbekistan and partly in Kyrgyzstan and Tajikistan, and is formed below the Tien Shan Mountains to the north and the Gissar Alay Mountains to the south. This has been the agricultural center of Central Asia for the last several thousand years. The basin is a major producer of cotton, fruits, and raw silk. It is one of the most densely populated regions of Central Asia, including the cities of Khujand, Kokand, Ferghana, Margilan, Namangan, Andijan, Osh, and Jalalabad.

Throughout its history, material and cultural wealth have made the valley a frequent target of conquest. Khujand, at the western edge of the valley, was once called "Alexandria the Far" as an outpost of Alexander the Great's army. From the third century the valley emerged as a Persian–Sogdian nexus and major stop along the Silk Road under the suzerainty of the Sassanids. The Chinese Tang Dynasty briefly exerted influence in the valley during the seventh and eighth centuries, followed by Arab conquest and Islamic conversions during the eighth and ninth centuries and Persian Samanid dominion during the tenth century. The rise of the Karakhanids brought lasting Turkicization of the Ferghana Valley during the eleventh century. The Chaghatay Ulus of the Mongol Empire during the thirteenth century and the Turkic Timur (Tamerlane) and his grandson Ulugh Bek during the fourteenth and fifteenth centuries introduced a period of burgeoning literature and Islamic erudition, followed by centuries of shifting local powers and instability under the various Turkic groups. Kokand khans ruled from the late eighteenth century until the Russian Empire annexed the valley as the Ferghana oblast to the Turkestan governor–generalship in 1876.

During the establishment of Soviet power in Central Asia (1920s and 1930s), the valley provided a fertile area for the Basmachi movement. In 1924, it was divided between the Uzbek SSR, the Tajik ASSR, and the Kirgiz ASSR. As a result, the valley inherited several cross border enclaves in a traditionally interwoven ethnic region. Despite a tradition of multiethnic cooperation, late–Soviet unrest and ethnic clashes erupted there in 1989 between

Uzbeks and Meshkhetian Turks, and in 1990 between Kyrgyz and Uzbeks in Osh. The famous Ferghana Canal was an early Soviet engineering project celebrated in prose, poetry, and film.

See also: BASMACHIS; CENTRAL ASIA; UZBEKISTAN AND UZBEKS

BIBLIOGRAPHY

Manz, Beatrice Forbes. (1987). "Central Asian Uprisings in the Nineteenth Century: Ferghana Under the Russians." *Russian Review* 46 (3):267–281.

Tabyshalieva, Anara. (1999). *The Challenge of Regional Cooperation in Central Asia: Preventing Ethnic Conflict in the Ferghana Valley.* Washington, DC: U.S. Institute of Peace.

MICHAEL ROULAND

FEUDALISM

According to the nearly unanimous consensus of Western scholars, pre–Soviet Russian scholars, and most Soviet scholars until the mid– to late–1930s, feudalism never appeared in Russia. By the end of the 1930s, however, it became the entrenched dogma in the Soviet Union that Russia had experienced a feudal period. Post–Soviet Russian historians have been unable to rid themselves of this erroneous interpretation of their own history, in spite of Western arguments to the contrary that have been advanced since 1991.

The fundamental issue is whether the term "feudalism" has any meaning other than "agrarian regime," that is, that most of the population lives in the countryside and makes its living from farming and that most of the gross domestic product is derived from agriculture. If that is all it means, then Russia was feudal until after World War II. Most definitions of feudalism, however, involve other criteria as well, which, as defined by George Vernadsky and others, typically encompass: (1) a fusion of public and private law; (2) a dismemberment of political authority and a parcellization of sovereignty; (3) an interdependence of political and economic administration; (4) the predominance of a natural, i.e., nonmarket, economy; (5) the presence of serfdom. Presumably all of these criteria, not just one or two, should be present for there to be feudalism in a locality.

The first historian to posit the existence of feudalism in Russia was Nikolai Pavlov–Silvansky (1869-1908), who based his theory primarily on the political fragmentation of Russia from the collapse of the Kievan Russian state in 1132 to the consolidation of Russia by Moscow by the early sixteenth century. The basic problem with that thesis is that there was no serfdom until the 1450s. Moreover, there were no fiefs. In 1912 Lenin defined feudalism as "land ownership and the privileges of lords over serfs." Mikhail Pokrovsky (1868-1932) worked out a "Soviet Marxist" understanding of Russian feudalism and traced its origin and major cause (large landownership) to the thirteenth century. "Feudalism" was necessary to legitimize the October Revolution and Soviet power. According to Marx, human history went through the stages of (1) primordial/primitive communism; (2) slave–owning; (3) feudalism; (4) capitalism; (5) imperialism; (6) socialism; (7) communism. The fact that Russia in reality never experienced "stages" two through five made it difficult to claim that the October Revolution was historically inevitable and therefore legitimate. Inventing "stages" three through five was therefore politically necessary.

A major problem for the Soviets was that Russia never knew a slave–owning stage (as in Greece and Rome). This "problem" was worked out in the early 1930s by a Menshevik historian, M. M. Tsvibak (who was liquidated a few years later in the Great Purges), with the claim that Russia had bypassed the slave–owning period entirely, that feudalism arose about the same time as the Kievan Russian state during the ninth century, or even earlier. Boris Grekov, the "dean" of Soviet historians between 1930 and 1953 (he allegedly had no use for Stalin), earlier had alleged that Russia had passed through a slave–owning stage, but he took the Tsvibak position in the later 1930s, and that remained the official dogma to the end of the Soviet regime. As a result, nearly all of Russian and Ukrainian history was deemed feudal and succeeded by "capitalism" with the freeing of the serfs from seignorial control in 1861.

See also: MARXISM; PEASANTRY; SLAVERY

BIBLIOGRAPHY

Hellie, Richard. (1971). *Enserfment and Military Change in Muscovy.* Chicago: University of Chicago Press.

Vernadsky, George. (1939). "Feudalism in Russia." *Speculum* 14:302-323.

RICHARD HELLIE

FILARET DROZDOV, METROPOLITAN

(1782–1867), Metropolitan of Moscow, theologian, and churchman.

Throughout his long career, Filaret (Vasily Mikhailovich Drozdov) played a central role in important matters of church, state, and society: as a moving force behind the Russian translation of the Bible, as a teacher of the Orthodox faith through his famous catechism, sermons, and textbooks, and as a reformer of the church, particularly its monasteries. His widespread reputation as a man of profound faith and great integrity made him the government's natural choice to compose the emancipation manifesto ending serfdom in 1861. When he died in 1867, the country went into mourning. As Konstantin Pobedonostsev, the future over-procurator of the Holy Synod, wrote on the day of the metropolitan's funeral: "The present moment is very important for the people. The entire people consider the burial of the metro[politan] a national affair."

Filaret's early career focused on reform of religious education, which he shifted from the Latin scholastic curriculum of the eighteenth century to a Russian and Bible-centered one during the early nineteenth century. He wrote two Russian textbooks in 1816 inaugurating a new Orthodox Biblical theology: *An Outline of Church-Biblical History* (*Nachertanie tserkovno-bibleiskoi istorii*) and *Notes on the Book of Genesis* (*Zapiski na knigu Bytiya*). By this time he was also heavily engaged in a contemporary Russian translation of the Bible that would carry the Christian message to the Russian people more effectively than the Slavonic Bible published during the previous century. He personally translated the Gospel of John. In 1823 he wrote a new Orthodox catechism with all of its Biblical citations in Russian. His abilities and work quickly advanced his career. He became a member of the Holy Synod in 1819 and archbishop of Moscow in 1821 (metropolitan in 1826).

Filaret's new Bible and catechetical initiatives provoked opposition in church and governing circles, who saw them as signs of Orthodoxy's deepening dependence on Protestantism. The critics soon stopped the Bible translation, burned its completed portions, and redirected church education on what Filaret called the "reverse course to scholasticism." His catechism was reissued in 1827 in revised form and in Slavonic. Under these circumstances, Filaret had to rethink his own position and ideas.

While he never departed from his belief that the church must communicate its teachings in a language people could understand (he finally won publication of a Russian translation of the Bible during the more liberal reign of Alexander II), Filaret now gave his ideas a more explicitly patristic underpinning, as evidenced in the dogmatic theology he eloquently and poetically expressed in his sermons. Moreover, he sponsored publication of the *Writings of the Holy Fathers in Russian Translation* (1843–1893). One eminent Russian theologian identifies the new work as the crucial moment in the "awakening of Orthodoxy" in modern times, the moment when Russian theology began to recover the teachings of the Eastern church fathers and to define itself with respect to both Roman Catholicism and Protestantism.

While many aspects of Filaret's activity as a leader of the Russian church for more than forty years bear mentioning, his efforts to reform and strengthen monasticism stand out. He promoted contemplative asceticism (*hesychasm*) on the territory of the Holy Trinity–St. Sergius monastery and elsewhere. Fully reformed monasteries, he believed, might inspire the return of the Old Ritualist and reconvert Byzantine Rite Catholics (Uniates) of Poland. He encouraged informal women's communities to become monasteries, and during the 1860s devised badly needed guidelines for all monasteries, stressing wherever possible that they follow the rule of St. Basil with its obligation for a common table, community property, work, and prayer. Filaret was canonized as a saint in 1992.

See also: METROPOLITAN; RUSSIAN ORTHODOX CHURCH; SAINTS

BIBLIOGRAPHY

Florovsky, Georges. (1979–1985). *Ways of Russian Theology*, vol. 1, chap. 5. Belmont, MA: Nordland.

Nichols, Robert L. (1990). "Filaret of Moscow as an Ascetic." In *The Legacy of St. Vladimir: Byzantium, Russia, America*, eds. J. Breck, J. Meyendorff, and E. Silk. Crestwood, NY: St. Vladimir's Seminary Press.

ROBERT NICHOLS

FILARET ROMANOV, PATRIARCH

(c. 1550–1633), Patriarch of Moscow and All Rus (1619–1633).

Born Fedor Nikitich Romanov, the future Patriarch Filaret came from an old boyar clan, known variously from the fourteenth century as the Koshkins, the Zakharins, the Iurevs, and finally as the Romanovs. The clan reached the height of power and privilege after 1547, when Tsar Ivan IV ("the Terrible") married Anastasia Iureva, Fedor Nikitich's aunt (Fedor was probably born after the wedding). During the reign of Ivan the Terrible's son and heir, Tsar Fedor Ivanovich (1584–1598), Fedor Nikitich Romanov succeeded his father, Nikita Romanovich Iurev, on a regency council that ruled along with Tsar Fedor. Fedor Nikitich had been a boyar since 1587. He was regional governor (*namestnik*) of Nizhnii Novgorod (1586) and later of Pskov (1590) and served in numerous ceremonial functions at court.

On the death of Tsar Fedor in 1598, Fedor Nikitich continued to hold important posts and retained his seniority among the boyars under the new tsar, Boris Godunov. In 1601, however, as part of a general attack by Boris on real and potential rivals to his power, Fedor was forcibly tonsured (made a monk) and exiled to the remote Antoniev-Siisky Monastery, near Kholmogory. His wife, Ksenia Ivanovna Shestova (whom he married around 1585), was similarly forced to take the monastic habit in 1601. She took the religious name Marfa and was sent in exile to the remote Tolvuisky Hermitage. Other Romanov relatives—Fedor's brothers and sisters and their spouses—similarly fell into disgrace under Boris Godunov, with only one of Fedor's brothers (Ivan) surviving his confinement.

That Fedor should be considered a rival to Boris was natural enough. He was the last tsar's first cousin, whereas Boris was merely a brother-in-law. There was also the more or less general belief, known even to foreign travelers in Russia at the time, that just before his death, Tsar Fedor had bequeathed the throne to his cousin Fedor, and that Boris Godunov had been elected to the throne only after the Romanovs had first refused it. While there is enough contemporary evidence to suggest that the Romanovs were genuinely thought of as candidates for the throne in 1598, many of the stories about Tsar Fedor's nomination of one of the Romanovs as his heir date from only after the Romanov ascension to the throne (in 1613) and therefore must be regarded with some suspicion.

Whatever the case, Fedor Nikitich, having taken the monastic name of Filaret, received some relief from his circumstances in 1605, when Boris Godunov died and was replaced by the First False Dmitry, who freed him (and his former wife, the nun Marfa) from his confinement and elevated him to the rank of Metropolitan of Rostov. After the fall of the First False Dmitry, Filaret took charge of the translation of the relics of Tsarevich Dmitry from Uglich to Moscow's Archangel Cathedral in the Kremlin. This was where Dmitry was interred and, shortly thereafter, where he was glorified as a saint. With the election of (St.) Germogen as patriarch, Filaret was sent back to Rostov; but when the Second False Dmitry captured the city in 1608, Filaret soon became one of his supporters in a struggle with Tsar Vasily Shuisky (r. 1606–1610), establishing himself in Dmitry's camp at Tushino, near Moscow. It was the Second False Dmitry, in fact, who elevated Filaret to be patriarch after (St.) Germogen was murdered by the Poles, who had intervened in Russian internal affairs.

Filaret briefly fell into Polish hands when Dmitry was defeated and put to flight, but he quickly made his way back to Moscow under the protection of Tsar Vasily Shuisky. However, military defeats brought Shuisky's regime down in 1610, and Shuisky was forcibly tonsured a monk. Political power rested then in a council of seven boyars who dispatched Filaret to Poland to invite Prince Wladislaw, son of Poland's King Sigismund III, to be tsar in Muscovy. During these negotiations, Filaret insisted that the young prince convert to Orthodoxy and to do so by rebaptism, a stipulation to which the Polish king was unwilling to concede. With the breakdown of these talks, Filaret was placed under house arrest, where he remained until after the Treaty of Deulino in 1618, which finally provided an end to Polish interests in the Russian throne.

In June 1619, Filaret returned to a Moscow and to a Russia ruled now by his son, Mikhail, who had been elected tsar by the Assembly of the Land (*Zemsky Sobor*) in February 1613. Within days, Filaret was consecrated patriarch and within days after that, he was proclaimed "Great Sovereign"—a title usually reserved for the ruler—signaling Filaret's unique position at the court. Filaret took the reins of government in his own hands, directing church and foreign policy with evidently little input from his son. In church matters, Filaret continued his previous position with regard to the non-Orthodox, insisting on the rebaptism of all converts and, in general, further hardening confessional lines with Muscovy's non-Orthodox neighbors and minorities. He also advocated for the Polish war that started in 1632, which turned against Muscovy with the failure of the siege of

Smolensk and the routing of the Russian army. Filaret died on October 1, 1633, amid the unfolding disasters of that war.

See also: ASSEMBLY OF THE LAND; CATHEDRAL OF THE ARCHANGEL; DMITRY, FALSE; GODUNOV, BORIS FYODOROVICH; IVAN IV; KREMLIN; METROPOLITAN; ROMANOV DYNASTY; ROMANOV, MIKHAIL FYODOROVICH; RUSSIAN ORTHODOX CHURCH; SHUISKY, VASILY IVANOVICH; TIME OF TROUBLES

BIBLIOGRAPHY

Dunning, Chester S.L. (2001). *Russia's First Civil War: The Time of Troubles and the Founding of the Romanov Dynasty.* University Park: Pennsylvania State University Press.

Keep, J.L.H. (1960). "The Regime of Filaret, 1619–1633." *The Slavonic and Easter European Review* 38:334–360.

Klyuchevsky, Vasily Osipovich. (1970). *The Rise of the Romanovs* tr. Liliana Archibald. London: Macmillan St. Martin's.

Platonov, Sergei Fyodorovich (1985). *The Time of Troubles,* tr. John T. Alexander. Lawrence: University of Kansas Press.

RUSSELL E. MARTIN

FINLAND

Finland, a country of approximately five million people, located in northeastern Europe, was part of the Russian Empire from 1809 to 1917. It gained its independence in the wake of the Bolshevik Revolution in 1917, and had a complex, close, and occasionally troubled relationship with the Soviet Union. After the collapse of the USSR, Finland began to turn more toward the West, joining the European Union in 1995.

Finns are not Slavs. They speak a Finno-Ugric language, closely related to Estonian and more distantly to Hungarian. The territory of modern-day Finland was inhabited as early as 7000 B.C.E., but there is no written record of the earliest historical period. During the ninth century C.E., Finns accompanied the Varangians on expeditions that led to the founding of Kievan Rus. The Finnish peoples maintained close trading ties with several early Russian cities, especially Novgorod, while from the west they were influenced by the nascent Swedish state.

UNDER SWEDISH RULE

Starting in the twelfth century, most of Finland was absorbed by the Swedish kingdom. Legend tells of a crusade led by King Erik in 1155 that established Christianity in Finland. The Swedes and Novgorod fought several conflicts in and around Finland during this time. The Peace of Noteborg in 1323 established a rough boundary between Swedish and Russian lands, with some Finns (Karelians) living on the eastern side of the border and adopting the Orthodox faith. Although the Swedes were Catholic at the time of the conquest, they broke with Rome under Gustavus Vasa (1523–1560), and Lutheranism was established as the official religion of Sweden and Finland in 1593. The Finnish lands enjoyed some local autonomy under the Swedes, and the Finnish nobility had certain political rights. Swedish was the language of the upper classes and remains an official language in Finland in the early twenty-first century.

During the mid-sixteenth century, Sweden became embroiled in several wars of religion and state expansion with Denmark, Poland, and Russia. Russia and Sweden fought over territory along the Arctic Ocean, and Sweden intervened during Russia's Time of Troubles (1598–1613). Later, under Gustavus Adolphus (1611–1632), the Treaty of Stolbova (1617) gave substantial territory on both sides of the Gulf of Finland to Sweden, thereby enabling it to control trade routes from the Baltic to Russia.

Under Charles XII (1697–1718) and Peter I (1682–1725), Sweden and Russia fought a major war for control of the Baltic. In 1714, Russia occupied Finland after the Battle of Storkro. However, in 1721, in the Treaty of Nystad (Uusikaupunki), the Russians withdrew from most of Finland (keeping the region of Karelia in the east) in return for control over Estonia and Livonia. More than 500,000 Finns, roughly half the population, died during this long conflict, and the national economy was ruined. Another war between Russia and Sweden from 1741 to1743 again resulted in the Russian occupation of Finland. However, in accordance with the Peace of Turku (1743), Russia withdrew from most of Finland, although it did annex some additional lands in the eastern part of the country. There were no further border changes after the third war between the two states from 1788 to 1790.

UNDER RUSSIAN RULE

In 1808, as a result of a Russian alliance with Napoleonic France, Russia attacked Sweden and again occupied Finland. This time, however, Finland was incorporated into the empire as an autonomous grand duchy, with Tsar Alexander I becoming its first grand duke. Under this arrangement, the Finns were to enjoy religious freedom, and Finland, in Alexander's words, would "take its place in the rank of nations, governed by its own laws." Russia returned land to the Finns, and most of them accepted Russian rule. During the nineteenth century Finland experienced a national awakening, spurred by developments in the arts, language, and culture, and political parties began to organize around national issues. By the end of the century, when Alexander III and Nicholas II tried to assert Russia's authority in Finland, there was resentment and resistance, culminating in the assassination of the Russian governor general in 1904.

Finland, 1992

INDEPENDENCE

Before and during the fateful events of 1917, many Russian revolutionaries, including Vladimir Lenin, took refuge in Finland, where there were active socialist and communist parties. After the Bolsheviks seized power, the Finns, taking advantage of the breakdown in central authority, declared independence on December 6, 1917. Later that month, Lenin recognized Finnish independence. Nonetheless, there was fighting in Finland during the Russian Civil War between Reds, backed by Moscow, and anti-communist Whites, backed by Sweden and Germany. The Whites prevailed, exacting vengeance on those Reds who did not flee to Russia. Finland made peace with Russia in 1920 with the Treaty of Tartu and adopted a constitution creating a democratic republic that continues to remain in effect. During the 1920s and 1930s Finnish democracy came under assault by both left-wing and right-wing groups, the former allied with the communists in the USSR and the latter attracted to Germany's Adolf Hitler and Italy's Benito Mussolini.

Finland's democracy survived, but a more serious threat was posed by Soviet military action. After the Germans and Soviets carved up Poland and the Baltic states during the fall of 1939, Finland found itself the target of territorial demands of Joseph Stalin. The Soviets demanded border changes around Leningrad and in the far north, islands in the Gulf of Finland, and a naval base in southern Finland. Diplomatic efforts to find a peaceful solution failed, and Soviet forces invaded Finland on November 30, 1939. Finland received assistance from Western countries, and its forces fought ferociously against the Soviets, who according to some accounts suffered 100,000 dead. Nonetheless, the Finns were outnumbered and outgunned. In March 1940 they agreed to the Soviet territorial demands, and more than 400,000 Finns left their homes rather than become citizens of the Soviet state. Continuing economic and military demands by the USSR eventually made Finland turn to Germany for assistance. Finnish troops advanced with the Germans in June 1941 when Germany attacked the USSR, precipitating, in effect, another war with the Soviets. In 1943 and 1944, as the tide of the war turned against Germany, Finland made

Soviet foreign minister Vyacheslav Molotov signs the Soviet-Finnish Non-Aggression Pact of 1939. Standing behind him are Andrei Zhdanov, Klimenty Voroshilov, Josef Stalin, and Otto Kuusinen. © HULTON-DEUTSCH COLLECTION/CORBIS

peace with the USSR and turned on the Germans, but it had to make additional territorial concessions to Moscow, most of which were incorporated into the USSR's Autonomous Republic of Karelia. Thus Finland enjoyed the dubious distinction of fighting both the Soviets and the Germans, and the country was devastated by years of war.

Although Finland was subjected to Russian influence during the war, the Finns avoided the fate of the East European states, which became communist satellites of the Soviet Union. Instead, in 1948, Finland signed an Agreement of Friendship, Cooperation and Mutual Assistance with the USSR that allowed it to keep its democratic constitution but prohibited it from joining in any anti-Soviet alliance. This agreement is sometimes derided as "Finlandization": Finland retained its constitutional freedoms but gave the USSR an effective veto over its foreign policy (e.g., it had close trade links with the USSR but did not join NATO or the European Community) and, on some questions, its domestic politics (e.g., anti-Soviet writers could not be published in Finland; Finnish politicians had to publicly affirm their confidence in Soviet policy). This was especially the case under President Urho Kekkonen (1956–1981), who had close ties with Moscow. Nonetheless, Finland was generally regarded as a nonaligned, neutral state. This culminated with the Conference on Security and Cooperation in Europe of 1975, which led, among other things, to the Helsinki Accords, an important human rights agreement that would later be used against the communist rulers of the Soviet Union and Eastern Europe. During the postwar period,

Finland, like the other Scandinavian states, developed a social-democratic welfare state, and Finns enjoyed one of the highest standards of living in the world.

After the Soviet Union collapsed, Finland and Russia signed a new treaty in 1992, which ended the "special relationship" between the two states. Trade ties have suffered because of Russia's economic collapse, and Finns increasingly have looked to the West for economic relationships. Finland joined the European Union in 1995, and enjoys close ties with the Baltic states, particularly Estonia.

See also: ESTONIA AND ESTONIANS; FINNS AND KARELIANS; NATIONALITIES POLICIES, TSARIST; NYSTADT, TREATY OF; SOVIET-FINNISH WAR

BIBLIOGRAPHY

Allison, Roy. (1985). *Finland's Relations with the Soviet Union, 1944–1984.* London: Macmillan.

Kirby, David G., ed. (1975). *Finland and Russia, 1808–1920: From Independence to Autonomy.* London: Macmillan.

Kirby, David G. (1979). *Finland in the Twentieth Century.* London: Hurst.

Singleton, Fred, and Upton, Anthony F. (1998). *A Short History of Finland.* Cambridge, UK: Cambridge University Press.

Tanner, Vaino. (1957). *The Winter War: Finland Against Russia, 1939–1940.* Stanford, CA: Stanford University Press.

Paul J. Kubicek

FINNS AND KARELIANS

Finns, Karelians (in Karelian Republic and eastern Finland), Izhorians (Ingrians) and Ingrian Finns (around St. Petersburg), Vepsians (southeast of St. Petersburg), near-extinct Votians (southwest of St. Petersburg), and Estonians speak mutually semi-intelligible Finnic languages. Novgorod absorbed many of them during the thirteenth century, without formal treaties. After defeating the Swedes and taking territory that included the present St. Petersburg, tsarist Russia subjugated all these peoples. Finns, Ingrian Finns, and most Estonians were Lutheran, while Karelians, Vepsians, Izhorians, and Votians were Greek Orthodox. Livelihood has extended from traditional forest agriculture to urban endeavors.

Finland and Estonia emerged as independent countries by 1920, while Karelia became an autonomous oblast (1920) and soon an Autonomous Soviet Socialist Republic (1923). Deportations, immigration, and other means of russification have almost obliterated the Izhorians, while reducing the Karelians, Finns, and Vepsians to 13 percent of Karelia's population (103,000 out of 791,000, in 1989). Altogether, the Soviet 1989 census recorded 131,000 Karelians (23,000 in Tver oblast), 18,000 Finns, and 6,000 Vepsians (straddling Karelia and the Leningrad and Vologda oblasts).

Karelia occupies a strategic location on the railroad to Russia's ice-free port of Murmansk on the Arctic Ocean. Much of the crucial American aid to the Soviet Union during World War II used this route. The Karelian Isthmus, seized by Moscow from Finland during that war, is not part of the Karelian republic, which briefly (1940 to 1956) was upgraded to a Karelo-Finnish union republic so as to put pressure on Finland.

The earliest surviving written document in any Finnic language is a Karelian thunder spell written on birch bark with Cyrillic characters. Karelia contributed decisively to the world-famous Finnish epic *Kalevala.* Finnish dialects gradually mutate to northern and western Karelian, to Aunus and Ludic in southern Karelia, and on to Vepsian. Given such a continuum, a common Karelian literary language has not taken root, and standard Latin-script Finnish is used by the newspaper *Karjalan Sanomat* (Karelian News) and the monthly *Karjala* (Karelia). A Vepsian periodical, *Kodima* (Homeland), uses both Vepsian (with Latin script) and Russian. Only 40,000 Karelians in Karelia and 22,000 elsewhere in the former Soviet Union consider Karelian or Finnish their main language. Among the young, russification prevails.

Karelia is an "urbanized forest republic" where agriculture is limited and industry ranges from lumber and paper to iron ore and aluminum. The capital, Petrozavodsk (Petroskoi in Karelian), includes 34 percent of Karelia's entire population. Ethnic Karelians have little say in political and economic management. Hardly any of the republic government leaders or parliament members speak Karelian or Finnish. The cultural interests of the indigenous minority are voiced by *Karjalan Rahvahan Liitto* (Union of the Karelian People), the

Vepsian Cultural Society, and the Ingrian Union for Finns in Karelia.

Economic and cultural interactions with Finland, blocked under the Soviet rule, have revived. Karelia's future success depends largely on how far a symbiosis with this more developed neighboring country can reach.

See also: FINLAND; NATIONALITIES POLICIES, SOVIET; NATIONALITIES POLICIES, TSARIST; NORTHERN PEOPLES

BIBLIOGRAPHY

Eskelinen, Heikki; Oksa, Jukka; and Austin, Daniel. (1994). *Russian Karelia in Search of a New Role.* Joensuu, Finland: Karelian Institute.

Kurs, Ott. (1994). "Indigenous Finnic Population of North-west Russia." *GeoJournal* 34(4):443–456.

Taagepera, Rein. (1999). *The Finno-Ugric Republics and the Russian State.* London: Hurst.

REIN TAAGEPERA

FIREBIRD

The Firebird (*Zhar–ptitsa*) is one of the most colorful legendary animal figures of Russian magical tales (fairy tales). With golden feathers and eyes like crystals, she is a powerful source of light, and even one of her feathers can illuminate a whole room. Sometimes she functions as little more than a magical helper who flies the hero out of danger; in other tales her feather and she herself are highly desired prizes to be captured. "Prince Ivan, the Firebird, and the Gray Wolf" depicts her coming at night to steal golden apples from a king's garden and becoming one object of a heroic quest by the youngest prince, Ivan. Helped by a gray wolf, he ends up with the Firebird as well as a noble steed with golden mane and golden bridle and Princess Yelena the Fair.

The tales became the narrative source for the first of two famous folklore ballets composed by Igor Stravinsky under commission from Sergei Diaghilev and his Ballets Russes. *L'Oiseau de feu,* with choreography by the noted Russian Michel Fokine, premiered at the Paris Opera on June 25, 1910, with great success and quickly secured the young Stravinsky's international reputation. Like his *Petrushka* that followed it, *The Firebird* impressed audiences with the colorfulness of both story and music and with its bold harmonic innovations. The two ballets also helped spread awareness of Russia's rich folk culture beyond its borders.

See also: BALLET, FOLKLORE

BIBLIOGRAPHY

Guterman, Norbert, tr. (1973). *Russian Fairy Tales,* 2d ed. New York: Pantheon Books.

Taruskin, Richard. (1996). *Stravinsky and the Russian Traditions: A Biography of the Works through Mavra.* 2 vols. Berkeley: University of California Press.

NORMAN W. INGHAM

FIRST SECRETARY, CPSU *See* GENERAL SECRETARY.

FIVE-HUNDRED-DAY PLAN

Proposals for reform of the Soviet economic system began to emerge during the 1960s, and some concrete reforms were introduced. All of these efforts, such as Alexei Kosygin's reforms in 1965, the new law on state enterprises in 1987, and the encouragement of cooperatives in 1988, basically involved tinkering with details. They did not touch the main pillars of the Soviet economy: hierarchical command structures controlling enterprise activity, detailed central decision-making about resource allocation and production activity, and fixed prices set by the government. The need for reform became ever more obvious in the "years of stagnation" under Leonid Brezhnev. When Mikhail Gorbachev came to power in 1985, reform proposals became more radical, culminating in the formulation of the Five-Hundred-Day Plan, put together at the request of Gorbachev and Boris Yeltsin by a group of able and progressive reform economists headed by Academician Stanislav Shatalin and presented to the government in September 1990.

The plan fully accepted the idea of a shift to a market economy, as indicated by its subtitle "transition to the market," and laid out a timetable of institutional and policy changes to achieve the transition. It described and forthrightly accepted the institutions of private property, market pricing, enterprise independence, competition as regulator, transformation of the banking system, macroeconomic stabilization, and the need to open the economy to the world market. It specified a timetable of steps to be taken and provided draft legislation to undergird the changes. One of its more radical elements was its acceptance of the desire of the republics for devolution of central power, and it endorsed their right to economic independence. This feature of the plan was fatal upon its acceptance, as Gorbachev was not ready to accept a diminution of central power.

Parallel with the Five-Hundred-Day Plan, a group in the government worked up an alternative, much less ambitious, proposal. Gorbachev asked the economist Abel Aganbegyan to meld the two into a compromise plan. Aganbegyan's plan accepted most of the features of the Five-Hundred-Day Plan, but without timetables. By then, however, it was too late. Yeltsin had been elected president of the Russian republic and had already started to move the RSFSR along the path of reform envisioned in the Shatalin plan. This was followed in August 1991 by the abortive coup to remove Gorbachev, and in December 1991 by the breakup of the Union, ending the relevance of the Five-Hundred-Day Plan to a unified USSR. But its spirit and much of its content were taken as the basis for the reform in the Russian republic, and many of the reformers involved in its formulation became officials in the new Russian government. The other republics went their own way and, except for the Baltic republics, generally rejected radical reform.

See also: AGANBEGYAN, ABEL GEZEVICH; COMMAND ADMINISTRATIVE ECONOMY; KOSYGIN REFORMS; SHATALIN, STANISLAV SERGEYEVICH

BIBLIOGRAPHY

Aslund, Anders. (1995). *How Russia Became a Market Economy.* Washington, DC: Brookings Institution.

Yavlinsky, G. (1991). *500 Days: Transition to the Market.* Trans. David Kushner. New York: St. Martin's Press.

ROBERT W. CAMPBELL

FIVE-YEAR PLANS

Russian economic planning had its roots in the late nineteenth century when tsarist explorers and engineers systematically found and evaluated the rich resources scattered all around the empire. Major deposits of iron and coal, as well as other minerals, were well documented when the Bolsheviks turned their attention to economic development. Initial attention focused on several centers in south Russia and eastern Ukraine, which were to be rapidly enlarged. Electric power was the glamorous new industry, and both Vladimir Lenin and Josef Stalin stressed it as a symbol of progress.

By 1927 the planners had prepared a huge three-volume Five-Year Plan, consisting of some seventeen hundred pages of description and optimistic projection. By 1928 Stalin had won control of the Communist Party from Leon Trotsky and other rivals, enabling him to launch Russia on a fateful new path.

The First Five-Year Plan (FYP) laid out hundreds of projects for construction, but the Party concentrated on heavy industry and national defense. In Germany Adolf Hitler was already calling for more "living room." In a famous 1931 speech Stalin warned that the USSR only had ten years in which to prepare against invasion (and he was right).

A 1950 propaganda poster urging farmers to fulfill the Five-Year Plan. The slogan reads, "Let us give to the country 127 million tons of grain per year." © HULTON ARCHIVE

The First Five-Year Plan was cut short as planning gave way to confusion. A Second Five-Year Plan was issued in one volume in 1934, already behind schedule. The planners were learning that one-year plans were more effective for managing the economy, leaving the five-year plans to serve as propaganda documents, especially effective abroad where the Great Depression seemed to signal the collapse of capitalism.

The Third Five-Year Plan had limited circulation, and the Fourth was only a pamphlet, issued as a special edition of the party newspaper, *Pravda*.

The Nazi invasion, starting June 22, 1941, required hasty improvisation, using previously prepared central and eastern bases to replace those quickly overrun by well-equipped German forces. The Nazis almost captured Moscow in December 1941.

After Soviet forces rallied, wartime planners organized hasty output increases, drawing on newly trained survivors of Stalin's drastic purges. Russian planners worked uneasily with U.S. and British officials as the long-delayed second front was opened, and abundant Lend-Lease supplies arrived.

After the war, improvisation gave way to Stalin's grim 1946 Five-Year Plan, which held the Soviet people to semi-starvation rations while he rebuilt heavy industry and challenged the United States in building an atomic bomb.

Fortunately for the Soviet people and the world, Stalin died in March 1953, and by 1957 Nikita Khrushchev was able to give Soviet planners a more humane agenda. The next Five-Year Plan was actually a seven-year plan with ambitious targets for higher living standards. Soviet welfare did improve markedly. However, Khrushchev was diverted by his efforts to control Berlin and by his ill-fated Cuban missile adventure. The Party leadership was furious, but instead of having him executed, they allowed him to retire.

This brilliant leader's successors were a dull lot. The planners returned to previous five-year plan procedures, which mainly cranked up previous targets by applying a range of percentage increases. Growth rates steadily declined.

In 1985 the energetic Mikhail Gorbachev looked for help from Soviet planners, but the planners were outweighed by the great bureaucracies running the system. In a final spasm, the last Five-Year Plan set overambitious targets like those of the first such endeavor.

Other Russians contributed greatly by creating new tools for economic management, especially Leonid Kontorovich, who invented linear programming; Wassily Leontief, who invented input-output analysis; and Tigran Khachaturov, who provided skillful political protection for several hundred talented economists as they improved Russian economics. These men rose above the barriers of the Russian planning system and thus deserve worldwide respect.

See also: ECONOMIC GROWTH, SOVIET; INDUSTRIALIZATION, SOVIET

BIBLIOGRAPHY

Bergson, Abram. (1964). *The Economics of Soviet Planning.* New Haven, CT: Yale University Press.

Gregory, Paul R., and Stuart, Robert C. (1990). *Soviet Economic Structure and Performance,* 4th ed. New York: Harper & Row.

Hunter, Holland, and Szyrmer, Janusz M. (1992). *Faulty Foundations.* Princeton, NJ: Princeton University Press.

HOLLAND HUNTER

FLORENCE, COUNCIL OF

In 1438 Pope Eugenius IV called a church council to consider reunion of the eastern and western churches. The Latin and Greek churches had been drifting apart for centuries and from the year 1054 onward had rarely been in communion with each other. The sack of the Byzantine capital of Constantinople by the western crusaders made it clear that they no longer considered the Greeks their co-religionists and proved to the Greeks of Byzantium that the Latins were not their brothers in faith. But by the fifteenth century, with the Ottoman Turks already in control of most of the territory of the Byzantine Empire and moving on its capital of Constantinople, reunion of the churches seemed to be a necessity if the Christian world were to respond with a united front to the Muslim threat to Europe.

The council convened in 1439 in the Italian city of Ferrara and then moved to Florence. Present were not only the Pope, the cardinals, and many western bishops and theologians, but also the Byzantine Emperor John VIII, the Patriarch of Constantinople, Joseph II, the foremost cleric of the eastern

Christian world, and a number of leading officials and clergy of the Byzantine world (including a Russian delegation). The main points of dispute between the two churches were the legitimacy of a western addition to the creed (the "filioque") and the nature of the church: whether it should be ruled by the Pope or by all the bishops jointly. After much discussion and debate, the delegates of the eastern church, under political pressure, accepted the western positions on the "filioque" and Papal supremacy, and reunion of the churches was solemnly proclaimed.

When the Greek representatives returned home, however, their decision was greeted with derision. Church union was never accepted by the masses of the Eastern Christian faithful. In any case, it became a dead letter with the 1453 Turkish conquest of Constantinople, renamed Istanbul by the Turks. When the Greek Isidore, Metropolitan of Kiev and presiding bishop of the Russian church, returned to Moscow where he normally resided and proclaimed the Pope as the head of the church, he was arrested on the orders of Grand Prince Basil II ("The Dark") and then diplomatically allowed to escape to Poland. In 1448 he was replaced as metropolitan by a Russian bishop, Jonah, without the consent of the mother church in Constantinople, which was deemed to have given up its faith by submitting to the Pope. From now on, the church of Russia would be an independent (autocephalous) Orthodox church.

The ramifications of the Council of Florence were significant. The rejection of its decisions in the East made it clear that the Roman Catholic and Orthodox churches were to be separate institutions, as they are today. Yet the concept of incorporating eastern ritual into Catholicism in certain places, a compromise that evolved at the council, became the model for the so-called uniate church created in Polish-governed Ukraine and Belarus in 1596, whereby the Orthodox church in those lands became part of the Catholic church while retaining its traditional eastern rites.

See also: BASIL II; METROPOLITAN; UNIATE CHURCH

BIBLIOGRAPHY

Cherniavsky, Michael M. (1955). "The Reception of the Council of Florence in Moscow." *Church History* 24:347–359.

Gill, Joseph. (1961). *The Council of Florence.* Cambridge, UK: Cambridge University Press.

GEORGE P. MAJESKA

FOLKLORE

Folklore has played a vital role in the lives of the Russian people and has exerted a considerable influence on the literature, music, dance, and other arts of Russia, including such major nineteenth- and twentieth-century writers and composers as Alexander Pushkin, Fyodor Dostoyevsky, Leo Tolstoy, Peter Tchaikovsky, and Igor Stravinsky.

A folklore tradition has existed and flourished in Russia for many centuries, has been collected and studied for well more than two hundred years, and is represented by a variety of large and small genres, including oral epic songs, folktales, laments, ritual and lyric songs, incantations, riddles, and proverbs.

A simple explanation for the survival of folklore over such a long period of time is difficult to find. Some possible reasons can be found in the fact that the population was predominately rural and unable to read and write prior to the Soviet era; that the secular, nonspiritual literature of the folklore tradition was for the most part a primary source of entertainment for Russians from all classes and levels of society; or that the Orthodox Church was unsuccessful in its efforts to repress the Russian peasant's pagan, pre-Christian folk beliefs and rituals, which over time had absorbed many Christian elements, a phenomenon commonly referred to as "double belief." The fact that the Russian peasant was both geographically and culturally far removed from urban centers and events that influenced the country's development and direction also played a role in folklore's survival. And Russia's geographical location itself was a significant factor, making possible close contact with the rich folklore traditions of neighboring peoples, including the Finns, the nomadic Turkic tribes, and the non-Russian peoples of the vast Siberian region.

Evidence of a folklore tradition appeared in Russian medieval religious and secular works of the eleventh through the fourteenth centuries, and conflicting attitudes toward its existence prior to the eighteenth century are well documented. The church considered it as evil, as the work of the devil. But memoirs and historical literature of the sixteenth and seventeenth centuries indicate that folklore, folktales in particular, was quite favorably regarded by many. Ivan the Terrible (1533–1584), for example, hired blind men to tell stories at his bedside until he fell asleep. Less than one hundred

***Prince Ivan and the Grey Wolf,* nineteenth-century engraving after a watercolor by Boris Zvorykin.** THE ART ARCHIVE/BIBLIOTHÈQUE DES ARTS DÉCORATIFS PARIS/DAGLI ORTI

years later, however, Tsar Alexis (1645–1676), son of Peter the Great (1696–1725), ordered the massacre of practitioners of this and other secular arts. Royal edict notwithstanding, tellers of tales continued to bring pleasure to people, and on the rural estates of noblemen and in high social circles of seventeenth- and eighteenth-century Moscow, skillful narrators were well rewarded.

The earliest collection of Russian folklore, consisting of some songs and tales, was made during the seventeenth century by two Oxford-educated Englishmen: Richard James, chaplain to an English diplomatic mission in Moscow (1619–1620), and Samuel Collins, physician to Tsar Alexei (during the 1660s).

The first important collection of Russian folklore by Russians was that of folksongs from the Ural region, made during the middle of the eighteenth century and published early during the nineteenth century. At about the same time a real foundation was laid for folklore research and scholarship in Russia, due largely to the influence of Western romanticism and widespread increase in national self-awareness. This movement, represented in particular by German romantic philosophers and folklorists such as Johann Herder (1744–1803) and the brothers Grimm (Jacob, 1785–1863; Wilhelm, 1786–1859), was mirrored in Russia during the early years of the nineteenth century among the Slavophiles, a group of Russian intellectuals of the 1830s, who believed in Russia's spiritual greatness and who showed an intense interest in Russia's folklore, folk customs, and the role of the folk in the development of Russian culture. Folklore now began to be seriously collected, and among the significant works published were large collections of Russian proverbs by V. I. Dal (1801-1872) and Russian folktales by A. N. Afanasev (1826-1871).

But the latter part of the nineteenth century signaled the most significant event in Russian folklore scholarship, when P.N. Rybnikov (1831–1885) and A.F. Hilferding (Gilferding, 1831–1872) uncovered a treasury of folklore in the Lake Onega region of northwestern Russia during the 1860s and 1870s, including a flourishing tradition of oral epic songs, which up to that time was believed to be almost extinct as a living folklore form. This discovery led to a systematic search for folklore that is still being conducted during the early twenty-first century.

During the Soviet period folklore was criticized for depicting the reality of the past and was even considered harmful to the people. Until the death of Stalin in 1953 folklore scholarship was under constant Party supervision and limited in scope, focusing on social problems and ideological matters. But folklore itself was recognized as a powerful means to promote patriotism and advance Communist ideas and ideals, and it became a potent instrument in the formation of Socialist culture. New Soviet versions of folklore were created and made public through a variety of media—concert hall, radio, film, television, and tapes and phonograph records. These new works included contemporary subject matter: for example, an airplane instead of the wooden eagle on whose back the hero often traveled, a rifle for slaying a modern dragon in military uniform, or marriage to the daughter of a factory manager rather than a princess.

Since the 1970s, Russian folklore has become free from government control, and the sphere of study has expanded. During the early twenty-first century, folklore of the far-flung regions of the former Soviet Union is being collected in the field. Many of the older, classic collections of Russian folklore are being republished, old cylinder recordings restored, and bibliographies published, mainly under the direction of the Folklore Committee of the Institute of Russian Literature (Pushkin House) of the Academy of Sciences of the USSR in St. Petersburg and the Folklore Section of the Gorky Institute of World Literature in Moscow.

Among the most important narrative folklore genres are Russian oral epic songs and folktales, which provide a rich diversity of thematic and story material. The oral epic songs are the major genre in verse. Many of them concern the adventures of heroes associated with Prince Vladimir's court in Kiev in southern Russia; the action in a second group of epic songs occurs on the "open plain," where Russians fight the Tatar invaders; and the events of a third group of songs take place near the medieval city of Novgorod in northern Russia. The stories are made up of themes of feasting, journeys, and combats; acts of insubordination and punishment; trials of skill in arms, sports, and horsemanship; and themes of courtship, marriage, infidelity, and reconciliation. Some popular songs are about the giant Svyatogor, the Old Cossack Ilya Muromets, the dragon-slayer Dobrynya Nikitich, Alyosha Popovich the priest's son, and the rich merchant Sadko.

The leading genre in prose, one that is well known beyond Russia, is the folktale, which includes tales of various kinds, such as animal and moral tales, as well as magic or so-called fairy tales, similar to the Western European fairy tales. Russian magic or fairy tales often tell a story about a hero who leaves home for some reason, must carry out one or several different tasks, encounters many obstacles along the way, accomplishes all of the tasks, and gains wealth or a fair maiden in the end. Among the popular heroes and villains of Russian folktales are Ivan the King's son, the witch Baba Yaga, Ivan the fool, the immortal Kashchey, Grandfather Frost, and the Firebird.

See also: FIREBIRD; FOLK MUSIC; PUSHKIN HOUSE

BIBLIOGRAPHY

Afanasev, Alexander. (1975). *Russian Fairy Tales.* New York: Random House.

Bailey, James, and Ivanova, Tatyana. (1998). *Russian Folk Epics.* Armonk, NY: M.E. Sharpe.

Ivanits, Linda J. (1989). *Russian Folk Beliefs.* Armonk, NY: M.E. Sharpe.

Miller, Frank J. (1990). *Folklore for Stalin: Russian Folklore and Pseudofolklore of the Stalin Era.* Armonk, NY: M.E. Sharpe.

Oinas, Felix J. (1985). *Essays on Russian Folklore and Mythology.* Columbus, OH: Slavica.

Oinas, Felix J., and Soudakoff, Stephen, eds. (1975). *The Study of Russian Folklore.* The Hague: Mouton.

Sokolov, Y.M. (1971). *Russian Folklore,* tr. Catherine Ruth Smith. Detroit, MI: Folklore Associates.

PATRICIA ARANT

FOLK MUSIC

Russian folk music is the indigenous vocal (accompanied and unaccompanied) and instrumental music of the Russian peasantry, consisting of songs and dances for work, entertainment, and religious and ritual occasions. Its origins lie in customary practice; until the industrial era it was an oral tradition, performed and learned without written notation. Common instruments include the *domra* (three- or four-stringed round bodied lute), *balalaika* (three-stringed triangular-bodied lute), *gusli* (psaltery), *bayan* (accordion), *svirel* (pennywhistle), and *zhaleyka* (hornpipe). Russian folk music includes songs marking seasonal and ritual events, and music for figure or circle dances (*korovody*) and the faster *chastye* or *plyasovye* dances. A related form, *chastushki* (bright tunes accompanying humorous or satirical four-line verses), gained rural and urban popularity during the late nineteenth century. The sung epic *bylina* declined during the nineteenth century, but *protyazhnye*—protracted lyric songs, slow in tempo and frequently sorrowful in content and tone—remain popular. Significant stylistic and repertoire differences exist among various regions of Russia.

Russian educated society's interest in folk music began during the late eighteenth century. Numerous collections of Russian folk songs were published over the next two centuries (notably N. L. Lvov and J. B. Práč, *Collection of Russian Folk Songs with Their Tunes,* St. Petersburg, 1790). From the nineteenth century onward, Russian composers used these as an important source of musical ma-

Russian peasants playing folk music, early-twentieth-century postcard. The Art Archive/Bibliothèque des Arts Décoratifs Paris/Dagli Orti

terial. During the nineteenth century, German philosopher Johann Herder's ideas of romantic nationalism and the importance of the folk in determining national culture inspired interest in and appreciation of native Russian musical sources, especially as they reflected notions of national pride. Mikhail Glinka, for his purposeful use of Russian folk themes in his 1836 opera *A Life for the Tsar*, is considered the founder of the "national" school of Russian music composition, most famously embraced by Mili Balakirev, Alexander Borodin, César Cui, Modest Mussorgsky, and Nikolai Rimsky-Korsakov. This designation had more political than musical significance, as composers not associated with the national school, such as Peter Tchaikovsky and Igor Stravinsky, also made use of folk music in their compositions.

Russian ethnographers of the late nineteenth and early twentieth centuries made efforts to record native folk music in the face of increasing urbanization. In 1896 Vasily Andreyev (1861–1918) organized an orchestra of folk instruments, and in 1911 Mitrofan Piatnitsky (1864–1927) founded a Russian folk choir. Originally consisting of peasant and amateur performers, both became well-known professional ensembles, providing folk music as entertainment for urban audiences.

During the Soviet era folk music had important symbolic importance as a form genuinely "of the people." During the 1930s, state support for socialist realism encouraged study and performance of folk music. Composers and amateur performers developed a new "Soviet folk song" that wedded traditional forms and styles with lyrics praising socialism and the Soviet state. Official support was demonstrated in the establishment of the Pyatnitsky choir and the Russian folk orchestra directed by Nikolai Osipov (1901–1945) as State ensembles. Russian folk music became a state-sanctioned performance genre characterized by organized amateur activities, notated music, academic study, and large professional performing ensembles that toured internationally. During the 1970s, Dmitry Pokrovsky (d. 1996) began a new effort to collect and perform Russian folk songs and tunes in authentic peasant village style, with local variations. This revival of Russian folk music received international attention as part of the world music movement.

See also: BALALAIKA; FOLKLORE; GLINKA, MIKHAIL; MUSIC; RIMSKY-KORSAKOV, NIKOLAI ANDREYEVICH

BIBLIOGRAPHY

Brown, Malcolm Hamrick. (1983). "Native Song and National Consciousness in Nineteenth-Century Russian Music." In *Art and Culture in Nineteenth-Century Russia*, ed. Theofanis George Stavrou. Bloomington: Indiana University Press.

Miller, Frank J. (1990). *Folklore for Stalin: Russian Folklore and Pseudofolklore in the Stalin Era.* Armonk, NY: M.E. Sharpe.

Rothstein, Robert A. (1994). "Death of the Folk Song?" In *Cultures in Flux: Lower-Class Values, Practices, and Resistance in Late Imperial Russia*, ed. Stephen P. Frank and Mark D. Steinberg. Princeton, NJ: Princeton University Press.

Taruskin, Richard. (1997). *Defining Russia Musically.* Princeton, NJ: Princeton University Press.

Susannah Lockwood Smith

FONDODERZHATELI

Literal translation: "fund holders."

In the Soviet economy, various organizations were holders and managers of inputs (*fondoderzhateli*). The principal fund holders were ministries and regional and local governments. In some instances, the state executive committees that directed construction organizations and local industry had fund-holding authority as well. Only fund holders were legally entitled to allocate funded resources, the most important of which were allocated by the State Planning Committee (Gosplan) and the State Committee for Material Technical Supply (Gossnab). Fund holders had to estimate input needs and their distribution among subordinate enterprises. They were obliged to allocate funds among direct consumers, such as enterprises, plants, and construction organizations within their jurisdiction. Fund holders also monitored the use of allocated funds. Funding (*fondirovanie*) was the typical form of centralized distribution of resources for important and highly "deficit" products. Such centrally allocated materials were called "funded" (*fondiruyumye*) commodities and were typically distributed among the enterprises by ministries. Enterprises were not allowed to exchange funded inputs legally. Material balances and distribution plans among fund holders were developed by Gosplan and then approved by the Council of Ministries. The ministries had their own supply departments that worked with central supply organizations. The enterprises related input requirements to their superiors through orders (*zayavki*), which were aggregated by the fund holder. At each stage of economic planning, requested inputs were compared to estimated input needs, and imbalances were corrected administratively without the use of prices. The process of allocating funded resources was characterized by constant bargaining between fund holders and consumers, where the latter were required to "defend" their needs.

See also: FUNDED COMMODITIES

PAUL R. GREGORY

FONVIZIN, DENIS IVANOVICH

(1744–1792), dramatist.

Denis Fonvizin, the first truly original Russian dramatist in the eighteenth century, is best known for two satirical plays written in prose: *The Brigadier-General* (*Brigadir*) and *The Minor* (*Nedorosl*). *Brigadir*, written in 1766, was not published until 1786. *Nedorosl* was first staged in 1783 and published the following year. Both are considered masterpieces combining Russian and French comedy.

Like all writers at the time, Fonvizin was born into a well-to-do family. His father, a strict disciplinarian, trained him to become a real "gentleman," and became the model for one of the characters—the father of Mr. Oldwise (*Starodum*)—in Fonvizin's play *The Minor.* Although thoroughly Russianized, the family's ancestor was a German or Swedish prisoner captured in the Livonian campaigns of Ivan the Terrible. At Moscow University Fonvizin participated actively in theatrical productions. Upon graduation in 1762 (when Catherine II became empress), Fonvizin entered the civil service. In St. Petersburg, he befriended Ivan Dmitrievsky, a prominent actor, and began to translate and adapt foreign plays for him. He wrote minor works, such as *Alzire, or the Americans* (1762) and *Korion* (1764), but tasted his first real success when Catherine summoned him to the Hermitage to read his comedy *The Brigadier* to her. In 1769 she then appointed him secretary to Vice-Chancellor Nikita Panin, Catherine's top diplomatic advisor.

Although faithful to the French genre in writing *The Brigadier,* Fonvizin was less inspired by Molière than by the Danish playwright Barin Ludvig Holberg, from whose play *Jean de France* Fonvizin's play was derived. A salon comedy, *The Brigadier* attacks the nobility's corruption and ignorance. After reading the play, Panin wrote to Fonvizin: "I see that you know our customs well, because the wife of your general is completely familiar to us. No one among us can deny having a grandmother or an aunt of the sort. You have written our first comedy of manners." The play also mocks the Russian gentry's "gallomania"; without French rules for behavior "we wouldn't know how to dance, how to enter a room, how to bow, how to perfume ourselves, how to put a hat on, and, when excited, how to express our passions and the state of our heart."

In 1782 Fonvizin finished *The Minor.* Since it was unthinkable that these lines could be read aloud to Catherine, he arranged a performance at Kniper's Theater in St. Petersburg with Dmitrievsky as the character, Mr. Oldwise. The audience, recognizing the play as original and uniquely Russian, signaled its appreciation by flinging purses onto the stage. The play condemns domestic tyranny and false education, while touching also on larger social questions, such as serfdom. The play concerns the stupid son in a noble family, the Prostakovs (a play on the word *prostoi* or "simple"), who refuses to study properly but still expects to receive privileges. The lad's name—Mitrofan (or Mitrofanushka in the diminutive)—is now a synonym in Russia for a dolt or fool. The composition of the family is telling. The mother, a bully, is obsessed with her son (that he get enough to eat and marry an heiress). Her brother resembles a pig more than a man (as his name, Skotina, suggests). Her husband acts sheepishly; the nurse spoils the boy; and the boy—wildly selfish and stupid—beats her. The play's basic action revolves around the conflict between the Prostakovs on the one hand and Starodum and his associates on the other. The formers' "coarse bestiality" (as Gogol termed it) contrasts sharply with the lofty morality that Starodum and his friends exhibit.

In 1782 Fonvizin's boss, Count Panin, had a stroke and summoned Fonvizin to write his Political Testament. He instructed the dramatist to deliver the testament, containing a blunt denunciation of absolute power, to Catherine after Panin's death. However, when Panin died the next year, Catherine impounded all his papers (not to be released from archives until 1905) and dismissed Fonvizin. Pushkin later wrote that Catherine probably feared him. The playwright's health declined after a seizure in 1785, and he died in 1792.

See also: THEATER

BIBLIOGRAPHY

Fonvizin, Denis Ivanovich, and Gleason, Walter J. (1985). *The Political and Legal Writings of Denis Fonvizin.* Ann Arbor, MI: Ardis.

Levitt, Marcus C. (1995). *Early Modern Russian Writers: Late Seventeenth and Eighteenth Centuries.* Detroit: Gale Research.

Moser, Charles A. (1979). *Denis Fonvizin.* Boston: Twayne.

Raeff, Marc, ed. (1966). *Russian Intellectual History: An Anthology.* New York: Harcourt, Brace & World.

JOHANNA GRANVILLE

FOOD

Russian food is typically hearty in taste, with mustard, horseradish, and dill among the predominant condiments. The cuisine is distinguished by the many fermented and preserved foods necessitated by the short growing season of the Russian North. Foraged foods, especially mushrooms, are important to Russian diet and culture. The Russians excel in the preparation of a wide range of fresh and cultured dairy products; honey is the traditional sweetener.

Russian cuisine is known for its extensive repertoire of soups and pies. The national soup (*shchi*) is made from cabbage, either salted or fresh. Soup is traditionally served at the midday meal, accompanied by an assortment of small pies, croutons, or dumplings. The pies are filled with myriad combinations of meat, fish, or vegetables, and are prepared in all shapes and sizes. The Russian diet tends to be high in carbohydrates, with a vast array of breads, notably dark sour rye, and grains, especially buckwheat.

Many of Russia's most typical dishes reflect the properties of the traditional Russian masonry stove, which blazes hot after firing and then gradually diminishes in the intensity of its heat. Breads and pies were traditionally baked when the oven was still very hot. Once the temperature began to fall, porridges could cook in the diminishing heat. As the oven's heat continued to subside, the stove was ideal for the braised vegetables and slow-cooked dishes that represent the best of Russian cooking.

The Orthodox Church had a profound influence on the Russian diet, dividing the year into feast days and fast days. The latter accounted for approximately 180 days of the year. Most Russians took fasting seriously, strictly following the proscriptions against meat and dairy products.

From the earliest times the Russians enjoyed alcoholic beverages, especially mead, a fermented honey wine flavored with berries and herbs, and *kvas*, a mildly alcoholic beverage made from fermented bread or grain. Distilled spirits, in the form of vodka, appeared only during the fifteenth century, introduced from Poland and the Baltic region.

The reforms carried out by Peter I greatly affected Russian cuisine. The most significant development was the introduction of the Dutch range, which relied on a cooktop more than oven chambers and resulted in more labor-intensive cooking methods. The vocabulary introduced into Russian over the course of the eighteenth century reveals influences from the Dutch, German, English, and ultimately French cuisines. By the close of the eighteenth century, Russia's most affluent families employed French chefs. With so much foreign influence, Russian cuisine lost its simple national character. The eighteenth-century refinements broadened Russian cuisine, ushering in an era of extravagant dining among the wealthy.

The sophistication of the table was lost during the Soviet period, when much of the populace subsisted on a monotonous diet low in fresh fruits and vegetables. Shopping during the Soviet era was especially difficult, with long lines even for basic foodstuffs. Hospitality remained culturally important, however, and the Soviet-era kitchen table was the site of the most important social exchanges.

The collapse of the Soviet state brought numerous Western fast-food chains, such as McDonald's, to Russia. With the appearance of self-service grocery stores, shopping was simplified, and food lines disappeared. However, food in post-Soviet Russia, while plentiful and widely available, was expensive during the early twenty-first century.

See also: AGRICULTURE; CAVIAR; PETER I; RUSSIAN ORTHODOX CHURCH; VODKA

BIBLIOGRAPHY

Glants, Musya, and Toomre, Joyce, eds. (1997). *Food in Russian History and Culture.* Bloomington: Indiana University Press.

Goldstein, Darra. (1999). *A Taste of Russia: A Cookbook of Russian Hospitality,* 2d ed. Montpelier, VT: Russian Life Books.

Herlihy, Patricia. (2002). *The Alcoholic Empire: Vodka and Politics in Late Imperial Russia.* New York: Oxford University Press.

Molokhovets, Elena. (1992). *Classic Russian Cooking: Elena Molokhovets' A Gift to Young Housewives,* tr. Joyce Toomre. Bloomington: Indiana University Press.

DARRA GOLDSTEIN

FOREIGN DEBT

The first stage in Russia's involvement with international capital markets was associated with the great drive for industrialization that marked the final decades of the nineteenth century. The backwardness of the country's largely rural economy implied substantial needs for imports, which in turn meant foreign borrowing. The epic railway construction projects in particular would not have been possible without such financing.

With growing volumes of Russian debt floating abroad, the country became increasingly vulnerable to speculative attacks, which could have proven highly damaging. The skillful policies of finance ministers Ivan Vyshnegradsky and Sergei Witte averted such dangers. By imposing harsh taxes on the rural economy, they also managed to promote exports from that sector, which made for a healthy trade surplus. As a result of the latter, by the end of the century the currency qualified for conversion to the gold standard.

Russia thus entered the twentieth century with a stable currency and in good standing on foreign capital markets. The Bolsheviks put an end to that. By deciding to default on all foreign debt of Imperial Russia, Vladimir Lenin effectively deprived the Soviet Union of all further access to foreign credit. Since the economy remained backward, all subsequent ambitions of achieving industrialization thus would have to be undertaken with domestic resources, or with the goodwill of foreign governments offering loan guarantees.

An early illustration of problems resulting from the latter scenario was provided during World War II, when the Soviet Union received substantial military assistance from its western allies, shipped via the famed Murmansk convoys. Known as "Lend-Lease," the program was not originally intended as a free gift, but during the subsequent Cold War the Soviet Union refused to make repayments. In 1972 the United States followed a previous British example in forgiving ninety percent of the debt. When Vladimir Putin became president in 2000, about $600 million of the remainder was still outstanding—and more had been added.

Toward the end of the Soviet era, much-needed modernization of the economy produced growing demands for imports of foreign technology, which in turn required foreign credits. Eager to have good relations with Mikhail Gorbachev, many Western governments gladly offered guarantees for such loans. By the end of 1991, with the Soviet Union in full collapse, those loans went into effective default. The total of all outstanding Soviet foreign debt came to almost $100 billion.

The first decade of Russia's post-Soviet existence was heavily marked by problems surrounding the handling of that debt. While foreign creditor governments remained insistent that it be repaid, they were also willing to offer substantial new credits in support of Russia's economic transition. The Russian government responded by evolving a strategy for debt management that rested on aggressively threatening default on old debt in order to obtain forgiveness, rescheduling, and fresh credits.

Much of the subsequent political wrangling would revolve around Russia's increasingly controversial relations with the International Monetary Fund (IMF). An initial credit of $1 billion was granted in July 1992, when Russia became a member of the Fund. In 1993, a further $1.5 billion was paid out, under a special "Systemic Transformation Facility" (STF). As Moscow failed to live up even to the soft rules of the STF, the IMF withheld disbursement of an agreed second $1.5 billion tranche.

Following severe criticism for having failed to offer proper support, in April 1994 the Fund decided to release the second tranche of the STF. The essentially political nature of the relation was now becoming evident. Despite Russia's continued problems in honoring its commitments, in April 1995 the IMF granted Russia a $6.5 billion twelve-month credit, and in March 1996 it agreed to a three-year $10.1 billion "Extended Fund Facility."

The latter was the second-largest commitment ever made by the Fund, and there was little effort made to hide its essentially political purpose. The objective was to secure the reelection of Boris Yeltsin to a second term as president, and the IMF was not alone in offering support. On a parallel track, France and Germany offered bilateral credits of $2.4 billion, and the "Paris Club" of foreign creditor governments agreed to a rescheduling of $38 billion in Soviet-era debt.

The latter was of particular importance, in that it opened the doors for Russia to the market for Eurobonds. Receiving its first sovereign credit rating in October 1996, in November the Russian government placed a first issue of $1 billion, which was to be followed, in March and June of the following year, by two further issues of DM2 billion and $2 billion, respectively. Up until the crash in August 1998, Russia succeeded in issuing a total of $16 billion in Eurobonds.

As the Russian government was gaining credibility as a debtor in good standing, other Russian actors, ranging from city governments to private enterprises, also began to venture into the market. Russian commercial banks in particular began securing substantial loans from their partners in the West.

Compounding the exposure, the Russian government was simultaneously saturating the market with ruble-denominated government securities, known as GKO and OFZ. While these instruments technically represented domestic debt, they became highly popular among foreign investors and therefore essential to the issue of foreign debt.

The final stage of Russia's financial bubble was heralded with the onset of the financial crisis in Asia, during the summer of 1997. At first believed to be immune to contagion by this "Asian flu," in the spring of 1998 Russia was becoming seriously ill. In May, the Moscow markets were in free fall, and by June the IMF was under substantial political pressure to take action. Some even warned of pending civil war in a country with nuclear capacities.

Following protracted negotiations, on July 13 the Fund announced a bailout package of $22.6 billion through December 1999, which was supported both by the World Bank and by Japan. A first disbursement of $4.8 billion was made on July 20, and the financial markets began to recover confidence. On August 17, however, the Russian government decided to devalue the ruble anyway and to declare a ninety-day moratorium on short-term debt service.

The potential losses were massive. The volume of GKO debt alone was worth about $40 billion. To this could be added $26 billion owed to multilateral creditors, and the $16 billion in Eurobonds. There also were additional billions in commercial bank credits, including about $6 billion in ruble futures contracts. And there still remained $95 billion in Soviet-era debt, some of which had been recently rescheduled.

In the spring of 1999, few believed that Russia would be able to stage a comeback within the foreseeable future. One foreign banker even stated that he would rather eat nuclear waste than lend any more money to Russia. The situation was aggravated by suspicions that the Russian Central Bank was clandestinely bailing out well-connected domestic actors, at the expense of foreign investors. It was also hard for many to accept the Russian government's unilateral decision to ignore its Soviet-era debt and to honor only purely "Russian" debt.

A year later, fuelled by the ruble devaluation and by rapidly rising oil prices, the Russian economy was making a spectacular recovery. In 2000, the first year of the Putin presidency, GDP grew by nine percent. The federal budget was finally in the black, with a good margin, and foreign trade generated a massive surplus of $61 billion. Despite this drastic improvement in economic performance, the Russian government nevertheless appeared bent on continuing its policy of threatening default in order to secure further restructuring and forgiveness of its old debts.

For the German government in particular, this finally proved to be too much. When the Russian prime minister Mikhail Kasyanov hinted that Russia might not be able to meet its full obligations in 2001, Chancellor Gerhard Schroeder informed Moscow that in case of any further trouble with Russian debt service, he would personally do all he could to isolate Russia. The effect was immediate and positive. From 2001 onward Russia has been current on all sovereign foreign debt (excluding the defaulted GKOs).

In support of its decision to fully honor its credit obligations, the Russian government made prudent use of its budget surplus. By accelerating repayments of debt to the IMF, it drew down the principal, and by introducing a strategic budget reserve to act as a cushion against future debt problems, it strengthened its credibility. The reward has been a series of upgrades in Russia's sovereign credit rating, and a calming of previous fears about further rounds of default.

While this has been positive indeed for Russia's international standing, it has not come without a price. Every billion that is paid out in foreign debt service effectively means one billion less in desperately needed domestic investment. In that sense, it will be a long time indeed before the Russian economy has finally overcome the damage that was done by foreign debt mismanagement during the Yeltsin years.

See also: BANKING SYSTEM, SOVIET; BANKING SYSTEM, TSARIST; ECONOMIC GROWTH, SOVIET; ECONOMY, CURRENT; INDUSTRIALIZATION; LEND LEASE.

BIBLIOGRAPHY

Hedlund, Stefan. (1999). *Russia's "Market" Economy: A Bad Case of Predatory Capitalism.* London: UCL Press.

Mosse, W.E. (1992). *Perestroika under the Tsars.* London: I.B. Taurus.

Stone, Randall W. (2002). *Lending Credibility: The International Monetary Fund and the Post-Communist Transition.* Princeton, NJ: Princeton University Press.

STEFAN HEDLUND

FOREIGN TRADE

Owing to its geographic size and diversity, Russia's foreign trade has always been relatively small, as compared to countries of Western Europe with whom it traded. Nevertheless, foreign trade has provided contacts with western technologies, ideas, and practices that have had considerable impact on the Russian economy, even during periods when foreign trade was particularly reduced. From earliest times Russia has typically traded the products of its forests, fields, and mines for the sophisticated consumer goods and advanced capital goods of Western Europe and elsewhere. Trade with Persia, China, and the Middle East, as well as more remote areas, has also been significant in certain times.

The first recorded Russian foreign trade contact was a treaty concluded in 911 by Prince Oleg of Kiev with the Byzantine emperor. During the medieval period most of the trade was conducted by *gostiny dvor* (merchant colonies), such as the Hanseatic League, resident in Moscow or at fairs at Novgorod or elsewhere. This practice was quite typical of the European Middle Ages because of the expense of travel and communication and the need to assure honest exchanges and payment.

During the early modern period Russian iron ore was very attractive to the British, but until the coking coal of Ukraine became available during the nineteenth century, Russia had to import much of its smelted iron and steel. Up to about 1891, when Finance Minister Ivan Vyshnegradsky raised the tariff, exports of grain and textiles did not suffice to cover imports, interest on previous loans, and the expenses of Russians abroad. Hence Russia had to depend on more foreign capital. Although Russia was known in this period as the "granary of Europe," prices were falling because of new supplies from North America. Nonetheless, Vyshnegradsky insisted, "Let them eat less, and export!"

One aspect of the state-promoted industrialization of 1880–1913 was an effort by the state bureaucracy to increase exports in support of the gold-backed ruble, introduced in 1897. To develop outlets for Russian manufactures, the next minister of finances, Count Sergei Witte, encouraged Russians consular officials to cultivate markets in China, Persia, and Turkey, where prior trade had been mostly in high-value goods such as furs. Witte's new railways, built for military purposes, made exchange of bulkier items economical for the first time. Subsidized sugar and cotton textiles would be sent to Persia and the East, with foreign competition foreclosed by prohibition on transit routes. Nonetheless, in 1913 fully sixty percent of Russian exports were foodstuffs and animals, another third lumber, petroleum, and other materials. Scarcely six percent were textiles, much of it from tsarist Poland. Russian imports were luxury consumer goods (including coffee and tea), equipment, and cotton fiber. Spurred by railroads, industrialization, and a convertible currency, foreign trade during the tsarist period reached a peak just before World War I with a turnover of $1.5 billion in prices of the time. This total was not matched after the Communist Revolution until the wartime imports of 1943, paid for largely by loans. Exports were approximately one-tenth of gross domestic product in 1913, a proportion hardly approached since. They were only four percent of GDP in 1977, for example.

Under the Bolsheviks, Russia conducted an off-and-on policy of self-sufficiency or autarky. According to Michael Kaser's figures, export volumes rose steadily from five percent of the 1913 level in 1922 to sixty-one percent by 1931. When Britain signed a trade agreement in 1922 and others followed, the Soviet government began to buy consumer goods to provide incentives for the workers. They also bought locomotives, farm machinery, and other equipment to replace those lost in the long war years. Exports also rose smartly.

With the beginnings of planning at the end of the 1920s, however, trade fell off throughout the 1930s and the first half of the 1940s, reflecting extreme trade aversion and suspicions of western intentions on Josef Stalin's part, as well as the general world depression, which adversely affected Russia's terms of trade. Russia wanted to be as self-sufficient as possible in case war cut off its supplies, as indeed occurred from 1939 to 1945. Imports of consumer goods fell precipitously, but so did some important industrial materials that were now produced domestically. Since 1928, Russian exports have averaged only about one to two percent of its national income, as compared with six to seven percent of that of the United States in a comparable period. Imports showed a similarly mixed pattern, with imports much exceeding exports during the long war years.

After World War II, Russia no longer pursued such an extreme policy of autarky. Export volumes rose every year, reaching 4.6 times the 1913 level by 1967. But they were still less than four percent of output. The statistical breakdown of Soviet trade was often censored. Its deficits on merchandise trade account and invisibles were financed in unknown part by sales of gold and by borrowings in hard currency. The latter resulted in a growing hard-currency debt to western creditors from 1970 onward, amounting to an estimated $11.2 billion by 1978. Neglect of comparative advantage and international specialization has probably been negative for economic growth and consumer welfare.

During the post–World War II period, most Soviet merchandise imports and exports were traded with the other Communist countries in bilateral deals concluded under the auspices of the Council of Mutual Economic Assistance (COMECON). Even though trade with the developed capitalist countries of the West and with less developed countries increased throughout this era, USSR trade with other "socialist" states still exceeded fifty percent of the total in 1979, while the share of the West was about one-third. Trade with COMECON members was nearly balanced year by year, but when it was not, the difference was credited in "transferable rubles," a book entry that hardly committed either side to future shipments. Franklyn Holzman termed this feature of Soviet trade "commodity inconvertibility," as distinct from currency inconvertibility, which also characterized intra-bloc trade and finance.

Trade with the developed western capitalist countries was always impeded by the deficient quality of Soviet manufactured goods, including poor merchandising and after-sales service. Furthermore, western countries also discriminated against Soviet exports by their tariff and strategic goods policies. Even so, some Russian-produced articles, like watches produced in military factories and tractors, entered a few markets. More significantly, the USSR was able to export tremendous quantities of oil, gas, timber, and nonferrous metals such as platinum and manganese, as well as some heavy chemicals. Notable imports included whole plants for the production of automobiles, tropical foodstuffs, and grain during periods of harvest failure.

Foreign trade was always a state monopoly in the USSR, even during the New Economic Policy (NEP). Under the control of the Minister of Foreign Trade, foreign-trade "corporations" conducted the buying and selling, though industrial ministries and even republic authorities could be involved in the negotiations. Barter deals at the frontiers and tourist traffic provide trivial exceptions to the rule. The object of the monopoly was to fit imports and exports into the overall plan regardless of changes in world prices and availabilities. Foreign trade corporations are not responsible for profits or losses caused by the difference between the prices they negotiate and the corresponding ruble price, given the arbitrary exchange rate. Exports must be planned to cover the cost of necessary imports—notably petroleum, timber, and natural gas during the last decades in exchange for materials, equipment, and foodstuffs during poor harvest years. Hence enterprise managers were told what to produce for export and what may be available from foreign sources. Thus, they had little or no knowledge of foreign conditions, nor interest in adjusting their activities to suit the international situation of the USSR. With internal prices unrelated to international scarcities, the planning agencies could not allow ministries or chief administration, still less enterprises, to decide on their own what to buy or sell abroad. Tariffs were strictly for revenue purposes. For instance, when the world market price of oil quadrupled in 1973–1974, the internal Soviet price did not change for nearly a decade. But trade with the outside world is conducted in convertible currencies, their volumes then translated into *valyuta* rubles at an arbitrary, overvalued rate for the statistics. Prices charged to or by COMECON partners were determined in many different ways, all subject to negotiation and dispute. Some effort was made during the 1970s to calculate a more efficient pattern of foreign trade for investment purposes, but in practice these calculations were little applied.

Given the shortage of foreign currency and underdeveloped trading facilities, Soviet trade corporations often engaged in "counterpart-trade," a kind of barter, where would-be western sellers were asked to take Soviet goods in return for possible resale. For instance, the sale of large-diameter gas pipes for West European customers would be repaid in gas over time. Obviously, these practices were awkward, and Soviet leaders tried a number of organizational measures to interest producers in increased exports, with little success.

One of the changes instituted under Mikhail Gorbachev's leadership was permission for Soviet enterprises to deal directly with foreign suppliers and customers. Given the short time perestroika had to work, it is impossible to tell whether these direct ties alone would have improved Soviet penetration of choosy markets in the developed world. After all, Soviet manufactures suffered from poor design, unreliability, and insufficient incentives, as well as substandard distribution and service.

During the years immediately after the dissolution of the Soviet Union, the Russian ruble became convertible for trade and tourist purposes, but exporters were required to rebate part of their earnings to the state for repayment of foreign debts. Further handicapping Russian exporters was the appreciating real rate of exchange, owing to continued inflation. The IMF also supported the overvalued ruble. By 1996 the ruble became fully convertible. All this made dollars cheap for Russians to accumulate and stimulated capital flight estimated at around $20 billion per year throughout the 1990s. It also made imports of food and luxuries unusually inexpensive, while making Russian exports uncompetitive. What is more, the former East European CMEA partner countries and most Commonwealth of Independent States (CIS) members now preferred to trade with the advanced western countries, rather than Russia. When in mid-1998 the government could no longer defend the overvalued ruble, it accepted a sixty percent depreciation to eliminate the large current account deficit in the balance of payments. This stimulated a recovery of Russian industry, particularly those firms producing import substitutes. Russian exports of oil and gas (which furnish about one-third of tax revenues) also recovered during the late 1990s. Rising energy prices likewise allowed the government to accumulate foreign exchange reserves, pay off much of its foreign debt, and finance still quite extensive central government operations. However, absent private investment, prospects for diversifying Russian exports beyond raw materials and arms were still unclear in the early twenty-first century.

See also: COUNCIL FOR MUTUAL ECONOMIC ASSISTANCE; ECONOMIC GROWTH, IMPERIAL; ECONOMIC GROWTH, SOVIET; FOREIGN DEBT; TRADE ROUTES; TRADE STATUTES OF 1653 AND 1667

BIBLIOGRAPHY

Erickson, P.G., and Miller, R.S. (1979). "Soviet Foreign Economic Behavior: A Balance of Payments Perspective." In *Soviet Economy in a Time of Change: A Compendium of Papers,* U.S. Congress, Joint Economic Committee, 3 vols. Washington, DC: U.S. Government Printing Office. 2:208–243.

Gregory, Paul R., and Stuart, Robert. (1999). *Comparative Economic Systems,* 6th ed. Boston: Houghton Mifflin.

Holzman, Franklyn D. (1974). *Foreign Trade under Central Planning.* Cambridge, MA: Harvard University Press.

Kaser, Michael. (1969). "A Volume Index of Soviet Foreign Trade." *Soviet Studies* 20(4):523–526.

Nove, Alec. (1986). *The Soviet Economic System,* 3d ed. Boston: Allen & Unwin.

Wiles, Peter. (1968). *Communist International Economics.* Oxford: Blackwell.

MARTIN C. SPECHLER

FRANCE, RELATIONS WITH

If the first official contact between France and Russia was established in 1049, when the daughter of Yaroslav, prince of Kiev, married Henri, King of France, bilateral relations were established with the treaty of friendship signed in 1613 by King Louis XIII and Tsar Mikhail Fyodorovich. Since then, cultural exchanges regularly expanded, most notably during the reigns of Peter the Great and Elizabeth. However, on political and economic grounds, the exchanges remained thus: England retained primacy in Russian foreign trade throughout the seventeenth and eighteenth centuries; and on the diplomatic scene, despite common geopolitical interests, France and Russia were quite often the victims of mutual hostile stereotypes. In 1793, embittered by France's radical revolution, Catherine II broke all diplomatic relations with the revolutionary state; and in 1804, despite the treaty of nonaggression concluded in 1801 with Napoleon, Alexander I joined the Third Coalition to defeat the "usurper," his political ambitions, and his expansionism. The war against Napoleon (1805–1813) was a national disaster, marked by several cruel defeats and by the fire of Moscow in 1812, but Alexander's victory, marked by his entrance into Paris in March 1814, gave him a decisive role during the Congress of Vienna.

The second half of the nineteenth century brought a major change in Russian-French relations. If France took part in the humiliating Crimean War in 1854–1856, during the late 1860s reconciliation began to take place and, in 1867 and 1868, the Russian Empire participated in the universal exhibitions organized in Paris. Political and military concerns motivated a decisive rapprochement during the last third of the century: France, traumatized by the loss of the provinces of Alsace and Lorraine, desperately needed an ally against Bismarck's Prussia, while for Alexander III's Russia, the goal was to gain an ally against the Austro-Hungarian Empire, which opposed the Russian pan-Slavic ambitions in the Balkans. In December 1888, the first Russian loan was raised in Paris and three years later, in August 1891, the two countries concluded a political alliance, followed by a military convention in December 1893. To sanctify the rapprochement, Tsar Nicholas II visited France three times, in October 1896, September 1901, and July 1909; and in July 1914, President Poincaré visited Russia to reinforce the alliance on the eve of World War I.

The October 1917 Revolution killed these privileged links. The Bolsheviks opted for a peace with no annexing and no indemnity—and refused to recognize the tsarist loans. As a result, the French state felt deceived, and in December 1917, it broke relations with Russia and engaged instead in a struggle against it. In the spring of 1918, France organized the unloading of forces to support the White Guard and took part in the Polish war against Russia (May–October 1920). However, these interventions failed to overthrow the Soviet regime and, by the end of 1919, French diplomacy opted for a policy of containment against the expansion of communism. By that time, French-Soviet contacts were reduced: the French presence in the USSR was limited to the settlement of a small group of radical intellectuals and to the visits of French Communists; similarly, there was no official Soviet presence in France, although communist intellectuals and artists continued actively promoting Soviet interests and values.

In 1924 Edouard Herriot, chief of the French government, decided to recognize the USSR. While he had no illusion about the authoritarian nature of the Soviet regime, he thought that France could no longer afford to ignore such an important country politically and that the signing of the Treaty of Rapallo in 1922 could be dangerous. Therefore, for geopolitical reasons, he chose to reestablish diplomatic relations.

This decision gave rise to a rapid growth of economic, commercial, and cultural exchanges. In particular, Soviet artists became increasingly present in France: Maxim Gorky and Ilya Ehrenburg, for example, became brilliant spokesmen for the Socialist literature. However, this improvement was a fragile one and remained subject to diplomatic turbulences, due to Fascism and Nazism. Foreign

French president Jacques Chirac shakes hands with Russian president Vladimir Putin as they meet in April 2003 to discuss the situation in Iraq. © AFP/CORBIS

Commissar Maxim Litvinov tried to bring the USSR closer to France and England, but French hesitation, demonstrated by the ambivalent French-Soviet treaty concluded in May 1935 and the lack of strong reaction to the Spanish Civil War, led Josef Stalin to conclude an alliance with Adolf Hitler instead. And on August 23, 1939, the conclusion of the Soviet-German Pact sanctified the collapse of the Soviet-French entente.

Bilateral relations were reestablished during World War II. In September 1941, three months after the beginning of the German invasion of the Soviet Union, Stalin decided to recognize General Charles de Gaulle officially as the "Chief of Free France"; in December 1944 in Moscow, de Gaulle and Stalin signed a treaty of alliance and mutual assistance. However, the Cold War, which began to spread over Europe in 1946, had deep consequences for Soviet-French relations, and in 1955 the Soviet state denounced the treaty of 1944.

In 1956 Nikita Khrushchev's proclaimed de-Stalinization was favorably received by French diplomacy, and in the same year the head of the French government, Guy Mollet, made a trip to the USSR. This trip reestablished contacts and led to a protocol on cultural exchanges. But from 1958 on, de Gaulle's return to power brought a new dynamic to relations with Moscow. De Gaulle wished to encourage "détente." In his view, this would restore France's international significance. In June 1966, he signed several important bilateral agreements with the USSR. Two committees were designed to improve economic cooperation; cooperation was also planned for space, civil nuclear, and television programs; and an original form of cooperation took place in the movie industry.

These agreements conferred a distinct flavor on bilateral relations: in contrast to the American-Soviet dialogue, which remained limited to strategic issues, the French-Soviet détente was in essence more global and covered a wide variety of areas of mutual interest. Political cooperation, economic and scientific exchanges, cultural exhibits, performers' tours, and movie festivals all contributed to build a bridge between the two countries.

Perestroika brought a new impulse to these relations. When Mikhail Gorbachev introduced drastic changes in March 1985, François Mitterrand's diplomacy first hesitated but, after a few months, provided strong support for the new leader; and in October 1990, a bilateral treaty of friendship—the first since 1944—was signed.

The collapse of the USSR imposed another yet another series of geopolitical and cultural changes on the new leaders. But these changes had little impact on the long-lasting structural bonds forged with France through the centuries.

See also: FRENCH INFLUENCE IN RUSSIA; FRENCH WAR OF 1812; NAPOLEON I; POLISH-SOVIET WAR; TILSIT, TREATY OF; WORLD WAR I; WORLD WAR II

BIBLIOGRAPHY

Shlapentokh, Dmitry. (1996). *The French Revolution in Russian Intellectual Life, 1865–1905.* Westport, CT: Prager.

MARIE-PIERRE REY

FREE ECONOMIC SOCIETY

The Free Economic Society for the Encouragement of Agriculture and Husbandry, established in 1765 to consider ways to improve the rural economy of the Russian Empire, became a center of scientific research and practical activities designed to improve agriculture and, after the emancipation of the serfs in 1861, the life of the peasantry. "Free" in the sense that it was not subordinated to any government department or the Academy of Sciences, the society served as a bridge between science, agriculture, and reform until shut down during World War I. It sponsored a wide variety of research in the natural and social sciences as well as essay competitions, publishing reports and essays in *Transactions of the Free Economic Society* (comprising 280 volumes by 1915), and nine other periodicals.

Founded under the sponsorship of Catherine the Great, who provided funds for a building and library, as well as a reformist agenda influenced by physiocratic ideas, the society brought together noble landowners, government officials, and scholars to study and disseminate information on advanced methods of agriculture and estate management, particularly as practiced abroad. Papers were presented on rural economic activities, new technologies, and economic ideas that could be applied to Russia. Young men were sent abroad to study agronomy. At the initiative of Catherine, the society's first essay competition examined the utility of serfdom for the commonweal, but the winning essay, which opposed serfdom, was ignored.

In the first half of the nineteenth century, the society's membership came to include more scientists, professionals, and officials, and fewer landowners. Its work focused on discussion of advanced ideas in agronomy, medicine, and the developing sciences of chemistry and biology. After 1830 the society concentrated on practical applications of technology to agriculture. Among its most important projects were research on the best varieties of plants to grow on Russian soil, efforts to improve crop yields and sanitary measures, and the introduction of smallpox vaccination into rural areas.

After the accession of Alexander II in 1855, the society threw itself into reform efforts and greatly expanded its activities. It offered popular lectures on physics, chemistry, and forestry. It entered the fight against illiteracy and in 1861 established a committee to study popular education. It supported research on soil science, agricultural economics, demography, and rural sociology, and carried out systematic geographic studies. To educate the newly freed peasantry, the society initiated a wide range of activities, mounting agricultural exhibits, establishing experimental farms, encouraging the use of chemical fertilizer and industrial crops, promoting scientific animal husbandry and beekeeping, and expanding its efforts to vaccinate the peasantry against smallpox. As part of its educational mission, the society published popular works on agriculture and distributed millions of pamphlets and books free of charge.

Increasingly, as the society became a forum for progressive economic thought critical of government policy toward the peasantry, its work took on political dimensions. The government revoked its charter in 1899, ordering it to confine its activities to agricultural research. Nonetheless, in 1905 the society supported the election of a constitutional assembly and after 1907 published surveys of peasant opinion on the land reforms proposed by Interior Minister Peter Stolypin that were implicitly critical of government policy. During World War I the tsarist government closed down the society because of its oppositional stance, and the new Soviet government formally abolished it in 1919.

See also: AGRARIAN REFORMS; AGRICULTURE; MOSCOW AGRICULTURAL SOCIETY; STOLYPIN, PETER ARKADIEVICH

BIBLIOGRAPHY

Pratt, Joan Klobe. (1983). "The Russian Free Economic Society, 1765–1915." Ph.D. diss., University of Missouri.

Pratt, Joan Klobe. (2002). "The Free Economic Society and the Battle Against Smallpox: A 'Public Sphere' in Action." *Russian Review* 61:560–578.

Vucinich, Alexander. (1963). *Science in Russian Culture.* Vol. 1: *A History to 1860.* Stanford, CA: Stanford University Press.

Vucinich, Alexander. (1970). *Science in Russian Culture.* Vol. 2: *1861–1970.* Stanford, CA: Stanford University Press.

CAROL GAYLE
WILLIAM MOSKOFF

FREEMASONRY

Freemasonry came to Russia as part of the eighteenth–century expansion that made the craft a global phenomenon. Although at first it was one of several social institutions, including salons, societies, and clubs, that made their way to Russia in the course of Westernization, Freemasonry soon acquired considerable importance, evolving into a widespread, variegated, and much vilified social movement.

Despite the legends that attributed the origins of Russian Freemasonry to Peter the Great (who purportedly received his degree from Christopher Wren), the first reliable evidence places the beginnings of the craft in Russia in the 1730s and early 1740s. The movement expanded in the latter half of the eighteenth century, especially between 1770 and 1790, when more than a hundred lodges were created in St. Petersburg, Moscow, and the provinces.

Freemasonry was an important element of the Russian Enlightenment and played a central role in the evolution of Russia's public sphere and civil society. The lodges were self-governed and open to free men (but not women) of almost every nationality, rank, and walk of life, with the notable exception of serfs. While many lodges were nothing but glorified social clubs, there were numerous brethren who saw themselves as on a mission to reform humankind and battle Russia's perceived "barbarity" by means of charity and self-improvement. They regarded the lodges as havens of righteousness and nurseries of virtue in a depraved world.

The history of Russian Freemasonry followed a tortuous path. Most of the lodges, especially in the provinces, were short–lived, and Russian Freemasonry was very fragmented. Some lodges were subordinated to the Grand Lodge of England; others belonged to the Swedish Rite, the Strict Observance, or some other jurisdiction. Contemporaries made a distinction between Freemasonry proper and Martinism, a mystical strand in the movement that claimed the famous mystic Claude Saint–Martin as its founder. A group of Moscow Rosicrucians headed by Johann–Georg Schwarz and Nikolai Ivanovich Novikov were the most important Martinists. Often referred to as "Novikov's circle," they enjoyed close ties with the university, the government, and even the local diocese and initiated numerous educational and charitable initiatives, such as the Friendly Learned Society, the Typographical Company, and the Philological Seminary. Novikov's circle was an important episode in the history of the Russian Enlightenment. Its activities, however, came to an end in 1792, when Novikov was arrested, interrogated, and sentenced to life in prison.

Many aspects of the so-called Novikov affair are still unclear. The government of Catherine II may have had political motives for arresting Novikov, given the Rosicrucians' ties to foreign powers as well as to the future Emperor Paul I and his entourage. The affair may also, in large part, have been caused by the fear of occult secret societies and anti–Masonic sentiment that was spreading through Europe. Anti–Masonry later became an important political factor in imperial and post-Soviet Russia.

Russian Freemasonry enjoyed a brief period of relatively unhampered existence in the eighteenth and early nineteenth centuries. The craft counted among its members practically every politician, military leader, and intellectual of note, including Mikhail Kutuzov and Alexander Pushkin; many of the Decembrists belonged to the Astrea lodge in St. Petersburg. After 1822, when Alexander I imposed a ban on all secret societies, the situation changed. The ban, confirmed by Nicholas I in 1826, signified the official end of Freemasonry, although some clandestine lodges continued to operate, particularly during a brief revival on the eve of World War I. Freemasonry was again outlawed in Soviet Russia in the early 1920s. The ban ended in the 1990s, when the French National Grand Lodge established lodges in Moscow, St. Petersburg, and Voronezh, and chapters of the Ancient and Accepted Scottish Rite were also organized.

See also: CATHERINE II; ENLIGHTENMENT, IMPACT OF; NOVIKOV, NIKOLAI IVANOVICH; PAUL I

BIBLIOGRAPHY

Smith, Douglas. (1999). *Working the Rough Stone: Freemasonry and Society in Eighteenth-Century Russia.* DeKalb: Northern Illinois University Press.

OLGA TSAPINA

FRENCH INFLUENCE IN RUSSIA

The first real manifestations of the influence of France in Russia date from Russia's first political opening toward Europe, undertaken by Peter the Great (r. 1682–1725) and further advanced by Catherine II (r. 1762–1796). In the first instance, this influence was cultural. The adoption of the French language as the language of conversation and correspondence by the nobility encouraged access to French literature. The nobility's preference for French governesses and tutors contributed to the spread of French culture and educational methods among the aristocracy. At the beginning of the nineteenth century, the Russian nobility still preferred French to Russian for everyday use, and were familiar with French authors such as Jean de la Fontaine, George Sand, Eugene Sue, Victor Hugo, and Honoré de Balzac.

The influence of France was equally strong in the area of social and political ideas. Catherine II's interest in the writings of the philosophers of the Enlightenment—Baron Montesquieu, Jean Le Rond d'Alembert, Voltaire, and Denis Diderot—contributed to the spread of their ideas in Russia during the eighteenth century. The empress conducted regular correspondence with Voltaire, and received Diderot at her court. Convinced that it was her duty to civilize Russia, she encouraged the growth of a critical outlook and, as an extension of this, of thought regarding Russian society and a repudiation of serfdom, which had consequences following her own reign.

The support of Catherine II for the spirit of the Enlightenment was nonetheless shaken by the French Revolution of 1789. It ceased entirely with the execution of King Louis XVI (January 1793). The empress was unable to accept such a radical challenge to the very foundations of autocratic rule. From the close of her reign onward, restrictions on foreign travel increased, and contacts were severely curtailed. Despite this change, however, liberal ideas that had spread during the eighteenth century continued to circulate throughout Russia during the nineteenth, and the French Revolution continued to have a persistent influence on the political ideas of Russians. When travel resumed under Alexander I (ruled 1801–1825), Russians once again began to travel abroad for pleasure or study. This stimulated liberal ideas that pervaded progressive and radical political thought in Russia during the nineteenth century. The welcome that France extended to political exiles strengthened its image as a land of liberty and of revolution.

During the nineteenth century, travel in France was considered a form of cultural and intellectual apprenticeship. Study travel abroad by Russians, as well as trips to Russia by the French, shared a common cultural space, encouraging exchanges most notably in the areas of fine arts, sciences, and teaching. Because they shared geopolitical interests *vis à vis* Germany and Austria-Hungary, France and Russia were drawn together diplomatically and economically after 1887. This resulted, in December 1893, in the ratification of a defensive alliance, the French-Russian military pact. At the same time, French investment capital helped finance the modernization of the Russian economy. Between 1890 and 1914, numerous French industrial and banking houses established themselves in Russia. French and Belgian capital supplied the larger part of the flow of investment funds, the largest share of which went into mining, metallurgy, chemicals, and especially railroads. The largest French banks, notably the Crédit Lyonnais, made loans to or invested in Russian companies. Public borrowing by the Russian state, totaling between eleven and twelve billion gold francs, was six times greater than direct investment on the part of the French.

On the eve of 1914, there were twelve thousand French nationals in Russia. Forty consuls were in the country looking out for French interests. French newspapers had permanent correspondents in St. Petersburg. In 1911, l'Institut Français (a French institute) was created there to help spread French culture in Russia. In fact, from the 1890s onward, France's cultural presence in Russia was consistently viewed as an adjunct to its policy of industrial and commercial implantation.

Following the close of the nineteenth century, the role of France as a land that welcomed political exiles and refugees had a reciprocal influence on the countries from which they came. When they returned to Russia, some of these individuals brought back ideas as well as social, pedagogical, and political experiences. For example, the experience acquired by Maxim Kovalevsky (1851–1916), professor of law and sociology, as the head of the Ecole supérieure russe des sciences sociales de Paris (the Russian Advanced School for Social Sciences in Paris), founded in 1901, served to organize the Université populaire Shanyavsky in Moscow (the Shanyavsky People's University), founded in 1908.

After the October Revolution of 1917, Paris, along with Berlin and Prague, was one of the three principal cities of Russian emigration in Europe. A hub of intellectual activity from the 1920s onward, the French capital was among the leading centers abroad for publishing Russian newspapers and books, of which a portion subsequently made its way into Russia, thereby helping to bind the emigrant population with Soviet Russians back home. The suspension of scientific and cultural relations between the USSR and the rest of the world, starting in the mid-1930s, put an end to this exchange.

The cultural influence of France did not disappear, however. Beginning in 1954, new attempts were made to bring France and the USSR closer together, beginning with cultural exchanges. During that year the Comédie française made a triumphant tour of the Soviet Union. Later, the trip by General Charles de Gaulle, in June of 1966, marked the beginning of a time of privileged relations between the two countries. A joint commission was created to foster exchange, and numerous cultural agreements were signed, some of which remained in effect during the early twenty-first century. French teaching assistants were appointed in Soviet universities, the teaching of French was expanded at the secondary school level, and agreements were signed for the distribution of French films in the USSR.

In the end, in the perception of the Russian people, France has remained the country of the Revolution of 1789 and the homeland of the Rights of Man. From the 1960s onward, French intellectuals outside of Russia strengthened this image by supporting the cause of Soviet dissidents. It is again in the name of human rights that France has attempted, since 1994, to soften the position of the Russian government with regard to Chechnya.

See also: CATHERINE II; ENLIGHTENMENT, IMPACT OF; FRANCE, RELATIONS WITH

BIBLIOGRAPHY

De Madariaga, Isabel. (1998). *Politics and Culture in Eighteenth-Century Russia.* London: Longman.

Kaufman, Peter H. (1994). *The Solidarity of a Philosophe: Diderot, Russia, and the Soviet Union.* New York: P. Lang.

Raeff, Marc. (1994). *Political Ideas and Institutions in Imperial Russia.* Boulder, CO: Westview Press.

Riasanovsky, Nicholas. (1999). *A History of Russia,* 6th ed. Oxford: Oxford University Press.

Shlapentokh, Dmitry. (1996). *The French Revolution in Russian Intellectual Life, 1865–1905.* Westport, CT: Praeger.

Voltaire. (1974). *Voltaire and Catherine the Great: Selected Correspondence.* Cambridge, MA: Oriental Research Partners.

Wesling, Molly W. (2001). *Napoleon in Russian Cultural Mythology.* New York: P. Lang.

MARTINE MESPOULET

FRENCH WAR OF 1812

The French war of 1812 was one of the most decisive conflicts of modern times. Napoleon crossed the Russian frontier on June 24, 1812, with more than 650,000 troops, and just a few months later recrossed the frontier, defeated, with less than one-tenth of that number. Although winter played a role in the deaths of tens of thousands of French soldiers during the retreat, Russia won the campaign through a skillful withdrawal and the careful selection of battlefields. Napoleon contributed to his own disaster by failing to provide adequately for an extended campaign in terms both of supplies and of reinforcements.

Originally Russia had contemplated an invasion of French-held Poland, but the Russian commander, Mikhail B. Barclay de Tolly, quickly changed the plan. When Napoleon crossed the frontier, Barclay de Tolly intended to have his First Army withdraw to a fortified camp at Drissa, luring

Napoleon's main body behind it. While Napoleon attacked the camp, Peter I. Bagration's Second Army was to fall on the French rear, destroying the invading army. The plan was abandoned and the retreat began when the Russians realized that Napoleon's force was more than twice as large as they had believed.

The Russian armies had been drawn up with a considerable gap between them, and Napoleon drove right through it, intending to keep them separated. Barclay de Tolly and Bagration naturally wished to link up before they accepted battle, but were unable to do so before reaching Smolensk in mid-August. Facing ever-increasing pressure from Tsar Alexander to fight, Barclay de Tolly prepared to accept battle supported by Smolensk's impressive walls. Napoleon, however, attempted to envelop the Russian position rather than attack head-on. As Barclay de Tolly became aware of this movement, he decided once again that discretion was the better part of valor and withdrew from Smolensk rather than risk losing his army.

Frustrated by this continued retreating and also by the bickering between Barclay de Tolly and Bagration, neither of whom was prepared to take orders from the other, Alexander appointed Mikhail I. Kutuzov as overall commander of what was now effectively an army group comprising two armies marching together. Despite Alexander's continued prodding, Kutuzov continued the retreat. As he neared Moscow, he recognized that he would have to give battle before abandoning Russia's ancient capital, and so he selected the field near Borodino, which he prepared with field fortifications.

Napoleon, chastened by his experience at Smolensk and desperate for a decisive battle, refused the advice of his subordinates to envelop the Russian position at Borodino and on September 7 launched a bloody frontal assault instead. The Russian army held, and Kutuzov mustered it to continue its retreat that night. Barely pausing in Moscow, Kutuzov withdrew to the south in order to prevent Napoleon from marching into the rich fields of Ukraine to replenish his supplies, and also to protect Russian reinforcements coming from those regions. Napoleon occupied Moscow on September 14 and remained in the city for more than a month before abandoning it on October 18. During the French occupation, the city was destroyed almost completely in an enormous fire, although the exact cause of the blaze remains unclear and controversial to this day.

Having decided to leave Moscow when Alexander refused to make any move toward peace, Napoleon tried to march southward but found Kutuzov's army arrayed against him at Maloyaroslavets. The bloody battle there on October 24–25 forced Napoleon back to the Warsaw-Moscow highway along which he had originally invaded, and he began the long retreat by the way he had come.

Napoleon's retreating forces suffered horribly. They had eaten most of the supplies along the road on their inward march, and the Russians had deliberately pursued a scorched-earth policy to destroy the remaining supplies. The burning of Moscow had also deprived Napoleon of valuable supplies, and when Kutuzov cut him off from Ukraine, the fate of the *Grande Armée* was sealed. All the way back to the Russian border, peasants, Cossacks, and Russian regular troops harried the French, who died in droves. The Russians attempted to cut off the French retreat altogether at the Battle of the Berezina on November 27–28. Although Napoleon managed to batter his way through, his casualties were staggering. When the remnants of the French army struggled across the Russian frontier, one of the most powerful armies ever assembled to that point in history had been virtually wiped out.

It is customary to credit the Russian winter with the destruction of the French army, but this notion is greatly exaggerated. The most critical events in the campaign—Napoleon's initial operations, the maneuver at Smolensk, the Battle of Borodino, the seizure of Moscow, and even the Battle of Maloyaroslavets—were fought before hard cold and snow set in. The Russian army was forced to confront the vast French force on its own without climatological aids for four months, and literally hundreds of thousands of French soldiers perished in that time. The hard winter that followed merely added to the misery and completed the destruction of a French force that had already been defeated by Russian arms.

The invasion of Russia set the stage for the collapse of Napoleon's hegemony in Europe. In the wake of Napoleon's flight, the Prussian auxiliary corps he had forced to advance into the Baltic States made peace with the Russia on its own accord and committed Prussia to fight against France. As Russian forces crossed their own frontier and marched westward, Austria, Britain, and Sweden were persuaded to join the now-victorious Russian army, and the final coalition against Napoleon was born. By catalyzing this last great and victorious coalition, the War of 1812 marked a profound turning point in European history and also in Russian history. Pursuing the French back to France, Russian troops found themselves in Paris itself. Alexander committed himself absolutely to a prominent role in the affairs of the entire European continent. Russian soldiers who had the unique chance to see the French capital, on the other hand, would ultimately become so frustrated with Alexander's conservative regime as to stage the Decembrist Rebellion in 1825. The costs of this greatest of Russian victories were, in every respect, staggering.

See also: BORODINO, BATTLE OF; DECEMBRIST MOVEMENT AND REBELLION; FRANCE, RELATIONS WITH; HOLY ALLIANCE; KUTUZOV, MIKHAIL ILARIONOVICH; QUADRUPLE ALLIANCE AND QUINTUPLE ALLIANCE

BIBLIOGRAPHY

Duffy, Christopher. (1973). *Borodino and the War of 1812.* New York: Scribner.

Tarle, Evgeny Viktorovich. (1942). *Napoleon's Invasion of Russia, 1812.* New York: Oxford University Press.

FREDERICK W. KAGAN

FRONTIER FORTIFICATIONS

Fortified lines played a major role in Muscovy's southern frontier defense strategy. The great scale of these fortifications projects testified to the Muscovite state's considerable powers of resource mobilization.

The defense of Muscovy's southern frontier relied heavily upon long fortified lines linking garrison towns and serving as stations for the corps of the southern frontier field army. These lines were never intended to be impermeable walls keeping out the Tatars, but rather a supporting infrastructure for reconnaissance patrols, signaling, and corps movements beyond or behind the defense line. The gradual extension of these defense lines deeper into the steppe over the course of the late sixteenth and seventeenth centuries reflected the Muscovite state's successes in the military colonization of its southern frontier and in its command and control of much larger field armies.

To stop the Crimean Tatars from invading central Muscovy, it had become necessary by 1512 to station several thousand troops along the Bank Line (Bereg), an especially vulnerable 250-kilometer (155.3-mile) stretch of the Oka between Kolomna and Kaluga, every spring and summer. By century's end the Abatis Line (Zasechnaya cherta), an additional network of forest abatis and fortifications almost 1,000 kilometers (620 miles) in span, had arisen another 100 kilometers (62 miles) farther south; the field army was restationed along it, providing central Muscovy with greater defense in depth and also encouraging military colonization of the forest-steppe zone. From 1637 to 1658 a new Belgorod Line was built along most of the southern edge of the forest-steppe, from Akhtyrka in northeastern Ukraine to Chelnavsk; it consisted of earthen fortifications built in the new Dutch manner, as well as abatis, and linked twenty-five garrison towns. From 1646 it became the new line of deployment for the corps of the southern field army as well as a place d'armes for aggressive operations down the Don (against the Crimean Khanate and the Ottoman fortress of Azov) and in Ukraine (against the Commonwealth during the Thirteen Years War). In 1679–1680 most of the steppe along the Northern Donets and Oskol rivers was enclosed behind yet another new line, the Izyuma Line, another 160 kilometers (99.42 miles) southeast of the Belgorod Line.

See also: CRIMEAN TATARS; MILITARY, IMPERIAL ERA; MUSCOVY; THIRTEEN YEARS' WAR

BRIAN DAVIES

FRUNZE, MIKHAIL VASILIEVICH

(1885–1925), military leader and theoretician.

Mikhail Vasilievich Frunze was a native of Semirchesk oblast, the son of an orderly, and a student in the Petersburg Polytechnic Institute, from which he failed to graduate. He joined the social democratic movement (1904) and led strikes in Ivanovo (May 1905). Arrested and twice sentenced to death, he was exiled instead and managed to escape. He did party work in Belorussia (1917), was head of the militia in Minsk, and was a member of the Party committee of the West Front. Frunze was head of the Party Soviet in Shuia (September 1917). Opposed to the Treaty of Brest-Litovsk, he joined the "Left-Communists." Frunze was military commissar of Yaroslavl Military District. From February 1919, he was at the front as commander of the Fourth and Turkestan Armies, then he was commander of the south wing of the East Front, fighting against Kolchak. From July 1919, Frunze was commander of the East Front deployed in the Urals, and from September 1919, he commanded the Turkestan Front. From September 1920, Frunze served as commander of the South Front deployed in Crimea and accepted the surrender of Pyotr Wrangel's remaining forces in the Crimea, who were later massacred by the Party and Cheka operatives, despite his disapproval. From December 1920, he headed the Revolutionary Military Soviet (RVS) and commanded the Crimea and Ukraine forces, which embarked on various punitive operations. He was elected to the Party Central Committee (1921), appointed as Deputy People's Commissar for Military and Naval Affairs (March 1924), and later (April 1924) served as the Chief of Staff of the Red Army. Frunze was a candidate member of the Politburo (1924). He authored a number of studies, including a guide on reorganizing the Red Army (1921), on military doctrine (1921, 1924), and on Vladimir Lenin and the Red Army (1925). He led the military reforms in 1924–1925. Frunze's ideas, formed in bruising battles with Leon Trotsky, involved a "unified doctrine" and setting up of a bureaucratically structured Red Army high command to meet wartime as well as peacetime needs. The necessity for an industrial defense base, as well as machinery for rapid mobilization, was also emphasized. These views were opposed by those who favored a militia-type Red Army.

On March 11, 1924, Frunze was appointed as Trotsky's deputy, and on January 1, 1925, Joseph Stalin named him Commissar of Military and Naval Affairs, replacing Trotsky. Frunze's death, as a result of an operation recommended by Stalin, has given rise to a number of claims that his demise was no accident and that it gave Stalin the opportunity to replace him with Kliment Voroshilov, about whose loyalty there was little doubt. Frunze is buried on Red Square. His son, fighter pilot Timur Frunze, was killed during the Battle of Stalingrad.

See also: MILITARY, SOVIET AND POST-SOVIET

BIBLIOGRAPHY

Gareev, M.A. (1987). *M.V. Frunze, Military Theorist.* Washington, DC: Pergamon-Brassey's.

Von Hagen, Mark (1990). *Soldiers in a Proletarian Leadership: The Red Army and the Soviet Socialist State.* Ithaca, NY: Cornell University Press.

MICHAEL PARRISH

FULL ECONOMIC ACCOUNTING

In the Soviet economy, industrial enterprises were treated as independent units from a financial management and economic accountability perspective. Under the system of full economic accounting (*polny khozrachet*) introduced by Mikhail Gorbachev, each enterprise was to be self-financing in the long run, meeting wage payments and other production costs from sales revenues. Investment requirements identified in the *techpromfinplan* were to be met from enterprise profits. Full economic accounting was a cornerstone of perestroika, regarded as an important measure to improve enterprise operations.

The *khozrachet* system used by Soviet enterprises during the 1980s was not new, but the attention paid to enterprise autonomy and accountability during the period of perestroika appeared more serious. Under the system of full economic accounting, unprofitable or "negative-value-added" firms were to go out of business either through a bankruptcy proceeding or by another enterprise taking over the loss-making firm's assets. Prior to perestroika, the *khozrachet* system gave lip service to self-financing and economic accountability, but in practice, loss-making firms routinely received subsidies from central authorities or industrial ministries redistributing profits from "winners" to "losers."

Gorbachev's full economic accounting system was supposed to end the automatic subsidies provided to loss-makers. It appeared to be the Soviet answer to the question of how to eliminate the "soft budget constraint" described by Janos Kornai as the primary contributing source of scarcity in a planned economy. However, centrally determined prices for inputs received by the firm and output sold by the firm made calculations of cost, revenue, and profit somewhat meaningless from an efficiency or economic accountability perspective. Centrally determined prices did not reflect scarcity, nor did they signal accurate information about the operation or performance of the Soviet industrial enterprise. Consequently, basing the full economic accounting system on these prices, in an environment of persistent and pervasive shortages, provided little opportunity to maneuver Soviet enterprises away from the production of shoddy goods and toward the production of goods that adequately captured the specifications or preferences of customers. Moreover, as planners maintained the bonus system that linked substantial monetary payments to the fulfillment of output targets rather than cost reductions, enterprise managers continued to over-order inputs and hoard labor in order to achieve the planned output targets. As planners continued to set output plan targets high relative to the firm's productive capacity, enterprise managers continued to disregard cost in efforts to fulfill planned output targets. In short, policies pursued by planners sustained the outcome that the extension to full economic accounting was to replace. The absence of bankruptcy law and established bankruptcy proceedings, plus the lack of a mechanism for one firm to acquire the assets of a second firm, also undermined the effectiveness of full economic accounting in improving enterprise operations.

See also: KORNAI, JANOS; PERESTROIKA; TECHPROMFINPLAN

BIBLIOGRAPHY

Gorbachev, Mikhail. (1987). *Perestroika: New Thinking for Our Country and the World.* New York: Harper & Row.

Gregory, Paul R. (1990). *Restructuring the Soviet Economic Bureaucracy.* New York: Cambridge University Press.

SUSAN J. LINZ

FUNDAMENTAL LAWS OF 1906

The Fundamental Laws, a 203-article compilation of existing laws on supreme rule, were first published in the Set of Laws of the Russian Empire (*Svod zakonov Rossyskoi impery*) in 1832. Unchanged since the edition published in 1892, they had to be revised in order to carry out the principles set forth in the October Manifesto of 1905. The revision was based on the principles established by the Manifesto of 1906, which made the State Council a second legislative chamber with the right to veto acts by the State Duma, thereby establishing that the Duma did not have the right to change the Fundamental Laws. The new revision of the Fundamental Laws was hurriedly accepted before the upcoming election of the Duma. Count Sergei Witte, one of the initiators of the October Manifesto and of the introduction of national representatives into Russian politics, warned that if the revision was issued before the election, the Duma would become the Constitutional Assembly, and this would lead to violence and the end of the new order.

There were three drafts of the Fundamental Laws: one liberal, one conservative, and one "moderate" (in fact closer to liberal). The latter, created at the State Chancellery by the deputy state secretary, Peter Kharitonov, was adopted as basis for the future document. The Japanese, Prussian, and Austro-Hungarian constitutions were studied in the process of creating and compiling the laws, as was a draft prepared by the Union of Liberation and published abroad. The draft prepared by the State Chancellery was discussed at five meetings of the Council of Ministers in March of 1906 under the chairmanship of Witte and was completed in a spirit of fortifying conservative principles. Such articles as "the restriction to punish in ways other than the court's ruling" and "the respected secrecy of private correspondence" were removed, and the tsar's prerogatives were strengthened. The project and its revisions were discussed at meetings on April 1906 in Tsarskoye Selo under the chairmanship of Tsar Nicholas II. After he approved the new edition of the Fundamental Laws, it was published on May 10 (April 27 O.S.), 1906, the day the State Duma opened. The new edition, containing 223 articles, transformed Russia into a constitutional monarchy.

Whereas the first article of the earlier version of the Fundamental Laws stated that "The Russian emperor is an autocratic monarch with unlimited power," article 4 now gave the tsar supreme autocratic power. The term "unlimited" was removed, and "autocratic" (*samoderzhavnyi*) was defined as declaring the independence of the country and the monarch. A special note by the historian Sergei Knazkov proved that the word "autocracy" had been used in this sense during the seventeenth century and had only assumed the meaning of unlimited power during the eighteenth. The new article proclaimed the unity and indivisibility of the Russian Empire. It noted that Finland was an "inseparable part" of Russia, but "was governed by special institutions on the basis of being a special legislative authority." Russian was declared the official language of the empire, and its use was required in the army, navy, and all state and civil institutions.

From then on, no law could be passed without the approval of the State Council and the State Duma. Members of the Duma were elected for five years. The State Council and the Duma could legislate on matters not covered by the Fundamental Laws. The chief innovation was the inclusion into the Fundamental Laws of articles that guaranteed identity rights and civil freedoms, specifically the protection of identity and residence, freedom of residence, activity, movement, protection of possessions, freedom of speech, press, unions, assembly, and religion. The declared rights and freedoms did not include Jews, for whom residential restrictions (the Jewish Pale of Settlement) and restrictions on civil service positions still existed.

These concessions notwithstanding, the tsar retained an enormous amount of power. He had the right of the legislative initiative, including the exclusive right to initiate revisions of the Fundamental Laws. Without his approval, laws approved by the legislative chambers could not be passed. Moreover, in emergency situations the tsar could promulgate laws when the Duma was not in session (article 87). These would be nullified, however, unless ratified by the Duma within two months. The tsar had supreme control of the country, including control over foreign policy, the power to declare war and peace, supreme command of the armed forces, the right to mint coins, the appointment and dissolution of the government, and the unlimited right to declare a state of war or emergency. The tsar had power over the Council of Ministers and could hold them accountable.

The State Council and the Duma were to be convened annually. The tsar determined the time span of their yearly activities and the duration of the "holidays" for legislative institutions. He appointed half of the members of the State Council and had the right to dissolve the Duma before the five-year mark. If he did so, he had to announce a date for new elections to the Duma. Nicholas II used this right twice, dissolving the first and second Dumas. In the second case, on June 3 (16), 1907, the electoral law was changed. This was a violation of the Fundamental Laws, because the new electoral law was not presented to the legislative institutions.

Under the second revision of the Fundamental Laws, Russia became a dualistic monarchy (Duma monarchy).

See also: DUMA; NICHOLAS II; OCTOBER MANIFESTO; STATE COUNCIL; WITTE, SERGEI YULIEVICH

BIBLIOGRAPHY

Ascher, Abraham. (1992). *The Revolution of 1905: Authority Restored.* Stanford, CA: Stanford University Press.

Harcave, Sidney, tr. and ed. (1990). *The Memoirs of Count Witte.* Armonk, NY: M.E. Sharpe.

Mehlinger, Howard D., and Tompson, John M. (1972). *Count Witte and the Tsarist Government in the 1905 Revolution.* Bloomington: Indiana University Press.

Szeftel, Marc. (1976). *The Russian Constitution of April 23, 1906: Political Institutions of the Duma Monarchy.* Brussels: Editions de la Librarie encyclopédique.

OLEG BUDNITSKII

FUNDED COMMODITIES

Funded commodities were a category of commodities considered so critical to the success of the annual plan that allocation was tightly controlled by Gosplan and the USSR Council of Ministers.

Soviet central planning aspired to comprehensive coverage of the supply and demand of all commodities and services in the economy. As there were millions of transactions in an economy the size of the USSR, this was not a realistic ambition. The system of materials balances was designed to replace market forces of supply and demand in attaining equilibrium in each market. This enormous task was subdivided by category in order to decentralize the burden of achieving balances to various administrative and territorial planning units.

Funded commodities represented a restricted list of critical commodities that were under the direct control and allocation of the Gosplan and required explicit approval by the USSR Council of Ministers. The number of commodities in this category varied considerably over time, reflecting various reorganizations of planning procedures, changes in priorities, and attempts to reform the process. According to Paul Gregory and Robert Stuart, the number of funded commodities varied from 277 in the beginning in 1928 to as many as 2,390. During the 1980s, the number was approximately 2,000. About 75,000 other commodities were also specifically planned and controlled either by Gosplan in conjunction with various centralized supply organizations, or by the ministries without explicit central oversight.

See also: FONDODERZHATELI; GOSPLAN

BIBLIOGRAPHY

Gregory, Paul R., and Stuart, C. Robert. (1990). *Soviet Economic Structure and Performance.* New York: HarperCollins.

Nove, Alec. (1965). *The Soviet Economy, An Introduction,* rev. ed. New York: Praeger.

James R. Millar

FUTURISM

A term coined by the Italian poet Filippo Tommaso Marinetti (1876–1944), Futurism emphasized discarding the static and irrelevant art of the past. It celebrated change, originality, and innovation in culture and society and glorified the new technology of the twentieth century, with emphasis on dynamism, speed, energy, and power. Russian Futurism, founded by Velimir Khlebnikov (1885–1922), a poet and a mystic, and Vladimir Mayakovsky (1893–1930), the leading poet of Russian Revolution of 1917 and of the early Soviet period, went beyond its Italian model with a focus on a revolutionary social and political outlook. In 1912 the Russian Futurists issued the manifesto "A Slap in the Face of Public Taste" that advocated the ideas of Italian futurism and attacked Alexander Pushkin, Fyodor Dostoyevsky, and Leo Tolstoy. With the Revolution of 1917, the Russian Futurists attempted to dominate postrevolutionary culture in hopes of creating a new art integrating all aspects of daily life within a vision of total world transformation; artists would respond to a call to transcend and remake reality through a revolutionized aesthetic, to break down the barriers that had heretofore alienated the old art and the old reality. Russian Futurism argued that art, by eliciting predetermined emotions, could organize the will of the masses for action toward desired goals. In 1923 Mayakovsky cofounded with Osip Brik the Dadaistic journal *LEF.* Soviet avant-garde architects led by Nikolai Ladovsky were also highly influenced by Futurism and the theory that humanity's "world understanding" becomes a driving force determining human action only when it is fused with world-perception, defined as "the sum of man's emotional values . . . created by sympathy or revulsion, friendship or animosity, joy or sorrow, fear or courage." Only by sensing the world through the "feeling of matter" could one understand, and thus be driven to change, the world. The Futurists were initially favored by Anatoly Lunacharsky, the Soviet commissar of education, and obtained important cultural posts. But by 1930 they had lost influence within the government and within most of the literary community.

See also: LUNACHARSKY, ANATOLY VASILIEVICH; MAYAKOVSKY, VLADIMIR VLADIMIROVICH; OCTOBER REVOLUTION

BIBLIOGRAPHY

Janecek, Gerald. (1996). *Zaum: The Transrational Poetry of Russian Futurism.* San Diego, CA: San Diego State University Press.

Markov, Vladimir. (1968). *Russian Futurism: A History.* Berkeley: University of California Press.

Hugh D. Hudson Jr.

FYODOR ALEXEYEVICH

(1661–1682), tsar of Russia, February 9, 1676 to May 7, 1682.

Fyodor was the ninth child of Tsar Alexis and his first wife, Maria Miloslavskaya. He became heir to the throne following the death of an elder brother in 1670. Fyodor is said to have studied Latin and Polish with the Belarusian court poet Simeon Polotsky, but sources indicate that his education was predominantly traditional, with some modern elements. Just fourteen on his accession in 1676, Fyodor ruled without a regent, but was supported by a number of advisors and personal favorites, notably his chamberlain Ivan Yazykov and the brothers Alexei and Mikhail Likhachev. Less intimate with the tsar, but highly influential, was Prince Vasily Golitsyn. Members of Fyodor's mother's family, the Miloslavskys, were less prominent, although they succeeded early in the reign in securing the banishment of Artamon Matveyev and several members of the rival Naryshkin clan. There were power struggles throughout the reign. There were also rumors that Fyodor's ambitious sister Sophia Alekseyevna regularly attended his sickbed. In fact, Fyodor, although delicate, was by no means the hopeless invalid depicted by some historians. Records show that he regularly participated in ceremonies and presided over councils. He married twice. His first wife Agafia Grushetskaya (of part-Polish extraction) and her newborn son died in July 1681. In February 1682 he married the noblewoman Marfa Apraksina.

The central event of Fyodor's reign was war with Turkey (1676–1681), precipitated by Turkish and Tatar incursions into Ukraine, compelling Russia to abandon the fort of Chigirin on the Dnieper. The treaty of Bakhchisarai (1681) established a twenty-year truce. War determined economic policy. In 1678 a major land survey was conducted in order to reassess the population's tax obligations, providing the only reliable, if partial, population figures for the whole century. In 1679 the household rather than land became the basis for taxation. Provincial reforms included abolition of some elected posts and wider powers for military governors. Fyodor's major reform was the abolition of the Code of Precedence (*mestnichestvo*) in 1682. An associated scheme to separate civil and military offices and create permanent posts was shelved, allegedly after the patriarch warned that such officials might accumulate independent power. In 1681 and 1682 a major church council sought to raise the caliber of priests and intensified the persecution of Old Believers.

Fyodor had his portrait painted, encouraged the introduction of part-singing from Kiev, and approved a charter for an academy modeled on the Kiev Academy (implemented only in the late 1680s). Polish fashions and poetry became popular with courtiers, but traditionalists regarded "Latin" novelties with suspicion. Tsar Alexis's theatre was closed down, and foreign fashions were banned. Historians remain undecided whether Fyodor was a sickly young nonentity manipulated by unscrupulous favorites or whether he showed promise of becoming a strong ruler. His reign is best viewed as a continuation of Russia's involvement in international affairs and of mildly Westernizing trends, especially via Ukraine and Poland.

See also: ALEXEI MIKHAILOVICH; GOLITSYN, VASILY VASILIEVICH; PETER I; SOPHIA

BIBLIOGRAPHY

Bushkovitch, Paul. (2001). *Peter the Great: The Struggle for Power, 1671–1725.* Cambridge, UK: Cambridge University Press.

Soloviev, Sergei. (1989). *History of Russia: Vol. 25, Rebellion and Reform: Fedor and Sophia, 1682–1689,* ed. and tr. Lindsey Hughes. Gulf Breeze, FL: Academic International Press.

LINDSEY HUGHES

FYODOR II

(1589–1605), Tsar of Russia and son of Boris Godunov.

Fyodor Borisovich Godunov was born in 1589 and eventually became tsar. His father, Boris Godunov, was the regent of the mentally retarded Tsar Fyodor I. Fyodor Godunov's mother, Maria, was the daughter of Tsar Ivan IV's favorite, Malyuta Skuratov (the notorious boss of the *oprichnina,* the tsar's hand-picked military and administrative elite). Upon the death of the childless Tsar Fyodor I in 1598, Boris Godunov became tsar, and Fyodor Borisovich became heir to the throne. Contemporaries described young Fyodor as handsome, athletic, and kind. Like his older sister Ksenya, Fyodor was well educated and learned from his father the art of government as he grew up. Fyodor was also an avid student of cartography, and he is credited with drawing a small map of Moscow, included on a well-known Dutch map of Russia published in 1614.

In April 1605 Tsar Boris died, and Fyodor was proclaimed Tsar Fyodor II. Although well prepared to rule, the sixteen-year-old tsar was soon overwhelmed by the civil war his father had been fighting against supporters of someone claiming to be Dmitry of Uglich (the youngest son of Tsar Ivan IV). Several of Fyodor's courtiers immediately began plotting to overthrow him, but it was the rebellion of the tsar's army on May 7, 1605, that sealed the fate of the Godunov dynasty. Tsar Fyodor II was toppled in a bloodless popular uprising in Moscow on June 1, 1605. Several days later he and his mother were strangled to death, and it was falsely reported that they had committed suicide. Almost no one mourned the death of Fyodor II; Moscow was too busy celebrating the arrival of Tsar Dmitry.

See also: DMITRY OF UGLICH; FYODOR ALEXEYEVICH; GODUNOV, BORIS FYODOROVICH; IVAN IV; OPRICHNINA

BIBLIOGRAPHY

Dunning, Chester (2001). *Russia's First Civil War: The Time of Troubles and the Founding of the Romanov Dynasty.* University Park: Pennsylvania State University Press.

Skrynnikov, Ruslan (1985). "The Rebellion in Moscow and the Fall of the Godunov Dynasty." *Soviet Studies in History* 24:137–54.

CHESTER DUNNING

FYODOR IVANOVICH

(1557–1598), Tsar of Russia reigned 1584–1598.

Fyodor Ivanovich was the second son of Ivan IV ("The Terrible" or *Ivan Grozny*). Ascending the throne in 1584, three years after his father killed his older brother Ivan in a fit of rage, Fyodor Ivanovich was nevertheless too mentally deficient to govern. His brother-in-law, Boris Godunov (the brother of his wife Irene), ruled instead as regent. Fyodor did not have children and thus was the last descendant of Rurik to occupy the Russian throne.

Fyodor's father Ivan IV had the longest reign in Russian history, from 1533 to 1584, and the first half of his reign was marked by constructive achievements in both foreign and domestic policy. His defeat of the Tartars of Kazan (1552) and Astrakhan (1556) opened the way southward and eastward to Russian expansion. He also welcomed the British explorer Richard Chancellor in 1553–1554 and established commercial relations with England. By 1560 Ivan IV had established the power and legitimacy of the tsar. He authorized reforms in the army and even established a consultative body known as the *zemsky sobor* to debate issues and provide advice (although only when he solicited it).

After the death in 1560 of his first wife Anastasia—whom he suspected had been poisoned—Ivan IV became moody and violent. Withdrawing from the boyars and the church, he insisted on personal control, exercised through the establishment of the *oprichnina*—the private police force he could order to kill his personal enemies. In 1591, just seven years after he killed his oldest son, Ivan's youngest son Dmitry died under mysterious circumstances, possibly by the hand of Boris Godunov, a member of the lesser nobility who had become Ivan's protegé. In 1584 when Ivan's second son Fyodor Ivanovich became tsar, Godunov shrewdly exploited Fyodor's feeble-mindedness to assume *de facto* power as regent. When Fyodor died in 1598, the *zemsky sobor* elected Godunov as tsar.

Godunov was an effective regent and tsar. Although he did nothing to ease the burden on the peasants (issuing a decree in 1601 limiting their rights to move from one estate to another), Godunov made strides in economic development and colonization of Siberia. He also established the patriarchate in 1589. Before then the Russian church recognized the patriarch of Constantinople (now Istanbul). Under Godunov's tutelage, Russia waged successful wars against the Tatars (1591) and Sweden (1595).

Plots, intrigues, and natural disasters soon undermined Godunov's power, however. A stranger appeared, claiming to be Ivan's youngest son, Dmitry (the first of three "False Dmitrys"). A famine from 1601 to 1603 stimulated rural unrest and opposition to Godunov's rule. Godunov was killed in 1605 while suppressing a revolt during the advance on Moscow of one of the False Dmitrys. His death ushered in a "Time of Troubles" (*Smutnoye vremya*), which lasted until the establishment of the Romanov dynasty in 1613.

See also: DMITRY, FALSE; GODUNOV, BORIS FYODOROVICH; IVAN IV; TIME OF TROUBLES

BIBLIOGRAPHY

Bobrick, Benson. (1987). *Fearful Majesty: The Life and Reign of Ivan the Terrible.* New York: Putnam.

Grey, Ian. (1973). *Boris Godunov: The Tragic Tsar.* New York: Scribner.

Lamb, Harold. (1948). *The March of Muscovy: Ivan the Terrible and the Growth of the Russian Empire, 1400–1648.* Garden City, NY: Doubleday.

Yanov, Alexander. (1981). *The Origins of Autocracy: Ivan the Terrible in Russian History.* Berkeley: University of California Press.

JOHANNA GRANVILLE

FYODOROV, BORIS GRIGORIEVICH

(b. 1958), economist, deputy prime minister (1992–1993), finance minister (1990, 1993), advocate of liberal economic reform.

Boris Fyodorov, an ambitious young economist who served briefly as deputy prime minister, found a business career more fruitful than politics. Fyodorov graduated from the Moscow Institute of Finance and went on to earn candidate and doctor's degrees at Moscow State University (1985) and the USA/Canada Institute (1990). From 1980 to 1987 he worked at Gosbank, and then at the Institute of World Economy and International Relations. He was part of the team led by Grigory Yavlinsky that prepared the Five-Hundred-Day Plan in 1990. In July 1990 he became finance minister in the Russian Federation government, but resigned in December. From April 1991 to October 1992 he worked for the European Bank for Reconstruction and Development, and then spent two months as Russian director at the World Bank. In December 1992 he became deputy prime minister in Boris Yeltsin's cabinet, taking on the job of finance minister in March 1993. In December 1993 he was elected to the State Duma from a Moscow constituency as a member of Yegor Gaidar's Russia's Choice party.

Fyodorov fell out with Prime Minister Viktor Chernomyrdin in January 1994, citing frustration with weak monetary and fiscal discipline. He then formed a liberal parliamentary fraction, Union of December 12, and in 1995 created his own party, Forward Russia, which mixed advocacy of market reform with patriotic slogans, including support for the war in Chechnya. He was reelected to the Duma in December 1995, famously publishing a book of blank pages entitled "The Economic Achievements of the Chernomyrdin Government." From May to September 1998 he headed the State Tax Administration, but his political career did not progress. In subsequent years he remained a prominent advocate of further liberal reforms and a defender of minority shareholder interests. In 2000 he was elected a member of the board of Gazprom and Unified Energy Systems, the two largest companies in Russia.

See also: CHERNOMYRDIN, VIKTOR STEPANOVICH; FIVE-HUNDRED-DAY PLAN; GAIDAR, YEGOR TIMUROVICH

BIBLIOGRAPHY

Kranz, Patricia Kranz. (1998). "No Tax Man Ever Had It Tougher." *Business Week* 3585:51.

PETER RUTLAND

FYODOROV, IVAN

(c. 1510–1583), the most celebrated among printers in old Rus.

Ivan Fyoderov (also called Ivan Fyodorovich, Fyodorov syn, Moskvitin, and drukar Moskvitin) was the initiator of printing in Muscovy and Ukraine, and was a printer also in Belarus. He produced the first printed Church Slavonic Bible (the "Ostroh Bible" of 1580–1581), the first Russian (or other East Slavic) textbook (Bukvar, 1574), and the first printed Russian alphabetical subject index, calendar, and poem. He was an accomplished craftsman in numerous trades, and a man of broad vision and great persistence. Altogether, Ivan played an important role in the promotion of literacy and Eastern Orthodox confessional unity, and he introduced a high level of content, design, and craftsmanship into a critically needed profession.

Born sometime around 1510 in Muscovy, he studied at Krakow University, where he probably received training in Greek and Latin, and from which he graduated in 1532. Subsequently, he worked as deacon in the St. Nikola Gostunsky church in the Moscow Kremlin, serving from some time after 1533 until 1565. He was selected by Tzar Ivan IV "Grozny" to initiate an official printing press in Moscow where, together with his partner Petr Mstislavets, he printed books that were needed for an expanding Russian Orthodox Church. These included the first dated Russian imprint, the *Apostol* of 1563–1564, and two editions of the *Chasovnik* (*Horologion*, 1565). Several anonymous Moscow editions from the immediately preceding period (c. 1553–1563) are also generally ascribed to Ivan. His Moscow activity was cut short by what he de-

Ivan Fyodorov, the first Russian printer. Painting by Alexander Moravov. © TASS/SOVFOTO

scribes in one of his later editions as the antagonism of narrow-minded people, and he moved to Zabludovo in Belarus together with his son (also named Ivan) and Petr Mstislavets. Here he opened a new print shop under the sponsorship of Hetman G. A. Khodkevich and produced several more editions, including the *Evangelie uchitelnoe* (1569, *Instructive Evangelary*) and a psalter (1570). Advised by his aging sponsor to retire to farming on land provided him, he declined, saying he was suited to sowing not seeds but the printed word. Instead, he moved to the city of Lviv (now in Ukraine), where with his son he printed more editions, including a reprint of his Moscow *Apostol* (1573–1574), and the *Bukvar* (1574, *Primer*).

Federov subsequently established one more print shop, on the estate of Prince Kostiantyn (Constantine) of Ostroh, participating in the latter's defense of Eastern Orthodoxy against increasing pressure from Western denominations. The major publication among the several issued there was the famous Ostroh Bible, which remains of prime historical, textual, and confessional importance. The first complete printed Church Slavonic Bible, it was issued in a large print-run and widely distributed among East Slavic lands and abroad, surviving in the early twenty-first century in some 300 copies. In 1581 Ivan left Ostroh to return to Lviv, where he died on December 15, 1583. He was buried in the Onufriev Monastery; his gravestone read, in part, "printer of books not seen before." The literature devoted to Ivan Fyodorov is vast, well exceeding two thousand titles, mostly in Russian and other Slavic languages.

See also: EDUCATION; IVAN IV

BIBLIOGRAPHY

"Ivan Fedorov's Primer of 1574: Facsimile Edition," with commentary by Roman Jakobson; appendix by William A. Jackson. (1955). *Harvard Library Bulletin* IX-1:1–44.

Mathiesen, Robert. (1981). "The Making of the Ostrih Bible." *Harvard Library Bulletin* 29(1): 71–110.

Thomas, Christine. (1984). "Two East Slavonic primers: Lvov 1574 and Moscow 1637." *British Library Journal* 10(1): 60–67.

HUGH M. OLMSTED

GAGARIN, YURI ALEXEYEVICH

(1934–1968), cosmonaut; first human to orbit Earth in a spacecraft.

The son of a carpenter on a collective farm, Yury Gagarin was born in the village of Klushino, Smolensk Province. During World War II, facing the German invasion, his family evacuated to Gziatsk (now called Gagarin City). Gagarin briefly attended a trade school to learn foundry work, then entered a technical school. He joined the Saratov Flying Club in 1955 and learned to fly the Yak-18. Later that year, he was drafted and sent to the Orenburg Flying School, where he trained in the MIG jet. Gagarin graduated November 7, 1957, four days after Sputnik 2 was launched. He married Valentina Goryacheva, a nursing student, the day he graduated.

Gagarin flew for two years as a fighter pilot above the Arctic Circle. In 1958 space officials recruited air force pilots to train as cosmonauts. Gagarin applied and was selected to train in the first group of sixty men. Only twelve men were taken for further training at Zvezdograd (Star City), a training field outside Moscow. The men trained for nine months in space navigation, physiology, and astronomy, and practiced in a mockup of the spacecraft Vostok. Space officials closely observed the trainees, subjecting them to varied physical and mental stress tests. They finally selected Gagarin for the first spaceflight. Capable, strong, and even-tempered, Gagarin represented the ideal Soviet man, a peasant farmer who became a highly trained cosmonaut in a few short years. Sergei Korolev, the chief designer of spacecraft, may have consulted with Nikita Khrushchev, Russia's premier, to make the final selection.

Gagarin was launched in Vostok 1 on April 12, 1961, from the Baikonur Cosmodrome near Tyuratam, Kazakhstan. The Vostok spacecraft included a small spherical module on top of an instrument module containing the engine system, with a three-stage rocket underneath. Gagarin was strapped into an ejection seat. He did not control the spacecraft, due to uncertainty about how spaceflight would affect his physical and mental reactions. He orbited the earth a single time at an altitude of 188 miles, flying for one hour and forty-eight minutes. He then ejected from the spacecraft at an altitude of seven kilometers, parachuting into a field near Saratov. His mission proved that humans could survive in space and return safely to earth.

Cosmonaut Yuri Gagarin prepares to be the first man to orbit the Earth. © BETTMANN/CORBIS. REPRODUCED BY PERMISSION.

Gagarin was sent on a world tour to represent the strength of Soviet technology. A member of the Communist Party since 1960, he was appointed a deputy of the Supreme Soviet and named a Hero of the Soviet Union. He became the commander of the cosmonaut corps and began coursework at the Zhukovsky Institute of Aeronautical Engineering. An active young man, Gagarin often felt frustrated in his new life as an essentially ceremonial figure. There were many reports of Gagarin's resulting depression and hard drinking. In 1967, however, he decided to train as a backup cosmonaut in anticipation of a lunar landing.

On March 27, 1968, Gagarin conducted a test flight with a senior flight instructor near Moscow. The plane crashed, killing both men instantly. Gagarin's tragic death shocked the public in the USSR and abroad. A special investigation was conducted amid rumors that Gagarin's drinking caused the crash. Since then, investigators have indicated other possible causes, such as poor organization and faulty equipment at ground level.

Gagarin received a state funeral and was buried in the Kremlin Wall. American astronauts Neil Armstrong and Edwin Aldrin left one of Gagarin's medals on the moon as a tribute. The cosmonaut training center where he had first trained was named after him. A crater on the moon bears his name, as does Gagarin Square in Moscow with its soaring monument, along with a number of monuments and streets in cities throughout Russia. At Baikonur, a reproduction of his training room is traditionally visited by space crews before a launch. Russians celebrate Cosmonaut Day on April 12 every year in honor of Gagarin's historic flight.

See also: SPACE PROGRAM

BIBLIOGRAPHY

Gagarin, Yuri. (1962). *Road to the Stars,* told to Nikolay Denisov and Serhy Borzenko, ed. N. Kamanin, tr. G. Hanna and D. Myshnei. Moscow: Foreign Languages Publishing House.

Gurney, Clare, and Gurney, Gene. (1972). *Cosmonauts in Orbit: The Story of the Soviet Manned Space Program.* New York: Franklin Watts.

Johnson, Nicholas L. (1980). *Handbook of Soviet Manned Space Flight.* San Diego, CA: Univelt.

Riabchikov, Evgeny. (1971). *Russians in Space,* tr. Guy Daniels. New York: Doubleday.

Shelton, William. (1969). *Soviet Space Exploration: The First Decade,* intro. by Gherman Titov. London: Barker.

PHYLLIS CONN

GAGAUZ

More than ten hypotheses exist about the origins of the Gagauz, although none of them has been proven decisively. In Bulgarian and Greek scholarship, the Gagauz are considered, respectively, to be Bulgarians or Greeks who adopted the Turkish language. The Seljuk theory is popular in Turkey. It argues that the Gagauz are the heirs of the Seljuk Turks who in the thirteenth century resettled in Dobrudja under the leadership of Sultan Izeddina Keikavus, and together with the Turkish-speaking Polovetsians of the southern Russian steppes (Kipchaks in Arabic, Kumans in European historiography) established the Oghuz state (Uzieialet).

In Russia scholars believe that the base of the Gagauz was laid by Turkish-speaking nomads

(Oghuz, Pechenegs, and Polovetsians) who settled in the Balkan Peninsula from Russia in the twelfth and thirteenth centuries, and there turned from nomadism into a settled population and adopted Christianity.

During the Russian-Turkish wars at the end of the eighteenth and beginning of the nineteenth centuries, the Gagauz resettled in the Bujak Steppe of southern Bessarabia, which had been emptied of the Nogai and annexed by the Russian Empire. From 1861 to 1862 a group of Gagauz settled in the Tauride province, a region that is today part of Ukraine. During the Stolypin agrarian reforms of 1906 to 1911, some of the Gagauz resettled in Kazakhstan, and in the 1930s, in protest against the collectivization imposed by Josef Stalin, they moved to Uzbekistan. There they stayed until the end of the 1980s under the name of Bulgars. At the end of the 1920s a few dozen families, in order to save themselves from the discriminatory policies of rumanization, migrated to Brazil and Canada.

The short-lived migration of some families to southern Moldavia, at the time of the Khrushchev Thaw at the end of the 1950s, was unsuccessful. According to the census of 1989, there were 198,000 Gagauz in the former Soviet Union, of whom 153,000 lived in Moldavia, 32,000 in Ukraine, and 10,000 in the Russian Federation. One-third of the Gagauz lived in cities.

Those Gagauz who are religious are Orthodox. The Gagauz language belongs to the southwestern (Oghuz) subgroup of the Turkish group of the Altaic language family. At the beginning of the nineteenth century, folklore texts were published in the Gagauz language, using the Cyrillic alphabet. In 1957 a literary language was established on the basis of the Russian alphabet. On January 26, 1996, by order of the People's Assembly of Gagauzia, writing switched to the Latin alphabet. The official languages in Gagauzia are Moldavian, Gagauz, and Russian.

The majority of the Gagauz are bilingual. In 1959, 94.3 percent of Gagauz spoke the language of their nationality; in 1989, 87.4 percent. The Gagauz speak fluent Russian. In 2000 the Gagauz language was taught in forty-nine schools, in Komrat State University, and in teachers' colleges and high schools.

The contemporary culture of the Gagauz is represented by the State Dramatic Theater (in the city of Chadyr-Lunga), the Kadynzha Ensemble, and musical and folklore groups.

On January 24, 1994, the parliament of the Republic of Moldova passed the law On the Special Legal Status of Gagauzia (*Gagauz Eri*), which established the autonomous region of Gagauzia. This new form of self-determination for the Gagauz was based on the two principles of ethnicity and territory and won great approval in Europe.

At the turn of the twentieth century cattle-raising and livestock husbandry dominated, this has been replaced by agriculture, viniculture, tobacco farming, and industrial production.

See also: MOLDOVA AND MOLDOVANS; NATIONALITIES POLICIES, SOVIET; NATIONALITIES POLICIES, TSARIST

MIKHAIL GUBOGLO

GAIDAR, YEGOR TIMUROVICH

(b. 1956), economist, prime minister.

The public face of shock therapy, Yegor Timurovich Gaidar was a soft-spoken economist who, at the age of thirty-six, became prime minister in the turbulent first year of Boris Yeltsin's administration. He came from a prominent family: his father was *Pravda*'s military correspondent, and his grandfather a war hero and author beloved by generations of Soviet children. Gaidar graduated from Moscow State University in 1980 with a thesis on the price mechanism, supervised by reform economist Stanislav Shatalin. He then worked as a researcher at the Academy of Sciences Institute of Systems Analysis. In 1983 he joined a commission on economic reform that advised General Secretary Yuri Andropov. In 1986, he formed an informal group, Economists for Reform, and from 1987 to 1990 he was an editor at the Communist Party journal *Kommunism*, under the reformist editor Otto Latsis. In 1990, he became a department head at *Pravda* and headed a new Institute of Economic Policy. Gaidar walked into the White House during the August coup and offered his services to Yeltsin aide Gennady Burbulis. With the support of the young democratic activists, Gaidar became a key player in Yeltsin's team, drafting his economic program and even the Belovezh accords, which broke up the Soviet Union. He later described himself as on a kamikaze mission to turn Russia into a market economy. As deputy prime minister (with Yeltsin serving as prime minister) and minister of finance and economics from November 1991, Gaidar oversaw the introduction of price liberal-

Yegor Gaidar directed Russia's 1992 shock-therapy program.
© KEERLE GEORGES DE/CORBIS SYGMA

ization in January 1992. Russia experienced a burst of hyper-inflation, but formerly empty store shelves filled with goods. Communist and nationalist opposition leaders unfairly blamed the collapsing economy on Yeltsin's policies and Gaidar's ideas. Gaidar was appointed acting prime minister in June 1992, but the Congress of People's Deputies refused to approve his appointment in December. He left the government, returning as economics minister and first deputy prime minister in September 1993, in the midst of Yeltsin's confrontation with the parliament. At one point in the crisis Gaidar appealed to people over television to take to the streets to defend the government. Gaidar took part in the creation of a liberal, progovernment electoral bloc, Russia's Choice, but it lost to red-brown forces in the December 1993 parliamentary elections, winning just 15.5 percent of the party list vote. Gaidar left the government in January 1994, although he stayed on as leader of Russia's Choice in Parliament. At the same time, Gaidar became head of his own think tank, the Institute of Transition Economies. In the December 1995 elections he led the renamed Russia's Democratic Choice, which failed to clear the five percent threshold. He spoke out against the war in Chechnya, but supported Yeltsin in the 1996 election. During the later 1990s Gaidar served more as an author and commentator than as a front-rank politician. He defended his record, advocated more liberal reform, and pursued business and academic interests. He was again elected to the Duma in December 1999 as head of the Union of Right Forces, an umbrella group uniting most of the fractured liberal leaders. The bloc went on to offer conditional support to President Vladimir Putin.

See also: GORBACHEV, MIKHAIL SERGEYEVICH; PERESTROIKA; PRIME MINISTER; PRIVATIZATION; SHOCK THERAPY; YELTSIN, BORIS NIKOLAYEVICH

BIBLIOGRAPHY

Gaidar, Yegor. (2000). *Days of Defeat and Victory.* Seattle, WA: University of Washington Press.

PETER RUTLAND

GAMSAKHURDIA, ZVIAD

(1931–1999), human rights activist and writer.

Born the son of Konstantin Gamsakhurdia, a famous Georgian writer and patriot, Zviad Gamsakhurdia became a leading Georgian dissident and human rights activist in the Soviet Union. In 1974, along with a number of fellow Georgian dissidents, he formed the Initiative Group for the Defense of Human Rights and in 1976, the Georgian Helsinki Group (later renamed the Helsinki Union). Active in the Georgian Orthodox church, during the 1970s he wrote and published a number of illegal *samizdat* (self-published) journals. The best-known were *The Golden Fleece* (*Okros sats'misi*) and *The Georgian Messenger* (*Sakartvelos moambe*). Arrested in 1977 for the second time (he was first imprisoned in 1957), after a public confession he was released in 1979 and resumed his dissident activities. After the arrival of *perestroika,* he participated in the founding of one of the first Georgian informal organizations in 1988, the Ilya Chavchavadze the Righteous Society. An active leader in major demonstrations and protests in 1988–1989, he became the most popular anticommunist national figure in Georgia and swept to power in October 1990 as leader of a coalition of nationalist parties called the Round Table-Free Georgia Bloc. Elected Chairman of the Georgian Supreme Soviet, after amendments to the constitution, he was elected the first president of the Georgian Republic in May 1991.

His period in office was brief and unsuccessful. Unable to make the transition from dissident activist to political mediator and statesman, his increasing authoritarianism alienated almost every interest group in Georgian society. A coalition of paramilitary groups, his own government's National Guard, intellectuals, and students joined to overthrow him in a fierce battle in the city center in January 1992. He made his base in neighboring Chechnya and in 1993 attempted to reestablish his power in Georgia, leading the country into civil war. Quickly defeated after his forces captured a number of major towns in west Georgia, he was killed, or committed suicide in December 1993 in the Zugdidi region, Georgia.

See also: GEORGIA AND GEORGIANS; NATIONALISM IN THE SOVIET UNION; PERESTROIKA

STEPHEN JONES

GAPON, GEORGY APOLLONOVICH

(1870–1906), Russian Orthodox priest led a peaceful demonstration of workers to the Winter Palace on Bloody Sunday, 1905; the event began the 1905 revolution.

Father Georgy Apollonovich Gapon was a Ukrainian priest who became involved with missionary activity among the homeless in St. Petersburg, where he was a student at the St. Petersburg Theological Academy. His work attracted the attention of police authorities, and when Sergei Zubatov began organizing workers in police-sponsored labor groups, Gapon was brought to his attention. Zubatov's efforts in Moscow ran into the opposition of industrialists who objected to police interference in business matters. In St. Petersburg Zubatov tried to tone down police involvement by recruiting clergy to provide direction to his workers. Gapon was reluctant to become involved, sensing opposition to Zubatov among the officials and the distrust of workers, but he began attending meetings and established contacts with the more influential workers. He also argued with Zubatov that workers should be allowed to decide for themselves what was good for them.

During the summer of 1903, Zubatov was dismissed and given twenty-four hours to leave the city. In this manner Gapon inherited an organization created and patronized by the police. On the surface Gapon seemed to justify the trust of the authorities. A clubroom was opened where meetings began with prayers and the national anthem. Portraits of the tsars hung on the wall. Ostensibly there were no reasons for the authorities to be concerned about the Assembly, as the organization was named, but beneath the surface, Gapon's ambitious plans began to unfold. Gathering a small group of the more active workers, he unveiled to them his "secret program," which advocated the winning of labor concessions through the strength of organized labor. His advocacy of trade unionism met with the enthusiastic support of the conferees, and he gained loyal supporters who would provide the leadership of the Assembly.

During the turbulent year of 1904, the Assembly grew rapidly. By the end of the year it had opened eleven branches. However, its rapid growth was causing concern among the factory owners, who feared the growing militancy of the workers and resented police interference on their behalf. Shortly before Christmas, four workers, all active members of the Assembly, were fired at the giant Putilov Works. Rumors spread that all members of the Assembly would be fired. When Gapon and police authorities tried to intercede, they were told that labor organizations were illegal and that the Assembly had no right to speak for its members. Faced with a question of survival, Gapon called a large meeting of his followers, at which it was decided to strike the Putilov Works—a desperate measure, since strikes were illegal.

The strike began on January 16, and by January 17 the entire working force in the capital had joined the strike. Branches turned into perpetual gatherings and rallies of workers. At one of the meetings, Gapon threw out an idea of a peaceful mass demonstration to present a workers' petition to the tsar himself. The idea caught on like fire. Gapon began preparing the petition. It essentially contained the more specific demands of his secret program and a vague compilation of the most popular demands of the opposition groups. Copies of the petition, "Most Humble and Loyal Address to be presented to the Tsar at 2 P.M. on the Winter Palace Square," were sent to various officials.

Meanwhile the march was prohibited, and reinforcements were brought to St. Petersburg. Police tried to arrest Gapon, but he could not be found. By then the workers were too agitated to abandon their hope to see the tsar; moreover, they did not think soldiers would fire on a peaceful procession that in some places was presented as a religious procession. But the soldiers opened fire in several locations, resulting in more than 130 casualties.

These events, known as Bloody Sunday, began the revolution of 1905.

Gapon called for a revolution, then escaped abroad. Becoming disillusioned with the revolutionary parties, he attempted to reconcile with the post-1905 regime of Sergei Witte. Upon his return to St. Petersburg, he tried to revive his organization but was killed by a terrorist squad acting on the orders of the notorious double agent, Evno Azef. To explain Gapon's murder, the perpetrators concocted a story of a workers' trial and execution.

See also: BLOODY SUNDAY; REVOLUTION OF 1905; RUSSIAN ORTHODOX CHURCH; ZUBATOV, SERGEI VASILIEVICH

BIBLIOGRAPHY

Ascher, Abraham. (1988). "Gapon and Bloody Sunday." *Revolution of 1905*, vol. 1. Stanford, CA: Stanford University Press.

Gapon, Georgy A. (1905). *The Story of My Life.* London: Chapman & Hall.

Sablinsky, Walter. (1976). *The Road to Bloody Sunday: Father Gapon and the St. Petersburg Massacre of 1905.* Princeton, NJ: Princeton University Press.

WALTER SABLINSKY

GASPIRALI, ISMAIL BEY

(1851–1914), Crimean Tatar intellectual, social reformer, publisher, and key figure in the emergence of the modernist, or jadid, movement among Russian Turkic peoples.

Ismail Bey Gaspirali was born March 8, 1851, in the Crimean village of Avci, but he spent most of his first decade in Bakhchisarai, the nearby town to which his family had moved during the Crimean War (1853–1856). Reared in the Islamic faith, his education began with tutoring in Arabic recitation by a local Muslim teacher (*hoca*), but then continued in the Russian-administered Simferopol gymnasium and Russian military academies in Voronezh and Moscow. In 1872 he embarked on a foreign tour that took him through Austria and Germany to France, where he remained for two years. A year followed in Istanbul, capital of the Ottoman Empire, before Gaspirali returned home during the winter of 1875. His observations abroad became the basis for one of his earliest and most important essays, *A Critical Look at European Civilization* (*Avrupa Medeniyetine bir Nazar-i Muvazene*, 1885), and inspired the urban improvement projects during the four years (1878–1882) that he served as mayor of Bakhchisarai.

By then, the importance of education and the modern press had become for Gaspirali the keys to improving the quality of life for Crimean Tatars and other Turkic peoples, who were mostly adherents of Islam. Nineteenth-century European military might, economic development, scientific advances, increased social mobility, political experimentation, and global expansion impressed upon him the need for reconsideration of Turkic cultural norms, perspectives, and aspirations. The narrow focus of education, inspired by centuries of Islamic pedagogy whose purpose was the provision of sufficient literacy in Arabic for reading and reciting the *Qur'an*, struck Gaspirali as unsuited for the challenges of modern life as defined by European experience. A new teaching method (*usul-i jadid*), emphasizing literacy in the child's native language, and a reformed curriculum that included study of mathematics, natural sciences, geography, history, and the Russian language, should be instituted in new-style primary schools where children would be educated in preparation for enrolling in more advanced, modern, and Russian-supported institutions. The survival of non-European societies such as his own, many already the victims of European hegemony and their own adherence to time-honored practices, depended upon a willingness to accept change and new information, open up public opportunities for women, mobilize resources and talents, and become involved with worldly affairs.

The medium by which Gaspirali propagandized his new method, both as pedagogue and social transformer, was the modern press. Beginning in April 1883, he published a dual-language newspaper in both Turkic and Russian entitled *The Interpreter* (*Tercüman* in Turkic, *Perevodchik* in Russian). It appeared without interruption until early 1918, becoming the longest surviving and most influential Turkic periodical within the Russian Empire. In later years, Gaspirali published other newspapers—*The World of Women* (*Alem-i Nisvan*), *The World of Children* (*Alem-i Sibyan*), and *Ha, Ha, Ha!* (*Kha, Kha, Kha!*), a satirical review—and numerous essays and didactic manuals on subjects ranging from Turkic relations with Russia to pedagogy, geography, hygiene, history, and literature.

Gaspirali's espousal of substantive social change raised opposition from both Russian and Turkic sources, but his moderate and reasoned tone won him important allies within local and national official circles, allowing him to continue his work with little interference. The intensification of ethnic controversy by the early twentieth century, however, increasingly marginalized him in relation to advocates of more strident nationalist sentiments and the politicization of Russian-Turkic relations. He died September 11, 1914 after a long illness.

See also: CRIMEAN TATARS; ISLAM; JADIDISM

BIBLIOGRAPHY

Fisher, Alan W. (1988). "Ismail Gaspirali, Model Leader for Asia." In *Tatars of the Crimea: Their Struggle for Survival*, ed. Edward Allworth. Durham: Duke University Press.

Kuttner, Thomas. (1975). "Russian Jadidism and the Islamic World: Ismail Gasprinskii in Cairo—1908. A Call to the Arabs for the Rejuvenation of the Islamic World." *Cahiers du monde russe et soviétique* 16:383–424.

Lazzerini, Edward J. (1988). "Ismail Bey Gasprinskii, the Discourse of Modernism, and the Russians." In *Tatars of the Crimea: Their Struggle for Survival*, ed. by Edward Allworth. Durham: Duke University Press.

Lazzerini, Edward J. (1992). "Ismail Bey Gasprinskii's *Perevodchik/Tercüman:* A Clarion of Modernism." In *Central Asian Monuments*, ed. by H.B. Paksoy. Istanbul: Isis Press.

EDWARD J. LAZZERINI

GATCHINA

One of the great imperial country palaces to the south of St. Petersburg, Gatchina was located near the site of a village known since 1499 as Khotchino. In 1708 Peter I granted the land to his beloved sister Natalia Alexeyevna, after whose death in 1717 the property belonged to a series of favored court servitors. In 1765 Catherine II purchased the estate from the family of Prince Alexander Kurakin and presented it to Grigory Orlov. She commissioned the Italian architect Antonio Rinaldi to design for Orlov a lavish palace-castle in a severe and monumental neoclassical style. Rinaldi, who had worked with the Neapolitan court architect Luigi Vanvitelli, created not only a grandiose palace ensemble but also a refined park.

The palace, begun in 1766 but not completed until 1781, was conceived as a three-story block with square, one-story service wings—designated the Kitchen and Stables—attached to either side of the main structure by curved colonnades. In order to project the appearance of a fortified castle, Rinaldi departed from the usual practice of stuccoed brick and surfaced the building in a type of limestone found along the banks of the nearby Pudost River. The flanking towers of the main palace and its restrained architectural detail further convey the appearance of a forbidding structure. On the interior, however, the palace contained a display of luxurious furnishings and decorative details, including lavish plaster work and superb parquetry designed by Rinaldi. Rinaldi also contributed to the development of the Gatchina park with an obelisk celebrating the victory of the Russian fleet at Chesme. The exact date of the obelisk is unknown, but presumably it was commissioned by Orlov no later than the mid-1770s in honor of his brother Alexei Orlov, general commander of the Russian forces at Chesme.

Following the death of Orlov in 1783, Catherine bought the estate and presented it to her son and heir to the throne, Paul. He in turn commissioned another Italian architect, Vincenzo Brenna, to expand the flanking wings of the palace. Brenna, with the participation of the brilliant young Russian architect Adrian Zakharov, added another floor to the service wings and enclosed the second level of a colonnade that connected them to the main palace. Unfortunately, these changes lessened the magisterial Roman quality of the main palace structure. Brenna also modified and redecorated a number of the main rooms, although he continued the stylistic patterns created by Rinaldi.

Grand Duke Paul was particularly fond of the Gatchina estate, whose castle allowed him to indulge his zeal for a military order based, so he thought, on Prussian traditions. The palace became notorious for military drills on the parade grounds in front of its grand facade. With the accession of Paul to the throne after the death of Catherine (November 1796), the Gatchina regime extended throughout much of Russia, with tragic results not only for the emperor's victims but also for Paul himself. After his assassination, in 1801, the palace reverted to the crown.

Among the many pavilions of the Gatchina park, the most distinctive is the Priory, the product of another of emperor Paul's fantasies. After their expulsion from the island of Malta, Paul extended to the Maltese Order protection and refuge, including the design of a small pseudo-medieval palace known as the Priory, intended for the prior of this monastic military order. In his construction of the Priory, the architect Nikolai Lvov made innovative use of pressed earth panels, a technique that Paul had observed during a trip to France. The relatively isolated location of the Priory made it a place of refuge in 1881–1883 for the new emperor, Alexander III, concerned about security in the wake of his father's assassination.

For most of the nineteenth century the palace drifted into obscurity, although it was renovated from 1845 to 1852 by Roman Kuzmin. After the building of a railway through Gatchina in 1853, the town, like nearby Pavlovsk, witnessed the development of dacha communities. Gatchina briefly returned to prominence following the Bolshevik coup on November 7, 1917. The deposed head of the Provisional Government, Alexander Kerensky, attempted to stage a return from Gatchina, but by November 14 these efforts had been thwarted. In the fall of 1919 the army of General Nikolai Yudenich also occupied Gatchina for a few weeks before the collapse of his offensive on Petrograd.

After the Civil War, the palace was nationalized as a museum, and in 1923 the town's name was changed to Trotsk. Following Trotsky's fall from power, the name was changed again, in 1929, to Krasnogvardeysk. With the liberation of the town from German occupation in January 1944, the imperial name was restored. Notwithstanding the efforts of museum workers to evacuate artistic treasures, the palace ensemble and park suffered catastrophic damage between September 1941 and 1944. Major restoration work did not begin until the 1970s, and in 1985 the first rooms of the palace museum were reopened.

See also: ARCHITECTURE

BIBLIOGRAPHY

Brumfield, William Craft. (1993). *A History of Russian Architecture.* New York: Cambridge University Press.

Orloff, Alexander, and Shvidovsky, Dmitri. (1996). *St. Petersburg: Architecture of the Tsars.* New York: Abbeville Press.

WILLIAM CRAFT BRUMFIELD

GENERAL SECRETARY

Top position in the Communist Party

Prior to the revolution, Vladimir I. Lenin, the head of the Bolshevik faction, had a secretary, Elena Stasova. After the Bolsheviks came to power in 1917, Lenin gave the position of secretary in the ruling Communist Party of Russia to Yakov Sverdlov, a man with a phenomenal memory. After Sverdlov's death in 1919, three people shared the position of secretary. In 1922, in recognition of the expanding party organization and the complexity of the newly formed USSR, a general secretary was appointed. Josef Stalin, who had several other administrative assignments, became general secretary, and used it to build a power base within the party. Lenin, before his death, realized Stalin had become too powerful and issued a warning in his Last Testament that Stalin be removed. However, skillful use of the patronage powers of the general secretary solidified Stalin's position. After Stalin's death in 1953, the position was renamed first secretary of the Communist Party (CPSU) in an attempt to reduce its significance. Nonetheless, Nikita S. Khrushchev (1953–1964) succeeded in using the position of first secretary to become the single most powerful leader in the USSR. Khrushchev's successor, Leonid I. Brezhnev (1964–1982) restored the title of general secretary and emerged as the most important political figure in the post-Khrushchev era. Mikhail S. Gorbachev, working as unofficial second secretary under general secretaries Yuri V. Andropov (1982–84) and Konstantin U. Chernenko (1984–85), solidified his position as their successor in 1985. Gorbachev subsequently reorganized the presidency in 1988–89, and transferred his attention to that post. After the 1991 coup, Gorbachev resigned as general secretary, one of several steps signaling the end of the CPSU.

The position of general secretary was the most influential role in leadership for most of the Soviet period. Its role was closely associated with the rise of Stalin and the end of the position was also a signal of the end of the Soviet system.

See also: COMMUNIST PARTY OF THE SOVIET UNION; SUCCESSION OF LEADERSHIP, SOVIET

BIBLIOGRAPHY

Hough, Jerry F. and Fainsod, Merle. (1979). *How the Soviet Union Is Governed.* Cambridge, MA: Harvard University Press.

Smith, Gordon B. (1988). *Soviet Politics: Continuity and Contradiction.* New York: St. Martin's Press.

NORMA C. NOONAN

GENETICISTS

Adherents of a prescriptive theoretical model for economic development planning in a controversy of the 1920s.

The geneticists participated in an important theoretical controversy with the teleologists over the nature and potential limits to economic planning. The issue was fundamental and cut to the heart of the very possibility of central planning. Would a central planning agency be constrained by economic laws, such as supply and demand, or by other fixed economic regularities, such as sector proportions, or could planners operate to shape the economic future according to their own preferences?

The geneticists argued that it was necessary to base economic plans on careful study of economic laws and historical determinants of economic activity. The past and certain general laws constrained any plan outcome. In this view, planning was essentially a form of forecasting. The teleologists argued on the contrary that planners should set their objectives independently of such constraints, that planning could seek to override market forces to achieve maximum results focused on decisive development variables, such as investment. Proponents of the geneticist view included Nikolai Kondratiev and Vladimir Groman and were well disposed to the New Economic Policy (NEP) of the 1920s. The teleologists included Stanislav Strumilin and Pavel Feldman who were less well disposed toward the NEP and believed it would be possible to force economic development through binding industrial and enterprising targets.

The argument became quite heated and oversimplified. The degree of freedom of action that the geneticists allowed planners was miniscule, and it appeared that planning would involve little more than filling in plan output cells based almost entirely on historical carryover variables. The teleologists claimed a degree of latitude to planners that was almost total. In the end the geneticists lost, and Soviet planning followed the teleologists' approach: it consisted of a set of comprehensive targets designed to force both the pace and the character of development. Soviet experience over the long run, however, suggests that the geneticists were closer to the mark concerning constraints on development.

See also: ECONOMIC GROWTH, SOVIET; KONDRATIEV, NIKOLAI DMITRIEVICH; NEW ECONOMIC POLICY; TELEOLOGICAL PLANNING

BIBLIOGRAPHY

Gregory, Paul R., and Stuart, Robert C. (1990). *Soviet Economic Structure and Performance*, 4th ed. New York: HarperCollins.

Millar, James R. (1981). *The ABCs of Soviet Socialism.* Urbana: University of Illinois Press.

JAMES R. MILLAR

GENEVA SUMMIT OF 1985

A summit meeting of U.S. president Ronald Reagan and Soviet leader Mikhail Gorbachev took place in Geneva, Switzerland, on November 19–20, 1985. It was the first summit meeting of the two men, and indeed of any American and Soviet leaders in six years. Relations between the two countries had become much more tense after the Soviet military intervention in Afghanistan at the end of 1979, and the election a year later of an American president critical of the previous era of détente and disposed to mount a sharp challenge, even a crusade, against the leaders of an evil empire. However, by 1985 President Reagan was ready to meet with a new Soviet leader and test the possibility of relaxing tensions.

Although the Geneva Summit did not lead to any formal agreements, it represented a successful engagement of the two leaders in a renewed dialogue, and marked the first step toward several later summit meetings and a gradual significant change in the relationship of the two countries. Both Reagan and Gorbachev placed a high premium on direct personal encounter and evaluation, and they developed a mutual confidence that helped steer national policies.

Gorbachev argued strongly at Geneva for a reconsideration of Reagan's Strategic Defense Initiative (SDI, or Star Wars), but to no avail. He did, however, obtain agreement to a joint statement that the two countries would "not seek to achieve military superiority" (as well as reaffirmation that "a nuclear war cannot be won and must never be fought"). This joint statement was given some prominence in Soviet evaluations of the summit, and was used by Gorbachev in his redefinition of Soviet security requirements. Although disappointed at Reagan's unyielding stance on SDI, Gorbachev had come to realize that it represented a personal moral commitment by Reagan and was not simply a scheme of the American military-industrial complex.

The Geneva summit not only established a personal bond between Reagan and Gorbachev, but for the first time involved Reagan fully in the execution of a strategy for diplomatic reengagement with the Soviet Union, a strategy that Secretary of State George Schultz had been advocating since 1983 despite the opposition of a number of members of the administration. For Gorbachev, the summit signified recognition by the leader of the other superpower. Although it was too early to predict the consequences, in retrospect it became clear that the renewed dialogue at the highest level would in time lead to extraordinary changes, ultimately contributing to the end of the Cold War.

See also: COLD WAR; STRATEGIC DEFENSE INITIATIVE; UNITED STATES, RELATIONS WITH

BIBLIOGRAPHY

Garthoff, Raymond L. (1994). *The Great Transition: American-Soviet Relations and the End of the Cold War.* Washington, DC: The Brookings Institution.

Shultz, George P. (1993). *Turmoil and Triumph: My Years as Secretary of State.* New York: Charles Scribner's Sons.

RAYMOND L. GARTHOFF

GENOA CONFERENCE

The Genoa Conference, convened in April and May 1922, was an international diplomatic meeting of twenty-nine states, including Britain, France, Italy, Germany, Russia, and Japan, but not the United States. It was summoned to resolve several problems in the postwar restructuring of Europe, including the desire to reintegrate Soviet Russia and Weimar Germany into the political and economic life of Europe on terms favorable to the dominant Anglo-French alliance. The Allies wanted Moscow to repay foreign debts incurred by previous Russian governments, compensate foreign owners of property nationalized by the Bolsheviks, and guarantee that revolutionary propaganda would cease throughout their empires.

The invitation for Soviet participation in the conference facilitated Moscow's drive for peaceful coexistence with the West and for the substantial foreign trade, technology, loans, and investment required by the New Economic Policy. Both sides failed to achieve their objectives. The Anglo-French side pressed for the broadest possible repayment of Russian obligations, but offered little in loans and trade credits. The Soviets pushed for as much Western financed trade and technological assistance as possible, but conditioned limited debt repayment on the recovery of the Soviet economy. Moreover, Foreign Commissar Georgy Chicherin angered the Western representatives by calling for comprehensive disarmament and representation for the colonial peoples in the British and French empires. The impasse between Russia and the West, combined with a similar stalemate between the Anglo-French side and Germany, caused Berlin and Moscow to conclude a political and economic pact, the Rapallo Treaty. Thus, the Genoa Conference ended in failure, though the USSR succeeded in gaining recognition as an integral part of European diplomacy and in bolstering its relationship with Germany.

See also: WORLD WAR I

BIBLIOGRAPHY

Fink, Carole. (1984). *The Genoa Conference: European Diplomacy, 1921–1922.* Chapel Hill: University of North Carolina Press.

White, Stephen. (1985). *The Origins of Detente: The Genoa Conference and Soviet-Western Relations, 1921–1922.* Cambridge, UK: Cambridge University Press.

TEDDY J. ULDRICKS

GENOCIDE

Genocide is a word coined after World War II to designate a phenomenon that was not new—the extermination, usually by a government, of a group of people for their ethnic, religious, racial, or political belonging. The term implies both a deliberate intent as well as a systematic approach in its implementation. Until international law came to terms with the Holocaust of the Jewish people in Europe, the extermination of such groups was considered as a crime against humanity or as a war crime, since wars tended to provide governments the opportunity to execute their designs. In a resolution adopted in 1946, the U.N. General Assembly declared genocide a crime under international law—its perpetrators to be held accountable for their actions. Two years later, with the full support of the USSR, the same body approved the Convention on the Prevention and Punishment of the Crime of Genocide that went into effect soon after.

Article II of the Convention defines genocide as "any of the following acts committed with intent to destroy, in whole or in part, a national, ethnical, racial, or religious group, as such: a) killing members of the group; b) causing serious bodily or mental harm to members of the group; c) deliberately inflicting on the group conditions of life calculated to bring about its physical destruction in whole or in part; d) imposing measures intended to prevent births within the group; and e) forcibly transferring children of the group to another." Article III of the Convention stipulated that those who commit such acts as well as those who support or incite them are to be punished. The Convention provided for an International Court of Justice to try cases of genocide. The Tribunal was established only in 2002. Meanwhile, the genocide of Ibos in Nigeria during the 1970s was not considered by any court; those responsible for the Cambodian genocide during the 1980s were tried by a domestic court some years later; the genocide during the mid 1990s of the Tutsis by the Hutus in Rwanda was finally considered by an international court in Tanzania, while an international tribunal in The Hague undertook a review of charges of genocide against Serb, Croat, and other leaders responsible for crimes during the Balkan crisis following the collapse of Yugoslavia during the early 1990s.

Two well-known cases of genocide have affected Russia and the Soviet Union. The Young Turk Government of the Ottoman Empire implemented a deliberate and systematic deportation and extermination of its Armenian population during World War I in the Western part of historic Armenia under its domination. Eastern Armenia had been integrated into the Russian Empire by 1828. Russia, along with other European powers, had pressed Ottoman governments to introduce reforms in Ottoman Armenia and Russian Armenians were involved in the efforts to produce change. Close to one million Armenians perished as a result. The Russian army, already at war with the Ottomans, was instrumental in saving the population of some cities near its border, assisted by a Russian Armenian Volunteer Corps. Many of the survivors of the Genocide ended up in Russian Armenia and southern Russia. Others emigrated after 1920 to Soviet Armenia, mainly from the Middle East during the years following World War II. A few of the Young Turk leaders responsible for the Armenian genocide were tried by a Turkish court following their defeat in the war and condemned, largely in absentia, but the trials were halted due to changes in the domestic and international environment.

During World War II Nazi advances into Soviet territory provided an opportunity to German forces to extend the policy of extermination of Jews into those territories. Nazi leaders responsible for the Holocaust were tried and condemned to various sentences at Nuremberg, Germany, following the war.

Russian and Soviet governments have tolerated or implemented policies that, while not necessarily qualified as genocides, raise questions relevant to the subject. Pogroms against Russian Jews during the last decades of the Romanov Empire and the deportation of the Tatars from Crimea, Chechens and other peoples from their Autonomous Republics within Russia, and Mtskhetan Turks from Georgia during and immediately following World War II on suspicion of collaboration with the Germans reflect a propensity on the part of Russia and Soviet governments to resolve perceived political problems through punishment of whole groups. Equally important, the politically motivated purges engineered by Josef Stalin and his collaborators of the Communist Party and Soviet government officials and their families and various punitive actions against whole populations claimed the lives of millions of citizens between 1929 and 1939.

In one case, Soviet policy has been designated as genocidal by some specialists. As a result of the forced collectivization of farms during the early 1930s, Ukraine suffered a famine, exacerbated by a severe drought, which claimed as many as five million lives. The Soviet government's refusal to recognize the scope of the disaster and provide relief is seen as a deliberate policy of extermination.

See also: NATIONALITIES POLICIES, SOVIET; NATIONALITIES POLICIES, TSARIST; WORLD WAR II.

BIBLIOGRAPHY

Courtois, Stéphane. (1999). *The Black Book of Communism: Crimes, Terror, Repression*, tr. Jonathan Murphy and Mark Kramer. Cambridge, MA: Harvard University Press.

Fein, Helen. (1979). *Accounting for Genocide: National Responses and Jewish Victimization during the Holocaust.* New York: The Free Press.

Walliman, Isidor, and Dobkowski, Michael N., eds. (1987). *Genocide and the Modern Age: Etiology and Case Studies of Mass Death.* New York: Greenwood Press.

Weiner, Amir. (2000). *Making Sense of War: The Second World War and the Fate of the Bolshevik Revolution.* Princeton, NJ: Princeton University Press.

GERARD J. LIBARIDIAN

GEOGRAPHY

Russia is the world's largest country, 1.7 times larger than second-place Canada, ten times larger than Alaska, and twenty-five times larger than Texas. It stretches from 19° E Longitude in the west to 169° W Longitude in the east, spanning 5,700 miles (9,180 kilometers) and eleven time zones. If Russia were superimposed on North America with St. Petersburg in Anchorage, Alaska, the Chukchi Peninsula would touch Oslo, Norway, halfway around the globe. Thus, when Russians are eating supper on any given day in St. Petersburg, the Chukchi are breakfasting on the next. From its southernmost point (42° N) to its northernmost islands (82° N), the width of Russia exceeds the length of the contiguous United States.

Russia's size guarantees a generous endowment of natural features and raw materials. The country contains the world's broadest lowlands, swamps, grasslands, and forests. In the Greater Caucasus Mountains towers Europe's highest mountain, Mt. Elbrus. Flowing out of the Valday Hills northwest of Moscow and into the world's largest lake, the Caspian Sea, is Europe's longest river, the "Mother Volga." Almost three thousand miles to the east, in Eastern Siberia, is Lake Baikal, the world's deepest lake. The Russian raw material base is easily the world's most extensive. The country ranks first or second in the annual production of many of the world's strategic minerals. Historically, Russia's size has ensured defense in depth. Napoleon and Hitler learned this the hard way in 1812 and in the 1940s, respectively.

Because Russia is such a northerly country, however, much of the land is unsuitable for human habitation. Ninety percent of Russia is north of the 50th parallel, which means that Russian farmers can harvest only one crop per field per year. Three-fourths of Russia is more than 250 miles (400 km) away from the sea. Climates are continental rather than maritime. Great temperature ranges and low annual precipitation plague most of the country. Therefore, only 8 percent of Russia's enormous landmass is suitable for farming. The quest for food is a persistent theme in Russian history. Before 1950, famines were harsh realities.

The Russian people thus chose to settle in the temperate forests and steppes, avoiding the mountains, coniferous forests, and tundras. The primary zone of settlement stretches from St. Petersburg in the northwest to Novosibirsk in Western Siberia and back to the North Caucasus. A thin exclave of settlement continues along the Trans-Siberian Railroad to Vladivostok in the Russian Far East. Except for random mining and logging, major economic activities are carried out in the settled area.

Russia's size evidences great distances between and among geographic phenomena. Accordingly, it suffers the tyranny of geography. Many of its raw materials are not accessible, meaning they are not resources at all. The friction of distance—long rail and truck hauls—accounts for high transportation costs. Although in its entirety Russia displays great beauty and diversity of landforms, climate, and vegetation, close up it can be very dull because of the space and time required between topographical changes. Variety spread thinly over a massive land can be monotonous. Three-fourths of the country, for example, is a vast plain of less than 1,500 feet (450 meters) in elevation. The typical Russian landscape is flat-to-rolling countryside, the mountains relegated to the southern borders and the area east of the Yenisey River. The Ural Mountains, which divide Europe from Asia, are no higher than 6,200 feet (1,890 meters) and form a mere inconvenience to passing air masses and human interaction. Russia's average elevation is barely more than 1,000 feet (333 meters).

Russia is a fusion of two geologic platforms: the European and the Asiatic. When these massive plates collided 250 million years ago, they raised a mighty mountain range, the low vestiges of which are the Urals. West of the Urals is the North European Plain, a rolling lowland occasioned by hills left by Pleistocene glaciers. One set of hills stretches between Moscow and Warsaw: The Smolensk-Moscow Ridge is the only high ground between the Russian capital and Eastern Europe and was the route used by Napoleon's and Hitler's doomed armies. Further north between Moscow and St. Petersburg are the Valday Hills, which represent the source of Russia's major river systems: Volga, Dnieper, Western Dvina, and so forth. Where it has not been cleared for agriculture, the plain nurtures a temperate forest of broadleaf trees, which dominate in the south, and conifers, which prevail in the north. The slightly leached gray and brown soils of this region were first cultivated by the early eastern Slavs.

In the south, the North European Lowland merges with the Stavropol Upland of the North Caucasus Foreland between the Black and Caspian seas. Here the forests disappear, leaving only grass-

Russia, 1992 © Maryland Cartographics. Reprinted with permission.

land, or steppe, the soils of which are Russia's fertile *chernozems*. Along the western and northern shores of the Caspian Sea, desert replaces the grasslands. Farther south, North Caucasia merges with the Greater Caucasus Mountains, the highest peak of which is Mt. Elbrus (18,481 feet [5,633 meters]).

The northern part of the European Lowland supports a northern coniferous forest, known as taiga. The largest continuous stand of conifers in the world, the taiga stretches from the Finnish border across Siberia and the Russian Far East to the Pacific Ocean. Even farther north, flanking the Arctic Ocean is the Russian tundra. Permafrost plagues both the taiga and tundra, limiting their use for anything other than logging and mineral development. Soils are highly infertile podzols. Virtually all of Siberia and the Russian Far East consist of either taiga or tundra, except in the extreme southeast, where temperate forest appears again.

East of the Urals is the West Siberian Lowland, the world's largest plain. The slow-moving Ob and Irtysh rivers drain the lowland from south to north. This orientation means that the lower courses of the rivers are still frozen as the upper portions thaw. The ice dam causes annual floods that create the world's largest swamp, the Vasyugan. The Ob region contains Russia's largest oil and gas reservoirs. In southeastern Western Siberia is Russia's greatest coal field, the Kuzbas. South of the Kuzbas are the mineral-rich Altai Mountains, which together with the Sayan, and the Yablonovy ranges, form the border between Russia, China, and Mongolia.

East of the Yenisey River is the forested Central Siberian Plateau, a broad, sparsely populated tableland that merges farther east with the mountain ranges of the Russian Far East. In the southeastern corner of the plateau is a great rift valley in which lies Lake Baikal, "Russia's Grand Canyon." Equal to Belgium in size, the world's deepest lake gets deeper with every earthquake.

See also: CLIMATE

BIBLIOGRAPHY

Lydolph, Paul E. (1990). *Geography of the USSR.* Elkhart Lake, WI: Misty Valley Publishing.

Mote, Victor L. (1994). *An Industrial Atlas of the Soviet Successor States.* Houston, TX: Industrial Information Resources.

Mote, Victor L. (1998). *Siberia Worlds Apart.* Boulder, CO: Westview.

Shaw, Denis J. B. (1999). *Russia in the Modern World: A New Geography.* Malden, MA: Blackwell.

VICTOR L. MOTE

GEORGIA AND GEORGIANS

Georgia [Sak'art'velo] is among the "Newly Independent States" to emerge from the collapse of the Soviet Union. Its territory covers 69,700 square kilometers, bordered by the North Caucasus republics of the Russian Federation on the north, Azerbaijan to the west, Armenia and Turkey to the south and southwest, and the Black Sea to the east. It includes three autonomous regions: Adjaria, Abkhazia, and South Ossetia. The latter two have maintained a quasi-independent status for most of the post-Soviet period, and have been the scenes of violence and civil war. The capital city of Tiflis, located on the Mtkvari (or Kura) River in the heart of Georgia, has a population of 1.2 million, approximately 22 percent of the republic's 5.4 million. Georgia's head of state is a president. A unicameral parliament is Georgia's legislative body.

The Georgians are historically Orthodox Christians, with some conversions to Islam during times of Muslim rule. Their language, with its own alphabet (thirty-three letters in the modern form), is a member of the Kartvelian family, a group distinct from neighboring Indo-European or Semitic languages. Speakers of Mingrelian and Svanetian, two of the other Kartvelian languages, also consider themselves Georgian. Laz, closely related to Mingrelian, is spoken in Turkey. Georgia has an ethnically diverse population: Georgian 70.1 percent, Armenian 8.1 percent, Russian 6.3 percent, Azeri 5.7 percent, Ossetian 3 percent, Abkhaz 1.8 percent, and other groups comprising 5 percent.

Georgian principalities and kingdoms began to appear in the last few centuries of the first millennium B.C.E, and existed alongside a well-traveled east-west route on the peripheries of both Persian and Greco-Roman civilizations. These influences were mediated through their Armenian neighbors who, with the Georgians, also maintained contacts with Semitic cultures.

Ancient Georgian culture was split into two major areas: east and west, divided by the Likhi mountains. The eastern portion, known as Kartli, or Iberia, had its center at Mtskheta, at the confluence of the Aragvi and Mtkvari Rivers. When not directly controlled by a Persian state, it still maintained ties with the Iranian political and cultural spheres. This connection lasted well into the Christian period, when the local version of Zoroastrianism vied with Christianity.

Western Georgia was known by different names, depending upon the historical source: Colchis, Egrisi, Lazica. It had more direct ties with Greek civilizations, as several Greek colonies had existed along the Black Sea coast from as early as the sixth century B.C.E. Western Georgia was eventually more directly under the control of the Roman Empire, in its successive incarnations.

The conversion of the Kartli to Christianity occurred in the fourth century as the Roman Empire was beginning its own transition to Christianity. As with other aspects of cultural life, Armenian and Semitic sources were important. Mirian and his royal family, after being converted by St. Nino, a Cappadocian woman, made Christianity the official religion. Dates in the 320s and 330s are argued for this event. The conversion of the west Georgians land owes itself more directly to Greek Christianity.

The conversion of the Georgians was accompanied by the invention of an alphabet in the early fifth century. Scripture, liturgy, and theological works were translated into Georgian. This association of the written language with the sacred is a vital aspect of Georgian culture.

The Georgian capital was transferred from Mtskheta to Tiflis in the fifth century, a process begun during the reign of King Vakhtang, called Gorgasali, and completed under his son Dachi. Vakhtang is portrayed in Georgian sources, in an

Georgian citizens wave flags and shout during an anti-government rally in Tiflis, May 26, 2001. © AFP/CORBIS

exaggerated fashion, as one of the important figures in transferring Kartli from an Iranian orientation to a Byzantine one. This was a complex time of struggle in the South Caucasus, not only between Byzantine and Persian Empires, but also among various Armenian, Caucasian Albanian, and Georgian states vying for power.

These currents of conflict were drastically altered in the seventh century when Islam asserted its military and political power. Tiflis was captured by an Arab army in 645, a mere thirteen years after the death of Muhammad, and would remain under Arab control until the time of David II/IV (the numbering of the Bagratid rulers differs according to one's perspective) in the eleventh century.

While Christianity was tolerated in Eastern Georgia, the political center shifted westward, where the Kingdom of Abkhazia grew to preeminence in the eighth century. This realm was one of mixed ethnic composition, including the Kartvelians of West Georgia (i.e. the ancestors of today's Mingrelians and Svanetians) and, toward the northwest, the ancestors of the Abkhazian people.

Meanwhile, a branch of the Bagratid family, which had ruled parts of Armenia, and who were clients of the Byzantine Empire, became prominent in the Tao-Klarjeti region of southwest Georgia. Because of Bagrat III (d. 1014), they became inheritors of the Kingdom of Abkhazia. From their capital Kutaisi they contemplated the re-conquest of Tiflis and the unification of Georgian lands. This was accomplished in 1122 by David II/IV, called the Builder, who reigned from 1089 to 1125. For nearly two centuries, through the reign of Tamar (1184–1212), the Georgians enjoyed a golden age,

Georgia, 1992 © Maryland Cartographics. Reprinted with permission.

when they controlled a multiethnic territory from the Black to the Caspian Seas and from the Caucasus Mountains in the north, toward the Armenian plateau in the south. It was also a time of great learning, with theological academies at Gelati, near Kutaisi, and in the east at Iqalto on the Kakhetian plain. The literary output of this time reached it zenith with Shota Rustaveli's epic tale of heroism and chivalry, *Knight in the Panther Skin*, written in the last quarter of twelfth century.

In the thirteenth century a succession of invasions by Turks and Mongols brought chaos and destruction upon the Georgians. These culminated in the devastating raids of Timur in the early fifteenth century. From these depredations Georgian society was very slow to recover, and for much of the next four centuries it remained under the sway of the Savafid Persian Empire and the Ottoman Empire. Georgians at this time were active at the Safavid court. The Bagratid dynasty continued to reign locally over a collection of smaller states that warred against one another. West European travelers who ventured through Georgia in these centuries give sad reports about the quality of life.

In the eighteenth century the Russian Empire's steady expansion brought it to the foothills of the Caucasus Mountains and along the Caspian Sea to the east of Georgia. Russians and Georgians had been in contact through earlier exchanges of embassies. Persian invasions in that century had been especially harsh, and the Georgians looked to their northern Orthodox neighbor for assistance. This assistance culminated first in the 1783 Treaty of Georgievsk, by which Irakle II's realm of Kartli-Kakheti became a protectorate of the Russian Empire. Then, in 1801, soon after his accession to the throne, Alexander I signed a manifesto proclaiming Kartli-Kakheti to be fully incorporated into Russia. Other parts of Georgia followed within the next decade, although not always willingly.

Despite Russification efforts during the nineteenth century, the Georgian language and culture underwent a renaissance that would undergird Georgian national aspirations in the twentieth century. The Society for the Spread of Literacy among the Georgians, founded by Iakob Gogebashvili, was important for fostering language acquisition, especially among children. Ilia Chavchavadze, Akaki Tsereteli, and Vazha Pshavela dominated the literary scene into the twentieth century.

Georgians joined with comrades throughout the Russian Empire in the revolutions of 1905 and 1917. When the Russian state began to shed its periphery in 1918, the Georgians briefly entered the Transcaucasian Republic. This political entity lasted from February until May 1918, but then split into its constituent parts. Georgia proclaimed its independence on May 26, 1918. The Democratic Republic of Georgia, beset by internal and external enemies, lasted less than three years, and on February 26, 1921, the Bolsheviks established Soviet power in Tiflis. Independent Georgia had been governed mainly by Mensheviks, an offshoot of the Russian Social Democratic Workers' Party. They were reluctant nationalists, led by Noe Zhordania, who served as president. These Mensheviks became the demonic foil for any number of aspects of Soviet historiography and remained so for the Abkhazians when they would press for greater autonomy.

The Soviet Socialist Republic of Georgia entered the USSR through the Transcaucasian Soviet Federative Socialist Republic in 1922 and remained a member of it until its dissolution in 1936. Afterward the Georgian Soviet Socialist Republic became one of the USSR's constituent republics. Three autonomous regions were created within Georgia, part of what some describe as a manifestation of the "divide and conquer" regime of ethnic pseudo-sovereignties. The South Ossetian Autonomous Oblast was established across the border from North Ossetia, and the Adjar A.S.S.R. was an enclave of historically Muslim Georgians in the southwest. The third, and most troubled, part of Georgia was Abkhazia. This region in the northwest along the Black Sea coast had been in an ambiguous federative, treaty status with Georgia, but was finally, in 1931, incorporated as an A.S.S.R.

Georgia fared generally no better or worse for having its "favorite son," Iosep Jugashvili (a.k.a. Josef Stalin), as the dictator of the Soviet Union. With other parts of the U.S.S.R., it suffered the depredations of party purges and the destruction of its national intelligentsia in the 1930s.

In the latter decades of the Soviet period, Georgia was held up as a sort of paradise within the Soviet system. Agriculture, with tea and citrus in the subtropical zone in the west, prospered, and the Black Sea coast was a favorite spot for vacationers from the cold north. The hospitality of the Georgians, seemingly uncooled by Soviet power, and always warmed by the quality of Georgia's famous wines, wooed Soviet and foreign guests alike.

The Georgians developed a vigorous dissident movement in the 1970s, with Zviad Gamsakhurdia and Merab Kostava playing leading roles. Tens of thousands came out into the streets of Tiflis in 1978 to protest the exclusion of the Georgian language from the new proposed Constitution of the Georgian S.S.R.

As Gorbachev's glasnost worked its effects, the Georgian independence movement gave rise to competing movements in South Ossetia and Abkhazia. In reaction to a communiqué issued by Abkhazian intellectuals in March 1989, the main streets of Tiflis again overflowed with protesters. On the morning of April 9, 1989, troops moved against the demonstration, killing at least twenty and injuring scores of others. This outburst of violence marked the beginning of the rapid devolution of Soviet power in Georgia.

Georgia voted for its independence on April 9, 1991, and elected its first president, Zviad Gamsakhurdia, in May. His rule was harsh, and his presidency barely survived the final collapse of the USSR by a few months into 1992. Eduard Shevardnadze, who had held power in Georgia under Communist rule, and who became Gorbachev's foreign minister, returned to Georgia, eventually to be elected twice to the presidency. His presidency was plagued by warfare and continuing conflict in South Ossetia and Abkhazia, both of which claimed independence. The ethnic conflict compounded the economic dislocations, although the proposed Baku-Tiflis-Ceyhan oil pipeline, the beginning of an east-west energy corridor, has brought the promise of some future prosperity.

See also: CAUCASUS; NATIONALITIES POLICIES, SOVIET; NATIONALITIES POLICIES, TSARIST; SHEVARDNADZE, EDUARD AMVROSIEVICH

BIBLIOGRAPHY

Allen, W. E. D. (1971). *A History of the Georgian People: From the Beginning down to the Russian Conquest in the Nineteenth Century.* New York: Barnes & Noble.

Aronson, Howard. (1990). *Georgian: A Reading Grammar*, 2nd ed. Columbus, OH: Slavica..

Braund, David. (1994). *Georgia in Antiquity: A History of Colchis and Transcaucasian Iberia, 550 BC–AD 562.* Oxford: Clarendon.

Lang, David Marshall. (1962). *A Modern History of Soviet Georgia.* New York: Grove.

Rapp, Stephen H., Jr. (1997). "Imagining History at the Crossroads: Persia, Byzantium, and the Architects of the Written Georgian Past." Ph.D. diss, University of Michigan. Ann Arbor.

Suny, Ronald G. (1994). *The Making of the Georgian Nation*, 2nd ed. Bloomington: Indiana University Press.

Toumanoff, Cyril. (1982). *History of Christian Caucasia.* Washington, DC: Georgetown University Press.

PAUL CREGO

GEORGIAN ORTHODOX CHURCH

The Orthodox Church of Georgia, an autocephalous church of the Byzantine rite Eastern Churches, is an ancient community. It dates from the fourth century, and stories of the evangelization of Kartli center around St. Nino, called Equal to the Apostles, who was born in Cappadocia, studied in Jerusalem, and made her way through Armenia to preach, heal, baptize, and convert the Georgian people. Later traditions add apostolic visits from St. Andrew and St. Simeon the Canaanite that reflect evangelization of western Georgia. Christians in Kartli continued to have a strong relationship with the Armenians until the seventh century, when these Christian people opted for different Christologies.

The autocephaly of the Orthodox Church is claimed from the fifth century, when the Archbishop of Mtskheta was given the title of Catholicos. There was later also a Catholicos in western Georgia, coinciding with the Kingdom of Abkhazia.

Western Georgia was evangelized more directly by Greeks, and, after the split from the Armenians, the entire Georgian Church strengthened its ties with the church in Constantinople. Of the family of Orthodox Churches that derive their liturgies from the Byzantine tradition, the liturgical language remains an archaic Georgian, not entirely intelligible to modern speakers.

The Georgians, for much of their history, have lived under the rule of Muslim states. Arab Muslims conquered Tiflis in 645, and it continued under Muslim rule until 1122. After a brief golden age the Georgians again came under Muslim control, alternating between Savifid Persians and Ottoman Turks. The church endured this period of time with difficulty and looked for assistance from their Orthodox neighbors in Russia toward the end of the eighteenth century. The identification of the Georgian nation with its Orthodox identity was strengthened in this period, as the church was often the guarantor of linguistic and national identity and the legal authority for the nation.

Soon after the Russians annexed Georgia (1801), the autocephaly of the Georgian Church was rescinded (1811) and it became a part of the Russian Orthodox Church. The Georgian Church became one of the institutions in Georgia through which the imperial government attempted its program of Russification.

The Georgian Church reclaimed its autocephaly in 1918, as Georgia was proclaiming its independence. This short period of breathing space was quickly constricted with the imposition of Soviet power, and nearly seven decades of atheist education and oppression took a devastating toll on the Georgian Church. As in the rest of the USSR, church buildings were closed, confiscated for other purposes, left to ruin, or destroyed. The role of the clergy was restricted, and many came under suspicion as possible KGB agents.

The reign of Catholicos-Patriarch Ilia II from December 1977 marked a new beginning in the life of the Georgian Church. Slowly, Ilia began to restore episcopal sees and reopen churches. In October 1988, the Tiflis Theological Academy was opened. With the changes of perestroika and glasnost and the collapse of the Soviet Union, the Georgian Church continued a dramatic revival. By the end of the 1990s dozens of churches had been rebuilt and many new ones built.

During the first decade of Georgia's new independence the church struggled to find its place in society and in relation to the state. Georgian politicians, especially the first president Zviad Gamsakhurdia, have used and misused their ties to the church. The new Georgian Constitution not only guarantees freedom of religion and conscience but gives the church a place of historical honor. This place of honor was given further definition and practical meaning by a Concordat signed by the government and the church on October 14, 2002.

The Georgian Church was encouraged to join the World Council of Churches (WCC) in 1961, and Ilia II has served as its president. Internal pressures from conservatives helped to further the decision of the Georgians to leave the WCC and other ecumenical bodies during the spring of 1997.

There has also been considerable persecution of non-Orthodox religious communities, including Baptists, Pentecostals, and Jehovah's Witnesses, in the post-Soviet period, some of it violent. The Orthodox responsible for this persecution are generally persons excommunicated by the Georgian Church. Some within the church, however, have participated either by direct violence or by an elevation of rhetoric against the non-Orthodox.

See also: BYZANTIUM, INFLUENCE OF; GEORGIA AND GEORGIANS; ORTHODOXY; RUSSIAN ORTHODOX CHURCH; RUSSIFICATION.

BIBLIOGRAPHY

Babian, Gorun. (2001). *The Relations Between the Armenian and Georgian Church: According to the Armenian Sources, 300–610.* Antelias, Lebanon: Armenian Catholicosate of Cilicia.

Mgaloblishvili, Tamila, ed. (1998). *Ancient Christianity in the Caucasus.* Surrey, England: Curzon.

PAUL CREGO

GERMAN DEMOCRATIC REPUBLIC

One of the unintended and initially unforeseen consequences of World War II was the division of Germany. At the end of the war, Western forces controlled and occupied Western Germany, while Soviet forces occupied Eastern Germany and Eastern Europe. The Allied powers, including Russia, agreed to divide Germany and Berlin into occupation zones. The tensions resulting from the joint administration of Germany, as well as the emergence of the Cold War, led in 1949 to the formal division of Germany into two separate states.

In 1949 occupied West Germany was transformed into the Federal Republic of Germany, a democratic state with close ties to the Western powers. In East Germany, the German Democratic Republic was founded. The Soviets had allowed political parties to form in their section of Germany as early as 1945, but had used pressure and coercive measures to achieve a merger between the socialist and communist parties during April of 1946. The result was the Socialist Unity Party (Sozialistische Einheitspartei Deutschlands) or SED, which came to exercise near-complete control in East Germany. The GDR, like other communist governments established in Eastern Europe, had a central committee, and power came from the party leadership, which also assumed key roles in the state bureaucracy. The government used repressive measures such as censorship and arrest, and began to require communist ideology to be taught in schools. Walter Ulbricht, the head of the German Democratic Republic, had been part of the German Communist Party from 1919, the year it was founded, and had served as a communist deputy in the Reichstag during the Weimar Republic. Ulbricht was flown from the Soviet Union to Germany after the Soviet army had invaded Germany. Ulbricht, a hard-line Stalinist, stated in 1952 that East Germany could pursue the construction of full socialism, further restricting workers and reducing the availability of consumer goods. Although the Soviet Union had been exerting considerable pressure upon Ulbricht to reform and alter his repressive policies, the Soviets used force to suppress the rebellion his policies provoked in 1953.

Since the Soviet occupation of East Germany had begun, hundreds of thousands of Germans had fled to the West. The desire to escape Soviet-occupied territory intensified during Ulbricht's tenure, a fact illustrated by the 400,000 Germans who left East Germany in 1953. The Soviet Union was able to lessen this massive emigration by patrolling the border between the two German states and making it impassable, but until 1961, Germans could take public transportation from East Berlin to West Berlin and then declare themselves to authorities. In 1961, the Soviets officially sealed off East Berlin, as well as the last breach in East Germany, by building the Berlin Wall.

The erection of the Berlin Wall led to a stabilization of the situation in East Berlin and the end to the constant drain on the population. Ulbricht introduced the New Economic System in 1963. The New Economic System did not succeed in substantially altering the centralized structure of the East Germany economy, but it allowed for a relaxation of the rigid economic policies and for some independent decisions. As a result of these changes, the East German economy became the strongest of all of those countries within the Soviet sphere of occupation, while still far below the economies of

Western Europe. Ulbricht appeared to be at the height of his power in 1968, but many of his policies were unpopular. In 1971 Soviet authorities forced Ulbricht to step down. Ulbricht died in 1973, and his death paved the way for improved relations between East and West Germany. The East German minister, Willie Stoph, negotiated and signed several treaties with the German Federal Republic. Stoph briefly served as the effective head of state but was replaced by Erich Honecker in 1976. In 1989 the changes and reforms initiated by Mikhail Gorbachev in the Soviet Union and the reluctance of the Soviet leader to use force to suppress rebellions elsewhere led to uprisings in Eastern Europe. In East Germany the Berlin Wall symbolized not just the repressive Soviet-style government that had been in place since 1949 but also the single largest cause of resentment among Germans. The Soviet control of East Berlin and East Germany necessitated the forced separation of family and friends who were unable to secure travel permits or permission to emigrate from the notoriously inefficient and reactionary bureaucracy in the East. The uprisings in Eastern Europe and the discontent in Germany led the SED to replace Honecker and to pass a new law regarding travel and emigration. It was too little too late, however, and crowds swarmed the crossing point arguing that restrictions had been relaxed. When Soviet guards, unsure of the situation, opened the gate and allowed them to pass, Germans began to dismantle the Wall, and it was not long until the communist government in East Germany collapsed. The noncommunist leadership of the German Democratic Republic immediately arranged to meet with authorities from the German Federal Republic. The initial focus of these talks was on the financial situation and the request for a loan to East Germany, but the question of German reunification also hung in the air. These developments led to the "Two plus Four" talks, encompassing the two German states and the four powers that had occupied Germany. The Two plus Four Treaty, concluded on September 12, 1990, dealt with all international issues regarding affairs in Germany, to the satisfaction of the major powers. The support of the president of the United States, George H.W. Bush, was instrumental in securing the approval of the French, who had grave concerns about the renewal of Germany. At 12:01 A.M. on October 3, 1990, the GDR ceased to exist, and the German Federal Republic became the sole authority for a reunified Germany. Reunification has greatly impacted all Germans socially, economically, and politically as the complicated process of reintegrating East and West Germany has taken place within both a national and an international context.

See also: COMMUNIST BLOC; COMMUNIST INTERNATIONAL; GERMANY, RELATIONS WITH

BIBLIOGRAPHY

Detwiler, Donald S. (1999). *Germany: A Short History*, 3rd edition. Carbondale: Southern Illinois University Press.

Turner, Henry Ashby, Jr. (1992). *Germany from Partition to Reunification.* Binghamton, NY: Vail-Ballou Press.

MELISSA R. JORDINE

GERMAN SETTLERS

German traders and missionaries began settling on the eastern shores of the Baltic Sea during the thirteenth century and eventually became the exclusive nobility in the region. The Germans ruled over the native Estonian and Latvian peasants and converted them first to Catholicism and then, after the Protestant Reformation, to Lutheranism. They were responsible for establishing merchant and artisan guilds in urban areas and feudal manors in rural areas. The Baltic Germans retained their privileged status even after Sweden decisively conquered the region during the 1620s. In 1721 the Russian Empire acquired the territories of Estland and Livland (equivalent to modern-day Estonia and northern Latvia) from Sweden. Germans became influential and loyal members of the Russian government and army, with some serving as generals, administrators, and diplomats. Baltic Germans fought simultaneously against the Bolsheviks and the Latvian nationalists during the late 1910s but did not succeed in establishing a permanent German-ruled state in the Baltics. The number of Germans living in the Baltics steadily decreased. Following a pact signed between the foreign ministers of Adolf Hitler and Josef Stalin in August 1939, almost all of the remaining Baltic Germans moved to German-ruled Poland over the next two years.

Germans arrived in the Russian Empire in several additional waves of immigration between 1763 and 1862. The areas in which these Germans initially settled included the Middle Volga Area, southern Ukraine, the Crimean peninsula, Bessarabia, Volhynia, and the Caucasus. Their religions included Lutheranism, Catholicism, and Mennonitism.

On July 22, 1763, the Russian Tsar Catherine the Great issued a manifesto that offered foreigners the opportunity to settle in Russia. The newcomers were promised land, self-governance, religious freedom, exemptions from taxes and military service, and other privileges. The manifesto particularly appealed to Germans, who had suffered during the Seven Years' War (1756–1763), a time of rampant famine and forced military conscription. From 1763 until 1767, approximately 25,000–27,000 Germans resettled in the Middle Volga river valley in 104 colonies in the provinces of Saratov and Samara, which later developed into 192 towns and villages. Most of the Volga Germans engaged in agriculture, harvesting such crops as rye, sunflowers, potatoes, and sugar beets, but some worked as tanners, sausage makers, millers, and craftspeople. Tsar Alexander II began drafting them into the Russian army in 1874. During the following decades, some Volga German families moved to Siberia, while others immigrated to the United States, Canada, and other countries. Volga Germans were afflicted by severe famines in 1891–1892, 1921–1922, and 1932–1933, the last one caused by Stalin's forced collectivization of farms. While the Volga Germans had been granted their own autonomous republic in 1924, it was abolished by Stalin on August 28, 1941, in the aftermath of Nazi Germany's invasion of the Soviet Union, and the Volga Germans were deported to Kazakhstan and Siberia and forced into slave labor.

Between 1783 and 1812, the Russian Empire annexed former Ottoman and Crimean Tatar territories on the northern Black Sea coast. In 1787 Germans began to settle in New Russia, which later became the provinces of Kherson, Yekaterinoslav, and Tauride. In 1813 Tsar Alexander I invited Germans to Bessarabia and offered them many privileges. The first German settlement in Bessarabia was founded in 1814, and in the following years, until 1842, many more Germans arrived and formed numerous other colonies. Many of the Bessarabian and Ukrainian Germans specialized in farming and grape growing, but others worked in trades like weaving, blacksmithing, shoemaking, and carpentry. Germans also founded factories and mills. Bessarabia became part of Romania in 1918, and its Germans departed in 1940.

The Russian Germans were very conscious of their identity, operating their own schools and churches and teaching their children the German language. Tsar Alexander III's Russification policies in the 1880s and 1890s made Russian the language of all schools and abolished the Germans' right to self-government. During World War I, with Germany an enemy of Russia, German organizations and newspapers were shut down by the Russian government, preaching in German was outlawed, and Germans from Volhynia were exiled to Siberia (1915). During the Soviet years, increasing numbers of young Germans became fluent in Russian rather than in German.

Whereas from the 1950s to the1970s few Soviet Germans were allowed to immigrate to Germany, during the late 1980s and 1990s a much larger number of Germans did so following the gradual easing of restrictions beginning in 1987. As of the 1989 census there were at least two million Germans living in the Soviet Union, but the majority of them left within a decade.

See also: NATIONALITIES POLICIES, SOVIET; NATIONALITIES POLICIES, TSARIST

BIBLIOGRAPHY

Brandes, Detlef. (1991). "A Success Story: The German Colonists in New Russia and Bessarabia: 1787–1914." *Acta Slavica Iaponica* 9:32–46.

Giesinger, Adam. (1981). *From Catherine to Khrushchev: The Story of Russia's Germans.* Lincoln, NE: American Historical Society of Germans from Russia.

Kern, Albert. (1998). *Homeland Book of the Bessarabian Germans.* Fargo, ND: Germans from Russia Heritage Collection, North Dakota State University Libraries.

Koch, Fred C. (1977). *The Volga Germans: In Russia and the Americas, from 1763 to the Present.* University Park: Pennsylvania State University Press.

Long, James W. (1988). *From Privileged to Dispossessed: The Volga Germans, 1860–1917.* Lincoln: University of Nebraska Press.

Pleve, Igor R. (2001). *The German Colonies on the Volga: The Second Half of the Eighteenth Century,* tr. Richard R. Rye. Lincoln, NE: American Historical Society of Germans from Russia.

KEVIN ALAN BROOK

GERMANY, RELATIONS WITH

The reign of Peter the Great (1682–1725) marked Russia's official entry into European diplomatic affairs. Around 1740 this was followed by the entry of another power, Prussia, transformed under Frederick the Great. Significant Russian-Prussian relations began during the reign of Catherine the Great

(1762–1796), a former German princess. Catherine's husband, Peter III, a great admirer of Frederick II, the king of Prussia, had withdrawn from the Seven Years' War, a decision that left Russia with no gains from a costly conflict that it had been waging successfully. After the coup removing Peter from the throne, Catherine repudiated his treaty with Prussia in order to demonstrate Russia's power and independence. By 1772, however, relations with Prussia had been reestablished, in part in connection with the negotiations leading to the partition of Poland by Russia, Prussia, and Austria. The French Revolution and the rise of Napoleon posed a direct threat to Prussia and Russia, and they both participated in the coalitions formed in opposition to the French emperor. The defeat of Napoleon led to the Congress of Vienna in 1815. The three most conservative of the attending powers (Russia, Austria, and Prussia) were determined to preserve a balance of power through the Concert of Europe and to preserve the old order by exercising the right to intervene militarily in order to preserve legitimate governments.

The next significant period in German-Russian relations occurred just prior to and during the unification of Germany under the leadership of King Wilhelm I of Prussia, and his iron chancellor, Otto von Bismarck. Bismarck was able to unite Germany in part by securing Russian nonintervention. Although Russia has been criticized for enabling the rise of Germany, there were practical considerations for its support of Bismarck, such as the possibility of increasing its influence in certain areas as a consequence of the Austro-Prussian War. Furthermore, the possible consequences of German unification under Prussia were not fully understood. During the immediate aftermath of the unification, Austria-Hungary, Russia, and Germany formed the Three Emperors' League (1872–1873), a defensive military alliance that attempted to revive and maintain the old order upheld at the Congress of Vienna. Difficulties and disagreements arising from the situation in the Crimea and in the Balkans brought about the league's collapse. It was revived and then allowed to lapse permanently in 1887 because of the impossibility of reconciling the differences between Austria-Hungary and Russia. Bismarck maintained relations with Austria and negotiated the Reinsurance Treaty with Russia, which guaranteed the neutrality of the signatories in case of war, except if Germany attacked France or Russia attacked Austria-Hungary. Wilhelm II's dismissal of Bismarck and refusal to renew the Reinsurance Treaty in 1890 led to the formation of new alliances. Russia, no longer tied to Germany or Austria-Hungary, and afraid of being diplomatically isolated and without allies, negotiated a treaty with France. Wilhelm II alienated the British, who maintained friendly relations with the French, and Germany found itself allied with only Italy and Austria-Hungary.

During the conflict between Austria-Hungary and Serbia that triggered World War I, Germany was compelled to support Austria-Hungary and Russia was similarly committed to support the Serbians. The resulting war led to a major conflict between Russia and Germany on the Eastern Front. Russia's poor performance in the war combined with the policies of Tsar Nicholas II led to defeat and revolution. The Bolshevik regime that replaced the Provisional Government ended Russia's participation in the war by the Treaty of Brest-Litovsk in 1917 which was bitterly resented by many Russian. The Versailles Treaty, signed by a defeated Germany, in 1919, overturned the earlier Russian-German agreement.

The refusal of the Allied powers to recognize the communist government and the diplomatic isolation of the Soviet Union were factors in German-Soviet relations during the interwar years. Even after the rise of Adolf Hitler and the violent suppression of the Communist Party in Germany, Josef Stalin continued to maintain relations with Germany. Although Hitler and Stalin gave considerable aid and support to different factions during the Spanish Civil War, no breach of their relationship occurred and negotiations for a nonaggression treaty were initiated. Stalin's primary reason for signing the Molotov-Ribbentrop Pact in 1939 is still uncertain. The Nazi-Soviet Pact included a nonaggression clause and a secret protocol calling for the division of Poland between the two countries. Whether Stalin believed a genuine alliance could be formed with Germany against the Allied powers or was merely attempting to gain time to further industrialize and prepare for war, it is clear that he did not expect the massive German invasion of the Soviet Union that was launched on June 22, 1941.

The defeat of Hitler and Germany by the Allied powers led to the occupation of Eastern Germany and East Berlin by the Soviet Union. Although divided and occupied, Germany played a role in the Cold War; the German Democratic Republic (East Germany) was allied with the Soviet Union, while the German Federal Republic (West Germany) was allied with the United States and the Western powers. The collapse of communism in Eastern Europe and the Soviet Union paved the way for the reunification of Germany in 1990. The republics of the former Soviet Union have established economic and diplomatic relations with unified Germany, which has become the Russian Federation's most important trading and financial partner in the post-communist era.

See also: GERMAN DEMOCRATIC REPUBLIC; GERMAN SETTLERS; NAZI-SOVIET PACT OF 1939; SOVIET-GERMAN TRADE AGREEMENT OF 1939; THREE EMPERORS' LEAGUE; WORLD WAR I; WORLD WAR II

BIBLIOGRAPHY

Jelavich, Barbara A. (1964). *A Century of Russian Foreign Policy, 1814–1914.* New York.

Smyser, W. R. (1999). *From Yalta to Berlin: The Cold War Struggle over Germany.* New York: St. Martin's Press.

Sodaro, Michael J. (1990). *Moscow, Germany, and the West from Khrushchev to Gorbachev.* Ithaca, NY: Cornell University Press.

Stent, Angela. (1999). *Russia and Germany Reborn: Unification, the Soviet Collapse, and the New Europe.* Princeton: Princeton University Press.

MELISSA R. JORDINE

GIGANTOMANIA

Gigantomania is the creation of abnormally large works. Gigantomania dominated different areas of political and cultural life in the Soviet Union and was a feature of other totalitarian societies (Nazi Germany, Fascist Italy, communist states of Eastern Europe, and modern China).

According to the Marxist theory, socialism must triumph historically over capitalism. Soviet rulers attempted to prove the superiority of the socialist system by the creation of gigantic industrial complexes, huge farms, colossal buildings, and enormous statues.

Enormous new cities and industrial centers were erected in the Soviet Union from the end of the 1920s through the 1930s. Historian Nicolas V. Riasanovsky wrote, "Gigantic industrial complexes, exemplified by Magnitostroi in the Urals and Kuznetsstroi in western Siberia, began to take shape. Entire cities arose in the wilderness. Magnitogorsk, for instance, acquired in a few years a population of a quarter of a million."

However, the execution of the Five-Year Plans, industrialization, and the forced collectivization of agriculture were accompanied by a huge number of human victims. Gulag prisoners working in terrible conditions built many of the huge projects.

Gigantism and monumental classicism became the typical features of Soviet architecture starting in the 1930s. All other architecture styles were suppressed in the Soviet Union. Historian Geoffrey Hosking points out that in the Soviet architecture ". . . neoclassical forms gradually became distorted, more extended in size . . .." As the result of this distortion, many large buildings were erected, as exemplified by the tasteless "wedding cake" style skyscrapers built in Moscow after World War II.

The same standard was used in Soviet sculpture and art. Huge monuments of Vladimir Lenin and Josef Stalin were erected in every sizable city. Many Soviet artists created paintings showing gigantic images of the communist leaders with tiny figures of the common people in the background.

Gigantomania began in Stalin's time, but continued after his death. During the 1960s to the 1980s two huge sculptures depicting the warrior "Motherland-Mother" were erected by sculptor Yevgeny Vuchetich near Kiev and Volgograd. According to Soviet doctrine, art should show the super-human accomplishments of the new socialist man, who was depicted as a huge muscular and overpowering human being. Even women were sculpted as enormous figures with rugged masculine physiques.

These works are now generally thought to be the vulgar creations of dilettante artists; showing the exceedingly poor taste of the all-powerful Soviet leaders who commanded their creation.

See also: ARCHITECTURE

BIBLIOGRAPHY

Bown, Matthew Cullerne, and Taylor, Brandon, eds. (1993). *Art of the Soviets: Painting, Sculpture, and Architecture in a One-party State, 1917–1992.* Manchester: Manchester University Press.

Groys, Boris. (1992). *The Total Art of Stalinism. Avant-Garde, Aesthetic Dictatorship, and Beyond,* tr. Charles Rougle. Princeton, NJ: Princeton University Press.

Hosking, Geoffrey. (2001). *Russia and the Russians.* Cambridge, MA: The Belknap Press of Harvard University Press.

London, Kurt. (1938). *The Seven Soviet Arts.* New Haven, CT: Yale University Press.

Riasanovsky, Nicolas V. (2000). *A History of Russia,* 6th ed. New York, Oxford: Oxford University Press.

Ryabushin, Alexander and Smolina, Nadia. (1992). *Landmarks of Soviet Architecture 1917–1991.* New York: Rizzoli.

VICTORIA KHITERER

GINZBURG, EVGENIA SEMENOVNA

(1904–1977), Stalin-era memoirist.

Evgenia Semenovna Ginzburg was one of the most well-known and respected memoirists of Josef Stalin's purges and life in the Soviet Gulag. She was born into a middle-class Jewish family in Moscow. She became a teacher and party activist in Kazan. She married Pavel Aksenov, a high-ranking party official in Kazan, and the couple had two sons. The eldest, Alyosha, would die during the Siege of Leningrad; the younger, Vasily, became a noted writer in his own right. In 1937 both Ginzburg and her husband were arrested. Ginzburg spent the next two years in solitary confinement before being sent to a labor camp in Kolyma. While in the camps, she undertook a variety of work, including nursing, and she met Anton Walter, a fellow prisoner who worked as a doctor. He became her second husband. In 1947 Ginzburg was released from captivity but chose to stay in the Magadan area to wait for Walter to finish his allotted prison sentence. She began teaching Russian language and literature. Ironically many of her students at the time worked for the security services. Ginzburg was rearrested in 1949. In 1955 she was released again. This time Ginzburg was allowed to return to Moscow and was officially rehabilitated. She began to write pieces for such Soviet periodicals as *Youth* (*Yunost*), the *Teacher's Newspaper* (*Uchitelskaya gazeta*), and the *News* (*Izvestiya*). Despite her rehabilitation, Ginzburg's background still made her a bit suspect in the eyes of the authorities, so she never joined the Soviet Writers' Union. In 1967 the first volume of her memoirs, *Journey into the Whirlwind,* was published in Italy. The book covers the 1934–1939 period of her life. In it, she describes how her mentality as a devoted party member changed once she realized the extent of the Purges, and she notes the kinds of things people had to do to survive their imprisonment. In Ginzburg's case, for instance, she took great solace from her vast knowledge of Russian poetry, and she would recite it at length for her fellow prisoners. The second volume of her memoirs, *Within the Whirlwind,* was published abroad in 1979 and describes her remaining years in prison as well as her life in Magadan and her eventual return to Moscow. There is a distinct difference in tone between the two volumes, with the second book being much harsher and honest in its criticisms. Many scholars have speculated that Ginzburg knew by then that her memoirs would not legally be published in the Soviet Union during her lifetime and that she chose not to temper her language in the hopes of publication. Both volumes of memoirs have been translated into an array of languages, and they remain among the best, most widely read accounts of Soviet prison life. In the Soviet Union, the books circulated widely in samizdat form among the dissident community and, finally, in 1989 they were published officially.

See also: DISSIDENT MOVEMENT; GULAG; PURGES, THE GREAT

BIBLIOGRAPHY

Heldt, Barbara. (1987). *Terrible Perfection.* Bloomington, IN: Indiana University Press.

Kelly, Catriona. (1994). *A History of Russian Women's Writing.* Oxford: Oxford University Press.

Kolchevska, Natasha. (1998). "A Difficult Journey: Evgeniia Ginzburg and Women's Writing of Camp Memoirs." In *Women and Russia: Projections and Self-Perceptions,* ed. Rosalind Marsh. New York: Berghahn Books.

Kolchevska, Natasha. (2003). "The Art of Memory: Cultural Reverence as Political Critique in Evgeniia Ginzburg's Writing of the Gulag." In *The Russian Memoir: History and Literature,* ed. Beth Holmgren. Evanston, IL: Northwestern University Press.

ALISON ROWLEY

GKOS

GKOs, *Gosudarstvennye Kratkosrochnye Obyazatelstva,* are short-term ruble-denominated treasury bills issued since 1993. They played a major role in Russia's August 1998 economic crisis.

In the 1990s Russia was unable to balance its budget. The general government budget deficit varied from 5 to as much as 25 percent of GDP without any declining trend. First the deficit was covered by money emission, which contributed to very high and variable inflation. The Russian government started in May 1993 to issue short-term zero-coupon bonds known as GKOs. This was meant as a non-inflationary method of financing the deficit. The GKO maturity is less than a year. Sometimes the average maturity has been as short as half a year. There are also ruble-denominated medium-term federal bonds known as OFZs (since 1995). Other government debt instruments were also issued, but GKOs remained the most important ones.

Russian inflation came down after 1995. The root problem, the budget deficit, was not addressed. It was believed that deficits could be financed by increasing debt. The government debt market was the fastest-growing market in 1996 and 1997. Domestic ruble-denominated debt remained very small until 1996 but rose to 13 percent of GDP in January 1997. This is still not an internationally high figure. But the high yields, short maturities, and large foreign ownership shares of GKOs made the situation explosive.

The GKO real interest rates were first highly negative due to unexpectedly high inflation. As inflation subsided but GKO nominal yields remained high—due to high inflation expectations, political uncertainty or other reasons—real interest rates shot up. They were 30–60 percent in 1996–1997. Later they decreased, only to reach new highs in early 1998, as the danger of default became evident. Interest payments rose to 27.6 percent of federal government revenue in 1995 and more than half in early 1998. Most GKOs were consequently issued to service earlier debt. By 1997 the GKO contribution to financing the deficit was actually negative. On the other hand, they had become the main revenue source for the larger Russian banks.

Access for foreigners to the GKO market was quite restricted until 1996. Due to the small size of the market relative to international capital flows and very high real interest rates, access was only liberalized gradually. Measures were used to keep the non-residents' earnings within limits. Still, by the end of 1997 their share in GKO stock was at least a third, perhaps more. The rest was basically owned by the Central Bank and the state-owned Sberbank. The risk of sudden exit of nonresident GKO holders was real. Nonresident behavior soon became a major source of the GKO market crisis in the spring of 1998.

After the crisis of August 1998, the government chose to restructure the GKOs and OFZs, which were to a large part frozen. Afterward, Russian government debt market has remained quite illiquid. With budget surpluses, the government has not needed new debt. Investors remain wary. GKO stock is less than 1 percent of GDP. However, debt instruments would be useful for liquidity control and protection from inflation.

See also: ECONOMY, POST-SOVIET; SBERBANK

BIBLIOGRAPHY

Gobbin, Niko, and Merleverde, Bruno. (2000). "The Russian Crisis: A Debt Perspective." *Post-Communist Economies* 12(2):141–163.

Malleret, Thierry, Orlova, Natalia, and Romanov, Vladimir. (1999). "What Loaded and Triggered the Russian Crisis?" *Post-Soviet Affairs* 15(2):107–129.

Willer, Dirk. (2001). "Financial Markets." *In Russia's Post-Communist Economy, eds. Brigitte Granville and Peter Oppenheimer.* Oxford: Oxford University Press.

PEKKA SUTELA

GLASNOST

Glasnost is a Russian word that proved fateful for the Soviet communist empire in its last years of existence. Variously translated as "openness," "transparency," or "publicity," its root sense is public voice or speech. Freedom of speech is a close Western equivalent.

Upon his rise to power in 1985 as General Secretary of the Communist Party of the Soviet Union, Mikhail Gorbachev introduced glasnost as one of a troika of slogans in his campaign to reform a faltering Soviet system. He called for glasnost (openness) in public discussion, perestroika (restructuring) in the economy and political system, and *novoye mneniya* (new thinking) in foreign policy. All three slogans broke away from the ideology-laden sloganeering of past Soviet leaders and suggested movement away from dictatorship to a more open and democratic Soviet future.

While Gorbachev made perestroika the troika's centerpiece, glasnost was the most potent in bringing new political forces and formerly silenced voices onto the political stage. The notion of a public voice distinct from the ruling power and the idea of open public debate ran hard against the Soviet ideological system.

Before Gorbachev, the regime recognized no public voice beyond the voice of the *nomenklatura*, the Communist Party hierarchy, speaking to its subjects through state-controlled media. All nonpolitical, literary, academic, and scientific publication was subject to the strictures of the party line and censorship.

Glasnost made its initial and unofficial appearance during the rule of Leonid Brezhnev, Gorbachev's predecessor. A small but vocal dissident movement (also known as the Democratic Movement) broke through the regime's facade of ideological conformity. It produced an underground press, *samizdat* (lit. self-publishing), which gave voice to a wide range of opinion and criticism at odds with the official line. A notable moment in samizdat came when Andrei Sakharov, the famed Soviet nuclear physicist and advocate of civil and democratic rights, published an unauthorized essay in 1968. He appealed to the top leaders to move toward glasnost and democracy as the path toward overcoming the country's urgent problems. Entitled *Progress, Coexistence and Intellectual Freedom*, the essay, written in typescript, circulated widely inside the USSR and was smuggled to the West. Sakharov's outspokenness led the Brezhnev regime to exile him in 1980 to the closed city Gorky, far from Moscow and Western media sources. In a symbolic gesture of his glasnost policy, Gorbachev freed Sakharov from exile six years later and allowed him to return to Moscow.

Though Sakharov's essay may well have influenced Gorbachev, Gorbachev's version of glasnost was limited and aimed at a controlled change and liberalizing reform of the Soviet system without destroying its foundations. Yet, despite his effort to keep glasnost within manageable limits, it opened the door ever wider to an intensifying and searching public debate challenging the Soviet order itself. Newspapers, journals, once-banned books, and revelations from archives appeared and found appreciative audiences. Glasnost as transparency brought to light what the regime had hidden. Revelation upon revelation of its record of mass repressions, abuses, lies, and corruption were publicized, deepening its disrepute among the public at large. Glasnost also gave voice to long-suppressed national independence movements within the empire, which contributed to its disintegration. Defenders of the old order warned Gorbachev that glasnost was a "two-edged sword" that could turn against its user. Yegor Ligachev, a fellow member of the Politburo, aimed a barb at Gorbachev that it was not wise to enter a room if you do not know the way out. And, in fact, the explosion of the nuclear reactor in Chernobyl, Ukraine, severely tested Gorbachev's commitment to glasnost.

Gorbachev's glasnost policy was a major factor precipitating and informing the political struggle developing in the leadership in the latter half of the 1980's and culminating in the coup of August 1991. The struggle began in earnest in the fall of 1987 with a split inside the ruling Politburo. Yegor Ligachev, former ally of Gorbachev, became his adversary on the right. Boris Yeltsin became his rival in the cause of reform on the left. Second in command in the Politburo, Ligachev defended the interests of the nomenklatura against Gorbachev's reforms. Yeltsin, who entered the Politburo under Gorbachev's patronage from provincial Sverdlovsk, pressed for a faster pace of reform than Gorbachev was then ready to promote. At a Central Committee meeting in October 1987, Yeltsin attacked Ligachev for sabotaging his reform efforts as Moscow party chief and accused Gorbachev of foot-dragging on perestroika. The upshot was Yeltsin's ouster from the Politburo and then as Moscow party secretary. His fall was a blessing in disguise for Yeltsin and freed him subsequently to rise as a popular leader untainted by association with the ruling group.

Despite his effort to control glasnost, Gorbachev soon found himself driven to more radical measures by the dynamic of the new political world that glasnost was bringing into play. First he proposed at a party plenum in January 1987 that party leaders be elected from below instead of by cooptation from above. He ran into a wall of resistance from local and regional party secretaries who feared losing power. He then turned to shifting his own base of power from the party to a new parliamentary body with constitutional powers beyond the reach of party control. In March 1989 he realized his project. A Congress of Peoples Deputies was instituted with two-thirds of its deputies popularly elected and a third selected from party and other official organizations. The Congress became a platform of open public debate televised to the whole country. Andrei Sakharov led the democratic grouping (Interregional Group) in opposition to the party nomenklatura. Sakharov lent his great prestige and the fire of his moral passion to the sharp and open debate in the body (often to Gorbachev's irritation as the presider) and galvanized public opinion against Communist Party abuses. Though conservative party elements held a large majority in the Congress, they found themselves on the defensive in the face of withering criticism from the Sakharov-led opposition. Glasnost was winning the day, but Gorbachev's grip on public debate and democratic reform began to slip. The introduction of popular elections was reversing the political thrust in the heart of the Soviet system. Power from above was increasingly challenged by power coming from below.

Yeltsin lost no time in using the electoral process Gorbachev brought into being. In Moscow he won a seat in the Congress by landslide, and after Sakharov's death in December, he assumed Sakharov's place as leader of the democratic faction. He also won a seat in the parliament of the Russian Federation, the body that elected Yeltsin its president in May 1990. At his initiative the Russian presidency was made into a national elective office, and in June 1991 he handily won that office in a national election, becoming the first Russian leader so chosen. Yeltsin became a powerful challenger to Gorbachev and to the Soviet system itself. Glasnost and democratic reform were no longer Gorbachev's preserve. What formerly had been a mere facade of Russian self-government now became a second center of authority in the land.

As rivalry between Gorbachev and Yeltsin unfolded, conservative elements inside the party were marshaling their forces to challenge Gorbachev and suppress glasnost and the democratic movement. Gorbachev now walked a tightrope between right-wing forces and the Yeltsin-led forces on the left. Gorbachev's effort to shore up his presidential powers and build his base in the Congress of Peoples Deputies and its Supreme Soviet was ineffectual. His popularity plummeted as Yeltsin's soared.

Leaders of the party's old guard finally struck in August 1991. They sought to employ all the Soviet agencies of repression against the developing democratic and national revolution. They organized an emergency committee, seized power in its name, declared martial law, sent an armada of tanks into Moscow, and put Gorbachev under house arrest in his vacation dacha in the Crimea. Yeltsin defied the perpetrators of the coup from atop a tank in front of the White House (the Russian parliament building), drawing a mass of supporters around him. The standoff ended when the military and special forces refused the emergency committee's orders to crush the opposition. The Russian democratic and national revolution under Boris Yeltsin's lead dissolved the emergency committee, arresting its members and the coup participants. The Russian Federation assumed full authority in its territories, abolished the Soviet Communist Party, and ushered the Soviet Union out of existence at the end of the year. The principal nations that had been subjected to the Soviet empire gained their independence. Gorbachev became a private citizen, and his rival, Yeltsin, went on to lead the resurrected Russian republic.

Before his death in December 1989, Sakharov, in a private encounter with Gorbachev, forewarned him that if he continued to seek unlimited power without standing for election, he would one day find himself without public support in a leadership crisis. Gorbachev was unwilling or unable to act on the clear implication that glasnost posed for his leadership, namely, that democratic legitimacy could only be secured through a process of public debate and popular election.

Though this was not his intention, Gorbachev paved the way for Russia's historical return as a nation-state and in the form of a democratic republic. His taking up of the cause of glasnost led to a renaissance of Russian intellectual and political life. Despite instability and a perilous transition from Soviet despotism to a fledgling republic, glasnost continued to be the rule in the new Russia's first decade, in the provisions of its new constitution, the existence of free public debate, and a series of orderly and reasonably fair parliamentary and presidential elections. Whether the spirit of glasnost prevails or wanes in the post-Yeltsin era was yet to be determined as the reborn Russia entered the twenty-first century. One thing was clear: glasnost would go down in the annals of Russian history as the potent word that brought down an empire.

See also: AUGUST 1991 PUTSCH; GORBACHEV, MIKHAIL SERGEYEVICH; LIGACHEV, YEGOR KUZMICH; PERESTROIKA; SAKHAROV, ANDREI DMITRIEVICH; SAMIZDAT; YELTSIN, BORIS NIKOLAYEVICH

BIBLIOGRAPHY

Gorbachev, Mikhail S. (1995). *Memoirs: Mikhail Gorbachev.* New York: Doubleday.

Gwertzman, B., and Kaufman, Michael T., eds. (1990, 1991). *The Collapse of Communism.* New York: Times Books.

Kaiser, Robert G. (1991). *Why Gorbachev Happened.* New York: Simon and Shuster.

Linden, Carl. (1997). "Gorbachev and the Fall of the Marxian Prince in Europe and Russia." In *Russia and China on the Eve of a New Millennium,* eds. Carl Linden and Jan S. Prybyla. New Brunswick, NJ: Transaction Publishers.

Tarasulo, Isaac J., ed. (1989). *Gorbachev and Glasnost: Viewpoints from the Soviet Press.* Wilmington, DE: Scholarly Resources Inc.

Walker, Rachael. (1993) *Six Years that Shook the World: Perestroika, the Impossible Project.* Manchester, UK: Manchester University Press.

CARL A. LINDEN

GLAVKI

Plural, short for glavnoye upravlenie, or chief administration.

Glavki are subordinate administrative units or departments of Soviet state planning and existed in economic, military, and cultural ministries, such as tourism. In the economy these subdivisions of central or local industrial ministries dealt with specific industrial branches in formulating and administering the annual and perspective plans.

These departments appeared originally as parts of the Supreme Council of National Economy (VSNKh or Vesenkha) controlling particular sectors, such as the match, soap, oil, and timber industries (*Glavspichki, Tsentromylo, Glavneft, Glovles,* and so forth). They replaced the corresponding People's Commissariats by early 1918. During the civil war period, the glavki controlled distribution of scarce materials and ordered new production of items for war, subject to interference from the Party's Politburo and without a national plan, wages, or bookkeeping. By 1921 this had become a bureaucratic chaos (called glavkism). Nevertheless, these units survived reorganizations during the New Economic Policy of the 1920s and thereafter, emerging once again in 1931. Now under the commissariats (called ministries after 1946) and Gosplan in the Stalinist planning period, they acquired direct power over their subordinate enterprises until Nikita Khrushchev's reorganization in 1957.

As a result of subdivisions, some glavki became new ministries, whose number in the industrial and construction branches alone reached thirty-three in 1946 and 1947, but about a year later the number was again reduced by unification. For instance, the Ministry of Textiles sometimes reverted to a chief administration within the Ministry of Light Industry, or the reverse. These continual organizational changes had questionable practical effect. Some of these *glavki*—such as those for finance or labor—were responsible for functional administration, and some were specialized subdivisions, such as the *glavki* for woolens in the Ministry of Textiles. Enterprises received their plans from the chief administration, usually in Moscow, and submitted their requirements to it. So-called funded inputs, which were especially scarce, were allocated to enterprises by the *glavki,* which set up their own supply arrangements to make sure their firms met the planned targets. They set up workshops to produce spare parts on an inefficiently small scale, a practice that also led to duplication. The chiefs of these chief administrations, usually called Deputy Ministers, became nonpolitical technical specialists, like most of the ministers over them, subject only to occasional intervention from party officials in the Kremlin. Their incentives were linked informally to the success of the enterprises under them, but not necessarily their profit or productivity. Accordingly, they could be relied on to support enterprises' requests for more investments and supplies and easier plans, even when they knew higher productivity would be possible. Sometimes they reallocated profits among their subordinated enterprises to allow all of them to meet their financial obligations. Even during the regional reorganization instituted by Khrushchev, the more important allocation decisions were made in the republican or sectoral glavki of the all-Union *Gossnab* (supply agency) in Moscow. This was necessary to prevent "localism," a preference for enterprises within one's region over the needs of enterprises elsewhere.

See also: GOSPLAN; INDUSTRIALIZATION, SOVIET

BIBLIOGRAPHY

Bergson, Abram. (1964). *The Economics of Soviet Planning.* New Haven: Yale University Press.

Carr, Edward Hallett, and Davies, R. W. (1969–[1978]). *Foundations of a Planned Economy, 1926–1929.* 3 vols. London: Macmillan.

Nove, Alec. (1961). *The Soviet Economy.* New York: Praeger.

MARTIN C. SPECHLER

GLAVLIT

The Main Directorate for Literary and Publishing Affairs (Glavnoe Upravlenie po Delam Literatury i Izdatelstv), known as Glavlit, was the state agency responsible for the censorship of printed materials in the Soviet Union. Although print was its main focus, it sometimes supervised the censorship of other media, including radio, television, theater, and film. Glavlit was created in 1922 to replace a network of uncoordinated military and civilian censorship agencies set up after the Bolshevik seizure of power. Although freedom of the press nominally existed in the Soviet Union, the government reserved the right to prevent the publication of certain materials. Glavlit was charged with preventing the publication of economic or military information believed to pose a threat to Soviet security; this included subjects as diverse as grain harvests, inflation, incidence of disease, and the location of military industries. Party and military leaders compiled a list of facts and categories deemed secret.

Glavlit was also charged with suppressing any printed materials deemed hostile to the Soviet state or the Communist Party. This ran the gamut from pornography to religious texts to anything that could be construed as critical of the party or state, whether implicitly or explicitly. Individual censors had a fair amount of discretion in this area, and often showed considerable creativity and paranoia in their work. The severity of censorship varied with the political climate. Glavlit was particularly strict in its supervision of the private publishers allowed to operate between 1921 and 1929.

Although some state publishing houses were initially exempted from Glavlit's supervision, by 1930 all printing and publishing in the Soviet Union was subject to pre-publication censorship. Everything from newspapers to books to ephemera, such as posters, note pads, and theater tickets, required the approval of a Glavlit official before it could be published; violation of this rule was a serious criminal offense.

Glavlit had several secondary functions, including the censorship of foreign literature imported to the Soviet Union. It also took part in purging materials associated with "enemies of the people" from libraries, bookstores, and museums.

Glavlit was part of the Russian Republic's Commissariat of Enlightenment until 1946, when it was placed under the direct authority of the All-Union Council of Ministers. Its official name changed several times after this point, usually to a variant of Main Directorate for the Protection of Military and State Secrets. Despite these changes, the acronym Glavlit continued to be used in official and unofficial sources. Technically a state institution, Glavlit answered directly to the Communist Party's Central Committee, which oversaw its work and appointed its leadership. Each Soviet Republic had its own Glavlit, with the Russian Republic's Glavlit setting the overall tone for Soviet censorship.

While most Soviet writers and editors learned to practice a degree of self-censorship to avoid problems, Glavlit served as a deterrent for those willing to question orthodox views. Its standards were relaxed in late 1988 as part of Mikhail Gorbachev's glasnost campaign. Glavlit was dissolved by presidential decree in 1991, essentially ending prepublication censorship in Russia, but other forms of state pressure on media outlets remained in effect.

See also: CENSORSHIP; GLASNOST; JOURNALISM; NEWSPAPERS; SAMIZDAT; TELEVISION AND RADIO; THEATER

BIBLIOGRAPHY

Fox, Michael S. (1992). "Glavlit, Censorship, and the Problem of Party Policy in Cultural Affairs, 1922–1928." *Soviet Studies* 44(6):1045–1068.

Plamper, Jan. (2001). "Abolishing Ambiguity: Soviet Censorship Practices in the 1930s." *Russian Review* 60(4):526–544.

Tax Choldin, Marianna, and Friedberg, Maurice, eds. (1989). *The Red Pencil: Artists, Scholars and Censors in the USSR*. Boston: Unwin-Hyman.

Brian Kassof

GLINKA, MIKHAIL IVANOVICH

(1804–1857), composer, regarded as founder of Russian art music, especially as creator of Russian national opera.

Mikhail Glinka, the musically gifted son of a landowner, gained much of his musical education during a journey to Europe (1830–1834). In Italy he became acquainted with the opera composers Vincenzo Bellini and Gaetano Donizetti, and in Berlin he studied music theory. After his return, Glinka channeled the spiritual effects of the trip into the composition of a work that went down in history as the first Russian national opera, "A Life for the Tsar" (1836). Three aspects of this opera were formative to operatic style in Russia: the national subject (here taken from the seventeenth century), the libretto in Russian, and the musical language, which combined the European basic techniques with Russian melodic patterns. The patriotic character of the subject fit extremely well into the conservative national attitudes of the 1830s under Tsar Nicholas I. In spite of Glinka's stylistic borrowings from European tradition, the Russian features of the music made way for a national art music apart form the dominant foreign models. Overnight, Glinka became famous and soon was admired as the father of Russian music. Whereas the "Life for the Tsar" marked the beginning of the historical opera in Russia, "Ruslan and Lyudmila" (1842) established the genre of the Russian fairy-tale opera. Thus, Glinka embodied the two strands of Russian opera that would flourish in the nineteenth century. Stylistically Glinka's Russian and Oriental elements exerted greatest influence on the following generations. Glinka became not only a creative point of reference for many Russian composers but also a national and cultural role model, and later a figure of cult worship with the reestablishment of Soviet patriotism under Josef Stalin.

See also: MUSIC; OPERA

BIBLIOGRAPHY

Brown, David. (1974). *Mikhail Glinka: A Biographical and Critical Study.* London: Oxford University Press.

Orlova, Aleksandra A. (1988). *Glinka's Life in Music: A Chronicle.* Ann Arbor: University of Michigan Research Press.

MATTHIAS STADELMANN

GLINSKAYA, YELENA VASILIEVNA

(d. 1538), the second wife of Grand Prince Basil III and regent for her son Ivan IV from 1533 to 1538.

Yelena Vasilievna Glinskaya was the daughter of Prince Vasily Lvovich Glinsky and his wife Anna, daughter of the Serbian military governor, Stefan Yakshich. After Basil III forced his first wife, Solomonia Saburova, to take the veil in 1525 because of her inability to produce offspring, he entered into a second marriage with Glinskaya in the following year. They bore two sons, the future Ivan IV and his younger brother Yury Vasilyevich.

Because Ivan IV was only three years old at the time of Basil III's death in 1533, Glinskaya became a regent of the Russian state during his minority. Although Basil III had entrusted the care of his widow and sons to relatives of Glinskaya and apparently had not made specific provisions for her regency, the royal mother used her pivotal dynastic position to defend her son's interests against those of rival boyar factions at court. Aided by her presumed lover, Prince Ivan Ovchina-Telepnev-Obolensky, and Metropolitan Daniel, Glinskaya headed up a government marked by efficient policies, both abroad and at home. Her government successfully fended off the efforts of Lithuania, the Crimean khan, and Kazan to encroach on Russian territories. At Glinskaya's death in 1538, Russia was at peace with its neighbors. Domestically, Glinskaya moved to eliminate the power of the remaining appanage princes, who presented a dynastic challenge to the Grand Prince. She initiated the creation and fortification of towns throughout the Russian realm, increasing the protection of the population and that of the realm substantially. In 1535 the regency government introduced a currency reform, adopting a single monetary system, which significantly improved economic conditions in Russia. Glinskaya's government also worked toward the institution of a system of local judicial officials, which was eventually realized in Ivan IV's reign. While Glinskaya managed to keep in check the various aristocratic factions, which sought to increase their influence vis-à-vis the young heir to the throne, the situation quickly reversed after her death. Without the protecting hand of his mother, the young Ivan IV was exposed to the political intrigues of the boyars until his ascendance to the throne in 1547.

As a royal wife, Glinskaya shared the problems of all Muscovite royal women, especially their concern about the production of children and their health. Glinskaya joined her husband on arduous pilgrimages to pray for offspring. Like her predecessor, Saburova, she seems to have believed that her womb could be divinely blessed. Five letters to Glinskaya attributed to Basil III portray the Grand Princess as a devoted mother who struggled to maintain her children's physical and emotional well-being.

Glinskaya's legitimacy and effectiveness as a regent have been the subject of scholarly debate. While earlier studies have treated the grand princess as a figurehead and her regency as a period of transition, recent work on the early sixteenth century stresses Glinskaya's political achievements in her own right. During the reign of her son, the Grand Princess's political and social status was enhanced in the chronicles produced at the royal court, and Glinskaya became a model for future tsars' wives.

See also: BASIL III; IVAN IV

BIBLIOGRAPHY

Miller, David. (1993). "The Cult of Saint Sergius of Radonezh and Its Political Uses." *Slavic Review* 52(4): 680–699.

Pushkareva, Natalia. (1997). *Women in Russian History from the Tenth to the Twentieth Century*, tr. and ed. Eve Levin. Armonk, NY: M. E. Sharpe.

Thyrêt, Isolde. (2001). *Between God and Tsar: Religious Symbolism and the Royal Women of Muscovite Russia.* DeKalb, IL: Northern Illinois University Press.

ISOLDE THYRÊT

GNEZDOVO

Located in the Upper Dnepr River, thirteen kilometers west of Smolensk, Gnezdovo was a key portage and transshipment point along the "Route to the Greeks" in the late ninth through the early eleventh centuries. The area provided easy access to the upper reaches of the Western Dvina, Dnepr, and Volga rivers. The archaeological complex consists of several pagan and early Christian cemeteries (17 hectares), one fortified settlement (1 hectare), and several unfortified settlements. More than 1,200 of the estimated 3,500 to 4,000 burial mounds have been excavated. While Balt and Slav burials are found in great number, the mounds with Scandinavian ethnocultural traits (cremations in boats and rich inhumations and chamber graves) receive the most attention. However, no more than fifty mounds can be positively identified as Scandinavian. Gnezdovo's burials are among the richest for European Russia in the tenth century and include glass beads, swords, horse riding equipment, silver and bronze jewelry, and Islamic, Byzantine, and western European coins.

Although much of Gnezdovo's settlement layers have perished, recent excavations reveal house foundations and pits containing the remains of iron smithing and the working of nonferrous metals into ornaments, not unlike production of the contemporaneous and better–preserved sites of Staraia Ladoga and Riurikovo gorodishche. Gnezdovo's most intense period of settlement dates to the period from 920 to the 960s, when its settlements had reached their maximum size and when many of the largest burial mounds were raised. Gnezdovo was abandoned in the early eleventh century, when a new center, Smolensk, assumed Gnezdovo's role in international and regional trade.

See also: KIEVAN RUS; ROUTE TO THE GREEKS; VIKINGS

BIBLIOGRAPHY

Avdusin D.A. (1969). "Smolensk and the Varangians according to Archaeological Data." *Norwegian Archaeological Review* 2:52-62.

HEIDI M. SHERMAN

GODUNOV, BORIS FYODOROVICH

(1552–1605), Tsar of Russia (1598–1605).

Tsar Boris Godunov, one of the most famous (or infamous) rulers of early modern Russia, has been the subject of many biographies, plays, and even an opera by Mussorgsky. Boris's father was only a provincial cavalryman, but Boris's uncle, Dmitry Godunov (a powerful aristocrat), was able to advance the young man's career. Dmitry Godunov brought Boris and his sister, Irina, to the court of Tsar Ivan IV, and Boris enrolled in Ivan's dreaded Oprichnina (a state within the state ruled directly by the tsar). Boris soon attracted the attention of Tsar Ivan, who allowed him to marry Maria, the daughter of his favorite, Malyuta Skuratov (the notorious boss of the Oprichnina). Boris and Maria had two children: a daughter named Ksenya and a son named Fyodor. Both children received excellent educations, which was unusual in early modern Russia. Boris's sister Irina was the childhood playmate of Ivan IV's mentally retarded son, Fyodor, and eventually married him. When Tsar Ivan died in 1584, he named Boris as one of Tsar Fyodor I's regents. By 1588, Boris triumphed over his rivals to become Fyodor's sole regent and the effective ruler of Russia.

Boris Godunov has been called one of Russia's greatest rulers. Handsome, eloquent, energetic, and extremely bright, he brought greater skill to the tasks of governing than any of his predecessors and was an excellent administrator. Boris was respected in international diplomacy and managed to make

Tsar Boris Godunov posed with the Russian regalia of state, to underscore his dubious claim to the throne. ARCHIVO ICONOGRAFICO, S.A./CORBIS. REPRODUCED BY PERMISSION.

peace with Russia's neighbors. At home he was a zealous protector of the Russian Orthodox Church, a great builder and beautifier of Russian towns, and generous to the needy. As regent, Boris was responsible for the elevation of his friend, Metropolitan Job (head of the Russian Orthodox Church), to the rank of Patriarch in 1589; and Boris's generosity to the Church was rewarded by the strong loyalty of the clergy. Boris continued Ivan IV's policy of rapidly expanding the state to the south and east; but, due to a severe social and economic crisis that had been developing since the 1570s, he faced a declining tax base and a shrinking gentry cavalry force. In order to shore up state finances and the gentry so that he could continue Russia's imperial expansion, Boris enserfed the Russian peasants in the 1590s, tied townspeople to their taxpaying districts, and converted short-term slavery to permanent slavery. Boris also tried to tame the cossacks (bandits and mercenary soldiers) on Russia's southern frontier and harness them to state service. Those drastic measures failed to alleviate the state's severe crisis, but they did make many Russians hate him.

Boris was accused by his enemies of coveting the throne and murdering his rivals. When it was reported that Tsar Ivan IV's youngest son, Dmitry of Uglich (born in 1582), had died by accidentally slitting his throat in 1591, many people believed Boris had secretly ordered the boy's death in order to clear a path to the throne for himself. (Several historians have credited that accusation, but there is no significant evidence linking Boris to the Uglich tragedy.) When the childless Tsar Fyodor I died in 1598, Boris was forced to fight for the throne. His rivals, including Fyodor Romanov (the future Patriarch Filaret, father of Michael Romanov), were unable to stop him from becoming tsar, but they did manage to slow him down. At one point, an exasperated Boris proclaimed that he no longer wanted to become tsar and retired to a monastery. Patriarch Job hastily convened an assembly of clergy, lords, bureaucrats, and townspeople to go to the monastery to beg Boris to take the throne. (This ad hoc assembly was later falsely represented as a full-fledged Assembly of the Land [or *Zemsky Sobor*] duly convened for the task of choosing a tsar.) In fact, Boris had enormous advantages over his rivals; he had been the ruler of Russia for a decade and had many supporters at court, in the Church, in the bureaucracy, and among the gentry cavalrymen. By clever maneuvering, Boris was soon accepted by the aristocracy as tsar, and he was crowned on September 1, 1598.

For most Russians, the reign of Tsar Boris was an unhappy time. Indeed, it marked the beginning of Russia's horrific Time of Troubles (1598–1613). By the end of the sixteenth century, Russia's developing state crisis reached its deepest stage, and a sharp political struggle within the ruling elite undermined Tsar Boris's legitimacy in the eyes of many of his subjects and set the stage for civil war. In his coronation oath, Tsar Boris had promised not to harass his political enemies, but he ended up persecuting several aristocratic families, including the Romanovs. That prompted some of his opponents to begin working secretly against the Godunov dynasty. Contemporaries described the fearful atmosphere that developed in Moscow and the gradual drift of Tsar Boris's regime into increasingly harsh reprisals against opponents and more frequent use of spies, denunciations, torture, and executions.

Early in Tsar Boris's reign catastrophe struck Russia. In the period 1601–1603, many of Russia's crops failed due to bad weather. The result was the worst famine in all of Russian history; up to one-third of Tsar Boris's subjects perished. In spite of Boris's sincere efforts to help his suffering people, many of them concluded that God was punishing Russia for the sins of its ruler. Therefore, when a man appeared in Poland-Lithuania in 1603 claiming to be Dmitry of Uglich, miraculously saved from Boris Godunov's alleged assassins back in 1591, many Russians were willing to believe that God had saved Ivan the Terrible's youngest son in order to topple the evil usurper Boris Godunov. When False Dmitry invaded Russia in 1604, many cossacks and soldiers joined his ranks, and many towns of southwestern Russia rebelled against Tsar Boris. Even after False Dmitry's army was decisively defeated in the battle of Dobrynichi (January 1605), enthusiasm for the true tsar spread like wildfire throughout most of southern Russia. Support for False Dmitry even began to appear in the tsar's army and in Moscow itself. A very unhappy Tsar Boris, who had been ill for some time, withdrew from public sight. Despised and feared by many of his subjects, Boris died on April 13, 1605. It was rumored that he took his own life, but he probably died of natural causes. Boris's son took the throne as Tsar Fyodor II, but within six weeks the short-lived Godunov dynasty was overthrown in favor of Tsar Dmitry.

See also: ASSEMBLY OF THE LAND; COSSACKS; DMITRY, FALSE; DMITRY OF UGLICH; FILARET ROMANOV, PATRIARCH; FYODOR IVANOVICH; IVAN IV; JOB, PATRIARCH; OPRICHNINA; ROMANOV, MIKHAIL FYODOROVICH; SLAVERY; TIME OF TROUBLES

BIBLIOGRAPHY

Barbour, Philip. (1966). *Dimitry Called the Pretender: Tsar and Great Prince of All Russia, 1605–1606.* Boston: Houghton Mifflin.

Crummey, Robert O. (1987). *The Formation of Muscovy, 1304–1613.* London: Longman.

Dunning, Chester. (2001). *Russia's First Civil War: The Time of Troubles and the Founding of the Romanov Dynasty.* University Park: Pennsylvania State University Press.

Margeret, Jacques. (1983). *The Russian Empire and Grand Duchy of Muscovy: A Seventeenth-Century French Account,* tr. and ed. Chester Dunning. Pittsburgh, PA: Pittsburgh University Press.

Perrie, Maureen. (1995). *Pretenders and Popular Monarchism in Early Modern Russia: The False Tsars of the Time of Troubles.* Cambridge, UK.: Cambridge University Press.

Platonov, S. F. (1973). *Boris Godunov, Tsar of Russia,* tr. L. Rex Piles. Gulf Breeze, FL: Academic International Press.

Skrynnikov, Ruslan. (1982). *Boris Godunov,* tr. Hugh Graham. Gulf Breeze, FL: Academic International Press.

Vernadsky, George. (1954). "The Death of Tsarevich Dimitry: A Reconsideration of the Case." *Oxford Slavonic Papers* 5:1–19.

CHESTER DUNNING

GOGOL, NIKOLAI VASILIEVICH

(1809–1852), short-story writer, novelist, playwright, essayist.

Nikolai Vasilievich Gogol, whose bizarre characters, absurd plots, and idiosyncratic narrators have both entranced and confounded readers worldwide and influenced authors from Fyodor Dostoyevsky to Franz Kafka to Flannery O'Connor, led a life as cryptic and circuitous as his fiction. He was born in 1809 in Sorochintsy, Ukraine. His father was a playwright; his mother, a highly devout and imaginative woman and one of Gogol's key influences. By no stretch a stellar student, Gogol showed theatrical talent, parodying his teachers and peers and performing in plays.

In 1828 Gogol moved to Petersburg with hopes of launching a literary career, His long poem *Hans Kuechelgarten* (1829), a derivative, slightly eccentric idyll, received only a brief and critical mention in the *Moscow Telegraph.* Dismayed, Gogol burned all the copies he could find and left for Lübeck, Germany, only to return several weeks later. In 1831 he met the poet Alexander Pushkin. His first collection *Evenings on a Farm Near Dikanka* (1831–1832), folk and ghost tales set in Ukraine and narrated by beekeeper Rudy Panko, reaped praise for its relative freshness and hilarity, and Gogol became a household name in Petersburg literary circles.

Gogol followed the *Dikanka* stories with two 1835 collections, *Arabesques* and *Mirgorod.* From *Mirgorod,* the "Tale of How Ivan Ivanovich Quarrelled with Ivan Nikiforovich" (nicknamed "The Two Ivans"), blends comedy with tragedy, prose with poetry, satire with gratuitous play. Describing the two Ivans through bizarre juxtapositions, the narrator explains how the fatal utterance of the word *gander* (*gusak*) severed their friendship for good.

Gogol's Petersburg tales, some included in *Arabesques*, some published separately, contain some of Gogol's best-known work, including "The Nose" (1835), about a nose on the run in full uniform; "Diary of a Madman" (1835), about a civil servant who discovers that he is the king of Spain; and "The Overcoat" (1842), about a copyist who becomes obsessed with the purchase of a new overcoat. In all these stories, as in the "Two Ivans," plot is secondary to narration, and the tension between meaning and meaninglessness remains unresolved.

In 1836 a poor staging and mixed reception of Gogol's play *The Inspector General* precipitated his second trip to Europe, where he stayed five years except for brief visits to Russia. While in Rome he wrote the novel *Dead Souls* (1842), whose main character, Pavel Ivanovich Chichikov, travels from estate to estate with the goal of purchasing deceased serfs (souls) to use as collateral for a state loan. Chichikov's travels can be considered a tour of Gogol's narrative prowess. With each visit, Chichikov encounters new eccentricities of setting, behavior, and speech.

In 1841 Gogol returned to Russia. There he began a sequel to *Dead Souls* chronicling Chichikov's fall and redemption. This marked the beginning of Gogol's decline: his struggle to establish a spiritual message in his work. His puzzling and dogmatic *Selections from Correspondence with Friends* (1847), in which he offers advice on spiritual and practical matters, dismayed his friends and supporters. Various travels, including a pilgrimage in 1848 to the Holy Land, failed to bring him the strength and inspiration he sought. Following the advice of his spiritual adviser and confessor, the fanatical Father Matthew, who told him to renounce literature, he burned *Dead Souls* shortly before dying of self-starvation in 1852.

See also: DOSTOYEVSKY, FYODOR MIKHAILOVICH; GOLDEN AGE OF RUSSIAN LITERATURE; PUSHKIN, ALEXANDER SERGEYEVICH

BIBLIOGRAPHY

Karlinsky, Simon. (1976). *The Sexual Labyrinth of Nikolai Gogol.* Cambridge, MA: Harvard University Press.

Maguire, Robert. (1994). *Exploring Gogol.* Stanford, CA: Stanford University Press.

Nabokov, Vladimir. (1961). *Nikolai Gogol.* New York: New Directions.

Senechal, Diana. (1999). "Diabolical Structures in the Poetics of Nikolai Gogol." Ph.D. diss., Yale University, New Haven, CT.

DIANA SENECHAL

GOLDEN AGE OF RUSSIAN LITERATURE

The Golden Age of Russian Literature is notably not a term often employed in literary criticism. It does not refer to any particular school or movement (e.g., Classicism, Romanticism, Realism); rather, it encompasses several of them. As such, it immediately falls prey to all the shortcomings of such literary categorizations, not the least of which is imprecision. The term furthermore demands, *eo ipso*, a pair of ungilded ages at either end, and might lead one to an easy and unstudied dismissal of works outside its tenure. Finally, those who wrote during its span were not particularly aware of living in an aureate age, and they certainly never consciously identified themselves as belonging to a unified or coherent faction—any similarity is adduced from the outside and puts in jeopardy the authors' particular geniuses. That said, the phrase "golden age of Russian literature" has gained currency and therefore, if for no other reason, deserves to be defined as carefully and intelligently as possible.

When they indulge in a yen for periodization, literary specialists tend to distinguish two contiguous (or perhaps slightly overlapping) golden ages: the first, a golden age of Russian poetry, which lasted (roughly) from the publication of Gavrila Derzhavin's Ossianic-inspired "The Waterfall" in 1794, until Aleksandr Pushkin's "turn to prose" around 1831 (or as late as Mikhail Lermontov's death in 1841); and the second, a Golden Age of Russian prose, which began with the nearly simultaneous publication of Nikolai Gogol's *Evenings on a Farm near the Dikanka* and Pushkin's *Tales of Belkin* (1831), and which petered out sometime during the last decades of the nineteenth century.

It is historians, with their professional inclination to divide time into discrete and digestible pieces, who most often make use of the term under discussion. Nicholas Riasanovsky, in *A History of Russia*, offers the following span: The golden age of Russian literature has been dated roughly from 1820 to 1880, from Pushkin's first major poems [his stylized, Voltairean folk-epic *Ruslan and Liudmila*] to Dostoevsky's last major novel [*Brothers*

Karamazov]. Riasanovsky's dates are notably narrower than those mentioned above. His span omits the first two decades of the century, and with them the late pseudo-classicism of Derzhavin, as well as the Sentimentalism and Ossianic Romanticism of Nikolai Karamzin and Vasily Zhukovsky—schools that constituted Pushkin's and Gogol's frame of reference and laid the verbal foundation for the later glorious literary output of Russia. On the far end, it disbars the final two decades of the nineteenth century, Anton Chekhov and Maksim Gorky notwithstanding. Ending the golden age in 1880 furthermore neatly excludes the second half of Tolstoy's remarkable sixty-year career.

1830S AND 1840S: ROMANTICISM

If one is to follow the historians in disregarding the first decades of the nineteenth century—to discount, so to say, the first blush and to wait until the flower has fully bloomed—then arguably a better date to initiate the golden age of literature would be 1831, which witnessed the debut of two uncontested masterpieces of Russian literature. In January, for the first time in its final form, *Woe from Wit*, Alexander Griboyedov's droll drama in verse (free iambs), was performed. A few months later, Pushkin put the final touches on *Eugene Onegin*, his unequaled novel in verse, which he had begun in 1823. The works are both widely recognized by Russians as the hallmarks of Russian literature, but they receive short shrift outside of their native land, a fate perhaps ineluctable for works of subtle and inventive poetry

The year 1831 also witnessed Gogol's successful entry into literary fame with his folksy *Evenings on a Farm near the Dikanka*. Gogol and Pushkin had struck up an acquaintance in that year, and Gogol claimed that Pushkin had given him the kernel of the ideas for his two greatest works: *Dead Souls* (1842), perhaps the comic novel *par excellence;* and the uproarious *Inspector General* (1836), generally recognized as the greatest Russian play and one that certainly ranks as one of the world's most stageable.

Pushkin also served as the springboard for another literato of the golden age, Lermontov, who responded to Pushkin's death (in a duel) in 1837 with his impassioned "Death of a Poet," a poem which launched Lermontov's brief literary career (he was killed four years later in a duel). Although his corpus is smallish—he had written little serious verse before 1837—and much of it was left unpublished until after his death (mostly for censorial reasons), Lermontov is generally considered Russia's second-greatest poet. He also penned a prose masterpiece, *A Hero of Our Time*, a cycle of short stories united by its jaded and cruel protagonist, Pechorin, who became a stock type in Russian literature.

In 1847 Gogol published his *Selected Passages from My Correspondence with Friends*, a pastiche of religious, conservative, and monarchical sermonettes—he endorses serfdom—that was met by an overwhelmingly negative reaction by critics who had long assumed that Gogol shared their progressive mindset. Vissarion Belinsky, perhaps the most influential critic ever in Russia, wrote a lashing rebuke that was banned by the censor, in part because it claimed that the Russian people were naturally atheists. The uproar surrounding *Selected Passages* effectively ended Gogol's career five years before the author's death in 1852.

REALISM

In 1849, the young writer Fyodor Dostoyevsky—who had created a sensation in 1845 with his parodic sentimentalist epistolary novel *Poor Folk*, but whose subsequent works had been coolly received—injudiciously read the abovementioned rebuke of Gogol and allowed his copy to be reproduced, for which he spent ten years in Siberia. When he returned to St. Petersburg, he published *Notes from the House of the Dead*, an engrossing fictionalized memoir of the years he had spent in penal servitude. The work was his first critical success since *Poor Folk*, and he followed it, during the 1860s and 1870s, with a series of novels that were both critical and popular successes, including *Notes from Underground* (1864) and *Crime and Punishment* (1866) —both, in part, rejoinders to the positivistic and utilitarian *Geist* of the time. His masterpiece *Brothers Karamazov* (1880) won him the preeminent position in Russian letters shortly before his death in 1881.

Gogol's death in 1852 moved Ivan Turgenev to write an innocuous commemorative essay, for which he was arrested, jailed for a month, and then banished to his estate. That year, his *Sportsman's Sketches* was first published in book form, and popular response to the vivid sketches of life in the countryside has been long identified as galvanizing support for the Emancipation. (Its upper-class readers were apparently jarred by the realization that peasants were heterogeneous and distinct individuals). Turgenev's prose works are united by their careful and subtle psychological depictions of highly self-conscious characters whose search for truth and a vocation reflects Russia's own vacillations during the decades of the 1860s and 1870s. His greatest work, *Fathers and Sons* (1862), depicted the nihilist and utilitarian milieu of Russia at the inception of Age of the Great Reforms. The clamor surrounding *Fathers and Sons*—it was condemned by conservatives as too liberal, but liberals as too conservative—pricked Turgenev's *amour propre*, and he spent the much of his remaining two decades abroad in France and Germany.

It was also in 1852 that Tolstoy's first published work, *Childhood*, appeared in *The Contemporary* (a journal Pushkin founded), under the byline L. N. (the initials of Tolstoy's Christian and patronymic names). The piece made Tolstoy an instant success: Turgenev wrote the journal's editor to praise the work and encourage the anonymous author, and Dostoyevsky wrote to a friend from faraway Siberia to learn the identity L. N., whose story had so engaged him. Along with Dostoyevsky, Tolstoy's prose dominated the Russian literary and intellectual spheres during the1860s and 1870s. *War and Peace* (1869), his magnum opus, describes the Russian victory over Napoleon's army. *Anna Karenina* (1878), a Russian version of a family novel, was published serially in *The Russian Messenger* (the same journal that soon thereafter published Dostoyevsky's *Brothers Karamazov*) and is generally considered one of the finest novels ever written.

THE END OF THE GOLDEN AGE

Although none of Tolstoy's works (before 1884) treated politics and social conflict in the direct manner of Dostoyevsky or Turgenev, they were nonetheless socially engaged, treating obliquely historical or philosophical questions present in contemporary debates. This circumspectness ended in the early 1880s after Tolstoy's self-described "spiritual restructuring," after which he penned a series of highly controversial, mostly banned works beginning with *A Confession*, (1884). Marking the end of golden age at the threshold of the 1880s—with Tolstoy's crisis and the deaths of Dostoyevsky (1881) and Turgenev (1883)—relies on the convenient myth of Tolstoy's rejection of literature in 1881, despite works such as *Death of Ivan Ilich, Resurrection, Kreutzer Sonata, Hadji Murad*, several excellent and innovative plays, and dozens of short stories—in brief, an output of belletristic literature that, even without *War and Peace* and *Anna Karenina*, would have qualified Tolstoy as a world-class writer. It also excludes Anton Chekhov, whose short stories and plays in many ways defined the genres for the twentieth century. Chekhov's first serious stories began to appear in the mid-1880s, and by the 1890s he was one of the most popular writers in Russia. Ending the golden age in the early 1880s likewise leaves out Maxim Gorky (pseudonym of Alexei Peshkov), whose half-century career writing wildly popular, provocative and much-imitated stories and plays depicting the social dregs of Russia began with the publication of "Chelkash" in 1895.

A better date to end the golden age, therefore, might well be 1899, a year that bore witness to the publication of Sergei Diagilev's and Alexander Benois's *The World of Art*, that herald of the silver age of Russian literature, with its bold, syncretic program of music, theater, painting, and sculpture, idealistic metaphysics, and religion. The same year Tolstoy published (abroad) his influential *What Is Art?*, an invective raging equally against the Realist, socially-engaged literature of the previous century and the esthete, *l'art pour l'art* school that then dominated the literary scene. In their stead, it promulgated an emotive art that would unify all of humankind into a mystical brotherhood—a program not at all irreconcilable with the silver age aesthetics, proving the lozenge that *les extrêmes se touchent*.

OVERVIEW

Although the golden age should in no way be seen as an internally, self-consciously united movement, several features marry the individual authors and their works. Russian literature of this period thrived independently of politics. Its prodigious growth was unchecked, perhaps encouraged, by autocracy (some flowers bloom best in poor soil): It set its roots during the stifling reign of Nicholas I, continued to grow during the Era of Great Reforms begun under the Tsar-Liberator Alexander II, blossomed profusely during the reactionarily conservative final years of his rule, and continued to bloom in fits under Alexander III. The literature of the period engaged and influenced the social debates of the era. It remained, however, above the fray, characteristically criticizing, as overly simplistic, the autocratic and conservative government and the utilitarian ideas of progressive critics alike, for which it was frequently condemned by all sides.

It was also, in many important ways, *sui generis*. One constant characteristic of all the works cited above is their distinctive Russian-ness. All of the authors were fluent in the conventions and heritage of Western European literature, but they frequently and consciously rejected and parodied its traditions. (This tendency explains why many early Western European readers and popularizers of Russian literature (e.g., Vogüé) considered Russians to be brilliant but unschooled savages.) What exactly constitutes the quiddity of this Russian-ness is a thorny issue, though one might safely hazard that one defining characteristic of Russian literature is its concern with elaborating the Russian idea.

Finally, the limited amount of Russian literature cannot be exaggerated. In the brief overview of the period given above, one might be surprised by the tightly interdigitated fates of Russian authors during the golden age. However, the world of Russian letters was remarkably small. As late as 1897, according to the census conducted that year, only 21.1 percent of the population was literate, and only 1 percent of the 125 million residents had middle or higher education. The Russian novelist and critic Vladimir Nabokov once noted that the entirety of the Russian canon, the generally acknowledged best of poetry and prose, would span 23,000 pages of ordinary print, practically all of it written during the nineteenth century—a very compact library indeed, when one figures that a handful of the works included in this anthological daydream are nearly a thousand pages each. Despite its slenderness, youth, and narrow base, in influence and artistic worth Russian literature rivals that of any national tradition.

See also: CHEKHOV, ANTON PAVLOVICH; DOSTOYEVSKY, FYODOR MIKHAILOVICH; GOGOL, NIKOLAI VASILIEVICH; LERMONTOV, MIKHAIL YURIEVICH; PUSHKIN, ALEXANDER SERGEYEVICH; TOLSTOY, LEO NIKOLAYEVICH

BIBLIOGRAPHY

Billington, James H. (1966). *The Icon and the Axe: An Interpretive History of Russian Culture.* New York: Vintage Books.

Brown, W.E. (1986). *A History of Russian Literature of the Romantic Period.* 4 vols. Ann Arbor: MI: Ardis.

Mirsky, D.P. (1958). *A History of Russian Literature from Its Beginnings to 1900,* ed. Francis Whitfield. New York: Vintage Books.

Proffer, Carl R., comp. (1989). *Nineteenth-Century Russian Literature in English: A Bibliography of Criticism and Translations.* Ann Arbor: MI: Ardis.

Terras, Victor. (1991). *A History of Russian Literature.* New Haven, CT: Yale University Press.

Terras, Victor, ed. (1985). *Handbook of Russian Literature.* New Haven, CT: Yale University Press.

Todd, William Mills, III, ed. (1978). *Literature and Society in Imperial Russia.* Stanford, CA: Stanford University Press.

MICHAEL A. DENNER

GOLDEN HORDE

An anachronistic and misleading term for an area more appropriately called the Ulus of Jochi or Khanate of Qipchaq (although Arabic sources at times refer to it as the Ulus of Batu or Ulus of Berke).

In Russian sources contemporary to the existence of the Golden Horde, the term *Orda* alone was used to apply to the camp or palace, and later to the capital city, where the khan resided. The term *Zolotaya Orda,* which has been translated as "Golden Horde," first appears in Russian sources of the late sixteenth to early seventeenth centuries, many decades after the end of the Qipchaq Khanate. In a travel account of 1624 concerning a journey he took to Persia, the merchant Fedot Afanasievich Kotov describes coming to the lower Volga River: "Here by the river Akhtuba [i.e., the eastern effluent of the Volga] stands the Zolotaya Orda. The khan's court, palaces, and [other] courts, and mosques are all made of stone. But now all these buildings are being dismantled and the stone is being taken to Astrakhan." Zolotaya Orda can be understood here to mean the capital city of the Qipchaq Khanate. Of the two capitals of that khanate—Old Sarai or New Sarai (referred to in the historiography as Sarai Batu and Sarai Berke, respectively)—Kotov's description most likely refers to New Sarai at the present-day Tsarev archaeological site.

In the *History of the Kazan Khanate* (*Kazanskaya istoriya*), which some scholars date to the second half of the sixteenth century and others to the early seventeenth century, the term *Zolotaya Orda* (or *Zlataya Orda*) appears at least fifteen times. Most of these references seem to be to the capital city—that is, where the khan's court was—but some can by extension be understood to apply to the entire area ruled by the khan. The problem with accepting the reliability of this work is its genre, which seems to be historical fiction. Given the popularity of the *History of the Kazan Khanate* (the text is extant in more than two hundred manuscript copies), one can understand how the term *Golden Horde* became a popular term of reference. It is more difficult to understand why.

Neither Kotov nor the author of the *History of the Kazan' Khanate* explains why he is using the term *Golden Horde.* It does not conform to the steppe color-direction system, such that black equals north, blue equals east, red equals south, white equals west, and yellow (or gold) equals center. The Qipchaq Khanate was not at the center of the Mongol Empire but at its western extremity, so one should expect the term *White Horde,* which does occur, although rarely, in sources contemporary to its existence. Even then the term seems to apply only to the khanate's western half, while the term *Blue Horde* identifies its eastern half. One could refer to the palace or the camp of any khan as "golden" in the sense that it was at the "center" of the khanate, but in no other case is it used to refer to a khanate as a whole.

In the eighteenth century, Princess Yekaterina Dashkova suggested that the term *Golden Horde* was applied to the Qipchaq Khanate "because it possessed great quantities of gold and the weapons of its people were decorated with it." But this conjecture seems to fall into the realm of folk etymology. Others have suggested that the term refers to the golden pavilion of the khan, or at least a tent covered with golden tiles (as the fourteenth-century traveler Ibn Battuta described the domicile of Khan (Özbek). Yet khans in other khanates had similar tents or pavilions at the time, so there was nothing that would make this a distinguishing trait of the Qipchaq khan or of his khanate, let alone a reason to call the khanate "golden." George Vernadsky proposed that Golden Horde may have been applied to the Khanate of Qipchaq (or Great Horde) only after the separation of the Crimean Khanate and Kazan Khanate from it in the mid-fifteenth century. It would have occupied, accordingly, a central or "golden" position between the two. Yet, neither of the other khanates, in the evidence available, was designated white or blue (or red or black) as would then be expected.

This leaves three intractable considerations: (1) there is no evidence that the Qipchaq Khanate was ever referred to as "Golden Horde" during the time of its existence; (2) the earliest appearance of the term in a nonfictional work is one written more than a hundred years after the khanate's demise and refers specifically to the capital city where the khan resided, not to the khanate as a whole; and (3) no better reason offers itself for calling the Qipchaq Khanate the Golden Horde than an apparent mistake in a late sixteenth- or early seventeenth-century Muscovite work of fiction.

The Khanate of Qipchaq was set up by Batu (d. 1255) in the 1240s after the return of the Mongol force that invaded central Europe. Batu thus became the first khan of a khanate that was a multiethnic conglomeration consisting of Qipchaqs (Polovtsi), Kangli, Alans, Circassians, Rus, Armenians, Greeks, Volga Bulgars, Khwarezmians, and others, including no more than 4000 Mongols who ruled over them. Economically, it was made up of nomadic pastoralists, sedentary agriculturalists, and urban dwellers, including merchants, artisans, and craftsmen. The territory of the khanate at its greatest expanse reached from Galicia and Lithuania in the west to present-day Mongolia and China in the east, and from Transcaucasia and Khwarezm in the south into the forest zone of the Rus principalities and western Siberia in the north. Some scholars dispute whether the Rus principalities were ever officially part of the Qipchaq Khanate or merely vassal states. These scholars cite the account of the fourteenth-century Arabic historian al-Umari to the effect that the Khanate consisted of four parts: Sarai, the Crimea, Khwarezm, and the *Desht-i Qipchaq* (the western Eurasian steppe). Since most Rus principalities were not in the steppe but in the forest zone north of the steppe, they would seem to be excluded. Other scholars argue that not too fine a point should be put on what al-Umari understood as the northern limit of the Desht-i Qipchaq, for, according to Juvaini, Jochi, the son of Chinghis Khan and father of Batu, was granted all lands to the west of the Irtysh River "as far in that direction as the hooves of Tatar horses trod," which would seem to include the Rus principalities conquered in campaigns between 1237 and 1240. In addition, a number of Rus sources refer to the Rus principalities as *ulus* of the khan.

The governmental structure of the Qipchaq Khanate was most likely the same as that of other steppe khanates and was led by a ruler called a "khan" who could trace his genealogical lineage back to Chinghis Khan. A divan of *qarachi beys* (called *ulus beys* in the thirteenth and fourteenth centuries), made up of four emirs, each of whom headed one of the major chiefdoms, constituted a council of state that regularly advised the khan. The divan's consent was required for all significant enterprises on the part of the government. All important documents concerning internal matters had to be countersigned (usually by means of a seal) by the *qarachi beys* for them to go into effect. Their witnessing was also required for all agreements with foreign powers to become official. The khan was not allowed to meet with foreign ambassadors without the presence of the qarachi beys, as representatives of the major chiefdoms. At times an assembly called a quriltai advised the khan but could also be called to choose a new khan or depose the reigning khan. Notable men from the ruling class made up the quriltai, and this included the khan's relatives and retinue, religious leaders, and other members of the nobility from the ruling class's lower ranks. The government was set up on a dual-administrative basis with a vizier in charge of civilian administration, including record-keeping and the treasury. The *beklaribek* (head of the qarachi beys) presided over military administration. The clan of each qarachi bey held the highest social and political status within its chiefdom, with people of every social status in descending order down to slaves beneath.

Six of the early khans of the Qipchaq Khanate were sky worshipers, the traditional religion of the Mongols. One of these khans, Sartaq (r. 1256–1257), may have been a Nestorian Christian and another, Berke (r. 1257–1267), was Muslim. But all the early khans followed policies of religious toleration. In the early fourteenth century, Khan Özbek (r. 1313–1341) converted to Islam, which from then on became the official religion of the elite of the Khanate and spread to most of the rest of the population. The Rus principalities, however, remained Christian, since the Rus Church enjoyed the protection of the khans as long as the Rus clergy prayed for the well-being of the khan and his family.

The Qipchaq Khanate had extensive diplomatic dealings with foreign powers, both as part of the Mongol Empire and independently. It maintained agreements with the Byzantine Empire and Mamluk Egypt. It fought incessantly with the Ilkhanate and maintained alternating periods of agreement and conflict with the Grand Dukes of Lithuania. It maintained extensive commercial dealings with Byzantium, Egypt, Genoa, Pisa, and Venice to the west, as well as with the other Mongol khanates and China to the east. During the fourteenth century, a high Islamic Turkic culture emerged in the Qipchaq Khanate.

At the end of the thirteenth century, the Qipchaq Khanate survived a devastating civil war between Khan Tokhta and the Prince Nogai. After the assassination of Khan Berdibek in 1359, the khanate went through more than 20 years of turmoil and endured another devastating civil war, this time between Khan Tokhtamish and the Emir Mamai. In 1395 Tamerlane swept through the khanate, defeated the army of Tokhtamish, and razed the capital cities. In the middle of the fifteenth century the Qipchaq Khanate began to split up, with the Crimean Khanate and Kazan Khanate separating off. Finally in 1502, the Crimean Khan Mengli Girey defeated the last khan of the Qipchaq Khanate, absorbed the western part of the khanate into his domains, and allowed the organization of the Khanate of Astrakhan to govern the rest. The Qipchaq Khanate, nonetheless, had lasted far longer as an independent political entity than any of the other *ulus* granted by Chinghis Khan to his sons.

See also: ASTRAKHAN, KHANATE OF; BATU; CENTRAL ASIA; CRIMEAN KHANATE

BIBLIOGRAPHY

Fedorov-Davydov, G. A. (1984). *The Culture of the Golden Horde Cities,* tr. H. Bartlett Wells. Oxford: B.A.R.

Fedorov-Davydov, G. A. (2001). *The Silk Road and the Cities of the Golden Horde.* Berkeley, CA: Zinat Press.

Halperin, Charles J. (1985). *Russia and the Golden Horde: Mongol Impact on Medieval Russian History.* Bloomington: Indiana University Press.

Schamiloglu, Uli. (1986). "Tribal Politics and Social Organization in the Golden Horde." Ph.D. diss., Columbia University, New York.

Schamiloglu, Uli. (2002). "The Golden Horde." In *The Turks,* 6 vols., ed. Hasan Celâl Güzel, C. Cem Oguz, and Osman Karatay, 2:819–835. Ankara: Yeni Türkiye.

Vernadsky, George. (1953). *The Mongols and Russia.* New Haven, CT: Yale University Press.

DONALD OSTROWSKI

GOLD STANDARD

A gold standard is a monetary system in which a country backs its currency with gold reserves and allows the conversion of its currency into gold. Tsarist Russia introduced the gold standard in January 1897 and maintained it until 1914. The policy was adopted both as a means of attracting foreign capital for the ambitious industrialization efforts of the late tsarist era, and to earn international respectability for the regime at a time when the world's leading economics had themselves adopted gold standards. Preparation for this move began under Russian Finance Minister Ivan Vyshnegradsky (1887–1892), who actively built up Russia's gold supply while restricting the supply of paper money. After a brief setback, the next finance minister, Sergei Witte (1892–1903), continued to amass gold reserves and restrict monetary growth through foreign borrowing and taxation. By 1896, Russian gold reserves had reached levels commensurate (in relative terms) with other major European nations on the gold standard. The gold standard proved so controversial in Russia that it had to be introduced directly by imperial decree, over the objections of the State Council (Duma). This decree was promulgated on January 2, 1897, authorizing the emission of new five- and ten-ruble gold coins. At this point the state bank (Gosbank) became the official bank of issue, and Russia pegged the new ruble to a fixed quantity of gold with full convertibility. This meant that the ruble could be exchanged at a stable, fixed rate with the other major gold-backed currencies of the time, which facilitated trade by eliminating foreign exchange risk.

Private foreign capital inflows increased considerably after the introduction of the gold standard, and currency stability increased as well. By World War I, Russia had been transformed from a state set somewhat apart from the international financial system to the world's largest international debtor. Proponents argue that the gold standard accelerated Russian industrialization and integration with the world economy by preventing inflation and attracting private capital (substituting for the low rate of domestic savings). They also point out that the Russian economy might not have recovered so quickly after the Russo-Japanese war and civil unrest in 1904 and 1905 without the promise of stability engendered by the gold standard. Critics, however, charge that the gold standard required excessively high foreign borrowing and tax, tariff, and interest rates to introduce. They further charge that once in place, the gold standard was deflationary, inflexible, and too preferential to foreign investment. Economist Paul Gregory argues that the entire debate may be moot, inasmuch as Russia had no choice but to adopt the gold standard in an international environment that practically required it for countries wishing to take advantage of the era's large-scale cross-border trade and investment opportunities. Russia abandoned the gold standard in 1914 under the financial pressure of World War I.

See also: FOREIGN TRADE; INDUSTRIALIZATION; VYSHNEGRADSKY, IVAN ALEXEYEVICH; WITTE, SERGEI YULIEVICH

BIBLIOGRAPHY

Drummond, Ian. (1976). "The Russian Gold Standard, 1897–1914." *Journal of Economic History* 36(4): 633–688.

Gerschenkron, Alexander. (1962). *Economic Backwardness in Historical Perspective: A Book of Essays.* Cambridge, MA: Belknap Press of Harvard University Press.

Gregory, Paul. (1994). *Before Command: An Economic History of Russia from Emancipation to the First Five-Year Plan.* Princeton, NJ: Princeton University Press.

Von Laue, Theodore. (1963). *Sergei Witte and the Industrialization of Russia.* New York: Columbia University Press.

JULIET JOHNSON

GOLITSYN, VASILY VASILIEVICH

(1643–1714), chief minister and army commander during the regency of Sophia Alekseyevna.

Prince Vasily Golitsyn was the eldest son of Prince Vasily Andreyevich Golitsyn and Tatiana Streshneva. Both his parents were from aristocratic clans with strong connections, which brought young Vasily the honorific posts of cup-bearer to Tsar Alexis in 1658 and coach attendant in 1666. In 1663 he married Avdotia Streshneva, who bore him six children. In 1675 he was posted to Ukraine, where he served intermittently during the Russo-Turkish war of 1676–1681, leading an auxiliary force, organizing fortification works and provisioning, and taking a major role in negotiations with Cossack leaders. He was appointed commander in chief of the southern army just before the truce of 1681. During visits to court, Golitsyn won the favor of Tsar Fedor (r. 1676–1682), who promoted him to the rank of boyar in 1676. He also held posts as director of the Artillery Chancellery and the Vladimir High Court. In 1681 he returned to Moscow to chair a commission on army reform, with special reference to regimental structure and the appointment of officers. The commission's proposals led to the abolition in January 1682 of the Code of Precedence, although its scheme for provincial vice-regencies was rejected.

Following Tsar Fedor's death in May 1682, Golitsyn rose further thanks to the patronage of

Tsarevna Sophia Alekseyevna, who became regent to the joint tsars Ivan V (r. 1682–1696) and Peter I (r. 1682–1725). Their relationship is said to have begun when Sophia was caring for the ailing Fedor, to whose bedchamber Golitsyn often reported, but contemporary Russian sources do not record any such meetings. The claim that the couple became lovers rests on hearsay and some coded letters dating from the later 1680s. Golitsyn was not closely involved in the intrigues with the Moscow militia (musketeers) that brought Sophia to power following a bloody revolt, but he remained close to the tsars during the so-called *Khovanshchina* and was appointed director of the important Foreign Office, and later accumulated the directorships of the Foreign Mercenaries, Cavalry, Little Russian (Ukrainian), Smolensk, Novgorod, Ustyug, and Galich chancelleries, which afforded him a substantial power base. In 1683 Sophia dubbed him "Guardian of the Tsar's Great Seal and the State's Great Ambassadorial Affairs."

Golitsyn's main talent was for foreign affairs. He was unusual among Russian boyars in knowing Latin and Greek and became known as a friend of foreigners. He was instrumental in negotiating the renewal of the 1661 Treaty of Kardis with Sweden (1684), trade treaties with Prussia (1689), and the important treaty of permanent peace with Poland (1686), by which Russia broke its truce with the Ottomans and Tatars and entered the Holy League against the infidels. In fulfillment of Russia's obligations to the League, Golitsyn twice led vast Russian armies to Crimea, in 1687 and 1689, on both occasions returning empty-handed, having suffered heavy losses as a result of shortages of food and water. Golitsyn's enemies blamed him personally for the defeats, but Sophia greeted him as a victor, thereby antagonizing the party of the second tsar Peter I, who objected to "undeserved rewards and honors." Following a stand-off between the two sides in August–September 1689, Golitsyn was arrested for aiding and abetting Sophia, bypassing the tsars, and causing "losses to the sovereigns and ruin to the state" as a result of the Crimean campaigns. He and his family were exiled to the far north, first to Kargopol, then to Archangel province, where he died in 1714.

Historians have characterized Golitsyn as a "Westernizer," one of a select band of educated and open-minded Muscovite boyars. His modern views were reflected not only in his encouragement of contacts with foreigners, but also in his library of books in foreign languages and his Moscow mansion in the fashionable "Moscow Baroque" style, which was equipped with foreign furniture, clocks, mirrors, and a portrait gallery, which included Golitsyn's own portrait. The French traveler Foy de la Neuville (the only source) even credited Golitsyn with a scheme for limiting, if not abolishing, serfdom, which is not, however, reflected in the legislation of the regency. Golitsyn's downfall was brought about by a mixture of bad luck and poor judgement in court politics. Peter I never forgave him for his association with Sophia and thereby forfeited the skills of one of the most able men of his generation.

See also: FYODOR ALEXEYEVICH; SOPHIA ALEXEYEVNA (TSAREVNA); WESTERNIZERS.

BIBLIOGRAPHY

Hughes, Lindsey. (1982). "A Seventeenth-century Westerniser: Prince V.V. Golitsyn (1643–1714)." *Irish Slavonic Studies* 3:47–58.

Hughes, Lindsey. (1984). *Russia and the West: The Life of a Seventeenth-Century Westernizer, Prince Vasily Vasil'evich Golitsyn (1643–1714).* Newtonville, MA: Oriental Research Partners.

Smith, Abby. (1995). "The Brilliant Career of Prince Golitsyn." *Harvard Ukrainian Studies* 19:639–645.

LINDSEY HUGHES

GONCHAROVA, NATALIA SERGEYEVNA

(1881–1962), artist, book illustrator, set and costume designer.

Natalia Sergeyevna Goncharova was born on June 21, 1881, in the village of Nagaevo in the Tula province; she died on October 17, 1962, in Paris. She lived in Moscow from 1892 and enrolled at the Moscow School of Painting, Sculpture, and Architecture in 1901 to study sculpture. She met Mikhail Larionov in 1900–1901 who encouraged her to paint and became her lifelong companion. They were married in 1957. In 1906 she contributed to the Russian Section at the Salon d'Automne, Paris. In 1908–1910 she contributed to the three exhibitions organized by Nikolai Riabushinsky, editor of the journal *Zolotoe runo* (*The Golden Fleece*) in Moscow. In 1910 she founded with Larionov and others the Jack of Diamonds group and participated in their first exhibition. In 1911 the group split and from 1911–1914 she participated in a series of rival exhibitions organized by Larionov: the "Donkey's Tail" (1912), the "Target "(1913), and the "No. 4" (1914). Throughout this period she worked in several styles— Primitivist, Cubist, and, in 1912–1913, Futurist and Rayist. Her work immediately became a lightning rod for debate over the legitimacy and cultural identity of new Russian painting. In 1910 a one-day exhibition of Goncharova's work was held at the Society for Free Esthetics. The nude life studies she displayed on this occasion led to her trial for pornography in Moscow's civil court (she was acquitted). Major retrospective exhibitions of Goncharova's work were organized in Moscow (1913) and St. Petersburg (1914). Paintings of religious subject matter were censored, and in the last exhibition temporarily banned as blasphemous by the Spiritual-Censorship Committee of the Holy Synod.

On April 29, 1914 Goncharova left with Larionov for Paris to mount Sergei Diagilev's production of Rimsky-Korsakov's Le Coq d'Or (a collaboration between herself and choreographer Mikhail Fokine). Also in 1914, the Galerie Paul Guillaume in Paris held her first commercial exhibition. During the 1920s and 1930s she and Larionov collaborated on numerous designs for Diagilev and other impresarios. Returning briefly to Moscow in 1915, she designed Alexander Tairov's production of Carlo Goldoni's *Il Ventaglio* at the Chamber Theater, Moscow. After traveling with Diagilev's company to Spain and Italy, she settled in Paris with Larionov in 1917. In 1920–1921 she contributed to the "Exposition internationale d'art moderne" in Geneva and in 1922 exhibited at the Kingore Gallery, New York. From the 1920s onward she continued to paint, teach, illustrate books, and design theater and ballet productions. After 1930, except for occasional contributions to exhibitions, Larionov and Goncharova lived unrecognized and impoverished. Through the efforts of Mary Chamot, author of Goncharova's first major biography, a number of their works entered museum collections, including the Tate Gallery, London, the National Gallery of Modern Art, Edinburgh, and the National Art Gallery in Wellington, New Zealand. In 1954 their names were resurrected at Richard Buckle's "The Diagilev Exhibition" in Edinburgh and London. In 1961 Art Council of Great Britain organized a major retrospective of Goncharova's and Larionov's works, and numerous smaller exhibitions were held throughout Europe during the 1970s. In 1995 the Musée national d'art moderne, Centre Georges Pompidou in Paris organized a large exhibition of their work in Europe. Exhibitions were also held at the State Tretyakov Gallery, Moscow (1999, 2000). The first retrospective of her Russian oeuvre since 1914 was held at the State Russian Museum in St. Petersburg in 2002.

See also: DIAGILEV, SERGEI PAVLOVICH

BIBLIOGRAPHY

Artcyclopedia Web site. (2003) <www.artcyclopedia.com/artists/goncharova_natalia.html>.

Chamot, Mary. (1972). *Gontcharova* Paris: La Bibliotheque des Arts.

Lukanova, Alla and Avtonomova, Natalia, eds. (2000). *Mikhail Larionov, Natalia Goncharova. Exhibition Catalogue.* Moscow: State Tretiakov Gallery.

Petrova, Evgeniia, ed. (2002). *Natalia Goncharova: the Russian Years. Exhibition Catalogue.* St. Petersburg: The State Russian Museum and Palace Editions.

JANE A. SHARP

GONCHAROV, IVAN ALEXANDROVICH

(1812–1891), writer.

Born in Simbirsk to a family of wealthy merchants, Ivan Goncharov moved to Moscow for his schooling in 1822 and then moved to St. Petersburg in 1835 where, with a few breaks, he remained until his death. He worked from 1855 to 1867 as government censor, a post that earned the criticism and mistrust of many of his contemporaries. Although his politics as a censor were clearly conservative when it came to reviewing Russian journals, he also used his position to allow many important and liberal works of literature into print, including works by Fyodor Dostoyevsky and Alexander Herzen. Goncharov's unfounded accusation of plagiarism against the novelist Ivan Turgenev in 1860 caused a scandal in the literary world; Goncharov suffered from bouts of neurosis and paranoia and lived most of his life in sedentary seclusion.

Goncharov is known primarily for three novels—*A Common Story* (1847), *Oblomov* (1859), and *The Precipice* (1869)—as well as a travel memoir of a government expedition to Japan, *The Frigate Pallas* (1855–1857). By far his best-known work is *Oblomov*, whose hero, an indolent and dreamy Russian nobleman, became emblematic of a Russian social type, the superfluous man. The figure of Oblomov made such a deep impression on readers that the radical critic Nikolai Dobrolyubov popularized the term *oblomovshchina* (oblomovitis) to describe the ineptitude of the Russian intelligentsia. Goncharov's novels rank him among the best Russian realist writers, yet his university years in Moscow at the height of the Russian romantic movement and his consequent attraction to its ideals places him within the era of the Golden Age of Russian literature.

See also: GOLDEN AGE OF RUSSIAN LITERATURE

BIBLIOGRAPHY

Ehre, Milton. (1974). *Oblomov and His Creator; the Life and Art of Ivan Goncharov.* Princeton, NJ: Princeton University Press.

Lyngstad, Alexandra, and Lyngstad, Sverre. (1971). *Ivan Goncharov.* New York: Twayne Publishers.

Setchkarev, Vsevolod. (1974). *Ivan Goncharov: His Life and Works.* Wurzburg: Jal-Verlag.

CATHERINE O'NEIL

GOODS FAMINE

The concept of the goods famine refers to excess demand (at prevailing prices) for industrial goods in the Soviet Union during the latter half of the 1920s. The importance of this excess demand can only be understood within the context of the New Economic Policy (NEP) of the 1920s and the underlying forces leading to excess demand. Specifically, the goods famine was an outgrowth of the Scissors Crisis and state policies relating to this episode.

Specifically, in the middle and late 1920s, the quicker recovery of agricultural production relative to industrial production meant that increases in the demand for industrial goods could not be met, an outcome characterized as the goods famine. State policy was ultimately successful in forcing a reduction of the prices of industrial goods. The concern was that a goods famine might drive rural producers, unable to purchase industrial goods, to reduce their grain marketings. This was viewed as a critical factor limiting the possible pace of industrialization.

The goods famine is important to the understanding of the changes implemented by Stalin in the late 1920s. Moreover, these events relate to economic issues such as the nature and organization of the industrial sector (e.g., monopoly power), state policies in a semi-market economy, and most important, the nature of peasant responses to market forces when facing the imperatives of an industrialization drive.

See also: AGRICULTURE; ECONOMIC GROWTH, SOVIET; INDUSTRIALIZATION, SOVIET; NEW ECONOMIC POLICY; PEASANT ECONOMY; SCISSORS CRISIS

BIBLIOGRAPHY

Gregory, Paul R. (1994). *Before Command: An Economic History of Russia from Emancipation to the First Five Year Plan.* Princeton, NJ: Princeton University Press.

Zaleski, Eugene. (1971). *Planning for Economic Growth in the Soviet Union, 1918–1932.* Chapel Hill: University of North Carolina Press.

ROBERT C. STUART

GORBACHEV, MIKHAIL SERGEYEVICH

(b. 1931), Soviet political leader, general editor of the CPSU (1985–1991), president of the Soviet Union (1990–1991), Nobel Peace Prize laureate (1990).

Mikhail Sergeyevich Gorbachev, the leader of the Soviet Union during a period of sweeping domestic and international change that saw the dismantling of communist systems throughout Europe and ended with the disintegration of the USSR itself, was born in the southern Russian village of Privolnoye in Stavropol province. His parents were peasants and his mother was barely literate.

Mikhail Gorbachev did not have an easy childhood. Born on March 2, 1931, he was just old enough to remember when, during the 1930s, both of his grandfathers were caught in the purges and arrested. Although they were released after prison, having been tortured in one case and internally exiled and used as forced labor in the other, young Misha Gorbachev knew what it was like to live in the home of an enemy of the people.

The war and early postwar years provided the family with the opportunity to recover from the stigma of false charges laid against the older generation, although the wartime experience itself was harsh. Gorbachev's father was in the army, saw action on several fronts, and was twice wounded. Remaining in the Russian countryside, Gorbachev and his mother had to engage in back-breaking work in the fields. For two years Gorbachev received no schooling, and for a period of four and one-half months the Stavropol territory, including Privolnoye, was occupied by the German army. In Josef Stalin's time, those who had experienced even short-lived foreign rule tended to be treated with grave suspicion.

Nevertheless, the Gorbachevs engaged as wholeheartedly in the postwar reconstruction of their locality as they had in the war effort. Exceptionally, when he was still a teenager, Gorbachev was awarded the Order of Red Banner of Labor for heroic feats of work. He had assisted his father, a combine operator (who was given the Order of Lenin) in bringing in a record harvest in 1948. The odds against a village boy gaining entry to Moscow State University in 1950 were high, but the fact that Gorbachev had been honored as an exemplary worker, and had an excellent school record and recommendation from the Komsomol, made him one of the exceptions. While still at high school during the first half of 1950, Gorbachev became a candidate member of the Communist Party. He was admitted to full membership in the party in 1952.

Although the Law Faculty of Moscow University, where Gorbachev studied for the next five years, hardly offered a liberal education, there were some scholars of genuine erudition who opened his eyes to a wider intellectual world. Prominent among them was Stepan Fyodorovich Kechekyan, who taught the history of legal and political thought. Gorbachev took Marxism seriously and not simply as Marxist-Leninist formula to be learned by rote. Talking, forty years later, about his years as a law student, Gorbachev observed: "Before the university I was trapped in my belief system in the sense that I accepted a great deal as given, assumptions not to be questioned. At the university I began to think and reflect and to look at things differently. But of course that was only the beginning of a long process."

Two events of decisive importance for Gorbachev occurred while he was at Moscow University. One was the death of Stalin in 1953. After that the atmosphere within the university lightened, and freer discussion began to take place among the students. The other was his meeting Raisa Maximovna Titarenko, a student in the philosophy faculty, in 1951. They were married in 1953 and remained utterly devoted to each other. In an interview on the eve of his seventieth birthday, Gorbachev described Raisa's death at the age of 67 in 1999 as his "hardest blow ever." They had one daughter, Irina, and two granddaughters.

After graduating with distinction, Gorbachev returned to his native Stavropol and began a rapid rise through the Komsomol and party organization. By 1966 he was party first secretary for Stavropol city, and in 1970 he became *kraikom* first secretary, that is, party boss of the whole Stavropol territory, which brought with it a year later membership in the Central Committee of the CPSU. Gorbachev displayed a talent for winning the good opinion of very diverse people. These included not only men of somewhat different outlooks within the Soviet Communist Party. Later they were also to embrace Western conservatives—most notably U.S. president Ronald Reagan and U.K. prime minister Margaret Thatcher—as well as European social democrats such as the former West German chancellor Willy Brandt and Spanish Prime Minister Felipe Gonzalez.

However, Gorbachev's early success in winning friends and influencing people depended not only on his ability and charm. He had an advantage in his location. Stavropol was spa territory, and leading members of the Politburo came there on holiday. The local party secretary had to meet them, and this gave Gorbachev the chance to make a good impression on figures such as Mikhail Suslov and Yuri Andropov. Both of them later supported his promotion to the secretaryship of the Central Committee, with responsibility for agriculture, when one of Gorbachev's mentors, Fyodor Kulakov, a previous first secretary of Stavropol territory, who held the agricultural portfolio within the Central Committee Secretariat (along with membership in the Politburo), died in 1978.

From that time, Gorbachev was based in Moscow. As the youngest member of an increasingly geriatric political leadership, he was given rapid promotion through the highest echelons of the Communist Party, adding to his secretaryship candidate membership of the Politburo in 1979 and full membership in 1980. When Leonid Brezhnev died in November 1982, Gorbachev's duties in the Party leadership team were extended by Brezhnev's successor, Yuri Andropov, who thought highly of the younger man. When Andropov was too ill to carry on chairing meetings, he wrote an addendum to a speech to a session of the Central Committee in December 1983, which he was too ill to attend in person. In it he proposed that the Politburo and Secretariat be led in his absence by Gorbachev. This was a clear attempt to elevate Gorbachev above Konstantin Chernenko, a much older man who had been exceptionally close to Brezhnev and a senior secretary of the Central Committee for longer than Gorbachev. However, Andropov's additions to his speech were omitted from the text presented to Central Committee members. Chernenko had consulted other members of the old guard, and they were united in wishing to prevent power from moving to a new generation represented by Gorbachev.

The delay in his elevation to the general secretaryship of the Communist Party did Gorbachev no harm. Chernenko duly succeeded Andropov on the latter's death in February 1984, but was so infirm during his time at the helm that Gorbachev frequently found himself chairing meetings of the Politburo at short notice when Chernenko was too ill to attend. More importantly, the sight of a third infirm leader in a row (for Brezhnev in his last years had also been incapable of working a full day) meant that even the normally docile Central Committee might have objected if the Politburo had proposed another septuagenarian to succeed Chernenko. By the time of Chernenko's death, just thirteen months after he succeeded Andropov, Gorbachev was, moreover, in a position to get his way. As the senior surviving secretary, it was he who called the Politburo together on the very evening that Chernenko died. The next day (March 11, 1985) he was unanimously elected Soviet leader by the Central Committee, following a unanimous vote in the Politburo.

General Secretary Mikhail Gorbachev waves to the crowd at Orly Airport in Paris. REUTERS/BETTMANN. REPRODUCED BY PERMISSION.

Those who chose him had little or no idea that they were electing a serious reformer. Indeed, Gorbachev himself did not know how fast and how radically his views would evolve. From the outset of his leadership he was convinced of the need for change, involving economic reform, political liberalization, ending the war in Afghanistan, and improving East-West relations. He did not yet believe that this required a fundamental transformation of the system. On the contrary, he thought it could be improved. By 1988, as Gorbachev encountered increasing resistance from conservative elements within the Communist Party, the ministries, the army, and the KGB, he had reached the conclusion that systemic change was required.

Initially, Gorbachev had made a series of personnel changes that he hoped would make a difference. Some of these appointments were bold and innovative, others turned out to be misjudged. One of his earliest appointments that took most observers by surprise was the replacement of the long-serving Soviet foreign minister, Andrei Gromyko, by the Georgian Party first secretary, Eduard Shevardnadze, a man who had not previously set foot in the Ministry of Foreign Affairs. Yet Shevardnadze became an imaginative and capable executor of a foreign policy aimed at ending the Cold War. At least as important a promotion was that given to Alexander Yakovlev, who was not even a candidate member of the Central Committee at the time when Gorbachev became party leader, but who by the summer of 1987 was both a secretary of the Central Committee and a full member of the Politburo. Yakovlev owed this extraordinarily speedy promotion entirely to the backing of Gorbachev. He, in turn, was to be an influential figure on the reformist wing of the Politburo during the second half of the 1980s.

Other appointments were less successful. Yegor Ligachev, a secretary of the Central Committee who had backed Gorbachev strongly for the leadership, was rapidly elevated to full membership in the

Politburo and for a time was de facto second secretary within the leadership. But as early as 1986 it was clear that his reformism was within very strict limits. Already he was objecting to intellectuals reexamining the Soviet past and taking advantage of the new policy of glasnost (openness or transparency) that Gorbachev had enunciated. Successive heads of the KGB and of the Ministry of Defense were still more conservative than Ligachev, and the technocrat, Nikolai Ryzhkov, as chairman of the Council of Ministers, was reluctant to abandon the economic planning system in which, as a factory manager and, subsequently, state official, he had made his career.

Gorbachev embraced the concept of *demokratizatsiya* (democratization) from the beginning of his General Secretaryship, although the term he used most often was perestroika (reconstruction). Initially, the first of these terms was not intended to be an endorsement of pluralist democracy, but signified rather a liberalization of the system, while perestroika was a useful synonym for reform, since the very term *reform* had been taboo in Soviet politics for many years. Between 1985 and 1988, however, the scope of these concepts broadened. democratization began to be linked to contested elections. Some local elections with more than one candidate had already taken place before Gorbachev persuaded the Nineteenth Party Conference of the Communist Party during the summer of 1988 to accept competitive elections for a new legislature, the Congress of People's Deputies, to be set up the following year. That decision, which filled many of the regional party officials with well-founded foreboding, was to make the Soviet system different. Even though the elections were not multiparty (the first multiparty elections were in 1993), the electoral campaigns were in many regions and cities keenly contested. It became plain just how wide a spectrum of political views lay behind the monolithic facade the Communist Party had traditionally projected to the outside world and to Soviet citizens.

While glasnost had brought into the open a constituency favorably disposed to such reforms, no such radical departure from Soviet democratic centralism could have occurred without the strong backing of Gorbachev. Up until the last two years of the existence of the Soviet Union the hierarchical nature of the system worked to Gorbachev's advantage, even when he was pursuing policies that were undermining the party hierarchy and, in that sense, his own power base. While there had been a great deal of socioeconomic change during the decades that separated Stalin's death from Gorbachev's coming to power, there was one important institutional continuity that, paradoxically, facilitated reforms that went beyond the wildest dreams of Soviet dissidents and surpassed the worst nightmares of the KGB. That was the power and authority of the general secretaryship of the Central Committee of the Soviet Communist Party, the post Gorbachev held from March 1985 until the dissolution of the CPSU in August 1991 and which—in particular, for the first four of his six and one-half years at the top of the Soviet political system—made him the principal policy maker within the country. Perestroika, which had originally meant economic restructuring and limited reform, came to stand for transformative change of the Soviet system. Both the ambiguity of the concept and traditional party norms kept many officials from revolting openly against perestroika until it was too late to close the floodgates of change.

A major impetus to Gorbachev's initial reforms had been the long-term decline in the rate of economic growth. Indeed, the closest thing to a consensus in the Soviet Union in 1985–1986 was the need to get the country moving again economically. A number of economic reforms introduced by Gorbachev and Ryzhkov succeeded in breaking down the excessive centralization that had been a problem of the unreformed Soviet economic system. For example, the Law on the State Enterprise of 1987 strengthened the authority of factory managers at the expense of economic ministries, but it did nothing to raise the quantity or quality of production. The Enterprise Law fostered inflation, promoted inter-enterprise debt, and facilitated failure to pay taxes to the central budget.

The central budget also suffered severely from one of the earliest policy initiatives supported by Gorbachev and urged upon him by Ligachev. This was the anti-alcohol campaign, which went beyond exhortation and involved concrete measures to limit the production, sale, and distribution of alcohol. By 1988 this policy was being relaxed. In the meantime, it had some measure of success in cutting down the consumption of alcohol. Alcohol-related accidents declined, and some health problems were alleviated. Economically, however, the policy was extremely damaging. The huge profits on which the state had relied from the sale of alcohol, on which it had a monopoly, were cut drastically not only because of a fall in consumption but also because, under conditions of semi-prohibition, moonshine took the place of state-manufactured vodka. Since the launch of perestroika had also coincided with a drop in the world oil price, this was a loss of revenue the state and its political leadership could not afford.

Gorbachev had, early in his general secretaryship, been ready to contemplate market elements within the Soviet economy. By 1989–1990 he had increasingly come to believe that market forces should be the main engine of growth. Nevertheless, he favored what he first called a "socialist market economy" and later a "regulated market." He was criticized by market fundamentalists for using the latter term, which they saw as an oxymoron. Although by 1993 Yegor Gaidar, a firm supporter of the market, was observing that "throughout the world the market is regulated." Gorbachev initially endorsed, and then retreated from, a radical but (as its proponents were later to admit) unrealistic policy of moving the Soviet Union to a market economy within five hundred days. The Five-Hundred-Day Plan was drawn up by a group of economists, chosen in equal numbers by Gorbachev and Boris Yeltsin (the latter by this time a major player in Soviet and Russian politics), during the summer of 1990. In setting up the working group, in consultation with Yeltsin, Gorbachev completely bypassed the Communist Party. He had been elected president of the Soviet Union by the Congress of People's Deputies of the USSR in March 1990 and was increasingly relying on his authority in that role. However, the presidency did not have the institutional underpinning that the party apparatus had provided for a General Secretary—until Gorbachev consciously loosened the rungs of the ladder on which he had climbed to the top. Ultimately, in the face of strong opposition from state and party authorities attempting to move to the market in a giant leap, Gorbachev sought a compromise between the views of the market enthusiasts, led by Stanislav Shatalin and Grigory Yavlinsky, and those of the chairman of the Council of Ministers and his principal economic adviser, Leonid Abalkin.

Because radical democrats tended also to be in favor of speedy marketization, Gorbachev's hesitation meant that he lost support in that constituency. People who had seen Gorbachev as the embodiment and driving force of change in and of the Soviet system increasingly in 1990–1991 transferred their support to Yeltsin, who in June 1991 was elected president of Russia in a convincing first-round victory. Since he had been directly elected, and Gorbachev indirectly, this gave Yeltsin a greater democratic legitimacy in the eyes of a majority of citizens, even though the very fact that contested elections had been introduced into the Soviet system was Gorbachev's doing. If Gorbachev had taken the risk of calling a general election for the presidency of the Soviet Union a year earlier, rather than taking the safer route of election by the existing legislature, he might have enhanced his popular legitimacy, extended his own period in office, and extended the life of the Soviet Union (although, to the extent that it was democratic, it would have been a smaller union, with the Baltic states as the prime candidates for early exit). In March 1990, the point at which he became Soviet president, Gorbachev was still ahead of Yeltsin in the opinion polls of the most reliable of survey research institutes, the All-Union (subsequently All-Russian) Center for the Study of Public Opinion. It was during the early summer of that year that Yeltsin moved ahead of him.

By positing the interests of Russia against those of the Union, Yeltsin played a major role in making the continuation of a smaller Soviet Union an impossibility. By first liberalizing and then democratizing, Gorbachev had taken the lid off the nationalities problem. Almost every nation in the country had a long list of grievances and, when East European countries achieved full independence during the course of 1989, this emboldened a number of the Soviet nationalities to demand no less. Gorbachev, by this time, was committed to turning the Soviet system into something different—indeed, he was well advanced in the task of dismantling the traditional Soviet edifice—but he strove to keep together a multinational union by attempting to turn a pseudo-federal system into a genuine federation or, as a last resort, a looser confederation.

Gorbachev's major failures were unable to prevent disintegration of the union and not improving economic performance. However, since everything was interconnected in the Soviet Union, it was impossible to introduce political change without raising national consciousness and, in some cases, separatist aspirations. If the disintegration of the Soviet Union is compared with the breakup of Yugoslavia, what is remarkable is the extent to which the Soviet state gave way to fifteen successor states with very little bloodshed. It was also impossible to move smoothly from an economic system based over many decades on one set of principles (a centralized, command economy) to a system based on another set of principles (market relations) without going through a period of disruption in which things were liable to get worse before they got better.

Gorbachev's failures were more than counterbalanced by his achievements. He changed Soviet foreign policy dramatically, reaching important arms control agreements with U.S. president Reagan and establishing good relations with all the Soviet Union's neighbors. Defense policy was subordinated to political objectives, and the underlying philosophy of *kto kogo* (who will defeat whom) gave way to a belief in interdependence and mutual security. These achievements were widely recognized internationally—most notably with the award to Gorbachev in 1990 of the Nobel Peace Prize. If Gorbachev is faulted in Russia today, it is for being overly idealistic in the conduct of foreign relations, to an extent not fully reciprocated by his Western interlocutors. The Cold War had begun with the Soviet takeover of Eastern Europe. It ended when one East and Central European country after another became independent in 1989 and when Gorbachev accepted the loss of Eastern Europe, something all his predecessors had regarded as non-negotiable. Gorbachev's answer to the charge from domestic hard-liners that he had "surrendered" Eastern Europe was to say: "What did I surrender, and to whom? Poland to the Poles, the Czech lands to the Czechs, Hungary to the Hungarians...."

After the failed coup against Gorbachev of August 1991, when he was held under house arrest on the Crimean coast while Yeltsin became the focal point of resistance to the putschists, his political position was greatly weakened. With the hard-liners discredited, disaffected nationalities pressed for full independence, and Yeltsin became increasingly intransigent in pressing Russian interests at the expense of any kind of federal union. In December 1991 the leaders of the Russian, Ukrainian, and Belorussian republics got together to announce that the Soviet Union was ceasing to exist. Gorbachev bowed to the inevitable and on December 25 resigned from the presidency of a state, the USSR, which then disappeared from the map.

During the post-Soviet period Gorbachev held no position of power, but he continued to be politically active. His relations with Yeltsin were so bad that at one point Yeltsin attempted to prevent him from travelling abroad, but abandoned that policy following protests from Western leaders. Throughout the Yeltsin years, Gorbachev was never invited to the Kremlin, although he was consulted on a number of occasions by Vladimir Putin when he succeeded Yeltsin. Gorbachev's main activities were centered on the foundation he headed, an independent think-tank of social-democratic leanings, which promoted research, seminars, and conferences on developments within the former Soviet Union and on major international issues. Gorbachev became the author of several books, most notably two volumes of memoirs published in Russian in 1995 and, in somewhat abbreviated form, in English and other languages in 1996. Other significant works included a book of political reflections, based on tape-recorded conversations with his Czech friend from university days, Zdeněk Mlynář, which appeared in 2002. He became active also on environmental matters as president of the Green Cross International. Domestically, Gorbachev lent his name and energy to an attempt to launch a Social Democratic Party, but with little success. He continued to be admired abroad and gave speeches in many different countries. Indeed, the Gorbachev Foundation depended almost entirely on its income from its president's lecture fees and book royalties.

Gorbachev will, however, be remembered above all for his contribution to six years that changed the world, during which he was the last leader of the USSR. Notwithstanding numerous unintended consequences of perestroika, of which the most regrettable in Gorbachev's eyes, was the breakup of the Union, the long-term changes for the better introduced in the Gorbachev era—and to a significant degree instigated by him—greatly outweigh the failures. Ultimately, Gorbachev's place in history is likely to rest upon his playing the most decisive role in ending the Cold War and on his massive contribution to the blossoming of freedom, in Eastern Europe and Russia itself.

See also: AUGUST 1991 PUTSCH; DEMOCRATIZATION; GLASNOST; GORBACHEV, RAISA MAXIMOVNA; NEW POLITICAL THINKING; PERESTROIKA; YELTSIN, BORIS NIKOLAYEVICH

BIBLIOGRAPHY

Braithwaite, Rodric. (2002). *Across the Moscow River: The World Turned Upside Down.* New Haven, CT: Yale University Press.

Breslauer, George. (2002). *Gorbachev and Yeltsin as Leaders.* New York: Cambridge University Press.

Brown, Archie. (1996). *The Gorbachev Factor.* Oxford: Oxford University Press.

Brown, Archie, and Shevtsova, Lilia, eds. (2001). *Gorbachev, Yeltsin, and Putin: Political Leadership in Russia's Transition.* Washington, DC: Carnegie Endowment for International Peace.

Chernyaev, Anatoly. (2000). *My Six Years with Gorbachev.* University Park: Pennsylvania State University Press.

Gorbachev, Mikhail. (1996). *Memoirs.* New York: Doubleday.

Gorbachev, Mikhail, and Mlynář, Zdeněk. (2001). *Conversations with Gorbachev.* New York: Columbia University Press.

Hough, Jerry F. (1997). *Democratization and Revolution in the USSR, 1985–1991.* Washington, DC: Brookings Institution Press.

Ligachev, Yegor. (1993). *Inside Gorbachev's Kremlin.* New York: Pantheon Books.

McFaul, Michael. (2001). *Russia's Unfinished Revolution: Political Change from Gorbachev to Putin.* Ithaca, NY: Cornell University Press.

Matlock, Jack F., Jr. (1995). *Autopsy of an Empire: The American Ambassador's Account of the Collapse of the Soviet Union.* New York: Random House.

Palazchenko, Pavel. (1997). *My Years with Gorbachev and Shevardnadze: The Memoir of a Soviet Interpreter.* University Park: Pennsylvania State University Press.

Archie Brown

GORBACHEV, RAISA MAXIMOVNA

(1932–1999), "first lady" of the Soviet Union, spouse of Mikhail Gorbachev.

Raisa Maximovna Titarenko was born on January 5, 1932, in Siberia and died at the age of 67 on September 21, 1999. She married Mikhail Gorbachev, a fellow student at Moscow State University in 1953 and achieved fame as the first spouse of a Soviet leader to accompany him on all his travels. This made a substantial contribution to the favorable impact the Gorbachevs had on their many foreign interlocutors.

Raisa Gorbachev became one of the best-known women in the world, partly because her attractive appearance, vivacity, and self-assurance were so much at odds with the image the wives of high-ranking Soviet politicians had projected hitherto. Her partnership with her husband was exceptionally close. It caused a sensation when Gorbachev revealed, in answer to a question from an American television interviewer, that he discussed everything with his wife, including high-level politics and the affairs of state.

Raisa, as she became universally known, was intellectually well equipped for the role she played. Though she had to attend many different schools as her father, a railway worker, moved from place to place, she gained a gold medal for maximum grades in all subjects and entered the philosophy department at Moscow State University in 1949. Later she did pioneering sociological research, gained the Russian equivalent of a Ph.D., and published a book in 1969 on the way of life of the peasantry in the Stavropol region (where her husband was the First Secretary of the Communist Party). Whereas many Soviet officials had books produced for them by hired hands, Raisa Gorbachev did her own field research and writing.

As a very visible "First Lady" in the Soviet Union between 1985 and 1991, she aroused envy and resentment at home (for her glamour and smart clothes) as well as admiration, but she was much more universally liked and respected abroad. She played a significant part in projecting both the new image and new reality of Soviet politics following the accession of her husband to the highest post in the Kremlin.

See also: GORBACHEV, MIKHAIL SERGEYEVICH

BIBLIOGRAPHY

Brown, Archie. (1996). *The Gorbachev Factor.* Oxford: Oxford University Press.

Gorbachev, Mikhail. (1996). *Memoirs.* London: Transworld.

Gorbachev, Raisa. (1991). *I Hope: Reminiscences and Reflections.* New York: HarperCollins.

Archie Brown

GORCHAKOV, ALEXANDER MIKHAILOVICH

(1798–1883), Chancellor and Foreign Minister of the Russian Empire, 1856–1881.

A descendant of an illustrious Russian aristocratic family, Alexander Gorchakov was educated at the lyceum in Tsarskoye Selo that is best known for his classmate, Alexander Pushkin. He excelled as a classical scholar and gained more than the usual fluency in Latin and French. He chose a diplomatic career, entering the foreign ministry under the tutelage of Count Karl Nesselrode, serving as minister to Stuttgart and Württemberg during the 1830s and 1840s and to the German Confederation, where he first met Otto von Bismarck. His promotion to Austrian ambassador during the Crimean War was a more serious test of his diplomatic ability and won his recognition as a worthy successor to Nesselrode. He was, nevertheless, a sharp critic, not only of the blunders that led to the war, but also of the peace terms that resulted. He consistently counseled caution on Russian involvement in the Balkans, a policy unheeded by his predecessors and successors, to Russia's and the world's misfortune.

As a true Russian following a German master, he rose to the occasion of the Russian defeat in the Crimean War to be Foreign Minister and Chancellor under Tsar Alexander II. In a period of vulnerability and weakness during the reforms of the tsar, he maintained a conservative-cautious front in European diplomacy, while gradually managing to nullify most of the ignominious restrictions of the Treaty of Paris (1856), such as the restrictions on warships in the Black Sea. His major subsequent accomplishments were to shield successfully the substantial Russian expansion in Central Asia (Turkistan) and the Far East (the acquisition of the Maritime Provinces) from European interference and to dispose of a costly and vulnerable territory in North America (Alaska) to the United States in 1867. His greatest accomplishment was the achievement of a dominant position for Russia in the Balkans through the treaty negotiations at San Stefano that concluded the Russo-Turkish War of 1877–1878 and at the Congress of Berlin that followed. His over-commitment to pan-Slavic and nationalist Russian goals, however, moved Russia into the center of Great Power rivalries in the late nineteenth and early twentieth centuries, sowing the seeds for the debacle of World War I.

Much of Gorchakov's success in advancing Russia's European interests, however, could also be credited to Bismarck, who promoted German-Russian collaboration, supported Gorchakov's initiatives, and whose paramount role in European diplomacy overshadowed Gorchakov's. In response, Gorchakov willingly supported German aggression in Holstein and in the Franco-Prussian War, thus promoting Bismarck's creation of the German Empire. They were partners in both waging limited wars for expansionist gains and in preserving general peace through aggressive diplomacy, but the Russian chancellor clearly resented the appearance of a German domination of Russian policy. While Bismarck suffered dismissal by his own government in 1879, Gorchakov overstayed his tenure, becoming a senile embarrassment by 1881. Unfortunately for both major European powers, none would follow with equal skill, international outlook, prestige, and ability to compromise and maintain peace. It is perhaps no surprise that Vladimir Putin's "new Russia" recognizes Gorchakov as a statesman who successfully promoted Russian interests in international relations and, in his honor, awarded the annual "Gorchakov peace prize," in 2002 to United Nations Secretary General Kofi Annan.

See also: ALEXANDER II; NESSELRODE, KARL ROBERT; PUSHKIN, ALEXANDER SERGEYEVICH

BIBLIOGRAPHY

Jelavich, Barbara.(1964). *A Century of Russian Foreign Policy, 1814–1914.* Philadelphia: Lippincott.

Kennan, George F.(1979). *The Decline of Bismarck's European Order: Franco-Russian Relations, 1875–1890.* Princeton, NJ: Princeton University Press.

NORMAN E. SAUL

GORDON, PATRICK LEOPOLD

(1635–1699), born in Cronden, Aberdeen, Scotland, died in Moscow.

Patrick Leopold Gordon, known in Russia as Petr Ivanovich Gordon, was a descendant of a Scottish Catholic aristocratic family and studied at Braunberg College in Danzig (Gdańsk) where he graduated in 1655. Gordon served in the Swedish and Polish armies, and then entered Russian service in 1661 with the rank of major, given the task of training New Formation regiments. Gordon was dispatched as an unofficial Russian envoy to England in 1666–1667 where he met with James II and played an important role in reviving Anglo-Russian relations, including trade which had been of marginal significance since the expulsion of the English from the Russian interior in 1649. He advised the English government and the Muscovy Company on strategies to adopt for negotiations with Russia. He also was an active participant in the Chyhyryn (Chigirin) campaign in 1677–1678 and the Crimean expeditions of 1687 and 1689. Gordon headed the Butyrskii Regiment, was promoted to general-major in 1678, and general-lieutenant in 1683.

Having supported the regime of Sof'ia Alekseevna, in 1689 he switched sides back to Peter I (the Great) who deposed his half-sister. Gordon became one of Peter's close associates and played a crucial role in the creation of a regular Russian army. He headed the Kozhukhov campaign of 1694 and obtained Peter's permission for the presence in Russia of a Roman Catholic clergy, and in 1694 founded a Catholic church in Moscow. Gordon was a leader of the Azov campaigns of 1695–1696, and was in charge of the seizure of the fortress in 1696. Gordon subdued the Strel'tsy (Musketeer) Uprising of 1698. He authored an extensive diary describing his experiences in Sweden, Poland, and Russia, 1655–1699, and also produced a large number of surviving letters pertaining to Anglo-Russian political and commercial relations, and late Muscovite political history.

See also: PETER I

BIBLIOGRAPHY

Gordon, Patrick.(1859). *Passages from the Diary of General Patrick Gordon of Auchleuchries, AD. 1635–AD. 1699.* Aberdeen: Printed for the Spalding Club.

Konovalov, Sergei. (1963). "England and Russia: Two Missions, 1666–8," *Oxford Slavonic Papers* 10:47–58.

Konovalov, Sergei. (1964). "Patrick Gordon's Dispatches from Russia, 1667." *Oxford Slavonic Papers* 11:8–16.

Konovalov, Sergei. (1967). "Sixteen Further Letters of Patrick Gordon," *Oxford Slavonic Papers* 13:72–95.

Poe, Marshall T. (2000). "A People Born to Slavery: Russia." In *Early Modern European Ethnography, 1476—1748.* Ithaca, NY: Cornell University Press.

JARMO T. KOTILAINE

GOREMYKIN, IVAN LONGINOVICH

(1839–1917), minister of interior and twice prime minister under Nicholas II.

Ivan Loginovich Goremykin was the prototypical bureaucrat and conservative leader of late tsarist times, and became, especially during World War I, a symbol of the old regime's outdatedness and resistance to change.

Born of a noble family, Goremykin spent his long life almost entirely in public service. During the 1860s, while an official in Russian Poland, he took a special interest in peasant affairs, and later he was involved in many studies of rural issues. Characteristic of his record, however, he never proposed any solutions. After various posts in the Senate, the Ministry of Justice, and the Ministry of Interior, Goremykin was appointed minister of Interior in October 1895 by the new tsar, Nicholas II, who valued him as a "safe" bureaucrat and a staunch supporter of the autocracy. Goremykin assured Nicholas that Russian society was basically stable and only some "completion and repair" was required to fix minor problems. Goremykin proposed extending the zemstvo system into the empire's western provinces plus a few borderlands, but Nicholas, fearing the spread of liberal ideas, decided in October 1899 to replace Goremykin.

After the tsar became disillusioned with Sergei Witte's reform efforts in 1905 and 1906, he fired Witte as prime minister in April 1906 and brought in Goremykin, then sixty-seven years old. Goremykin discarded the program Witte had intended to submit to the First Duma and stonewalled the Duma's demands. Having decided to dismiss the Duma and seeking a stronger leader, the tsar sent Goremykin into retirement in July 1906, replacing him with Peter Stolypin.

But in January 1914 Goremykin, at the age of seventy-four, again became prime minister. Because of his frailty and lack of initiative and because he rebuffed public attempts to improve the government's war effort, Goremykin came to symbolize the regime's incompetence and callousness. Despite public pressure, Nicholas II stuck by his decrepit prime minister until January 1916, when Goremykin was finally replaced.

See also: NICHOLAS II; STOLYPIN, PETER AKRADIEVICH; WITTE, SERGEI YULIEVICH

BIBLIOGRAPHY

Hosking, Geoffrey. (1973). *The Russian Constitutional Experiment: Government and Duma, 1907–1914.* Cambridge, UK: Cambridge University Press.

Kokovtsov, V. N. (1935). *Out of My Past.* Stanford, CA: Stanford University Press.

Lincoln, W. Bruce. (1986). *Passage through Armageddon: The Russians in War and Revolution, 1914–1918.* New York: Simon and Schuster.

JOHN M. THOMPSON

GORKY, MAXIM

(1868–1936), renowned writer and playwright.

Maxim Gorky (Maxim the Bitter) was born Alexei Maximovich Peshkov in Nizhny Novgorod during the reign of Tsar Alexander II and died in the Stalinist Soviet Union. Gorky was orphaned at an early age, and his formal education ended when he was ten because his impoverished grandparents could not support him. He was self-taught in many areas, including literature, philosophy, and history, both Russian and Western.

Gorky rose to prominence early in life and made his mark as a writer, playwright, publicist, and publisher in Russia and abroad. His literary career began in 1892 with the publication of the story "Makar Chudra." His articles and stories were soon appearing in provincial newspapers and journals. His ideas of the writer's involvement in the social, political, and economic problems facing Russia were close to those of Leo Tolstoy and Vladimir G. Korolenko, who became his mentor and friend. Some of his literary works had important political significance, such as the poem *Burevestnik* (*The Stormy Petrel*), which in 1901 prophesied the oncoming storm of revolution. While visiting the United States in 1906 on a mission to win friends for the revolution and raise funds for the Russian Social Democratic Workers' Party (RSDWP), he wrote the novel *Mat* (*Mother*). Gorky's revolutionary ideology lay in his insistence on the inevitability of radical change in Russian society.

Writer Maxim Gorky established the Socialist Realism genre.
ARCHIVE PHOTOS, INC./HERBERT. REPRODUCED BY PERMISSION.

Disillusioned with the passivity and ignorance of the peasant, Gorky gradually abandoned *narodnik* (populist) ideology in favor of social democracy. He financed Vladimir Lenin's *Iskra* (*The Spark*). At the same time he supported other parties, such as the Socialist Revolutionaries and the Liberals.

The events of Bloody Sunday and the Revolution of 1905 induced Gorky to become involved, for the only time in his life, in revolutionary work. He wrote articles for the first legal Bolshevik newspaper, *Novaia zhizn* (*New Life*), gave financial assistance, and criticized the tsar's October Manifesto for its conservatism. Warned of his imminent arrest, Gorky left Russia for the Italian island of Capri and did not return until 1913. Alienated by the Lenin and the RSDWP, Gorky joined a group led by Alexander A. Bogdanov, who shared his belief in mass education. With Bogdanov and Anatoly V. Lunacharsky, he organized a school for underground party workers. This was also the time of the emergence of a new religion called *Bogostroitelstvo* (*God-building*), best defined as a theory of the divinity of the masses. Gorky's *Ispoved* (*Confession*), written in 1908, served as an exposition of this belief and led to a break with Lenin.

On his return to Russia in 1913, Gorky devoted his time, ability, and resources to advancing Russian education and culture, projects brought to an end by World War I and the revolutions of 1917. Gorky was enthusiastic about the February Revolution, hoping that Russia would become a liberal democratic state. Soon after Lenin's return to Russia in April 1917, Gorky, writing in *Novaia zhizn* (*New Life*), criticized the Bolshevik propaganda for a socialist revolution. These views appeared in articles called *Nesvoevremennye mysli* (*Untimely Thoughts*). Russia, wrote Gorky, was not ready for the socialist revolution envisioned by the Bolsheviks.

Under Lenin and the Bolsheviks, Gorky saw it as his task to save Russia's cultural treasures and intellectual elite. In 1921, horrified by the cruelty and bloodshed of the civil war, he decided to leave Soviet Russia but not before he succeeded in obtaining American aid for the country's famine victims.

His second exile was spent mostly in Sorrento, Italy. Among his political writings of this period is the essay *O russkom krestianstve* (*On the Russian Peasantry*), which appeared in 1922 in Berlin and during the 1980s in the Soviet Union. A bitter indictment of the Russian peasantry, it was resented by both the Russian émigré community and Soviet leaders. In 1928, under pressure from Josef Stalin, Gorky returned to the Soviet Union. The years from 1928 to1936 were trying for him, for he could see but not speak of the realities of Stalinist Russia. He became an icon and cooperated with the regime, apparently believing that socialism would modernize Russia.

The cause of Gorky's death in 1936 is still debated, some maintaining that he died of natural causes, others that he was a victim of a Stalinist purge. Similarly, opinion in today's Russia is divided on the question of Gorky as a political activist. Gorky was a great political activist and writer of short stories, plays, memoirs, and novels such as *Foma Gordeev*, *The Artamonovs*, the trilogy *My Childhood*, *In the World*, and *My Universities*, and *The Life of Klim Samgin*.

See also: KOROLENKO, VLADIMIR GALAKTIONOVICH; SOCIAL DEMOCRATIC WORKERS PARTY; SOCIALIST REALISM; TOLSTOY, LEO NIKOLAYEVICH

BIBLIOGRAPHY

Scherr, Barry P. (1988). *Maxim Gorky*. Boston: Twayne.

Weil, Irwin. (1966). *Gorky: His Literary Development and Influence on Soviet Intellectual Life*. New York: Random House.

Yedlin, Tovah. (1999). *Maxim Gorky: A Political Biography*. Westport, CT: Praeger.

TOVAH YEDLIN

GOSBANK

Gosbank (the State Bank of the USSR) was the Soviet Union's monobank. Characteristic of command economies, monobanks combine central and commercial banking functions into a single state-owned institution. Gosbank's primary tasks were to issue cash and credit according to government directives, and to operate the payments and clearing system. The Soviet government created Gosbank in October 1921 as the State Bank of the Russian Federation and changed its name to the State Bank of the USSR (Gosbank) in July 1923. The Soviet government permitted communal and cooperative banks to exist separately during the New Economic Policy period of the 1920s, but a series of banking reforms from 1930 to 1932 ended these last vestiges of commercial activity.

Several organizational changes ensued in the following years, and by the mid-1960s Gosbank's structure had crystallized. The USSR Council of Ministers directly controlled Gosbank. Gosbank's director sat on the Council of Ministers, and the Council nominated the members of Gosbank's board. Besides its main branches in each of the fifteen union republics and sub-branches in autonomous republics, territories, and regions, Gosbank controlled three subordinate banks: Stroibank USSR (the All-Union Bank for Investment Financing), Sberbank USSR (the Savings Bank), and Vneshtorgbank (the Foreign Trade Bank). In addition, Gosbank and Vneshtorgbank controlled foreign subsidiary banks in London, Paris, Frankfurt, Luxembourg, and Vienna. The oldest and most prominent were Moscow Narodny Bank, founded in London in 1919, and Eurobank, founded in Paris in 1925.

As a part of General Secretary Mikhail Gorbachev's perestroika (restructuring) program, the Soviet government dismantled the monobank in January 1988 and created a two-tiered banking system. Gosbank became a central bank, and retained only its major offices in the republics, large cities, and oblasts. The state foreign trade bank (now renamed Vneshekonombank) and Sberbank remained under Gosbank's direct control. The rest of Gosbank split off into three specialized banks. Agroprombank (the Agro-Industrial Bank) and Zhilsotsbank (the Housing and Social Development Bank) emerged from Gosbank proper, while Stroibank became Promstroibank (the Industrial-Construction Bank).

In 1990 the Russian government transformed a Moscow branch of Gosbank into the Central Bank of Russia (CBR) during the battle for sovereignty between the Soviet and Russian governments. The CBR and Gosbank operated in parallel until after the failed coup attempt against Gorbachev in August 1991, when the Soviet governing bodies lost their hold on power. On August 23, Russian president Boris Yeltsin ordered the USSR Council of Ministers to complete the transfer of Union-level organizations on Russian territory to the custody of the Russian state by the end of the year. On November 15, Yeltsin took over, by decree, the USSR Ministry of Finance and the USSR Chief Administration for the Production of State Bank Notes, Coins, and Medals. The Presidium of the Russian Supreme Soviet then unilaterally passed a resolution dissolving Gosbank and transferring its "facilities, documents, and specialists" to the CBR. On January 1, 1992, the CBR officially took over the rest of Gosbank's resources in Russia, and Gosbank ceased to exist.

See also: BANKING SYSTEM, SOVIET; CENTRAL BANK OF RUSSIA; SBERBANK; STROIBANK

BIBLIOGRAPHY

Garvy, George. (1977). Money, Financial Flows, and Credit in the Soviet Union. New York: National Bureau of Economic Research.

Hellman, Joel. (1993). Breaking the Bank: The Political Economy of Banking Reform in the Soviet Union. Ph.D. dissertation, Department of Political Science, Columbia University, New York.

Kuschpèta, Olga. (1978). The Banking and Credit System of the USSR. Leiden, Netherlands: Nijhoff Social Sciences Division.

Zwass, Adam. (1979). Money, Banking, and Credit in the Soviet Union and Eastern Europe. White Plains, NY: M. E. Sharpe.

JULIET JOHNSON

GOSIZDAT

State publishing house of the Russian Republic.

Gosizdat was the most important publishing house in Soviet Russia between 1919 and 1930, and played an important role in the creation of the Soviet publishing system. After coming to power, the Bolsheviks nationalized most private book publishers and printers, transferring their assets to local party and state organizations, which used them to set up their own publishing operations. When the new publishing system proved too disorganized and chaotic, Gosizdat was founded in May 1919 to provide a centralized alternative. Gosizdat started as a contract-printer, receiving most of its editorial content from other Soviet institutions, though it did produce some titles independently. It also acted as a regulatory body overseeing the work of remaining local publishing houses, controlling their access to raw materials and enforcing political censorship. Gosizdat's production during this period consisted primarily of short agitational and military titles, though it also published some longer scientific works. These books and pamphlets were state-funded and distributed at no charge. Gosizdat's output was almost entirely in the Russian language.

With the onset of the New Economic Policy (NEP) in 1921, the Soviet publishing industry and Gosizdat underwent dramatic changes. Publishing was decentralized, as Soviet institutions were permitted to open their own publishing operations, and books became priced commodities. Gosizdat lost its regulatory functions and focused on producing its own books, though it continued to do some contract printing. Unlike most Russian-language publishing houses, whose production was specialized (at least in theory), Gosizdat remained a universal publishing house, issuing works on a wide variety of subjects, including fiction, children's literature, scientific texts, propaganda, and works on Marxism and Leninism. It had monopolies on the publication of Russian literary classics and textbooks. Gosizdat issued between 25 and 40 percent of Soviet Russian-language book production (measured by pages) each year in the 1920s. Gosizdat also published a number of important periodicals. During the 1920s, Gosizdat absorbed a number of prominent Soviet publishing houses, including *Krasnaya nov*, *Priboy*, and *Zemlya i fabrika*.

Gosizdat was techically part of the Commissariat of Enlightenment, though in practice it answered directly to the Communist Party's Central Committee, which appointed its board of directors, reviewed editorial appointments, and monitored its work. Gosizdat acted as the Central Committee's main book publisher and was afforded special privileges, including large state subsidies and freedom from external ideological censorship.

In August 1930, Gosizdat provided the foundation for a new, centralized publishing conglomerate, the Association of State Publishing Houses (OGIZ), into which most existing Soviet publishing houses were merged. Even after this time, it was not uncommon for Soviet sources to use the term *gosizdat* to describe the Russian Republic's main publishing operation, whatever its official name. Variants of the term were also used to describe the main publishing house serving some republics or languages: The Tatar State Publishing House, for instance, was known as Tatizdat or Tatgiz. Specialized Russian-language publishing houses were also popularly known by similar acronyms; for example, the State Technical Publishing House was Gostekhizdat.

See also: CENSORSHIP; CENTRAL COMMITTEE; SAMIZDAT

BIBLIOGRAPHY

Friedberg, Maurice. (1962). *Russian Classics in Soviet Jackets.* New York: Columbia University Press.

Kassof, Brian Evan. (2000). "The Knowledge Front: Politics, Ideology, and Economics in the Soviet Book Publishing Industry, 1925–1935." Ph. D. diss., University of California, Berkeley.

Kenez, Peter. (1985). *The Birth of the Propaganda State: Soviet Methods of Mass Mobilization, 1917–1929.* Cambridge, UK: Cambridge University Press.

BRIAN KASSOF

GOSKOMSTAT

The term *Goskomstat* is the abbreviation used to designate the State Committee for Statistics (Gosudarstvennyi Komitet Statistiki, or Goskomstat), which, in July 1997, replaced the Central Statistical Agency (TsSU). Founded in 1918, the Soviet office for statistics went through various institutional transformations starting in January 1930, when central planning was established. The office lost its institutional independence that year and was subsumed under Gosplan, the State Planning Administration. Its missions were redefined. From then on its main task would be to supply Gosplan with the numbers it needed to create the indicators necessary to the planned management of the Soviet economy and society. Conflicts erupted as early as the end of the 1920s between TsSU statisticians and the political leadership on a number of issues, particularly on the measurement of crop levels and the analysis of social differences in the countryside. During the 1930s, disagreements on population numbers led to the purges that touched most of the officials in charge of the census of 1937. In 1948, TsSU once again became independent from Gosplan, but its activity remained essentially focused on the production of numbers for the planning and improvement of indicators.

Following the launching of perestroika policies, in 1985, a decree dated July 17, 1987, stated the necessity to "rebuild the foundations for statistical activity in the country." Nevertheless, planned management of the economy was not abandoned right away. The year 1991 marked a breaking off in this respect with Goskomstat entering a period of reforms clearly oriented toward the abandonment of planning and the transition to a market economy. First, the disappearance of the Soviet state caused the breakup of USSR's Goskomstat followed by the transfer of its various services to each new state born out of the former USSR: each created its own statistics committee or department. After the founding of the Commonwealth of Independent States (CIS), on December 30, 1991, a statistics committee was created to coordinate the activities of statistics committees of CIS member states.

Adjustment to the new constraints imposed upon the production of statistical data resulting from the transition to a market economy brought about a number of different programs affecting Goskomstat starting in 1992. The recasting of economic indicators, the elaboration of new monitoring tools—notably for trade and financial activities—and methods for gathering economic data from a growing number of companies outside the state sector, as well as the construction of a new national accounting system, were all accomplished thanks to the support of experience from statistical administrations of Western countries. Concern for the ability to compare Russian statistical data with those released by other countries explains the attention that was given to the elaboration of principles for the calculation of GNP and such indicators as price, population, labor, foreign trade, and financial activity statistics that match the practices adopted by Western nations in this domain.

See also: CENTRAL STATISTICAL AGENCY; ECONOMY, CURRENT; GOSPLAN

MARTINE MESPOULET

GOSPLAN

Gosplan SSSR (*Gosudarstvenny planovy komitet SSSR*—the State Planning Committee of the USSR), the core state committee of the Soviet economic bureaucracy, was created in 1921. During the first Five-Year Plan (1928–1932) Valerian Kuybyshev headed Gosplan. Gosplan was responsible for executing the directives of the Council of Ministries, translating general directives into operational plans for the ministries, and advising the Council of Ministries on a wide range of issues. Gosplan planned for the ministries, not for enterprises, although some large enterprises were planned directly by Gosplan. Gosplan communicated extensively with the ministries in the process of drafting the plan. It was subdivided into industrial departments, such as coal, ferrous metals, and machine building, and also had summary departments, such as finance, to deal with functions that crossed functional bodies. The early recognition of Gosplan's importance came in 1925 and 1926, when it began to prepare the annual preliminary plan targets, or so-called control figures. During the 1930s the principle of guidance of economic policy on an annual basis was established, although much publicity was devoted to nonoperational five-year plans. Annual plans, including production and financial targets, so-called *promfinplany,* were drawn up sector by sector. By 1926 and 1927, promfinplany that were originated by ministries became dependent on the control figures. Formally, the plan era began in 1928 with the First Five-Year Plan for intensive economic growth. The Five-Year Plan was a comprehensive plan that set the major economic goals for a five-year period. The five-year goals were not put into operation in the shorter-term operational plans. Once the Soviet regime stipulated the plan figures, all levels of the economy from individual enterprises to the national level were theoretically obliged to meet those goals ("The plan is the law"). During the period from 1928 to 1932, the basic principles of Soviet planning were established. Gosplan was to be the central coordinating body to which all other planning bodies were to submit their proposals. The control figures would provide the general direction for the economy. The actual detailed operational plans for enterprises (*promfinplany*) were to conform to the control figures. Materials were to be allocated through a system of balances, which would elaborate the sources and uses of basic industrial materials. The long-term planning horizon was set at five years, the average period required for the completion of investment projects. Operational plans were prepared in cooperation with the planning departments of ministries, the most important of which were the all-union ministries. In day-to-day operations, inter-ministry cooperation was limited in such matters as equipment delivery and construction planning. Soviet law gave Gosplan substantial responsibilities concerning supply planning. Gosplan was charged with preparing and confirming plans for the distribution of production among ministries. It was Gosplan who prepared general material limits (*limityu*) for the ministries. Later these material limits would be broken down into product profiles by the State Committee for Material Technical Supply, Gossnab, which was formed in 1947 to assist in supply planning. Gosplan remained the primary planning body of the Soviet Union until its collapse in December 1991.

See also: ECONOMIC GROWTH, SOVIET; FIVE-YEAR PLANS

BIBLIOGRAPHY

Gregory, Paul R., and Stuart, Robert C. (2001). *Russian and Soviet Economic Performance and Structure.* Boston, MA: Addison Wesley.

Hewett, Edward A. (1988). *Reforming the Soviet Economy: Equality Versus Efficiency.* Washington, DC: Brookings Institution.

PAUL R. GREGORY

GOSTI

The gosti (singular: gost) were great merchants who enjoyed high social status. They are encountered in the Kievan and later Mongol period, but are best known as a corporate group that emerged in the sixteenth century and figured prominently in the economic, political, administrative, and court life of seventeenth-century Russia.

In the last half of the sixteenth century, the leading merchants of Muscovy were organized into three privileged corporations: the gosti, the *gostinnaya sotnya,* and the *sukonnaya sotnya.* They were obliged to render services to the government and were compensated with certain privileges. The gosti, whose number averaged around thirty throughout the seventeenth century, stood at the top of the merchant hierarchy. The rank was not hereditary, so the government periodically designated replacements for those who had died or became incapable of rendering service.

They were obliged, among other burdensome duties, to serve as the tsar's factors, to collect customs at the port of Archangel and at Moscow, to oversee the state liquor monopoly, and to participate in ceremonial functions at the court. In return for the exercise of these duties, the gosti were freed of the obligation to quarter troops, and permitted to brew and keep stocks of liquor. They were not required to pay taxes imposed on other townsmen, and they were the only Russian merchants permitted to travel abroad on business.

Representatives of the gosti participated in the land assemblies (zemskie sobory) and advised the rulers on questions of war and peace. They were leaders of a long-running campaign to abolish privileges granted to foreign merchants and to secure uncontested control of the domestic market. Peter the Great, dissatisfied with their perceived want of dynamism, phased them out in the first quarter of the eighteenth century.

See also: GOSTINAYA SOTNYA; MERCHANTS; SUKKONNAYA SOTNYA

BIBLIOGRAPHY

Baron, Samuel H. (1980). "The Fate of the Gosti in the Reign of Peter the Great." In *Muscovite Russia: Collected Essays*, ed. Samuel H. Baron. London: Variorum.

Baron, Samuel H. (1980). "Who Were the Gosti?" In *Muscovite Russia: Collected Essays*, ed. Samuel H. Baron. London: Variorum.

SAMUEL H. BARON

GOSTINAYA SOTNYA

Literally "Guest Hundred," a privileged corporation of Russian merchants between the late sixteenth and early eighteenth centuries.

The name Gostinaya sotnya derives from the word *gost* (guest), which was used to refer to prosperous merchants in medieval Russia. The Gostinaya sotnya was the second most important corporation of elite merchants after the *gosti* (pl. of *gost*). Members of the Gostinaya sotnya tended to be relatives of gosti, former members of the *Sukonnaya sotnya* (a lower corporation of merchants), prominent local merchants, and prosperous peasant-traders. Three categories of Gostinaya sotnya members were defined in terms of wealth.

Members of the Gostinaya sotnya performed official duties for the government, usually once every six years for half a year at a time. They typically served as heads or officials of local customs and taverns. They assisted gosti in large cities and conducted similar functions independently in smaller towns. They sold treasury goods at fairs and abroad. In return, Gostinaya sotnya members were exempted from direct taxes, minor customs duties, and the responsibility to quarter soldiers. They were excluded from the jurisdiction of local authorities and granted other privileges, including the right to distill liquor for personal consumption. Elevated fines of ten to twenty rubles were assessed in cases of dishonor committed against Gostinaya sotnya members. Unlike the status of a gost, membership in the Gostinaya sotnya was hereditary and typically shared with other family members engaged in a joint enterprise.

A 1613 charter issued to members of the Gostinaya sotnya closely resembled the charter of the gosti; however, it did not authorize travel abroad. Foreign travel was subsequently permitted through government-issued passes. The Gostinaya sotnya typically sent two representatives to Assemblies of the Land (*zemskie sobory*).

The Gostinaya sotnya had 345 members in 1601 and 1602; membership fell to 185 in 1630 and 158 in 1649. A total of 2,100 individuals joined the Gostinaya sotnya during the seventeenth and early eighteenth centuries, with a particular marked growth in the 1680s. With the introduction of the poll tax in the 1720s, members of the Gostinaya sotnya, along with townsmen, joined the stratum of merchants.

See also: GOSTI; FOREIGN TRADE; MERCHANTS; SUKONNAIA SOTNYA; TAXES

BIBLIOGRAPHY

Hellie, Richard. "The Stratification of Muscovite Society: The Townsmen." *Russian History* 5(2):119–175.

Hittle, J. Michael. (1979). *The Service City: State and Townsmen in Russia, 1600–1800.* Cambridge, MA: Harvard University Press.

JARMO T. KOTILAINE

GOSUDARYEV DVOR

Literally, "sovereign's court," a hierarchical institution made up of the ruler's elite servitors during the late twelfth through seventeenth centuries.

Courts of east Slavic princes usually included close members of the retinue, service cavalrymen, and household officials. Members of boyar families with established ties to the prince of Moscow formed the basis of the Muscovite court during the fourteenth century. The growing political power of the Muscovite ruler attracted numerous distinguished newcomers, including members of the Lithuanian and Tatar ruling families, to his court in the fourteenth through sixteenth centuries. Muscovite rulers also incorporated the princes of territories annexed by Moscow into their court, although some of them, known as service princes, retained some organizational autonomy within the court until the end of the sixteenth century.

As a result of the reforms of the 1550s, the sovereign's court functioned on the basis of a mixture of hierarchical and territorial principles. During the second half of the sixteenth century, the court acquired a clear hierarchy of ranks: boyars, *okolnichie*, counselor cavalrymen, counselor secretaries, the household ranks and chancellery secretaries, the ruler's personal guard (*stolniki, stryapchie, zhiltsy*), service princes, and the lowest ranks (*dvorovye deti boyarskie*, later *vybornye dvoryane*). Service relations between courtiers were subject to rules of precedence (*mestnichestvo*), a complex system that defined the status of a courtier on the basis of the prominence and service appointments of his ancestors and relatives. Territoriality was crucial to the court's lowest strata, which included members of collateral branches of boyar families, people who had advanced through faithful service, and newcomers of lower status. The people who held the lowest court ranks were leading members of local cavalrymen communities and were listed by the town where they had service lands. They served in Moscow on a rotating basis. Secretaries entered the court thanks to their literacy and the patronage of the ruler or influential courtiers. A servitor's career at court thus dependent on his pedigree, his position in the local cavalrymen community, his personal skills and merits, and the favor of his patrons.

The princes of Moscow used a variety of means to secure the integrity of their court. Members of the court swore an oath of allegiance and received land grants on condition that they served the prince. Muscovite rulers secured the loyalty of distinguished newcomers by granting them superior status over the boyars, manipulating their land possessions, encouraging marriages with members of the royal family and the local elite, and subjecting the disloyal to disgrace and executions. Ivan IV's reign saw the climax of repressions against members of the court, which was divided in two parts during the Oprichnina. The social and genealogical composition of the court, however, remained stable until the middle of the seventeenth century, when people of lower origin began entering the court's upper strata. At the same time, the leaders of local cavalrymen communities were excluded from the court. Peter I stopped making appointments to the upper court ranks during the early 1690s.

The sovereign's court included the most combatworthy Muscovite troops and provided cadres for administrative and diplomatic tasks. An efficient military and administrative institution, the sovereign's court was vital to the victory of the princes of Moscow over their opponents and to the functioning of the Russian state during the sixteenth and seventeenth centuries.

See also: BOYAR; CHANCELLERY SYSTEM; IVAN III; IVAN IV; OPRICHNINA

BIBLIOGRAPHY

Alef, Gustave. (1986). *The Origins of Muscovite Autocracy: The Age of Ivan III.* Forschungen zur Osteuropäischen Geschichte, vol. 39. Berlin: Osteuropa-Institut; Wiesbaden: Otto Harrassowitz.

Poe, Marshall T. (2003). *The Russian Elite in the Seventeenth Century*, 2 vols. Helsinki: The Finnish Academy of Science and Letters.

SERGEI BOGATYREV

GOVERNING SENATE

The Governing Senate was founded in 1711. Its initial primary responsibility was to govern the empire when the emperor was on military campaigns. The establishment of the Senate was also part of a government re-organization undertaken by Peter I (1689–1725) who wished to make the government structure more responsive to his wishes and more effective at tapping society's resources for military purposes. In 1722 it was transformed from a higher governing organ to a higher supervisory one responsible for resolving legal and administrative disputes. Catherine II (1763–1796) further systemized the Senate by dividing it into six departments with relatively clear institutional responsibilities related to administrative oversight.

The governmental reforms undertaken by Alexander I (1801–1825) fundamentally changed the role of the Senate. According to his decrees of 1801 and 1802 the Senate had the right to judicial review and supervision of the highest governmental organs, including the newly established ministries. No legislative bill could become law without the Senate's approval. However, one year later a new decree stripped the Senate of these powers. The founding of the ministerial system and the State Council (1810) fatally weakened the Senate's role in practice. For the remainder of the nineteenth century it played the role of a High Court of Review and along with other institutions exercised limited administrative supervision. Until 1905 the Senate, whose forty or fifty members were chosen by the tsar, rarely met, except on ceremonial occasions. Six departments that dealt with a myriad of judicial, social, and political issues continued to work under the supervision of the Senate.

After the Revolution of 1905 the role of the Senate changed once again. It became the High Criminal Court dealing with corruption in the bureaucracy. Its first department played a role in the preparations for the formation of the First Duma, while its Second Department became the supreme appellate court for land-related issues.

See also: ALEXANDER I; CATHERINE II; PETER I

BIBLIOGRAPHY

Seton-Watson, Hugh. (1991). *The Russian Empire 1801–1917.* Oxford: Oxford University Press.

Yaney, George. (1973). *The Systemization of Russian Government.* London: University of Illinois Press.

ZHAND P. SHAKIBI

GRAIN CRISIS OF 1928

The Grain Crisis of 1928 was economic and political in nature and was a turning point in the Soviet regime's policy toward the peasantry, a preview of Josef Stalin's harsh methods of collectivization. Ten years after the Revolution, agriculture was still based on individual farming, with peasants cultivating more than ninety-seven percent of the land and selling their product to the state at set procurement prices in order to meet their tax obligations. The most important product was grain, and the system of state procurement supplied grain to feed the cities and the military, and for export. Under the New Economic Policy (NEP), the existence of a free market for agricultural products helped keep procurement prices competitive. Most peasants were at or near the subsistence level. A small number of richer peasants (the so-called kulaks) supplied most of the grain sold on the free market. Prices for industrial products produced by the state sector were kept relatively high in order to accumulate capital. In December 1927, the Fifteenth Party Congress of the Communist Party endorsed the idea of planned economic development, requiring the state to accumulate even more capital from domestic sources, principally the peasantry, while maintaining exports. Grain procurement prices were lowered in order to keep state expenditures down. A war scare in 1927 led people to hoard food.

Within this context, the grain crisis began to take shape toward the end of 1927. Although it was an average harvest, grain procurements fell precipitously at the end of the year; in November and December of 1927, procurements were about half of what they had been during the same months of the previous year. The problem was especially acute in Siberia, the Volga, and the Urals, even though the harvest had been good in these areas. Richer peasants withheld grain from the market, waiting for prices to rise. Peasants also switched from producing grain to other agricultural commodities. For example, in the Urals, while peasant grain sales to the state declined by a third, the sale of meat rose by fifty percent, egg sales doubled, and bacon sales went up four times.

Stalin insisted that the kulaks were withholding grain from the market to sabotage the regime, creating as much a political problem as an economic problem. He argued that the class struggle was intensifying. In January 1928 he visited the Urals and West Siberia and called for a series of emergency measures to extract grain from the recalcitrant peasantry. In direct opposition to the views of Nikolai Bukharin and other moderates in the Politburo, quotas for compulsory grain deliveries were imposed on kulaks and also on middle peasants. Peasants responded by decreasing grain production during 1928, but this simply intensified the crisis. For the year October 1927–October 1928, grain procurements fell by fourteen percent relative to the same period a year earlier, although the harvest was down by only seven to eight percent.

The grain crisis of 1928 was a critical turning point in Soviet economic and political history. Applying compulsion to the peasants rather than using economic incentives meant that NEP was dead. Most significantly, the events of 1928 showed that Stalin saw the peasantry as the enemy and established the context of a warlike crisis that would justify violence. The outlines of the harsh collectivization drive were already visible.

See also: COLLECTIVIZATION OF AGRICULTURE; KULAKS; NEW ECONOMIC POLICY

BIBLIOGRAPHY

Nove, Alec. (1969). *An Economic History of the U.S.S.R.* London: Allen Lane.

Tucker, Robert. (1990). *Stalin in Power.* New York: Norton.

CAROL GAYLE
WILLIAM MOSKOFF

GRAIN TRADE

In Russia the dynamics of the grain trade depended on demand in the domestic and foreign markets. Before 1762 the export of grain was conducted under government supervision and depended on the domestic price level. If local prices exceeded an established level, export of grain was prohibited because of fears of further price rises. But even in the years of low prices, permission for the export of grain was required. The government considered grain a strategic commodity and gave this permission reluctantly. As a result, before 1762 grain trade was limited mainly to the empire's frontiers. Only after the declaration of freedom of grain trade in 1762 did a systematic growth of grain exports begin. Before the 1780s the export of grain was prohibited only in case of a substantial price rise, and by the 1790s export became virtually free. Domestic demand for grain came from the urban population, the army, industry (mainly distillation), and the rural population of provinces that experienced a grain deficit.

The demand for marketable grain was comparatively small because nearly 75 percent of the population, even as late as 1897, was engaged in agriculture and able to satisfy its need for grain with its own production. The urban population was not large (in 1914 only 15.3% of the population lived in towns, and a portion of the townspeople engaged in agriculture). The regular army was comparatively small (in 1719, 2.9% of the country's total population; in 1795, 2.5%; in 1850, 1.5%; in 1913, 0.8%). The consumption of vodka was limited physiologically (in 1913 in Russia the consumption of vodka converted to spirit was only 3.1 liters per capita) and the technology of distillation was improving. A constant demand for grain was felt only in the vicinity of big cities, industrial centers, and where arable land was scarce or soil poor. According to rough estimates, during the 1800s the urban population consumed 4.7 percent of all grain produced; in 1851–1860, 5.6 percent; and in 1912–1913, 9.1 percent; with industry consuming 4.1, 3.5, and 0.5 percent correspondingly; the army, 2.1, 2.1, and 1.2 percent; and exports 1.0, 3.8, and 15.7 percent. During the 1800s the share of marketable grain was nearly 12 percent of the gross yield of grain; during the 1850s, 15 percent; and in 1892–1913, 26.4 percent.

The grain trade began to grow markedly after the abolition of serfdom. Domestic and, even more, foreign demand increased, both of which were stimulated by extension of the railway network. Of three most important factors stimulating the demand for grain, export was in the first place, industrialization the second, and urbanization the third. The export of marketable grain constituted 7 percent of the total grain trade during the early 1800s, 26 percent during the 1850s, and 60 percent in 1892–1893; in terms of weight the average annual export of grain amounted to 0.2 million tons, 1.1 million tons, and 10.7 million tons correspondingly. The export of grain acquired vital importance for Russia. The main export cereals were wheat, rye, barley, and oats. In the mass of exported grain in 1762–1802 the share of wheat was 48 percent; rye, 45 percent; barley, 3.9 percent; oats, 2.8 percent; other cereals, 0.3 percent; in 1841–1850, 66, 17, 4, 6, and 7 percent correspondingly; in 1912–1913, 37, 8, 41, 11, and 3 percent. Russian grain was mainly exported to Western European countries. Germany, Holland, Switzerland, and Italy imported mainly Russian grain, while England, Belgium, and France imported U.S. grain. Russia and the United States competed mainly in exports of red cereals: wheat and some barley. Grey cereals, rye and oats, were chiefly delivered from Russia and did not encounter U.S. competition.

During the post-reform period considerable success was achieved in the organization of the grain trade: A whole army of trade agents appeared; credit for marketable grain was created; great amounts of capital were mobilized; means of communication, ports, and the merchant navy were improved; a tariff system was designed; a fairly dense network of elevators and granaries was formed; a corporative organization of grain tradesmen emerged; grain ex-

Laborers in Odessa walk among the cattle-driven wagons laden with sacks of wheat, 1878. © CORBIS

changes were founded in major centers of grain trade (St. Petersburg, Moscow, Voronezh, Elizavetgrad, Borisoglebsk); information on crops, grain exports, stocks, prices, and freights became widely available. Western European commercial ethics and trade customs were gradually adopted. Despite indisputable progress, the organization of Russian grain trade did not attain the high level of development that it did in the United States, Russia's main competitor in the world grain market. Elevators and granaries served merely as storehouses in Russia; classification of grains was not practiced there. Railways were not equipped with proper warehouses, rolling stock, and double track sections. Consequently, in good years, grain piled up at railway junctions, waiting for loading in the open, sometimes for up to two months. The quality of grain deteriorated, making it difficult for tradesmen to meet the conditions of contracts. The state of the roads along which grain was delivered to railway stations was unsatisfactory. Macadamized roads were few. In European Russia in 1912, there were

6 kilometers (3.7 miles) of them per 1,000 square kilometers (386.1 square miles); in the United States, 53 kilometers (33 miles); in Germany, 516 kilometers (320.6 miles); in Great Britain, 819 kilometers (508.9 miles); and in France, 1,073 kilometers (666.7 miles). Grain was brought to the stations not when it was profitable to sell it but when roads permitted. In ports there was a lack of warehouses for grain storage as well as a lack of facilities for grain reloading. All this raised overhead expenses and prices, and reduced the competitive capacity of Russian grain.

In Russia, foreign grain trade was in the hands of Western European tradesmen, and domestic trade remained in the hands of native tradesmen, mainly Jews, who purchased grain in the country and delivered it to ports for foreign exporters who gave credits and therefore dictated the conditions. The buyers-up were interested only in expanding and accelerating their turnovers. They did not attach much importance to the price level, since they made money on the difference between purchase and sale price. The sellers were peasants overburdened with various payments and landowners with big debts. They were short of liquid capital and, because of transportation conditions, not free to choose the moment of sale. Russian grain producers could neither wait for a favorable situation in the market nor exert influence upon prices, the level of which depended on crops and market competition of the sellers themselves. Inadequate organization of the grain trade resulted in the sale of Russian grain on world markets at less of a profit than U.S. grain. U.S. producers and sellers were to some extent able to regulate grain supplies to the world market, restraining the fall in prices in case of surplus grain supplies and maintaining high prices in a profitable market situation.

On account of great export (during the nineteenth and early twentieth centuries grain played the same role as did oil and gasoline during the late twentieth and early twenty-first centuries) the level of prices was of great significance for Russia. Incomes and solvency of peasants and landlords, the country's trade balance, and earnings from customs duties depended on the price level. From the eighteenth century to the early twentieth century, the situation in the world grain markets was for the most part advantageous to Russia. Russian local grain prices, expressed in grams of gold, rose 10.2 times from 1,707 grams (60.2 ounces) to 1,914 grams (67.5 ounces) (5.7 times during the eighteenth century), while the general index of prices for domestic goods rose 6.6 times (five times during the eighteenth century). By contrast, in European countries, despite cyclic fluctuations, grain prices and the general price index had a tendency to decline in this period. In eighteenth-century Russia, a phenomenal rise in grain prices (and generally in all prices) occurred. During the sixteenth and seventeenth centuries Russia had stood apart from the price revolution in Europe, but during the eighteenth century Russia entered world trade, and a belated price revolution took place. The Russian price revolution resulted in a leveling of Russian and world prices. At the turn of the eighteenth century, Russian prices were about nine to ten times lower than world prices, and at the turn of the twentieth century only 20 to 30 percent lower.

The leveling of Russian and world prices occurred under the influence of the market economy laws, which required, first of all, that prices for Russian goods correspond not only with national but also with world production costs, and, second, that they be determined by the relations between demand and supply both in the Russian and world markets. As Russia was joining the world market, local grain prices were becoming less dependent on local crops and local demand, and more dependent on the situation in the world market. During the late nineteenth and early twentieth centuries the dynamics of Russian grain prices were largely determined by the world market situation, and red grain prices were fully dependent on it. All of this attests that from the beginning of the eighteenth century Russia joined the international division of labor and gradually turned into a full member of the world economy and world market, and that the principles of the market economy penetrated the Russian national economy as early as the eighteenth century, long before the reforms of the 1860s. Hence, from the eighteenth to the early twentieth century the general line of Russia's socioeconomic evolution remained unchanged and consisted in commercialization of the economy and enhancement of the role of the market as a production regulator. Serfdom hampered and slowed down but did not prevent the development of capitalism in Russia, just as prior to 1865 slavery did not stop the development of capitalism in the United States. Grain prices exerted substantial influence upon numerous aspects of the economic, social, and political life of the country. They played an important part in the modernization of the national economy, development of social stratification of the peasantry, destruction of the peasant commune, and urbanization and industrialization of the country.

See also: AGRICULTURE; ECONOMY, TSARIST; FOREIGN TRADE; PEASANT ECONOMY.

BIBLIOGRAPHY

Herlihy, Patricia. (1986). *Odessa: A History, 1794–1914.* Cambridge, MA: Distributed by Harvard University Press for the Harvard Ukrainian Research Institute.

Mironov, Boris N. (1992). "Consequences of the Price Revolution in Eighteenth-Century Russia." *Economic History Review* 45(3):457–478.

BORIS N. MIRONOV

GRAND ALLIANCE

Officially termed the Anti-Hitlerite Coalition by the Soviet Union, the Grand Alliance (1941–1945) was a military and political coalition of countries fighting against the Axis (Nazi Germany, Fascist Italy, Imperial Japan), and their satellites. The alliance evolved during World War II through common understandings and specific formal and informal agreements negotiated between the Big Three (United States, Soviet Union, and Great Britain) at wartime conferences, ministerial meetings, and periodic summits between the respective heads of state. In addition to the Big Three, the alliance included China, members of the British Commonwealth, France, and many other countries. While some formal agreements and modest liaison and coordinating bodies existed within the context of these agreements, particularly between the United States and Great Britain, the alliance as a whole formed few formal official policy organs.

Evolving step by step after the German invasion of the Soviet Union, the alliance was a virtual marriage of necessity between the two Western democracies and Stalin's communist government, impelled by the reality of war and a common threat to all three powers, as well as the necessity of joining military and political forces to achieve victory in the war. The motives and attitudes of alliance members varied over time according to the military situation and the member states' political aims. To varying degrees, the Big Three shared certain wartime goals in addition to victory: for instance, mutual military assistance, formulation of a common unified wartime military strategy, establishment of a postwar international security organization, and elimination of any future threats from Germany and Japan.

The decisive stage in the formation of the Grand Alliance occurred after the German invasion of the Soviet Union in June 1941, when, prompted by fear that Germany might win the war, British Prime Minister Winston Churchill and U.S. President Franklin D. Roosevelt declared their support for the Soviet Union as "true allies in the name of the peoples of Europe and America." Great Britain and the Soviet Union signed a mutual aid treaty in July 1941, and Stalin endorsed the peace aims of Roosevelt's and Churchill's Atlantic Charter in September. In November the United States solidified the alliance by extending lend-lease assistance to the Soviet Union. Thereafter, a steady stream of agreements and periodic meetings between unofficial representatives, ministers, and heads of state of the three countries formalized the alliance. The most important ministerial meetings took place in London (September–October 1941) and Moscow (October 1941 and October 1943) and at the Big Three summits at Tehran (November 1943–January 1944), Yalta (Crimea) (February 1945), and Potsdam (July–August 1945). During wartime, tensions emerged within the alliance over such vital issues as the adequacy of lend-lease aid, military coordination among Allied armies, the opening of a second front on mainland Europe, the postwar boundaries of the Soviet Union, the political structure of liberated European countries, Soviet participation in the war against Japan, European reconstruction, and the shape and nature of postwar peace.

See also: CHINA, RELATIONS WITH; FRANCE, RELATIONS WITH; GREAT BRITAIN, RELATIONS WITH; UNITED STATES, RELATIONS WITH; WORLD WAR II

BIBLIOGRAPHY

Churchill, Winston S. (1950). *The Grand Alliance.* Boston: Houghton Mifflin.

Feis, Herbert. (1957). *Churchill, Roosevelt, Stalin: The War They Waged and the Peace They Sought.* Princeton, NJ: Princeton University Press.

Kimball, Warren F. (1997). *Forged in War: Roosevelt, Stalin, Churchill and the Second World War.* New York: Morrow.

Stoler, Mark A. (2000). *Allies and Adversaries: The Joint Chiefs of Staff, the Grand Alliance, and U.S. Strategy in World War II.* Chapel Hill: University of North Carolina Press.

DAVID M. GLANTZ

GRAND PRINCE

The title of "grand prince" designated the senior prince of the Rurikid dynasty in Rus principalities from the era of Kievan Rus until 1721.

In scholarly literature on Kievan Rus the term *grand prince* is conventionally used to refer to the prince of Kiev. Succession to the position of grand prince was determined by principles associated with the rota system, according to which the position passed laterally from the eldest member of the senior generation of the dynasty to his younger brothers and cousins. When all members of that generation died, those members of the next generation whose fathers had actually held the position of grand prince of Kiev became eligible to inherit the position in order of seniority.

Despite common usage of the term in scholarly literature, the absence of the title "grand prince" and even the title "prince" in contemporary sources, including chronicles, treaties, charters, diplomatic documents, seals, and coins, suggests that they were rarely used during the Kievan era. The title "grand prince" in tenth-century treaties concluded between the Rus and the Byzantines has been interpreted as a translation from Greek formulas rather than a reflection of official Rus usage. The title also occurs in chronicle accounts of the deaths of Yaroslav the Wise (1054), his son Vsevolod (1093), and Vsevolod's son Vladimir Monomakh (1125), but this usage is regarded as honorific, borrowed from Byzantine models, and possibly added by later editors.

"Grand prince" was first used as an official title not for a prince of Kiev, but for Vsevolod "the Big Nest" of Vladimir-Suzdal (ruled 1176–1212). Within their principality it was applied to his sons Konstantin and Yuri as well. Outside of Vladimir-Suzdal, however, recognition of Vsevolod as grand prince, despite his dynastic seniority, was inconsistent, and during the very late twelfth and early thirteenth centuries the title was occasionally attributed to rulers of Kiev.

The title "grand prince" came into more common and consistent use during the fourteenth century. In addition to its use by the prince of Vladimir, it was also adopted by the princes of Tver, Riazan, and Nizhny Novgorod by the second half of the century. The princes of Moscow, who acquired an exclusive claim to the position of grand prince of Vladimir during this period, joined the title to the phrase "of all Rus" to elevate themselves above the other grand princes. During the fifteenth and sixteenth centuries, as they absorbed the other Rus principalities into Muscovy and subordinated their princes, they not only monopolized the title "grand prince," but also began to use other titles conveying the meaning of sovereign (gosudar or gospodar). From 1547, when Ivan IV "the Terrible" was coronated, until 1721, when Peter I "the Great" adopted the title "emperor," the rulers of Muscovy used "grand prince and tsar" as their official titles.

See also: KIEVAN RUS; ROTA SYSTEM; RURIKID DYNASTY

BIBLIOGRAPHY

Poppe, Andrzej. (1989). "Words That Serve the Authority: On the Title of 'Grand Prince' in Kievan Rus." *Acta Poloniae Historica* 60:159–184.

JANET MARTIN

GREAT BRITAIN, RELATIONS WITH

Russia's relations with Great Britain have been marked by chronic tension. During the nineteenth century, the British were keenly aware of tsarist Russia's expansion into Central Asia and of the menace it might hold for lands in the British Commonwealth, particularly India. Twice during that century the British invaded Afghanistan to forestall what they perceived as a Russian threat to occupy the country and use it as a staging area for an attack on India. Prophetic of George Kennan's "X" telegram of 1946 and the U.S. policy of containment, the British foreign minister Lord Palmerston said in 1853: "The policy and practice of the Russian government has always been to push forward its encroachments as fast and as far as the apathy or want of firmness of other governments would allow it to go, but always to stop and retire when it was met with decided resistance and then to wait for the next favorable opportunity." That same year the British decided to resist the effort by Tsar Nicholas I (1796–1855) to enhance Russian power and influence over the Black Sea region and the Ottoman Empire. War broke out between Russia and Turkey in October 1853 over a dispute about religious rights in the Holy Land. Great Britain and France joined forces with Turkey and laid siege to Sevastopol, Russia's naval base in the Crimea, and in September 1855 the Russians were forced to accept defeat. The Treaty of Paris (March 30, 1856), ending the war, was a serious diplomatic setback for Russia, because it guaranteed the integrity of Ottoman Turkey and obliged Russia to surrender southern Bessarabia, at the mouth of the Danube. The Crimean War failed to settle the Russian-British rivalry, but it impressed upon Nicholas's successor, Alexander II, the need to overcome Russia's backwardness in order to compete successfully with Britain and the other European powers.

As a further result of the Crimean War, Austria, which had sided with Great Britain and France, lost Russia's support in Central European affairs. Russia joined the Triple Entente with Britain and France in 1907, more as a result of the widened gap between it and the two Germanic powers and improved relations with Britain's ally, Japan, than out of any fondness for Britain and France. When Archduke Franz Ferdinand was assassinated (June 28, 1914), Russia was not prepared to see Austria-Hungary defeat Serbia, a Slavic country, and the mobilization systems and interlocking alliances of the great powers undermined all attempts to avert a general war. The general disruption caused by World War I contributed to the revolutions in February and October 1917.

The Bolshevik Revolution enraged the British. Vladimir Lenin and other communists called on the workers in all countries to overthrow their capitalist oppressors and characterized the war as caused by rivalries between capitalist and imperialist countries like Britain. Lenin withdrew Russia from the war and signed a separate peace treaty with Germany at Brest-Litovsk in 1918. In the aftermath, Soviet support for national liberation movements in the empire, and of anti-British sentiment and activity in the Middle East, was a special source of annoyance to Britain. To avenge the Brest-Litovsk treaty, and alarmed that the Germans might transfer troops to the Western Front, the British, French, and Japanese intervened in Russia's Civil War, deploying troops to Murmansk, Arkhangelsk, and Vladisvostok, and later funneling material and money to the White armies opposing the Red Army. Winston Churchill (minister of munitions in 1917) made no secret of his antipathy toward Bolshevism, aiming to "strangle the infant in its crib."

Soviet policy toward Britain during the 1920s and 1930s was marked by contradictions. On the one hand, Josef Stalin tried to expand his diplomatic and commercial contacts with this archetypical imperialist power, as part of an effort to win recognition as a legitimate regime. On the other hand, he and his colleagues in the Kremlin remained wary of an anti-Soviet capitalist alliance and worked for the eventual demise of the capitalist system. Then, with the League of Nations weakened by the withdrawal of Japan and Germany, the Versailles Peace Treaty openly flaunted by Adolf Hitler's rearming of Germany, and the world economy crashing in the Great Depression, Stalin began thinking of an alliance with Britain as protection against Germany. When Prime Minister Neville Chamberlain capitulated to Hitler at Munich in 1938, Stalin decided to make a pact with the Nazis and did so the following year. But on June 22, 1941, Hitler renounced the nonaggression treaty and invaded the Soviet Union, thus precipitating the Grand Alliance between Britain, the Soviet Union, and United States. Churchill's cynical words reveal his true feelings about Stalin and the Slavic country to the east: "If Hitler had invaded Hell, I would find something nice to say about the Devil in the House of Commons."

The USSR lost twenty million lives and suffered incalculable destruction during World War II. The conflict ended in the total defeat of the Axis powers, with the Red Army occupying Albania, Czechoslovakia, Poland, Yugoslavia, Bulgaria, Romania, and Hungary. Relations between Britain and the Soviet Union chilled rapidly. Churchill warned of the hazards of growing Soviet domination of Europe (a descending "iron curtain") in a historic March 5, 1946, speech at Westminster College in Fulton, Missouri. The formation of two military alliances, NATO (1949) and the Warsaw Pact (1955). solidified the Cold War, which lasted until 1989.

In the postwar era, the Soviet Union perceived Britain as an imperialist power in decline, especially after it relinquished most of its colonies. Nevertheless, Britain remained an important power in Soviet eyes because of its nuclear forces, its leadership of the British Commonwealth, and its close ties with the United States. In general, however, Soviet relations with Britain took a back seat to Soviet relations with France (especially during the presidency of Charles de Gaulle) and West Germany (especially during the administration of Willy Brandt). This may have been because Britain, unlike West Germany, was a united country and thus not susceptible to Soviet political pressure exerted through the instrument of a divided people, and because the British Communist Party, because of its small size, had less influence in electoral politics than the French Communist Party. Given its close trade ties with the United States, Britain was less dependent economically than other West European states on

Soviet and East European trade and energy resources. Britain also fulfilled its obligations as a NATO member, whereas France withdrew in 1966 from the military side of the alliance.

Even after the collapse of communist regimes throughout Eastern Europe in 1989 and the end of the Soviet Union in December 1991, the Soviet-era division of Europe continued to influence Russia's foreign policy toward Britain and other West European countries. Although the Warsaw Pact was disbanded, NATO extended its reach, admitting three former Soviet allies (Hungary, Poland, and the Czech republic) in 1999. Some Russian hardliners feared that NATO would embrace all of Russia's former allies and deprive it of its traditional European buffer zone. Nevertheless, the al Qaeda terrorist attack on New York's World Trade Center on September 11, 2001 fostered closer ties between Russian president Vladimir Putin and other Western leaders, including British prime minister Tony Blair. New security threats that transcend state borders, such as global networks of suicidal terrorists, chemical and biological warfare, international organized crime, cyberwar, and human trafficking, all underscore the need for greater cooperation among sovereign states.

See also: CRIMEAN WAR; GRAND ALLIANCE; NORTH ATLANTIC TREATY ORGANIZATION; WORLD WAR II

BIBLIOGRAPHY

Adams, Ralph James Q. (1993). *British Politics and Foreign Policy in the Age of Appeasement, 1935–39.* Stanford, CA: Stanford University Press.

Blackwell, Michael. (1993). *Clinging to Grandeur: British Attitudes and Foreign Policy in the Aftermath of the Second World War.* Westport, CT: Greenwood Press.

Eudin, Xenia Joukoff, and Slusser, Robert. (1967). *Soviet Foreign Policy, 1928–1934; Documents and Materials.* University Park: Penn State University Press.

Keeble, Curtis. (1990). *Britain and the Soviet Union, 1917–1989.* New York: St. Martin's Press.

Kennan, George F. (1960). *Soviet Foreign Policy, 1917–1941.* Princeton, NJ: Van Nostrand.

Pravda, Alex, and Duncan, Peter J. S., eds. (1990). *Soviet-British Relations since the 1970s.* New York: Cambridge University Press.

Ross, Graham. (1984). *The Foreign Office and the Kremlin: British Documents on Anglo-Soviet Relations, 1941–45.* New York: Cambridge University Press.

Ulam, Adam B. (1968). *Expansion and Coexistence: The History of Soviet Foreign Policy, 1917–67.* New York: Praeger.

Ullman, Richard. (1961–1972). *Anglo-Soviet Relations, 1917–1921,* 3 vols. Princeton, NJ: Princeton University Press.

JOHANNA GRANVILLE

GREAT NORTHERN WAR

The Great Northern War (1700–1721) was the main military conflict of Peter the Great's reign, ending in a Russian victory over Sweden that made Russia an important European power and expanded Russia's borders to the Baltic Sea, including the site of St. Petersburg. The war began in the effort of Denmark and Poland-Saxony to wrest control of territories lost to Sweden during the seventeenth century, the period of Swedish military hegemony in northern Europe. When the rulers of those countries offered alliances to Peter in 1698 and 1699, he saw an opportunity to recover Ingria, the small territory at the eastern end of the Gulf of Finland that Russia had lost to Sweden in 1618. Possession of Ingria would once again give Russia access to the Baltic Sea, which seems to have been Peter's principal aim. To achieve this aim Peter built a European-style army and a navy based in the Baltic. The war also served as a major stimulus to Peter's reforms.

The initial phase of the war (1700–1709) was marked by Swedish successes. Peter's attempt to capture the port of Narva in Swedish-held Estonia ended in catastrophic defeat on November 30, 1700, at the hands of Charles XII, king of Sweden. The defeat meant the destruction of most of Peter's new army, which he then had to rebuild. Fortunately, Charles chose to move south into Poland, hoping to unseat August II from the throne of Poland and expand Swedish influence. In 1706 Charles succeeded in forcing August II to surrender and leave the war and to recognize Stanislaw Leszczynski, a Swedish puppet, as king of Poland. In 1707 Charles moved east through Poland toward Russia, apparently hoping to both defeat and overthrow Peter and replace him with a more compliant tsar from among the Russian boyars. Charles also managed to convince Ivan Mazepa, the Hetman of the Ukrainian Cossacks, to join him against Peter, but in Russia itself there was no move in favor of Charles. Instead, the Russian army retreated before the Swedes, acquiring experience and mounting ever more effective resistance. Charles was forced south into Ukraine during the fall of

The Battle of Poltava in 1709 marked the turning point in the Great Northern War. © BETTMANN/CORBIS

1708, and Peter's defeat of the Swedish relief column at Lesnaya (October 9, 1708) left him without additional food and equipment.

The battle of Poltava (July 8, 1709) proved the turning point of the war. The Swedish army suffered heavy casualties and fled the field southwest toward the Dnieper River. When they reached the banks with the Russians in hot pursuit, they found too few boats to carry them across and had to surrender. Only Charles, his staff, and some of his personal guard escaped into Ottoman territory. Thus the way was clear for Peter to occupy the Baltic provinces and southeast Finland, then a Swedish possession, in 1710.

By the end of 1710 Peter had achieved his principal war aims, for these conquests secured the approaches to St. Petersburg. In 1711 the outbreak of war with the Turks provided an unwelcome distraction, and he was able to turn his attention to the Northern War only in 1712. His allies now included the restored August II of Poland-Saxony, as well as Denmark and Prussia. Russian troops moved into northern Germany to support these allies, and Sweden's German possessions, Bremen, Stralsund, and Stettin, fell by 1714. In 1713 Peter managed to occupy all of Finland, which he hoped to use as a bargaining chip in the inevitable peace negotiations. Charles XII, who returned to Sweden from Turkey in 1714, would not give up. Ignoring Sweden's rapidly deteriorating economic situation, he refused to acknowledge defeat. Peter's small but decisive naval victory over the Swedish fleet at Hangö peninsula on the Finnish coast in 1714 preserved Russian control over Finland and allowed Peter to harass the Swedish coast. A joint Russo-Danish project to invade Sweden in 1716 came to nothing, and the war continued until 1721 with a series of Russian raids along the Swedish coast. The death of Charles XII in 1718 even prolonged the war, for Great Britain, worried over Russian influence in the Baltic region and northern Germany, began to support Sweden, but it was too late. In 1721 the treaty of Nystad put an end to the war, allowing Russia to keep southeast Finland (the town of Viborg), Ingria, Estonia, and the province of Livonia (today southern Estonia and Latvia north of the Dvina river).

Peter's victory in the Great Northern War radically altered the balance of power in northern and eastern Europe. The defeat of Sweden and the loss of most of its overseas territories other than Finland and Stralsund, as well as the collapse of Swedish absolutism after 1718, rendered Sweden a minor power once again. The events of the war revealed for the first time decisively the political and military weakness of Poland. Russia, by contrast, had defeated the formerly hegemonic power of the region, recovered Ingria, acquired the Baltic provinces and part of Finland, and founded St. Petersburg as a new city and new capital. These acquisitions gave Russia a series of seaports to support both trade and a naval presence in the Baltic Sea, as well as a shorter route to Western Europe. Victory in the war justified Peter's military, administrative, and economic reforms and the Westernization of Russian culture. It also enormously reinforced his personal prestige and power.

See also: LESNAYA, BATTLE OF; PETER I; NARVA, BATTLES OF; POLTAVA, BATTLE OF; SWEDEN, RELATIONS WITH

BIBLIOGRAPHY

Bushkovitch, Paul. (2001). *Peter the Great.* Lanham, MD: Rowman and Littlefield.

Hatton, Ragnhild. (1968). *Charles the Twelfth.* London: Weidenfeld and Nicholson.

Frost, Robert I. (2000). *The Northern Wars: War, State, and Society in Northeastern Europe.* Harlow, UK: Longman.

PAUL A. BUSHKOVITCH

GREAT PATRIOTIC WAR *See* WORLD WAR II.

GREAT REFORMS

At the accession of Alexander II in 1855, some twenty-two million Russian peasants were serfs; their status was like slavery. "State peasants" were similarly constrained. In 1861, serfdom was abolished. Other reforms followed. Together they are called the "great reforms." How did they emerge from a conservative regime? How did they relate one to another? What was their impact on Russia's development?

The explanations most often given for the abolition of serfdom do not work. Russia's defeat in the Crimean War left the regime discredited and impoverished, ill positioned to challenge the serfholding elite. The regime believed that peasant rebellions were more likely a result of reform. It expected economic growth if serfdom were abolished, but dreaded economic disruption. It understood that serfdom was outmoded, but it seemed to work. When, in August 1857, a secret committee pronounced that "not only the peasants but even the Government itself is not prepared for a general emancipation" of the serfs, Alexander expressed satisfaction.

Three months later, the government began to reform serfdom. The turnabout occurred because serfdom was weak. The serfholders were dependent upon the state, to which they had mortgaged two-thirds of their serfs and on which they relied to keep the serfs subordinate. They had no political experience. Most of them shared a culture oriented to western Europe, where serfdom had disappeared. No articulate voice in Russia could praise serfdom. Thanks to censorship, nothing critical or supportive of serfdom, appeared in print. Russia had no Garrison, but also no Calhoun; serfdom had no ideology.

The breakthrough took the form of directives to the governor-general of three northwestern provinces. These incoherent documents were the by-product of an abandoned initiative, but their publication committed the government to the reform of serfdom. And they contained the germ of a resolution to the key problem. The government believed that a noble's land was inalienable private property; peasants believed the land was theirs because they tilled it. Freedom without land would, from a peasant perspective, be a monstrous injustice. To give privately-owned land to the peasants would, from an elite perspective, be no less monstrous. The directives reaffirmed the serfholders' property rights, but provided peasant households with the use of allotments of land.

Ostensibly, the nobility of each province was to participate in drafting the reform. The government learned that there was no flim-flam the nobility would not tolerate. It made a series of promises to the nobility and withdrew or ignored each one. The nobles barely responded, confident because most top positions in government were held by men as hostile to reform as they were.

The abolition legislation was not created by these dignitaries, but by a group of zealous reformers assembled in an Editorial Commission. They had enormous energy and guile. They managed to convince Alexander that their critics were actually challenging his autocratic prerogatives.

The legislative process was epitomized when the commission's draft came before the Council of State in early 1861. The council was composed of Alexander's friends and confidants. It voted down each section of the draft by large margins. The members were counting on the emperor's sympathy and his distrust of reformers. These dignitaries could not, however, come up with a coherent alternative. Furthermore, the council was not a legislature. With each section of the draft, the emperor used his prerogative to endorse the minority position, and the Editorial Commission's version became law without significant change. The result was a cautious reform that was nonetheless much more radical than anyone in authority had contemplated.

The terms of the legislation promulgated on February 19, 1861, varied from province to province. The reformers wanted to accommodate the nobility. Hence, in the North the allotments of land assigned to the ex-serfs were relatively large but costly; since the land was of little value, the squires would rather have cash. To the south, where land was valuable, the allotments were smaller but not so costly. The complexity of the legislation is compounded by special cases, some involving millions of peasants. The commune was unknown in Ukraine and was not imposed there. State peasants would be more generously treated than serfs when the reform was extended to them in 1866; the regime was more willing to sacrifice its interests than those of serfholders. If one focuses on a majority of Great Russian serfs, one can grasp the reform by comparing it to the system of serfdom.

(1) Authority: The essence of serfdom was the subjection of the serfs to the arbitrary power of their master or mistress. Serfholders could buy and sell serfs and subject them to physical or sexual abuse. The laws limiting the squires' powers were vague and rarely enforced. This arbitrary power of the serfholding noble was utterly abolished by the legislation of 1861. The ex-serfs found themselves subject in a new way, however, to the nobles as a class, because they dominated local administration. And most ex-serfs were dependent, as renters, wage-laborers, or sharecroppers, on a squire in the neighborhood.

(2) Ascription: A second element of serfdom was ascription, or fastening. The reform left peasants ascribed, but transferred the power to regulate their comings and goings from the squire to the village commune, which now issued the passports that enabled peasants to go in search of wage work. The government retained ascription as a security measure.

(3) Economics: It was the economic elements of the reform that most severely restricted the freedom of ex-serfs. Most peasants received (through the commune) an allotment of land and had to meet the obligations that went with the allotment. It was almost impossible to dispose of the allotment. Few peasants who wanted to pull up stakes and start afresh could do so.

Servile agriculture was linked to the repartitional commune. Plowland was held by the commune and subject to periodic repartition among households. The objective of repartition was to match landholding to the labor-power of each household, since the commune allocated and reallocated burdens, such as taxes, as well as plowland. The reform, like the serfholders before, imposed a system of mutual responsibility. If one household did not meet its obligations, the others had to make up the difference. It was in the interests of the commune that each household have plowland proportional to its labor power.

Also characteristic of the servile economy was "extraeconomic compulsion." Under serfdom, it was not the market but the serfholders's arbitrary authority that determined the size of the serfs' allotments and the dues they had to render. After the reform, these were determined not by the market, but by law.

These characteristics of the servile economy broke down slowly because, to minimize disruption, the reformers took the elements of serfdom as their point of departure. The size of the allotments set by statute derived from the size under serfdom. In the interests of security, the reformers retained the commune, although it impeded agricultural progress. The statutes sought to minimize the economic dependence of ex-serfs on their former masters. They provided that peasants could redeem their allotments over a forty-nine-year period. Redemption entailed an agreement between the squire and his ex-serfs, which was hard to achieve. Until the redemption process began in a village, the ex-serfs were in a state of "temporary obligation," subject to yesterday's serfholder. Within limits set by statute, they had to render dues in cash or in labor in return for their allotments.

The abolition of serfdom regulated more than it changed, but regulation represented an enormous change: The arbitrary power of the serfholder had been the essence of serfdom. The reform could not provide an immediate stimulus to economic development. The regime set a higher value on stability, on the prosperity of the nobility, and on the welfare of the peasantry, than on development. It feared chaos more than it wanted progress. So it imposed stability and opened the way for a slow passage out of the structures of serfdom.

It is argued that the other great reforms followed from the abolition of serfdom, but the peasant reform reordered the Russian village, while the other reforms addressed the opposite end of the social spectrum. For example, the education reform (1863) restored autonomy to Russia's universities, permitting the rector and faculty to run them; the minister of education, however, had broad authority to interfere. It also provided for technical secondary schools. However, only graduates of the traditional, classical schools could enter the universities; the regime supposed that Greek and Latin had a sobering effect on the young. The reform also gave new authority, but little money, to local agencies to establish primary schools. Finally, it allowed some education to women, provided that they would get an education "appropriate for the future wife and mother."

The censorship was reformed in 1865. Under the old system, a censor went over every word of a book or magazine, deleting or changing anything subversive. This system had been supportive of serfdom, but useful publications had been impeded, and pre-censorship had not prevented the dissemination of radical ideas. The emperor wanted knowledge to flourish, but he was suspicious of intellectuals. He observed, "There are tendencies which do not accord with the views of the government; they must be stopped." The censorship reform did that. It eliminated the prepublication censorship of books and most journals. Editors and publishers were responsible for everything they printed, however, and subject to heavy fines, criminal penalties, and the closing of periodicals. The regime appreciated that publishers dreaded financial loss. The result was self-censorship, more exacting than precensorship.

The Judicial Reform (1864) was not closely related to the abolition of serfdom, since peasants were not usually subject to the new courts. Under the old system, justice had been a purely bureaucratic activity. There were no juries, no public trials, and no legal profession. Corruption and delay were notorious. Commercial loans were available only on short terms and at high interest because the courts could not protect the interests of creditors.

The new system provided for independent judges with life tenure; trial by jury in criminal cases; oral and public trials; and an organized bar of lawyers to staff this adversary system. Peasants were formally eligible to serve on juries, but property qualifications for jury service excluded all but a few peasants. Here, as elsewhere, distinctions linked to the system of estates of the realm (*soslo-viya*) were retained by other means.

The reform of the courts had long been under discussion. Officials who shared the emperor's suspicion of lawyers and juries were unable to produce any workable alternative to the chaos they knew. Hence the task of drafting the new system passed to a group of younger men with advanced legal training. With the task came powers of decision making. The reformers acted in the spirit of the cosmopolitan legal ethos they had acquired with their training. They, alone of the drafters of reform statutes, avowedly followed western models and produced the most thorough-going of the reforms.

The zemstvo, or local government, reform (1864) provided for elective assemblies at the district and provincial levels; the electorate was divided into three curias: landowners (mostly nobles), peasant communities, and towns. Voting power was proportional to the value of real estate held by each curia, but no curia could have more than half the members.

The zemstvo's jurisdiction included the upkeep of roads, fire insurance, education, and public health. Squires and their ex-serfs sat together in the assemblies, if not in proportion to their share of the population. Public-spirited squires found a sphere of activity in the boards elected by the assemblies. These boards, in turn, hired health workers, teachers, and other professionals. The zemstvo provided an arena of public service apart from the state bureaucracy, where liberal landowners and dissidents interacted. The accomplishments of the zemstvo were remarkable, given their limited resources and the government control over them. The provincial governor could suspend any decision taken by a zemstvo. The zemstvo had only a limited power to tax, and as much as half the total it collected went to functions performed for the state.

Why didn't the government do more? It cherished autocracy and realized that genuine constitutional change would favor the rich and the educated, not the peasants; many nobles sought a national zemstvo as compensation for their supposed losses. Most important, to let authority pass to judges, juries, editors, and others not under direct bureaucratic discipline required a trust in which the regime was deficient. Many bureaucrats feared that the reforms would come back to haunt the regime. They were right. The bar did become a rallying point for dissidents, the economic and social position of the nobility did decline, and the zemstvo eventually protested. Cautious officials can be good prophets, even if the solutions they offer are ineffective.

See also: ALEXANDER II; EMANCIPATION ACT; PEASANTRY; SERFDOM

BIBLIOGRAPHY

Bushnell, John; Eklof, Ben; and Zakharova, Larisa, eds. (1994). *Russia's Great Reforms.* Bloomington: Indiana University Press.

Field, Daniel. (1976). *The End of Serfdom: Nobility and Bureaucracy in Russia, 1855–1861.* Cambridge, MA: Harvard University Press.

Mironov, Boris. (1999). *A Social History of Imperial Russia, 1700–1917,* 2 vols., ed. Ben Eklof. Boulder, CO: Westview.

Wortman, Richard. (1976). *The Development of a Russian Legal Consciousness.* Chicago: University of Chicago Press.

DANIEL FIELD

GREECE, RELATIONS WITH

Ideas originating in Greece, a country in southeastern Europe that occupies the southernmost part of the Balkan Peninsula and is bordered by the Aegean, Mediterranean, and Ionian seas, first influenced Russian culture as early as the tenth century, during the golden age of Kievan Rus. Prince Vladimir (978–1015) adopted Eastern Orthodoxy, which reflected his close personal ties with Constantinople, a city that dominated both the Black Sea and the Dnieper River, Kiev's busiest commercial route. Adherence to the Eastern Orthodox Church had long-range political, cultural, and religious consequences for Russia. The church liturgy was written in Cyrillic, and a corpus of translations from the Greeks had been produced for the South Slavs. The existence of this literature facilitated the East Slavs' conversion to Christianity and introduced them to rudimentary Greek philosophy, science, and historiography without the necessity of learning Greek. Russians began to look to the Greeks for religious inspiration and came to regard the Catholics of Central Europe as schismatics. This tendency laid the foundation for Russia's isolation from the mainstream of Western civilization.

Seeking warm-water ports, Russian explorers were attracted to Greece. No part of mainland Greece is more than 100 kilometers (60 miles) from water, and islands constitute about one-fifth of the country's land area. By the nineteenth century, as the Russian Empire expanded to the southwest, its population grew more diverse and began to include Greek Orthodox peoples.

After Russia's defeat by Japan in 1905, the government began to take a more active interest in the Balkans and the Near East. The decline of the Ottoman Empire ("the sick man of Europe") encouraged nationalist movements in Greece, Serbia, Romania, and Bulgaria. In 1912 the Balkan League, which included Greece, defeated the Ottoman Empire in the First Balkan War. A year later, the alliance split, and the Greeks, Serbs, and Romanians defeated Bulgaria in the Second Balkan War. Russia tried to extend its influence over the new nations. Greco-Russian relations became strained when Russia sided with Serbia in the conflict between Serbia and Greece for control of Albania.

Greece fought on the side of the Western allies and Russia in World War I, and similarly on the side of the Allies, including the Soviet Union, in World War II. In the immediate aftermath of the war, tensions arose between the legitimate Greek government and the Soviet Union. The Greek resistance movement during World War II, the National Liberation Front (EAM) and its army (ELAS), were dominated by the Communist Party. When the Greek government-in-exile returned to Athens in late 1944 shortly after the liberation, the communists tried to overthrow it, and in the ensuring civil war they were supported by Josef Stalin's USSR and (more enthusiastically) Tito's Yugoslavia. Britain funded the non-communists, but when the economic commitment exceeded its postwar capabilities, the United States took on the burden with the Truman Doctrine. Thanks to massive military and economic aid from the United States, which came just in time, the communists, who had established a provisional government in the northern mountains, were ultimately defeated.

Relations between Greece and the USSR cooled with the former's admission to NATO in 1952. Beginning in the mid-1950s, NATO's southeastern flank experienced periodic cycles of international tension. The problem in Cyprus, where the population is split between Greek-Cypriots (approximately 78%) and Turkish-Cypriots (18%) led eventually to a Turkish invasion of the island on July 20, 1974, to protect the Turkish-Cypriot minority.

Nevertheless, Greek-Soviet ties established during the 1980s not only survived the political upheaval that ended the Soviet Union, they even improved. In 1994 Greece signed new protocols with Russia for delivery of natural gas from a pipeline to run from Bulgaria to Greece. In 2002, during its fourth presidency of the European Union (EU), Greece repeatedly called for improved relations with Russia. At the Russia-EU summit in Brussels on November 11, 2002, Prime Minister Costas Simitis emphasized the importance of implementing the Brussels agreement on the Kaliningrad region, an enclave on the Baltic Sea that would be cut off from the rest of Russia by the Schengen zone when Poland and Lithuania joined the EU. Greece also prepared a new strategy for greater cooperation between Russia and the EU, which is Russia's largest trading partner.

See also: BALKAN WARS; KIEVAN RUS; ORTHODOXY; ROUTE TO GREEKS

BIBLIOGRAPHY

Gerolymatos, André. (2003). *The Balkan Wars: Conquest, Revolution, and Retribution from the Ottoman Era to the Twentieth Century and Beyond.* New York: Basic Books.

Gvosdev, Nicholas. (2001). *An Examination of Church-State Relations in the Byzantine and Russian Empires with an Emphasis on Ideology and Models of Interaction.* Lewiston, NY: Edwin Mellen Press.

Joseph, Joseph S. (1999). *Cyprus Ethnic Conflict and International Politics: From Independence to the Threshold of the European Union.* New York: Palgrave Macmillan.

Koliopoulos, John S. (1999). *Plundered Loyalties: World War II and Civil War in Greek West Macedonia.* New York: New York University Press.

Prousis, Theophilus. (1994). *Russian Society and the Greek Revolution.* DeKalb: Northern Illinois University Press.

JOHANNA GRANVILLE

GREEKS

As early as 1000 B.C.E., pre-Hellenic Greeks, in search of iron and gold, explored the southeast shores of the Black Sea. Beginning in the fifth and sixth centuries B.C.E., Greeks established fishing villages at the mouths of the Danube, Dnieper, Dniester, and Bug Rivers. They founded the colony of Olbia between the eighth and sixth centuries B.C.E. near the South Bug River and carried on trade in metals, slaves, furs, and later grain. Greek jewelry, coins, and wall paintings attest to the presence of Greek colonies during the Scythian, Sarmatian, and Roman domination of the area.

During the late tenth century C.E., Prince Vladimir of Kievan Rus accepted the Orthodox Christian religion after marrying Anna, sister of Greek Byzantine Emperor Basil II. With the conversion came the influence of Greek Byzantine culture including the alphabet, Greek religious literature, architecture, icon painting, music, and crafts. The East Slavs carried on a vigorous trade with Byzantium following the famous route "from the Varangians to the Greeks"—from the Baltic to the Black Sea.

With the fall of Constantinople to the Turks in 1453, many Greeks, fleeing onerous taxes, emigrated to Russia. Ivan III (1462–1505) married Sophia, the niece of the last Byzantine emperor, giving rise to the Muscovite claim that Moscow was the "Third Rome." Ivan, like many future Russian rulers, employed Greeks as architects, painters, diplomats, and administrators.

The opening of the Black Sea grain trade with Western Europe and the Near East during the early nineteenth century gave impetus to a large Greek immigration to the Black Sea coast. Greek merchant families prospered in Odessa, which was the headquarters of the Philiki Etaireia Society, advocating the liberation of Greece from Turkey (1821–1829).

In 1924 some 70,000 Greeks left the Soviet Union for Greece. Of the estimated 450,000 Greeks at the time of Stalin, 50,000 Greeks perished during the collectivization drive and Purges of the

1930s. Greeks, especially from the Krasnodar Region, were sent to the Solovki Gulag and to Siberia. In 1938 all Greek schools, theaters, newspapers, magazines, and churches were closed down. In 1944 Crimean and Kuban Greeks were exiled to Kazakhstan. Between 1954 and 1956 Greek exiles were released, but they could not return to the Crimea until 1989. The last major immigration of Greeks to the Soviet Union began in 1950 with the arrival of about 10,000 communist supporters of the Greek Civil War of 1949. The Soviet census for 1970 showed 57,800 persons of Greek origin. The Soviet census for 1989 had 98,500 Greeks in Ukraine and 91,700 Greeks in Russia. The 2001 census for Ukraine reported 92,500 Greeks.

See also: NATIONALITIES POLICIES, SOVIET; NATIONALITIES POLICIES, TSARIST; ORTHODOXY

BIBLIOGRAPHY

Herlihy, Patricia. (1979–1980). "Greek Merchants in Odessa in the Nineteenth Century." *Eucharisterion: Essays Presented to Omeljan Pritsak on His Sixtieth Birthday by his Colleagues and Students. Harvard Ukrainian Studies* 3–4(1):399–420.

Herlihy, Patricia. (1989). "The Greek Community in Odessa, 1861–1917." *Journal of Modern Greek Studies* 7:235–252.

Prousis, Theophilus C. (1994). *Russian Society and the Greek Revolution.* DeKalb: Northern Illinois University Press.

Rostovtzeff, Michael I. (1922). *Iranians and Greeks in South Russia.* Oxford: Clarendon Press.

PATRICIA HERLIHY

GREEN MOVEMENT

Green Movement is the term used to describe peasant resistance to the Bolshevik government during the Russian Civil War.

The first rebellions against the Bolshevik government began in 1918 and increased with frequency and intensity through the civil war period. In 1918 and 1919 peasant rebellions were poorly organized and localized affairs, easily suppressed by small punitive expeditions. In 1920, however, after the defeat of the White armies, the Bolsheviks faced large, well-organized peasant insurgent movements in Tambov, the Volga and Urals regions, Ukraine, and Siberia.

The causes of the rebellions were similar. After the failure of Committees of the Rural Poor to bring a reliable government to the countryside, the Bolshevik regime relied on armed detachments to procure grain and recruits, and to stop the black market in food and consumer goods. The depredations of these detachments, the only representatives of the Soviet government that most peasants saw, became increasingly severe as war communism ground down the Russian economy. By 1920, many peasants had little grain left, even as communist food supply organizations made greater demands on them. Large numbers of young men—deserters and draft-dodgers from the Red Army—hid in villages and the surrounding countryside from armed detachments sent to gather them.

The Soviet-Polish war, beginning in August 1920, increased the demands on peasants for food and recruits, and stripped the provinces of trained, motivated troops. This allowed peasant uprisings that were initially limited to a small area to grow, with armed bands finding willing recruits from the mass of deserters and draft-dodgers. By early 1921 much of the countryside was unsafe even for large Red Army detachments.

The Green Movement of 1920 and 1921 was qualitatively different from the peasant rebellions the communist government had faced in 1918 or 1919. While many peasant insurgents fought in small independent bands, Alexander Antonov's Insurgent Army in Tambov and Nestor Makhno's forces in Ukraine were organized militias whose members had military training. Enjoying strong support from political organizations (often made up of local SRs [Socialist Revolutionists], Anarchists, or even former Bolsheviks), they established an underground government that provided food, horses, and excellent intelligence to the insurgents, and terrorized local communists and their supporters. They were much harder to defeat.

By February 1921 the communist government suspended grain procurements in much of Russia and Ukraine, and in March, at the Tenth Party Congress, private trade in grain was legalized. The end of the Soviet-Polish war in March also freed elite armed forces to turn against the insurgents. In the summer of 1921 hundreds of thousands of Red Army soldiers, backed by airplanes, armored cars, and artillery, attacked the insurgent forces. In their wake followed the Cheka, who eliminated support for the insurgents by holding family members hostage, making villages collectively responsible for guerilla attacks, shooting suspected supporters of the insurgents, and sending thousands more to concentration camps. Facing drought and terror, and with the abolition of forced grain procurement and military conscription, support for the Green Movement collapsed by September 1921. A few leaders, such as Makhno, slipped across the border, but most were hunted down and killed, such as Antonov, who died in a shootout in June 1922.

See also: CIVIL WAR OF 1917-1922; COMMITTEES OF THE VILLAGE POOR; SOCIALIST REVOLUTIONARIES; WAR COMMUNISM

BIBLIOGRAPHY

Brovkin, Vladimir, ed. (1997). *The Bolsheviks in Russian Society.* New Haven, CT: Yale University Press.

Figes, Orlando. (1989). *Peasant Russia, Civil War: The Volga Countryside in Revolution, 1917–1921.* Oxford: Oxford University Press.

Malet, Michael. (1982). *Nestor Makhno in the Russian Civil War.* London: Macmillan.

Radkey, Oliver. (1976). *The Unknown Civil War in Soviet Russia.* Stanford, CA: Hoover Institution Press.

A. DELANO DUGARM

GRIBOEDOV, ALEXANDER SERGEYEVICH

(1795–1829), dramatist and diplomat.

Alexander Griboedov is best known as the author of *Woe from Wit* (*Gore ot uma*). The first Russian comedy of manners, the play was written in 1823, but not published until 1833 because of censorship.

Born in Moscow as the son of a military officer, Griboedov showed talent at an early age in a number of areas. He was admitted to Moscow University at the age of eleven. By the age of sixteen he had graduated in literature, law, mathematics, and natural sciences. He also had a gift for music. The Napoleonic invasion prevented him from pursuing a doctorate. He served in the military from 1812 to 1816. After the war he entered the civil service in the ministry of foreign affairs. In 1818 he was sent to Persia (Iran) as secretary to the Russian mission. There Griboedov added Arabic and Persian to the long list of foreign languages he had mastered (French, German, Italian, and English). In 1821 he transferred to service in the Caucasus, but took a leave of absence in St. Petersburg and Moscow from February 1823 to May 1825 to write *Woe from Wit.* Although Griboedov was back in the Caucasus by December of 1825, he was nevertheless summoned under arrest for his alleged involvement in the abortive Decembrist uprising of that time. After extensive interrogations, however, he was cleared of suspicion and returned to his diplomatic post. Griboedov negotiated the peace treaty of 1828 that ended the Russo-Persian War. As a reward for his wits, he was appointed Russian minister in Tehran in 1828, where—in ironic mockery of his own play's title—he was murdered in January 1829 by religious fanatics who attacked the Russian embassy. The twentieth-century novelist Yuri Tynianov wrote about Griboedov's death in *Death and Diplomacy in Persia* (1938).

Woe from Wit, composed in rhymed verse, is a seminal work in Russian culture. Many lines from the play have entered everyday Russian speech as quotations or aphorisms. Its hero, Chatsky, is the prototype of the so-called superfluous man, who criticizes social and political conditions in his country but does nothing to bring about a change. In addition to the gap between generations, the concept of service is a key theme. In a monolithic country with minimal private enterprise, a man's career choices were either civil or military. Griboedov mocks as shallow and morally irresponsible the character Famusov, who says in the play: "For me, whether it is business matters or not, my custom is, once it's signed, the burden is off my shoulders." As for military service, the hero Chatsky prefers to serve the cause and not specific personalities. He says to Famusov: "I should be pleased to serve, but worming oneself into one's favor is sickening" (Sluzhit' by rad, prisluzhivat'sia toshno). Famusov rejects such serious loyalty to a higher cause, reminiscing fondly of his uncle who stumbled and hurt himself while in court. When Catherine the Great showed amusement, the uncle deliberately fell again as a way to please her. Here Griboedov appears to counter the poet Gavryl Romanovich Derzhavin's ode to Catherine ("Felitsa"), written in 1789, in which Catherine is praised as someone who treats subordinates respectfully. The play contains an extensive gallery of satirical portraits that continue to hold relevance to contemporary audiences in Russia and around the world.

See also: THEATER

BIBLIOGRAPHY

Tynianov, Iurii Nikolaevich. (1975). *Death and Diplomacy in Persia,* 2nd ed. Westport, CT: Hyperion.

JOHANNA GRANVILLE

Reddaway, Peter. (1972). *Uncensored Russia: Protest and Dissent in the Soviet Union.* New York: American Heritage Press.

JONATHAN WEILER

GRIGORENKO, PETER GRIGORIEVICH

(1907–1987), leading Soviet human rights activist.

Born in Ukraine, Peter Grigorenko was a decorated war hero during World War II. He rose to the rank of Major General in 1959. In 1964 Grigorenko was arrested for participation in the Society for the Restoration of Leninist Principles, which warned of the reemergence of a Stalinist cult of personality. For fifteen months he was in psychiatric hospitals and prisons before being released in 1965. Stripped of a military pension, denied professional work, Grigorenko, at age 58, emerged as a tireless campaigner for human rights. He became a mythic figure among Crimean Tatars for aiding their fight for national rights. He organized demonstrations at dissident trials in the late 1960s and wrote and signed petitions on behalf of dissidents. He attacked the use of psychiatric confinement as a method of punishing political prisoners. For his troubles, he was arrested again, in Tashkent on May 7, 1969, and held in psychiatric confinement until 1974. He subsequently became one of the founding members of the Moscow Helsinki Group, established after the signing of the Helsinki Accords in 1975. On November 30, 1977, Grigorenko flew to New York with his wife and a son for emergency surgery. While there, he was stripped of his Soviet citizenship. Peter Reddaway, writing in 1972 about the Soviet human rights movement, said "if one person had to be singled out as having inspired the different groups within the Democratic movement more than anyone else, then it would surely be [Grigorenko]. Indeed he became, while free, in an informal way the movement's leader." Grigorenko died in New York City in 1987.

See also: DISSIDENT MOVEMENT

BIBLIOGRAPHY

Alexeyeva, Lyudmila. (1985). *Soviet Dissent: Contemporary Movements for National, Religious and Human Rights.* Middletown, CT: Wesleyan University Press.

Grigorenko, Petr. (1982). *Memoirs.* New York: Norton.

GRISHIN, VIKTOR DMITRIEVICH

(1914–1992), member of the Politburo of the Communist Party of the Soviet Union.

Twice decorated Hero of Socialist Labor (1974, 1984), Viktor Grishin was one of the highest-ranking members of the Communist Party of the Soviet Union (CPSU) on the eve of Michael S. Gorbachev's selection as party leader. Born in Moscow, he received his degree in geodesy in 1932. From 1938 to 1940 he served in the Red Army, during which time he became a member of the CPSU. Following his discharge from the army in 1941, he was assigned to duties in the Moscow Party organization.

Grishin entered the upper echelons of the party when he was made a member of the Central Committee of the CPSU in 1952. He took on additional responsibilities as the head of Soviet professional unions in 1956, a position he held until 1967. In 1961 he was made a candidate of the Politburo, and in 1967 he became First Secretary of the Moscow Party organization, one of the most powerful posts in the CPSU. By 1971, he was a full member of the Politburo.

Grishin was one of Gorbachev's rivals for the post of General Secretary in 1985. In order to ensure the loyalty of the Moscow Party organization, Gorbachev had Grishin removed from both the Politburo and the Moscow Party organization in 1986. He was replaced in both posts by Boris Yeltsin. Grishin was retired from the CPSU and lived on a party pension until his death in 1992.

See also: CENTRAL COMMITTEE; GORBACHEV, MIKHAIL SERGEYEVICH; MOSCOW; POLITBURO

BIBLIOGRAPHY

Mawdsley, Evan, and White, Stephen. (2000). *The Soviet Elite from Lenin to Gorbachev: The Central Committee and Its Members, 1917–1991.* Oxford: Oxford University Press.

TERRY D. CLARK

GRIVNA

A Russian monetary and weight unit used from the ninth or tenth century to the eighteenth century.

Initially the grivna was a unit of account (twenty-five dirhams or Islamic silver coins) and a unit of weight (c. 68 grams, or 2.4 ounces), used interchangeably for denominating imported coined silver. Since foreign coins fluctuated in weight and fineness and diminished in import frequency, by the late tenth century the grivna weighed around 51.2 grams (1.8 ounces) and equaled fifty cut dirhams. By the eleventh century, the ratio of coins to weight of a grivna was further altered with the appearance of a rodlike, or Novgorodian type, silver ingot in northern Rus, weighing around 200 grams (7 ounces). This unit, called mark in German, like the silver itself, was imported from western and central Europe to northern Russia via the Baltic. Consequently, in Novgorod there developed a 1:4 relationship between the silver ingot, called grivna of silver, and the old grivna, or grivna of kunas. Both units diffused outside of Novgorod to other parts of Russia, including the Golden Horde, but the relationship of the grivna of kunas to the grivna of silver fluctuated throughout the lands until the fifteenth century, when the ingots were replaced by Russian coins. However, the term grivna (grivenka) and the 200 grams (7 ounces) it represented remained in Russian metrology until the eighteenth century.

The southern Rus lands also manufactured and used silver grivna ingots, but they were hexagonal in shape and, following the weight of the Byzantine litra, weighed around 160 grams (5.6 ounces). These Kievan-type ingots were known in southern Rus from the early eleventh century until the Mongol conquest.

See also: ALTYN; DENGA; KOPECK; RUBLE

BIBLIOGRAPHY

Noonan, Thomas S. (1987). "The Monetary History of Kiev in the pre-Mongol Period." *Harvard Ukrainian Studies* 11:384–443.

Pritsak, Omeljan. (1998). *The Origins of the Old Rus' Weights and Monetary Systems.* Cambridge, MA: Harvard Ukrainian Research Institute.

Spassky, Ivan Georgievich. (1967). *The Russian Monetary System: A Historico-Numismatic Survey*, tr. Z. I. Gorishina and rev. L. S. Forrer. Amsterdam: Jacques Schulman.

ROMAN K. KOVALEV

GROMOV, BORIS VSEVOLODOVICH

(b. 1943), Commander of Fortieth Army in Afghanistan, Deputy Minister of Internal Affairs, Deputy Minister of Defense, Member of the State Duma, and Governor of Moscow Oblast (District).

Boris Gromov had a distinguished career as a professional soldier in the Soviet Ground Forces. In 1962 he graduated from the Suvorov Military School in Kalinin. From there he attended the Higher Combined Arms Command School in Leningrad and was commissioned in the Soviet Army in 1965. From 1965 Gromov held command and staff assignments. In 1974 he graduated from the Frunze Military Academy. From 1980 to 1982 he commanded a motorized rifle division in Afghanistan; on his return to the Soviet Union, he attended the Voroshilov Military Academy of the General Staff, graduating in 1984. In 1987 Gromov returned to Afghanistan as Commander of the Fortieth Army and led the withdrawal of Soviet forces from Afghanistan, which was completed in February 1989. His next assignment was that of Commander of the Kiev Military District, a post he held until November 1990, when, in an unexpected move, he was named First Deputy Minister of Internal Affairs and Commander of Internal Troops. He held that post until August 1991. In the aftermath of the unsuccessful coup against Gorbachev, Gromov was appointed First Deputy Commander of Soviet (later Commonwealth of Independent States) Conventional Forces. In May 1992 he was appointed Deputy Minister of Defense of the Russian Federation. In 1994 Gromov joined a group of senior Russian officers who broke with Minister of Defense Pavel Grachev and publicly warned against military intervention in Chechnya when Russian forces were unprepared. In the aftermath of that act, Gromov was moved to the Ministry of Foreign Affairs. In 1995 he stood for election to the State Duma on the My Fatherland Party ticket and won. In January 2000 he was elected Governor of the Moscow Oblast. Gromov received the Hero of the Soviet Union award for his service as army commander in Afghanistan.

See also: AFGHANISTAN, RELATIONS WITH; MILITARY, SOVIET AND POST-SOVIET

BIBLIOGRAPHY

Baev, Pavel K. (1996). *The Russian Army in a Time of Troubles*. London: Sage Publications.

Gromov, Boris. (2001). "Wounds of a Bitter War." *New York Times*, No. 2767 (October 01, 2001), Op-Ed.

Jacob W. Kipp

GROMYKO, ANDREI ANDREYEVICH

(1909–1989), Soviet foreign minister and president.

Andrei Gromyko was born into a peasant family in the village of Starye Gromyki in Belorussia. He joined the Communist Party in 1931. He completed study at the Minsk Agricultural Institute in 1932 and gained a Candidate of Economics degree from the All-Union Scientific Research Institute of Agronomy in 1936. From 1936 to 1939 he was a senior researcher in the Institute of Economics of the Academy of Sciences and the executive editorial secretary of the journal *Problemy ekonomiki;* he later gained a doctorate of Economics in 1956. In 1939 Gromyko switched to diplomatic work and became section head for the Americas in the People's Commissariat of Foreign Affairs. Later that year he became counselor in the Soviet Embassy in Washington. Between 1943 and 1946 he was Soviet ambassador to the United States and Cuba. During this time, he was involved in the Dumbarton Oaks Conference (1944) called to produce the UN Charter and the 1945 San Francisco conference establishing the United Nations. He also played an organizational role in the Big Three wartime conferences. From 1946 to 1948 he was the permanent representative in the UN Security Council as well as deputy (from 1949 First Deputy) minister of foreign affairs. Except for the period 1952–1953 when he was ambassador to Great Britain, he held the First Deputy post until he was promoted to foreign minister following the anti-party group affair of 1957. Gromyko remained foreign minister until July 1985, when he became chairman of the Presidium of the Supreme Soviet, effectively Soviet president.

Throughout his career, Gromyko was neither highly ambitious nor a major political actor on the domestic scene. Although a full member of the Central Committee from 1956, he did not become a full member of the Politburo until 1973. He developed his diplomatic skills and became the public face of Soviet foreign policy, gaining a reputation as a tough negotiator who never showed his hand. He was influential in the shaping of foreign policy, in particular détente, but he was never unchallenged as the source of that policy; successive leaders Nikita Khrushchev and Leonid Brezhnev both sought to place their personal stamp upon foreign policy, while there was always competition from the International Department of the Party Central Committee and the KGB. Gromyko formally nominated Mikhail Gorbachev as General Secretary in March 1985, and three months later was moved from the Foreign Ministry to the presidency. The foreign policy for which he was spokesperson during the Brezhnev period now came under attack as Gorbachev and his Foreign Minister Eduard Shevardnadze embarked on a new course. Gromyko's most important task while he was president was to chair a commission that recommended the removal of restrictions on the ability of Crimean Tatars to return to Crimea. Gromyko was forced to step down from the Politburo in September 1988, and from the presidency in October 1988, and was retired from the Central Committee in April 1989. He was the author of many speeches and articles on foreign affairs.

Soviet foreign ministry Andrei Gromyko, nicknamed "Mr. Nyet" by his Western counterparts, addresses the U.N. General Assembly. United Nations

See also: BREZHNEV, LEONID ILICH; GORBACHEV, MIKHAIL SERGEYEVICH

BIBLIOGRAPHY

Edmonds, Robin. (1983). *Soviet Foreign Policy: The Brezhnev Years.* Oxford: Oxford University Press.

Gromyko, Andrei. (1989). *Memories,* tr. Harold Shukman. London: Arrow Books.

The Tauris Soviet Directory. The Elite of the USSR Today. (1989). London: I. B. Tauris.

Graeme Gill

GROSSMAN, VASILY SEMENOVICH

(1905–1964), one of the most important Russian novelists of the twentieth century who became increasingly disillusioned with the Soviet system.

Vasily Grossman was born in 1905 in the town of Berdichev in Ukraine. He spent the years from 1910 to 1914 in Switzerland with his mother and attended high school in Kiev. He received a degree in chemical engineering from Moscow University in 1929 and worked in various engineering jobs until becoming a full-time writer in 1934. He published his first news article in 1928 and his first short story in 1934 and became a prolific writer of fiction during the 1930s. He published a long novel about the civil war entitled *Stepan Kolchugin* between 1937 and 1940. In 1938, his wife was arrested, but Grossman wrote to Nikolai Yezhov and achieved her release.

During World War II, Grossman served as a correspondent for *Red Star* (*Krasnaya Zvezda*) and spent the entire war at the front. His writing during the war years was immensely popular, and his words are inscribed on the war memorial at Stalingrad (now Volgograd). He also began writing short stories, which were collected in titles such as *The People are Immortal.* However, from that perspective, he also began to doubt the abilities of the systems that organized the war effort.

Grossman's postwar projects were often challenging to the Soviet system, and several were not published until long after their completion. Beginning in 1943, Grossman and Ilya Ehrenburg began to collect personal accounts of the Holocaust on the territories of the Soviet Union, entitled the *Black Book of Russian Jewry.* Grossman became the editor of the collection in 1945 and continued to prepare it for publication. The printing plates were actually completed, but in 1946, as anti-Semitism began to increase and Josef Stalin turned against the Jewish Anti-Fascist Committee, they were removed from the printing plant. The book would not be published in any part of the former USSR until 1994.

His postwar fiction about the war generated intense criticism from Soviet officials. His novel *For a Just Cause* (*Za pravoye delo*), published in 1952, led to attacks for its lack of proper ideological focus. His most contemplative piece about the war, *Life and Fate* (*Zhizn i sudba*) was arrested by the KGB in 1961. Although they seized Grossman's copy of the manuscript, another had already been hidden elsewhere and preserved. Often compared to Leo Tolstoy's *War and Peace,* the novel bitterly attacks Stalin and the Soviet system for failures. He focuses on the suffering of one family at the hands of large forces outside of their control. In it he touches upon the Gulags, the Holocaust, and the repressions that accompanied the heroism of ordinary Soviets. After twenty years, it was smuggled out of the Soviet Union on microfilm and published in the West. His last novel, *Everything is in Flux* (*Vse techet*), is an angry indictment of Soviet society and was distributed only in Samizdat.

On his death from cancer in 1964, Grossman disappeared from public Soviet literary discussions, only reappearing under Mikhail Gorbachev. In retrospect, Grossman's writing has been acknowledged as some of the most significant Russian literature of the twentieth century.

See also: CENSORSHIP; JEWS; SAMIZDAT; STALIN, JOSEF VISSARIONOVICH; WORLD WAR II

BIBLIOGRAPHY

Ehrenburg, Ilya, and Grossman, Vasily. (2002). *The Complete Black Book of Russian Jewry,* tr. David Patterson. New Brunswick, NJ: Transaction Publishers.

Garrard, John, and Garrard, Carol. (1996). *The Bones of Berdichev: The Life and Fate of Vasily Grossman.* New York: Simon and Schuster.

Grossman, Vasily. (1985). *Life and Fate,* tr. Robert Chandler. New York: Harper & Row

Karl E. Loewenstein

GUARDS, REGIMENTS OF

The Russian Imperial Guards regiments originated in the two so-called play regiments that the young Tsar Peter I created during the 1680s. They took their names, Preobrazhensky and Semonovsky, from the villages in which they had originally taken form. Peter used those regiments to seize power from Sophia Alexeyevna, then ruling as regent, and establish himself in sole rule. Unlike the streltsy musketeer units that had been the elite element in the Russian army to that point, the guards were trained and equipped in the style of Western European armies, and drilled by Western officers.

Their original complements were entirely noble, including the enlisted ranks, and the guards regiments served as the principal training ground for officers for the line units. The guards, especially the Preobrazhensky regiment, often provided escorts for the tsar, even accompanying him on his tour of Europe. They also fought in his wars, playing an important role at the Battle of Narva in 1700 and throughout the Northern War. The guards served a political function under Peter as well, participating in the arrests of nobles and other governmental activities.

With Peter's death, the guards regiments increased in political significance. A demonstration by both regiments played a role in bringing Peter's wife, Catherine I, to power peacefully. They also brought Anna and Elizabeth to power through forceful *coup d'état*, and participated in Catherine II's seizure of the throne and murder of her husband, Peter III. Although they continued to participate in the smaller wars of the eighteenth century against Poland, Sweden, and Turkey, they did not play an important role in the Seven Years' War. Their numbers were nevertheless expanded, including the formation of the Izmailovsky Regiment by Anna and the Cavalier-Guard Cavalry Regiment, as well as the Guard Horse Regiment, among others.

The political significance of the guards regiments fell between Catherine the Great's reign and the end of the Napoleonic wars, while the guards' combat role increased. They accompanied Alexander I to battle in the war of 1805 and played an important role on the Austerlitz battlefield. They also participated in the 1812 campaign, including a prominent role in the Battle of Borodino, and they fought throughout the following two years of conflict against France. The Napoleonic Wars saw a significant reorganization of the guards similar to that which occurred throughout the Russian army at that time. In 1806 a guards division was formed of the three guards infantry regiments. In 1811 an Independent Guards Corps was formed, which persisted in various forms until the end of the empire.

The years after Napoleon's defeat saw a resurgence in the guards' political importance. In 1820 the Semenovsky Guards Regiment mutinied, and the rebellion had to be suppressed by other, loyal, troops. And in 1825, during the interregnum following the death of Alexander I, guards troops participated in the abortive Decembrist Rebellion, likewise suppressed by troops loyal to Nicholas I, the new tsar. Although the individuals who participated in the rebellions were punished, the guards as a whole were not. Indeed, the number of guards units mushroomed through the nineteenth century, so that in 1914 there were seventeen infantry and fourteen cavalry regiments with four artillery brigades, in addition to smaller detachments. The guards also spread into the navy in the form of individual units and ships.

Guards units participated in the Russo-Turkish Wars of 1828–1829 and 1877–1878, and individual guards officers participated as volunteers in the Russo-Japanese War. The guards units were used to help put down the Revolution of 1905. The guards regiments then played a prominent role in all of the major campaigns of World War I. Their ranks were decimated by the casualties they incurred, however, and by 1917 most guards units were filled with simple conscripts. Their political reliability, therefore, was no greater than that of any other army units. As a result, guards regiments garrisoned in Petrograd participated in the February Revolution against the government and helped bring down the tsarist regime. Guards units also helped the Bolsheviks to power in October.

Throughout the imperial period, members of the guards units received a number of significant privileges. In particular, guards officers were granted an additional one or two steps on the Table of Ranks, depending upon which units they belonged to (this benefit was reduced by one step toward the end of the nineteenth century). The tsars and tsaritsas and their favorites frequently served as the colonels of the guards regiments, and appointments in those regiments were keenly sought as a step toward political, social, and, of course, military advancement. On the whole, guards regiments did not perform better in combat than most good, well-trained regiments of the regular army.

With the advent of communist rule the guards regiments were disbanded. In 1941, however, Josef Stalin reestablished the concept of "guards" in a new form. Following the Battle of Smolensk, five rifle divisions were redesignated the First through the Fifth Guards Infantry Divisions for extraordinary valor as units in combat. Thereafter other units, including divisions, corps, and armies, received the designation "guards" as a reward for valor in battle.

See also: MILITARY, IMPERIAL ERA; PETER I

FREDERICK W. KAGAN

GUBA ADMINISTRATIVE SYSTEM

The guba system made communities partially responsible for their own policing and entrusted the investigation and partial adjudication of felony cases to local elected officials.

In the early sixteenth century the local administration of criminal justice was in the hands of vicegerents *(namestniki)* appointed by the grand prince and remunerated with the right to collect their own feeding maintenance (*kormlenie*). An increasing number of community complaints that the vicegerents were corrupt or unable to deal decisively with banditry led the government of Grand Prince Ivan IV to begin issuing in 1538 and 1539 ordinance charters permitting petitioning communities to remove criminal justice affairs from their vicegerents' jurisdiction and entrust them to criminal justice chiefs (*gubnye golovy*) elected from the local middle service class and criminal justice elders (*gubnye starosty*) elected from the more prosperous local peasants and taxpaying townsmen. A guba was the territorial jurisdiction of an elected criminal justice chief or elder, be it an urban posad commune or a rural canton. The elected guba executives and their deputies (*tselovalniki*) were made responsible for hunting down and arresting bandits and other felons, investigating and trying felony cases, and carrying out the sentences upon them.

This guba reform appears to have been motivated less by the need to respond to sharpening class conflict than by Moscow's interest in achieving greater specialization in and central control over provincial criminal justice matters than had been possible with the vicegerents. The degree of genuine administrative autonomy it conceded to the recipient communities was limited in that the communities, once given the privilege of electing guba officials, were under collective responsibility for their performance, and their guba officials were required to submit reports and accounts to a supervising commission of boyars at Moscow. By 1555 this supervising commission had evolved into the Robbery Chancellery (*Razboyny prikaz*). It is unclear whether guba officials themselves ever had the authority to pronounce death sentences upon felons, or whether the right of verdict in capital cases had to be reserved for the Robbery Chancellery. Some see in the 1550 Sudebnik law code Moscow's intent of universalizing the guba system, but there is no evidence this was accomplished.

The development of norms for guba policing, investigations, and hearings is reflected in a series of sources: the first guba community charters of the 1530s through the 1550 Sudebnik code; the 1555 Ordinance Book of the Robbery Chancellery; the revisions of this Ordinance book produced between 1617 and 1631; Chapter Twenty-One of the 1649 Ulozhenie law code; and the 1669 New Decree Statutes on Theft, Robbery, and Murder Cases. Some elements of traditional diadic justice remained to the end: for example, continued partial reliance on community hue and cry to apprehend criminals, and some continued reliance on community polling (*povalny obysk*) to establish guilt on the basis of reputation in the community's eyes. But in these successive ordinances, the shift to a more triadic criminal justice system became more apparent, especially from 1617 on, as seen in increasing emphasis placed on proactive struggle against brigandage and greater use of torture to produce confessions and name accomplices. In the 1669 New Decree Statutes, the guba organs are instructed in how to cooperate with special inquistors sent from Moscow to conduct mass dragnets. The tendency after the Time of Troubles was also to subordinate most guba offices to the offices of the chancellery-appointed town governors (*voyevodas*). In 1679 the guba offices were abolished and the town governors given full authority over felony cases. The purpose was apparently to simplify the financing of local government and reduce the number of elective offices in which men might take refuge from military duty. But it had the effect of increasing the workload of the town governors and providing more opportunities to corrupt them, so the guba system was restored in 1684.

See also: COLLECTIVE RESPONSIBILITY; IVAN IV; LAW CODE OF 1649; SUDEBNIK OF 1550; TIME OF TROUBLES

BRIAN DAVIES

GUBERNIYA

The highest unit of administrative-territorial division in prerevolutionary Russia.

In 1708 Peter I decreed the organization of Russian territory into eight large administrative regions (Petersburg, Moscow, Arkhangelsk, Smolensk, Kiev, Kazan, Azov, and Siberia), each under the jurisdiction of a centrally appointed governor. Between 1713 and 1719, each government was subdivided into *provintsii* (provinces) and *uezdy* (districts). By the time of Catherine II's accession in 1762, Russian territory had been reorganized into twenty governments. During the first decade of her reign, Catherine resolved to rationalize the territorial division and administration of imperial territory. Her "Constitution for the Administration of Governments" of 1775 established forty *guberny*, each with a male population of between 300,000–400,000 (by the end of her reign the number of governments had increased to fifty-one). Each government was subdivided into several *okrugy* or uezdy of between twenty and thirty thousand male inhabitants. This system was retained in European Russia throughout the nineteenth century, but the new territories of the imperial periphery were organized into general-governorships and, later, *oblast* (regions). The 1864 *zemstvo* reform established assemblies in many provinces, elected on a narrow, indirect franchise, which were responsible for nominating an executive board with responsibility for regional economic administration. Judicial and policing matters remained the responsibility of the governor, who also ratified the appointment of the president of the executive board. After the February Revolution of 1917, the Provisional Government replaced governors with commissars and after the Bolshevik Revolution authority passed to the executive committee of the regional soviet. Between 1924 and 1929 the new regime dissolved governments and replaced them with oblast and *kraya*.

See also: COMMUNIST PARTY OF THE SOVIET UNION; LOCAL GOVERNMENT AND ADMINISTRATION; UEZD; ZEMSTVO

NICK BARON

GUILDS

Organizations of merchants in groups called a "hundred" (*sto* or *sotnya*) existed in medieval Novgorod and in Muscovy. The first organization of merchants in guilds (*gildy*; singular *gildia*) occurred in December 1724, when Peter I divided the urban population into a first guild, composed of wealthy merchants, doctors, pharmacists, ship captains, painters, and the like; a second guild, comprising retail traders and artisans; and all others, called the "common people."

Although the word *guild* was borrowed from medieval European practice, guilds in Russia had purely administrative functions: to categorize merchants according to the extent of their economic activities and to collect fees from them. Merchants also bore heavy responsibilities of unpaid state service, such as tax collection and service on municipal boards, law courts, and other local institutions.

A decree issued on January 19, 1742, specified three merchant guilds. In a decree of March 17, 1775, Catherine II freed merchants from the soul tax and set 500 rubles of declared capital as the minimum requirement for enrollment in the merchant estate, subject to the payment of 1 percent of declared capital each year. A law issued on May 25, 1775, set specific minimum amounts: 10,000 rubles for the first guild, 1,000 rubles for the second, and 500 rubles for the third. In her Charter to the Cities, promulgated on April 21, 1785, Catherine II increased the minimum capital requirements to 5,000 rubles for the second guild and 1,000 rubles for the third. By abolishing the merchants' former monopoly on trade and industry, Catherine allowed the gentry and serfs to engage in ruinous competition with the merchants, free of the annual guild payment. Many enterprising merchants fled this precarious situation by rising into the gentry. The merchant estate therefore remained small and weak.

In 1839 a first-guild certificate, costing 600 rubles, entitled a merchant with at least 15,000 rubles in assets to own ships and factories, to offer banking services, and to trade in Russia and abroad. Second-guild certificates, sold for 264 rubles, entitled merchants whose stated wealth surpassed 6,000 rubles to manage factories and engage in wholesale or retail trade in Russia. Members of the third guild were permitted to conduct retail trade in the city or district where they resided, provided they owned assets worth 2,400–6,000 rubles and purchased certificates costing 1.25 percent of the declared amount.

The third guild was abolished in 1863 and a new fee structure established, but the link between large-scale economic activity and membership in the merchant estate was already dissolving. Laws issued in 1807, 1863, and 1865 allowed non-merchants engaged in manufacturing and wholesale commerce to enroll in a merchant guild while maintaining their membership in another social estate as well. From 1863 onward, anyone, regardless of social status or even citizenship, could create and manage a corporation. Still, many industrialists and traders enrolled in merchant guilds, as their fathers and grandfathers had done, to demonstrate their commitment to a group identity separate from the gentry.

See also: CAPITALISM; CHARTER OF THE CITIES; MERCHANTS; RUSSIA COMPANY

BIBLIOGRAPHY

Baron, Samuel H. (1980). *Muscovite Russia: Collected Essays.* London: Variorum.

Bushkovitch, Paul. (1980). *The Merchants of Moscow, 1580–1650.* New York: Cambridge University Press.

Hittle, J. Michael. (1979). *The Service City: State and Townsmen in Russia, 1600–1800.* Cambridge, MA: Harvard University Press.

THOMAS C. OWEN

GULAG

Stalinist labor camps.

The prison camp system of the Stalin era, whose acronym in Russian (GULag—hereafter Gulag) stood for *Glavnoye upravlenie lagerei*, or Main Camp Administration, grew into an enormous network of camps lasting into the mid-1950s. Other penal institutions, including prisons, labor colonies, and special settlements, supplemented the labor camps to form a vast number of sites available to the Soviet government for the incarceration and exile of its enemies. While much larger than both its tsarist and Soviet antecedents in size and scope, Stalin's prison empire evolved along lines clearly established over centuries of Russian rule. But the gulag far outpaced all predecessor systems and became an infamous symbol of state repression in the twentieth century.

Although unprecedented in reach, the labyrinth of Stalinist camps had its roots in both the tsarist and early Soviet periods. The secret police under the tsars, ranging from the *oprichniki* at the time of Ivan the Terrible in the sixteenth century to the Third Section and *Okhranka* of later years, established the broad historical outlines for Stalinist institutions. Imprisonment, involuntary servitude, and exile to Siberia formed a long and well-known experience meted out by these prerevolutionary organs of state security. Soon after the October Revolution, however, the new government under the leadership of Vladimir Lenin also issued key resolutions on incarceration, forced labor, and internal exile that explicitly set the stage for the gulag. The Temporary Instructions on Deprivation of Freedom (July 1918) and the Decree on Red Terror (September 1918) took aim at class enemies of the new regime to be sent to prison for various offenses. Other Bolshevik decrees from as early as January 1918 stipulated arrest and hard labor for political opponents of the new state as well as workers who had violated the labor code. The initial Soviet secret police agency, the Cheka (acronym for the Extraordinary Commission for Combatting Counterrevolution and Sabotage), controlled many but not all of the camps, which would in time be reintegrated with other prison structures and grow to an immense scale.

Other than proportion, one of the critical differences between this embryonic camp system under Lenin and its successor under Stalin concerned the problem of jurisdiction. In Lenin's time, the Soviet government lacked a centralized administration for its prison organizations. The Cheka, People's Commissariat of the Interior, and People's Commissariat of Justice all oversaw various offshoots of the penal camp complex. In 1922 and 1923, the GPU (State Political Administration) and then the OGPU (Unified State Political Administration) replaced the Cheka as the main secret police organization and assumed command over many of the labor camps. The first and largest cluster of prison camps under its authority, the primary ones of which existed on the Solovetski Islands in the White Sea to the north of Petrograd (renamed Leningrad in 1924), became known at this time as SLON (Northern Camps of Special Designation). While Lenin left no blueprint for a future camp leviathan under Stalin, the infamous archipelago of Gulag sites that lasted until the time of Nikita Khrushchev clearly grew out of these early variants. In 1930, the gulag was officially established just as the parameters of the labor camp network began to expand greatly after Stalin's consolidation of power.

The tremendous growth in inmate numbers throughout the 1930s proved a defining feature of Stalinism, and certainly one that sets it apart from previous eras. Whereas prisoner counts of the Stalin era would rise into the millions, neither the tsars nor Soviet leaders before 1929 incarcerated

Perm-35, the last Soviet gulag. © P.Perrin/CORBIS SYGMA

more than a few hundred thousand inmates. The collectivization of agriculture and the dekulakization campaign in the early 1930s began new trends in the Soviet Union, ushering in much higher rates of imprisonment. The Great Purges later in the decade again increased these statistics, particularly in the number of political prisoners sentenced to the Gulag. Other events, such as signing of the Nazi-Soviet Nonaggression Pact in August 1939, led to further waves of inmates, including Polish and Baltic citizens who joined their Soviet counterparts in remote camp zones across the USSR. By the 1940s, the Stalinist labor camps contained a multinational assortment of prisoners.

The *troika,* or three-person extrajudicial panel that could both try and sentence the accused even in absentia, became infamous in the late 1930s as a common mechanism for dispatching enemies of the state to widespread gulag regions. Comprising fourteen sections, Article 58 of the well-worn Soviet Criminal Code found extensive and arbitrary application throughout the Stalin era as the labor camps began to stretch to all corners of the nation. The organs of state security became preoccupied with the shipment of prisoners to penal sites across the country. One of the most legendary in the early 1930s involved construction of the Baltic–White Sea Canal. Other inmates labored under similarly hostile conditions on the Solovetski Islands, or at gulag sites in and around Vorkuta, Magadan, Pechora, and Karaganda.

Throughout its history, the gulag served both a punitive and economic function. From its very origins, Soviet prisons and camps had been repositories for enemies of the regime. Useful both for isolating and punishing real and imagined opponents, the labor camps in particular became a tool of repressive state policy. But while inefficient and substandard in many respects, the gulag fulfilled a vital economic role as well. Russia had long wrestled with the question of adequate labor in remote parts of the empire, which only compounded the intractable problems of a cash-poor economy nationwide. Although the roots of serfdom can in part be found in such conditions, Peter the Great in later years addressed numerous shortcomings with ever-increasing levels of coercion that expanded the realm of forced labor to include large prisoner contingents and peasants ascribed to factories. Political exile and hard labor became synonymous with Siberia in particular, and provided a blueprint for the Stalin era.

Although going far beyond Petrine goals, Stalin employed similar methods in the twentieth century. Inmates offered a bottomless pool of workers to be sent to areas historically poor in labor supply. The most famous and important gulag zones, focused upon the procurement of lumber and minerals, were located in remote northern and eastern regions of the USSR far from population centers. Leaving aside the question of productivity and efficiency, both of which registered at exceedingly low levels in the camps, the Soviet state sought a fulfillment of industrialization targets in such areas through the widespread application of prison contingents. But the labor camps soon grew beyond this scope, and began to fill economic functions within a larger national framework. Some gulag sites in time even appeared in and around major cities and industries. The Soviet government expanded the use of inmates in numerous large-scale construction projects, particularly involving railroad, canal, and highway plans. Eventually, the secret police concentrated inmate scientists in special prison laboratories known as sharashkas, where vital technical research proceeded under the punitive eye of the state.

While circumstances proved much better in such special design bureaus, most inmates throughout the gulag system both lived and worked under grueling conditions. Aside from enervating physical labor in extreme winter climates, prisoners suffered as well from poor living arrangements and minimal food rations. Hard labor in the mines and forests of Siberia was backbreaking and required a stamina that few inmates could maintain over long periods. Turning Marxism on its head, inmates also received caloric norms based upon a sliding scale of labor output that penalized low production levels even from the least healthy. Moreover, prisoners were subject to the whims of an unpredictable camp hierarchy that meted out harsh punishments for offenses, however minor. The threat of the isolator or lengthier terms of incarceration hung over every inmate and made the camp population dread the seemingly wanton authority of the camp bosses.

As a rule, conditions within the camps worsened over time up through the end of the 1930s and early 1940s. The brunt of this fell on the politicals, who as a result of the Great Purges had begun to arrive in the gulag in significant numbers by this time. Constituting the most dangerous element in the view of the Soviet government, political prisoners occupied the lowest rung in the camps. Moreover, prison bosses favored actual criminals convicted for far lesser economic crimes, and placed them in positions of authority within the informal camp structure. The result was an inverted universe in which normal societal mores were suspended and the rules of the criminal world came to the fore. For many inmates, such moral corrosion proved even more onerous than the physical hardships of camp life.

The gulag incarcerated several million inmates over the length of its existence. Archival records reveal that the numbers were not as high as those posited by Alexander Solzhenitsyn and others in previous years, although exact counts remain elusive for several reasons. In terms of the gulag proper, the highest camp figures for any one time were to be found in the late 1940s and early 1950s. Even then, there were not much more than two million prisoners on average within the camps at any given moment. Additional totals from internal exile, special settlement, and labor colonies augmented this number. But statistics convey only a narrow viewpoint on the reality of the gulag, which proved to be one of the most repressive mechanisms in the history of the Soviet Union.

See also: BERIA, LAVRENTI PAVLOVICH; PRISONS; PURGES, THE GREAT; STATE SECURITY, ORGANS OF; YEZHOV, NIKOLAI IVANOVICH

BIBLIOGRAPHY

Applebaum, Anne. (2003). *Gulag: A History.* New York: Broadway Books.

Ginzburg, Evgeniia. (1967). *Journey into the Whirlwind,* tr. Paul Stevenson and Max Hayward. New York: Harcourt, Brace, and World.

Ivanovna, Galina Mikhailovna. (2000). *Labor Camp Socialism: The Gulag in the Soviet Totalitarian System,* ed. Donald J. Raleigh, tr. Carol Flath. Armonk, NY: M. E. Sharpe.

Khlevniuk, Oleg. (2003). *History of the Gulag.* New Haven, CT: Yale University Press.

Solzhenitsyn, Aleksandr. (1974–1978). *The Gulag Archipelago, 1918–1956: An Experiment in Literary Investi-*

gation, 3 vols. tr. Thomas P. Whitney and H. Willetts. New York: Harper and Row.

David J. Nordlander

GUM

The acronym GUM stands for Main Department Store (Glavnyi universal'nyi magazin), and indeed, from the time it opened in 1953, GUM was the Soviet Union's largest and busiest retail establishment. Located on the northeast corner of Red Square, GUM occupies the historic premises of Moscow's Upper Trading Rows. This enormous glass-roofed complex, completed in 1893, might be considered an early shopping mall; in the late imperial period, it housed between three hundred and one thousand shops at a time. The Upper Trading Rows were nationalized along with other commercial businesses in the aftermath of the Bolshevik Revolution, and were almost immediately converted into office space for the new Soviet bureaucracy. The New Economic Policy of the 1920s brought a brief revival of trade in the building when the municipal government established a five-and-dime emporium there, but it soon reverted to administrative use.

When the premises were refurbished for retailing during the early 1950s, the emphasis was no longer on discounted sales. GUM became the Soviet capital's most prestigious store, with specialized departments for such luxuries as Central Asian rugs, televisions, crystal stemware, and fur coats. Another department, Section 200, sold luxury wares exclusively to the Soviet elite; entry into this department was by permit only.

In 1992 GUM was reorganized as a joint-stock company. According to a 1991 formula, one-quarter of the shares went to the Moscow city government and one-quarter to employees, while the balance was sold to private investors.

See also: RED SQUARE

Julie Hessler

GUMILEV, LEV NIKOLAYEVICH

(1912–1992), dissident historian, geographer, and ethnographer in the Soviet Union.

Lev Gumilev belonged to the old Russian intelligentsia. His father, Nikolai Gumilev, was a prominent poet of the Silver Age and a victim of Bolshevik terror. His mother, Anna Akhmatova, was one of the greatest Russian women poets. Lev Gumilev's ties with the old intelligentsia led to frequent imprisonments from the 1920s to the 1950s in Josef Stalin's Gulag (prison camp system). Gumilev joined a punishment battalion in 1944 and fought in the Battle of Berlin. In spite of this, he became a major intellectual figure in Leningrad and developed an international reputation for his studies of the ancient Turkic and Mongol peoples. He combined historical and archeological research with historical geography to develop a new discipline, ethnography (*narodovedenie*) in the Department of Oriental Studies of Leningrad State University. Soviet scholar circles found thought anti-Marxist in his research and publications. He was accused of ignoring the role of the class struggle in history. Gumilev was particularly concerned with the relationship between culture and nation and the impact of biological energy and morals upon the development of ethnic groups. He advanced a theory of ethnogenesis to explain the rise and decline of particular ethnic groups in terms of biological and not social factors. He stressed the absence or presence of drive (*passionarnost*) in a particular people as manifest in the personalities of leaders to explain the people's role in the unfolding of the nation's history. These ideas have had a profound influence on Russian nationalist thought and the development of Eurasianism in contemporary Russia.

See also: DISSIDENT MOVEMENT; NATIONALISM IN THE SOVIET UNION

BIBLIOGRAPHY

Shnirelman, Viktor, and Panarin, Sergei. (2001). "Lev Gumilev: His Pretensions as a Founder of Ethnology and his Eurasian Theories." *Inner Asia* 3:1–18

Jacob W. Kipp

GUMILEV, NIKOLAI STEPANOVICH

(1886–1921), poet executed by the Bolsheviks.

Born in Kronstadt and educated at the Tsarskoye Selo Gymnasium, Nikolai Stepanovich Gumilev was a major Silver Age poet and a victim of

Bolshevik repression. Gumilev, his first wife, Anna Akhmatova, and Osip Mandelstam were the foremost representatives of acmeism, a movement emphasizing concrete personal experience that arose in response to the dominant symbolist school of poetry during the 1910s. Gumilev also played a central role in the St. Petersburg–based Guild of Poets, a literary organization intermittently active between 1910 and 1921.

As a monarchist and self-styled "poet-warrior," Gumilev volunteered to serve in the Russian army in August 1914. In 1918 he returned to Petrograd, where he worked as an editor and translator for the World Literature series.

Gumilev was arrested by the Bolsheviks in August 1921 for his alleged part in an anti-Soviet plot. Although the charges were almost certainly fabricated, Gumilev and sixty others were executed within weeks, over the protest of many writers. His execution was part of a sustained campaign against intellectuals by the Bolsheviks, who hoped to stifle potential dissent while loosening economic and social controls during the New Economic Policy. Gumilev's execution is frequently cited as evidence that the systematic use of state terror was an integral part of communist rule, not an aberration associated with Stalinism. Many contemporaries viewed the deaths of Gumilev and the poet Alexander Blok, just twelve days apart, as symbolic of the destruction of the prerevolutionary intelligentsia.

Gumilev's work was banned in the Soviet Union from 1923 until 1986. His poetry has become very popular in Russia since that time, with more than forty editions of his works appearing. Major collections included *Romantic Flowers* (1908), *Alien Sky* (1912), *Quiver* (1916), and *The Pillar of Fire* (1921). Gumilev also wrote several plays.

See also: AKHMATOVA, ANNA ANDREYEVNA; BLOK, ALEXANDER ALEXANDROVICH; MANDELSHTAM, OSIP EMILIEVICH; SILVER AGE

BIBLIOGRAPHY

Gumilev, Nikolai. (1999). *The Pillar of Fire and Other Poems*, trans. Richard McKane, intro. by Michael Basker. London: Anvil Poetry Press.

Sampson, Earl D. (1970). "Nikolay Gumilev: Towards a Reevaluation." *Russian Review* 29(3):301–311.

BRIAN KASSOF

GYPSY

Gypsies (*tsygane* in Russian, while *Roma* is the name preferred by this group) have been one of the most visible and yet least powerful of ethnic groups in Russia. The population is considerably larger than the 153,000 in the Russian Federation who were listed as Gypsies in the 1989 census. This is due to underreporting, a high birth rate, and immigration from former Soviet republics. Roma leaders claim a population of at least one million. As is true of Roma populations all over Europe, little is known of their ethnic origins and history as a people, though it is theorized that Gypsies originated in India. Many migrated to Russia by way of Germany and Poland during the eighteenth century after suffering persecution there. Romani, the language spoken by most gypsies, has Indo-European roots with some links to ancient Sanskrit.

Gypsies are widely dispersed across Russia, with communities in Moscow, St. Petersburg, Samara, Komi Republic, Sverdlovsk, Vologda, Volgograd, Voronezh, Yaroslavl, and elsewhere. Following long-standing cultural traditions, Roma have resisted assimilation and exist on the margins of society. Geographic dispersal and social marginalization meant that the Roma did not enjoy the state support that often characterized Soviet nationality policy. Gypsies had no territorial entity of their own, no schools offering instruction in their own language, and no newspapers. The first Roma newspaper in Russia began publication in Samara only in 2001. Even under Josef Stalin, however, the cultural role of gypsies in Soviet society was recognized. In 1931 the Romen Theater opened in Moscow. It was the first theater in the world to showcase gypsy culture, and gypsy actors and musicians performed and were trained there. The theater continues to be active in post-Soviet Russia. Gypsy themes have been prominent in Russian culture, particularly through the popular film *Tabor Goes to Heaven* (*Tabor ukhodit v nebo*) which was released in 1976.

In Russia as in the rest of Eastern Europe, gypsies have been the object of public scorn and official repression. Many have traditionally engaged in illegal or semilegal occupations such as black marketeering, petty theft, fencing stolen goods, and organized begging. This is both a cause and effect of the lack of acceptance of gypsies in Russian society. During the Soviet period, gypsies often engaged in black-market selling of alcohol and perfume, as well as fortune-telling and other occult arts. State repression of the gypsies reached a new height during the Nikita Khrushchev period. New regulations issued in 1957 attempted to restrict their movements outside of places where they were registered. This attempt to prevent the movement of gypsies has continued in post-Soviet Russia, with the police sometimes tearing down illegal gypsy settlements and forcing residents to return to their home region. With the expansion of private enterprise in post-Soviet Russia, the Roma reportedly have been squeezed out of their traditional commercial occupations, with even fortune-telling taken over by non-gypsy entrepreneurs who had an easier time dealing with the authorities. There has been an increasing incidence of gypsies involved in more serious crimes, such as the drug trade, a tendency bemoaned by leaders of the Roma community.

In 2000 the Russian government officially recognized the need for gypsies to have a political voice, and it authorized the creation of a council that would defend gypsy interests. Its leaders have campaigned against frequent stereotyping of gypsies in the media and have condemned police harassment based solely on ethnic identity.

See also: GYPSYMANIA; NATIONALITIES POLICIES, SOVIET; NATIONALITIES POLICIES, TSARIST

BIBLIOGRAPHY

Crowe, David M. (1994). *A History of Gypsies of Eastern Europe and Russia.* New York: St. Martin's Press.

European Roma Rights Center (2003). "Written Comments of the European Roma Rights Center Concerning the Russian Federation for Consideration by the United Nations Committee on the Elimination of Racial Discrimination at its Sixty-second Session, March 3–21, 2003." <http://www.errc.org/publications/legal/CERD-Russia_Feb_2003>

DARRELL SLIDER

GYPSYMANIA

Gypsymania took both literary and musical forms during the early nineteenth century. The gypsy theme—imagined scenes from their life and customs—captivated Russian poets. Alexander Pushkin's contributions gained popularity and immediately entered the literary canon. Gypsymania in music (*tsyganshchina*) outlasted the literary genres. Its sources—choirs comprising free, serf, and state peasant ethnic gypsies (Roma) and Russian composers who adapted gypsy motifs to popular romances—were blended by star performers such as Stesha (Stepanida Sidorovna Soldatova, 1784–1822) and her successors. Tsyganshchina's attraction rested on lyrics, music, and performance style. Song lyrics represented gypsies as hot-blooded, wild in love, cruel in hatred, and enamored of freedom and the open road. The music was marked by sharp contrasts and sudden changes of tempo. The critic Apollon Grigorev wrote in 1847: "If you seek sounds, if you seek expression for those undefined, incomprehensible, sorrowful 'blues' (*khandra*), you make off to the Gypsies, immerse yourself in the hurricane of these wild, passionate, oppressively passionate songs." An English visitor to a Moscow cafe during the 1850s described the performance of a gypsy choir wearing expensive and gaudy garments. They sat or lay on the floor; the soloist was joined by the company who drank and smoked as they strolled from table to table, stamping their feet. As cafes, restaurants, and phonograph records proliferated during the early twentieth century, gypsymania launched the careers of a half dozen superstars of the era who often emulated in life the emotional turbulence of their songs. Most Russians found them irresistible.

Critics accepted both the traditional music of the Roma, because it bore a folkish spirit, and the stylizations of composers at play like Franz Liszt and Johannes Brahms. The middle range, by far the most popular, invited rancor: the local vernacular adorned with gypsy devices of rhythm, sonority, instrumentation, and phrasing. In Russia, songs composed in the gypsy manner, such as "Two Guitars" and "Dark Eyes," evoked repugnance among some critics. Ironically, genuine gypsies when playing Roma music also borrowed from local styles, and this habit accounts for the huge variety among the various authentic gypsy styles from Spain to Finland. Under Bolshevism, hostility to tsyganshchina took on a political edge. During the 1920s, classical musicians lamented its vulgarity, and proletarian composers charged the music with inciting decadence, bourgeois values, and miscreant sexuality. The gypsy genre disappeared during the Cultural Revolution (1928–1931), and a form of gypsy music was partially revived, in a sanitized form, with the founding of the Teatr Romen in 1931 where something like genuine Roma performances were mounted. Recordings by other Soviet singers of selected gypsy songs were released under the watchful eye of the censors. With the coming of glasnost under Mikhail Gorbachev, every kind of previously taboo gypsy songs resurfaced, only to be drowned out soon by Western rock and hip-hop.

See also: FOLK MUSIC; GYPSY; PUSHKIN, ALEXANDER SERGEYEVICH

BIBLIOGRAPHY

Stites, Richard. (1992). *Russian Popular Culture: Entertainment and Society since 1900.* Cambridge, UK: Cambridge University Press.

RICHARD STITES

HAGIOGRAPHY

Various types of narratives with documentary and commemorative functions for the Orthodox Church are also regarded as important literary works in the medieval Russian canon. Sacred biographies (*vitae*) were written about persons who had followed Christ's example in life and shown evidence of powers after death to intercede for believers, attributes that qualified them for sainthood. A short summary of the saint's life was read initially at the ceremonial inauguration of the feast day and thereafter to honor the saint's memory. Longer vitae circulated in religious anthologies of devotional readings. Eulogistic biographies of rulers, initially written for the funeral service, were recorded in chronicles, then revised for hagiographical anthologies. Tales from the Patericon record episodes from the lives of holy monks, their teachings, or the history of a monastic community. The vitae also include extended accounts of miracles worked by icons, some of which are viewed as local or national symbols, as well as tales of individual miracles.

When the Kievans converted to Christianity during the reign of Vladimir I (d. 1015), they received Greek Orthodox protocols for the recognition and veneration of saints, as well as a corpus of hagiographical texts. Beginning in the eleventh century, Kievan monks produced their own records of native saints. Veneration for the appanage princes Boris and Gleb, murdered in the internecine struggles following the death of their father Vladimir, inspired three extended lives that are regarded as literary classics. Also influential was the life of Theodosius (d. 1074), who became a monk and helped to found the renowned Kiev Cave Monastery. His biography, together with stories of the monastery's miraculous founding and of its monks, was anthologized in the *Kiev Cave Monastery Patericon.* The earliest hagiographical works from the city-state of Novgorod, surviving in thirteenth-century copies, focus on the bishops and abbots of important cloisters. Lives of Suzdalian saints, such as the Rostov bishops Leontius, Isaiah, and Ignatius, and the holy monk Abraham, preserve collective memories of clerics who converted the people of the area to Christianity.

In the fourteenth and early fifteenth centuries, Russian monks fled the cities, moving into wilderness areas to live as hermits, then founded monasteries to house their disciples. The writings produced in these monastery scriptoria promoted asceticism as the highest model to which a Christian could aspire. Biographies of saints were supplemented with long prefaces, prayers, laments, and digressive praises employing the poetic imagery and complex syntactic structures characteristic of hymnography. An introductory commonplace, declaring the writer's wish to write an account that will be a fitting crown or garland of praise for the saint, has inspired some scholars to group these lives into a hagiographical school whose trademark is "word-weaving" (*pletenie sloves*). The most prominent writers of this school include Metropolitan Cyprian (c. 1330–1406), identified by some as a Bulgarian and others as a Serb, who wrote a revised life of the holy Metropolitan Peter in 1381; Epiphanius the Wise (second half of the fourteenth century to the first quarter of the fifteenth century), author of the first life of St. Sergius of Radonezh and St. Stephen of Perm (1390s); and Pachomius the Logothete, an Athonian monk sometimes identified as a Serb, who was commissioned to rewrite the lives of widely venerated holy men from Novgorod, Moscow, and leading monasteries between 1429 and 1484.

Sixteenth-century Muscovite hagiographers composed expansive narratives celebrating saints and icons viewed as protectors of the Russian tsardom. The most influential promoter of the Muscovite school was Macarius. While serving as archbishop of Novgorod (1537–1542), Macarius ordered the collection of saints' lives and icon legends, as well as other translated and original religious texts, for a twelve-volume anthology known as the *Great Menology* (*Velikie Minei Chetii*). The first "Sophia" version was donated to the Novgorod Cathedral of Holy Wisdom in 1541. During his tenure as metropolitan of Moscow (1542–1563), Macarius commissioned additional lives of saints who were recognized as national patrons at the Church Councils of 1547 and 1549, for a second expanded version of this anthology, which he donated to the Kremlin Cathedral of the Dormition in 1552. A third fair copy was prepared between 1550 and 1554 for presentation to Tsar Ivan the Terrible. Between 1556 and 1563, expanded sacred biographies of Kievan rulers Olga and Vladimir I, appanage princes and princesses and four Moscow metropolitans, as well as an ornate narrative about the miracles of the nationally venerated icon Our Lady of Vladimir, were composed for Macarius's *Book of Degrees*. These lives stressed the unity of the Russian metropolitan see and the theme that the line of Moscow princes had prospered because they followed the guidance of the Church.

In the seventeenth century, two twelve-volume hagiographical anthologies were produced by clerics affiliated with the Trinity-Sergius Monastery: the Trinity monk German Tulupov and the priest Ioann Milyutin. Their still unpublished menologies preserve lives of native Russian saints and legends of local wonder-working icons not included in earlier collections. In 1684 the Kiev Cave Monastery monk Dmitry (Daniel Savvich Tuptalo), who would be consecrated metropolitan of Rostov and Yaroslavl in 1702, began to research Muscovite, Western, and Greek hagiographical sources. Dmitry's goal was to retell the lives of saints and legends of wonder-working icons in a form accessible to a broad audience of Orthodox readers. The first version of his reading menology was printed in 1705 at the Kiev Cave Monastery. In 1759, a corrected edition printed in Moscow became the authorized collection of hagiography for the Russian Orthodox Church. Also noteworthy as sources on the spirituality of the seventeenth century are the lives of Old Believer martyrs (Archpriest Avvakum, burned as a heretic on April 1, 1682, and Lady Theodosia Morozova who died in prison on November 2, 1675) and the life of the charitable laywoman Yulianya Osorina, written by her son Kallistrat, district elder (*gubnaya starosta*) of Murom between 1610 and 1640.

See also: KIEVAN CAVES PATERICON; ORTHODOXY; RUSSIAN ORTHODOX CHURCH; SAINTS

BIBLIOGRAPHY

Bosley, Richard. (1997). "The Changing Profile of the Liturgical Calendar in Muscovy's Formative Years." In *Culture and Identity in Muscovy: 1359–1584*, eds. A. M. Kleimola and G. D. Lenhoff. Moscow: ITZ-Garant.

Ebbinghaus, Andreas. (1997). "Reception and Ideology in the Literature of Muscovite Rus." In *Culture and Identity in Muscovy: 1359–1584*, eds. A. M. Kleimola and G. D. Lenhoff. Moscow: ITZ-Garant.

Fennell, John. (1995). *A History of the Russian Church to 1448*. New York: Longman.

Hollingsworth, Paul, tr. and ed. (1992). *The Hagiography of Kievan Rus'*. Harvard Library of Early Ukrainian Literature II. Cambridge, MA: Harvard University Press.

Lenhoff, Gail D. (1997). *Early Russian Hagiography: The Lives of Prince Fedor the Black* (Slavistiche Veröffentlichungen 82). Berlin-Wiesbaden: Harrassowitz Verlag.

Prestel, David K. (1992). "Biblical Typology in the Kievan Caves Patericon." *The Modern Encyclopedia of Religions in Russia and the Soviet Union* 4:97–102. Gulf Breeze, FL: Academic International Press.

GAIL LENHOFF

HAGUE PEACE CONFERENCES

Tsar Nicholas II summoned peace conferences at The Hague in the Netherlands in 1899 and 1907. His gestures appealed to pacifist sentiments in the West, but his primary motives were quite pragmatic. He hoped the 1899 conference would ban the rapid-fire artillery being developed by Austria-Hungary, Russia's rival in the Balkans. Russia could neither develop nor purchase such weapons except at great expense. Finance Minister Serge Witte urged that such money be spent instead on modernizing Russia's economy. Having called the conference, the Imperial government found itself tied in knots. Its war minister warned that Russia would need more and better arms to achieve its goals in the Far East against Japan and in the Black Sea region against Ottoman Turkey. Russia's major ally, France, objected to any limitations because it sought new arms to cope with Germany. Before the conference even opened, St. Petersburg assured Paris that no disarmament measures would be adopted.

The 1899 Hague Conference did not limit arms, but it did refine the laws of war, including the rights of neutrals. It also established an international panel of arbiters available to hear cases put before it by disputing nations.

A second Hague conference was planned five years after the first, but did not convene then because Russia was fighting Japan. Nicholas did summon the meeting in 1907, after Russia began to recover from its defeat by Japan and from its own 1905 revolution. It was during the 1905 upheaval that Vladimir Ilich Lenin first articulated his view on disarmament. The revolutionary task, he said, is not to talk about disarmament (*razoruzhenie*) but to disarm (*obezoruzhit'*) the ruling classes.

The Russian delegation in 1907 proposed less sweeping limits on armaments than in 1899. However, when some governments proposed a five-year ban on dirigibles, Russia called for a permanent ban. Nothing came of these proposals, and the second Hague conference managed only to add to refinements to the laws of war.

See also: LENIN, VLADIMIR ILICH; NICHOLAS II

BIBLIOGRAPHY

Clemens, Walter C., Jr. "Nicholas II to SALT II: Change and Continuity in East-West Diplomacy." *International Affairs* 3 (July 1973):385–401.

Rosenne, Shabtai, comp. (2001). *The Hague Peace Conferences of 1899 and 1907 and International Arbitration: Reports and Documents.* The Hague: T.M.C. Asser.

Van den Dungen, Peter. (1983) *The Making of Peace: Jean de Bloch and the First Hague Peace Conference.* Los Angeles: Center for the Study of Armament and Disarmament, California State University.

WALTER C. CLEMENS, JR.

HANSEATIC LEAGUE

The Hanseatic League was an association of north European towns that dominated trade from London in the west to Flanders, Scandinavia, Germanic Baltic towns, and Novgorod in the east. There is no precise date for the beginning of the Hansa, but during the twelfth century German merchants established a commercial center at Visby on the island of Gotland, and by the early thirteenth century founded Riga, Reval (Tallinn), Danzig (Gdansk), and Dorpat (Tartu).

German and Scandinavian merchants established the Gothic Yard (*Gotsky dvor*) and the Church of St. Olaf on Novgorod's Trading Side. Toward the end of the twelfth century, Lübeck built the German Yard (*Nemestsky dvor*, or *Peterhof* for the Church of St. Peter) near the Gothic Yard. At the same time Novgorodian merchants frequented Visby, Sweden, Denmark, and Lübeck.

During the thirteenth century Lübeck gradually replaced Visby as the commercial center of the League, and during the fourteenth century the Gothic Yard became attached to Peterhof. In 1265 the north German towns accepted the "law of Lübeck" and agreed for the common defense of the towns. The League's primary concern was to ensure open sea-lanes and the safety of its ships from piracy. In addition to Novgorod, the League founded counters or factories in Bruges, London, and Bergen. At its height between the 1350s and 1370s, the League consisted of seventy or more towns; perhaps thirty additional towns were loosely associated with the Hansa. The cities met irregularly in a diet (or *Hansetage*) but never developed a central political body or common navy. The League could threaten to exclude recalcitrant towns from its trade.

A Novgorod-Hansa agreement of 1269 laid the basic structure of commercial relations. German and Scandinavian merchants from Lübeck, Reval, Riga, and Dorpat traveled twice per year, in summer and winter, to Novgorod. German merchants were under their own jurisdiction within Peterhof, but disputes involving Novgorodians fell to a joint court that included the mayor and chiliarch (military commander). During the thirteenth century the German Yard elected its own aldermen, but during the fourteenth century Lübeck and Visby chose the aldermen. During the fifteenth century the Livonian towns selected a permanent official who resided in Novgorod.

Novgorod supplied the Hansa with furs, wax, and honey, and received silver ingots (the source of much of medieval Rus's silver), as well as Flemish cloth, salt, herring, other manufactured goods, and occasionally grain. In 1369 the League imposed duties on its silver exports to Novgorod; in 1373 it halted silver exports for two years, and in 1388 for four years. Novgorod turned to the Teutonic Order for silver, but exports stopped after 1427. During the 1440s war broke out between Novgorod and the Teutonic Order and the League, closing the German Yard from 1443 to 1448.

Novgorod's fur trade declined in the second half of the fifteenth century. After conquering Novgorod in 1478, Moscow closed the German Yard in 1494. The Yard reopened in 1514, but Moscow developed alternative trading routes through Ivangorod, Pskov, Narva, Dorpat, and Smolensk. During the sixteenth century Dutch and English traders further undermined the League's commercial monopolies. In 1555 the English obtained duty-free privileges to trade manufactured goods for Russian furs.

See also: FOREIGN TRADE; GERMANY, RELATIONS WITH; NOVGOROD THE GREAT

BIBLIOGRAPHY

Dollinger, Philippe. (1970). *The German Hansa*, tr. D. S. Ault. Stanford, CA: Stanford University Press.

LAWRENCE N. LANGER

HARD BUDGET CONSTRAINTS

In market economies, firms face hard budget constraints. This means that they must cover their costs of production using revenues generated either from the sales of their product or from other financial sources. In the short term, firms facing hard budget constraints may borrow to cover their operating costs. In the long term, however, if firms cannot cover their costs from their revenues, they fail, which means they must declare that the company is bankrupt or they must sell their assets to another firm. Hard budget constraints coincide with a situation where government authorities do not bail out or subsidize poorly performing or loss-making firms.

Soviet industrial enterprises did not face hard budget constraints. Unlike their counterparts in market economies, Soviet firms' primary objective was to produce output, not to make a profit. In many respects, planners controlled the financial performance of firms, because planners set the prices of labor, energy, and other material inputs used by the firm and also set the prices on products sold by the firm. Centrally determined prices in the Soviet economy did not facilitate an accurate calculation of costs, because they were not based on considerations of scarcity or efficient resource utilization. Nor did prices reflect demand conditions. Consequently, Soviet firms were not able to accurately calculate their financial condition in terms that would be appropriate in a market economy. More importantly, however, Soviet planners rewarded the fulfillment of output targets with large monetary bonuses and continually pressured Soviet industrial enterprises to produce more. With quantity targets given highest priority, managers of Soviet firms were not concerned with costs, nor were they faced with bankruptcy if they engaged in ongoing loss-making activities. Without the constraint to minimize or reduce costs, and given the emphasis on fulfilling or expanding output targets, Soviet firms were encouraged to continually demand additional resources in order to increase their production. In contrast to hard budget constraints faced by profit-maximizing firms in market economies, Soviet industrial enterprises faced soft budget constraints.

See also: NEW ECONOMIC POLICY; VALUE SUBTRACTION; VIRTUAL ECONOMY

BIBLIOGRAPHY

Kornai, Janos. (1986). *Contradictions and Dilemmas: Studies on the Socialist Economy and Society*, tr. Ilona Lukacs, et al. Cambridge, MA: MIT Press.

Kornai, Janos. (1992). *The Socialist System: The Political Economy of Communism.* Princeton, NJ: Princeton University Press.

SUSAN J. LINZ

HAYEK, FRIEDRICH

(1899–1992), leading proponent of markets as an evolutionary solution to complex social coordination problems.

One of the leaders of the Austrian school of economics in the twentieth century, Friedrich Hayek received the Nobel Memorial Prize in Economic Science in 1974. Born to a distinguished family of Viennese intellectuals, he attended the University of Vienna, earning doctorates in law and economics in 1921 and 1923. He became a participant in Ludwig von Mises's private economics seminar and was greatly influenced by von Mises's treatise on socialism and his argument about the impossibility of economic rationality under socialism due to the absence of private property and markets in the means of production. Hayek developed a theory of credit-driven business cycles, discussed in his books *Prices and Production* (1931) and *Monetary Theory and the Trade Cycle* (1933). As a result he was offered a lectureship, and then the Tooke Chair in Economics and Statistics at the London School of Economics and Politics (LSE) in 1931. There he worked on developing an alternative analysis to the nascent Keynesian economic system, which he published in *The Pure Theory of Capital* in 1941, by which point the Keynesian macro model had already become the accepted and dominant paradigm of economic analysis.

In the 1930s and 1940s, Hayek made his major contribution to the analysis of economic systems, pointing out the role of markets and the price system in distilling, aggregating, and disseminating usable specific knowledge among participants in the economy. The role of markets as an efficient discovery procedure, generating a spontaneous order in the flux of changing and unknowable specific circumstances and preferences, was emphasized in his "Economics and Knowledge" (1937), "The Use of Knowledge in Society" (1945), and *Individualism and Economic Order* (1948). These arguments provided a fundamental critique of the possibility of efficient economic planning and an efficient socialist system, refining and redirecting the earlier Austrian critique of von Mises. They have also provided the basis for a substantial theoretical literature on the role of prices as a conveyor of information, and for the revival of non-socialist economic thought in the final days of the Soviet Union.

Hayek worked at LSE until 1950 when he moved to Chicago, joining the Committee of Social Thought at the University of Chicago. There Hayek moved beyond economic to largely social and philosophic-historical analysis. His major works in these areas include his most famous defense of private property and decentralized markets, *The Road to Serfdom* (1944), *New Studies in Philosophy, Politics and Economics* (1978), and the compilation *The Fatal Conceit: The Errors of Socialism* (1988). These works, more than his economic studies, provided much of the intellectual inspiration and substance behind the anti-Communist and economic liberal movements in eastern Europe and the Soviet Union in the 1980s and 1990s. In 1962 Hayek left Chicago for the University of Freiburg in Germany, and subsequently for Salzburg, where he spent the rest of his life. The Nobel Prize in 1974 significantly raised interest in his work and in Austrian economics.

See also: LIBERALISM; SOCIALISM

BIBLIOGRAPHY

Bergson, Abram. (1948). "Socialist Economics." In *A Survey of Contemporary Economics,* ed. H. S. Ellis. Homewood, IL: Irwin.

Blaug, Mark. (1993). "Hayek Revisited." *Critical Review* 7(1):51–60.

Caldwell, Bruce. (1997). "Hayek and Socialism." *Journal of Economic Literature,* 35(4):1856–1890.

Foss, Nicolai J. (1994). *The Austrian School and Modern Economics: A Reassessment.* Copenhagen, Denmark: Handelshojskolens Forlag.

Lavoie, Don. (1985). *Rivalry and Central Planning: The Socialist Calculation Debate Reconsidered.* Cambridge, UK: Cambridge University Press.

Machlup, Fritz. (1976). "Hayek's Contributions to Economics." In Buckley, William F., et al., *Essays on Hayek,* ed. Fritz Machlup. Hillsdale, MI: Hillsdale College Press.

O'Driscoll, Gerald P. (1977). *Economics as a Coordination Problem: The Contribution of Friedrich A. Hayek.* Kansas City: Sheed, Andrews and McMeel.

RICHARD E. ERICSON

HEALTH CARE SERVICES, IMPERIAL

Prior to the reign of Peter the Great there were virtually no modern physicians or medical programs in Russia. The handful of foreign physicians employed by the *Aptekarskyi prikaz* (Apothecary bureau) cared almost exclusively for the ruling family and the court. Peter himself took a serious interest in medicine, including techniques of surgery and dentistry. His expansion of medical services and medical practitioners focused on the armed forces, but his reformist vision embodied an explicit concern for the broader public health.

As of 1800 there were still only about five hundred physicians in the empire, almost all of them foreigners who had trained abroad. During the eighteenth century schools in Russian hospitals provided a growing number of Russians with limited training as surgeons or surgeons' assistants. The serious training of physicians in Russia itself began in the 1790s at the medical faculty of Moscow University and in medical-surgical academies in Moscow and St. Petersburg. Later these were joined by medical faculties at universities in St. Petersburg, Dorpat, Kazan, and elsewhere. The early medical corps in Russia also included auxiliary medical personnel such as feldshers (physicians' assistants), midwives, barbers, bonesetters, and vaccinators. Much of the population relied upon traditional healers and midwives well into the twentieth century.

Catherine the Great made highly visible efforts to improve public health. In 1763 she created a medical college to oversee medical affairs. She had herself and her children inoculated against smallpox in 1768 and sponsored broader vaccination programs. She established foundling homes, an obstetric institute in St. Petersburg, and several large hospitals in the capitals. Her provincial reform of 1775 created Boards of Public Welfare, which built provincial hospitals, insane asylums, and almshouses. In 1797, under Paul I, provincial medical boards assumed control of medicine at the provincial level, and municipal authorities took over Catherine's Boards of Public Welfare. With the establishment of ministries in 1803, the Medical College was folded into the Ministry of Internal Affairs and its Medical Department.

The paucity of medical personnel made it difficult to provide modern medical care for a widely dispersed peasantry that constituted over eighty percent of the population. During the 1840s the Ministry of State Domains and the Office of Crown Properties initiated rural medical programs for the state and crown peasants. The most impressive advances in rural medicine were accomplished by zemstvos, or self-government institutions, during the fifty years following their creation in 1864. District and provincial zemstvos, working with the physicians they employed, developed a model of rural health-care delivery that was financed through the zemstvo budget rather than through payments for service. By 1914 zemstvos had crafted an impressive network of rural clinics, hospitals, sanitary initiatives, and schools for training auxiliary medical personnel. The scope and quality of zemstvo medicine varied widely, however, depending upon the wealth and political will of individual districts. The conferences that physicians and zemstvo officials held at the district and provincial level were a vital dimension of Russia's emerging public sphere, as was a lively medical press and the activities of professional associations such as the Pirogov Society of Russian Physicians.

By 1912 there were 22,772 physicians in the empire, of whom 2,088 were women. They were joined by 28,500 feldshers, 14,000 midwives, 4,113 dentists, and 13,357 pharmacists. The fragmentation of medical administration among a host of institutions made it difficult to coordinate efforts to combat cholera and other epidemic diseases. Many tsarist officials and physicians saw the need to create a national ministry of public health, and a medical commission headed by Dr. Georgy Ermolayevich Rein drafted plans for such a ministry. Leading zemstvo physicians, who prized the zemstvo's autonomy and were hostile to any expansion of central government control, opposed the creation of such a ministry. The revolutions of 1917 occurred before the Rein Commission's plans could be implemented.

See also: FELDSHER; HEALTH CARE SERVICES, SOVIET

BIBLIOGRAPHY

Alexander, John T. (1980). *Bubonic Plague in Early Modern Russia: Public Health and Urban Disaster.* Baltimore and London: Johns Hopkins University Press.

Conroy, Mary Schaeffer. (1994). *In Health and in Sickness: Pharmacy, Pharmacists, and the Pharmaceutical Industry in Late Imperial, Early Soviet Russia.* Boulder, CO: East European Monographs.

Frieden, Nancy. (1981). *Russian Physicians in an Era of Reform and Revolution, 1856–1905.* Princeton, NJ: Princeton University Press.

Hutchinson John F. (1990). *Politics and Public Health in Revolutionary Russia, 1890–1918.* Baltimore: Johns Hopkins University Press.

McGrew, Roderick E. (1965). *Russia and the Cholera, 1823–1832.* Madison: University of Wisconsin Press.

Ramer, Samuel C. (1982). "The Zemstvo and Public Health." In *The Zemstvo in Russia: An Experiment in*

Local Self-Government, ed. Terence Emmons and Wayne S. Vucinich. Cambridge, UK: Cambridge University Press.

Solomon, Susan, and Hutchinson, John F., eds. (1990). *Health and Society in Revolutionary Russia.* Bloomington: Indiana University Press.

Samuel C. Ramer

HEALTH CARE SERVICES, SOVIET

Soviet socialized medicine consisted of a complex of measures designed to provide free medical care to the entire population, at the time of service, at the expense of society. The Soviet Union was the first country in the world to grant every citizen a constitutional right to medical care. This commitment was one of the few brighter (and redeeming) aspects of an otherwise bleak totalitarian system and often held as an example to emulate by other nations. The promise of universal, free (though not necessarily equal) care was held as the fulfillment of an age-long dream of providing care to those who needed it regardless of their station in life and ability to pay. It thus promised to eliminate the commercial aspects of the medical encounter that, in the eyes of many, had turned the physician into a businessman concerned primarily with his income and his willingness to treat only those who were affluent.

In the first decade of the Soviet regime, the official ideology held that illness and premature mortality were the products of a faulty socioeconomic system (i.e., capitalism) and that the establishment of a socialist society (eventually to become communist) would gradually eliminate most of the social causes of disease and early deaths by creating improved conditions (better nutrition, decent standard of living, good working conditions, housing, and prevention). This approach was set aside when Stalin took power at the end of the 1920s. He launched a program of forced draft industrialization and militarization at the expense of the standard of living, with an emphasis on medical and clinical or remedial approach, rather than prevention, to maintain and repair the working and fighting capacity of the population. The number of health personnel and hospital beds increased substantially, though their quality was relatively poor, except for the elites.

Soviet socialized medicine was essentially a public and state enterprise. It was the state that provided the care. It was not an insurance system, nor a mix of public and private activities, nor was it a charitable or religious enterprise. The state assumed complete control of the financing of medical care. Soviet socialized medicine became highly centralized and bureaucratized, with the Health Ministry USSR standing at the apex of the medical pyramid. Physicians and other health personnel became state salaried employees. The state also financed and managed medical education, all health facilities from clinics to hospitals to rest homes, medical research, the production of pharmaceuticals, and medical technology. The system thus depended entirely on budgetary allocations as line items in the budget. More often than not, the health care system suffered from low priority and was financed on what came to be known as the residual principle. After all other needs had been met, whatever was left would go to health care. Most physicians (the majority of whom were women) were poorly paid compared to other occupations, and many medical facilities were short of funds to purchase equipment and supplies or to maintain them.

Access to care was stratified according to occupation, rank, and location. Nevertheless the population, by and large, looked upon the principle of socialized medicine as one of the more positive achievements of the Soviet regime and welfare system, and held to the belief that everyone was entitled to free care. Their major complaint was with the implementation of that principle. Soviet socialized medicine could be characterized as having a noble purpose, but with inadequate resources, flawed execution, and ending in mixed results.

See also: FELDSHER; HEALTHCARE SERVICES, IMPERIAL

BIBLIOGRAPHY

Field, Mark G. (1957). *Doctor and Patient in Soviet Russia.* Cambridge, MA: Harvard University Press.

Field, Mark G. (1967). *Soviet Socialized Medicine: An Introduction.* New York: The Free Press.

Field, Mark G., and Twigg, Judyth L., eds. (2000). *Russia's Torn Safety Nets: Health and Social Welfare During the Transition.* New York: St. Martin's Press.

Ryan, Michael. (1981). *Doctors and the State in the Soviet Union.* New York: St. Martin's Press.

Sigerist, Henry E. (1947). *Medicine and Health in the Soviet Union.* New York: Citadel Press.

Solomon, Susan Gross, and Hutchinson, John F., eds. (1990). *Health and Society in Revolutionary Russia.* Bloomington: Indiana University Press.

Mark G. Field

HEGEL, GEORG WILHELM FRIEDRICH

(1770–1831), leading nineteenth-century philosopher.

Georg Wilhem Friedrich Hegel was one of the most influential idealist philosophers of the nineteenth century. In German philosophical thought, Hegel was rivaled in his own times perhaps only by Immanuel Kant.

Hegel developed a sweeping spectrum of thought embracing metaphysics, epistemology, logic, historiography, science, art, politics, and society. One branch of his philosophy after his death was reworked and fashioned into an "algebra of revolution," as developed by Karl Marx and Friedrich Engels, Russian Marxists and socialists, and later by Vladimir I. Lenin, the founder of Bolshevism.

For Hegel, reality, which progresses dynamically through a process, or phases, of thesis, antithesis, and synthesis—his triadic concept of logic, inspired by the philosophy of Heraclitus—is essentially spiritual. Ultimate, determinant reality, according to Hegel, is the absolute World Spirit (*Weltgeist*). This spirit acts in triadic, dialectical fashion universally throughout world history. For Hegel, the state was the principal embodiment, or bearer, of this process.

Georg Wilhelm Friedrich Hegel influenced the writings of Karl Marx. © BETTMANN/CORBIS

Because of its occasional obscurity and complexity, Hegelianism as a social and political philosophy soon split into various, contrasting branches. The primary ones were the extremes widely known as Right and Left Hegelianism. There was also a middle, or moderate, form of Hegelianism that in some ways influenced English, Italian, American, and other branches of late-nineteenth-century idealism and pragmatism.

Right (or Old) Hegelianism regarded reality more or less passively, as indubitably rational. Whatever is real is rational, as seen in the status quo. Spirit, it alleged, develops on a grand, world scale via the inexorable, dialectical processes of history. Wherever this process leads must be logical since spirit is absolute and triadically law-bound. In the milieu of contrasting European politics of the nineteenth century, Right Hegelianism translated into reactionary endorsement of restorationism (restoring the old order following the French Revolution and the Napoleonic Wars) or support for monarchist legitimacy.

By contrast, however, Left (or Young) Hegelianism, which influenced a number of thinkers, including Marx and Engels together with Russian Marxists and socialists, stressed the idea of grasping and understanding, even wielding, this law-bound process. It sought thereby to manipulate reality, above all, via society, politics, and the state. For revolutionaries, the revolutionary movement became such a handle, or weapon.

Hegel had taught that there was an ultimate reality and that it was spiritual. However, when the young, materialist-minded Marx, under the influence of such philosophers as Feuerbach, absorbed Hegel, he "turned Hegel upside down," to use his collaborator Friedrich Engels's apt phrase. While retaining Hegelian logic and the historical process of the triadic dialectic, Marx, later Engels, and still later Lenin, saw the process in purely nonspiritual, materialistic, historical, and socioeconomic terms. This became the ideology, or science, of historical materialism and dialectical materialism as embraced by the Russian Marxist George Plekhanov and, thence, by Lenin—but in an interpretation of the ideology different from Plekhanov's.

In the Marx-Engels-Lenin-Stalin interpretation of Left Hegelianism, historical change, the motor of history as determined by the forces and processes within the given social and economic system, is law-bound and strictly predictable. As presented in historical materialism, the history of societies develops universally by stages—namely, from slavery, to feudalism, to capitalism, and finally to socialism, whose final stage is full-fledged communism.

Each stage, except the merged last two (socialism/communism), contains the seeds of its own destruction (or "contradictions") as the dialectical process of socioeconomic development spirals upward to the next historical stage. For instance, capitalism's antithesis is seen in the seeds of its own destruction together with the anticipation of the new synthesis of socialism/communism. Such seeds, said the Marxists, are capitalism's impoverishment of a majority of the exploited population, overproduction, unemployment, class struggle, economic collapse, and, inevitably, revolution.

Progressive elements of the former, capitalist order are then continued in new form in the final, socialist/communist phase. This assumes the form of industrialization, mass production, a just sociopolitical order (under a workers' dictatorship of the proletariat). In this formulation the Marxists developed the theory of base and superstructure. The base is the economic system; the superstructure are such facets of society as government, laws, religion, literature, and the arts. The superstructure both reflects and rationalizes the base.

Ultimately, under the dictatorship of the proletariat, state power, as described in the Marxist Critique of the Gotha Program, gradually withers away. The society is thence led into the final epoch of communism. In this final stage, a virtual millennium, there are no classes, no socioeconomic inequality, no oppression, no state, no law, no division of labor, but instead pure equality, communality, and universal happiness. Ironically, in contrast to Marx's formulation, the ultimate phase in Hegel's own interpretation of the dialectic in history was the Prussian state.

In Lenin's construction of Marxism, Hegelianism was given an extreme left interpretation. This is seen, among other places, in Lenin's "Philosophical Notebooks." In this work Lenin gives his own interpretation of Hegel. He indicates here and in other writings that absolute knowledge of the inevitable historical process is attainable—at least by those equipped to find it scientifically.

The leaders of the impending proletarian revolution, Lenin says in his 1903 work, *What Is to Be Done?*, become a select circle of intellectuals whose philosophy (derived from Marx and Hegel) equips them to assume exclusive Communist Party leadership of the given country. Lenin could imagine that such knowledge might allow a nation's (namely, Russia's) socioeconomic development to skip intermediate socioeconomic phases, or at least shorten them. In this way, the Russian Bolsheviks could lead the masses to the socialist/communist stage of development all but directly. This could be accomplished by reducing or suppressing the phase of bourgeois capitalism. (This Leninist interepretation of the dialectic has been criticized by other Marxists as running counter to Hegel's, and Marx's, own explanations of the dialectic.)

Thus, in Lenin's interpretation of Hegel and Marx, the dictatorship of the proletariat becomes the leader and teacher of society, the single indoctrinator whose absolute power (based on the people) saves the masses from the abuses of the contradictions of capitalist society, whether in rural or urban society, while guiding society to the final, communist phase.

See also: DIALECTICAL MATERIALISM; ENGELS, FRIEDRICH; LENIN, VLADIMIR ILICH; MARXISM

BIBLIOGRAPHY

Gregor, A. James. (1995). "A Survey of Marxism." In *The Oxford Companion to Philosophy*, ed. Ted Honderich. Oxford: Oxford University Press.

Hegel, Georg Wilhem Friedrich. (1967). *The Philosophy of Right*. Oxford: Clarendon.

Marx, Karl, and Engels, Friedrich. (1962). *Selected Works*. 2 vols. Moscow: Foreign Languages Pub. House.

Possony, Stefan T. (1966). *Lenin: The Compulsive Revolutionary*. London: Allen & Unwin.

Tucker, Robert C. (1972). *Philosophy and Myth in Karl Marx*, 2nd ed. Cambridge, UK: Cambridge University Press.

Weeks, Albert L. (1968). *The First Bolshevik: A Political Biography of Peter Tkachev*. New York: New York University Press.

Albert L. Weeks

HELSINKI ACCORDS

Signed at the Finnish capital of Helsinki on August 1, 1975, the Helsinki Accords were accepted by thirty-five participating nations at the first Conference on Security and Cooperation in Europe. The conference included all of the nations of Europe (excluding Albania), as well as the Soviet Union, the United States, and Canada. The Helsinki Accords had two noteworthy features. First, Article I formally recognized the post-World War II borders of Europe, which included an unwritten acknowledgement of the Soviet Union's control over the Baltic states of Estonia, Latvia, and Lithuania, which the USSR had annexed in 1940. Second, Article VII stated that "the participating States recognize the universal significance of human rights and fundamental freedoms." This passage, in theory, held the Soviet Union responsible for the maintenance and protection of basic human rights within its borders.

Although the Soviet government was never serious about conforming to the human rights parameters defined by the Helsinki Accords, the national leadership under General Secretary Leonid I. Brezhnev believed that its signing of the document would improve the Soviet Union's diplomatic position with the United States and other Western countries. Specifically, the state wished to foster the perception that it was as an equal player in the policy of *détente,* in which both superpowers sought to relax Cold War tensions. What the regime did not anticipate, however, was that those outside the Soviet Union, as well as many of the USSR's own citizens, would take the Accords seriously. Soon after the Soviet delegation returned from Finland, a number of human rights watchdog groups emerged to monitor the USSR's compliance with the Accords.

Among those organizations that arose after the signing of the accords was Helsinki Watch, founded in 1978 by a collection of Soviet dissidents including the notable physicist Andrei D. Sakharov and other human rights activists living outside the USSR. Helsinki Watch quickly became the best-known and most outspoken critic of Soviet human rights policies. This collection of activists and intellectuals later merged with similar organizations to form an association known as Human Rights Watch. Many members of both Helsinki Watch and Human Rights Watch who were Soviet citizens endured state persecution, including trial, arrest, and internal exile (e.g., Sakharov was exiled to the city of Gorky) from 1977 to 1980. Until the emergence of Mikhail S. Gorbachev as Soviet general secretary in 1985, independent monitoring of Soviet compliance with the accords from within the USSR remained difficult, although the dissidents of Helsinki Watch were never completely silenced. After the introduction of openness (glasnost) and restructuring (perestroika) under Gorbachev in the late 1980s, however, these individuals' efforts received much acclaim at home and abroad. The efforts of Helsinki Watch and its successor organizations served notice in an era of strict social control that the Soviet Union was accountable for its human rights obligations as specified by the Helsinki Accords.

See also: BREZHNEV, LEONID ILICH; DÉTENTE; DISSIDENT MOVEMENT; HUMAN RIGHTS

BIBLIOGRAPHY

Civnet: A Website of Civitas International. (2003). "The Helsinki Accords." <http://www.civnet.org/resources/document/historic/helsinki.htm>

Luxmoore, Jonathan. (1990). *Helsinki Agreement: Dialogue or Discussion?* New York: State Mutual Book and Periodical Service.

Nogee, Joseph and Donaldson, Robert, eds. (1992) *Soviet Foreign Policy since World War II,* 4th ed. New York: Macmillan.

Sakharov, Andrei D. (1978). *Alarm and Hope.* New York: Knopf.

CHRISTOPHER J. WARD

HERZEN, ALEXANDER IVANOVICH

(1812–1870), dissident political thinker and writer, founder of Russian populism.

Alexander Ivanovich Herzen was born in Moscow, the illegitimate son of a Russian aristocrat and his German-born mistress. His family name, derived from the German *herz* ("heart"), was given to him by his father. In 1825 Herzen was deeply affected by the Decembrist revolt that fueled his rejection of the Russian status quo. His early commitments were developed in the companionship he formed with a young relative, Nikolai Ogarev. In 1828 on the Vorobyevy Hills, they took a solemn oath of personal and political loyalty to each other.

While a student at Moscow University, Herzen became the center of gravity for a circle of critically-minded youth opposed to the existing social and moral order; in 1834 both Herzen and Ogarev were arrested for expressing their opinions in private. Herzen was exiled to Perm and later to Vyatka, where he worked as a clerk in the governor's office. A surprise encounter with the future tsar Alexander Nikolayevich (later Alexander II) led to his transfer to the city of Vladimir. There he found work as a journalist, and later received permission to reside in St. Petersburg. This, however, was soon followed by another period of exile that lasted until 1842. Meanwhile, Herzen's study and propagation of Hegelian philosophy became the cornerstone of his debates and intellectual alliances with radical Westernizers such as Vissarion Grigorievich Belinsky, moderates such as Timofey Nikolayevich Granovsky, and the early Slavophiles. He established himself as a prolific writer on issues such as the perils of excess specialization of knowledge, the promises and defaults of utopian socialism exemplified by Robert Owen (1771–1858) and Charles Fourier (1772–1837), the libertarian anarchism of Pierre-Joseph Proudhon (1809–1865), and, most of all, the purportedly socialist promise of the Russian peasant commune. This latter subject became the centerpiece of his thought and worldview; as set forth in his key work, *From the Other Shore* (1847–1848, coinciding with the appearance of Marx's *Communist Manifesto*), Herzen laid out the key arguments of Russian populism, arguing that the primordial collective morality of the commune must be preserved against the inroads of capitalism, and extolling Russia's opportunity to overtake the West on the path of social progress toward a just and equitable organization of society, without having to pass through the capitalist stage. Populism, as envisioned by Herzen, was to become one of the two main currents of Russia's revolutionary thought, alongside with Marxism. Each of these philosophical strains cross-fertilized and competed with the other.

In 1847, urged by Ogarev from abroad to escape the dictatorial regime of Nicholas I, Herzen managed to overcome political obstacles to his emigration and leave Russia, as it later turned out, forever. He traveled across continental Europe, witnessed the failure of the French Revolution of 1848, and invested in a radical newspaper edited by Proudhon that was soon to be shut down. He developed a bitter critique of European capitalism, which he denounced for its Philistine depravity and wickedness. In his view, even the promise of socialism was hardly a cure for corruption of what one would call today the consumer society. This new outlook reinforced the Russo-centric element of his populism (although never reconciling him with Russian domestic oppression), and was reflected in his major writings of the period, including *Letters from France and Italy*, published over the period from 1847 to 1854; *On the Development of Revolutionary Ideas in Russia*, published in 1851; and *Russian People and Socialism*, published in 1851.

In 1852 Herzen moved from Nice to London, which became his home until the end of his life. He set up the first publishing house devoted to Russian political dissent, printing revolutionary leaflets, his journal *Polyarnaya zvezda* (Polar Star), and, finally, his pivotal periodical, *Kolokol* (The Bell), which he published between 1857 and 1867. This brought Herzen great fame in Russia, where the liberal atmosphere of Alexander II's Great Reforms allowed Herzen's works to be distributed, albeit illicitly, across the country. *Kolokol*'s initial agenda advocated the emancipation of the serfs and played a major role in shaping social attitudes such that emancipation became inevitable.

Although living in London, Herzen often spoke out publicly on key issues of the day, addressing his remarks directly to Tsar Alexander II, at times positioning himself as a mediator between the authorities and the liberal and radical elements of Russian society, but identifying firmly with the latter. After 1861, however, his émigré politics were rapidly overtaken by growing radicalism within Russia, and he was increasingly treated with condescension by the younger activists as being out of touch with the new realities. The crackdown on the Polish rebellion by tsarist troops in 1863 and the ensuing conservative tilt in Russia marked the twilight of Herzen's public career. He died in Paris in 1870, and was buried in Nice. Over time he became a symbolic founding figure of Russia's democratic movement, broadly conceived to include its different and often widely divergent ideological and political traditions. In this, his reputation is similar to Pushkin's standing within Russian literature. He is best remembered for his ability to synthesize a variety of anti-authoritarian currents, from liberal and libertarian to revolutionary-socialist and Russophile populist, whose mutual contradictions were not as clearly evident in his time as they became in later years.

Among his many literary works, which range from fiction to philosophy and politics, the central place is occupied by *My Past and Thoughts*, which was written between 1852 and 1866. This is a personal, political, and intellectual autobiography, into which he injected a wide-ranging discussion and analysis of the major developments of his time in Russia and Europe.

See also: DISSIDENT MOVEMENT; POPULISM; SOCIALIST REVOLUTIONARIES; WESTERNIZERS

BIBLIOGRAPHY

Herzen, Alexander. (1979). *The Russian People and Socialism*, tr. Richard Wollheim. Oxford: Oxford University Press.

Herzen, Alexander. (1989). *From the Other Shore*, tr. Moura Budberg. Oxford: Oxford University Press.

Herzen, Alexander. (1999). *My Past and Thoughts*, tr. Constance Garnett. Berkeley: University of California Press.

Herzen, Alexander, and Zimmerman, Judith E. (1996). *Letters from France and Italy, 1847-1851.* Pitt Series in Russian and East European Studies, No 25. Pittsburgh: University of Pittsburgh Press.

Malia, Martin. (1961). *Alexander Herzen and the Birth of Russian Socialism, 1812–1855.* Cambridge: Harvard University Press.

Venturi Franco. (2001). *Roots of Revolution*, revised ed., tr. Francis Haskell. London: Phoenix Press.

Walicki, Andrzej. (1969). *The Controversy over Capitalism: Studies in the Social Philosophy of the Russian Populists.* Oxford: Clarendon Press.

DMITRI GLINSKI

HIGHER PARTY SCHOOL

The Higher Party School was created in 1939 under the Central Committee of the Communist Party of the Soviet Union. It was tasked with training future leaders (known in Soviet parlance as "cadres") for Party and state positions. The purpose was to prepare them for propaganda work with the masses and for supervising managers and state officials, while ensuring their political loyalty or *partynost* (Party-mindedness). In 1978 it was merged with the Academy of Social Sciences, which provided more advanced training. A similar Higher School was created for the Young Communist League (Komsomol) in 1969. Party officials under the age of forty were selected by the Communist Party and came to the main school in Moscow from across the Soviet Union for a two-year training program that was long on Marx, Lenin, and the latest Party edicts and short on practical skills. For leaders from the non-Russian republics, attendance provided important exposure to life in the Soviet capital. With the general erosion of ideology in the Brezhnev era, the Party became increasingly concerned about the efficacy of its ideological training, so funding for Party education was increased.

Selection for the school was an important step in the career ladder for would-be members of the higher Party *nomenklatura*. Living conditions at the school were comfortable, and it provided an opportunity to meet senior Party officials and to network with one's peers, connections that could be useful in one's future career. The Moscow school had about 120 faculty and 300 students per year; it also had 22 regional branches that ran shorter seminars and correspondence courses for Communist leaders at every level in the Party hierarchy, including the heads of regional and city councils (soviets). Some of these schools provided remedial education for Party cadres who had missed out on higher education. In the 1980s one in three of the regional (*obkom*) party secretaries had passed through the Higher Party School; its graduates included General Secretary Yuri Andropov. Ironically Vyacheslav Shostakovsky, the school's rector, was one of the leaders of the Democratic Platform movement that in 1990 called for the Communist Party to relinquish its monopoly of power. After the collapse of the Soviet Union, the network of Party schools turned themselves into colleges of management and public administration. The premises of the Higher Party School itself are now occupied by the Russian State Humanities University.

See also: CADRES POLICY; COMMUNIST PARTY OF THE SOVIET UNION

BIBLIOGRAPHY

Rutland, Peter. (1992). *The Politics of Economic Stagnation in the Soviet Union.* New York: Cambridge University Press.

PETER RUTLAND

HILARION, METROPOLITAN

(Eleventh century; exact dates unknown), first native of Rus to be metropolitan of Kiev, author of the *Sermon on Law and Grace.*

Very little biographical information is known about Hilarion. In the *Russian Primary Chronicle* under 1051 it is reported that Prince Yaroslav of Kiev assembled the bishops in St. Sophia Cathedral and appointed Hilarion, a Carpatho-Rusyn (native of Rus), as metropolitan bishop. He is described as a devout man, learned in the Scriptures, and an ascetic, who served as one of Yaroslav's priests in the church of the Holy Apostles at Berestovo, a favorite princely residence located just south of Kiev.

While a priest, Hilarion selected a spot on a hill above the Dnieper not far from Berestovo where he dug a small cave in which to chant the hours and pray to God in solitude. This cave was later occupied by Anthony of the Caves and served as the foundation for the Caves Monastery of Kiev. Hilarion was the first native of Rus to be metropolitan. The only other Carpatho-Rusyn to serve as metropolitan in Kievan Rus was Klim Smolyatich in the twelfth century. Scholars have long debated Yaroslav's motives for appointing Hilarion, and many maintain that the decision reflects an anti-Byzantine bias. There is no condemnation of the appointment in Byzantine sources, however, and Yaroslav's purpose remains unclear. There is much speculation but no concrete information for Hilarion's biography after his appointment. All that is known is that the *First Novgorod Chronicle* mentions a new metropolitan by 1055. Whether Hilarion's tenure survived his patron Yaroslav (d. 1054) is not known.

Hilarion's most significant contribution to Kievan culture is his *Sermon on Law and Grace.* A master of rhetoric and the oratorical tradition, Hilarion expressed the pride of his newly converted nation as it joined the Christian community, and celebrated its past achievements. Utilizing the familiar Biblical contrast between law and grace, Hilarion began by emphasizing the gift of grace through Christ, which ended humankind's subservience to the law and through which Rus was converted. In the second part of the sermon, Hilarion turned his attention to the apostle of Rus, Vladimir I, as well as to the works of his son, Yaroslav.

Scholars have often seen an anti-Jewish bias or evidence of a struggle with Byzantium in the sermon. There is little evidence of either, however, and it is best read as a sophisticated and effective attempt to establish the place of Rus in sacred history by moving from theological doctrine to the specific pious actions of the Kievan princes.

Although a number of works have been attributed to Hilarion, only the sermon and a confession of faith followed by a postscript can with any certainty be ascribed to his pen.

See also: CAVES MONASTERY; YAROSLAV VLADIMIROVICH

BIBLIOGRAPHY

Franklin, Simon. (1991). *Sermons and Rhetoric of Kievan Rus'.* Cambridge, MA: Ukrainian Research Institute of Harvard University.

The Russian Primary Chronicle: Laurentian Text. (1953). Edited and translated by Samuel Hazzard Cross and Olgerd. P. Sherbowitz-Wetzor. Cambridge, MA: The Mediaeval Academy of America.

David K. Prestel

HIS MAJESTY'S OWN CHANCERY

His Majesty's Own Chancery was formally founded by Paul I (r. 1796–1801) in 1796. Centralizing power further, Nicholas I (r. 1825–1855) greatly expanded the Chancery's power and role in government, placing it above the regular bureaucracy and under his direct control. As the Russian bureaucracy grew during the nineteenth century, the emperors struggled to maintain personal control over it and to have it carry out the imperial will. The Chancery was one solution to this problem. It provided a mechanism for greater monarchical control over government and society, and it gave the emperor the opportunity to bypass bureaucratic inertia.

In 1826 two departments were added to the Chancery. The First Section prepared documents and papers for the emperor's review and supervised the bureaucracy's personnel. The Second Section worked on the codification of the empire's laws, resulting in the publication in 1832 of *The Fundamental Laws of the Russian Empire.* After the death of Empress Maria Fedorovna in 1828, a Fourth Section was established to handle her sizeable charitable endowments. In 1836, a Fifth Section studied the conditions under which the state peasants lived, and implemented reforms designed to improve them. In contrast to serfs, who were owned by the nobility, state peasants belonged to the emperor, which gave the government greater flexibility in regard to reform. More importantly, its research became the basis for the emancipation of the serfs legislation that was passed by Alexander II in 1861. In 1842, a Sixth Section was charged with the establishment of Russian administrative control in the Caucasus. These last two sections had a relatively short existence, and were closed when the tasks assigned to them were completed.

The Third Section, founded in 1826, became the most famous—or infamous—part of the Chancery, because of its police and supervisory functions that were equivalent to an internal intelligence service. It was a relatively effective state organ for the collection and analysis of information and for the implementation of the emperor's will. Five subsections handled wide ranging duties. The first of these was the most secret, and probably the most important from the government's point of view. It conducted investigations into political crimes, and maintained surveillance of society, and it kept watch on groups and individuals that were deemed politically unreliable. After the revolutions of 1848 in several European countries, its activities intensified, reflecting the government's, and Nicholas's, growing fear of penetration of radical revolutionary ideas into Russia. A second subsection handled corruption and crime within the state apparatus. The third kept an eye on foreigners living in Russia. The fourth managed and controlled relations between peasants and landowners. Censorship and control over printed matter was assigned to the fifth subsection.

The Third Section also had an executive body known as the Gendarme Corps, who were personal representatives of the emperor. Members of the corps were assigned to individual governorships and large cities, where they played the role of arbiter between society and local governments while supervising both. The corps provided the emperor with reliable information on the condition of his empire. Nicholas could not completely control the bureaucratic machine that was his Chancery, however. For example, the Third Section maintained surveillance on the heir to the throne, Grand Duke Konstantin Nikolaevich, illegally and without his or the emperor's knowledge.

In the 1880s, the Chancery underwent serious reorganization. Many of its functions were transferred to the ministries and the central bureaucracy. The Ministry of the Interior took over many of the responsibilities of the Third Section. The Gendarme Corps remained in existence until 1917 as an elite police force, but its central position did not survive after the death of Nicholas I. By the reign of Nicholas II, His Majesty's Own Chancery handled only questions related to promotions and pensions of bureaucrats.

See also: NICHOLAS I

BIBLIOGRAPHY

Lincoln, W. Bruce. (1978). *Nicholas I: Emperor and Autocrat of all the Russias.* London: Indiana University Press.

Saunders, David. (1992). *Russia in the Age of Reaction and Reform.* London: Routledge.

Seton-Watson, Hugh. (1991). *The Russian Empire 1801–1917.* Oxford: Oxford University Press.

Yaney, George. (1973). *The Systemization of Russian Government.* Urbana: University of Illinois Press.

ZHAND P. SHAKIBI

HISTORICAL SONGS

Folklorists apply this term to certain Russian oral epic songs tracing to a later period than the type of the bylina and dealing with known historical persons and events. Although Soviet specialists attempted to find earlier examples, the historical song as people know it most probably arose in Muscovy in the sixteenth century; the first clear examples have to do with the reign of Tsar Ivan IV but appear to have been composed somewhat after it. Historical songs are typically shorter than the bylina but continue many features of oral epic composition, including prosody. In place of the larger-than-life *bogatyr*, the hero of a historical song is often a common soldier or cossack. In this folklore genre from a relatively late period observers have one of their best opportunities to see how historical events became adapted and transformed in the minds of simple Russian people. What they produced were imaginative, poetic treatments of problems, persons, and happenings.

Two outstanding songs concerning Ivan the Terrible and known in many collected variants are those called "The Conquest of Kazan" and "The Wrath of Ivan the Terrible against His Son." Both stress the dangerous anger of the tsar, which may explode suddenly like the gunpowder that breached the wall of Kazan during the Russian siege of 1552. In the second instance it is turned against his own son, a tsarevich whom he suspects of treason. The offending parties have to be saved by a third person who risks his own life by speaking up to the tsar and is the real hero of the song. Historians have tried to associate "The Wrath of Ivan the Terrible against His Son" with the sack of Novgorod in 1570, but the imperfect fit with history brings out the fact that songs often embodied only a popular conception of the spirit of events. Ivan IV emerges as both a fearful and a respected ruler.

Seventeenth-century historical songs include themes associated with the Time of Troubles: the supposed murder of Tsarevich Dmitry, a lament of Ksenia Godunova, the rise of pretender Grishka Otrepiev, the assassination of Mikhailo Skopin-Shuisky. Stenka Razin's reputation naturally inspired a number of songs later in the century. From the eighteenth century, there is a cycle about Peter the Great that depicts him as a people's tsar who mingled with the common folk. A development from the historical songs were the so-called cossack songs and soldier songs, usually still shorter and sung rather than chanted. Although examples of historical songs are claimed even from the mid-nineteenth century, the genre was clearly dying out.

See also: BYLINA; FOLKLORE; FOLK MUSIC; MUSIC

BIBLIOGRAPHY

Chadwick, N. Kershaw. (1964). *Russian Heroic Poetry*, reprint ed. New York: Russell & Russell.

Stief, Carl. (1953). *Studies in the Russian Historical Song.* Copenhagen: Rosenkilde & Bagger.

NORMAN W. INGHAM

HISTORIOGRAPHY

Historiography is the writing of history, the aggregation of historical compositions. The establishment of history as a modern scholarly discipline in Russia dates back to the end of the seventeenth and the first half of the eighteenth centuries. At the order of Peter the Great, the accumulation of historical sources began with the translation of works of Western European historians such as Samuel Pufendorf. Compositions that justified the tsar's activity and, in particular, the reasons behind the Northern War were recounted by Peter's companions, including Feofan Prokopovich and Petr Shafirov. The eminent Russian statesman and Historian of the first half of the eighteenth century, Vassily Tatischev, was influenced by rationalism. He understood history as a political history of the country. In *Istoriia Rossiiskaia* (Russian History, published after his death), he provided, for the first time, the classification of the periods of Russian history.

German historians were invited to work at the Academy of Sciences in the 1730s and 1740s, and they had a great impact on Russian historiography. Three of these Germans were particularly important: Gerhard Friedrich Müller and Gottlieb Siegfried Bayer, who formulated what is known as Norman theory, and August Ludwig Schlözer, who tried to reconstruct the original text of the earliest Russian chronicle, *Povest Vremennykh Let* (The Primary Russian Chronicle), in his work titled *Nestor*.

Also important were the works of Major General Ivan Boltin, written in the 1780s and 1790s. Boltin proposed the idea of a comparative method of studying history, an approach that would take into account the cause-and-effect connection between historical events. A great impact on social conscience was made by Nikolai Karamzin's *Istoriia Gosudarstva Rossiiskogo* (The history of the Russian state), published in twelve volumes between 1816 and 1829. This work was sold in enormous quantities, according to the time's standards. While working on the *History*, Karamzin developed the modern Russian language. According to Alexander Pushkin, Russia was discovered by Karamzin, like America was discovered by Columbus. Methodologically, however, the belles-lettres style of Karamzin's work did not suit the standards of historical science of the time. Karamzin proved that autocracy was vital for Russia, having proposed the thesis that the history of the people belongs to the tsar.

As a counterweight to Karamzin's history of the state, publisher and journalist Nikolai Polevoi tried to create *Istoriia Russkogo Naroda* (A History of the Russian People), but he could not cope with the task. Instead of the history of society, his six-volume work, published between 1829 and 1833, was yet another version of the history of state power. He was unable to break away from the convention of organizing the material by ruling periods.

In the nineteenth century, historiography became professional, and a majority of historical works were now created by scholars at universities. The development of Russian historiography was greatly affected by the philosophy of Georg Hegel and the works of German historians, especially the representatives of the German historical law school. From 1840 through the 1860s, in the works of Konstantin Kavelin, Sergei Soloviev, and Boris Chicherin, the Russian state (judicial) school of historiography was formed. According to the views of the historians of the Russian state school, Russia differed markedly from the West, where social development came from the bottom. In Russia, according to this view, the organizer of society, classes, and the relations between classes was the state. The society was typically weak, unorganized, and movable, which was supported by the geographical distribution of Russian people on the Western European plain, a circumstance that provided for no natural borders. For Kavelin, the state acted as a creator of history.

The theoretical views of historians of the state school were most fully embodied in the *Istoriia*

Rossii S Drevneishikh Vremen (History of Russia from Ancient Times), published in twenty-nine volumes between 1851 and 1879. This work was written by the greatest Russian historian, Sergei Mikhailovich Soloviev. His conception was characterized by the perception of the inner organic pattern of the historical process, defined by objective, primarily geographical, factors and of the state, as the supreme embodiment of the history of the people. He believed the most important factor of Russian history to be its colonization, and he saw the breakthrough in Russian history to be the reign of Peter the Great, who put Russia on the path to Europeanization.

As a counterweight to the members of the state school, referred to as Westernizers, who believed that Russia was developing the same way as Western Europe, Slavophiles (among them Ivan and Konstantin Aksakov and Ivan and Petr Kireyevsky) believed that Russia's development was independent and self-directed, and that Peter the Great's reforms were artificial. They believed that it was necessary to return to the policies of the seventeenth century, when the tsar had the power of rule and the people had the power of opinion. They were influenced by German Romanticism, especially as expressed in Friedrich Schelling's philosophy. Slavophiles did not create any significant historical works other than Ivan Belyaev's *Krestiane na Rusi* (Peasants in Russia), published in 1860.

In the second half of the nineteenth century, more and more works of Russian historians concerned the socioeconomic problems, the history of peasants and serfdom, and peasant communes. The eminent historian of this time period was Vasily Osipovich Klyuchevsky, who replaced his teacher, Soloviev, in the Department of Russian History at the Moscow University. Klyuchevsky believed that Russian history developed under the influence of various factors, geographical, economic, social, and political. Klyuchevsky's great influence is partly explained by the brilliant style of his works, especially his lectures *Kurs Russkoii Istorii* (A Course of Russian History), first printed in 1880 as lithographs, appearing in five bound volumes between 1904 and 1921. He was known for his deeply psychological approach, and his portraits of Russian historical figures are still unmatched. Klyuchevsky was skeptical of Peter the Great's reforms, believing them to be chaotically organized and prompted by the needs of the Northern War.

Klyuchevsky's school became the leading school in Russian historiography of the late nineteenth and early twentieth centuries. The members of this school included Paul Milyukov, Alexander Kizevetter, Mikhail Lubavsky, Mikhail Bogoslovsky, and others. Methodological searches were typical for Russian historians of that time: they were affected by ideas of neopositivism (Miliukov), neokantianism (Alexander Lappo-Danilevsky), and Marxism (Mikhail Tugan-Baranovksy, Petr Struve). The more popular general work on the history of Russia published in this period was Milyukov's *Ocherki Po Istorii Russkoii Kultury* (Essays on the History of Russian Culture), which came out in several parts from 1896 to 1903. Milyukov formed a thesis about the simplicity and slowness of Russia's historical process, and of the structure of Russian history as having been built from the top down. Standing apart from the supporters of Russia's independent historical process, Nikolai Pavlov-Silvansky tried to prove its similarity to the Western European experience, postulating the presence of feudalism in medieval Russia in his *Feodalizm v Drevnei Rusi* (Feudalism in Old Russia) published in 1907.

For the Moscow school generalizations were typical, but the historians of the St. Petersburg school (Konstantin Bestuzhev-Riumin, Sergei Platonov, Lappo-Danilevsky, and others) paid special attention to publication and the analysis of earlier historical sources.

In general, Russian historiography of the early twentieth century blossomed early, but this ended abruptly with the October Revolution of 1917. After the Bolsheviks prohibited the teaching of history in schools and dismantled the historical departments in universities, the last citadel of non-Marxist historiography was the Academy of Sciences, but after the so-called Academic Affair and mass repressions against historians from 1929 to 1931, the Marxist-Leninist school of historiography became supreme in the USSR.

See also: KARAMZIN, NIKOLAI MIKHAILOVICH KLYUCHEVSKY, VASILY OSIPOVICH

BIBLIOGRAPHY

Byrnes, Robert F. (1995). *V. O. Kliuchevsky: Historian of Russia.* Bloomington: Indiana University Press.

Mazour, Anatole. (1975). *Modern Russian Historiography.* Westport, CT: Greenwood Press.

Sanders, Tomas, ed. (1999). *Historiography of Imperial Russia.* Armonk, NY: M. E. Sharp.

Vernadsky, George. (1978). *Russian Historiography: A History.* Belmont, MA: Nordland.

OLEG BUDNITSKII

HOLY ALLIANCE

The Holy Alliance is the name given to the treaty signed on September 26, 1815, in Paris by the monarchs of Austria, Prussia, and Russia. Its maker and prime mover was Tsar Alexander I. In 1815 after the downfall of Napoleon, Alexander was at the height of his powers. A romantic, an idealist, indeed something of an evangelical who had experienced a religious conversion in 1812, Alexander had fallen under the influence of a spiritualist, Baroness Julie von Krüdener, the wife of one of his diplomats, and the alliance was the product of nightly prayer meetings between the two. The alliance called upon the three powers to deal with one other and with their peoples on the basis of the Christian Gospel so there could emerge a fraternal union of rulers and peoples that would forever rid the earth of the scourge of war. At the insistence of the Austrian chancellor, Klemens von Metternich, Alexander's ally in the war against Napoleon, "fraternal" was struck out and changed to "a paternal alliance of monarchs over their peoples," lest the former clause be interpreted by Russia in a manner that would conflict with the language of other treaties under negotiation at this time.

Two common criticisms of the Holy Alliance are that its members (which in time included most the sovereigns of Europe) forged it into an instrument of oppression against their subjects, and, more important, that Alexander used it as a base to attain hegemony in Europe. Neither criticism is persuasive. The first can be challenged on factual grounds. The aspirations of the overwhelming majority of Europeans in the aftermath of the devastation of the Napoleonic Wars ran to one thing and one thing only: peace. National rights, national liberties, and the like were at this time simply not matters of priority. Moreover, the Holy Alliance powers exercised considerable restraint after 1815, as demonstrated by the extent to which they allowed multiple revolutionary fuses to be lit before they stepped in—in a real sense they allowed revolutions to explode (the Spanish and Italian revolutions of 1820–1821; the revolutions in France, Belgium, the Papal States, and Poland in 1830–1831; those in France, Germany, Austria, and Italy in 1848). Similarly, the argument that Alexander was bent on expansion in Europe overlooks the many things he did that pulled the opposite way. With a combination of threats and persuasion, he forced Prussia from the path of aggrandizement in Poland and onto that of cooperation with Austria. He resisted repeated appeals from the smaller German states for an anti-Austrian alliance—a move that he believed would be inimical to the interests of the general peace. Finally, he continually urged Russians to respect Turkish interests in the Balkans and especially in Greece. The fact is that Alexander was a committed moderate statesman who happened to believe what he said, and what he said illustrates a point often forgotten by historians and political scientists—that there is a place in the international system for principles and moral values.

See also: NAPOLEON I; VIENNA, CONGRESS OF

BIBLIOGRAPHY

Knapton, Ernest John. (1939). *The Lady of the Holy Alliance: The Life of Julie de Krüdener.* New York: Columbia University Press.

Nicolson, Harold. (1946). *The Congress of Vienna: A Study in Allied Unity, 1812–1822.* New York: Harcourt, Brace.

Schroeder, Paul. (1994). *The Transformation of European Politics, 1763–1848.* Oxford: Oxford University Press.

DAVID WETZEL

HOLY SYNOD

The governing body of the Russian Orthodox Church from 1721 to 1917.

On January 25, 1721, Peter the Great formally established an Ecclesiastical College to rule and reform the Russian Orthodox Church. This new governing body was renamed the Most Holy Governing Synod at its first session in February and replaced the former office of Patriarch, which had been in abeyance since the death of the last incumbent, Adrian, in 1700. The creation of the Synod, modeled after the state-controlled synods of the Lutheran church, was an integral part of Peter's wider program for the reform of Russia's secular administrative and military machine, a program aimed at improving efficiency, eradicating abuses, and, above all, increasing the Sovereign's control of revenue.

The Synod was entrusted with the administration of all church affairs. A governing statute called the Ecclesiastical Regulation was written by Archbishop Feofan Prokopovich, with amendments by Peter. According to the statute, the Synod was to have twelve clerical members appointed by the tsar, although in practice there were always fewer. Despite the powers granted by the statute, ecclesiastical authority was effectively reduced in 1722 when Peter created the office of over-procurator to oversee the Synod. The over-procurator was to be a lay official whose chief duty was to be the Sovereign's "eye," to "ensure that the Synod does its duty." In theory the Synod was meant to be equal to its secular counterpart, the Senate, but in reality ecclesiastical government had very little autonomy and was firmly subordinate to the tsar. Collegial administration guaranteed the Sovereign firmer control over the church than patriarchal administration had allowed, and removed the challenge to the tsar's authority that a patriarch had represented.

Despite the formal recognition of the Synod in 1723 by four Eastern patriarchs, Russian clergy resented the abolition of Russia's patriarchate, the domination of the Synod by Peter's handpicked foreign clergy, and the interference in church affairs by the over-procurator. Nonetheless, attempts to restore the patriarchate after Peter's death in 1725 failed. Instead, the office of over-procurator (in abeyance from 1726) was restored in 1741, gaining exclusive access to the tsar in 1803. From 1824 the over-procurator exercised effective authority over all aspects of church administration and held ministerial rank. The best-known incumbent, Konstantin Petrovich Pobedonostsev (1880–1905), was able to wield far-reaching influence during his procuratorship.

After the election of the First Imperial Duma in 1905, deputies began to voice concern over the Synod's subservience to the procurator and tsar, but only after Nicholas II's abdication could steps be taken to restore the autonomy of the church. In July 1917 the Provisional Government abolished the post of over-procurator and invited the Synod to call elections to a council to decide the future of church administration. In November 1917 a council of 564 delegates reestablished the patriarchate and elected Metropolitan Tikhon of Moscow as Patriarch of All Russia, thus bringing to an end Peter the Great's system of Synodal governance.

See also: ORTHODOXY; PETER I; POBEDONOSTSEV, KONSTANTIN

BIBLIOGRAPHY

Cracraft, James. (1971). *The Church Reform of Peter the Great.* Stanford, CA: Stanford University Press.

Freeze, Gregory. (1983). *The Parish Clergy in the Nineteenth Century.* Princeton, NJ: Princeton University Press.

Hughes, Lindsey. (1998). *Russia in the Age of Peter the Great.* New Haven, CT: Yale University Press.

DEBRA A. COULTER

HOMELESS CHILDREN

Homeless children, or *besprizorniki*, constituted one of the most vexing social problems facing the new Soviet state, caused by cumulative effects of World War I (1914–1917), the Russian Revolution and Civil War (1918–1921), and cold, hunger, and disease, which claimed the lives of millions of parents. The catastrophic famine of 1921 and 1922 produced millions of additional orphaned and abandoned children. Divorce, single motherhood, unemployment, and economic dislocation pushed surviving children out on the streets. By 1922, historian Alan Ball estimates, there were seven million homeless children in Russia.

These homeless children represented a profound crisis for the Bolshevik government. They roamed the country alone and in groups, often following rail arteries to Moscow, Rostov-on-the-Don, Samara, Saratov, Tashkent, and other cities. Seemingly omnipresent waifs begged for food in train stations and other public places. Most resorted to stealing, petty crimes, and prostitution. The state sent children to special homes (*detdoma*), long-term boarding institutions run by the Commissariat of Enlightenment (Narkompros). Initially intended to offer programs capable of instilling in the waifs an instinct for the collective and preparing them to join the ranks of the proletariat, these children's homes were overwhelmed by the sheer volume of homeless children. Many children's homes lacked food and heat and were rife with dysentery, scurvy, and syphilis. Countless children escaped from these institutions, preferring to take their chances on the streets. Labor communes, most notably the secret police's Dzerzhinsky Labor Commune run by Anton Makarenko, sought to rehabilitate young delinquents and met with mixed success.

Convinced that socialized child rearing was an impossible ideal, the state, beginning in 1925, shifted its focus back to the family as the basic unit for social structure. The 1926 Family Code emphasized the family as a unit for effecting social change rather than the state; thousands of besprizorniki left state-funded children's homes and were adopted. By 1927 besprizorniki were considered less a pedagogical than a social problem stemming from the breakdown of the Soviet family. Increasingly, the state relied on punishment rather than pedagogy to clear the streets of besprizorniki, ordering militia sweeps of the children in the 1930s. The problem of homeless children did not go away; collectivization and the famine of 1932 and 1933 produced another wave of homeless children. Most of these besprizorniki were placed in children's homes and special schools for young delinquents. The number of homeless children continued to increase during times of severe social strain, notably World War II and the collapse of the Soviet Union, though not on the scale that the country witnessed in the 1920s.

See also: FAMILY CODE OF 1926

BIBLIOGRAPHY

Ball, Alan M. (1994). *And Now My Soul Is Hardened: Abandoned Children in Soviet Russia, 1918–1930.* Berkeley: University of California Press.

Goldman, Wendy. (1993). *Women, the State and Revolution: Soviet Family Policy and Social Life, 1917–1936.* Cambridge, UK: Cambridge University Press.

Stevens, Jennie. (1982). "Children of the Revolution: Soviet Russia's Homeless Children (Besprizorniki) in the 1920s." *Russian History* 9(2–3):242–264.

Stolee, Margaret Kay. (1988). "Homeless Children in the USSR, 1917–1957." *Soviet Studies* 40:64–83.

JACQUELINE M. OLICH

HONOR AND DISHONOR *See* BESCHESTIE.

HRUSHEVSKY, MIKHAIL SERGEYEVICH

(1866–1934), prominent Ukrainian historian and statesman.

In 1890 Mikhail Hrushevsky graduated from Kiev University, where he studied under Volodymyr Antonovych. In 1894 he was appointed to the newly created chair of Ukrainian history at Lviv University (at the time, in the Austro-Hungarian Empire). While in Lviv, Hrushevsky reorganized the Shevchenko Scientific Society (est. 1873) into an equivalent of a Ukrainian Academy of Sciences, founded new scholarly journals, and established his school of Ukrainian history. After the 1905 Revolution Hrushevsky lived in St. Petersburg and Kiev, where he became increasingly involved in liberal politics. In Kiev he founded the Ukrainian Scientific Society (1907), as well as a cluster of journals and newspapers. Arrested and exiled to eastern Russia during World War I, Hrushevsky emerged after the February Revolution as a recognized leader of moderate Ukrainian nationalists. In March 1917 he was elected president of the Central Rada (Council), which eventually developed into a Ukrainian parliament. During the Revolution Hrushevsky moved to the left and joined the Ukrainian Party of Socialist Revolutionaries, which had a majority in the Rada. On the last day of its existence, April 29, 1918, the Rada elected Hrushevsky president of the Ukrainian People's Republic.

Hrushevsky lived abroad after 1919, but returned to Soviet Ukraine in 1924 and soon resumed his role as the dean of Ukrainian historians. But the authorities increasingly criticized his scholarship as nationalistic and in 1931 transferred him to Moscow. By the time of his death in 1934, his school in Soviet Ukraine was destroyed by arrests and condemnations. Hrushevsky's main scholarly achievement is his monumental *History of Ukraine-Rus'* (10 vols., 1898-1937) covering the period until 1658. He also authored several short surveys of Ukrainian history and a five-volume *History of Ukrainian Literature.* Rejecting the history of state formations in favor of the history of the people, Hrushevsky criticized traditional Russian historical models and was influential in claiming Kievan Rus as a part of Ukrainian history. In contrast to Hrushevsky's denigration by the Soviet ideologues as a bourgeois nationalist, in post-Soviet Ukraine Hrushevsky is lauded as the nation's greatest historian and statesman.

See also: UKRAINE AND UKRAINIANS

BIBLIOGRAPHY

Hrushevs'kyi, Mykhailo. (1993–). *History of Ukraine-Rus'*, vols. 1, 7, 8. Edmonton: Canadian Institute of Ukrainian Studies Press.

Hrushevs'kyi, Mykhailo (1941). *A History of Ukraine.* New Haven, CT: Yale University Press.

Prymak, Thomas M. (1987). *Mykhailo Hrushevsky: The Politics of National Culture.* Toronto: University of Toronto Press.

SERHY YEKELCHYK

HUMAN RIGHTS

Human rights are the rights individuals are said to have as human beings. They are claims on society—its members and government (Henkin, 1996). They are spelled out in international law, drawing on the norms of the Universal Declaration of Human Rights (1948) (Steiner and Alston, 2000). Russia has a long history of authoritarian rule and human rights abuses. Nikolai Berdyayev went so far as to connect the depth and longevity of Russian communism, a system inimical to human rights, to this persistent culture of despotism (1960). In the vivid phrasing of Alexander Radishchev, an eighteenth-century dissident, in his *Journey from Saint Petersburg to Moscow* (which landed him in Siberia), the rigid censorship under Catherine the Great resembled a restrictive nursemaid who stunts children's growth toward self-reliant maturity.

Human rights improved somewhat thanks to the liberating effects of Russia's rapid industrialization after the emancipation of the serfs in 1861 and the judicial and local government reforms in 1864. In Tsarist Russia by 1914, a liberal and democratic socialist professional class of educators, lawyers, judges, social workers, women's rights advocates, and rapidly growing and mainly non-Bolshevik political parties increasingly demanded the protection of individual rights and a law-governed state. That meant broadening the selective westernization, launched two hundred years earlier by Peter the Great and aimed at strengthening Russia, to include the rights and freedoms he and his successors generally sought to exclude.

Following the abdication of Nicholas II in March 1917, the Provisional Government of March–November 1917 produced what the Bolshevik leader Vladimir Lenin himself called the freest country in Europe, before he and his minority party of Bolsheviks forcibly ended that freedom by sharply curbing human rights.

The Bolsheviks socially cleansed Russia's reformed courts, democratic professionals, and growing autonomous civil society. They held Russia to the constitutional principles that rights must serve the cause of socialism as interpreted by the Communist Party. Vladimir Lenin's death in 1924 opened the way to the consolidation of total power by Josef Stalin, his forced collectivization of the peasants, his five-year plans for heavy industrialization, and his purges of alleged enemies of the people.

The cultural thaw after Stalin's death in March 1953 ended with the ousting of Party leader Nikita Khrushchev in 1964. Ensuing trials of social satirists and critics sparked a courageous dissident movement in Russia, Ukraine, and elsewhere. Its members, who were promptly imprisoned or exiled, included Andrei Sakharov, proponent of East-West convergence; Yuri Orlov and the Moscow Helsinki Group; and Alexander Solzhenitsyn, chronicler of Soviet labor camps.

Mikhail Gorbachev, Soviet leader from March 1985 to December 1991, introduced *glasnost*—openness or free expression—and soon after, *perestroika*—attempts at economic and political reform. Gorbachev freed political prisoners and exiles between 1986 and 1989. His UN speech of December 7, 1988, praised the once spurned Universal Declaration of Human Rights and revised the 1977 Constitution accordingly. But he reformed too little too late. Four months after his near-overthrow in the August 1991 coup by his own reactionary appointees, the Soviet Union split into three once-again independent Baltic republics and twelve newly independent states, including the Russian Federation.

Boris Yeltsin, Russian president from 1991 until his resignation in 1999, forced on Russia the 1993 Constitution increasing presidential power but also containing Article 2: "The individual and his rights and freedom are the highest value. The recognition, observance and defense of the human rights and freedoms of the individual and the citizen are the obligation of the state." The Constitution proclaims a broad range of civil, political, social, and economic rights. Contrasting realities under overbearing and corrupt state administrations infringed on freedom of expression, religion, fair and humane justice, freedom of movement, and freedom from racial, ethnic, and homophobic bigotry, and hate crimes. Moreover, during the wars to retain Chechnya just about every human right was violated. Inequality, poverty, and homelessness haunted the land while the new rich lived high. Women experienced inequality and exploitation in employment, widespread divorce, abandonment, and domestic violence, and trafficking into prostitution. Life expectancy fell to third-world levels, especially among men, owing to stress, accidents, alcoholism, and the pervasive inadequacy of health care (Juviler, 2000; Human Rights Watch).

Such political and social human rights violations prompted the formation of numerous free but under-funded human rights advocacy groups—

nongovernmental organizations. They ranged from Russian Soldiers' Mothers, who were against the wide abuses of military recruits, to the anti-Stalinist and pro-rights Memorial Society, to Muslim cultural and aid societies.

Seventy years of Communist social and legal cleansing are not overcome in a decade or two. In Ken Jowitt's words, "We must think of a 'long march' rather than a simple transition to democracy" (Jowitt, 1992, 189), with all sorts of human rights to redeem.

See also: DISSIDENT MOVEMENT; GULAG; SAKHAROV, ANDREI DMITRIEVICH; SOLZHENITSYN, ALEXANDER ISAYEVICH

BIBLIOGRAPHY

Berdiaev, Nicolas. (1960). *The Origin of Russian Communism.* Ann Arbor: University of Michigan Press.

Henkin, Louis. (1996). *The Age of Rights*, 2nd ed. New York: Columbia University Press.

Human Rights Watch World Report. (2003). <http://www.hrw.org/wr2kr/europe11.html>.

Jowitt, Ken. (1992). *New World Disorder: The Leninist Extinction.* Berkeley: University of California Press.

Juviler, Peter. (1998). *Freedoms Ordeal: The Struggle for Human Rights and Democracy in Post-Soviet States.* Philadelphia: University of Pennsylvania Press.

Juviler, Peter. (2000). "Political Community and Human Rights in Post-Communist Russia." In *Human Rights: New Perspectives, New Realities*, ed. Adamantia Pollis and Peter Schwab. Boulder, CO: Lynne Reinner.

Steiner, Henry, and Alston, Philip. (2000). *International Human Rights in Context: Law, Politics, Morals*, 2nd ed. New York: Oxford University Press.

PETER JUVILER

HUNGARIAN REVOLUTION

The Hungarian Revolution of 1956 was the first major anti-Soviet uprising in Eastern Europe and the first shooting war to occur between socialist states. In contrast to earlier uprisings after the death of Soviet leader Joseph Stalin in March 1953, such as the workers' revolt in East Berlin (1953) and the Polish workers' rebellion in Poznan, Poland (October 1956), the incumbent Hungarian leader, Imre Nagy, did not summon Soviet military troops to squelch the revolution. Instead, he attempted to withdraw Hungary from the Warsaw Pact. Hence, the Hungarian revolution symbolizes perhaps the first major "domino" to fall in a process that ultimately resulted in the Soviet Union's loss of hegemony over Eastern Europe in 1989.

When Stalin's successor, Nikita Khrushchev, delivered his Secret Speech at the Twentieth Party Congress in February 1956, he not only exposed Stalin's crimes, but also presented himself as a proponent of different paths to socialism, a claim that would later prove hard to fulfill. All over Eastern Europe, hardline Stalinist leaders wondered fearfully how far destalinization would go. Meanwhile, their opponents, who criticized Stalinist policies, suddenly gained in popularity. In Hungary, Nagy was one such critic and reformer. He had served as Hungary's prime minister from July 4, 1953, to April 18, 1955. In the spring of 1955, however, Nagy was dislodged by a hard-line Stalinist leader, Mátyás Rákosi, who had been forced to cede that post to Nagy in mid-1953.

Social pressures continued to build in Hungary under the leadership of Rákosi, called Stalin's "best disciple" by some. He had conducted the anti-Yugoslav campaign in 1948 and 1949 more zealously than other East European party leaders. Hundreds of thousands of Hungarian communists had been executed or imprisoned after 1949. By late October 1956 the popular unrest in Hungary eluded the control of both the Hungarian government led by Rákosi's successor, Ernõ Gerõ, and the USSR.

On October 23, 1956, several hundred thousand people demonstrated in Budapest, hoping to publicize their sixteen-point resolution and to show solidarity with Poland where, in June, an industrial strike originating in Poznan turned into a national revolt. The Budapest protesters demanded that Nagy replace Gerõ, the Hungarian Communist Party's first secretary from July 18 to October 25, 1956. Fighting broke out in Budapest and other Hungarian cities and continued throughout the night.

It is now known that Soviet leaders decided on October 23 to intervene militarily. Soviet troops executed Plan *Volna* ("Wave") at 11:00 P.M. that same day. The next morning a radio broadcast announced that Nagy had replaced András Hegedüs as prime minister. On October 25, János Kádár, a younger, centrist official, replaced Gerõ as first secretary. However, this first Soviet intervention did not solve the original political problem in the country. New documents have revealed that the Kremlin initially decided on October 28 against a

Russian tanks and armored vehicles surround the Hungarian parliament building in Budapest. © HULTON ARCHIVE

second military intervention. But on October 31, they reversed course and launched a more massive intervention (Operation *Vikhr*, or "Whirlwind"). During the night of November 3, sixteen Soviet divisions entered Hungary. Fighting continued until mid-November, when Soviet forces suppressed the resistance and installed a pro-Soviet government under Kádár.

See also: HUNGARY, RELATIONS WITH; KHRUSHCHEV, NIKITA SERGEYEVICH;

BIBLIOGRAPHY

Békés, Csaba; Rainer, János M.; and Byre, Malcolm. (2003). *The 1956 Hungarian Revolution: A History in Documents.* Budapest: Central European University Press.

Cox, Terry, ed. (1997). *Hungary 1956—Forty Years On.* London: Frank Cass.

Granville, Johanna. (2003). *The First Domino: International Decision Making in the Hungarian Crisis of 1956.* College Station: Texas A & M University Press.

Györkei, Jenõ, and Horváth, Miklós. (1999). *The Soviet Military Intervention in Hungary, 1956.* Budapest: Central European University Press.

Litván, György, and Bak, János M. (1996). *The Hungarian Revolution of 1956: Reform, Revolt and Repression, 1953–1963.* New York: Longman.

JOHANNA GRANVILLE

HUNGARY, RELATIONS WITH

Russian and Soviet relations with Hungary, in contrast to those with other east central European countries, have been especially tense due to factors such as Hungary's monarchical past, historical rivalry with the Russians over the Balkans, Russia's invasion of Hungary in 1848, Hungary's alliances in both world wars against Russia or the USSR, the belated influence of communism in the interwar period, the Soviet invasion in 1956 to crush the nationalist revolution, and Hungary's vastly different language and culture in general.

No part of Hungary had ever been under direct Russian rule. Instead, Hungary formed part of the Habsburg Empire, extending over more than 675,000 square kilometers in central Europe. Both empires—the tsarist and Habsburg—fought for hegemony over Balkan territories. The Habsburg empire included what is now Austria, Hungary, Slovakia, and the Czech Republic, as well as parts of present-day Poland, Romania, Italy, Slovenia, Croatia, Bosnia and Herzegovina, and the Federal Republic of Yugoslavia. In July 1848 the Hungarians, led by Lajos Kossuth, fought for liberation from Austria. However, upon the Austrians' request in 1849, Tsar Nicholas I sent Russian troops to crush the rebellion. Nevertheless, Kossuth's initiative paved the way for the compromise in March 1867 (known in German as the *Ausgleich*), which granted both the Austrian and Hungarian kingdoms separate parliaments with which to govern their respective internal affairs. It also established a dual monarchy, whereby a single emperor (Francis Joseph I) conducted the financial, foreign, and military affairs of the two kingdoms.

By the late 1800s and early 1900s, ethnic groups within the empire clamored for self-rule. On June 28, 1914, Gavrilo Princip, a member of a secret nationalist movement, Mlada Bosna ("Young Bosnia"), shot Austrian Archduke Francis Ferdinand and his wife in Sarajevo, thus precipitating World War I. Austro-Hungary fought with Germany against Great Britain, France, and Russia. Throughout the fall of 1918 the Austro-Hungarian Empire collapsed as its armies retreated before enemy forces.

On March 21, 1919, Béla Kun established a communist regime in Hungary that lasted four months. Given their monarchical past, Hungarians resented communists, who seized their farms and factories and sought to form a stateless society. After a brief transition, Admiral Miklós Horthy became Regent of Hungary, heading a new monarchy that lasted twenty-five years.

Defeated in World War I, Hungary lost more than two-thirds of its territory in the 1920 peace settlement ("Treaty of Trianon"). In 1914 Hungary had 21 million inhabitants; Trianon Hungary had less than 8 million. German Nazi leader Adolf Hitler was able to coax Hungary to fight on the Axis side in World War II by promising the return of some of the territory Hungary lost in 1920. Despite its gradual alliance with Germany and Italy against the Soviet Union in the war, the German army (Wehrmacht) occupied Hungary on March 19, 1944. Hitler put Ferenc Szálasi (leader of the fascist Arrow Cross Party) in charge as prime minister. By mid-April 1945, however, the Soviet Red Army expelled the Germans from Hungary. The Soviet troops remained in Hungary until 1990.

Another element of Hungary's particularly anti-Soviet history is the belated influence of communism in the interwar period. While most other East European countries turned authoritarian after 1935, Hungary remained relatively liberal until 1944. After a short democratic period, the Communist Party took over in 1948. The Hungarian Communist Party never did win an election, but gained control due to the presence of Soviet troops and their hold over government posts. Its first secretary was Matyás Rákosi, a key figure in the international communist movement who had returned with other Hungarian communists from exile in the Soviet Union. These include Imre Nagy (later prime minister during the Hungarian Revolution in 1956) and József Révai who became the key ideologist in the 1950s. Other communists remained in Hungary and organized the Communist Party illegally during the war, such as János Kádár (who became general secretary after 1956) and László Rajk (the first key victim of the purges in 1949).

The Soviet Union also established its hegemony over Eastern Europe in commercial and military spheres. In 1949 Stalin had established the Council for Mutual Economic Cooperation (CMEA or Comecon) to counter President Truman's Marshall Plan, which Stalin prevented Hungary and other East European countries from joining. In Comecon the member states were expected to specialize in particular industries; for example, Hungary focused on bus and truck production.

The East European satellites were expected to copy the Stalinist model favoring heavy industry at the expense of consumer goods. In doing so, Rákosi's economic plans contradicted Hungary's genuine interests, as they required the use of obsolete Soviet machinery and old-fashioned methods. Unrealizable targets resulted in a flagrant waste of resources and the demoralization of workers.

Meanwhile, fearing a World War III against its former ally, the United States, the Soviet leadership encouraged the Hungarian army to expand. Having failed to prevent West Germany's admission into NATO, the USSR on May 14, 1955, established the Warsaw Pact, which subordinated the satellites' armies to a common military command. Austria was granted neutrality in the same year. In 1956 the first major anti-Soviet uprising in Eastern Europe—the Hungarian Revolution—took place. It is not surprising that Hungary, given its history, culture, and language (a non-Slavic tongue, Magyar), was the first satellite to challenge Moscow directly by declaring neutrality and withdrawing from the Warsaw Pact.

Despite the restlessness of the population after the crushed revolution and the repression of 1957-1958, Kádár's regime after normalization differed sharply from Rákosi's style of governance. Kádár's brand of lenient ("goulash") communism earned grudging respect from the Hungarian people. Kádár never trumpeted his moderate New Economic Mechanism (NEM) of 1968 as a socioeconomic model for other satellites, lest he irritate Moscow.

Hungary's overthrow of its Communist regime in 1989-1990 and independence today prove that the nationalist spirit of the revolution was never extinguished. The Soviet collapse in 1991 led to the demise of the Warsaw Pact and Comecon. In March 1999 NATO admitted Hungary, Poland, and the Czech Republic as members.

See also: HUNGARIAN REVOLUTION

BIBLIOGRAPHY

Békés, Csaba; Rainer, János M.; and Byrne, Malcolm. (2003). *The 1956 Hungarian Revolution: A History in Documents.* Budapest: Central European University Press.

Deák, István. (2001). *Phoenix: Lawful Revolution: Louis Kossuth and the Hungarians, 1848–1849.* London: Phoenix Press.

Felkay, Andrew. (1989). *Hungary and the USSR, 1956–1988: Kadar's Political Leadership.* New York: Greenwood Press.

Fenyo, Mario. (1972). *Hitler, Horthy, and Hungary: German-Hungarian Relations, 1941–1944.* New Haven, CT: Yale University Press.

Gerö, András. (1997). *The Hungarian Parliament (1867–1918): A Mirage of Power,* tr. James Patterson. New York: Columbia University Press.

Granville, Johanna. (2003). *The First Domino: International Decision Making in the Hungarian Crisis of 1956.* College Station: Texas A & M University Press.

Györkei, Jenő, and Horváth, Miklos. (1999). *The Soviet Military Intervention in Hungary, 1956.* Budapest: Central European University Press.

Kann, Robert A. (1980). *History of the Habsburg Empire, 1526–1918.* Berkeley: University of California Press.

Litván, György, and Bak, János M. (1996). *The Hungarian Revolution of 1956: Reform, Revolt, and Repression, 1953–1963.* New York: Longman.

O'Neill, Patrick H. (1998). *Revolution from Within: The Hungarian Socialist Workers' Party and the Collapse of Communism.* Cheltenham, UK: Edward Elgar.

JOHANNA GRANVILLE

HUNS

The Huns (the word means "people" in Altaic) were a confederation of steppe nomadic tribes, some of whom may have been the descendants of the Hsiung-nu, rulers of an empire by the same name in Mongolia. After the collapse of the Hsiung-nu state in the late first century C.E., the Huns migrated westward to Central Asia and in the process mixed with various Siberian, Ugric, Turkic, and Iranian ethnic elements. Around 350, the Huns migrated further west and entered the Ponto-Caspian steppe, from where they launched raids into Transcaucasia and the Near East in the 360s and 370s. Around 375, they crossed the Volga River and entered the western North Pontic region, where they destroyed the Cherniakhova culture and absorbed much of its Germanic (Gothic), Slavic, and Iranian (Sarmatian) ethnic elements. Hun movement westward initiated a massive chain reaction, touching off the migration of peoples in western Eurasia, mainly the Goths west and the Slavs west and north-northeast. Some of the Goths who escaped the Huns' invasion crossed the Danube and entered Roman territories in 376. In the process of their migrations, the Huns also altered the linguistic makeup of the Inner Eurasian steppe, transforming it from being largely Indo-European-speaking (mainly Iranian) to Turkic.

From 395 to 396, from the North Pontic the Huns staged massive raids through Transcaucasia into Roman and Sasanian territories in Anatolia, Syria, and Cappadocia. By around 400, Pannonia (Hungary) and areas north of the lower Danube became the Huns' staging grounds for attacks on the East and West Roman territories. In the 430s and 440s, they launched campaigns on the East Roman Balkans and against Germanic tribes in central Europe, reaching as far west as southern France.

The Huns' attacks on territories beyond the North Pontic steppe and Pannonia were raids for booty, campaigns to extract tribute, and mercenary fighting for their clients, not conquests of their wealthy sedentary agricultural neighbors and their lands. Being pastoralists, they wielded great military powers, but only for as long as they remained in the steppe region of Inner Eurasia, which provided them with the open terrain necessary for their mobility and grasslands for their horses. Consequently, Hun attacks west of Pannonia were minor, unorganized, and not led by strong leaders until Attila, who ruled from about 444 or 445 to 453. However, even he continued the earlier Hun practice of viewing the Roman Empire primarily as a source of booty and tribute.

Immediately after Attila's sudden death in 453, the diverse and loosely-knit Hun tribal confederation disintegrated, and their Germanic allies revolted and killed his eldest son, Ellac (d. 454). In the aftermath, most of the Huns were driven from Pannonia east to the North Pontic region, where they merged with other pastoral peoples. The collapse of Hun power can be attributed to their inability to consolidate a true state. The Huns were always and increasingly in the minority among the peoples they ruled, and they relied on complex tribal alliances but lacked a regular and permanent state structure. Pannonia simply could not provide sufficient grasslands for a larger nomadic population. However, the Hun legacy persisted in later centuries. Because of their fierce military reputation, the term "Hun" came to be applied to many other Eurasian nomads by writers of medieval sedentary societies of Outer Eurasia, while some pastoralists adopted Hun heritage and lineage to distinguish themselves politically.

See also: CAUCASUS; CENTRAL ASIA; UKRAINE AND UKRAINIANS

BIBLIOGRAPHY

Christian, David. (1998). *A History of Russia, Central Asia and Mongolia, Vol. 1: Inner Asia from Prehistory to the Mongol Empire.* Oxford: Blackwell.

Golden, Peter B. (1992). *An Introduction to the History of the Turkic Peoples.* Wiesbaden, Germany: Harrassowitz Verlag.

Maenchen-Helfen, O. J. (1973). *The World of the Huns: Studies in Their History and Culture.* Berkeley: University of California Press.

Sinor, Denis. (1990). "The Hun Period." In *The Cambridge History of Early Inner Asia,* ed. Denis Sinor. Cambridge, UK: Cambridge University Press.

ROMAN K. KOVALEV

ICONS

Icons are representations, usually on wood, of sacred figures—Christ and the Virgin Mary, the apostles, saints, and miraculous events. The Greek term *eikon* (Russian, *obraz*) denotes "semblance," indicating that the icon does not incarnate but only represents sacred objects. As such it serves to facilitate spiritual communion with the sacred; the distinctive two-dimensional flatness symbolizes an immateriality and hence proximity to the otherworldly. In rare cases this mediating role reaches miraculous proportions when the faithful believe that a "miracle-working" (*chudotvornaya*) icon has interceded to save them from harm, such as the depredations of war and disease.

The evolution of icons in Russia paralleled the development of Eastern Orthodoxy itself. Initially, after Grand Prince Vladimir embraced Eastern Orthodoxy in 988, icons were produced by Greek masters in Byzantium; few in number, they were restricted to the urban elites that actually practiced the new faith. The most venerated icon in Russia, the "Vladimir Mother of God," was actually a twelfth-century Greek icon imported from Constantinople. Revered for its representation of the Virgin's tender relationship to Christ, it became the model of the *umilenie* (tenderness) style that dominated Marian representation in most Russian iconography.

The Crusades from the West and the Mongol invasion from the East suddenly disrupted the Byzantine predominance in the mid-thirteenth century. The new indigenous icons showed a marked tendency toward not only simplification but also regionalization. As Kiev Rus dissolved into separate principalities under Mongol suzerainty, icon-painting acquired distinctive styles in Vladimir-Suzdal, Novgorod, Pskov, Yaroslavl-Rostov, Tver, and Moscow. Some icons also bore a distinctive local theme, such as the "Battle between the Novgorodians and Suzdalians," a mid-fifteenth century icon with unmistakable overtones for Novgorod's life-and-death struggle with Moscow.

The evolution of icon painting also derived from external influences. One phase began with the resumption of ties to Byzantium in the mid-fourteenth century and culminated in the icons and frescoes of Theophanes the Greek (c. 1340–after 1405). His indigenous co-workers included the most venerated Russian icon-painter, Andrei Rublev (c. 1360–1430), whose extant creations include the celebrated "Trinity" icon. A second phase came in the late fifteenth century, when Italian masters—imported to construct an awe-inspiring Kremlin—helped introduce some Western features (for example, the clothing and gestures of the Virgin). That was but a foreshadowing of the far greater Western influence in the seventeenth century, when the official icon-painting studios in the Kremlin Armory (under Simon Ushakov, 1626–1686) used Western paints and techniques to produce more naturalistic, monumental icons. Such innovations elicited sharp criticism from traditionalists such as Archpriest Avvakum, but they heralded tendencies ever more pronounced in Imperial Russia.

Even as Moscow developed an official style, the production of icons for popular consumption became much more widespread. The Church Council of 1551 complained about the inferior quality of such images and admonished painters not to "follow their own fancy" but to emulate the ancient icons of "the Greek icon-painters, Andrei Rublev, and other famous painters." That appeal did nothing to stem the brisk production of popular icons, with some small towns (e.g., Palekh, Kholuy, Shuya, and Mstera) gaining particular renown. Popular icons were not only simpler (indulging fewer details and fewer colors), but also incorporated folkish elements alien to both traditional Byzantine and newer official styles. Although authorities sought to suppress such icons (e.g., a 1668 edict restricting the craft to certified icon-painters), such decrees had scant effect.

Indeed, both popular and elite icon-painting continued to coexist in the eighteenth and nineteenth centuries. Popular icons flourished and proliferated; while some centers (such as the specialized producers in Vladimir province) exhibited artistic professionalization, the expanding production of amateur icons aroused the concern of both Church and state. But attempts to regulate the craft (e.g., decrees of 1707 and 1759) did little to restrict production or to dampen demand. A far greater threat eventually came from commercialization—the manufacture of brightly colored, cheap lithographs that pushed artisanal icons from the marketplace in the late nineteenth century. Seeking to protect popular icon painting, Nicholas II established a Committee for the Stewardship of Russian Icon Painting in 1901, which proposed a broad set of measures, such as the establishment of icon-painting schools to train craftsmen and to promote their work through special exhibitions.

Icon production for elites took a quite different path. After Peter the Great closed the icon-painting studio of the Armory in 1711, its masters scattered to cities throughout the realm to ply their trade. By the late eighteenth century, however, the Academy of Arts became the main source of icons for the major cathedrals and elites. By the mid-nineteenth century the Academy had not only developed a distinct style (increasingly naturalistic and realistic) but also significantly expanded its formal instruction in icon painting, including the establishment of a separate icon-painting class in 1856.

At the same time, believers and art connoisseurs showed a growing taste for ancient icons. By mid-century this interest began to inspire forgeries as well as orders for icons in the old style. The meaning of that old style underwent a revolutionary change in the early twentieth century: As art restorers peeled away the layers of paint and varnish applied in later times, they were astonished to discover that the ancient icons were not dark and somber, but bright and clear. The All-Russian Congress of Artists in 1911 held the first exhibition of restored icons; the new Soviet regime would devote much attention to the process of restoration.

While placing a high priority on icon restoration, the Soviet regime repressed production of new icons: It closed traditional ecclesiastical producers (above all, monasteries), and redirected popular centers of icon production such as Palekh to specialize in secular folk art. Although Church workshops continued to produce icons (by the early 1980s more than three million per year—an important source of revenue), not until 1982 did the Church establish an elite patriarchal icon-painting studio. The subsequent breakup of the Soviet Union not only generated a sharp surge in demand (from believers and reopened churches), but enabled the Church to establish a network of icon-painting schools specifically devoted to the revival of traditional iconography.

See also: ACADEMY OF ARTS; BYZANTIUM, INFLUENCE OF; DIONISY; ORTHODOXY; PALEKH PAINTING; RUBLEV, ANDREI; THEOPHANES THE GREEK; USHAKOV, SIMON FEDOROVICH

BIBLIOGRAPHY

Onasch, Konrad, and Schneiper, Annemarie. (1995). *Icons: The Fascination and the Reality.* New York: Riverside Book Company.

Ouspensky, Leonid, and Lossky, Vladimir. (1982). *The Meaning of Icons,* 2nd. ed. Crestwood, NY: St. Vladimir's Seminary Press.

GREGORY L. FREEZE

IDEALISM

The debates regarding Russia's national identity and historical destiny were always vital to the work of the prominent Russian thinkers, who were also preoccupied with moral issues and closely involved with literature. Due to its location between Europe and Asia, Russia belongs to both cultural worlds, having inherited different and often contradictory value standards that played a significant role in the course of its history. This marginal cultural situation of the country resulted in two competing approaches to its role in world history: national isolationism and openness to Europe, both trends still present in the national consciousness. During the Kievan Rus period, affiliation with Europe was a strong feature of culture. The Tatar invasion and the development of the Moscow Kingdom generated a strong tide of alienation from the West. After the fall of the Byzantine Empire, the Moscow Kingdom was the proclaimed "the third Rome" (by monk Filotius)—the vanguard force in world history inheriting the grandeur of the Roman Empire and at the same time opposed to the declining West. Peter the Great made a radical attempt to bridge the gap between Russia and the West by assimilating European values and life standards on Russian soil. However, his attempt to create a new cultural synthesis brought about contradictory results: superficial reception of the Western standards in economic, social, political, and cultural spheres on the one hand, and reinforcement of traditional non-European Russian values on the other. As Nikolai Berdyayev noted, Russia never knew the Renaissance and never accepted the humanism and individualism produced within this cultural paradigm. Although European civilization created the disciplinary society (Michel Foucault) in the modern period, it preserved the sphere of individual rights and liberties that was gradually expanding in parallel with rational standards of social control and coercion. Communal and authoritarian tendencies of Russian culture had no real counterbalance in personal values such as those commonly accepted in Europe. Even in the period of Russian Enlightenment that started under Catherine II, the critical efforts of such leading intellectuals as Nikolai Novikov, Mikhail Shcherbatov, or Alexander Radishchev did not bring radical change to tsarist rule and the prevailing cultural climate of the country.

The understanding of national history throughout the nineteenth and early twentieth centuries was considerably influenced by the Enlightenment, German idealism, and the philosophy of Romanticism. Whatever their value systems, Russian thinkers of the first part of the nineteenth century interpreted history in view of the tragic events of the French Revolution and Napoleon's invasion of Russia. This is the reason why, as Vasily Zenkovsky pointed out, Russian thinkers were highly critical of the results of Western historical development. The structure of Russian thought from the Enlightenment to the beginning of the twenty-first century was based on binary oppositions lacking synthetic reconciling units. Oppositions deeply embedded in Russian thought included communitarianism and democracy versus imperial autocracy; egalitarianism versus social hierarchy; progress versus traditionalism; and so forth. The deficiency of synthesis of contradictions inherent in Russian thought constitutes its difference from the Western intellectual paradigm.

RUSSIA AND THE WEST: THE DILEMMA OF NATIONAL SELF-IDENTITY

At the beginning of the nineteenth century, Westernized Russian thought found its expression in two different trends: the moderate conservatism of historian and writer Nikolai Karamzin, who defended autocracy of the Catherine II variety against the chaos of the French Revolution, and the Decembrist movement, which idealized the democratic traditions of Novgorod and Pskov republics and intended to put constitutional limits on the autocracy of the tsar. Famous poet Alexander Pushkin (according to Berdyayev, the only Russian man of the Renaissance) vigorously supported the ideas of the Decembrists. At the opposite pole, Vladimir Odoyevsky, Dmitry Venevitinov, and other members of the Wisdom-lovers society, who represented the anti-Enlightenment trend and were convinced followers of Schelling, believed in the leading role of Russia and its mission to save European civilization. Although Pyotr Chaadayev's thought was also nourished by Schelling and other representatives of German idealism, he took a more critical approach to Russia. According to Chaadayev, Russia lacked a true heritage of historical tradition and should therefore assimilate the European cultural legacy before assuming a leadership role in tackling humanity's problems.

These discussions evolved into the debate of the Slavophiles and the Westernizers. Despite their criticism of serfdom and the existing political order, Ivan Kireyevsky, Alexei Khomyakov, Konstantin Aksakov, and other Slavophiles, highly disparaging of Catholicism and Protestantism, European individualism, and the rationalist culture of the Enlightenment, proclaimed the necessity of finding a particularly Russian path of cultural and political development. While critical of the West, German idealism, and Hegelian doctrine as its utmost expression, the Slavophiles were nevertheless nourished conceptually by Schelling's philosophy. They believed in the superiority of Russian civilization based on the Russian Orthodox vision of the unity of human and God, the special harmonic order of relations existing among the believers (*sobornost*), and the peasant commune organization of social life as a paradigm of organic relations that should replace the external coercion of state power.

In contrast to the Slavophiles, the Westernizers believed in the productive role of humanity's rational development and progress, the positive significance of the modernization process initiated by Peter the Great, and the necessity to unify Russia with the European West. Unlike the Slavophiles, this movement had no homogeneous philosophy and ideology, representing rather a loose alliance of different trends of literary and philosophical thought that were strongly influenced by German idealism and, in particular, by Hegel. Radical democrats, such as Vissarion Belinsky, Alexander Herzen, or Nikolai Ogarev, proposed ideas that differed from the liberal persuasions of Timofei Granovsky, Konstantin Kavelin, and Boris Chicherin. Moderate criticism of the European West and nascent mass society, common to many Westernizers, found its utmost expression in the peasant socialism of Herzen and Ogarev, who, like the Slavophiles, idealized the peasant commune as a pattern of organic social life needed by Russia.

Nikolai Chernyshevsky and other revolutionary democratic enlighteners of the 1860s, who further developed the Westernizers' ideas while upholding the value of the communal foundations of Russian peasant society, paved the way for the radical populist ideology of Pyotr Lavrov, Pyotr Tkachev, and Mikhail Bakunin and the liberal populism of Nikolai Mikhailovsky. Radical populist ideology influenced the Russian version of Marxism considerably. The "return to the soil" movement, headed by Fyodor Dostoevsky, Nikolai Strakhov, and Apollon Grigoriev, was a reaction to this trend of thought. In the 1870s, Nikolai Danilevsky developed his philosophical theory of historical–cultural types inspired by the ideal of Pan–Slavic unity with the leadership of Russia. Skeptical of both the Pan–Slavic ideal and the contemporary stage of European liberal egalitarian society, Konstantin Leontiev proposed, in his version of the conservative theory of historical–cultural types, the ideal of Byzantinism preserving the communal and hierarchical traditional foundations of Russian culture and society in isolation and opposition to the liberal–individualistic European West.

THE SEARCH FOR THE UNIVERSAL VISION OF HISTORY AND THE CHALLENGE OF THE TWENTIETH CENTURY

The end of the nineteenth century and the beginning of the twentieth century were marked by the growing popularity of Friedrich Nietzsche, Karl Marx, Leo Tolstoy, and Vladimir Soloviev in Russian intellectual circles. As one of the prophets of his time, Tolstoy, in the tradition of Rousseau, put forward a criticism of industrial civilization and state power in the capitalist age and proposed his utopian ideal of Christian anarchism glorifying the archaic peasant way of life as a radical denial of the existing social order and alienation. Based on the ideas of Plato and the neo–Platonists Leibniz and Schelling, Soloviev's doctrine of absolute idealism interpreted history as a field of human creativity, a realization of Godmanhood—that is, the permanent cooperation of God and human. In his philosophy of history, Soloviev moved from the understanding of Russia's role as the intermediary link between the East and West to the ideal of theocratic rule unifying the Church power (the pope) with earthly rule of the Russian tsar, and finally came to a profound criticism of theocratic rule. On the final stage of his philosophical career, he gave a very critical evaluation of the autocratic tradition of the Moscow Kingdom and the Russian Empire that became the source of inspiration for Dmitry Merezhkovsky, Nikolai Berdyayev, Vyacheslav Ivanov, and other Silver Age religious philosophers who revealed the negative traits of the alliance between the Orthodox Church and the State and called for the free creativity of religious laymen in order to bring about radical change in Russian social and cultural life.

After the Bolshevik Revolution the majority of prominent Russian thinkers had to migrate abroad. Berdyayev, Georgy Fedotov, and Merezhkovsky continued there the tradition of the philosophy of history based on the idea of unity of Russia and Europe. At the opposite pole, national conservative isolationism found its expression in the works of Pyotr Alexeyev, Pyotr Bicilli, Nikolai Trubetskoy, Pyotr Savitsky, Lev Karsavin, and other representatives of the Eurasian movement. The liberal and conservative nationalist visions of Russian history are still present in contemporary thought. The liberal paradigm coined by Andrei Sakharov was preserved in the writings of Yegor Gaidar, Boris Fyodorov, Grigory Yavlinsky, and others. Alexander Solzhenitsyn's vision of Russian history based on Berdyayev's legacy is moderately conservative, while Alexander Dugin and other neo–Eurasians form the extreme right wing, advocating an isolationist nationalist approach to Russia's past and present.

See also: BERDYAYEV, NIKOLAI ALEXANDROVICH; CHAADAYEV, PETER YAKOVLEVICH; DECEMBRIST MOVEMENT AND REBELLION; ENLIGHTENMENT, IMPACT OF; HEGEL, GEORG WILHELM FRIEDRICH; KARAMZIN, NIKOLAI MIKHAILOVICH; LOVERS OF WISDOM, THE; SLAVOPHILES; TOLSTOY, LEO NIKOLAYEVICH; WESTERNIZERS

BIBLIOGRAPHY

Berlin, Isaiah. (1978). *Russian Thinkers.* London: Hogarth.

Florovsky, Georges. (1979–1987). *Ways of Russian Theology.* 2 vols., tr. Robert L. Nichols. Belmont, MA: Nordland.

Glatzer-Rosenthal, Bernice, ed. (1986). *Nietzsche in Russia.* Princeton, NJ: Princeton University Press.

Kline, George. (1968). *Religious and Anti-Religious Thought in Russia.* Chicago: University of Chicago Press.

Lossky, Nicholas. (1951). *History of Russian Philosophy.* New York: International Universities Press.

Pipes, Richard, ed. (1961). *The Russian Intelligentsia.* New York: Columbia University Press.

Raeff, Marc. (1966). *The Origins of the Russian Intelligentsia: The Eighteenth-Century Nobility.* New York: Harcourt, Brace & World.

Riasanovsky, Nicholas. (1952). *Russia and the West in the Teaching of the Slavophiles: A Study of Romantic Ideology.* Cambridge, MA: Harvard University Press.

Walicki, Andrzej. (1979). *A History of Russian Thought from the Enlightenment to Marxism,* tr. Helen Andrews-Rusiecka. Stanford, CA: Stanford University Press.

Zenkovsky, Vasilii. (1953). *A History of Russian Philosophy,* 2 vols., tr. George L. Kline. New York: Columbia University Press.

BORIS GUBMAN

IGOR

(d. 945), second grand prince of Kiev, who, like his predecessor Oleg, negotiated treaties with Constantinople.

Igor, the alleged son of Ryurik, succeeded Oleg around 912. Soon after, the *Primary Chronicle* reports, the Derevlyane attempted to regain their independence from the prince of Kiev. Igor crushed the revolt and imposed an even heavier tribute on the tribe. In 915, when the Pechenegs first arrived in Rus, Igor concluded peace with them, but in 920 he was forced to wage war. After that, nothing is known of his activities until 941 when, for unexplained reasons, he attacked Byzantium with 10,000 boats and 40,000 men. His troops ravaged the Greek lands for several months. However, when the Byzantine army returned from Armenia and from fighting the Saracens, it destroyed Igor's boats with Greek fire. In 944 Igor sought revenge by allegedly launching a second attack. When the Greeks sued for peace, he conceded, sending envoys to Emperor Romanus Lecapenus to confirm the agreements that Oleg had concluded in 907 and 911. The treaty reveals that Igor had Christians in his entourage. They swore their oaths on the Holy Cross in the Church of St. Elias in Kiev, while the pagans swore their oaths on their weapons in front of the idol of Perun. In 945 the Derevlyane once again revolted against Igor's heavy-handed measures; when he came to Iskorosten to collect tribute from them, they killed him. His wife, the esteemed Princess Olga from Pskov, then became regent for their minor son Svyatoslav.

See also: GRAND PRINCE; KIEVAN RUS; PECHENEGS; PRIMARY CHRONICLE; RURIKID DYNASTY

BIBLIOGRAPHY

Vernadsky, George. (1948). *Kievan Russia.* New Haven, CT: Yale University Press.

MARTIN DIMNIK

ILMINSKY, NIKOLAI IVANOVICH

(1822–1891), professor of Turkic Languages at Kazan University and lay Russian Orthodox missionary, known as "Enlightener of Natives."

Nikolai Ilminsky gave up a brilliant academic career to devote himself to missionary work among the non-Russians. He was convinced that only through the mother tongue and native teachers and clergy could the nominally baptized and animists become true Russian Orthodox believers and thus resist conversion to Islam. This conviction was at the heart of what became known as the "Ilminsky System."

In 1863, while still holding the chair of Turkic languages at both Kazan University and Kazan Theological Academy, Ilminsky established the Kazan Central Baptized-Tatar School, which served as his showcase and model for non-Russian schools and whose thousands of graduates spawned numerous village schools. In 1867 Ilminsky founded the Gurri Brotherhood, which supported the growing network of native schools, and set up the Kazan Translating Commission. By 1891 the Commission had produced 177 titles in over a dozen languages; by 1904 the Commission had produced titles in twenty-three languages. For most of the languages, this required the creation of alphabets, grammars, primers, and dictionaries. Starting with the baptized Tatars of the Kazan region, Ilminsky's activities extended to the multinational Volga-Ural area, to Siberia, and to Central Asia. But disciples carried his system further: Ivan Kasatkin, for example, founded the Orthodox Church of Japan.

Ilminsky's system encountered strong opposition from Russian nationalists who saw in the Russian language the "cement of the Empire" and feared that his approach encouraged national self-esteem among the minorities. Yet by demonstrating the fervent piety of his students and above all stressing that the alternative was defection to Islam, he was able to obtain the backing of powerful figures in the government and the Church, including Konstantin Pobedonostev. Ilminsky even became a quasi-official advisor on nationality affairs and as such promoted strict censorship, unfavorable appointments, and restrictive laws for Muslims and Buddhists.

The impact of Ilminsky's system on preliterate nationalities was revolutionary, as these peoples, equipped with a written language and the beginnings of a national intelligentsia, experienced a national awakening. Such national leaders as the Chuvash Ivan Yakovlev and the Kazakh Ibrai Altynsarin were Ilminsky's disciples and protégés, while Lenin's father worked closely with Ilminsky in promoting non-Russian education in Simbirsk Province. This may explain why Lenin's nationality policy, summarized as "national in form, socialist in content" was remarkably similar to Ilminsky's system, which was defended by his supporters as "national in form, Orthodox in content."

See also: EDUCATION; NATIONALITIES POLICIES, TSARIST; RUSSIAN ORTHODOX CHURCH; TATARSTAN AND TATARS

BIBLIOGRAPHY

Dowler, Wayne. (2001). *Classroom and Empire: The Politics of Schooling Russia's Eastern Nationalities, 1860–1917.* Montreal: McGill-Queen's University Press.

Kreindler, Isabelle. (1977). "A Neglected Source of Lenin's Nationality Policy." *Slavic Review* 36:86–100.

ISABELLE KREINDLER

IMMIGRATION AND EMIGRATION

To paraphrase the nineteenth-century historian of Russia, Vasily Klyuchevsky, the history of Russia is the history of migration. The Kievan polity itself was founded by Varangian traders in the ninth century, then populated by the steady migration and population growth of Slavic agriculturalists. By the sixteenth century the attempt to control population movement became one of the most important tasks of the Muscovite state. Serfdom (i.e., elimination of the right of peasants to move from one lord to another) was entrenched in the late sixteenth and early seventeenth centuries by the tsars of Muscovy in order to ensure that their servitors could feed their horses and buy sufficient weaponry. Serfdom's logic led to an elaborate system of controls over movement within the country and of course precluded any possibility of legal emigration for the vast majority of the population. The Muscovite polity also developed mechanisms to prevent the departure of its servitors and elites. Peasant flight—often to join the Cossacks in border regions—was not a negligible phenomenon, and there were several exceptional mass emigrations. Most notable was the departure of an estimated 400,000 Crimean Tatars, Nogai, and Kalmyks in the late eighteenth century after the annexation of their lands by the Russian Empire, and another mass emigration in the 1850s and 1860s of Adygs, Cherkess, Nogai, and others after the completion of the conquest of the Caucasus. But regular yearly emigration did not occur on a significant scale until the 1860s.

Russian Jewish exiles arrive in New York City. © BETTMANN/CORBIS

Thus it would be logical to link the first appearance of steady yearly emigration with the emancipation of the serfs in 1861. But this relationship is not so clear. Of the four million emigrants from the Russian Empire from 1861 to 1914, less than 3 percent were Russians. The vast majority were Jews and Germans, neither of which had been under serfdom. It was probably not serfdom so much as the commune, with its systems of collective responsibility and partible inheritance, that kept emigration figures so low for Russians. A massive emigration of Germans began in the 1870s in reaction to the abolition of their exemption from military conscription and continued due to the increasingly serious shortage of fertile lands in the Russian Empire as a result of population growth. Nearly 1.5 million Jews emigrated from 1861 to 1914, both in reaction to ongoing government repression and pogroms and in order to take advantage of civic equality and economic opportunities available in the United States and elsewhere. The sudden and massive increase in emigration also had a great deal to do with the transportation revolution, which brought cheap railroad and steamship tickets, making intercontinental travel possible for those of modest means.

While the tsar selectively recruited and encouraged immigrants from Europe to serve as soldiers, technicians, architects, and engineers on a fairly extensive scale by the sixteenth and seventeenth centuries, the second half of the eighteenth century was the heyday of immigration to the Russian Empire. Inspired by physiocratic notions that the population is the fundamental source of wealth, and eager to populate the vast, fertile, untilled southern steppe that they had conquered, empresses Elizabeth and Catherine created very favorable conditions for immigrants in the mid-eighteenth century. These included free grants of land, permanent exemption from military service, temporary exemption from taxes, and even a degree of religious freedom. The result was a rapid and massive immigration that slowed only in the mid- to late nineteenth century as the amount of free land declined. By the late nineteenth century, as a result of rapid population growth after the emancipation of the serfs, a shortage of land led the regime to reverse its encouragement of immigration and impose some serious restrictions upon it.

Immigration did not take place on a major scale at any period under Soviet rule. While technical experts were recruited from the West in the 1930s, and workers came to the Soviet Union in relatively small numbers in the 1920s, and then again in the 1950s, on the whole, immigration was remarkably small in scale throughout the entire Soviet period.

Likewise, emigration was illegal throughout the Soviet era, and it occurred on a significant scale only on an exceptional basis. During the Civil War, before the Bolsheviks established firm control over the entire territory of the state, a major emigration of political opponents of the regime and others occurred. By some estimates roughly 2 million people left from 1918 to 1922. The next major exodus occurred as a result of World War II, which left millions of Soviet civilians and soldiers as displaced peoples in areas occupied by Russia's allies. Millions were returned after the war—often against their will—as a result of allied agreements. But at least a half million were able to emigrate permanently.

The next major wave of emigration came in the 1970s when Soviet Jews were allowed to leave in relatively substantial numbers. While only about 10,000 Soviet Jews emigrated from the Soviet Union from 1954 to 1970, an average of 22,800 emigrated per year from 1971 to 1980. Soviet Jewish emigration was sharply curtailed in the 1980s, but when restrictions were first eased in 1988 and then effectively removed in 1990, a mass emigration of roughly a million Jews occurred. Soviet German emigration followed a similar pattern, though fewer Germans were allowed to emigrate prior to 1988. A mass emigration of nearly 1.5 million Soviet Germans, encouraged by the German policy of automatically granting citizenship (and generous access to welfare and public services), occurred from 1988 to 1996. In the 1990s economic difficulties led to large emigrations of Russians and other groups as well. This wave of emigration began to slow by the end of the 1990s, but it remained important and a matter of concern at the beginning of the twenty-first century, especially considering the continuing high rates of emigration among well-educated and highly trained young people.

See also: DEMOGRAPHY; GERMAN SETTLERS; JEWS; NATIONALITIES POLICY, SOVIET; NATIONALITIES POLICY, TSARIST

BIBLIOGRAPHY

Bartlett, Roger P. (1979). *Human Capital: The Settlement of Foreigners in Russia, 1762–1804.* Cambridge, UK: Cambridge University Press.

ERIC LOHR

IMPERIAL RUSSIAN GEOGRAPHICAL SOCIETY

Legend holds that the idea for the Russian Geographical Society (RGS) arose at a dinner party thrown by A. F. Middendorf in St. Petersburg in 1845. Middendorf had just returned from his famous expedition to Eastern Siberia. He, along with Fyodr Litke, Karl Ber, and Ferdinand Wrangel, conceived the society, which ultimately attracted seventeen charter members, including the most prominent Russian explorers, scientists, and public officials of their day. The goal was systematically to expand and quantify the understanding of their country, which was still relatively unknown. Geographical societies elsewhere in the world (England, France, Prussia, and so on) were mainly concerned with general geography, whereas homeland geography (*domashnyaya geografiya*) was for them secondary. The early founders of the RGS thus were leading proponents of the nationalist reform-minded movement that perfused Russia in the mid-1800s. The emphasis would be upon Russia's special place in the world: its diversity of climates, languages, customs, peoples, and so forth.

Although, early on, members wished to call it the "Russian Geographical-Statistical Society," on August 18, 1845, Tsar Nicholas I declared that it would be named the "Russian Geographical Society"; this remained the official name for the next five years. In October 1845, the majority of the charter members held their first meeting and selected 51 active members from throughout Russia. After 1850 the society was renamed the Imperial Russian Geographical Society (*Imperatorskoye russkoye geograficheskoye obshchestvo* [IRGS]), an appellation that would persist until 1917.

Almost immediately after its founding, the RGS became a polestar for opponents of Nicholas I. It became one of the ideological centers of the struggle against serfdom and had direct links to Russian utopian socialists, such as the Petrashevsky Circle. Its titular leader was the tsar's second son, Grand Prince Constantine, who represented the most "progressive" (i. e., nationalistic) ideas of that time. Within the society, conflict arose between the largely non-Russian founders (the Baltic Germans) and the ethnically pure Russian contingent. Throughout the rest of the nineteenth century, the IRGS stressed Russia's messianic mission in Asia, and most of the society's sponsored expeditions, including the famous Amur expedition of 1855–1863, were indeed carried out in Asia. By 1917 the IRGS had compiled a legacy of 1,500 volumes of scholarly literature.

See also: GEOGRAPHY; RUSSIAN GEOGRAPHICAL SOCIETY

BIBLIOGRAPHY

Bassin, Mark. (1983). "The Russian Geographical Society, the 'Amur Epoch,' and the Great Siberian Expedition, 1855–1863." *Annals of the Association of American Geographers* 73:240–256.

Harris, Chauncey D., ed. (1962). *Soviet Geography: Accomplishments and Tasks*, tr. Lawrence Ecker. New York: American Geographical Society.

VICTOR L. MOTE

IMPERIAL RUSSIAN TECHNOLOGICAL SOCIETY

In the era before the revolution, the Imperial Russian Technical Society (IRTS) was the most important and oldest technical organization in Russia. Founded in 1866 in St. Petersburg on the model of similar societies across Europe, it brought together scientists, engineers, and other people interested in promoting technological development. Subsidized by the Ministry of Public Education, the Ministry of Finances, and other government agencies, and by industry, it focused on inventions and the application of technology in order to further the development of Russia's manufacturing and production industries and foster the country's overall industrial and economic growth. Headed by scientists such as chemist Dmitry I. Mendeleyev and military engineer and chemist Count Kochubei, IRTS encouraged greater cooperation between government and the world of science, technology, and industry.

The members of IRTS were concerned about the output of Russia's weak private sector and felt that the technology policy of the tsarist state was inadequate, especially in the military sphere. This view was confirmed by the Russo-Japanese War (1904–1905), and in fact it was not until then that the government began to encourage IRTS in its support of aviation. World War I provided IRTS with another opportunity to demand greater state support for scientific and technological research.

From the outset IRTS was strongly committed to the dissemination of technical education, favoring the polytechnic model at the university level rather than specialized institutes, because students in schools of the former type would be more creative and flexible in their future jobs. In addition to technical schools and special classes, it conducted night schools for adults. It also tried to popularize technological development by organizing a technical library, a technical museum, and an itinerant museum, and by publishing science books for technical schools. As early as 1867 IRTS started publishing a magazine, *Notes from the Imperial Russian Technical Society* (*Zapiski IRTO*), and organizing meetings on technical subjects and on technical and professional training. Finally, it distributed awards and medals in support and reward of inventions and research and applications in the field of technology.

IRTS was a national organization and had a network of correspondents throughout Russia. Starting in the 1860s it had offices in many provinces. By 1896 there were twenty-three of these, some of which published their own magazines. In 1914 IRTS had two thousand members, four times as many as when it began. The Russian Technical Society continued its activities until 1929, when it was eliminated on the grounds that it was an organization of bourgeois specialists.

See also: ACADEMY OF SCIENCES; MENDELEYEV, DMITRY IVANOVICH; MOSCOW AGRICULTURAL SOCIETY; SCIENCE AND TECHNOLOGY POLICY

BIBLIOGRAPHY

Bailes, Kendall E. (1978). *Technology and Society under Lenin and Stalin. Origins of the Soviet Technical Intelligentsia, 1917-1941*. Princeton: Princeton University Press.

Balzer, Harley D. (1980). "Educating Engineers: Economic Politics and Technical Training in Tsarist Russia." Ph.D. diss., University of Pennsylvania.

Balzer, Harley D. (1983). "The Imperial Russian Technical Society." In *The Modern Encyclopedia of Russian and Soviet History*, edited by Joseph L. Wieczynski, Vol. 32, 176-180. Gulf Breeze, FL: Academic International Press.

Balzer, Harley D. (1996). "The Engineering Profession in Tsarist Russia." In *Russia's Missing Middle Class: The Professions in Russian History*, edited by Harley D. Balzer, 55-88. Armonk, NY: M. E. Sharpe.

Blackwell, William. (1968). *The Beginning of Russian Industrialization.* Princeton: Princeton University Press.

MARTINE MESPOULET

INDEX NUMBER RELATIVITY

The period of the first Five-Year Plans and the rapid collectivization of Soviet agriculture, 1929–1937, witnessed rapid economic growth accompanied by radical changes in the structure of the Soviet economy—first, from a predominantly agricultural towards an industrial one, and second, within industry, from a predominantly smaller-scale economy of light and consumer industries, to heavy industry, machinery, construction, and transportation. The vast expansion and mass production of heavy manufacturing goods reduced their cost of production, relative to those of light industry and of agricultural products. This phenomenon of simultaneous changes in the structure of production and relative prices during periods of rapid economic growth in the Soviet context was discovered and analyzed by Alexander Gerschenkron when he estimated the rate of economic growth of Soviet manufacturing during this period. Growth of the national product (GNP) of a country is estimated by a quantity index, aggregating the growth of production of individual sectors by assigning to each sector a "weight" corresponding to the average price of the products of this sector at a certain point of time during the period under investigation. It has been demonstrated that when the relative prices of the expanding sector are declining, as in the Soviet Union during the 1930s, the index produces a much higher rate of growth when prices of the initial period are used as weights than the index that uses prices at the end of the period. The first is called a Laspeyres index and the second a Paasche index, both named after their developers. Under the Laspeyres index, relatively higher prices, and hence larger weights, are assigned to faster growing sectors, thus producing a higher aggregate rate of growth, and vice versa. Hence the term "index number relativity."

One commonly quoted calculation of the two indexes for the period 1928 to 1937 is Abram Bergson's: According to his estimates Soviet GNP grew over that period by 2.65 times according to the Laspeyres variant but only by 1.54 times according to the Paasche index (1961, Table 18, p. 93). The two measures apparently present two very different views on the achievements of the Soviet economy during this crucial period, as well as on the estimates of economic growth over the longer run. However, since both are "true," they must be telling the same story. One commonly used "solution" to dealing with this relativity was to use the (geometric) average of the two estimates. An alternative was to replace both measures by a Divisia index (also named after its developer) that calculates growth for every year separately using prices of that year as weights, and then add up all growth rates for the entire period. The outcome is usually not far away from the average of the Laspeyres and Paasche indexes. Subsequent estimates of Soviet GDP growth over this period offered a variety of amendments to the original ones; some among them narrowed the gap between the two indices. During the rest of the Soviet period, the second half of the twentieth century, index number relativity did not play an important role, mostly because the major structural changes were accomplished already before World War II.

See also: COLLECTIVIZATION OF AGRICULTURE; ECONOMIC GROWTH, SOVIET; FIVE-YEAR PLANS

BIBLIOGRAPHY

Bergson, Abram. (1961). *The Real National Income of Soviet Russia since 1937.* Cambridge, MA: Harvard University Press.

Gerschenkron, Alexander. (1947). "The Soviet Indexes of Industrial Production." *Review of Economics and Statistics* 29:217–226.

GUR OFER

INDICATIVE PLANNING

As distinct from directive planning, as practiced in the Soviet Union from 1928 onward, indicative planning is a set of consistent numerical projections of the economic future without specific incentives for their fulfillment. Rather, the indicative plan is conceived as coordinated information that guides the choices of separate entities in the market economy.

The first indicative plans were those made up by Gosplan in the USSR during the mid-1920s. These were soon integrated into mandatory instructions issued by the Supreme Council of the National Economy (VSNKh), later by Gosplan itself. The output plans were supplemented by material balances, inspired by German experience during World War I and generalized as input-output analysis in the work of Wassily Leontief and others.

During and immediately after World War II economists in Continental Europe developed the idea of indicative planning as a guide to recovery and to ongoing short-term economic policy making. Notable were the Central Planning Bureau in the Netherlands, led by Jan Tinbergen, the French Commissariat Général du Plan, inspired by Jean Monnet, and the Japanese Economic Planning Agency. In all of these, government agencies play a role in collecting and developing the information necessary to build a multi-sectoral econometric model. Such a model allows alternative policy instruments to be tested for their effects on such targets as inflation, the growth rate, and the balance of payments. While indicative planning assumes a primarily private market economy with competition from outside the country, the *concertation* (unofficial collusion) of private investment plans—as practiced in France and Japan—is supposed to avoid duplication of effort, increase investment volumes, and perhaps reduce cyclical instability. Japanese and French bureaucrats have also guided investment funds from state-controlled sources into favored projects. In practice, however, it is doubtful that indicative planning has had much positive influence on the economic performance of these economies, particularly as they opened themselves up to international trade and capital flows.

Communist Yugoslavia adopted a kind of indicative planning in the 1950s. The main purpose was to guide the distribution of capital to self-managed enterprises throughout the republics of that country. After the fall of Communism, indicative planning was also adopted in Poland. The theoretical basis for indicative planning in a socialist context was developed by Janos Kornai and his coauthors, but practice never conformed to such rational schemes.

Indicative planning should be distinguished from so-called "indirect planning," embodied in the New Economic Mechanism in Hungary in 1968 and contemplated by Soviet reformers of the late 1980s. Instead of establishing a mixed or regulated market economy, as in Western Europe, the Communist authorities continued to dominate the economy through investment and supply planning, as well as subsidies. In both Hungary and Gorbachev's Russia, a weak budget constraint on wages and other costs led to inflationary pressure and shortages, along with rising external debts. These problems contributed to the collapse of indirect planning.

See also: GOSPLAN; INPUT-OUTPUT ANALYSIS

BIBLIOGRAPHY

Ellman, Michael. (1990). "Socialist Planning." In *Problems of the Planned Economy*, edited by John Eatwell, Murray Milgate, and Peter Newman. New York: Norton.

Kornai, Janos. (1980). *Economics of Shortage*. Amsterdam. North-Holland.

MARTIN C. SPECHLER

INDUSTRIALIZATION

The concept of industrialization implies the movement of an economy from a primarily agricultural basis to a mixed or industrial/service basis with an accompanying increase in output and output per capita. Although the early stages of industrialization require systemic and policy measures to steer resources into the productive process, eventually the growth of output must be generated through the growth of productivity. During the process of successful industrialization, measurement of the importance of the agricultural and industrial sectors, characterized for example by output shares in GDP, will indicate a relative shift away from agricultural production towards industrial production along with the sustained growth of total output. The analysis of these changes differs if cast within the framework of neoclassical economics (and its variations) as opposed to the Marxist-Leninist framework. Much of our analysis of the Russian economy during the Tsarist era and the subsequent events of the Soviet era have focused on the process of industrialization under varying institutional arrangements, policy imperatives, and especially changing ideological strictures.

To the extent that Lenin and the Bolshevik Party wished to pursue the development of a socialist and ultimately a communist economic system after the Bolshevik revolution of 1917, the relevant issue for the Bolshevik leadership was the degree to which capitalism had emerged in prerevolutionary Russia. Fundamental to industrialization in the Marxist-Leninist framework is the development of capitalism as the engine of progress, capable of building the economic base from which socialism is to emerge. Only upon this base can industrial socialism, and then communism, be built. From the perspective of classical and neoclassical economic theory, by contrast, the prerequisites for industrialization are the emergence of a modern agriculture capable of supporting capital accumulation, the growth of industry, the transformation of population dynamics, and the structural transformation of the Russian economy placing it on a path of sustained economic growth.

While there is considerable controversy surrounding the events of the prerevolutionary era when cast in these differing models, the level of economic development at the time of the Bolshevik revolution was at best modest, and industrialization was at best in early stages. From the standpoint of neoclassical economic theory, structural changes taking place were consistent with a path of industrialization. However, from a Marxist-Leninist perspective, capitalism had not emerged. The relevance of disagreements over these issues can be observed if we examine the abortive period, just after the Revolution of 1917, of War Communism. While indeed an attempt was made during this period to move towards the development of a socialist economy, these efforts contributed little, if anything, to the long-term process of industrialization.

Although during the New Economic Policy (NEP) a number of approaches to industrialization were discussed at length, the outcome of these discussions confirmed that ideology would prevail. The Marxist-Leninist framework would be used, even in a distorted manner, as a frame of reference for industrialization, albeit with many institutional arrangements and policies not originally part of the ideology. While the institutional arrangements based upon nationalization and national economic planning facilitated the development and implementation of socialist arrangements and policies, priority was placed nonetheless on the rapid accumulation of capital, a part of the process of industrialization that should have occurred during the development of capitalism, according to Marx. Thus, while an understanding of the elements of Marxism-Leninism is useful for the analysis of this era, most Western observers have used the standard tools of neoclassical economic theory to assess the outcome.

During the command era (after 1929), industrialization was initially rapid, pursued through a combination of command (nonmarket) institutions and policies within a socialist framework. The replacement of private property with state ownership facilitated the development of state institutions, which, in combination with command planning and centralized policy-making, ensured a high rate of accumulation and rapid expansion of the capital stock. In effect, the basic components of industrialization traditionally emerging though market forces were, in the Soviet case, implemented at a very rapid pace in a command setting, effectively replacing consumer influence with plan prerogatives. The pace and structural dimensions of industrialization could, with force, therefore be largely dictated by the state, at least for a limited period of time. Private property was eliminated, national economic planning replaced market arrangements, and agriculture was collectivized.

For some, the emergence of Soviet economic power and its ultimate collapse presents a major contradiction. While there is little doubt that a major industrial base was built in the Soviet Union, it was built without respect for basic economic principles. Specifically, because the command economy lacked the flexibility of market arrangements and price messages, resources could be and were allocated largely without regard to long-term productivity growth. The command system lacked the flexibility to ensure the widespread implementation of technological change that would contribute to essential productivity growth. Finally, and significantly, the socialization of incentives failed, and the consumer was largely not a part of the industrial achievements. Even the dramatic changes of perestroika during the late 1980s were unable to shift the Soviet economy to a new growth path that favored rational and consumer-oriented production.

Industrialization in the post-1990 transition era was fundamentally different from that of earlier times. First, the ideological strictures of the past were largely abandoned, though vestiges may have remained. Second, to the extent that the command era led to the development of an industrial base in-

The five-tiered iconostasis or altar screen in the Kremlin Cathedral of the Dormition, Moscow. This unique collection of icons ranging from the eleventh to the seventeenth centuries is of immense historical and artistic value. © ARCHIVO ICONOGRAPHICO, S.A./CORBIS

THE ARTS

Top: **Icon painter Andrei Rublev's best-known work, *The Old Testament Trinity Prefiguring the Incarnation* was commissioned by Patriarch Nikon in 1411 in honor of St. Sergius. Unlike most Byzantine-era icons, the *Trinity* used bright colors to help convey its complex theme.**

Bottom: ***The Face of Christ* (c. 1660) with scenes from the Holy Shroud by Simon Ushakov. Using the traditional style of Russian iconography, Ushakov was also influenced by the colors and details of the Western European artistic tradition.**

Top left: ***Saint Procopius Praying for the Passing Seafarers*** **(1914) by Nicholas Konstantinovich Roerich. Before emigrating from Russia, Roerich was known for his scenes of Slavic prehistory.** © THE STATE RUSSIAN MUSEUM/CORBIS

Below: **Study of Seated Woman from the** ***Tomb of Mikhail Kozlovsky*** **by Stepan Pimenov, 1802. Pimenov, a noted sculptor in his own right, created this piece for the burial site of his mentor Kozlovsky.** © THE STATE RUSSIAN MUSEUM/CORBIS

Below: The Threshing Floor (1821–1822), one of several paintings depicting everyday peasant life by Alexei Venetsianov. Peasant agriculture flourished among the Slavic population of the Russian Empire.

Top: **Natalia Goncharova's interest in religious iconography is evident in the outlining and presentation of the figures in her painting *Peasants* (1911).** © THE STATE RUSSIAN MUSEUM/CORBIS

Bottom: ***Haymaking* (1909) by Kasimir Malevich, the founder of the Suprematist school of abstract painting, typifies the earliest works of Futurism. Malevich's images are often compared to biblical figures.** © ARCHIVO ICONOGRAFICO, S.A./CORBIS

*Top: **Portrait of Leo Tolstoy*** **(1873) by Ivan Nikolayevich Kramskoy, painted as the author began to write *Anna Karenina*.**

Bottom: **Portrait of famous poet Anna Akhmatova by Natan Altman, 1914.**

Top left: **1783 portrait of Catherine II by Dmitri Levitsky depicts her as *Legislatress in the Temple of the Goddess of Justice.***

Below right: **Vasily Kuptsov's 1934 rendering of the ANT-20 *Maxim Gorky* airplane celebrates socialism's achievements in aviation.**

Bottom: ***Lenin in Razliv* (1934) by Arkady Rylov. Painted ten years after the death of Vladimir Lenin, this heroic painting is an indication of the public's veneration of the Bolshevik leader and founder of the Soviet state. A later version of this painting became a staple of the Lenin Cult, as it depicts him awaiting the Revolution in the village of Razliv, outside Petrograd.**

Top right: **Late eighteenth-century ivory and wood wedding chest. By the era of Catherine the Great, the Russian upper classes had adopted many European cultural traditions.** © MASSIMO LISTRI/CORBIS

Middle: **Matryoshka (nesting) dolls for sale.** © WOLFGANG KAEHLER/CORBIS

Below: **Dancers in the corps de ballet of the Maryinsky Ballet, formerly the Kirov Ballet, perform *Swan Lake,* 1997.** © STEVE RAYMER/CORBIS

appropriate for sustaining long term economic growth and economic development, the task at hand became the modification of that industrial base. Third, the modification of the industrial base required the development of new institutions and new policies capable of implementing necessary changes that would place the contemporary Russian economy on a long-term sustainable growth path. It is this challenge that separated the early stages of industrialization from the process of industrialization during transition, since the latter implies changes to an existing structure rather than the initial development of that structure.

The process of industrialization is necessarily modified and constrained by a variety of environmental factors. In the case of Russia, those environmental factors should be largely positive insofar as Russia is a country of significant natural wealth and human capital.

See also: ECONOMIC GROWTH, SOVIET; INDUSTRIALIZATION, RAPID; INDUSTRIALIZATION, SOVIET

BIBLIOGRAPHY

Gregory, Paul R., and Stuart, Robert C. (2001). *Russian and Soviet Economic Performance and Structure*, 7th ed. New York: Addison Wesley Longman.

Millar, James R. (1981). The *ABCs of Soviet Socialism*. Urbana: University of Illinois Press, 1981.

Nove, Alec. (1981). *The Soviet Economic System*. London: Unwin Hyman.

ROBERT C. STUART

INDUSTRIALIZATION, RAPID

Soviet growth strategy was focused on fast growth through intensive industrialization. It involved the self-development of an industrial base, concentrated in capital goods or "means of production," also dubbed "Sector A" according to Marxian jargon. It became the official strategy of the Soviet leadership as a resolution of the Soviet Industrialization debate that occupied communist thinkers and politicians during the mid-1920s. The industrialization debate considered two growth strategies. One, supported by moderates and led by Nikolai Bukharin, advocated an extension of the New Economic Policy (NEP), centered on industrialization but based on the initial development of agriculture, mostly by individual and independent farmers. A prospering agricultural sector would create demand on the part of both consumers and producers for industrial goods, as well as surplus resources in terms of savings, to finance this industrialization. While all sectors of manufacturing would be developed, surplus agricultural products would be used as exports in order to import machinery and technology from the West. Advocates of the alternative strategy, including leaders of the left such as Leon Trotsky, preferred a more rapid state-led industrialization drive, concentrated in large state-owned heavy industrial enterprises financed by forced savings, extracted from collectivized (thus supposedly more productive) agriculture and from the population. While machinery and technology would be imported, the main thrust would be to build an indigenous heavy industrial base and early self-sufficiency in all industrial goods, and more autarky. The high level of forced savings would minimize consumption and hence provide for higher rate of investment, faster growth, and a relatively smaller "Sector B" of consumer goods and light industry; in contrast with a normal path of early development of light and consumer goods industries, followed by gradual move toward the production of machinery and capital goods. The more radical variant was also more consistent with Marxian doctrine and teaching.

Josef Stalin used the industrialization debate as a leverage to gain control, first by siding with the moderates to oust Trotsky and his followers, and then by ousting the moderates and adopting an even more extreme variant of forced industrialization. Other motivations for his choice of the heavy industrialization route were the Soviet Union's rich endowment of natural resources (coal, iron ores, oil, and gas), and the need (facing external threats), or desire, to develop a strong military capability.

This strategy guided the industrialization drive throughout, with only some easing off toward the end of the Soviet period. The 1930s were characterized by the construction of a large number of giant industrial, power, and transportation projects that involved moving millions of people to new and old cities and regions. This was also the period when collectivized agriculture was expected to provide surplus products and resources to feed the growing industrial labor force and to export in exchange for modern technology. Students of the period differ on the extent to which this really happened, and some claim that most of the extracted surplus through food procurements had to be reinvested in machinery and other inputs needed to make the new collective and state farms work. With the increasing threat of war toward the end of the 1930s, manufacturing became more oriented toward military production. Much of the industrial effort during the war years was directed toward the production of arms, but it was also characterized by a gigantic transfer of many hundreds of enterprises from the western parts of the USSR eastward to Siberia and the Far East in order to protect them from the advancing German army. This transfer happened to be consistent with an explicit goal of the regime to develop the east and northeast, the main concentration of natural resources, an effort that was facilitated over the years through the exploitation of millions of forced labor workers.

The rate of industrial growth in the Soviet Union was higher than that of agriculture and services, and the share of industry in total output and in the labor force increased over time as in any developing country. Except that in the Soviet Union these trends were stronger: The gaps in favor of industry were wider, also due to the deliberate constraint on the development of the service sector, considered nonproductive according to Marxian doctrine. Thus the share of industrial output in GNP climbed to more than 40 percent in the 1980s, significantly above the share in other countries of similar levels of economic development. The share of industrial labor was not exceptionally high due to the concentration of capital and of labor-saving technology. This over-industrialization, including noncompetitive industries, even some creating negative value, was recognized in the 1990s as a drag on the ability of former Communist states to adjust to a normal market structure and an open economy during the transition. The autarkic policy of industrialization pursued over most of the Soviet period contributed to a technological noncompatibility with the West, which further hurt the competitiveness of Soviet industry.

The bias of Soviet industrialization toward Sector A of investment and capital, as well as military goods, is apparent in the internal structure of industry. The share of Sector A industry grew fast to almost half of total industry and stayed at approximately that level throughout the entire period. It was also estimated that during the 1970s and 1980s military-related production occupied a substantial share of the output of the machine-building and metalworking sector as well as more than half the entire activities of research and development. The development of consumer and light industry ("Sector B," under Marxian parlance) was not only limited in volume; it also suffered from a low priority in the planning process and thus from low quality and technological level. "Sector A" industries, including the major military sector, enjoyed preferential treatment in the allocation of capital and technology, of high-quality labor resources and materials, and of more orderly and timely supplies. Hence some of the technological achievements in the spheres of defense and space. Hence also the very high costs of these achievements to the economy at large and to Sector B consumer industries in particular, which were characterized by low-quality and lagging technology, limited assortment, and perennial shortages. This policy of priorities also explains the very limited construction resources allocated to housing and to urban development, causing housing shortages, as well as the very low production of private cars and (to a lesser extent) household appliances. The biased structure of industry became also a serious barrier for restructuring under the transition.

See also: COLLECTIVIZATION OF AGRICULTURE; ECONOMIC GROWTH, SOVIET; INDUSTRIALIZATION

BIBLIOGRAPHY

Bergson, Abram. (1961). *The Real National Income of Soviet Russia since 1928.* Cambridge, MA: Harvard University Press.

De Melo, Martha; Denizer, Cevdet; Gelb, Alan; and Tenev, Stoyan. (1997). "Circumstance and Choice: the Role of Initial Conditions and Policies in Transition Economies." World Bank, *Policy Research Working Paper* no. 1866.

Domar, Evsey. (1953). "A Soviet Model of Growth." In his *Essays in the Theory of Economic Growth.* New York: Oxford University Press.

Easterly, William, and Fischer, Stanley. (1995). "The Soviet Economic Decline: Historical and Republican Data." *World Bank Economic Review,* 9(3):341–371.

Erlich, Alexander. (1960). *The Soviet Industrialization Debate, 1924–1928.* Cambridge, MA: Harvard University Press.

Millar, James R. (1990) *The Soviet Economic Experience.* Urbana, University of Illinois Press.

Ofer, Gur. (1987). "Soviet Economic Growth, 1928–1985." *Journal of Economic Literature* 25(4):1767–1833.

GUR OFER

INDUSTRIALIZATION, SOVIET

The industrialization of the Soviet Union proceeded at a rapid pace between the two World Wars, starting in 1929. Within an historically short period of twelve to fifteen years, an economically backward agrarian country achieved rapid economic growth, created a more modern industrial sector, and acquired new technologies that changed it from an agrarian to an industrial economy.

At the turn of the century Imperial Russia was lagging behind its neighbors to the west in practically all aspects of economic development. Weakened by World War I and the civil war that followed, Russia was in ruins in 1918. The Communist Party that seized power after the Bolshevik revolution in 1917 initially proclaimed a world revolution as its goal. The first socialist revolution occurred in Russia, the weakest link among the world capitalist states. However, later failures to propagate communist rule in Germany, Hungary, and Poland demonstrated that the export of revolution required not an ideological dogma, but a powerful economy and military might. Both required powerful industry.

Soviet industrialization was organized according to five-year plans. The first five-year plan was launched by the Soviet dictator Joseph Stalin in 1928. It was designed to industrialize the USSR in the shortest possible time. The plan, put into action ruthlessly, aimed to make the USSR self-sufficient and emphasized heavy industry at the expense of consumer goods. The first plan covered the period from 1928 to 1933 but was officially considered completed in 1932, although its achievements were greatly exaggerated. One objective of the plan was achieved, however: the transformation of agriculture from predominantly individual farms into a system of large collective farms. The communist regime thought that the resources for industrialization could only be squeezed out of agriculture. Moreover, they believed that collectivization would improve agricultural productivity and produce sufficient grain reserves to feed the growing urban labor force caused by the influx of peasants seeking industrial work. Forced collectivization also enabled the party to extend its political dominance over the peasantry, eliminating the possibility of resurrection of market relations in agriculture. The traditional Russian village was destroyed and replaced by collective farms (*kolkhoz*) and state farms (*sovkhoz*), which proved to be highly inefficient.

Although the first five-year plan called for the collectivization of only 20 percent of peasant households, by 1940 some 97 percent of all peasant households had been collectivized, and private ownership of property was virtually eliminated in trade. Forced collectivization helped Stalin achieve his goal of rapid industrialization, but the human costs were huge. Stalin focused particular hostility on the wealthier peasants or kulaks. Beginning in 1930 about one million kulak households (some five million people) were deported and never heard from again. Forced collectivization of most of the remaining peasants resulted in a disastrous disruption of agricultural production and a catastrophic famine in 1932 and 1933 in Ukraine, one of the richest agricultural regions in the world, which exacted a toll of millions of lives. The rationale for collectivization in the Soviet Union, with all of its negative consequences, was its historic necessity in communist terms: Russia had to engage in rapid industrialization in order to create a massive heavy industry and subsequently powerful modern armed forces.

The second five-year plan (1933–1937) continued and expanded the first, albeit with more moderate industrial goals. The third plan (1938–1942) was interrupted by World War II. The institution of the five-year plan was reinforced in 1945, and five-year plans continued to be published until the end of the Soviet Union.

From the very beginning of industrialization, the Communist Party placed the main emphasis on the development of heavy industry, or, as it was called in the Soviet literature, "production of means of production." Metallurgical plants that included the whole technological chain from iron ore refining to furnaces and metal rolling and processing facilities were constructed or built near the main coal and iron ore deposits in Ukraine, the Ural Mountains, and Siberia. Similarly, production plants for aluminum and nonferrous metals were constructed at a rapid pace. Electric energy supply was ensured through the construction of dozens of hydroelectric and fuel-operated power stations; one of them, a Dnieper plant, was canonized as a symbol of Soviet industrialization. Railroads and waterways were modernized and built to ensure uninterrupted flow of resources. Automobile and aviation industries were built from scratch. Whole plants were purchased in the West, mostly from the United States, and put in operation in the Soviet Union. Stalingrad Tractor Plant and Gorki Automotive Plant began production in the early

1930s. Many American engineers were lured by promises of high wages to work at those plants and contributed to a rapid technology transfer to Russia.

New weapon systems were developed and put into production at the expense of consumer goods. On the eve of World War II the Red Army had more than twenty-three thousand tanks—six times more than Fascist Germany. Similar ratios applied for artillery, aircraft, navy vessels, and small arms. Substantial resources were materialized and frozen in the stockpiles of weapons. Nonetheless, World War II did not begin according to Stalin's plans. The USSR was unprepared for Hitler's invasion.

During the first period of war a substantial portion of the European territory was lost to Germany. During the second half of 1941 and the beginning of 1942, industrial facilities were relocated to the east (beyond the Volga river and the Urals) from European Russia, Central and Eastern Ukraine (including major industrial centers of Kharkov, Dniepropetrovsk, Krivoy Rog, Mariupol and Nikopol, Donbass), and the industrial areas of Moscow and Leningrad; this relocation ranks among the most difficult organizational and human achievements of the Soviet Union during World War II. The industrial foundation laid between 1929 and 1940 proved sufficient for victory over Fascist Germany in World War II.

See also: INDUSTRIALIZATION; INDUSTRIALIZATION, RAPID

BIBLIOGRAPHY

Gregory, Paul R., and Stuart, Robert C. (2001). *Russian and Soviet Economic Performance and Structure.* Boston, MA: Addison Wesley.

Nove, Alec. (1965). *The Soviet Economy: An Introduction,* rev. ed. New York: Praeger.

PAUL R. GREGORY

INORODTSY

Any non-Slavic subject of the Russian Empire, such as Finns, Germans, or Armenians.

By the beginning of the twentieth century, the term *inorodtsy* carried pejorative overtones. First used in a legislative project of 1798, the word was given a precise legal definition by a legal statute of 1822. Here it was used to refer to groups of Russian subjects for whom the fundamental laws of the Empire were deemed inappropriate and who therefore required a special, protected status. While under the protection of the state, they would be gradually "civilized," becoming more like the settled Russian population. Initially applied to peoples living in Siberia, the category also came to include newly–annexed peoples of Middle Asia (Kazaks, Kyrgyz, Turkmen), some of whom had a long tradition of permanent settlement and high culture.

With the exception of the Jews, the inorodtsy were indigenous peoples who inhabited areas of Siberia and Central Asia. (Thus, the common translation of this term in English as "aliens" is misleading; "natives" might better convey what the term implied to Russian colonizers.) They included the Kyrgyz; the Samoyeds of Archangel province; the nomads of Stavropol province; the nomanic Kalmuks of Astrakhan and Stavropol provinces; and the Kyrgyz of the Internal Hordes of Middle Asia (the regions of Akmolin, Semipalatinsk, Semirech, and the territory beyond the Ural mountains).

The Statute on the Inorodtsy of 1822, associated with Mikhail Speransky's enlightened administration of Siberia, sought to protect the traditional hunting and grazing areas of native peoples from encroachment by Russian settlers. The Statute placed all inorodtsy into one of three categories: settled, nomadic, and wandering hunter–gatherer–fishermen. Each category received special prerogatives and levels of protection thought appropriate for its level of culture and its economic pursuits. The inorodtsy were permitted local self–administration, which included police duties, administration of justice (based on customary law), and the collection of taxes in money or in kind, as appropriate. Administration was placed in the hand of the local elites, generally tribal elders and chieftains.

With a few exceptions, such as some groups of Buryats, inorodtsy were generally exempted from military service. The military reform of 1874 began to erode this privilege. A Bashkir cavalry squadron was created in Orenburg province in 1874, while in the 1880s a growing number of native peoples in Siberia were subject to some form of service. Some groups were permitted to substitute service with a monetary tax, while others were recruited on an individual basis, with the assurance that they would be assigned to specific regiments. An attempt, announced on June 25, 1916, to end the tradition of a general exemption from military service of many Middle Asian peoples and to draft

390,000 inorodtsy into the army for support duties, triggered a vast anticolonial revolt in Middle Asia, which was put down with great brutality.

Jews were included in the category of inorodtsy by a statute of 1835. This categorization was entirely anomalous. The general tendency of Russian legislation towards the Jews was to promote their *sliyanie* (merger) with the non-Jewish population, yet their designation as inorodtsy placed them in a special, unique category. All other inorodtsy received special privileges and exemptions as a result of this status, while for the Jews it was a vehicle for the imposition of liabilities. The inorodtsy of Siberia in particular were viewed as living at a lower cultural level, as followers of animistic, pagan belief systems. (Many of the inorodtsy of Middle Asia were Muslims.) The Jews, in contrast, were adherents of a "higher" religion. Most inorodtsy were in the eastern regions of the Empire; the Jews were resident in the Russian–Polish borderlands; indeed, they were largely barred from settlement in those areas where most inorodtsy were to be found. The most distinctive privileges of the inorodtsy were their own institutions of government, and exemption from military service; the Jews were made liable for military service in 1827, and the autonomous Jewish community, the *kahal*, was abolished in 1844. There was an ethnic component of inorodets status, since any inorodets who converted from paganism to Christianity retained all the rights and privileges of an inorodets; Jewish converts to Christianity lost the legal status of "Jew" and the disabilities that it carried. Nonetheless, this bizarre anomaly endured until the demise of the Russian Empire, when the Provisional Government not only granted full equality to the Jews, but also abolished all special legislation for the inorodtsy.

See also: JEWS; NATIONALITIES POLICIES, TSARIST

BIBLIOGRAPHY

Baumann, Robert, F. (1987). "Subject Nationalities in the Military Service of Imperial Russia: The Case of the Bashkirs." *Slavic Review* 46:489-502.

Baumann, Robert F. (1986). "Universal Military Service Reform and Russia's Imperial Dilemma." *War and Society* 4(2):31-49

Kappeler, Andreas. (2001). *The Russian Empire: A Multi-Ethnic History.* Harlow, UK: Longman.

Klier, John D. (1989). "The Concept of 'Jewish Emancipation' in a Russian Context." In *Civil Rights in Imperial Russia*, eds. Olga Crisp and Linda Edmondson. Oxford: Clarendon Press.

Sokol, Edward Dennis. (1954). *The Revolt of 1916 in Russian Central Asia.* Baltimore: Johns Hopkins Press.

JOHN D. KLIER

INPUT-OUTPUT ANALYSIS

Input-output analysis is a methodology for investigating production relations among primary factors, intersectoral flows, final demands, and transfers. Primary and intermediate factors are the "inputs," and final demands and transfers are the "outputs." Aggregate input values equal "gross national income" and aggregate output "gross domestic product." Consequently, input-output is best conceptualized as a map, or flowchart, of intersectoral activities that underlie the standard aggregate measures of national income and product. It permits analysts to quantify precisely and assess the matrix of intersectoral relationships, often hidden or overlooked in more aggregative methodologies. Sometimes this serves an informative purpose. For example, Soviet leaders suppressed data on the USSR's military-industrial production level, and the delivery of weapons to final demand, but this information was contained in its input-output tables, and could be ferreted out by Western scholars and intelligence agencies in principle. Input-output tables also shed light on the internal consistency of Soviet statistics. If these data were a patchwork, either of truths or lies, latent inconsistencies should be visible in the flow relationships.

Soviet economists were concerned with the latter application of the technique, and viewed input-output analysis as a useful adjunct to "materials balance" planning. Gosplan (the state planning agency) constructed its plans from the late 1920s onward on a sector-by-sector basis, taking inadequate account of intersectoral dependencies. Soviet input-output tables, first introduced for 1959, provided a sophisticated check, enabling planners to discern whether adjustments were required in specific instances to their simpler procedures.

The construction of input-output tables is a laborious task that could not be completed swiftly enough to displace material balancing as the method of choice for developing annual and five-year plans. Nonetheless, it did serve as a valuable tool for perspective planning. The great strength of the methodology was its lucid theoretical foundation, which permitted analysts to grasp the hidden assumptions affecting the reliability of their forecasts.

Wassily Leontiev, Nobel Laureate and the father of input–output analysis, hypothesized that production technologies for practical purposes could be conceived as approximately linear homogeneous functions, with constant returns to scale, and rectangular isoquants, even though he knew that this would not always be true. The working assumption implied that both "socialist" and "capitalist" economies were strongly determined by their technological structure (supply side economics) because factor proportions were fixed and could not be altered by competitive negotiations. Nor did planners and entrepreneurs have to fret about diminishing returns to proportional investment, because a doubling of all inputs would always result in a doubling of output. Some economists contended before the demise of communism that this strong determinism proved that markets were superfluous, but this is no longer fashionable. During the early twenty-first century input-output in post-Soviet Russia serves primarily as a guide to indicative perspective planning, that is, a tool used by policy makers to evaluate various development scenarios. Whereas it once was an adjunct to material balance planning, it became a tool for managing market-based development.

See also: GOSPLAN

BIBLIOGRAPHY

Carter, Anne. (1970). *Structural Change in the American Economy.* Cambridge, MA: Harvard University Press.

Leontief, Wassily. (1951). *The Structure of the American Economy 1919–1939*, 2nd ed. New York: Oxford University Press.

Miernyk, William. (1965). *The Elements of Input–Output Analysis.* New York: Random House.

Rosefielde, Steven. (1975). *The Transformation of the 1966 Soviet Input–Output Table from Producers to Adjusted Factor Cost Values.* Washington: G.E. TEMPO.

Treml, Vladimir; Gallik, Dimitri; Kostinsky, Barry; and Kruger, Kurt. (1972). *The Structure of the Soviet Economy: Analysis and Reconstruction of the 1966 Input–Output Table.* New York: Praeger Publishers.

STEVEN ROSEFIELDE

INSTITUTE OF RED PROFESSORS

The Institute of Red Professors (*Institut Krasnoy professury*, or IKP) was founded by government decree on February 11, 1921, in order to train a new generation of Marxist cadres for careers in education and elsewhere in the Party, state, and scientific establishment. Along with the Communist Academy, the IKP was launched as an alternative to the "bourgeois" Academy of Sciences and universities that the Bolsheviks had inherited from the old regime. Headed between 1918 and 1932 by Mikhail Pokrovsky, the IKP was formally affiliated with the Commissariat of the Enlightenment. In practice it was also subordinate to the party's Central Committee—specifically, the Politburo, Orgburo, Secretariat, and department of agitation and propaganda.

At its launch the IKP was designed to be an interdisciplinary body. But by 1922 it had been divided into three departments—history, economics, and philosophy—that were augmented in 1924 by a preparatory program for less-qualified students. Four more departments were added in 1928 that concerned party history, law, literature, and the natural sciences. After an abortive merger with the Communist Academy between 1930 and 1931, the IKP was broken up into separate institutes devoted to history, Communist Party history, economics, philosophy, and the natural sciences. These divisions, in turn, were quickly flanked by six more institutes after the IKP assumed responsibility for the Communist Academy's graduate program in 1931.

Although the IKP was initially designed to be an elite institution of the red intelligentsia, it was transformed in the mid-1920s by repeated reorganizations, the dismissal of former Trotskyites and Mensheviks, and ongoing efforts to proletarianize the IKP community as a whole. Personal ambition and the turbulence of the so-called cultural revolution between 1928 and 1932 further divided the IKP. Although wholly Marxist, the faculty and student body split repeatedly along generational, class, and educational lines during these years. These tensions led faculty and students to seek positions elsewhere, a trend encouraged by the Sovietization of the universities and the Academy of Sciences that was underway at this time. Indeed, the Stalinist cooption of these educational institutions—facilitated by a merciless purge of the old bourgeois professorate—left the IKP without a clear mandate and ultimately led to its closure in 1938.

Over the course of its existence, the IKP was frequented by both party officials and Marxist scholars. Some of the most prominent among them included Vladimir Adoratsky, Andrey Bubnov, Nikolai Bukharin, Abram Deborin, Sergey Dubrovsky,

Emilian Yaroslavsky, Bela Kun, Nikolai Lukin, Anatoly Lunacharsky, Vladimir Nevsky, Mikhail Pokrovsky, Yevgeny Preobrazhensky, Karl Radek, Leon Trotsky, Yevgeny Varga, and Vyacheslav Volgin. IKP graduates who went on to serve in prominent positions in party, state, and scientific institutions included Grigory Alexandrov, Isaak Mints, Mark Mitin, Militsa Nechkina, Anna Pankratova, Boris Ponomarev, Pyotr Pospelov, Nikolai Rubinshtein, Arkady Sidorov, Mikhail Suslov, Pavel Yudin, and Nikolai Voznesensky.

See also: ACADEMY OF SCIENCES; COMMUNIST ACADEMY; EDUCATION

BIBLIOGRAPHY

David-Fox, Michael. (1997). *Revolution of the Mind: Higher Learning Among the Bolsheviks, 1918–1929.* Ithaca, NY: Cornell University Press.

Fox, Michael S. (1993). "Political Culture, Purges, and Proletarianization at the Institute of Red Professors, 1921–1929." *Russian Review* 52(1):20 42.

DAVID BRANDENBERGER

INSTRUCTION, LEGISLATIVE COMMISSION OF CATHERINE II

In July of 1767 the Legislative Commission met in Moscow and was presented with Catherine II's *Instructions.* The lengthy *Instructions* (twenty chapters and 526 articles) were intended to guide the work of the Commission as they came together to discuss the grievances of their electors and the nature of government and the laws in Russia. The *Instructions* borrowed heavily from writers such as Baron de Montesquieu (*The Spirit of the Laws*), Cesare Beccaria (*An Essay on Crimes and Punishments*), William Blackstone (*Commentaries on the Laws of England*), and Baron Bielfeld (*Political Institutions*), as well as from Catherine's correspondence with such enlightenment thinkers as Voltaire and Diderot.

The *Instructions* themselves were neither a law code nor a blueprint for a constitution (as some historians have claimed), but rather a kind of guide as to the type of government and society Catherine hoped to mold in Russia. Catherine may have been inspired by Frederick II of Prussia, who had also promulgated his own visions as to the proper role of the monarch and the organization of the bureaucracy; when Catherine finished writing and editing her *Instructions,* she sent a German translation to Frederick II. Certainly one goal of the *Instructions* was to proclaim Russia's place as a modern European state rather than the Asiatic despotism Montesquieu had named it. The *Instructions* deal with political, social, legal, and economic issues, and in 1768 Catherine issued a supplement that dealt with issues of public health, public order, and urban life.

Catherine's reasons for promulgating the *Instructions* as well as her success in achieving the stated goals have been the subject of considerable debate. The Legislative Commission disbanded in 1768 as war broke out between Russia and Turkey, and the Commission never succeeded in finalizing a draft of a law code. Several partial codes were issued later, and some refer back directly to Catherine's *Instructions.* However, a complete body of law code was never produced in Catherine's time. The other perceived failure of the *Instructions* was the fact that it did not deal with serfdom. Catherine's criticisms of serfdom were deleted from her final draft after consultations with her advisers. Chapter 11 of the *Instructions* does note that a ruler should avoid reducing people to a state of slavery. However, Catherine had originally included a proposal that serfs should be allowed to accumulate sufficient property to buy their freedom and that servitude should be limited to six years.

Because Catherine did not abolish serfdom, reduce the power of the nobility, draft a constitution, or promulgate a complete law code, Catherine's *Instructions* have often been considered a failure. Many people have assumed that Catherine was simply vain or a hypocrite or that she hoped to dazzle the west with visions of Russia's political progress. De Madariaga disagrees, noting that the *Instructions* were never intended to limit Catherine's power. Catherine made it clear that she saw absolutism as the only government suitable for Russia, but that even in an absolute government fundamental laws could and should be obeyed. In states ruled by fundamental laws (a popular concept in the eighteenth century), citizens could not be deprived of their life, liberty, or property without judicial procedure. In her *Instructions* Catherine made the case for the importance of education, for abolishing torture, and for very limited capital punishment. Perhaps just as importantly, the *Instructions* disseminated a great deal of important legal thinking from the West and created a language in which political and social discussions could be held.

See also: CATHERINE II; ENLIGHTENMENT, IMPACT OF

BIBLIOGRAPHY

Alexander, John. (1989). *Catherine the Great: Life and Legend.* Oxford: Oxford University Press.

Catherine II, Empress of Russia. (1931). *Documents of Catherine the Great: The Correspondence with Voltaire and the Instruction of 1767, in the English text of 1768,* ed. W. F. Reddaway. Cambridge, UK: Cambridge University Press.

De Madariaga, Isabel. (1990). *Catherine the Great: A Short History.* New Haven, CT: Yale University Press.

Dukes, Paul. (1977). *Catherine the Great's Instructions to the Legislative Commission.* Newtonville, MA: Oriental Research Partners.

Raeff, M. (1966). *Plans for Political Reform in Imperial Russia, 1730–1905.* Englewood Cliffs, NJ: Prentice Hall.

MICHELLE DENBESTE

INTELLIGENTSIA

The intelligentsia were a social stratum consisting of people professionally engaged in intellectual work and in the development and spread of culture.

The term *intelligentsia* was introduced into the Russian language by the minor writer Boborykin in the 1860s and it soon became widely used. According to Martin Malia, the word intelligentsia has had two primary overlapping uses: either all people who think independently, whom the Russian literary critic Dmitry Pisarev called "critically thinking realists," or the more narrow meaning, "the intellectuals of the opposition, whether revolutionary or not." However, the second definition, which is often found in historical literature, is too narrow and unjustifiably excludes important thinkers, philosophers, writers, public figures, and political rulers. For example, the famous Russian philosopher Nikolai Berdiaev called Tsar Alexander I "a Russian *intelligent* on the throne." Thus one may consider as intelligentsia well-educated and critical-thinking people of all political spectrums of society, not just radicals and liberals.

THE INTELLIGENTSIA IN THE RUSSIAN EMPIRE

Historians have different opinions about the time of the appearance of the Russian intelligentsia as a historical phenomenon. Some of them consider people who were opposed to the Russian political regime since the end of the eighteenth century as intelligentsia. According to this chronology the first representatives of Russian intelligentsia were writers Alexander Radischev and Nikolai Novikov, who protested against serfdom and the existing regime, as well as the first Russian revolutionaries, the Decembrists. They were either separated individuals or small groups of people without significant influence on Russian society. Their ideas foreshadowed important future intellectual trends. Because of this, most historians considered them as a proto-intelligentsia.

In the 1830s–1850s philosophical debates largely divided Russian intellectuals into Westernizers and Slavophiles, in line with their opinion about how Russian society should develop. Westernizers advocated a West European way for the development of Russia, while Slavophiles insisted on Russian historical uniqueness. Both these groups of Russian proto-intelligentsia had their distinguished representatives. The most famous Slavophiles were the writers Ivan and Konstantine Aksakov and the thinkers Ivan Kiryevsky and Alexsei Khomiyakov. The most distinguished Westernizers of this time were Peter Chaadayev and writer and radical publicist Alexander Herzen. Since there was strict censorship in Russia, Herzen established the Russian publishing house "Free Russian Press" in London in 1852, where he published the journal *Kolokol (The Bell).*

The most radical faction of Russian intellectuals began to adopt Western socialist ideas at this time. Among the famous radical intelligentsia were publicist Vissarion Belinsky, anarchist Mikhail Alexandrovich Bakunin, and the radical Mikhail Petrashevsky's circle, which discussed the necessity of the abolition of serfdom in Russia and reform of the Russian monarchy in a democratic, federal republic.

The circle of Russian intellectuals remained very small before the 1860s. Higher education was available only to the noble elite of society; consequently most of the Russian proto-intelligentsia was from the gentry.

The majority of western historians agree that the Russian intelligentsia appeared as an actual social stratum in the 1860s. There were several reasons for its appearance, among them the period of Great Reforms in Russia under Tsar Alexander II with the liquidation of serfdom, liberalization of society, and awakening of public opinion. Also, the development of capitalism in Russia and the beginning of industrialization demanded more educated people. At this time the technical intelligentsia appeared in Russia, while education became more widespread among the population.

In the 1860s there appeared a current among Russian intelligentsia called "nihilism" (from the Latin *nihil* meaning reject). Some historians believe that nihilism was a reaction of part of Russian society to the failure of the government in the Crimean War. The term *nihilism* was popularized by the Russian author Ivan Turgenev in his novel *Fathers and Sons* in 1862, where he described the conflict between two generations. Historian Philip Pomper wrote: the "Nihilist denied not only traditional roles of women but also the family, private property, religion, art—in a word, all traditional aspects of culture and society." According to Pomper the doctrinal bases of Russian nihilism were materialism, utilitarianism, and scientism. The most famous writers and literary critics, who more or less shared nihilistic ideas, were Nikolai Chernyshevsky, Nikolai Dobrolubov, and Dmitry Pisarev.

Populism became the ideology of a large segment of the Russian intelligentsia in the 1870s–1880s. This was a reaction to the nihilist's rationalistic elitism on one side, and the continuation of the ideas of the Slavophiles on the other. Populists had great sympathy for the suffering peasant masses and, like Slavophiles, they believed in the uniqueness of the Russian peasant commune and saw in it the germ of the future socialist society. They created the movement "Going to the people." The many admirers of this movement lived among peasants, attempting to educate them and spread their ideas about a future just society. Peasants usually looked suspiciously at these intelligent agitators from the cities and sometimes physically attacked them.

When "Going to the people" failed, Russian populists rejected this tactic and instead created several secret societies to struggle against the government. One of these groups of Russian radical intelligentsia, Zemlya i Volya, was established in Petersburg in 1876. In 1878 this organization split into two parts. Extreme members founded the new group Narodnaya Volya that chose political terror as their primary tactic. In 1881 members of Narodnaya Volya assassinated Tsar Alexander II. Moderate members of Zemlya i Volya founded Chernyi Peredel, which continued anti-government agitation. The most noted member of Chernyi Peredel was the future Marxist Georgy Plekhanov.

Marxism and other socialist movements became popular in Russia in the 1890s with the development of industry and the rise in the number of industrial workers. The first Marxist and socialist groups in Russia were composed almost entirely of intellectuals. The writings of Karl Marx and the other ideologists of socialism were too complicated for comprehension by barely literate workers. The Russian radical intelligentsia took on the mission of spreading these socialist ideas among the proletariat. Their motivation was similar to their radical predecessors of the 1860s: the search for social justice and dreams about equality for all members of society. But unlike in earlier times, these political groups transformed into large political parties with well-formed programs of political struggle against the government. Among these political parties were the Russian Social-Democratic Party that split in 1903 into the Bolsheviks and Mensheviks, the Socialist Revolutionaries, various anarchist groups, etc. These political parties used a variety of methods to struggle against the government: from political agitation and propaganda to terror, organization of political strikes, and attempts to overthrow the government. Members of these parties were from disparate sections of society, but Russian radical intelligentsia led all of these groups.

These political movements had support in their struggle with the existing regime from the movements of national minorities in the Russian empire. The best representatives of the Ukrainian and Polish intelligentsia were persecuted by the tsarist regime for expression of their national feelings and calling for the independence of their nations. Thus the celebrated Ukrainian poet and artist Taras Shevchenko was sent by order of Tsar Nicolas I to a ten-year term in a labor battalion in Siberia "under the strictest supervision" and was forbidden to write and sketch. Use of the Ukrainian language was forbidden several times in the Russian empire. Russian governments severely suppressed Polish uprisings and sent thousands of people who participated in them to exile in Siberia.

Jews were the most oppressed group in the Russian empire. Their restriction to the Pale of Settlement, the "percentage norm" (i.e., limitation on numbers admitted) in Russian universities and gymnasiums for Jewish students, and the policy of state anti-Semitism made the life of the Jewish intelligentsia miserable in the empire. Revolutionary and nationalist moods were widely spread among the Jewish intelligentsia. Thus Jews comprised a percentage of revolutionaries far higher than the proportion of Jews in the Russian population.

Conservatives in the Russian intelligentsia always opposed Russian radicals and revolutionaries. Russian conservatives did not create their political parties until the beginning of the twentieth century. They usually supported the Russian monarchy and government, and expressed their ideas in philosophical and literary works, and in the Russian conservative press. Among them were famous thinkers (Konstantin Leontiev), writers (Feodor Dostoyevsky), and publicists (Mikhail Katkov, Vasily Shulgin). All of them warned Russian society about the danger of the socialists' ideas and the impending revolution. Their ideas were shared by a significant part of the Russian intelligentsia.

After the first Russian revolution in 1905 the volume of essays *Vekhi* (*Landmarks*, 1909) argued against the revolutionary inclinations of the Russian intelligentsia. Among the authors was a group of famous Russian religious philosophers and publicists (philosophers Nicolai Berdiaev, Sergei Bulgakov, publicist Peter Struve, and others). Some of the authors of this book were former socialists and Marxists who were greatly disillusioned after the first Russian revolution. *Vekhi* was one of the most famous books in Russia in the early 1900s, it was reprinted five times during its first year.

The Liberal movement appeared comparatively late among the Russian intelligentsia, on the eve of the First Russian Revolution of 1905. During the First Russian Revolution, Russian liberals created the Constitutional Democratic Party (Cadets), with the goal of transforming the absolute monarchy into a constitutional monarchy. The ideas of liberalism were not widely spread among the Russian population; thus the Constitutional Democratic Party never had a large influence on political events in the country. The Constitutional Democratic Party was often called the party of Russian intelligentsia, because they dominated the party, although intelligentsia led most political parties and movements in Russia.

The Russian intelligentsia was responsible for what is arguably the greatest achievement of Russian culture: Russian literature. The majority of Russian writers, artists, scholars, and scientists lived a quiet everyday life and pursued their aesthetic, scholarly, and scientific tasks. The apolitical Russian intelligentsia believed that literature and art should have only aesthetic goals. These ideas were shared by many celebrated writers, poets, and artists of the Silver Age of the Russian culture (at the beginning of the twentieth century).

A large part of the intelligentsia greeted the February revolution as an attempt at the liberalization of the country. Many of them favored the provisional government. However, at the time of the October revolution only an insignificant minority of the Russian intelligentsia supported the Bolsheviks.

THE INTELLIGENTSIA IN THE SOVIET UNION

The Russian intelligentsia felt responsible for the future of the country, and some of them had the naïve illusion that they could persuade the Bolshevik leaders to stop terror. However, such attempts by the Russian writers Maxim Gorky and Vladimir Korolenko, who appealed personally to the Bolshevik leader Vladimir Lenin, were unsuccessful. Bolsheviks did not forgive the counter-revolutionary mood of the intelligentsia and soon began repression against it. One of the first victims was the famous poet of the Silver Age of Russian culture Nikolai Gumilev. In 1921 he was accused of conspiracy against the Soviet regime and was executed. Many of the intelligentsia emigrated from Russia after the October revolution. The elite of the Russian intelligentsia, including famous philosophers (among them was an author of *Vekhi*, Nicolai Berdiaev) and writers, were expelled from the country by the order of the Bolshevik leaders in the fall of 1922.

The Bolsheviks attempted to spread Marxist ideology among the entire population and to control the development of culture in the Soviet Union. They declared war on illiteracy. Thousands of new schools were opened in the Soviet Union, and education became obligatory. The children of peasants and workers received the right to enter technical schools and universities. In contrast members of formerly rich bourgeois families were deprived of many rights, and the Soviet universities were very reluctant to accept them. The educational system in the Soviet Union was under the absolute control of the Communist Party, and communist ideology was the core of the educational curriculum.

The majority of the new Soviet intelligentsia consisted of technically trained personnel who, according to Richard Pipes, had ". . . mere nodding acquaintance with the liberal arts, once considered the essence of a higher education." Thus Pipes characterized these people as semi-intelligentsia or "white collar." However, people educated in this way were most devoted to the political system. They did not know any other ideology beside the Communist. The Soviet government exterminated all other sources of knowledge except the apolitical and pro-Soviet. Many authors and books, and all press except the Bolsheviks', were forbidden in the Soviet Union. All publications appeared only after approval under strict Soviet censorship. In literature, the Russian Association of Proletarian Writers (RAPP), with its dogmatic party approach controlled all works of Soviet writers. The communications of Soviet citizens with foreigners was severely restricted. Thus was created the Soviet intelligentsia, completely devoted to the communist regime.

Soviet propaganda even influenced the minds of some Russian emigrants. Among the Russian emigrant intelligentsia there appeared a movement called "left wing Smenovekhism." Members of this movement criticized the authors of *Vekhi* for ". . . their inability to accept the great Russian Revolution." The authors of the volume of essays *Smena Vekh (Change Landmarks)* proclaimed their pro-Soviet position.

During Josef Stalin's regime many thousands of intelligentsia became the innocent victims of political repression. Only a small percentage of them dared to resist the regime. Most of the repressed intelligentsia were loyal to the Soviet system. Among them were talented writers (Boris Pil'niak, Isaac Babel), poets (Osip Mandelshtam), scientists, and scholars. Others, such as the poet Marina Tsvetaeva, were pushed to commit suicide.

Nevertheless, the Communist government needed the creators of weapons and ideologies, as well as musicians and artists. Thus in the Soviet Union there always existed an intellectual elite that made distinguished achievements in many areas of scientific and scholarly life, and in art and culture. The other part of the Soviet intelligentsia actively collaborated with the state in the hope of promoting their careers, with the expectation of receiving some state privileges. Thus at the same time, when some Soviet writers, poets, artists, and musicians created masterpieces, others created works devoted to the Soviet political leaders. Huge portraits of Stalin and Lenin decorated every state office and their statues were erected in each city.

Some change in the political climate appeared after the secret speech of Nikita Khrushchev to the twentieth Congress of the Communist Party of the Soviet Union (1956) about the crimes of Stalin's regime. The time from this speech through the first part of the 1960s was called the period of cultural "Thaw." At that time political executions were stopped, and the intelligentsia felt freer to express their ideas and feelings. During this period many political prisoners were released, including many intellectuals. The Thaw brought a new approach to culture and art, which became more humane. During these years many masterpieces of Russian literature were published, many of them devoted to the recent past: Stalin's repression and World War II. Among these works was *One Day in the Life of Ivan Denisovich* by Alexander Solzhenitsyn, the poetry of Anna Akhmatova and Boris Pasternak, and Pasternak's novel *Doctor Zhivago,* for which he won the Nobel Prize for Literature in 1958. However, the treatment of Pasternak in the Soviet Union was appalling and hastened his death. Thus Khrushchev's cultural policy was contradictory: he united some cultural liberalization with the continuation of some repression. During the cultural Thaw the Communist Party did not release culture from ideological control, but only extended the limits on the creativity of the intelligentsia.

The period of Leonid Brezhnev's leadership (1964–1982) was a time of political and cultural stagnation. Stalin and his policies were somewhat rehabilitated, which led to increased repression against the intelligentsia. In 1965 two writers, Andrey Sinyavsky and Yuli Daniel, were arrested for publishing satirical works in the West. But the Soviet intelligentsia were not completely silent as in the past. Prominent intellectuals protested against the arrest of Sinyavsky and Daniel. The period of Thaw, with the humanization of the society and the rethinking of the recent historical past, changed the social atmosphere in the Soviet Union. Soviet intellectuals began the dissident and "human rights" movements. They avoided state censorship by *samizdat* (self-publishing) printings that gave freedom of self-expression to their authors. The Soviet regime did not surrender its ideological positions and continued the persecution of nonconformist intellectuals. In 1974 the famous writer Alexander Solzhenitsyn was forcibly deported from the Soviet Union. In 1980 the hydrogen bomb physicist and progressive thinker Andrei Sakharov was sent to internal exile to Gorky. These people who participated in the dissident and Human rights movements were the forerunners of glasnost and the transformation of the communist regime into a democratic society.

Mikhail Gorbachev began his leadership in 1985 with an initiative for "democratization of social and economic life." He did not want to undermine the communist regime, but intended to improve it and make it more effective. However, the liberalization of society and diminishing of the censorship opened the press and mass media for political discussions and public exposure of historical reality. In a short time this changed public opinion, social values, and the attitude of the majority of the society against the communist regime. After a long break the intelligentsia had revived their influence on public opinion. The former dissidents Andrey Sakharov, Alexander Solzhenitsyn, and hundreds of others returned from emigration, exile, and prisons to lead movements opposing the communists. All these processes, combined with the economic crisis, undermined the communist government. The Soviet Union collapsed in December 1991 with the intelligentsia playing an important role in the destruction of the Soviet empire.

The post-Soviet years, however, have not become years of the flourishing of arts and sciences in the former Soviet states. In most of the new countries the intelligentsia have received freedom of expression, but have lost almost all government financial support. The new post-Soviet states are unable to adequately finance scientific projects and development of culture and art. Many intellectuals have lost their jobs, and some emigrated from the former Soviet states to the West in the 1990s. The future of the intelligentsia in the post-Soviet countries depends entirely upon political and economic developments.

See also: AKSAKOV, IVAN SERGEYEVICH; AKSAKOV, KONSTANTIN SERGEYEVICH; BAKUNIN, MIKHAIL ALEXANDROVICH; BELINSKY, VISSARION GRIGORIEVICH; BULGAKOV, SERGEI NIKOLAYEVICH; DISSIDENT MOVEMENT; HERZEN, ALEXANDER IVANOVICH; JOURNALISM; PISAREV, DMITRY IVANOVICH; SOLZHENITSYN, ALEXANDER ISAYEVICH.

BIBLIOGRAPHY

Acton, Edward. (1997). "Revolutionaries and Dissidents: The Role of the Russian Intellectual in the Downfall of Tsarism and Communism." In *Intellectuals in Politics: From the Dreyfus Affair to Salman Rushdie,* edited by Jeremy Jennings and Anthony Kemp-Welch. London and New York: Routledge.

Fisher, George. (1969). *Russian Liberalism from Gentry to Intelligentsia.* Cambridge, MA: Harvard University Press.

Hosking, Geoffrey. (2001). *Russia and the Russians.* Cambridge, MA: The Belknap Press of Harvard University Press.

Kagarlitsky, Boris. (1994). *The Thinking Reed: Intellectuals and the Soviet State, 1917 to the Present,* tr. Brian Pierce. London, New York: Verso.

Pipes, Richard, ed.(1961). *The Russian Intelligentsia.* New York: Columbia University Press.

Pomper, Philip. (1970). *The Russian Revolutionary Intelligentsia.*New York: Thomas Y. Crowell Company, Inc.

Read, Christopher. (1990). *Culture and Power in Revolutionary Russia: The Intelligentsia and the Transition from Tsarism to Communism.* Houndmills, Basingstoke, Hampshire and London: The Macmillan Press LTD.

Slapentokh, Vladimir. *Soviet Intellectuals and Political Power: The Post-Stalin Era.* Princeton, NJ: Princeton University Press.

Tompkins, Stuart Ramsay. (1957). *The Russian Intelligentsia: Makers of the Revolutionary State.* Norman: University of Oklahoma Press.

VICTORIA KHITERER

INTERMEDIATE RANGE NUCLEAR FORCES TREATY

In 1987 Soviet President Mikhail Gorbachev and U.S. President Ronald Reagan signed the first major Soviet-U.S. disarmament agreement—the Intermediate-Range Nuclear Forces (INF) Treaty. The pact broke precedent in three ways. Previous treaties limited weapons, but the INF Treaty stipulated abolition of top-of-the-line missiles. Second, the deal was highly asymmetrical: Moscow gave up more than Washington. Third, the treaty's provisions were to be verified not just by "national means" (mainly, spy satellites), but also by on-site inspections by Soviets in the United States and Americans in the USSR.

Demand for such a treaty arose in the 1970s when the USSR began to deploy what the West called SS-20 missiles. These were two-stage, intermediate-range missiles, many of them mobile, hard for the United States to track or attack. Since most SS-20s targeted Europe (some aimed at China), they were intimidating to America's NATO partners.

The Reagan administration proposed a "zero option." If the USSR abolished all its SS-20s, the United States would not build an equivalent. After

Moscow refused, the United States deployed in Europe two kinds of INF: cruise missiles that could fly in under Soviet radar, and ballistic missiles with warheads able to reach Kremlin bomb shelters.

Seeking better relations with the West, Gorbachev put aside his objections to the U.S. quest for antimissile defenses. Gorbachev and Reagan in 1987 signed a treaty that obliged both countries to destroy all their ground-based missiles, both ballistic and cruise, with a range of 500 to 5,500 kilometers. To reach zero, the Kremlin had to remove more than three times as many warheads and destroy more than twice as many missiles as Washington, a process both sides completed in 1991. Skeptics noted that each side retained other missiles able to do the same work as those destroyed and that INF warheads and guidance systems could be recycled.

See also: COLD WAR; STRATEGIC ARMS LIMITATION TREATIES; STRATEGIC DEFENSE INITIATIVE; ZERO-OPTION

BIBLIOGRAPHY

Clemens, Walter C., Jr. (1990). *Can Russia Change? The USSR Confronts Global Interdependence.* New York: Routledge.

FitzGerald, Frances. (2000). *Way Out There in the Blue: Reagan, Star Wars, and the End of the Cold War.* New York: Simon & Schuster.

Herf, Jeffrey. (1991). *War by Other Means: Soviet Power, West German Resistance, and the Battle of Euromissiles.* New York: Free Press.

Talbott, Strobe. (1985). *Deadly Gambits.* New York: Vintage/Random House.

Wieczynski, Joseph L., ed. (1994). *The Gorbachev Encyclopedia: Gorbachev, the Man and His Times.* Los Angeles: Center for Multiethnic and Transnational Studies.

Wieczynski, Joseph L., ed. (1994). *The Gorbachev Reader.* Los Angeles: Center for Multiethnic and Transnational Studies.

WALTER C. CLEMENS JR.

INTERNATIONAL SPACE STATION

The United States in 1984 initiated a program to build a space station—a place to live and work in space—and invited its allies in Europe, Japan, and Canada to participate in the project, which came to be called "Freedom." In 1993 the new presidential administration of Bill Clinton seriously considered canceling the station program, which had fallen behind schedule and was over budget. Space officials in Russia suggested as an alternative that the United States merge its space station program with the planned Russian Mir-2 program.

The United States accepted this suggestion and made it a key element of the redesign of what came to be called the International Space Station (ISS). The existing partners in the Freedom program issued a formal invitation to Russia to join the station partnership, which Russia accepted in December 1993.

There were both political and technical reasons for welcoming Russia into the station program. The Clinton administration saw station cooperation as a way of providing continuing employment for Russian space engineers who otherwise might have been willing to work on improving the military capabilities of countries hostile to the United States. Cooperation provided a means to transfer funds into the struggling Soviet economy. It was also intended as a signal of support by the White House for the administration of President Boris Yeltsin.

In addition, Russia brought extensive experience in long-duration space flight to the ISS program and agreed to contribute key hardware elements to the redesigned space station. The U.S. hope was that the Russian hardware contributions would accelerate the schedule for the ISS, while also lowering total program costs.

Planned Russian contributions to the ISS program include a U.S.-funded propulsion and storage module, known as the Functional Cargo Block, built by the Russian firm Energia under contract to the U.S. company Boeing. Russia agreed to pay for a core control and habitation unit, known as the service module; Soyuz crew transfer capsules to serve as emergency escape vehicles docked to the ISS; unmanned Progress vehicles to carry supplies to the ISS; two Russian research laboratories; and a power platform to supply power to these laboratories.

The Functional Cargo Block (called *Zarya*) was launched in November 1998, and Russia continued to provide a number of Soyuz and Progress vehicles to the ISS program. However, Russia's economic problems delayed work on the service module (called *Zvezda*), and it was not launched until July 2000, two years behind schedule. As of

January 2002, it was unclear whether Russia would actually be able to fund the construction of its two promised science laboratories and the associated power platform.

With the launch of Zvezda, the ISS was ready for permanent occupancy, and a three-person crew with a U.S. astronaut as commander and two Russian cosmonauts began a 4.5 month stay aboard in November 2000. Subsequent three-person crews are rotating between a Russian and a U.S. commander, with the other two crew members being from the other country. The crew size aboard ISS is planned to grow to six or seven after the European and Japanese laboratory contributions are attached to ISS sometime after 2005.

The sixteen-nation partnership in the ISS is the largest ever experiment in technological cooperation and provided a way for Russia to maintain its involvement in human space flight, which dates back to 1961, the year of the first person in space, Russian cosmonaut Yuri Gagarin.

See also: MIR SPACE STATION, SPACE PROGRAM

BIBLIOGRAPHY

National Aeronautics and Space Administration. (2002). "International Space Station." http://spaceflight.nasa.gov/station.

Progressive Management. (2001). "2001—The International Space Station Odyssey Begins: The Complete Guide to the ISS with NASA and Russian Space Agency Documents." CD-ROM. Mount Laurel, New Jersey: Progressive Management.

JOHN M. LOGSDON

INTOURIST *See* TOURIST.

INTER-REGIONAL DEPUTIES' GROUP

The Inter-Regional Deputies' Group (IRDG) took shape in June 1989 as a loose democratic grouping in the first USSR Congress of People's Deputies. But its main historical achievements were the propagation of democratic ideas to the Soviet public, and its catalytic role as a focus and example for democratic groups. Its period of intense activity lasted less than a year. Its functions were soon superseded, primarily by the rise of the Democratic Russia movement.

At the time of IRDG's spontaneous emergence, its spokespersons took pains to deny that it was a faction that might divide the congress. However, by the time it held its founding conference on July 29–30, 1989, Soviet miners had launched a strike that put forward political as well as economic demands and radicalized political thinking among Soviet democrats. The IRDG realized that its original goal of merely pressuring the Communist Party into conducting reforms no longer fit the mood of those elements in a society that favored change. Now it needed to campaign for what the former dissident Andrei Sakharov had demanded at the congress: the repeal of Article Six of the Soviet Constitution, which legitimized the political monopoly of the Communists. Only such repeal would allow the emergence of a variety of constitutionally legitimate parties, and thus open the door to radical change.

This principle, coupled with the IRDG's insistence on the right of the union republics to exercise the sovereignty to which they were already entitled on paper, became the two main planks of the IRDG's initial program. Later, principles such as support for a market economy and private property were added.

The founding conference, attended by 316 of the congress's 2,250 deputies, saw much debate on whether the IRDG should constitute itself as a faction, and whether it should define itself as an opposition. The majority, convinced by historian Yuri Afanasiev's proposition that Marxism-Leninism was unreformable, was inclined to answer these questions in the affirmative. Organizationally, 269 of those present joined the new group and elected as their leaders five co-chairmen and a coordinating council of twenty. The co-chairmen comprised Afanasiev; Sakharov; the politically reascendant Boris Yeltsin; the economist and future mayor of Moscow, Gavriil Popov; and—to symbolize the IRDG's commitment to the sovereignty of the union republics—the Estonian Viktor Palm.

Over the next months the IRDG held meetings at which numerous speeches were made and many draft laws proposed. However, partly because its most ambitious politician, Yeltsin, usually chose to act independently of the IRDG, the group proved unable to channel all this activity into practical action. Soon it realized that factional activity in the congress was not feasible for a small group that never numbered more than four hundred. Some of its members, notably Yeltsin, saw that the upcoming elections to the fifteen new republican congresses, scheduled for early 1990, held out more promise of real political change than did the USSR congress. Others, such as Sakharov and Afanasiev, rejected this approach, which was inevitably tinged with ethnic nationalism, in favor of uniting democrats and promoting democratization throughout the whole of the USSR.

In sum, the IRDG's brief but bold example of self-organization in the often hostile environment of the USSR congress, and the enormous publicity generated by the televised speeches of IRDG members at the first two congresses and other public meetings, had major repercussions for the democratic groups and candidates who organized themselves for the 1990 elections, and thus, also, for the development of Russian democracy.

See also: ARTICLE 6 OF 1977 CONSTITUTION; CONGRESS OF PEOPLE'S DEPUTIES; POPOV, GAVRIIL KHARITONOVICH; SAKHAROV, ANDREI DMITRIEVICH; YELTSIN, BORIS NIKOLAYEVICH

BIBLIOGRAPHY

Reddaway, Peter, and Glinski, Dmitri. (2001). *The Tragedy of Russia's Reforms: Market Bolshevism Against Democracy.* Washington, DC: U.S. Institute of Peace Press.

Urban, Michael; Igrunov, Vyacheslav; and Mitrokhin, Sergei. (1997). *The Rebirth of Politics in Russia.* Cambridge, UK: Cambridge University Press.

PETER REDDAWAY

IRAN, RELATIONS WITH

During the period of the Shah, Soviet-Iranian relations were cool, if not hostile. Memories of the 1946 Soviet occupation of Northern Iran, the activities of the Iranian Communist Party, and the increasingly close U.S.-Iranian alliance kept Moscow and Tehran diplomatically far apart, although there was a considerable amount of trade between the two countries. Following the overthrow of the Shah, Moscow initially hoped the Khomeini regime would gravitate toward the Soviet Union. However, the renewed activities of the Iranian communist party, together with Tehran's anger at Moscow for its support of Baghdad during the Iran-Iraq war, kept the two countries apart until 1987, when Moscow increased its support for Iran. By 1989 Moscow had signed a major arms agreement with Tehran, and the military cooperation between the two countries continued into the post-Soviet period.

After the collapse of the Soviet Union, Iran emerged as Russia's primary ally in the Middle East. Moscow became Iran's most important supplier of sophisticated military equipment, including combat aircraft, tanks, and submarines, and began building a nuclear reactor for Tehran. For its part, Iran provided Moscow with important diplomatic assistance in combating the Taliban in Afghanistan and in achieving and maintaining the ceasefire in Tajikistan, and both countries sought to limit U.S. influence in Transcaucasia and Central Asia.

The close relations between Russia and Iran, which had begun in the last years of the Soviet Union under Gorbachev, developed steadily under both Yeltsin and Putin, with Putin even willing to abrogate the Gore-Chernomyrdin agreement, negotiated between the United States and Russia in 1995, which would have ended Russian arms sales to Iran by 2000.

Moscow was also willing, despite U.S. objections, to aid Iran in the development of the Shihab III intermediate-range ballistic missile and to supply Iran with nuclear reactors. However, there were areas of conflict in the Russian-Iranian relationship. First, the two countries were in competition over the transportation routes for the oil and natural gas of Central Asia and Transcaucasia. Iran claimed it provided the shortest and safest route for these energy resources to the outside world, while Russia wished to control the energy export routes of the states of the former Soviet Union, believing that these routes lay in the Russian sphere of influence. Second, by early 2001 Russia and Iran had come into conflict over the development of the energy resources of the Caspian Sea. Russia sided with Azerbaijan and Kazakhstan in their call for the development of their national sectors of the Caspian Sea, while Iran demanded either joint development of the Caspian Sea or a full 20 percent of the Caspian for itself. A third problem lay on the Russian side. Throughout the 1990s the conservative clerical regime in Iran became increasingly unpopular, and while it held the levers of power (army, police, and judiciary), the election of the Reformist Mohammed Khatami as Iran's President in 1997 (and his overwhelming reelection in 2001), along with the election in 2000 of a reformist Parliament (albeit one with limited power), led some in the Russian leadership to fear a possible Iranian-American rapprochement, which would have limited Russian influence in Iran. The possibilities of economic cooperation between the United States and Iran dwarfed those of Russia and Iran, particularly because both Russia and Iran throughout the 1990s encountered severe economic problems. Fortunately for Moscow, the conservative counterattack against both Khatami and the reformist Parliament at least temporarily prevented the rapprochement, as did President George W. Bush's labeling of Iran as part of the "axis of evil" in January 2002. On the other hand, Russian-Iranian relations were challenged by the new focus of cooperation between Russia and the United States after the terrorist attacks of September 11, 2001, and by Russia's acquiescence in the establishment of U.S. bases in central Asia.

In sum, throughout the 1990s and into the early twenty-first century, Russia and Iran were close economic, military, and diplomatic allies. However, it was unclear how long that alliance would remain strong.

See also: IRAQ, RELATIONS WITH; UNITED STATES, RELATIONS WITH

BIBLIOGRAPHY

Freedman, Robert O. (2001). *Russian Policy Toward the Middle East Since the Collapse of the Soviet Union: The Yeltsin Legacy and the Challenge for Putin (The Donald W. Treadgold Papers in Russian, East European, and Central Asian Studies,* no. 33). Seattle: Henry M. Jackson School of International Studies, University of Washington.

Nizamedden, Talal. (1999). *Russia and the Middle East.* New York: St. Martin's.

Rumer, Eugene. (2000). *Dangerous Drift: Russia's Middle East Policy.* Washington, DC: Washington Institute for Near East Policy.

Shaffer, Brenda. (2001). *Partners in Need: The Strategic Relationship of Russia and Iran.* Washington, DC: Washington Institute for Near East Policy.

Vassiliev, Alexei. (1993). *Russian Policy in the Middle East: From Messiasism to Pragmatism.* Reading, UK: Ithaca Press.

Robert O. Freedman

IRAQ, RELATIONS WITH

Following the signing of its Treaty of Friendship and Cooperation with the Soviet Union in 1972, Iraq became Moscow's primary ally in the Arab world. The warm Soviet-Iraqi relationship came to an end, however, in 1980, when Iraq invaded Iran, thereby splitting the Arab world and creating serious problems for Moscow's efforts to create anti-imperialist Arab unity. During the Iran-Iraq war Moscow switched back and forth between Iran and Iraq, but by the end of the war, in 1988, Gorbachev's new thinking in world affairs had come into effect, and the United States and USSR had begun to cooperate in the Middle East. That cooperation reached its peak when the United States and USSR cooperated against the Iraqi invasion of Kuwait in 1990.

When the Soviet Union collapsed, Yeltsin's Russia inherited a very mixed relationship with the Iraqi regime of Saddam Hussein. Although Iraq had been a major purchaser of Soviet arms, Saddam's invasion of Iran in 1980 and Kuwait in 1990 had greatly complicated Soviet foreign policy in the Middle East and led to the erosion of Moscow's influence in the region. At the beginning of his period of rule as Russia's President, Boris Yeltsin adopted an anti-Iraqi position and even contributed several ships to aid the United States in enforcing the anti-Iraqi naval blockade to prevent contraband from reaching Iraq.

However, beginning in 1993 when Yeltsin came under attack from the increasingly powerful parliamentary opposition, he began to improve relations with Iraq, both to gain popularity in parliament and to demonstrate he was not a lackey of the United States. Thus Yeltsin began to criticize the periodic U.S. bombings of Iraq, even when it was in retaliation for the assassination attempt against former President George Bush.

By 1996, when Yevgeny Primakov became Russia's Foreign Minister, Russia had three major objectives in Iraq. The first was to regain the more than seven billion dollars in debts that Iraq owed the former Soviet Union. The second was to acquire business for Russian companies, especially its oil companies. The third objective by 1996 was to enhance Russia's international prestige by opposing what Moscow claimed was Washington's efforts to create an American-dominated unipolar world.

Moscow, however, ran into problems with its Iraqi policy in 1997 and 1998 when U.S.-Iraqi tension escalated over Saddam Hussein's efforts to interfere with U.N. weapons inspections. While Russian diplomacy helped avert U.S. attacks in November 1997, February 1998, and November 1998, Moscow, despite a great deal of bluster, was unable to prevent a joint U.S.–British attack against suspected weapons sites in December 1998.

Following the attack, Moscow sought a new U.N. weapons inspection system, and when Putin became Prime Minister in 1999, Russia succeeded in pushing through the U.N. Security Council the UNMOVIC inspection system to replace the UNSCOP inspection system. Unfortunately for Moscow, which, under Iraqi pressure, abstained on the vote, Iraq refused to accept the new system, which linked Iraqi compliance with the inspectors with the temporary (120-day) lifting of U.N. sanctions on civilian goods. This meant that most of the Russian oil production agreements that had been signed with the Iraqi government remained in limbo, although Moscow did profit from the agreements made under the U.N.–approved "oil-for-food" program.

When the George W. Bush administration came to office, it initially sought to toughen sanctions against Iraq, especially on "dual-use" items with military capability, such as heavy trucks (which could carry missiles). Russia opposed the U.S. policy, seeking instead to weaken the sanctions. The situation changed, however, after September 11, 2001, when there was a marked increase in U.S.-Russian cooperation, and the two countries worked together to work out a mutually acceptable list of goods to be sanctioned. Russia, however, ran into problems when the U.S. attacked Iraq in March 2003. Russia condemned the attack, and U.S.-Russian relations deteriorated as a result, although there was a rapprochement at the end of the war when Russia supported the U.S.–sponsored UN Security Council resolution 1483 that confirmed U.S. control of Iraq.

See also: IRAN, RELATIONS WITH; PERSIAN GULF WAR; UNITED STATES, RELATIONS WITH

BIBLIOGRAPHY

Freedman, Robert O. (2001). *Russian Policy Toward the Middle East Since the Collapse of the Soviet Union: The Yeltsin Legacy and the Challenge for Putin (The Donald W. Treadgold Papers in Russian, East European, and Central Asian Studies,* no. 33). Seattle: Henry M. Jackson School of International Studies, University of Washington.

Nizamedden, Talal. (1999). *Russia and the Middle East.* New York: St. Martin's.

Rumer, Eugene. (2000). *Dangerous Drift: Russia's Middle East Policy.* Washington, DC: Washington Institute for Near East Policy.

Shaffer, Brenda. (2001). *Partners in Need: The Strategic Relationship of Russia and Iran.* Washington, DC: Washington Institute for Near East Policy.

Vassiliev, Alexei. (1993). *Russian Policy in the Middle East: From Messiasism to Pragmatism.* Reading, UK: Ithaca Press.

ROBERT O. FREEDMAN

IRON CURTAIN

"From Stettin in the Baltic to Trieste in the Adriatic, an iron curtain has descended across the Continent." With these words on March 5, 1946, former British Prime Minister Winston Churchill marked out the beginning of the Cold War and a division of Europe that would last nearly forty-five years. Churchill's metaphorical iron curtain brought an end to the uncomfortable Soviet-Anglo-American alliance against Nazi Germany and began the process of physically dividing Europe into two spheres of influence. In his speech Churchill recognized the "valiant Russian people" and Josef Stalin's role in the destruction of Hitler's military, but then asserted that Soviet influence and control had descended across Eastern Europe, thereby threatening the safety and security of the entire continent through "fifth columns" and "indefinite expansion of [Soviet] power and doctrines." In even more provocative language Churchill equated Stalin with Adolph Hitler by telling his American audience that the Anglo-American alliance must act swiftly to prevent another catastrophe, this time communist instead of fascist, from befalling Europe.

In response, Stalin also equated Churchill with Hitler. Stalin rebuked Churchill for using odious Nazi racial theory in his suggestion that the nations of the English-speaking world must unite against this new threat. For Stalin this smacked of racial domination of the rest of the world. He noted that Soviet casualties (which he grossly undercounted) far outweighed the deaths of the other allies combined and that therefore Europe owed a debt to the USSR, not to the United States as Churchill claimed, for saving the continent from Hitler. Stalin explained his intentions in occupying what would become known as the Eastern Bloc: After such devastating losses, was it not logical, he asked, to try to find peaceful governments on the Soviet border? Stalin conceded Churchill's point that communist parties were growing, but argued that this was due to the failures of the West, not Soviet occupation. The people for whom Churchill had such disdain, according to Stalin, were moving toward leftist parties because the communists throughout Europe were some of the first and fiercest foes of fascism. Moreover, he noted that this was precisely why British citizens voted Churchill out of power in favor of the Labor Party.

By linking the other to Hitler, both men sought to demonize their one-time ally and convince their audiences that a new war against an equal evil was on the horizon. This set the tone for the rest of the Cold War as the western powers established the Truman Doctrine, Marshall Plan, and NATO, to which the USSR responded in quick succession. The chief battleground was divided Germany and Berlin. Any escalation by one side was quickly met by the other, as both sides operated on mistaken assumptions that a war for world dominance (or at least regional dominance) was at hand. In short, the "Iron Curtain" speech, the real title of which was "Sinews of Peace," created a metaphorical division of Europe that soon became a reality. This division only began to erode in 1989 with the destruction of the Berlin Wall and the 1991 dissolution of the Soviet Union.

See also: COLD WAR; GERMANY, RELATIONS WITH; STALIN, JOSEF VISSARIONOVICH; WORLD WAR II

BIBLIOGRAPHY

Alperovitz, Gar. (1965). *Atomic Diplomacy: Hiroshima and Potsdam; The Use of the Atomic Bomb and the American Confrontation with Soviet Power.* New York: Simon and Schuster.

Gaddis, John Lewis. (1997). *We Now Know: Rethinking Cold War History.* Oxford: Oxford University Press.

Kort, Michael. (1998). *The Columbia Guide to the Cold War.* New York: Columbia University Press.

McCauley, Martin. (1995). *The Origins of the Cold War, 1941–1949.* New York: Longman.

KARL D. QUALLS

ISLAM

From the beginning, Rus and its successors have interacted with Muslims as neighbors, rulers, and subjects. Long-distance trade in silver from Muslim lands provided the impetus for the establishment of the first Rus principalities, and Islam arrived in the lands of Rus before Christianity. The rulers of the Volga Bulghar state converted to Islam at the turn of the tenth century, several decades before Vladimir's conversion to Christianity in 988 C.E. The Bulghar state was destroyed between 1236 and 1237 by the Mongols, who then went on to subjugate the principalities of Rus. The conversion to Islam in 1327 of Özbek Khan, the ruler of the Golden Horde, meant that political overlordship of the lands of Rus was in the hands of Muslims for over a century. As the power relationship between Muscovy and the Golden Horde began to shift, Muscovite princes found themselves actively involved in its succession struggles. In 1552 Ivan IV conquered Kazan, the most prominent of the successor states of the Golden Horde, and began a long process of territorial expansion, which brought a diverse group of Muslims under Russian rule by the end of the nineteenth century.

THE TSARIST STATE AND ITS MUSLIM POPULATION

Muscovy acquired its first Muslim subjects as early as 1392, when the so-called Mishar Tatars, who inhabited what is now Nizhny Novgorod province, entered the service of Muscovite princes. The khans of Kasymov, a dynasty that lost out in the succession struggles of the Golden Horde, came under Muscovite protection in the mid-fifteenth century and became a privileged service elite. Nevertheless, the conquest of Kazan was a turning point, for it opened up the steppe to gradual Muscovite expansion. Over the next two centuries Muscovy acquired numerous Muslim subjects as it asserted suzerainty over the Bashkir and Kazakh steppes. In 1783 Catherine II annexed Crimea, the last of the successors of the Golden Horde, and late-eighteenth-century expansion brought Russia to the Caucasus. While the annexation of the Transcaucasian principalities (including present-day Azerbaijan) was accomplished with relative ease, the conquest of the Caucasus consumed Russian energies for the first half of the nineteenth century. The final subjugation of Caucasian tribes was complete only with the capture of their military and spiritual leader, Shamil, in 1859. Finally, in the last major territorial expansion of its history, Russia subjugated the Central Asian khanates of Khiva, Bukhara, and Kokand in a series of military campaigns between 1864 and 1876. Kokand was abolished entirely, and large parts of the territory of Khiva and Bukhara were also annexed to form the province of Turkestan. The remaining territories of Khiva and Bukhara were turned into Russian pro-

Muslims pray at Moscow's principal mosque, March 5, 2001. © REUTERS NEWMEDIA INC./CORBIS

tectorates in which traditional rulers enjoyed wide-ranging autonomy in internal affairs, but where external economic and political relations were under the control of Russia. The conquest of Central Asia dramatically increased the size of the empire's Muslim population, which stood at more than fourteen million at the time of the census of 1897.

The Russian state's interaction with Islam and Muslims varied greatly over time and place, and it is fair to say that no single policy toward Islam may be discerned. In the immediate aftermath of the conquest of Kazan, the state followed a policy of harsh repression. Repression was renewed in the early eighteenth century, when Peter and his successors began to see religious uniformity as a desirable goal. In 1730 the Church opened its Office of New Converts and initiated a campaign of conversion in the Volga region. While its primary target were the animists inhabiting the region, the Office also destroyed many mosques. As many as 7,000 Tatars may have converted to Orthodoxy, thus laying the foundation of the Kräshen community of Christian Tatars. For much of the rest of the imperial period, however, the state's attitude is best characterized as one of "pragmatic flexibility" (Kappeler). Service to the state was the ultimate measure of loyalty and the source of privilege. Those Tatar landlords who survived the dispossession of the sixteenth century were allowed to keep their land and were even able to own Orthodox serfs.

The reign of Catherine II (1762–1796) marks a turning point in the state's relationship with its Muslim subjects. She made religious tolerance an official policy and set about creating a basis for loyalty to the Russian state in the Tatar lands. She affirmed the rights of Muslim nobles and even sought to induct the Muslim clerisy in this endeavor. In 1788, she established a "spiritual assembly" at Orenburg. The Orenburg Muslim Spiritual Assembly was an attempt, unique in the Muslim world, by the state to impose an organizational structure on Islam. Islam was for Catherine a higher form of religion than shamanism, and she hoped that the Kazakhs would gradually be brought into the fold of Islam through the efforts of the Tatars. This was of course intertwined with the goal of bringing the Kazakh steppe under closer Russian control and outflanking Ottoman diplomacy there. Headed by a mufti appointed by the state, the assembly was responsible for appointing and licensing imams as teachers throughout the territory under its purview, and overseeing the operation of mosques.

While the policies enacted by Catherine survived until 1917 in their broad outline, her enthusiasm for Islam did not. The Enlightenment had also brought to Russia the concept of fanaticism, and it tended to dominate Russian thinking about Islam in the nineteenth century. Islam was now deemed to be inherently fanatical, and the question now became one of curbing or containing this fanaticism. If Catherine had hoped for the Islamization of the Kazakhs as a mode of progress, nineteenth century administrators sought to protect the "natural" religion of the Kazakhs from the "fanatical" Islam of the Tatars or the Central Asians.

Conquered in the second half of the nineteenth century and having a relatively dense population, Central Asia came closer than any other part of the Russian empire to being a colony. The Russian presence was thinner, and the local population not incorporated into empire-wide social classifications. Not only was there was no Central Asian nobility, but the vast majority (99.8%) of the local population were defined solely as *inorodtsy* (alien, i.e., non-Russian, peoples). The region was ruled by a governor-general possessing wide-ranging powers and answerable directly to the tsar. The first governor-general, Konstantin Kaufman (in office 1867–1881), laid the foundations of Russian policies in the region. For Kaufman, Islam was irredeemably connected with fanaticism, which could be provoked by thoughtless policies. Such fanaticism could be lessened by ignoring Islam and depriving it of all state support, while the long-term goal of assimilating the region into the Russian empire was to be achieved through a policy of encouraging trade and enlightenment. Kaufman therefore did not allow the Orenburg Muslim Assembly to extend its jurisdiction into Turkestan. The policy of ignoring Islam completely was modified after Kaufman's death, but the Russian presence was much more lightly felt in Central Asia than in other Muslim areas of the empire.

ISLAM UNDER RUSSIAN RULE

Islam is an internally diverse religious system in which many traditions and ways of belonging to the community of Muslims coexist. As Devin DeWeese has shown, Islam became a central aspect of the communal identities of Muslims in the Golden Horde. Conversion was remembered in sacralized narratives that defined conversion as the moment that the community was constituted. Shrines of saints served to Islamize the very territory on which Muslims lived. Until the articulation in the late nineteenth and early twentieth centuries of modern national identities among the various Muslim communities of the Russian empire, communal identities were a composite of ethnic, genealogical, and religious identities, inextricably intertwined.

The practice of Islam, its reproduction, and its transmission to future generations took place in largely autonomous local communities. Each community was centered around a mosque and (especially in Central Asia) a shrine. The servants of the mosques were selected by the community, and the funding provided by local notables or through endowed property (*waqf*). Each community also maintained a *maktab*, an elementary school in which children acquired basic knowledge of Islamic ritual and belief. Higher religious education took place in *madrasas*, both locally and in neighboring Muslim countries. Unlike the Christian clergy, Muslim scholars, the ulama, were a self-regulating group. Entry into the ranks of the ulama was contingent upon education and insertion into chains of discipleship. Islamic religious practice required neither the institutional framework nor the property of a church. This loose structure meant that the fortunes of Islam and its carriers were not directly tied to the vicissitudes of Muslim states.

The process of Islamization continued after the Russian conquest of the steppe and was at times even supported by the Russian state. The state settled Muslim peasants in the trans-Volga region in the eighteenth and nineteenth centuries, but the main agent of the Islamization of the steppe was the Tatar mercantile diaspora. As communities of Tatar merchants appeared throughout the steppe beginning in the late eighteenth century, Tobolsk, Orenburg, and Troitsk became major centers of Islamic learning. Tatar merchants began sending their sons to study in Central Asia, and Sufi linkages with Central Asia and the lands beyond were strengthened.

VARIETIES OF REFORM

In the early nineteenth century, reform began to emerge as a major issue among Tatar ulama. The initial issues, as articulated by figures such as Abdunnasir al-Qursavi (1776–1812) and Qayyum Nasiri (1825–1902), related to the value of the tradition of interpretation of texts as it had been practiced in Central Asia and in the Tatar lands since Mongol times. Qursavi, Nasiri, and their followers questioned the authority of traditional Islamic theology and argued for creative reinterpretation through recourse to the original scriptural sources of Islam. This religious conception of reform was connected to developments in the wider Muslim world through networks of education and travel. By the turn of the twentieth century, Tatar scholars such as Musa Jarullah Bigi, Alimjan Barudi, and Rizaetdin Fakhretdin were prominent well beyond the boundaries of the Russian empire.

A different form of reform arose around the reform of Muslim education. Its initial constituency was the urban mercantile population of the Volga region and the Crimea, and its origins are connected with the tireless efforts of the Crimean Tatar noble Ismail Bey Gaspirali (1851–1914). Gaspirali had been educated at a military academy but became involved in education early on in his career. Muslims, he felt, lacked many skills important to full participation in the mainstream of imperial life. The fault lay with the *maktab*, which not only did not inculcate useful knowledge, such as arithmetic, geography, or Russian, but failed, moreover, in the task of equipping students with basic literacy or even a proper understanding of Islam itself. Gaspirali articulated a modernist critique of the *maktab*, emanating from a new understanding of the purposes of elementary education. The solution was a new method (*usul-i jadid*) of education, in which children were taught the Arabic alphabet using the phonetic method of instruction and the elementary school was to have a standardized curriculum encompassing composition, arithmetic, history, hygiene, and Russian. Gaspirali's method found acceptance among the Muslim communities of the Crimea, the Volga, and Siberia, and eventually appeared in all parts of the Russian empire inhabited by Muslims. New-method schools quickly became the flagship of a multifaceted movement of cultural reform, which came to be called "Jadidism" after them.

Jadidism was an unabashedly modernist discourse of cultural reform directed at Muslim society itself. Its basic themes were enlightenment, progress, and the awakening of the nation, so that the latter could take its own place in the modern, civilized world. Given the lack of political sovereignty, however, it was up to society to lift itself up by its bootstraps through education and disciplined effort. Jadid rhetoric was usually sharply critical of the present state of Muslim society, which the Jadids contrasted unfavorably to a glorious past of their own society and the present of the civilized countries of Europe. The single most important term in the Jadid lexicon was *taraqqi*, progress. Progress and civilization were universal phenomena for the Jadids, accessible to all societies on the sole condition of disciplined effort and enlightenment. There was nothing in Islam that prevented Muslims from joining the modern world; indeed, the Jadids argued that only a modern per-

Sixteenth-century manuscript illustration showing Bahram Gur, legendary Sassanian king in Persian mythology, and the Russian princes in the Red Pavilion. © THE ART ARCHIVE/BODLEIAN LIBRARY OXFORD/THE BODLEIAN LIBRARY

son equipped with knowledge "according to the needs of the age" could be a good Muslim. In this, Jadidism differed sharply from other currents of reform among the ulama. The debate between the Jadids and their traditionalist opponents was the defining feature of the last decades of the Tsarist period.

In Central Asia, the distinct social and political context imparted Jadidism a distinct flavor. The ulama retained much greater influence in Central Asia, while the new mercantile class was weaker. Central Asian Jadids, therefore, tended to be more strongly rooted in Islamic education than their counterparts elsewhere. Nevertheless, they faced resolute opposition from within their own society, as well as from a Russian state always suspicious of unofficial initiatives.

THE "MUSLIM QUESTION" IN LATE IMPERIAL POLITICS

For the Jadids, the nation was an integral part of modernity, and they set out to define the parameters of their nation. The new identity was not foreordained, however, for the nation could be defined along any of several different axes of solidarity. For some, all Muslims of the Russian empire constituted a single national community. Gaspirali argued that the Muslims needed "unity in language, thought, and deeds," and his newspaper sought to show this through example. In 1905 a number of Tatar and Azerbaijani activists organized an All-Russian conference for Muslim representatives to work out a common plan of action. The conference established the Ittifaq-i Müslimin (Union of Muslims) as a quasi-political organization. Delegates resolved to work for greater political, religious, and cultural rights for their constituency. During the elections to the Duma, the Ittifaq aligned itself with the Kadets. Two further conferences were held in 1905 and 1906, but Muslim political activity was curbed after the Stolypin coup of 1907, which reduced the representation of Muslims and denied the Ittifaq permission to register a political party.

Muslim unity was threatened by regional and ethnic solidarities. The discovery of romantic notions of identity by the Jadids led them to articulate the identity of their community along ethnonational lines. Here too, visions of a broad Turkic unity coexisted with narrower forms of identity, such as Tatar or Kazakh. The appeal of local ethnic identities proved too strong for broader Islamic or Turkic identities to surmount. This was the case in 1917, when the All-Russian Muslim movement was briefly resurrected and Tatar leaders organized a conference in Moscow to discuss a common political strategy for Muslims. Divisions between representatives from different regions quickly appeared, and the various groups of Muslims went their separate ways.

Although Muslim activists continually professed their loyalty to the state, their activity aroused suspicion both in the state and among the Russian public, which construed it as pan-Islamism and connected it with alleged Ottoman intrigues to destabilize the Russian state. The rise of ethnic self-awareness was likewise seen as pan-Turkism and also connected to outside influences. Russian administrators had hoped that enlightenment would be the antidote to fanaticism. Now the fear of pan-Islamism and pan-Turkism, both articulated by modern-educated Muslims, led to a reappraisal. The fanaticism of modernist Islam was deemed much more dangerous than that of the traditional Islam, since it led to political demands. This perception led the state to intensify its support for traditional Islam.

THE SOVIET PERIOD

The Russian revolution utterly transformed the political and social landscape in which Islam existed in the Russian empire. The new regime was radically different from its predecessor in that it actively sought to intervene in society and to reshape not just the economy, but also the cultures of its citizens. It was hostile to religion, perceiving it as both an alternate source of loyalty and a form of cultural backwardness. As policies regarding Soviet nationalities emerged in the 1920s, the struggle for progress acquired a prominent role, especially among nationalities deemed backward (and all Muslim groups were so classified). Campaigns for cultural revolution began with the reform of education, language, and the position of women, but quickly extended to religion. The antireligious campaign eventually led to the closure of large numbers of mosques (many were destroyed, others given over to "more socially productive" uses, such as youth clubs, museums of atheism, or warehouses). *Waqf* properties were confiscated, *madrasas* closed, and large numbers of ulama arrested and deported to labor camps or executed. The only Muslim institution to survive was the spiritual assembly, now stationed in Ufa.

The campaign was effective in its destructiveness. Islam did not disappear, but the infrastructure which reproduced Islamic religious and cultural knowledge was badly damaged and links with the outside Muslim world cut off. Islam was forced into isolation. The most important consequence of this isolation was that "Islam" was rendered synonymous with "tradition". Official channels of socialization, such as the school system and the army, which reached very deep into society, were not just secular, but atheistic. With *maktabs* and *madrasas* abolished, the ranks of the carriers of Islamic knowledge denuded, and continuity with the past made difficult by changes in script, religious knowledge was vastly circumscribed and the site of its reproduction pushed into private or covert realms. The public sphere were stripped of all references to Islam.

During World War II, as the state's hostility to religion abated briefly, it sought to permit limited practice of religion under close supervision. To this end, it created three new Muslim spiritual administrations in addition to the one at Ufa to oversee the practice of Islam. Of the four, the one based in Tashkent and responsible for Central Asia soon emerged as the most significant. The spiritual assemblies had to tread a thin line between satisfying the requirements of the state and ensuring a space in which Islamic institutions could exist officially. A great deal of religious activity existed beyond the control of the assemblies, but it was at home in a specifically Soviet context. Islam in the postwar decades was subordinated to powerful national identities formed for the most part in the Soviet period. Islam and its rituals were celebrated as part of one's national heritage even as Islamic knowledge shrunk greatly.

Since the collapse of the Soviet Union, Islam has become more prominent in public life as Muslims have engaged in a recovery of their national and cultural heritage. Mosques have been reopened or rebuilt and contacts with Muslims abroad established, and a there has been a general increase in personal piety. Nevertheless, the Soviet-era connections between Islam and national heritage remain intact, and as post-Soviet regimes undertake nation-building, Islam retains its strong cultural definitions.

See also: CENTRAL ASIA; GASPIRALI, ISMAIL BEY; GOLDEN HORDE; NATIONALITIES POLICIES, SOVIET; NATIONALITIES POLICIES, TSARIST; RELIGION

BIBLIOGRAPHY

Bennigsen, Alexandre, and S. Enders Wimbush. (1979). *Muslim National Communism: a Revolutionary Strategy for the Colonial World*. Chicago: University of Chicago Press.

Carrère d'Encausse, Hélène. (1988). *Islam and the Russian Empire: Reform and Revolution in Central Asia*, tr. Quintin Hoare. Berkeley: University of California Press.

DeWeese, Devin. (1995). *Islamization and Native Religion in the Golden Horde: Baba Tükles and Conversion to Islam in Historical and Epic Tradition*. University Park: Pennsylvania State University Press.

Frank, Alan J. (1998). *Islamic Historiography and "Bulghar" Identity among the Tatars and Bashkirs of Russia*. Leiden, Netherlands: Brill.

Frank, Alan J. (2001). *Muslim Institutions in Imperial Russia: The Islamic World of Novouznesensk District and the Kazakh Inner Horde, 1780–1920*. Leiden, Netherlands: Brill.

Gammer, Moshe. (1994). *Muslim Resistance to the Tsar: Shamil and the Conquest of Chechnia and Daghestan*. London: Frank Cass.

Geraci, Robert. (2001). *Window on the East: National and Imperial Identities in Late Imperial Russia*. Ithaca, NY: Cornell University Press.

Kamp, Marianne R. (1998). "Unveiling Uzbek Women: Liberation, Representation, and Discourse, 1906–1929." Ph.D. diss., University of Chicago.

Kappeler, Andreas. (1992). "Czarist Policy Toward the Muslims of the Russian Empire." In *Muslim Communities Reemerge: Historical Perspectives on Nationality, Politics, and Opposition in the Former Soviet Union and Yugoslavia*, ed. Andreas Kappeler et al. Durham, NC: Duke University Press.

Keller, Shoshana. (2000). *To Moscow, not Mecca: Soviet Campaigns against Islam in Central Asia, 1917–1941*. Westport, CT: Praeger.

Khalid, Adeeb. (1998). *The Politics of Muslim Cultural Reform: Jadidism in Central Asia*. Berkeley: University of California Press.

Khalid, Adeeb. (2000). "Society and Politics in Bukhara, 1868–1920." *Central Asian Survey* 19: 367–396.

Ro'i, Yaacov. (2000). *Islam in the Soviet Union: From the Second World War to Gorbachev*. New York: Columbia University Press.

Steinwedel, Charles. (1999). "Invisible Threads of Empire: State, Religion, and Ethnicity in Tsarist Bashkiria, 1773–1917." Ph.D. dissertation, Columbia University, New York.

Swietochowski, Tadeusz. (1995). *Russia and Azerbaijan: A Borderland in Transition*. New York: Columbia University Press.

Adeeb Khalid

ISRAEL, RELATIONS WITH

During most of the Soviet period, Soviet-Israeli relations were strained if not broken. Although Moscow gave diplomatic and even military support (via Czechoslovakia) to Israel during its war of independence (1948–1949), by 1953 it had shifted to a pro-Arab position and it broke diplomatic relations with Israel during the June 1967 Six-Day War. From the mid-1960s until Mikhail Gorbachev came to power, the USSR, seeking to align the Arab world against the United States, called Israel the "lynchpin of U.S. imperialism in the region." Under Gorbachev, however, the USSR made a major shift in policy, taking an even-handed position in the Arab-Israeli conflict, and by 1991 had reestablished full diplomatic relations with Israel.

In the period since the collapse of the Soviet Union, relations between Moscow and Jerusalem, already warming in the final years of the Soviet Union when Gorbachev was in power, continued to improve. Trade between the two countries rose to a billion dollars per year, Jews were free to emigrate from Russia to Israel, and the two countries even cooperated in the production of military equipment such as helicopters and airborne command-and-control aircraft (AWACS). On the diplomatic front, under both Yeltsin and Putin, Russia took a balanced position, unlike the pre-Gorbachev Soviet government, which consistently took a pro-Arab, anti-Israeli stand. However, during the period when Yevgeny Primakov was Russia's Foreign Minister and Prime Minister (1996–1999), there was a marked tilt toward the Arab position. Following Primakov's ouster and the renewed Russian involvement in a war against Islamic rebels in Chechnya (where Israel supported Russia diplomatically), Russia under Putin's leadership switched back to a balanced position. Some Russian leaders even compared the Islamic-based terrorism Israel faced, from Hamas and Islamic Jihad, to the Islamic-based opposition Russia was battling in Chechnya.

The major problem in the Russian-Israeli relationship was the supply of Russian arms and military technology—including missile technology—to Iran. Given the fact that the clerical leadership of Iran called for Israel's destruction and supplied weapons to both Hezbollah and to the Palestinian Authority to fight Israel, Israel bitterly opposed the Russian sales. However, after the collapse of the Soviet Union, Iran became Russia's number one ally in the Middle East, and Russia continued to supply Iran with arms.

One of the dynamic aspects of the Russian-Israeli relationship after 1991 was the role of the million-plus Jews from the former Soviet Union (FSU) who emigrated to Israel. They formed the largest Russian-speaking diaspora outside the FSU and constituted a major cultural bond between Israel and Russia. As the Russian vote became increasingly important in Israeli elections, candidates for the post of Israeli Prime Minister sought to cultivate this electorate by announcing their wish to improve ties with Russia. For its part, Moscow, especially under Putin, developed a special relationship with the Russian community in Israel and saw that community as a tool to enhance Russian-Israeli trade and hence improve the Russian economy. Below the level of official relations, the Russian mafia created ties (including money-laundering ties) with its Russian counterparts in Israel, and this led to joint efforts by the Russian and Israeli governments to fight crime, occasioning frequent mutual visits of the Ministers of the Interior of both countries to deal with this problem.

Another major change from Soviet times was Russia's willingness to follow the U.S. lead in seeking to end the Israeli-Arab conflict. Thus Russia supported the OSLO I and OSLO II peace agreements in tandem with U.S. efforts to end the Al-Aksa intifada through the U.S.–backed Mitchell Report. Such action was facilitated in part by the decreasing importance to Russia of the Arab-Israeli conflict, which was pivotal to Moscow's policy in the Middle East during Soviet times, and in part by Russia's desire, especially under Putin, to demonstrate cooperation with the United States.

See also: JEWS; IRAN, RELATIONS WITH; IRAQ, RELATIONS WITH; REFUSENIKS; UNITED STATES, RELATIONS WITH

BIBLIOGRAPHY

Freedman, Robert O. (2001). *Russian Policy Toward the Middle East Since the Collapse of the Soviet Union: The Yeltsin Legacy and the Challenge for Putin (The Donald W. Treadgold Papers in Russian, East European, and Central Asian Studies*, no. 33). Seattle: Henry M. Jackson School of International Studies, University of Washington.

Nizamedden, Talal. (1999). *Russia and the Middle East.* New York: St. Martin's.

Rumer, Eugene. (2000). *Dangerous Drift: Russia's Middle East Policy.* Washington, DC: Washington Institute for Near East Policy.

Shaffer, Brenda. (2001). *Partners in Need: The Strategic Relationship of Russia and Iran.* Washington, DC: Washington Institute for Near East Policy.

Vassiliev, Alexei. (1993). *Russian Policy in the Middle East: From Messiasism to Pragmatism.* Reading, UK: Ithaca Press.

Robert O. Freedman

ITALY, RELATIONS WITH

From the time of Italy's unification in the mid-nineteenth century through the post-Soviet era, schizophrenic collaboration and competition in the Balkans and Danubian Europe has marked Italo-Russian relations, with national interests consistently trumping shifting ideologies in both countries.

The schizophrenia was there from the beginning. Although Tsar Alexander II, for example, objected to Italy's unification, the wars fought to that end could not have been arranged and contained without the Tsar's complicity. By the late 1870s liberal Italy was becoming enmeshed in the Triple Alliance with Austria and Germany. Although it was primarily directed against France, the Italians hoped the alliance would also blunt autocratic Russia's penetration of the Balkans. Later, Russia's defeat at Japanese hands in 1905 removed the counterbalance to Austria's influence in the Balkans, and Italy became every bit as aggrieved as Russia by Austria's conduct during the First Bosnian Crisis (1908–1909). The result was the Italo-Russian Racconigi Agreement (1909). Of the European powers, only Italy supported Russia on the Straits Question. Although Rome promised several times to stand by its obligations taken at Racconigi, Russia proved unable to use the Italo-Turkish War (1911–1912) as an excuse to reexamine the Straits Question.

During World War I, both Rome and Petrograd feared Austro-German advances into the Balkans. Rome, however, was no more eager to see Germanic dominance replaced by Russian-led Panslavism than Russia was to see it replaced by Italian influence. The complex, multilateral negotiations that brought Italy into the war (1915) required the uneasy compromise of Russian and Italian ambitions in the Balkans. These compromises seriously eroded Russia's political situation and betrayed Serbia, Russia's ally and *caucasus belli.* After the war, Italy generally refrained from supporting the anti-Bolshevik White armies during Russia's civil war, although Rome did provide small contingents to the Allied intervention in Vladivostok and briefly planned to intervene in Georgia.

Thereafter, Italo-Soviet relations fell into the old grooves of *Realpolitik.* Even Benito Mussolini's rise to power (1922) had little effect on diplomatic directions. Despite the presumed ideological antipathies dividing communist Russia and fascist Italy, the Duce exploited Italy's position between the Allies and the Soviets to reintroduce Russia into Europe and to arbitrate among the great powers. Although commercial aspirations motivated Italy's recognition of the Soviets (1924), the fascists and soviets also drew together in common hostility to responsible parliamentary systems of government. By 1930, the Soviet Union, Italy, and Germany were tending to ally against France and its allies.

With Hitler's rise to power (1933), Moscow and Rome sought ways to contain the threat of a resurgent Germany. Through extensive cooperation, both began to support the status quo to block German expansion, especially in the Balkans. Russia's nonaggression pact with Italy (1933) marked a significant step in its Collective Security policy directed against Germany. Italy's successful defense of Austria (1934)—the one successful example of Collective Security before World War II—seemed to vindicate Soviet policy.

Good relations, despite Moscow's extraordinary efforts at appeasement, collapsed during the Italo-Ethiopian War (1935–1936) and the Spanish Civil War (1936–1939). Afterward the Italo-Soviet economic agreements (February 1939) began a rapprochement and presaged the Nazi-Soviet Pact of August. Even after World War II began, Moscow continued to hope to split the Italo-German alliance and to use Italy to block German penetration into the Balkans: for example, by encouraging Italy's plan for a bloc of Balkan neutrals in the Fall and Winter of 1939. These plans came to naught when Germany and then Italy attacked Russia in June 1941. The Italian expeditionary army on the Eastern Front met horrific disaster in 1943.

The Allies signed an armistice with Italy in 1943, and the following year the USSR recognized the new Italy. In 1947, the two signed a peace treaty. Italo-Russian relations were again subsumed in the struggles between larger alliance systems, this time with Italy playing a crucial role in the North Atlantic Treaty Organization, which stood against the Soviet-led Warsaw Pact. Particularly interesting was the rise of the Italian Communist Party (PCI). After the brutal crushing of the Hungarian Revolt (1956), however, the PCI began to distance itself from the USSR and to promote an "Italian Road to Socialism." In March 1978, the PCI entered a governmental majority for the first time. Stung by the Soviet invasion of Afghanistan, the PCI increasingly promoted Eurocommunism, which ultimately played a large role in delegitimizing Soviet Russia's imperial satellite system in Eastern Europe. After the collapse of Communism in Russia in the early 1990s, the main point of cooperation and conflict between Russia and Italy remained focused in the Balkans and Danubian regions.

See also: BALKAN WARS; WORLD WAR I; WORLD WAR II

BIBLIOGRAPHY

Clarke, J. Calvitt. (1991). *Russia and Italy against Hitler: The Bolshevik-Fascist Rapprochement of the 1930s.* New York: Greenwood Press.

Corti, Eugenio. (1997). *Few Returned: Twenty-Eight Days on the Russian Front, Winter 1942–1943*, tr. Peter Edward Levy. Columbia: University of Missouri Press.

Nobile, Umberto. (1987). *My Five Years with Soviet Airships*, tr. Frances Fleetwood. Akron, OH: Lighter-Than-Air Society.

Toscano, Mario. (1970). *Designs in Diplomacy: Pages from European Diplomatic History in the Twentieth Century.* Translated and edited by George A. Carbone. Baltimore: The Johns Hopkins Press.

Urban, Joan Barth. (1986). *Moscow and the Italian Communist Party: From Togliatti to Berlinguer.* Ithaca, NY: Cornell University Press.

J. CALVITT CLARKE III

IVAN I

(d. 1340), prince of Moscow and sole grand prince of Vladimir.

By collaborating with the Tatar overlords in Saray, Ivan I overcame his rivals in Tver and made Moscow the most important domain in northeast Russia. He was nicknamed "Moneybag" ("Kalita") to reflect his shrewd money handling practices.

Ivan Danilovich was the son of Daniel and grandson of Alexander Yaroslavich "Nevsky." In 1325, when he succeeded his brother Yury as prince of Moscow, he continued Moscow's fight with Tver for supremacy. Two years later the people of Tver, the town ruled by Grand Prince Alexander Mikhailovich, revolted against the Tatars. In 1328 Ivan visited Khan Uzbek, who gave him the patent for the grand princely throne and troops to punish the insurgents. After Ivan devastated Tver and forced Alexander to flee, the town and its prince never regained their position of power. Significantly, in his rivalry with Tver, Ivan won the support of the Metropolitan, who chose Moscow for his residence. In the 1330s, as Grand Prince Gedimin increasingly threatened Russia, Ivan also fought to suppress pro-Lithuanian factions in the northwestern towns. His greatest challenge was to subdue Novgorod, which used its association with Lithuania against him, and which challenged him when he levied Tatar tribute on it. By faithfully collecting the tribute, however, and by visiting the Golden Horde on nine occasions and winning the khan's trust, he persuaded the Tatars to stop raiding Russia. Moreover, by currying the khan's favour, Ivan was able to keep the title of grand prince and secure succession to it for his son Simeon. Ivan died on March 31, 1340.

See also: GOLDEN HORDE; GRAND PRINCE; MOSCOW

BIBLIOGRAPHY

Fennell, John L. I. (1968). *The Emergence of Moscow 1304–1359.* London: Secker and Warburg.

Martin, Janet. (1995). *Medieval Russia 980–1584.* Cambridge, UK: Cambridge University Press.

MARTIN DIMNIK

IVAN II

(1326–1359), prince of Moscow and grand prince of Vladimir.

In the 1340s Lithuania encroached into western Russia and challenged the Golden Horde for control of Russian towns. Thus the prince of Moscow and other princes had to establish relations with both foreign powers. Ivan's elder brother Simeon and father Ivan I Danilovich "Kalita" ("Moneybag") had collaborated with the Tatars to promote Moscow's interests against princely rivals and against Lithuania. Ivan, a weak ruler under whose reign Moscow's authority declined, charted a different course. After Simeon died in 1353, Ivan traveled to Saray, where Khan Jani-Beg, against the objections of Novgorod and Suzdal-Nizhny Novgorod, gave him the patent for the grand princely throne of Vladimir. Later, however, he was persuaded to establish cordial relations with Lithuania and to decrease Moscow's subordination to the khan. He formed a treaty with pro-Lithuanian Suzdal, arranged a marriage alliance with Lithuania, and prevented Tatar envoys from entering Muscovite lands. His change of policy kindled serious opposition. Many of his councilors fled to pro-Tatar Ryazan, thus weakening Moscow's internal solidarity. Metropolitan Alexei also sided with the defectors. When the khan himself challenged Ivan, he yielded to the pressure. In 1357 he submitted to Berdi-Beg, the new khan, and was reconciled with his disgruntled boyars. But he failed to increase Moscow's territories, and Novgorod ignored him. Moreover, in the testament he issued before his death, he confirmed the practice of hereditary appanages, which his brother Simeon had first espoused, and which further fragmented the Moscow principality. He died on November 13, 1359.

See also: GOLDEN HORDE; MOSCOW

BIBLIOGRAPHY

Fennell, John L. I. (1968). *The Emergence of Moscow 1304–1359.* London: Secker and Warburg.

Martin, Janet. (1995). *Medieval Russia 980–1584.* Cambridge, UK: Cambridge University Press.

MARTIN DIMNIK

Eighteenth-century portrait of Ivan III.

IVAN III

(1440–1505), grand prince of Moscow (1462–1505), sovereign of "all Russia" (from 1479).

Ivan Vasilyeich was the eldest son and successor to Basil II, co-regent in the last years of his blind father. Ivan's youth coincided with the dynastic war, in which he took part at age twelve, leading the campaign against Dmitry Shemyaka (1452). Thereafter, Ivan became a steady champion of autocratic rule.

Under Ivan III's reign, the uniting of separate Russian principalities into a centralized state made great and rapid progress. Some of these principalities lost their independence peacefully (Yaroslavl, 1463–1468; Rostov, 1474); others tried to resist and were subjugated by military force (Great Novgorod, 1471–1478; Tver, 1485; Vyatka, 1489).

The incorporation of Great Novgorod into the emerging Muscovite state took especially dramatic form. When Novgorodian boyars questioned the sovereignty of the grand prince over their city-state, Ivan III led his troops to Great Novgorod. In the battle on the Shelon River, July 14, 1471, the Novgorodian army was completely defeated. Four boyars who had been captured (including Dmitry Boretsky, one of the leaders of anti-Muscovite party in Novgorod) were executed by the grand prince's order. In the peace treaty of August 11, 1471, the city acknowledged the lordship of the grand prince and gave up the right of independent foreign relations. Six years later, Ivan III found a pretext to start a new campaign against Novgorod; this time the city-state surrendered without a struggle. In January 1478, Great Novgorod lost its autonomy completely: The *veche* (people's assembly) and the office of *posadnik* (the head of the city government) were abolished, and the assembly's bell, the symbol of Novgorod's sovereignty, was taken away to Moscow. In the 1480s, having confiscated the domain of the archbishop of Great Novgorod and the estates of local boyars, Ivan III began to distribute these lands among his military men on condition of loyal service. Thus the pomestie system was established, which became the basis of the social and military organization in Muscovy.

Soon after the conquest of Great Novgorod, Ivan III assumed the title of the sovereign of all Russia (*gosudar vseya Rusi*). Not only did the title reflect the achievements of the grand prince in uniting the Russian lands, but it also implied claims to the rest of the territories with eastern Slavic population, which at that time lived under the rule of Lithuanian princes. So conflict with the Grand Duchy of Lithuania became imminent.

In the 1480s, some princes from the Upper Oka region (Vorotynskies, Odoyevskies, and others) left Lithuanian service for Moscow, and Ivan III accepted them and their patrimonies (towns Vorotynsk, Peremyshl, Odoev, and so forth). During the war of 1492 to 1494, the Muscovite army occupied an important town of Vyazma (in the Smolensk region). The peace treaty signed on February 5, 1494, legalized all the acquisitions of Ivan III. Peace, though ensured by the marriage of Ivan's daughter, Elena, to the grand duke of Lithuania, Alexander, turned out to be a short-term armistice: In 1500 another Russian-Lithuanian war began.

First, the princes of Novgorod Seversk and Starodub went over to the grand prince of Moscow. Then Ivan III sent his troops to defend his new vassals. In the battle at Vedrosha River (July 14, 1500), which decided the outcome of the war, Muscovite commanders defeated the Lithuanian army and captured its leader, hetman Konstantin Ostrozhsky. During the summer campaign of 1500 Muscovite forces occupied Bryansk, Toropets, Putivl, and other towns. According to the armistice of 1503, the border with Lithuania moved far in the southwestern direction.

Ivan III was the first Russian ruler to gain full independence from the Golden Horde. From about 1472 he paid no tribute to the khan. Twice, in 1472 and 1480, khan Ahmad invaded Russia, trying to restore his sovereignty over the Russian land and its ruler, but both times he failed. The withdrawal of Ahmad from the banks of Ugra River in November 1480 symbolized the overthrow of the yoke.

The unified Russian state played an increasingly visible role on the international scene: Ivan III established relations with Crimea (1474), Venice (1474), Hungary (1482), the German empire (1489), Denmark (1493), and the Ottoman empire (1496). To meet the needs of his expanded state, Ivan III began to recruit engineers and military specialists from the West. The towers and walls of the Kremlin were built in the 1480s and 1490s by Italian architects and remain one of the most visible material signs of Ivan III's reign.

The contours of the Russian foreign policy, shaped in Ivan's reign, remained stable for generations to come. In the west, Ivan III left to his heir the incessant struggle with the Polish and Lithuanian rulers over the territories of the eastern Slavs. In the east and south, a more differentiated policy was pursued toward the khanates that had succeeded the Golden Horde. This policy included attempts to subjugate the khanate of Kazan in the middle Volga and efforts aimed at neutralizing Crimea.

In his last years Ivan III faced a serious dynastic crisis after the unexpected death in 1490 of his heir, also Ivan (the "Young"), the son of the first Ivan's III wife, Maria of Tver (d. 1467). In 1472 Ivan III married Sophia Paleologue, a Byzantine princess brought up in Rome. This marriage also produced children, including Basil (Vasily). Ivan the Young, married to Yelena, the daughter of Moldavian prince, left a son, Dmitry. So, after 1490, Ivan III was to choose between his grandson (Dmitry) and son (Basil). At first, he favored the grandson: In February 1498, Dmitry was crowned as grand prince and heir to his grandfather. But later Dmitry and his mother Yelena fell into disgrace and were taken into custody; Basil was proclaimed the heir (1502). The reasons for these actions remain unclear. In July 1503, Ivan III experienced a stroke and real power passed into the hands of Basil III.

Contemporaries and later historians agree in depicting Ivan III as a master politician: prudent, cautious, efficient, and very consistent in his policy of constructing a unified and autocratic Russian state.

See also: GOLDEN HORDE; MUSCOVY; NOVGOROD THE GREAT

BIBLIOGRAPHY

Alef, Gustave. (1986). *The Origins of Muscovite Autocracy: The Age of Ivan III.* Berlin: Osteuropa-Institut.

Crummey, Robert O. (1987). *The Formation of Muscovy, 1304–1613.* London: Longman.

Fennell, John L. (1961). *Ivan the Great of Moscow.* London: Macmillan.

Kollmann, Nancy Shields. (1986). "Consensus Politics: The Dynastic Crisis of the 1490s Reconsidered." *Russian Review* 45:235–267.

Vernadsky, George. (1959). *Russia at the Dawn of the Modern Age.* New Haven, CT: Yale University Press.

MIKHAIL M. KROM

IVAN IV

(1530–1584), "The Terrible" (Grozny), grand prince of Moscow and tsar of all Russia.

The long reign of Ivan IV saw the transformation of Muscovy into a multiethnic empire through ambitious political, military, and cultural projects, which revolved around the controversial figure of the monarch.

IVAN IV AND THE RURIKID DYNASTY

Born to the ruling Moscow branch of the Rurikid dynasty, Ivan nominally became grand prince at the age of three after the death of his father, Grand Prince Vasily III. During the regency of Ivan's mother, Yelena Glinskaya, from 1533 to 1538, ruling circles strengthened Ivan's position as nominal ruler by eliminating Prince Andrei Ivanovich of Staritsa and Prince Yury Ivanovich of Dmitrov, representatives of the royal family's collateral branches. Ivan's status as dynastic leader was reinforced during his coronation as tsar on January 16, 1547. Drawing extensively on Byzantine and Muscovite coronation rituals and literary texts to reveal the divine sanction for Ivan's power, the ceremony posited continuity between his rule and the rule of the Byzantine emperors and Kievan princes. Ivan continued the aggressive policy of his ancestors toward the collateral branches of the dynasty by eliminating his cousin, Prince Vladimir Andreyevich of Staritsa (1569).

Ivan was married several times. His wives were from Muscovite elite clans (Anastasia Zakharina Romanova, Maria Nagaya) and from relatively obscure gentry families (Marfa Sobakina, Anna Koltovskaya, Anna Vasilchikova). He also tried to raise the status of the dynasty by establishing matrimonial ties with foreign ruling houses, but succeeded only in marrying the Caucasian Princess Maria (Kuchenei) (1561). Throughout his reign, Ivan sought to secure the succession of power for his sons, although he accidentally killed his elder son Ivan (1581). The tsar's other son, the reportedly mentally challenged Fyodor, eventually inherited the throne.

Ivan the Terrible stands before St. Basil's Cathedral, erected to commemorate his victory over the Kazan khanate. THE BETTMANN ARCHIVE. REPRODUCED BY PERMISSION.

IVAN IV AND HIS COURT

When Ivan was a minor, power was in the hands of influential courtiers. Under Yelena Glinskaya, Prince Mikhail Lvovich Glinsky competed for power with Yelena's favorite, Prince Ivan Fyodorovich Ovchina-Obolensky. Yelena's death (1538) was followed by fierce competition between the princely clans of Shuyskys, Belskys, Kubenskys, and Glinskys, and the boyar Vorontsov clan. After his coronation, Ivan attempted to stabilize the situation at court through improving the registry of elite military servitors, providing them with prestige landholdings around Moscow, and regulating service relations among the elite during campaigns. The authorities limited the right of some princely families to dispose of their lands in order to pursue the lands policy. Ivan granted top court ranks to a wide circle of elite servitors, which especially benefited the tsarina's relatives, the Zakharins-Yurevs. Ivan also favored officials of lower origin, Alexei Fyodorovich Adashev and Ivan Mikhaylovich Viskovaty, though some experts question their influence at court. Historians sometimes call the ruling circles of the 1550s "the chosen council," but this vague literary term is apparently irrelevant to governmental institutions.

Beginning in 1564, Ivan IV subjected his court to accusations of treason, executions, and disgraces by establishing the *Oprichnina*. Despite the subsequent abolition of the *Oprichnina* in 1572, Ivan continued to favor some of its former members. Among them were the elite Nagoy and Godunov families, including Ivan's relative and would-be tsar Boris Godunov. The established princely Shuysky and Mstislavsky clans and the Zakharin-Yurev boyar family retained their high positions at court throughout Ivan's reign.

Ivan's court also included Tatar servitors, including prominent members of the Chingissid dynasty, who received the title of tsar. Ivan granted the last survivor of those Tatar tsars, Simeon Bekbulatovich (Sain-Bulat), the title of grand prince of Moscow and official jurisdiction over a considerable part of the realm. Historians usually interpret the reign of Simeon (1575–1576) as a parody of the Muscovite political system. It may be that Ivan, in granting Simeon the new title, sought to deprive Simeon of the title of tsar and thereby eliminate a possible Chingissid succession to the throne.

IVAN IV AND HIS REALM

In the 1550s, Ivan IV and his advisors attempted to standardize judicial and administrative practices across the country by introducing a new law code (1550) and delegating routine administrative and financial tasks to the increasingly structured chancelleries. The keeping of law and order and control of the local population's mobility became the tasks of locally elected officials, in turn accountable to the central chancelleries. The remote northern territories enjoyed a greater autonomy in local affairs than the central parts of the country.

Albeit limited and inconsistent, these reforms allowed Ivan to maintain an approximately 70,000-man army and to pursue an aggressive foreign policy. With the capture of the Tatar states of Kazan (1552) and Astrakhan (1556), Ivan acquired vast territories populated with a multiethnic, predominantly Muslim population with distinctive cultural and economic traditions. The conquest of those lands, whose peoples remained rebellious throughout Ivan's reign, contributed to the tension between Muscovy and the powerful Muslim states of Crimea and Turkey, which jointly attacked Astrakhan in 1569. The Crimean khan devastated Moscow in 1571, but Ivan's commanders inflicted a defeat on him in 1572. Ivan failed to avoid simultaneous involvement in military conflicts on several fronts. Without settling the conflict in the south, he launched a war against his western neighbor, Livonia, in 1558. Historians traditionally interpret the Livonian War (1558–1583) in geopolitical terms, asserting that Ivan was looking for passage to the Baltic Sea to expand overseas trade. Revisionists explain the war's origins in terms of Ivan's short-range interest in getting tribute. The Livonian war only resulted in human and material losses for Muscovy. Ivan supported commercial relations between Muscovy and England, but attempts to conclude a political union with the queen of England were in vain. The war, famines, epidemics, and the *Oprichnina* caused a profound economic crisis in Muscovy, especially in the Novgorod region. By the end of Ivan's reign, peasants abandoned 70 to 98 percent of arable land throughout the country. Many of them fled to the periphery of the realm, including Siberia, whose colonization intensified in the early 1580s.

IVAN IV AND THE ORTHODOX CHURCH

Ivan IV cultivated a close relationship with the Orthodox Church through regular pilgrimages and generous donations to monasteries. The symbolism of court religious rituals, in which the tsar participated with the metropolitan, and the semiotics of Ivan's residence in the Kremlin stressed the divine character of the tsar's power and the prevailing harmony between the tsar and the church. In 1551, Ivan participated in a church council that attempted to systematize religious practices and the jurisdiction of church courts. Metropolitan Macarius, head of the church and a close advisor to the tsar, sponsored an ideology of militant Orthodoxy that presented the tsar as champion and protector of the true faith. Macarius also played a part in conducting domestic and foreign policy. Contrary to traditional views, the court priest Silvester apparently did not exert political influence on the tsar. Ivan demonstrated a flexible attitude toward the landownership of the church and its tax privileges.

Ivan often played ecclesiastical leaders off each other and even deposed disloyal hierarchs.

CONTROVERSY OVER IVAN'S PERSONALITY AND HISTORICAL ROLE

Ivan is credited with writing diplomatic letters to European monarchs, epistles to elite servitors and clerics, and a reply to a Protestant pastor. Dmitry Likhachev, J. L. I. Fennell, and other specialists describe Ivan as an erudite writer who developed a peculiar literary style through the use of different genres, specific syntax, irony, parody, and mockery of opponents. According to his writings, Ivan, traumatized by childhood memories of boyar arbitrariness, sought through terror to justify his autocratic rule and to prevent the boyars from regaining power. Edward Keenan argues that Ivan was illiterate, never wrote the works attributed to him, and was a puppet in the hands of influential boyar clans. The majority of experts do not share Keenan's view. All information on the influence of particular individuals and clans on Ivan comes from biased sources and should be treated with caution.

Nikolay Karamzin created an influential romantic image of an Ivan who first favored pious counselors but later became a tyrant. Many historians have explained Ivan's erratic policy in psychological terms (Nikolay Kostomarov, Vasily Klyuchevsky); some have assumed a mental disorder (Pavel Kovalevsky, D. M. Glagolev, Richard Hellie, Robert Crummey). The autopsy performed on Ivan's remains in 1963 suggests that Ivan might have suffered from a spinal disease, but it is unclear how the illness affected his behavior. The probability that Ivan was poisoned should be minimized. Other historians sought to rationalize Ivan's behavior, presuming that he acted as a protector of state interests in a struggle with boyar hereditary privileges (Sergei Solovyov, Sergei Platonov). According to Platonov, Ivan was a national democratic leader whose policy relied on the nonaristocratic gentry. This concept was revived in Stalinist historiography, which implicitly paralleled Ivan and Stalin by praising the tsar for strengthening the centralized Russian state through harsh measures (Robert Vipper, Sergei Bakhrushin, Ivan Smirnov). Stepan Veselovsky and Vladimir Kobrin subjected Platonov's concept to devastating criticism. Beginning in the 1960s, Soviet historians saw Ivan's policy as a struggle against various elements of feudal fragmentation (Alexander Zimin, Kobrin, Ruslan Skrynnikov). The political liberalization of the late 1980s evoked totalitarian interpretations of Ivan's rule (the later works of Kobrin and Skrynnikov). Boris Uspensky, Priscilla Hunt, and Andrei Yurganov explain Ivan's behavior in terms of the cultural myths of the tsar's power.

See also: AUTOCRACY; BASIL III; GLINSKAYA, ELENA VASILYEVNA; KIEVAN RUS; KURBSKY, ANDREI MIKHAILOVICH; MAKARY, METROPOLITAN; MUSCOVY; OPRICHNINA; OTHRODOXY

BIBLIOGRAPHY

Bogatyrev, Sergei. (1995). "Grozny tsar ili groznoe vremya? Psikhologichesky obraz Ivana Groznogo v istoriografii." *Russian History* 22:285–308.

Fennell. J.L.I. ed., tr. (1955). *The Correspondence between Prince Kurbsky and Tsar Ivan IV of Russia.* Cambridge, UK: Cambridge University Press.

Fennell, John. (1987). "Ivan IV As a Writer." *Russian History* 14:145–154.

Kalugin, V.V. (1998). *Andrey Kurbsky i Ivan Grozny. Teoreticheskie vzglyady i literaturnaya tekhnika drevnerusskogo pisatelya.* Moscow: Yazyki russkoy kultury.

Keenan, Edward L. (1971). *The Kurbskii–Groznyi Apocrypha: The Seventeenth-Century Genesis of the "Correspondence" Attributed to Prince A. M. Kurbskii and Tsar Ivan IV,* with an appendix by Daniel C. Waugh. Cambridge, MA: Harvard University Press.

Kliuchevsky, V.O. (1912). *A History of Russia,* tr. C. J. Hogarth, vol. 2. London: J. M. Dent and Sons.

Hunt, Priscilla. (1993). "Ivan IV's Personal Mythology of Kingship." *Slavic Review* 52:769–809.

Perrie, Maureen. (2001). *The Cult of Ivan the Terrible in Stalin's Russia.* Basingstoke, NY: Palgrave.

Platonov, S.F. (1986). *Ivan the Terrible,* ed. and tr. Joseph L. Wieczynski, with "In Search of Ivan the Terrible" by Richard Hellie. Gulf Breeze, FL: Academic International Press.

Rowland, Daniel. (1995). "Ivan the Terrible As a Carolingian Renaissance Prince." In *Kamen Kraeugln, Rhetoric of the Medieval Slavic World: Essays Presented to Edward Keenan on His Sixtieth Birthday by His Colleagues and Students. Harvard Ukrainian Studies,* vol. 19, ed. Nancy Shields Kollmann; Donald Ostrowski; Andrei Pliguzov; and Daniel Rowland. Cambridge, MA: The Ukrainian Research Institute of Harvard University.

Skrynnikov, Ruslan G. (1981). *Ivan the Terrible,* ed. and tr. Hugh F. Graham. Gulf Breeze, FL: Academic International Press.

Sergei Bogatyrev

IVAN V

(1666–1696), Tsar Ivan Alexeyevich, third son of Tsar Alexei Mikhailovich.

Ivan V, who suffered from physical and perhaps mental impairments, ruled jointly with his younger brother Peter (the Great). There is no evidence that Ivan ever exercised power or made any independent decisions during his lifetime. Virtually nothing is known about his early life in the Kremlin Palace. He suddenly came into prominence in April 1682 with the death of his older brother, Tsar Fyodor (r. 1676–1682). Though the boyars and the church passed him over in favor of his half-brother Peter, the revolt of the musketeers compelled them to appoint Ivan as co-tsar and soon made possible the emergence of Ivan's sister Sophia as regent of Russia. Despite having been often portrayed as merely the unhappy tool of Sophia and her Miloslavsky relatives against Peter and his family, the Naryshkins, it seems that Ivan's household soon distanced itself from Sophia and in 1689 supported the coup d'etat that removed Sophia from the regency. In 1684 Sophia had Ivan married to Praskovya Saltykova, a young noblewoman from a clan Sophia believed to be friendly to her aims. Ultimately the Saltykovs supported Peter and became an important element in Peter's court. Ivan and Praskovya's daughter, Anna Ivanovna, ruled Russia from 1730 to 1740.

See also: PETER I; SOPHIA; STRELTSY

PAUL A. BUSHKOVITCH

IVAN VI

(1740–1764), emperor of Russia, October 28, 1740 to December 6, 1741.

Ivan was born in August 1740, the son of Duke Anton-Ulrich of Brunswick and Anna Leopoldovna (1718–1746), niece of the childless Empress Anna (reigned 1730–1740), who nominated Anna's as yet unborn child as her heir. The infant Ivan succeeded Anna in October 1740, first with Ernst J. Biron, then with Anna Leopoldovna as regent. A cabinet equally composed of Russians and Germans was formed. Supported by the very capable B. C. Münnich and Heinrich Osterman, the regime continued policies inaugurated during Empress Anna's reign. It fell as a result of its vulnerability more than its inadequacy. The emperor's mother, the twenty-two year old regent, Anna Leopoldovna, became the target of gossip and scandal. In November/December 1741, on the eve of the departure of troops for war against Sweden, Peter I's daughter Elizabeth seized her chance to overthrow Ivan, with the support of guard regiments and the French and Swedish ambassadors. Elizabeth's proclamations emphasized the service she was doing Russia by bringing "German" rule to an end. Osterman and Münnich were sentenced to death, then reprieved and banished to Siberia. The deposed imperial family was moved to the far north and the ex-emperor Ivan was imprisoned in Schlüsselburg fortress to prevent him from becoming a rallying point for opposition to the throne. His mental health was severely damaged by years of incarceration. In 1764 a supporter devised an ill-conceived plan to release him and restore him to the throne, which had been seized by Catherine II in 1762. The ex-emperor was killed by his guards, who were acting on orders from St. Petersburg to take extreme measures in the event of an escape attempt.

See also: ELIZABETH; GERMANY, RELATIONS WITH

BIBLIOGRAPHY

Anisimov, Evgeny. (1995). *Empress Elizabeth: Her Reign and Her Russia*, ed. and tr. John T. Alexander. Gulf Breeze, FL: Academic International Press.

LINDSEY HUGHES

IVAN THE TERRIBLE *See* IVAN IV.

IVASHKO, VLADIMIR ANTONOVICH

(b. 1932), Ukrainian Communist Party leader.

Vladimir Antonovich Ivashko was born in the Poltava region of Ukraine and made his career in politics. He graduated from the Kharkiv Mining Institute in 1956 and joined the Communist Party in 1960. In 1978 he was appointed secretary of the Kharkiv oblast (provincial) committee of the Party, and by 1986 he had been promoted to the Party secretariat. In 1987 Ivashko became the first secretary of the Dnipropetrovsk Party organization in Ukraine (a very significant power base of the Soviet Union, and the area in which Leonid Brezhnev had made his career). At the same time, he became the deputy party leader of the Communist Party of

Ukraine (CPU) under Volodymyr Shcherbytsky (1918–1989). In early 1980, following the Soviet invasion of Afghanistan, Ivashko was sent temporarily to Kabul, where he played the role of advisor to Soviet puppet ruler Babrak Karmal. Subsequently, however, he remained in Ukraine. After the resignation of Shcherbytsky in September 1989, Ivashko was elected first secretary of the Central Committee (CC) of the CPU. During the summer of 1990, he resigned suddenly after Mikhail Gorbachev requested that he take up a newly created position in Moscow as deputy general secretary of the CC of the Communist Party of the Soviet Union on July 11, 1990. At the Twenty-Eighth Party Congress of the same month, he defeated Yegor Ligachev in an election to take on this role. Analysts continue to debate Ivashko's role in the failed putsch of August 1991 in Moscow, in which he appeared to have adopted a middle role between the plotters and Gorbachev.

See also: UKRAINE AND UKRAINIANS

BIBLIOGRAPHY

Kuzio, Taras. (2000). *Ukraine: Perestroika to Independence.* New York: St. Martin's Press.

Solchanyk, Roman. (2001). *Ukraine and Russia: The Post-Soviet Transition.* Lanham, MD: Rowman & Littlefield.

Wilson, Andrew. (1997). *Ukrainian Nationalism in the 1990s: A Minority Faith.* Cambridge, UK: Cambridge University Press.

DAVID R. MARPLES

IZBA

Izba is the Russian word for "peasant hut."

The East Slavic (Russian, Ukrainian) izba remained fundamentally unchanged as the Slavs migrated into Ukraine sometime after 500 C.E., then moved north to Novgorod and the Finnish Gulf by the end of the ninth century, and finally migrated east into the Volga-Oka mesopotamia between 1000 and 1300. Primarily the Slavs settled in forested areas because predatory nomads kept them north of the steppes. In forested regions the izba typically was a log structure with a pitched, thatched roof. The dimensions of the huts depended on the height of the trees out of which they were constructed. In the few non-forested areas where East Slavs lived prior to the construction of fortified lines (especially the Belgorod Line in 1637–1653), which walled the steppe off from areas to the north of it, people inhabited houses constructed of staves, wattle, and mud. From time to time people also lived in semi-pit dwellings, dugouts in the ground covered over with branches and other materials to keep out the rain and snow.

The interiors of the izba were fundamentally the same everywhere, though the precise layouts depended on locale. In the North and in central Russia, when one entered through the door, the stove (either immediately adjacent to the wall or with a space between the stove and the wall) was immediately to the right, and the stove's orifice was facing the wall opposite the entrance. In southeastern Russia the stove was along the wall opposite the entrance, with the orifice facing the entrance. Other variations could be found in western and southwestern Russia. Because the fundamental problem of the izba was heating it, conservation of heat during the six months of the heating season (primarily October through March) was the major structural issue. There were several solutions. One was to chink the spaces between the logs with moss and mud. The second was the so-called "Russian stove," typically a large, three-chambered object made of various combinations of stone, mud, brick, and cement. Its three chambers extracted most of the heat before it reached the smoke hole and radiated it out into the room. The third solution for saving heat was not to have any form of chimney (and only a few small windows), because typically eighty percent of the heat generated by a stove or an open hearth in the middle of the room will be lost if there is a chimney venting the stove or a hole in the roof to exhaust the smoke. Such a large percentage of heat is lost because of the requirement of a "draw" to pull the smoke upward and out of the izba.

The consequences of this third form of izba heating were numerous. For one, there was soot scattered throughout the izba, typically with a line around the walls, about waist-high, marking where the bottom of the smoke typically was. The smoke had two basic harmful constituents: carbon monoxide gas and more than two hundred varieties of particulate matter. The harm this did to peasant health and the amount by which it reduced residents' energy have not been calculated. Government officials beginning at least as early as the reign of Nicholas I were concerned about the health impact of the smoky hut, and by 1900 most were gone, though some lingered on into the 1930s. That peasants thereafter were able to afford the fuel to compensate for the heat lost through chimneys indicates that peasant incomes were rising.

The other features of the izba were benches around the room, on which the peasants sat during the day and on which many of them slept at night. The most honored sleeping places were on top of the stove. These places were reserved for the old people, an especially relevant issue after the introduction of the household tax in 1678, which forced the creation of the extended Russian family household and increased the mean household size from four to ten. This packing of so many people into the izba must have increased the communication of diseases significantly, another consequence of the izba that remains to be calculated.

The Russian word for "table" (*stol*) is old, going back to Common Slavic, whereas the word for chair (*stul*) only dates from the sixteenth century. These facts correspond with historians' general understandings: most peasant *izby* had tables, but many probably did not have chairs. Ceilings were introduced in some huts around 1800, pushing the smoke all the way down to the floor. Before 1800 the huts all had pitched roofs and the smoke would rise up under the roof and fill the space from the underside of the roof down to where the smoke line was. With the introduction of the ceiling, that cavity was lost and the smoke went down to the floor. Goods were stored in trunks.

See also: PEASANTRY; SERFDOM

BIBLIOGRAPHY

Hellie, Richard. (2001). "The Russian Smoky Hut and Its Probable Health Consequences." *Russian History* 28(1–4):171–184.

RICHARD HELLIE

IZVESTIYA

The newspaper *Izvestiya* was first published on February 28, 1917, by the Petrograd Soviet of Workers and Soldiers' Deputies formed during the February Revolution. The paper's name in Russian means "Bulletin," and it first appeared under the complete title "Bulletin of the Petrograd Soviet of Workers' Deputies." Immediately upon seizing power in October 1917, the Bolsheviks appointed their own man, Yuri Steklov, editor-in-chief. In March 1918 the newspaper's operations were transferred to Moscow along with the Bolshevik government. From an official standpoint the newspaper became the organ of the Central Executive Committee of the Soviets-the leading organ of the Soviet government, as opposed to the Communist Party.

For the first ten years of its existence, the paper relied heavily on the equipment and personnel from the prerevolutionary commercial press. In Petrograd, *Izvestiya* was first printed at the former printshop of the penny newspaper *Copeck* (*Kopeyka*), and until late 1926 many of its reporters were veterans of the old *Russian Word* (*Russkoye slovo*).

Throughout the Soviet era *Izvestiya*, together with the big urban evening newspapers such as *Evening Moscow* (*Vechernaya Moskva*) was known as a less strident, less political organ than the official party papers such as *Pravda*. Particularly in the 1920s but also later, the paper carried miscellaneous news of cultural events, sports, natural disasters, and even crime. These topics were almost entirely missing from the major party organs by the late 1920s. In the late 1920s head editor Ivan Gronsky pioneered coverage of "man-against-nature" adventure stories such as the Soviet rescue of the crew of an Italian dirigible downed in the Arctic. Later dubbed "Soviet sensations" by journalists, such ideologically correct yet thrilling stories spread throughout the Soviet press in the 1930s.

In part as a result of its less political role in the Soviet press network, Josef Stalin and other Central Committee secretaries tended to be suspicious of *Izvestiya*. The editorial staff was subjected to a series of purges, beginning with the firing of "Trotskyite" journalists in 1925, and continuing in 1926 with the firing of veteran non-Communist journalists from *Russkoye slovo*. In 1934 the Party Central Committee appointed Stalin's former rightist political opponent Nikolai Bukharin to the head editorship. However in 1936 and 1937, Bukharin, former editor Gronsky, and many other senior editors were purged in the Great Terror. Bukharin was executed; Gronsky and others survived the Stalinist prison camps.

During the Thaw of the late 1950s and early 1960s, the editor-in-chief of *Izvestiya* was Alexei Adzhubei, Nikita Khrushchev's son-in-law, who used the paper to advocate de-Stalinization and Khrushchev's reforms. Under Adzhubei, *Izvestiya* writers practiced a "journalism of the person," which presented "heroes of daily life" and exposed the problems of ordinary Soviet subjects. Adzhubei was removed from the editorship in 1964 when Khrushchev fell, but Thomas Cox Wolfe has argued that the "journalism of the person" laid important ideological groundwork for Mikhail Gorbachev's perestroika reform program in the second half of the 1980s.

After the collapse of the Soviet Union, *Izvestiya* made a successful transition to operation as a private corporation.

See also: ADZHUBEI, ALEXEI IVANOVICH; JOURNALISM; UNIVERSITIES

BIBLIOGRAPHY

Kenez, Peter. (1985). *The Birth of the Propaganda State: Soviet Methods of Mass Mobilization, 1917–1929.* Cambridge, UK: Cambridge University Press.

Lenoe, Matthew. (1997). "Stalinist Mass Journalism and the Transformation of Soviet Newspapers, 1926–1932." Ph.D. dissertation, University of Chicago.

Wolfe, Thomas Cox. (1997). "Imagining Journalism: Politics, Government, and the Person in the Press in the Soviet Union and Russia, 1953–1993." Ph.D. diss., University of Michigan, Ann Arbor.

MATTHEW E. LENOE

IZYASLAV I

(1024–1078), grand prince of Kiev and progenitor of the Turov dynasty.

Before Yaroslav Vladimirovich "the Wise" died in 1054, he designated his eldest living son, Izyaslav, as grand prince of Kiev. Izyaslav and his younger brothers Svyatoslav and Vsevolod ruled as a triumvirate for some twenty years. During that time they asserted their authority over all the other princes and defended Rus against the nomadic Polovtsy (Cumans). However, Izyaslav's rule in Kiev was insecure. In 1068, after he was defeated by the Polovtsy and refused to arm the Kievans, the latter rebelled, and he fled to the Poles. Because his brother Svyatoslav refused to occupy the throne, Izyaslav returned to Kiev in 1069 with the help of Polish troops. Two noteworthy events occurred during his second term of rule. In 1072 he and his brothers transported the relics of Saints Boris and Gleb into a new church that he had built in Vyshgorod. They also compiled the so-called "Law Code of Yaroslav's Sons" (*Pravda Yaroslavichey*). In 1073, however, Izyaslav quarreled with his brothers. They drove him out of Kiev and forced him to flee once again to Boleslaw II of the Poles. Failing to obtain help there, he traveled to Western Europe, where he sought aid unsuccessfully from the Holy Roman Emperor Henry IV and from Pope Gregory VII. He finally returned to Kiev after his brother Svyatoslav died there in 1076. His last sojourn in Kiev was also short: on October 3, 1078, he was killed in battle fighting his nephew Oleg, Svyatoslav's son.

See also: GRAND PRINCE; KIEVAN RUS; YAROSLAV VLADIMIROVICH

BIBLIOGRAPHY

Dimnik, Martin. (1994). *The Dynasty of Chernigov 1054–1146.* Toronto: Pontifical Institute of Mediaeval Studies.

Franklin, Simon, and Shepard, Jonathan. (1996). *The Emergence of Rus 750–1200.* London: Longman.

MARTIN DIMNIK

IZYASLAV MSTISLAVICH

(c. 1096–1154), grandson of Vladimir Vsevolodovich "Monomakh" and grand prince of Kiev.

Between 1127 and 1139, when his father Mstislav and his uncle Yaropolk ruled Kiev, Izyaslav received, at different times, Kursk, Polotsk, southern Pereyaslavl, Turov, Pinsk, Minsk, Novgorod, and Vladimir in Volyn. In 1143 Vsevolod Olgovich, grand prince of Kiev, gave him southern Pereyaslavl again, but his uncle Yuri Vladimirovich "Dolgoruky" of Suzdalia objected, fearing that he would use the town as a stepping-stone to Kiev. After Vsevolod died in 1146, the Kievans, despite having pledged to accept his brother Igor as prince, invited Izyaslav to rule Kiev because he belonged to their favorite family, the Mstislavichi. But his reign was insecure, because the Davidovichi of Chernigov and Yuri challenged him. In 1147, in response to a plot by the Davidovichi to kill Izyaslav and reinstate Igor, whom Izyaslav was holding captive, the Kievans murdered Igor. Meanwhile Yuri argued that Monomakh's younger sons, Izyaslav's uncles, had prior claims to Izyaslav, in keeping with the lateral system of succession to Kiev that Yaroslav Vladimirovich "the Wise" had allegedly instituted in his so-called testament. Yuri and his allies waged war on Izyaslav and expelled him on two occasions. Finally, in 1151, Izyaslav invited Vyacheslav, Yuri's elder brother, to rule Kiev with him. Yuri acknowledged the legitimacy of Vyacheslav's reign and allowed Izyaslav to remain co-ruler of Kiev until his death on November 13, 1154. Izyaslav's reign was exceptional in that, in 1147, he ordered a synod of bishops to install Klim (Kliment) Smolyatich as the second native metropolitan of Kiev.

See also: KIEVAN RUS; YAROSLAV VLADIMIROVICH.

BIBLIOGRAPHY

Hanak, Walter K. (1980). "Iziaslav Mstislavich." *The Modern Encyclopedia of Russian and Soviet History*, ed. Joseph L. Wieczynski, 15:88–89. Gulf Breeze, FL: Academic International Press.

Martin, Janet. (1995). *Medieval Russia 980–1584*. Cambridge, UK: Cambridge University Press.

Martin Dimnik

J

JACKSON-VANIK AGREEMENT

The Jackson-Vanik Amendment to the U.S.-Soviet Trade Bill, which became law in 1974, was to play a major role in Soviet-American relations until the collapse of the Soviet Union in 1991. The Jackson-Vanik Amendment had its origins in 1972. In response to the sharp increase in the number of Soviet Jews seeking to leave the Soviet Union, primarily because of rising Soviet anti-Semitism, the Brezhnev regime imposed a prohibitively expensive exit tax on educated Jews who wanted to leave. In response, Senator Henry Jackson of the State of Washington introduced an amendment to the Soviet-American Trade Bill, linking the trade benefits Moscow wanted (most favored nation treatment for Soviet exports and U.S. credits) to the exodus of Soviet Jews. Jackson's amendment quickly got support in Congress, as Representative Charles Vanik of Ohio introduced a similar amendment in the U.S. House of Representatives. The Soviet leadership, which might have thought that a trade agreement with the Nixon Administration would conclude the process, belatedly woke up to the growing Congressional opposition. After initially trying to derail the Jackson-Vanik amendment by threatening that it would lead to an increase in anti-Semitism both in the Soviet Union and the United States, the Soviet leaders began to make concessions. At first they said there would be exemptions to the head tax, and then they put the tax aside as the Soviet-American Trade Bill neared passage in Congress in 1974. At the last minute, however, Senator Adlai Stevenson III, angry at Soviet behavior during the Yom Kippur War of 1973 when Moscow had cheered the Arab oil embargo against the United States, introduced an amendment limiting U.S. credits to the Soviet Union to only $300 million over four years, and prohibiting U.S. credits for developing Soviet oil and natural gas deposits. The Soviet leadership, which had been hoping for up to $40 billion in U.S. credits, then repudiated the trade agreement. However, the impact of the Jackson-Vanik Amendment remained. Thus whenever Moscow sought trade and other benefits from the United States, whether in the 1978–1979 period under Brezhnev, or in the 1989–1991 period under Gorbachev, Jewish emigration from the Soviet Union soared, reaching a total of 213,042 in 1990 and 179,720 in 1991.

See also: JEWS; UNITED STATES, RELATIONS WITH

BIBLIOGRAPHY

Freedman, Robert O., ed. (1984). *Soviet Jewry in the Decisive Decade, 1971–1980.* Durham: Duke University Press.

Freedman, Robert O., ed. (1989). *Soviet Jewry in the 1980s.* Durham: Duke University Press.

Korey, William. (1975). "The Story of the Jackson Amendment." *Midstream* 21(3):7–36.

Orbach, William. (1979). *The American Movement to Aid Soviet Jews.* Amherst: University of Massachusetts Press.

Stern, Paula. (1979). *Water's Edge: Domestic Politics and the Making of American Foreign Policy.* Westport, CT: Greenwood Press.

ROBERT O. FREEDMAN

JADIDISM

The term *jadidism* is used to describe a late-nineteenth and early-twentieth-century project to modernize Turkic Islamic cultures within or indirectly influenced by the Russian Empire. Emerging between the 1840s and 1870s among a small number of intellectuals as a fragmented but spirited call for educational reform and wider dissemination of practical knowledge by means of the modern press, jadidism became by the early twentieth century a socially totalizing movement that was epistemologically rationalist and ultimately revolutionary in its expectations and consequences.

The successes of European and Russian advances into all of the historic centers of world civilization, beginning with the Portuguese explorations of the fifteenth century and lasting through the final stage of the Russian conquest of Central Asia in the 1880s, instigated reactions abroad that ranged from indifference to multiple forms of resistance and accommodation.

In those regions with historically deep literate cultures (China, India, and the Islamic lands from Andalusia to Central Eurasia and beyond), interaction with the West encouraged some intellectuals to question the efficacy for the unfolding modern age of arguably timeless cultural canons, centuries of commentaries, and classical forms of education, as well as political, economic, and social norms and practices. They concluded that modernity, as defined by what Europeans were capable of accomplishing and how they made their lives, was a goal toward which all peoples had to strive, and that its pursuit required reform of indigenous cultures, if not their abandonment, with at least a degree of imitation of Western ways.

Within the Turkic communities of the Russian Empire, beginning with groups inhabiting the Volga-Ural region, Crimea, the Caucasus, and the Kazakh Steppe, the lures of modernity stimulated such reformist sentiments. The early advocates, all Russophiles, included Mirza Muhammad Ali Kazem Beg (1802–1870), Abbas Quli Aga Bakikhanli (1794–1847), Mirza Fath-Ali Akhundzade (1812–1878), Hasan Bey Melikov Zardobi (1837–1907), Qokan Valikhanov (1835–1865), Ibrai Altynsarin (1841–1889), Abdul Qayyum al-Nasyri (1824–1904), and Ismail Bey Gaspirali (1851–1914). These men, for the most part isolated from one another temporally and geographically, articulated critiques of the Islamic tradition that held intellectual and institutional sway over their separate societies. This critique did not decry Islamic ethics, nor did it deny historic achievements wherever Islam had taken root. Rather, it approached Islam from a rationalist perspective that reflected the influence of Western intellectual tendencies, through a Russian prism, emanating from the seventeenth and eighteenth centuries. This perspective viewed religion as socially constructed and not divinely ordained, as one more aspect of human experience that could and should be subjected to scientific inquiry and reexamination, and as a private, personal matter rather than a public one. For these men, who represent the first jadidists, the properly functioning, productive, competitive, and modern society was secular, guided but not trumped at every turn by religion.

The popular appeal of jadidism remained limited and diffused prior to the turn of the twentieth century. Projects for educational reform and publishing ventures were either short-lived or unfulfilled. The persistence of Ismail Bey Gaspirali in both areas proved a turning point, with his new-method schools (the first opened in 1884) establishing a model and his newspaper *Perevodchik/Tercuman* (The Interpreter, 1883-1918) becoming the first Turkic-language periodical in the Russian Empire to survive more than two years. These successes and the effects of social, economic, and political turmoil, which gained momentum across the empire between 1901 and 1907, helped expand the social base and influence of jadidism, leading to a proliferation of publications, regional and imperial-wide gatherings, and involvement in the newly created State Duma.

For a brief period, jadidism seemed to have come of age, but its apparent triumph disguised underlying confusion over its long-term goals and meaning. First, growing participation in the movement by Islamic clerics, some remarkably educated and attuned to early-twentieth-century realities, seemed fortuitous, but their attempts to reconcile Islam with the modern age, to draw analogies with the Christian Reformation and raise the specter of Martin Luther, and to persist in the goal of keeping Islam at the center of society ran against the fundamentally secular spirit of jadidism. Second, the jadidist founding fathers had accepted, for practical reasons if not genuine sympathy, Russian political authority and the need for close cooperation with the dominant Russian population. After 1905, such political accommodation seemed less persuasive to a new generation enervated by the patent weaknesses of the monarchy and the equally visible power of the people to influence imperial affairs. Finally, jadidism always spoke to a universal way of life that transcended the limitations of any particular religion, intellectual tradition, culture, or time. In post-1905 Russia, the appeal of local and regional ethnic identities overwhelmed this universalism and its moderating spirit, replacing it with romantic notions of primordial ethnicity, nationalism, and the nation-state. Against such forces, jadidism, as conceived by its putative founders, proved inadequate; by 1917, it had all but disappeared from the public discourse of Central Eurasia.

See also: CENTRAL ASIA; ISLAM

BIBLIOGRAPHY

Jersild, Austin. (1999). "Rethinking from Zardob: Hasan Melikov Zardabi and the 'Native' Intelligentsia." *Nationalities Papers* 27:503–517.

Khalid, Adeeb. (1998). *The Politics of Muslim Cultural Reform: Jadidism in Central Asia.* Berkeley: University of California Press.

Lazzerini, Edward J. (1992). "Beyond Renewal: The Jadid Response to Pressure for Change in the Modern Age." In *Muslims in Central Asia: Expressions of Identity and Change,* ed. Jo Ann Gross. Durham, NC: Duke University Press.

EDWARD J. LAZZERINI

JAPAN, RELATIONS WITH

Russian-Japanese relations throughout the twentieth century were characterized by hostility, mutual suspicion, and military conflict. Foreign policy perceptions, policies, and behaviors shaped the relationship, as did personalities, issues, and disputes—most notably the dispute over the four Kuril islands, or northern territories, in Japanese parlance. Japan and the USSR emerged from World War II with radically different views of security: the former inward-looking and defensive, with constrained military capabilities; the latter outward-looking, offensive, and militaristic. The Japanese were convinced that internal law and justice dictated the return of the southern Kurils, while the Soviets asserted that territory acquired by war could not be relinquished. Post-Soviet Russia has been more amenable to discussing the territorial issue, but progress has been glacial.

Russian explorers first pushed southward from Kamchatka into the Kuril island chain, encountering Japanese settlers in the late seventeenth and early eighteenth centuries. The two countries eventually agreed on a border, with the 1855 Treaty of Shimoda granting Etorofu and the islands south of it to Japan. Russia's push into Manchuria and construction of the Chinese Eastern Railway late in the nineteenth century threatened Japan's growing

Russian president Vladimir Putin and Japanese prime minister Yoshiro Mori confer in Irkutsk, Russia, March 25, 2001.

imperial interests in China and led to the Russo-Japanese War of 1904–1905. The 1905 Treaty of Portsmouth, brokered by U.S. president Theodore Roosevelt, ended the war and gave Japan control of coal-rich Sakhalin south of the fiftieth parallel along with the adjacent islands.

Formally Russia's ally during World War I, Japan became alarmed at the Bolshevik coup in 1917 and subsequently deployed some 73,000 troops to protect its interests in the Russian Far East. Japan withdrew from Russia in 1922 but negotiated concessions for natural resources in northern Sakhalin. Tensions remained high during most of the interwar period, and there were armed clashes along the Soviet border with Japanese-occupied Manchuria between 1937 and 1939. Moscow and Tokyo negotiated a neutrality pact in April 1941. The two armies clashed only during the final days of the war, as the Red Army swept through Manchuria and occupied all of Sakhalin and the Kurils. Nearly 600,000 Japanese soldiers and civilians were captured and interned in Soviet labor camps; roughly one-third of them perished in Siberia.

Relations between Japan and the USSR during the Cold War were tense and distant. The Soviet government refused to sign the Japanese Peace Treaty at the 1951 San Francisco Conference, which in any event failed to specify ownership of Sakhalin and the Kurils. Differing interpretations over sovereignty of the islands would preclude a Russo-Japanese peace treaty well into the twenty-first century. The Soviet-Japanese Joint Declaration of 1956 normalized relations and proposed the return of Shikotan and the Habomais (an idea quashed by U.S. secretary of state John Foster Dulles), but it failed to solve the territorial issue. Moscow objected to the U.S.-Japan security relationship, and from the 1960s through the 1980s targeted part of its substantial military force deployed in the Russian Far East toward Japan.

For much of the postwar era Russo-Japanese relations reflected the competition between the Soviet Union and the United States. For Washington, Japan was the key ally against Communist expansion in the western Pacific. The Soviet leadership in the Nikita Khrushchev and Leonid Brezhnev eras seems to have regarded Japan as merely an extension of the United States, and consistently blamed Japan for the poor state of Russo-Japanese relations. Stalemate on the territorial issue served American interests by maintaining confrontation between Japan and Russia, ensuring the Soviets would need to commit resources to protect their sparsely populated eastern borders.

Moscow's leadership refused to acknowledge Japan as a significant international actor in its own right, even as the country developed into an export powerhouse with the world's second largest economy. Moscow's approach to Japan must be viewed in the context of Soviet global and regional considerations, especially the Cold War competition with America and, after 1961, the deterioration of ties with Communist China. The Kremlin's foreign policy architects generally viewed Japan with disdain. They seldom relied on the considerable expertise of the USSR's Japan specialists and frequently pursued contradictory goals with regard to Japan.

Cultural distance also may explain part of the antipathy between Russia and Japan. Public opinion surveys indicate that Russia consistently ranks at the top of countries most disliked by Japanese. Russians are considerably more favorably inclined to Japan, but in many respects their two civilizations are very different. Tellingly, the collapse of the Soviet Union was not enough to provoke a sudden upsurge of pro-Russian sentiment, as it did in much of Europe and the United States.

Not until Mikhail Gorbachev's "new thinking" did Soviet foreign policy show much flexibility toward Japan. Gorbachev and his foreign minister Eduard Shevardnadze were more attentive to their Asia specialists, but they ranked Japan relatively low on the list of foreign policy priorities, after ties with the United States, Europe, and China. By the time Gorbachev visited Tokyo in April 1991, his freedom to maneuver was constrained by a backlash from conservatives in Moscow that, combined with growing nationalist and regional opposition, made any progress on the territorial issue virtually impossible.

Russo-Japanese relations did not improve markedly after the collapse of the Soviet Union. Russian president Boris Yeltsin's 1993 meeting with Prime Minister Kiichi Miyazawa produced the Tokyo Declaration, in which the two sides pledged to negotiate the territorial issue on the basis of historical facts and the principles of law and justice. But the two sides interpreted these terms differently. Prime Minister Ryutaro Hashimoto (1996–1998) tried a package approach to relations, bundling a wide range of issues including trade, energy, security, and cultural exchanges, and he came closer to reaching an accord than had any previous Japanese leader. But the flurry of informal summits and intensified diplomatic activity in the late 1990s failed either to deliver a peace treaty or to enhance economic cooperation.

Prospects for trade and investment improved early in the twenty-first century as Tokyo urged Moscow to approve a Siberian oil pipeline to the eastern coast, competing with a Chinese bid for a route to Daqing. Relations were said to be entering a new, businesslike phase following the January 2003 summit between President Vladimir Putin and Prime Minister Junichiro Koizumi. But as in the latter half of the twentieth century, the territorial dispute remained the touchstone for Russo-Japanese relations.

See also: KURIL ISLANDS; RUSSO-JAPANESE WAR

BIBLIOGRAPHY

Ivanov, Vladimir I., and Smith, Karla S., eds. (1999). *Japan and Russia in Northeast Asia: Partners in the 21st Century.* Westport, CT: Praeger.

Kimura, Hiroshi. (2000). *Distant Neighbors, Vol. 1: Japanese-Russian Relations under Brezhnev and Andropov; Vol. 2: Japanese-Russian Relations under Gorbachev and Yeltsin.* Armonk, NY: M. E. Sharpe.

Nimmo, William F. (1994). *Japan and Russia: A Reevaluation in the Post-Soviet Era.* Westport, CT: Greenwood.

Rozman, Gilbert, ed. (2000). *Japan and Russia: The Tortuous Path to Normalization, 1949-1999.* New York: St. Martin's Press.

Charles E. Ziegler

JASSY, TREATY OF

During the eighteenth century, Russia and Turkey fought repeatedly for hegemony on the Black Sea and in adjacent lands, including the Pontic steppe. Russia's growing power became truly dominant during Catherine II's Second Turkish War, when the military-administrative talents of Grigory Alexandrovich Potemkin and the generalship of Alexander Vasilievich Suvorov and Nikolay Vasilyevich Repnin finally brought Turkey to its knees. In a treaty negotiated successively by Potemkin and Aleksandr Andreyevich Bezborodko at Jassy in modern Romania, Sultan Selim III's representative, Yusof Pasha, agreed with terms that essentially acknowledged Russia's stature as a Black Sea power.

Potemkin died before the treaty was signed on January 9, 1792, but his absence did not affect the outcome. Russia agreed to withdraw its troops from south of the Danube, and Turkey recognized Russian annexation of the Crimea and lands between the Bug and Dniester rivers. Both parties recognized the Kuban River as their mutual boundary in the foothills of the Caucasus, while Turkey agreed to restrain raids on Georgia and Russia's Kuban territories. The southern steppe now came under full Russian control, with a subsequent blossoming of settlement and commercial activities. The Russians now also had both naval bases on the Black Sea and a territorial springboard for further military action, either in the Caucasus or in the Balkans. The Treaty of Jassy thus marked a major milestone in the titanic struggle between Russia and Turkey for empire in the Black Sea basin.

See also: POTEMKIN, GRIGORY ALEXANDROVICH; RUSSO-TURKISH WARS; TURKEY, RELATIONS WITH

BIBLIOGRAPHY

Alexander, John T. (1989). *Catherine the Great: Life and Legend.* New York: Oxford University Press.

Menning, Bruce W. (2002). "Paul I and Catherine II's Military Legacy, 1762–1801." In *The Military History of Tsarist Russia,* eds. Frederick W. Kagan and Robin Higham. New York: Palgrave.

Bruce W. Menning

JEWS

The Russian Empire acquired a Jewish population through the partitions of Poland in 1772, 1793, and 1795. By 1800 Russia's Jewish population numbered more than 800,000 persons. During the nineteenth century the Jews of the Russian Empire underwent a demographic explosion, with their population rising to more than five million in 1897 (a number that does not include the approximately one million persons who emigrated from the empire prior to 1914). Legislation in 1791, 1804, and 1835 required most Jews to live in the provinces acquired from Poland and the Ottoman Empire in the eighteenth and early nineteenth centuries, the so-called Pale of Jewish Settlement. There were also some residence restrictions within the Pale, such as a ban on settlement in most districts of the city of Kiev, and restrictions on settlement within fifty kilometers of the foreign borders. The Temporary

Laws of May 1882 forbade new Jewish settlement in rural areas of the Pale. Before 1882 the Russian state progressively permitted privileged categories of Jews (guild merchants, professionals, some army veterans, students, and master-craftsmen) to reside outside the Pale. Larger in size than France, the Pale included areas of dynamic economic growth, and its restrictions were widely evaded,

Jewish bystanders are attacked by an angry mob after someone throws a bomb during the Christian Corpus Domini procession in Bielostok, June 1906. © Mary Evans Picture Library

but it was nonetheless considered the single greatest legal liability on Russian Jews. The regulations of the Pale, including the May Laws, did not apply to Jews in the Kingdom of Poland, although they too were barred from settlement in the Great Russian provinces.

ECONOMIC LIFE

Jews were primarily a trade-commercial class, serving in the feudal economy as the link between the peasants and the market, and as agents of the noble landowners and leasees of the numerous monopolies on private estates. They were particularly active in the production and sale of spirits, as agents of noble and state monopolies on this trade. Individual Jewish families lived in peasant villages, while larger communities were found in market towns, the shtetl of Jewish lore.

The Jewish population increase and internal migration contributed to the growth of urban centers such as Odessa, Kiev, Vilna, Warsaw, and Lodz. In the second half of the nineteenth century, Jews moved into occupations in urban-based factory work. A small elite gained prominence as tax farmers, bankers, railway contractors, and industrial entrepreneurs. A number of Jews had successful careers in the professions, chiefly law, medicine, and journalism. Most Jews, however, lived lives of relative poverty.

RELIGION AND CULTURE

The vernacular of Jews in the empire comprised various dialects of Yiddish, a Germanic language with a substantial admixture of Hebrew and Slavic languages. Hebrew and Aramaic were languages of prayer and study. In the all-Russian census of 1897 more than 97 percent of Jews declared Yiddish their native language, although this figure obscures the high level of multi-lingualism among East European Jewry.

The empire's Jews were, with very few exceptions, Ashkenazi-a Yiddish-speaking cultural community that shared common rituals and traditions. It was a highly literate culture that valorized learning and the study of legal and homiletic texts, the Talmud. Ashkenazi culture also included elements of the Jewish mystical tradition, the Kabbalah. The main division between adherents to religious traditionalism in Eastern Europe was between the so-called Mitnagedim, (The Opponents) and the Hasidim (The Pious Ones). The latter contained many strands, each grouped around a charismatic leader, or *tzaddik* (righteous man). There was also a small band of *maskilim*, the adherents of Haskalah, which was the Jewish version of the European Enlightenment movement. They advocated religious reform and intellectual and linguistic acculturation.

In an effort to reach the non-acculturated masses, followers of the Russian Haskalah wrote literary works in Yiddish and Hebrew, helping to create standardized and modernized versions of both languages. The most notable of these writers were Abraham Mapu, Perez Smolenskin, and Reuven Braudes in modern Hebrew; Sholem Yakov Abramovich (pen name, Mendele Moykher-Sforim) in Hebrew and Yiddish; and Sholem Rabinovich (Sholem Aleichem) and Yitsak Leybush Perets in Yiddish. Avraam Goldfaden was the foremost creator of a Yiddish-language theater, although its growth was stunted by a governmental ban in 1883. The turn of the century saw the emergence of a number of outstanding Hebrew poets, most notably Khaim Nakhman Bialik and Shaul Chernikhovsky. There was a vigorous Jewish press in Hebrew, Yiddish, Russian, and Polish.

In response to the challenges of modernity, religious movements such as Israel Lipkin Salanter's Musar Movement, which penetrated traditional study centers (yeshivas), sought ways to preserve a vigorous traditional style of life. While women were not expected to be scholars, many were literate. Both religious and secular literature aimed at a female audience was published in Yiddish.

All young males were expected to study in religious schools known as the *cheder*. A state initiative of 1844 created a state-sponsored Jewish school system with primary and secondary levels, offering a more modern curriculum. Total enrollment was low, but the schools served Jews as a point of entry into Russian culture and higher education. Most *maskilim* and acculturated Jews in the mid-nineteenth century had some connection with this school system. By the 1870s Jews in urban areas began to enter Russian schools in large numbers. Concerned that the Jews were swamping the schools, the state imposed quotas on the admission of Jews to secondary and higher education. A number of Jews became prominent artists in Russia, most notably the painter Isaac Levitan and the sculptor Mark Antokolsky.

INTERNAL GOVERNMENT

Until 1844 the internal government of the Jews comprised the *kahal* (*kagal* in Russian), a system of autonomous local government inherited from

Russian Jews under assault while police look on with indifference, 1880s. © BETTMANN/CORBIS

the Polish-Lithuanian Commonwealth. The *kahal,* dominated by local elites, exercised social control, selected the religious leadership (rabbis), and assessed and collected taxes under a system of collective responsibility. After 1827 the *kahal* also oversaw the selection of recruits for the army. A number of taxes were unique to the Jews, most notably a tax on kosher meat (*korobochka*) and a tax on sabbath candles. Jews in Poland and Lithuania created a number of national bodies, the *va'adim* (the singular form is *va'ad*), which assessed taxes on communities, negotiated with the secular authorities, and attempted to set social standards. Although similar bodies were abolished in Poland in 1764, the Russian state allowed Jews to create them on a regional basis. These included provincial kahals, and the institution of Deputies of the Jewish People, which lasted until 1825. Seen as an obstacle to Jewish integration, the kahal system was technically abolished in 1844, but virtually all of its functions endured unchanged.

Within each community existed a wide variety of societies (*hevrah,* plural: *hevrot*) that oversaw an extensive range of devotional, educational, and charitable functions. The most important of these was the burial brotherhood, the *hevrah kaddisha.*

LEGAL STATUS

The defining characteristic of a Jew in Russian law was religious confession; a convert from Judaism to any other faith ceased legally to be a Jew. In other respects Russian law possessed numerous and contradictory provisions that applied only to Jews. In Russia's social-estate based system, almost all Jews were classed as townspeople (*meshchane*) or merchants (*kuptsy*), and the general regulations for these groups applied to them, but with many exceptions. Confusingly, all Jews were also placed in the social category of aliens (*inorodtsy*), which included groups such as Siberian nomads, who were under the special protection of the state. A huge body of exceptional law existed for all aspects of Jewish life, including tax assessment, military recruitment, residence, and religious life. Jewish emancipation in Russia would have had to encompass the removal of all such special legislation.

THE "JEWISH QUESTION" IN RUSSIA

The guiding principles of Russia's Jewish policy were not based on traditional Russian, Orthodox Christian anti-Semitism, nor was there ever a sustained and coordinated effort to convert all Jews to Russian Orthodoxy, with the exception of conversionary pressures on Russian army recruits. Russian policy was influenced by the Enlightenment-era critique of the Jews and Judaism that saw them as a persecuted minority, but also isolated and backward, economically unproductive, and religious fanatics prone to exploit their Christian neighbors. In 1881 Russian policy was broadly aimed at the acculturation and integration of the Jews into the broader society. The anti-Jewish riots (pogroms) of 1881 and 1882 led to a reversal of this policy, inspiring efforts to segregate Jews from non-Jews through residence restrictions (the May Laws of 1882) and restricted access to secondary and higher education. Much of Russian legislation towards the Jews after 1889 lacked a firm ideological basis, and was ad hoc, responding to the political concerns of the moment.

Following the emancipation of the serfs in 1861, Russian public opinion, fearful of Jewish exploitation of the peasantry, grew increasing critical of the Jews. These critical attitudes were characterized as Judeophobia. Originally based on concrete, albeit exaggerated, socioeconomic complaints (exploitation, intoxication of the peasantry), Russian Judeophobia acquired fantastic elements by the end of the century, exemplified by forgeries like *The Protocols of the Elders of Zion*, which claimed to expose a Jewish plot bent on world domination. The presence of Jews in the revolutionary movement led the state to attribute political disloyalty to Jews in general. Right-wing political parties were invariably anti-Semitic, exemplified by their rallying cry, "Beat the Yids and Save Russia!"

Jews made significant contributions to all branches of the Russian revolutionary movement, including Populism, the Social Revolutionaries, and Marxist Social Democracy, which included a Jewish branch, the Bund, that concentrated on propaganda among the Jewish working class. Lev Pinsker, author of the 1882 pamphlet *Auto-Emancipation!*, and Ahad Ha'am were major ideologues of the early Zionist movement. East European Jews were the mainstay of Theodor Herzl's movement of political Zionism.

See also: BUND, JEWISH; JUDAIZERS; NATIONALITIES POLICIES, SOVIET; NATIONALITIES POLICIES, TSARIST PALE OF SETTLEMENT; POGROMS

BIBLIOGRAPHY

Aronson, I. Michael. (1990). *Troubled Waters: The Origins of the 1881 Anti-Jewish Pogroms in Russia.* Pittsburgh, PA: University of Pittsburgh Press.

Dubnow, S. M. (1916–1920). *History of the Jews in Russia and Poland,* 3 vols. Philadelphia, PA: Jewish Publication Society of America.

Frankel, Jonathan. (1981). *Prophecy and Politics: Socialism, Nationalism, and the Russian Jews, 1862–1917.* Cambridge, UK: Cambridge University Press.

Klier, John D. (1985). *Russia Gathers Her Jews: The Origins of the Jewish Question in Russia.* DeKalb, IL: Northern Illinois University Press.

Klier, John D. (1995). *Imperial Russia's Jewish Question, 1885–1881.* Cambridge, UK: Cambridge University Press.

Klier, John D., and Lambroza, Shlomo, eds. (1991). *Pogroms: Anti-Jewish Violence in Modern Russian History.* Cambridge, UK: Cambridge University Press.

Mendelsohn, Ezra. (1970). *Class Struggle in the Pale.* Cambridge, UK: Cambridge University Press.

Miron, Dan. (1996). *A Traveler Disguised: The Rise of Modern Yiddish Fiction in the Nineteenth Century.* Syracuse, NY: Syracuse University Press.

Nathans, Benjamin. (2002). *Beyond the Pale: The Jewish Encounter with Late Imperial Russia.* Berkeley and Los Angeles: University of California Press.

Rogger, Hans. (1986). *Jewish Policies and Right-Wing Politics in Imperial Russia.* London and New York: Macmillan.

Stanislawski, Michael. (1983). *Tsar Nicholas I and the Jews: The Transformation of Jewish Society in Russia, 1825–1855.* Philadelphia: Jewish Publication Society of America.

Tobias, Henry J. (1972). *The Jewish Bund in Russia.* Stanford, CA: Stanford University Press.

Zipperstein, Steven J. (1986). *The Jews of Odessa: A Cultural History.* Stanford, CA: Stanford University Press.

JOHN D. KLIER

JOAKIM, PATRIARCH

(1620–1690), Ivan "Bolshoy" Petrovich Savelov (as a monk, Joakim) was consecrated Patriarch Joakim of Moscow and All Russia on July 26, 1674.

When Patriarch Joakim assumed the post, the Russian Church was experiencing increasing opposition. Joakim moved firmly but tactfully to rationalize the administrative structure of the church, to bolster patriarchal finances, and to bring the institution under his control. Joakim's administrative reforms were complemented by efforts to revitalize the reform program begun at mid-century, which included both liturgical and spiritual reform. During Joakim's tenure, liturgical reform continued, and sermons and other simple religious tracts were composed, printed, and distributed in increasing numbers. Joakim was also committed to a program of education, under the control of the church. Joakim's ardent conviction that the church alone could define doctrine and should control education generated opposition. Individuals and groups, ranging from the original opponents of Patriarch Nikon and their followers to disparate dissenters who did not conform to new practices, vocally and sometimes violently opposed the liturgical and administrative changes effected by Patriarch Joakim and the church he led. When teaching, preaching, and persuasion failed to convince opponents, the state stepped in to persecute and repress. In the 1680s Joakim's determination that a proposed academy of higher learning be under patriarchal control led to a clash with the monk Sylvester Medvedev and a faction that enjoyed the sympathy of the regent, Sophia Alexeyevna. This conflict ripened into a dispute about the Eucharist that drew in learned members of the clerical elite in Ukraine. The debate threatened plans to subordinate the Kievan see to the Moscow patriarchate. Quickly it degenerated into polemics. The palace coup of 1689 that brought Peter to the throne ended the dispute. Patriarch Joakim's support of Peter assured his victory in this affair. Sylvester Medvedev was arrested, then, almost a year after Patriarch Joakim's death, tried and executed. This was a crude political resolution to what had begun as a learned debate. As such, it undermined the legitimacy of the church in the eyes of the educated. Joakim died on March 17, 1690, shortly after the coup, leaving a testament that manifested profound anxiety for the future of both church and state.

Joakim has attracted little scholarly attention. Discussions that relate to his patriarchate focus on the increasing influence of Ukrainian churchmen in Moscow, the struggle over the opening of an academy in Moscow, the Eucharistic controversy of the late 1680s, and the subordination of the Kievan church to the Russian patriarch. Until recently, the dominant theme in this literature was the growing tension in Moscow as Old Muscovite culture confronted Ukrainian Culture and as supporters of a Greek direction for the Russian Church came into conflict with those favoring an allegedly Latin direction. Joakim traditionally was placed on the side of the conservative, Old Muscovite, Greek faction opposed to a progressive, Ukrainian, Latin faction. An emerging body of related scholarship questions this binary analysis, suggesting the need for a more complex approach to the period and the man.

See also: MEDVEDEV, SYLVESTER AGAFONIKOVICH; NIKON, PATRIARCH; PATRIARCHATE; PETER I; RUSSIAN ORTHODOX CHURCH; SOPHIA

BIBLIOGRAPHY

Potter, Cathy Jean. (1993). "The Russian Church and the Politics of Reform in the Second Half of the Seventeenth Century." Ph.D. diss. Yale University, New Haven, CT.

Vernadsky, George, ed. and tr. (1972). "Testament of Patriarch Ioakim." In *A Source Book for Russian History.* New Haven, CT: Yale University Press.

CATHY J. POTTER

JOB, PATRIARCH

(d. 1607), first patriarch of the Russian Orthodox Church.

Tonsured in the Staritsky Monastery around 1553, Job was appointed archimandrite by Tsar Ivan IV in 1569. In 1571 he was transferred to Moscow as prior of the Simonov Monastery, then as head of the Novospassky Monastery (1575–1580). Job was consecrated Bishop of Kolomensk in April 1581, Archbishop of Rostov in 1586, and Metropolitan of Moscow in December 1586. On January 26, 1589, he was raised to the position of Patriarch of All Russia by Patriarch Jeremiah of Constantinople.

Job's consecration as Russia's first patriarch was an event of national significance. The Russian Church had formerly been under the jurisdiction of Constantinople with the status of a metropolitanate, but by the sixteenth century many Russians believed that Moscow was the last bastion of true faith, a "Third Rome." Hence the establishment of an autocephalous church was considered necessary for national prestige. During Russia's civil war in 1605, Job played a leading role by declaring the Pretender "False Dmitry" a heretic and calling on the people to swear allegiance to Tsar Boris Godunov and his son Fyodor. Consequently, when Dmitry became tsar in June 1605 Job was deposed and exiled to Staritsky monastery. He died in 1607.

Although sometimes criticized by contemporaries and historians for his support of the Godunovs, Job was known as a humble man of impeccable morals, learned for his times, who worked for the good of the church and the promotion of Orthodox Christianity. In 1652 Job was canonized as a saint by Patriarch Nikon, with the approval of Tsar Alexei Mikhaylovich.

See also: DMITRY, FALSE; FYODOR IVANOVICH; GODUNOV, BORIS FYODOROVICH; IVAN IV; METROPOLITAN; NIKON, PATRIARCH; ORTHODOXY; PATRIARCHATE; SIMONOV MONASTERY

BIBLIOGRAPHY

Dunning, Chester. (2001). *Russia's First Civil War.* University Park: Pennsylvania State University Press.

Vernadsky, George. (1969). *The Tsardom of Moscow 1547–1682.* 2 vols. New Haven, CT: Yale University Press.

DEBRA A. COULTER

JOSEPH OF VOLOTSK, ST.

(c. 1439–1515), coenobiarch and militant defender of Orthodoxy.

Of provincial servitor origin, Ivan Sanin became the monk Joseph (Iosif) around 1460 under the charismatic Pafnuty of Borovsk. Having a robust body, superb voice, powerful will, clear mind, excellent memory, and lucid pen, Joseph was forced by Ivan III to succeed as abbot in 1477. They soon quarreled over peasants, and in 1479 Joseph returned with six seasoned colleagues to Volotsk to start his own cloister under the protection of Ivan's brother Boris. Joseph attracted additional talent and quickly developed his foundation into a center of learning rivaling its model, Kirillov-Beloozersk. Dionisy, the leading iconographer of the day, painted Iosif's Dormition Church gratis.

Joseph joined Archbishop Gennady's campaign against the Novgorod Heretics in the late 1480s. Masterminding the literary defense of Orthodoxy, Joseph personally persuaded Ivan III to sanction the synod (1504), which condemned a handful of dissidents to death and others to monastery prisons. The celebrated quarrel with Nil Sorsky's disciple Vassian Patrikeyev and the "Kirillov and Trans-Volgan Elders" erupted soon after these executions, which, the latter argued, were not canonically justifiable.

In 1507, claiming oppression by his new local prince, Joseph placed his monastery under royal protection. He was then excommunicated by his new spiritual superior, Archbishop Serapion of Novgorod (r. 1505–1509), for failing to consult him. Basil III, Metropolitan Simon (r. 1495–1511), and the Moscow synod of bishops backed Joseph and deposed Serapion, but Joseph was tainted as the courtier of the grand prince and as a slanderer, while Vassian's star rose. Nevertheless, the monastery continued to flourish. As Joseph physically weakened, he formally instituted the cogoverning council, which ensured continuity under his successors.

Joseph's chief legacies were the Iosifov-Volokolamsk Monastery and his *Enlightener* (*Prosvetitel*) or *Book Against the Novgorod Heretics.* Under his leadership the cloister innovated and rationalized the lucrative commemoration services for the dead, patronized religious art, initiated one of the country's great libraries and scriptoria, and became a quasi-academy, nurturing prelates for half a century. Among his disciples and collaborators were the outstanding ascetic Kassian Bosoi (d. 1531), who had taught Ivan III archery and lived to help baptize Ivan IV; a nephew, Dosifey Toporkov, who composed the *Russian Chronograph* in 1512; the book-copyist Nil Polev, who donated to Iosifov the earliest extant copies of both Nil Sorsky's and Joseph's writings; and Joseph's enterprising successor, the future Metropolitan Daniel.

The *Enlightener,* produced before 1490 and revised through the year of Joseph's death, was his most authoritative and copied work. It served simultaneously as the foundation of Orthodoxy for militant churchman and as a doctrinal and ethical handbook for laity and clergy. Its dramatic and distorted introductory "Account of the New Heresy of the Novgorod Heretics" sets the tone of diabolic Judaizers confronted by heroic defenders of the faith. The eleven polemical-didactic discourses that follow justify Orthodoxy's Trinitarian and redemptive doctrines (1–4), the veneration of icons and other holy objects (5–7), the unfathomability of the Second Coming and the authority of Scripture and patristics (8–10), and monasticism (11). The standard concluding part, either appended epistles composed before the 1504 synod in the brief redaction, or the four or five extra discourses of the post-1511 extended redaction, defend the repression and execution of heretics. Joseph's conscious rhetorical strategy of lumping all dissidence together allows him to impute to the heretics the objections by fellow Orthodox to inquisitorial measures. Among his notable assertions are that one should resist unto death the blasphemous commands of a tyrant; that killing a heretic by prayer or hands is equivalent; that one should entrap heretics with divinely wise tricks; and, most famous, that the Orthodox Tsar is like God in his authority.

Joseph's extended, fourteenth-discourse and nine-tradition *Monastic Rule*, adumbrated in a brief, eleven-sermon redaction, was Russia's most detailed and preaching work of its kind, but chiefly an in-house work for his cloister. The blueprint for the monastery's success is contained in his polemical claim to represent native traditions and his insistence on attentiveness to rituals, modesty, temperance, total obedience, labor, responsibility of office, precise execution of commemorations, protection of community property, pastoral care, and the council's authority. In addition, ten of his extant epistles defend the monastery's property in concrete ways. Questionable sources from the 1540s and 1550s, connected with his followers' struggles, also link him to the generic defense of monastic property, supposedly at a church council in 1503. He composed a variety of other admonitions, including a call for price-fixing during a local famine.

Canonized in 1591, Joseph was venerated also by the Old Believers. The Russian Church today invokes him as the "Russian star," but some observers since the 1860s have considered his ritualism and inquisitorial intolerance an unfortunate phenomenon and legacy.

See also: BASIL III; CHURCH COUNCIL; DANIEL, METROPOLITAN; DIONISY; IVAN III; JUDAIZERS; ORTHODOXY; POSSESSORS AND NON-POSSESSORS

BIBLIOGRAPHY

Goldfrank, David. (2000). *The Monastic Rule of Iosif Volotsky*, rev. ed. Kalamazoo, MI: Cistercian Publications.

Luria, Jakov S. (1984). "Unresolved Issues in the History of the Ideological Movements of the Late Fifteenth Century." In *Medieval Slavic Culture*, eds. Henrik Birnbaum and Michael S. Flier, vol. 1 of 2. *California Slavic Studies* 12:150–171.

DAVID M. GOLDFRANK

JOURNALISM

Russian journalism, both under the tsars and since, has more often responded to state requirements than it has exemplified the freedom of the press. Moreover, not until a decade or so before the 1917 Revolution did a number of newspapers win mass readerships by lively and extensive daily reporting of domestic and foreign news.

Peter I (r. 1682–1725) started the first newspaper in a small format, the *St. Petersburg Bulletin*, and wrote for it himself to advance his reform program. Later in the eighteenth century journals appeared as outlets for literary and didactic works, but they could not escape the influence of the state. As part of her effort to enlighten Russia, Catherine II (r. 1762–1796) launched *All Sorts of Things* in 1769. This was a weekly publication modeled on English satirical journals. Nicholas Novikov, a dedicated Freemason, published his well-known *Drone* on the presses of the Academy of Sciences, providing outlet for pointedly critical comments about conditions in Russia, including serfdom, but he went too far, and the Empress closed down his publishing activities.

In the early, reformist years of the reign of Alexander I (1801–1825), a number of writers promoted constitutional ideas in periodicals controlled or subsidized by the government. Between 1804 and 1805, an education official named I. I. Martynov edited one such newspaper, *Northern Messenger*, and promoted Western ideas. He portrayed Great Britain as an advanced and truly free society. Nikolai Mikhailovich Karamzin, the tsar's unofficial historian, founded *Messenger of Europe* (1802–1820) to introduce Russian readers to European developments.

Among the reign's new monthlies, those issued by the Ministries of War, Public Education, Justice, the Interior, and the Navy continued until the 1917 Revolution. The Ministry of Foreign Affairs published a newspaper in French. After the Napoleonic wars, Alexander I backed a small newspaper, *Messenger of Zion*, its main message being that the promoters of Western European Enlight-

A student browses through newspapers for sale at a St. Petersburg University kiosk, 1992. © STEVE RAYMER/CORBIS

enment were plotting to subvert the Russian church and state.

The reign of Nicholas I (1825–1855) saw commercial successes by privately owned but progovernment periodicals. For example, the *Library for Readers*, founded by Alexander Filippovich Smirdin, reached a peak circulation of seven thousand subscribers in 1837. As the first of the so-called thick journals that dominated journalism for about three decades, each issue ran about three hundred pages and was divided into sections on Russian literature, foreign literature, science, art, and the like. Its size and content made it especially appealing in the countryside, where it provided a month's reading for landlord families. Works by virtually all of Russia's prominent writers appeared in serial form in such journals.

Smirdin also acquired Russia's first popular, privately owned daily newspaper, *Northern Bee*, which was essentially a loyalist publication that had permission to publish both foreign and domestic political information. The *Bee* also had the exclusive right to publish news of the Crimean War, but only by excerpting it from the Ministry of War's official newspaper, *Russian War Veteran*. During the war, the *Bee* achieved the unprecedented readership of ten thousand subscribers.

Another major development was the growing success in the 1840s of two privately owned journals, *Notes of the Fatherland* and *The Contemporary*. Each drew readers largely by publishing the literary reviews of a formidable critic, Vissarion Belinsky, who managed to express his moral outrage at human wrongs, despite the efforts of censors. However, journalism turned from a literary emphasis to a more political one during the reign of the tsar-reformer Alexander II (r. 1855–1881), who emancipated some 50 million serfs and effected reforms in education, local government, the judiciary, and the military, and relaxed the practice of preliminary, or pre-publication, censorship. One of his first steps in this regard was, in 1857, to permit journalists to publicize the peasant emancipation question, a topic previously forbidden. The next was allowing journalists to comment on how best to reform the courts and local government.

Journalists seized what was, on the whole, a genuine expansion of free speech about public affairs. They had as their ideal Alexander Herzen, the emigre whose banned words they read in *The Bell*, a Russian-language paper he produced in London and smuggled into Russia. By keeping informed on developments in Russia through correspondence and visitors, Herzen published authoritative information and liberal arguments, especially on the emancipation of the serfs, and influenced many who served under Alexander II. Meanwhile, Nikolai Gavrilovich Chernyshevsky, an erudite man who read several languages, became Russia's leading political journalist through the pages of *The Contemporary*; and he, like Herzen, wove in relevant events from Western Europe to shape public and government opinion on reform issues. Another such journalist, Dmitry Pisarev, wrote many of his major pieces in prison, and published them in the other major radical journal within the Empire, *Russian Word*; however, he espoused the nihilist position of accepting nothing on faith but, rather, testing all accepted truths and practices by the critical tools of reason and science. In line with the view of a liberal censor at that time, Alexander Vasilevich Nikitenko, higher censorship officials suspended both journals for eight months in 1862 and later permanently closed them.

Through his new censorship statute of 1865, widely hailed as a reform, Alexander II unleashed a major expansion of the commercial daily press, which was concentrated in Moscow and the capital, St. Petersburg. During the last decade of the previous reign, only six new dailies (all in the special-interest category) had been allowed, but officials now approved sixty new dailies in the first decade under Alexander II, and many of these were granted permission to publish not just general news but also a political section. In 1862, private dailies received permission to sell space to advertisers, a right that allowed lower subscription fees. The new income source prompted the publisher of *Son of the Fatherland* to change it from a weekly to a daily, and it soon acquired twenty thousand subscribers, well over half of them in the provinces.

By Western standards, however, overall circulation levels remained modest, even as more and more newspapers became commercially successful in the 1860s. Andrei Alexandrovich Kraevsky's moderate daily, *Voice*, saw profits grow as readers increased to ten thousand by the close of the 1860s. *Moscow Bulletin*, edited by Michael Katkov, who leased it in 1863 and changed it from a weekly to a daily, doubled its circulation to twelve thousand in two years' time, in part because of its ardently nationalistic leaders, which were front-page opinion pieces modeled on French *feuilletons* and written by Mikhail Nikiforovich Katkov, known as the editorial "thunderer." Just as outspoken and popular were the leaders written in the capital for the daily, *St. Petersburg Bulletin*, by Alexei Sergeyevich Suvorin, who kept that conservative paper's circulation high. Readers preferring nationalistic and slavophile journalism critical of the government bought Ivan Aksakov's *Day* (1865–1866) and then his *Moscow* (1867–1869), its end coming when the State Council banned his daily and barred him from publishing, citing his unrelenting defiance of censorship law.

Another boon for newspapers under Alexander II was their new right, granted in the early 1860s, to buy foreign news reports received in Russia by the Russian Telegraph Agency (RTA, run by the Ministry of Foreign Affairs), after such dispatches had been officially approved. In this period, too, publishers improved printing production by buying advanced equipment from Germany and elsewhere in Europe, including typesetting machines and rotary presses that that permitted press runs in the tens of thousands. Publishers also imported photographic and engraving tools that made possible the pictorial magazines and Sunday supplements.

Following the politically-motivated murder of Alexander II, his son and heir Alexander III (r. 1881-1894) gave governors full right to close publications judged to be inciting a condition of alarm in their provinces, without the approval of the courts. But there were still possibilities for critical journalists even at a time of conservative government policies. Nicholas K. Mikhailovsky, who espoused a radical populist viewpoint, published in *Notes of the Fatherland* until the government closed it in 1884. Most of the staff moved to *Northern Messenger*, which began publishing in 1885. After spending a period in exile, Mikhailovsky joined the *Messenger* staff and wrote later for two other populist journals, *Russian Wealth* and *Russian Thought*. He was one of the outstanding examples of the legal populist journalists and led the journalistic critique of the legal Marxists.

During the early years of Nicholas II (r. 1894–1917), some Russian journalists promoted anti-government political and social views in the papers printed abroad by such illegal political parties as the Social Democrats, the Socialist Revolutionaries, and the Union of Liberation. The Social Democrats, led by Vladimir Ilich Lenin, began *Spark* in 1902 in London, its declared purpose being to unseat the tsar and start a social revolution. Those who backed *Spark* in Russia had to accept *Spark*'s editorial board as their party's leaders. When the various anti-autocracy factions cohered as legal parties in Russia following the Revolution of 1905, each published its own legal newspaper. The Mensheviks launched *Ray* in 1912 and Lenin's Bolsheviks started *Pravda* (Truth) in 1912, but the government closed the latter in 1914. (*Pravda* emerged again after the Revolution of 1917 as the main outlet for the views of the ruling Communist Party). Another type of journalism was that of Prince V. P. Meshchersky, editor of the St. Petersburg daily, *The Citizen*. Meshchersky accepted money from a secret government "reptile" fund. His publishing activities were completely venal, but both Alexander II and Nicholas II supported him because of his pro-autocracy, nationalistic views.

With mass publishing commonplace in the big cities of Russia by 1900, publishers in those centers continued to increase readerships, some with papers that primarily shocked or entertained. In the first category was *Rumor* of St. Petersburg; in the second, *St. Petersburg Gazette*, for which Anton Chekhov wrote short stories pseudonymously. The copeck newspapers of Moscow and St. Petersburg provided broad coverage at little cost for urban readers. Making a selling point of pictures and fiction, by 1870 Adolf Fyodorovich Marks lined up nine thousand paid subscriptions to meet the initial costs of his illustrated magazine, *The Cornfield*, which was the first of the so-called thin journals, and increased readership to 235,000 by century's turn. The government itself entered into mass production of its inexpensive newspaper for peasants, *Village Messenger*, and achieved a press run of 150,000.

High reporting standards set by long-time publisher Alexei Sergeyevich Suvorin, on the other hand, won a large readership for the conservative *New Times*, the daily he had acquired in 1876. Reputedly the one paper read by members of the Imperial family, *New Times* merited respect for publishing reporters such as Vasily Vasilevich Rozanov, one of the best practitioners of the cryptic news style typical in modern journalism. Imperial funding to friendly publishers like Suvorin, regardless of need, continued to 1917 through subsidies and subscription purchases. (Other recipients of lesser stature were *Russian Will*, *Contemporary Word*, *Voice of Moscow*, and *Morning of Russia*.) Another paper receiving help from the government was *Russian Banner*, the organ of the party of the extreme right wing in Russia after 1905, the Union of the Russian People. On the other end of the political spectrum, satirical publications targeting high officials and Tsar Nicholas II flourished in the years 1905 through 1908, though many were short-lived. One count shows 429 different titles of satirical publications during these years.

One outstanding newspaper, *Russian Word* of Moscow, became Russia's largest daily. Credit goes to the publisher of peasant origins, Ivan D. Sytin, who followed the journalistic road urged on him by Chekhov by founding a conservative daily in 1894 and transforming it into a liberal daily outside party or government affiliations. Sytin was no writer himself, but in 1901 he hired an excellent liberal editor, Vlas Doroshevich, who became one of Russia's most imitated journalists and a prose stylist whom Leo Tolstoy ranked as second only to Chekhov. Doroshevich gained the title king of *feuilletonists* by dealing with important issues in an engaging, chatty style. As editor of *Word*, he ordered each reporter to make sense of breaking events by writing as if he were the reader's informative and entertaining friend. At the same time he barred intrusion by the business office into the newsroom, and kept Sytin to his promise not to interfere in any editorial matters whatsoever. Through these journalistic standards, Doroshevich built *Russian Word* into the only million-copy daily published in Russia prior to the Revolution of 1917.

Pravda, not *Russian Word*, however, would be the paper that dominated the new order established by Lenin's Bolsheviks. In the early twenty-first century, the front section of the building that housed *Word* abuts the building of *Izvestiia*, another Bolshevik paper from 1917 that has, in its post-communist incarnation, become one of Russia's great newspapers. *Pravda*, the huge Soviet-era daily with a press-run of more than six million, was first and foremost the organ of the Central Committee of the Communist Party of the USSR and it perpetuated Lenin's idea that the press in a socialist society must be a collectivist propagandist, agitator, and organizer. Other newspapers during the Soviet era were bound to follow *Pravda*'s political line, expressed in the form of long articles and the printing of speeches of high officials, and to promote the achievements of Soviet life. Regional and local papers, little distinguishable from *Pravda* in format, had leeway to cover local news, and specialized papers had scope to introduce somewhat different coverage, as well. In any event, the agitational purpose of Soviet papers meant that Western concepts of independent reporting and confidentiality of sources had no place in journalism in the USSR.

Since the collapse of the Soviet Union in 1991, the new Constitution of the Russian Federation, approved by popular referendum on December 12, 1993, recognized freedom of thought and speech, forbade censorship, and guaranteed "the right to freely seek, obtain, transmit, produce, and disseminate information by any legal method." The Constitution prohibited the creation of a state ideology that could limit the functioning of the mass media. Within months, in June of 1994, the Congress of Russian Journalists insisted that journalists resist pressure on the reporting of news from any source.

Russian journalists, working to these high standards, have sometimes paid a price for their commitment to objective reporting. Journalist Anna Politkovskaya, for writing critical dispatches from Chechnya for the small, biweekly newspaper *New Gazette*, was detained for a period by the FSB, the federal security service, and received numerous threats to her personal security. When Gregory Pasco, the naval officer turned journalist, exposed nuclear waste dumping in the Pacific Ocean by the Russian fleet, a court convicted him of treason. Other Russian journalists who engaged in forthright reporting have been killed under mysterious circumstances.

Major Russian newspapers have not managed to establish their own financial independence, because they are owned by wealthy banks and resource companies closely connected to the federal government. Most newspapers outside of Moscow and St. Petersburg (from 95 to 97% of them, according to the Glasnost Foundation) are owned or controlled by governments at the provincial or regional level. One of their tasks is to assist in the reelection of local officials. Overall, only a handful of newspapers in Russia are independent journalistic voices in the early twenty-first century. On the other hand, controls on journalism in Russia are no longer monolithic, as in the Soviet era, and citizens of the Russian Federation had access to varied sources of news reports in the print and electronic media. The Internet newspaper *lenta.ru*, for instance, offers coverage comparable to a Western paper.

See also: BELINSKY, VISSARION GRIGORIEVICH; CENSORSHIP; CHERNYSHEVSKY, NIKOLAI GAVRILOVICH; HERZEN, ALEXANDER IVANOVICH INTELLIGENTSIA; KATKOV, MIKHAIL NIKIFOROVICH; MIKHAILOVSKY, NIKOLAI KONSTANTINOVICH; NEWSPAPERS; SUVORIN, ALEXEI SERGEYEVICH; SYTIN, IVAN DMITRIEVICH; THICK JOURNALS

BIBLIOGRAPHY

Ambler, Effie. (1972). *Russian Journalism and Politics: The Career of Aleksei S. Suvorin, 1861–1881*. Detroit: Wayne State University Press.

McReynolds, Louise. (1991). *The News under Russia's Old Regime: The Development of a Mass Circulation Press.* Princeton, NJ: Princeton University Press.

Norton, Barbara T., and Gheith, Jehanne M., eds. (2001). *An Improper Profession: Women, Gender, and Journalism in Late Imperial Russia.* Durham, NC: Duke University Press.

Ruud, Charles A. (1982). *Fighting Words: Imperial Censorship and the Russian Press, 1804–1906.* Toronto: University of Toronto Press.

CHARLES A. RUUD

JUDAIZERS

A diverse group of heretics in Novgorod (c. 1470–1515), sometimes referred to as the Novgorod-Moscow heretics.

The Judaizing "heresy" arose in Novgorod in the years 1470 and 1471, after a Kievan Jew named Zechariah (Skhary) proselytized the priest Alexei, who in turn enticed the priest Denis and many others, including the archpriest Gavril, into Judaism. Around 1478, Ivan III, who had just subjugated Novgorod, installed them in the chief cathedrals of the Moscow Kremlin. In 1484 or 1485, the influential state secretary and diplomat Fyodor Kuritsyn and the Hungarian "Martin" joined with Alexei and Denis and eventually attracted, among others, Metropolitan Zosima (r. 1490–1494), as well as Ivan III's daughter-in-law Elena of Moldavia, Meanwhile, Archbishop Gennady of Novgorod (r. 1484–1504) discovered the Novgorod heretics and started a campaign against them, which was later taken up by Joseph of Volotsk. Synods were held in Moscow in 1488 and 1490, leading to an auto-da-fé in Novgorod and to the imprisonment of Denis and several others. Alexei had already died, however, and several others, like the historiographer-copyist Ivan Cherny, fled. Joseph's faction forced

Zosima from office and convened another Moscow synod in 1504, which condemned five heretics to death, including the late Kuritsyn's brother Ivan Volk, a state secretary expert in the law, and Archimandrite Kassian of Novgorod's Yurev Monastery. Others, like the merchant Semon Klenov, were imprisoned.

The accusations against the "heretics" reveal a hodgepodge of tenets rather than a coherent sect. The dissidents allegedly elevated Old Testament law, denigrated Christian scripture and patristic writings, attacked icons and monasticism, and denied the Trinity and the Incarnation. They dissimulated in the presence of steadfast adherents of Orthodoxy, practiced astrology and black magic, and after the end of the Russian Orthodox year 7000 (1492 C.E.) ridiculed Christian writings that had predicted the Second Coming around that time, and especially the New Testament for describing its own era as the last epoch. They also opposed the condemnation of heretics and demanded that repentant heretics not be punished.

Whatever Jewishness lies behind these accusations may go back to the scriptural, astronomical, and philosophical interchanges between Jews and Orthodox Christians in western Rus during the fifteenth century. Fyodor Kuritsyn's "Laodician Epistle," a chain poem, is reminiscent of Jewish wisdom literature. In addition, the dissidents were more open to secular culture and rationalism than most representatives of the official church. Some of the accusations of heresy may have derived from issues pertaining to specific icons, to various Novgorodian practices, to the use of Jewish astronomical knowledge, to Moscow's treatment of conquered Novgorod, and even to church lands. Whatever the case, when a similar outbreak of dissidence occurred in Novgorod and Moscow during the 1550s, it was attributed to Protestant, not Jewish, influences. The phenomenon of dissidence prompted Archbishop Gennady to assemble a coterie of Orthodox and Catholic experts to compile the first complete Slavonic Bible and make other useful translations.

See also: IVAN III; JOSEPH OF VOLOTSK, ST.; KURITSYN, FYODOR VASILEVICH; NOVGOROD THE GREAT; ORTHODOXY; POSSESSORS AND NON-POSSESSORS

BIBLIOGRAPHY

Klier, John. (1997). "Judaizing without Jews? Moscow-Novgorod, 1470–1504." In *Culture and Identity in Muscovy, 1359–1584*, ed. Ann M. Kleimola and Gail D. Lenhoff. Moscow: ITZ-Garant.

Tauber, Moishe. (1995). "The Kievan Jew Zacharia and the Astronomical Works of the Judaizers." In *Jews and Slavs*, vol. 3, ed. Wolf Moskovich, Shmuel Shvarzbard, and Anatoly Alekseev. Jerusalem: Hebrew University Press.

DAVID M. GOLDFRANK

JULY DAYS OF 1917

Abortive Bolshevik uprising in Petrograd in July 1917.

On July 3–5, 1917, in Petrograd, militant soldiers, sailors, and factory workers staged an abortive uprising. For weeks, local Bolshevik, Anarchist, and Left Socialist Revolutionary organizers had agitated against the Provisional Government and for immediate transfer of power to the Soviets of Workers and Soldiers Deputies. This call to action resonated with workers engaged in bitter labor conflicts and among garrison soldiers facing deployment to the front. July 3 witnessed a flurry of meetings, demonstrations, and strikes. That evening tens of thousands of soldiers and workers, led by left socialist agitators, marched on the city center and insisted that the Soviet assume power. However, the Soviet's Menshevik and Socialist Revolutionary leaders, already engulfed in a crisis in the government coalition, refused.

The Bolshevik Military Organization and Petersburg Committee pushed for an uprising while the Central Committee wavered. Leon Trotsky, Grigory Zinoviev, and Lev Kamenev initially urged restraint but tentatively endorsed the demonstrations in the early hours of July 4. The party's leader, Vladimir Lenin, remained absent from Petrograd until midday.

On July 4 huge crowds of armed workers, soldiers, and sailors controlled the city's streets; nearly four hundred people died in scattered fighting and random shootings. Crowds again demanded that unwilling Soviet leaders accept power. Lenin and the Central Committee meanwhile debated the possibility of a successful seizure of power. By evening, the tenor of events had changed dramatically. When the government publicly alleged that Lenin was a German agent, several garrison units turned against the demonstrations. Rumor spread that soldiers were marching on Petrograd to defend the government. By morning on July 5, the inchoate seizure of power collapsed. The government arrested several Bolshevik leaders, on whom it blamed the uprising. Lenin went into hiding, and his party suffered a significant temporary decline.

The July Days resonated throughout Russia—rallies for Soviet power, for instance, took place in Moscow, Saratov, Krasnoyarsk, and other provincial cities—but its chief significance lay in exposing the fragility of the Provisional Government and in accelerating the polarization of Russian politics and society.

BIBLIOGRAPHY

Rabinowitch, Alexander. (1968). *Prelude to Revolution: The Petrograd Bolsheviks and the July 1917 Uprising.* Bloomington: Indiana University Press.

Wade, Rex A. (2000). *The Russian Revolution, 1917.* New York: Cambridge University Press.

Michael C. Hickey

KABARDIANS

Kabardians are one of the titular nationalities of the north Caucasian Republic of Kabardino-Balkaria in the Russian Federation. The population of the republic, whose capital city is Nalchik, is 790,000, of whom 48 percent are Kabardian. Of these, 55 percent are rural and engaged in agriculture, animal husbandry, and metallurgy, as well as in health services in the well-known spa resorts of the region. Kabardians also live in the adjacent Stavropol Krai, the Krasnodar Krai, and in North Ossetia.

Kabardian is linguistically classified as East Circassian, and the Kabardians belong to the same ethnolinguistic family as the Adyge and the Cherkess who live in neighboring republics. Policies on nationalities during the Soviet era established these three groups as separate "peoples" and languages, but historical memory and linguistic affinity, as well as post-Soviet ethnic politics, perpetuate notions of ethnic continuity. An important element in this has been the contact, since the break-up of the Soviet Union, with Kabardians living in Turkey, Syria, Israel, Jordan, western Europe, and the United States. These are the descendents of migrants who left for the Ottoman Empire in the late nineteenth century after the Russian conquest of the Caucasus. In the 1990s a number of Kabardian families from the diaspora settled in Nalchik, but integration remains fraught with social and legal problems.

The Kabardians are largely Muslim, though a small Kabardian Russian Orthodox group inhabits the city of Mozdok in Ossetia. Other religious influences, including Greek Orthodox Christianity and indigenous beliefs and rituals, can still be discerned in cultural practices. The Soviet state discouraged Islamic practice and identity but supported cultural nation-building. Kabardian folk-dance groups (i.e., "Kabardinka") have achieved widespread fame.

In the post-Soviet period, interethnic tensions led, in the early 1990s, to an attempted partition of the republic between the two nationalities, but this did not come to pass. The wars in Abkhasia (between 1992 and 1993) and Chechnya (1994–1997; 1999–2000) affected Kabardian sympathies and politics, causing the Russian state to intermittently infuse the republic with resources to prevent the spreading of conflict. Islamic movements, generally termed "Wahhabism," are in some evidence, and mosque building and religious instruction and practice are on the increase.

See also: ABKHAZIANS; ADYGE; CAUCASUS; CHERKESS; CHECHNYA AND CHECHENS; ISLAM; NATIONALITIES POLICIES, SOVIET; NATIONALITIES POLICIES, TSARIST

BIBLIOGRAPHY

Baddeley, John F. (1908). *The Russian Conquest of the Caucasus.* London: Longmans, Green & Co.

Borxup, Marie Bennigsen, ed. (1992). *The North Caucasus Barrier: The Russian Advance towards the Muslim World.* New York: St. Martin's Press.

Gammer, Moshe. (1994). *Muslim Resistance to the Tsar: Shamil and the Conquest of Chechnia and Daghestan.* London: Frank Cass.

Jaimoukha, Amjad. (2001). *The Circassians: A Handbook.* London: Curzon Press.

Jersild, Austin. (2002). *Orientalism and Empire: North Caucasus Mountain Peoples and the Georgian Frontier, 1854–1917.* Montreal and Kingston: McGill-Queens University Press.

Matveeva, Anna. (1999). *The North Caucasus: Russia's Fragile Borderland.* Great Britain: The Royal Institute of International Affairs.

SETENEY SHAMI

KADETS *See* CONSTITUTIONAL DEMOCRATIC PARTY.

KAGANOVICH, LAZAR MOYSEYEVICH

(1893–1991), Stalinist; deputy prime minister of the Soviet Union from 1944 to 1957.

Known for his viciousness, Lazar Kaganovich was a staunch Stalinist and a ruthless participant in the purges of the 1930s. Born near Kiev, Ukraine, Kaganovich became active in the Social Democratic Party from 1911 and served as the first secretary of the Ukrainian Communist Party from 1925 to 1928. A brilliant administrator, Kaganovich served on the Presidium of the CPSU from 1930 to 1957 and held numerous important posts, including first secretary in the Moscow Party Organization (1930–1935), key administrator of the Agricultural Department of the Central Committee (1933), people's commissar of transport (1935), and people's commissar of heavy industry (1935). In December 1944 he was appointed deputy prime minister of the Soviet Union.

An influential proponent of forced collectivization, Kaganovich advocated harsh repression of the rich peasants, or kulaks, in the late 1920s. During the grain procurement campaign of 1932, Kaganovich headed a commission that was sent to the North Caucasus to speed up grain collection. On November 2 his commission adopted a resolution that called for the violent breakup of kulak sabotage networks and the use of terror to break the resistance of rural communists. The result was the arrest of thousands and the deportation of tens of thousands of rural inhabitants.

His belief in the efficacy of coercion led him to develop a strategy that called for indiscriminate mass repression of workers as a way to increase productivity and punish what he considered anti-Soviet actions in industry. As commissar of transport, Kaganovich was particularly hard on railway men, calling for the death sentence for various offenses that might lead to the breakdown of Soviet transport plans. He devised the so-called theory of counterrevolutionary limit setting on output that he used to destroy hundreds of engineering and technical cadres.

In the Great Purges (1936–1938) Kaganovich took the extreme position that the Party's interests justified everything. In the summer of 1937 Kaganovich was sent to carry out purges of local Party organizations in Chelyabinsk, Yaroslavl, Ivanovo, and Smolensk. Throughout 1936 and 1937 he also had all his deputies, nearly all road chiefs and political section chiefs, and many other officials in transport arrested without any grounds whatsoever. In August 1937 he demanded that the NKVD (secret police) arrest ten officials in the People's Commissariat of Transport because he thought their behavior suspicious. All were arrested as spies and shot. He ultimately had thirty-eight transport executives and thousands of Party members arrested.

Following Stalin's death in 1953, Kaganovich opposed Nikita Khrushchev's proposal to admit errors committed by the Party under Stalin's leadership. He remained an oppositionist, eventually allying with Georgy Malenkov, Vyacheslav Molotov, and Dmitry Shepilov, in the so-called Anti-Party Group that attempted to remove Khrushchev from power in 1957. Following the failed coup, Kaganovich was removed from his position as deputy prime minister and assigned to managing a potash works in Perm oblast. He died there of natural causes in 1991.

See also: COLLECTIVIZATION OF AGRICULTURE; KULAKS; PURGES, THE GREAT; STALIN, JOSEF VISSARIONOVICH

BIBLIOGRAPHY

Conquest, Robert. (1990). *The Great Terror: A Reassessment.* New York: Oxford University Press.

Courtois, Stephane, et al. (1999). *The Black Book of Communism: Crimes, Terror, Repression.* Cambridge, MA: Harvard University Press.

Crankshaw, Edward. (1970). *Khrushchev Remembers.* Boston: Little, Brown.

Kahn, Stuart. (1987). *The Wolf of the Kremlin.* New York: Morrow.

KATE TRANSCHEL

KAL 007

On September 1, 1983, a Soviet SU-15 shot a Korean civilian 747 airliner from the sky. All 269 passengers on board perished. Korean authorities publicly stated the plane had mistakenly strayed off its intended course by some 365 miles. This was caused by a technical error programmed into the inertial navigation system by the plane's pilot, according to Korean authorities. Unfortunately, the plane entered Soviet territory over the Kamchatka peninsula where submarines were located and, on the night of the flight, a secret test of an SS-25 Soviet missile reportedly was planned. A U.S. RC-135 spy plane was in the area, and it is assumed the Soviets believed they were destroying the RC-135 or a civilian version of a spy plane. Soviet Colonel Gennadi Osipovich was the pilot given the responsibility of challenging and eventually shooting and destroying Korean Airlines flight 007. Osipovich recalled in a 1996 interview in the *New York Times* how he pulled alongside the airliner and recognized in the dark the configuration of windows indicating a civilian airliner. He believed this civilian airliner could have a military use and believes to this day, according to the interview, that the plane was on a spy mission. He regrets not shooting the plane down over land so that such proof could be recovered. If Osipovich had waited another twenty to twenty-five seconds to destroy the plane, KAL 007 would have been over neutral territory, which most likely would have averted the incident. A serious U.S.-Soviet diplomatic fallout ensued.

See also: KOREA, RELATIONS WITH

TIMOTHY THOMAS

KALININGRAD

At the 1945 Potsdam Conference, the Western allies acceded to Josef Stalin's demand that the northern third of East Prussia be awarded to the Soviet Union. He provided two justifications for the transfer of the territory that would be renamed Kaliningrad: The USSR needed an ice-free port on the Baltic Sea, and, through the annexation, the Germans would compensate the Soviet people for the millions of lives they lost at the hands of the Nazi invaders. The American president, Franklin D. Roosevelt, and the British prime minister, Winston Churchill, said in the Potsdam Protocol that the transfer of territory was contingent upon a final peace treaty; this treaty was never signed by the Allied and Axis powers.

The Prussians, who originally occupied the area, lost their lands after the Teutonic Knights invaded the southern shores of the Baltic littoral in the thirteenth century. By the seventeenth century, the Prussians—cousins to the Latvians and Lithuanians, all of whom spoke a closely related language—disappeared as a nation, and the German invaders henceforth adopted the name "Prussians."

Russians never lived in East Prussia, although in 1758, during the Seven Years War, Russian troops briefly occupied the capital Königsberg and some surrounding territory. After World War I, the German province of East Prussia was created on this territory but was separated from the rest of Germany by the Polish Corridor. Poland was awarded the southern two-thirds of old East Prussia after World War II, and the Soviet Union took control of its northern third, about the size of Northern Ireland. Henceforth most of the German residents fled, or were forced from the area, and their farms and cities were occupied by migrants from other areas of the Soviet Union. Most were Russians and by the mid-1990s this westernmost Russian region had about 930,000 residents. About 80 percent lived in urban areas, the rest in the countryside.

During the Cold War, Kaliningrad was a closed territory with a heavy military presence: The USSR's Baltic Sea fleet was located there along with contingents of ground and air defense units. It was the first line of defense against an attack from the west and could be used simultaneously for offensive operations in a westward coup de main.

With the collapse of the Soviet Union in 1991, Kaliningrad became an "exclave" of the Russian Federation (i.e., a geographical anomaly, since it was a political entity of Russia but surrounded by Lithuania, Poland, and the Baltic Sea). All land and rail routes to and from Kaliningrad to Russia henceforth had to traverse foreign borders.

In the 1990s Kaliningrad was perceived simultaneously as a flash point of conflict with its neighbors and a gateway to Europe. The first perspective was based on the presence of large numbers of Russian troops, and on Russian fears that foreign interests (in Germany and Lithuania) claimed the oblast. By the late 1990s none of these latent points of conflict became manifest. According to U.S. government estimates, there were 25,000 Russian military personnel in the oblast, and no foreign government had claims on it.

But Kaliningrad did not become a gateway to Europe either. On the contrary: Afflicted by daunting economic, political, and social problems, Kaliningrad was described by Western observers as a "black hole" in the center of Europe. Today the oblast no longer receives the heavy subsidies it enjoyed during the Soviet era, and it has experienced greater dips in its agricultural and manufacturing sectors than other Russian regions. To make matters worse, the region's residents and political leadership complained that the authorities in Moscow have ignored them, or have adopted conflicting policies that have exacerbated the oblast's economic problems.

To attract domestic and foreign investment, first a "free" and then a "special" economic zone was created. But Moscow's failure to enact enabling legislation, or to change existing laws, have undercut the zones. After Russia's August 1998 fiscal crisis, Kaliningrad's economic situation deteriorated further. By 2000 the European Union indicated that it was prepared to address the "Kaliningrad Question" through its Northern Dimension—a development plan for Russia's northwestern regions—but they received mixed signals from Moscow.

Russian authorities expressed concern that Kaliningraders would suffer once Poland and Lithuania entered the EU and adopted stricter border controls. Also, while President Vladimir Putin indicated that he desired closer ties with Europe, his representatives in Moscow and Kaliningrad were slow to adopt a common approach toward the oblast's problems. By the fall of 2002, however, the EU and Russia reached an agreement on providing transit documents (and a sealed train) to facilitate travel to and from Kaliningrad to Russia through Lithuania.

Many European and American analysts believe that Kaliningrad can serve as a test case and demonstrate how the West might help Russia in its drive to build a democratic and capitalist society.

See also: ECONOMY, POST-SOVIET; PRUSSIA, RELATIONS WITH

BIBLIOGRAPHY

Fairlie, Lyndell D., and Sergounin, Alexander. (2001). *Are Borders Barriers?* Helsinki: The Finnish Institute of International Affairs.

Joenniemi, Perti, and Prawitz, Ian, eds. (1998). *Kaliningrad: The European Amber Region*. Aldershot, UK: Ashgate.

Krickus, Richard J. (2002). *The Kaliningrad Question*. Lanham, MD: Rowman and Littlefield.

RICHARD J. KRICKUS

KALININ, MIKHAIL IVANOVICH

(1875–1946), Bolshevik, president of the USSR in 1922.

Active in the Russian Social Democratic Party from 1898, Mikhail Kalinin was an Old Bolshevik who held numerous important positions, including chairman of the All-Russian Central Executive Committee (1919) and president of the USSR (1922).

Born of peasant parents in Tver Province, Kalinin moved to St. Petersburg in 1889 and found employment at the Putilov factory. Kalinin's peasant origins and experience as a skilled industrial worker made him an attractive representative of the Communist Party. After the October Revolution in 1917, he became the chief administrator in Petrograd. He quickly rose to prominence as a member of the party's Central Committee from 1919, a full member of the Politburo from 1925, and chair of commissions to prepare Soviet constitutions in 1923 and 1936.

In defense of the New Economic Policy (NEP), Kalinin allied with Josef Stalin against Leon Trotsky and the Left Opposition in struggles for power following Vladimir Lenin's death. When Stalin switched sides, adopting the Left's program of forced collectivization of agriculture, Kalinin sided with Nikolai Bukharin in advocating moderation. Urging a conciliatory approach toward the peasantry, Kalinin opposed harsh treatment of the kulaks. While never publicly criticizing Stalin, Kalinin expressed reservations about the terror of the 1930s. He continued to serve the party as a propagandist until the end of World War II, and was one of the few Old Bolsheviks to survive the Stalinist purges. On June 3, 1946, Kalinin died of cancer.

See also: BOLSHEVISM; CONSTITUTION OF 1936

BIBLIOGRAPHY

Kalinin, M. I. (1950). *On Communist Education: Selected Speeches and Articles.* Moscow: Foreign Languages Pub. House.

KATE TRANSCHEL

KALMYKS

The Kalmyks, who call themselves the Khalmg, are descendants of the Oyrats people originating from western Mongolia (Jungaria). These were nomadic tribes, kindred to the Mongols in material culture, language, and religion. Today, most Kalmyks live in Kalmykia (the Republic of Kalmykia), which is one of the twenty-one nationality based republics of the Russian Federation recognized in the 1993 Russian Constitution. Kalmykia (about 29,400 square miles) is located in southeastern Russia on the northwestern shore of the Caspian Sea. Its capital, Elista, has more than 90,000 residents. Salt lakes abound in the region, but Kalmykia lacks permanent waterways. Lying in the vast depression of the north Caspian lowland, the territory consists largely of steppe and desert areas.

In 2000 roughly 314,300 people lived in Kalmykia. Its population was 45 percent Kalmyk, 38 percent Russian, 6 percent Dagestani, 3 percent Chechen, 2 percent Kazak, and 2 percent German. Representatives of the Torgut, Dorbet, and Buzawa tribes also inhabit the republic. In contrast to some of the other non-Russian languages spoken in the Russian Federation, the Kalmyk language (Kalmukian) has been classified as an "endangered language" by UNESCO due to the declining number of active speakers. Very few children learn the language, and those who do are not likely to become active users.

Another characteristic that distinguishes the Kalmyks from many non-Russian nationalities is their long and tortuous past. Due to the deficit of pasture lands and to feudal internecine dissension, the Oyrat tribes migrated westward from Chinese Turkistan to the steppes west of the mouth of the Volga River in the late sixteenth and early seventeenth centuries. Between 1608 and 1609, the Oyrats pledged their allegiance to the Russian tsar. As allies, they guarded the Russian Empire's eastern frontier during the reign of Peter I (the Great), from 1682 to 1725. Under Catherine II, however, the Kalmyks' fortune changed, and they became vassals. Unhappy with this situation, about 300,000 Kalmyks living east of the Volga began to return to China, but were attacked en route by Russian, Kazakh, and Kyrgyz warriors. Another group residing west of the Volga had remained in Russia, adopting a seminomadic lifestyle and practicing Lamaist Buddhism. They became known as the Kalmyk, which in Turkish means "remnant," referring to those who stayed behind.

In 1920 the Kalmyk autonomous oblast (province) was established, which became the Kalmyk Autonomous Soviet Socialist Republic (ASSR) in 1934. However, the Kalmyks' status shifted radically again when, in 1943, Josef Stalin dissolved the republic and deported some 170,000 Kalmyks to Siberia. He sought to punish the Kalmyk units who had fought the Russians in collaboration with the Germans. Stalin forcibly resettled a total of more than 1.5 million people, including the Volga Germans and six other nationalities of the Crimea and northern Caucasus: the Crimean Tatars, Chechens, Ingush, Balkars, Karachai, and Meskhetians. Other minorities evicted from the Black Sea coastal region included Bulgarians, Greeks, and Armenians.

Things improved for the Kalmyks when in 1956 Stalin's successor, Nikita Khrushchev, denounced the earlier deportation as criminal and permitted about 6,000 Kalmyks to return the following year. The Kalmyk ASSR was officially reestablished in 1958. Thirty-five years later, the Russian Constitution of 1993 officially recognized the Republic of Kalmykia (Khalmg Tangch). That year, Kirsan Ilyumzhinov won the first presidential elections in the new republic. His program focused on socioeconomic improvements and the revival of Kalmyk language.

See also: CONSTITUTION OF 1993; NATIONALITIES POLICIES, SOVIET; NATIONALITIES POLICIES, TSARIST

BIBLIOGRAPHY

Amitai-Preiss, Reuven, and David Morgan. (2000). *The Mongol Empire and Its Legacy.* Leiden: E. J. Brill.

Bormanshinov, Arash. (1991). *The Lamas of the Kalmyk People: The Don Kalmyk Lamas.* Bloomington: Indiana University, Research Institute for Inner Asian Studies.

Hammer, Darrell P. (1997). *Russia Irredenta: Soviet National Policy Reappraised.* Washington, DC: National Council for Soviet and East European Research.

Kappeler, Andreas. (2001). *The Russian Empire: A Multiethnic History.* New York: Longman.

Nekrich, A. M. (1978). *The Punished Peoples: The Deportation and Fate of Soviet Minorities at the End of the Second World War.* New York: Norton.

Warhola, James W. (1996). *Politicized Ethnicity in the Russian Federation: Dilemmas of State Formation.* Lewiston, ME: Edwin Mellen Press.

JOHANNA GRANVILLE

KAMENEV, LEV BORISOVICH

(1883–1836), Bolshevik leader, Soviet state official, purged and executed under Stalin.

Born July 18, 1883, in Moscow and raised in Tbilisi, Lev Borisovich Rosenfeld entered the revolutionary movement while studying law at Moscow University. In 1901 he joined the Russian Social Democratic Labor Party (RSDLP) and adopted the pseudonym Kamenev ("man of stone"). In 1903 the RSDLP split into two factions, and Kamenev aligned himself with the Bolsheviks and Vladimir Ulyanov (Lenin). Kamenev's revolutionary activities brought several arrests and brief periods of exile. During the 1905 Revolution, Kamenev proved an outstanding orator and organizer. In 1908 he joined Lenin's inner circle in exile, then led the Bolshevik faction in Russia's State Duma. In November 1914, tsarist police arrested Kamenev for endorsing Lenin's "defeatist" position on the war and exiled him to Siberia.

The February 1917 Revolution brought Kamenev back to Petrograd. He initially rejected Lenin's "April Thesis" and on the Bolshevik Central Committee (CC) opposed the idea of seizing power. Instead he endorsed an all-socialist coalition government. On October 23, 1917, the CC endorsed Lenin's call for insurrection; Kamenev balked. He resigned from the CC on October 29, but rejoined it during the October Revolution and became chair of the Central Executive Committee of Soviets (CEC). Still he pursued an all-socialist coalition. Because the CC rejected these efforts, Kamenev again quit on November 17, 1917. He also resigned from the CEC, on November 21, 1917, after the Council of People's Commissars (Sovnarkom) issued decrees without CEC approval. Kamenev recanted on December 12, 1917, and rejoined the CC in March 1918.

Afterward, Kamenev held high-level government and Party positions, including chair of the Moscow Soviet (1919–January 1926), and memberships on the Sovnarkom (1922–1926), the Council of Labor and Defense (1922–1926), the CC (1918–1926), and the Politburo (1919–1926). A "triumvirate" of Kamenev, Grigory Zinoviev, and Josef Stalin assumed tacit control of the Party and state in 1923, as Lenin lay dying, and engaged in a fierce campaign of mutual incrimination against Leon Trotsky over economic policy and bureaucratization. By January 1925 the triumvirate had defeated Trotsky's Left Opposition, but a rift emerged pitting Kamenev and Zinoviev against Stalin and the Politburo's right wing. In December 1925, Kamenev criticized Stalin's dictatorial tendencies at the Fourteenth Party Congress; this led to his condemnation as a member of the New Opposition. Demoted to candidate Politburo status, Kamenev was stripped of important state posts. In the spring of 1926, he and Zinoviev joined Trotsky in a United Opposition, criticizing the CC majority's "pro-peasant" version of the New Economic Policy. The majority stripped him of Politburo membership in October 1926. The United Opposition continued in vain through 1927; the majority removed Kamenev from the CC on November 14, and the Party's Fifteenth Congress expelled him on December 2, 1927. In ritual self-abnegation, he recanted and was readmitted to the Party in June 1928. He subsequently held minor posts, and faced the threat of arrest.

Kamenev was arrested, again expelled from the Party, and exiled to Siberia in October 1932, for purported association with Martemian Ryutin's oppositionist group. Released, then readmitted to the Party in December 1933, he briefly served in Moscow bureaucratic publishing posts. On December 16, 1934, he was arrested once more, for alleged complicity in the murder of Sergei Kirov. At a January 16, 1935, secret trial he was falsely convicted for conspiring to kill Kirov and sentenced to five years imprisonment; an additional five-year sentence was added after a second secret trial in July 1935, for allegedly plotting to kill Stalin. In

Lev Kamenev rose through the Bolshevik ranks to become a member of the Politburo, only to be later executed on Stalin's orders. © BETTMANN/CORBIS

July 1936, Kamenev conceded to Stalin's demand for a public show trial. This August 1936 spectacle concluded with sixteen "Trotskyist-Zinovievist plotters" convicted on a range of fantastic charges, including spying for the Nazis. Despite Stalin's promise to spare the lives of Old Bolsheviks, all were condemned to death. On August 24, 1936, Kamenev was executed alongside Zinoviev.

See also: SHOW TRIALS; STALIN, JOSEF VISSARIONOVICH; ZINOVIEV, GRIGORY YEVSEYEVICH

BIBLIOGRAPHY

Rabinowitch, Alexander. (1976). *The Bolsheviks Come to Power: The Revolution of 1917 in Petrograd.* New York: Norton.

Schapiro, Leonard. (1971). *The Communist Party of the Soviet Union,* 2nd ed. New York: Vintage.

Tucker, Robert C. (1990). *Stalin in Power: The Revolution From Above, 1928–1941.* New York: Norton.

Voskresensky, Lev. (1989). *Names That Have Returned: Nikolai Bukharin, Alexei Rykov, Grigori Zinovyev, Lev Kamenev, Grigori Sokolnikov, Martemyan Ryutin.* Moscow: Novosti.

MICHAEL C. HICKEY

KANDINSKY, VASSILY VASSILIEVICH

(1866–1944), artist.

In 1889, after studying at Moscow University in law and economics, Vassily Vasilievich Kandinsky participated in an expedition to the Vologda province in the north of Russia, sponsored by the Imperial Society for Natural Sciences, Ethnography, and Anthropology. The folk art, music, and rituals of the far north were influences that prompted his later decision to abandon his law profession for art at the age of thirty.

In 1897 Kandinsky moved to Munich to study at the private art school of Anton Abè, where he met Alexei von Jawlensky and Marianne Werefkin. After finishing his studies in the Munich Academy in 1901, Kandinsky joined the Expressionist association, Phalanx, where he met Gabrielle Münther, a student at the Phalanx school. Although Kandinsky maintained Munich as his principle place of residence, he exhibited in Moscow at the Moscow Association of Artists, at the Izdebsky Salon in Odessa, and with the Neue Künstlerveriningung in Munich, all the while maintaining and strengthening the contacts between Russian artists and their German counterparts.

By 1911 Kandinsky was the leading representative of the Russian avant-garde, participating in the Jack of Diamonds show and organizing the Blaue Reiter group with Franz Marc, inviting David Burliuk and the Hyleans to participate in the exhibition and the Blaue Reiter Almanac. In 1912 he published his theory of art, *Concerning the Spiritual in Art,* in Munich. After the outbreak of World War I, he returned to Russia and actively participated in Russian cultural life. After the Revolution of 1917, he served in IZO Narkompros (The Visual Arts Section of the People's Commissariat for Enlightenment). From 1918 he taught at the SVOMAS (Free Art Studio), and in 1920 he became director of INKhUK (The Institute of Artist Culture). By 1921 the art establishment began to turn away from abstraction in art toward more realistic representation, and a disillusioned Kandinsky returned to Germany to participate in Bauhaus.

See also: CHAGALL, MARC

BIBLIOGRAPHY

Bowlt, John E., and Long, Rose-Carol Washton, eds. (1980). *The Life of Vasilii Kandinsky in Russian Art: A Study of On the Spiritual in Art.* Newtonville, MA: Oriental Research Partners.

Hahl-Koch, Jelena. (1993). *Kandinsky.* New York: Rizzoli.

Weiss, Peg. (1995). *Kandinsky and Old Russia: The Artist as Ethnographer and Shaman.* New Haven, CT: Yale University Press.

MARK KONECNY

KANTOROVICH, LEONID VITALIYEVICH

(1912–1986), Soviet mathematician and economist; founder of the theory of optimal planning and of linear programming.

Kantorovich showed early promise as a mathematical scientist, entering Leningrad University at the age of fourteen and graduating at eighteen. There he did research in set theory and soon met other great Soviet mathematicians, among them Andrey Nikolaevich Kolmogorov. By 1934 Kantorovich was made a full professor. After the war, he played an important role in the new Siberian Branch of the Academy of Sciences, moving to Novosibirsk in 1960.

During the 1930s Kantorovich contributed to the developing theory of partially ordered functional spaces. In 1938 he began his applied work in economics when he was asked by the Laboratory of the Plywood Trust to solve the problem of distributing raw materials to maximize equipment productivity under quantitative restrictions. This problem proved to be mathematically similar to that of optimizing a sown area or the distribution of transportation flows. Kantorovich solved this by using a kind of functional analysis he called the "method of resolving multipliers." By 1939 he had published a small book laying out the main ideas and algorithms of linear programming, later advanced independently by Tjalling Koopmans, George Dantzig, and others. Subsequently, Kantorovich combined linear programming with the idea of dynamic programming to advance methods for calculating wholesale prices and transportation tariffs, a norm for the effectiveness of capital investments and depreciation allowances, and other payments. This work, generalized to planning problems on the industrial, regional, or national level, led to his receiving the Bank of Sweden Prize in Economic Sciences in Memory of Alfred Nobel in 1975, the only Soviet economist ever so honored. A full member of the USSR Academy of Sciences from 1960, Kantorovich received the Lenin Prize and many other honors in Russia and abroad.

See also: ACADEMY OF SCIENCES

BIBLIOGRAPHY

Campbell, Robert W. (1961). "Marx, Kantorovich, and Novozhilov: Stoimost versus Reality." Slavic Review 20(3): 402–18.

Kantorovich, Leonid V. (1965). The Best Use of Economic Resources. Oxford: Pergamon.

MARTIN C. SPECHLER

KAPLAN, FANYA

(1887–1918), anarchist-terrorist; arrested and executed for a failed attempt on Lenin's life.

Born into the family of a Jewish teacher in Ukraine, Fanya Kaplan (also known as Feiga Kaplan, Feiga Roitblat, Dora Kaplan) joined a local anarchist terrorist organization during the 1905 Revolution. For her participation in a bomb-making operation in Kiev, she spent ten years in the Nerchinsk penal complex in Siberia. Here she became acquainted with other female terrorists, most notably the Socialist Revolutionaries (SRs) Maria Spiridonova and Anastasia Bitsenko. A number of her prison comrades maintain that Kaplan went blind during her early years in Nerchinsk but partially recovered her vision in 1913; one memoirist also noted Kaplan's deafness. Released by the Provisional Government's amnesty for political prisoners following the February Revolution of 1917, Kaplan was receiving medical treatment in Ukraine when the Bolsheviks came to power in October 1917. Kaplan later stated that she was a supporter not of the Bolshevik-Left SR coalition government, but rather of the Constituent Assembly promoted by the SRs and their leader Victor Chernov. In the spring of 1918 Kaplan returned to Moscow and there visited her former prison comrade, Bitsenko, who, like Spiridonova, had joined the Left SRs. Kaplan, however, appears to have had nothing to do with the Left SR

Party and little to do with the SRs. When Lenin was wounded in August 1918, Kaplan's nervous behavior at the scene led to her arrest, although it subsequently emerged that no one had actually witnessed her role in the shooting. She was executed within days of being apprehended. Bolshevik authorities labeled Kaplan an SR and the attempt on Lenin's life an SR terrorist conspiracy; SR leaders strongly denied both accusations during their show trial in 1922.

See also: ANARCHISM; LENIN, VLADIMIR ILICH; SHOW TRIALS; SOCIALIST REVOLUTIONARIES; TERRORISM

BIBLIOGRAPHY

Jansen, Marc. (1982). *A Show Trial under Lenin: The Trial of the Socialist Revolutionaries, Moscow 1922*, tr. Jean Sanders. The Hague: Martinus Nijhoff Publishers.

Lyandres, Semion. (1989). "The 1918 Attempt on the Life of Lenin: A New Look at the Evidence." *Slavic Review* 48(3):432–48.

SALLY A. BONIECE

KARACHAI

The Karachai are a small Turkic nationality of the central North Caucasus. They speak a language from the Kypchak group of the Altaic language family and are closely related to the Balkars. They inhabit high-elevation mountain valleys of the upper Kuban and Teberda river basins, and their pastures once stretched up to the peaks and glaciers of the northern slope of the Great Caucasus mountain range.

Their remote origins can be traced to Kypchak-speaking pastoralist groups such as the Polovtsians, who may have been forced to take refuge high in the mountains by the Mongol invasions in thirteenth century. At some point before the sixteenth century, the Karachai came under the domination of the princes in Kabarda. The Crimean khanate claimed nominal jurisdiction over much of the northwest Caucasus and, correspondingly, Karachai territories, until its demise in 1782. Conversion to Islam took place gradually, gaining momentum during the eighteenth and nineteenth centuries. A series of military incursions into their territories motivated several Karachai elders to sign a capitulation agreement and nonaggression pact with Russian forces in 1828. Although they were officially considered subjects of the tsar from that moment, various forms of resistance to Russian rule continued until 1864. A Karachai-Cherkess autonomous region was established in 1922 and in 1926 was divided into two distinct units. Karachai territories were occupied by the forces of Nazi Germany between July 1942 and January 1943. While many Karachai men served in the Red Army, others joined bandit and anti-Soviet partisan groups. In the fall of 1943 the Supreme Soviet of the USSR ordered the deportation of the Karachai people for alleged cooperation with the Germans and participation in organized resistance to Soviet power. The Karachai autonomous region was abolished in 1944 and virtually the entire Karachai population was deported to Kyrgyzstan and Kazakhstan. In 1956 party members and Red Army veterans were allowed to return to their homeland, and in 1957 others were legally given the right to return. In 1957 the joint Karachai-Cherkess autonomous region was reestablished and the mass return of the Karachai was initiated. After the fall of the Soviet Union, the Karachai-Cherkess autonomous region became a republic of the Russian Federation.

Traditionally, Karachais subsisted on a combination of agriculture and stock-raising. As late as the first decades of the twentieth century, only one-fourth of all Karachai had adopted a completely stationary lifestyle. The rest of the population seasonally relocated from summer to winter pastures with their herds of horses, cattle, sheep, and goats. During the Soviet period, the Karachai remained one of the least urbanized groups: Less than 20 percent lived in cities. Clans were a central component of traditional Karachai social organization. Although some clans and their elders could be recognized as more prominent or senior than others, the Karachai did not have a powerful princely elite or nobility. In the twentieth century the Karachai population grew from about 30,000 to about 100,000. A Karachai literary language was developed and standardized in the 1920s.

See also: CAUCASUS; CHERKESS; ISLAM; NATIONALITIES POLICIES, SOVIET; NATIONALITIES POLICIES, TSARIST

BIBLIOGRAPHY

Wixman, Ronald. (1980). *Language Aspects of Ethnic Patterns and Processes in the North Caucasus.* Chicago: University of Chicago.

BRIAN BOECK

KARAKALPAKS

Karakalpaks are a Turkic people who live in Central Asia. Of the nearly 500,000 Karakalpaks, more than 90 percent live in northwestern Uzbekistan, in the Soviet-created Karakalpak Autonomous Republic (KAR). Other Karakalpaks live elsewhere in Uzbekistan, as well as in Kazakhstan, Turkmenistan, Russia, and Afghanistan. Most adhere to Sunni Islam, although Sufi sects have also attracted many followers. They speak a language that is closely related to Kazakh and Kyrgyz.

Most historians trace the Karakalpaks' origins to Persian and Mongolian peoples living on the steppes of Central Asia and Southern Russia. Their name literally meets "black hatted," and mention of a tribe thought to be ancestral to today's Karakalpaks first appears in Russian chronicles (as Chorniye Kolbuki) in 1146. Renowned for their military prowess, this group allied themselves with the Kievan princes in their battles with other Russian princes and tribes of the steppes. In the 1200s some Karakalpaks joined the Mongol Golden Horde, and by the 1500s they enjoyed a short-lived independence. Over time, however, they became subjects of other Central Asian peoples and eventually the Russians, who pushed into Central Asia in the 1800s.

In 1918 they were included with other Central Asian peoples in the Turkistan Autonomous Republic, and in 1925 a Karakalpak Autonomous Oblast was created in the Kazakh Autonomous Soviet Socialist Republic. This oblast eventually became the KAR, and in 1936 it became part of the Uzbek Soviet Socialist Republic. Under Soviet rule, Karakalpaks were encouraged to move to the KAR, their nominal homeland.

The post-Soviet period found most Karakalpaks desperately poor, living in an environmentally devastated area adjacent to the rapidly shrinking Aral Sea. Serious health problems such as hepatitis, typhoid, and cancer are widespread. Despite their nomadic traditions, their economy is dominated by agriculture, especially cotton production, which has suffered due to water shortages, soil erosion, and environmental damage. Because of lack of investment in the region, the KAR's relations with the central Uzbek government have been strained.

See also: CENTRAL ASIA; ISLAM; NATIONALITIES POLICIES, SOVIET; NATIONALITIES POLICIES, TSARIST; UZBEKISTAN AND UZBEKS

BIBLIOGRAPHY

Hanks, Reuel. (2000). "A Separate Peace? Karakalpak Nationalism and Devolution in Post-Soviet Uzbekistan." *Europe-Asia Studies* 52: 939–53.

PAUL J. KUBICEK

KARAKHAN DECLARATION

In the Karakhan Manifesto of 1919, the Soviet government offered to annul the unequal treaties imposed on China by Imperial Russia. The declaration, signed by Deputy Commissar of Foreign Affairs Lev M. Karakhan , included rights of extraterritoriality for Russians in China, economic concessions, and Russia's share of the Boxer rebellion indemnity. Though dated July 25, 1919, it was not actually published for another month. Civil war prevented its delivery to China, but the Beijing authorities soon learned its substance.

Controversy arose because the document was prepared in two versions. One variant contained the statement that "the Soviet Government returns to the Chinese people, without any compensation, the Chinese Eastern Railway [CER]. . . ." The version published in Moscow in August 1919 did not include this provision, but the copy that was delivered to Chinese diplomats in February 1920 did incorporate the offer to return the CER. However, a Soviet proposal on September 27, 1920, for a Sino-Russian agreement made no mention of returning the Chinese Eastern Railway, but requested a new agreement for its joint administration by the two nations. All subsequent Soviet reprintings of the Karakhan Manifesto omit the offer to return the CER, while a Chinese reprinting of the document in 1924 included the offer. The existence of two versions manifests the ambiguity in Soviet policy toward the Far East in 1919 and 1920, arising from the unpredictable course of the civil war and foreign intervention. Thereafter, the consolidation of Bolshevik power in Siberia, combined with continuing instability in China, led Moscow to seek some degree of control over the economically and strategically important CER.

See also: CHINA, RELATIONS WITH; CIVIL WAR OF 1917–1922; RAILWAYS

BIBLIOGRAPHY

Degras, Jane, ed. (1951). *Soviet Documents on Foreign Policy, Vol. 1: 1917–1924.* London: Oxford University Press.

Leong, Sow-theng. (1976). *Sino-Soviet Diplomatic Relations, 1917–1926.* Honolulu: University Press of Hawaii.

TEDDY J. ULDRICKS

KARAMZIN, NIKOLAI MIKHAILOVICH

(1766–1826), writer, historian, and journalist.

Born in the Simbirsk province and educated in Moscow, Nikolai Karamzin served only briefly in the military before retiring to devote himself to intellectual pursuits. In 1789 he undertook a journey to western Europe, visiting several luminaries, including Immanuel Kant, on his way. Reaching Paris in the spring of 1790, he witnessed history in the making. He described his trip in his *Letters of a Russian Traveler,* published upon his return in 1790 in a series of journals he founded himself. The *Letters* display an urbane, westernized individual in command of several languages and behavioral codes and are meant to signal Russia's coming of age. They demonstrate a keen interest in history, but primarily as a collection of anecdotes.

The short stories Karamzin wrote in the 1790s exerted tremendous influence on the development of nineteenth-century fiction. Karamzin's main purpose in literature and journalism was to promote a culture of politeness. History became one of the main themes of his works, which grappled with the paradoxes of modernity: The systematic debunking of myths, inspired by a commitment to reason, clashed with a need to mythologize the past to throw into relief the moral and intellectual emancipation enabled by the Enlightenment.

Karamzin elaborated a new political stance while editing the *Messenger of Europe* in 1802 and 1803. A professed realist, he argued for a strong central government, whose legitimacy would lie in balancing conflicting interests and preventing the emergence of evil. Karamzin grew disenchanted with Napoleon, who had first seemed to bring forth peace and stability, but his infatuation with consolidated political power endured.

In October 1803, Karamzin became official historiographer to Tsar Alexander I. He uncovered many yet unknown sources on Russian history, including some that subsequently perished in the Moscow fire of 1812. In 1811 Karamzin submitted his *Memoir on Ancient and New Russia,* which contained a biting critique of the policies of Alexander I, but vindicated autocracy and serfdom. The *Memoir* signaled Karamzin's turn away from an Enlightenment-inspired universalist notion of history and affirmed the distinctness of Russia's historical path.

In 1818 Karamzin published the first eight volumes of his *History of the Russian State,* an instant bestseller. The *History* consists of two parts: a naive-sounding account of events, close in style to the Chronicles, with minimal narratorial intrusions and an apparent lack of overriding critical principle; and extensive footnotes, which display considerable skepticism in the handling of sources and sometimes contradict the main narrative. The narrative rests on the notion that the course of events is vindicated by their outcome—the consolidation of the Russian autocratic state—but it lets stories speak for themselves.

Due to this narrative and political stance, the immediate reception of the *History* was mostly negative. Yet after the publication of three more volumes from 1821 to 1824, which included a condemnation of the reign of Ivan the Terrible, the reception began to shift (the last volume was published posthumously in 1829). Alexander Pushkin called the *History* "the heroic deed of an honest man," and Karamzin's stance of moral independence came to the foreground. The *History* continued to be read in the nineteenth century, primarily as a storehouse of patriotic historical tales. It fell into disfavor during Soviet times, yet met an intense period of renewed interest in the perestroika years as part of an exhumation of national history.

See also: ENLIGHTENMENT, IMPACT OF; HISTORIOGRAPHY; NATIONALISM IN THE ARTS

BIBLIOGRAPHY

Black, J.L., ed. (1975). *Essays on Karamzin: Russian Man-of-Letters, Political Thinker, Historian, 1766–1826.* The Hague: Mouton.

Wachtel, Andrew Baruch. (1994). *An Obsession with History: Russian Writers Confront the Past.* Stanford, CA: Stanford University Press.

ANDREAS SCHÖNLE

KASYANOV, MIKHAIL MIKHAILOVICH

(b. 1957), prime minister of the Russian Federation.

Kasyanov graduated from the Moscow Automobile and Road Institute and worked for the State

Construction Committee and Gosplan, State Planning Committee, from 1981 to 1990. He moved to the economics ministry, and in 1993 Boris Fyodorov brought him to the Finance Ministry to take charge of negotiations over Russia's foreign debts. Fluent in English, Kasyanov became deputy finance minister in 1995 and finance minister in May 1999. In January 2000 he was appointed first deputy prime minister under prime minister and acting president Vladimir Putin. Katyanov, praised by Putin as a "strong coordinator, " was named prime minister of the government in May 2000, winning easy confirmation from the State Duma in a vote of 325 to 55. The calm, gravel-voiced Kasyanov was seen as a figure with close ties to Boris Yeltsin's inner circle—the owners of large financial industrial groups.

Despite repeated rumors of his impending dismissal, Kasyanov was still in office in mid-2003. He oversaw cautious but substantial reforms in taxation and the legal system, but liberals criticized him for failing to tackle the "natural monopolies" of gas, electricity, and railways. This led to some embarrassing criticism from members of his own administration, such as economy minister German Gref and presidential economic advisor Andrei Illarionov, not to mention public admonition from President Putin in spring 2003 for failing to deliver more rapid economic growth. In Russia's super-presidential system, the job of prime minister is a notoriously difficult one. Although the prime minister has to be approved by the State Duma, once in office he answers only to the president, and has no independent power beyond that which he can accumulate through skillful administration and discreet political maneuvering.

See also: GOSPLAN; PUTIN, VLADIMIR VLADIMIROVICH

BIBLIOGRAPHY

Shevtsova, Lilia. (2003). *Putin's Russia.* Washington, DC: Carnegie Endowment for International Peace.

PETER RUTLAND

KATKOV, MIKHAIL NIKIFOROVICH

(1818–1887), Russian journalist and publicist.

The son of a minor civil servant, Mikhail Nikiforovich Katkov graduated from Moscow University in 1838 and attended lectures at Berlin University in 1840–1841. From 1845 to 1850 Katkov was an assistant professor of philosophy at Moscow University. In 1851 he became editor of the daily *Moskovskie Vedomosti* (*Moscow News*), and in 1856 he also became editor of the journal *Russky Vestnik* (*Russian Messenger*).

Katkov changed his political preferences several times during his life. In the 1830s he shared the ideas of the Russian liberal and radical intelligentsia and was close to the Russian literary critic Vissarion Belinsky, radical thinker Alexander Herzen, and the anarchist Mikhail Bakunin. In the early 1840s Katkov broke his connections with the radical intelligentsia, instead becoming an admirer of the British political system. During his early journalistic career, he supported the liberal reforms of Tsar Alexander II and wrote about the necessity of transforming the Russian autocracy into a constitutional monarchy.

The Polish uprising had a great impact on the changing of Katkov's political views from liberalism to Russian nationalism and chauvinism. He published a number of articles favoring reactionary domestic policies and aggressive pan-Slavic foreign policies for Russia. The historian Karel Durman wrote, "Katkov claimed to be the watchdog of the autocracy and this claim was widely recognized." As one of the closest advisors of Tsar Alexander III, Katkov had a great impact on Russian policies. According to the Ober-Procurator of the Holy Synod Constantine Pobedonostsev, "there were ministries where not a single important action was undertaken without Katkov's participation." Durman points out that in no other country could a mere publicist standing outside the official power structure exercise such an influence as had Katkov in Russia.

See also: ALEXANDER II; ALEXANDER III; INTELLIGENTSIA; JOURNALISM

BIBLIOGRAPHY

Durman, Karel. (1988). *The Time of the Thunderer. Mikhail Katkov, Russian Nationalist Extremism and the Failure of the Bismarckian System, 1871–1887.* New York: Columbia University Press.

Katz, Martin. (1966). *Mikhail N. Katkov. A Political Biography 1818–1887.* Paris: Mouton & Co.

VICTORIA KHITERER

KATYN FOREST MASSACRE

Katyn Forest, a wooded area near the village of Gneizdovo outside the Russian city of Smolensk, was the scene in early 1940 of a wholesale killing by the Soviet NKVD (Narodny Komissariat Vnutrennykh Del), or secret police, of 4,143 Polish servicemen, mostly Polish Army officers. These victims, who had been incarcerated in the Kozielsk Soviet concentration camp, constituted only part of the genocide perpetrated against Poles by the NKVD in 1939 and 1940.

The Poles fell as POWs into Soviet hands just after the Soviet Red Army occupied the eastern half of Poland under the terms of two notorious Molotov-Ribbentrop pacts: the Nazi-Soviet agreements signed between the USSR and Nazi Germany in August and September 1939. The crime, committed on Stalin's personal orders at the opening of World War II, is often referred to as the Katyn Massacre or the Katyn Forest Massacre.

The incident was not spoken of for sixty years. Even such Western leaders as President Franklin D. Roosevelt and British Prime Minister Winston Churchill placed little or no credence in reports of the crime at the time, despite the fact that informed Poles had provided proof. For his part, Churchill urged exiled Polish officials such as Vladislav Sikorski to keep the incident quiet lest the news upset the East-West alliance of the Soviet and Western powers fighting Nazi Germany.

These first deaths came after one of the most notorious of several repressions by the Stalin regime against Poles. In 1939, notes Robert Conquest, besides the 440,000 Polish civilians sent to Soviet concentration camps as a result of the Soviet occupation of eastern Poland beginning in September, the Soviets took 200,000 POWs during the Red Army's campaign in Poland. Most of these officers and enlisted men of the Polish Army wound up in camps at Kozielsk, Starobelsk, and Ostachkov. Of these, only forty-eight were ever seen alive again. Later Stalin promised Polish officials that the Soviet government would "look into" the disappearance of these men. But Soviet officials refused to discuss the matter whenever it was again raised.

With the coming of World War II, that is, the war between Germany and the USSR after June 21, 1941, the German Army swept into eastern Poland. In 1943 the Germans, as occupiers of Poland, came across the Polish corpses at Katyn. They duly publicized their grim discovery to a skeptical world press, blamed the Soviets for the terror, and shared their find with a neutral European medical commission based in Switzerland. The members of this commission were convinced that the mass graves were the result of Soviet genocide, but they voiced their findings discreetly, sometimes refusing even to give an opinion.

In 1944, when the Red Army retook the Katyn area from the Wehrmacht, Soviet forces exhumed the Polish dead. Again they blamed the Nazis. Many people throughout the world supported the Soviet line.

It was not until near the end of communist rule in Russia in 1989 with the unfurling of the new policy of glasnost (openness) in the USSR, that partial admission of the crime was acknowledged in Russia and elsewhere. Later, after the demise of communist rule in Russia, two further sites were found where Poles, including Jews, were executed. The number of victims of the killings at all three sites totaled 25,700.

See also: SOVIET-POLISH WAR; STALIN, JOSEF VISSARIONOVICH; WORLD WAR II

BIBLIOGRAPHY

Conquest, Robert. (1990). *The Great Terror: A Reassessment.* New York: Oxford University Press.

Crozier, Brian. (1999). *The Rise and Fall of the Soviet Empire.* Rocklin, CA: Prima Publishing.

Crozier, Brian. (2000). "Remembering Katyn." <http://www-hoover.stanford.edu/publications/digest/002/crozier.html>.

ALBERT L. WEEKS

KAUFMAN, KONSTANTIN PETROVICH

(1818–1882), Russian general (of Austrian ancestry) who became governor–general (viceroy) of Turkestan following its conquest.

Konstantin Petrovich Kaufman's fame came as the ruler of Russia's new colony in Central Asia. His previous military experience had scarcely prepared him for his career as creator of colonial Turkestan. He trained as a military engineer and served for fifteen years in the Russian army fighting the mountain tribes in the Caucasus. His achievements during his service there called him to the attention of a fellow officer, General Dimitri Milyutin. When Milyutin became minister of war in the 1860s, he needed a trustworthy, experienced officer to govern Turkestan. Kaufman was his choice.

At the time Kaufman received his appointment in 1867, the conquest of Turkestan had only begun. He became commander of the Russian frontier forces there and had authority to decide on military action along the borders of his territory. When neighboring Turkish principalities began hostile military action against Russia, or when further conquests appeared feasible, Kaufman assumed command of his troops for war. By the end of his rule, Russia's borders enclosed much of Central Asia to the borders of the Chinese Empire. Only Khiva and Bukhara remained nominally independent khanates under Russian control. Turkestan's borders with Persia (Iran) and Afghanistan were for many years a subject of dispute with Great Britain, which claimed a sphere of domination there.

Kaufman had charge of a vast territory far removed from European Russia. Its peoples practiced the Muslim religion and spoke Turkic or Persian languages. It so closely resembled a colony, like those of the overseas possessions of European empires, that he took example from their colonial policies to launch a Russian civilizing mission in Turkestan. He ended slavery, introduced secular (nonreligious) education, promoted the scientific study of Turkestan's various peoples (even sending an artist, Vasily Vereshchagin, to paint their portraits), encouraged the cultivation of improved agricultural crops, and even attempted to emancipate women from Muslim patriarchal control. Kaufman's means to achieve these ambitious goals were meager, because of the lack of sufficient funds and the paucity of Russian colonial officials. Also, he feared that radical reforms would stir up discontent among his subjects. His fourteen-year period as governor-general brought few substantial changes to social and economic conditions in Turkestan. However, it ended the era of rule by Turkish khans and left Russia firmly in control of its new colony.

See also: TURKESTAN

BIBLIOGRAPHY

Barooshian, Voohan. (1993). *V. V. Vereshchagin: Artist at War.* Gainsville: University Press of Florida.

Brower, Daniel. (2002). *Turkestan and the Fate of the Russian Empire.* Richmond, UK: Curzon Press.

MacKenzie, David. (1967). "Kaufman of Turkestan: An Assessment of His Administration (1867–1881)." *Slavic Review* 25 (2): 265–285.

DANIEL BROWER

KAZAKHSTAN AND KAZAKHS

Kazakhstan, a Eurasian region inhabited since the mid-1400s by the Kazakh people, comprises an immense stretch of steppe that runs for almost 3,200 kilometers (2,000 miles) from the Lower Volga and Caspian Sea in the west to the Altai and Tien Shan mountain ranges in the east and southeast. In the early twenty-first century, the Kazakh republic serves as a bridge between Russian Siberia in the north and the Central Asian republics of Kirghizia/Kyrgyzstan, Uzbekistan, and Turkmenia/Turkmenistan in the south. To the east it is bounded by the region of the People's Republic of China that is known as Xinjiang (Sinkiang) or Chinese Turkestan. With an area of some 2,71,500 square kilometers (1,050,000 square miles), Kazakhstan is almost twice the size of Alaska. As the Kazakh SSR it was the largest republic in the USSR next to the Russian Federation and was sometimes known as the Soviet Texas. The climate is severely continental, with January's mean temperatures varying from –18 degrees Celsius (0 degrees Fahrenheit) in the north to –3 degrees C (27 degrees F) in the south, and July's from 19 degrees C (66 degrees F) in the north to 28–30 degrees C (83–86 degrees F) in the south. Annual precipitation in the north averages 300 millimeters (11.7 inches), in the mountains 1,600 millimeters (62 inches), and in the desert regions less than 100 millimeters (3.9 inches). Fortunately, the region is one of inland drainage with a number of rivers, the Irtysh, Ili, Chu, and Syr Darya included, that flow into the Aral Sea and Lake Balkhash. This permits the extensive irrigation that now threatens the Aral Sea with extinction.

Originally peopled by the Sacae or Scythians, by the end of the first century B.C.E. the area of Kazakhstan was populated by nomadic Turkic and Mongol tribes. Known to the Chinese as the Usun, they were the ancestors of the later Kazakhs. First, however, these tribes formed a succession of loose, tribal-based confederations known as khaganates (later khanates). Of these the most powerful was the Turgesh (or Tiurkic) of the sixth century C.E. Other nomadic empires followed its collapse in the 700s, beginning with the Karakhanids who ruled southern Kazakhstan or Semireche from the 900s to the 1100s. They were replaced by the Karakitai (Kara Khitai), who succumbed to the Mongols during 1219–1221. Subsequently these tribes were included in the semiautonomous White Horde, which was established by Orda, the eldest son of Genghis

Public square in Astana, the new post-Soviet capital of Kazakhstan. © LIBA TAYLOR/CORBIS

Khan's eldest son Dzhuchi, as a component of the more extensive Mongol Golden Horde. Having established itself between the Altai Mountains and Syr Darya River, the White Horde quickly gained control of Semireche and East Turkestan as well. But if its rulers were descendants of the Mongol royal line, most of its populace were ethnically Turkic.

With the collapse of that empire, these tribes at first were subject to the Nogai Tatars, formerly of the Golden Horde, and then of the Uzbeks. By 1447 the latter had conquered the territory between the Syr Darya and Irtysh Rivers, the inhabitants of whom became known as the Uzbek Kazakhs. Yet the White Horde lingered, civil strife and fights for power were constant, and in 1465 two of its princes, the brothers Janibek (Dzhanibek) and Gerei, led a number of Turkic tribes in a migration southeast to Mogulstan (Mogolistan), which once was part of the domain of Genghis Khan's second son Chagatai, and which now was an independent state. They were welcomed by its ruler and given lands on the Chu and Talas Rivers, where they formed a powerful Kazakh khanate. By the late 1400s this had extended its power over much of the formerly Uzbek-controlled *Desht-i Kipchak,* or Kipchak Steppe. Over the next few decades most of the Kazakh tribes—the Kipchaks, Usuns, Dulats, and Naimans included—were united briefly under Kasym Khan (1511–1518). He extended their power southward while giving his subjects a period of relative calm. Internal strife then reemerged after his death, and the Kazakh state began disintegrating as its components joined with other tribes arriving from the collapsing Nogai Horde. Having merged during the 1600s they formed themselves into three nomadic confederations known as "hordes" or *zhuzy* (dzhuzy): the *Ulu* (Large, Great, or Senior) in Semireche, the *Kishiu* (Small, Lesser, or Junior) between the Aral and Caspian Seas, and the *Orta* (Middle) in the central steppe. But taken together, they were now an ethnically distinct people, known to the Russians since the latter 1500s as the Kirgiz-Kazakhs, with a social system based on the families and clans that continued to influence Kazakh politics into the twenty-first century.

A woman lights candles during a Russian Orthodox ceremony in northern Kazakhstan, a region heavily populated by ethnic Russians. © AFP/CORBIS

By the mid-1600s the Kazakhs were again under pressure, this time from the Jungarian (Dzhungarian) Oriots or Kalmyks who attacked westward from Mongolia. Divided as they were, the Kazakhs at first had difficulty in opposing the invaders, and the conflict dragged on into the 1700s. Although the Kazakhs then did unite briefly to win some major victories, the menace only lifted after the Manchus decisively vanquished the Oriot-Kalmyks in 1758. In the interim, the Kazakhs had drifted gradually but steadily into the orbit of Imperial Russia. Consequently, some leaders began seeking support from the Russians in their struggles. Thus the khans and other leaders of the Small Horde in 1731, of the Middle Horde in 1740, and of part of the Great Horde in 1742, agreed to accept Russian suzerainty. But matters were not that straightforward, and while Russian scholars generally regard such treaties as evidence of the Kazakhs' "voluntary union" with their empire, subsequent Kazakh historians disagree. They argue that this was a mere tactic in a larger game of playing Russia off against Manchu China, maintain that the khans lacked the requisite authority to make such concessions, and as evidence point to the frequent cases of resistance to and uprisings against the Russian colonizers. A textbook appearing in the new Republic of Kazakhstan charges that the tsarist authorities even encouraged the Oriot-Kalmyk attacks as a means of driving the Kazakhs into Russian arms. So, as elsewhere, history has become a major weapon in modern Kazakhstan's bitter ethnic and nationalist debates.

From 1730 to 1840 St. Petersburg's rule was exercised through the governor-general of Orenburg. As Russian expansion southward became progressively more organized and effective, the authorities were able to abolish the traditional Kazakh

Kazakhstan, 1992 © MARYLAND CARTOGRAPHICS. REPRINTED WITH PERMISSION

forms of leadership. They deposed the khan of the Middle Horde in 1822, that of the Small Horde in 1824, and that of the Large Horde in 1848. Meanwhile, they also created the new Bukei (Bukej) or Inner Horde in 1812. Then Bukei, younger son of the Small Horde's Khan Nurali, received permission to move some 1,600 tents into lands between the Urals and Volga, which had been abandoned by the western Oriot-Kalmyks, who had fled to China. These Kazakhs eventually settled in the Province of Astrakhan and by the mid-1800s had some 150,000 tents. At this time the Large Horde meanwhile had some 100,000 tents, the Small Horde 800,000, and the Middle Horde 406,000 tents.

In the mid-1800s St. Petersburg organized the governor generalships of the Steppe and of Turkestan to manage the Kazakhs and Central Asians to the south. During the late 1800s a growing wave of Russian and other Slavic (largely Ukrainian) peasant immigrants flowed into the region's northern sections and began settling on Kazakh lands. The resulting discontent of the Kazakhs and other Central Asians boiled over in the great revolt of 1916 and reemerged again during the civil strife between 1917 and 1920.

During that conflict the intellectuals of the Alash Orda sought to establish a Western-style Kazakh state. Many eventually supported the Communists in the creation of the Kirghiz (Kazakh) Autonomous Soviet Socialist Republic (ASSR) as part of Soviet Russia in 1920. Reorganized as the Kazakh ASSR in 1925, it became a constituent republic under Josef

Stalin in 1936 and remained so until December 1991. But despite its "democratic" constitution, during the 1930s Kazakhstan underwent the horrors of collectivization, of the forced settlement of the nomadic stockbreeders, of the resulting famine and epidemics, and of deportations and executions. Meanwhile, the purges decimated the Kazakh intelligentsia and political leadership. The result was a reported 2.2 million Kazakh deaths (a 49% loss), so that there were fewer Kazakhs in the USSR in 1939 than in 1926. Equally disturbing, by the decade's end the republic was being flooded by deportees from elsewhere, converted into a basic element of Stalin's Gulag Archipelago, and from 1949 into a testing ground for nuclear weapons as well.

Although a new Soviet Kazakh educated elite slowly emerged after 1938, their position in their own nominal state was threatened further by the new influx of hundreds of thousands of Russian, Ukrainian, and German immigrants during Nikita Khrushchev's Virgin Lands agricultural program in the 1950s. The mixed results of this effort, the problems raised by nuclear testing on the republic's territory, and the fact that by 1979 the Kazakhs reportedly were outnumbered by Russians (41% to 36%), further fueled their ethnic resentments. These exploded in riots that gripped the capital of Alma-Ata in December 1986 when Dinmukhammed Kunayev, the ethnic Kazakh longtime head of the republican Communist Party, was replaced by a Russian in December 1986. But in April 1990 Nursultan Nazarbayev, another ethnic Kazakh, assumed the post of Party chief. With the collapse of the USSR in 1991, he charted the course that established the Republic of Kazakhstan and brought it into the new CIS. Emerging as virtual president-for-life from the votes of 1995 and 1999, and backed by his own and his wife's families and elements of his Large Horde clan, he has preserved the unity of his ethnically, religiously, and culturally diverse state, which awaits the development of the Caspian oil reserves as a means of alleviating the crushing poverty that afflicts many of its citizens, Kazakhs and others alike.

See also: CENTRAL ASIA; ISLAM; KUNAYEV, DINMUKHAMMED AKHMEDOVICH; NATIONALITIES POLICIES, SOVIET; NATIONALITIES POLICIES, TSARIST; NAZARBAYEV, NURSULTAN ABISHEVICH

BIBLIOGRAPHY

Akiner, Shirin. (1986). *Islamic Peoples of the Soviet Union*, 2nd ed. London: KPI.

Bremmer, Ian, and Taras, Ray, eds. (1993). *Nations and Politics in the Soviet Successor States*. Cambridge, UK: Cambridge University Press.

Grousset, Rene. (1970). *The Empire of the Steppes: A History of Central Asia*. New Brunswick, NJ: Rutgers University.

Hildinger, Erik. (1997). *Warriors of the Steppe: A Military History of Central Asia, 500 BC–1700 AD*. New York: Sarpedon.

Krader, Lawrence. (1963). *Peoples of Central Asia*. Bloomington: Indiana University Press.

Olcott, Martha Brill. (1995). *The Kazakhs*, 2nd ed. Stanford, CA: Hoover Institution Press.

Olcott, Martha Brill. (2002). *Kazakhstan: Unfulfilled Promise*. Washington, DC: Carnegie Endowment for International Peace.

Wixman, Ronald. (1984). *The Peoples of the USSR: An Ethnographic Handbook*. London: Macmillan.

DAVID R. JONES

KAZAN

Kazan is the capital and major historic, cultural, and economic center of the autonomous republic of Tatarstan, Russia. It is located on the left bank of the Volga River where the Kazanka River joins it, eighty-five kilometers north of the Kama tributary. In 2002 it had an estimated population of 1,105,300.

The traditional understanding is that the name comes from the Turkic and Volga Tatar word *qazan*, meaning "kettle." A rival theory has been proposed that it derives from the Chuvash *xusan/xosan*, meaning "bend" or "hook," referring to the bend of the Volga near which Kazan is located. The Bulgars founded Iski Kazan in the thirteenth century as one of the successors to their state, which had been destroyed by the Mongols. At that time, it was located forty-five kilometers up the Kazanka. Around the year 1400, it was moved to its present location. Ulu Muhammed, who had been ousted from the Qipchaq Khanate in 1437, defeated the last ruler of the principality of Kazan to establish a khanate by 1445. It was an important trading center, with an annual fair being held nearby.

During the first half of the sixteenth century, the khanate of Kazan was involved in a three-cornered struggle with Muscovy and the Crimean khanate for influence in the western steppe area. Ivan IV conquered the city in 1552, ending the

Khanate of Kazan. Muscovy then used Kazan as an advanced staging area for further expansion down the Volga. In 1555 the archepiscopal see of Kazan was established.

From the late sixteenth century on, Kazan was the gateway to Siberia, as people and supplies were funneled through the town en route to the east, and furs and minerals were brought west. It was made capital of the Volga region in 1708, and Peter I had the ships for his Persian campaign built there. The Slavonic-Latin Academy, which became the Kazan Theological Academy, was founded in 1723 but abolished after 1917. From 1723 to 1726 the Cathedral of Saints Peter and Paul was built in Kazan. The first lay provincial secondary school was founded there in 1758.

Kazan was sacked by Emelian Pugachev in 1774, but Catherine II rebuilt the city on a gridiron design and named it a provincial capital in 1781. During the eighteenth century, light industry and food production developed, as well as a theater, which led to a number of similar theaters being founded in the nineteenth century. In 1804 the University of Kazan was founded, which helped to establish the city as an intellectual center. The first provincial newspaper was published there in 1811. Kazan was also considered a major manufacturing center, the products of which included prepared furs, leather manufacture, shoes, and soap. In the 1930s heavy industry developed, such as aircraft production and transportation and agricultural machinery. More recent industries include the production of chemicals, electrical engineering, and precision equipment, as well as oil refining. In 1945 the Kazan branch of the Academy of Sciences was established. Presently, Kazan has a philharmonic society, a museum of Tatar culture, and a theater devoted to the production of Tatar operas and ballets.

See also: MUSCOVY; TATARSTAN AND TATARS

BIBLIOGRAPHY

Bukharaev, Ravil. (1995). *Kazan: The Enchanted Capital.* London: Flint River.

Keenan, Edward L. (1979–1980). "Kazan—The Bend." *Harvard Ukrainian Studies* 3/4: 484–96.

Matthews, David J., and Ravil Bukharaev, eds. (2000). *Historical Anthology of Kazan Tatar Verse: Voices of Eternity.* Richmond, England: Curzon Press.

Pelenski, Jaroslaw. (1974). *Russia and Kazan: Conquest and Imperial Ideology (1438–1560s).* The Hague: Mouton.

DONALD OSTROWSKI

KELLOGG-BRIAND PACT

The Kellogg-Briand Pact, also known as the Pact of Paris, was the creation of French Foreign Minister Aristide Briand and U.S. Secretary of State Frank B. Kellogg in 1928. Parties to this treaty pledged themselves to "renounce the resort to war as an instrument of national policy in their mutual relations" and to resolve all international disputes by "peaceful means alone." This agreement was signed in Paris on August 27, 1928, by France, the United States, and thirteen other powers. Soon it was endorsed by almost every country in the world, including the Soviet Union, Britain, Germany, and Japan. The treaty contained no enforcement mechanism and was, therefore, merely a pious promise to avoid war.

Soviet ratification of the pact on August 29, 1928, was part of a "peace offensive" spearheaded by Deputy Commissar of Foreign Affairs Maxim M. Litvinov. Beyond attempts to improve bilateral relations with the great powers and Russia's smaller neighbors, this campaign included efforts to promote broad measures of disarmament and to involve the USSR in the multilateral diplomacy of Europe. The pact was also supplemented by the Litvinov Protocol, signed on February 9, 1929, by the USSR, Poland, Rumania, and Latvia (and subsequently by Lithuania, Iran, and Turkey), pledging the peaceful resolution of all disputes among the signatories. Soviet participation in the pact and the protocol represented a victory for Litvinov's policy of constructive engagement with the dominant Western powers and a defeat for his nominal chief, Foreign Commissar Georgy Chicherin. It also marked a temporary victory for Nikolai Bukharin and other moderate Politburo members who supported the New Economic Policy and advocated security through peace and cooperation with the great powers.

See also: BUKHARIN, NIKOLAI IVANOVICH; LITVINOV, MAXIM MAXIMOVICH; NEW ECONOMIC POLICY

BIBLIOGRAPHY

Ferrell, Robert H. (1952). *Peace in Their Time: The Origins of the Kellogg-Brian Pact.* New Haven, CT: Yale University Press.

Jacobson, Jon. (1994). *When the Soviet Union Entered World Politics.* Berkeley: University of California Press.

TEDDY J. ULDRICKS

KERENSKY, ALEXANDER FYODOROVICH

(1881–1970), leading figure of the Provisional Government in 1917.

Alexander Kerensky was born on May 4, 1881, in Simbirsk, Russia. He studied history and law at St. Petersburg University. In 1906 he became a defense lawyer in political cases and soon became a well-known public figure. In 1912, Kerensky was elected to the Fourth Duma. Although he described himself as a socialist and associated with the Socialist Revolutionary Party (SRs), he was the mildest of socialists, his views constituting a blend of moderate socialism with left-wing liberalism.

During the February Revolution he seemed to be everywhere—giving a speech here, haranguing soldiers there, scurrying in and out of meetings, issuing orders, dramatically arresting members of the old regime and equally dramatically rescuing others from mob violence. A young man of thirty-five, he emerged as the popular hero of the February Revolution and the new government, the object of public adulation; his face adorned postcards and store windows. When the Petrograd Soviet was formed on March 27, he was elected vice-chairman. He was the only Socialist to enter the Provisional Government when it was formed on March 2 and more and more became its key figure, serving in succession as minister of justice (March–May), minister of war (May–September), and minister-president (July–November), and adding the title of commander in chief of the army in September. Indeed, more than any other political figure of 1917 he identified completely with the Provisional Government and in turn came to be identified with it, both in 1917 and after.

In May and June 1917 he became the government's focal point for preparing a major military

Prime Minister Alexander Kerensky salutes while inspecting his troops in 1917. © HULTON-DEUTSCH COLLECTION/CORBIS

offensive, taking long tours of the front to stimulate fighting enthusiasm among soldiers. Despite the unpopularity and disastrous outcome of the offensive, Kerensky's personal reputation survived, and he became minister-president of the new, second coalition government. Moreover, as other leading political figures left the government, Kerensky became more and more dominant within it. Even as Kerensky achieved complete leadership of the government, however, both its and his own popularity eroded as the government failed to solve problems and to fulfill popular aspirations (despite its substantial achievements). The Kornilov Affair in September, a conflict growing out of the complex relation between Kerensky and General Lavr Kornilov that many saw as a counterrevolutionary attempt, earned Kerensky the enmity of both left and right and completed the destruction of his reputation. Crowds that earlier had cheered him as the hero of the revolution now cursed him Kerensky remained head of the government after the Kornilov Affair, but his popularity was gone, and his personal authority swiftly declined. His fateful decision was to move against the Bolsheviks on the eve of the Second Congress of Soviets; this sparked the October Revolution, which swept him from power.

After the Bolshevik Revolution, Kerensky spent several weeks underground, trying unsuccessfully to organize an anti-Bolshevik movement. In May 1918, he made his way out of the country and lived the rest of his life in exile, where he was active in emigré politics, delivered lectures, and wrote several accounts of the revolution and his role in it. He died on June 11, 1970, in the United States.

Kerensky was both the heroic and the tragic figure of the Russian Revolution of 1917. Thin, pale, with flashing eyes, theatrical gestures, and vivid verbal imagery, he was a dramatic and mesmerizing speaker with an incredible ability to move his listeners. Huge crowds turned out to hear him. As the year wore on, however, Kerensky's oratory could not compensate for the government's failures. The same speech-making that had made him a hero in the spring earned him scorn and a reputation as an empty babbler by autumn's end. The new paper currencies issued by the Provisional Government under his leadership were popularly called "Kerenki," and because inflation quickly made them worthless, his name thus took on something of that meaning as well. It was a tragic fall for the hero of February.

Alexander Kerensky, leader of the 1917 Provisional Government. THE ART ARCHIVE/MUSÉE DES 2 GUERRES MONDIALES PARIS/DAGLI ORTI

See also: FEBRUARY REVOLUTION; KORNILOV AFFAIR; OCTOBER REVOLUTION; PROVISIONAL GOVERNMENT

BIBLIOGRAPHY

Abraham, Richard. (1987). *Alexander Kerensky: The First Love of the Revolution.* New York: Columbia University Press.

Kerensky, Alexander. (1965). *Russia and History's Turning Point.* New York: Duell, Sloan and Pearce.

Kolonitskii, Boris I. (1997). "Kerensky." In *Critical Companion to the Russian Revolution, 1914–1921.* Bloomington: Indiana University Press.

REX A. WADE

K.G.B. *See* STATE SECURITY, ORGANS OF.

KHABAROV, YEROFEI PAVLOVICH

(c. 1610–1667), adventurer, explorer of Siberia.

Born in Vologda region, Yerofei Khabarov began his career managing a saltworks for the famed Stroganov clan. He traveled throughout western Siberia in the 1620s. He moved on to the Yenisei River, then the Lena, in the 1630s. He invested in farmlands and local saltworks. He also developed useful ties to Vasily Poyarkov, the administrator of Yakutsk and an early explorer of the Amur River basin.

In 1649 Khabarov turned to exploration. His goal was to follow up on Poyarkov's earlier forays into the Amur region, seeking an easier and more reliable route than Poyarkov had been able to find. In March, Khabarov left Yakutsk with 150 men, following the Olekma River.

Over the winter of 1650, Khabarov crossed the Yablonovy Range, reaching the Amur River soon after. He ruthlessly pacified the local tribe, the Daurs. He also established a garrison on the Amur. In his reports to Yakutsk and Moscow, Khabarov advocated conquest of the Amur, both for the river's strategic importance and the region's economic assets: grain, fish, and fur.

In 1650 and 1651, Khabarov launched further assaults against the Daurs, expanding Russian control over the area, but with great violence. Khabarov founded Achansk, captured Albazin, and made his way down the Amur until the summer of 1651. By this point, he was encroaching on territory that China's recently founded Manchu (Qing) Dynasty considered to be its sphere of influence. When the Daurs appealed to China for assistance, the Manchus attacked Achansk in the spring of 1652. Khabarov's garrison was forced to withdraw, but for the moment, the Manchus did not press their advantage. Nonetheless, Russia and China would engage in many frontier struggles until the signing of the Treaty of Nerchinsk (1689).

Meanwhile, word of Khabarov's cruel treatment of the Daurs reached Russian authorities, and he was arrested in the fall of 1653. Khabarov was put on trial, but his services were considered valuable enough to have outweighed the abuses he had committed. He was exonerated and placed in command of the Siberian fortress of Ilimsk. In 1858 Russia's new city at the juncture of the Amur and Ussuri rivers, Khabarovsk, was given his name.

See also: CHINA, RELATIONS WITH; SIBERIA

BIBLIOGRAPHY

Bassin, Mark. (1999). *Imperial Visions: Nationalist Imagination and Geographical Expansion in the Russian Far East, 1840–1865.* Cambridge, UK: Cambridge University Press.

Bobrick, Benson. (1992). *East of the Sun: The Epic Conquest and Tragic History of Siberia.* New York: Poseidon.

Lincoln, W. Bruce. (1993). *Conquest of a Continent: Siberia and the Russians.* New York: Random House.

JOHN MCCANNON

KHAKASS

The Khakass Republic or Khakassia (23,855 square miles, 61,784 square kilometers) is an autonomous republic within the Russian Federation. Located in Krasnoyarsk Krai at the far northwestern end of the Altay Range in south-central Siberia, it differs from other Siberian republics in at least two ways. First, the Khakass, while Turkic speaking, are actually Orthodox Christians, not Muslims, Buddhists, or shamanists. Second, ethnic Russians outnumber the Khakass. In 1959, 48,000 Khakass were living in Khakassia, forming 12 percent of the total population. By 1979 there were 57,300 Khakass, forming 11.4 percent of the population. Ethnic Russians now constitute the remaining 80 to 90 percent of the population of Khakassia.

The Khakass Republic extends along the left bank of the Yenisey River, upon the wooded slopes of Kuznetsk Ala-Tau and the Sayans, in the western portion of the Minusinsk depression. Lake Baikal lies 1,000 kilometers to the east. The Abakan (a tributary of the Yenisey) and Chulym rivers drain the area. The capital is Abakan and the next largest city is Chernogorsk (a coal-mining center). While the terrain in the southern and western regions is hilly, the northern and eastern parts of the region are flat, black-earth steppelands (the Abakan-Minusinsk Basin). The climate is continental, with the average temperatures between –15 and 21 degrees Celsius in January, and between 17 and 19 degrees Celsius in July.

The origin of the name Khakass is in the word *hagias (hjagas)*, which was used by the Chinese for an ancient tribe in the Sayan Mountains. Historically, the Khakass have gone by several different names: the Tatars of Minusinsk, the Tatars of Abakan, the Turks of Abakan, the Turks of the

Yenisey. The Khakass themselves call themselves by their own tribal names, including *sagai, khas, peltyr, shor, koybal,* and *hyzyl-kizhi.*

The Khakass language belongs to the Uighur-Oguz group in the Eastern Hun branch of the Turkic languages. While the structure and the basic vocabulary of the Khakass language are of Turkic-Tatar origin, the language contains many loan words from the Chinese, Mongolian, and Russian languages.

The first Russians arrived in Khakassia in the seventeenth century. The Khakass Autonomous Region was established in 1930. In 1992 the region became an official autonomous republic in the Russian Federation. Formerly nomadic herders, the Khakass now farm, hunt, or breed livestock. The republic produces timber, copper, iron ore, barite, gold, molybdenum, and tungsten.

See also: NATIONALITIES POLICIES, SOVIET; SIBERIA

BIBLIOGRAPHY

Berdahl, Daphne, and Matti Bunzl. (2000). *Altering States: Ethnographies of Transition in Eastern Europe and the Former Soviet Union.* Ann Arbor: University of Michigan Press.

Gorenburg, Dmitry P. (2003). *Minority Ethnic Mobilization in the Russian Federation.* New York: Cambridge University Press.

Petroff, Serge. (2000). *Remembering a Forgotten War: Civil War in Eastern European Russia and Siberia, 1918–1920.* New York: Columbia University Press.

Raleigh, Donald J. (2001). *Provincial Landscapes: Local Dimensions of Soviet Power, 1917–1953.* Pittsburgh: University of Pittsburgh Press.

JOHANNA GRANVILLE

KHALKIN-GOL, BATTLE OF

In the late 1930s, as events pushed the world inexorably toward war, the Soviet Union and Japan clashed several times over the precise location of their borders. The most serious of these incidents, occurring from May to September of 1939, took place in Mongolia, by a river named Khalkhin-Gol. Soviet forces crossed the river to assert their sovereignty over a disputed tract of land and ran into serious resistance from the Japanese Sixth Army. The Japanese believed that the river marked the border and had just been ordered to treat any incursions with the utmost severity. They launched a series of attacks against the Mongolian and Soviet troops and eventually managed to push back the initial advance. Stalin and his advisors, already convinced that the Japanese army wanted to seize Siberia for its natural resources, decided that this was the great attack they feared. In response, they gave the commander on the scene, Georgy Konstantinovich Zhukov, all the tanks, aircraft, and manpower he would need to deal with the threat.

Zhukov put together a major offensive that would not only drive the Japanese from Mongolia, but also take the disputed land irrevocably for the Soviet satellite. By the time he was ready for his attack, at the end of August, his forces outnumbered the Japanese two to one, and he had far more tanks and artillery than the Japanese could muster. His strategy, which called for the envelopment and destruction of the enemy, worked as planned, and the Japanese army suffered heavy casualties. The Japanese commander, Michitaro Komatsubara, refused to accept the outcome of the battle, however, and had prepared a counteroffensive. This was canceled when a cease-fire was signed in Moscow. War had broken out in Europe, and neither country could afford to be distracted by minor clashes on their borders. The battle at Khalkhin-Gol convinced the Japanese army that a fight with the Soviets would be a long, drawn-out affair, and helped the Japanese empire make the decision to turn southward in 1941, rather than attack Siberia.

See also: JAPAN, RELATIONS WITH; ZHUKOV, GEORGY KONSTANTINOVICH

BIBLIOGRAPHY

Coox, Alvin. (1985). *Nomonhan. Japan against Russia, 1939.* Stanford: Stanford University Press.

Zhukov, Georgy. (1971). *The Memoirs of Marshal Zhukov.* New York: Delacorte Press.

MARY R. HABECK

KHANTY

The Khanty people live in western Siberia from the Arctic Circle in the north to the conflux of the Irtysh and Tavda rivers in the south. The Khanty are mainly concentrated in the Khanty-Mansiysk autonomous okrug, with the administrative center Khanty-Mansiysk (population 34,300 in 1995).

The Khanty also live in the Yamal-Nenets autonomous okrug and in Tomsk oblast. According to the Soviet 1989 census, the total population of the Khanty numbered 22,521.

In the beginning of the eighteenth century, Khanty were baptized by Russian Orthodox missionaries. However, Khanty have followed their native religion until the present time. According to Khanty cosmology, there exist several layers of Heaven and Underworld and seven main gods, the most powerful of whom is Numi Torum. Shamans are mediators between gods and humans.

The Khanty language belongs to the Ob-Ugrian branch of the Finno-Ugric language family of Uralic language stock. Standardized written language based on the Latin alphabet was introduced in the 1930s. In 1940 it was transferred into the Cyrillic system. According to the All-Union census data as of 1989, the knowledge of native language among the Khanty was 60.5 percent.

Traditionally, the Khanty were divided between two phratries and several clans. Political leaders of the Khanty were clan elders and princes who collected taxes for Tsarist authorities and were responsible for native administration and court. During the Soviet period this native political structure was abolished.

The Khanty are seminomadic hunters, fishers, and reindeer breeders. During the Soviet period, animal husbandry, fur farming, and agriculture were introduced as small-scale enterprises.

From the eleventh century, the Khanty traded and had armed conflicts with Russians from Novgorod. Between the thirteenth and sixteenth centuries, the Khanty payed tribute to the Siberian Khanate. At the end of the sixteenth century the Khanty were conquered by Russia. The most serious change in Khanty recent history was the collectivization campaign in the 1930s. Between 1933 and 1934, the Khanty rebelled against the Soviets in what is known as the Kazym War. After the 1980s the native political movement expanded, mainly concentrating around the Association for the Salvation of the Ugra (founded in 1989).

See also: NATIONALITIES POLICIES, SOVIET; NATIONALITIES POLICIES, TSARIST; NORTHERN PEOPLES; SIBERIA

BIBLIOGRAPHY

Balzer, Marjorie Mandelstam. (1999). *The Tenacity of Ethnicity: A Siberian Saga in Global Perspective.* Princeton, NJ: Princeton University Press.

Prokof'yeva, E. D.; Chernetsov, V. N.; and Prytkova, N. E. (1964). "The Khants and Mansi." In *The Peoples of Siberia*, ed. M. G. Levin, L. P. Potapov. Chicago: University of Chicago Press.

Taagepera, Rein. (1999). *The Finno-Ugric Republics and the Russian State.* London: Hurst.

ART LEETE

KHASBULATOV, RUSLAN IMRANOVICH

(b. 1942), economist, Russian legislator.

Ruslan Khasbulatov studied at Kazakh State University and Moscow State University (MGU), where he was active in the Komsomol and joined the Communist Party of the Soviet Union (CPSU) in 1966. He earned a doctorate in economics from MGU in 1970. Khasbulatov spent the 1970s and 1980s working at the Academy of Sciences's Institute of Scientific Information and the Scientific Research Institute for Questions of Secondary Schools. He transferred to the Plekhanov Institute for Economic Management in 1979, eventually becoming chair of the division of Economy of Foreign Countries.

In 1990 Khasbulatov was elected to the first RSFSR (Russian Soviet Federated Socialist Republic) Congress of People's Deputies. When the Congress elected Yeltsin as chair, he picked Khasbulatov as his first deputy (May 1990). Following Yeltsin's election to the newly created Russian presidency, Khasbulatov became speaker of parliament (October 1991).

Khasbulatov opposed the amount of power that devolved to Yeltsin after the collapse of the Soviet Union. He also opposed Yeltsin's economic policy of shock therapy and the privatization campaigns. As Yeltsin's team drafted a new Russian constitution, Khasbulatov spearheaded a parliamentary effort to reduce Yeltsin's authority and more equitably redistribute powers between the Russian executive and legislative branches.

The power struggle culminated in Yeltsin's dissolution of parliament in September 1993. Led by Khasbulatov and Russian Vice President Alexander Rutskoi, legislators barricaded themselves in the parliamentary building. Yeltsin responded by firing on the building the night of October 3–4, 1993. Khasbulatov was led from the building in handcuffs and sent to prison. In February 1994, the Russian State Duma amnestied Khasbulatov along with all the participants in the parliamentary rebellion.

An ethnic Chechen, Khasbulatov became involved in the domestic politics of the rebellious republic. He unsuccessfully ran for president in 1996 and has been involved in negotiations to end the second Chechen war. As of 2003, Khasbulatov teaches at the Plekhanov Institute in Moscow.

See also: CHECHNYA AND CHECHENS; OCTOBER 1993 EVENTS; PRIVATIZATION; YELTSIN, BORIS NIKOLAYEVICH

BIBLIOGRAPHY

Dunlop, John B. (1993). *The Rise of Russia and the Fall of the Soviet Empire.* Princeton, NJ: Princeton University Press.

ANN E. ROBERTSON

KHAZARS

A nomadic Turkic-speaking tribal confederation and an offshoot of the Turk kaghanate, the Khazars established one of the earliest and most successful states in medieval eastern Europe. Khazar history is divided into two periods: the Crimean–North Caucasus (c. 650–750) and the Lower Volga (c. 750–965) phases. Politically focused on the northern Black Sea region, during the first phase the Khazars were locked in endless wars against the Arabs over the control of the Caucasus. After a major defeat in 737, the Khazars relocated their political focus to the north and established their capital of Atil/Itil in the Volga delta around 800. The next one hundred years of Khazar history (known as Pax Chazarica) brought security to the Russian steppe and the surrounding regions, permitting cross-continental trade to flourish via Khazaria and providing it with the necessary stability for the formation of a unique material culture, known to archaeologists as Saltovo.

Khazaria was an empire or kaghanate, the highest form of Turkic political organization. The kaghan or its leader was apparently of Turkic origin and had supreme secular and sacred functions. During the ninth century, his political-religious role was split: He retained his religious sacred function, while the governor or *beg* ruled the state.

At its height in the first half of the ninth century, Khazar territories stretched from the middle Dnieper in the west to the Volga-Ural steppe in the east, and from the middle Volga in the north to the Crimea in the south. It was populated by Turkic and Iranian nomads, Finno-Ugrian foragers, Slavic agriculturalists, and urban Crimean Greeks, making the kaghanate a multiethnic, multilingual, and multireligious state. Khazar economy was diverse and included animal husbandry, agriculture, hunting and gathering, fishing, craft production, agriculture, viniculture, and domestic and international trade. Khazars traded locally manufactured goods as well as the furs, slaves, honey, and wax they obtained as tribute from the Slavic and Finno-Ugrian tribes of the north. Khazaria also acted as an intermediary for Rus-Arab trade and received a tithe from the bypassing merchants. Millions of Islamic silver coins (dirhams) were exported via the "Khazar Way" (lower Volga-Don-Donets-Oka-upper Volga) trade route to northwestern Russia in exchange for Rus commodities.

Most Khazars practiced shamanist-Täri religion. In the late eighth to early ninth century (but perhaps as late as 861), the Khazar ruling elite converted to Judaism. While many questions remain concerning this conversion and its pervasiveness, it is clear that by accepting Judaism, the ruling class made Khazaria a religious neutral zone for its warring Christian and Islamic neighbors. Religious tolerance and Khazaria's international commercial interests brought Christians, Muslims, Jews, pagans, and others to trade and live within the kaghanate.

Pax Chazarica came to an end by the early tenth century. Already in the 890s, Pechenegs and Magyars infiltrated Khazaria from the east, while the Rus annexed Khazarian territories in the northwest. Concurrently, the Khazar Way declined and the Rus-Islamic trade shifted to the lands of the Volga Bulghars, thereby bypassing Khazar toll collectors. Greatly weakened, Khazaria was destroyed in 965 by the Rus and their Torky allies.

See also: ISLAM; JEWS; RELIGION; TORKY

BIBLIOGRAPHY

Dunlop, D. M. (1967). *The History of the Jewish Khazars.* New York: Schocken Books.

Golden, Peter B. (1980). *Khazar Studies: An Historico-Philological Inquiry into the Origins of the Khazars, Vol. 1.* Budapest: Akadémiai Kiadó.

Golden, Peter B. (1990). "The Peoples of the South Russian Steppe." In *The Cambridge History of Early Inner Asia*, ed. Denis Sinor. Cambridge, UK: Cambridge University Press.

Golden, Peter B. (1992). *An Introduction to the History of the Turkic Peoples*. Wiesbaden, Germany: Harrassowitz Verlag.

Noonan, Thomas S. (1997). "The Khazar Economy." *Archivum Eurasiae Medii Aevi* 9:253–318.

Zuckerman, C. (1995). "On the Date of the Khazars' Conversion to Judaism and the Chronology of the Kings of the Rus Oleg and Igor: A Study of the Anonymous Khazar *Letter* from the Genizah of Cairo." *Revue des Études Byzantines* 53:237–270.

Roman K. Kovalev

KHIVA

Khiva, a city in northwestern Uzbekistan and the name of a khanate in existence prior to and during the rule of the Russian Empire, is located in the midst of the deserts of Central Asia. Early in human history, farming peoples settled in the region, relying on irrigation to bring water to their fields from the nearby Amu River (Amu-Darya), known in antiquity as the Oxus. Its sources in the great glacial fields of the Pamir and Hindu Kush mountains to the southeast assured a steady supply of water sufficient to sustain agriculture and human settlement. Long-distance commerce began with the opening of the great trade routes (collectively known as the Silk Route) between Asia, the Middle East, and Europe. Nomadic tribes frequently invaded the territory, conquering the lands of Khorezm (as Khiva was then called) and destroying the cities. Settlers founded the city of Khiva in the tenth century, during a period of prosperity. That time of peace came to an end with the Mongol invasion of the thirteenth century. Two centuries later, Turkic tribes in turn conquered the region.

One Turkic leader (khan) founded the Khanate of Khiva shortly afterward. The strongest unifying force among its peoples was the Islamic religion. All the peoples living there belonged to the Sunni branch of Islam. The hot climate permitted the Khivan farmers to grow cotton. It was woven into beautiful rugs, which Khiva's merchants transported for sale to the Middle East and to Russia. Slavery was common, for nomads brought captives for sale in Khiva whom they had captured in Persia (Shiite Muslims), and in the Siberian plains (Russians). The Khivan peoples were divided by clan and tribal loyalties, and spoke several Turkic languages. The most important division was between the nomadic tribes of the desert and those who lived in towns or farmed the irrigated land. Nomadic raids and revolts unsettled the principality. Frequent wars with neighboring rulers (especially Bukhara) also kept Khiva weak.

The Russian Empire conquered the khanate in the 1870s. In the eighteenth century, it had begun to expand into the plains of southern Siberia and northern Central Asia, with the goal of colonial domination of the area. In the 1860s its armies began their offensive against the khanates of the southern oasis lands. The khanate forces were poorly armed and quickly capitulated. Khiva surrendered to a Russian army after a brief war in 1873. Some khanates were absorbed into the empire. Khiva (and Bukhara) remained as Russian protectorates, independent in their internal affairs but forced to accept the empire's control over their foreign affairs. The Khanate of Khiva was left with a shrunken territory within the borders imposed by Russia. Its trade with Russia grew rapidly, for its cotton was in great demand for Russian textile manufacturing.

Following the collapse of the Russian Empire in 1917, the khanate briefly regained its full independence. But in 1918 armies under the command of the Communist Party from the revolutionary state of Soviet Russia invaded Central Asia. The Communists won the support of a group of Khivan reformers, who took charge of a tiny state that they called the Khorezm People's Republic. It lasted only until 1924, when the Soviet government ordered Khorezm's leaders to agree to the annexation of their state by the new Union of Soviet Socialist Republics. Its lands were divided between the Soviet Republics of Uzbekistan and Turkmenistan. The Communists believed that their new ethnoterritorial republics, grouped around one majority ("titular") nationality, would assist in bringing socialism to the Central Asian peoples. Uzbek and Turkmen communists assumed command of the peoples once ruled by the Khivan khan. The city of Khiva became a small regional center. Its ancient walled city was a picturesque reminder of its pre-Russian past.

See also: CENTRAL ASIA; TURKMENISTAN AND TURKMEN; UZBEKISTAN AND UZBEKS

Ichan-Kala, the ancient inner city of Khiva, was designated a UNESCO World Heritage Site for its many monuments and oriental architecture. © LUDOVIC MAISANT/CORBIS

BIBLIOGRAPHY

Becker, Seymour. (1968). *Russia's Protectorates in Central Asia: Bukhara and Khiva, 1865–1924.* Cambridge, MA: Harvard University Press.

Glazebrook, Philip. (1937). *Journey to Khiva.* London: Harvill Press.

Naumkin, Vitaly. (1992). *Khiva.* Caught in Time: Great Photographic Archives. Reading, UK: Garnet Publishing.

DANIEL BROWER

KHMELNITSKY, BOHDAN

(c. 1595–1657), hetman of the Zaporozhian Cossack Host (1648–1657) and founder of the Hetmanate (Cossack state).

Born into a family of Orthodox petty gentry, Khmelnitsky fought at the Battle of Cecora (1620) and was taken prisoner to Istanbul for two years. Enrolled as a registered Cossack, he was a military chancellor during the Cossack revolts of 1637 and 1638. In 1646 he took part in a Cossack delegation to King Wladyslaw IV, who sought to win the Cossacks over to his secret plans for a war against the Ottomans. In 1647 a magnate's servitor attacked Khmelnitsky's estate. Khmelnitsky found no redress. Arrested in November 1647, he escaped and fled to the traditional Cossack stronghold, or *Sich*, where he was proclaimed hetman in February 1648. He received support from the Crimean Khanate, and in May Khmelnitsky defeated the Polish armies sent against him. The king died in that month, throwing the Polish-Lithuanian Commonwealth, an elective monarchy, into crisis.

Throughout 1648, as an uprising raged in Ukraine with attacks on landholders, Catholic clergy, and Jews, Khmelnitsky energetically organized a military force and a civil administration. Defeating what remained of the Commonwealth's forces in September, he influenced the election of Jan Kazimierz as a propeace candidate. At the end of the year, Khmelnitsky marched east, entering

Kyiv to the acclamation that he was a Moses liberating his people from the "Polish bondage." He declared his intentions to rule as an autocrat as far as Western Ukrainian Lviv.

A renewed war (the Battle of Zboriv) proved inconclusive because of the desertion of the Crimean khan. From mid-1649 Khmelnitsky searched for foreign allies against the Commonwealth, but the Tatars remained his only ally. Initially the Ottoman Empire seemed the most likely supporter, but the extension of Ottoman protection in 1651 did not bring the required military assistance. Khmelnitsky sought to gain a status for Ukraine similar to the Ottoman vassal Moldavia, in part by marrying his son into its ruling family. Having been defeated by the Poles at Berestechko in June 1651, he in turn defeated them in June 1652. His Danubian intervention ended in fiasco with his son Tymish's death in September 1653. The weakened Khmelnitsky then turned more seriously to the Muscovite tsar, and after the Russian decision to take him under "tsar's high hand" in 1653, he convened a Cossack council at Pereyaslav and took an oath of loyalty to the tsar in January 1654 , but failed to receive an oath from his emissaries. Retaining far greater power in Ukraine than the terms negotiated, Khmelnitsky came to be disillusioned with Muscovy, especially after the truce between Muscovy and the Commonwealth in November 1656. He joined a coalition with Sweden and Transylvania against the Commonwealth (and against Muscovite wishes), but a Transylvanian-Ukrainian invasion had failed just before his death.

Evaluations of Khmelnitsky and his policies vary greatly, with some seeing him as a great statesman and others as a destructive rebel. The nature of the Pereyaslav Agreement has been the subject of controversy; in Soviet historiography it was viewed as the "reunification" of Ukraine with Russia.

See also: COSSACKS; UKRAINE AND UKRAINIANS

BIBLIOGRAPHY

Basarab, John. (1982). *Pereiaslav 1654: A Historiographical Study.* Edmonton: Canadian Institute of Ukrainian Studies Press.

Hrushevsky, Mykhailo. (2002). *History of Ukraine-Rus'',* vol. 8. Edmonton: Canadian Institute of Ukrainian Studies Press.

Stow, Kenneth, and Teller, Adam, eds. (2003). "*Gezeirot Ta''h* Jews, Cossacks, Poles, and Peasants in 1648 Ukraine." *Jewish History* 17(2).

Sysyn, Frank E. (1985). *Between Poland and Ukraine: The Dilemma of Adam Kysil, 1600–1653.* Cambridge, MA: Harvard University Press for HURI.

Sysyn, Frank E. (1995). "The Changing Image of the Hetman: On the 350th Anniversary of the Khmel''nyts''kyi Uprising." *Jahrbücher für Geschichte Osteuropas* 46: 531–45.

Vernadsky, George. (1941). *Bohdan, Hetman of Ukraine.* New Haven, CT: Yale University Press.

FRANK E. SYSYN

KHOMYAKOV, ALEXEI STEPANOVICH

(1804–1860), slavophile philosopher, theologian, poet, and playwright.

Alexei Khomyakov was born in Moscow of an old noble family. He was well educated in a pious, traditional, cultivated household, under the particular influence of his devout mother. He was tutored in French, English, and Latin in his childhood and youth, and later added Greek and German. The Khomyakov house burned to the ground in the Moscow fire of 1812, and the family was forced to take refuge on one of their country estates near Ryazan. When Khomyakov first saw St. Petersburg in 1815, the pious young Muscovite allegedly found it a pagan and thoroughly un-Russian place. At the University of Moscow, Khomyakov studied philosophy and theology, but took his kandidat (master's; in some cases equivalent of Ph.D.) degree in mathematics in 1821.

Between 1822 and 1825, Khomyakov served in the military, to which he briefly returned in 1828 as the captain of a regiment, when Emperor Nicholas I appealed for volunteers to fight in the Turkish War. In the early 1820s he also had relations with the so-called Lovers of Wisdom (*Obshchestvo Lyubomudriya*) and published several poems in the *Moscow Messenger.* Following his first stint in the army, he briefly studied painting in Paris and visited Switzerland and Italy before returning to Russia.

In the 1820s and the 1830s, Khomyakov was known primarily as a playwright (*Ermak, the False Dmitry*) and a poet. His poetry is "characterized by rhetorical pathos, a lofty view of the poet's calling, and a preview of his later Slavophile ideas." In 1829 he retired from government service to devote himself to literature and his estates, and in 1834 he married Yekaterina Yazykov, the sister of the poet.

Unlike most of his Slavophile contemporaries, Khomyakov had strong practical and scientific interests: He concerned himself with the practical pursuit of profitable agriculture on his estates and followed developments in modern science and even engineering. In addition to his growing theological and practical pursuits, he followed contemporary social and political issues closely. Nevertheless, from his childhood on, he felt that science and politics must always be subordinated to religious values.

Khomyakov and Ivan Kireyevsky had known each other since the early 1820s, but in the mid-1830s they became close friends. Khomyakov's "On the Old and New," followed by Kireyevsky's "An Answer to Khomyakov" (1839) are the earliest surviving written documents of Slavophilism, as these traditionally minded aristocrats groped for an answer to Peter Chaadayev's "Philosophical Letter." Khomyakov was more willing than other Slavophiles to admit that the Russian state had been an important factor in Russian history. He thought the Russian state that arose in the wake of Mongol domination showed an "all-Russian" spirit, and he regarded the history of Russia between the Mongol period and the death of Peter the Great as the consolidation of the idea of the state—a dreadful process because of the damage it did to Russian society, but necessary. Only through Peter's reforms could the "state principle" finally triumph over the forces of disunity. But now the harmony, simplicity, and purity of pre-Petrine Russia, which had been so badly damaged, must be recovered for future generations.

If Ivan Kireyevsky may be described as the philosopher of Slavophilism, Khomyakov was surely its theologian. His introduction of the concept of *sobornost* (often translated as "concialiarity" or "conciliarism") as a fundamental distinction between the Orthodox Church and the Western confessions took a long time to be recognized in Russia but has become a fundamental aspect of Orthodox theology since his death. Opposing both Catholic hierarchy and Protestant individualism, Khomyakov defined the church as a free union of believers, loving one another in mystical communion with Christ. Thus *sobornost* is the consciousness of believers in their collectivity. Contrasting with Catholic authority, juridical in nature, was the creative role of church councils, but only as recognized over time by the entire church. Faith, for Khomyakov, was not belief in or commitment to a set of crystallized dogmas, but a prerational, collective inner knowledge or certainty. An excellent brief statement of Khomyakov's theology can be found in his influential essay *The Church Is One*, written in the mid-1840s but published only in 1863. He also published three theological treatises in the 1850s entitled "Some Words of an Orthodox Christian about Western Creeds."

Clearly Khomyakov's idea of *sobornost* had its social analogue in the collective life of the Russian peasant in his village communal council (*obshchina*), which recognized the primacy of the collectivity, yet guaranteed the integrity and the well-being of the individual within that collective. Sobornost was particularly associated with Khomyakov, but his view of the centrality of the peasant commune was generally shared by the first-generation Slavophiles, especially by Ivan Kireyevsky. In addition, Khomyakov distinguished in his posthumously published *Universal History* between two fundamental principles, which, in their interaction, determine "all thoughts of man." The "Iranian" principle was that of freedom, of which Orthodox Christianity was the highest expression, while the Kushite principle, its opposite, rested on the recognition of necessity and had clear associations with Asia.

Khomyakov, unlike Kireyevsky or the Aksakovs, had a special sense of Slav unity, which may have originated in his travels through south Slavic lands in the 1820s. In that limited sense he represented a bridge between Slavophilism and pan-Slavism. As early as 1832 he wrote a poem called "The Eagle," in which he called on Russia to free the Slavs. At the beginning of the Crimean War, he wrote an even more famous poem entitled "To Russia," in which he excoriated his country for its many sins but called upon it to become worthy of its sacred mission: to fight for its Slavic brothers. The message of his "Letter to the Serbs" (1860) was similar. Khomyakov died suddenly of cholera in 1860.

See also: PANSLAVISM; SLAVOPHILES; THEATER

BIBLIOGRAPHY

Christoff, Peter. (1961). *An Introduction to Nineteenth-Century Russian Slavophilism: A Study in Ideas, Vol. 1: A. S. Khomiakov.* The Hague: Mouton.

Riasanovsky, Nicholas. (1952). *Russia and the West in the Teaching of the Slavophiles: A Study of Romantic Ideology.* Cambridge, MA: Harvard University Press.

Walicki, Andrzej. *The Slavophile Controversy: History of a Conservative Utopia in Nineteenth-Century Russian Thought.* Oxford: Clarendon.

ABBOTT GLEASON

KHOVANSHCHINA

The Khovanshchina originated in the struggle over the succession following the death of Tsar Fyodor Ivanovich in 1682. Strictly speaking, the term refers to the period following the musketeer revolt of May 1682, when many leading boyars and officials in the Kremlin were massacred, and the creation of the dual monarchy of Tsars Ivan and Peter under the regency of Tsarevna Sophia Alexeyevna, although some historians use the term loosely as a general heading for all the unrest of 1682. The musketeers demanded that Sophia's government absolve them of all guilt and erect a column on Red Square to commemorate their service in eliminating "wicked men." The government duly complied but failed to prevent a new wave of unrest associated with religious dissidents and with the musketeers' continuing dissatisfaction with pay and working conditions.

The troops were encouraged to air their grievances by the new director of the Musketeers Chancellery, Prince Ivan Khovansky, a veteran of campaigns against Poland in the 1650s and 1660s. He had shown sympathy for Old Believers while governor in Novgorod and was angered by the prominence of many new men at court whom he, of ancient lineage, regarded as upstarts. Acting as the musketeers' self-styled "father," Khovansky made a show of mediating on their behalf and also organized a meeting between the patriarch and dissidents to debate issues of faith. When the defrocked dissident priest Nikita assaulted an archbishop, he was arrested and executed, but his sponsor Khovansky remained too popular with the musketeers for the government to touch him. Instead, they tried to reduce the power of the Khovansky clan by reshuffling chancellery personnel. Sophia took the tsars on tours of estates and monasteries, leaving Khovansky precariously in charge in Moscow and increasingly isolated from other boyars.

Khovansky's failure to obey several orders allowed Sophia further to isolate him. His fate was sealed by the discovery of an anonymous—and probably fabricated—letter of denunciation. In late September Khovansky and his son Ivan were lured to a royal residence outside Moscow, where they were charged with plotting to use the musketeers to kill the tsars and their family to raise rebellion all over Moscow and snatch the throne. Lesser charges included association with "accursed schismatics," embezzlement, dereliction of military duty, and insulting the boyars. The charges were full of inconsistencies, but the Khovanskys were beheaded on the spot. The musketeers prepared to barricade themselves into Moscow, but eventually they were reduced to begging Sophia and the tsars to return. They were forced to swear an oath of loyalty based on a set of conditions, the final clause of which threatened death to anyone who praised their deeds or fomented rebellion. The government's victory consolidated Sophia's regime and marked a stage in the eventual demise of the musketeers.

These events provided material for Mussorgsky's opera *Khovanshchina* (1872–1880), which treats the historical facts fairly loosely and culminates in a mass suicide of Old Believers.

See also: FYODOR IVANOVICH; OLD BELIEVERS; SOPHIA

BIBLIOGRAPHY

Bushkovitch, Paul. (2001). *Peter the Great. The Struggle for Power, 1671–1725.* Cambridge, UK: Cambridge University Press.

Hughes, Lindsey. (1990). *Sophia Regent of Russia 1657–1704.* New Haven, CT: Yale University Press.

Soloviev, Sergei. (1989). *History of Russia.* Volume 25: *Rebellion and Reform. Fedor and Sophia, 1682–1689,* ed. and trans. Lindsey Hughes. Gulf Breeze, FL: Academic International Press.

LINDSEY HUGHES

KHOZRASCHET

Within the planned economy, Soviet industrial enterprises operated on an independent economic accounting system called *khozraschet*. In principle, enterprises were to operate according to the principle of self-finance, which meant they were to cover their production costs from sales revenue, as well as earn a planned profit. A designated portion of the planned profit was turned over to the industrial ministry to which the firm was subordinate. However, prices paid by firms for input as well as prices earned by firms from the sales of their output were centrally determined and not based upon scarcity or efficiency considerations. Consequently, calculations of costs, revenues, and profit had little practical significance in evaluations of the need to adjust present or future activities of the firm. For example, firms operating with persistent losses were not subject to bankruptcy or closure; firms earning profits did not willingly offer to increase production. Under khozraschet, profits and losses did not serve either a signaling role or disciplinary role, as they tend to do for firms in a market economy.

The khozraschet system enabled Soviet enterprise managers to monitor their operations and overall plan performance, and to have financial relations with the State bank, Gosbank. Funds earned by the enterprise were deposited at Gosbank; enterprises applied to Gosbank for working capital loans. Given the enterprise autonomy granted by the khozraschet system, financial relations with other external administrative units, such as the industrial ministry to which the firm was subordinate, also occurred when conditions warranted. Under the khozraschet system, enterprise managers were able to exercise some degree of flexibility and initiative in fulfilling plan targets.

The khozraschet system was applied to work brigades in the construction industry in the early 1970s and expanded to work brigades introduced in other industries in the mid-1970s and early 1980s. State farms, called *sovkhozy*, operated under the khozraschet system of independent financial management, as did the Foreign Trade Organizations (FTOs) operating under the supervision of the Ministry of Foreign Trade. The khozraschet system vanished with the end of central planning.

See also: COMMAND ADMINISTRATIVE ECONOMY; GOSBANK

BIBLIOGRAPHY

Conyngham, William J. (1982). *The Modernization of Soviet Industrial Management.* New York: Cambridge University Press.

Gregory, Paul R., and Stuart, Robert C. (2001). *Russian and Soviet Economic Performance and Structure,* 7th ed. New York: Addison Wesley.

SUSAN J. LINZ

KHRUSHCHEV, NIKITA SERGEYEVICH

(1894–1971), leader of the USSR during the first decade after Stalin's death.

Nikita Khrushchev rose from obscurity into Stalin's inner circle, unexpectedly triumphed in the battle to succeed Stalin, equally unexpectedly attacked Stalin and embarked on a program of de-Stalinization, and was suddenly ousted from power after his reforms in internal and foreign policy proved erratic and ineffective.

Khrushchev was born in the poor southern Russian village of Kalinovka, and his childhood there profoundly shaped his character and his self-image. His parents dreamed of owning land and a horse but achieved neither goal. His father, who later worked in the mines of Yuzovka in the Donbas, was a failure in the eyes of Khrushchev's mother, a strong-willed woman who invested her hopes in her son.

In 1908 Khrushchev's family moved to Yuzovka. By 1914 he had become a skilled, highly paid metalworker, had married an educated woman from a fairly prosperous family, and dreamed of becoming an engineer or industrial manager. Ironically, the Russian Revolution "distracted" him into a political career that culminated in supreme power in the Kremlin.

Between 1917 and 1929, Khrushchev's path led him from a minor position on the periphery of the revolution to a role as an up-and-coming apparatchik in the Ukrainian Communist party. Along the way he served as a political commissar in the Red Army during the Russian civil war, assistant director for political affairs of a mine, party cell leader of a technical college in whose adult education division he briefly continued his education, party secretary of a district near Stalino (formerly Yuzovka), and head of the Ukrainian Central Committee's organization department.

In 1929 Khrushchev enrolled in the Stalin Industrial Academy in Moscow. Over the next nine years his career rocketed upward: party leader of the academy in 1930; party boss of two of Moscow's leading boroughs in 1931; second secretary of the Moscow city party organization itself in 1932; city party leader in 1934; party chief of Moscow Province, additionally, in 1935; candidate-member of the party Central Committee in 1934; and party leader of Ukraine in 1938. He was powerful enough not only to have superintended the rebuilding of Moscow, but to have been complicit in the Great Terror that Stalin unleashed, particularly in the Moscow purge of men who worked for Khrushchev and of whose innocence he must have been convinced.

Fidel Castro and Nikita Khrushchev sign the January 1964 Soviet-Cuban Trade Agreement. © BETTMANN/CORBIS

Between 1938 and 1941, Khrushchev was Stalin's viceroy in Ukraine. During these years, he grew more independent of Stalin while at the same time serving Stalin ever more effectively. Even as he developed doubts about the purges, Khrushchev grew more dedicated to the cause of socialism and proud of his own service to it, particularly of conquering Western Ukrainian lands and uniting them with the rest of Ukraine as part of Stalin's 1939 deal with Hitler.

Khrushchev's role in World War II blended triumph and tragedy. A political commissar on several key fronts, he was involved in, although not primarily responsible for, great victories at Stalingrad and Kursk. But he also contributed to disastrous defeats at Kiev and Kharkov by helping to convince Stalin that the victories the dictator sought were possible when in fact they proved not to be. After the war in Ukraine, where Khrushchev remained until 1949, his record continued to be contradictory: on the one hand, directing the rebuilding of the Ukrainian economy, and attempting to pry aid out of the Kremlin when Stalinist policies led to famine in 1946; on the other hand, acting as the driving force in a brutal, bloody war against the Ukrainian independence movement in Western Ukraine.

In 1949 Stalin called Khrushchev back to Moscow as a counterweight to Georgy Malenkov and Lavrenti Beria in the Kremlin. For the next four years, Khrushchev seemed the least likely of Stalin's men to succeed him. Yet, when Stalin died on March 5, 1953, Khrushchev moved quickly to do so. After leading a conspiracy to oust Beria in June 1953, he demoted Malenkov and then Vyacheslav Molotov in 1955.

By the beginning of 1956, Khrushchev was the first among equals in the ruling Presidium. Yet a mere year and half later, he was nearly ousted in an attempted Kremlin coup. His near-defeat resulted from a variety of factors, of which the most important were the consequences of Khrushchev's Secret Speech attacking Stalin at the Twentieth

Party Congress in February 1956. This speech, the content of which became widely known, sparked turmoil in the USSR, a political upheaval in Poland, and a revolution in Hungary, which Soviet troops crushed in November 1956. Khrushchev's aims in unmasking Stalin ranged from compromising Stalinist colleagues to expiating his own sins. The result of the speech, however, was to begin the process of undermining the Soviet system while at the same time undermining himself.

Khrushchev's opponents, primarily Malenkov, Molotov, and Lazar Kaganovich, took advantage of the disarray to try to oust him in June 1957. With their defeat, he might have been expected to intensify his anti-Stalin campaign. Instead, his policies proved contradictory, as if the tumultuous consequences of the Secret Speech had taught Khrushchev that his own authority depended on Stalin's not being totally discredited.

Even before Khrushchev was fully in charge, improving Soviet agriculture had been perhaps his highest priority. In 1953 he had endorsed long-needed reforms designed to increase incentives: a reduction in taxes, an increase in procurement prices paid by the state for obligatory collective farm deliveries, and encouragement of individual peasant plots, which produced much of the nation's vegetables and milk. By 1954, however, he was pushing an ill-conceived crash program to develop the so-called Virgin Lands of western Siberia and Kazakhstan as a quick way to increase overall output. Another example of Khrushchev's impulsiveness was his wildly unrealistic 1957 pledge to overtake the United States in the per capita output of meat, butter, and milk in only a few years, a promise that counted on a radical expansion of corn-growing even in regions where that ultimately proved impossible to sustain.

That all these policies failed to set Soviet agriculture on the path to sustained growth was visible in the disappointing harvests of 1960 and 1962. These setbacks led Khrushchev to raise retail prices for meat and poultry products in May 1962, breaking with popular expectations. The move triggered riots, including those in Novocherkassk, where nearly twenty-five people were killed by troops brought in to quell the disturbances. Khrushchev's next would-be panacea was his November 1962 proposal to divide the Communist Party itself into agricultural and industrial wings, a move that alienated party officials while failing to improve the harvest, which was so bad in 1963 that Moscow was forced to buy wheat overseas, including from the United States.

First Secretary Nikita Khrushchev wears his two Hero of the Soviet Union medals. © BETTMANN/CORBIS

The party split was the latest in a series of reorganizations that characterized Khrushchev's approach to economic administration. In 1957 he replaced many of the central Moscow ministries that had been running the economy with regional "councils of the national economy," a change that alienated the former central ministers who were forced to relocate to the provinces.

Housing and school reform were also on Khrushchev's agenda. To address the dreadful urban housing shortage bequeathed by Stalin, Khrushchev encouraged rapid, assembly-line construction of standardized, prefabricated five-story apartment houses, which proved to be a quick fix, but not a long-term solution. Khrushchev's idea of school reform was to add a year to the basic ten-year program, to be partly devoted to learning a manual trade at a local factory or farm, an idea that reflected his own training but met widespread resistance from parents, teachers, and factory and farm directors loath to take on new teenage charges.

The Thaw in Soviet culture began before Khrushchev's Secret Speech but gained momentum from it. The cultural and scientific intelligentsia was a natural constituency for a reformer like Khrushchev, but he and his Kremlin colleagues feared the Thaw might become a flood. His inconsistent actions alienated all elements of the intelligentsia while deepening Khrushchev's own love-hate feelings toward writers and artists. On the one hand, he authorized the 1957 World Youth Festival, for which thousands of young people from around the world flooded into Moscow. On the other hand, he encouraged the fierce campaign against Boris Pasternak after the poet and author of *Dr. Zhivago* was awarded the Nobel Prize in Literature in 1958. The Twenty-second Party Congress in October 1961, which was marked by an eruption of anti-Stalinist rhetoric, seemed to recommit Khrushchev to an alliance with liberal intellectuals, especially when followed by the decision to authorize publication of Alexander Solzhenitsyn's novel about the Gulag, *One Day in the Life of Ivan Denisovich*, and Yevgeny Yevtushenko's poem "The Heirs of Stalin." But after the Cuban missile crisis ended in defeat, Khrushchev turned to chastising and browbeating the liberal intelligentsia at a series of ugly confrontations in the winter of 1962 and 1963.

As little as his minimal education prepared him to run the internal affairs of a vast, transcontinental empire, it prepared him even less for foreign policy. For the first fifty years of his life he had little exposure to the outside world and almost none to the great powers, and after Stalin's death, he initially remained on the foreign policy sidelines. Even before defeating the Anti-Party Group, however, he began to direct Soviet foreign relations, and afterward it was almost entirely his to command. Stalin's legacy in foreign affairs was abysmal: When he died, the West was mobilizing against Moscow, and even allies (in Eastern Europe and China) and neutrals had been alienated. All Stalin's heirs sought to address these problems, but Khrushchev did so most boldly and energetically.

To China Khrushchev offered extensive economic and technical assistance of the sort for which Stalin had driven a hard bargain, along with benevolent tutelage that he assumed Mao would appreciate. Initially the Chinese were pleased, but Khrushchev's failure to consult them before denouncing Stalin in 1956, his fumbling attempts to cope with the Polish and Hungarian turmoil of the same year, and his requests for military concessions in 1958 led to two acrimonious summit meetings with Mao (in August 1958 and September 1959), after which he precipitously withdrew Soviet technical experts from China in 1960. The result was an open, apparently irrevocable Sino-Soviet split.

Khrushchev tried to bring Yugoslavia back into the Soviet bloc, the better to tie the Communist camp together by substituting tolerance of diversity and domestic autonomy for Stalinist terror. Khrushchev's trip to Belgrade in May 1955, undertaken against the opposition of Molotov, gave him a stake in obtaining Yugoslav President Tito's cooperation. But if Tito, too, was eager for reconciliation, it was on his own terms, which Khrushchev could not entirely accept. As with China, therefore, Khrushchev's embrace of a would-be Communist ally ended not in new harmony but in new stresses and strains.

Whereas Stalin had mostly ignored Third World countries, since he had little interest in what he could not control, Khrushchev set out to woo them as a way of undermining "Western imperialism." In 1955 he and Prime Minister Nikolai Bulganin traveled to India, Burma, and Afghanistan. In 1960 he returned to these three countries and visited Indonesia as well. He backed the radical president of the Congo, Patrice Lumumba, and reached out to support Fidel Castro in Cuba. Yet, despite these and other moves, Khrushchev also tried to ease Cold War tensions with the West, and particularly with his main capitalist rival, the United States. As Khrushchev saw it, he had opened up the USSR to Western influences, abandoned the Stalinist notion that world war was inevitable, made deep unilateral cuts in Soviet armed forces, pulled Soviet troops out of Austria and Finland, and encouraged reform in Eastern Europe.

The Berlin ultimatum that Khrushchev issued in November 1958—that if the West didn't recognize East Germany, Moscow would give the German Communists control over access to West Berlin, thus abrogating Western rights stipulated in postwar Potsdam accords—was designed not only to ensure the survival of the beleaguered German Democratic Republic, but to force the Western allies into negotiations on a broad range of issues. And at first the strategy worked. It secured Khrushchev an invitation to the United States in

September 1959, the first time a Soviet leader had visited the United States, after which a four-power summit was scheduled for Paris in May 1960. But in the end, Khrushchev's talks with Eisenhower produced little progress, the Paris summit collapsed when an American U-2 spy flight was shot down on May 1, 1960, and his Vienna summit meeting with President John F. Kennedy in June 1961 produced no progress either. Instead of a German agreement, he had to settle for the Berlin Wall which was constructed in August 1961.

By deploying nuclear missiles in Cuba in October 1962, Khrushchev aimed to protect Fidel Castro from an American invasion, to rectify the strategic nuclear imbalance, which had swung in America's favor, and just possibly to prepare the way for one last diplomatic offensive on Berlin. After he was forced ignominiously to remove those missiles, not only was Khrushchev's foreign policy momentum spent, but his domestic authority began to unravel. With so many of his domestic and foreign policies at dead ends, with diverse groups ranging from the military to the intelligentsia alienated, and with his own energy and confidence running down, the way was open for his colleagues, most of them his own appointees but by now disillusioned with him, to conspire against him. In October 1964, in contrast to 1957, the plotters prepared carefully and well. Led by Leonid Brezhnev, they confronted him with a united opposition in the Presidium and the Central Committee, and forced him to resign on grounds of age and health.

From 1964 to 1971 Khrushchev lived under de facto house arrest outside Moscow. Almost entirely isolated, he at first became ill and depressed. Later, he mustered the energy and determination to dictate his memoirs; the first ever by a Soviet leader, they also served as a harbinger of glasnost to come under Mikhail Gorbachev. Called in by party authorities to account for the Western publication of his memoirs, Khrushchev revealed the depth not only of his anger at his colleagues-turned-tormentors, but his deep sense of guilt at his complicity in Stalin's crimes. By the very end of his life, to judge by a Kremlin doctor's recollections, he was even losing faith in the cause of socialism.

After his death, Khrushchev became a "nonperson" in the USSR, his name suppressed by his successors and ignored by most Soviet citizens until the late 1980s, when his record received a burst of attention in connection with Gorbachev's new round of reform. Khrushchev's legacy, like his life, is remarkably mixed. Perhaps his most long-lasting bequest is the way his efforts at de-Stalinization, awkward and erratic though they were, prepared the ground for the reform and then the collapse of the Soviet Union.

See also: BREZHNEV, LEONID ILICH; COLD WAR; CUBAN MISSILE CRISIS; DE-STALINIZATION; STALIN, JOSEF VISSARIONOVICH; THAW, THE

BIBLIOGRAPHY

Breslauer, George. (1982). *Khrushchev and Brezhnev as Leaders: Building Authority in Soviet Politics.* Boston: Allen and Unwin.

Khrushchev, Nikita S. (1970). *Khrushchev Remembers,* tr. and ed. Strobe Talbott. Boston: Little, Brown.

Khrushchev, Nikita S. (1974). *Khrushchev Remembers: The Last Testament,* tr. and ed. Strobe Talbott. Boston: Little, Brown.

Khrushchev, Nikita S. (1990). *Khrushchev Remembers: The Glasnost Tapes,* tr. and ed. Jerrold L. Schecter with Vyacheslav Luchkov. Boston: Little, Brown.

Khrushchev, Sergei. (1990). *Khrushchev on Khrushchev,* tr. and ed. William Taubman. Boston: Little, Brown.

Khrushchev, Sergei N. (2000). *Nikita Khrushchev and the Creation of a Superpower,* tr. Shirley Benson. University Park: Penn State University Press.

Medvedev, Roy. (1983). *Khrushchev,* tr. Brian Pearce. Garden City, NY: Doubleday/Anchor.

Taubman, William. (2003). *Khrushchev: The Man and His Era.* New York: W. W. Norton.

Taubman, William; Khrushchev, Sergei; and Gleason Abbott, eds. (2000). *Nikita Khrushchev.* New Haven: Yale University Press.

Tompson, William J. (1995). *Khrushchev: A Political Life.* New York. St. Martin's.

William Taubman

KHUTOR

Although there were proposals dating from the early 1890s to establish small-scale farming based on the establishment of the khutor, it was not until the 1911 Stolypin rural reforms that the khutor came into existence as part of the land settlement provisions for "individual enclosures." The khutor lasted for three decades before it was eliminated by the Soviets. In contrast to the long-standing system of land ownership under which farms were held and worked in common by an entire village, under the Stolypin reforms an individual could now own a plot of land on which was also located his house and farm buildings. This totally self-contained farm unit was the khutor.

Never important as an agricultural institution either under the tsars or during the Soviet period, khutors, along with the closely related *otrub* (where only the farmland was enclosed), accounted for less than 8 percent of total farm output at its height before the Bolshevik Revolution and for a mere 3.5 percent of all peasant land as of January 1, 1927. Only in the northwest and western parts of the Russian Republic were khutors an important part of peasant agriculture—11 percent and 19 percent of all households, respectively.

Before collectivization in 1929, there were two forces causing the number of khutors to fluctuate in number. On the one hand, as a result of the revolution and the civil war that followed, many of the khutors once again became part of a communal mir. But, on the other hand, the 1922 Land Code permitted peasants to leave the mir, and in some places peasants were encouraged to create khutors. As a consequence, the number of khutors increased in the western provinces as well as the central industrial region of Russia.

In spite of its relative numerical unimportance, the khutor remained a thorn in the side of the Soviet leadership, who rightly saw the often prosperous khutor as inconsistent with the larger effort to socialize Soviet agriculture. The khutor, which existed alongside collective farm agriculture in the 1930s, was finally dissolved at the end of the decade. All peasant homes located on the khutors were to be destroyed by September 1, 1940, without compensation to the peasants who lived in them. Nearly 450,000 rural households were transferred to the collective farm villages. The khutor as a form of private agriculture in Russia became extinct.

See also: COLLECTIVIZATION OF AGRICULTURE; MIR; PEASANT ECONOMY; STOLYPIN, PETER ARKADIEVICH

BIBLIOGRAPHY

Danilov, V. P. (1988). *Rural Russia under the New Regime*. Bloomington: Indiana University Press.

Fitzpatrick, Sheila. (1994). *Stalin's Peasants: Resistance and Survival in the Russian Village after Collectivization*. New York: Oxford University Press.

WILLIAM MOSKOFF
CAROL GAYLE

KIEVAN CAVES PATERICON

The *Kievan Caves* Patericon is a monastic collection of tales about monks of the Caves Monastery of Kiev. It reflects the rich monastic practice and theology of the learned monks of the Kievan Caves Monastery. The core of the patericon is the epistolary works of Bishop Simon of Vladimir-Suzdal, a former Caves monk, and the monk Polikarp, to whom Simon addresses an epistle and accompanying stories, written between 1225 and his death in 1226. Ostensibly, Simon writes to Polikarp because he is appalled at the latter's ambition for a see and feels he must instruct him to remain in the holy Monastery of the Caves. Attempting to convince Polikarp to stay at the Caves, Simon attaches nine stories to his letter, which are intended to illustrate the holiness of the monastery and its inhabitants. There is no recorded response to Bishop Simon, but sometime prior to 1240, Polikarp wrote to his superior, the archimandrite Akindin, and attached to his brief missal eleven tales recounting the exploits of thirteen more monks.

To this core were added in various editions a number of disparate works associated with the Caves Monastery, including the *Life of Theodosius*. It is not clear when the collection began to be called a patericon (*paterik*), a word used to designate a number of Byzantine monastic collections translated into Slavic, but this title was not used in the oldest extant manuscript, the *Berseniev Witness*, which was copied in 1406 at the request of Bishop Arseny of Tver. A printed version appeared in 1661, which, though seriously flawed, was apparently quite popular, as it was reprinted many times up to the nineteenth century.

See also: CAVES MONASTERY; KIEVAN RUS

BIBLIOGRAPHY

Fedotov, George P. (1965). *The Russian Religious Mind*. New York: Harper Torchbooks.

The Paterik of the Kievan Caves Monastery. (1989). Tr. and intro. Muriel Heppell. Cambridge, MA, Harvard Ukrainian Research Institute.

DAVID K. PRESTEL

KIEVAN RUS

Kievan Rus, the first organized state located on the lands of modern Russia, Ukraine, and Belarus, was ruled by members of the Rurikid dynasty and centered around the city of Kiev from the mid-ninth century to 1240. Its East Slav, Finn, and Balt population dwelled in territories along the Dnieper, the Western Dvina, the Lovat-Volkhov, and the upper Volga rivers. Its component peoples and territories were bound together by common recognition of the Rurikid dynasty as their rulers and, after 988, by formal affiliation with the Christian Church, headed by the metropolitan based at Kiev. Kievan Rus was destroyed by the Mongol invasions of 1237–1240. The Kievan Rus era is considered a formative stage in the histories of modern Ukraine and Russia.

The process of the formation of the state is the subject of the Normanist controversy. Normanists stress the role of Scandinavian Vikings as key agents in the creation of the state. Their view builds upon archeological evidence of Scandinavian adventurers and travelling merchants in the region of northwestern Russia and the upper Volga from the eighth century. It also draws upon an account in the *Primary Chronicle*, compiled during the eleventh and early twelfth centuries, which reports that in 862, Slav and Finn tribes in the vicinity of the Lovat and Volkhov rivers invited Rurik, a Varangian Rus, and his brothers to bring order to their lands. Rurik and his descendants are regarded as the founders of the Rurikid dynasty that ruled Kievan Rus. Anti-Normanists discount the role of Scandinavians as founders of the state. They argue that the term Rus refers to the Slav tribe of Polyane, which dwelled in the region of Kiev, and that the Slavs themselves organized their own political structure.

According to the *Primary Chronicle*, Rurik's immediate successors were Oleg (r. 879 or 882 to 912), identified as a regent for Rurik's son Igor (r. 912–945); Igor's wife Olga (r. 945–c. 964), and their son Svyatoslav (r. c. 964–972). They established their authority over Kiev and surrounding tribes, including the Krivichi (in the region of the Valdai Hills), the Polyane (around Kiev on the Dneper River), the Drevlyane (south of the Pripyat River, a tributary of the Dneper), and the Vyatichi, who inhabited lands along the Oka and Volga Rivers.

The tenth-century Rurikids not only forced tribal populations to transfer their allegiance and their tribute payments from Bulgar and Khazaria, but also pursued aggressive policies toward those neighboring states. In 965 Svyatoslav launched a campaign against the Khazaria. His venture led to the collapse of the Khazar Empire and the destabilization of the lower Volga and the steppe, a region of grasslands south of the forests inhabited by the Slavs. His son Vladimir (r. 980–1015), having subjugated the Radimichi (east of the upper Dnieper River), attacked the Volga Bulgars in 985; the agreement he subsequently reached with the Bulgars was the basis for peaceful relations that lasted a century.

The early Rurikids also engaged their neighbors to the south and west. In 968, Svyatoslav rescued Kiev from the Pechenegs, a nomadic, steppe Turkic population. He devoted most of his attention, however, to establishing control over lands on the Danube River. Forced to abandon that project by the Byzantines, he was returning to Kiev when the Pechenegs killed him in 972. Frontier forts constructed and military campaigns waged by Vladimir and his sons reduced the Pecheneg threat to Kievan Rus.

Shortly after Svyatoslav's death, his son Yaropolk became prince of Kiev. But conflict erupted between him and his brothers. The crisis prompted Vladimir to flee from Novgorod, the city he governed, and raise an army in Scandinavia. Upon his return in 980, he first engaged the prince of Polotsk, one of last non-Rurikid rulers over East Slavs. Victorious, Vladimir married the prince's daughter and added the prince's military retinue to his own army, with which he then defeated Yaropolk and seized the throne of Kiev. Vladimir's triumphs over his brothers, competing non-Rurikid rulers, and neighboring powers provided him and his heirs a monopoly over political power in the region.

Prince Vladimir also adopted Christianity for Kievan Rus. Although Christianity, Judaism, and Islam had long been known in these lands and Olga had personally converted to Christianity, the populace of Kievan Rus remained pagan. When Vladimir assumed the throne, he attempted to create a single pantheon of gods for his people, but soon abandoned that effort in favor of Christianity. Renouncing his numerous wives and consorts, he married Anna, the sister of the Byzantine Emperor Basil. The Patriarch of Constantinople appointed a metropolitan to organize the see of Kiev and all Rus, and in 988, Byzantine clergy baptized the population of Kiev in the Dnieper River.

After adopting Christianity, Vladimir apportioned his realm among his principal sons, sending each of them to his own princely seat. A bishop accompanied each prince. The lands ruled by Rurikid princes and subject to the Kievan Church constituted Kievan Rus.

During the eleventh and twelfth centuries Vladimir's descendants developed a dynastic political structure to administer their increasingly large and complex realm. There are, however, divergent characterizations of the state's political development during this period. One view contends that Kievan Rus reached its peak during the eleventh century. The next century witnessed a decline, marked by the emergence of powerful autonomous principalities and warfare among their princes. Kiev lost its central role, and Kievan Rus was disintegrating by the time of the Mongol invasion. An alternate view emphasizes the continued vitality of the city of Kiev and argues that Kievan Rus retained its integrity throughout the period. Although it became an increasingly complex state containing numerous principalities that engaged in political and economic competition, dynastic and ecclesiastic bonds provided cohesion among them. The city of Kiev remained its acknowledged and coveted political, economic, and ecclesiastic center.

The creation of an effective political structure proved to be an ongoing challenge for the Rurikids. During the eleventh and twelfth centuries, princely administration gradually replaced tribal allegiance and authority. As early as the reign of Olga, her officials began to replace tribal leaders. Vladimir assigned a particular region to each of his sons, to whom he also delegated responsibility for tax collection, protection of communication and trade routes, and for local defense and territorial expansion. Each prince maintained and commanded his own military force, which was supported by tax revenues, commercial fees, and booty seized in battle. He also had the authority and the means to hire supplementary forces.

When Vladimir died in 1015, however, his sons engaged in a power struggle that ended only after four of them had died and two others, Yaroslav and Mstislav, divided the realm between them. When Mstislav died (1036), Yaroslav assumed full control over Kievan Rus. Yaroslav adopted a law code known as the Russkaya Pravda, which with amendments remained in force throughout the Kievan Rus era.

He also attempted to bring order to dynastic relations. Before his death he issued a "Testament" in which he left Kiev to his eldest son Izyaslav. He assigned Chernigov to his son Svyatoslav, Pereyaslavl to Vsevolod, and lesser seats to his younger sons. He advised them all to heed their eldest brother as they had their father. The Testament is understood by scholars to have established a basis for the rota system of succession, which incorporated the principles of seniority among the princes, lateral succession through a generation, and dynastic possession of the realm of Kievan Rus. By assigning Kiev to the senior prince, it elevated that city to a position of centrality within the realm.

This dynastic system, by which each prince conducted relations with his immediate neighbors, provided an effective means of defending and expanding Kievan Rus. It also encouraged cooperation among the princes when they faced crises. Incursions by the Polovtsy (Kipchaks, Cumans), Turkic nomads who moved into the steppe and displaced the Pechenegs in the second half of the eleventh century, prompted concerted action among Princes Izyaslav, Svyatoslav, and Vsevolod in 1068. Although the Polovtsy were victorious, they retreated after another encounter with Svyatoslav's forces. With the exception of one frontier skirmish in 1071, they then refrained from attacking Rus for the next twenty years.

When the Polovtsy did renew hostilities in the 1090s, the Rurikids were engaged in intradynastic conflicts. Their ineffective defense allowed the Polovtsy to reach the environs of Kiev and burn the Monastery of the Caves, founded in the mid-eleventh century. But after the princes resolved their differences at a conference in 1097, their coalitions drove the Polovtsy back into the steppe and broke up the federation of Polovtsy tribes responsible for the aggression. These campaigns yielded comparatively peaceful relations for the next fifty years.

As the dynasty grew larger, however, its system of succession required revision. Confusion and recurrent controversies arose over the definition of seniority, the standards for eligibility, and the lands subject to lateral succession. In 1097, when the intradynastic wars became so severe that they interfered with the defense against the Polovtsy, a princely conference at Lyubech resolved that each principality in Kievan Rus would become the hereditary domain of a specific branch of the dynasty. The only exceptions were Kiev itself, which in 1113 reverted to the status of a dynastic possession, and Novgorod, which by 1136 asserted the right to select its own prince.

The settlement at Lyubech provided a basis for orderly succession to the Kievan throne for the next forty years. When Svyatopolk Izyaslavich died, his cousin Vladimir Vsevolodich Monomakh became prince of Kiev (r. 1113–1125). He was succeeded by his sons Mstislav (r. 1125–1132) and Yaropolk (r. 1132–1139). But the Lyubech agreement also acknowledged division of the dynasty into distinct branches and Kievan Rus into distinct principalities. The descendants of Svyatoslav ruled Chernigov. Galicia and Volynia, located southwest of Kiev, acquired the status of separate principalities in the late eleventh and twelfth centuries, respectively. During the twelfth century, Smolensk, located north of Kiev on the upper Dnieper river, and Rostov-Suzdal, northeast of Kiev, similarly emerged as powerful principalities. The northwestern portion of the realm was dominated by Novgorod, whose strength rested on its lucrative commercial relations with Scandinavian and German merchants of the Baltic as well as on its own extensive empire that stretched to the Ural mountains by the end of the eleventh century.

The changing political structure contributed to repeated dynastic conflicts over succession to the Kievan throne. Some princes became ineligible for the succession to Kiev and concentrated on developing their increasingly autonomous realms. But the heirs of Vladimir Monomakh, who became the princes of Volynia, Smolensk, and Rostov-Suzdal, as well as the princes of Chernigov, became embroiled in succession disputes, often triggered by attempts of younger members to bypass the elder generation and to reduce the number of princes eligible for the succession.

The greatest confrontations occurred after the death of Yaropolk Vladimirovich, who had attempted to arrange for his nephew to be his successor and had thereby aroused objections from his own younger brother Yuri Dolgoruky, the prince of Rostov-Suzdal. As a result of the discord among Monomakh's heirs, Vsevolod Olgovich of Chernigov was able to take the Kievan throne (r. 1139–1146) and regain a place in the Kievan succession cycle for his dynastic branch. After his death, the contest between Yuri Dolgoruky and his nephews resumed; it persisted until 1154, when Yuri finally ascended to the Kievan throne and restored the traditional order of succession.

An even more destructive conflict broke out after the death in 1167 of Rostislav Mstislavich, successor to his uncle Yuri. When Mstislav Izyaslavich, the prince of Volynia and a member of the next generation, attempted to seize the Kievan throne, a coalition of princes opposed him. Led by Yuri's son Andrei Bogolyubsky, it represented the senior generation of eligible princes, but also included the sons of the late Rostislav and the princes of Chernigov. The conflict culminated in 1169, when Andrei's forces evicted Mstislav Izyaslavich from Kiev and sacked the city. Andrei's brother Gleb became prince of Kiev.

Prince Andrei personified the growing tensions between the increasingly powerful principalities of Kievan Rus and the state's center, Kiev. As prince of Vladimir-Suzdal (Rostov-Suzdal), he concentrated on the development of Vladimir and challenged the primacy of Kiev. Nerl Andrei used his power and resources, however, to defend the principle of generational seniority in the succession to Kiev. Nevertheless, after Gleb died in 1171, Andrei's coalition failed to secure the throne for another of his brothers. A prince of the Chernigov line, Svyatoslav Vsevolodich (r. 1173–1194), occupied the Kievan throne and brought dynastic peace.

By the turn of the century, eligibility for the Kievan throne was confined to three dynastic lines: the princes of Volynia, Smolensk, and Chernigov. Because the opponents were frequently of the same generation as well as sons of former grand princes, dynastic traditions of succession offered little guidance for determining which prince had seniority. By the mid-1230s, princes of Chernigov and Smolensk were locked in a prolonged conflict that had serious consequences. During the hostilities Kiev was sacked two more times, in 1203 and 1235. The strife revealed the divergence between the southern and western principalities, which were deeply enmeshed in the conflicts over Kiev, and those of the northeast, which were relatively indifferent to them. Intradynastic conflict, compounded by the lack of cohesion among the components of Kievan Rus, undermined the integrity of the realm. Kievan Rus was left without effective defenses before the Mongol invasion.

When the state of Kievan Rus was forming, its populace consisted primarily of rural agriculturalists who cultivated cereal grains as well as peas, lentils, flax, and hemp in natural forest clearings or in those they created by the slash-and-burn method. They supplemented these products by fishing, hunting, and gathering fruits, berries, nuts, mushrooms, honey, and other natural products in the forests around their villages.

Commerce, however, provided the economic foundation for Kievan Rus. The tenth-century Rurikid princes, accompanied by their military retinues, made annual rounds among their subjects and collected tribute. Igor met his death in 945 during such an excursion, when he and his men attempted to take more than the standard payment from the Drevlyane. After collecting the tribute of fur pelts, honey, and wax, the Kievan princes loaded their goods and captives in boats, also supplied by the local population, and made their way down the Dnieper River to the Byzantine market of Cherson. Oleg in 907 and Igor, less successfully, in 944 conducted military campaigns against Constantinople. The resulting treaties allowed the Rus to trade not only at Cherson, but also at Constantinople, where they had access to goods from virtually every corner of the known world. From their vantage point at Kiev the Rurikid princes controlled all traffic moving from towns to their north toward the Black Sea and its adjacent markets.

The Dnieper River route "from the Varangians to the Greeks" led back northward to Novgorod, which controlled commercial traffic with traders from the Baltic Sea. From Novgorod commercial goods also were carried eastward along the upper Volga River through the region of Rostov-Suzdal to Bulgar. At this market center on the mid-Volga River, which formed a nexus between the Rus and the markets of Central Asia and the Caspian Sea, the Rus exchanged their goods for oriental silver coins or dirhams (until the early eleventh century) and luxury goods including silks, glassware, and fine pottery.

The establishment of Rurikid political dominance contributed to changes in the social composition of the region. To the agricultural peasant population were added the princes themselves, their military retainers, servants, and slaves. The introduction of Christianity by Prince Vladimir brought a layer of clergy to the social mix. It also transformed the cultural face of Kievan Rus, especially in its urban centers. In Kiev Vladimir constructed the Church of the Holy Virgin (also known as the Church of the Tithe), built of stone and flanked by two other palatial structures. The ensemble formed the centerpiece of "Vladimir's city," which was surrounded by new fortifications. Yaroslav expanded "Vladimir's city" by building new fortifications that encompassed the battlefield on which he defeated the Pechenegs in 1036. Set in the southern wall was the Golden Gate of Kiev. Within the protected area Vladimir constructed a new complex of churches and palaces, the most imposing of which was the masonry Cathedral of St. Sophia, which was the church of the metropolitan and became the symbolic center of Christianity in Kievan.

The introduction of Christianity met resistance in some parts of Kievan Rus. In Novgorod a popular uprising took place when representatives of the new church threw the idol of the god Perun into the Volkhov River. But Novgorod's landscape was also quickly altered by the construction of wooden churches and, in the middle of the eleventh century, by its own stone Cathedral of St. Sophia. In Chernigov Prince Mstislav constructed the Church of the Transfiguration of Our Savior in 1035.

By agreement with the Rurikids the church became legally responsible for a range of social practices and family affairs, including birth, marriage, and death. Ecclesiastical courts had jurisdiction over church personnel and were charged with enforcing Christian norms and rituals in the larger community. Although the church received revenue from its courts, the clergy were only partially successful in their efforts to convince the populace to abandon pagan customs. But to the degree that they were accepted, Christian social and cultural standards provided a common identity for the diverse tribes comprising Kievan Rus society.

The spread of Christianity and the associated construction projects intensified and broadened commercial relations between Kiev and Byzantium. Kiev also attracted Byzantine artists and artisans, who designed and decorated the early Rus churches and taught their techniques and skills to local apprentices. Kiev correspondingly became the center of craft production in Kievan Rus during the eleventh and twelfth centuries.

While architectural design and the decorative arts of mosaics, frescoes, and icon painting were the most visible aspects of the Christian cultural transformation, Kievan Rus also received chronicles, saints' lives, sermons, and other literature from the Greeks. The outstanding literary works from this era were the *Primary Chronicle* or *Tale of Bygone Years*, compiled by monks of the Monastery of the Caves, and the "Sermon on Law and Grace," composed (c. 1050) by Metropolitan Hilarion, the first native of Kievan Rus to head the church.

During the twelfth century, despite the emergence of competing political centers within Kievan Rus and repeated sacks of it (1169, 1203, 1235), the city of Kiev continued to thrive economically.

Its diverse population, which is estimated to have reached between 36,000 and 50,000 persons by the end of the twelfth century, included princes, soldiers, clergy, merchants, artisans, unskilled workers, and slaves. Its expanding handicraft sector produced glassware, glazed pottery, jewelry, religious items, and other goods that were exported throughout the lands of Rus. Kiev also remained a center of foreign commerce, and increasingly re-exported imported goods, exemplified by Byzantine amphorae used as containers for oil and wine, to other Rus towns as well.

The proliferation of political centers within Kievan Rus was accompanied by a diffusion of the economic dynamism and increasing social complexity that characterized Kiev. Novgorod's economy also continued to be centered on its trade with the Baltic region and with Bulgar. By the twelfth century artisans in Novgorod were also engaging in new crafts, such as enameling and fresco painting. Novgorod's flourishing economy supported a population of twenty to thirty thousand by the early thirteenth century. Volynia and Galicia, Rostov-Suzdal, and Smolensk, whose princes vied politically and military for Kiev, gained their economic vitality from their locations on trade routes. The construction of the masonry Church of the Mother of God in Smolensk (1136–1137) and of the Cathedral of the Dormition (1158) and the Golden Gate in Vladimir reflected the wealth concentrated in these centers. Andrei Bogolyubsky also constructed his own palace complex of Bogolyubovo outside Vladimir and celebrated a victory over the Volga Bulgars in 1165 by building the Church of the Intercession nearby on the Nerl River. In each of these principalities the princes' boyars, officials, and retainers were forming local, landowning aristocracies and were also becoming consumers of luxury items produced abroad, in Kiev, and in their own towns.

In 1223 the armies of Chingis Khan, founder of the Mongol Empire, first reached the steppe south of Kievan Rus. At the Battle of Kalka they defeated a combined force of Polovtsy and Rus drawn from Kiev, Chernigov, and Volynia. The Mongols returned in 1236, when they attacked Bulgar. In 1237–1238 they mounted an offensive against Ryazan and then Vladimir-Suzdal. In 1239 they devastated the southern towns of Pereyaslavl and Chernigov, and in 1240 conquered Kiev.

The state of Kievan Rus is considered to have collapsed with the fall of Kiev. But the Mongols went on to subordinate Galicia and Volynia before invading both Hungary and Poland. In the aftermath of their conquest, the invaders settled in the vicinity of the lower Volga River, forming the portion of the Mongol Empire commonly known as the Golden Horde. Surviving Rurikid princes made their way to the horde to pay homage to the Mongol khan. With the exception of Prince Michael of Chernigov, who was executed, the khan confirmed each of the princes as the ruler in his respective principality. He thus confirmed the disintegration of Kievan Rus.

See also: OLGA; PRIMARY CHRONICLE; ROUTE TO GREEKS; VIKINGS; YAROSLAV VLADIMIROVICH

BIBLIOGRAPHY

Chronicle of Novgorod, 1016–1471, tr. Robert Michell and Nevill Forbes. (1914). London: Royal Historical Society.

Dimnik, Martin. (1994). *The Dynasty of Chernigov 1054–1146.* Toronto: Pontifical Institute of Mediaeval Studies.

Fennell, John. (1983). *The Crisis of Medieval Russia 1200–1304.* London: Longman.

Franklin, Simon, and Shepard, Jonathan. (1996). *The Emergence of Rus 750–1200.* London: Longman.

Kaiser, Daniel H. (1980) *The Growth of Law in Medieval Russia.* Princeton, NJ: Princeton University Press.

Martin, Janet. (1995). *Medieval Russia 980–1584.* Cambridge, UK: Cambridge University Press.

Poppe, Andrzej. (1982). *The Rise of Christian Russia.* London: Variorum Reprints.

The Russian Primary Chronicle, Laurentian Text, tr. Samuel Hazzard Cross and Olgerd P. Sherbowitz-Wetzor. (1953). Cambridge, MA: Medieval Academy of America.

Shchapov, Yaroslav Nikolaevich. (1993). *State and Church in Early Russia, Tenth–Thirteenth Centuries.* New Rochelle, NY: Aristide D. Caratzas.

Vernadsky, George. (1948). *Kievan Russia.* New Haven, CT: Yale University Press.

JANET MARTIN

KIPCHAKS *See* POLOVTSY.

KIREYEVSKY, IVAN VASILIEVICH

(1806–1856), the most important ideologist of Russian Slavophilism, along with Alexei Khomyakov.

The promulgation of Slavophilism in the middle third of the nineteenth century marked the turn from Enlightenment cosmopolitanism to the fixation on national identity that has dominated much of Russian culture since that time. No life better suggests that crucial change in Russian cultural consciousness than Kireyevsky's. He first ventured into publicism as the editor of a journal that he called *The European.* The journal appeared in 1830, but was suppressed by the government after only two issues, almost entirely on the basis of a fanciful reading of Kireyevsky's important essay, *The Nineteenth Century*, in the inflamed atmosphere created by the European revolutions of that year. This traumatic event helped to end the Western orientation of Kireyevsky's earlier career and led to a series of new relationships, which, taken together, constituted a conversion to romantic nationalism.

Kireyevsky's childhood was spent in Moscow and on the family estate (Dolbino) in the vicinity of Tula and Orel, where the Kireyevsky family had been based since the sixteenth century. His father died of cholera during the French invasion of 1812, and he, his brother Peter, and their sisters were raised by their beautiful and intelligent mother, A. P. Elagina, who was the hostess of one of Moscow's most influential salons during the 1830s and 1840s. The poet Vasily Zhukovsky, her close friend, played some role in Kireyevsky's early education and he had at least a nodding acquaintance with other major figures in Russian culture, including Pushkin.

Kireyevsky studied with Moscow University professors in the 1820s, although he did not actually attend the university. There, under the influence of Professor Mikhail Grigorevich Pavlov, his interests shifted from enlightenment thinkers to the metaphysics of Friedrich Wilhelm Schelling. After graduation he became one of the so-called archive youth, to whom Pushkin refers in *Eugene Onegin*; he also frequented an informal grouping known as the Raich Circle, as well as a kind of inner circle drawn from it, called the Lovers of Wisdom (*Obshchestvo Liubomudriya*), devoted to romantic and esoteric knowledge.

After producing some literary criticism for the *Moscow Messenger*, Kireyevsky spent ten months in Germany, cultivating his new intellectual interest in German philosophy. He was entertained by Hegel in Berlin and attended some of Schelling's lectures in Munich, but, like many a Russian traveler, he was homesick for Russia and returned earlier than he had planned. The outbreak of cholera in Moscow was the official reason for his hasty return.

After the fiasco of the *European*, Kireyevsky underwent an intellectual and spiritual crisis from which he emerged, at the end of the 1830s, a considerably changed man: married, converted to Orthodoxy, and purged of many Western aspects of his former outlook. His wife's religiosity; his brother's interest in Russian peasant culture, and his new friend Alexei Khomyakov's belief in the superiority of Orthodox practice over the Western confessions all worked on him profoundly.

The immediate catalyst for the first Slavophile writings, however, was the famous "First Philosophical Letter" of Peter Chaadayev, which appeared in a Moscow journal in 1836. Chaadayev famously found Russia's past and present stagnant, sterile, and ahistorical, largely because Russia had severed itself from the Roman and Catholic West. The discussion between Kireyevsky, Khomyakov, and their younger followers over the next several decades constituted a collective "answer to Chaadayev." Orthodox Christianity, according to the Slavophiles, actually benefited from its separation from pagan and Christian Rome. Orthodoxy had been spared the rationalism and legalism which had been taken into the Roman Catholic Church, from Aristotle, through Roman legalism, to scholasticism and Papal hierarchy. Russian society had thus been able to develop harmoniously and communally. Although, since Peter the Great, the Russian elite had been seduced by the external power and glamor of secular Europe, the Russian peasants had preserved much of the old, pre-Petrine Russian culture in their social forms, especially in the peasant communal structure. Kireyevsky and the other Slavophiles hoped that these popular survivals, combined with an Orthodox revival in the present, could restore Russian culture to its proper bases. Kireyevsky expressed these ideas in a series of short-lived journals, which appeared under the editorship of various Slavophile individuals and groups. The Slavophile sketch of the patrimonial and traditional monarchy of the pre-Petrine period is largely fanciful, as is that of the social and political life dominated by a variety of communal forms, but such sketches constituted a highly effective indirect attack on the Russia of Nicholas I and on the development of European industrialism. Kireyevsky's Slavophilism, with its curious blend of traditionalism, libertarianism, and communalism, has left unmistakable marks on virtually all variants of Russian nationalism and social romanticism since his time. Although his written legacy was limited to a few articles, Ivan Kireyevsky was the philosopher of Slavophilism, just as Khomyakov was its theologian.

See also: KHOMYAKOV, ALEXEI STEPANOVICH; SLAVOPHILES

BIBLIOGRAPHY

Christoff, Peter. (1972). *An Introduction to Nineteenth-Century Russian Slavophilism: A Study in Ideas, Vol. 2: I. V. Kireevsky.* The Hague: Mouton.

Gleason, Abbott. (1972). *European and Muscovite: Ivan Kireevsky and the Origins of Slavophilism.* Cambridge, MA: Harvard University Press.

Walicki, Andrzej. (1975). *The Slavophile Controversy: History of a Conservative Utopia in Nineteenth-Century Russian Thought.* Oxford: Clarendon.

ABBOTT GLEASON

KIRILL-BELOOZERO MONASTERY

The Kirill-Beloozero Monastery was founded in 1397 in the far Russian north as a hermitage dedicated to the Dormition of the Virgin. Its founder was Cyril of Belozersk, conversant of Sergius of Radonezh, hesychast (mystical hermit), and former abbot of Simonov Monastery. It rapidly gained brethren, land, and renown. At Cyril's death in 1427, its patron was the prince of Belozersk-Mozhaisk, and its titular head was the Archbishop of Rostov, to whom Kirillov was administratively subordinated by 1478.

Social and administrative reforms occurred under Abbot Trifon, who lived from about 1434 to about 1517. Trifon was a monk of the Athos-linked St. Savior Monastery on the Rock, and later became Archbishop of Rostov (1462–1467). At this point the monastery gained the name "Kirillov" and, probably, its strict cenobitic (communal-disciplinarian) rule. It entered a relationship with the Moscow authorities. During the civil wars, Trifon loosed Basil II from his cross oath to Dmitry Shemyaka (1446); Cyril was canonized in 1448 and his *vita* (life) was written by Pachomius the Logothete in 1462. Trifon's successor and fellow St. Savior monk, Abbot Cassian, who lived from about 1447 until about 1469, went on a Moscow embassy to the ecumenical patriarch in Constantinople.

During Trifon's abbacy, a Byzantine-influenced school flourished, where basic texts of grammar, logic, cosmology, and history circulated. Its legacy was a bibliographical trend whose representatives (such as Efrosin, fl. 1463–1491) compiled and catalogued much of the literary inheritance of Bulgaria, Kievan Rus, and Serbia, and edited important works of Muscovite literature (such as the epic *Zadonshchina*) and chronography (the *First Sophia Chronicle*). Kirillov's great library (1,304 books by 1621) has survived almost intact.

From 1484 to 1514, Kirillov was a focal point for the Non-Possessors, abbots and monks—including Gury Tushin, Nilus Sorsky, and Vassian Patrikeev—who rejected monastic estates and promoted hesychast ideals of mental prayer and hermitism. After 1515, Kirillov followed the Possessor trend, whose first leader, Joseph of Volok, had praised the cenobitic discipline of several of its early abbots. Kirillov's sixteenth-century abbots achieved high rank, such as Afanasy (1539–1551), later bishop of Suzdal, whom Andrew Kurbsky called "silver-loving," and from 1530 to 1570 their landholdings expanded terrifically (at mid-seventeenth century Kirillov was the fifth-largest landowner in Muscovy).

Attracting wealth, privileges, and pilgrims from the central government as well as the boyar aristocracy, Kirillov lost self-governance to Moscow. Ivan IV, whose birth was ascribed to St. Cyril's intervention and who expressed a wish to join Kirillov's brethren in 1567, took over its administration, lecturing its abbot and boyar monks (such as Ivan-Jonah Sheremetev) on piety in a letter of 1573. (Boris Godunov later selected Kirillov's abbot, and the False Dmitry chose its monks.) By the mid-sixteenth century, Kirillov had become fiscally subject to the bishop of Vologda, and by century's end to the patriarch.

In the 1590s Kirillov was transformed from a cultural center into a fortress, with stone towers and walls that withstood Polish-Lithuanian attacks during the Time of Troubles. Its infirmary treated monks and laymen, and its icon-painting and stonemasonry workshops sold their wares to Muscovites. Kirillov was also used as a prison. Its most illustrious detainee, Patriarch Nikon, was held in solitary confinement from 1676 to 1681 without access to his library, paper, or ink.

From the eighteenth century, Kirillov lost its military importance, and an economic and spiritual decline began. It was closed by Soviet authorities in 1924 and transformed into a museum. In 1998 monastic life at Kirillov was partly restored.

See also: CAVES MONASTERY; SIMONOV MONASTERY; TRINITY ST. SERGIUS MONASTERY

BIBLIOGRAPHY

Fedotov, George P. (1966). *The Russian Religious Mind.* Vol. II: *The Middle Ages. The Thirteenth to the Fifteenth Centuries.* Cambridge, MA: Harvard University Press.

ROBERT ROMANCHUK

KIRIYENKO, SERGEI VLADILENOVICH

(b. 1962), former prime minister of the Russian Federation and a leader of the liberal party Union of Right Forces.

Kiriyenko was born in Sukumi, which is presently in Abkhazia, nominally a part of the Republic of Georgia. In 1993 he received a degree in economic leadership from the Academy of Economics. Soon he founded a bank, Garantiya, in Nizhny Novgorod. He was so successful that the governor, Boris Nemtsov, recommended that he take over the nearly bankrupt oil company, Norsi. He succeeded once again, breaking the apathy that allowed a bad situation to fester. He first threatened to close the company, hoping this would spur workers' efficiency. It did not. So he worked out a complicated restructuring plan that involved tax breaks and new negotiations with workers, suppliers, and buyers. Kiriyenko managed to convince all parties that it was in their joint interests to increase production, and within a year production increased about 300 percent.

Kiriyenko now had a national reputation, and Russian President Boris Yeltsin made him minister for fuel and energy in 1997. In this capacity he favorably impressed American President Bill Clinton's Russian specialist Strobe Talbott. In March 1998 Yeltsin shocked Russia and the world when he fired his long-time prime minister, Viktor Chernomyrdin, and announced his intention to replace him with Kiriyenko. There ensued a bitter battle between Yeltsin and the Duma over Kiriyenko's appointment. Only on the third and last vote did the Duma confirm Kiriyenko. In his first speech as prime minister, Kiriyenko pointed out that Russia faced "an enormous number of problems."

Despite his talents, Kiriyenko could not change some basic facts. By July 1998 unpaid wages totaled 66 billion rubles ($11 billion); service of the government debt consumed almost 50 percent of the budget; the price of oil, one of Russia's chief exports, was falling; and a financial crisis in Asia had investors fleeing "emerging markets," Russia included. In June a desperate Yeltsin telephoned Clinton to ask him to intervene in the deliberations of the International Monetary Fund on Russia's behalf. It was too late. In August the Russian government in effect declared bankruptcy, and Yeltsin dismissed the Kiriyenko government. As of June 2003, Kiriyenko was president of Russia's chemical weapons disarmament commission.

See also: NEMTSOV, BORIS IVANOVICH; UNION OF RIGHT FORCES; YELTSIN, BORIS NIKOLAYEVICH

BIBLIOGRAPHY

Aron, Leon. (2000). *Yeltsin: A Revolutionary Life.* London: HarperCollins.

Talbott, Strobe. (2002). *The Russia Hand: A Memoir of Presidential Diplomacy* New York: Random House.

HUGH PHILLIPS

KIROV, SERGEI MIRONOVICH

(1886–1934), Leningrad Party secretary and Politburo member.

Born in 1886 as Sergei Mironovich Kostrikov in Urzhum, in the northern Russian province of Viatka, Kirov was abandoned by his father and left orphaned by his mother. He spent much of his childhood in an orphanage before training as a mechanic at a vocational school in the city of Kazan from 1901 to 1904. He became involved in radical political activity during his student years, after which he moved to Tomsk and joined the Social Democratic Party, garnering attention as a local party activist before the age of twenty. Kirov joined the Bolshevik Party and was arrested in 1906 for his activities in the revolutionary events of 1905 in Tomsk. After his release in 1909, he moved to Vladikavkaz and resumed his career as a professional revolutionary, taking a job with a local liberal newspaper and changing his last name to Kirov. He continued his party activities in the Caucasus in the years before the October Revolution, serving in various capacities as one of the leading Bolsheviks in the Caucasus during the Revolution and civil war eras. Kirov occupied the post of secretary of the Azerbaijan Central Committee from 1921 to 1926. In 1926 he became a candidate mem-

Sergei Kirov, the popular leader of the Leningrad Party Committee, was assassinated in 1934. © BETTMANN/CORBIS

ber of the Politburo and took the position of first secretary of the Leningrad Provincial Party organization, playing a major role in the political defeat of Grigory Zinoviev by Josef Stalin. Kirov gained full Politburo membership in 1930 and retained his position as head of the Leningrad Party organization until his death in 1934.

On December 1, 1934, a lone gunman named Leonid Nikolaev murdered Kirv at the Leningrad party headquarters. Kirov's murder served as a pretext for a wave of repression that was carried out by Stalin in 1935 and 1936 against former political oppositionists, including Zinoviev and Lev Kamenev, and against large sectors of the Leningrad population. The connection between Kirov's death and the coordinated repression of 1935 and 1936 has led numerous contemporary observers, as well as later scholars, to speculate that Stalin himself arranged the murder in order to justify an attack on his political opponents. Proponents of this theory argue that Kirov represented a moderate opposition to Stalin in the years 1930 to 1933, in particular as an opponent to Stalin's demand in 1932 for the execution of the oppositionist Mikhail Riutin; they also argue that provincial-level party bosses wanted to replace Stalin with Kirov as general secretary of the Bolshevik Party at the Seventeenth Congress in 1934. Archival research carried out after the fall of the USSR has generally failed to support these claims, suggesting instead that Kirov was a dedicated Stalinist and that Kirov's murderer was a disgruntled party member working without instruction from higher authorities. Stalin's repressive response to the Kirov murder was likely a cynical use of the assassination for his own political ends as well as a genuine response of shock at the murder of a high-level Bolshevik official. Proponents of Stalin's responsibility, however, have not conceded the argument, and the debate is unlikely to be resolved without substantial additional evidence.

See also: CIVIL WAR OF 1917–1922; OCTOBER REVOLUTION; PURGES, THE GREAT; SOCIAL DEMOCRATIC WORKERS PARTY; STALIN, JOSEF VISSARIONOVICH

BIBLIOGRAPHY

Conquest, Robert. (1989). *Stalin and the Kirov Murder.* New York: Oxford University Press.

Knight, Amy. (1999). *Who Killed Kirov?* New York: Hill and Wang.

Lenoe, Matt. (2002). "Did Stalin Kill Kirov and Does It Matter?" *The Journal of Modern History* 74: 352–80.

PAUL M. HAGENLOH

KLYUCHEVSKY, VASILY OSIPOVICH

(1841–1911), celebrated Russian historian.

Vasily Klyuchevsky was born to the family of a priest of Penza province. In 1865 he graduated from the Moscow University (Historical-Philological Department). In 1872 he earned a master's degree and in 1882 a doctorate. In 1879 he became associate professor, and in 1882 professor, of Russian history at Moscow University. He was named corresponding member of the Russian Academy of Sciences in 1889 and academician of history and Russian antiquities in 1900. Klyuchevsky was connected with government and church circles. From 1893 to 1895 he taught history to Grand Duke Georgy, son of Alexander II. In 1905 he took part in a conference organized by Nicholas II on the new press regulations and also participated in conferences on designing the state Duma. He was the holder of many decorations and in 1903 was given the rank of Privy Councilor. After legalization of political parties in October 1905, Klyuchevsky ran for election to the First State Duma on the Constitutional Democratic ticket, but lost.

Klyuchevsky was a pupil and follower of Sergei Solovev and his successor in the Department of Russian History at Moscow University. His main works are: (1) *Drevne-russkie zhitiya sviatykh kak istorichesky istochnik* (*The Old Russian Hagiography as a Historical Source*), published in 1872, in which he proved that hagiography did not contain reliable historical facts; (2) *Boiarskaya Duma drevnei Rusi* (*The Boyar Duma of Old Russia*), published in 1882, in which he studied the history of the most important government institution in pre-Petrine Russia; (3) *Proiskhozhdenie krepostnogo prava v Rossii* (*The Genesis of Serfdom in Russia*), published in 1885, in which he suggested a new conception of the origin of serfdom according to which serfdom was engendered by peasants' debts to landowners and developed on the basis of private-legal relations, the state only legalizing it; (4) *Podushnaya podat i otmena kholopstva v Rossii* (*Poll-Tax and the Abolition of Bond Slavery in Russia*), published in 1885, in which he showed that a purely financial reform had serious socio-economic consequences; and (5) *Sostav predstavitelstva na zemskikh soborakh drevnei Rusi* (*The Composition of Representatives at Assemblies of the Land in Old Russia*), published in 1892, in which he substantiated the point of view that the assemblies were not representative institutions. Klyuchevsky prepared a number of special courses on source study, historiography of the eighteenth century, methodology, and terminology and wrote many articles on the history of Russian culture.

Starting in 1879 Klyuchevsky taught a general course on Russian history from the ancient times to the Great Reforms of the 1860s and 1870s. This course is regarded as a summation of his research findings and interpretations. Klyuchevsky believed that world history developed in accordance with certain objective regularities, "peoples consecutively replacing one another as successive moments of civilization, as phases of the development of humankind," and that in the history of an individual country these regularities play out under the influence of particular local conditions. He analyzed Russian history through three principal categories: the individual, society, and environment. In his opinion, these elements determined the process of a country's historical development. The objective of his course was to discover the "secret" of Russian history: to assess what had been done and what had to be done to put the developing Russian society into the first rank of European nations. In his opinion, a student who mastered his course should become "a citizen who acts consciously and conscientiously," capable of rectifying the shortcomings of the social system of Russia.

Klyuchevsky was a positivist and tried to attain positive scientific knowledge in his course. However, from the point of view of his admirers, the most valuable and attractive feature of his course consisted in his artistic descriptions of historical events and phenomena, replete with vivid images and everyday scenes of the past; his original analysis of sources and psychological analysis of historical figures; and his skeptical and liberal judgments and evaluations—in other words, in his figurative and intuitive comprehension and artistic representations of the past. He spoke ironically of the shortcomings of the social system, social institutions, manners, and customs, and censured the faults of tsars and statesmen. All these qualities attracted crowds of students who understood his ideas of the past as comments on current conditions. His course exhibited such mastery of literary style that in 1908 he was named an honorary member of Russian Academy of Sciences in belles lettres.

At the Moscow University Klyuchevsky created his own school, which prepared such prominent historians as Alexander Kizevetter, Matvei Lyubavskii, Yuri Got'e, Pavel Milyukov, and others. Klyuchevsky's works continue to enjoy popularity and to influence historiography in Russia to this day.

See also: EDUCATION; HISTORIOGRAPHY; UNIVERSITIES

BIBLIOGRAPHY

Byrnes, Robert F. (1995). *V. O. Kliuchevskii: Historian of Russia*. Bloomington: University of Indiana Press.

Kliuchevskii, V. O. (1960). *A History of Russia*, tr. C. J. Hogarth. New York: Russell and Russell.

Kliuchevskii, V. O. (1961). *Peter the Great*, tr. Liliana Archibald. New York: Vintage.

Kliuchevskii, V. O. (1968). *Course in Russian History: The Seventeenth Century*, tr. Natalie Duddington. Chigago: Quadrangle Books.

BORIS N. MIRONOV

KOKOSHIN, ANDREI AFANASIEVICH

(b. 1946), member of the State Duma; deputy chairman of the Duma Committee on Industry, Construction, and High Technologies; chairman of Expert Councils for biotechnologies and information technologies; director of the Institute for International Security Studies of the Russian Academy of Sciences; chairman of the Russian National Council for the Development of Education.

A graduate of Bauman Technical Institute, Kokoshin worked for two decades with the Institute of the United States and Canada of the Academy of Sciences (ISKAN), rising to the position of deputy director and establishing a reputation as one of the leading experts on U.S. defense and security policy. He received his doctorate in political science and is a member of the Academy of Natural Sciences.

In the late 1980s Kokoshin collaborated on a series of articles that promoted a radical change in Soviet defense policy, supporting international disengagement, domestic reform, and the technological-organizational requirements of the Revolution in Military Affairs. In 1991 he opposed the August Coup. With the creation of the Russian Ministry of Defense in May 1992, he was appointed first deputy minister of defense with responsibility for the defense industry and research and development. In May 1997 Russian President Boris Yeltsin named him head of the Defense Council and the State Military Inspectorate. In March 1998 Yeltsin appointed him head of the Security Council. In the aftermath of the fiscal crisis of August 1998, Yeltsin fired Kokoshin. In 1999 Kokoshin ran successfully for the State Duma.

Kokoshin has written extensively on U.S. national security policy and Soviet military doctrine. He championed the intellectual contributions of A. A. Svechin to modern strategy and military art. His *Soviet Strategic Thought, 1917–1991*, was published by MIT Press in 1998.

See also: SVECHIN, ALEXANDER

BIBLIOGRAPHY

Kipp, Jacob W. (1999). "Forecasting Future War: Andrei Kokoshin and the Military-Political Debate in Contemporary Russia." Ft. Leavenworth: Foreign Military Studies Office.

Kokoshin, A. A., and Konovalov, A. A. eds. (1989). *Voenno-tekhnicheskaia politika SShA v 80-e gody.* Moscow: Nauka.

Larionov, Valentin, and Kokoshin, Andrei. (1991). *Prevention of War: Doctrines, Concepts, Prospects.* Moscow: Progress Publishers.

Jacob W. Kipp

KOLCHAK, ALEXANDER VASILIEVICH

(1873–1920), admiral, supreme ruler of White forces during the Russian civil war.

Following his father's example, Alexander Kolchak attended the Imperial Naval Academy, and graduated second in his class in 1894. After a tour in the Pacific Fleet and participation in scientific expeditions to the Far North, he saw active duty during the Russo-Japanese War (1904–1905). By July 1916 he merited promotion to vice-admiral and command of the Russian Black Sea Fleet.

Kolchak continued to serve under the Provisional Government following the February Revolution of 1917, but resigned his command when discipline broke down in his ranks. At the time of the Bolshevik seizure of power in October, Kolchak was abroad. But he responded with alacrity to the invitation of General Dimitry L. Horvath, manager of the Chinese Eastern Railway, to help coordinate the anti-Bolshevik forces in Manchuria.

White resistance to Soviet rule was also mounting along the Volga and in western Siberia, as well as in the Cossack regions of southern Russia. During May and June 1918 in Samara, KOMUCH (Committee of Members of the Constituent Assembly)—a moderate socialist government with pretensions to national legitimacy—emerged to compete with the even more anti-Bolshevik but autonomist-minded Provisional Siberian Government (PSG) in Omsk for leadership of the White cause. Under pressure from the Allies, KOMUCH agreed to merge with PSG into a five-man Directory as a united front against the Bolsheviks in September 1918. But the short-lived Directory lasted only until November 18. On that day, Kolchak was appointed dictator with the ambitious title of supreme ruler of Russia—and in due course recognized as such by the two other main White military commanders, Anton Denikin in the south and Nikolai Yudenich in the Baltic region.

The arrival of French General Maurice Janin, as commander-in-chief of all Allied forces in Russia, complicated the issue of the chain of command

and authority. Its significance became obvious when Janin and the "Czechoslovak Legion" (prisoners-of-war from the Austro-Hungarian Army who were in the process of being repatriated with Allied assistance) took over guarding the Trans-Siberian railway and proceeded at their discretion to block the passage of the supreme ruler's echelons.

While Kolchak's British-trained army came to number approximately 200,000 men (with a very high proportion of officers), it was never an effective fighting machine. Moreover, the admiral failed to implement a popular political program. Indeed, he was unable to unite the White forces completely, even in Siberia and the Far East. The Russian heartland remained under control of the Bolsheviks, and their depiction of the admiral as a tool of the old regime and foreign interests had enough of the ring of truth.

For Kolchak the military tide turned decisively in the summer of 1919. In mid-November his capital in Omsk fell. By late December, the chastened supreme ruler was in the less-than-sympathetic custody of Janin and the hastily departing Czech Legion. Consequently, even his safe passage to Irkutsk—where the moderate socialist Political Center had just taken over—could not be guaranteed. When the Center demanded Kolchak as the price of letting the Legion and Janin go through, the Admiral was unceremoniously surrendered on January 15, 1920. To forestall Kolchak's rescue by other retreating White forces, he was shot early on February 7. His dignified conduct at the end has long been admired by White emigrés, and since the collapse of the Soviet Union, Kolchak's reputation has undergone a dramatic rehabilitation in Russia as well.

See also: CIVIL WAR OF 1917–1922; WHITE ARMY

BIBLIOGRAPHY

Dotsenko, Paul. (1983). *The Struggle for a Democracy in Siberia, 1917–1921*. Stanford, CA: Hoover Institution Press.

Pereira, N. G. O. (1996). *White Siberia*. Montreal: McGill-Queens University Press.

Smele, Jonathan D. (1996). *Civil War in Siberia*. Cambridge, UK: Cambridge University Press.

Varneck, Elena, and Fisher, H. H., eds. (1935). *The Testimony of Kolchak and Other Siberian Materials*. Stanford, CA: Stanford University Press.

N. G. O. PEREIRA

KOLKHOZ *See* COLLECTIVE FARM; COLLECTIVIZATION OF AGRICULTURE.

KOLLONTAI, ALEXANDRA MIKHAILOVNA

(1872–1952), theoretician of Marxist feminism; founder of Soviet Communist Party's Women's Department.

Kollontai was born Alexandra Domontovich. Her father, Mikhail Domontovich, was a politically liberal general. Her mother, Alexandra, shared Domontovich's free-thinking attitudes and supported feminism as well. They provided their daughter a comfortable childhood and good education, including college-level work at the Bestuzhevsky Courses for Women. When Alexandra was twenty-two, she married Vladimir Kollontai. Within a year she had given birth to a son, Mikhail, but the matronly life soon bored her. She dabbled in volunteer work and then decided in 1898 to study Marxism so as to become a radical journalist and scholar.

Between 1900 and 1917 Kollontai participated in the revolutionary underground in Russia, but mostly she lived abroad, where she made her reputation as a theoretician of Marxist feminism. To Friedrich Engels' and Avgust Bebel's economic analysis of women's oppression Kollontai added a psychological dimension. She argued that women internalized society's values, learning to accept their subordination to men. There was hope, however, for the coming revolution would usher in a society in which women and men were equals and would therefore create the conditions for women to emancipate their psyches. In the meantime socialists should work hard to draw working-class women to their movement. Kollontai was a severe critic of feminism, which she considered a bourgeois movement, but she shared with the feminists a deep commitment to women's emancipation as a primary goal of social reform.

In the prerevolutionary period Kollontai also became known as a skilled journalist and orator. She was a Menshevik, but in 1913, when Bolsheviks Konkordia Samoilova, Inessa Armand, and Nadezhda Krupskaya launched a newspaper aimed at working-class women, they invited Kollontai to be a contributor. She responded enthusiastically. In 1915 she came over to their faction because she believed that Vladimir Lenin was the only Russian Social-Democratic leader who was resolute in his opposition to World War I.

Kollontai returned to Russia in the spring of 1917. She spent the revolutionary year working with other Bolshevik feminists on projects among working-class women. She also became one of the Bolsheviks' most effective speakers; her popularity earned her election to the Central Committee. After the party seized power in October, Kollontai became Commissar of Social Welfare, and in that capacity she laid the foundation for socialized obstetrical and newborn care. In early March 1918 she resigned her post to protest the Brest-Litovsk Treaty with Germany, and for the next two years she divided her energies between agitation on the front, writing, and organizing activities with working-class women. In fall 1920 she was appointed head of the Zhenotdel, the Communist Party's Women's Department.

Kollontai had argued for a woman's department since before the revolution. When she became its head she worked diligently to build up the organization, which suffered from poor funding and lack of support. She managed to stave off efforts to abolish the Zhenotdel and also publicized widely the party's program for women's emancipation. Kollontai's tenure in this office was short, however, because in 1921 she joined the Workers Opposition, a group critical of Party authoritarianism. She was fired from the Zhenotdel the next year.

In the following two decades Kollontai became a distinguished Soviet diplomat. She served as Soviet ambassador to Sweden from 1930 to her retirement in 1945. Her most important contribution was as mediator in negotiations to end the Winter War between the USSR and Finland (1939–1940). In the 1920s she also published novels and essays that analyzed the gender and sexual liberation that would come with the construction of a communist society. These works drew strong criticism from more conservative communists, and Kollontai ceased to publish on her favorite subject after the Stalinist leadership consolidated power in the late 1920s. Thereafter she wrote multiple versions of her memoirs. She survived the party purges in the 1930s, probably because she was a respected diplomat who lived far away from party politics.

Kollontai died in Moscow on March 9, 1952. With the revival of feminism in the 1960s, her writings were rediscovered, and she came again to be seen an important Marxist feminist.

Diplomat, feminist, and revolutionary, Alexandra Kollontai was the world's first female ambassador.

See also: ARMAND, INESSA; BOLSHEVISM; FEMINISM; KRUPSKAYA, NADEZHDA; SAMOILOVA, KONKORDIA; ZHENOTDEL

BIBLIOGRAPHY

Clements, Barbara Evans. (1979). *Bolshevik Feminist: the Life of Aleksandra Kollontai.* Bloomington: Indiana University Press.

Clements, Barbara Evans. (1997). *Bolshevik Women.* Cambridge: Cambridge University Press.

Farnsworth, Beatrice. (1980). *Alexandra Kollontai: Socialism, Feminism, and the Bolshevik Revolution.* Stanford, CA: Stanford University Press.

Holt, Alix, ed. (1977). *Selected Writings of Alexandra Kollontai.* Westport, CT: Lawrence Hill.

Kollontai, Alexandra. (1978) *The Love of Worker Bees,* tr. Cathy Porter. Chicago: Academy Press Limited.

BARBARA EVANS CLEMENTS

KOMBEDY *See* COMMITTEES OF THE VILLAGE POOR.

KOMI

The Komi are an indigenous Arctic people. Of the 497,000 Komi (1989 census), the majority (292,000) live in the Komi Republic, which extends to the Arctic Circle, and in the contiguous Permian Komi Autonomous okrug within the Perm oblast (Komi population 95,000). Their language belongs to the Finno-Ugric family and is mutually semi-intelligible with Udmurt, farther south. In the 1300s the Komi were the merchants of the Far North and had a unique alphabet. Most Komis have Caucasian features. Distinguished U.S. sociologist Pitrim Sorokin (1889–1968) was a Komi cultural activist in his youth.

The northern Komi partly converted to Greek Orthodoxy in the late 1300s, prior to the Novgorod conquest, and maintained Komi-language liturgies up to 1700. The Permian Komi Duchy of Great Perm converted under duress just before Novgorod was seized (1472) by Moscow, which allowed the duke to stay as a vassal but dismissed his son. Cultural renaissance was strong by 1900.

Despite Komi pleas, Moscow excluded the Permian Komi from the Komi Autonomous *oblast*, formed in 1921 and upgraded to Autonomous Republic in 1936. The Permian Komi National okrug (district), formed in 1925, remains a "periphery of a periphery" within the Perm oblast. Two separate literary languages were developed. Numerous slave labor camps were located in Komi lands. Russian immigration has reduced the Komi from 92 percent of the population in 1926 to 23 percent in 1989. In the okrug the drop has been from 77 percent to 60 percent.

The huge and flat Komi Republic (population 1.3 million) produces 10 percent of Russia's paper, 7 percent of its coal, and also oil and gas. Indigenous Komi live mainly in the southern agricultural zone. Those who have shifted to Russian as their main language (25%) participate actively in the economic life. The Permian Komi okrug is a depressed area where the only resource, lumber, has been depleted.

In 1989 the First Komi National Congress established a Komi National Revival Committee, which succeeded in having Komi and Russian declared coequal state languages in the Republic. The impact has been real but limited, leading to the creation of a more activist organization, Doriam Asnõmös (Let's Defend Ourselves).

See also: FINNS AND KARELIANS; NATIONALITIES POLICIES, SOVIET; NATIONALITIES POLICIES, TSARIST

BIBLIOGRAPHY

Lallukka, Seppo. (1995). "Territorial and Demographic Foundations of Komi-Permiak Nationality." *Nationalities Papers* 23:353–371.

Taagepera, Rein. (1999). *The Finno-Ugric Republics and the Russian State.* London: Hurst.

REIN TAAGEPERA

KOMUCH

The Committee of the Constituent Assembly (Komitet Uchreditelnogo Sobraniya) or KOMUCH the first constitutional alternative to the Soviet rule in Russia, emerged during the spring of 1918. The alternative derived its legitimacy from the Constituent Assembly, whose nine hundred deputies had been elected in late 1917 to draft a new constitution for the Russian Republic, proclaimed by the Provisional Government on September 9. The electoral victory of the Party of Socialist Revolutionaries (PSR or SRs)—which won 58 percent of the popular vote and 440 seats in the assembly, compared to the Bolsheviks' 25 percent of the vote and 175 seats—augured well for the possibility of a constitutional and peaceful evolution of Russia into a modern democratic republic.

This possibility was thwarted, however, when Lenin dissolved the Assembly on January 6. However, the SRs convened a secret conclave in Petrograd at the end of January and decided to organize an armed uprising on behalf of the Assembly to divest the Bolsheviks of power. They aimed to reconvene the Assembly as the only source of legitimate authority in the country on the territories liberated from the Bolsheviks; to renew the Assembly's work on drafting a new constitution; and to enact land and other reforms. To implement these policies the party decided to shift the center of its activities from Petrograd to Samara, Saratov, and other strongholds in the Volga region. In Samara the party established a Revolutionary Center early in February 1918, to organize the uprising as soon as twenty of its deputies from that region returned to their home constituencies. The center entrusted B. K. Fortunatov with organizing the military forces, while P. D. Klimushkin and I. M. Brushvit engaged in political work to secure cooperation with the deputies of other political parties and other anti-Bolshevik forces in the region.

When the Czechoslovak Legion captured Samara on June 8, 1918, the Revolutionary Center assumed power in the name of the KOMUCH, in order to govern, on behalf of the Constituent Assembly, not only that city but also other cities liberated by the joint forces of the Legion and the KOMUCH. These joint operations captured Nikolayevsk on July 20, Khvalinsk on July 11, Kunzetsk on July 15, Syzran on July 10, Simbirsk on July 22, Sterlitamak on July 15, and Kazan on August 6. As a result, a beachhead more than 300 miles long was established on the western bank of the Volga. The objective was to hold it until the arrival of the Allied forces from Vladivostok to reestablish the Eastern Front in Russia, according to the decision of the Allied Supreme War Council of July 2. While this was a feasible project—the entire Trans-Siberian Railway from the Volga to that port was under the control of the Czechs—the Allied forces never came, because of President Woodrow Wilson's opposition.

Although by the beginning of October the Legion and the KOMUCH deployed on this beachhead 62,370 men, they were outnumbered by Trotsky's 93,500 troops, a large number of them composed of former German, Hungarian, and Austrian prisoners of war serving now in the Bolshevik ranks. Samara was evacuated on October 8. The evacuation of the administrative and political activities of KOMUCH from Samara to Ufa terminated its four-month-long effort to establish the constitutional alternative to the Soviet rule in the Volga region. And in Ufa, by accepting the authority, although grudgingly, of the All Russia Provisional Government established there on September 23, 1918, the Komuch ceased to exist.

See also: ALLIED INTERVENTION; CIVIL WAR OF 1917–1922; PROVISIONAL GOVERNMENT; SOCIALIST REVOLUTIONARIES

BIBLIOGRAPHY

Fic, Victor M. (1998). *The Rise of the Constitutional Alternative to Soviet Rule. Provisional Governments of Siberia and All-Russia: Their Quest for Allied Intervention.* Boulder, CO: East European Monographs; New York: Columbia University Press.

VICTOR M. FIC

KONDRATIEV, NIKOLAI DMITRIEVICH

(1892–1938), agricultural economist and business cycle analyst.

Internationally renowned for his work on long-run economic cycles, Nikolai Kondratiev was born in 1892 in Ivanovskaya region. He studied economics under Mikhail Tugan-Baranovsky and became an important member of the Socialist Revolutionary (SR) Party. His first major work was a detailed study of the Russian grain market, and in 1921 he created the world-famous Conjuncture Institute in Moscow. In 1922 he published his first account of long cycles. These were approximately fifty-year economic cycles, revealed in price levels and trade statistics, which appeared to provoke (or be provoked by) technological innovations and social upheavals, and which were caused by the periodic renewal of basic capital goods. This idea, subsequently called the Kondratiev cycle, has been very influential among non-mainstream economists and is even employed by historians and stock market analysts, but it is fundamentally questioned by more orthodox economists.

From within the People's Commissariat of Agriculture, Kondratiev also wrote insightful commentary on the economic development of Russia, particularly on agriculture and planning methodology, and advocated a market-led industrialization strategy for the USSR. This involved specializing in the export of agricultural produce in the short term in order to fund industrial development in the medium term, in line with the Ricardian idea of comparative advantage. This approach received impetus from Kondratiev's trip overseas in 1924 and 1925, and was crystallized in Kondratiev's plan for agriculture and forestry from 1924 to 1928. Such thinking was anathema to Josef Stalin, who had Kondratiev arrested in 1930, jailed for eight years, and finally shot. While in jail, Kondratiev wrote a book on economic methodology as well as moving letters to his wife on the human condition.

See also: AGRICULTURE; ECONOMIC GROWTH, SOVIET; INDUSTRIALIZATION, SOVIET

BIBLIOGRAPHY

Barnett, Vincent. (1998). *Kondratiev and the Dynamics of Economic Development: Long Cycles and Industrial Growth in Historical Context.* London: Macmillan.

Makasheva, Natalia; Samuels, Warren J.; and Barnett, Vincent, eds. (1998). *The Works of Nikolai D. Kondratiev*. London: Pickering and Chatto.

VINCENT BARNETT

KONEV, IVAN STEPANOVICH

(1897–1973), military leader and marshal of the Soviet Union.

Born to a peasant family in Viatsky, Konev entered the Old Army in 1916 and rose to the rank of junior officer before joining the Party and the Red Army in 1918 and being appointed commissar of Nikolskii District. During the civil war, he was commander of Armored Train No. 105, attached to the 5 Rifle Brigade, and fought in Siberia and the Far East. From 1921 to 1922 he took part in putting down the Kronshtadt Rebellion and was appointed commissar in the staff in the National Revolutionary Army of the Far East Republic.

Konev attended a higher course in the military academy in 1926 and graduated from the Frunze Academy in 1934. During the 1920s and 1930s he commanded the 2 Rifle Division and later a corps. Untouched by the purges, he was elected to the Supreme Soviet in 1937, and in 1938 he took over as the commander of the newly formed 2 Independent Red Banner Far East Army. Despite rumors to the contrary, Konev was not involved in fighting the Japanese in Lake Khasan or Khalkhin Gol. In 1939 he was elected as a candidate member of the Central Committee. During 1940 and 1941, he commanded the Transbaikal and North Caucasus Military Districts. The latter was reinstituted shortly before World War II as the 19 Army and was transferred to the Western Special Military District to be mauled by the blitzkrieg.

In September, 1941, Konev took over the command of the Western Front, which was pushed back in the Battles of Orel and Viasma by the Germans, and for a few anxious days in October contact was lost with him. Josef Stalin threatened to courtmartial him but was persuaded by Zhukov to appoint Konev as commander of the newly formed neighboring Kalinin Front, which played a significant part in finally stopping the German advance toward Moscow. In August 1942 Konev replaced Zhukov as commander of the Western Front, which failed to defeat the now well-entrenched Germans. For a brief period in March 1943 Konev commanded the Northwest Front before being appointed commander of the Steppe Military District (later Steppe Front), the massive reserve force formed by the Russians in anticipation of the German attack against the Kursk Bulge. Konev's units were deployed sooner than planned, but managed, with enormous losses, to persuade the Germans to break off their offensive. With the German defeat at Kursk, which Konev called the swan song of the German panzers, the Red Army went on the offensive with Konev commanding the 2 Ukraine (October 1943) and later 1 Ukraine (May 1944) Fronts.

Konev was involved in most of the major battles of the last two years of the war, which included the crossing of several major rivers, including the Dnepr and Vistula-Oder. During the Battle of Berlin, Stalin used the rivalry between Konev and Georgy Zhukov, who now commanded the neighboring 1 Belorussian Front, to advance his military and political goals. In the last phase of the campaign, forces commanded by Konev captured Prague. In both 1944 and 1945 Konev received the title Hero of the Soviet Union. After the war, Konev was appointed commander of the Central Group of Forces, and in 1946 he took over the ground forces, as well as being appointed Deputy Minister of the Armed Forces. He lost the former position in 1950. In 1951 he was appointed commander of the Carpathian Military District.

In late 1952 Konev wrote to Stalin claiming that he had been a victim of the Doctor's Plot. In December 1953 Konev presided over the military court that sentenced to death Laurenti Beria and his colleagues. In 1955–1956 Konev was once again commander of the Ground Forces. From 1955 to 1960, he was also the first deputy minister of the Armed Forces, and from May 1955 to June 1960 commander of the Warsaw Pact Forces, taking part in putting down the 1956 revolution in Hungry. In 1961–1962 Konev was commander of Soviet forces in Germany before being transferred to the military inspectorate. In 1965 he represented the USSR at Winston Churchill's funeral. Konev himself is buried at the Kremlin Wall. Konev was a typical Soviet commander in his indifference to losses and was one of Stalin's favorites.

See also: MILITARY, SOVIET AND POST-SOVIET; WORLD WAR II; ZHUKOV, GEORGY KONSTANTINOVICH

BIBLIOGRAPHY

Polevoi, N. (1974). *Polkovodets.* Moscow: Politizdat.

Portugal'skii, R. M. (1985). *Marshal I. S. Konev.* Moscow: Voenizdat.

MICHAEL PARRISH

KONSTANTIN NIKOLAYEVICH

(1827–1892), political and naval figure, second son of Tsar Nicholas I, brother of Tsar Alexander II, and an advocate of liberal reform.

Because Konstantin Nikolayevich was not the tsarevich, his designation as a general admiral at the age of four marked him early for a career in the Imperial Russian Navy. In 1853 he actually began to discharge the functions of his rank, and between 1855 and 1881 he simultaneously headed the Naval Ministry and served as commander–in–chief of Russian naval forces. A reformer of broad vision and originality, he bore responsibility for modernizing the navy, overseeing the transition from sail to steam. After 1845 he was also honorary president of the Imperial Russian Geographic Society, from whose membership sprang a number of future Russian reformers. Characteristically, the grand duke viewed his own naval bailiwick as an engine of change, in contemporary parlance "a ministry of progress," engaged in training personnel for service in other branches of government. His reform–minded protégés were known as the *konstantinovtsy.*

Grand Duke Konstantin Nikolayevich, second son of Nicholas I. © HULTON ARCHIVE

An opponent of serfdom and government censorship, Konstantin Nikolayevich spurned his father's legacy to advocate openness, reform, and the cause of liberal bureaucrats such as Nikolai Milyutin and Alexander Golovnin. The grand duke believed that peasants should receive title to their own private holdings. In 1857, to speed deliberations over serf emancipation, Tsar Alexander II appointed him president of the Secret Committee on the peasant question. Following emancipation in 1861, Konstantin Nikolayevich served for two decades as president of the Main Committee on Peasant Affairs, which oversaw implementation of peasant–related reform legislation.

Meanwhile, as a counter to growing Polish opposition to Russian rule, the grand duke in March 1862 also received appointment to Warsaw as viceroy and commander–in–chief. He was removed in August 1863, after his liberal "policy of pacification" had failed to forestall open rebellion. Nevertheless, throughout the 1860s and 1870s he remained a staunch advocate of his brother's Great Reforms, supporting them from various influential governmental positions, including presidency of the State Council between 1865 and 1881. In general, the grand duke also backed the military policies of war minister Dmitry Milyutin, while resisting the reactionary policies of Dmitry Tolstoy, the minister of education. In 1866 Konstantin Nikolayevich unsuccessfully sponsored moderate legislation that would have introduced into the State Council representatives from both zemstvo and noble assemblies. During the last years of his brother's reign, he sided with the liberal policies of Mikhail Loris–Melikov, Minister of the Interior. Upon the accession of Tsar Alexander III in 1881, the grand duke left state service.

A cultivated man, Konstantin Nikolayevich read widely, maintained diverse interests, and played the cello. He was accepted in intellectual circles and maintained honorary membership in a number of learned societies. He left important memoirs and an impressive correspondence, much of which has been published.

See also: ALEXANDER II; GREAT REFORMS; MILITARY, IMPERIAL; MILITARY REFORMS; PEASANTRY

BIBLIOGRAPHY

Lincoln, W. Bruce. (1990). *The Great Reforms: Autocracy, Bureaucracy, and the Politics of Change in Imperial Russia.* DeKalb: Northern Illinois University Press.

LARISSA ZAKHAROVA

KOPECK

The kopeck (*kopeyka*)—equal to one-hundredth of the ruble—was first introduced as part of a 1534 monetary reform as equal to 0.68 grams of silver.

The silver coin was twice as heavy as the Muscovite *denga* (*moskovka*) and known as *denga kopeynaya*, because—like its Lithuanian model—it depicted a rider carrying a lance (*kope*). The name *novgorodka*, initially much more common, reflected the fact that it equaled in value the old Novgorod denga. In spite of the reform, the Muscovite denga and *altyn* (the latter equal to three kopecks) remained the basic units of accounting until the eighteenth century. The kopeck was the largest denomination minted until the 1654 monetary reform, along with the *denga* and the *polushka* (one-quarter kopeck). Vasily Shuisky briefly minted gold kopecks, and during Alexei Mikhailovich's currency reform from 1655 to 1663, kopecks were minted of copper. Alexei also began to mint ruble, *poltina* (50 kopecks), and altyn coins, as well as, experimentally, the grosh (two kopecks). In 1701 the *polupoltinnik* (25 kopecks), the *grivna* (10 kopecks), and the *polugrivna* (5 kopecks) were introduced.

Peter I's monetary reform of 1704 introduced a decimal system with the copper kopeck as the basic subdivision of the silver ruble, although silver kopecks continued to be minted until 1718. Fifteen- and twenty-kopeck coins were introduced in 1760. Coins of up to 5 kopecks during the rest of the Imperial Era tended to be minted of copper, regardless of transition between silver, gold, and paper rubles. During the Soviet period, kopecks were minted of an alloy of copper and zinc.

See also: ALEXEI MIKHAILOVICH; ALTYN; COPPER RIOTS; DENGA; RUBLE; SHUISKY, VASILY IVANOVICH

BIBLIOGRAPHY

Spassky, Ivan Georgievich. (1968). *The Russian Monetary System: A Historico-Numismatic Survey*, tr. Z. I. Gorishina and rev. L. S. Forrer. Amsterdam: J. Schulman.

JARMO T. KOTILAINE

KOREANS

Korean emigration to Russia began in 1864 and continued until the late 1920s, when the Communist authorities managed to close the border. This migration was driven largely by the abundance of arable land in the Russian Maritime Province, as well as by political reasons. By 1917 there were some 100,000 ethnic Koreans residing in the Russian far east.

During the Russian Civil War, Koreans actively supported the Reds. However, in 1937 all Soviet Koreans in the far east were forcefully relocated to Central Asia, allegedly to undermine the Japanese espionage networks within their ranks. Until the late 1950s, Soviet Koreans largely engaged in farming, but after Stalin's death they began to move to the cities. By the 1980s Koreans had become one of the best-educated ethnic groups in the USSR.

In 1945 the USSR acquired southern Sakhalin from Japan. The area included a number of Korean workers who had been moved there by the Japanese colonial administration. Most of these workers came from the southern provinces of Korea. Until the 1970s they were not allowed to become citizens of the USSR, and held either North Korean citizenship or no citizenship at all. Within the Soviet Korean community, these Sakhalin Koreans have formed quite a distinct group.

Most of the Korean migrants initially spoke the Hamgyong (northwestern) dialect, which is quite different from standard Korean, although the Soviet Korean schools taught the standard Seoul dialect. From the late 1950s young Soviet Koreans switched to the exclusive use of Russian. Most Korean schools were closed in the late 1930s, but two Korean-language newspapers and a Korean theater survived. Korean was also taught as a second language in some schools in Korean villages. In Sakhalin secondary education in Korean was available until 1966 and a part of the Korean community still uses Korean.

After the collapse of the USSR, most Koreans remained in Uzbekistan (some 200,000) and Kazakhstan (100,000). The Russian Federation has an estimated 140,000 ethnic Koreans. Their numbers are rapidly increasing due to migration from Central Asia, where Koreans are often discriminated against. There is almost no return migration to South Korea.

See also: CENTRAL ASIA; FAR EASTERN REGION; KOREA, RELATIONS WITH; NATIONALITIES POLICIES, SOVIET; NATIONALITIES POLICIES, TSARIST

BIBLIOGRAPHY

Kho, Songmu. (1987). *Koreans in Soviet Central Asia.* Helsinki: Finnish Oriental Society.

ANDREI LANKOV

KOREAN WAR

Following the defeat of Japan in 1945, the Soviet Union and the United States jointly occupied Korea, which had been ruled by Japan for four decades. After the United States and USSR failed to agree on the composition of a government for the country, separate states were established in 1948 in the two occupation zones, each aspiring to extend its rule over the remainder of the country. In 1949 North and South Korea engaged in serious fighting along their border, and on June 25, 1950, the North Korean army launched a massive conventional assault on South Korea, led by Soviet-made tanks.

Because North Korea was closely controlled by the Soviet Union and heavily dependent on Soviet assistance, Western leaders unanimously viewed the attack on South Korea as an act of Soviet aggression. Fearing that a failure to repel such aggression would encourage Moscow to mount similar invasions elsewhere, leading possibly to a third world war, the United Nations (UN) for the first time in its history authorized the creation of a multinational force to defend South Korea. The United States commanded the UN forces and contributed the overwhelming majority of troops, supplemented by units from Canada, the United Kingdom, France, Belgium, the Netherlands, Luxembourg, Greece, Turkey, Ethiopia, South Africa, Thailand, Australia, the Philippines, New Zealand, and Colombia.

The invasion of South Korea also prompted the United States to take a series of actions that shaped the Cold War for the remainder of the USSR's existence. The United States sent naval forces to protect Taiwan from an attack from the mainland, strengthened its support for the French in Indochina, solidified NATO, moved toward the rearmament of Germany, signed a separate peace treaty with Japan, tripled its military spending, and began to station troops overseas indefinitely.

After UN forces advanced into North Korean territory in October 1950, the People's Republic of China sent massive numbers of troops to prevent a North Korean defeat. The Soviet Air Force also intervened, thinly disguised as Chinese, beginning an undeclared air war with the United States that was the only sustained military engagement between the two superpowers. By the spring of 1951 the war had become a stalemate along a front roughly following the prewar border. Negotiations for an armistice began in the summer of 1951, but the war was prolonged another two years, at the cost of massive casualties and intensification of the East-West conflict worldwide. The armistice signed in July 1953 left intensely hostile states on the Korean peninsula, the North backed by the Soviet Union and China, and the South by the United States and its allies.

Russian archival documents made available in the 1990s show that Western leaders were correct in assuming that the decision to attack South Korea was made by Josef Stalin. His chief aim was to prevent a Japanese attack on the Soviet Union through the Korean peninsula, and he concluded that the U.S. failure to prevent a communist victory in China indicated that it would not intervene to prevent a similar victory in Korea. He was never willing to commit Soviet ground forces but urged the Chinese and North Koreans to keep fighting. Immediately after Stalin's death the new leadership in Moscow decided to bring the war to an end.

See also: CHINA, RELATIONS WITH; COLD WAR; KOREANS; KOREA, RELATIONS WITH; UNITED NATIONS; UNITED STATES, RELATIONS WITH

BIBLIOGRAPHY

Stueck, William. (1995). *The Korean War: An International History.* Princeton, NJ: Princeton University Press.

Weathersby, Kathryn. (1995). "To Attack, or Not to Attack? Stalin, Kim Il Sung and the Prelude to War." *Cold War International History Project Bulletin* 5:1–9.

Weathersby, Kathryn. (1995–1996). "New Russian Documents on the Korean War." *Cold War International History Project Bulletin* 6–7:30–84.

Weathersby, Kathryn. (1998). "Stalin, Mao, and the End of the Korean War." In *Brothers in Arms: The Rise and Fall of the Sino-Soviet Alliance, 1945–1963,* ed. Odd Arne Westad. Washington, DC, and Stanford, CA: Woodrow Wilson Center Press/Stanford University Press.

KATHRYN WEATHERSBY

KOREA, RELATIONS WITH

The first contact between Russia and Korea can be traced to the seventeenth century, but it was only from 1858 to 1861, when Russia established its control over the lower Amur River and acquired a short (8.7-mile [14-kilometer]) land border with Korea that the interaction of the two countries began in earnest. Formal diplomatic relations were established on July 7, 1884, when a Russo-Korean Treaty of Amity and Commerce was signed in Seoul.

From 1890 to 1905, Korea featured prominently in Russian diplomatic designs as a major target of economic and political expansion in the Far East. Russia was also heavily involved in Korean domestic politics. Attempts to increase the Russian influence in Korea and Manchuria were among the reasons for the Russo-Japanese War of 1904 to 1905.

After the October Revolution in 1917, Soviet-Korean exchanges remained limited in scope. The Soviet Union was instrumental in the creation of the local communist movement in Korea. Moscow promoted the unification of leftist groups into the short-lived Korean Communist Party (created in 1925 and disbanded in 1928). In the 1930s the USSR also provided support to Korean communist guerrillas in Manchuria.

World War II led to a dramatic change in the situation. On August 11, 1945, the Soviet Army crossed the Korean border and within a week established control over the territory north of the 38th parallel (this parallel had been agreed upon with the U.S. command as a provisional demarcation line). Meanwhile, the southern half of Korea was occupied by U.S. forces in September. From 1945 to 1947 the Soviet and American governments made some progress toward a compromise over the future government of a united Korea. At the same time, the Soviet military administration was actively establishing a communist regime in the north.

The Soviet administration backed Kim Il Sung, a former Manchurian guerrilla commander who had served in the Red Army since 1942. After the Democratic People's Republic of Korea (DPRK) was declared in September 1948, Russia was the first country to establish diplomatic relations with the new state (October 12, 1948). Relations with the south, where the Republic of Korea was proclaimed in 1948, were meanwhile completely frozen.

From 1948, Kim Il Sung lobbied Moscow for permission to attack the South. Initially these suggestions were rejected, but in late 1949 Josef Stalin approved the proposal. Russian advisers were sent to Pyongyang to plan the operations, which commenced on July 26, 1950. The North Korean armed forces were trained by Soviet advisers and equipped with Soviet weapons. During the war, the USSR also dispatched several units of fighter jets to fight on the North Korean side.

After the Korean War, Russia remained the main source of military and economic aid for North Korea. On July 6, 1961, a Treaty of Friendship, Cooperation, and Mutual Assistance was signed in Moscow. According to this treaty, Russia was obliged to protect the DPRK militarily in the event of a war (this clause was deleted from a new treaty signed in 2000).

In the late 1950s Kim Il Sung refused to follow the new policies of de-Stalinization. He skillfully used the Sino-Soviet rivalry to extricate North Korea from Soviet control and proceeded with the construction of his own brand of national Stalinism. North Korea remained neutral in the Sino-Soviet conflict and was more politically distant from the USSR than any other communist state apart from China and Albania. However, strategic considerations forced Moscow to continue with its economic aid to the North.

With the advent of perestroika, the changing strategic outlook led the USSR to seek rapprochement with the Republic of Korea (ROK), which was seen as an important trading partner. In the late 1980s the USSR engaged in numerous unofficial exchanges with Seoul, and on September 30, 1990, official diplomatic relations between the USSR and the ROK were finally established.

After the collapse of the USSR, the new Russian government refused to subsidize the trade with its erstwhile ally. Trade collapsed (from 2.3 billion USD in 1990 to 0.1 billion USD in 1995) and has remained insignificant ever since (0.1 billion USD in 2000). At the same time, attempts to influence the security situation in northeast Asia and other strategic considerations prompted Russia in the late

1990s to increase its diplomatic exchanges with the DPRK (including a visit by President Vladimir Putin in 2000).

Meanwhile Russian exchanges with the ROK were developing rapidly. By 2001 the trade volume between the two countries had reached $2.9 billion. South Korean companies imported raw materials, scrap metal, and seafood from Russia while selling finished goods, including consumer electronics, textiles, and cars.

See also: KAL 007; KOREANS; KOREAN WAR; PUTIN, VLADIMIR VLADIMIROVICH; RUSSO-JAPANESE WAR

BIBLIOGRAPHY

Il Yung Chung, ed. (1992). *Korea and Russia: Toward the 21st Century.* Seoul: Sejong Institute.

Lensen George. (1982). *Balance of Intrigue: International Rivalry in Korea & Manchuria, 1884–1899.* Tallahassee: University Presses of Florida.

Ree, Erik van. (1989). *Socialism in One Zone: Stalin's Policy in Korea, 1945–1947.* Oxford: Berg Publishers.

Andrei Lankov

KORENIZATSYA

The USSR's founding agreement of 1922 and its Constitution of 1924 gave it the form of a federal state that was organized according to national principles. This marked the beginning of a phase of limited autonomy for the non-Russian ethnic groups living in Soviet Russia and the blossoming of nationalism, which sometimes went as far as the actual formation of nations. Not only the large nationalities, but even the smaller, scattered peoples were given the opportunity to form their own national administrative territories. The will of the Communist Party—which was expressed in the program of the Twelfth Party Congress in 1923—was that all Soviet institutions in non-Russian areas, including courts, administrative authorities, all economic bodies, the labor unions, even the party organs themselves, should consist as much as possible of local nationality cadres. *Korenizatsya* was supposed to protect and nurture the autochthonous population's way of life, its customs and traditions, and its writing system and language. Up to the middle of the 1930s, korenizatsya was a central political slogan whose program was diametrically opposed to a policy of Russification and national repression.

Especially in the 1920s and the beginning of the 1930s, korenizatsya (which is also referred to in research literature as indigenization or Stalin's nativization campaign) achieved significant success. Forty-eight nationalities, including the Turkmen, Kirgiz, Komi, and Yakut peoples, received a written language for the first time. The status of the Ukrainian language greatly increased. In Belarus a strong and lasting national awakening occurred. The use of the national languages in schools and as administrative languages was, without a doubt, a nation-forming factor. The proportion of national cadres greatly increased in all sectors. Attributes of nation states, such as national academies of science, national theater, national literature, national historical traditions, and the like, were established or consolidated and staffed by indigenous personnel.

However, with the social revolution that started in 1929, the policy of korenizatsya got into a conflict that some researchers consider to have caused its end. The forced industrialization promoted centralization and Russification. The modernization demand of the Bolsheviks collided with the promise of korenizatsya to respect local customs. The women's policy in Central Asia is an example of this conflict. Collectivization was even more strongly perceived as an attack on the nationalities. National autonomy, which could have provided a framework for organized resistance to collectivization, was revoked by the Stalinist state power and increasingly relegated to formal elements. National communists were eliminated. Many of the indigenous elites produced by the korenizatsya program frequently did not survive the purges of 1937 and 1938. However, they were replaced by new, compliant cadres of the same ethnic group.

Especially when viewed against the background of the rigid Russification policy of tsarist Russia, the korenizatsya policy can be considered to represent significant progress in the treatment of the nationalities. In the cultural area the achievements of korenizatsya still continue to have an effect up to the present day. They provided an important foundation for the relatively smooth emergence of independent national states after the breakup of the USSR in 1991. Of course, it should be noted that the federal structure of the Soviet State had a centrally organized Communist Party opposite it, which, together with the state security organs, was always in a position to limit national autonomy, or, if the party required it, even to eliminate it entirely. Thus, in the time after 1935, the blossoming of the nationalities was purely a propaganda backdrop, in front of which the Father of Nations (that is, Stalin) staged his increasingly Great Russia–oriented policy.

See also: KOMI; NATIONALISM IN THE SOVIET UNION; NATIONALITIES POLICIES, SOVIET; SAKHA AND YAKUTS; TURKMENISTAN AND TURKMEN; UKRAINE AND UKRAINIANS

BIBLIOGRAPHY

Martin, Terry. (2001). *The Affirmative Action Empire. Nations and Nationalism in the Soviet Union, 1923–1939*. Ithaca and London: Cornell University Press.

Simon, Gerhard. (1991). *Nationalism and Policy toward the Nationalities in the Soviet Union: From Totalitarian Dictatorship to Post-Stalinist Society*. Boulder, CO: Westview Press.

Smith, Jeremy. (1999). *The Bolsheviks and the National Question, 1917–1923*. New York: St. Martin's Press.

ROBERT MAIER

KORMCHAYA KNIGA

The *Kormchaya Kniga,* also known as the Navigator's Chart (Map) or The Pilot's Book, is the Slavic version of the Greek laws known as the *Nomocanon*. The first Slavic translation of the Greek *Nomocanon* was probably made by St. Methodius in the second half of the ninth century. It included the canons found in the "Syntagma of Fifty Titles" and the first Slavic manual of laws called the "Court Law of the People" (Zakon sudny lyudem). The *Kormchaya* usually contained information such as Apostolic canons, decrees of the first four Ecumenical Councils, resolutions of local synods, instructions of the Church Fathers, and imperial edicts on church issues. It became the guide for ecclesiastical courts and church affairs in Rus. Before the seventeenth century, no single copy of the *Kormchaya* served as the official code of the Russian Church. A copy assumed local authority when a bishop made it the law of his eparchy. Consequently, by the beginning of the seventeenth century, the diversity of materials in the many existing copies created confusion. Around 1649 Patriarch Joseph, concerned by this ambiguity, arranged for a correct version of church laws to be published. In 1650, the first printed Kormchaya appeared, but three years later Patriarch Nikon published a revised version, which, although severely criticized by the Old Believers, remained the official code. The Holy Synod reprinted Nikon's version in 1787 and reissued it in 1804, 1810, 1816, and 1834. In 1889 Patriarch Joseph's *Kormchaya* was reprinted and used by a sect of Old Believers. It was reprinted again in St. Petersburg in 1912 and 1913.

See also: NIKON, PATRIARCH; OLD BELIEVERS; PATRIARCHY; ORTHODOXY; RUSSIAN ORTHODOX CHURCH

BIBLIOGRAPHY

Dewey, H. W., and Kleimola, Ann M., tr. (1977). "Zakon sudnyi liudem." *Michigan Slavic Studies* 14.

Žužek, Ivan. (1964). *Kormčaja* kniga: Studies on the Chief Code of Russian Canon Law. *Rome: Pont. Institutum Orientalium Studiorum.*

MARTIN DIMNIK

KORMLENIE

Old Russian term that describes a specific system of remunerating state officials.

Loosely translated as "feeding," *Kormlenieu* meant that princes awarded their servitors lands from which tribute could be extracted. Part of what was taken would be passed on to the prince, and the remainder would be kept.

In a situation of general poverty, where there was insufficient money to pay for needed troops, it may have seemed rational to offer kormlenie, but as that system came to form the basis for financing an emerging state bureaucracy, its serious drawbacks became apparent.

One problem was the lack of effective controls over how much was extracted; another, that the subjects would be drawn into complex patterns of personalized relations, where all distinctions between public and private were eroded. Above all, kormlenieu constituted a serious obstacle to the introduction of a money economy.

Under Tsar Peter the Great an attempt was made to replace kormleniei by the payment of wages, but under his successors persistent shortages of money caused a reversal to the old policies of allowing officials to live off the land.

Even in the Soviet era, one might well interpret the positions of local party bosses as similar to those of the holders of old kormlenie, who were allowed to help themselves to whatever they felt that their fiefdoms could offer.

See also: ECONOMY, TSARIST

BIBLIOGRAPHY

Pipes, Richard. (1974). *Russia Under the Old Regime.* New York: Charles Scribner's Sons.

STEFAN HEDLUND

KORMOVYE KNIGI *See* FEAST BOOKS.

KORNAI, JANOS

(b. 1928), economist.

Janos Kornai was educated in Budapest and became professor of economics in the Institute of Economics of the Hungarian Academy of Sciences in 1967 and at Harvard University in 1986.

In *Overcentralization in Economic Administration* (1957) Kornai was one of the first in the Soviet bloc to show the defects of central planning and argue for more decentralization and use of financial and market methods in guiding the socialist economy. His *Mathematical Planning of Structural Decisions* (1967; second edition 1975) developed the idea of two-level planning.

Kornai attempted to apply organizational and information theory, as well as management science, to analyze the advanced socialist economy in his *Anti-Equilibrium* (1971). He employed nonequilibrium concepts to replace the Walrasian market-clearing of standard neoclassical theory. Along these lines, his *Economics of Shortage* (2 vols., 1980) pictured an economy, like Hungary's or Soviet Russia's, with chronic excess demand and limited price flexibility. Supply would be allocated to meet excess demand by nonprice, quantitative methods. Tautness would show up as queues for consumer goods, indicating inefficiency and underutilization of resources.

During this period, Kornai developed his famous concept of the "soft budget constraint." Socialized enterprises were not required to cover costs, as ad hoc subsidies and credits would invariably be made available by state institutions so that the firm would not have to close. Loss-making enterprises were a cause of excess demand in the economy.

Following the democratic revolution in Hungary, Kornai argued for fiscal restraint, particularly in the payment of pensions, so that Hungary could invest more for growth.

See also: ECONOMIC GROWTH, SOVIET

MARTIN C. SPECHLER

KORNILOV AFFAIR

The Kornilov Affair was the main counterrevolutionary episode of the Russian Revolution of February 1917. It grew out the general political and socioeconomic crises of the summer, including the failure of the military offensive, government instability, economic disintegration, and, in particular, the emergence in July and August of a more assertive political right demanding a "restoration of order." Attention increasingly centered on General Lavr Kornilov, who emerged as the potential Napoleon of the Russian Revolution.

After the summer 1917 offensive failed, Kornilov vigorously advocated using harsh measures to restore discipline in the army. This drew the attention of a wide range of people interested in restoration of order, mostly conservatives and liberals but also some socialists, who found him more acceptable than most generals (he had a reputation for being more "democratic" because of his modest background and good relations with his troops). They pressured Alexander Kerensky, now head of government, to appoint Kornilov supreme commander-in-chief of the army, which Kerensky did on July 31. The problems that lay ahead were signaled by Kornilov's remarkable acceptance conditions, especially that he would be "responsible only to [his] own conscience and to the whole people," and his insistence on a free hand to restore military discipline. Kerensky did not really trust Kornilov, but hoped to use him both to appease the right and to counterbalance the left. Kornilov in turn disdained the Petrograd politicians. Intermediaries, especially Boris Savinkov, a former Socialist Revolutionary terrorist who was now the assistant minister of war, tried to convince Kerensky and Kornilov that the salvation of the country rested on their cooperation.

During August, tensions surrounding Kornilov's presumed intentions grew. Leftist newspapers and orators warned that he was a potential counterrevolutionary military dictator, while conservative newspapers and speakers hailed him as the prospective savior of Russia. People looking to break the power of the soviets and change the political structure began to organize around him. The degree of his knowledge and approval of these efforts remains unclear, but he clearly saw himself as a key figure in the regeneration of Russia and the reconstruction of Russian politics, perhaps by force.

By September political tensions in Petrograd were high. Kerensky and Kornilov groped toward some sort of agreement, despite mutual distrust. An exchange of messages, mostly through intermediaries (Kornilov was at military front headquarters), explored restructuring the government and discussed the respective roles of the two men. These also revealed their suspicions of each other. Kerensky became convinced that the general planned a coup and, on September 9, he suddenly dismissed Kornilov. Outraged, Kornilov denounced Kerensky and launched army units toward Petrograd. This quickly collapsed as delegates from the Petrograd Soviet convinced the soldiers that they were being used for counterrevolution. By September 12 the Kornilov revolt had foundered, and Kornilov and some other generals were arrested.

The Kornilov Affair had enormous repercussions. Kerensky, the moderate socialists, and the liberals were discredited because of their earlier support of Kornilov. The Bolsheviks and radical left, in contrast, had warned against the danger of a military coup and now seemed vindicated. Their political stock soared, and they soon took over the Petrograd and other soviets, preparing the way for the October Revolution.

See also: FEBRUARY REVOLUTION; KERENSKY, ALEXANDER FYODOROVICH; OCTOBER REVOLUTION; PROVISIONAL GOVERNMENT

BIBLIOGRAPHY

Ascher, Abraham. (1953). "The Kornilov Affair." *Russian Review* 12:235–352.

Asher, Harvey. (1970). "The Kornilov Affair: A History and Interpretation." *Russian Review* 29:286–300.

Munck, J. L. (1987). *The Kornilov Revolt: A Critical Examination of the Sources and Research.* Aarhus, Denmark: Aarhus University Press.

White, James D. (1968–1969). "The Kornilov Affair: A Study in Counter Revolution." *Soviet Studies* 20: 187–205.

REX A. WADE

KOROLENKO, VLADIMIR GALAKTIONOVICH

(1853–1921), noted Russian short-story writer, publicist, and political activist.

When Korolenko was arrested in 1879 for alleged populist activities and exiled to Siberia, he used the time to write many lyrical tales, exceptional for their descriptions of human sadness and desolate nature. His existential sufferings in Yakutsk, during which he often contemplated suicide, find expression in his writings.

One of Korolenko's famous short stories, "Makar's Dream" (1885), is also set in Siberia. In it, Makar, a poor little peasant who has become half-savage by his association with the Yakutsk people, dreams of a better future. Normally he has no time for dreaming; his days are consumed by hard physical labor—chopping, ploughing, sowing, and grinding. He only dreams when he is drunk. One Christmas Eve, Makar drifts off in a drunken sleep and dreams that the god of the woods, Tayon, has judged him harshly for his former deeds and has decided to transform him into a post-horse. Makar ends up convincing Tayon of his innate goodness.

In another famous story, "The Blind Musician" (1886), a blind youth overcomes his painful self-pity to become a sensitive violinist whose music takes on universal resonance. As his uncle watches the captivated audience, he thinks about his nephew. "He understands suffering. He has had his share, and that is why he can change it into music for this happy audience." Korolenko's talent thus lies in his expressions of the emotional and sentimental dimensions of life, his compassion for the downtrodden, as well as his masterful depictions of nature, which have much in common with Turgenev's.

Like many Russian writers, Korolenko felt that literature should play a leading role in advancing human progress; that a writer should not stand idly by in the face of injustice. He sought to create works that would unite realism and romanticism. In one historical story about the revolt of the Jews against the Romans ("A Tale about Florus, Agrippa, and Menachem, the Son of Jehudah"), Korolenko rebuts Tolstoy's doctrine of nonviolent resistance to evil. In works such as "The Day of Atonement" (first entitled "Iom-Kipur," 1890) and later in "House Number 13," Korolenko also took issue with anti-Semitism. Korolenko condemned the Bolshevik regime and the Red Terror he witnessed in indignant letters that he wrote to Anatoly Lunacharsky, the People's Commissar for Education.

See also: INTELLIGENTSIA; SIBERIA

BIBLIOGRAPHY

Korolenko, Vladimir Galaktionovich. (1972). *The History of My Contemporary.* New York: Oxford University Press.

Korolenko, Vladimir Galaktionovich. (1971). *Makar's Dream, and Other Stories.* Freeport, NY: Books for Libraries Press.

Korolenko, Vladimir Galaktionovich, and Antony Lambton. (1986). *Bad Company and Other Stories.* London: Quartet.

JOHANNA GRANVILLE

KORSH THEATER

Founded in 1882 by entrepreneur F. A. Korsh (1852–1923), this was the first successful private, commercial theater established after the repeal of the government's monopoly on theaters in the two capitals, Moscow and St. Petersburg. Built in the heart of Moscow's bustling theater district, the Korsh Theater was designed to meet four professional objectives: to respond to audiences' changing aesthetic demands; to increase performance opportunities for provincial actors; to present productions of new plays, which led to special Friday night performances of experimental works; and to make both the Russian and the international dramaturgy available to students, which Korsh accomplished by offering free Sunday morning performances. The playwrights whose works played in Russia first at the Korsh included Hermann Sudermann, Edmond Rostand, Henrik Ibsen, August Strindberg, George Bernard Shaw, and, perhaps most significantly, Anton Chekhov. Performers who advanced their careers here included comedian Vladimir Davydov, heartthrob Alexander Lensky, and light opera celebrities Lidia Yavorskaya and Maria Blyumental-Tamarina. The theater itself, designed by nationalist architect M. N. Chichagov, was the first to use electric lighting.

Korsh could afford his artistic innovations because of the extent to which he catered to the crowd, exemplifying the "dictatorship of the box office." The most popular, and prolific, playwright in his employ was I. I. Myasnitsky (Baryshev), who kept Korsh supplied with farces, comedies of topical issues with protagonists from all social backgrounds, such as "The Old Woman Makes a Fool of Herself." The theater's most famously popular production was the 1892 staging of Victorien Sardou's comedy about Napoleon's ex-washer woman, *Madame Sans-Gene,* translated by Korsh himself, and featuring the latest fashions directly from Paris.

Until its incorporation by the Soviet government in 1925, the Korsh Theater offered a central locale where new ideas about Russian culture were contested, reshaped, sometimes vulgarized, but always celebrated.

See also: CHEKHOV, ANTON PAVLOVICH; THEATER

BIBLIOGRAPHY

McReynolds, Louise.(2003). *Russia at Play: Leisure Activities at the End of the Tsarist Era.* Ithaca, NY: Cornell University Press.

LOUISE MCREYNOLDS

KORYAKS

The Koryaks (*Koryaki*) are an indigenous Paleo-Asiatic people living in northeast Siberia, on the northern part of the Kamchatka Peninsula and on the adjoining mainland from the Taigonos Peninsula to the Bering Sea (a total of 152,000 square miles, or 393,680 square kilometers). The traditional roaming area of the nomadic Koryaks has been west of the Kamchatka Central Range, up to the Itelmen settlements. In addition to Koryaks, Itelmens, Chukchi, and Evenki have also lived on this territory for centuries. Administratively the Koryaks live in the Koryak Autonomous Region (*okrug*), a territory approximately the size of Arizona and which is one of the ten autonomous regions recognized in the Russian Constitution of 1993.

The Koryak Autonomous Region is just one part of the larger Kamchatka Peninsula, which includes the Karaginsky and Komandorsky islands in the Bering Sea. With an area of about 490,425 square miles, the countries England, Portugal, Belgium, and Luxembourg together could be placed on the territory of Kamchatka. The peninsula contains many volcanoes, some of them active. The Koryak territory is mostly forest tundra, as well as tundra in the subarctic climate belt. The highest temperature in the summer is 34° centigrade and the lowest in the winter (in the central and northern parts of the peninsula) falls to about –49° centigrade.

The term *koryak* derives from the word for reindeer (*kor*). When combined with its prepositional suffix, korak means "with (or at) the reindeer." This is not surprising, given the Koryak's heavy reliance on reindeer for a wide range of bare essentials, including meat, transportation, household articles, fat (to light indoor lamps), materials for constructing mobile dwellings (*yarangas*), bones (for tools and household items), and hides (to make clothes, footwear, and even diapers and sanitary napkins). When referring to themselves, however, the Koryaks do not use the term. Instead, they call themselves either *nimilany* ("residents of a settled village") or *chavchuvens* (nomadic reindeer people).

In contrast to some other non-Russian nationalities, such as the Tuvinians, the Koryaks are a minority in their own region. Russians and Ukrainians make up more than 75 percent of the total population. The remaining 25 percent are Koryaks, Chukchi, Itelmens, and Evenki. Koryaks make up only one-fifth of the indigenous Siberian population.

See also: EVENKI; NORTHERN PEOPLES; NATIONALITIES POLICIES, SOVIET; SIBERIA

BIBLIOGRAPHY

Berdahl, Daphne, and Bunzl, Matti. (2000). *Altering States: Ethnographies of Transition in Eastern Europe and the Former Soviet Union.* Ann Arbor: University of Michigan Press.

Humphrey, Caroline. (2002). *The Unmaking of Soviet Life: Everyday Economies after Socialism.* Ithaca, NY: Cornell University Press.

Keay, John. (2002). *The Mammoth Book of Explorers.* New York: Carroll & Graf.

Reid, Anna. (2003). *The Shaman's Coat: A Native History of Siberia.* New York: Walker & Company.

Whybrow, Helen. (2003). *Dead Reckoning: Great Adventure Writing from the Golden Age of Exploration, 1800–1900.* New York: W. W. Norton.

JOHANNA GRANVILLE

KORZHAKOV, ALEXANDER VASILIEVICH

(b. 1950), aide to President Boris Yeltsin.

Alexander Vasilievich Korzhakov was the most trusted aide of President Boris Yeltsin until Yeltsin dismissed him in 1996. From 1970 until 1989 he worked in Administration 9 of the KGB, which provided personal security for senior Soviet officials. From 1985 to 1987 he was a bodyguard to Yeltsin, and remained loyal to him after Yeltsin was politically disgraced in 1987. For this the KGB dismissed him in 1989. During Yeltsin's political resurrection Korzhakov resumed work as his bodyguard. From 1991 he headed the Presidential Security Service (PSS) with the rank of major general, and increasingly became a close political adviser to Yeltsin. In August 1991 he played an important role in Yeltsin's successful defeat of the three-day hardline coup.

In October 1993, Korzhakov apparently played a key role in persuading the defense minister to have the military storm the parliament. Also, he personally arrested the leaders of the armed opposition.

Later he turned the PSS into what Yeltsin called his personal "mini-KGB." He built up departments for personal surveillance, political dirty tricks, and political and economic analysis. He encouraged Yeltsin to become politically more authoritarian and less liberal on economic reform, and even advocated specific policies on oil. As he freely admitted in his revealing memoir about Yeltsin, he played a major role in recruiting Boris Berezovsky and other rich businessmen to support Yeltsin financially and through their media. Thus he helped turn them into oligarchs with political clout. In 1995 he even arranged for Berezovsky to control, financially and otherwise, the newly created television company, Public Russian Television. It was important, he argued, to have a major channel that was firmly pro-administration and would counter the widespread criticism of the Kremlin in the existing media.

In 1996 Yeltsin appointed Korzhakov to one of the two teams that organized his reelection bid, the team headed by Oleg Soskovets. But Korzhakov feared that Yeltsin would lose, and therefore urged him to find a pretext to postpone the election and close down the parliament, or Duma. In March, Yeltsin took his advice, but opposition in the cabinet thwarted his plans at the last minute. In May he named Korzhakov his first adviser. In June, however, when Korzhakov and his allies clashed with the second election team in a fierce struggle for influence over Yeltsin, the latter suddenly opted for the second team, headed by Anatoly Chubais, and dismissed Korzhakov.

In February 1997 Korzhakov was elected to the Duma as an independent from Tula. In 1999 he was reelected on a Fatherland ticket and served on the Defense Committee. During the late 1990s he gave lengthy interviews detailing numerous allegedly corrupt activities of Yeltsin, his family, Chubais, and others, but did not discuss his own business affairs. He was never sued for libel or slander, apparently because the people he exposed believed he had evidence for what he said. Of special significance were his repeated accounts of how Berezovsky gave Yeltsin three million dollars in 1994, claiming this was a payment of royalties on Yeltsin's memoirs, when in fact the book had earned negligible royalties.

In 2001 Korzhakov was instrumental in launching the monthly investigative newspaper *Stringer.*

See also: AUGUST 1991 PUTSCH; OCTOBER 1993 EVENTS; SOSKOVETS, OLEG NIKOLAYEVICH; STATE SECURITY, ORGANS OF; YELTSIN, BORIS NIKOLAYEVICH

BIBLIOGRAPHY

Reddaway, Peter, and Glinski, Dmitri. (2001). *The Tragedy of Russia's Reforms: Market Bolshevism against Democracy.* Washington, DC: U.S. Institute of Peace Press.

PETER REDDAWAY

Zoya Kosmodemyanskaya hanged by the Nazis. © HULTON ARCHIVE

KOSMODEMYANSKAYA, ZOYA

(1923–1941), partisan girl known as "Tanya" in World War II and canonized as Russian war heroine; also known as the Soviet Joan of Arc, she was posthumously awarded the honorary title Hero of the Soviet Union.

At the outbreak of war in June 1941, Zoya Kosmodemyanskaya, member of the Moscow Komsomol (Communist Youth), volunteered for the partisan movement. According to the official Soviet version, in December 1941, while carrying out a military assignment behind the front line, she was caught by the Germans, arrested, tortured, and finally hanged.

The young girl's tragic end was used as propaganda to arouse hatred for the cruel enemy and convey the necessity for vengeance. Written for this purpose, the numerous reports, which emphasized her courage, steadfastness, and exceptional strength of resistance, portrayed her as a true Soviet model and saint who had endured torture and chosen death over betraying her comrades—a model example for sacrificial death in the "Holy War" against fascism.

She shared the fate of many other daring and fearless compatriots who were popularized as heroes and heroines in the same manner. Yet Kosmodemyanskaya differed in that the public responded with compassion and affection, even abroad. Her unusual popularity cannot be explained by her heroic exploit alone, being that many others were called heroes for the same or similar behavior in fighting the enemy. Rather the visual and verbal depiction of her short life and tragic fate by several outstanding artists, poets, and filmmakers contributed to the unusually high degree of veneration.

In additon to dozens of publications on her exemplary life, bearing true hagiographic qualities, including poems (one by Margarita Aliger), songs, paintings, plays, it was a documentary photograph published in the newspaper *Pravda* on the occasion of her death that drew the public's attention because it broke with the traditional Soviet style of visual representation. Most influential, however, was the film *Zoya* directed by Lev Arnshtam (1944). The beauty and the performance of the actress Galina Vodyanitskaya in the role of Kosmodemyanskaya left a lasting impression in popular consciousness that turned the partisan heroine into a symbol of identity for more than one postwar generation of young Soviet women imitating her in dress, hairdo, and manner.

In the post-Soviet debate on the legend and reality of Soviet war heroes, some voices turned her into a henchman of Stalin's plan of "scorched earth," killed by the villagers, not by the Germans; others raised questions about her identity. Still, Kosmodemyanskaya is one of the few members of the Soviet pantheon of heroes who did not fall victim to the strong iconoclastic movement of the 1990s. Kosmodemyanskaya's place in history lies beyond historical truth; it is founded on her power as a legend that became part of collective memory.

Her grave can be found in the Moscow Novodevishche Cemetery, a special museum and a monument by M. G. Manizer in the village Petrishchevo, the place of her execution, near Moscow.

See also: WORLD WAR II

BIBLIOGRAPHY

Kosmodemyanskaya, Liubov. (1942). *My daughter Zoya*. Moscow: Foreign Language Press.

Sartorti, Rosalinde. (1995). "On the Making of Heroes, Heroines, and Saints." In *Culture and Entertainment in Wartime Russia*, ed. Richard Stites. Bloomington: Indiana University Press.

ROSALINDE SARTORTI

KOSYGIN, ALEXEI NIKOLAYEVICH

(1904–1980), Soviet prime minister.

Alexei Kosygin was born into a worker's family in St. Petersburg. After finishing schooling at the Leningrad Cooperative Technical School in 1924, he moved to Siberia and worked in a series of positions in the cooperative movement. It was while in Siberia, in 1927, that he joined the Communist Party. After returning to Leningrad he completed further studies at the Leningrad Textile Institute in 1935. Reflecting the opportunities opened up by the Stalinist terror and the patronage of Leningrad party boss Andrei Zhdanov, Kosygin moved rapidly from being a foreman and shop superintendent in the Zhelyabov factory through a series of industrial, city, and party posts, until in 1939 he became people's commissar for the textile industry. From April 1940 until March 1953 he was deputy chairman of the Council of People's Commissars (from 1946 Council of Ministers), or deputy prime minister; from June 1943 until March 1946 he was also prime minister of Russia. During this period, he likewise held a series of ministerial appointments, principally in the light industry and consumer goods industry areas. Kosygin had become a full member of the Party's Central Committee in 1939, a candidate member of the Politburo in March 1946, and a full member in February 1948.

Kosygin's upward trajectory was halted in connection with the fall of Zhdanov and the Leningrad Affair. Although one of the intended victims of this affair, Kosygin survived, but at the Nineteenth Party Congress in 1952 he was dropped to candidate status in the Presidium (as the Politburo was then called). Following Stalin's death and the consolidation of the position of one of Kosygin's enemies, Georgy Malenkov, Kosygin was dropped altogether from the enlarged Presidium in March 1953. At the same time, he was removed as deputy prime minister. He retained a ministerial position in the consumer goods/light industry sector and was restored as deputy prime minister in December 1953. He held this post until December 1956 when he became deputy chair (and from 1959 chair) of the state planning body. With Malenkov's fall as part of the Antiparty Group, in June 1957 Kosygin was restored to candidate membership of the Presidium and in the following month to the deputy prime ministership. He retained this post, from May 1960 as first deputy chairman, until October 1964, when he became chairman of the Council of Ministers, or prime minister. In May 1960 he also became a full member of the Central Committee Presidium.

The fluctuations in Kosygin's official positions in the early to mid-1950s reflect the vicissitudes of factional politics in the late-Stalin and early post-Stalin periods. In particular, Kosygin's fortunes seem to have been related inversely to those of Malenkov. Khrushchev's triumph over the Antiparty Group consolidated Kosygin's position near the apex of Soviet politics, but it was Kosygin's turning against Khrushchev that later allowed Kosygin to attain prime ministership. When the Soviet leadership tired of Khrushchev, they turned to Kosygin and Brezhnev. In the initial post-Khrushchev period, there seemed to be a general balance both between these two leaders and within the broader party leadership. Initially Kosygin was actively involved in foreign policy, including overseeing the Tashkent Agreement between India and Pakistan in 1965, negotiating with U.S. President Lyndon B. Johnson at Glassboro in 1967, and conducting key talks with the Chinese in 1965 and 1969. He was the sponsor of the so-called Liberman economic reforms (also known as the Kosygin reforms) in September 1965, which sought to generate greater autonomy from party control for the economic managers, although he also tightened central direction of the economy by eliminating the regional economic councils. Kosygin basically sought the more efficient management of the economy, but with the hostile Soviet reaction to the Prague Spring, the likelihood of liberalizing moves in the economy was eliminated. The suppression of the Prague Spring marked the ascendancy of Brezhnev and the clear subordination of Kosygn, who remained prime minister until his retirement in October 1980, and therefore through most of the period that Gorbachev would later call the "era of stagnation". He was more a technocrat than a politician, but bears some of the responsibility for the Soviet Union's perilous economic situation during the 1980s.

See also: BREZHNEV, LEONID ILICH; KOSYGIN REFORMS; LENINGRAD AFFAIR; MALENKOV, GEORGY MAXIMILYANOVICH; ZHDANOV, ANDREI ALEXANDROVICH

BIBLIOGRAPHY

Breslauer, George W. (1982). *Khrushchev and Brezhnev as Leaders: Building Authority in Soviet Politics.* London: Allen & Unwin.

Gelman, Harry. (1984). *The Brezhnev Politburo and the Decline of Détente.* Ithaca, NY: Cornell University Press.

Tatu, Michel. (1968). *Power in the Kremlin: From Khrushchev to Kosygin.* New York: Viking.

GRAEME GILL

KOSYGIN REFORMS

After Nikita S. Khrushchev was removed in October 1964, Alexei N. Kosygin (1904–1980) became chairman of the USSR Council of the Ministers, as part of a duumvirate with Leonid Brezhnev. Within months the new leadership restored the industrial ministerial structure, which Khrushchev had replaced with regional *sovnarkhozy* (economic councils). Gosplan regained its prime role in economic planning.

In September 1965, Kosygin announced a comprehensive planning reform that implemented some of the ideas of the Kharkov economist Yevsey Liberman and many other industrial economists who had urged relying on the profit indicator instead of detailed and numerous directives, which often conflicted with each other. Profitability had for some time been one of the indicators of plan fulfillment, though the main indicator was still gross output (*valovaya produktsia*, or*val* for short), as compared with planned levels. Now the directives would be seven in number, with profitability on capital (at controlled prices, not market ones)—or sales, for consumer goods firms—to constitute the main bonus-forming indicator. Instead of four standard indicators for use of labor, there would be only one: the wage fund.

Other obligatory tasks were to be sales (*realizatsiya*), assortment, payments to the budget, centralized investments, new techniques to be introduced, and mandatory supply tasks. The infamous *val* would be abandoned, along with the cost reduction target, both of which jeopardized quality of production. Depending on the enterprise's success in increasing sales and the profit rate—and subject to fulfillment of the other tasks in plan—retained profits would go to new investments, social facilities and housing, and extra worker bonuses. This provision was intended to enhance material incentives for those engaged at the enterprise. Though differentiated and quite complicated, these norms were supposed to be stable. After paying a new capital charge of 6 percent, more than half of net profits usually went to the state, however, not to enterprise funds. New enterprise whole prices would be announced by 1967 but still based on costs, not market scarcity. This would permit the end to subsidies for loss-making enterprises.

One advantage of the sovnarkhozy system was retained: The regional inter-industrial supply depots were preserved under the State Committee on Material Supplies (*Gossnsab*). Wholesale trade was thereby to be expanded. Several other state committees were also established for price setting and for science and technology. Concern for technological change was also reflected in the creation of science-production associations, intended to make a better connection between research, technology, and the introduction of new goods.

No sooner were these reforms implemented than significant modifications had to be introduced to regulate the size and distribution of enterprise funds. New targets were added for consumer goods and quality; later in the 1970s, labor productivity, gross output, and other targets returned to the mandatory list. Supply problems persisted; little wholesale trade occurred.

Most specialists believe that the Kosygin reforms failed because of continuing imbalances between feasible supplies and the demands of the Party-controlled government, the unwillingness to release prices, and bureaucratic resistance to any radical change. But tinkering and experiments continued until 1982. Perestroika would revive many of the basic ideas of the Kosygin reforms, with a very different denouement: chaos and collapse rather than reversal and stagnation.

See also: ECONOMIC GROWTH, SOVIET; KOSYGIN, ALEXEI NIKOLAYEVICH; LIBERMAN, YEVSEI GRIGOREVICH; PERESTROIKA; SOVNARKHOZY

BIBLIOGRAPHY

Gregory, Paul R., and Stuart, Robert C. (1998). *Russian and Soviet Economic Performance and Structure,* 6th ed. Reading, MA: Addison-Wesley.

Nove, Alec. (1986). *The Soviet Economic System,* 3rd ed. Boston: Allen & Unwin.

MARTIN C. SPECHLER

KOTOSHIKHIN, GRIGORY KARPOVICH

(c. 1630–1667), Muscovite official, émigré, and author.

As an under-secretary of the Muscovite Chancery for Foreign Affairs, Grigory Kotoshikhin was one of the few seventeenth-century Russians allowed to travel to the West, on diplomatic missions to Poland and Sweden. In 1663 he began to give information on foreign policy to the Swedish agent in Moscow. The following year he fled abroad, finally settling in Stockholm. At the behest of the Swedish government he compiled a lengthy description of the Muscovite state. Fatally injuring his landlord in a drunken quarrel, Kotoshikhin was sentenced to death. On the eve of his execution he embraced the Lutheran faith.

Kotoshikhin's manuscript was soon translated into Swedish but then forgotten. Rediscovered in the late 1830s, it was published in Russia in 1840 under the title *On Russia in the Reign of Alexis Mikhailovich.* Though its importance as a historical source was immediately recognized, the evaluation of Kotoshikhin's account in Russia and the Soviet Union would long be influenced by ideological considerations. In the nineteenth century, Westernizers praised Kotoshikhin for exposing Muscovite backwardness, while Slavophiles condemned him for blackening Muscovite reality. In the late Stalin period and beyond, the dictates of hyper-nationalism obligated scholars to excoriate Kotoshikhin as a traitor who defamed his country to please his Swedish hosts.

There are indeed a few passages in which Kotoshikhin lashes out at Muscovite ignorance, dishonesty, superstition, and xenophobia and lauds the "blessed freedom" of the West. But these passionate outbursts, almost certainly interpolations in the original text, are in striking contrast with the content and tone of the rest of the account, which is severely factual and almost entirely free of broad generalizations and value judgments. The level of accuracy is remarkably high, particularly for someone writing in a foreign country with no sources other than the Law Code of 1649. Kotoshikhin emphasized those topics that were of interest to the Swedish government; these corresponded well with what he knew best. There are lengthy descriptions of the central administrative institutions, diplomatic protocol, and court ceremonial; somewhat shorter discussions of the nobility, the army, provincial administration, merchants and trade, and the marriage customs of the upper class; and virtually nothing on the peasantry or the Orthodox Church. Kotoshikhin portrays a government of legal norms and bureaucratic process, and provides strong though not unimpeachable evidence on the constitutional role of the estates of the realm in electing or confirming each tsar from 1584 to 1645.

On Russia in the Reign of Alexis Mikhailovich has been republished a number of times (1859, 1884, 1906, 1984, and twice in 2000; Pennington, 1980, is the definitive edition of the text, with exhaustive linguistic commentaries). It remains a uniquely valuable source. No other Muscovite ever wrote anything comparable, and no Western traveler ever had Kotoshikhin's expert knowledge.

Kotoshikhin was born ahead of his time. From the reign of Peter the Great onward, Russians were able to adopt Western ways and values while remaining loyal to their native land. In Kotoshikhin's generation this was not yet possible.

See also: ALEXEI MIKHAILOVICH; LAW CODE OF 1649; SLAVOPHILES; WESTERNIZERS

BIBLIOGRAPHY

Weickhardt, George. (1990). "Kotoshikhin: An Evaluation and Interpretation." *Russian History* 17: 127–154.

BENJAMIN UROFF

KOVALEV, SERGEI ADAMOVICH

(b. 1930), dissident, politician, human rights activist.

Sergei Kovalev became famous as a dissident in the 1970s and later as a politician working for human rights in post-communist Russia. Trained as a biologist, he spent much of his early career at Moscow State University. In 1969 he was dismissed for dissident activity. From 1970 to 1974 he worked in a research station.

In 1967 Kovalev became involved in human rights circles, and soon developed a close friendship with fellow dissident Andrei Sakharov. Like Sakharov, he believed in the strategy of insisting on strict application by the authorities of the existing laws, and also of working for law reform. In 1968 he was one of the anonymous founders and editors of the *samizdat* (typewritten self-published) journal *A Chronicle of Current Events*, which documented violations of human rights and circulated covertly from hand to hand. In 1969 he was a founding member of the Action Group to Defend Civil Rights in the USSR.

In 1974 he was arrested and eventually tried in closed court. Sentenced to seven years in a strict-regime labor camp, he served his whole term, taking part in numerous protests and hunger strikes by prisoners. On his release he was forced to live from 1984 to 1987 in the remote town of Kalinin.

In the late 1980s Kovalev took part in various initiatives aimed at creating a civil society. In 1990 he was elected on a Democratic Russia ticket to the RSFSR's Congress of People's Deputies and its Supreme Soviet. He chaired the latter's Human Rights Committee, which passed important legislation on refugees, citizenship, procedures for emergency rule, the exculpation of political prisoners, and parliamentary supervision of the security services.

In the fall of 1993 he opposed Yeltsin's proroguing of the parliament, but did not support the parliamentary opposition. In October Yeltsin appointed him chair of his Commission on Human Rights, and the political movement Russia's Choice elected him chair of its council. In December he was elected to the new parliament, and as of 2003 has remained a deputy, switching his allegiance in 2001 from the successor of Russia's Choice to Yabloko.

In 1996 Kovalev resigned from Yeltsin's Human Rights Commission, in protest against his increasing authoritarianism and the war crimes committed by the military in Chechnya. He continues to be active in a variety of forums, and is widely seen in the early twenty-first century as the leading champion of human rights in Russia.

See also: DISSADENT MOVEMENT; MEMORIAL; SAKHAROV, ANDREI DMITRIEVICH; SAMIZDAT

PETER REDDAWAY

KOVALEVSKAYA, SOFIA VASILIEVNA

(1850–1891), mathematician and writer.

Sofia Korvin-Krukovskaya, growing up on an estate in Vitebsk province, displayed unusual mathematical ability from childhood. Desperate to escape the strictures of gentry womanhood, at eighteen she contracted a "fictive" marriage with the paleontologist and social activist Vladimir Kovalevsky, who took her to western Europe to study. In 1874 Kovalevskaya, mentored by the eminent German mathematician Karl Weierstrass, received a doctorate from Göttingen University. Afterward, the Kovalevskys, now married in fact, returned to St. Petersburg, where their daughter was born in 1878. In 1883 Kovalevsky, embroiled in financial scandal connected with an oil company scheme, committed suicide. Unable to find suitable teaching work in Russia, Kovalevskaya, at the urging of Weierstrass and the Swedish mathematician Gustav Mittag-Leffler, accepted a professorship in the newly established Stockholm University, becoming the first woman in modern Europe to hold such a post. In Sweden the homesick Kovalevskaya wrote her vivid reminiscences of girlhood; a novella based on a true incident, *The Nihilist Girl*; two plays written in Swedish with writer Anna Charlotte Leffler under the title *Struggle for Happiness*, concerning the contrast between real and ideal fates in life; and some journalistic articles. In 1888 Kovalevskaya received the prestigious French Prix Bordin for mathematics in blind competition. Death from pneumonia in 1891 cut short Kovalevskaya's dual careers as mature scientist and budding author. In the early twentieth century her story served as inspiration for science-minded girls throughout Europe. Her mathematics—in particular, equations describing the motions of rotating solids over time ("Kovalevsky's top")—has particular relevance in the space age.

BIBLIOGRAPHY

Koblitz, Ann Hibner. (1993). *A Convergence of Lives: Sofia Kovalevskaia, Scientist, Writer, Revolutionary.* New Brunswick, NJ: Rutgers University Press.

Kovalevskaya, Sonya. (1979). *A Russian Childhood*, tr., ed., and intro. Beatrice Stillman; with an analysis of Kovalevskaya's Mathematics by P. Y. Kochina. New York: Springer-Verlag.

Kovalevskaya, Sonya. (2001). *Nihilist Girl*, tr. Natasha Kolchevska with Mary Zirin. New York: Modern Language Association of America.

MARY ZIRIN

KOZLOV, FROL ROMANOVICH

(1908–1965), top Communist party leader during the 1950s and early 1960s.

Frol Kozlov's path to power was typical for party leaders of his generation of Soviet. Born in a village in Ryazan Province, Kozlov became a worker and assistant foreman at a textile plant where he also served as Communist Youth League secretary. After studying at the Leningrad Polytechnical Institute and working as an engineer, he rose through the ranks: secretary of the Izhevsk city party committee (1940–1941), second secretary of Kuibyshev Province (1947–1949), a party leader of Leningrad (1949–1957), candidate member of the Central Committee's Presidium (1957), and a Central Committee secretary in 1960.

Presidium colleague Alexander Shelepin later described Kozlov as a "very limited man." Anastas Mikoyan labeled him an "unintelligent, pro-Stalinist reactionary and careerist." Yet Kozlov backed Khrushchev in his battle with the Antiparty Group in 1957, and according to Khrushchev, he seemed knowledgeable about economic matters, and "firm, not someone who can be easily swayed."

By 1963, when Kozlov was de facto second secretary of the Soviet Communist party, he seemed to Western Kremlinologists to be leading conservative resistance to Khrushchev's reforms. In all probability, however, there was no organized opposition, and in fact, Kozlov soon began to irritate Khrushchev, for example, when he allowed the Soviet Communist Party's ritual May Day 1963 greetings to other Communist parties to imply an unauthorized change of line on Yugoslavia. Shortly after Khrushchev berated Kozlov for this mistake (but not necessarily because of Khrushchev's tirade), Kozlov suffered a stroke, which removed him from participation in the Presidium, although he formally remained a member until Khrushchev's ouster in October 1964.

See also: KHRUSHCHEV, NIKITA SERGEYEVICH

BIBLIOGRAPHY

Khrushchev, Sergei. (1990). *Khrushchev on Khrushchev*, tr. and ed. William Taubman. Boston: Little, Brown.

Tatu, Michel. (1969). *Power in the Kremlin: From Khrushchev to Kosygin*, tr. Helen Katel. New York: Viking Press.

WILLIAM TAUBMAN

KOZYREV, ANDREI VLADIMIROVICH

(b. 1951), Russian foreign minister.

Andrei Kozyrev served as post-Communist Russia's first foreign minister, from 1990 to 1996. He was well known as an advocate of pro-Western policies, but by the mid-1990s, as these views fell out of favor, he was forced from office.

Kozyrev was born in Belgium in 1951, where his father, a Soviet diplomat, was then serving. He was educated at Moscow State Institute of International Relations, and he joined the Soviet Ministry of Foreign Affairs, becoming head of the Department of International Organizations in 1986. He is fluent in English, Spanish, and French.

In 1990, when Russia declared its sovereignty, Kozyrev was named foreign minister, and he was one of the leading advocates for reform in Boris Yeltsin's circle. After the collapse of the Soviet Union, he helped spearhead Russia's pro-Western turn in foreign policy, pursuing cooperation with the United States on issues such as disarmament, the Middle East, Yugoslavia, and trade and economic relations. He was also viewed by many as one of the most important voices for liberalism and democracy in post-Communist Russia.

However, the incipient partnership between Moscow and Washington began to flounder in 1993 over such issues as the war in Yugoslavia and NATO (North Atlantic Treaty Organization) expansion. Critics began to push for a more forceful and aggressive Russian foreign policy, and Kozyrev's language also became more bellicose on occasion, including threats against Russia's neighbors and an assertion of special rights for Russia in the former Soviet space—the Near Abroad. Nonetheless, this was not enough, and by 1995 Yeltsin let it be known that he was no longer satisfied with the course of Russia's foreign policy. In January 1996 Yevgeny Primakov, a career Soviet diplomat known for more conservative views, replaced Kozyrev, who then served as a member of the Russian Duma (parliament) until the end of 1999. He has written numerous articles and books on international politics.

See also: NEAR ABROAD; PERESTROIKA; YELTSIN, BORIS NIKOLAYEVICH

BIBLIOGRAPHY

Kozyrev, Andrei. (1995). "Partnership or Cold Peace?" *Foreign Policy* 99: 3–14.

Talbott, Strobe. (2002). *The Russia Hand: A Memoir of Presidential Diplomacy.* New York: Random House.

PAUL J. KUBICEK

KRASNOV, PYOTR NIKOLAYEVICH

(1869–1947), Cossack ataman, anti-Bolshevik leader, and author.

Son of a Cossack general, Pyotr Krasnov was born in St. Petersburg and educated at Pavlovsk Military School, graduating in 1888. During World War I, he rose to the rank of lieutenant-general and to the command of the Third Cavalry Corps in August 1917. After the October Revolution, in uneasy collaboration with Alexander Kerensky (whom, as a monarchist, he despised), Krasnov was among the first to take military action against the Bolsheviks, attempting to lead Cossack forces from Gatchina toward Petrograd. However, the Bolsheviks dissuaded his Cossacks from becoming involved in "Russian affairs," and Krasnov himself was taken prisoner near Pulkovo. Remarkably, he was released after swearing not to oppose the Soviet government further. He immediately moved to the Don territory, was elected ataman of the Don Cossack Host in May 1918, and, assisted by Germany, cleared the Don of Red forces over the summer of that year. After the armistice, his former collaboration with Germany made his position difficult. Following defeats at the hands of the Reds and quarrels with the pro-Allied General Denikin, in early 1919 Krasnov resigned his post and emigrated to Germany. He subsequently became a prolific writer of forgettable historical novels but also worked with various anti-Bolshevik groups in interwar Europe, eventually allying himself with the Nazis and helping them, from 1941 to 1945, to form anti-Soviet Cossack units from Soviet POWs. In 1945 he joined the Cossack puppet state that the Nazis established in the Italian Alps. Surrendering to the British in May 1945, he was among those forcibly repatriated to the Soviet Union, in accordance with provisions of the Yalta agreement. In January 1947, accused of treason, he was hanged, by order of the Military Collegium of the USSR Supreme Court.

See also: CIVIL WAR OF 1917–1922; COSSACKS; KERENSKY, ALEXANDER FYODOROVICH

BIBLIOGRAPHY

Tolstoy, Nikolai. (1977). *Victims of Yalta.* London: Hodder & Stoughton.

JONATHAN D. SMELE

KRAVCHUK, LEONID MAKAROVICH

(b. 1934), Ukrainian politician and first president of post-Soviet Ukraine.

Elected president of Ukraine on December 1, 1991—the same date as the historic referendum on Ukrainian independence—Kravchuk won decisively, garnering 61.6 percent of the popular vote in a six-way contest. His primary political achievement was to establish Ukraine's sovereignty and maintain peace and social order with a minimum of violence and almost no ethnic conflict. It is impossible to overemphasize the importance of this accomplishment. However, he appears to have misunderstood the relationship between state building and economic reforms. This failure would cost him the presidency in early elections in July 1994.

A consummate politician, Kravchuk gained for himself the nickname "sly fox" because of his ability to maneuver in predicaments that he himself had created. His political shrewdness manifested itself in the events of 1991 when, as chairman of the Ukrainian Supreme Soviet, he publicly vacillated during the Moscow coup attempt of August 19–21. While other Ukrainian officials supported Russian President Boris Yeltsin, Kravchuk urged caution. With the failure of the coup and with public opinion turning against him, Kravchuk led the Communist Party of Ukraine (CPU) to join the democratic opposition on August 24 and to adopt Ukraine's Declaration of Independence by a vote of 346 to 1. Kravchuk also redeemed himself by resigning from the CPU and the CPSU.

Clearly, the CPU strategy was to retain power in an independent Ukraine. The democratic opposition was too weak and disorganized to take power on its own; for this, they needed the Communists. It is ironic that, as the former ideology chief of the CPU, Kravchuk persecuted nationalist groups, such as the Popular Front for Perestroika in Ukraine (*Rukh*), only to appropriate their goals and program in his 1991 bid for the newly established presidency. As president, however, Kravchuk effectively postponed economic and political reforms in favor of nation building. A notable aspect of his leadership was a continuing reliance on officials of the former Communist *apparat* in key governmental positions. Consequently, the simultaneous pursuit of political stability and economic reform was all but ruled out.

Confused and contradictory economic policies emanated from Kravchuk's government. He publicly supported radical reforms even as he worked to strengthen the hold of the former *nomenklatura* over the state and economy. The saga of Kravchuk's management of the economy was the massive emission of cheap credits and budget subsidies to industry, coupled with the imposition of administrative controls over prices and currency exchange rates. Major price increases in January and July 1992 drove Ukraine from the ruble zone in November of that year. But Ukrainian authorities proved no better at controlling inflation, plunging the nation into hyperinflation throughout 1993, when prices increased by more than 10,000 percent. Industrial output also plunged precipitously as the economic crisis widened and deepened.

Throughout 1992 and into 1993, Kravchuk was locked in a struggle with Prime Minister Leonid D. Kuchma for authority to reform the economy. Consequently, Kravchuk dismissed his errant premier in September 1993. The president made a halfhearted attempt to renew the command economy in late 1993, but by then the economic decline severely damaged Kravchuk's credibility. In response to pressure from heavily industrialized eastern Ukraine, Kravchuk agreed to early elections, to be held in July 1994. Facing his one-time premier, Leonid Kuchma, Kravchuk was defeated in the second round, garnering but 45.1 percent of the popular vote. The former president did not retire from politics, however; he was elected a member of parliament in a special election in September 1994, replacing a people's deputy who died before taking office. He was reelected in 1998 and 2002 from the party lists of the Social Democratic Party of Ukraine, and from 1998 onward has been a member of the parliamentary Committee on Foreign Relations.

See also: PERESTROIKA; UKRAINE AND UKRAINIANS

BIBLIOGRAPHY

Kravchuk, Robert S. (2002). *Ukrainian Political Economy: The First Ten Years.* New York: Palgrave Macmillan.

Kuzio, Taras, and Andrew Wilson. (1994). *Ukraine: Perestroika to Independence.* Edmonton: Canadian Institute of Ukrainian Studies Press.

Wilson, Andrew. (1997). "Ukraine: Two Presidents and Their Powers." In *Postcommunist Presidents*, ed. Ray Taras. New York: Cambridge University Press.

ROBERT S. KRAVCHUK

KREMLIN

Few architectural forms have acquired greater resonance than the Moscow Kremlin. In actuality many medieval Russian towns had a "kremlin," or fortified citadel, yet no other kremlin acquired the fame of Moscow's. The Kremlin structure, a potent symbol of Russian power and inscrutability, owes much of its appearance to the Russian imagination—especially the tower spires added in the seventeenth century by local architects. Yet the main towers and walls are the product of Italian fortification engineering of the quattrocento, already long outdated in Italy by the time of their construction in Moscow. Nonetheless, the walls proved

The Moscow Kremlin at twilight. © ROYALTY-FREE/CORBIS

adequate against Moscow's traditional enemies from the steppes, whose cavalry was capable of inflicting great damage on unwalled settlements, but had little or no heavy siege equipment.

In the 1460s the Kremlin's limestone walls, by then almost a century old, had reached a dangerous state of disrepair. Local contractors were hired for patchwork; as for reconstruction, Ivan III turned to Italy for specialists in fortification. Between 1485 and 1516 the old fortress was replaced with brick walls and towers extending 2,235 meters and ranging in thickness from 3.5 to 6.5 meters. The height of the walls varied from eight to nineteen meters, with the distinctive Italian "swallowtail" crenelation. Of the twenty towers, the most elaborate were placed on the corners or at the main entrances to the citadel. Among the most imposing is the Frolov (later Spassky, or Savior, Tower), built between 1464 and 1466 by Vasily Ermolin and rebuilt in 1491 by Pietro Antonio Solari, who arrived in Moscow from Milan in 1490. The decorative crown was added in 1624 and 1625 by Bazhen Ogurtsov and the Englishman Christopher Halloway. At the southeast corner of the walls, the Beklemishev Tower (1487–1488, with an octagonal spire from 1680) was constructed by Marco Friazin, who frequently worked with Solari. This and similar Kremlin towers suggest comparisons with the fortress at Milan. The distinctive spires were added by local architects in the latter part of the seventeenth century.

Although he built no cathedrals, Pietro Antonio Solari played a major role in the renovation of the Kremlin. He is known not only for his four entrance towers—the Borovitsky, the Constantine and Helen, the Frolov, and the Nikolsky (all 1490–1493)—as well as the magnificent corner Arsenal Tower and the Kremlin wall facing the Red Square, but also for his role in the completion of the Faceted Chambers (*Granovitaya palata*), its name due to the diamond-pointed rustication of its limestone main facade. Used for banquets and state receptions within the Kremlin palace complex, the building was begun in 1487 by Marco Friazin, who designed the three-storied structure with a great hall whose vaulting was supported by a central pier. Much of the ornamental detail, however, was modified or effaced during a rebuilding of the Chambers by Osip Startsev in 1682.

The rebuilding of the primary cathedral of Moscow, the Dormition of the Virgin, began in the early 1470s with the support of Grand Prince Ivan III and Metropolitan Philip, leader of the Russian Orthodox Church. Local builders proved incapable of so large and complex a task. Thus when a portion of the walls collapsed, Ivan obtained the services of an Italian architect and engineer, Aristotle Fioravanti, who arrived in Moscow in 1475. He was instructed to model his structure on the Cathedral of the Dormition in Vladimir; and while his design incorporates certain features of the Russo-Byzantine style, the architect also introduced a number of technical innovations. The interior—with round columns instead of massive piers—is lighter and more spacious than any previous Muscovite church. The same period also saw the construction of smaller churches in traditional Russian styles, such as the Church of the Deposition of the Robe (1484–1488) and the Annunciation Cathedral (1484–1489).

The ensemble of Kremlin cathedrals commissioned by Ivan III concludes with the Cathedral of the Archangel Mikhail, built in 1505–1508 by Aleviz Novy. The building displays the most extravagantly Italianate features of the Kremlin's Italian Period, such as the scallop motif, a Venetian feature soon to enter the repertoire of Moscovy's architects. The wall paintings on the interior date from the mid-seventeenth century and contain, in addition to religious subjects, the portraits of Russian rulers, including those buried in the cathedral from the sixteenth to the end of the seventeenth centuries.

The culminating monument in the rebuilding of the Kremlin is the Bell Tower of Ivan the Great, begun in 1505, like the Archangel Cathedral, and completed in 1508. Virtually nothing is known of its architect, Bon Friazin, who had no other recorded structure in Moscow. Yet he was clearly a brilliant engineer, for his bell tower—60 meters high, in two tiers—withstood the fires and other disasters that periodically devastated much of the Kremlin. The tower, whose height was increased by an additional 21 meters during the reign of Boris Godunov, rests on solid brick walls that are 5 meters thick at the base and 2.5 meters on the second tier.

The most significant seventeenth-century addition to the Kremlin was the Church of the Twelve Apostles, commissioned by Patriarch Nikon as part of the Patriarchal Palace in the Kremlin. This large church was originally dedicated to the Apostle Philip, in implicit homage to the Metropolitan Philip, who had achieved martyrdom for his opposition to the terror of Ivan IV.

During the first part of the eighteenth century, Russia's rulers were preoccupied with the building of St. Petersburg. But in the reign of Catherine the Great, the Kremlin once again became the object of autocratic attention. Although little came of Catherine's desire to rebuild the Kremlin in a neoclassical style, she commissioned Matvei Kazakov to design one of the most important state buildings of her reign: the Senate, or high court, in the Kremlin. To create a triangular four-storied building, Kazakov masterfully exploited a large but awkward lot wedged in the northeast corner of the Kremlin. The great rotunda in its center provided the main assembly space for the deliberations of the Senate. To this day the rotunda is visible over the center of the east Kremlin wall.

During the nineteenth century, Nicholas I initiated the rebuilding of the Great Kremlin Palace (1839–1849), which had been severely damaged in the 1812 occupation. In his design the architect Konstantin Ton created an imposing facade for the Kremlin above the Moscow River and provided a stylistic link with the Terem Palace, the Faceted Chambers, and the Annunciation Cathedral within the Kremlin. Ton also designed the adjacent building of the Armory (1844–1851), whose historicist style reflected its function as a museum for some of Russia's most sacred historical relics.

With the transfer of the Soviet capital to Moscow in 1918, the Kremlin once again became the seat of power in Russia. That proved a mixed blessing, however, as some of its venerable monuments, such as the Church of the Savior in the Woods, the Ascension Convent, and the Chudov Monastery, were destroyed in order to clear space for government buildings. Only after the death of

Josef Stalin was the Kremlin opened once again to tourists. The most noticeable Soviet addition to the ensemble was the Kremlin Palace of Congresses (1959–1961, designed by Mikhail Posokhin and others). It has the appearance of a modern concert hall (one of its uses), whose marble-clad rectangular outline is marked by narrow pylons and multistoried shafts of plate glass. The one virtue of its bland appearance is the lack of conflict with the historic buildings of the Kremlin, which remain the most important cultural shrine in Russia.

See also: ARCHITECTURE; ARMORY; CATHEDRAL OF THE ARCHANGEL; CATHEDRAL OF THE DORMITION; MOSCOW; RED SQUARE

BIBLIOGRAPHY

Brumfield, William Craft. (1993). *A History of Russian Architecture.* New York: Cambridge University Press.

Hamilton, George Heard. (1983). *The Art and Architecture of Russia.* New York: Penguin Books.

WILLIAM CRAFT BRUMFIELD

KREMLINOLOGY

Close analysis of the tense power struggles among the Soviet leadership. A term coined during the last days of the Stalin regime with the onset of the Cold War.

Usually more than just a study of contending personalities, or a "who-whom" (who is doing what to whom), Kremlinology was an indispensable analysis of Soviet policy alternatives and their implications for the West. It also turned out to be a point of departure for any serious political history, inevitably connected to the ideas that drove the Soviet regime and in the end determined its fate. Western intelligence experts, academics, and journalists all made contributions to this pursuit. Attention was often focused on "protocol evidence," such as the order in which leaders' names might appear on various official lists, or the way they were grouped around the leader in photographs. However, since factional rivalry was usually expressed in ideological pronouncements and debates, the most widely respected practitioners of Kremlinology were emigré writers who had direct experience of the ways of the Soviet communists. The most famous of these was the Menshevik Boris Nikolayevsky. Initially Kremlinologists centered on quarrels among Josef Stalin's subordinates in order to get an idea of his policy alternatives and turns. After Stalin's death, Kremlinology mapped out the succession struggle that occasioned the rise of Nikita Khrushchev. It was again useful in understanding the politics of the Gorbachev reform era and the destruction of Soviet power.

The domestic and foreign policy issues were debated in the ideological language of the first great Soviet succession struggle in the 1920s that brought Stalin from obscurity to supreme power. After his defeat and exile, Leon Trotsky explained Stalin's rise to the Western public as the victory of a narrow insular national Communism, according to the slogan "socialism in one country," over his own internationalist idea of "permanent revolution." Materials from three Trotsky archives in the West later showed these extreme positions to have been less crucial to Stalin's ascent than his complex maneuvers for a centrist position between right and left factions. Trotsky continued to analyze Soviet politics during the Great Purge of 1936–1938 in his *Byulleten oppozitsy* (Bulletin of the Opposition). This was matched by the commentary of the well-connected Moscow correspondents of the Menshevik *Sotsialistichesky vestnik* (Socialist Courier).

For various reasons, the émigré writings had to be read with caution. Often they were employed to establish a position in the debate over the Russian Question: What is the nature of the Soviet regime, and has it betrayed the revolution? In 1936 Nikolayevsky published the *Letter of an Old Bolshevik,* presumably the confessions of Nikolai Bukharin interviewed in Paris. It contained important information indicating the origins of Stalin's purges in a 1932 dispute over the anti-Stalin platform document of Mikhail Ryutin. However, the *Letter* was dramatized and embellished by Nikolayevsky's gleanings from other sources. Some historians later rejected it as spurious and even denied the existence of a Ryutin Program. But during Mikhail Gorbachev's glasnost campaign the full text was published, reading quite as Nikolayevsky had described it.

In Stalin's last days, Nikolayevsky tried to interpret the antagonism between Leningrad chief Andrei Zhdanov and Stalin's protégé Georgy Malenkov by linking Zhdanov to Tito and the Yugoslav Communists and Malenkov to Mao and the Chinese. Later studies bore this out. The rise of Khrushchev as successor to Stalin was charted by Boris Meissner, Myron Rush, Wolfgang Leonhard, and Robert Conquest. Michel Tatu described Khrushchev's fall in 1964 and the central role played by Mikhail Suslov, the ideological secretary.

Suslov loomed large in Soviet politics from this point until his death at the end of the Brezhnev regime in 1982. The ideological post was the center of gravity for a regime of collective leadership under the rubric of "stabilization of cadres." That Suslov died a few months before Brezhnev in 1982 meant he could not oversee the succession in the interests of the Kremlin gerontocracy. The result was a thorough housecleaning by Yuri Andropov in his brief tenure. An even more thorough shakeup by Mikhail Gorbachev followed. This would have been unlikely had Suslov lived.

In defense of the Suslov pattern of collective leadership, the Politburo tried its best to shore up Yegor Ligachev in the ideological post as a limit on Gorbachev. But Gorbachev managed to destroy all the party's fetters on his power by 1989, just as he lost the East European bloc. After that, he behaved like a conscious student of Soviet succession and proclaimed himself a centrist, balancing between the radical Boris Yeltsin and the weakened consolidation faction of the Communist Party of the Soviet Union (CPSU). The last stand of the latter was the attempted putsch of August 1991, the failure of which left Gorbachev alone with a vengeful Yeltsin.

Commentary on the Yeltsin leadership of post-Soviet Russia echoed some themes of Kremlinology, especially in analysis of the power of the Yeltsin group ("The Family") and its relation to well-heeled post-Soviet tycoons ("The Oligarchs"). However, power in the Kremlin could no longer be read in Communist ideological language and had to be studied as with any other state. Kremlinology, or analysis of Soviet power struggles, nevertheless retains its value for political historians who can take note of a recurrent programmatic alternance between a leftist Leningrad tendency and a rightist Moscow line. The centrist who defeated the others by timely turns was able to triumph in the three great Soviet succession struggles.

See also: HISTORIOGRAPHY; STALIN, JOSEF VISSARIONOVICH; SUSLOV, MIKHAIL ANDREYEVICH; UNITED STATES, RELATIONS WITH

BIBLIOGRAPHY

Conquest, Robert. (1961). *Power and Policy in the USSR.* New York: Macmillan.

D'Agostino, Anthony. (1998). *Gorbachev's Revolution, 1985–1991.* Basingstoke, UK: Macmillan.

Gelman, Harry. (1984). *The Brezhnev Politburo and the Decline of Détente.* Ithaca, NY: Cornell University Press.

Leonhard, Wolfgang. (1962). *The Kremlin Since Stalin,* tr. Elizabeth Wiskemann. New York: Praeger.

Linden, Carl A. (1966). *Khrushchev and the Soviet Leadership, 1957–1964.* Baltimore: Johns Hopkins.

Nicolaevsky, Boris. (1965). *Power and the Soviet Elite.* New York: Praeger..

Rush, Myron. (1974). *How Communist States Change Their Rulers.* Ithaca, NY: Cornell University Press.

Anthony D'Agostino

KRITZMAN, LEV NATANOVICH

(1890–c. 1937), Soviet economist and agrarian expert.

Born in 1890, Kritzman became a Menshevik in 1905. After a long period in exile, he returned to Russia in early 1918 when he joined the Bolshevik Party. An expert in economic policy and a strong advocate of planning, he held various posts in the Supreme Council for the National Economy and in 1921 joined the Presidium of Gosplan (State Planning Agency).

In addition to his professional duties, he published numerous works on planning and the economy in which he argued for introducing a single economic plan. He was criticized by Lenin for this position. After the introduction of the New Economic Policy in 1921, Kritzman, together with Ya. Larin, Leon Trotsky, and Yevgeny Preobrazhensky, continued to advocate an extension of state planning. During the 1920s, Kritzman produced a number of important works, including a major study of war communism, *Geroichesky period velikoi russkoi revolyutsy* (*The Heroic Period of the Great Russian Revolution*), still one of the key analyses of economic policy in the early Soviet period. As director of the Agrarian Institute of the Communist Academy from 1925 and editor of its journal *Na Agrarnom Fronte* (*On the Agricultural Front*), he promoted empirical research into class differentiation among the peasantry and called for greater state support for socialized agriculture. He also served during his career as assistant director of the Central Statistical Administration and a member of the editorial boards of *Pravda, Problemy Ekonomiki* (*Problems of Economics*) and the *Great Soviet Encyclopedia.* Stalin's launch of mass collectivisation and dekulakization in late 1929 rendered Kritzman's work and ideas obsolete by eradicating the individual household farm. After some years conducting private research, he was arrested and died in prison either in 1937 or 1938.

See also: COLLECTIVIZATION OF AGRICULTURE; NEW ECONOMIC POLICY; PEASANT ECONOMY; WAR COMMUNISM

BIBLIOGRAPHY

Cox, Terry. (1986). *Peasants, Class and Capitalism. The Rural Research of L.N. Kritzman and his School.* Oxford: Clarendon Press.

Solomon, Susan Gross. (1977). *The Soviet Agrarian Debate: A Controversy in Social Science 1923–1929.* Boulder, CO: Westview Press.

NICK BARON

KRONSTADT UPRISING

The Kronstadt Uprising was a well-known revolt against the Communist government from March 1 to 18, 1921, at Kronstadt, a naval base in the Gulf of Finland, base of the Russian Baltic Fleet, and a stronghold of radical support for the Petrograd Soviet in 1917.

By early 1921 the Bolshevik government had defeated the armies of its White opponents, but had also presided over a collapse of the economy and was threatened by expanding Green rebellions in the countryside. The Kronstadt garrison was disillusioned by reports from home of the depredations of the food requisitioning detachments, and by the corruption and malfeasance of Communist leaders. In response to strikes and demonstrations in Petrograd in February 1921, a five-man revolutionary committee took control of Kronstadt. It purged local administration, reorganized the trade unions, and prepared for new elections to the soviet, while preparing for a Communist assault. It called for an end to the Communist Party's privileges; for new, free elections to soviets; and an for end to forced grain requisitions in the countryside.

Communist reaction was quick. A first attack on March 8 resulted only in bloodshed; however, on March 18 a massive assault across the ice by 50,000 troops, stiffened by Communist detachments and several hundred delegates to the Tenth Party Congress and led by civil war hero Mikhail Tukhachevsky, captured the island stronghold. Thousands of Kronstadt activists died in the assault or in the repression that followed.

The Kronstadt rebellion, along with the Green Movement, presented a direct threat to Communist control. While the rebellions were put down, their threat led to important policy changes at the Tenth Party Congress, including the abandonment of War Communism (the grain monopoly and forced grain requisitions) and a ban on factions within the Communist Party.

See also: CIVIL WAR OF 1917–1922; GREEN MOVEMENT; SOCIALIST REVOLUTIONARIES

BIBLIOGRAPHY

Avrich, Paul. (1970). *Kronstadt 1921.* Princeton, NJ: Princeton University Press.

Getzler, Israel. (1983). *Kronstadt, 1917–1921: The Fate of a Soviet Democracy.* Cambridge, UK: Cambridge University Press.

A. DELANO DUGARM

KROPOTKIN, PYOTR ALEXEYEVICH

(1842–1921), Russian revolutionary.

Born into a family of the highest nobility, Kropotkin (the "Anarchist Prince," according to his 1950 biographer George Woodcock) swam against the current of convention all his life. He received his formal education at home and then at the Corps of Pages in St. Petersburg, graduated in 1862, and, to the tsar's astonishment, requested a posting to Siberia rather than the expected court career. There he remained until 1867. Siberia was a liberation for Kropotkin, contrary to the experience of others. He participated as a geographer and naturalist in expeditions organized by the Imperial Russian Geographical Society (IRGS). He was also entering his parallel career as a revolutionary: for him, Russia's Age of Great Reforms was that of the discovery of unchanging corruption among Siberian state officials.

In 1867 Kropotkin returned to St. Petersburg where he enrolled at the University (he never graduated), supporting himself by working for the IRGS. His scientific reputation grew and in 1871 he was offered the post of IRGS secretary, which he rejected. Events in his own life (the death of his tyrannical father), in Russia (the growth of a revolutionary student movement), and in the world (the Paris Commune) strengthened his revolutionary feelings. In 1872 he visited Switzerland for the first time to discover more about the International Workingmen's Association and on his return to Russia began to frequent the Chaikovsky Circle. As his 1976 biographer Martin Miller revealed, Kropotkin authored the Circle's principal pamphlet, "Must We Examine the Ideal of the Future Order?" (1873).

Kropotkin was by this time (though the title was yet to be invented) an anarchist-communist—that is, he advocated the destruction of state tyranny over society (as anarchist predecessors like William Godwin, Pierre Proudhon, and Mikhail Bakunin had done) on one hand, while on the other he sought a communist, egalitarian transformation of society (like Karl Marx, only without using the authority of the state). This paradox required the dissolution of national government and its post-revolutionary replacement by a free federation of small communes, a local government freely administered from below rather than national and imposed from above. Revolutionaries from privileged backgrounds must organize the preceding popular revolt by propaganda and persuasion only: Workers and peasants must make the revolution themselves.

In March 1874 Kropotkin was arrested for his revolutionary activities and interrogated over a two-year period. Moved to a military hospital, he was liberated in a complex, sensational escape organized by his comrades. Kropotkin continued his revolutionary career in the Jura Federation, Switzerland, comprising the anarchist sections of the International, and from early 1877 began for the first time to take part in public political life: demonstrating, making speeches, attending congresses, writing articles. This activity is chronicled in detail in Caroline Cahm's 1983 biography. Around 1880, the issue of terrorism or "propaganda by the deed," as was the expression of the time, arose. This was crystalized by the assassination of Alexander II in 1881. Although not approving assassination as a political method, Kropotkin was unwilling to condemn the assassins, explaining their actions as the result of impotent desperation. At the end of 1882 he was arrested in France for revolutionary activity in which, for once, he had not participated. Sentenced to five years' imprisonment, he was released following international pressure in early 1886 and settled in London, England.

For a living and for the cause, Kropotkin now lectured throughout Britain and wrote for numerous publications. His principal fame during the British period derived from his books, including *In Russian and French Prisons* (1887), *Memoirs of a Revolutionist* (1899), *Fields, Factories, and Workshops* (1899), *Mutual Aid* (1902), *Modern Science and Anarchism* (1903), *Russian Literature* (1905), *The Terror in Russia* (1909), and *The Great French Revolution* (1909). With British comrades, he launched the anarchist journal *Freedom*. He wrote frequently for political publications in several languages. He was greatly encouraged by the 1905 revolution in Russia.

Kropotkin's writings during these years of exile are parts of an ongoing argument with those hegemonic Victorian thinkers Thomas Malthus, Herbert Spencer, and Charles Darwin. He takes issue with Malthus's bleak vision to argue that humanity's future is not limited by its reproductive success, but by science and equality. Nature shows the role of mutual aid in its evolution, analogous to the freely cooperating communes of postrevolutionary humanity. Anarchist communism is not merely desirable, but inevitable. Kropotkin's optimistic view of science no longer commands respect, but to many his works beckon us to a wonderful future.

In 1917, in old age, Kropotkin was able to return to revolutionary Russia. He worked for a while on various federalist projects and died in Dmitrov, a Moscow province. His last major work, *Ethics*, was published posthumously and incomplete in 1924.

See also: ANARCHISM; BAKUNIN, MIKHAIL ALEXANDROVICH; IMPERIAL RUSSIAN GEOGRAPHICAL SOCIETY

BIBLIOGRAPHY

Cahm, Caroline. (1989). *Kropotkin and the Rise of Revolutionary Anarchism 1872–1886.* Cambridge, UK: Cambridge University Press.

Cahm, Caroline, Colin Ward, and Ian Cook. (1992). *P. A. Kropotkin's Sesquicentennial: A Reassessment and Tribute.* Durham: University of Durham, Centre for European Studies.

Miller, Martin A. (1976). *Kropotkin.* Chicago: University of Chicago Press.

Slatter, John (ed.). (1984). *From the Other Shore: Russian Political Emigrants in Britain 1880–1917.* London: Frank Cass.

Woodcock, George, and Ivan Avakumovic. (1950). *The Anarchist Prince: A Biographical Study of Peter Kropotkin.* London: Boardman.

JOHN SLATTER

KRUPSKAYA, NADEZHDA KONSTANTINOVNA

(1869–1939), revolutionary, educator, head of Glavpolitprosvet (the Chief Committee for Political Education) and deputy head of the Commissariat of Enlightenment, full member of the Central Committee of the Communist Party (1927–1939), wife of Vladimir Ilich Lenin.

A native of St. Petersburg, Nadezhda Krupskaya developed an early and lifelong interest in education, especially that of adults. Beginning in the 1890s, she taught in workers' evening and adult education schools. In Marxist circles she met Vladimir Ilich Ulyanov (Lenin). When she and Lenin were both arrested in 1895 and 1896, she followed him to Siberia as his fiancée and later as his wife. While in exile, Krupskaya wrote her most famous work, *The Woman Worker* (first published in 1901 and 1905). Here she explored the problems faced by women as workers and mothers.

From 1901 to 1917 Krupskaya shared Lenin's life in exile abroad, helping to direct his correspondence and build up the organization of the Party. She worked on the editorial boards of the journals *Rabotnitsa, Iskra, Proletary,* and *Sotsial-Demokrat.* She also began writing about theories of progressive American and European education, especially those of John Dewey. In the 1920s these ideas on education were to have some impact on Soviet schooling, though they were then reversed in the 1930s.

After 1917 she headed the newly created Extra-Curricular Department of the Commissariat of Education, which was later replaced by the Chief Committee on Political Education (*Glavpolitprosvet*). She also worked in the *zhenotdel* (the women's section of the Party), editing the journal *Kommunistka,* but never heading the section.

In 1922 and 1923, when Lenin was seriously incapacitated with illness, Krupskaya quarreled badly with Josef Stalin, whom she found rude and boorish. When Lenin died in January 1924, Krupskaya found herself isolated and increasingly drawn to side with the Leningrad Opposition led by Grigory Zinoviev and Lev Kamenev. By the fall of 1926, however, she had defected from the Opposition. From 1927 to 1939 she served as a full member of the (now much weakened) Central Committee of the Party. During the height of the Purges, she tried to save some of Stalin's victims,

Nadezhda Krupskaya, wife of Vladimir Lenin, seated at her desk. © HULTON-DEUTSCH COLLECTION/CORBIS

including Yuri Pyatakov, but without success. Although Stalin gave a eulogy at her funeral in 1939, her works were suppressed until Nikita Khrushchev's Thaw.

Historians have tended to minimize Krupskaya's importance, viewing her primarily as Lenin's wife. Yet she played a crucial role in establishing the Party, building up the political education apparatus that reached millions of people, and keeping women's issues on the political agenda.

See also: ARMAND, INESSA; EDUCATION; LENIN, VLADIMIR ILICH; ZHENOTDEL

BIBLIOGRAPHY

McNeal, Robert H. (1972). *Bride of the Revolution.* Ann Arbor: University of Michigan Press.

Noonan, Norma C. (1991). "Two Solutions to the Zhenskii Vopros in Russia and the USSR, Kollontai and

Krupskaia: A Comparison." *Women and Politics* 2(3):77–100.

Stites, Richard. (1975). "Kollontai, Inessa, and Krupskaia: A Review of Recent Literature." *Canadian-American Slavic Studies* 9(1):84–92.

Stites, Richard. (1978). *The Women's Liberation Movement in Russia: Feminism, Nihilism, and Bolshevism, 1860–1930.* Princeton, NJ: Princeton University Press.

Wood, Elizabeth A. (1997). *The Baba and the Comrade: Gender and Politics in Revolutionary Russia.* Bloomington: Indiana University Press.

ELIZABETH A. WOOD

KRYLOV, IVAN ANDREYEVICH

(1769–1844), writer, especially of satirical fables, who is often called the "Russian Aesop."

The son of a provincial army captain who died when he was ten, Krylov had little formal education but significant artistic ambitions. Entering the civil service in Tver, Krylov was subsequently transferred to the imperial capital of St. Petersburg in 1782, which gave him access to the most prominent of cultural circles. Although he began his literary career penning comic operas, when he joined Nikolai Novikov and Alexander Radishchev on the editorial board of the satirical journal *Pochta dukhov* (Mail for Spirits) in 1789, he became recognized as a leading figure in Russia's Enlightenment. When the French Revolution made enlightened principles particularly dangerous during the last years of the reign of Catherine the Great, Krylov left St. Petersburg to escape the more severe fates suffered by his coeditors. He spent five years traveling and working in undistinguished positions.

In 1901, with the assumption of the throne by Catherine's liberally minded grandson, Alexander I, Krylov moved to Moscow and resumed his literary career. Five years later, he returned to St. Petersburg, returning also to satire. He began translating the works of French storyteller Jean La Fontaine, and in the process discovered his own talents as a fabulist. Moreover, his originality coincided with the intellectual movement to create a national literature for Russia. His new circle was as illustrious as the old, including the poet Alexander Pushkin, who was the guiding spirit behind the evolution of Russian into a literary language.

Krylov's fables, which numbered more than two hundred, featured anthropomorphized animals who made political statements about contemporary Russian politics. This satirical style allowed him to describe repressive aspects of the autocracy without suffering the wrath of Catherine's heirs. He received government sinecure with a position in the national public library, where he worked for thirty years. Many of his characters and aphorisms continue to resonate in Russian popular culture.

See also: CATHERINE II; ENLIGHTENMENT, IMPACT OF; PUSHKIN, ALEXANDER SERGEYEVICH

BIBLIOGRAPHY

Krylov, Ivan. (1977). *Krylov's Fables*, tr. with a preface by Sir Bernard Pares. Westport, CT: Hyperion Press.

Stepanov, N. L. (1973). *Ivan Krylov.* New York: Twayne.

LOUISE MCREYNOLDS

KRYUCHKOV, VLADIMIR ALEXANDROVICH

(b. 1924), Soviet police official; head of the KGB from 1988 to 1991.

Born in Volgograd, Russia, Vladimir Kryuchkov joined the Communist Party in 1944 and became a full-time employee of the Communist Youth League (*Komsomol*). In 1946 Kryuchkov embarked on a legal career, working as an investigator for the prosecutor's office and studying at the All-Union Juridical Correspondence Institute, from which he received a diploma in 1949. Kryuchkov joined the Soviet Ministry of Foreign Affairs in 1951 and enrolled as a student at the Higher Diplomatic School in Moscow. He received his first assignment abroad in 1955, when he was sent to Hungary to serve under Soviet Ambassador Yuri Andropov. Kryuchkov was in Budapest during the Soviet invasion in 1956 and was an eyewitness to the brutal suppression of Hungarian nationalists by Soviet troops. After returning to Moscow in 1959, he worked in the Central Committee Department for Liaison with Socialist Countries, which his former supervisor Andropov now headed. In 1967, when Andropov was appointed to the leadership of the KGB, the Soviet police and intelligence apparatus, he brought Kryuchkov, who rose to the post of chief of the KGB's First Chief Directorate (foreign intelligence) in 1977. In 1988 Soviet party leader Mikhail Gorbachev appointed Kryuchkov chairman of the KGB. Although Kryuchkov voiced public support for Gorbachev's liberal reforms, he grew increasingly alarmed by the threats to Soviet unity posed by the non-Russian republics. In August 1991, Kryuchkov and his hard-line colleagues in the government declared a state of emergency in the country, hoping that Gorbachev, who was vacationing in the Crimea, would support them. When Gorbachev refused, they backed down and were arrested. Kryuchkov was released from prison in 1993 and in 1996 published his memoirs, *A Personal File* (*Lichnoye delo*), where he defended his attempt to keep the Soviet Union together and accused Gorbachev of weakness and duplicity.

See also: ANDROPOV, YURI VLADIMIROVICH; AUGUST 1991 PUTSCH; GORBACHEV, MIKHAIL SERGEEVICH; INTELLIGENCE SERVICES; STATE SECURITY, ORGANS OF

BIBLIOGRAPHY

Knight, Amy. (1988). *The KGB: Police and Politics in the Soviet Union*. Boston: Allen and Unwin.

Knight, Amy. (1996). *Spies Without Cloaks: The KGB's Successors.* Princeton, NJ: Princeton University Press.

AMY KNIGHT

KUCHUK KAINARJI, TREATY OF

The first war between Russia and Turkey during the reign of Catherine the Great began in 1768. After the Russians won a series of victories and advanced beyond the Danube River deep into Ottoman territory in the Balkans, Field Marshal Peter Rumyantsev and Turkish plenipotentiaries met in an obscure Bulgarian village and signed a peace treaty on July 10, 1774. The war was a major victory for Catherine's expansionist policy and a realization of the goals of Peter the Great in the south. The Russian Empire gained permanent control of all the fortress-ports on the Sea of Azov and around the Dneiper-Bug estuary, the right of free navigation on the Black Sea, including the right to maintain a fleet, and the right of passage through the Bosphorus and the Dardanelles for merchant vessels. The Tatar khanate of the Crimean Peninsula was recognized as independent, thus removing the Ottoman presence from the northern shore of the Black Sea and essentially bringing the area under Russia control (it was peacefully annexed in 1783), and the Turks paid an indemnity of 4.5 million rubles, which covered much of the Russian costs of the war.

The treaty also gave Russia the right to maintain consulates throughout the Ottoman Empire and to represent the interests of the Orthodox Church in the Holy Land. Because Russia no longer needed an alliance with an independent Zaporozhian Cossack host, this military and diplomatic success led to its destruction and the end of any notion of an autonomous Ukraine for more than a hundred years. The treaty symbolized the consolidation of Russian control of the southern steppe, the rise of Russia as a great European and Middle Eastern power, and the beginning of the end of Turkish supremacy in the area. No wonder there were great celebrations in Moscow a year later, during which the foremost Russian military heroes were lavishly rewarded and Rumyantsev was given the honorific *Zadunyasky* ("beyond the Danube"). More than any other event, the treaty established Catherine II as "the Great" in terms of Russian expansion. The Ottoman loss, however, left a vacuum in the eastern Mediterranean open for the ambitions of Napoleon I twenty-five years later, and many more battles in the eastern Mediterranean would result. Perhaps the shattering international impact of the treaty is the ghost behind the Middle Eastern and Balkan problems of the twentieth century and beyond.

See also: CATHERINE II; RUMYANTSEV, PETER ALEXANDROVICH; RUSSO-TURKISH WARS

BIBLIOGRAPHY

Alexander, John T. (1989). *Catherine the Great: Life and Legend.* Oxford: Oxford University Press.

Madariaga, Isabel de. (1981). *Russia in the Age of Catherine the Great.* New Haven: Yale University Press.

NORMAN SAUL

KULAKS

The term *kulak* came into use after emancipation in 1861, describing peasants who profited from their peers. While kulak connotes the power of the fist, the nearly synonymous term *miroyed* means "mir-eater." At first the term "kulak" did not refer to the newly prosperous peasants, but rather to village extortioners who consume the commune, men of special rapacity, their wealth derived from usury or trading rather than from agriculture. The term never acquired precise scientific or economic definition. Peasants had a different understanding of the kulaks than outsiders; however, both definitions focused on social and moral aspects. During the twentieth century Lenin and Stalin defined the kulaks in economic and political terms as the capitalist strata of a polarized peasantry. Exploitation was the central element in the peasants' definition of the *miroyed* as well as in outsiders' definition of the kulak. Peasants, by contrast, attributed power to the kulak and limited their condemnation to peasants who exploited members of their own community. The kulaks also played an important political role in self-government of the peasant community. In the communal gathering they controlled decision making and had great influence on the opinion of the rest of the peasants.

The meaning of the term changed after the October Revolution, as the prerevolutionary type of kulak seldom survived in the village. In the 1920s the kulaks were in most instances simply wealthier peasants who, unlike their predecessors, were incontestably devoted to agriculture. They often were only slightly distinguishable from the middle peasants. Thus many Bolshevik leaders denied the existence of kulaks in the Soviet countryside. When in the mid-1920s the question of differentiation of the peasantry became part of the political debate, the statisticians had to provide a picture based on Lenin's assumption of class division. As social differentiation was still quite weak, it was impossible to define a clear class of capitalist peasants. The use of hired laborers and the leasing of land was under control of the rural soviets. Traditional forms of exploitation in the countryside, such as usury and trading, had lost their significance due to the growing cooperative organization of the peasantry. Since the use of hired laborers—a sign of capitalist exploitation—made it difficult to find a significant number of peasant capitalists for statistical purposes, a mixture of signs of wealth and obscure indicators of exploitation came into use in definition of the kulak: for example, ownership of at least three draught animals, sown area of more than eleven hectares, ownership of a trading establishment even without hired help, ownership of a complex and costly agricultural machine or of a considerable quantity of good quality implements, and hiring out of means of production. In general, the existence of one criterion was enough to define the peasant household as kulak. The statisticians thus determined that 3.9 percent of the peasantry consisted of kulaks.

It was exactly its indefiniteness that allowed the Bolsheviks to use the term *kulak* to initiate class war in the Soviet countryside toward the end of the 1920s. In order to force the peasants into the kolkhoz, the Politburo declared the almost nonexistent group of kulaks to be class enemies. Every peasant who was unwilling to join the kolkhoz had to fear being classified as kulak and subjected to expropriation and deportation. The justification lay in the political role the stronger peasants played in the communal assemblies. Together with the bulk of the peasants they were skeptical of any ideas of collective farming. The sheer existence of successful individual peasants ran counter to the Bolshevik aim of collectivization.

Due to the political pressure of new regulations for disenfranchisement in the 1927 election campaign and expropriation by the introduction of an excessive and prohibitive individual taxation in 1928, the number of kulaks started to decrease. This process was called self-dekulakization, meaning the selling of means of production, reducing the rent of land, and the leasing of implements to poorer farms. It was easy for the kulak to bring himself socially and economically down to the situation of a middle peasant. He only had to sell his agricultural machine, dismiss his *batrak* (hired laborer), or close his enterprise for there to be nothing left of the kulak as defined by the law. Several kulaks sought to escape the blows by flight to the towns, to other villages, or even into the kolkhozy if they were admitted.

On December 27, 1929, Stalin announced the liquidation of the kulaks as a class, that is, their expropriation and deportation. For the sake of the general collectivization the kulaks were divided into three different groups. The first category, the so-called "counterrevolutionary kulak-activists, fighting against collectivization" should be either arrested or shot on the spot; their families were to be deported. The second category, "the richest kulaks," were to be deported together with their families into remote areas. The rest of the kulaks were to be resettled locally. The Politburo not only planned the deportation of kulaks, ordering between 3 to 5 percent of the peasant farms to be liquidated and their means of production to be given to the kolkhoz, but also fixed the exact number of deportees and determined their destinations. The kulaks were clearly needed as class enemies to drive the collectivization process forward: After the liquidation of the kulaks in early 1930, and during the second major wave of collectivization in 1931, the Politburo ordered a certain percentage of the remaining peasant farms to be defined as kulaks and liquidated. Even if a peasant was obviously not wealthy, the term *podkulak* (walking alongside the kulaks) enabled the worker brigades to expropriate and arrest him.

Between 1930 and 1933, some 600,000 to 800,000 peasant households consisting of 3.5 to 5 million people, were declared to be kulaks, expropriated, and turned out of their houses. As local resettlement proved difficult, deportation hit more families than originally planned. By the end of 1931, about 380,000 to 390,000 kulak households consisting of about two million people were deported and brought to special settlements in remote areas, mostly in northern Russia or Siberia. Between 1933 and 1939, another 500,000 people reached the special settlements, mostly deportees from the North Caucasus during the famine of 1933. About one-fourth of the deportees did not survive the transport or the first years in the special settlements. After the new constitution of 1936, the term *kulak* fell out of use. At the beginning of 1941, 930,000 people were still registered in the special settlements. They were finally reinstated with their civilian rights during or shortly after World War II.

See also: CLASS SYSTEM; COLLECTIVE FARM; COLLECTIVIZATION OF AGRICULTURE; COOPERATIVE SOCIETIES; EMANCIPATION ACT; PEASANTRY; STALIN, JOSEF VISSARIONOVICH

BIBLIOGRAPHY

Frierson, Cathy Anne. (1992). *From Narod to Kulak: Peasant Images in Russia, 1870–1885*. Ph.D. diss., University of Michigan, Ann Arbor.

Lewin, Moshe. (1966/1967). "Who was the Soviet Kulak?" *Soviet Studies* 18:189–212.

Merl, Stephan. (1990). "Socio-economic Differentiation of the Peasantry." In *From Tsarism to the New Economic Policy: Continuity and Change in the Economy of the USSR*, ed. Robert W. Davies. London: Macmillan Press.

Viola, Lynne. (1996). *Peasant Rebels under Stalin: Collectivization and the Culture of Peasant Resistance*. New York: Oxford University Press.

STEPHAN MERL

KULESHOV, LEV VLADIMIROVICH

(1899–1970), film director and theorist.

Along with Sergei Eisenstein, Vsevolod Pudovkin, and Dziga Vertov, Lev Kuleshov revolutionized the art of filmmaking in the 1920s. One of the few Young Turks to have had significant prerevolutionary experience in cinema, Kuleshov was employed by the Khanzhonkov studio as an art director in 1916 and worked with the great Russian director Yevgeny Bauer until Bauer's death in 1917. Kuleshov's first movie as a director was *Engineer Prite's Project* (1918). During the Russian Civil War he organized newsreel production at the front.

In 1919 he founded a filmmaking workshop in Moscow that came to be known as the Kuleshov collective. Because of the shortage of film stock during the civil war, the collective shot "films without film," which is to say that they staged rehearsals. Several important directors and actors emerged from the collective, including Boris Barnet, Vsevolod Pudovkin, Alexandra Khokhlova, Sergei Komarov, and Vladimir Fogel.

Kuleshov also became known as the leading experimentalist and theorist among the Soviet Union's future cinema artists, and published his ideas extensively. His most famous was known as the "Kuleshov effect." By juxtaposing different images with the same shot of the actor Ivan Mozzhukhin, Kuleshov demonstrated the relationship between editing and the spectator's perception. Although there is some debate about the validity of the experiment in the early twenty-first century, at the time it was widely reported that viewers insisted that Mozzhukhin's expression changed according to the montage. His published his film theories in 1929 as *The Art of the Cinema*.

Kuleshov made a series of brilliant but highly criticized movies in the 1920s, most important among them *The Extraordinary Adventures of Mr. West in the Land of the Bolsheviks* (1924) and *By the Law* (1926). Even before the Cultural Revolution (1928–1931), Kuleshov had been attacked as a "formalist," and his career as a director essentially ended in 1933 with *The Great Consoler*. In 1939 Kuleshov joined the faculty of the All-Union State Institute of Cinematography and taught directing to a new generation of Soviet filmmakers.

See also: BAUER, YEVGENY FRANTSEVICH; CULTURAL REVOLUTION; EISENSTEIN, SERGEI MIKHAILOVICH; MOTION PICTURES

BIBLIOGRAPHY

Kuleshov, Lev.(1974). *Kuleshov on Film: Writings*. Berkeley: University of California Press.

Youngblood, Denise J. (1991). *Soviet Cinema in the Silent Era, 1918–1935.* Austin: University of Texas Press.

DENISE J. YOUNGBLOOD

KULIKOVO FIELD, BATTLE OF

On September 8, 1380, Rus forces led by Grand Prince Dmitry Ivanovich fought and defeated a mixed (including Tatar, Alan, Circassian, Genoese, and Rus) army led by the Emir Mamai on Kulikovo Pole (Snipe's Field) at the Nepryadva River, a tributary of the Don. As a result of the victory, Dmitry received the sobriquet "Donskoy." Estimates of numbers who fought in the battle vary widely. According to Rus chronicles, between 150,000 and 400,000 fought on Dmitry's side. One late chronicle places the number fighting on Mamai's side at 900,030. Historians have tended to downgrade these numbers, with estimates ranging from 30,000 to 240,000 for Dmitry and 200,000 to 300,000 for Mamai.

The circumstances of the battle involved politics within the Qipchaq Khanate. Mamai attempted to oust Khan Tokhtamish, who had established himself in Sarai in 1378. In order to raise revenue, Mamai intended to require tribute payments from the Rus princes. Dmitry organized the Rus princes to resist Mamai and, in effect, to support Tokhtamish. As part of his strategy, Mamai had attempted to coordinate his forces with those of Jagailo, the grand duke of Lithuania, but the battle occurred before the Lithuanian forces arrived. After fighting most of the day, Mamai's forces left the field, presumably because he was defeated, although some historians think he intended to conserve his army to confront Tokhtamish. Dmitry's forces remained at the scene of the battle for several days, and on the way back to Rus were set upon by the Lithuania forces under Jagailo, which, too late to join up with Mamai's army, nonetheless managed to wreak havoc on the Rus troops.

Although the numbers involved in the battle were immense, and although the battle led to the weakening of Mamai's army and its eventual defeat by Tokhtamish, the battle did not change the vassal status of the Rus princes toward the Qipchaq khan. A cycle of literary works, including *Zadonshchinai* (Battle beyond the Don) and *Skazanie o Mamaevom poboishche* (Tale of the Rout of Mamai), devoted to ever-more elaborate embroidering of the bravery of the Rus forces, has created a legendary aura about the battle.

See also: DONSKOY, DMITRY IVANOVICH; GOLDEN HORDE; KIEVAN RUS

BIBLIOGRAPHY

Halperin, Charles J. (1986). *The Tatar Yoke.* Columbus, OH: Slavica Publishers.

DONALD OSTROWSKI

KULTURNOST

The term *kulturnost* ("culturedness") originates from the Russian *kultura* (culture) and can be translated as "cultured behavior," "educatedness," or simply "culture."

Kulturnost is a concept used to determine the level of a person's or a group's education and culture, which can be purposefully transferred and individually adopted. It first appeared in the 1870s when the *narodniki* (group of liberals and intellectuals) tried to bring education and enlightenment to the working and peasant masses. A "cultured person" (*kulturnyi chelovek*) was one who mastered culture.

The meanings of kulturnost can differ with time, place, and context. It became a strategy of the Soviet regime in the 1930s, when millions of peasants poured into the cities and new construction sites, and their *nekulturnost* (uncultured behavior) seemed to endanger public order. Cultural policy aimed to transform them into disciplined Soviet citizens by propagandizing kulturnost, which in this context demanded good manners, personal hygiene (e.g. cleaning teeth), dressing properly, but also a certain educational background, level of literacy, and basic knowledge of communist ideology.

Kulturnost was thus part of a broader Soviet civilizing mission addressing the Russian peasants, but also native "backward" peoples. In the creation of a new Soviet middle class, kulturnost centered on individual consumption. Values and practices that were formerly scorned as bourgeois could be reestablished on the basis of kulturnost in the 1930s.

As an integration strategy used by the regime and as a reference point for various parts of the population, kulturnost gained significance in the formation of Russian and Soviet identities.

See also: NATIONALITIES POLICY, SOVIET; PEASANTRY

BIBLIOGRAPHY

Fitzpatrick, Sheila. (1992). *The Cultural Front. Power and Culture in Revolutionary Russia.* Ithaca, NY: Cornell University Press.

Volkov, Vadim. (2000). "The Concept of *Kul'turnost'*. Notes on the Stalinist Civilizing Process." In *Stalinism. New Directions*, ed. Sheila Fitzpatrick. London and New York: Routledge.

JULIA OBERTREIS

KUNAYEV, DINMUKHAMMED AKHMEDOVICH

(1912–1993), second ethnic Kazakh to lead the Kazakh Communist Party, member of the Soviet Politburo.

Born in Alma-Ata, Dinmukhammed Kunayev became a mining engineer after graduating from Moscow's Kalinin Metals Institute in 1936. He joined the Communist Party in 1939 and soon became chief engineer, and then director, of the Kounrad Mine of the Balkhash Copper-Smelting Combine. Between 1941 and 1945 he was deputy chief engineer and head of the technical section of the Altaipolimetall Combine, director of the Ridder Mine, and then director of the extensive Leninogorsk Mining Administration. From 1942 to 1952 he also was deputy chairman of the Kazakh Council of People's Commissars. Having obtained a candidate's degree in technical sciences in 1948, he became a full member of the Kazakh Academy of Sciences in 1952 and served as its president until 1955 and as chairman of the Kazakh SSR's Council of Ministers from 1955 to 1960.

By now a regular delegate to both the Kazakh and Soviet Party Congresses and Supreme Soviets, Kunayev progressed within the Communist hierarchy as well. In 1949 he became a candidate, and in 1951 a full member, of the Kazakh Central Committee, and in 1956 a member of the Central Committee of the CPSU. A member of the Kazakh Party's Bureau, he first served as the powerful first secretary from 1960 to 1962 and, after chairing the ministerial council from 1962 to 1964, served again as first secretary from 1964 to 1986. In 1966 he also became a candidate member of the Soviet Central Committee's Politburo, in 1971 he was promoted to full membership, and he was twice named a Hero of Socialist Labor (1972, 1976). Much of his success was due to the patronage of the Soviet leader Leonid Brezhnev, who himself earlier had been the Kazakh Party's first secretary. Critics charged that Kunayev showered Brezhnev with gifts and cash, but left politics to Party officials while he focused on the interests of his large and corrupt Kazakh clan. Even so, he did promote the concept of Kazakhstani citizenship and, in December 1986, his dismissal for corruption and replacement by the Russian Gennady Kolbin sparked the Alma-Ata riots. Despite Kunayev's ejection from the Politburo in January 1987, in 1989 his supporters secured his election to the Kazakh parliament, and he remained a deputy until he died near Alma-Ata in 1993. In late 1992 his clan and former Kazakh officials honored him by establishing a Kunayev International Fund in Alma-Ata. It had the proclaimed goals of strengthening the Kazakh Republic's sovereignty, improving its living standards, and reviving the Kazakh cultural heritage.

See also: CENTRAL COMMITTEE; COMMUNIST PARTY OF THE SOVIET UNION; KAZAKHSTAN AND KAZAKHS

BIBLIOGRAPHY

Olcott, Martha Brill. (1995). *The Kazakhs*, 2nd ed. Stanford, CA: Hoover Institution.

DAVID R. JONES

KURBSKY, ANDREI MIKHAILOVICH

(1528–1583), prince, boyar, military commander, emigré, writer, and translator.

A scion of Yaroslav's ruling line, Kurbsky began his career at Ivan IV's court in 1547. From 1550 on, Kurbsky participated in military campaigns, including the capture of Kazan (1552). In 1550 he was listed among the thousand elite military servitors in Muscovy. In 1556 Kurbsky received the highest court rank, that of boyar. During the Livonian war, Kurbsky became a high-ranking commander (1560). In 1564 Kurbsky fled to Sigismund II Augustus, ruler of Poland and Lithuania, fearing persecution in Muscovy. Kurbsky's defection resulted in the confiscation of his lands and the repression of his relatives in Muscovy.

Receiving large estates from Sigismund II, Kurbsky served his new lord in a military capacity, even taking part in campaigns against Muscovy (1564, 1579, 1581). Kurbsky tried to integrate himself into Lithuanian society through two marriages to local women and participation in the work of local elective bodies. At the same time, he was involved in numerous legal and armed conflicts with his neighbors.

A number of literary works and translations are credited to Kurbsky. Among them are three letters to Ivan IV, in which Kurbsky justified his flight and accused the tsar of tyranny and moral corruption. His "History of the Grand Prince of Moscow" glorifies Kurbsky's military activities and condemns the terror of Ivan IV. Kurbsky is sometimes seen as the first Russian dissident, though in fact he never questioned the political foundations of Muscovite autocracy. Continuing study of Kurbsky's works has overturned traditional descriptions of him as a conservative representative of the Muscovite aristocracy. Together with his associates, Kurbsky compiled and translated in exile works from various Christian and classical authors. Kurbsky's literary activities in the Polish-Lithuanian Commonwealth are a striking example of contacts between Renaissance and Eastern Orthodox cultures in the second half of the sixteenth century. Kurbsky's interest in theological and classical writings, however, did not make him part of Renaissance culture or alter his Muscovite cultural stance.

Edward L. Keenan argues that the texts attributed to Kurbsky were in fact produced in the seventeenth century and that Kurbsky was functionally illiterate in Slavonic. Keenan's hypothesis is based on the dating and distribution of the surviving manuscripts, on textual similarities between works credited to Kurbsky and those by other authors of later origin, and on his idea that members of the sixteenth-century secular elite, including Kurbsky, remained outside the tradition of church Slavonic religious writing. Most experts reject Keenan's ideas. His opponents offer an alternative textual analysis and detect circumstantial references to Kurbsky's letters to Ivan IV in sixteenth-century sources. Scholars have discovered an earlier manuscript of Kurbsky's first letter to Ivan IV and have provided considerable information on Kurbsky's life in exile, on his political importance as an opponent of Ivan IV, and on the cultural interaction between the church and secular elites in Muscovy. Though Kurbsky claimed he could not write Cyrillic, this statement is open to different interpretations. Other Muscovites, whose ability to write is well documented, also made similar declarations. Kurbsky's major works were translated into English by J. L. I. Fennell: *The Correspondence between Prince Kurbsky and Tsar Ivan IV of Russia* (1955); *Prince A. M. Kurbsky's History of Ivan IV* (1963).

See also: IVAN IV; LIVONIAN WAR; YAROSLAV VLADIMIROVICH

BIBLIOGRAPHY

Auerbach, Inge. (1997). "Identity in Exile: Andrei Mikhailovich Kurbskii and National Consciousness in the Sixteenth Century." In *Culture and Identity in Muscovy, 1359–1584 / Moskovskaya Rus (1359–1584): Kultura i istoricheskoe soznanie* (*UCLA Slavic Studies. New Series*, vol. 3), ed. Ann M. Kleimola and Gail L. Lenhoff. Moscow: ITZ-Garant.

Filyushkin, A. I. (1999). "Andrey Mikhaylovich Kurbsky." *Voprosy istorii* 1:82–96.

Halperin, Charles J. (1998). "Edward Keenan and the Kurbskii-Groznyi Correspondence in Hindsight." *Jahrbücher für Geschichte Osteuropas* 46:376–403.

Keenan, Edward L. (1971). *The Kurbskii-Groznyi Apocrypha: The Seventeenth-Century Genesis of the "Correspondence" Attributed to Prince A. M. Kurbskii and Tsar Ivan IV*, with an appendix by Daniel C. Waugh. Cambridge, MA: Harvard University Press.

Sergei Bogatyrev

KURDS

The Kurds (or *kurmandzh*, as they call themselves) are a people of Indo-European origin who claim as their homeland (Kurdistan) the region encompassing the intersection of the borders of Turkey, Iran, Iraq, and Syria. The name "Kurd" has been officially used only in the Soviet Union; the Turks call them Turkish Highlanders, while Iranians call them Persian Highlanders. Although the Kurdish diaspora throughout the world numbers 30 to 40 million, most Kurds live in the mountains and uplands of the above mentioned countries and number between 10 and 12 million.

The Kurds have never had their own sovereign country, but for a short period in the early 1920s a Kurdish autonomous region existed in Azerbaijan. Although most Kurds live in Turkey, Iran, Iraq,

Lithograph depicting Kurds fighting Tatars, c. 1849. © HISTORICAL PICTURE ARCHIVE/CORBIS

and Syria, two types of Kurdish peoples lived in the Soviet Union before its collapse: the Balkano-Caucasian Caspian type of the European race akin to the Azerbaijanis, Tats, and Talysh (living in Transcaucasia), and the Central-Asian Kurds such as the Baluchis (living in Tajikistan). Most Muslims of the former Soviet Union resided in Central Asia, but some also lived on the USSR's western borders, as well as in Siberia and near the Chinese border. Ethnically Soviet Muslims included Turkic, Caucasian, and Iranian people. The Kurds, along with the Tats, Talysh, and Baluchis, are Iranian people. In Transcaucasia the Kurds live in enclaves among the main population: in Azerbaijan (in Lyaki, Kelbadjar, Kubatly, and Zangelan); in Armenia (in Aparan, Talin, and Echmiadzin); and in Georgia (scattered in the eastern parts). In Central Asia they lived in Kazakhstan, Tajikistan, and Turkmenistan (along the Iranian border, as well as in Ashkhabad).

The Kurds of Caucasia and Central Asia were isolated for so long from their brethren in the Middle East that their development in the Soviet Union has diverged enough that some consider the Soviet Kurds to be a separate ethnic group. Kurdish is an Indo-European language belonging to the Northwestern Iranian branch and is divided into several dialects. The Kurds of Caucasia and Central Asia speak the *kurmandzh* dialect. Younger generations of Soviet Kurds in larger cities grew up bilingual, speaking Russian as well. In the main, the Kurds are followers of Islam. The Armenian Kurds are Sunnites, while the Central Asian and Azerbaijani Kurds are Shiite.

In the Russian Federation in the twenty-first century, Kurds are frequently the targets of ethnic violence. Skinheads, incited by Eduard Limonov (a right-wing author and journalist) and Alexander Barkashov (former head of the Russian National Unity Party who openly espouses Nazi beliefs) have assaulted Kurds, Yezids, Meskheti Turks, and other non-Russians, particularly those from the Caucasus. Racism has prevailed even among Russian officials, who have stated that non-Russian ethnic groups such as the Kurds can only be guests in the Krasnodar territory (in the Russian southwest), but not for long.

See also: CAUCASUS; CENTRAL ASIA; ISLAM

BIBLIOGRAPHY

Bulloch, John, and Harvey Morris. (1992). *No Friends but the Mountains: The Tragic History of the Kurds.* New York: Oxford University Press.

Chaliand, Gerard. (1993). *A People without a Country: The Kurds and Kurdistan.* New York: Olive Branch Press.

Izady, Mehrdad R. (1992). *The Kurds: A Concise Handbook.* Washington DC: Crane Russak.

Kreyenbroek, Philip G. (1992). *The Kurds: A Contemporary Overview.* London: Routledge.

Randal, Jonathan C. (1997). *After Such Knowledge, What Forgiveness? My Encounters with Kurdistan.* New York: Farrar, Straus and Giroux.

JOHANNA GRANVILLE

KURIL ISLANDS

The Kurils form an archipelago of more than thirty mountainous islands situated in a curving line running north from Japanese Hokkaido to Russia's Kamchatka peninsula, enclosing the Sea of Okhotsk and occupying an area of 15,600 square kilometers. The Kurils have numerous lakes and rivers, with a harsh monsoon climate, and are highly seismic, with some thirty-five active volcanoes. Russians in search of furs first moved into the islands from Kamchatka early in the eighteenth century, thus coming into contact with the native Ainu and eventually with the Japanese, who were expanding northward. The 1855 Treaty of Shimoda divided the islands; those north of Iturup were ceded to Russia, while Japan controlled the four southern islands. In the 1875 Treaty of St. Petersburg, Japan ceded Sakhalin to Russia in exchange for the eighteen central and northern islands; the 1905 Treaty of Portsmouth granted Japan sovereignty over southern Sakhalin and all neighboring islands. The USSR reoccupied the Kurils after World War II, and in 1948 expelled 17,000 Japanese inhabitants. Since then the southern four islands (Kunashiri, Shikotan, Iturup, and the Habomais group) have been disputed territory.

The Kuril islands are administered by Russian Sakhalin. Never large, the population declined to about 16,000 following a major earthquake in 1994. Some 3,500 border troops, far fewer than in Soviet times, remain to guard the territory. During the Soviet period the islands were considered a vital garrison outpost. The military valued the island chain's role in protecting the Sea of Okhotsk, where Soviet strategic submarines were located. The major industries are fish processing, fishing, and crabbing, much of which is illegal. Once pampered and highly paid by the Soviet government, the Kuril islanders were neglected by Moscow after the collapse of the Soviet Union. Of necessity, the inhabitants are developing closer ties with northern Japan.

See also: JAPAN, RELATIONS WITH; RUSSO-JAPANESE WAR

BIBLIOGRAPHY

Cobb, Charles E., Jr. (1996). "Storm Watch Over the Kurils." *National Geographic* 190(4):48–67.

Stephan, John J. (1974). *The Kuril Islands: Russo-Japanese Frontier in the Pacific.* Oxford: Clarendon Press.

CHARLES E. ZIEGLER

KURITSYN, FYODOR VASILEVICH

(died c. 1502), state secretary (*diak*) and accused heretic under Ivan III.

From an unknown family, but recognized for his linguistic, literary, and administrative talents, Fyodor Vasilevich Kuritsyn was one of Ivan III's chief diplomats in the 1480s and 1490s. Kuritsyn's most important mission was to Matthias Corvinas of Hungary and Stefan the Great of Moldavia from 1482 to 1484 to arrange an alliance against Poland-Lithuania. Kuritsyn then became one of the sovereign's top privy advisors and handled several affairs with Crimea and European states, including secret matters. Fixer of the first official Russian document with the two-headed eagle, Kuritsyn was also involved in Muscovy's initial land cadastres. The disappearance of his name from the written sources after 1500 may have been connected with the fall of Ivan III's half-Moldavian grandson and crowned co-ruler Dmitry.

The traces of Kuritsyn's intellectual life are intriguing. According to testimony obtained from a Novgorod priest's son under torture, Kuritsyn returned from Hungary and formed a circle of clerics and scribes that "studied anti-Orthodox material." Other "heretics" found refuge at his home, so Archbishop Gennady concluded that Kuritsyn was the "protector . . . and . . . leader of all those scoundrels." According to Joseph of Volotsk's exaggerated *Account*, the Novgorodian heresiarch-archpriest Alexei and Kuritsyn "studied astronomy, lots of literature, astrology, sorcery, and secret knowledge, and therefore many people inclined toward them and were mired in the depths of apostasy." Kuritsyn's milieu probably did have access to some philosophical and astronomical treatises.

The only work with Kuritsyn's name as conveyor or translator-copyist is a brief poem with an attached table of letters and coded alphabet, sharing the deceptive, New Testament-Apocryphal title, "Laodician Epistle." The poem is of the chain type, on the theme of the sovereign soul enclosed in faith, linking wisdom, knowledge, the prophets, fear of God, and virtue. The table gives phonetic and, where appropriate, grammatical characteristics of the letter symbols in their dual function as letters and numbers. It uses both Greek and Slavic terms—the latter having the metaphorical symmetry of vowel-soul and consonant-body—and may contain some hidden meanings or utility for divination. An anonymous explanatory introduction is close to the likewise anonymous "Outline of Grammar," both possibly by Kuritsyn. They promote the sovereignty of the literate mind and treat letters as God's redemptive gift to humanity and the source of wisdom, science, memory, and predictive powers. Not strictly heretical, but akin to Jewish wisdom literature, these works sat on the humanist fringe of the acceptable in Muscovy.

Kuritsyn also may have composed, redacted, or simply conveyed from Moldavia the underlying text of the Slavic "Tale of Dracula." This string of semi-folklorish anecdotes about the "evil genius" Wallachian *voevoda* Vlad the Impaler recounts the just and unjust beastly reprisals of this self-styled "great sovereign" without moral commentary—except in the description of his purported apostasy to Catholicism. Implicitly "Dracula" teaches that despots must be humored and envoys trained and smart.

Kuritsyn probably died around 1501. In 1502 or 1503 Ivan III reportedly knew "which heresy Fyodor Kuritsyn held," and in 1504 allowed Fyodor's brother, the diplomat-jurist state secretary Ivan Volk, to be burned as a heretic or apostate. Fyodor's son Afanasy was also a state secretary.

See also: IVAN III; RUSSIAN ORTHODOX CHURCH

BIBLIOGRAPHY

Taube, Moshe. (1995). "The 'Poem on the Soul' in the *Laodicean Epistle* and the Literature of the Judaizers." *Harvard Ukrainian Studies* 19:671–685.

DAVID M. GOLDFRANK

KUROPATKIN, ALEXEI NIKOLAYEVICH

(1848–1925), adjutant general, minister of war, commander during the Russo-Japanese War, colonial administrator, and author.

Born in Sheshurino, Pskov Province, in 1848 to a retired officer with liberal inclinations, Alexei Kuropatkin received a superb military education, graduating from the Paul Junker Academy in 1866 and the Nicholas Academy of the General Staff in 1874. Much of Kuropatkin's career was linked to the empire's eastern frontier. Beginning as an infantry subaltern in Central Asia, he saw active duty during the conquest of Turkestan (1866–1871, 1875–1877, 1879–1883) and the Russo-Turkish War (1877–1878). Kuropatkin's close association with the flamboyant White General Mikhail Dimitriyevich Skobelev, earned him a misleading reputation as a decisive commander in combat (a deception Kuropatkin actively promoted by writing popular campaign histories). Kuropatkin was best suited for administration and intelligence, and he enjoyed a rapid rise in the military bureaucracy, including posts in the army's Main Staff (1878–1879, 1883–1890), head of the Trans-Caspian Oblast (1890–1898), and minister of war (1898–1904).

Kuropatkin assumed command of the ministry in a climate of strategic vulnerability, as growing German military power combined with a weakening economy. Accordingly, his top priority was to strengthen the empire's western defenses against the Central Powers. However, Nicholas II's adventures on the Pacific drew him back to the East, albeit reluctantly. Well aware of the threat posed by Japan's modern armed forces, Kuropatkin opposed the Russian emperor's increasingly aggressive course in Manchuria. Nevertheless, he loyally resigned his post as minister to command Russia's land forces in East Asia when Japan attacked in 1904. Insecurity and indecision hobbled his performance in the field. Reluctant to risk his troops in a decisive contest, Kuropatkin chose instead to order retreats whenever the outcome of a clash seemed in doubt. As a result, while he never lost a major battle, his repeated pullbacks fatally corroded Russian morale, and constituted one of the leading reasons for tsarist defeat in 1905.

After the war, Kuropatkin published prolifically in an effort to restore his tarnished reputation. During World War I, he returned to the colors on the northwestern front in 1915, but his leadership proved to be equally undistinguished. In July 1916 Nicholas II reassigned him as Turkestan's governor-general, where he suppressed a major nationalist rebellion later that year. Although he was relieved of his post and even briefly arrested by the Provisional Government in early 1917, Kuropatkin avoided the postrevolutionary fate of many other prominent servants of the autocracy. He spent his remaining years as a schoolteacher in his native Sheshurino until his death of natural causes on January 26, 1925. Kuropatkin does not figure prominently in the pantheon of great Russian generals, but his many published and unpublished writings reveal one of the more perceptive minds of the tsarist military.

See also: CENTRAL ASIA; RUSSO-JAPANESE WAR; RUSSO-TURKISH WARS; SKOBELEV, MIKHAIL DIMITRIYEVICH; TURKESTAN

BIBLIOGRAPHY

Kuropatkin, Aleksei N. (1909). *The Russian Army and the Japanese War*, tr. A. B. Lindsay. 2 vols. New York: E. P. Dutton.

Romanov, Boris A. (1952). *Russia in Manchuria*, tr. Susan Wilbur Jones. Ann Arbor, MI: Edwards Press.

Schimmelpenninck van der Oye, David H. (2001). *Toward the Rising Sun: Russian Ideologies of Empire and the Path to War with Japan.* DeKalb, IL: Northern Illinois University Press.

DAVID SCHIMMELPENNINCK VAN DER OYE

KURSK, BATTLE OF

The Battle of Kursk (July 5–August 23, 1943) resulted in the Soviet defeat of the German Army's last major offensive in the East and initiated an unbroken series of Red Army victories culminating in the destruction of Hitler's Third Reich. The battle consisted of Operation *Zitadelle,* (Citadel), the German Army's summer offensive to destroy Red Army forces defending the Kursk salient, and the Red Army's Operations Kutuzov and Rumyantsev against German forces defending along the flanks of the Kursk salient. More than seven thousand Soviet and three thousand German tanks and self-propelled guns took part in this titanic battle, making it the largest armored engagement in the war.

The defensive phase of the battle began on July 5, 1943, when the 9th Army of Field Marshal Guenther von Kluge's Army Group Center and the 4th Panzer Army and Army Detachment Kempf of Field Marshal Erich von Manstein's Army Group South launched concentric assaults against the northern and southern flanks of the Kursk salient. In seven days of heavy fighting, the 13th and 70th Armies and 2nd Tank Army of General K. K. Rokossovsky's Central Front fought three German panzer corps to a virtual standstill in the Ponyri and Samodurovka regions, seven miles deep into the Soviet defenses. To the south, during the same period, three panzer corps penetrated ten to twenty miles through the defenses of the Voronezh Front's 6th and 7th Guards and 69th Armies, as well as the dug in 1st Tank Army, before engaging the Steppe Front's counterattacking 5th Guards Army and 5th Guard Tank Armies in the Prokhorovka region. Worn down by constant Soviet assaults against their flanks, the German assault faltered on the plains west of Prokhorovka. Concerned about the deteriorating situation in Italy and a new Red Army offensive to the north, Hitler ended the offensive on July 13.

The day before, the Red Army commenced its summer offensive by launching Operation Kutuzov, massive assaults by five Western and Bryansk Front armies against German Second Panzer Army defending the Orel salient. Red Army forces, soon joined by the 3rd Guards and 4th Tank Armies and most of the Central Front, penetrated German defenses around Orel within days and began a steady advance, which compelled German forces to abandon the Orel salient by August 23. On August 5, three weeks after halting German forces at Prokhorovka, the Voronezh and Steppe Fronts commenced Operation Rumyantsev, a massive offensive by ten armies toward Belgorod and Kharkov. Spearheaded by the 1st and 5th Guards Tank Armies and soon reinforced by three additional armies, for the first time in the war the advancing forces defeated counterattacks by German operational reserves, and captured Kharkov on August 23.

The defeat of Hitler's last summer offensive at Kursk marked the beginning of the Red Army summer-fall campaign, which by late September collapsed the entire German front from Velikie Luki to the Black Sea and propelled Red Army forces forward to the Dnieper River. After Kursk the only unresolved questions regarded the duration and final cost of Red Army victory.

See also: WORLD WAR II

BIBLIOGRAPHY

Erickson, John. (1983). *The Road to Berlin.* Boulder, CO: Westview Press .

Glantz, David M., and House, Jonathan M. (1999). *The Battle of Kursk.* Lawrence: University Press of Kansas.

Glantz, David M., and Orenstein, Harold S, eds. (1999). *The Battle for Kursk 1943: The Soviet General Staff Study.* London: Frank Cass.

Manstein, Erich von. (1958). *Lost Victories.* Chicago: Henry Regnery.

Zetterling Niklas, and Frankson, Anders. (2000). *Kursk 1943: A Statistical Analysis.* London: Frank Cass.

DAVID M. GLANTZ

KURSK SUBMARINE DISASTER

On Saturday, August 12, 2000, the nuclear-powered cruise-missile submarine Kursk (K-141), one of Russia's most modern submarines, was lost with all 118 crewmembers during a large-scale exercise of the Russian Northern Fleet in the Barents Sea. The Kursk sank just after its commander, Captain First Rank Gennady Lyachin, informed the exercise directors that the submarine was about to execute a mock torpedo attack on a surface target. Exercise controllers lost contact with the vessel and fleet radio operators failed to reestablish communication. Shortly after the Kursk's last communication, Russian and Western acoustic sensors recorded two underwater explosions, one smaller and a second larger (the equivalent of five tons of TNT).

Russian surface and air units began a search for the submarine and in the early evening located a target at a depth of 108 meters (354.3 feet) and about 150 kilometers (93 miles) from the Northern Fleet's base at Murmansk. Russian undersea rescue units were dispatched to the site. The command of the Northern Fleet was slow to announce the possible loss of the submarine or to provide reliable information on the event. On August 13 Admiral Vyacheslav Popov, commander of the Northern Fleet, conducted a press conference on the success of the exercise but did not mention the possible loss of the Kursk. A Russian undersea apparatus reached the Kursk on Sunday afternoon and reported that the submarine's bow had been severely damaged by an explosion. The rescue crews suggested three hypotheses to explain the sinking: an internal explosion connected with the torpedo firing, a possible collision with another submarine or surface ship, or the detonation of a mine left over from World War II.

On Monday, August 14, the Northern Fleet's press service began to report its version of the disaster. The reports emphasized the absence of nuclear weapons, the stability of the submarine's reactors, and the low radioactivity at the site. It also falsely reported that communications had been reestablished with the submarine. The Northern Fleet and the Naval High Command in Moscow reported the probable cause of the disaster as a collision with a foreign submarine. While there were reports of evidence supporting this thesis, none was ever presented to confirm the explanation, and both the United States and Royal navies denied that any of their submarines had been involved in any collision with the Kursk. The Russian Navy was also reluctant to publish a list of those on board the submarine. The list, leaked to the newspaper *Komsomolskaya pravda* (Komsomol Truth), was published on August 18. The Russian Navy's initial unwillingness to accept foreign assistance in the rescue operation and failure to get access to the Kursk undermined its credibility.

When President Vladimir Putin learned of the crisis while on vacation in Sochi, he created a State Commission under Deputy Prime Minister Ilya Klebanov to investigate the event. Putin invited foreign assistance in the rescue operation. British and Norwegian divers successfully entered the Kursk on August 21 and found no survivors. Putin had kept a low profile during the rescue phase and did not directly address the relatives of the crew until August 22. At that time Putin vowed to recover the crew and vessel. In the fall of 2001 an international recovery team lifted the Kursk, minus the damaged bow. The hull was brought back to a dry dock at Roslyakovo. In December 2001, on the basis of information regarding the preparation for the exercise in which the Kursk was lost, President Putin fired fourteen senior naval officials, including Admiral Popov. Preliminary data from the Klebanov commission seems to confirm that the submarine sank as a result of a detonation of an ultra high-speed torpedo, *skval*-type. On June 18, 2002, Ilya Klebanov confirmed that the remaining plausible explanation for the destruction of the submarine was an internal torpedo explosion.

See also: MILITARY, SOVIET AND POST-SOVIET; PUTIN, VLADIMIR VLADIMIROVICH

BIBLIOGRAPHY

Burleson, Clyde. (2002). *Kursk Down*. New York: Warner Books.

JACOB W. KIPP

KUSTAR

Cottage worker, home worker; a peasant engaged in cottage industry (*kustarnaya promyshlennost*) to earn cash, usually in combination with agricultural production.

Cottage industry became an important source of income for rural peasants in some parts of Russia by the sixteenth century and developed extensively during the nineteenth century, producing a wide range of wooden, textile, metal, and leather goods. It was usually a family enterprise, although some peasants formed producer cooperatives and worked under the supervision of an elected elder. Some cottage workers independently produced and sold their production, while others participated in a putting-out system in which they worked for a middleman who furnished them with raw or semi-finished materials and collected and marketed the finished products. By the beginning of the twentieth century, the state, zemstvos, and cooperatives had established schools, credit banks, and warehouses to assist cottage workers in producing and marketing a wide variety of goods.

The socioeconomic position of Russian cottage workers was the subject of many debates in the decades preceding the revolution. Populists argued that most cottage workers remained peasant agriculturists and engaged in cottage industry only to supplement their earnings from agriculture, while Marxists contended that cottage workers were becoming proletarianized and wholly dependent on the income they earned from selling manufactured goods to middlemen.

Despite increasing competition from factories, cottage industry continued to account for a large share of Russian manufactured goods until the end of the tsarist regime, and enjoyed a brief revival in the 1920s under the New Economic Policy. Notwithstanding the importance of cottage industry in the Russian economy, there is no reliable data for the number of cottage workers in the country as a whole. Estimates range from 2.5 million to 15 million peasants engaged in cottage industry at the end of the nineteenth century.

See also: PEASANT ECONOMY; PEASANTRY

BIBLIOGRAPHY

Blum, Jerome. (1961). *Lord and Peasant in Russia from the Ninth to the Nineteenth Century.* Princeton, NJ: Princeton University Press.

Crisp, Olga. (1976). *Studies in the Russian Economy Before 1914.* London: Macmillan.

Gatrell, Peter. (1986). *The Tsarist Economy, 1850–1914.* London: Batsford.

Salmond, Wendy R. (1996). *Arts and Crafts in Imperial Russia: Reviving the Kustar Art Industries, 1970–1917.* Cambridge, UK: Cambridge University Press.

E. ANTHONY SWIFT

KUTUZOV, MIKHAIL ILARIONOVICH

(1745–1813), general, renowned for his victory over Napoleon.

At the age of sixty-seven, Mikhail Kutuzov led the Russian armies to victory over Napoleon in the War of 1812 and created the preconditions for their final victory in the campaigns of 1813 and 1814. Kutuzov first distinguished himself in extensive service against the Turks during the reign of Catherine II. He served in the Russo-Turkish War of 1768–1774, first on the staff of Petr Rumyantsev's army, and then in line units with Vasily Dolgorukov's Crimean Army. In combat in the Crimea in 1774 he was shot through the head and lost an eye. When he returned to service, he took command of the Bug Light Infantry Corps of Field Marshal Alexander Suvorov's army. He led his corps into combat with the Turks once again when war broke out in 1788. He was wounded again at the siege of Ochakov in that year, but continued to command troops throughout the war, serving under Grigory Potemkin and Alexander Suvorov. Following the end of hostilities, Kutuzov served in a number of senior positions, including ambassador to Turkey, commander of Russian forces in Finland, and military governor of Lithuania. It seemed that his days as an active commander had passed. In September 1801 he retired.

The Napoleonic Wars put a quick end to Kutuzov's ease. When war threatened in 1805, Alexander I designated Kutuzov, now a field marshal, commander of the leading Russian expeditionary army sent to cooperate with the Austrians. On the way to the designated rallying point of Braunau, on the Austrian border with Bavaria, Kutuzov learned of the surrender of the Austrian army at Ulm on October 20. Now facing French forces four times stronger than his army, Kutuzov began a skillful and orderly withdrawal to the east, hoping to link up with reinforcements on their way from Russia. Desperate rearguard actions made possible this retreat, which included even a brief victory over one of Napoleon's exposed corps at the Battle of Dürnstein. Despite Napoleon's best efforts, Kutuzov managed to withdraw his army and link up with reinforcements, headed by the tsar himself, at Olmütz in Moravia in late November. Fooled into thinking that Napoleon was weak, Alexander overruled the more cautious Kutuzov repeatedly in the days that followed, ordering the field marshal to launch an ill-advised attack on the French at Austerlitz on December 2. Wounded once again while trying to rally his men to hold a critical position, Kutuzov helped Alexander salvage what could be saved from the wreckage, and then commanded the army during its retreat back to Russian Poland.

Blaming Kutuzov for his own mistakes, Alexander relegated Kutuzov to the post of military governor general of Kiev. It was not long before Kutuzov returned to battle, however, for he joined the Army of Moldavia in 1808 and commanded large units in the war against the Turks (1806–1812). In 1809 he was relieved once more and sent to serve as governor general of Lithuania, but in 1811 Alexander designated Kutuzov as the commander of the Russian army fighting the Turks. In the shadow of the impending Franco-Russian war, Kutuzov waged a skillful campaign that resulted in the Peace of Bucharest bare weeks before the French invasion began.

The War of 1812 was Kutuzov's greatest campaign. Alexander relieved Mikhail Barclay de Tolly after his retreat from Smolensk and appointed Kutuzov, hoping thereby to see a more active resistance to the French onslaught. Kutuzov, however, continued Barclay de Tolly's program of retreating in the face of superior French numbers, until he stood to battle at Borodino. Following that combat, Kutuzov continued his withdrawal, eventually abandoning Moscow and retreating to the south. He defeated Napoleon's attempt to break out to the richer pastures of Ukraine at the Battle of Maloyaroslavets, and then harried the retreating French forces all the way to the Russian frontier and beyond. He died on April 28, 1813, a few weeks after having been relieved of command of the Russian armies for the last time.

See also: ALEXANDER I; AUSTERLITZ, BATTLE OF; BORODINO, BATTLE OF; BUCHAREST, TREATY OF; FRENCH WAR OF 1812; MILITARY, IMPERIAL ERA; NAPOLEON I; RUSSO-TURKISH WARS

BIBLIOGRAPHY

Parkinson, Roger. (1976). *The Fox of the North: The Life of Kutuzov, General of War and Peace.* London: P. Davies.

FREDERICK W. KAGAN

KUYBYSHEV, VALERIAN VLADIMIROVICH

(1888–1935), Bolshevik, politician, Stalinist, active in civil war and subsequent industrialization initiatives.

Active in the Social Democratic Party from 1904, Valerian Kuybyshev was an Old Bolshevik who played a major role in the Russian Civil War as a political commissar with the Red Army. Having fought on the Eastern Front against the forces of Admiral Kolchak, he was instrumental in consolidating Soviet power in Central Asia following the civil war. Kuybyshev subsequently held several important political posts: chairman of the Central Control Commission (1923); chairman of the Supreme Council of the Soviet Economy (1926); member of the Politburo (1927); chairman of Gosplan (1930); and deputy chairman of both the Council of People's Commissars and Council of Labor and Defense (1930).

A staunch Stalinist throughout the 1920s, Kuybyshev advocated rapid industrialization and supported Stalin in the struggle against the Right Opposition headed by Nikolai Bukharin. Kuybyshev's organizational skills and boundless energy were critical in launching the First Five-Year Plan in 1928. However, in the early 1930s Kuybyshev became associated with a moderate bloc in the Politburo who opposed some of Stalin's more repressive political policies.

Kuybyshev died suddenly on January 26, 1935, ostensibly of a heart attack, but there is some speculation that he may have been murdered by willful medical mistreatment on the orders of Genrich Yagoda—an early purge following the assassination of Sergei Kirov. Whatever the actual circumstances of his death, he was given a state funeral, and the city of Samara was renamed in his honor.

See also: CIVIL WAR OF 1917–1922; INDUSTRIALIZATION, RAPID; RED ARMY; RIGHT OPPOSITION; STALIN, JOSEF VISSARIONOVICH.

BIBLIOGRAPHY

Conquest, Robert. (1990). *The Great Terror: A Reassessment.* New York: Oxford University Press.

Kuibyshev, V. V. (1935). *Personal Recollections.* Moscow.

KATE TRANSCHEL

KUZNETSOV, NIKOLAI GERASIMOVICH

(1904–1974), commissar of the navy and admiral of the fleet of the Soviet Union.

A native of the Vologda area, from a peasant background, Kuznetsov was born on July 11, 1904. He joined the Red Navy in 1919, served during the civil war with North Dvina Flotilia, and fought against the Allied Expeditionary Force and the Whites. He served in the Black Sea Fleet beginning in 1921, became a Communist Party member in 1925, and graduated from the Frunze Naval School in 1926 and the naval Academy in 1932. He served as assistant commander of the cruiser *Krasnyi Kavkaz* (1932–1934), and as commander of the cruiser *Chervona Ukraina* (1934–1936). Kuznetsov served as naval attaché in Spain and was the Soviet advisor to the Republican Navy during the Spanish Civil War from 1936 to 1937. After returning from Spain, he served as the first deputy commander of the Pacific Fleet (commissioned August 15, 1937) and as commander of the Pacific Fleet from 1938 to 1939.

Kuznetsov was recalled to Moscow in March of 1939 and was appointed as the first deputy. Days later, on March 12, 1939, he was appointed commissar of the Navy. He held this position until 1946, leading the Soviet Navy during World War II with mixed results. The Navy did not perform well against an enemy whose naval interests were elsewhere, and it remained in a defensive mode for most of the war, suffering heavily at the hands of the Luftwaffe. The Soviet retreat from the Baltics proved to be a fiasco, but the Navy performed better in the evacuation of Odessa and Sevastopol. Two landings in Kerch in 1942 and 1943 ended in disaster, but the blame was not confined to the Navy. The Volga Flotilla played a significant part in the defense of Stalingrad, and the stationary Baltic Fleet provided artillery support in the Battle of Leningrad. Throughout 1944 and 1945, a number of landings took place behind the enemy lines, which resulted in little gain and heavy losses.

The outspoken Kuznetsov may have offended Stalin, although he blamed the Navy's shortcomings on Andrei Alexandrovich Zhdanov, the political commissar of the Navy before the war. In February 1946, Stalin divided the Baltic and Pacific Fleets into four separate units, a decision Kuznetsov opposed. The end result was the removal of Kuznetsov. He was forced to face a Court of Honor, where several admirals were accused of passing naval secrets to the Allies during the war. Kuznetsov was reduced to the rank of rear admiral on February 3, 1948, and was sent to the reserves, but was called back and appointed as deputy commander in chief in the Far East for the Navy on June 12, 1948. On February 20, 1950, he was reappointed to his old job of commander of the Pacific Fleet. Stalin, encouraged by Lavrenti Beria (head of the secret police), also recalled him, and once again named him commissar of the Navy on July 20, 1951. He kept this position even after Stalin's death.

On the night of October 29, 1955, the Soviet Navy suffered its greatest peacetime disaster when the battleship *Novorossisk* blew up in Sevastopol, with the loss of 603 lives. Kuznetsov was blamed for this disaster, and was removed from his position. On February 15, 1956, he was once again reduced in rank and forcibly retired. Kuznetsov's reputation was rehabilitated only in 1988, fourteen years after his death and after a long campaign by his widow. During his roller-coaster career, he was rear admiral twice, vice admiral three times, and admiral of the Fleet of the Soviet Union twice. He was deputy to the Supreme Soviet three times, and served the Eighteenth Party Congress in 1939. He was also declared a Hero of the Soviet Union on

September 14, 1945. The Soviet naval policy changed after Kuznetsov, who was mainly a surface-ship admiral, to emphasize an oceanic navy that was heavily dependent on a large fleet of submarines, missile cruisers, and even the occasional aircraft carrier.

See also: BALTIC FLEET; BLACK SEA FLEET; MILITARY, IMPERIAL; PACIFIC FLEET

MICHAEL PARRISH

KYRGYZSTAN AND KYRGYZ

The Kyrgyz are a nomadic people of Turkic descent living in the northern Tien Shan mountain range. Originally chronicled as living in the region of what is today eastern Siberia and Mongolia, the Kyrgyz migrated westward more than a thousand years ago and settled in the mountains of Central Asia. At the beginning of the twenty–first century, ethnic Kyrgyz live in the countries of Kazakhstan, China, Russia, Uzbekistan, and Tajikistan. The majority of the Kyrgyz live in the country of the Kyrgyz Republic (known as Kyrgystan), a former republic of the Soviet Union that received its independence in 1991 when the Soviet Union collapsed. With an area of 76,000 square miles (198,500 square kilometers), the mountainous, landlocked republic is nestled between Kazakhstan, China, Tajikistan, and Uzbekistan. The Kyrgyz Republic's population is 4,822,166, of which 2,526,800 (52.4%) are ethnic Kyrgyz. Significant minority groups include Russians (18%), Uzbeks (12.9 percent), Ukrainians (2.5%), and Germans (2.4%). The capital city of Bishkek has an estimated population of 824,900, although the number may be closer to one million if illegal immigrants are considered.

Sunni Islam of the Hanafi School is the dominant faith among the Kyrgyz. However, when Islam was introduced to the people, many kept their indigenous beliefs and customs. The force of Islam was further weakened during the Soviet period when active religious adherence was discouraged. During the early twenty-first century, the Kyrgyz government espouses strong support for maintaining a secular state and any sympathy for radical Islam has been marginalized.

Linguistically, Kyrgyz is a Turkic language that is mutually intelligible with Kazakh. Throughout the past several centuries, it has been written in the Arabic, Latin, and Cyrillic scripts, with the latter two dominant during the Soviet period. The government is shifting the language back to the Latin script, with an effort to emulate the Turkish model.

The early history of the Kyrgyz is shrouded in mythology, particularly the founding legend of the Manas, an epic poem of more than one million lines that is still presented orally, through song. Kyrgyz have had, in the past, their own forms of government, although more often they have been under the rule of outside forces: Mongol, Chinese, Timurid, and Russian, to name the most significant. During the period of the Russian Empire, the Kyrgyz were often called Kara-Kyrgyz. There is a common history with the Kazakhs, who were confusingly called the Kyrgyz by Russian ethnographers for most of the nineteenth century. Although they were incorporated into the Khanate of Kokand in the eighteenth century, the Kyrgyz were not always content with being controlled by others. Kyrgyz clans rebelled four times between 1845 and 1873. When the Khanate of Kokand was incorporated into the Russian province of Semirech'e in 1876, the same ire was directed against the new overlords.

Through the rest of the nineteenth century and into the early twentieth century, the region of the Kyrgyz was firmly entrenched in the Russian Empire. In 1916, there was a large-scale uprising in the region against the threat of drafting ethnic Kyrgyz and other Central Asians into the Russian Army, to support the effort against Germany and Austria-Hungary. The regional turmoil only deepened with the Bolshevik Revolution of 1917 and the subsequent civil war, both of which had direct effects on the Kyrgyz people. Significant fighting took place on Kyrgyz soil, and the anti-Bolshevik Basmachi Rebellion was partially based in the regions of southern Kyrgyzstan, around the city of Osh. By the early 1920s the region was pacified, but at a high cost: Perhaps a third of all residents of the region either died in the fighting and in the famine that plagued Central Asia in those years, or fled to China.

In the National Delimitation of 1924, the territory of the Kyrgyz was incorporated in the Kazakh Soviet Socialist Republic and was dubbed an Autonomous Republic. The region was elevated to full Union-Republic status in 1936 and was officially called the Kirgiz Soviet Socialist Republic (Kir.S.S.R.). This entity lasted until 1991, when the

Kyrgyzstan, 1992. © Maryland Cartographics. Reprinted with permission

Soviet Union was officially dissolved. At the time of independence, the name was changed to the Republic of Kyrgyzstan, and later the Kyrgyz Republic. With independence, the former president of the Kirgiz Soviet Socialist Republic, Askar Akayev, was elected president of the new country. He continued to hold that position in 2003, and has consolidated his authority over the years. The Kyrgyz Republic has the institutions associated with a democracy—a legislature, a judiciary, a president, and a constitution—but the conditions for democratic development remain weak.

Economically, the Kyrgyz have traditionally been nomadic herders, and pastoral activity remains important for the Kyrgyz. With more than 80 percent of the territory being mountainous, pastoral habits include bringing the herds to high-elevation fields during the summer and back to the valleys during the winter months. There are also mineral deposits in the country, particularly of gold and some strategic minerals that can be exploited. Overall, the economy remains poor, with a gross national product (GDP) of approximately $13.5 billion dollars. While the purchasing power parity (PPP) of the country is $2,800 per capita, typical incomes often fall to less than $100 per month per person.

Making matters worse is the fact that the country has borrowed heavily from the international community during the first decade of independence. The national budget is actually exceeded by the amount owed to organizations such as the World Bank and the International Monetary Fund, totaling more than $1.6 billion as of 2003. In addition, corruption is rampant and most international companies and observers view the business conditions in the country in a negative light. These problems will continue to plague any effort at economic reform that the current government, or its successor, might try to implement.

While there are ethnic Kyrgyz in neighboring Uzbekistan, Kazakhstan, Tajikistan, and China, the respective populations are relatively modest and do not cause much concern. Regardless, the Kyrgyz feel it necessary to establish positive relations with these neighboring states, in large part because of the difficult borders and the fact that the Kyrgyz Republic is a relatively small neighbor in this region. Thus, it is not surprising to see the Kyrgyz government participate in a number of multilateral security and trade agreements. It is an active member of the Commonwealth of Independent States, the Shanghai Cooperation Organization (which includes China, Russia, Tajikistan, Kazakhstan, and Uzbekistan), the Collective Security Agreement (with six CIS states), as well as a number of regional initiatives. It is also a member of the NATO Partnership for Peace Program and, as a result of the U.S.-led Global War on Terrorism, agreed to have NATO forces establish a military airbase outside of the capital city Bishkek in 2001. During 2002, the Kyrgyz government allowed the Russian Air Force to base jets at a second airbase, and in 2003 the army of Kyrgyzstan conducted military exercises with the People's Liberation Army of China.

Foreign relations ultimately are less of a concern than the day-to-day domestic problems that plague the country. Economic development, employment difficulties, crime, corruption, and social problems continue to exist in the Kyrgyz Republic.

See also: CENTRAL ASIA; ISLAM; KAZAKHSTAN AND KAZAKHS; NATIONALITIES POLICIES, SOVIET; NATIONALITIES POLICIES, TSARIST; POLOVTSY

BIBLIOGRAPHY

Achylova, Rakhat. (1995). "Political Culture and Foreign Policy in Kyrgyzstan." In *Political Culture and Civil Society in Russia and the New States of Eurasia*, ed. Vladimir Tismaneanu. Armonk, NY: M. E. Sharpe.

Allworth, Edward, ed. (1994). *Central Asia: 130 Years of Russia Dominance, A Historical Overview.* Durham, NC: Duke University Press.

Anderson, John. (1999). *Kyrgyzstan: Central Asia's Island of Democracy.* New York: Harwood Academic Publishers.

Bennigsen, Alexandre and Wimbush, S. Enders. (1985). *Muslims of the Soviet Empire: A Guide.* London: C. Hurst.

Cummings, Sally, ed. (2002). *Power and Change in Central Asia.* London: Routledge.

Huskey, Eugene. (1997). "Kyrgyzstan: The Fate of Political Liberalization." In *Conflict, Cleavage, and Change in Central Asia and the Caucasus*, ed. Karen Dawisha and Bruce Parrott. Cambridge, UK: Cambridge University Press.

Stewart, Rowan and Weldon, Susie. (2002). *Kyrgyzstan: An Illustrated Guide.* New York: Odyssey Publications.

ROGER KANGAS

LABOR

Labor commonly refers to the work people do in the employ of others. In its history, labor in Russia has taken a wide variety of forms, from slavery to labor freely exchanged for wages, and the full gamut of possibilities between those extremes. The fates of both peasants and workers have been tightly bound together through most of Russian history.

FROM KIEV THROUGH PETER I

While slavery was common through the reign of Peter I, perhaps accounting for 10 percent of the population around 1600, it was never the dominant factor in the economy. In Kievan Rus, labor was generally free in both the vibrant cities and the countryside. Although information is scarce, manufacturing throughout the Kievan and Muscovite periods seems to have been generally on a small-scale, artisanal basis; for a variety of reasons a European-style guild system never developed. The free-hire basis of labor only began to become seriously restricted with the centralization of the Muscovite state. The slow but steady imposition of serfdom on peasants was matched by a similar reduction in the urban population's mobility. Both peasants and city dwellers were permanently tied to their locations by the Law Code of 1649. Constraints on movement became even more severe when Peter I instituted the poll tax as a communal obligation, firmly binding all nonnobles to their communal organization, whether rural or urban.

Before 1700, urban manufacture was artisanal, carried out in very small enterprises, which makes it difficult to speak of an urban working class. Large-scale manufacturing began in the countryside, close to natural resources, either on noble-owned land, with nobles utilizing their own peasants, or on land granted by the government for specifically industrial purposes. In the latter case, although labor was hired at times, the work force was more usually peasants who had been assigned either temporarily or permanently to that particular enterprise. The binding of the entire population to specific locations after 1649 made freely hirable labor difficult to find. This problem was exacerbated after Peter the Great began large-scale industrialization, most notably in the Urals metallurgical complex.

FROM PETER TO THE GREAT REFORMS

During the course of the 1700s, however, the role of hired labor became more important, as the increasing importance of money in the economy made industrial labor an attractive option for both cash-starved serf owners and peasant households. This was true especially in northern Russia, where the soil was less fertile, the growing season shorter, and agriculture less viable. These regions would also experience a new kind of industrial growth, as peasant entrepreneurs, under the protection of financially interested owners, slowly exploited local craft traditions and began to build industries using hired labor. The two Sheremetev-owned villages of Ivanovo and Pavlovo are examples of this trend, becoming major textile and metalworking centers, respectively.

The first decades of the nineteenth century witnessed an increased acceleration in the factory and mining workforce, from 224,882 in 1804 to 860,000 in 1860. Although less than 10 percent of workers in 1770 were hired as opposed to assigned, by 1860 well over half were hired. Not all of this labor was free, however, since it included hiring contracts forced upon peasants by serf owners or even village communes. In addition, hired labor was concentrated in the greatest growth industry of the period, textiles, especially in the central provinces of Moscow and Vladimir. Forced labor still comprised the great majority of the metallurgical and mining work forces on the eve of the Great Reforms.

PEASANT OR PROLETARIAN?

Although peasants remained tied to their commune as a result of the emancipation of the serfs, this hindered the labor market as little as serfdom had. By 1900, 1.9 million Russians worked in factories and mines; by 1917, 3.6 million did so. In addition, the total number of those earning any kind of wage, either full or part time, increased from 4 million to 20 million between 1860 and 1917. The bulk of this increase in the factory and mining work force came from the peasantry. For a century, historians have debated whether the Russian industrial worker was more a peasant or a proletarian, an argument rendered more acute by the coming to power in 1917 of a regime claiming to rule in the name of the proletariat. This argument has never been satisfactorily resolved. Most industrial peasants remained juridical peasants, with financial obligations to the village commune. More than that, they usually identified themselves as peasants. A few historians have claimed that with an unceasing influx of peasants into the work force, the Russian working class was simply the part of the peasantry who worked in factories, and some see the Bolshevik Revolution as the successful manipulation by intellectuals of naïve peasant-workers. Others, on the other hand, have carefully traced the development of a hereditary work force, as the children of migrants themselves went to work in the factories, lost their ties to the countryside, and came to identify themselves not as peasants, but as workers. The archetype of this is the iconic St. Petersburg skilled metalworker, a second or third-generation worker, literate, born and raised in the city, with a sophisticated understanding of political matters and consciously supporting a socialist path in the recasting of Russian society. The truth is certainly somewhere between these poles, but there is no consensus on where. Certainly through the 1930s most of the industrial workforce consisted of first-generation workers. However, on the eve of the revolution, possibly a third of workers were hereditary.

What it meant to be a hereditary worker is not clear. Many workers grew up in the countryside, worked in a factory for several years, then returned to the village to take over the family plot. Their children grew up in the village, might themselves die in the village, would work in factories for a decade or so, and could thus be considered both peasants and hereditary workers. In addition, well over half of Russia's factory workers labored in mills located in the countryside. Thus, although they worked in a factory, they were still in and of the village.

LABOR IN REVOLUTIONARY RUSSIA

Regardless of whether they were peasant or proletarian, there was a continually increasing quantity of factory workers, who constituted growing proportions of the two rapidly expanding capitals, St. Petersburg and Moscow, where workers would play a political role beyond their numerical weight in the general population. Throughout the imperial period, working conditions were horrible, with seventy-hour work-weeks and little concern for worker health.

Although strikes remained illegal through most of the imperial period, they are recorded as early as the 1600s. However, the size of the industrial sector was not large enough to produce strikes of major concern to the state until the 1880s, with larger strike waves occurring in the mid-1890s and

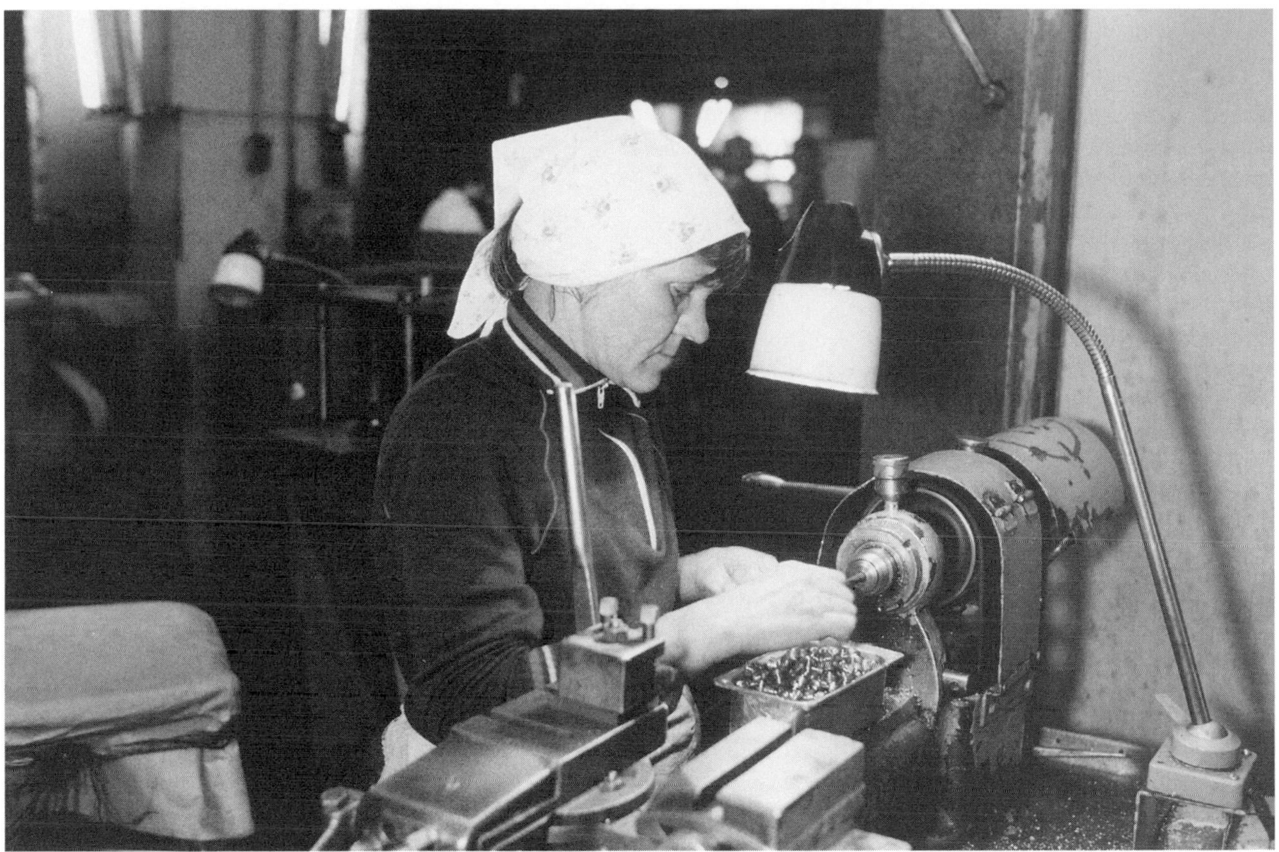

Woman working in Soviet electronics factory in Moscow. © Peter Turnley/CORBIS

the first years of the twentieth century. Socialist activists began large-scale efforts to organize the industrial labor force in the 1890s, and many historians have seen the steady fall in violence and increase in political demands during strikes as the result of politically motivated organizers. Whether workers were more led by the political parties, or rather utilized the parties' organizational capabilities for their own ends, remains a debatable issue.

Independent labor unions have never played a large role in Russia, in part because they were illegal until 1905. The state attempted to organize some unions before 1905 to counteract the influence of the socialists. This backfired in January 1905, when one of these officially sanctioned worker organizations led protests that were repressed by the state in the massacre known as Bloody Sunday. During the subsequent year of revolution, workers played a visible role. Their participation in a general strike in the fall led directly to the October Manifesto. In 1917, industrial workers, especially in Petrograd, help set the tone for the revolution. This was especially apparent in their support of the soviets as an institution and, eventually for the Bolsheviks, who not only advocated soviet power, but also spoke out for the workers' favorite parochial concern: worker control of the factories.

THE SOVIET PERIOD AND BEYOND

During the Civil War, however, working class influence weakened significantly. The regime banned strikes, and natural worker leaders were co-opted into the party and state bureaucracies and the military. Furthermore, economic collapse caused most workers with peasant ties to flee the starving cities. General strikes in Moscow and Petrograd in early 1921 helped usher in the New Economic Policy (NEP), although the NEP would produce its own labor discontent. Workers resented that prewar technical elites retained supervisory roles and the state's attempts to increase worker productivity. There was chronic underemployment and peasant competition for jobs.

This discontent provided much popular support for the radical measures of the First Five-Year

Plan, which in turn brought millions more peasants into new factories. The chaos of the early 1930s led to the imposition of very strict labor laws, removing strikes as a viable weapon for labor until the late 1980s. The stabilization of the planned economy produced the first unmistakably hereditary working class in Russian history, as migration from the countryside slowed significantly and educational policies restricted social mobility. This was also a very docile period in labor relations, with very few strikes or viable protests. One major wave of labor discontent did occur from 1962 to 1964, which helped bring down Nikita Khrushchev when he tried to attack the status quo with price hikes and demands for increased productivity. Workers were guaranteed a job, were rarely fired, and were seldom threatened with demands for greater productivity, while being granted a lifestyle that could be considered comfortable by historical standards. As a popular epigram expressed it, "We pretend to work, and they pretend to pay us." This situation changed in the Mikhail Gorbachev era. The massive dislocations that accompanied the shift from a planned to free market economy at first produced massive strikes, followed by sullen quiescence, as those who still had jobs did not feel secure enough to strike. Labor discontent in the 1990s manifested itself primarily in a steady sizable vote for the Communist Party. Political and economic stability in the early twenty-first century led to normalization of labor markets and more consistent payment of wages than after the shock therapy of the early 1990s.

See also: FIVE-YEAR PLANS; NEW ECONOMIC POLICY; PEASANTRY; SERFDOM; SLAVERY

BIBLIOGRAPHY

Chase, William J. (1987). *Workers, Society, and the Soviet State: Labor and Life in Moscow, 1918–1929.* Urbana: University of Illinois Press.

Ekonomakis, Evel G. (1998). *From Peasant to Petersburger.* London: Macmillan Press Ltd.

Filtzer, Donald. (1992). *Soviet Workers and De-Stalinization: The Consolidation of the Modern System of Soviet Production Relations, 1953–1964.* Cambridge, UK: Cambridge University Press.

Haimson, Leopold. (1964–1965). "The Problem of Social Stability in Urban Russia, 1905–1914." *Slavic Review* 23:619–642, 24:1–22.

Johnson, Robert Eugene. (1979). *Peasant and Proletarian: The Working Class of Moscow in the Late Nineteenth Century.* New Brunswick, NJ: Rutgers University Press.

Kuromiya, Hiroaki. (1988). *Stalin's Industrial Revolution: Politics and Workers, 1928–1932.* Cambridge, UK: Cambridge University Press.

McDaniel, Tim. (1988). *Autocracy, Capitalism, and Revolution in Russia.* Berkeley: University of California Press.

Zelnik, Reginald E. (1968). "The Peasant and the Factory." In *The Peasant in Nineteenth-Century Russia,* ed. Wayne S. Vucinich. Stanford, CA: Stanford University Press.

Zelnik, Reginald E. (1971). *Labor and Society in Tsarist Russia. The Factory Workers of St. Petersburg, 1855–1870.* Stanford, CA: Stanford University Press.

David Pretty

LABOR BOOKS

Labor Books were issued to all officially employed persons in the Soviet Union and were used to keep a written record of the daily work behavior of each worker. These labor books were introduced in the Soviet Union in late 1938. Labor books are of historical interest as one of several drastic changes in labor regulations implemented in the late 1930s in an effort to develop and to sustain labor discipline. Moreover, these regulations, which included the requirement of internal passports, limitations on mobility, and the organized and controlled placement of labor, were significant elements of the general process of labor allocation reducing the influence of market-type forces and incentives and were more generally important as restrictions on the freedom of the population.

Throughout the Soviet era, the mix of mechanisms used for labor allocation changed considerably. Beginning in the 1930s, the system of controls was expanded in many directions. These controls, including the widespread use of forced labor, were a fundamental systemic component of the Soviet economic system. However, during the post-Stalin era, the use of direct controls over labor allocation was reduced and began to be replaced by market-type forces and direct incentive arrangements. These incentives were increasingly used to allocate labor in a variety of dimensions, for example by sector and region of the economy.

The use of labor books in the Soviet Union is an important component of the more general process of replacing market mechanisms with state directed nonmarket mechanisms during the command era. The impact of these controls on labor allocation and labor productivity in an economy artificially characterized as a full employment economy (an economy with a "job right constraint") remain controversial in the overall judgement of labor allocation procedures and results during the Soviet era.

See also: LABOR

BIBLIOGRAPHY

Bergson, Abram. (1964). *The Economics of Soviet Planning.* New Haven, CT: Yale University Press.

Gregory, Paul R., and Stuart, Robert C. (2001). *Russian and Soviet Economic Performance and Structure,* 7th ed. New York: Addison Wesley Longman.

Nove, Alec. (1982). *An Economic History of the USSR.* New York: Penguin Books.

ROBERT C. STUART

LABOR CAMPS *See* GULAG.

LABOR DAY

The labor day (*trudoden*) was a mechanism for calculating the labor payment of peasants belonging to collective farms. In theory the collective farm was a cooperative form of organization, and thus peasants divided among themselves a residual payment for work rather than a contractual wage. The latter was reserved for the payment of state workers (*rabochii*) in industrial enterprises and on state farms.

Each daily task on a collective farm was assigned a number of labor days, according to the nature of the task, its duration, difficulty, and so forth. Peasants accumulated labor days, which were recorded in a labor book. Although a peasant might have some sense of the value of a labor day from past experience, the value of a labor day in terms of money or product would not be known until the end of the agricultural season. Valuation would be determined by the following general formula: To calculate the value of a labor day, the compulsory deliveries to the state would be subtracted from the farm output, and the result divided by the total number of labor days.

After the completion of the harvest, the value of each labor day could be known, and each peasant rewarded in kind (for example, grain) or in money (rubles). With the magnitude of compulsory deliveries at low fixed prices set by the state, the state wielded significant power by extracting products from the farm. Moreover, even though changes in the frequency and form of payment were made over time, the labor day system was a very crude mechanism of payment, with severe limitations as an incentive system.

See also: COLLECTIVE FARM; PEASANTRY

BIBLIOGRAPHY

Davies, R. W. (1980). *The Soviet Collective Farm, 1929–1930.* Cambridge, MA: Harvard University Press.

Stuart, Robert C. (1972). *The Collective Farm in Soviet Agriculture.* Lexington, MA: D.C. Heath.

ROBERT C. STUART

LABOR THEORY OF VALUE

The labor theory of value may be traced to the writings of John Locke, an English philosopher of the late 1600s. While Locke assumed that all the resources that were found in nature had been provided by God and therefore were common property, he argued that when people took things that had been present in a natural state and reshaped them into products of use for human beings, they mixed their labor with the raw materials, and thus had the right to personal ownership of the resulting products. Indeed, the products that a worker produced became an extension of that worker. Locke employed the labor theory of value to justify private ownership of property, the cornerstone principle of capitalism. He planted the seeds of the ideas that human labor is the unique factor that creates value in commodities, and that the value of any product is approximately determined by the amount of labor that is necessary to produce it.

Karl Marx became familiar with the labor theory of value through his extensive reading of the works of British economists, including Adam Smith and David Ricardo, whose works reflected the pervasive influence of Locke's ideas and accepted the labor theory of value. Ironically, in Marx's hands, the Lockean premises became the basis for an radical critique of capitalism and an implicit justification of socialism. In Marx's theoretical model of a capitalist economy, the workers or proletarians labor with means of production, such as industrial plant and machinery, which are owned by a capitalist. Since the workers own no share of the means of production, they are driven by necessity to work for someone who does own productive property. During the hours of each worker's labor, the worker produces commodities, or products that are bought and sold in the market. The capitalist sells those commodities in order to receive income. The price for which each commodity is sold is called "exchange value" in Marxist terminology. The capitalist must return some of that value to the worker in the form of wages, since workers will not work without some material reward. It is axiomatic in Marx's theory that the value that is returned to the worker is less than that which has been created by the worker's labor. That portion of the value that has been created by the labor of the proletarian, but is not returned to the proletarian, obviously flows to the capitalist, and constitutes "surplus value" in Marx's words.

In Marx's view, surplus value is the excess of the value the proletarian has produced above what it takes to keep the proletarian working, and surplus value is the source of profit for the capitalist. Marx argued that with the development of capitalism, competition would force capitalists to strive relentlessly to extract as much surplus value as possible from their workers. Initially the capitalists would simply increase the hours of labor of their workers and decrease the workers' pay, but that kind of simple intensification of exploitation would soon reach physical limits. The capitalists would then adopt the strategy of increasing the mechanization of production, substituting machine power for human muscle power to an ever-growing degree, with the objective of getting more products out of fewer laborers. Mechanization, by throwing ever larger numbers of workers out of the factories, would ensure the growth of unemployment, which would guarantee that the wages of those who continued to work would be driven down to the subsistence level. Marx believed that he was describing the inexorable tendency of the increasing misery of the proletariat, which would give rise to a progressively sharpening struggle between the proletariat and the bourgeoisie, which, with the final crisis of capitalism, would result in proletarian revolution and the elimination of capitalism.

In the first volume of *Capital*, which he published in 1867, Marx clearly suggested that the exchange value or market price of a commodity was determined, at least on the average, by the labor which had gone into producing it. Until the end of his intellectual career, Marx continually struggled with the attempt to reconcile the conception of the intrinsic value of a product, which supposedly represented the amount of labor embodied in it, and its exchange value, which in actuality reflected supply and demand. It could be argued that in the third volume of *Capital*, edited by Friedrich Engels and published after Marx's death, that problem was still unresolved, as indeed it could not be resolved on the basis of Marx's fundamental assumptions.

The labor theory of value was wholly accepted by Soviet Marxist-Leninst ideology as a fundamental theoretical assumption. The premises of that theory explain why Soviet leaders from Lenin to Gorbachev were extremely suspicious of the practice of hiring laborers for wages in private enterprises, since any employment of workers on privately owned property was automatically considered exploitation, the essential source of class struggle. In fact, with the proclamation by Stalin that the foundations of socialism had been constructed in the Soviet Union by 1936, hiring people to work for private employers was prohibited by law. In socialist society, the payment of wages to workers and peasants in collective enterprises was not thought to present any problem, since in theory the means of production in the Soviet Union belonged to those same workers and peasants. In light of the labor theory of value, it is not difficult to understand why, in the late 1980s, when Mikhail Gorbachev finally began to allow limited, small-scale private enterprises, such endeavors were officially termed "individual labor activity" and "cooperatives," avoiding the admission of a relationship between employers and employees in the private sector.

See also: MARXISM; SOCIALISM

BIBLIOGRAPHY

Baradat, Leon P. (1984). *Political Ideologies: Their Origins and Impact*, 5th ed. Englewood Cliffs, NJ: Prentice-Hall.

Evans, Alfred B., Jr. (1993). *Soviet Marxism-Leninism: The Decline of an Ideology*. Westport, CT: Praeger.

McClellan, David. (1980). *The Thought of Karl Marx*, 2nd ed. London: Macmillan.

ALFRED B. EVANS JR.

LAKE BAIKAL

Known as the "Pearl of Siberia," Lake Baikal is the oldest and deepest lake on earth. Home to more than one thousand endemic species of aquatic life, it is a focal point for environmental activism and Siberian national pride.

Located in south central Siberia, Baikal is 636 kilometers (395.2 miles) long, 80 kilometers (49.71 miles) wide, and 1,637 meters (5,371 feet) deep. A watershed of 55,000 hectares (212.4 square miles) feeds the lake through more than three hundred rivers. Only the Angara River drains Baikal, flowing northwest from the southern tip of the lake. The lake probably began to form about 25 million years ago, at the site of a tectonic rift. The fault continues to widen and there are thermal vents in the lake's depths.

Baikal's zooplankton, called epishura, is at the base of a unique food chain, with the prized Omul salmon and the nerpa, the world's only freshwater seal, at its top. Epishura is also a biological filter, contributing to the lake's extraordinary clarity and purity. The Baikal Ridge along the northwest shore of the lake is heavily populated by birds and animals and contains deposits of titanium, lead, and zinc. The Khamardaban range, lying to the south of the lake, contains gold, tungsten, and coal.

Humans have inhabited the area around Baikal at least since the Mesolithic period (ten to twelve thousand years ago). The dominant native peoples in the area since the twelfth to fourteenth centuries C.E. are Buryat Mongols. Another local tribe is the Evenks, a Tungus clan of traditional reindeer nomads of the taiga. Many native peoples consider Baikal sacred, and some believe that Olkhon Island, the largest on the lake, was the birthplace of Genghis Khan.

Russian explorers first came to the shores of Baikal in 1643, and by 1650 Russia had completed its annexation of the area around the lake. Russians met little resistance from indigenous peoples in the area, and Russian populations gradually increased over the following centuries, attracted by the fur trade and mining. The city of Irkutsk, on the Angara River, was a destination for convicts, including political exiles, during the nineteenth century. The Trans–Siberian Railway, which runs around the south tip of the lake, brought more settlers and more rapid economic development to the area during the 1890s. A Circum–Baikal Railway opened in 1900. Construction of the Baikal–Amur Mainline (BAM), a second trans–Siberian rail line that passes just north of the lake, took place from 1943 to 1951 and resumed in the 1974.

The fragile ecology of Lake Baikal faces many threats. The two large rail lines at either end of the lake have compromised the watersheds through logging and erosion. Lumber mills and factories near Ulan–Ude send thousands of tons of contaminants annually into the lake. The Baikalsk cellulose combine has altered the ecology of the southern part of the lake, killing off epishura and accounting for high concentrations of PCBs and other toxins. Large die–offs of nerpa seals have been attributed to dioxin contamination. Environmental activists have vigorously opposed industrial development, and have focused international attention on the lake. Two nature reserves (*zapovedniks*) and two national parks protect portions of the lakeshore. The entire lake and its coastal protection zone became a UNESCO World Natural Heritage Site in 1996.

See also: BURYATS; ENVIRONMENTALISM; EVENKI

BIBLIOGRAPHY

Matthiessen, Peter. (1992). *Baikal: Sacred Sea of Siberia*. San Francisco: Sierra Club Books.

Mote, Victor L. (1998). *Siberia: Worlds Apart*. Boulder, CO: Westview Press.

United Nations Environment Programme World Conservation Monitoring Center (UNEP–WCMC). (1996). "Protected Areas Programme: Lake Baikal." <http://www.unep–wcmc.org/sites/wh/baikal.htm>.

RACHEL MAY

LAND AND FREEDOM PARTY

There were two revolutionary groups named "Land and Freedom" (Zemlya i Volya). The first was a phenomenon of the early 1860s, with a membership largely of intellectuals in Moscow and the Russian provinces. It maintained contacts with émigrés living abroad (most notably Alexander Herzen) and was supported in Russia by the anarchists Prince Peter Kropotkin and Mikhail Bakunin. Repressed by the government, it ceased to exist by 1863 or 1864.

The second and better-known Land and Freedom group emerged after the failure of the "Going to the People" experiments in the early 1870s.

Forced to review their strategy and activities, Russian populists realized that the peasants were hostile to intellectuals and that the state would not change of its own accord. In 1876, in St. Petersburg, they organized a new Land and Freedom group as a secret political organization. The leaders of the group, whose members included Mark Natanson, Alexander Mikhailov, and Lev Tikomirov, reasoned that revolutionaries would have to go among and work through the Russian people (*narod*). They were well aware, however, that many Russian activists had idealized the peasants and overestimated their willingness to revolt. Thus, if Land and Freedom was to achieve its goals of giving peasants collective ownership of the land through the *obshchina*, promoting freedom of the individual so that the peasants would be able to regulate their own affairs, and bringing about the abolition of private property, it would have to be better organized (through a more centralized structure) and, above all, would have to use *agitprop* (agitation and propaganda) in both word and deed to win the people over.

To this end, members of Land and Freedom went out in the Russian countryside, concentrating on the Volga region, where there had been peasant uprisings in the past. They also agitated among rebellious students in the winter of 1877 to 1878. In the late 1870s, Land and Freedom decided to disrupt the Russian state by carrying out terrorist acts targeting landowners, the police, and government officials. When the state responded by restricting its activities and arresting many of its members, Land and Freedom split into two other groups, Narodnaia Volya (People's Will) and Chernyi Peredel (Black Petition), both of which left a mark on Russian history when Alexander II was assassinated in 1881.

See also: AGITPROP; ANARCHISM; PEASANTRY; PEASANT UPRISINGS; TERRORISM

BIBLIOGRAPHY

Hardy, Deborah. (1987). *Land and Freedom: The Origins of Russian Terrorism, 1876–1879.* Westport, CT: Greenwood Press.

Kelly, Aileen. (1982). *Mikhail Bakunin: A Study in the Psychology and Politics of Utopianism.* New York: Oxford University Press.

Offord, Derek. (1987). *The Russian Revolutionary Movement in the 1880s.* Cambridge, UK: Cambridge University Press.

CHRISTOPHER WILLIAMS

LAND CAPTAIN

Land captains were representatives of the administrative and judicial authority in Russian villages from 1889 to 1917.

The Statute Concerning Land Captains was passed on July 12, 1889, and was one of the counterreforms made during the rule of Emperor Alexander III. The purpose of this law was the partial restoration of the control of provincial nobility over the peasants. In 40 provinces, 2,200 land districts, headed by land captains, were formed. Land captains were appointed by the Minister of Interior, usually from local hereditary nobles at the recommendation of governors and provincial marshals of nobility. They had extensive administrative and judicial power, controlled the activity of peasant communities, and formed the primary judicial authority for peasants and other taxpayers. A land captain had to have a higher education and three years of experience in serving as a peace mediator (*mirovoy posrednik*), a mirian (mir-peasant commune) judge, or member of a provincial council of peasant affairs. Moreover, he had to possess at least 200 desiatinas (approximately 540 acres of land) or real estate worth at least 7.5 thousand rubles. When candidates with records sufficient for the position were unavailable, local hereditary nobles with primary and secondary education were eligible. In special cases any local noble could be appointed. A land captain had the right to cancel any decision made by the village or the *volost* gathering (*skhod*) of the district, order the physical punishment of a taxpayer for minor misdemeanors, and order a three–day arrest or a six–ruble fine. The land captain appointed *volost* courts, which had been previously elected by the peasants, from a number of candidates selected by village communities (the *volost* was the smallest administrative unit in tsarist Russia). He could cancel any decision of a *volost* court, remove a judge, arrest, fine, or order physical punishment. The decisions of a land captain were considered final and did not allow for revision or complaints. In accordance with the reform of 1889, District (*Uyezd*) Bureaus of Peasant Affairs and *mir* (communal) courts were cancelled. The *mir* courts were reinstalled in 1912. The post of a land captain was cancelled by a decision of the Provisional Government on October 14, 1917.

See also: AUTOCRACY; PEASANTRY

BIBLIOGRAPHY

Zaionchkovskii, Petr Andreevich. (1976). *The Russian Autocracy under Alexander III.* Gulf Breeze, FL: Academic International Press.

OLEG BUDNITSKII

LANDSBERGIS, VYTAUTAS

(b. 1932), Lithuanian musicologist and political leader.

Vytautas Landsbergis, a musicologist by training, emerged as a political leader in Lithuania in the fall of 1988. One of the founding members of the Movement for Perestroika in Lithuania, better known as Sajudis, he quickly became one of the Sajudis Initiative Group's most prominent public spokespersons. In the fall of 1988 he became Sajudis's President when the organization began openly to advocate political goals and to demand the restitution of the independent Lithuanian state. In 1989 he won note throughout the Soviet Union as a deputy in the Soviet Congress of People's Deputies, where he led the campaign to force the Soviet government to recognize the existence of the Secret Protocols to the Nazi-Soviet Non-Aggression Pact of August 23, 1939, and to renounce them as having been immoral. As an uncompromising Lithuanian leader, he became one of Mikhail Gorbachev's best-known political opponents, and for a time he found common cause with Gorbachev's major Russian opponent, Boris Yeltsin.

In March 1990, after Sajudis had won an overwhelming majority in the elections to the Lithuanian parliament, Landsbergis was elected President of the Supreme Council's Presidium, and as such became the Lithuanian chief of state. On March 11, 1990, the Supreme Council proclaimed Lithuania's reestablishment as an independent state, and Landsbergis focused on Lithuania's drive to win international recognition of its independence. Toward this goal he followed a policy of harsh confrontation with the Soviet government, and he traveled widely abroad seeking support. Posing the question of Lithuanian independence as a moral more than a political issue, he appealed to world public opinion over the heads of what he saw as unresponsive foreign governments. In January 1991, when Soviet troops seized key buildings in Vilnius, Landsbergis remained at his office in the parliament and became the prime symbol of Lithuanian resistance to Soviet rule.

After the collapse of the Soviet Union in the fall of 1991, Landsbergis's political fortunes began to wane, although he continued to be a popular figure among Lithuanian émigrés in the United States, from whom he received considerable moral and financial support. A referendum aimed at strengthening his authority failed in the spring of 1992, and in the fall he was forced out of office by the overwhelming victory of the Lithuanian Democratic Labor Party (the former Communist Party) in the elections to the new parliament, now called the Seimas. For the next four years, Landsbergis held the post of Leader of the Opposition. In 1996, after the victory of his political party, the Homeland Union, in parliamentary elections, he became President of the Presidium of the Seimas, a post he held until new elections in 2000. In 1997 he failed in his bid to become President of the Republic.

See also: LITHUANIA AND LITHUANIANS; NATIONALISM IN THE SOVIET UNION

BIBLIOGRAPHY

Landsbergis, Vytautas. (2000). *Lithuania Independent Again.* Seattle: University of Washington Press.

Lieven, Anatole. (1993). *The Baltic Revolution: Estonia, Latvia, Lithuania, and the Path to Independence.* New Haven, CT: Yale University Press.

Senn, Alfred Erich. (1995). *Gorbachev's Failure in Lithuania.* New York: St. Martin's Press.

ALFRED ERICH SENN

LAND TENURE, IMPERIAL ERA

Two themes predominate in historical literature on land tenure in the imperial era: first, the fragility of private property rights and their association with Russian economic "backwardness"; and, second, the problem of agrarian reform after the abolition of serfdom in 1861. From the medieval era, two competing conceptions of property coexisted in Russian law. The first concerned inherited (patrimonial) forms of landed property, which privileged the rights of the kin group, or clan (*rod*), over those of the individual. Although individuals controlled inherited property, their right to alienate patrimonial land was restricted. Proprietors acted as custodians, rather than absolute owners, of immovable assets: If they chose to sell an estate without the consent of family members, the latter enjoyed the right to redeem the estate at its purchase price. Testamentary freedom over patrimonial estates was also severely circumscribed.

Alongside the institution of patrimonial property, a second conception of property emerged in the early modern era that invested far greater rights of ownership in the individual. Muscovite law codes allowed for the special status of the acquired estate, or land purchased from another clan. Proprietors of acquired land could alienate and bequeath such assets as they wished. After a family member inherited acquired property, however, this land became patrimonial and was subject to the laws governing lineage land. The notion of acquired property surfaced as early as the twelfth century; nonetheless, many legal historians argue that the concept of private property was not fully elaborated in the law until the reign of Catherine II, when the empress confirmed the status of acquired property in her Charter of the Nobility in 1785.

Yet even the Charter of the Nobility stopped short of granting the nobility unfettered rights over their landed estates. Patrimonial property continued to be governed by the rules of partible inheritance, according to which surviving spouses received one-seventh and daughters claimed one-fourteenth of the immoveable estate of the deceased; sons then divided the remaining land equally. In the absence of sons, each daughter received an equal share of the estate. The result of partible inheritance was estate fragmentation: In contrast to landowners in Western Europe, Russian proprietors often held land in small parcels, scattered in several districts, rather than consolidated holdings.

Some historians maintain that partible inheritance was instrumental in the decline of the Russian nobility and discouraged individual proprietors from improving their estates. Certainly this was the view of Peter the Great, who attempted to overturn inheritance practice with the Law of Single Inheritance in 1714. The new law instructed parents to bequeath land in its entirety to one son or daughter. From the perspective of the nobility, the Law of Single Inheritance not only violated centuries of tradition but also undermined their children's welfare. Many nobles circumvented the decree through illegal transactions, fabricating debts and selling land in order to redistribute the proceeds among their heirs. When Anna Ivanovna ascended the throne in 1730, she quickly succumbed to noble demands to reinstitute partible inheritance. Devotion to partible inheritance did not preclude acknowledgement of its harmful effects, however. Until the eve of the Revolution, tension persisted between the nobility's conviction that landed property should be divided among all sons and daughters, and the conflicting desire to prevent disintegration of their patrimony.

Historians also blame absentee ownership and the insecurity of property for poor productivity on noble estates. The broad consensus is that Russian nobles were chronically in debt, preferred life in the city to residing on their estates, and were far more likely to engage in conspicuous consumption than to invest in the development of their holdings. Moreover, until the late eighteenth century, Russian nobles risked confiscation of their land for a whole series of misdemeanors. Although Catherine II's Charter of the Nobility stipulated that nobles could not be deprived of their estates without due process, the charter nonetheless defined crimes meriting confiscation as broadly as possible. The abolition of serfdom in 1861 dealt a further blow to noble property rights, as proprietors lost their unpaid labor and were compelled to relinquish approximately half of their land to their former serfs. Although the government guaranteed the nobility generous redemption payments for the land they had sacrificed, the response of many nobles in the post-Emancipation era was to sell their land and seek other sources of income. Some ambitious proprietors moved to the country and devoted their energies to modernizing their estates. By the beginning of the twentieth century, however, the vast majority of noble landowners were unable to support their families on the proceeds of their estates alone.

While the nobility campaigned to bolster the institution of private property, the notion of individual property rights was largely alien to Russian peasants, even after the abolition of serfdom in 1861. The majority of Russian peasants lived in villages in which arable land was controlled by the repartitional commune (mir). Although regional variations existed, in most villages individual peasants owned their tools and livestock, while households controlled the land upon which they built their houses and cultivated their gardens. Arable land, however, was held jointly by the commune, which periodically redistributed strips of land among the village households. The goal of redistribution was to provide each household in the village with an equal share of resources and to ensure that each would fulfill its fiscal obligations. Redistribution by no means created perfect equality among commune members, but it allowed peasants some measure of security in an environment characterized by a short growing season, severe weather, poor soil, and primitive transportation.

For Russian intellectuals—in particular, the Slavophiles—the peasant commune represented the true collectivist and egalitarian nature of the Russian people, which they contrasted with Western veneration of the individual. Yet the repartitional commune did not become a feature of peasant life until the eighteenth century, when the fiscal pressures of the Petrine reforms encouraged noble proprietors to impose collective responsibility on their villages to meet tax obligations. Collective ownership nonetheless impeded the development of the notion of private property among the peasantry. While historians continue to debate what the long-term consequences of the Stolypin reforms (1906–1914) might have been, if they had not been interrupted by war and revolution, when Petr Stolypin, advisor to Nicholas II, sought to transform the Russian countryside by allowing peasant households to separate from the commune and claim a consolidated holding, only a minority of villages took advantage of this opportunity. Educated Russians were convinced that collective ownership caused low agricultural productivity, but for the majority of Russian peasants the commune offered far more benefits than private ownership. Furthermore, although land hunger remained a constant among the peasantry in the years following Emancipation, historians have begun to question the existence of an agrarian crisis in the years leading up to the Revolution and to suggest that collective cultivation of land was by no means the major obstacle to economic innovation. The village commune remained central to the peasant way of life, not only until 1917, but until Stalin succeeded in destroying rural tradition with collectivization. Significantly, when peasants during the October Revolution seized the estates of noble proprietors, they claimed the land not for individual peasants, but in the name of the village commune.

Ultimately, the concept of private property was fraught was inconsistencies in imperial Russia, for nobles and peasants alike. As Richard Wortman has noted, property rights remained "an attribute of privilege " (p. 15), associated with despotism and oppression, rather than the foundation for political and civil rights. Educated Russians on the eve of Revolution remained divided in their belief that peasant loyalty to the repartitional commune was a sign of their "backwardness," and their own suspicion that the defense of private property would benefit only the landowning nobility. Under these conditions, the Bolshevik agenda to nationalize the land in 1917 initially met with little opposition.

See also: DVORIANSTVO; EMANCIPATION ACT; LAND TENURE, SOVIET AND POST-SOVIET; SERFDOM

BIBLIOGRAPHY

Blum, Jerome. (1961). *Lord and Peasant in Russia from the Ninth to the Nineteenth Century.* Princeton, NJ: Princeton University Press.

Crisp, Olga. (1989). "Peasant Land Tenure and Civil Rights Implications before 1906." In *Civil Rights in Imperial Russia,* ed. Olga Crisp and Linda Edmondson. Oxford: Oxford University Press.

Kingston-Mann, Esther, and Mixter, Timothy, eds. (1991). *Peasant Economy, Culture, and the Politics of European Russia, 1800–1921.* Princeton, NJ: Princeton University Press.

Marrese, Michelle Lamarche. (2002). *A Woman's Kingdom: Noblewomen and the Control of Property in Russia, 1700–1861.* Ithaca, NY: Cornell University Press.

Wagner, William G. (1994). *Marriage, Property, and Law in Late Imperial Russia.* Oxford: Oxford University Press.

Wortman, Richard. (1989). "Property Rights, Populism, and Russian Political Culture." In *Civil Rights in Imperial Russia,* ed. Olga Crisp and Linda Edmondson. Oxford: Oxford University Press.

Yaney, George. (1982). *The Urge to Mobilize: Agrarian Reform in Russia, 1861–1930.* Urbana: University of Illinois Press.

MICHELLE LAMARCHE MARRESE

LAND TENURE, SOVIET AND POST-SOVIET

A central idea of communist ideology was opposition to private ownership of the means of production. This prohibition against private property was manifest first and foremost in land relations. Guided by their ideological beliefs, the new Bolshevik regime, the day after seizing power from the Provisional Government in October 1917, issued a decree "On Land" that abolished private ownership of land and introduced the nationalization of land. The October decree was followed by land legislation in January 1918 that forbade the renting or exchange of land.

Following the end of the Russian Civil War (1917–1921), the first Soviet Land Code was adopted in 1922. It regulated land use and stayed in force until the early 1990s. The first Soviet Land Code affirmed the nationalization of land and abolished private ownership of land, minerals under the soil, water, and forests. Article 27 of the 1922 Land Code forbade the purchase, sale, bequeathing, or mortgaging of land. The 1922 Land Code did allow land leasing from the state until 1928. Starting in 1928, legal changes were introduced that eroded the liberties contained in the 1922 Land Code. Restrictions on land leasing laid the basis for the collectivization of agricultural land starting in 1929. Family farms, which were based on leased land, were aggregated into large state and collective farms based on state ownership of land. Restrictions on land leasing remained in force until the late 1980s.

The prohibition on private land ownership did not mean, however, that Soviet citizens were deprived of land use. Rural and urban households were able to use small land plots, which were used for the growing of food for family consumption and to supplement family income. These plots of land were called "auxiliary plots," sometimes translated as personal subsidiary plots or simply "private plots." In general, food production and food sales from state and collective farms were planned and regulated by the central government. Auxiliary plots were not based upon private ownership of land, but they did lie outside the scope of state planning. Auxiliary plots could be assigned to a family or an individual. Although communist ideology was opposed to these private uses of land and considered those land plots remnants of capitalism, the food produced from these plots contributed significant percentages of the nation's food, in particular meat, milk, eggs, vegetables, and potatoes. For rural dwellers, the food produced from auxiliary plots and sold at urban food markets accounted for nearly one-half of the family income well into the 1950s. Given these circumstances, the Soviet leadership had to put pragmatism above ideology and permit auxiliary plots to exist. Successive Soviet leaders had different ideas concerning the treatment of auxiliary plots. During difficult economic times, the Soviet regime adopted more lenient attitudes. However, among the political elite the supremacy of large-scale collective agriculture was not and could not be doubted, and, prior to the coming to power of Mikhail Gorbachev in 1985, no Soviet leader considered allowing independent farms based on land leasing.

When Gorbachev became General Secretary, he wanted to revitalize Soviet agriculture, which had experienced stagnation in its food production during the early 1980s. His idea was to allow individuals who desired to start independent farms to lease land from state and collective farms. In February 1990, the USSR Law on Land was adopted. It legalized the leasing of agricultural land in order to create independent individual farms, but did not legalize land ownership. In April 1991, a new Land Code was adopted, replacing the 1922 Land Code, and this new version codified the right of land leasing.

The Law on Land also allowed individual republics of the USSR to pass their own land laws. In December 1990, the Russian Republic reversed the 1922 legislation regarding land ownership by adopting a Law on Property that distinguished between private (*chastnaya*) and state ownership of land. The passage of a number of other laws, including On Land Reform, meant that, for the first time since the Communists came to power in 1917, private ownership of land was permitted, although the purchase of land was heavily regulated and a ten-year moratorium placed on land sales.

When the Soviet Union dissolved in late December 1991, Russian President Boris Yeltsin moved decisively to reaffirm his commitment to private land ownership, which had already been legalized during the Soviet period. In late December 1991, Yeltsin issued government resolutions and presidential decrees ordering large farms to reorganize and distribute land shares to all farm members and allocate actual land plots to those who wanted to leave the parent farm. He also restated the right to private ownership of land and encouraged the rise of a new class of private farmers based on private ownership of land. Despite these steps, during the 1990s the issue of private land ownership and the right to buy and sell land were heavily contested and were key aspects of the policy conflict between reformers and conservatives.

Following the dissolution in October 1993 of the Supreme Soviet and Congress of People's Deputies—the leftover Soviet era legislature—Yeltsin continued to shape land relations. On October 27, 1993, Yeltsin issued a decree entitled "On the Regulation of Land Relations and the Development of Agrarian Reform in Russia," which had an important impact on land relations until the end of the decade. This decree provided for the distribution of land deeds to owners of land and land shares, thereby creating the legal foundation for a land market. In December 1993, the new Russian Constitution guaranteed the right to private ownership of land. This right was reaffirmed in the Civil Code, adopted in 1994.

Starting in 1994, a rudimentary land market arose, involving the buying and selling of land, including agricultural land. The land market was somewhat restricted in that agricultural land was to be used only for agricultural purposes. But the decree was an important first step and had the desired effect: By the end of the 1990s, millions of land transactions were being registered annually (although most were lease transactions).

After seven years of heated political disagreement, a post-Soviet Land Code was passed and signed into law by President Vladimir Putin in October 2001. For the first time since 1917, a Land Code existed that allowed Russian citizens to possess, buy, and sell land. The most contentious issue, the right to buy and sell agricultural land, was omitted from the new Land Code.

Following the passage of the Land Code, the Putin administration moved quickly to enact a law regulating agricultural land sales. By June 2002, a government-sponsored bill on the turnover of agricultural land passed three readings in the State Duma and was sent to the upper chamber, the Federation Council, where it was approved in July 2002. Near the end of July 2002, President Putin signed the bill into law, the first law since 1917 to regulate agricultural land sales in Russia.

The law that was signed into force was very conservative, requiring that agricultural land be used for agricultural purposes. With the exception of small plots of land, such as household subsidiary plots, if the owner of privately owned land wished to sell his land, he was required to offer it to local governmental bodies, who had one month to exercise their right of first refusal before the land could be offered to third parties. If the land was offered to a third party, it could not be at a price lower than was originally offered to the local government. Owners of land shares were required to offer their shares first to other members of the collective, then to the local government, both of which had one month to exercise their right of first refusal. Only if this right was not used could the shares be sold to a third party, but not at a price lower than was originally offered to the local government. If the owner changed the price of his land (or his land shares), then the local government had to be given the right of first refusal again at the new price. The law established minimum size limits on land transactions and maximum size limits on land ownership. Finally, the law provided for land confiscation (as did the Land Code) if the land was not used, or was not used for its intended purpose, or if use resulted in environmental degradation.

See also: AGRICULTURE; COLLECTIVE FARMS; LAND TENURE, IMPERIAL ERA

BIBLIOGRAPHY

Danilov, Viktor P. (1988). *Rural Russia under the New Regime.* Bloomington: Indiana University Press.

Medvedev, Zhores A. (1987). *Soviet Agriculture.* New York: Norton.

Wadekin, Karl-Eugen. (1973). *The Private Sector in Soviet Agriculture.* 2nd ed. Berkeley: University of California Press.

Wegren, Stephen K. (1998). *Agriculture and the State in Soviet and Post-Soviet Russia.* Pittsburgh, PA: University of Pittsburgh Press.

STEPHEN K. WEGREN

LANGUAGE LAWS

The issue of language question has been the subject of recurring political, social, and ideological controversy in Russia since the fifteenth century. Both the intellectual elite and the state were involved in discussions of the issue. Until the 1820s they were primarily concerned with the formation and functions of the Russian literary language.

EIGHTEENTH AND EARLY NINETEENTH CENTURIES

Peter the Great's educational and cultural reforms were the first direct state involvement in the language question in Russia. During the early eighteenth century, governmental orders systematically regulated and resolved the language system, which at this time was characterized by the progressive penetration of original Russian elements into the established Church Slavonic literary norm and by a significant increase in the influence of foreign languages. Peter's program envisioned the creation of a civil idiom based on various genres of the spoken language, and the modernization and secularization of elevated Church Slavonic, whose resources were insufficient for adequate description of the vast new areas of knowledge. At the same time, the language of the epoch was oriented toward Western European languages as sources of novel information and terminology, and thus there were many foreign borrowings. The tsar tackled this problem personally, requiring that official documents were to be written in plain Russian that avoided the use of obscure foreign words and terms. Peter's nationalization of language culminated in the 1707 orthography reform. He decreed the creation of the so-called civil alphabet and removed eight obsolete letters from Church Slavonic script. However, in 1710, partly in response to criticism from the church, Peter reintroduced certain letters and diacritic signs into the civil alphabet. In spite of its limitations, Peter's orthographic reform was a first step toward the creation of a truly secular, civil Russian writing system. It paved the way for three consecutive reforms by the Imperial Academy of Sciences in 1735, 1738, and 1758 that further simplified the alphabet.

Throughout the eighteenth century, the language question dominated intellectual debate in Russia. During the first decades of the nineteenth century, linguistic polemics intensified with the emergence of Nikolai Karamzin's modernizing program aimed at creating an ideal literary norm for Russian on the basis of the refined language of high society. Karamzin's plan met with a heated response from conservatives who wanted to retain Church Slavonic as a literary language. His opponents were led by Admiral Alexander Shishkov. In December 1812, Emperor Alexander I encouraged the Imperial Russian Bible Society to translate and publish the scriptures in the empire's many languages to promote morality and religious peace between its peoples. The society distributed tens of thousands of Bibles in Church Slavonic, French, German, Finnish, Estonian, Latvian, Lithuanian, Polish, Armenian, Georgian, Kalmyk, and Tatar in the first year of its existence. The publication of the scriptures in Russian, however, aroused strong opposition from the conventional Orthodox clergy, who eventually persuaded Alexander to change his position. In 1824 he appointed Admiral Shishkov to head the Ministry of Education. Shishkov terminated the publication of the Russian Bible and reestablished Church Slavonic as the sole language of scripture for Russians.

1860s TO 1917

Starting in the second half of the nineteenth century, imperial policy promoted Russian national values among the non-Russian population of the empire and established Russian as the official language of the state. The government exercised administrative control over the empire's non-Russian languages through a series of laws that considerably, if not completely, restricted their functions and spheres of usage.

These laws primarily concerned the Polish and Ukrainian languages, which were feared as sources and instruments of nationalism. Russification had been adopted as the government's official policy in Poland in response to the first Polish uprising. After the second uprising, in 1863, Polish was banished from education and official usage. Russian became the language of instruction. Harsh censorship ensured that most of the classics of Polish literature could be published only abroad; thus, for instance, the dramas of the national poet, Adam Mickiewicz, were not staged in Warsaw.

The suppression of Ukrainian culture and language was also a consequence of the 1863 uprising. Ukrainian cultural organizations were accused of promoting separatism and Polish propaganda, and in July 1863 Peter Valuev, the minister of internal affairs, banned the publication of scholarly, religious, and pedagogical materials in Ukrainian. Only belles–lettres were to be published in the "Little Russian" dialect. In 1875, renewed Ukrainophile activity again aroused official suspicion. An imperial special commission recommended that the government punish Ukrainian activists and ban the publication and importation of Ukrainian books, the use of Ukrainian in the theater and as a language of instruction in elementary schools, and the publication of Ukrainian newspapers. Alexander II accepted these ruthless recommendations and encoded them in the Ems Decree, signed in the German town of Ems on May 18, 1876.

Belorusian was also regarded as a dialect of Russian, but was not officially prohibited because of the limited scope of its literature. Georgian was subjected to a number of severe restrictions. Imperial language policy was not liberalized until after the Revolution of 1905, and then only under enormous public pressure. From 1904 there had also been democratic projects for alphabet reform, championed by such famous scholars as Jan Baudouin de Courtenay and Filipp Fortunatov. In 1912 the orthography commission submitted its propositions to the government, but they were never approved, due to strong opposition in intellectual and clerical circles. The implementation of the orthography reform, which again removed certain superfluous letters from the alphabet, came only in October 1918, when the Bolshevik government adopted the commission's recommendations.

REVOLUTIONARY AND SOVIET LANGUAGE POLICY

The language question had always been high on the Bolshevik political and cultural agenda. Soon after the Revolution, the Bolshevik government declared a new language policy guaranteeing the complete equality of nationalities and their languages. Formulated in a resolution of the Tenth Communist Party Congress in March 1921, this policy emphasized that the Soviet state had no official language: everyone was granted the right to use a mother tongue in private and public affairs, and non-Russian peoples were encouraged to develop educational, administrative, cultural, and other institutions in their own languages. In practice, this meant that the more than one hundred languages of the non-Russian population, of which only twenty had a written form, had to be made as complete and functional as possible. The revolutionary language policy was indisputably democratic in stance, but some observers argue that its real driving force was the new government's need to establish its power and ideology in ethnically and linguistically diverse parts of the country. In any case, the language reform of the 1920s and early 1930s was unprecedented in scale. More than forty unlettered languages received a writing system, and about forty-five had their writing systems entirely transformed. During the 1920s a Latinization campaign created new alphabets and transformed old ones onto a Latin (as opposed to a Cyrillic or Arabic) basis. In February 1926 the First Turcological Congress in Baku adopted the Latin alphabet as a basis for the Turkic languages. Despite a few instances of resistance, the language reform was remarkably successful, and during the early 1930s education and publishing were available in all the national languages of the USSR. Between 1936 and 1937 a sharp change in Soviet nationalities policy led to a sudden decision to transform all of the country's alphabets onto a Cyrillic basis. Complete Cyrillization was implemented much faster than the previous alphabet reforms. From the late 1930s until the late 1980s, Soviet language policy increasingly promoted russification. National languages remained equal in declarations, but in practice Russian became the dominant language of the state, culture, and education for all the peoples of the USSR. It was only at the end of the 1980s, when a measure of political and cultural self-determination was restored, that the various Soviet nations and their languages acquired a higher status.

THE RUSSIAN FEDERATION

Article 68 of the 1993 constitution of the Russian Federation declares that Russian is the state language. Federal subunits of Russia have the constitutional right to establish their own state languages along with Russian. The state guarantees protection and support to all the national languages, with emphasis on the vernaculars of small ethnic groups. On December 11, 2002, however, President Vladimir Putin introduced amendments to the Law on Languages of the Russian Federation that established the Cyrillic alphabet as a compulsory norm for all of the country's state languages. Supported by both chambers of the Russian parliament, this amendment was strongly opposed by local officials in Karelia and Tatarstan. Russian lawmakers are also concerned about the purity of the Russian language. In February 2003 a draft law prohibiting the use of jargon, slang, and vulgar words, as well as the use of foreign borrowings instead of existing Russian equivalents, was adopted by the lower chamber of the Duma but was rejected by the Senate. The language issue clearly remains as topical as ever in Russia, and state language policy may be entering a new phase.

See also: CYRILLIC ALPHABET; EDUCATION; KARAMZIN, NIKOLAI MIKAILOVICH; NATIONALITIES POLICIES, SOVIET; NATIONALITIES POLICIES, TSARIST

BIBLIOGRAPHY

Buck, Christopher D. (1984). "The Russian Language Question in the Imperial Academy of Sciences." In *Aspects of the Slavic Language Question*, Vol. 2: *East Slavic*, ed. Riccardo Picchio and Harvey Goldblatt. New Haven, CT: Yale Concilium on International and Area Studies.

Comrie, Bernard. (1981). *The Languages of the Soviet Union*. Cambridge, UK: Cambridge University Press.

Gasparov, Boris M. (1984). "The Language Situation and the Linguistic Polemic in Mid-Nineteenth-Century Russia." In *Aspects of the Slavic Language Question*. Vol. 2: *East Slavic*, ed. Riccardo Picchio and Harvey Goldblatt. New Haven, CT: Yale Concilium on International and Area Studies.

Hosking, Geoffrey. (2001). *Russia and the Russians: A History*. London: Allen Lane.

Kirkwood, Michael, ed. (1989). *Language Planning in the Soviet Union.* London: Macmillan.

Kreindler, Isabelle. (1982). "The Changing Status of Russian in the Soviet Union." *International Journal of the Sociology of Language* 33:7–41.

Kreindler, Isabelle, ed. (1985). *Sociolinguistic Perspectives on Soviet National Languages: Their Past, Present and Future.* Berlin: Mouton de Gruyter.

Uspenskij, Boris A. (1984). "The Language Program of N. M. Karamzin and Its Historical Antecedents." In *Aspects of the Slavic Language Question.* Vol. 2: *East Slavic,* ed. Riccardo Picchio and Harvey Goldblatt. New Haven, CT: Yale Concilium on International and Area Studies.

VLADISLAVA REZNIK

LAPPS *See* SAMI.

LATVIA AND LATVIANS

The Republic of Latvia is located on the eastern littoral of the Baltic Sea, and the vast majority of the world's Latvians (est. 1.5 million in 2000) live in the state that bears their name. They occupy this coastal territory together with the the other two Baltic peoples with states of their own, the Estonians and the Lithuanians, as well as a substantial number of other nationality groups, including Russians. The complex relationship between this region and the Russian state goes back to medieval times. The modern history of this relationship, however, can be dated to the late eighteenth century, when the Russian Empire, under Catherine the Great, concluded the process (begun by Peter the Great) of absorbing the entire region. From then until World War I, the Latvian population of the region was subject to the Russian tsar. The disintegration of the empire during the war led to the emergence of the three independent Baltic republics in 1918 (Latvia, Estonia, Lithuania), which, however, were annexed by the USSR in 1940. They were formally Soviet Socialist Republics until the collapse of the USSR in 1991. Since then, Latvia and the other two Baltic republics have been independent countries, with strong expectations of future membership in both NATO and the European Community. The notion among political leaders in Russia that the Baltic territories, among others, were the Russian "near abroad," however, remained strong during the 1990s.

Before they were united into a single state in 1918, the Latvian-speaking populations of the Baltic region lived for many centuries in different though adjacent political entities, each of which had its own distinct cultural history. The Latvians in Livonia (Ger. Livland) shared living space with a substantial Estonian population in the northern part of the province. Those in the easternmost reaches of the Latvian-language territory were, until the eighteenth century, under the control of the Polish-Lithuanian Commonwealth, and afterward part of Vitebsk province of the Russian Empire. The Latvians of Courland (Ger. Kurland), until 1795, were residents of the semi-independent duchy of Courland and Semigallia, the dukes owing their loyalty to the Polish king until the duchy became part of the Russian Empire. The final acquisition of all these territories by the Russian Empire was not accompanied by an internal consolidation of the region, however, and most of the eighteenth-century administrative boundaries remained largely unchanged. Also remaining unchaged throughout the nineteenth century was the cultural and linguistic layering of the region. In the Latvian-language territories, social and cultural dominance remained in the hands of the so-called Baltic Germans, a subpopulation that had arrived in the Baltic littoral as political and religious crusaders in the thirteenth century and since then had formed seemingly unchanging upper orders of society. The powerful Baltic German nobility (Ger. Ritterschaften) and urban patriciates (especially in the main regional city of Riga) continued to mediate relations between the provincial lower orders and the Russian government in St. Petersburg.

Most historians hold that a national consciousness that transcended the provincial borders was starting to develop among the Latvian-speakers of these provinces during the eighteenth century. The main national awakening of the Latvians, however, took place from the mid-1800s onward, and by the time of World War I had produced a strong sense of cultural commonality that manifested itself in a thriving Latvian-language literature, a large number of cultural and social organizations, and a highly literate population. Challenging provincial Baltic German control, some Latvian nationalists sought help in the Russian slavophile movement; this search for friends ended, however, with the systematic russification policies under Alexander III in the late 1880s, which restricted the use of the

Latvia, 1992 © Maryland Cartographics. Reprinted with permission

Latvian language in the educational and judicial systems and thus affected everyday life. Henceforth, both the Baltic German political elite and the Russian government seemed to many Latvian nationalists to be forces inimical to Latvian aspirations for independence.

The main events in the region during the twentieth century changed the nature of the inherited antagonisms of the Latvian area, but did not solve them. The emergence of a Latvian state capped the growth of Latvian nationalism, but created in the new state the need to resolve the problems of economic development, national security, and minority nationalities. The Russian population in Latvia in the interwar years remained in the range of 7 to 10 percent. In the fall of 1939 virtually the entire Baltic German population of Latvia emigrated to the lands of the Third Reich. World War II, however, brought annexation by the Soviet Union in 1940, occupation by the Third Reich from 1941 to 1945, and from 1945 the continued sovietization of the Latvian state that had begun in 1940 and 1941. As a constituent republic of the USSR, the Latvian SSR from the mid-1940s onward experienced, over the next four decades, an influx of Russians and Russian-speakers that entirely changed its nationality structure. Simultaneously, the Latvian language was downgraded in most spheres of public life and education, and resistance to these trends was attacked by the Latvian Communist Party as bourgeois nationalism. The Latvian capital, Riga, became the headquarters of the Baltic Military District, vastly enlarging the presence of the Soviet military. For many Latvians all these developments seemed to endanger their language, national culture, and even national autonomy. Thus

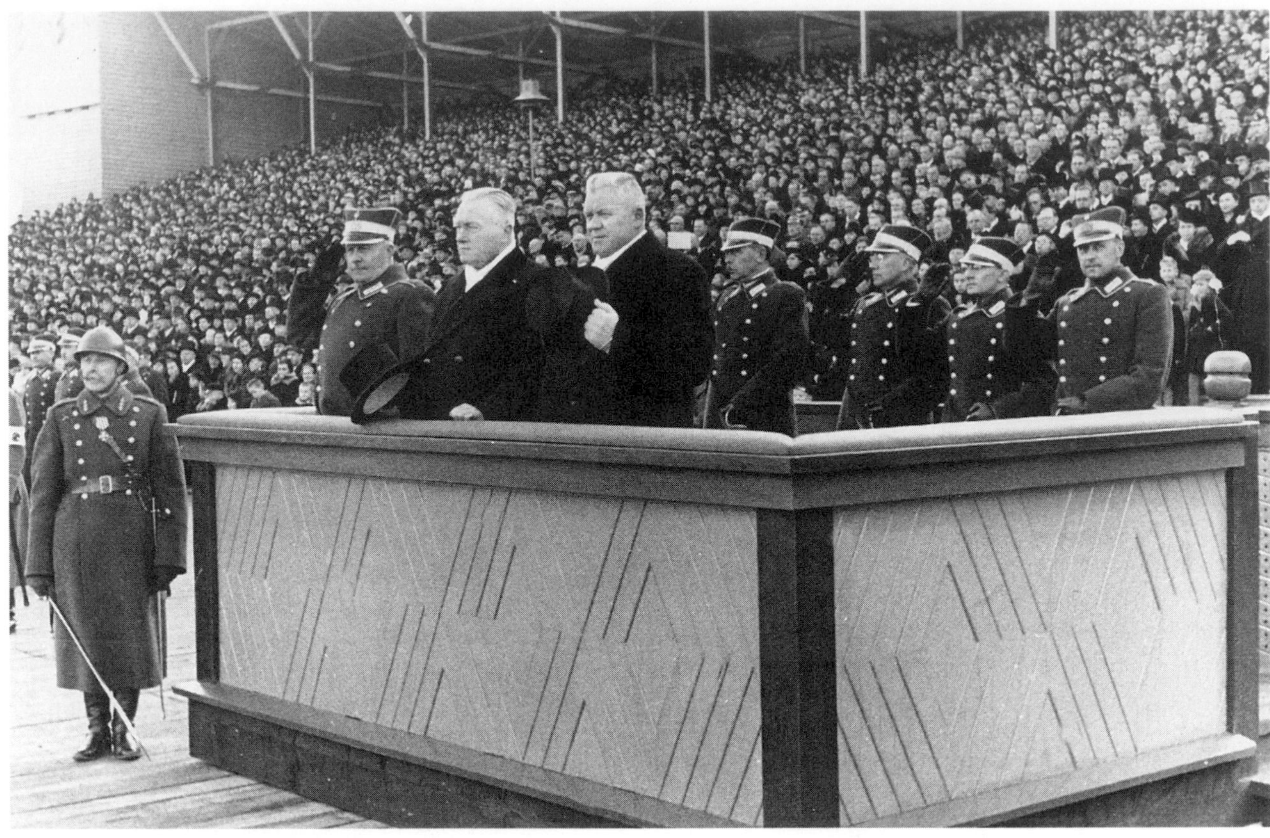

President Karlis Ulmanis reviews troops at an Independence Day parade (c. 1935). His great-nephew Guntis Ulmanis was the first president of post-Soviet Latvia. © HULTON ARCHIVE

the large-scale participation of Latvians (even Communist Party members) in the Latvian Popular Front in the Gorbachev period was not surprising, and the view that Latvia should reclaim its independence became a powerful political force from 1989 onward.

The collapse of the USSR and the return of Latvian independence left the country with a population of about 52 percent ethnic Latvians and 48 percent Russians, Ukrainians, Belorussians, and others. In 2001 the proportion of Latvians stood at 57.9 percent, the other nationalties having been reduced by emigration and low fertility rates. About 40 percent of the Slavic minority populations were Latvian citizens, leaving the social and political integration of other members of these populations as one of the principal problems as the country became integrated into Western economic, social, and security organizations.

See also: CATHERINE I; ESTONIA AND ESTONIANS; NATIONALITIES POLICIES, SOVIET; NATIONALITIES POLICIES, TSARIST

BIBLIOGRAPHY

Misiunas, Romuald, and Taagepera, Rein. (1993). *The Baltic States: Years of Dependence, 1940–1990.* Berkeley: University of California Press.

Plakans, Andrejs. (1995). *The Latvians: A Short History.* Stanford, CA: Hoover Institution Press, 1995.

Plakans, Andrejs. (1997). *Historical Dictionary of Latvia.* Lanham, MD: Scarecrow Press.

Rauch, Georg von. (1974). *The Baltic States: The Years of Independence, 1917–1940.* Berkeley: University of California Press.

ANDREJS PLAKANS

LAW CODE OF 1649

The Russian/Muscovite law code of 1649, formally known as the *sobornoye ulozhenie* (or *Ulozhenie*, the name of the code, which will be used in the article), was one of the great legal monuments of all time. Historically, in Russia, it is probably the second most important literary monument composed between 882 and at least 1800, outranked only by the various redactions of the Russian chronicle.

Like some other major legal monuments in Russian history, the Law Code of 1649 was the product of civil disorder. Tsar Alexei Mikhailovich had come to the throne at age 16 in 1645. His former tutor, Boris Morozov, was ruling in his name. Morozov and his clique, at the pinnacle of corruption, aroused great popular discontent. A crowd formed in Moscow on June 2, 1648, and presented a petition to Tsar Alexei, whose accompanying bodyguards tore it up and flung it back into the faces of the petitioners, who, joined by others, then went on a looting and burning rampage. The rebellion soon spread to a dozen other Russian towns. Inter alia, the petitioners cited judicial abuses by the Morozov clique, mentioned that great rulers in Byzantium had compiled law codes, and demanded that Alexei follow suit.

To calm the mob, Alexei agreed that a new law code should be compiled and on July 16 appointed one of the leading figures of the seventeenth century, Nikita Odoyevsky, to head a commission of five to compile it. Three of them were experienced bureaucrats who together had decades of experience working in the Moscow central governmental chancellery system (the *prikazy*). The Odoyevsky Commission set to work immediately, and the preamble to the Law Code explains how they worked. They asked the major chancelleries (about ten of the existing forty) for their statute books (*ustavnye/ukaznye knigi*), the decisions of the chancelleries on scrolls. The scrolls summarized the cases and contained the resolutions for each case. The Odoyevsky Commission selected the most important resolutions and tried to generalize them by removing the particulars of each case as well as put them in logical order (on the scrolls they were in chronological order). Depending on how frequently the resolutions had been used and how old they were, the fact that many of the Law Code's articles were summaries from the statute books is more or less apparent. When seeking precedents to resolve a case, the chancelleries frequently wrote to each other asking for guidance, with the result that similar resolutions sometimes can be found in several statute books. Fires during the Time of Troubles had destroyed most of the chancellery records; the chancelleries restored some of these by writing to the provinces requesting legal materials sent from Moscow before 1613. The same approach was used after a fire in 1626 again had destroyed many of the chancellery records.

The chancelleries had other sources of precedents, some of which are mentioned in the Law Code itself (in the preamble and rather often in marginalia on the still-extant original scroll copy of the Law Code) and others that can be found by comparing the chancellery scrolls and other laws with the Law Code. Major sources were Byzantine law, which circulated in Russia in the Church Statute Book (the *Kormchaya kniga*, a Russian version of the Byzantine *Nomocanon*) and the *Lithuanian Statute* of 1588 (which had been translated from West Russian into Muscovite Middle Russian around 1630). In addition to the chancellery records, the *Sudebnik* (Court Handbook) of 1550 was a source for the chancelleries and for the 1649 monument.

By October 3, 1648, the Odoyevsky Commission had prepared a preliminary draft of half of the new code. In response to the June riots, Tsar Alexei changed the personnel of his government and summoned an Assembly of the Land to consider the new law code. The Odoyevsky Commission draft was read to the delegates to the Assembly of the Land, who apparently voted up or down each article. In addition, the delegates brought their own demands, which were incorporated into the new code and comprised about eighty-three articles of all the 968 articles in the code. From 77 to 102 articles originated in Byzantium, 170 to 180 in the *Lithuanian Statute* of 1588. From 52 to 118 came from the *Sudebnik* of 1550, and 358 can be traced to post-1550 (primarily post-1613) practice.

The code's 968 articles are grouped into twenty-five chapters. The *Sudebniki* of 1497, 1550, and 1589 had been arranged one article after another, but the Composite *Sudebnik* of 1606 was grouped into chapters (twenty-five of them), as was the *Lithuanian Statute* of 1588. The architecture of the code is also interesting, from "the highest, the sublime" (the church, religion: chapter 1; the tsar and his court: chapters 2 and 3) to "the lowest, the gross" (musketeers: chapter 23; cossacks: chapter 24; and illicit taverns: chapter 25). Although there are a handful of codification defects in the code, they are few in number and trivial. The entire document was considered by the Assembly of the Land and signed by most of the delegates on January 29, 1649. Those who withheld their signatures were primarily churchmen who objected to the code's semi-secularization of the church (see below). Almost immediately the scroll copy was sent to the printer, and twelve hundred copies were manufactured between April and May 20. The *Ulozhenie* was the second lay book published in Muscovy. (The first was Smotritsky's *Grammar*, published in 1619.) The price was high (one ruble; the median daily wage was four kopeks), but the book sold out almost immediately, and another twelve hundred copies were printed, with some minor changes, between August 27 and December 21, 1649. They also sold out quickly. The *Ulozhenie* was subsequently reprinted eight times as an active law code, and it served as the starting point for the famous forty-five-volume Speransky codification of the laws in 1830. It has been republished eight times after 1830 because of its enormous historical interest. In 1663 it was translated into Latin and subsequently into French, German, Danish, and English.

Commentators have marveled that the Odoyevsky Commission was able to produce such a remarkable monument at all, let alone in so short a time. Until 1830, other codification attempts were made, but they all failed. Certainly the success of the code can be attributed largely to the preparation on the part of the Odoyevsky Commission: They brought a nearly finished document to the Assembly of the Land for approval and amendment. In contrast, Catherine II's Legislative Commission of 1767 failed miserably because it had no draft to work from, but started instead from abstract principles and went nowhere. The speed of the Odoyevsky Commission is also easy to account for: Each chapter is based primarily on an extraction of the laws from a specific chancellery's statute book or demands made at the Assembly of the Land. The Odoyevsky Commission made no attempt to write law itself or to fill lacunae in existing legislation.

The Law Code of 1649 is a fairly detailed record of its times, practices, and major concerns. Most noteworthy are the additions insisted on by the delegates to the Assembly of the Land, amendments which the government was too weak and frightened to oppose. Three areas are especially significant: the completion of the enserfment of the peasantry (chapter 11), the completion of the legal stratification of the townsmen (chapter 19), and the semi-secularization of the church (chapters 13, 14, and 19).

While the peasants were enserfed primarily at the demands of others (the middle service class provincial cavalry), the townsmen were stratified into a caste at their own insistence. Urban stratification and enserfment proceeded in parallel from the early 1590s on, but the resolutions in the *Ulozhenie* were different. Serfs could be returned to any place of which there was record of their having lived in the past, but townsmen were enjoined to remain where they were in January 1649 and could be returned only if they moved after that time. Enserfment was motivated by provincial cavalry rent demands, while townsmen stratification was motivated by state demands for taxes, which were assessed collectively and were hard to collect when those registered in a census (taken most recently in 1646–1647) moved away. The townsmen got monopolies on trade and manufacturing, as well as on the ownership of urban property (this primarily dispossessed the church). Roughly the same rules applied to fugitive townsmen as fugitive serfs, especially when they married.

If one thinks in terms of victimization, the primary "victim" of the Law Code of 1649 (after the serfs) was the Orthodox Church. As mentioned, much of its urban property was secularized. Its capacity to engage in trade and manufacturing was compromised. The state laid down provisions for protecting the church in chapter 1, but this in and of itself states which party is superior and limits the "harmony" (from the Byzantine Greek *Epanogoge*) of the two. Chapter 12 discusses the head of the church, the patriarch, thus obviously making him subordinate to the state. Worst of all for the church was chapter 13, which created the Monastery Chancellery, a state office which in theory ran all of the church except the patriarchate. This measure especially secularized much of the church, and though it was repealed on Alexei's death in 1676, it was revitalized with a vengeance by Peter the Great's creation of the Holy Synod in 1721, when all of the church became a department of the state. The *Ulozhenie* also forbade the church from acquiring additional landed property, the culmination of a process which had begun with the confiscation of all of Novgorod's church property after its annexation by Moscow in 1478.

The Law Code of 1649 is a comprehensive document, the product of an activist, interventionist, maximalist state that believed it could control many aspects of Russian life and the economy (especially the primary factors, land and labor). Chapters 2 and 3 protected the tsar and regulated life at his court. The longest chapter, 10, is quite detailed on procedure. The major forms of landholding, service lands (*pomestye*) and hereditary estate lands, are discussed in chapters 16 and 17, respectively. Slavery is the subject of the code's second longest chapter, 20. Criminal law is covered in two chapters, 21 (mostly of Russian origin) and 22 (mostly of Lithuanian and Byzantine origin), which were combined in the 1669 Felony Statute and represented the peak of barbarous punishments in Russia. Other subjects covered are forgers and counterfeiters (chapters 4 and 5), travel abroad (typically forbidden, chapter 6), military service (chapter 7), the redemption of Russians from foreign military captivity (chapter 8), various travel fees (chapter 9) and seal fees (chapter 18), the oath (chapter 14), and the issue of reopening resolved cases (chapter 15). Codes as comprehensive and activist as this one did not appear in Austria, Prussia, or France until more than a century later.

See also: ALEXEI MIKHAILOVICH; ASSEMBLY OF THE LAND; KORMCHAYA KNIGA; MOROZOV, BORIS IVANOVICH; PEASANTRY; SERFDOM; SUDEBNIK OF 1497; SUDEBNIK OF 1550; SUDEBNIK OF 1589

BIBLIOGRAPHY

Hellie, Richard. (1965). "Muscovite Law and Society: The *Ulozhenie* of 1649 as a Reflection of the Political and Social Development of Russia since the *Sudebnik* of 1589." Ph.D. diss., University of Chicago.

Hellie, Richard. (1979). "The Stratification of Muscovite Society: The Townsmen." *Russian History* 6(2): 119–175.

Hellie, Richard. (1988–1991). "Early Modern Russian Law: The *Ulozhenie* of 1649." *Russian History* 2(4): 115–224.

Hellie, Richard. (1989–1990). "Patterns of Instability in Russian and Soviet History." *Chicago Review of International Affairs,* 1(3):3–34; 2(1):3–15.

Hellie, Richard. (1992). "Russian Law from Oleg to Peter the Great." Foreword to *The Laws of Rus': Tenth to Fifteenth Centuries,* tr. and ed. Daniel H. Kaiser. Salt Lake City, UT: Charles Schlacks.

Hellie, Richard, ed. and tr. (1967, 1970). *Muscovite Society: Readings for Introduction to Russian Civilization.* Chicago: University of Chicago.

Hellie, Richard, ed. and tr. (1988). *The Muscovite Law Code (Ulozhenie) of 1649.* Irvine, CA: Charles Schlacks.

RICHARD HELLIE

LAY OF IGOR'S CAMPAIGN

A twelfth-century literary masterpiece, the *Lay of Igor's Campaign* was probably composed soon after the unsuccessful 1185 campaign of Prince Igor of Novgorod–Seversk and his brother Vsevolod of Kursk against the Cumans (Polovtsians) of the steppe. The *Lay* (*Slovo o polku Igoreve*), by an anonymous author, minimizes narrative of facts (which were presumably fresh in the minds of the audience, and which are known to scholars from the Hypatian Chronicle and others) and instead evokes the heroic spirit of the time and the need for unity among the princes. Hence its title, Slovo, meaning a speech or discourse, not a story and not verse (the English translation "Lay" is misleading).

Though the text was heavily influenced by East Slavic folklore, it is nonetheless a sophisticated literary work. Its rhythmical prose approaches poetry in the density of its imagery and the beauty of its sound patterns. The images are taken mainly from nature and Slavic mythology. A solar eclipse, the calls of birds of omen, and creatures of myth (the Div) foreshadow Igor's defeat on the third day of battle. Trees and grass droop in sorrow for human disaster.

The technique is that of mosaic, of sparkling pieces juxtaposed to create a brilliant whole. Scenes and speeches shift with hardly any explicit transitions. To understand the message requires paying strict attention to juxtaposition. For example, the magic of Vseslav followed immediately by the magic of Yaroslavna and the apparent sorcery of Igor.

Very few Christian motifs appear; those that do are primarily toward the close. Instead, there are the frequent mentions of pagan gods and pre–Christian mythology. Even so, the *Lay* should not be considered a neo–pagan work; rather its bard seems to use this imagery to create an aura of olden times, the time of the grandfathers and their bard, Boyan. The principle of two historical levels, repeatedly invoked, serve the purpose of creating the necessary epic distance impossible for recent events by themselves, and also sets up a central theme: The princes of today should emulate the great deeds of their forefathers while avoiding the mistakes. Extolling Igor and his companions as heroes, the bard, mostly through the central speech of Grand Prince Svyatoslav, also calls for replacing their drive for personal glory with a new ethic of common defense.

The *Lay* was first published in 1800, reportedly from a sole surviving North Russian copy of the fifteenth or sixteenth century acquired by Count Alexei Musin–Pushkin. The supposed loss of the manuscript in the fire of Moscow in 1812 has made it possible for some skeptics over the years to challenge the work's authenticity, speculating that it was a fabrication of the sixteenth century (Alexander Zimin) or even the 1790s (Andrÿea Mazon). Up to a point, this has been a classic confrontation of historians and philologists, each group claiming priority for its own method and viewpoint. Much depends on how one views its relationship with *Zadonshchina,* which clearly bears some genetic connection to it, almost certainly as a later imitation of the *Lay.*

Despite the unproven doubts and suspicions of a few, the *Slovo o polku Igoreve,* in its language, imagery, style, and themes, is perfectly compatible with the late twelfth century, as was demonstrated by leading scholars such as Roman Jakobson, Dmitry Likhachev, Varvara Adrianova–Peretts, and many others. It remains one of the masterpieces of all East Slavic literature.

See also: FOLKLORE; ZADONSHCHINA

BIBLIOGRAPHY

Zenkovsky, Serge A., tr. and ed. (1974). *Medieval Russia's Epics, Chronicles, and Tales,* 2nd ed. rev. New York: Dutton.

NORMAN W. INGHAM

LAZAREV INSTITUTE

The Lazarev Institute (*Lazarevskii institut vostochnykh iazykov*) was founded in Moscow in 1815 by the wealthy Armenian Lazarev (Lazarian) family primarily as a school for their children. In 1827 the school was named the Lazarev Institute of Oriental Languages (Oriental in the nineteenth-century sense, including the Middle East and Northern Africa) by the State and placed under the supervision of the Ministry of Public Education. For the next twenty years the Lazarev Institute functioned as a special gymnasium that offered language courses in Armenian, Persian, Turkish, and Arabic, in addition to its regular curriculum in Russian. The student body was composed mostly of Armenian and Russian boys aged ten to fourteen. In 1844 there were 105 students: seventy-three Armenians, thirty Russians, and two others. In 1848 the Institute was upgraded to a lyceum and offered classes in the aforementioned languages for the upper grades. The Institute trained teachers for Armenian schools, Armenian priests, and, most importantly, Russian civil servants and interpreters. The government, responding to the importance of the Institute's role in preparing men to administer the diverse peoples of the Caucasus, funded and expanded the program. Many Armenian professionals and Russian scholars specializing in Transcaucasia received their education at the Lazarev Institute. In 1851 Armenians, Georgians, and even a few Muslims from Transcaucasia were permitted to enroll in the preparatory division, where, in addition to various subjects taught in Russian, they also studied their native tongues. The Russian conquest of Daghestan and plans to expand further into Central Asia made the Lazarev Institute even more necessary. In 1872, following the Three-Emperors' League, Russia was once again free to pursue an aggressive policy involving the Eastern Question. The State divided the institution into two educational sections. The first served as a gymnasium, while the second devoted itself to a three-year course in the languages (Armenian, Persian, Arabic, Turkish, Georgian), history, and culture of Transcaucasia.

The Lazarev Institute had its own printing press and, beginning in 1833, published important works in thirteen languages. It also published two journals, *Papers in Oriental Studies* (1899–1917) and the *Emin Ethnographical Anthology* (six issues). Its library had some forty thousand books in 1913.

Following the Bolshevik Revolution, on March 14, 1919, the Council of the People's Commissars of the Russian Soviet Federated Socialist Republic (RSFSR) renamed the Institute the Armenian Institute and, soon after, the Southwest Asian Institute. In 1920 it was renamed the Central Institute of Living Oriental Languages. A year later it was renamed the Moscow Oriental Institute. In October 1921, a section of the Institute was administered by Soviet Armenia and became a showcase devoted to Armenian workers and peasants. By the 1930s the Institute lost its students to the more prestigious foreign language divisions in Moscow and Leningrad. Its library collection was transferred to the Lenin Library of Moscow. In the last four decades of the USSR, the building of the Institute was home to the permanent delegation of Soviet Armenia to the Supreme Soviet. Following the demise of the USSR, the building of the Institute became the Armenian embassy in Russia.

See also: ARMENIA AND ARMENIANS; EDUCATION; NATIONALITIES POLICIES, TSARIST

BIBLIOGRAPHY

Bournoutian, George. (1998). *Russia and the Armenians of Transcaucasia, 1797–1889: A Documentary Record.* Costa Mesa, CA: Mazda Press.

Bournoutian, George. (2001). *Armenians and Russia, 1626–1796: A Documentary Record.* Costa Mesa, CA: Mazda Press.

GEORGE BOURNOUTIAN

LAZAREVSKAYA, YULIANYA USTINOVNA

See OSORINA, YULIANYA USTINOVNA.

LEAGUE OF ARMED NEUTRALITY

Already annoyed by American privateer interference with Anglo-Russian maritime trade in the 1770s, Catherine the Great was even more frustrated by British countermeasures that intercepted and confiscated neutral shipping suspected of aiding the rebellious American colonies. In March 1780 she issued a Declaration of Armed Neutrality that became the basic doctrine of maritime law regarding neutral rights at sea during war. It defined, simply and clearly, the rights of neutral vessels, contraband (goods directly supportive of a military program), and the conditions and restrictions of an embargo, and overall defended the rights of neutrals (the flag covers the cargo) against seizure and condemnation of nonmilitary goods. Having already established herself in the forefront of enlightened rulers, Catherine invited the other nations of Europe to join Russia in arming merchant vessels against American or British transgression of these rights. Because of the crippling of American commerce, most of the infractions were by the British.

Coming at this stage in the War for Independence, the Russian declaration boosted American morale and inspired the Continental Congress to dispatch Francis Dana to St. Petersburg to secure more formal recognition and support. Although Russia had little in the way of naval power to back up the declaration, it encouraged France and other countries to aid the American cause. Britain reluctantly stood by while a few French and Dutch ships under the Russian flag entered American ports, bringing valuable supplies to the hard-pressed colonies. Even more supplies entered the United States via the West Indies with the help of a Russian adventurer, Fyodor Karzhavin. The military effect was minimal, however, because the neutral European states hesitated about making commitments because of fear of British retaliation. By 1781, however, the United Provinces (the Netherlands), Denmark, Sweden, Austria, and Prussia had all joined the league.

The league was remembered in the United States, somewhat erroneously, as a mark of Russian friendship and sympathy, and bolstered Anglophobia in the two countries. More generally, it affirmed a cardinal principle of maritime law that continues in effect in the early twenty-first century. Indirectly, it also led to a considerable expansion of Russian-American trade from the 1780s through the first half of the nineteenth century.

See also: CATHERINE II; ENLIGHTENMENT, IMPACT OF

BIBLIOGRAPHY

Bolkhovitinov, Nikolai N. (1975). *The Beginnings of Russian-American Relations, 1775–1815.* New Haven: Yale University Press.

Madariaga, Isabel de. (1963).*Britain, Russia and the Armed Neutrality of 1780.* London: Macmillan.

Saul, Norman E. (1991). *Distant Friends: The United States and Russia, 1763–1867.* Lawrence: University Press of Kansas.

NORMAN E. SAUL

LEAGUE OF NATIONS

Formed by the victorious powers in 1919, the League of Nations was designed to enforce the Treaty of Versailles and the other peace agreements that concluded World War I. It was intended to replace secret deals and war, as means for settling international disputes, with open diplomacy and peaceful mediation. Its charter also provided a mechanism for its members to take collective action against aggression.

Soviet Russia and Weimar Germany initially were not members of the League. At the time of the League's founding, the Western powers had invaded Russia in support of the anticommunist side in the Russian civil war. The Bolshevik regime was hostile to the League, denouncing it as an anti-Soviet, counterrevolutionary conspiracy of the imperialist powers. Throughout the 1920s, Soviet Commissar of Foreign Affairs Georgy Chicherin aligned the USSR with Weimar Germany, the other outcast power, against Britain, France, and the

League. German adherence to the Locarno Accords with Britain and France in 1925, and Germany's admission to the League in 1926, dealt a blow to Chicherin's policy. This Germanophile, Anglophobe, anti-League view was not shared by Deputy Commissar of Foreign Affairs Maxim Litvinov, who advocated a more balanced policy, including cooperation with the League. Moreover, the USSR participated in the Genoa Conference in 1922 and several League-sponsored economic and arms control forums later in the decade.

Chicherin's retirement because of ill health, his replacement as foreign commissar by Litvinov, and, most importantly, the rise to power of Adolf Hitler in Germany served to reorient Moscow's policy. The Third Reich now replaced the British Empire as the main potential enemy in Soviet thinking. In December 1933 the Politburo adopted the new Collective Security line in foreign policy, whereby the USSR sought to build an alliance of anti-Nazi powers to prevent or, if necessary, defeat German aggression. An important part of this strategy was the attempt to revive the collective security mechanism of the League. To this end, the Soviet Union joined the League in 1934, and Litvinov became the most eloquent proponent of League sanctions against German aggression. Soviet leaders also hoped that League membership would afford Russia some protection against Japanese expansionism in the Far East. Unfortunately, the League had already failed to take meaningful action against Japanese aggression in Manchuria in 1931, and it later failed to act against the Italian attack on Ethiopia in 1935. Soviet collective security policy in the League and in bilateral diplomacy faltered against the resolution of Britain and France to appease Hitler.

When Stalin could not persuade the Western powers to ally with the USSR, even in the wake of the German invasion of Czechoslovakia, he abandoned the collective security line and signed the Nazi-Soviet Pact with Hitler on August 23, 1939. Subsequent Soviet territorial demands on Finland led to the Winter War of 1939–1940 and to the expulsion of the USSR from the League as an aggressor. However, Hitler's attack on Russia in 1941 accomplished what Litvinov's diplomacy could not, creating an alliance with Britain and the United States. The USSR thus became in 1945 a founding member of the United Nations, the organization that replaced the League of Nations after World War II.

See also: CHICHERIN, GEORGY VASILIEVICH; LITVINOV, MAXIM MAXIMOVICH; NAZI-SOVIET PACT OF 1939; UNITED NATIONS; WORLD WAR I; WORLD WAR II

BIBLIOGRAPHY

Buzinkai, Donald I. (1967). "The Bolsheviks, the League of Nations, and the Paris Peace Conference, 1919." *Soviet Studies* 19:257–263.

Haigh, R.H.; Morris, D.S.; and Peters, A.R. (1986). *Soviet Foreign Policy: The League of Nations and Europe, 1917–1939.* Totowa, N.J.: Barnes and Noble.

Haslam, Jonathan. (1984). *The Soviet Union and the Struggle for Collective Security in Europe, 1933–39.* New York: St. Martin's Press.

Jacobson, Jan. (1994). *When the Soviet Union Entered World Politics.* Berkeley: University of California Press.

TEDDY J. ULDRICKS

LEAGUE OF THE MILITANT GODLESS

One of the early Soviet regime's most ambitious attempts at social engineering, the League of the Militant Godless (*Soyuz voinstvuyushchikh bezbozhnikov*) was also one of its most dismal failures. Founded in 1925 as the League of the Godless, it was one of numerous volunteer groups created in the 1920s to help extend the regime's reach into Russian society. These organizations hoped to attract nonparty members who might be sympathetic to individual elements of the Bolshevik program. The word "militant" was added in 1929 as Stalin's Cultural Revolution gathered speed, and at its peak in the early 1930s, the League claimed 5.5 million dues-paying *bezbozhniki* (godless).

Organized like the Communist Party, the League consisted of cells of individual members at factories, schools, offices, and living complexes. These cells were managed by local councils subordinated to regional and provincial bodies. A League Central Council presided in Moscow. Despite the League's nominal independence, it was directed at each level by the corresponding Communist Party organization.

The League's mandate was to disseminate atheism, and, to achieve this goal, it orchestrated public campaigns for the closure of churches and the prohibition of church bell pealing. It staged demonstrations against the observance of religious holidays and the multitude of daily Orthodox practices.

The League also arranged lectures on themes such as the existence of God, Biblical miracles, astronomy, and so forth. The League's Central Council published a raft of antireligious publications in Russian and in the languages of national minorities. Larger provincial councils issued their own antireligious periodicals.

The League's rapid organizational rise seemed to embody the Bolshevik success in transforming Holy Russia into the atheistic Soviet Union. But appearances were misleading. In ironic obeisance to Marxist dialectics, the League reached its organizational peak in the early 1930s before collapsing utterly a few years later when, consolidation taking priority over Cultural Revolution, the Party withdrew the material support that had sustained the League's rise. The League's disintegration cast its earlier successes as a "Potemkin village" in the Russian tradition. In the League's case, the deception was nearly complete: Only a fraction of the League's nominal members actually paid dues. Many joined the League without their knowledge, as a name on a list submitted by a local party official. Overworked local party officials often viewed League activities as a last priority. The population largely ignored the League's numerous publications. Local antireligious officials often succeeded in drawing the ire of the local community in their ham-handed efforts to counter Orthodoxy. Indeed, the local versions of debates in the early and mid-1920s between leading regime propagandists and clergymen went so poorly that they were prohibited by the late 1920s.

The final irony was that whatever secularization occurred in the 1920s and 1930s, little of it can be attributed to the League. Orthodoxy's retreat in this period was due to the raw exercise of state power that resulted in the closure of tens of thousand of churches and the arrest of many priests. Urbanization and industrialization played their part, as did the flood of new spaces, images, and associations that accompanied the creation of Soviet culture. Only in this final element did the League play a role, and it was a very minor one. The League may have been a symbol of secularization but was hardly an agent of it.

After a brief revival in the late 1930s, the League faded once again into the background as World War II brought an accommodation with religion. It was formally disbanded in 1947, four years after the death of its founder and leader, Emilian Yaroslavsky. Yaroslavsky, an Old Bolshevik, had been a leading propagandist in the 1920s and 1930s. An ideological chameleon, he survived two decades of ideological twists and turns and died a natural death in 1943 at the age of sixty-five.

Despite its ultimate failure, the League put into clear relief the regime's fundamental approach to the task of social transformation. Highlighting Bolshevism's faith in the power of organization and building on the tradition of Russian bureaucracy, the regime emphasized the organizational manifestation of a desired sentiment to such an extent that it eventually superseded the actual sentiment. The state of atheism in Soviet Russia was essentially the same as the state of the League, as far as the regime was concerned. As long as the League was visible, the regime assumed that it had achieved one of its ideological goals. Moreover, the atheism promoted by the League looked a great deal like a secular religion. Here the regime appeared to be taking the path of least resistance, by which fundamental culture was not changed but simply given a new gloss. This approach boded ill for the long-term success of the Soviet experiment with culture and for the Soviet Union itself.

See also: BOLSHEVISM; RUSSIAN ORTHODOX CHURCH

BIBLIOGRAPHY

Husband, William. (1998). "Soviet Atheism and Russian Orthodox Strategies of Resistance, 1917–1932." *Journal of Modern History* 70(1):74–107.

Husband, William. (2000). *Godless Communists: Atheism and Society in Soviet Russia, 1917–1932.* DeKalb: Northern Illinois University Press.

Peris, Daniel. (1995). "Commissars in Red Cassocks: Former Priests in the League of the Militant Godless." *Slavic Review* 54(2):340–364.

Peris, Daniel. (1998). *Storming the Heavens: The Soviet League of the Militant Godless.* Ithaca, NY: Cornell University Press.

DANIEL PERIS

LEBED, ALEXANDER IVANOVICH

(1950–2002), Soviet, airborne commander, Afghan veteran, commander of the Fourteenth Army, Secretary of the Russian security council, and governor of Krasnoyarsk oblast.

Alexander Lebed graduated from the Ryazan Airborne School in 1973 and served in the Airborne

Forces. From 1981 to 1982 he commanded an airborne battalion in Afghanistan, and then attended the Frunze Military Academy from 1982 to 1985. In 1988 he assumed command of an airborne division, which deployed to various ethno-national hot spots within the USSR, including Tbilisi and Baku. An associate of General Pavel Grachev, the Commander of Airborne Forces, Lebed was appointed Deputy Commander of Airborne Forces in February 1991. In August, Lebed commanded the airborne troops sent to secure the Russian White House during the attempted August coup against Gorbachev. In a complex double game, Lebed neither secured the building nor arrested Yeltsin. In 1992 Pavel Grachev appointed him commander of the Russian Fourteenth Army in Moldova. Lebed intervened to protect the Russian population in the self-proclaimed Transdneistr Republic, which was involved in an armed struggle with the government of Moldova. Lebed became a hero to Russian nationalists. But in 1993 Lebed refused to support the Red-Browns opposing Yeltsin. In 1994 he spoke out against the Yeltsin government's military intervention in Chechnya, calling it ill prepared and ill conceived. In 1995 Lebed was retired from the military at President Yeltsin's order. In December 1995 he was elected to the State Duma. He then ran for president of Russia on the Congress of Russian Communities ticket with a nationalist and populist program and finished third (14.7% of the vote) in the first round of the 1996 election, behind Yeltsin and Zyuganov. Yeltsin brought Lebed into his administration as Secretary of the Security Council to ensure his own victory in the second round of voting. But Lebed proved an independent actor, and in August, when the war in Chechnya reerupted, Lebed sought to end the fighting to save the Army, accepted a cease-fire, and signed the Khasavyurt accords with rebel leader Aslan Maskhadov. The accords granted Chechnya autonomy but left the issue of independence for resolution by 2001. Lebed's actions angered Yeltsin's close associates, including Minister of Internal Affairs Anatoly Kulikov, who engineered Lebed's removal from the government in October 1996. Yeltsin justified the removal on the grounds that Lebed was a disruptive force within the government. In 1998 Lebed ran successfully for the post of Governor of Krasnoyarsk Oblast. On April 28, 2002, he was killed in a helicopter crash outside Krasnoyarsk.

See also: MILITARY, SOVIET AND POST-SOVIET; TRANSDNIESTER REPUBLIC

BIBLIOGRAPHY

Kipp, Jacob W. (1996). "The Political Ballet of General Aleksandr Ivanovich Lebed: Implications for Russia's Presidential Elections." *Problems of Post-Communism* 43:43–53.

Kipp, Jacob W. (1999). "General-Lieutenant Aleksandr Ivanovich Lebed: The Man, His Program and Political Prospects in 2000." *Problems of Post-Communism* 46:55–63.

Lebed, Alexander. (1997). *General Alexander Lebed: My Life and My Country.* Washington, DC: Regnery Pub.

Petrov, Nikolai. (1999). *Alexander Lebed in Krasnoyarsk Krai.* Moscow: Carnegie Center.

JACOB W. KIPP

LEFORTOVO

Lefortovo is a historic area in the eastern part of Moscow, on the left bank of the Yauzy River, named for the Lefortovsky infantry regiment, commanded by Franc Yakovlevicz Lefort, a comrade of Peter the Great, which was quartered there toward the end of the seventeenth century. In the 1770s and 1780s the soldiers occupied sixteen wooden houses. Nearby were some slaughterhouses and a public courtyard, where in 1880 the Lefortovo military prison was constructed (architect P. N. Kozlov). At the time it was intended for low-ranking personnel convicted of minor infringements. St. Nikolai's Church was built just above the entrance to the prison. Over the next hundred years several new buildings were added to the prison complex.

In tsarist times Lefortovo was under the jurisdiction of the Main Prison Administration of the Ministry of Justice. After the revolution it became part of the network of prisons run by the Special Department of the Cheka. In the 1920s Lefortovo was under the OGPU (United Main Political Administration). In the 1930s, together with the Lubyanka Internal Prison and the Butyrskoi and Sukhanovskoi prisons, it was under the GUGB (Central Administrative Board of State Security) of the NKVD (People`s Commissioner's Office for Internal Affairs) of the USSR. Suspects were tortured and shot in the former church of the prison, and tractor motors were run to drown out the awful sounds. With the closing of the Lubyanka Internal Prison in the 1960s, Lefortovo attained its present status as the main prison of the state security apparatus. In October 1993, Alexander Rutskoi and

Roman Khasbulatov, the organizers of the abortive putsch against Boris Yeltsin, were held in the Lefortovo detention isolator (solitary confinement) of the Ministry of Safety (MB) of the Russian Federation. In December 1993 and January 1994 the Lefortovo isolator passed from the jurisdiction of the Ministry of Safety to the Ministry of Internal Affairs (MVD). By the end of 1994 the FSB again created an investigatory administration, and in April 1997, after an eight-month struggle between the Ministry of Internal Affairs and the FSB, the isolator was again transferred to FSB jurisdiction.

The three-tier complex of the FSB's Investigative Administration, unified with the prison, is located adjacent to the Lefortovo isolator. According to the testimony of former inmates, there are fifty cells on each floor of the four-story cellblock. As of 2003 there were about two hundred prisoners in Lefortovo. The exercise area is located on the roof of the prison. Most of the cells are about 10 meters square and hold two inmates; there are also some cells for three, and a few for one. Lefortovo differs from other Russian detention prisons not only in its relatively good conditions but also for its austere regime. The inmates held here have been arrested on matters that concern the FSB, such as espionage, serious economic offenses, and terrorism, rather than ordinary crimes.

See also: GULAG; LUBYANKA; PRISONS; STATE SECURITY, ORGANS OF

BIBLIOGRAPHY

Krakhmalnikova, Zoya. (1993). *Listen, Prison! Lefortovo Notes: Letters from Exile.* Redding, CA: Nikodemos Orthodox Publication Society.

GEORG WURZER

LEFT OPPOSITION

Headed by Leon Trotsky, the Left Opposition (1923–1927) rallied against Bolshevik Party discipline on a wide array of issues. It became one of the last serious manifestations of intra-Party debate before Josef Stalin consolidated power and silenced all opposition.

Following the illness and death of Vladimir Lenin, the formation of the Left Opposition centered on Trotsky and the role he played in the struggle for Party leadership and the debates over the future course of the Soviet economy. Throughout 1923, after three strokes left Lenin incapacitated, Stalin actively strengthened his position within the Party leadership and moved against several oppositionist tendencies. In October that same year, Trotsky struck back with a searing condemnation of the ruling triumvirate (Grigory Zinoviev, Lev Kamenev, and Stalin), publicly charging them with "secretarial bureaucratism" and demanding a restoration of Party democracy.

At the same time, proponents of Trotsky's theory of permanent revolution, including such luminaries as Yevgeny Preobrazhensky, Grigory Pyatakov, Timofey Sapronov, and V. V. Osinsky, coalesced around the Platform of the Forty-Six. Representing the position of the left, they attributed the Party's ills to a progressive division of the Party into functionaries, chosen from above, and the rank-and-file Party members, who did not participate in Party affairs. Further, they accused the leadership of making economic mistakes and demanded that the dictatorship of the Party be replaced by a worker's democracy.

Formulating a more comprehensive platform, Trotsky published a pamphlet entitled *The New Course* in January 1924. By this time, the Left Opposition had gained enough public support that the leadership made some concessions in the form of the Politburo's adoption of the New Course Resolution in December. Nonetheless, at the Thirteenth Party Congress in May 1924, the Left Opposition was condemned for violating the Party's ban on factions and for disrupting Party unity.

The Left Opposition's economic platform focused on the goals of rapid industrialization and the struggle against the New Economic Policy (NEP). Left Oppositionists, also known as Trotskyites because of Trotsky's central role, argued that encouraging the growth of private and peasant sectors of the economy under the NEP was dangerous because it would create an investment crisis in the state's industrial sector. Moreover, by favoring trade and private agriculture, the state would make itself vulnerable to the economic power of hostile social classes, such as peasants and private traders. In 1925, Preobrazhensky, the left's leading theoretician, proposed an alternative course of action with his theory of primitive socialist accumulation. Arguing that the state should shift resources through price manipulations and other market mechanisms, he believed that peasant producers and consumers should bear the burden of capital accumulation for the state's industrialization drive. According to his plan, the government could achieve this end by regulating prices and taxes.

In a polity where loyalty and opposition were deemed incompatible, the Left Opposition was doomed from the start. Following the Thirteenth Party Congress denunciation, Trotsky renewed his advocacy of permanent revolution as Stalin promoted his theory of socialism in one country. The result was Trotsky's removal from the War Commissariat in January 1925 and his expulsion from the Politburo the following year. At the same time, Kamenev and Zinoviev broke with Stalin over the issue of socialism in one country and continuation of the NEP. In mid-1926, in an attempt to subvert Stalin's growing influence, Trotsky joined with Kamenev and Zinoviev in the Platform of the Thirteen, forming the United Opposition.

By 1926, however, it was already too late to mount a strong challenge to Stalin's growing power. Through skillful maneuvering, Stalin had been able increasingly to secure control over the party apparatus, eroding what little power base the oppositionists had. In 1927 Trotsky, Kamenev, and Zinoviev were removed from the Central Committee. By the end of that year the trio and all of their prominent followers, including Preobrazhensky and Pyatakov, were purged from the Party. The next year, Trotsky and members of the Left Opposition were exiled to Siberia and Central Asia. In February 1929 Trotsky was deported from the country, thus beginning the odyssey that ended with his murder by an alleged Soviet agent in Mexico City in 1940. Despite recantations and pledges of loyalty to Stalin, the remaining so-called Trotskyites could never free themselves of the stigma of their past association with the Left Opposition. Nearly all of them perished in the purges of the 1930s.

See also: RIGHT OPPOSITION; TROTSKY, LEON DAVIDOVICH; UNITED OPPOSITION

BIBLIOGRAPHY

Carr, Edward Hallett, and Davies, R. W. (1971). *Foundations of a Planned Economy, 1926–1929,* 2 vols., New York: Macmillan.

Deutscher, Isaac. (1963). *The Prophet Unarmed: Trotsky, 1921–1929.* New York: Oxford University Press.

Erlich, Alexander. (1960). *The Soviet Industrialization Debate, 1924–1928.* Cambridge, MA: Harvard University Press.

Graziosi, Andrea. (1991). "'Building the First System of State Industry in History': Piatakov's VSNKh and the Crisis of NEP, 1923–1926." *Cahiers du monde russe et sovietique* 32:539–581.

Trotsky, Leon. (1975). *The Challenge of the Left Opposition, 1923–1925.* New York: Pathfinder Press.

KATE TRANSCHEL

LEFT SOCIALIST REVOLUTIONARIES

The Left Socialist Revolutionaries (Left SRs) were an offshoot of the Socialist Revolutionary (SR) Party, a party that had arisen in 1900 as an outgrowth of nineteenth-century Russian populism. Both the SRs and their later Left SR branch espoused a socialist revolution for Russia carried out by and based upon the radical intelligentsia, the industrial workers, and the peasantry. After the outbreak of World War I in August 1914, some party leaders in the emigration, such as Yekaterina Breshko-Breshkovskaya, Andrei A. Argunov, and Nikolai D. Avksentiev, offered conditional, temporary support for the tsarist government's war efforts. Meanwhile, under the guidance of Viktor Chernov and famous populist leader Mark Natanson, the Left SRs or SR–Internationalists, as they were variously called, insisted that the party maintain an internationalist opposition to the world war. These developments, mirrored along Social Democrats, caused conflicts within and almost split the party inside Russia. By mid-1915, the antiwar forces began to predominate among SR organizations that were just beginning to recover from police attacks after the war's outbreak. Much of the party's worker, peasant, soldier, and student cadres turned toward leftist internationalism, whereas prowar (defensist) support came primarily from the party's intelligentsia. By 1916, many SR (in effect Left SR) organizations poured out antigovernment and antiwar propaganda, took part in strikes, and agitated in garrisons and at the fronts. In all these activities, they cooperated closely with Bolsheviks, Left Mensheviks, and anarchists of similar outlook. This coalition and the mass movements it spurred wore down the incompetent tsarist state and overthrew it on March 12 (February 27, O.S.), 1917.

As SR leaders returned to the Russian capital, they reunified leftist and rightist factions and emphasized the party's multi–class approach. Chernov, who in 1914-1915 had helped form the Left

SR movement, now sided with the party moderates by approving SR participation in the Provisional Government and the Russian military offensive of June 1917. Until midsummer the party's inclusive strategy seemed to work, as huge recruitments occurred everywhere. The SRs seemed poised to wield power in revolutionary Russia. Simultaneously, leftists such as Natanson, Boris Kamkov, and Maria Spiridonova, noting the growing worker-soldier uneasiness with the party's policies, began to reshape the leftist movement and cooperated with other leftist parties such as the Bolsheviks and Left Mensheviks. In this respect, they helped recreate the wartime leftist coalition that had proved so effective against the tsarist regime. By late summer and fall, the Left SRs, acting as a de facto separate party within the SR party and working at odds with it, were doing as much as the Bolsheviks to popularize the idea of soviet and socialist power. During October–November, they opposed Bolshevik unilateralism in overthrowing the Provisional Government, instead of which they proposed a multiparty, democratic version of soviet power.

Even after the October Revolution, the Left SRs hoped for continued coexistence with other SRs within a single party, bereft, they hoped, only of the extreme right wing. When the Fourth Congress of the SR Party (November 1917) dashed those hopes by refusing any reconciliation with the leftists, the Left SRs responded by convening their own party congress and officially constituting themselves as a separate party. In pursuit of multiparty soviet power, during December 1917 they reaffirmed their block with the communists (the Bolsheviks used this term after October 1917) and entered the Soviet government, taking the commissariats of justice, land, and communications and entering the supreme military council and the secret police (*Cheka*). They favored the Constituent Assembly's dismissal during January 1918 but sharply opposed other communist policies. Daily debates between communist and Left SR leaders characterized the high councils of government. When Lenin promulgated the Brest–Litovsk Peace with Germany in March 1918 against heavy opposition within the soviets and his own party, the Left SRs resigned from the government but remained as a force in the soviets and the all–Russian soviet executive committee.

Having failed to moderate communist policies by working within the government, the Left SRs now appealed directly to workers and peasants, combining radical social policy with democratic outlooks on the exercise of power. Dismayed by Leninist policy toward the peasantry, the economic hardships imposed by the German peace treaty, and blatant communist falsification of elections to the Fifth Congress of Soviets during early July 1918, the Left SR leadership decided to assassinate Count Mirbach, the German representative in Moscow. Often misinterpreted as an attempt to seize power, the successful but politically disastrous assassination had the goal of breaking the peace treaty. The Left SRs hoped that this act would garner wide enough support to counter–balance the communists' hold on the organs of power. Regardless, Lenin managed to placate the Germans and propagate the idea that the Left SRs had attempted an antisoviet coup d'état. Just as SRs and Mensheviks had already been hounded from the soviets, now the Left SRs suffered the same fate and, like them, entered the anticommunist underground. In response, some Left SRs formed separate parties (the Popular Communists and the Revolutionary Communists) with the goal of continuing certain Left SR policies in cooperation with the communists, with whom both groups eventually merged. Throughout the civil war, the Left SRs charted a course between the Reds and Whites as staunch supporters of soviet rather than communist power. They maintained a surprising degree of activism, inspiring and often leading workers' strikes, Red Army and Navy mutinies, and peasant uprisings. They helped create the conditions responsible for the introduction of the 1921 New Economic Policy, some of whose economic compromises they opposed. During the early 1920s they succumbed to the concerted attacks of the secret police. The Left SRs' chief merit, their reliance on processes of direct democracy, turned out to be their downfall in the contest for power with communist leaders willing to use repressive methods.

See also: CIVIL WAR OF 1917–1922; FEBRUARY REVOLUTION; OCTOBER REVOLUTION; SOCIALISM; SOCIALIST REVOLUTIONARIES

BIBLIOGRAPHY

Melancon, Michael. (1990). *The Socialist Revolutionaries and the Russian Anti–War Movement, 1914-1917.* Columbus: Ohio State University Press.

Mstislavskii, Sergei. (1988). *Five Days That Shook the World.* Bloomington: Indiana University Press.

Radkey, Oliver. (1958). *The Agrarian Foes of Bolshevism: Promise and Default of the Russian Socialist Revolutionaries, February-October 1917.* New York: Columbia University Press.

Radkey, Oliver. (1963). *The Sickle under the Hammer: The Russian Socialist Revolutionaries in the Early Months of Soviet Rule.* New York: Columbia University Press.

Steinberg, I.N. (1935). *Spiridonova: Revolutionary Terrorist.* London: Methuen.

Steinberg, I.N. (1953). *In the Workshop of the Revolution.* New York: Rinehart.

MICHAEL MELANCON

LEGAL SYSTEMS

The Russian legal system—the judicial institutions and laws—has been shaped by many different influences, domestic as well as foreign. It constitutes just one of several legal systems at work within Russia. As befits any large, multiethnic society, many different legal systems have coexisted in Russia at various points in history. Prior to the twentieth century especially, many of the non-Slavic peoples of the Russian empire as well as Russian peasants relied on their religious or customary laws and institutions to regulate important aspects of life (e.g., family, marriage, property, inheritance).

PRINCIPALITIES AND MUSCOVY

As in Western Europe, the early history of Russian law is marked by an initial reliance on oral customary legal norms giving way in time to written law codes and judicial institutions heavily influenced by religious sources. The oldest documentary records of Russian customary law are several treaties concluded by Kievan Rus in the tenth century with Byzantium. These treaties included Russian principles of criminal law that, like their counterparts in Western Europe, were heavily reliant on a system of vengeance and monetary compensation for harm committed against another. One interesting feature of Russian customary law was that women enjoyed a higher, more independent status under Russian law than under contemporary Byzantine law.

The introduction of Christianity to Kievan Rus exposed the Russians both to the notion of written law as well as canon law principles imported from Byzantium. In the eleventh century, Russian customary law was set down in writing comprehensively for the first time in the *Russkaya Pravda,* which focused on criminal law and procedure and incorporated principles of blood feud and monetary compensation for damages. Later versions of the *Russkaya Pravda* included elements of civil and commercial law, which were heavily drawn from German and Byzantine sources. Courts under the *Russkaya Pravda* consisted of tribunals of the elder members of the local community, rather than genuine state-sponsored courts. While some scholars maintain that the *Russkaya Pravda* was in force over all of ancient Russia, others argue that its effect was much more limited to only a few principalities. Where it was enforced, the *Russkaia Pravda* remained in effect until the seventeenth century.

During the fifteenth through seventeenth centuries, Russian law was modified to support the emerging Muscovite autocracy. In particular, the legal status of the peasants was reduced to serfdom. During this same period, several important written collections of law were adopted dealing with criminal, civil, administrative, and commercial law and procedure. Under the *Sudebnik* of 1497, torture was institutionalized as a normal tool of criminal investigations. The *Ulozhenie* of 1649, which remained the principal basis for much of Russian law for two centuries, consisted of 967 articles covering most areas of the law. The criminal law sections of the *Ulozhenie* were noted for introducing more severe punishments into Russian law (burying alive, burning, mutilation). These documents were not well-organized, systematized codes of law, but were merely collections of existing laws, decrees, and administrative regulations.

RUSSIAN EMPIRE

Beginning with Peter the Great, several tsars attempted to rationalize the Russian legal system by introducing Western innovations and bolstering their autocratic rule by improving the efficiency with which Russian courts went about their business. Toward this end, Peter established the Senate to supervise the courts and punish corrupt or incompetent judges as well as the office of the procurator-general, which was established in 1722 to oversee the Senate and to supervise the enforcement of laws and decrees. The office of the Russian procurator-general continues to this day.

One of the most intractable problems facing Russian legal reformers was the morass of unorganized and undifferentiated laws and decrees in effect. The Russian legal system sat on a foundation of out-of-date or half-forgotten laws, decrees, and procedures, and judges and government officials were hard-pressed to know which laws were in effect at any given moment. In the nineteenth cen-

A guard stands by the defendant in a 1992 murder trial in St. Petersburg. The accused is kept in a cage inside the courtroom.

tury, Russian specialists under the direction of M. M. Speransky attempted to rationalize this material by collecting and distilling it into a fifteen-volume digest, the *Svod zakonov rossiiskoi imperii*, published in 1832.

The most significant tsarist-era legal reforms were adopted in 1864, when a modern, Western-style judicial system was introduced in the aftermath of the emancipation of the serfs. The new judicial system introduced professional judges and lawyers, trial by jury, modern evidentiary rules, justices of the peace, and modern criminal investigation procedures drawn from Continental models. Reaction to these liberal judicial reforms set in during the reign of Alexander II after the acquittal of several famous dissidents, including the assassin Vera Zasulich, and the independence of the courts in political cases was significantly eroded after the assassination of Alexander II in 1881. Despite this reaction, the institutions established by the Judicial Reforms of 1864 remained in effect until 1917.

SOVIET REGIME

A decree adopted in late 1917, On the Court, abolished the tsarist judicial institutions, including the courts, examining magistrates, and bar association. However, during the first years following the Bolshevik Revolution, legal nihilists such as E. Pashukanis, who advocated the rapid withering away of the courts and other state institutions, contended with more pragmatic leaders who envisioned the legal system as an important asset in asserting and defending Soviet state power. The latter group prevailed. Vladimir Lenin, during the New Economic Policy, sought to re-establish laws, courts, legal profession, and a new concept of socialist legality to provide more stability in society and central authority for the Party hierarchy. The debate between the legal nihilists and their opponents was definitively resolved by Josef Stalin in the early 1930s. As Stalin asserted control over the Party and initiated industrialization and collectivization, he also asserted the importance of stabilizing the legal system. This process culminated in the 1936 constitution, which strengthened law and legal institutions, especially administrative law, civil, family, and criminal law.

The broad outlines of the legal system established by Stalin in the 1930s remained in effect until the late 1980s. Reforms introduced by Mikhail Gorbachev in the late 1980s, however, made significant changes in the Soviet judicial system. Gorbachev sponsored a lengthy public discussion of how to introduce *pravovoe gosudarstvo* (law-based state) in the USSR and introduced legislation to improve the independence and authority of judges and to establish the Committee for Constitutional Supervision, a constitutional court.

POST-SOVIET REFORMS

In the years since the collapse of the Soviet Union, Russia has adopted a wide array of legislation remaking many aspects of its judicial system, drawing heavily on foreign models. Most of the legislation that has been adopted was foreshadowed in the 1993 constitution and includes new laws and procedure codes for the ordinary courts and the arbitrazh courts, which are courts devoted to matters arising from business and commerce, new civil and criminal codes, and a new land code, finally adopted in 2001.

See also: COOPERATIVES, LAW ON; FAMILY LAW OF 1936; FUNDAMENTAL LAWS OF 1906; GOVERNING SENATE; PROCURACY; RUSSIAN JUSTICE; STATE ENTERPRISE, LAW OF THE; SUCCESSION, LAW ON; SUDEBNIK OF 1497

MICHAEL NEWCITY

LEGISLATIVE COMMISSION OF 1767–1768

In December 1766, Catherine II called upon the free "estates" (nobles, townspeople, state peasants, Cossacks) and central government offices to select deputies to attend a commission to participate in the preparation of a new code of laws. The purpose of the commission was therefore consultative; it was not intended to be a parliament in the modern sense. The Legislative Commission opened in Moscow in July 1767, then moved to St. Petersburg in February 1768. Following the outbreak of the Russo-Turkish War in January 1769, it was prorogued and never recalled. The selection of deputies was a haphazard affair. The social composition of the assembly was: nobles, 205; merchants, 167; *odnodvortsy* (descendants of petty servicemen on the southern frontiers), 42; state peasants, 29; Cossacks, 44; industrialists, 7; chancery clerks, 19; tribesmen, 54. Deputies brought instructions, or *nakazy,* from the bodies that selected them. Catherine's *Nakaz* (*Great Instruction*) was read at the opening sessions and provided a basis for some of the discussion that followed. The commission met in 203 sessions and discussed existing laws on the nobility, on the Baltic nobility, on the merchant estate, and on justice and judicial procedure. No decisions were made by the commission on these matters, and no code of laws was produced. The Legislative Commission was nevertheless significant: It gave Catherine an important source of information and insight into concerns and attitudes of different social groups, through both the nakazy and the discussions which took place, including a discussion on serfdom; it provided an opportunity for the discussion and dissemination of the ideas in Catherine's Nakaz; it led to the establishment of several subcommittees, which continued to meet after the prorogation of the commission, and which produced draft laws that Catherine utilized for subsequent legislation.

See also: CATHERINE II; INSTRUCTION TO THE LEGISLATIVE COMMISSION OF CATHERINE II

BIBLIOGRAPHY

Dukes, Paul. (1967.) *Catherine the Great and the Russian Nobility.* Cambridge, UK: Cambridge University Press.

Madariaga, Isabel de. (1981). *Russia in the Age of Catherine the Great.* London: Weidenfeld and Nicolson.

JANET HARTLEY

LEICHOUDES, IOANNIKIOS AND SOPHRONIOS

Greek hieromonks, Ioannikios (secular name: Ioannes, 1633–1717) and Sophronios (secular name: Spyridon, 1652–1730).

The two brothers Leichoudes were born on the Greek island of Kephallenia. They studied philosophy and theology in Greek-run schools in Venice. Sophronios received a doctorate in philosophy from the University of Padua in 1670. Between 1670 and 1683, they worked as preachers and teachers in Kephallenia and in Greek communities of the Ottoman Empire. In 1683 they reached Constantinople, where they preached in the Patriarchal court. Following a Russian request for teachers, they arrived in Moscow in 1685. There they established the first formal educational institution in Russian history, the Slavo-Greco-Latin Academy, and participated in a heated debate known as the Eucharist conflict, principally against Sylvester Medvedev. They taught in the Academy until 1694, when they were removed for attempted flight after a scandal involving one of their relatives. After a brief stint as translators in the Muscovite Printing Office and as tutors of Italian, they were accused of heresy by one of their former students. Between 1698 and 1706, they were transferred to various monasteries, both in Moscow and in other towns, where they continued their authorial activities. In 1706 they were sent to Novgorod and established a school under the supervision of Metropolitan Iov. In 1707 Sophronios was recalled to Moscow to work in a Greek school there. Ioannikios taught in Novgorod until 1716, when he joined his brother in Moscow. After his brother's death, Sophronios continued his teaching activities until 1723, when he became archimandrite of the Solotsinsky monastery in Ryazan until his death. The two brothers authored or coauthored many polemical (anti-Catholic and anti-Protestant), philosophical, and theological works, sermons, panegyrics, orations, and, most important, textbooks for their students. A large part of these textbooks were adaptations of those used in Jesuit colleges. Through their educational activities, the Leichoudes, though Orthodox, imparted to their students the Jesuit interpretation of Aristotelian philosophy, and the Baroque culture of contemporary Europe. As such, they contributed to the Russian elite's westernization and its preparedness to accept Peter the Great's own westernizing reforms.

See also: ORTHODOXY; RUSSIAN ORTHODOX CHURCH; SLAVO-GRECO-LATIN ACADEMY; WESTERNIZERS

BIBLIOGRAPHY

Chrissidis, Nikolaos A. (2000). "Creating the New Educated Elite: Learning and Faith in Moscow's Slavo-Greco-Latin Academy, 1685–1694." Ph.D. dissertation, Yale University, New Haven, CT.

NIKOLAOS A. CHRISSIDIS

LEIPZIG, BATTLE OF

The "Battle of Nations" near Leipzig between allied Russian, Prussian, Austrian, and Swedish armies against Napoleon's army from October 16 to 19, 1813.

Napoleon's army (approximately 200,000 troops, 747 field guns), concentrated near Leipzig, faced four allied armies, totaling 305,000 troops—125,000 of them Russian, 90,000 Austrian, 72,000 Prussians, 18,000 Swedes—and 1,385 field guns. The battle took place on a plain near Leipzig on October 16, mainly on the grounds of the Bohemian army (133,000 men, commanded by the Austrian field marshal Karl Schwarzenberg), which approached the city from the south. Napoleon tried to defeat the coalition armies one by one. He concentrated 122,000 men against the Bohemian army, and 50,000 under the command of marshal Michel Ney against the Silesian army (60,000 men, commanded by the Prussian general Gebhardt Blücher), attacking from the north.

The opposing sides' positions did not suffer much change by the end of the day. Casualties turned out to be relatively even (30,000 each), but the allies' casualties were compensated with the arrival of the North army (58,000 men, commanded by Karl–Juhan Bernadotte) and the Polish army (54,000 men, commanded by Russian general Leonty Bennigsen) on October 17. Meanwhile, Napoleon's army received a mere 25,000 men as a reinforcement.

On the morning of October 18, the allies attacked Napoleon's positions. As a result of a fierce battle, they gained no significant territorial advantage. The allies, however, sent only 200,000 men to battle, while 100,000 more were kept in reserve. The French, meanwhile, had nearly exhausted their ammunition. On the night of October 18, Napoleon's armies were drawn back to Leipzig, and began their retreat in the morning. In the middle of the day on October 19, the allies entered Leipzig.

Napoleon's losses at Leipzig amounted to 100,000 men killed, wounded, and taken captive, and 325 field guns. The allies lost approximately 80,000 men, of them 38,000 Russians. The allied victory at Leipzig led to the cleansing of the territories of Germany and Holland of Napoleon's forces.

See also: NAPOLEON I

BIBLIOGRAPHY

Nafziger, George F. (1996). *Napoleon at Leipzig: the Battle of Nations, 1813*. Chicago, IL: Emperor's Press.

Smith, Digby George. (2001). *1813, Leipzig: Napoleon and the Battle of the Nations.* London: Greenhill Books; Mechanicsburg, PA: Stackpole Books.

OLEG BUDNITSKII

LENA GOLDFIELDS MASSACRE

The Lena Goldfields Massacre of April 4, 1912, shook Russian society and rekindled the revolutionary and workers' movements after the post–1905 repression. The shooting occurred during a strike at the gold fields on the upper branches of the Lena River to the northeast of Lake Baikal. The Lena Goldfields Company, owned by prominent Russian and British investors, had recently established a monopoly of the region's mines, which produced most of Russia's gold. Individuals of the highest government rank held managerial positions in the company. The fact that Russia's currency was on the gold standard further enhanced the company's significance. Especially after the joint shocks of the Russo–Japanese War and the Revolution of 1905, the ruble's health in association with renewed economic expansion vitally concerned the imperial government. When the strike broke out during late February 1912 in protest of generally poor conditions, the government and company officials in St. Petersburg naturally wished to limit the strike. These hopes were frustrated by a group of employees and workers, political exiles with past socialist and strike experience, who provided careful advice to the strikers. Consequently, the workers avoided overstepping the boundaries of legal strike activity. Company officials refused to meet the main strike demands, including a shorter workday and higher pay. Workers, whose patience had been tried by repeated company violations of the work contract and existing labor laws, as confirmed by the chief mining inspector and the governor of Irkutsk province, refused to end the strike without real concessions.

Working closely with company officials, the government sent a company of soldiers to join the small contingent already on duty near the mines and finally, after all negotiations failed, decided to break the five–week impasse by arresting the strike leaders. This ill–advised action carried out on April 3 only strengthened the workers' resolve. On April 4, a large crowd of unarmed miners headed for the administration building to petition for the release of the leaders. Alarmed by the sudden appearance of four thousand workers, police and army officers ordered the soldiers to open fire. Roughly five hundred workers were shot, about half mortally. Subsequently, the official government investigative commission under Senator Sergei Manukhin blamed the company and high government officials both for the conditions that underlay the strike and for the shooting.

The shooting unleashed a firestorm of protest against the government and the company, including in the press and in the State Duma. Especially damaging were accusations of collusion between state and company officials aimed at using force to end the peaceful strike. Even groups normally supportive of the government levied a barrage of criticism. On a scale not seen since 1905, strikes broke out all over Russia and did not cease until the outbreak of World War I. The revolutionary parties also swung into action with leaflets and demonstrations. The oppositionist movement found its cause inadvertently aided when Minister of the Interior Nikolai Makarov asserted to the State Duma about the shooting: "Thus it has always been and thus it will always be." This phrase, which caused an additional firestorm of protest, seemed to symbolize the government's stance toward laboring Russia. Spurred by the shooting and the government's attitude, revolutionary activities again plagued the tsarist regime, now permanently stamped as perpetrator of the Lena Goldfields Massacre.

See also: OCTOBER REVOLUTION; REVOLUTION OF 1905; WORKERS

BIBLIOGRAPHY

Melancon, Michael. (1993). "The Ninth Circle: The Lena Goldfield Workers and the Massacre of 4 April 1912." *Slavic Review* 53(3):766-795.

Melancon, Michael. (2002). "Unexpected Consensus: Russian Society and the Lena Massacre, April 1912." *Revolutionary Russia* 15(2):1-52.

MICHAEL MELANCON

LEND LEASE

Lend-lease was a system of U.S. assistance to the Allies in World War II. It was based on a bill of March, 11, 1941, that gave the president of the United States the right to sell, transfer into property, lease, and rent various kinds of weapons or materials to those countries whose defense the president deemed vital to the defense of the United States itself. According to the system, the materials destroyed, lost, or consumed during the war should not be subject to payment after the war. The materials that were not used during the war and that were suitable for civilian consumption should be paid in full or in part, while weapons and war materials could be demanded back. After the United States entered the war, the concept of *lend lease*, originally a system of unidirectional U.S. aid, was transformed into a system of mutual aid, which involved pooling the resources of the countries in the anti-Hitler coalition (known as the concept of "pool"). Initially authorized for the purpose of aiding Great Britain, in April 1941 the Lend-Lease Act was extended to Greece, Yugoslavia, and China, and, after September 1941, to the Soviet Union. By September, 20, 1945, the date of cancellation of the Lend-Lease Act, American aid had been received by nearly forty countries.

During World War II, the U.S. spent a total of $49.1 billion on the Lend-Lease Act. This included $13.8 billion in aid to Great Britain and $9.5 billion to the USSR. Repayment in kind—called "reverse lend-lease"—was estimated at $7.8 billion, of which $2.2 million was the contribution of the USSR in the form of a discount for transport services.

The Soviet Union received aid on lend-lease principles not only from the United States, but also from the states of the British Commonwealth, primarily Great Britain and Canada. Economic relations between them were adjusted by mutual aid agreements and legalized by special Allies' protocols, renewable annually. The First Protocol was signed in Moscow on October, 1, 1941; the second in Washington (October 6, 1942); the third in London (September 1, 1943); and the fourth in Ottawa (April, 17, 1945). The Fourth Protocol was added by a special agreement between the USSR and the United States called the "Program of October 17, 1944" (or "Milepost"), intended for supplies for use by the Soviet Union in the war against Japan.

On the basis of those documents, the Soviet Union received 18,763 aircraft, 11,567 tanks and self-propelled guns, 7,340 armored vehicles and armored troop-carriers, more than 435,000 trucks and jeeps, 9,641 guns, 2,626 radar, 43,298 radio stations, 548 fighting ships and boats, and 62 cargo ships. The remaining 75 percent of cargoes imported into the USSR consisted of industrial equipment, raw material, and foodstuffs. A significant portion (up to seven percent) of supplies was lost during transportation.

Most of the cargoes sent to the USSR were delivered by three main routes: via Iran, the Far East, and the northern ports Arkhangelsk and Murmansk. The last route was the shortest but also the most dangerous.

After the war the United State cancelled all lend-lease debts except that of the USSR. In 1972 the USSR and the United States signed an agreement that the USSR would pay $722 million of its debt by July 1, 2001.

See also: FOREIGN DEBT; WORLD WAR II; UNITED STATES, RELATIONS WITH, NORTHERN CONVOYS

BIBLIOGRAPHY

Beaumont, Joan. (1980). *Comrades in Arms: British Aid to Russia, 1941–1945.* London: Davis-Poynter.

Hall, H. Duncan; Scott, J. D., and Wrigley, C. C. (1956). *Studies of Overseas Supply.* London: H. M. Stationery Off.

Herring, George C. (1973). *Aid to Russia, 1941–1946: Strategy, Diplomacy, the Origins of the Cold War.* New York: Columbia University Press.

Jones, Robert Huhn. (1969). *The Roads to Russia: United States Lend-Lease to the Soviet Union.* Norman: University of Oklahoma Press.

Van Tuyll, Hubert P. (1989). *Feeding the Bear: American Aid to the Soviet Union, 1941–1945.* New York: Greenwood Press.

MIKHAIL SUPRUN

LENIN ENROLLMENT *See* COMMUNIST PARTY OF THE SOVIET UNION.

LENINGRAD AFFAIR

The "Leningrad Affair" refers to a purge between 1949 and 1951 of the city's political elite and of nationally prominent communists who had come from Leningrad. More than two hundred Leningraders, including many family members of those directly accused, were convicted on fabricated political charges, and twenty-three were executed. Over two thousand city officials were fired from their jobs. Hundreds from many other cities were jailed during this purge.

The "Leningrad Affair" derived largely from a power struggle between Soviet leader Josef Stalin's two leading potential successors: Andrei Zhdanov, Leningrad's party chief during the city's lengthy wartime siege, and Georgy Malenkov, supported by the head of the political police, Lavrenti Beria. Zhdanov's sudden death of apparent natural causes in the late summer of 1948 left his protégés from Leningrad vulnerable. In early 1949 Malenkov charged that the Leningraders were trying to create a rival Communist Party of Russia in conspiracy with another former Leningrad party chief, Alexei Kuznetsov. Malenkov used as pretexts a wholesale trade market that had been set up in Leningrad without Moscow's permission, as well as alleged voting irregularities in a Leningrad party conference. The Leningrad party members were also charged with treason.

Aside from Kuznetsov, the most prominent victims of the "Leningrad Affair" were Politburo member and Gosplan chairman Nikolai Voznesensky and first secretary of the Leningrad party committee Pyotr Popkov. The three were shot along with others on October 1, 1950. The purge signaled a return to the violent and conspiratorial politics of the 1930s. It eliminated the Leningraders as contenders for national power and downgraded Leningrad essentially to the status of a provincial city within the USSR.

See also: BERIA; LAVRENTI PAVLOVICH; MALENKOV, GEORGY MAKSIMILYANOVICH; ZHDANOV, ANDREI ALEXANDROVICH; STALIN, JOSEF VISSARIONVICH

BIBLIOGRAPHY

Knight, Amy. (1993). *Beria: Stalin's First Lieutenant.* Princeton, NJ: Princeton University Press.

Volkogonov, Dmitri. (1991). *Stalin: Triumph and Tragedy,* ed. and tr. Harold Shukman. New York: Grove Weidenfeld.

Zubkova, Elena. (1998). *Russia After the War: Hopes, Illusions, and Disappointments, 1945-1957,* tr. and ed. Hugh Ragsdale. Armonk, NY: M. E. Sharpe.

RICHARD BIDLACK

LENINGRAD, SIEGE OF

For 872 days during World War II, German and Finnish armies besieged Leningrad, the Soviet Union's second largest city and important center for armaments production. According to recent estimates, close to two million Soviet citizens died in Leningrad or along nearby military fronts between 1941 and 1944. Of that total, roughly one million civilians perished within the city itself.

The destruction of Leningrad was one of Adolf Hitler's strategic objectives in attacking the Soviet Union on June 22, 1941. On September 8, 1941, German Army Group North sealed off Leningrad. It advanced to within a few miles of its southern districts and then took the town of Schlisselburg along the southern shore of Lake Ladoga. That same day, Germany launched its first massive aerial attack on the city. Germany's ally, Finland, completed the blockade by retaking territory north of Leningrad that the Soviet Union had seized from Finland during the winter war of 1939–1940. About 2.5 million people were trapped within the city. The only connection that Leningrad maintained with the rest of the Soviet Union was across Lake Ladoga, which German aircraft patrolled. Finland refused German entreaties to continue its advance southward along Ladoga's eastern coast to link up with German forces.

Hitler's plan was to subdue Leningrad through blockade, bombardment, and starvation prior to seizing the city. German artillery gunners, together with the Luftwaffe, killed approximately 17,000 Leningraders during the siege. Although supplies of raw materials, fuel, and food dwindled rapidly within Leningrad, war plants within the city limits produced large numbers of tanks, artillery guns, and other weapons during the fall of 1941 and continued to manufacture vast quantities of ammunition throughout the rest of the siege.

Most civilian deaths occurred during the winter of 1941–1942. Bread was the only food that was regularly available, and between November 20 and December 25, 1941, the daily bread ration for most Leningraders dropped to its lowest level of 125 grams, or about 4.5 ounces. To give the appearance of larger rations, inedible materials, such as saw dust, were baked into the bread. To make matters worse, generation of electrical current was sharply curtailed in early December because only one city power plant operated at reduced capacity. Most Leningraders thus lived in the dark; they lacked running water because water pipes froze and burst. Temperatures during that especially cold winter plummeted to -40 degrees Farenheit in late January. Residents had to fetch water from central mains, canals, and the Neva River. The frigid

Soviet troops launch a counterattack during the Nazi siege of Leningrad. © HULTON-DEUTSCH COLLECTION/CORBIS

winter, however, brought one advantage: Lake Ladoga froze solid enough to become the "Road of Life" over which food was trucked into the city, and some 600,000 emaciated Leningraders were evacuated.

During the spring and summer of 1942, those remaining in Leningrad cleaned up debris and filth from the previous winter, buried corpses, and planted vegetable gardens in practically every open space they could find. A fuel pipeline and electrical cable were laid under Ladoga, and firewood and peat stockpiled in anticipation of a second siege winter. The evacuation over Ladoga continued, and by the end of 1942 the city's population was pared down to 637,000. Repeated attempts were made in 1942 to lift the siege; yet it was not until January 1943 that the Red Army pierced the blockade by retaking a narrow corridor along Ladoga's southern coast. A rail line was extended into the city, and the first train arrived from "the mainland" on February 7. Nevertheless, the siege would endure for almost another year as German guns continued to pound Leningrad and its tenuous rail link from close range. On January 27, 1944, the blockade finally ended as German troops retreated all along the Soviet front.

Leningrad's defense held strategic importance for the Soviet Union. Had the city fallen in the autumn of 1941, Germany could have redeployed larger forces toward Moscow and thereby increased the chances of taking the Soviet capital. Leningraders who endured the horrific ordeal were motivated by love of their native city and country, fear of what German occupation might bring, and the intimidating presence of Soviet security forces. In just the first fifteen months of the war, 5,360 Leningraders were executed for a variety of alleged crimes, including political ones.

Relations between Leningrad's leadership and the Kremlin were tempestuous during the siege ordeal. The city's isolation gave it a measure of autonomy from Moscow, and the suffering Leningrad endured promoted the growth of a heroic reputation for the city. From 1949 to 1951 many of Leningrad's political, governmental, industrial, and cultural leaders were fired, and some executed, on orders from the Kremlin during the notorious Leningrad Affair.

See also: LENINGRAD AFFAIR; WORLD WAR II

BIBLIOGRAPHY

Glantz, David M. (2002). *The Battle for Leningrad, 1941–1944.* Lawrence: University of Kansas Press.

Goure, Leon. (1962). *The Siege of Leningrad.* Stanford, CA: Stanford University Press.

Petrovskaya Wayne, Kyra. (2000). *Shurik: A Story of the Siege of Leningrad.* New York: The Lyons Press.

Salisbury, Harrison. (1969). *The 900 Days: The Siege of Leningrad.* New York: Harper & Row.

Simmons, Cynthia and Perlina, Nina, eds. (2002). *Writing the Siege of Leningrad: Women's Diaries, Memoirs, and Documentary Prose.* Pittsburgh, PA: University of Pittsburgh Press.

Skrjabina, Elena. (1971). *Siege and Survival: The Odyssey of a Leningrader.* Carbondale: Southern Illinois University Press.

RICHARD BIDLACK

LENIN LIBRARY *See* RUSSIAN STATE LIBRARY.

LENIN'S TESTAMENT

Lenin's so-called Political Testament was actually a letter dictated secretly by Vladimir Ilich Lenin in late December 1922, which he intended to discuss at the Twelfth Party Congress in April 1923. The letter was initially known only to Lenin's wife Nadezhda Krupskaya and the two secretaries who took down its contents. Unfortunately, on March 10, 1923, Lenin suffered a stroke, which put an end to his active role in Soviet politics. It is widely believed that Krupskaya, fearing that its contents might cause further Party disunity, kept the testament under lock and key, until Lenin's death in January 1924. She then felt it safe enough to be read to delegates at the Thirteenth Congress. All those attending this Congress were sworn to keep the contents of the letter a secret. It was then suppressed in the Soviet Union, and so the document did not appear in English until 1926.

A number of versions are currently in circulation, each of which has been manipulated for political purposes, especially by those who wish to criticize Josef Stalin or show how positively Leon Trotsky was viewed by Lenin. Nevertheless it is clear that Lenin was concerned in the Testament with potential successors and that most of all he favored Trotsky rather than his actual successor Stalin. The Testament of December 29 indicates it clear that Lenin wanted to avoid an irreversible split in the Party and provides a balanced assessment of all prospective candidates. With regard to Trotsky, Lenin notes that "[as] his struggle against the CC [Central Committee] on the question of the People's Commissariat has already proved, [he] is distinguished not only by outstanding ability. He is personally perhaps the most capable man in the present CC, but he has displayed excessive self-assurance and shown preoccupation with the purely administrative side of the work." Concerning Stalin, by contrast, Lenin points out that he "is too rude, and this defect, although quite tolerable in our midst and in dealings among us Communists, becomes intolerable in a general secretary. That is why I suggest that the comrades think about a way of removing Stalin from that post and appointing (sic) another man in his stead who in all other respects differs from Comrade Stalin in having only one advantage, namely, that of being more tolerant, more loyal, less capricious, and so forth." In a postscript dated March 5, 1923, Lenin criticizes Stalin for insulting Lenin's wife and adds that unless they receive a retraction and apology then "relations between us should be broken off." In relation to other members of the CC, Lenin points to the October episode in which Zinoviev and Kamenev objected to the idea of an immediate armed insurrection against the Provisional Government and also to Trotsky's Menshevik past, but he adds that neither should suffer any blame or personal consequence.

Lenin was therefore extremely worried about the degree of power Stalin had attained and thought this was dangerous for the future of the Party and Russia insofar as he was capable of abusing this power. He advocated that Stalin be removed from the post of general secretary. It is generally agreed by historians that Trotsky's failure to use the Testament was a major political mistake and an error that allowed Stalin to rise to power. But it is also conceded that Trotsky, in agreeing not to use it in this manner, was abiding by Lenin's wishes to avoid a split. Trotsky therefore put Party unity before his own ambitions.

See also: LENIN, VLADIMIR ILICH; STALIN, JOSEF VISSARIONOVICH; TROTSKY, LEON DAVIDOVICH

BIBLIOGRAPHY

Buranov, Yuri. (1994). *Lenin's Will: Falsified and Forbidden.* Amherst, NY: Prometheus.

Volkogonov, Dmitri. (1994). *Lenin: A New Biography.* New York: Free Press.

Wolfe, Bertram D. (1984). *Three Who Made a Revolution: A Biographical History.* New York: Stein and Day.

CHRISTOPHER WILLIAMS

LENIN'S TOMB

Shortly after the death of Vladimir Ilich Lenin in 1924, and despite the opposition of his wife, Nadezhda Krupskaya, Soviet leaders built a mausoleum on Moscow's Red Square to display his embalmed body. The architect Alexei V. Shchusev designed two temporary cube-shaped wooden structures and then a permanent red granite pyramid-like building that was completed in 1929. The top of the mausoleum held a tribune from which Soviet leaders addressed the public. This site became the ceremonial center of the Bolshevik state as Stalin and subsequent leaders appeared on the tribune to view parades on November 7, May 1, and other Soviet ceremonial occasions. When Josef V. Stalin died in 1953, his body was placed in the mausoleum next to Lenin's. In 1961, as Nikita Khrushchev's attack on Stalin's cult of personality intensified, Stalin's body was removed from the mausoleum and buried near the Kremlin wall. Lenin and his tomb, however, remained the quintessential symbols of Soviet legitimacy.

Because of Lenin's status as unrivaled leader of the Bolshevik Party, and because of Russian traditions of personifying political power, a personality cult glorifying Lenin began to develop even before his death. The Soviet leadership mobilized the legacy of Lenin after 1924 to establish its own legitimacy and gain support for the Communist Party. Recent scholarship has disproved the idea that it was Stalin who masterminded the idea of embalming Lenin, instead crediting such figures as Felix Dzerzhinsky, Leonid Krasin, Vladimir Bonch-Bruevich, and Anatoly Lunacharsky. It has also been suggested that the cult grew out of popular Orthodox religious traditions and the philosophical belief of certain Bolshevik leaders in the deification of man and the resurrection of the dead through science. The archival sources underscore the contingency of the creation of the Lenin cult. They show that Dzerzhinsky and other Bolshevik leaders consciously manipulated popular sentiment about Lenin for utilitarian political goals. Yet this would not have created such a powerful political symbol if it had not been rooted in the spiritual, philosophical, and political culture of Soviet leaders and the Soviet people. More than a decade after the fall of communism, Lenin's Tomb continued to stand on Red Square even though there were periodic calls for his burial.

See also: CULT OF PERSONALITY; KREMLIN; KRUPSKAYA, NADEZHDA KONSTANTINOVNA; LENIN, VLADIMIR ILICH; RED SQUARE

BIBLIOGRAPHY

Tucker, Robert C. (1973). *Stalin as Revolutionary, 1879–1929.* New York: Norton.

Tumarkin, Nina. (1983). *Lenin Lives! The Lenin Cult in Soviet Russia.* Cambridge, MA: Harvard University Press.

KAREN PETRONE

LENIN, VLADIMIR ILICH

(1870–1924), revolutionary publicist, theoretician, and activist; founder of and leading figure in the Bolshevik Party (1903–1924); chairman of the Soviet of People's Commissars of the RSFSR/USSR (1917–1924).

The reputation of Vladimir Ilich Lenin (pseudonym of V.I. Ulyanov) has suffered at the hands of both his supporters and his detractors. The former turned him into an idol; the latter into a demon. Lenin was neither. He was born on April 22, 1870, into the family of a successful school inspector from Simbirsk. For his first sixteen years, Lenin lived the life of a child of a conventional, moderately prosperous, middle-class, intellectual family. The ordinariness of Lenin's upbringing was first disturbed by the death of his father, in January 1886 at the age of 54. This event haunted Lenin, who feared he might also die prematurely, and in fact died at almost exactly the same age as his father. Then, in March 1887, Lenin's older brother was arrested for terrorism; he was executed the following May. The event aroused Lenin's curiosity about what had led his brother to sacrifice his life. It also put obstacles in his path: As the brother of a convicted terrorist, Lenin was excluded from Kazan University. He eventually took a law degree,

Soviet leader Vladimir Lenin sitting alone at his desk.
© BETTMANN/CORBIS

with distinction, by correspondence from St Petersburg University in January 1892. However, his real interests had already turned to serving the oppressed through revolution rather than at the bar.

All the indications suggest that Lenin was initially attracted to populism, and only later came under the sway of Marxism. He joined a number of provincial Marxist study circles, but first began to attract attention when he moved to the capital, St. Petersburg, and engaged in illegal political activities among workers and intellectuals. In February 1894, he met fellow conspirator Nadezhda Konstantinovna Krupskaya, who became his lifelong companion. After his first visit to Western Europe, in 1895, to meet the exiled leaders of Russian Marxism, Lenin returned to St. Petersburg and helped set up the League of Struggle for the Emancipation of the Working Class. He was arrested in December 1896 and, after prison interrogation in St. Petersburg, was exiled to the village of Shushenskoe, in Siberia. Krupskaya, who was exiled separately, offered to share banishment with him. The authorities agreed, providing they married, which they did in July 1898. Siberian exile, though rigorous in many respects, was an interlude of relative personal happiness in Lenin's life. His lifelong love of nature asserted itself in long walks, observation of social and animal life of the area, and frequent hunting expeditions. He read a great deal, communicated widely by letter with other socialists, and undertook research and writing. Direct political activity was not possible, and Lenin played no part in the formation, in 1898, of the Russian Social Democratic Workers' Party (RSDLP), to which he at first adhered to but from which he later split. His term of exile ended in February, 1900. In July of that same year, he left Russia for five years.

Up until that point much of Lenin's political writing, from his earliest known articles to his first major treatise, *The Development of Capitalism in Russia*, written while he was in Siberia, revolved around the dispute between Marxists and populists. The populists had proposed that Russia, given its commune-based peasant class and underdeveloped industry, could pass from its current condition of "backwardness" to socialism without having to first undergo the rigors of capitalist industrialization. Such a notion was an anathema to Lenin, who believed the Marxist axiom that socialist revolution could only follow from the overdevelopment of capitalism, which would bring about its own collapse. Lenin attacked the populist thesis in several articles and pamphlets. The main theme of his treatise on *The Development of Capitalism in Russia* was that, in fact, capitalism was already well-entrenched in Russia, and therefore the question of whether it could be avoided was meaningless. Nonetheless, it remained obvious that Russia had only a small working class, and much of the rest of Lenin's life could be seen as an attempt to reconcile the actual weakness of proletarian forces in Russia with the country's undoubted potential for some kind of popular revolution, and to ensure Marxist and proletarian dominance in any such revolution.

THE EMERGENCE OF BOLSHEVISM (1902–1914)

Lenin worked to develop theoretical and practical means to accomplish these closely related tasks. The core of Lenin's activity revolved around the organization and production of a series of journals. He frequently described himself on official papers as a journalist, and he did, in fact, write a prodigious number of articles, as well as many longer works. In 1902, Lenin produced one of his most widely read and, arguably most misunderstood, pamphlets, *What Is to Be Done?*, which has been widely taken to be the founding text of a distinctive Lenin-

Lenin rallies the masses in this 1921 photo. ASSOCIATED PRESS. REPRODUCED BY PERMISSION.

ist understanding of how to construct a revolutionary party on the basis of what he called "professional revolutionaries." When it was first published, however, it was read as a statement of Marxist orthodoxy. Lenin asserted the primacy of political struggle, opposing the ideas of the economists, who argued that trade union struggle would serve the workers' cause better than political revolution.

It was only in the following year, 1903, that Lenin began to break with the majority of the social-democratic movement. Again, received opinion, which claims Lenin split the party at the 1903 social-democratic party congress, oversimplifies the nature of the break. Lenin's key resolution at the congress, in which he attempted to narrow the definition of party membership, was voted down. Later, by means many have judged foul, he garnered a majority vote on the issue of electing members to the editorial board of the party journal, *Iskra*, on which Lenin and his supporters predominated. It was from this victory that the terms *Bolshevik* (majoritarians) and *Menshevik* (minoritarians) began to slowly come into vogue. However, the split of the party was only fully completed over the next few months, even years, of arid but fierce party controversies. Lenin's bitter polemic *One Step Forward, Two Steps Back: The Crisis in Our Party*, published in Geneva in February 1904, marks a clearer division and catalog of contentious issues than did *What Is to Be Done.* It was criticized not only by its target, Yuli Osipovich Martov, but also by Georgy Valentinovich Plekhanov, Pavel Axelrod, Vera Zasulich, Karl Kautsky, and Rosa Luxemburg. Lenin's remaining allies of the time included Alexander Bogdanov, Anatoly Lunacharsky, Grigory Zinoviev, and Lev Kamenev.

So much energy was involved in the dispute that the development of an actual revolutionary situation in Russia went almost unnoticed by the squabbling exiles. Even after Bloody Sunday (January 22, 1905) Lenin's attention remained divided between the revolution and the task of splitting the social democrats. With the latter aim in view, he convened a Third Party Congress (London, April 25 to May 10) consisting entirely of Bolsheviks. Only in August did Lenin's main pamphlet on revolutionary strategy, *Two Tactics of Social Democracy in the Russian Revolution,* appear. Inevitably, the wrong tactic—the identification of the revolution as bourgeois—was attributed to the Mensheviks. The correct, Bolshevik, tactic, was the recognition of "a democratic dictatorship of the proletariat and the peasantry," which put less reliance on Russia's weak bourgeoisie. It also marked a significant effort by Lenin to incorporate the peasantry into the revolutionary equation. This was another way in which Lenin strove to compensate for the weakness of the working class itself, and the peasantry remained part of his strategy, in a variety of forms, for the rest of his life.

In the atmosphere of greater freedom prevailing after the issuing of the October Manifesto, which was squeezed out of the tsarist authorities under extreme duress and appeared to promise basic constitutional rights and liberties, Lenin returned to Russia legally on November 21, 1905. Even so, by December 17, police surveillance had driven him underground. He supported the heroic but catastrophically premature workers' armed uprising in Moscow in December. As conditions worsened he retreated to Finland and then, in December 1907, left the Russian Empire for another prolonged west European sojourn that lasted until April 1917. Even before the failure of the 1905 revolution, the party split continued to attract an inordinate amount of Lenin's attention. The break with Leon Trotsky in 1906 and Bogdanov in 1908 removed the last significant thinkers from the Bolshevik movement, apart from Lenin himself, who seemed constitutionally incapable of collaborating with people of his own intellectual stature. The break with Bogdanov was consummated in Lenin's worst book, *Materialism and Empiriocriticism* (1909), a naïve and crudely propagandistic blunder into the realm of philosophy.

Politically, Lenin had wandered into the wilderness as leader of a small faction that was situated on the fringe of Russian radical politics and distinguished largely by its dependence on Lenin and its refusal to contemplate a compromise that might reunite the party. Lenin was also distinguished by a ruthless morality of only doing that which was good for the revolution. In its name friendships were broken, and re-made, at a moment's notice. Later, when in power, he urged occasional episodes of violence and terror to secure the revolution as he understood it, although, like a sensitive war leader, he did so reluctantly and only when he thought it absolutely necessary.

For the next few years Lenin was at his least influential. Had it not been for the backing of the novelist Maxim Gorky, it is unlikely the Bolsheviks could have continued to function. He had close support from Grigory Yevseyevich Zinoviev, Lev Borisovich Kamenev, Inessa Armand (with whom he may have had a brief sexual liaison), and from his wife Nadezhda Krupskaya. He also remained close to his family. When possible, he vacationed with them by the beaches of Brittany and Arcachon, or in the Swiss mountains. Lenin's love of nature, of walking and cycling, frequently counteracted the immense nervous stresses occasioned by his political battles. He was prone to a variety of illnesses, which acted as reminders of his father's early death, convincing him that he had to do things in a hurry. However, the second European exile was characterized by frustration rather than achievement.

FROM OBSCURITY TO POWER (1914–1921)

The onset of the First World War began the transformation of political fortune which was to bring Lenin to power. His attitude to the war was characteristically bold. Despite the collapse of the Second International Socialist Movement and the apparent wave of universal patriotism of August 1914, Lenin saw the war as a revolutionary opportunity and declared, as early as September 1914, that socialists should aim to turn it into a Europe-wide civil war. He believed that the basic class logic of the situation, that the war was fought by the masses to serve the interests of the imperialist bourgeoisie, would eventually become clear to the troops who, being trained in arms, would then turn on their oppressors. He also wrote a major pamphlet, *Imperialism: The Highest Stage of Capitalism. A Popular Outline* (1916). Returning to the theme of justifying a Marxist revolution in "backward" Russia, he argued that Russia was a component part of world capitalism and therefore the initial assault on capital, though not its decisive battles, could be conducted in Russia. Within months, just such an opportunity arose.

Lenin's transition from radical outcast to revolutionary leader began after the fall of tsarism in February 1917. A key moment was his declaration, in the so-called *April Theses,* enunciated immediately on his return to Russia (April 16–17, 1917), that the party should not support the provisional government. By accident or design, this was the key to Bolshevik success. As other parties were sucked into supporting the provisional government, they each lost public support. After the Kornilov Affair, when the commander-in-chief, Lavr Kornilov, appeared to be spearheading a counter-revolution in August and September of 1917, it was the Bolsheviks who were the main beneficiaries because they were not tainted by association with the discredited provisional government which, popular opinion believed, was associated with Kornilov's apparent coup. Even so, it took immense personal effort by Lenin to persuade his party to seize their opportunity. Contrary to much received opinion and Bolshevik myth, the October Revolution was not carefully planned but, rather, improvised. Lenin was in still in hiding in Finland following proscription of the party after the July Days, when armed groups of sailors had failed in an attempt to overthrow the provisional government and the authorities took advantage of the situation to move against the Bolsheviks. He had been vague about details of the proposed revolution throughout the crucial weeks leading up to it, suggesting, at different moments, that it might begin in Moscow, Petrograd, Kronstadt, the Baltic Fleet, or even Helsinki. Only his own emergence from hiding, on October 23rd and 29th and during the seizure of power itself (November 6–7 O.S.) finally brought his party in line behind his policy. The provisional government was overthrown, and Lenin became Chairman of the Soviet of People's Commissars, a post he held until his death.

October was far from the end of the story. The tragic complexity of the seizure of power soon became apparent. The masses wanted what the slogans of October proclaimed: soviet power, peace, land, bread, and a constituent assembly. Lenin, however, wanted nothing less than the socialist transformation not only of Russia but of the world. Conflict was inevitable. By early 1918, autonomous workers and peasants organizations, including their political parties and the soviets themselves, were losing all authority. Ironically, at this moment one of Lenin's most libertarian, almost anarchist, writings, *State and Revolution,* written while he was in Finland, was published. In it he praised direct democracy and argued that capitalism had so organized and routinized the economy that it resembled the workings of the German post office. As a result, he wrote, the transition to socialism would be relatively straightforward.

However, reality was to prove less tractable. Lenin began to talk of "iron discipline" as an essential for future progress, and in *The Immediate Tasks of the Soviet Government* (March–April 1918) proclaimed the concept of productionism—the maximization of economic output as the preliminary to building socialism—to be a main goal of the Soviet government. Productionism was an ideological response to Russia's Marxist paradox, a worker revolution in a "backward" peasant country. Indeed, the weakness of the proletariat was vastly accentuated in the first years of Soviet power, as industry collapsed and major cities lost up to two-thirds of their population through disease, hunger, and flight to the countryside.

Like the events of October, early Soviet policy was also improvised, though within the confines of Bolshevik ideology. Lenin presided over the nationalization of all major economic institutions and enterprises in a crude attempt to replace the market with allocation of key products. He also oversaw the emergence of a new Red Army; the setting up of a new state structure based on Bolshevik-led soviets; and a system of direct appropriation of grain from peasants, as well as the revolutionary transformation of the country. This last entailed the taking over of land by peasants and the disappearance from Soviet territory of the old elites, including the aristocracy, army officers, capitalists, and bankers. To the chaos of the early months of revolution was added extensive protest within the party from its left wing, which saw productionism and iron discipline as a betrayal of the libertarian principles of 1917. The survival of Lenin's government looked improbable. However, the outbreak of major civil war in July 1918 gave it a new lease of life, forcing people to choose between imperfect revolution, represented by the Bolsheviks, or out-and-out counter-revolution, represented by the opposition (called the Whites). Most opted for the former but, once the Whites were defeated in 1920, tensions re-emerged and a series of uprisings against the Soviet government took place.

THE FINAL YEARS (1922–1924)

Lenin's solution to the post–civil war crisis was his last major intervention in politics, because his health began to fail from 1922 onwards, exacerbated by the bullet wounds left after an assassination attempt in August 1918. The key problem in the crisis was peasant disaffection with the grain appropriation system. Lenin replaced requisitioning by a tax-in-kind, which in turn necessitated the partial restoration of market relations. Nonetheless, the state retained the commanding heights of the economy, including large factories, transport, taxation, and foreign trade. The result was known as the New Economic Policy. It was Lenin's third attempt at a form of transition. The first, outlined in the *April Theses*, was based on "Soviet supervision of production and distribution," a system that had collapsed within the first months of Bolshevik power. The second, later called war communism, was based on iron discipline, state control of the economy, and grain requisitioning. Lenin believed his third solution was the correct one, arrived at through the test of reality. It was accompanied by intellectual and political repression and the imposition of a one-party state on the grounds that concession to bourgeois economic interests gave the revolution's enemies greater power that had to be counteracted by greater political and intellectual control by the party. Lenin remained enthusiastic about the NEP, and did not live to see the complications that ensued in the mid-1920s.

In his last writings, produced during his bouts of convalescence from a series of increasingly severe strokes beginning in May 1922, Lenin laid down a number of guidelines for his successors. These included a cultural revolution to modernize the peasantry (*On Co-operation*, January 1923) and a modest reorganization of the bureaucracy to get it under control ("Better Fewer but Better," March 1923, his last article). In his "Testament" (*Letter to the Congress*, December 1922), Lenin argued that the party should not, in future, antagonize the peasantry. Most controversially, however, he summed up the candidates for succession without clearly supporting any one of them. His criticism of Stalin—that he had accumulated much power and Lenin was not confident that he would use it wisely—was strengthened in January of 1923, after Stalin argued with Krupskaya. Lenin called for Stalin to be removed as General Secretary, a post to which Lenin had only promoted him in 1922. There was no suggestion that Stalin should be removed from the Politburo or Central Committee. In any case, Lenin was too ill to follow through on his suggestions, thereby opening up vast speculation as to whether he might have prevented Stalin from coming to power had he lived longer.

Lenin's last year was spent at his country residence near Moscow. In the company of Nadezhda Krupskaya and his sisters, he lived out his last months being read to and taken on walks in his wheelchair. In October 1923 he even had enough energy to return for a last look around his Kremlin office, despite the guard's initial refusal to admit him because he did not have an up-to-date pass. However, his health continued to deteriorate, and he died on the evening of January 21, 1924.

See also: BOLSHEVISM; FEBRUARY REVOLUTION; JULY DAYS OF 1917; KORNILOV AFFAIR; KRUPSKAYA, NADEZHDA KONSTANTINOVNA; LENIN'S TESTAMENT; LENIN'S TOMB; NEW ECONOMIC POLICY; OCTOBER MANIFESTO; OCTOBER REVOLUTION; POPULISM; WAR COMMUNISM; WHAT IS TO BE DONE?

BIBLIOGRAPHY

Carrère d'Encausse, Hélène. (1982). *Lenin: Revolution and Power.* London: Longman.

Claudin-Urondo, Carmen. (1977). *Lenin and the Cultural Revolution.* Sussex and Totowa, New Jersey: Harvester Press/Humanities Press.

Harding, Neil. (1981). *Lenin's Political Thought.* 2 vols. London: Macmillan.

Harding, Neil. (1991). *Leninism.* London: Macmillan.

Krupskaya, Nadezhda. (1970). *Memories of Lenin.* London: Panther.

Lenin, Vladimir Ilich (1960-1980) *Collected Works.* 47 vols. Moscow: Progress Publishers.

Lenin, Vladimir Ilich. (1967). *Selected Works.* 3 vols. Moscow: Progress Publishers.

Lewin, Moshe. (1968). *Lenin's Last Struggle.* New York: Random House.

Pipes, Richard. (1996). *The Unknown Lenin.* New Haven and London: Yale University Press.

Read, Christopher. (2003). *Lenin: A Revolutionary Life.* London: Routledge.

Service, Robert. (1994). *Lenin: A Political Life.* 3 vols. London: Macmillan.

Service, Robert. (2000). *Lenin: a Biography.* Cambridge, MA: Harvard University Press.

Shub, David. (1966). *Lenin.* Harmondsworth: Penguin.

Ulam, Adam. (1969). *Lenin and the Bolsheviks.* London: Fontana/Collins.

Volkogonov, Dmitril. (1995). *Lenin: Life and Legacy,* ed. Harold Shukman. London: Harper Collins.

Weber, Gerda, and Weber, Hermann. (1980). *Lenin: Life and Work.* London: Macmillan.

White, James. (2000). *Lenin: The Practice and Theory of Revolution.* London: Palgrave.

Williams, Beryl. (2000). *Lenin.* London: Harlow Longman.

CHRISTOPHER READ

LEONTIEV, KONSTANTIN NIKOLAYEVICH

(1831–1891), social philosopher, literary critic, and novelist.

Konstantin Nikolayevich Leontiev occupied a unique place in the history of nineteenth-century Russian social thought. He was a nationalist and a reactionary whose position differed in significant respects from the thinking of both the Slavophiles and the Pan-Slavists. Some historians refer to Leontiev's social philosophy as Byzantinism.

Leontiev led a varied life, in which he was in turn a surgeon, a diplomat, an editor, a novelist, and a monk. He was raised on a small family estate in the province of Kaluga. After studying medicine at the University of Moscow, he served as a military surgeon during the Crimean War. Following his military service, he returned to Moscow to continue the practice of medicine and to write a series of novels that enjoyed little success. He married a young, illiterate Greek woman in 1861, but continued to engage in a series of love affairs. His wife gradually descended into madness.

In 1863 Leontiev entered the Russian diplomatic service, which led to his assignment to posts in the Balkans and Greece. While serving in that region, he developed an admiration for Byzantine Christianity, which was to remain a dominant theme in his thinking. He was irresistibly attracted to the Byzantine monasticism that he observed during a stay at Mount Athos in 1871 and 1872. Leontiev arrived at the conviction that aesthetic beauty, not happiness, was the supreme value in life. He rejected all humanitarianism and optimism; the notion of human kindness as the essence of Christianity's social teaching was utterly alien to him. His stance was anomalous in that he lacked strong personal religious faith, yet advocated strict adherence to Eastern Orthodox religion. He believed that the best of Russian culture was rooted in the Orthodox and autocratic heritage of Byzantium, and not the Slavic heritage that Russia shared with Eastern Europeans. He thought that the nations of the Balkans were determined to imitate the bourgeois West. He hoped that despotism and obscurantism could save Russia from the adoption of Western liberalism and constitutionalism, and could give Russia and the Orthodox Christians of the Balkans the opportunity to unite on the basis of their common traditions, drawn from the Byzantine legacy.

Leontiev accepted Nikolai Danilevsky's conception that each civilization develops like an organism, and argued that each civilization necessarily passes through three phases of development, from an initial phase of primary simplicity to a second phase, a golden era of growth and complexity, followed at last by "secondary simplification," with decay and disintegration. He despised the rationalism, democratization, and egalitarianism of the West of his day, which he saw as a civilization fully in the phase of decline, as evident in the domination of the bourgeoisie, whom he held in contempt for its crassness and mediocrity. He thought it desirable to delay the growth of similar tendencies in Russia, but he concluded, with regret, that Russia's final phase of dissolution was inevitable, and saw some signs that it had already begun.

Leontiev did not hesitate to endorse harshly repressive, authoritarian rule for Russia in order to stave off the influence of the West and slow the decline as long as possible. He saw Tsarist autocracy and Orthodoxy as the powerful forces protecting tradition in Russian society from the dangerous tendencies toward leveling and anarchy. He glorified extreme social inequality as characteristic of a civilization's phase of flourishing complexity. Unlike the Slavophiles, Leontiev had little admiration for the Russian peasants, who in his view inclined toward dishonesty, drunkenness, and cruelty, and he repudiated the heritage of the reforms adopted by Alexander II. Toward the end of his life, he became increasingly pessimistic about the possibility of preserving autocracy and aristocracy in Russia.

After leaving the diplomatic service, Leontiev suffered from constant financial stringency, despite finding a position as an assistant editor of a provincial newspaper. His stories about life in Greece did not find a wide audience, although late in his life he did attract a small circle of devoted admirers. In 1891 he took monastic vows and assumed the name of Clement. He died in the Trinity Monastery near Moscow in the same year.

Leontiev was one of the most gifted literary critics of his time, though he was not widely appreciated as a novelist. In *Against the Current: Selections from the Novels, Essays, Notes and Letters of Konstantin Leontiev* (1969), George Ivask says that in Leontiev's long novels, "his narration is often capricious, elliptic, impressionistic, and full of lyrical digression depicting the vague moods of his superheroes, who express his own narcissistic ego." After Leontiev's death Vladimir Soloviev contributed to the recognition of Leontiev's erratic brilliance, stimulating a revival of interest in Leontiev in the early twentieth century.

See also: BYZANTIUM, INFLUENCE OF; DANILEVSKY, NIKOLAI; NATIONALISM IN THE ARTS

BIBLIOGRAPHY

Ivask, George, ed. (1969). *Against the Current: Selections from the Novels, Essays, Notes and Letters of Konstantin Leontiev.* New York: Weybright and Talley.

Roberts, Spencer, ed. and tr. (1968). *Essays in Russian Literature: The Conservative View: Leontiev, Rozanov, Shestov.* Athens: Ohio University Press.

Thaden, Edward C. (1964). *Conservative Nationalism in Nineteenth-Century Russia.* Seattle: University of Washington Press.

ALFRED B. EVANS JR.

LERMONTOV, MIKHAIL YURIEVICH

(1814–1841), leading nineteenth-century Russian poet and prose writer.

Mikhail Yurievich Lermontov became one of Russia's most prominent literary figures. Based on the quality and evolution of his writing, some believe that if he had lived longer he would have surpassed the greatness of Alexander Pushkin. Lermontov's reputation is rooted equally in his poetry and prose. Fame came to him in 1834 when he wrote *Death of a Poet,* in which he accuses the Imperial Court of complicity in Pushkin's death in a duel.

The evolution of Lermontov's poetry reflected a change in emphasis from the personal to wider social and political issues. *The Novice* (1833) is known for its tight structure and elegant language. *The Demon* (1829–1839) became his most popular poem. Taking place in the Caucasus, it describes the love of a fallen angel for a mere mortal. *The Circassian Boy* (1833) reflects his strong scepticism in regard to religion and admiration of premodern life. *The Song of the Merchant Kalashnikov* (1837) is his greatest poem set in Russia. His best-known play is *The Masquerade* (1837), a stinging commentary on St. Petersburg high society.

Lermontov is considered to be the founder of the Russian realistic psychological novel, further developed by Fyodor Dostoyevsky and Leo Tolstoy. *A Hero of Our Time,* which is partly autobiographical, is his greatest work in this genre. The main character, Pechorin, is an example of a disenchanted and superfluous man, and his story provides a bitter critique of Russian society. In this novel Lermontov masterfully and realistically described the landscape of the Caucasus, the everyday life of the various tribes there, and a wide range of characters.

Lermontov was killed in a duel with a former classmate in 1841.

See also: GOLDEN AGE OF RUSSIAN LITERATURE; PUSHKIN, ALEXANDER SERGEYEVICH

BIBLIOGRAPHY

Garrard, John. (1982). *Mikhail Lermontov.* Boston: Twayne.

Kelly, Laurence. (2003). *Tragedy in the Caucasus.* London: Tauris.

ZHAND P. SHAKIBI

LESKOV, NIKOLAI SEMENOVICH

(1831–1895), prose writer with an unmatched grasp of the Russian popular mentality; supreme master of nonstandard language whose stories and novels often contrast societal brutality against the decency of "righteous men" (*pravedniki*).

Nikolai Semenovich Leskov spent his youth in part on his father's estate and in part in the town of Orel, interacting with a motley cross-section of provincial Russia's population. Although lacking a completed formal education, he later boasted professional experiences ranging from criminal investigator to army recruiter and sales representative. His first short stories appeared in 1862.

From the beginning, Leskov's prose conveyed deep compassion for the underdog. Aesthetically, he brought the narrative tool of *skaz*—relating a story in colorful, quasi-oral language marked as that of a personal narrator—to a new degree of perfection. Among his best works are the novellas *Ledi Makbet Mtsenskogo uyezda* (*Lady Macbeth of Mtsensk,* 1865) and *Zapechetlenny angel* (*The Sealed Angel,* 1873); the former is a gritty tale of raw passions leading to cold-blooded murders, including infanticide, while the latter is the story of errant icon painters who encounter a miracle. *Soboryane* (Cathedral Folk, 1867-1872), a masterful novel-chronicle, depicts the Russian clergy in a respectful manner uncommon for its time; however, a subsequent spiritual crisis caused Leskov's ultimate break with the Orthodox Church. His fairytale "Levsha" (The Lefthander, 1881) became an instant popular classic, praising the rich talents of Russian rank-and-file folk while bemoaning their pathetic lot at the hands of an indifferent ruling class.

Leskov's unique, first-hand knowledge of Russian reality, in combination with uncompromising ethical standards, alienated him from both the liberal and the conservative mainstream. Throughout his career, he opposed nihilism and remained a "gradualist," insisting that Russia needed steady evolution rather than an immediate revolution.

Leo Tolstoy aptly called Leskov "the first Russian idealist of a Christian type."

See also: SKAZ

BIBLIOGRAPHY

Lantz, Kenneth. (1979). *Nikolay Leskov.* Boston: Twayne.

McLean, Hugh. (1977). *Nikolai Leskov: The Man and His Art.* Cambridge, MA: Harvard University Press.

PETER ROLLBERG

LESNAYA, BATTLE OF

The battle of Lesnaya, fought on October 9, 1708, between the Russian army of Peter the Great and a Swedish column under General Adam Ludvig Lewenhaupt, played an important role in the campaign of that year through its weakening of the Swedish army. Russia's aim was to resist the attempt of Charles XII, King of Sweden, to invade Russia. Charles marched through Poland, reaching Grodno (now western Belarus) by January 1708, and resumed the march eastward toward Moscow the following June. Peter's army retreated before him, laying waste the land and offering occasional resistance. At the Russian-Polish border, Charles realized that he could go no further east, as he was running out of supplies, so he turned south toward the Ukraine. At the same time, General Lewenhaupt was moving southeast from Riga to join his king with 12,500 men, sixteen guns, and several thousand carts filled with supplies for the Swedish army. As Lewenhaupt approached the village of Lesnaya, on the small river Lesyanka southeast of Mogilev (now southeast Belarus), Peter brought up a flying corps of 5,000 infantry and 7,000 dragoons. Peter divided his forces into two columns, one commanded by himself, the other by his favorite, Alexander Menshikov. In a fortified camp made of the wagons, Lewenhaupt defended himself from noon on, until the Russian general Reinhold Bauer came up with another 5,000 dragoons. Around 7:00 P.M. the fighting stopped, and Lewenhaupt retreated south toward the main Swedish army, losing half his force and most of the supplies. Peter estimated the Russian losses at 1,111 killed and 2,856 wounded. The battle played an important role in sapping the strength of the Swedish army and provided Russia with an important psychological victory as well. To the end of his life Peter celebrated the day with major festivities at court.

See also: GREAT NORTHERN WAR; PETER I

PAUL A. BUSHKOVITCH

LEZGINS

The Lezgins are an ethnic group of which half resides in the Dagestani Republic. According to the 1989 census they numbered 240,000 within that republic, a little more than 11 percent of the population. All told, some 466,006 Lezgins lived in the Soviet Union, with most of the rest residing in Azerbaijan. Of the total, 91 percent regarded Lezgin as their native language and 53 percent considered themselves to be fluent in Russian as a second language. Within Dagestan the Lezgins are concentrated mainly in the south in the mountainous part of the republic.

The Lezgin language is a member of the Lezgin group of the Northeast Caucasian languages. In Soviet times they were gathered in the larger category of the Ibero-Caucasian family of languages. The languages within this family, while geographically close together, are not closely related outside of its four major groupings. This categorization has become understood more as a part of the Soviet ideology of *druzhba narodov* (friendship of peoples). The other Lezgin languages are spoken in Azerbaijan and Dagestan. They are generally quite small groups, and the term "Lezgin" as an ethnic category has sometimes served to cover the entire group. Ethnic self-identity, calculated with language and religion, has been a fluid concept.

The Lezgin language since 1937 has been written in a modified Cyrillic alphabet. Following the pattern of other non-Slavic languages in the Soviet Union, it had a Latin alphabet from 1928 to 1937. Before that it would have been written in an Arabic script. A modest number of books have been published in the Lezgin language. From 1984 to 1985, for example, fifty titles were published. This compares favorably with other non-jurisdictional ethnic groups, such as their fellow Dagistanis, the Avars, but less so with some nationalities that possessed some level of ethnic jurisdiction, such as the Abkhazians.

The Lezgins long gained a reputation as mountain raiders among people to their south, particularly the Georgians. Again, precision of identity was not necessarily a phenomenon in naming raiders as Lezgins. The Lezgins and the Lezgin languages were likely a part of the diverse linguistic composition of the Caucasian Kingdom of Albania. Much has been said of Udi in this context.

In the post-Soviet world the Lezgins have been involved in ethnic conflict in both Azerbaijan and Dagestan. They form a distinct minority in the former country and experience difficulty in the context of this new nation's attempt to define its own national being. In Dagestan the Lezgins, located in the mountains and constituting only 15 percent of the population, find themselves generally alienated from the centers of power. They are also in conflict with some of the groups that live more closely to them.

See also: DAGESTAN; ETHNOGRAPHY, RUSSIAN AND SOVIET; NATIONALITIES POLICIES, SOVIET; NATIONALITIES POLICIES, TSARIST

BIBLIOGRAPHY

Karny, Yo'av. (2000). *Highlanders: a Journey to the Caucasus in Quest of Memory.* New York: Farrar, Straus and Giroux.

PAUL CREGO

LIBERAL DEMOCRATIC PARTY

The Liberal Democratic Party of Russia (LDPR; known as the LDPSU during the last months of the Soviet period) was created in the spring of 1990, with active participation of the authorities and special services, as a controllable alternative to the growing democratic movement. In the 1991 presidential elections, the liberal democratic leader, the political clown Vladimir Zhirinovsky, won a surprising 6.2 million votes (7.8%) and took third place after victorious Boris Yeltsin and the main Communist candidate Nikolai Ryzhkov. In the 1993 Duma elections, the victories of the LDPR became a sensation; Zhirinovsky alone, capitalizing on sentiments of protest, secured 12.3 million votes (22.9%). From there the LDPR was able to advance five candidates in single-mandate districts. Such resounding success—both on the party list and in the districts—would not befall the LDPR again, although in 1994 and 1995 Zhirinovsky stirred up considerable energy for party formation in the provinces. In the 1995 elections, the LDPR registered candidates in 187 districts (more than the Communist Party of the Russian Federation, or KPRF) but received only one mandate and half its previous vote: 7.7 million votes (11.2%, second to the KPRF). In the 1996 presidential elections, Zhirinovsky received 4.3 million votes (5.7%, fifth place). The LDPR held approximately fifty seats in the Duma from 1996 to 1999 which helped repay, with interest, the resources invested earlier in the party's publicity since, with the domination of the left in the Duma, these votes were able to tip the scales in favor of government initiatives. The LDPR turned into an extremely profitable political business project.

In the 1999 elections, the Central Electoral Commission played a cruel joke on the Liberal Democrats. The LDPR list, consisting of a large number of commercial positions, filled by quasi-criminal businessmen, was not registered. On the very eve of the elections, when Zhirinovsky, hurriedly assembling another list and registering as the "Zhirinovsky Bloc," launched the advertising campaign "The Zhirinovsky Bloc Is the LDPR," the Central Electoral Commission registered the LDPR, but without Zhirinovsky. The Liberal Democrats were saved from this fatal split (LDPR without Zhirinovsky as a rival of the Zhirinovsky Bloc) only by the intervention of the Presidium of the Supreme Court. In the 1999 elections, the Zhirinovsky Bloc received 6 percent of the vote and finished fifth; half a year later, in the 2000 presidential elections, Zhirinovsky himself finished fourth with 2.7 percent. The LDPR fraction in the Duma from 2000 to 2003 was the smallest; it began with 17 delegates and ended with 13. It was headed by Zhirinovsky's son Igor Lebedev, as the party's head had become vice-speaker of the Duma.

Actively exploiting the nostalgia for national greatness (and for the USSR with its powerful army and special services, but without "Party nomenklatura"), "enlightened nationalism," and anti-Western sentiments; castigating the "radical reformers" and denouncing efforts at breaking the country both from without and within, the LDPR enjoys significant support from surviving groups and strata that do not share the communist ideology. The populist brightness, spiritedness, and outstanding political and acting abilities of Zhirinovsky play an important role, bringing him into sharp contrast with ordinary Russian politicians. The LDRP has especially strong support among the military and those Russian citizens who lived in Russia's national republics and SNG (Union of Independent States) countries among residents of bordering nations. The LDPR had its greatest success in regional elections from 1996 to 1998, when its candidates won as governor in Pskov oblast, mayor in the capital Tuva, parliament in Krasnodar Krai, and the Novosibirsk city assembly; a LDPR candidate came close to victory in the presidential elections in the Mari Republic as well. The LDPR results in the 1999–2002 term were significantly weaker, but with the expansion of NATO, the war in Iraq, and so forth, the LDPR ratings rose again. At its reregistration in April 2002, the LDPR declared nineteen thousand members and fifty-five regional branches.

See also: CONSTITUTION OF 1993; ZHIRINOVSKY, VLADIMIR VOLFOVICH

BIBLIOGRAPHY

McFaul, Michael. (2001). *Russia's Unfinished Revolution: Political Change from Gorbachev to Putin.* Ithaca, NY: Cornell University Press.

McFaul, Michael, and Markov, Sergei. (1993). *The Troubled Birth of Russian Democracy: Parties, Personalities, and Programs.* Stanford, CA: Hoover Institution Press.

McFaul, Michael and Petrov, Nikolai, eds. (1995). *Previewing Russia's 1995 Parliamentary Elections.* Washington, DC: Carnegie Endowment for International Peace.

McFaul, Michael; Petrov, Nikolai; and Ryabov, Andrei, eds. (1999). *Primer on Russia's 1999 Duma Elections.* Washington, DC: Carnegie Endowment for International Peace.

Reddaway, Peter, and Glinski, Dmitri. (2001). *The Tragedy of Russia's Reforms: Market Bolshevism Against Democracy.* Washington, DC: U.S. Institute of Peace Press.

NIKOLAI PETROV

LIBERALISM

Any discussion of Russian liberalism must start with a general definition of the term. The online *Stanford Encyclopedia of Philosophy* emphasizes liberals' advocacy of individual liberty and freedom from unjustified restraint. In the nineteenth century, liberalism had a strong economic strain, stressing industrialization and laissez-faire economics. With one notable exception, Russia's first liberals were little concerned with economic affairs, as the country remained mired in a semi-feudal agrarian economy. And at all times, the quest for political liberty was at the heart of Russian liberalism.

While it is impossible to select a starting point that will satisfy everyone, an early figure in the quest for freedom was Alexander Radishchev, a well-educated and widely traveled Russian nobleman. He is best known for his *A Journey from Petersburg to Moscow* (1790) that vividly exposed the evils of Russian serfdom, an institution little different from slavery in the American south of the time. An enraged Empress Catherine the Great (r. 1762–1796) demanded his execution but settled for Radishchev's banishment to Siberia. Pardoned in 1799, he was nonetheless a broken man who committed suicide in 1802. Yet Radishchev served as an inspiration to both radicals and liberals for decades to come.

In particular he inspired the Decembrist movement of 1825. This group of noble military officers attempted to seize power in an effort so confusing that they are known simply by the month of their failed coup. Five of the conspirators were executed, but many of them advocated the abolition of serfdom and autocracy, two hallmarks of early Russian liberalism.

Under Emperor Nicholas I (r. 1825–1855), virtually all talk of real reform earned the attention of the secret police. Yet some Russians found a way to express themselves; most important was the historian, Timofei Granovsky, who used his lectern to express his hostility to serfdom, advocacy of religious intolerance, and his admiration for parliamentary regimes. His influence was largely limited, however, to his pupils, including one of Russia's most famous liberals, the philosopher and historian Boris Chicherin.

Chicherin's political career began under the reform-minded Emperor Alexander II (r. 1855–1881) and included both theoretical and practical pursuits. The author of several books and innumerable articles and reviews, Chicherin was also a professor and an active politician. His liberalism included a vigorous defense of personal liberties protected by law and a consistent rejection of violence to achieve political change. He was the first prominent Russian liberal to defend a free market as a prerequisite for political liberty, squarely breaking with the emerging socialist movement.

Another important liberal was Ivan Petrunkevich. Following two attempts on the life of Emperor Alexander II, the government issued an appeal for public support against terrorism. In response, Petrunkevich declared in 1878 that the people must resist not only terror from below, but also terror from above. That same year, he met with five terrorists in an effort to unite all opponents of the status quo, an effort that failed because the terrorists rejected Petrunkevich's demand that they disavow violence. In an 1879 pamphlet he insisted upon the convocation of a constituent assembly to guarantee basic civil liberties. Despite frequent clashes with the government, Petrunkevich remained active in politics even after his exile following the Bolshevik revolution.

At the turn of the century, Russia was on the eve of revolution. Rapid industrialization under appalling conditions fostered a radical working class movement, while a surge in the peasant population produced widespread land hunger. At the same time a middle class of capitalists and professionals was emerging, and from it came many of Russia's leading liberals.

The last emperor, Nicholas II (1894–1917), proved singularly incapable of handling the Herculean task of ruling Russia. He quickly dashed any hopes liberals may have entertained for reform when he dismissed notions of diluting his autocratic power as "senseless dreams." Nonetheless, the liberals remained active.

In 1901 they established their own journal, *Liberation*, and two years later an organization, the Union of Liberation. When Russia exploded in the Revolution of 1905, the Union coordinated a movement that ranged from strikes to terrorist assassinations. Nicholas made concessions that only fueled the rebellion and in April, liberals were demanding the convocation of a constituent assembly to create a new order. In October, Nicholas issued the October Manifesto, guaranteeing basic civil liberties and the election of a national assembly, the Duma, with real political power. By then the liberals had their own political party, the Constitutional Democrats (Cadets).

It seemed that liberalism's great opportunity had arrived. At the very least, several liberals achieved national prominence in the years after 1905. Pyotr Struve, an economist and political scientist, originally embraced Marxism, but by 1905, he espoused a radical liberalism that called for full civil liberties and the establishment of a constitutional monarchy. He was elected to the Second Duma and supported Russia's entrance into the World War I. When the Bolsheviks seized power in 1917, Struve joined the unsuccessful opposition and soon left Russia for good.

The most prominent liberal of the late imperial period was the historian, Pavel Milyukov. In 1895 his political views cost him a teaching position, and he used the time to travel abroad, visiting the United States. His public lectures emphasized the need to abolish the autocracy and the right to basic civil liberties. But Milyukov also realized that liberalism was doomed if it failed to address the land issue in an overwhelmingly agrarian nation.

Milyukov supported Russia's participation in World War I, but by 1916 he was so exasperated with the catastrophic prosecution of the war that he publicly implied that treason had penetrated to the highest levels of the government. When the autocracy collapsed in February 1917, Milyukov became the foreign minister of the provisional government, the highest office ever reached by a Russian liberal. It did not last long. Under great pressure, in May he issued a promise to the allies that Russia would remain in the war to the bitter end. Antiwar demonstrations ensued, and Milyukov was forced to resign. He died in France in 1943.

Despite the efforts of Milyukov, Struve, and others, Russian liberalism increasingly fell between two stools. On the one hand were the revolutionaries who had nothing but contempt for liberals with their willingness to compromise with the imperial system. The regime's supporters, on the other hand, saw the liberals as little better than bomb-throwing revolutionaries. In a society as polarized as Russia was in 1914, with a political system as archaic as its leader was incompetent, any form of political moderation was likely doomed.

The Communists thoroughly crushed all opposition, but some brave individuals continued to call for human freedom, the most important being Andrei Sakharov. A physicist by training, he was a man of extraordinary intelligence and courage.

Admitted as a full member of the Soviet Academy of Sciences at the age of thirty-two, he was deprived of the lavish privileges accorded the scientific elite of the USSR on account of his subsequent advocacy of human rights and civil liberties. Under Mikhail Gorbachev, Sakharov returned to national prominence; he died almost exactly two years before the demise of the Soviet Union on Christmas 1991.

In the Russian Federation of the early twenty-first century, political terms such as *liberal, conservative, radical,* and so on are almost meaningless. But liberalism in its more traditional sense won a major victory in the 1996 presidential election when Boris Yeltsin defeated the Communist candidate Gennady Zyuganov. Yeltsin's liberal credentials were later much criticized, but he successfully defended freedom of speech, the press, and religion, and he initiated free market reforms. At the very least, liberalism became more powerful in Russia than any time in the past.

See also: CONSTITUTIONAL DEMOCRATIC PARTY; DECEMBRIST MOVEMENT AND REBELLION; MILYUKOV, PAUL NIKOLAYEVICH; NICHOLAS II; RADISHCHEV, ALEXANDER NIKOLAYEVICH; SAKHAROV, ANDREI DMITRIEVICH

BIBLIOGRAPHY

Fischer, George. (1958). *Russian Liberalism: From Gentry to Intelligentsia.* Cambridge, MA: Harvard University Press.

Hamburg, Gary. (1992). *Boris Chicherin and Early Russian Liberalism.* Stanford, CA: Stanford University Press.

Roosevelt, Patricia. (1986). *Apostle of Russian Liberalism: Timofei Granovsky.* Newtonville, MA: Oriental Research Partners.

Stockdale, Melissa K. (1996). *Paul Miliukov and the Quest for a Liberal Russia, 1880–1918.* Ithaca, NY: Cornell University Press.

Timberlake, Charles, ed. (1972). *Essays on Russian Liberalism.* Columbia: University of Missouri Press.

Walicki, Andrzej. (1986). *Legal Philosophies of Russian Liberalism.* Oxford: Clarendon.

HUGH PHILLIPS

LIBERMAN, YEVSEI GRIGOREVICH

(1897–1983), economist who proposed making profit the main success indicator for Soviet enterprises.

Yevsei Grigorevich Liberman's education and career were erratic and undistinguished. He graduated from the law faculty at Kiev University in 1920 and then earned a candidate of sciences degree at the Institute of Labor in Kharkov. In 1930 he began to work in the Kharkov Engineering-Economics Institute. During World War II he was evacuated to Kyrgyzstan, where he held positions in the Ministry of Finance and the Scientific Research Institute of Finance. He returned to the Kharkov Engineering-Economics Institute after the war and in 1963 became a professor of statistics at Kharkov University. At various times he was also the director of a machinery plant and a consultant to machinery plants.

Liberman's personal experience in actual enterprises helped him to understand the shortcomings of the Soviet incentive system. As early as his doctoral dissertation in 1957, he suggested reducing the number of planning indicators for firms and focusing on profit instead. In 1962 he became a *cause célèbre* when he published an article in *Pravda* that proposed making profit the sole success indicator in evaluating enterprise performance. Since Liberman was not a significant player in economic reform circles, it is thought that others, such as Vasily Sergeyevich Nemchinov, engineered publication of this article as a trial balloon. Thus he was more significant as a lightning rod around which controversy swirled than as a thinker with a sophisticated understanding of economics or of the complex task of transforming the Soviet administrative command system.

See also: NEMCHINOV, VASILY SERGEYEVICH

BIBLIOGRAPHY

Liberman, E. G. (1971). *Economic Methods and the Effectiveness of Production.* White Plains, NY: International Arts and Sciences Press.

Treml, Vladimir G. (1968). "The Politics of Libermanism." *Soviet Studies* 29:567–572.

ROBERT W. CAMPBELL

LIGACHEV, YEGOR KUZMICH

(b. 1920), a secretary of the Central Committee of the Communist Party of the Soviet Union (December 1983 to mid-1990), and member of the Politburo (April 1985 to mid-1990).

Yegor Ligachev criticized Gorbachev's reforms and Yeltsin's leadership style. PACH/CORBIS-BETTMANN. REPRODUCED BY PERMISSION..

Yegor Ligachev was a leading orthodox critic of many aspects of General Secretary Mikhail Gorbachev's program of reforms. From 1985 until late 1988 he served as the party's informal second secretary responsible for the supervision of official ideology and personnel management. During this period, he clashed with Secretary Alexander Yakovlev over cultural and ideological policies and openly assailed the cultural liberalization fostered by glasnost and the growing public criticism of the USSR's past.

While Ligachev publicly endorsed perestroika in general terms, he opposed Gorbachev's efforts to limit party officials' responsibilities and to expand the legislative authority of the soviets. He was widely identified with the orthodox critique of perestroika provided by Nina Andreyeva in early 1988. At the Nineteenth Conference of the Communist Party of the Soviet Union (CPSU) in mid-1988, Ligachev refused to publicly endorse Gorbachev's reform of the Secretariat and its subordinate apparat. In September 1988 he lost his position as second secretary and was named director of the newly created agricultural commission of the Central Committee.

Ligachev was deeply disturbed by the collapse of Communist power in Eastern Europe and the flaccid response to those events on the part of the Gorbachev regime. Nor did he support the general secretary's decision to end the CPSU's monopoly of power in February 1990. In the spring of 1990 he moderated his critique of the regime in an apparent effort to win election as deputy general secretary at the Twenty-eighth Party Congress, but he lost the election by a wide margin. Following the reform of the Secretariat and Politburo at the congress he retired from both bodies. He did not fully condemn the attempted coup against Gorbachev in August 1991, but he vigorously denied charges of direct involvement in these events.

See also: ANDREYEVA, NINA ALEXANDROVNA; AUGUST 1991 PUTSCH; GLASNOST; GORBACHEV, MIKHAIL SERGEYEVICH; PERESTROIKA

BIBLIOGRAPHY

Harris, Jonathan. (1989). "Ligachev on Glasnost and Perestroika." In *Carl Beck Papers in Russian and East European Studies,* no. 706. Pittsburgh, PA: University Center for Russian and East European Studies.

Ligachev, Egor. (1993). *Inside Gorbachev's Kremlin.* New York: Pantheon Books.

JONATHAN HARRIS

LIKHACHEV, DMITRY SERGEYEVICH

(1906–1999), cultural historian, religious philosopher.

Dmitry Sergeyevich Likhachev was known as a world-renowned academic, literary and cultural historian, sociologist, religious philosopher, prisoner of the gulag, and preservationist of all kinds of Russian culture. But he was much more. By the end of his life he had become one of the most respected citizens of Russia. As an academic, Likhachev was the preeminent expert of his generation on medieval Russian culture, and the literature of the tenth through seventeenth centuries in particular, perhaps the most prolific writer and researcher on Russian culture in the twentieth century. One of his obituaries described him as "one of the symbols of the twentieth century . . . [whose] life was devoted to education . . . the energetic service of the highest ideals of humanism, spirituality, genuine patriotism, and citizenship . . . consistently preaching eternal principles of morality and conscientiousness . . . a person of the rarest erudition and generous spirit, who educated a whole galaxy of worthy students" (*Kultura* No. 36, 7–13 October, 1999, 1). Another said, "[He] took the helm of the ship of Russian culture and steered it to a hopefully better world." He was a greatly talented historian and many of his more than one thousand publications were known throughout the world's academic community. By his life's end he had been granted honorary titles by sixteen national academies and European universities, as well as several high honors from his native land, including Hero of Soviet Labor. He served as a researcher in various Soviet academic institutions of renown, gained the title of university professor, and for his seminal work on the Russian classic, *Lay of Igor's Campaign*, was received into the Soviet Academy of Sciences. His very active life also led him to membership in the Russian Duma after the fall of the Soviet Union.

See also: ACADEMY OF SCIENCES; HISTORIOGRAPHY; LAY OF IGOR'S CAMPAIGN

BIBLIOGRAPHY

Likhachev, Dmitry S. (2000). *Reflections on the Russian Soul: A Memoir.* Budapest, Hungary: Central European University Press.

JOHN PATRICK FARRELL

LISHENTSY *See* DISENFRANCHIZED PERSONS.

LITHUANIA AND LITHUANIANS

Located on the southeastern shore of the Baltic Sea, Lithuania has been an independent republic since 1991. Encompassing 66,200 square kilometers, it has a population (2001) of 3,491,000 inhabitants, of whom 67.2 percent live in cities and 32.8 percent in rural areas. Over 80 percent of the population is Lithuanian, about 9 percent Russian, and 7 percent Polish.

Lithuanians first established a government in the thirteenth century to resist the Teutonic Knights attacking from the West. In 1251 the Lithuanian ruler Mindaugas accepted Latin Christianity, and in 1253 received the title of king, but his successors were known as Grand Dukes. When Tatars overran the Russian principalities to the East, the Grand Duchy expanded into the territory that today makes up Belarus and Ukraine. At its height, at the end of the fourteenth century, although the Lithuanians are a Baltic and not a Slavic people, Lithuania had a majority of East Slavs in its population, and for a time it challenged the Grand Duchy of Moscow as the "collector of the Russian lands."

Faced by Moscow's growing strength, Lithuanian leaders turned to Poland for help, and through a series of agreements made between 1385 and 1387, the two states formed a union, solidified by the marriage of the two rulers, Jagiello and Jadwiga, and by the reintroduction of Latin Christianity through the Polish structure of the Roman Catholic church. (Lithuania had reverted to paganism after Mindaugas's abdication in 1261.) Reinforced by the Union of Lublin in 1569, the Polish-Lithuanian Commonwealth continued until the Partitions of Poland at the end of the eighteenth century. In 1795 the Third Partition of Poland brought Russian rule to most of what today constitutes Lithuania.

Russian authorities attempted to wean the Lithuanians from the Polish influences that had dominated during the period of the Commonwealth. The Russians banned the use of the name "Lithuania" (Litva) and administered the territory as part of the "Northwest Region." After the Polish uprisings of 1831 and 1863, the authorities helped Lithuanians in some ways but also tried to force them to adopt the Cyrillic alphabet. At the same time, the authorities limited the economic development of the region, which lay on the Russian-German border. Under these conditions, a Lithuanian national consciousness emerged, and with it the goal of cultural independence from the Poles and eventual political independence from Russia.

The Lithuanians received their opportunity in the course of World War I. On February 16, 1918, after almost three years of German occupation, the Lithuanian Council (Taryba) declared the country's independence, but a provisional government began to function only after the German defeat in November 1918. Russian efforts in 1919 to reclaim the region in the form of a Lithuanian Soviet Socialist Republic failed, and in May 1920 a Constituent Assembly met and formalized the state structure.

The First Republic's foreign policy focused on Lithuania's claim to the city of Vilnius as its historic capitol. The Poles had seized the city in 1920, and as a result, Lithuania tended to align itself with

Lithuania, 1992 © Maryland Cartographics. Reprinted with permission

Germany and the Soviet Union as part of an anti-Versailles camp. In 1939, by the terms of the Nazi-Soviet Non-Aggression pact, Germany and the Soviet Union were to divide Eastern Europe, and Lithuania fell into the Soviet orbit. In 1940 Soviet forces overthrew the authoritarian regime that had ruled Lithuania since 1926, and Moscow directed the country's incorporation into the Soviet Union as a constituent republic.

The 1940s brought destruction and havoc to Lithuania. In 1940 and 1941, Soviet authorities deported thousands of Lithuanian citizens of all nationalities into the interior of the USSR. When the Germans invaded in 1941, some local people joined with the Nazi forces in the massacre of the vast majority of the Jewish population of Lithuania. (In 1940 and 1941 Jews had constituted almost 10 percent of Lithuania's population.) When the Soviet army returned in 1944 and 1945, Lithuanian resistance erupted and continued into the early 1950s. Thousands died in the fighting, and Soviet authorities deported at least 150,000 persons to Siberia. (The exact number of killings and deportations is subject to considerable dispute.)

Under Soviet rule the Lithuanian social structure changed significantly. Before World War II, the majority of Lithuanians were peasants, and even at the beginning of the twenty-first century, many urban dwellers still maintained some sort of psychological link with the land. The Soviet government, however, collectivized agriculture and pushed industrialization, moving large numbers of people into the cities and developing new industrial centers. By the 1960s, after the violent resistance had failed, more Lithuanians began to enter the Soviet system, becoming intellectuals, economic leaders, and party members. Emigré Lithuanian scholars often estimated that only 5 to 10 percent of Lithuanian party members were "believers," while the majority had joined out of necessity.

In 1988, after Mikhail Gorbachev had loosened Moscow's controls throughout the Soviet Union, the Lithuanians became a focus of the process of ethno-regional decentralization of the Soviet state. Gorbachev's program of reform encouraged local initiative that, in the Lithuanian case, quickly took on national coloration. The Lithuanian Movement for Perestroika, now remembered as *Sajudis*, mobilized the nation first around cultural and ecological issues, and later, in a political campaign, around the goal of reestablishment of independence.

Gorbachev quickly lost control of Lithuania, and he successively resorted to persuasion, economic pressure, and finally violence to restrain the Lithuanians. After the Lithuanian Communist Party declared its independence of the Soviet party in December 1989, worldwide media watched Gorbachev travel to Lithuania in January to persuade the Lithuanians to relent. He failed, and after *Sajudis* led the Lithuanian parliament on March 11, 1990, to declare the reconstitution of the Lithuanian state, Gorbachev imposed an economic blockade on the republic. This, too, failed, and in January 1991, world media again watched as Soviet troops attacked key buildings in Vilnius and the Lithuanians passively resisted Moscow's efforts to reestablish its authority. The result was a stalemate. Finally, after surviving the so-called "August Putsch" in Moscow, Gorbachev, under Western pressure, recognized the reestablishment of independent Lithuania.

See also: BRAZAUSKAS, ALGIRDAS; LANDSBERGIS, VYTAUTAS; NATIONALITIES POLICIES, SOVIET; NATIONALITIES POLICIES, TSARIST; POLAND; VILNIUS

BIBLIOGRAPHY

Eidintas, Alfonsas, and Zalys, Vytautas. (1997). *Lithuania in European Politics: The Years of the First Republic, 1918–1940.* New York: St. Martin's Press.

Misiunas, Romuald, and Taagepera, Rein. (1992). *The Baltic States: Years of Dependence, 1940–1990,* expanded and updated ed. Berkeley: University of California Press.

Senn, Alfred Erich. (1959). *The Emergence of Modern Lithuania.* New York: Columbia University Press.

Senn, Alfred Erich. (1990). *Lithuania Awakening.* Berkeley: University of California Press.

Senn, Alfred Erich. (1995). *Gorbachev's Failure in Lithuania.* New York: St. Martin's Press.

Vardys, V. Stanley. (1978). *The Catholic Church, Dissent, and Nationality in Soviet Lithuania.* Boulder, CO: East European Quarterly.

Alfred Erich Senn

LITVINOV, MAXIM MAXIMOVICH

(1876–1951), old Bolshevik, leading Soviet diplomat, and commissar for foreign affairs.

Maxim Maximovich Litvinov was born Meer Genokh Moisevich Vallakh in Bialystok, a small city in what is now Poland. He joined the socialist movement in the 1890s and sided with Vladimir Lenin when the Social Democratic Party split into Bolshevik and Menshevik factions. From 1898 to 1908, he smuggled guns and propaganda into the empire, but having achieved little, he emigrated to Britain. There he married an English woman and led a quiet, conventional life, even becoming a British subject. During the October Revolution, he served briefly as the Soviet representative to London but was expelled from Britain for "revolutionary activities" in October 1918. In Moscow he became a deputy commissar for foreign affairs and frequently negotiated with the Western powers for normal diplomatic relations, to little success. However, Litvinov did conclude a 1929 nonaggression pact with the USSR's western neighbors, including Poland and the Baltic states.

From 1930 to 1939 Litvinov served as commissar for foreign affairs. In 1931 he negotiated a nonaggression treaty with France, an extremely anti-Soviet state that had become worried about an increasingly unstable Germany. Soon after Adolf Hitler came to power, Litvinov initiated alliance talks with France, finding a partner in Louis Barthou, the foreign minister. In December 1933, the Soviet Communist Party leadership formally approved Litvinov's proposal both for a military alliance with France and for the Soviet Union's entrance into the League of Nations. Talks took a tortuous course, but in June 1934, Barthou and Litvinov agreed on a eastern pact of mutual assistance that would be guaranteed by a separate Franco-Soviet treaty of mutual assistance.

For several reasons, however, these treaties proved ineffectual. First of all, Barthou was assassinated in October 1934, and Pierre Laval, an advocate of good relations with Germany, replaced him. Moreover, the British were hostile to close relations with Moscow, and France was generally unwilling to act without London's support. Finally, in 1937, Stalin ordered the decimation of the Red Army's leadership at the same time he was terrorizing the entire nation. To the already suspicious West, it seemed clear that the USSR could not possibly be a reliable ally. Litvinov realized the damage the Great Terror wrought on Soviet foreign policy but was powerless in domestic politics. Ignored and rebuffed at virtually every turn by the West, Litvinov was replaced by Stalin's close associate, Vyacheslav Molotov, in May 1939, four months before the signing of the Nazi-Soviet Pact.

With the German invasion of the USSR in June 1941, Stalin appointed Litvinov ambassador to the United States. For the next two years, Litvinov constantly urged the West to open a second front in France. Angered at Litvinov's lack of success, Stalin recalled him in 1943. He served as a deputy commissar for foreign affairs, making many proposals to Stalin advocating Great Power cooperation after the war. This effort failed, and Litvinov eventually understood that Stalin saw security not in terms of cooperation with the West, but in the building of a bulwark of satellite states on the USSR's western border. Two months before his final dismissal in August 1946, Litvinov told the American journalist Richard C. Hottelet that it was pointless for the West to hope for good relations with Stalin. Perhaps the most remarkable and mysterious fact of Litvinov's long career is that he died a natural death.

See also: BOLSHEVISM; FRANCE, RELATIONS WITH

BIBLIOGRAPHY

Phillips, Hugh. (1992). *Between the Revolution and the West: A Political Biography of Maxim M. Litvinov.* Boulder, CO: Westview.

Sheinis, Zinovii. (1990). *Maxim Litvinov.* Moscow: Progress Publishers.

HUGH PHILLIPS

LIVING CHURCH MOVEMENT

Also known as the Renovationist Movement, the Living Church Movement, a coalition of clergy and laity, sought to combine Orthodox Christianity with the social and political goals of the Soviet government between 1922 and 1946. The movement's names reflected fears that Orthodoxy faced extinction after the Bolshevik Revolution. Renovationists hoped to renew their church through reforms in liturgy, practice, and the rules on clergy marriage.

The movement began in response to the revolutions of 1905 and 1917. Parish priests in Petrograd formed the Group of Thirty-Two in 1905 and proposed a liberal program for church administration that would allow married parish priests, not just celibate monastic priests, to become bishops. This group joined advocates of Christian socialism in a Union for Church Regeneration that advocated the separation of church and state, greater democracy within the church, and the use of modern Russian instead of medieval Old Church Slavonic in the Divine Liturgy. Repressed after 1905, the reform movement reappeared in 1917 only to wither from lack of widespread Orthodox support.

The Living Church Movement appeared during the famine of 1921–1922, thanks in large part to Bolshevik suspicions that Orthodox bishops were plotting counterrevolution. The Politburo approved a plan for splitting the church through a public campaign to seize church treasures for famine relief. Bolshevik leaders secretly wanted to strip the church of valuables that might be used to finance political opposition. Patriarch Tikhon Bellavin and other bishops opposed the government's plan to seize sacred icons, chalices, and patens. A small group of clergy led by Alexander Vvedensky, Vladimir Krasnitsky, and Antonin Granovsky used covert government aid to set up a rival national Orthodox organization that supported confiscation of church valuables, expressed loyalty to the Soviet regime, and promoted internal church reforms.

When Patriarch Tikhon unexpectedly abdicated in May 1922, Living Church leaders formed a Supreme Church Administration and pushed for revolution in the church by imitating the successful tactics of the Bolsheviks. Renovationists tried to force the church to accept radical reforms in liturgy, administration, leadership, and doctrine. Parish clergy responded favorably to proposed changes; bishops and laity overwhelmingly rejected them. Government authorities threatened, arrested, and exiled opponents to the Living Church, thereby further eroding popular support for reform.

Internal divisions within the Supreme Church Administration also weakened the movement. Three competing renovationist parties emerged. The Living Church Group of Archpriest Krasnitsky promoted church revolution led by parish priests. This group was more interested in giving greater power to parish priests by allowing them to remarry and to become bishops than in changing canons and dogma. Bishop Granovskii organized a League for Church Regeneration that espoused democracy in the church. The league appealed to conservative lay believers because it promised them a greater voice in church affairs and defended traditional Orthodox beliefs and practices. A third renovationist party, the League of Communities of the Ancient Apostolic Church led by Archpriest Vvedensky, combined Granovsky's democratic principles and Krasnitsky's reform proposals with Vvedensky's passion for Christian socialism.

Infighting among renovationist groups threatened to destroy the movement, so the Soviet government forced them to reconcile. The reunified Living Church gained control over nearly 70 percent of Russian Orthodox parish churches by the time their national church council convened in May 1923. The council defrocked Patriarch Tikhon and condemned his anti-Soviet activity. It also approved limited church reforms, including the abolition of the patriarchate and the ordination of married bishops, and proclaimed the church's loyalty to the regime.

By June 1923 the Soviet government became worried over the strength of renovationism. The Politburo decided to release Tikhon from jail after he agreed in writing to acknowledge his crimes and to promise loyalty to the government. Orthodox believers and clergy immediately rallied to him. The reformers reorganized in order to stop defections to the patriarchate. All renovationist parties were banned, most reforms were abandoned, and the Supreme Church Administration became the Holy Synod led by monastic bishops. Granovsky and Krasnitsky refused to accept these changes and were pushed aside. Vvedensky joined the Holy Synod in a reduced role.

The Renovationist Movement lost support throughout the 1920s, despite this reorganization and an attempt to reunite the church by calling a second renovationist national church council in October 1925. Most Orthodox believers saw everyone in the Living Church Movement as traitors who had sold out to the Communists. The movement declined dramatically throughout the 1930s as did the Orthodox church in general. The Living Church Movement experienced a short lived revival during the first years of World War II, when Soviet persecution of religion eased and Vvedensky became leader of the movement. In September 1943 Josef Stalin permitted senior patriarchal bishops to reinstate a national church administration. A month later, he approved a plan to merge renovationist parishes with the Moscow patriarchate. Vvedensky opposed this decision, but his death in July 1946 officially ended the Living Church Movement. For decades afterward, however, Orthodox believers used "Living Church" and "Renovationist" as synonyms for religious traitors.

See also: FAMINE OF 1921–1922; ORTHODOXY; RUSSIAN ORTHODOX CHURCH; TIKHON, PATRIARCH

BIBLIOGRAPHY

Curtiss, John S. (1952). *The Russian Church and the Soviet State, 1917–1950.* Boston: Little, Brown.

Freeze, Gregory L. (1995). "Counter-reformation in Russian Orthodoxy: Popular Response to Religious Innovation, 1922–1925." *Slavic Review* 54:305–339.

Roslof, Edward E. (2002). *Red Priests: Renovationism, Russian Orthodoxy, and Revolution, 1905–1946.* Bloomington: Indiana University Press.

Walters, Philip. (1991). "The Renovationist Coup: Personalities and Programmes." In *Church, Nation and State in Russia and Ukraine*, ed. Geoffrey A. Hosking. London: MacMillan.

EDWARD E. ROSLOF

LIVONIAN WAR

The Livonian War (1558–1583), for the possession of Livonia (historic region that became Latvia and Estonia) was first between Russia and the knightly Order of Livonia, and then between Russia and Sweden and the Polish–Lithuanian Commonwealth.

The outbreak of war was preceded by Russian–Livonian negotiations resulting in the 1554 treaty on a fifteen–year armistice. According to this treaty, Livonians were to pay annual tribute to the Russian tsar for the city of Dorpat (now Tartu), on grounds that the city (originally known as "Yuriev") belonged formerly to Russian princes, ancestors of Ivan IV. Using the overdue payment of this Yuriev tribute as a pretext, the tsar declared war on Livonia in January 1558.

As for Ivan IV's true reasons for beginning the war, two possibilities have been suggested. The first was offered in the 1850s by Russian historian Sergei Soloviev, who presented Ivan the Terrible as a precursor of Peter the Great in his efforts to gain harbors on the Baltic Sea and thus to establish direct economic relations with European countries. Until 1991 this explanation remained predominant in Russian and Soviet historiography; it was also shared by some Swedish and Danish scholars.

However, from the 1960s on, the thesis of economic (trade) interests underlying Ivan IV's decision to make war on Livonia has been subjected to sharp criticism. The critics pointed out that the tsar, justifying his military actions in Livonia, never referred to the need for direct trade with Europe; instead he referred to his hereditary rights, calling Livonia his patrimony (*votchina*). The alternative explanation proposed by Norbert Angermann (1972) and supported by Erik Tiberg (1984) and, in the 1990s, by some Russian scholars (Filyushkin, 2001), emphasizes the tsar's ambition for expanding his power and might.

It is most likely that Ivan IV started the war with no strategic plan in mind: He just wanted to punish the Livonians and force them to pay the contribution and fulfil all the conditions of the previous treaty. The initial success gave the tsar hope of conquering all Livonia, but here his interests clashed with the interests of Poland–Lithuania and Sweden, and thus a local conflict grew into a long and exhaustive war between the greatest powers of the Baltic region.

As the war progressed, Ivan IV changed allies and enemies; the scene of operations also changed. So, in the course of the war one can distinguish four different periods: 1) from 1558 to 1561, the period of initial Russian success in Livonia; 2) the 1560s, the period of confrontation with Lithuania and peaceful relations with Sweden; 3) from 1570 to 1577, the last efforts of Ivan IV in Livonia; and 4) from 1578 to 1582, when severe blows from Poland–Lithuania and Sweden forced Ivan IV to give up all his acquisitions in Livonia and start peace negotiations.

During the campaign of 1558, Russian armies, encountering no serious resistance, took the important harbor of Narva (May 11) and the city of Dorpat (July 19). After a long pause (an armistice from March through November 1559), in 1560 Russian troops undertook a new offensive in Livonia. On August 2 the main forces of the Order were defeated near Ermes (now Ergeme); on August 30 an army led by prince Andrei Kurbsky captured the castle of Fellin (now Vilyandy).

As the collapse of the enfeebled Livonian Order became evident, the knighthood and cities of Livonia began to seek the protection of Baltic powers: Lithuania, Sweden, and Denmark. In 1561 the country was divided: The last master of the Order, Gottard Kettler, became vassal of Sigismund II Augustus, the king of Poland and grand duke of Lithuania, and acknowledged sovereignty of the latter over the territory of the abolished Order; simultaneously the northern part of Livonia, including Reval (now Tallinn), was occupied by the Swedish troops.

Regarding Sigismund II as his principal rival in Livonia and trying to ally with Erik XIV of Sweden, Ivan IV declared war on Lithuania in 1562. A large Russian army, led by the tsar himself, besieged the city of Polotsk on the eastern frontier of the Lithuanian duchy and seized it on February 15, 1563. In the following years Lithuanians managed to avenge this failure, winning two battles in 1564 and capturing two minor fortresses in 1568, but no decisive success was achieved.

By the beginning of the 1570s the international situation had changed again: A coup d'état in Sweden (Erik XIV was dethroned by his brother John III) put an end to the Russian–Swedish alliance; Poland and Lithuania (in 1569 the two states united into one, Rzecz Pospolita), on the contrary, adhered to a peaceful policy during the sickness of King Sigismund II Augustus (d. 1572) and periods of interregnum (1572–1573, 1574–1575). Under these circumstances Ivan IV tried to drive Swedish forces out of northern Livonia: Russian troops and the tsar's vassal, Danish duke Magnus (brother of Frederick II of Denmark), besieged Revel for thirty weeks (August 21, 1570–March 16, 1571), but in vain. The alliance with the Danish king proved its inefficiency, and the raids of Crimean Tartars (for instance, the burning of Moscow by Khan Devlet–Girey on May 24, 1571) made the tsar postpone further actions in Livonia for several years.

In 1577 Ivan IV made his last effort to conquer Livonia; his troops occupied almost the entire country (except for Reval and Riga). Next year the war entered its final phase, fatal to the Russian cause in Livonia.

In 1578 Russian troops in Livonia were defeated by combined Polish–Lithuanian and Swedish forces near the fortress Venden (now Tsesis), and the tsar's vassal, duke Magnus, joined the Polish side. In 1579 the Polish king, Stephen Bathory, a talented general, recaptured Polotsk; the following year, he invaded Russia and devastated the Pskov region, having taken the fortresses of Velizh and Usvyat and having burned Velikiye Luky. During his third Russian campaign in August 1581, Bathory besieged Pskov; the garrison led by prince Ivan Shuisky repulsed thirty–one assaults. At the same time the Swedish troops seized Narva. Without allies, Ivan IV sought peace. On January 15, 1582, the treaty concluded in Yam Zapolsky put an end to the war with Rzecz Pospolita: Ivan IV gave up Livonia, Polotsk, and Velizh (Velikiye Luky was returned to Russia). In 1583 the armistice with Sweden was concluded, yielding Russian towns Yam, Koporye, and Ivangorod to the Swedish side.

The failure of the Livonian war spelled disaster for Ivan IV's foreign policy; it weakened the position of Russia towards its neighbors in the west and north, and the war was calamitous for the northwestern regions of the country.

See also: IVAN IV

BIBLIOGRAPHY

Esper, Thomas. (1966). "Russia and the Baltic, 1494-1558." *Slavic Review* 25:458-474.

Kirchner, Walter. (1954). *The Rise of Baltic Question.* Newark: University of Delaware Press.

MIKHAIL M. KROM

LOBACHEVSKY, NIKOLAI IVANOVICH

(1792–1856), mathematician; creator of the first non-Euclidean geometry.

Nikolai Lobachevsky was born in Nizhny Novgorod to the family of a minor government official. In 1809 he enrolled in Kazan University, selecting mathematics as his major field. From Martin Bartels and Franz Bronner, German immigrant professors, he learned the fundamentals of trigonometry, analytical geometry, celestial mechanics, differential calculus, the history of mathematics, and astronomy. Bronner also introduced him to the current controversies in the philosophy of science.

In 1811 Lobachevsky was granted a magisterial degree, and three years later he was appointed instructor in mathematics at Kazan University. His first teaching assignment was trigonometry and number theory as advanced by Carl Friedrich Gauss. In 1816 he was promoted to the rank of associate professor. In 1823 he published a gymnasium textbook in geometry and, in 1824, a textbook in algebra.

Lobachevsky's strong interest in geometry was first manifested in 1817 when, in one of his teaching courses, he dwelt in detail on his effort to adduce proofs for Euclid's fifth (parallel) postulate. In 1826, at a faculty meeting, he presented a paper that showed that he had abandoned the idea of searching for proofs for the fifth postulate; in contrast to Euclid's claim, he stated that more than one parallel could be drawn through a point outside a line. On the basis of his postulate, Lobachevsky constructed a new geometry including, in some opinions, Euclid's creation as a special case. Although the text of Lobachevsky's report was not preserved, it can be safely assumed that its contents were repeated in his "Elements of Geometry," published in the *Kazan Herald* in 1829–1830. In the meantime, Lobachevsky was elected the rector of the university, a position he held until 1846.

In order to inform Western scientists about his new ideas, in 1837 Lobachevsky published an article in French ("Geometrie imaginaire") and in 1840 a small book in German (*Geometrische Untersuchungen zur Theorie der Parallellinien*). His article "Pangeometry" appeared in Russian in 1855 and in French in 1856, the year of his death. At no time did Lobachevsky try to invalidate Euclid's geometry; he only wanted to show that there was room and necessity for more than one geometry. After becoming familiar with the new geometry, Carl Friedrich Gauss was instrumental in Lobachevsky's election as an honorary member of the Gottingen Scientific Society.

After the mid-nineteenth century, Lobachevsky's revolutionary ideas in geometry began to attract serious attention in the West. Eugenio Beltrami in Italy, Henri Poincare in France, and Felix Klein in Germany contributed to the integration of non-Euclidean geometry into the mainstream of modern mathematics. The English mathematician William Kingdon Clifford attributed Copernican significance to Lobachevsky's ideas.

On the initiative of Alexander Vasiliev, professor of mathematics, in 1893 Kazan University celebrated the centennial of Lobechevsky's birth. On this occasion, Vasiliev presented a lengthy paper explaining not only the scientific and philosophical messages of the first non-Euclidean geometry but also their growing acceptance in the West. At this time, Kazan University established the Lobachevsky Prize, to be given annually to a selected mathematician whose work was related to the Lobachevsky legacy. Among the early recipients of the prize were Sophus Lie and Henri Poincaré.

In 1926 Kazan University celebrated the centennial of Lobachevsky's non-Euclidean geometry. All speakers placed emphasis on Lobachevsky's influence on modern scientific thought. Alexander Kotelnikov advanced important arguments in favor of close relations of Lobachevsky's geometrical propositions to Einstein's general theory of relativity. Lobachevsky also received credit for a major contribution to modern axiomatics and for proving that entire sciences could be created by logical deductions from assumed propositions.

See also: ACADEMY OF SCIENCES

BIBLIOGRAPHY

Kagan, V. N. (1952). *N. I. Lobachevsky and His Contributions to Science.* Moscow: Foreign Languages Publishing House.

Vucinich, Alexander. (1962). "Nikolai Ivanovich Lobachevskii: The Man Behind the First Non-Euclidean Geometry." *ISIS* 53:465–481

ALEXANDER VUCINICH

LOCAL GOVERNMENT AND ADMINISTRATION

The history of local government in Russia and Soviet Union can be characterized as a story of grand plans and the inability to fully implement these plans. The first serious attempt to establish this branch of government in Russia came during the reign of Peter I. Between 1708 and 1719 Peter introduced provincial reforms, in which the country was divided into fifty *guberniiu* (provinces). Each of the provinces was then subdivided into *uyezdy* (districts). Appointed administrators governed the provinces, while district administrators and councils assisting provincial administrators were elected among local gentry. Provincial and district government was to be responsible for local health, education, and economic development. In 1720–1721 Peter introduced his municipal reform. This was the continuation of the earlier, 1699 effort to reorganize municipal finances. Municipal administration was to be elected from among the townspeople, and it was to be responsible for day-to-day running of a town or city.

The results of Peter's reforms of local and municipal government were uneven. The basic subdivisions for the country (provinces and districts) survived the imperial period and were successfully adopted by Soviet authorities. The substance of the reforms—the elective principle and local responsibility—fell victim to local apathy and inability to find suitable officials.

Another attempt to reform local government in Russia took place during the reign of Catherine II. Catherine followed the policy of strengthening of gentry as a class, and under her Charter of Nobility of 1785, the gentry of each province was given a status of legal body with wide-ranging legal and property rights. The gentry, together with the centrally appointed governor, constituted local government in Russia under Catherine. In the same year, Catherine II granted a charter to towns, which provided for limited municipal government, controlled by wealthy merchants.

The truly wide-ranging local and municipal reforms were instituted during the reign of Alexander II. The 1864 local government reform established local (zemstvo) assemblies and boards on provincial and district levels. Representation in district Zemstvos was proportional to land ownership, with allowances for real estate ownership in towns. Members of district Zemstvos elected, among themselves, a provincial assembly. Assemblies met once per year to discuss basic policy and budget. They also elected Zemstvo boards, which, together with professional staff, dealt with everyday administrative matters. The Zemstvo system was authorized to deal with education, medical and veterinary services, insurance, roads, emergency food supplies, local statistics, and other matters.

Wide-ranging municipal reforms started in the early 1860s, when several cities were granted, on a trial basis, the right to draft their own municipal charter and elect a city council. The result of these experiments was the 1870 Municipal Charter. Under its provision, a town council was elected by all property owners or taxpayers. The council elected an administrative board, which ran a town between the elections.

The local government reforms of 1860s and 1870s were wide-ranging and significant. However, they still left significant inequalities in the system. Electoral rights were based on property ownership, and largest property owners—the gentry in the rural areas and the wealthy merchants in the cities—had the greatest representation in the local government. These inequalities increased under the successors of Alexander II—Alexander III and Nicholas II—when peasants and the non-Orthodox religious minorities were denied rights to elect and be elected.

The February Revolution of 1917 brought local and municipal government reforms of 1860s and 1870s to their widest possible extent. The lifting of all class-, nationality-, and religion-based restrictions on citizens' participation in government considerably widened local government electorate. The temporary municipal administration law of June 9 formulated accountability, conflicts of interest, and appeal mechanisms. As central government weakened between February and October Revolutions, the role of local government in providing services and basic security to the citizens increased. At the same time, the soviets, the locally based umbrella bodies of socialist organizations, came into existence. The soviets and old local administrations coexisted throughout the Russian Civil War. As Bolsheviks consolidated power, however, the old local administrations were dissolved, and local soviets assumed their responsibilities. Throughout early 1920s the local soviets were purged of non-Bolshevik representatives and, by the time of Lenin's death, they lost their practical importance as a seat of power in the Soviet Union. The structure of local soviets was similar to that of the provincial and district Zemstvos. They consisted of standing and plenary committees, which discussed matters before them and elected presidium and the chair of the soviet. Local soviets were tightly intertwined with local Communist Party structures and representatives of central government. This, together with their inability to raise taxes and tight central control, severely curtailed their effectiveness in such areas as public housing, municipal transport, retail trade, health, and welfare. Following the collapse of the Soviet Union, there was a move away from soviets and toward Western models of local government. However, the shape of this branch of government is yet to be decided in the post-Communist Russian Federation.

See also: ASSEMBLY OF THE LAND; GUBERNIYA; SOVIET; TERRITORIAL-ADMINISTRATIVE UNITS; ZEMSTVO

BIBLIOGRAPHY

Kenez, Peter. (1999). *A History of the Soviet Union from the Beginning to the End.* Cambridge, UK: Cambridge University Press.

Riasanovsky, Nicholas V. (2000). *A History of Russia.* New York: Oxford University Press.

Sakwa, Richard. (1998). *Soviet Politics in Perspective*, 2nd ed. London; New York: Routledge.

IGOR YEYKELIS

LOMONOSOV, MIKHAIL VASILIEVICH

(1711–1765), chemist, physicist, poet.

Mikhail Lomonosov was born in a small coastal village near Arkhangelsk. His father was a prosperous fisherman and trader. At age nineteen Lomonosov enrolled in the Slavic-Greek-Latin Academy in Moscow, a religious institution where he learned Latin and was exposed to Aristotelian philosophy and logic. In 1736 he was one of sixteen students selected to continue their studies at the newly established secular university at the St. Petersburg Academy of Sciences. Immediately the Academy sent him to Marburg University in Germany to study the physical sciences under the guidance of Christian Wolff, famous for his versatile interest in the links between physics and philosophy. He also spent some time in Freiberg, where he studied mining techniques. He sent several scientific papers to St. Petersburg. After five years in Germany, he returned to St. Petersburg and began immediately to present papers on physical and chemical themes. In 1745 he was elected full professor at the Academy.

Lomonosov drew admiring attention not only as "the father of Russian science" but also as a major modernizer of national poetry. He introduced the living word as the vehicle of poetic expression. According to Vissarion Belinsky, who wrote in the middle of the nineteenth century: "His language is pure and noble, his style is precise and powerful, and his verse is full of glitter and soaring spirit." According to Evelyn Bristol: "Lomonosov created a body of verse whose excellence was unprecedented in his own language."

Lomonosov's work in science was of an encyclopedic scope; he was actively engaged in physics, chemistry, astronomy, geology, meteorology, and navigation. He also contributed to population studies, political economy, Russian history, rhetoric, and

Portrait of poet and scientist Mikhail Lomonosov from the State Hermitage Museum collection. © REPRODUCED BY PERMISSION OF THE STATE HERMITAGE MUSEUM, ST. PETERSBURG, RUSSIA/CORBIS

grammar. He brought the most advanced scientific theories to Russia, commented on their strengths and weaknesses, and advanced original ideas. He sided with Newton's atomistic views on the structure of matter; questioned the existence of the heat-generating caloric, a popular crutch of eighteenth-century science; and endorsed and commented on Huygens's clearly manifested inclination toward the wave theory of light. He raised the question of the scientific validity of the notion of instantaneous action at a distance that was built into Newton's notion of universal gravitation, conducted experimental research in atmospheric electricity, made the first steps toward the formulation of conservation laws, suggested a historical orientation in the study of the terrestrial strata, and claimed the presence of atmosphere at the planet Venus. In the judgment of Henry M. Leicester, Lomonosov's scientific papers revealed "a remarkable originality and . . . ability to follow his theories to their logical ends, even though his conclusions were sometimes erroneous."

In a series of odes, Lomonosov combined his poetic gifts with his scientific engagement to produce scientific poetry. These odes dealt with scientific themes and were dedicated to the popularization of rationalist methods in obtaining socially valuable knowledge. "A Letter on the Uses of Glass," one such ode, relied on rich and poignant metaphors to portray the invincible power of scientific ideas of the kind advanced by Kepler, Huygens, and Newton. This poem, an ode in praise of the scientific world outlook, is the first Russian literary work to hail Copernicus's heliocentrism.

The appearance of Lomonosov's papers on physical and chemical themes in the St. Petersburg Academy of Sciences journal *Novy Kommentary* (*New Commentary*) during the 1750s marked the beginning of a new epoch in Russia's cultural history. They were the first publications of scientific papers by a native Russian scholar to appear in the same journal with contributions by established naturalists and mathematicians of Western origin and training. The papers, presented in Latin, dealt with major scientific problems of the day and were noticed by reviewers in Western scholarly journals.

Few of his Russian contemporaries understood the intellectual and social significance of Lomonosov's achievements in science and of his enthusiastic advocacy of Baconian views on science as the commanding source of social progress. His relations with the members of the St. Petersburg Academy and with distinguished members of the literary community were punctuated by stormy conflicts, personal and professional. He showed a tendency to magnify the animosity, overt or latent, of German academicians toward Russian personnel and Russia's cultural environment. Particularly noted were his outbursts against G. F. Müller, A. L. Schlozer, and G. Z. Bayer, the founders of the Norman theory of the origin of the Russian state. On one occasion, he was sent to jail as a result of complaints by foreign colleagues regarding his abusive language at scientific sessions of the Academy. In the face of mounting complaints about his behavior, Catherine II signed a decree in 1763 forcing Lomonosov to retire; however, before the Senate could ratify the decree, the empress changed her mind. Part of Lomonosov's obstinacy stemmed from his desire to see increased Russian representation in the administration of the Academy. In fairness to Lomonosov, it must be noted that he had high respect for and maintained cordial relations with most German members of the Academy.

Lomonosov went through a series of skirmishes with theologians who protected the irrevocability of canonized belief from the challenges launched by science, and even wrote a hymn lampooning the theologians who stood in the way of scientific progress. While attacking theological zealots, he never deviated from a candid respect for religion—and he never alienated himself from the church. Small wonder, then, that two archimandrites and a long line of priests officiated at his burial rites. After his death, the church recognized him as one of Russia's premier citizens, and many learned theologians took an active part in building the symbolism of the Lomonosov legend.

In his time, and shortly after his death, Lomonosov was known almost exclusively as a poet; only isolated contemporaries grasped the intellectual and social significance of his achievements in science. A good part of his main scientific manuscripts languished in the archives of the St. Petersburg Academy until the beginning of the twentieth century. Lomonosov was known for having made little effort to communicate with Russian scientists in and outside the Academy. On his death, a commemorative session was attended by eight members of the Academy, who heard a short encomium delivered by Nicholas Gabriel de Clerc, a French doctor of medicine, writer on Russian history, newly elected honorary member of the Academy, and personal physician of Kirill Razumovsky, president of the Academy. While de Clerc praised Lomonosov effusively, he barely mentioned his work in science.

See also: ACADEMY OF ARTS; ACADEMY OF SCIENCES; EDUCATION; ENLIGHTENMENT, IMPACT OF; SLAVIC-GREEK-LATIN ACADEMY

BIBLIOGRAPHY

Leicester, Henry M. (1976). *Lomonosov and the Corpuscular Theory.* Cambridge, MA: Harvard University Press.

Menshutkin, B. N. (1952). *Russia's Lomonosov, Chemist, Courtier, Physicist, Poet*, tr. I. E. Thal and E. J. Webster, Princeton, NJ.: Princeton University Press.

Pavlova, G. E., and Fedorov, A. S. (1984). *Mikhail Vasil'evich Lomonasov: His Life and Work*, Moscow: Mir.

ALEXANDER VUCINICH

LORIS-MELIKOV, MIKHAIL TARIELOVICH

(1825–1888), Russian general and minister, head of Supreme Executive Commission in 1880–1881.

Mikhail Loris-Melikov was born in Tiflis into a noble family. He studied at the Lazarev Institute of Oriental Languages in Moscow and at the military school in St. Petersburg (1839–1843). In 1843 he started his military service as a minor officer in a guard hussar regiment. In 1847 he asked to be transferred to the Caucasus, where he took part in the war with highlanders in Chechnya and Dagestan. He later fought in the Crimean War from 1853 to 1856. From 1855 to 1875 he served as the superintendent of the different districts beyond the Caucasus and proved a gifted administrator. In 1875 Loris-Melikov was promoted to cavalry general. From 1876 he served as the commander of the Separate Caucasus Corps. During the war with Turkey of 1877–1878 Loris-Melikov commanded Russian armies beyond the Caucasus, and distinguished himself in the sieges of Ardagan and Kars. In 1878 he was awarded the title of a count.

In April of 1879, after Alexander Soloviev's assault on emperor Alexander II, Loris-Melikov was appointed temporary governor-general of Kharkov. He tried to gain the support of the liberal community and was the only one of the six governor-generals with emergency powers who did not approve a single death penalty. A week after the explosion of February 5, 1880, in the Winter Palace, he was appointed head of the Supreme Executive Commission and assumed almost dictator-like power. He continued his policy of cooperation with liberals, seeing it as a way of restoring order in the country. At the same time, he was strict in his tactics of dealing with revolutionaries. In the underground press, these tactics were called "the wolf's jaws and the fox's tail." In April 1880 Loris-Melikov presented to Alexander II a report containing a program of reforms, including a tax reform, a local governing reform, a passport system reform, and others. The project encouraged the inclusion of elected representatives of the nobility, of *zemstvos*, and of city government institutions in the discussions of the drafts of some State orders.

In August 1880 the Supreme Executive Commission was dismissed at the order of Loris-Melikov, who believed that the commission had done its job. At the same time, the Ministry of Interior and the Political Police were reinstated. The third division of the Emperor's personal chancellery (the secret police) was dismissed, and its functions were given to the Department of State Police of the Ministry of the Interior. Loris-Melikov was appointed minister of the interior. In September 1880, at the initiative of Loris-Melikov, senators' inspections were undertaken in various regions of Russia. The results were to be taken into consideration during the preparation of reforms. In January 1880 Loris-Melikov presented a report to the emperor in which he suggested the institution of committees for analyzing and implementing the results of the senators' inspections. The committees were to consist of State officials and elected representatives of *zemstvos* and city governments. The project later became known under the inaccurate name of "Loris-Melikov's Constitution." On the morning of March 13, 1881, Alexander II signed the report presented by Loris-Melikov and called for a meeting of the Council of Ministers to discuss the document. The same day the emperor was killed by the members of People's Will.

At the meeting of the Council of Ministers on March 20, 1881, Loris-Melikov's project was harshly criticized by Konstantin Pobedonostsev and other conservators, who saw this document as a first step toward the creation of a constitution. The new emperor, Alexander III, accepted the conservators' position, and on May 11 he issued the manifesto of the "unquestionability of autocracy," which meant the end of the reformist policy. The next day, Loris-Melikov and two other reformist ministers, Alexander Abaza and Dmitry Miliutin, resigned, provoking the first ministry crisis in Russian history.

Having resigned, but remaining a member of the State Council, Loris-Melikov lived mainly abroad in Germany and France. He died in Nice.

See also: ALEXANDER II; AUTOCRACY; LOCAL GOVERNMENT AND ADMINISTRATION; ZEMSTVO

BIBLIOGRAPHY

Zaionchkovskii, Petr Andreevich. (1976). *The Russian Autocracy under Alexander III.* Gulf Breeze, FL: Academic International Press.

Zaionchkovskii, Petr Andreevich. (1979). *The Russian Autocracy in Crisis, 1878-1882.* Gulf Breeze, FL: Academic International Press.

OLEG BUDNITSKII

LOTMAN, YURI MIKHAILOVICH

(1922–1993), scholar, founder of the Tartu-Moscow Semiotic School.

Yuri Lotman was a widely cited scholar of Soviet literary semiotics and structuralism. He established the Tartu-Moscow Semiotic School at Tartu University in Estonia. This school is famous for its *Works on Sign Systems* (published in Russian as *Trudy po znakovym systemam*). Unusually prolific, he published some eight hundred works on a high scholarly level. He is sometimes compared to Mikhail Bakhtin, another well-known Russian scholar.

Lotman began teaching at the University of Tartu in 1954. Starting as a historian of Russian literature, Lotman focused on the work of Radishchev, Karamzin, and Vyazemsky and the writers linked to the Decembrist movement. His later books covered all major literary works, from the *Lay of Igor's Campaign* to the classic nineteenth-century authors such as Pushkin and Gogol, to Bulgakov, Pasternak, and Brodsky. From traditional philology Lotman shifted in the early sixties to cultural semiotics. His first key publication of that time, *Lectures on Structural Poetics* (1964), introduced the abovementioned series *Trudy po znakovym sistemam,* which was one of the main initiatives of the Tartu-Moscow school.

Lotman's theory of literature rests upon two closely related sets of fundamental concepts—those of semiotics and structuralism. Semiotics is the science of signs and sign systems, which studies the basic characteristics of all signs and their combinations: the words and word combinations of natural and artificial languages, the metaphors of poetic language, and chemical and mathematical symbols. It also treats systems of signs such as those of artificial logical and machine languages, the languages of various poetic schools, codes, animal communication systems, and so on. Each sign contains: a) the signifying material (perceived by the sense organs), and b) the signified aspect (meaning). For words of natural (ordinary) language, pronunciation or writing is the signifying aspect while content is the signified aspect. The signs of one system (for example, the words of a language) can be the signifying aspect for complex signs of another system (such as that of poetic language) superimposed on them.

Lotman defined structuralism as "the idea of a system: a complete, self-regulating entity that adapts to new conditions by transforming its features while retaining its systematic structure." He argued that any chosen object of investigation must be viewed as an interrelated, interdependent system composed of units and rules for their possible combinations. He defined culture itself as "the whole of uninherited information and the ways of its organization and storage." From the point of view of semiotics, anything linked with meaning in fact belongs to culture. Since natural language is the central operator of culture, Lotman and the Tartu-Moscow school deemed natural language to be a primary modeling system containing a general picture of the world. Language was the most developed, universal means of communication—the "system of systems." Lotman took keen interest in the way philosophical ideas, world views, and social values of a given period are enacted in its literature (via language). For Lotman, a period's literary and ideological consciousness and the aesthetics of its trends and currents have a systemic quality. These categories are not a hodgepodge of convictions about the world and literature, but a hierarchic group of cognitive, ethical, and aesthetic values.

Critics might object to perceived "scientific optimism," reductionism, and polemics of the Tartu-Moscow School. The ideological pressures within the USSR with which the school coped probably discouraged internal debates and explicit criticism of its own views.

See also: BAKHTIN, MIKHAIL MIKHAILOVICH; EDUCATION; ESTONIA AND ESTONIANS

BIBLIOGRAPHY

Lotman, Iu. M.; Ginzburg, Lidiia; et al. (1985). *The Semiotics of Russian Cultural History: Essays.* Ithaca, NY: Cornell University Press.

Lotman, Iu. M. (2001). *Universe of the Mind: A Semiotic Theory of Culture (The Second World)*, tr. Ann Shukman. Bloomington: Indiana University Press.

Staton, Shirley F. (1987). *Literary Theories in Praxis.* Philadelphia: University of Pennsylvania Press.

JOHANNA GRANVILLE

LOVERS OF WISDOM, THE

The Lovers of Wisdom (*Liubomudry*), writers based in Moscow during the 1820s, were strongly influenced by Romanticism and set out to explore the philosophical, religious, aesthetic and cultural implications of German Idealist philosophy. The Society for the Love of Wisdom met secretly in the apartment of its president, Vladimir Odoyevsky (ca. 1803–1869) from 1823 to 1825. While the Society formally disbanded following the Decembrist uprising, its members' works continued to display unity of interest and purpose through the late 1820s. The group's core consisted of Odoyevsky, Dmitry Venevitinov (1805–1827), Ivan Kireyevsky (1806–1856), Alexander Koshelev (1806–1883), and Nikolai Rozhalin (1805–1834). But the number of people generally considered Lovers of Wisdom is much broader, including Alexei Khomyakov (1804–1860), Stepan Shevyrev (1806–1864), Vladimir Titov (1807–1891), Dmitry Struisky (1806–1856), Nikolai Melgunov (1804–1867), and Mikhail Pogodin (1800–1875).

In secondary literature, the Lovers of Wisdom have long been overshadowed by the Decembrists. While the Decembrists pursued political and military careers in St. Petersburg and allegedly conspired to force political reform, the Lovers of Wisdom bided their time at comfortably undemanding jobs at the Moscow Archive of the Ministry of Foreign Affairs. They indulged in speculation on the most abstract issues, with a bent toward mysticism. Even their choice of name, "Lovers of Wisdom" as opposed to "philosophers", or *philosophes*, is thought to have marked their opposition to the progressive tradition of the radical Enlightenment.

Yet the Lovers of Wisdom thought of themselves as enlighteners in the broader sense. They aimed to reinvigorate Russian high culture by attacking the moral corruption of the nobility and promoting creativity and the pursuit of knowledge. They contrasted the superstition and petty-mindedness of the nobility to the moral purity of the "lover of wisdom," who often appeared in their satires and oriental tales in the guise of a magus, dervish, brahmin, Greek philosopher, or sculptor, or a misunderstood Russian writer. Whether in short stories, metaphysical poetry, or quasi-philosophical prose works, Odoyevsky, Venevitinov, Khomyakov and Shevyrev emphasized the great spiritual and even religious importance of the young, creative individual, or genius. The special status of such individuals was only highlighted by their apparent moral fragility and vulnerability in a hostile environment.

The group was heavily indebted to Romanticism and to German Idealist philosophy. Admittedly, Friedrich Wilhelm Joseph Schelling's philosophy seems to have appealed in part because it was difficult to understand. As Koyré (1929) remarked, their Romanticism was characterized by a "slightly puerile desire to feel 'isolated from the crowd,' the desire for the esoteric, which is complemented by the possession of a secret, even if that secret consists only in the fact that one possesses one." (p. 37). But their works also display a genuine commitment to principles such as the fundamental unity of matter and ideas, and the notion that these achieve higher synthesis in the absolute, the spirit that guides the world. To them, creating a work of art, or striving for any kind of knowledge, brought the individual into contact with the absolute, lending the artist or intellectual special religious status.

Such views did not accord with Orthodox Christianity. The political authorities did not welcome them either. Yet the Lovers of Wisdom found ways of promoting their views in poetry and prose they published in journals and almanacs, especially in *Mnemozina* (1824–1825), edited by Odoyevsky with the Decembrist Wilgelm Kyukhelbeker, and *Moskovsky vestnik* (1827–1830), edited by Pogodin. They also published translations from leading voices of Romanticism such as Goethe, Byron, Tieck and Wackenroder.

The closure of *Moskovsky vestnik* in 1830 marked the end of the Lovers of Wisdom as a group. But the death of Venevitinov, often considered their most talented member, in 1827, had already dealt them a blow, as did the departure of many key members from Moscow in the late 1820s. In the early 1830s, the group's members developed in new directions. Some of them, such as Kireyevsky and Khomyakov, eventually became leaders of the Slavophile movement, arguably the most coherent and original strain in nineteenth-century Russian thought.

See also: DECEMBRIST MOVEMENT AND REBELLION; KHOMYAKOV, ALEXEI STEPANOVICH; KIREYEVSKY, IVAN VASILIEVICH; ODOYEVSKY, VLADIMIR FYODOROVICH; POGODIN, MIKHAIL PETROVICH

BIBLIOGRAPHY

Gleason, Abott. (1972). *European and Muscovite: Ivan Kireevsky and the Origins of Slavophilism.* Cambridge, MA: Harvard University Press.

Koyré, Alexandre. (1929). *La philosophie et le problème national en Russie au début du XIXe siècle.* Paris: Librairie Ancienne Honoré Champion.

VICTORIA FREDE

LUBOK

Broadsides or broadsheet prints (pl. *lubki*).

Broadsides first appeared in Russia in the seventeenth century, probably inspired by German woodcuts. Subjects were depicted in a native style. Captions complemented the printed images. The earliest *lubki* represented saints and other religious figures, but humorous illustrations also circulated that captured the parody spirit of *skomorok* (minstrel) performances of the era—especially the wacky wordplay of the theatrical entr'actes.

In the 1760s prints began to be made from metal plates, facilitating production of longer texts. Lithographic stone supplanted copper plates, but in turn gave way to cheaper and lighter zinc plates in the second half of the nineteenth century. Pedlars bought the pictures in bulk at fairs or in Moscow and sold them in the countryside. Originally acquired by nobles, the images were taken up by the merchantry, officials, and tradesmen before becoming the province of the peasantry in the nineteenth century, at which point *lubok,* in its adjectival form, came to mean "shoddy." It was also in the nineteenth century that the term came to refer to cheap printed booklets aimed at popular audiences.

Lubki depicted historical figures, characters from folklore, contemporary members of the ruling family, festival pastimes, battle scenes, judicial punishments, and hunting and other aspects of everyday life, along with religious subjects. The prints decorated peasant huts, taverns, and the insides of lids of trunks used by peasants when they moved to cities or factories to work. The native style of the prints was adapted by Old Believers in the nineteenth century in their manuscript printing. Avant-garde artists in the early twentieth century drew inspiration from the style in their neo-primitivist phase. An "Exhibition of Icons and Lubki" was held in Moscow in 1913.

See also: CHAPBOOK LITERATURE; OLD BELIEVERS

BIBLIOGRAPHY

Bowlt, John E. (1998). "Art." In *The Cambridge Companion to Modern Russian Literature,* ed. Nicholas Rzhevsky. Cambridge, UK: Cambridge University Press.

Brooks, Jeffrey. (1985). *When Russia Learned to Read: Literacy and Popular Literature, 1861–1917.* Princeton, NJ: Princeton University Press.

Farrell, Dianne E. (1991). "Medieval Popular Humor in Russian Eighteenth Century *Lubki.*" *Slavic Review* 50:551–565.

GARY THURSTON

LUBYANKA

The All-Russian Extraordinary Commission on the Struggle Against Counter-Revolution, Sabotage, and Speculation (VCHk, or Cheka) was founded by the Bolsheviks in December 1917. Headed by Felix Dzerzhinsky, it was responsible for liquidating counterrevolutionary elements and remanding saboteurs and counter-revolutionaries to be tried by the revolutionary-military tribunal. In February 1918 it was authorized to shoot active enemies of the revolution rather than turn them over to the tribunal.

In March 1918 the Cheka established its headquarters in the buildings at 11 and 13 Great Lubyanka Street in Moscow. Between the 1930s and the beginning of the 1980s, a complex of buildings belonging to the security establishment grew up along Great Lubyanka Street. The building at No. 20 was constructed in 1982 as the headquarters of the KGB (Committee of State Security), now the FSB (Federal Security Bureau), for Moscow and the Moscow area.

The famous Lubyanka Internal Prison was situated in the courtyard of what is now the main building of the FSB on Lubyanka Street. Closed in the 1960s, it is at present the site of a dining room, offices, and a warehouse. All its prisoners were transferred to Lefortovo. In the time of mass reprisals, prisoners were regularly shot in the courtyard of the Lubyanka Prison. Automobile engines were run to drown out the noise. Suspects were brutally interrogated in the prison's basement.

In addition to the FSB headquarters, the buildings on Lubyanka Street also include a museum of the history of the state security agencies. The office of Lavrenty Beria, long-time chief of the Soviet security apparatus, has been kept unchanged and is open to visitors.

See also: BERIA, LAVRENTI PAVLOVICH; DZERZHINSKY, FELIX EDMUNDOVICH; GULAG, LEFORTOVO; MINISTRY OF THE INTERIOR; PRISONS; STATE SECURITY, ORGANS OF

A statue of Felix Dzerzhinsky—the first head of the Soviet secret police—looms over Lubyanka Prison in Moscow. Following the failed August 1991 coup attempt by Communist Party hard-liners, this statue was torn down. © NOVOSTI/SOVFOTO

BIBLIOGRAPHY

Burch, James. (1983). *Lubyanka: A Novel.* New York: Atheneum.

GEORG WURZER

LUKASHENKO, ALEXANDER GRIGORIEVICH

(b. 1954), president of Belarus.

Alexander Grigorievich Lukashenko became president of Belarus on July 10, 1994, when he defeated Prime Minister Vyachaslav Kebich in the country's first presidential election, running on a platform of anti-corruption and closer relations with Russia. He established a harsh dictatorship as president, amending the constitution to consolidate his authority.

Lukashenko was born in August 1954 in the village of Kopys (Orshanske Rayon, Vitebsk Oblast), but most of his early career was spent in Mahileu region, where he graduated from the Mahileu Teaching Institute (his speciality was history) and the Belarusian Agricultural Academy. From 1975 to 1977, he was a border guard in the Brest area. He then spent five years in the army before returning to Mahileu, and the town of Shklau, where he worked as manager of state and collective farms, and also in a construction materials combine. He was elected to the Belarusian Supreme Soviet in 1990, where he founded a faction called Communists for Democracy. In the early 1990s he chaired a commission investigating corruption.

In April 1995, several months into his presidency, Lukashenko organized a referendum that replaced the country's state symbols and national flag with others very similar to the Soviet ones and elevated Russian to a state language. A second referendum in November 1996 considerably enhanced the authority of the presidency by reducing the parliament to a rump body of 120 seats (formerly there were 260 deputies), establishing an upper house closely attached to the presidency, and curtailing the authority of the Constitutional Court. Lukashenko then dated his presidency from late 1996 rather than the original election date of July 1994.

By April 1995, Lukashenko had established a community relationship with Boris Yeltsin's Russia, which went through several stages before being formalized as a Union state in late 1999. Under Vladimir Putin, however, Russia distanced itself from the agreement and in the summer of 2002 threatened to incorporate Belarus into the Russian Federation.

Lukashenko clamped down on opposition movements and imposed tight censorship over the media. His contraventions of human rights in the republic have elicited international concern.

See also: BELARUS AND BELARUSIANS

BIBLIOGRAPHY

Marples, David R. (1999). *Belarus: A Denationalized Nation.* Amsterdam: Harwood Academic Publishers.

Zaprudnik, Jan. (1995). *Belarus: At a Crossroads in History.* Boulder, CO: Westview Press.

DAVID R. MARPLES

LUKYANOV, ANATOLY IVANOVICH

(b. 1930), chair of the USSR Supreme Soviet during the August 1991 coup attempt.

Anatoly Lukyanov studied law at Moscow State University, graduating in 1953. While at the university, he chaired the University Komsomol branch, and Mikhail Gorbachev was deputy chair. Lukyanov joined the Party in 1955 and began a career within the Party apparatus. He was appointed to the Central Committee Secretariat in 1987. By 1988, Lukyanov was named a candidate member of the Politburo and first deputy chair of the Presidium of the USSR Supreme Soviet.

The first USSR Congress of People's Deputies elected Lukyanov chairman of the newly reconfigured Supreme Soviet in 1990. This post allowed him to control the parliamentary agenda. He was repeatedly accused of stonewalling legislation he did not like and putting bills he supported to vote multiple times if they were voted down.

Despite his close personal links with Gorbachev, Lukyanov sided with opponents of Gorbachev's policies. The hard-line Soyuz faction particularly favored Lukyanov over Gorbachev. During his December 1990 resignation speech to the Congress, Foreign Minister Eduard Shevardnadze specifically criticized Lukyanov for interfering in Soviet-German relations and for his desire for a dictatorship.

As Gorbachev's new Union Treaty neared ratification in summer 1991, hard-line members of the Soviet leadership hierarchy staged a coup to overthrow Gorbachev and prevent adoption of the treaty. Though Lukyanov was not a member of the State Committee for the State of Emergency that briefly seized power August 19–21, 1991, he supported their efforts. Lukyanov was arrested following the coup's collapse, then amnestied in February 1994 and elected to the Russian Duma in 1995 and 1999, where he chaired the parliamentary committee on government reform.

See also: AUGUST 1991 PUTSCH

BIBLIOGRAPHY

Wishnevsky, Julia. (1991). "Anatolii Luk'yanov: Gorbachev's Conservative Rival?" *RFE/RL Report on the USSR* 3(23):8–14.

ANN E. ROBERTSON

LUNACHARSKY, ANATOLY VASILIEVICH

(1875–1933), Bolshevik intellectual and early Soviet leader.

Born the son of a state councilor, Anatoly Lunacharsky joined the Social Democratic movement in 1898 and was soon arrested. As an exile in Vologda, he met Alexander Bogdanov. In Paris in 1904 both men joined the Bolshevik faction, but they left it again in 1911 after clashes with Lenin over philosophy. Bogdanov advocated empiriocriticism, claiming that only direct experience could be relied on as a basis for knowledge. Lunacharsky promoted God–building, an anthropocentric religion striving toward the moral unity of mankind. Lunacharsky rejoined the Bolshevik Party in August 1917 and became the first People's Commissar of Enlightenment (*Narkom prosveshcheniya*, or *Narkompros*), serving from October 1917 to 1929. A prolific writer on literature and the arts and an important patron of the intelligentsia, Lunacharsky was often regarded within the party as too "soft" for a Bolshevik. From the mid–1920s he was increasingly marginalized, and his last years at Narkompros were marked by fierce battles over education and culture as his soft line in policy was discredited with the onset of the Cultural Revolution. After his resignation from Narkompros, he held various second–rank positions in cultural administration and spent much time abroad, partly for health reasons. In 1933 he was appointed ambassador to Spain, but died before assuming the position. His reputation plummeted after his death, but from the 1960s to the 1980s, thanks partly to the untiring work of his daughter, Irina Lunacharskaya, he became a symbol of a (pre–Stalinist) humanistic Bolshevism protective of the intelligentsia and committed to the advancement of high culture.

See also: BOLSHEVISM; CULTURAL REVOLUTION; EDUCATION; PROLETKULT

BIBLIOGRAPHY

Fitzpatrick, Sheila. (1970). *The Commissariat of Enlightenment: Soviet Organization of Education and the Arts under Lunacharsky, October 1917-1921.* Cambridge, UK: Cambridge University Press.

O'Connor, Timothy Edward. (1983). *The Politics of Soviet Culture: Anatolii Lunacharskii.* Ann Arbor, MI: UMI Research Press.

SHEILA FITZPATRICK

LUZHKOV, YURI MIKHAILOVICH

(b. 1936), Russian politician and mayor of Moscow.

Yuri Luzhkov became a member of the Communist Party of the Soviet Union (CPSU) in 1968 and remained a member until the party was outlawed in the wake of the failed coup of August 1991. He left a management career in the chemical industry to become a deputy to the Moscow City Council (Soviet) in 1977. In 1987, his political career took a great stride forward when Boris Yeltsin became First Secretary of the Moscow Communist Party organization. In keeping with the Soviet practice of assigning party members to multiple responsibilities, Luzhkov was appointed deputy to the Supreme Soviet of the Russian Soviet Federated Socialist Republic (RSFSR) and first deputy to the chair of the Moscow City Executive Committee.

Luzhkov was appointed chair of the City Executive Committee following Gavriil Popov's election as mayor of Moscow in 1990. The following year he was elected Popov's vice mayor. During the August 1991 coup, he helped organize the defense

Yuri Luzhkov is sworn in for his second term as mayor of Moscow, December 29, 1996. © REUTERS NEWMEDIA INC./CORBIS

of the White House, the parliament building of the Russian Federation from which Boris Yeltsin organized the resistance to the efforts of conservatives within the CPSU to undo the Gorbachev reforms.

Following the collapse of the coup and the subsequent dissolution of the Soviet Union, a struggle emerged between Russian President Boris Yeltsin and the legislature over the course of reform. Luzhkov, owing to his strong support for Yeltsin in the conflict, was made mayor by presidential decree when Popov was forced to resign. The decree was met with opposition within the Moscow City Council, which tried unsuccessfully on two occasions to unseat Luzhkov.

As his predecessor had done, Luzhkov threw his support behind Yeltsin in the confrontation with the Russian parliament. At the height of the conflict following Yeltsin's September 1993 decree dissolving the legislature, which resulted in an armed standoff, the mayor cut off utilities and services to the parliament and deployed the city's police to forcibly disband meetings and demonstrations organized in support of the legislature.

Luzhkov remained mayor of Moscow, but his regime has not been without controversy. He has come under particular criticism for the manner in which privatization of municipal property has been carried out. On several occasions the press has charged the mayor with corruption, favoritism, and using his position for personal gain. Despite this, the city's relatively good economic situation in comparison with the rest of the country has made Luzhkov enormously popular with Muscovites. He was reelected with 88 percent of the vote in 1996.

However, the mayor's efforts to rid the city of those without residency permits has undermined his popularity with the rest of the country. When Luzhkov announced his candidacy to the 2000 presidential elections and formed the bloc Fatherland-All Russia, supporters of Vladimir Putin were able to organize a negative ad campaign, which quickly marginalized the mayor's bloc. Following Putin's electoral victory, Luzhkov moved to defend his political position by declaring his loyalty to the new president.

See also: AUGUST 1991 PUTSCH; FATHERLAND-ALL RUSSIA; MOSCOW; YELTSIN, BORIS NIKOLAYEVICH

BIBLIOGRAPHY

Luzhkov, Yuri M. (1996). *Moscow Does Not Believe in Tears: Reflections of Moscow's Mayor.* Chicago: James M. Martin.

TERRY D. CLARK

LYSENKO, TROFIM DENISOVICH

(1898–1976), agronomist and biologist.

Trofim Denisovich Lysenko was born in Karlovka, Ukraine, to a peasant family. He attended the Kiev Agricultural Institute as an extramural student and graduated as doctor of agricultural science in 1925. A disciple of horticulturist Ivan Michurin's work, Lysenko worked at the Gyandzha Experimental Station between 1925 and 1929 and coined his theory of vernalization in the late 1920s. His vernalization theory described a process where

Soviet geneticist Trofim Lysenko measures the growth of wheat in a collective farm near Odessa, Ukraine. © HULTON-DEUTSCH COLLECTION/CORBIS

winter habit was transformed into spring habit by moistening and chilling the seed.

During the agricultural crisis of the 1930s, Soviet authorities started supporting Lysenko's theories. By the mid-1930s Lysenko's dominance in agricultural sciences was clearly established as he founded agrobiology, a pseudoscience that promised to increase yields rapidly and cheaply. He became president of the Lenin All-Union Academy of Agricultural Sciences in 1938 and director of the Institute of Genetics at the Academy of Sciences in 1940. Lysenko and his followers, Lysenkoites, have long been thought to have had a direct line to the Stalinist terror apparatus as they targeted geneticists that they thought opposed Lysenkoism, most famously noted scientist Nikolai Vavilov.

As Lysenko's political influence increased, he expressed his views more forcefully. His view of genetics was irrational and based neither on reason nor scientific experimentation. His theory of heredity rejected established principles of genetics, and he believed that he could change the genetic constitution of strains of wheat by controlling the environment. For example, he claimed that wheat plants raised in the appropriate environment produced seeds of rye.

By 1948 education and research in traditional genetics had been completely outlawed in the Soviet Union. The 1948 August Session of the Lenin Academy of Agricultural Sciences gave the Lysenkoites official endorsement for these views, which were said to correspond to Marxist theory. From that moment, and until Josef Stalin's death, Lysenko was the total autocrat of Soviet biology. His position as Stalin's henchman in Soviet science has been compared to Andrei Zhdanov's role in culture during this time of high Stalinism.

In April 1952 the Ministry of Agriculture withdrew its support of Lysenko's cluster method of planting trees, but Lysenko was not publicly rebuked until after Stalin's death in 1953. Nikita Khrushchev tolerated criticism of Lysenkoism, but it took eleven years to completely confirm the uselessness of agrobiology. It was only with Khrushchev's ousting from power in 1964 that Lysenko was fully discredited and research in traditional genetics accepted. He resigned as president of the All-Union Academy of Agricultural Sciences in 1956, and his removal from the position of director of the Institute of Genetics in 1965 signified the full return of scientific professionalism in Soviet science. Lysenko kept the title of academician and held the position of chairman for science at the Academy of Science's Agricultural Experimental Station, located not far from Moscow, until he died in November 20, 1976.

See also: AGRICULTURE; SCIENCE AND TECHNOLOGY POLICY; STALIN, JOSEF VISSARIONOVICH; VAVILOV, NIKOLAI IVANOVICH

BIBLIOGRAPHY

Joravsky, David. (1970). *The Lysenko Affair.* Cambridge, MA: Harvard University Press.

Medvedev, Zhores A. (1969). *The Rise and Fall of T. D. Lysenko.* New York: Columbia University Press.

Medvedev, Zhores A. (1978). *Soviet Science.* New York: Norton.

RÓSA MAGNÚSDÓTTIR